To Jan,
who lit the spark of love within
for whom the flames still burn.

CONCEPTS OF
CHEMICAL DEPENDENCY

NINTH EDITION

HAROLD E. DOWEIKO

Gundersen-Lutheran Medical Center

La Crosse, WI

CENGAGE
Learning®

Australia • Brazil • Mexico • Singapore • United Kingdom • United States

![CENGAGE Learning logo]

Concepts of Chemical Dependency, Ninth Edition

Harold E. Doweiko

Product Director: Jon-David Hague

Product Manager: Julie Martinez

Associate Content Developer: Amelia Blevins

Content Coordinator: Sean Cronin

Product Assistant: Kyra Kane

Associate Marketing Manager: Shanna Shelton

Art and Cover Direction, Production Management, and Composition: PreMediaGlobal

Manufacturing Planner: Judy Inouye

Rights Acquisitions Specialist: Thomas McDonough

Cover Images: beer in a dark room: Yellowj/Shutterstock.com; closeup of many dirty cigarettes butts background: maximult/Shutterstock.com; colored pills, tablets and capsules on a white background: Ziablik/Shutterstock.com; injecting heroin: Photo Graphic Room/Shutterstock.com; marijuana plants: Ijansempoi/Shutterstock.com; mushroom: Kina/Shutterstock.com

For product information and technology assistance, contact us at **Cengage Learning Customer & Sales Support, 1-800-354-9706.**

For permission to use material from this text or product, submit all requests online at **www.cengage.com/permissions.** Further permissions questions can be e-mailed to **permissionrequest@cengage.com.**

Library of Congress Control Number: 2013955319

ISBN-13: 978-1-285-45513-6

ISBN-10: 1-285-45513-4

Cengage Learning
200 First Stamford Place, 4th Floor
Stamford, CT 06902
USA

Cengage Learning is a leading provider of customized learning solutions with office locations around the globe, including Singapore, the United Kingdom, Australia, Mexico, Brazil, and Japan. Locate your local office at **www.cengage.com/global.**

Cengage Learning products are represented in Canada by Nelson Education, Ltd.

To learn more about Cengage Learning Solutions, visit **www.cengage.com.**

Purchase any of our products at your local college store or at our preferred online store **www.cengagebrain.com.**

Printed in the United States of America
2 3 4 5 6 7 18 17 16 15 14

CONTENTS

PREFACE

The world of the neurosciences is constantly changing. New discoveries about the process of neurotransmission, how neurotransmitter receptor sites are distributed throughout the brain, how certain chemicals damage neurons or aid in their recovery, how the brain experiences and recovers from trauma all conspire to make a textbook such as this exceptionally difficult to keep current. Many long-cherished theories have been discarded, whereas new information leads to the formation of new theories or suggests new directions for theoretical inquiry. An excellent example is Koob's (2009) assertion that scientists are only now starting to explore the role of glial[1] cells in the brain. The glial cells comprise 90% of the brain's mass, play roles in the process of neurogenesis, provide metabolic support of the neurons, and are involved in the process of neurotransmission itself.

Over the years, there have been a number of changes made to this text, and this process has continued with the current edition. New research is cited, and the process of publishing journal articles online before the publication of the printed version has resulted in the citation of numerous journal articles that were "published online prior to print." Further, because research suggests that substance use patterns between young adults who go on to attend college and those who do not might differ, a new chapter that focuses just on substance use issues in the college student population has been added to the text. Information about the synthetic THC-like compounds that became popular drugs of abuse in the first months of this decade has also been reviewed. Several of the chapters have been rewritten in an attempt to avoid duplication of material. Out of curiosity, I tried to count every change made to the manuscript from the addition or deletion of a reference to the addition of new material and deletion of material not thought relevant, movement of a section to another part of a chapter so that it would be more appropriate there, and so on, and gave up at 600.

With the publication of the *Diagnostic and Statistical Manual of Mental Disorders* (5th Edition) *(DSM-5)* (American Psychiatric Association, 2013), it was necessary to include a new section in each chapter devoted to a drug(s) of abuse integrating the *DSM-5* diagnostic criteria for that substance into the text in addition to the substance-induced disorders that might accompany the abuse of each compound. A new appendix has also been added to explore the changes between the diagnostic criteria utilized in the *DSM-5* and those of its predecessors and how the *DSM-5* does not have separate categories for substance abuse and substance addiction as was true in the previous edition of the *Diagnostic and Statistical Manual of Mental Disorders*.

Over the years, several instructors have contacted the author to inquire about the chapter sequence decisions. It is difficult to write a text that will be used across a range of diverse fields of study in the order that will meet the demands of that class (psychology, sociology, nursing, and substance abuse counseling to name a few of the college classes that have used earlier editions of this text). I do believe that it is important to review the drugs of abuse and their effects first so that

---

[1]See Glossary.

the student might understand why the abuse of these compounds is so appealing and to ground the student in the world of substance *abuse* and not other fields of study. The author of this text was, for example, speaking at a seminar about the total amount of amphetamine that an addict might inject in a "speed run"[2] when a nurse blurted out that the hypothetical person could not *possibly* be injecting that much methamphetamine because it was dangerous and potentially fatal. "Welcome to the world of amphetamine abuse" was the author's response. Substance abuse is a different reality than the one, pharmaceutical sciences, taught in nursing schools, psychology programs, sociology programs, or even medical school. On more than one occasion, the author of this text has been approached by a trauma surgeon to explain why a person would knowingly expose themselves to such high doses of anabolic steroids, and how would this affect their behavior? On many occasions, students or seminar participants have expressed surprise at some of the contaminants or adulterants found in illicit drugs. The average person does not understand that persons with a substance use disorder (SUD) frequently view contaminants as part of the cost of abuse of their desired drug(s). For these reasons, the author of this text has adopted the philosophy that to understand and treat the SUDs, you need to first understand the chemicals being abused and their effects.

Supplements

- *Online Instructor's Manual contains information to assist the instructor in designing the course, including chapter outlines, key terms, discussion questions, teaching and learning activities, learning objectives, and additional online resources.*
- *Cengage Learning Testing Powered by COGNERO is a flexible, online system that allows instructors to author, edit, and manage test bank content from multiple Cengage Learning solutions; create multiple test versions in an instant; and deliver tests from your LMS, your classroom, or wherever you want. A Microsoft Word version of the Test Bank is also available to instructors.*
- *Online PowerPoint® Slides for each chapter assist you with your lecture by providing concept coverage using images, figures, and tables directly from the textbook.*

- *CourseMate for Concepts of Chemical Dependency brings course concepts to life with interactive learning, study, and exam preparation tools that support the printed textbook. Access an integrated e-Book, glossary, quizzes, and more in the CourseMate for Concepts of Chemical Dependency. Go to CengageBrain.com to register or purchase access.*

Acknowledgments

It is not possible to thank all of those people who have provided so much support and feedback during the preparation of this edition. Most certainly my late wife, Jan, continues to be deserving of my thanks for reading each edition of this text over and over to ensure clarity. Her valuable input and her feedback continues to be missed. I would like to thank Dr. David Metzler for his willingness to part company with many copies of various journals over the years. This allowed me to access many of the references cited in this text, and his kindness is appreciated. In addition I would like to thank the following reviewers: Jason Florin (College of DuPage), Walter Chung (Eastern University), Carol Lynn Hulce (UW-Superior), Debra Murray (Viterbo University), Frankie Tack (Central Piedmont Community College), Carla Wozniak (Pueblo Community College), Kananur Chandras (Fort Valley State University), Suzanne Whitehead (Northern State University), and Theresa Johnson (Ohio University Lancaster). The production team should also be thanked for their assistance, for their behind-the-scenes labor helped this edition see the light of day.

Disclaimer

The clinical examples used in this text are based on a wide variety of sources, including (but not limited to) characters as portrayed in various movies, books, or television programs, news stories from the media, clinical examples provided in various references cited at the end of this text, or as portrayed by presenters at various workshops that the author has attended. *All examples provided are hypothetical in nature. Any resemblance to any person, living or dead, is entirely because of chance and should not be inferred by the reader.* Further, the practice of substance abuse counseling or psychotherapy is very complex and the practitioner should be familiar with a wide range of resources in conducting their practice. *Neither the author nor the publisher shall be liable or responsible for any harm, loss, or damage allegedly arising from any information or suggestion made in or omitted from this text.*

---

[2]Discussed in the chapter on amphetamine abuse and addiction.

CHAPTER 1

Why Worry about Substance Abuse or Addiction?

Introduction

Historical evidence would suggest that substance abuse has been a problem for society for thousands of years, and substance use disorders (SUDs) collectively remain the most prevalent mental health issue facing society today (Kilts, 2004; Vuchinich, 2002). Substance use disorders[1] might take any number of forms, including the subset of SUDs known as alcohol use disorders (AUDs) and nicotine use disorders (NUDs). Another subform of SUDs is composed of those who abuse prescription drugs. The most prominent form of SUDs is the abuse of illegal drugs such as the hallucinogens, cocaine, narcotics, and marijuana.[2] Finally, there are those who abuse compounds not normally intended for human use such as the inhalants or anabolic steroids.[3]

The face of SUDs has changed over time as one compound or another gains widespread acceptance among those who wish to abuse such a substance and then is replaced by the next popular drug of abuse. However, alcohol and nicotine hold a unique position in this process: Their use is legal for persons above a certain age. This contributes to the stable levels of alcohol or tobacco use in the United States in spite of widespread acknowledgment of the physical, social, and financial toll that each causes to society. There have been initiatives to ban the use of these compounds over the years with arguable success. In contrast to the patterns of alcohol or tobacco use, the illicit drugs follow a curious cycle: First one compound becomes a popular drug of abuse, and then it is slowly replaced by another, "better" illicit drug of abuse. After the physical and emotional dangers of that substance are discovered, drug abusers switch to another, purportedly "better" and "safer" drug of abuse. In this chapter we will begin to examine the impact of SUDs on society.

---

[1]Because the term *alcoholic* has been found to actually deter many in need of treatment for their alcohol use problem from seeking rehabilitation (Keyes et al., 2010), the term "alcohol use disorder" will be used to indicate persons who abuse or are addicted to alcohol, while the more inclusive term "substance use disorder" is used to address the entire spectrum of drug use disorders.

[2]This is because most people are loath to classify alcohol abuse or addiction as a *substance* use disorder. After all, it is only alcohol, right?

[3]While many of the steroid compounds being abused were indeed intended for human use, they are used at dosage levels far in excess of what is deemed medically acceptable, and thus could be said not to be intended for human use. Further, many of the steroid compounds being abused were not intended for use with humans, but were designed for use with animals, and diverted to the illicit market.

Substance Use Disorders as Unsuspected Influences on Society

It is difficult to identify every way in which SUDs influence society. It has been estimated that the direct and indirect costs of SUDs consume *over 15 percent* of the average state's budget[4] (National Center on Addiction and Substance Abuse at Columbia University, 2009a). Society's response to this problem is somewhat ambivalent as evidenced by the fact that each year in the United States $264 billion is spent purchasing illicit drugs, whereas another $200 billion is spent annually fighting the "war on drugs." Politicians hide the full cost of this "war" by sliding part of the expense from one budgetary column to the next (National Center on Addiction and Substance Abuse at Columbia University, 2009a). For example, the cost of incarcerating those who are convicted of drug-related offenses is part of the Department of Corrections budget, whereas the cost of providing health care and social support for those convicted of drug-related offenses is part of the Human Services budget, and so on (Cafferty, 2009).

In the second decade of the 21st century the rising cost of health care in the United States has become hotly debated. Politicians speak at length about the rising cost of health care, but ignore the impact of SUDs, as evidenced by the following facts:

- *Approximately 25% of patients seen by the primary care physician have an SUD (Jones, Knutson, & Haines, 2004).*
- *Excessive alcohol use was a factor in 50% of all deaths from acute traumatic injuries (Baron, Garbely, & Boyd, 2009).*
- *Approximately 1 million hospital emergency room visits are the result of illicit drug abuse (Centers for Disease Control and Prevention, 2010b).*
- *Approximately 40% of all hospital admissions can be tied either directly or indirectly to alcohol use/ abuse (Baron et al., 2009; Greenfield, 2007; Greenfield & Hennessy, 2008).*

- *Hospitalized persons with an SUD are more likely to require rehospitalization within 30 days of discharge than nonusers (Walley et al., 2012).*
- *Approximately 25% of those individuals on Medicaid have an SUD. As this group ages, their medical costs increases at a higher rate than for age matched individuals without an SUD (Clark, Samnaliev, & McGovern, 2009).*

The SUDs are frequently intertwined with psychiatric problems, further contributing to the rising cost of health care as evidenced by the facts that:

- *Substance Use Disorders are a factor in 50–75% of all psychiatric hospital admissions (Miller, 2004).*
- *Substance Use Disorders are the second most common cause of suicide in this country.*
- *One-third of those persons who commit suicide had alcohol disorders (Karch, Dahlberg, & Patel, 2010).*
- *Between 40 and 60% of those individuals who do commit suicide were intoxicated at the time of their deaths,[5] and 10% had evidence of other drugs of abuse in their bodies at the time of their death (Karch, Cosby, & Simon, 2006; Scott & Marcotte, 2010).*
- *Traumatic brain injury (TBI) accounts for almost one-third of trauma-related deaths in the United States each year, and between 29 and 52% of who survive the TBI have alcohol in their body at the time of admission (Miller & Adams, 2006).*

Substance Use Disorders and Interpersonal Violence

There is a well-documented relationship between SUDs and violent behavior that has remained relatively constant over the years. Half of all perpetrators of a violent crime have been found to have been drinking before the commission of that crime (Coghlan, 2008; Parrott & Giancola, 2006). It has also been found that substance-abusing adults were 2.7 times as likely to have physically abused a child, and 4.2 times as likely to have neglected a child as were their non-substance-abusing peers (Ireland, 2001). Alcohol is a

---

[4]Alcohol-related disease results in approximately 20,700 deaths each year in this country, a figure that does not include persons who die in alcohol-related accidents or who are killed in an alcohol-related homicide (Johnson, 2010).

[5]The discrepancy between these two figures is explained by the fact that many of those who commit suicide consume alcohol as a way to steel their courage before taking their own lives, while others commit suicide impulsively while intoxicated.

factor in 40–86% of all homicides committed in the United States (Parrott & Giancola, 2006)[6] and 40% of homicide cases in Europe (Coghlan, 2008). Illicit drug use increases the woman's chance of being murdered by her significant other by as much as 28-fold, even if she was not abusing chemicals herself at the time of her death (Parrott & Giancola, 2006).

The Scope of the Problem of the Substance Use Disorders

At least half of the world's population has used at least one psychoactive substance at least once with alcohol being the most commonly used psychoactive chemical (Leamon, Wright, & Myrick, 2008). However, only about 200 million people, or about 5% of the entire population of the world, has abused an *illicit* substance (United Nations, 2012). The majority of those who use a psychoactive substance do so on a short-term experimental basis and rarely present the problems to society seen in cases of substance *addiction*. Addiction develops only in a minority of persons who abuse a compound(s). However, a thriving "black market"[7] has evolved to meet the demand for illicit drugs created by the curious user, the infrequent abuser, the heavy abuser or the person who is addicted to a chemical(s). The worldwide illicit drug trade is estimated to be an $800 billion/year industry, making it larger than the annual gross domestic product of 90% of the world's countries (United Nations, 2012; Vital Signs, 2007).

In a sense, illicit drug use might be said to be an "American way of life." Sixteen percent of the entire population over the age of 12 is addicted to nicotine, alcohol, or illegal drugs (Winerman, 2013). This figure is deceptive however since it is possible for a person who is addicted to nicotine to also be addicted to another compound such as alcohol. Still, with just under 5% of the world's total population the United States consumes 60% of the illicit drugs produced on this planet ("Drug War Success Claims Challenged," 2006). Each day in the United States, approximately 8,000 people try an illicit drug for the first time (Lemonick & Park, 2007; Substance Abuse and Mental Health Services Administration, 2009). Many of these individuals probably only experiment with illicit drugs

out of curiosity for <12 months[8] and then discontinue or curtail further use of that compound (Center for Substance Abuse Research, 2008).

The most commonly abused illicit substance is marijuana, with 75.7% of illicit drug users abusing marijuana, and 57.3% of illicit drug abusers using only marijuana (Substance Abuse and Mental Health Services Administration, 2009). This figure still means that 8.6 million people over the age of 12 abused an illicit compound other than marijuana in the month preceding the survey (Substance Abuse and Mental Health Services Administration, 2009). An interesting research study conducted by Banta-Greene, Field, Chiala, and Sudakin (2009) revealed that waste water from both rural and urban areas contained measurable amounts of cocaine and methamphetamine metabolites, underscoring the widespread abuse of these compounds in this country. In the next section, we will more closely examine the scope of the problem of SUDs in this country.

Alcohol Use, Abuse, and Addiction

As the estimated 119 million people in the United States who ingest alcohol at least once each year can attest alcohol is a popular recreational chemical (Office of National Drug Control Policy, 2006). For most of these people alcohol will not become a problem in any sphere of their lives. However, between 8 and 16 million persons in the United States do become physically dependent on alcohol, whereas another 5.6 million are believed to abuse it on a regular basis (Bankole & Alt-Daoud, 2005). This may underestimate the total number of persons with an alcohol use disorder, since many high-functioning persons with an AUD are able to successfully hide this fact from friends, family, and coworkers, possibly for decades (Benton, 2009).

For the average person alcohol might represent a pleasant diversion from the stress of daily living; however, a minority of those who drink consume a disproportionate amount of the alcohol produced. Ten percent of drinkers consume 60% of the alcohol consumed in the United States, whereas the top 30% of drinkers consume 90% of the alcohol consumed in this country (Kilbourne, 2002). If their drinking has resulted in their suffering social, physical, emotional, or vocational

---

[6]These different estimates reflect the different methodologies used in different research studies.

[7]See Glossary.

[8]However, it is important to keep in mind that even those who are merely curious about the effects of an illicit drug(s) run the risk of becoming addicted.

consequences[9] then they are said to have an AUD. The majority of those in the United States who do develop an AUD are male by a ratio of approximately 2–3 men to every woman (Kranzler & Ciraulo, 2005a). These figures underscore the danger of alcohol use and abuse in spite of its legal status as a socially acceptable recreational compound for adults.

Estimates of the Problem of Opiate Abuse and Addiction[10]

When many people in the United States hear the term *narcotics* they immediately think of heroin, a drug that does indeed account for 71% of the opiate use disorders around the world (United Nations, 2012). Globally, it has been estimated that 15.6 million people either abuse, or are addicted to, heroin (United Nations, 2012). In the United States current estimates suggest that approximately 3 million people have abused heroin at some point in their lives and that there are between 810,000 and 1 million people currently dependent on it (Jaffe & Strain, 2005). The states with the largest numbers of opioid abusers are thought to be California, New York, Massachusetts, and New Jersey, although heroin use disorders are found in every state of the union (Jaffe & Strain, 2005), with a male to female ratio of 4 to 1 (Krambeer, von McKnelly, Gabrielli, & Penick, 2001).

Unfortunately, heroin is only one of a wide range of opioids that might be obtained and abused.[11] In the United States is a growing number of people who are addicted to prescription narcotic analgesics either prescribed for the user, or obtained from illicit sources. An estimated 33 million persons are thought to have used a narcotic analgesic not prescribed to them at some point in their lives, and 5 million are thought to have done so in just the past year. The problem of medication diversion is an ongoing one in the United States with the result that many opioid addicts support their opioid abuse almost exclusively on prescribed medications either obtained from a physician or obtained from illicit sources. Thus the estimate of 800,000 to 1 million heroin addicts *underestimates* the total number of people addicted to an opiate in this country by an unknown margin.

Estimates of the Problem of Stimulant Abuse and Addiction[12]

Globally, the problem of central nervous system (CNS) stimulant abuse[13] has apparently reached a plateau with approximately 25 million people around the world abusing a CNS stimulant at least once each year (United Nations, 2012). In North America,[14] the demand for the most potent of the CNS stimulants, the amphetamines (especially methamphetamine), has been stable, with about 3.8 million people in North America abusing these compounds at least once each year (United Nations, 2012). Much of the methamphetamine in the United States enters the country from other countries, although there are still local "labs" making small amounts of methamphetamine for local consumption. The media in the United States often focuses on local CNS stimulant use disorders; however, in reality only 15% of CNS stimulant abusers live in North America (United Nations, 2012). As is true for narcotic analgesics, an unknown percentage of prescribed CNS stimulants are diverted to the illicit market, providing a pool of unrecognized stimulant abusers/addicts who rely on these.

Estimates of the Problem of Cocaine Abuse and Addiction

The number of cocaine abusers/addicts has remained relatively stable around the globe over the past decade (United Nations, 2012). Globally, approximately 14 million people are cocaine abusers or addicts, the vast majority of whom are thought to live in North America[15] (United Nations, 2012). In the United States, it has been estimated that there are perhaps 2.5 million people who are addicted to cocaine, and an unknown number of people who have abused it at some point in their lives (Grinfeld, 2001). The true scope of cocaine abuse/addiction in the United States is confused by the fact that in spite of its reputation, researchers during the last wave of cocaine abuse in the

---

[9]The topic of determining whether a person has an AUD will be discussed later in this book.

[10]For the purpose of this text, the terms "opioid," "opiate," and "narcotic" will be used interchangeably, although, as will be discussed in Chapter 14, there are technical differences between these terms.

[11]The topic of opioid abuse and addiction is discussed in Chapter 14.

[12]This topic is discussed in more detail in Chapter 12.

[13]Which includes the abuse of methylphenidate and the various amphetamines.

[14]Which, as noted earlier in this chapter, includes both Canada and the United States.

[15]The United Nations defines "North America" as including both Canada and the United States.

United States concluded that only 3–20% of those who abused cocaine would go on to become addicted to it[16] (Musto, 1991).

Estimates of the Problem of Marijuana Use, Abuse, and Addiction

Globally, it is estimated that at least 160 million people have used marijuana in the past 12 months (United Nations, 2012). Just under 30 million people are thought to be current users of marijuana in North America[17] (United Nations, 2012). Approximately 25% of the entire population of the United States is thought to have abused marijuana at least once, and of this number 3 million people are thought to be addicted to it (Grinfeld, 2001).[18]

Estimates of the Problem of Hallucinogen Abuse[19]

Many researchers question whether it is possible to become *addicted* to hallucinogens. But it is thought that perhaps 10% of the population of the United States has abused hallucinogen at least once in their lives (Sadock & Sadock, 2007). It is estimated that 1.1 million persons in the United States have abused a hallucinogenic compound in the past month (Substance Abuse and Mental Health Services Administration, 2009).

Estimates of the Problem of Tobacco Abuse and Addiction

Tobacco is a special product: It might be legally purchased by adults, yet is acknowledged to be destructive and addictive. Unfortunately, tobacco products are easily available to adolescents, and in some cases to children. Researchers estimate that approximately 20.8% of the entire population of the United States are current cigarette smokers, 25% are former smokers, and 50% have never smoked (Hays et al., 2011; Sadock & Sadock, 2007).

The Cost of Chemical Abuse/Addiction

Globally, the drug use disorders are the sixth leading cause of disease in adults (Leamon et al., 2008). Illicit drug use is thought to cost the global economy $880 billion/year, with the AUDs costing the world economy another $880 billion/year (Vital Signs, 2007). In the United States, the alcohol and drug use disorders are thought to drain at least $375 billion/year from the economy (Falco, 2005). The annual toll from the various diseases associated with illicit drug use in the United States, combined with the number of drug related infant deaths, suicides, homicides, and motor vehicle accidents, is estimated to be approximately 12,000–17,000 people a year (Donovan, 2005; Miller & Brady, 2004; Mokdad, Marks, Stroup, & Gerberding, 2004).

All of the estimates cited in the last paragraph are in addition to the 440,000 persons who are thought to die each year from smoking-related illness brought on by their own tobacco use, and the additional 35,000 to 56,000 persons each year in the United States who are thought to lose their lives to illness brought on by exposure to "secondhand" or "environmental" tobacco smoke (Benson & Sacco, 2000; Bialous & Sarna, 2004; Mokdad et al., 2004). Further, approximately 100,000 people die each year in the United States as a direct result of their alcohol use (Niami et al., 2003; Small, 2002). Notice that the last sentence stated "as a *direct* result" of the individual's alcohol use. The alcohol use disorders contribute to or exacerbate 60 different disorders (Room, Babor, & Rehm, 2005). A person might die from one of the disease states exacerbated by their drinking, but the disease state will be identified on the death certificate as the primary cause of death, not their alcohol abuse. If one were to include these "indirect" alcohol-related deaths, it becomes clear that alcohol either directly or indirectly causes as many deaths each year in the United States as do tobacco products (Room et al., 2005).

---

[16]The danger, as will be discussed again in Chapter 12, is that it is impossible to predict at this time *which* individual will go on to become addicted to cocaine, and thus the use of this compound is discouraged, if only for this reason. Other dangers associated with cocaine use/abuse/addiction will be discussed in Chapter 12.

[17]Remember, again, that this includes *both* the United States and Canada.

[18]Although most people do not think of marijuana as a potentially addictive substance, as will be discussed in Chapter 13, some abusers do indeed become addicted to it.

[19]This is a difficult subject to discuss in depth since some researchers classify MDMA as a hallucinogen, others classify it as an amphetamine, and still others call it an hallucinogenic amphetamine compound. For the sake of this text it will be classified as a hallucinogen. See Chapter 15 for more details on this issue.

The Cost of Alcohol Use/Abuse/Addiction

Globally, alcohol use is thought to be a direct factor in 10–11% of all deaths each year (Stevenson & Sommers, 2005). In the United States, alcohol dependence ranks third as the most common cause of preventable death (Johnson, 2010). The annual economic impact of alcohol use/abuse/addiction in the United States is thought to be at least $185 billion/year, of which $26 billion is for direct health care costs, and $37 billion as a result of lost productivity brought on by alcohol-related premature death (Belenko, Patapis, & French, 2005; Gilpin & Kolb, 2008; Petrakis, Gonzalez, Rosenheck, & Krystal, 2002; Smothers, Yahr, & Ruhl, 2004). To state this data in other, more personal terms, the alcohol use disorders cost every man, woman, and child in the United States $638 per year (Grant et al., 2006).

It has been estimated that the complications brought on by alcohol use account for 15–25% of the annual total expenditure for health care each year in the United States (Anton, 2005; Swift, 2005). Although only 5–10% of the population in this country has an AUD, they consume a disproportionate amount of the yearly health care expenditure in the United States as evidenced by the fact that between 15 and 30% of those individuals in nursing homes are thought to be there either as a direct or indirect result of their AUD (Schuckit, 2006a). Alcohol abuse is also a factor in numerous motor vehicle accidents, which collectively cost the U.S. economy an estimated $24.7 billion/year (Craig, 2004). Alcohol is thought to be involved in approximately 40% of all motor vehicle accidents and 40–60% of all traumatic injury cases involve patients with an SUD (Craig, 2004; Savage, Kirsh, & Passik, 2008).

The Cost of the Tobacco Use Disorders

Although it is legally produced, purchased, and used by adults without restriction, tobacco use extracts a terrible toll around the globe. Globally, more than 3 million people/year die around the world as a direct result of their use of tobacco products, of whom about 442,000 live in the United States (Hays et al., 2011). The annual economic losses from in just the United States alone amounts to $157 billion/year (Hays et al., 2011). One in every five deaths in this country can be directly traced to smoking-related illness (Sadock & Sadock, 2007). This figure does not include those persons who die as a result of exposure to "secondhand" or "environmental" tobacco smoke each year in this country.

The Cost of the Substance Use Disorders

It has been calculated that when one totals the cost of premature death and illness, lost wages, financial losses by victims of substance-related crime, who were hurt by others combined with the cost of law enforcement activities directly aimed at the problem of SUDs, illicit substance use costs at least $900 for every person 18 years or older in the United States each year (Heyman, 2009). When the cost of disability, accidental injuries, health care, and absenteeism from work are added together, the total economic impact of SUDs on the U.S. economy each year is estimated to be $428 billion (Gonzalez, Vasisileva, & Scott, 2009).

The health care problem has received much publicity in recent years, although the role of SUDs in this problem has received surprisingly little media attention. The negative impact of SUDs on health care was illustrated by the team of Santora and Hutton (2008) who concluded that hospitalized alcohol abusers had average hospital care expenses that were 120% higher than for the person who was not an abuser, and that opioid abusers who are hospitalized require health care expenditures that are 482% higher than for nonabusers. As will be discussed in the next section, society's response to this crisis has arguably been haphazard, piecemeal, and frequently inadequate.

Who Treats Persons with an SUD?

Having established that SUDs are a legitimate problem we are left with the question: Who treats those people with such disorders? The various state governments spend only four cents of every dollar on programs devoted to the prevention and treatment of persons with an SUD (Grinfeld, 2001). Health care professionals in general are woefully ill-prepared to work with substance abusers. Although between 15 and 30% of patients seen by the typical primary care physician have an SUD, most physicians are still undertrained (or not trained) to recognize substance abusers (O'Connor, Nyquist, & McCellan, 2011). Less than one-fifth of the physicians surveyed reported that they thought that they were trained to treat patients with the most common form of SUDs, AUDs, whereas less than 17% thought that their training was sufficient to enable them to work with patients with other forms of SUDs (Clay, Allen, & Parran, 2008).

Further, most physicians emerge from graduate training with a negative attitude toward individuals with an SUD (Renner, 2004a). Possibly as a result of this deficit in their training and their preconceptions about persons with an SUD, fewer than one-third of physicians carefully screen for SUDs among their patients (Greenfield & Hennessy, 2008b). Less than 50% of patients who go to see a physician about alcohol-related problems are even *asked* about their alcohol or drug use by their physician (Pagano, Graham, Frost-Pineda, & Gold, 2005). This failure to inquire about a patient's substance use habits might be a major reason why SUDs are both under-diagnosed and under-treated (Clay et al., 2008; Greenfield & Hennessy, 2008a, 2008b). This conclusion is supported by the observation that less than 1% of internal medicine and family practice physicians, and only 5.1% of psychiatric consultations result in an accurate diagnosis of an SUD when it is present (Banta & Montgomery, 2007).

Physicians are taught that the addictions are chronic, treatable disorders, yet "more often than not [will] view the addicted patient as challenging at best and not worthy of customary compassion" (Brown, 2006, p. 5). Physician postgraduate educational programs do attempt to address this problem; however, the average length of such training in the addictions is only about 8 hours (Renner, 2004a). Nor is this professional blindness limited to physicians. Although nursing professionals frequently have more contact with patients than do physicians, "the majority of nursing schools … required only 1 to 5 clock hours of instruction on alcohol and drug abuse content during their entire undergraduate curricula" (Stevenson & Sommers, 2005, p. 15). Thus those health professionals who will have the most contact with the patient, the nursing staff, are as ill-prepared to work with patients with SUDs as is the average physician.

Marriage and family therapists are another group of health care professionals that, as a whole, are ill prepared to recognize much less deal with SUDs. Such problems are rarely identified, vital clues to the nature of the disorder within the family are missed, and therapy might be rendered ineffective. If these disorders are identified, they are usually addressed by a referral to another therapist of another discipline by the marriage or family therapist. This interrupts the continuity of care and therapy is often carried out in a haphazard manner with little communications between treatment professionals. Further, if there is a dual diagnosis situation (substance abuse with co-occurring mental illness) there is a definite need for family therapy, although this is rarely initiated (Minkoff, 2008).

In spite of the obvious relationship between SUDs and various forms of psychopathology, "most clinical psychologists are not well prepared to deal with issues involving substance use or abuse" (Sobell & Sobell, 2007, p. 2). Seventy-four percent of psychologists surveyed admitted that they had no formal training in the identification or treatment of the addictions, and rated their graduate school training in this area as being inadequate (Aanavi, Taube, Ja, & Duran, 2000). Only professional substance abuse counselors are required to have a high level of professional training in the recognition and treatment of SUDs, with national standards for individuals working in this field having recently been established. Because such counselors make up only a minority of those in the health care industry, the most common response to the question of who treats those individuals who are addicted to alcohol or drugs is all too often "nobody."

Chapter Summary

The problem of excessive alcohol use, and illicit drug, has plagued society for generations. Solutions to the problem of SUDs that have proven inadequate include banishment, execution, castration, incarceration, religious intervention, and various forms of treatment. The United States, with a minority of the world's population, is the largest consumer of illicit drugs, which drains an estimated $428 billion from the economy each year. Alcohol use disorders drain an additional $400 billion/year from the U.S. economy, yet society's response to the problem of SUDs has been poor at best, if virtually entirely ineffective.

CHAPTER 2

The Nature of the Beast
(Being an Examination of the Problem of SUDs)

Introduction

There are multiple perspectives on substance use disorders (SUDs) in the United States. Biologists have documented episodes where at least some mammals appear to intentionally seek out compounds such as fermented fruits or mushrooms that can alter that creature's perceptions of the world. Such episodes have been captured on film, and many are available for viewing as public entertainment over the "Internet." Domestic cat owners have supplied their pets with "cat nip," often doing so on a regular basis much to the delight of their four-legged family members. It would appear that we share the desire to chemically alter our perception of the world with our mammal cousins.

The American Society of Addiction Medicine (ASAM) has suggested a model of SUDs that integrates the biological, psychological, and sociological theories of the addictions into one unified model.[1] This model attempts to address the various forces that exacerbate or inhibit the individual's substance use behaviors, and although it is not the grand unified theory (GUT) of addictions that has long been sought, it is a major step in the formulation of a GUT. However, until this GUT is advanced, we are left with the question: What are SUDs, and why are they a problem?

Why Do People Choose to Use Drugs or Alcohol?

There are many answers to this question because substance abstinence/use/abuse is a common endpoint of the various forces that help to shape that individual's life and decisions. An individual might choose to initiate substance use for a variety of reasons. The individual might use chemicals to express a previously forbidden impulse, cope with emotional or physical pain, explore alternative realities, substitute a substance-induced feeling of euphoria for the less mundane reality in which they live, as a way to escape from the pain of their social status, or as a sign of rebellion, just to mention a few of the reasons why a person might initiate substance use (Rasmussen, 2008). Why they continue to use alcohol or drugs is possibly quite different and the reason(s) for the continuation of substance use should be explored on a case-by-case basis.

Our hedonistic society would seem to encourage at least the explorational use of the drugs of abuse which have become so pervasive in our culture that every one of us must make a conscious choice every day to

---

[1]Discussed in Chapter 25.

use/not use a recreational chemical(s).[2] A possible reflection of this decision making process is seen in Figure 2-1. Admittedly, for most of us this decision is so automatic that it does not even require conscious thought. However the decision to initiate substance use is influenced by a wide range of factors including:

Blindness to the Compound's Effects: Unfortunately, one side effect of alcohol, the drugs of abuse, and some prescription medications is substance-induced "blindness," for want of a better term. The person will report that they *feel* better, when an objective observer would say that they have actually decompensated in terms of their interpersonal behaviors, ability to handle finances, ability to maintain cognitive function, and attend to the necessary activities of daily living (Breggin, 2008). Many abusers of narcotic analgesics are wrongfully told that they cannot become addicted to a substance that they simply "snort," and they believe this myth in spite of the libraries of data that argues the exact opposite. Often, the price for this ignorance is the development of a physical addiction to what was once a recreational substance.

Pharmacological Reward Potential: The reward potential of a compound depends upon its chemical structure, the individual's biochemistry, and the route of administration (Budney et al., 2003; O'Brien, 2006). Those compounds that have a rapid onset of action or *immediacy of effect* (Kalivas, 2003) and that induce a greater sense of pleasure have the highest reward potential for abuse (O'Brien, 2011).

The basic laws of behavioral psychology hold that if something (a) increases the individual's sense of pleasure, or (b) decreases his/her discomfort, then s/he is likely to repeat the behavior (in this case using alcohol or a drug). In contrast, if a compound were to (c) increase the individual's sense of discomfort, or, (d) reduce the individual's sense of pleasure, s/he would be less likely to repeat that behavior. Arguably, although the reward potential of the drugs of abuse might be a powerful incentive for repeated use, it is not sufficient in itself to induce addiction to that compound (Kalivas, 2003).

Social Learning: The role of social learning is a form of psychological learning that is discussed in Chapter 25. It is mentioned here because social learning is involved in the development of the individual's expectations for each potential recreational substance.

Individual Expectations: Substance use expectations begin to evolve in childhood or early adolescence, and evolve over time as a result of such influences as peer groups, childhood exposure to advertising, parental substance use behaviors, and past experiences (Monti, Kadden, Rohsenow, Cooney, & Abrams, 2002; Sher, Wood, Richardson, & Jackson, 2005). The individual's expectations for a substance are also strongly influenced by the context and cultural traditions in which s/he uses that chemical (Lindman, Sjoholm, & Lang, 2000; Sher et al., 2005). The topic of how individual expectations about the effects of a substance overlap the topic of learning theory is discussed in more detail in Chapter 25.

Cultural/Social Influences: Each individual lives in a cultural matrix that both helps shape his or her behavior and is affirmed by that person's adherence to those norms. The topic of the social/cultural factors that influence substance use behaviors will be discussed in more detail in Chapter 25.

Legal Sanctions: In today's society the job of enforcing social rules is often carried out by the judicial system. If the individual should elect to use a drug(s) whose use is not approved of by society or a drug that is socially accepted, in an unacceptable manner,[3] the legal system steps in to punish this unacceptable behavior (Szasz, 2009). However, the perspective of SUDs as reflecting a "disease" state as advocated by the health care establishment is often at conflict with that of the legal system, which adheres to the premise that the individual must be held accountable for his or her socially inappropriate behaviors deemed unacceptable to the parent society, including the use of chemicals. This topic will be explored further in Chapter 25.

---

[2]In response to those of you who wish to argue this past point, consider the following: Where is the nearest liquor store, or bar? If you wanted to do so, would you know where to buy some marijuana? If you did not know, would you know the name of a person to ask who would know? Are there certain people that you know of (co-workers, friends, and others) whose company you avoid because you do not approve of their substance use? You see: We are not so removed from the problem of recreational drug use as we would like to believe, are we?

[3]Even in this category, there are contradictions. For example, the recreational use of a narcotic is illegal, and a matter for the courts to handle. However, if the person were to have a valid prescription from a physician, s/he now becomes a "patient" for whom the use of the same compound is sanctioned.

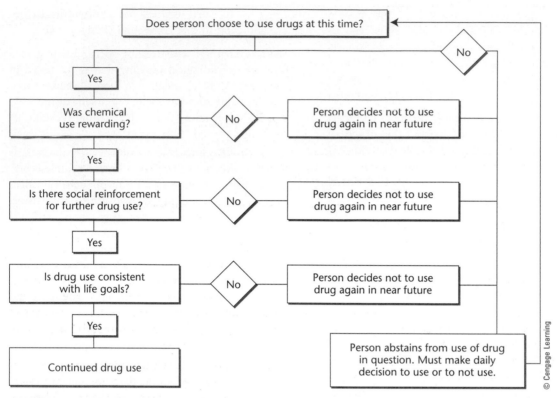

FIGURE 2-1 The Chemical Use Decision-Making Process.

Drug Abuse Cycles

Bennett and Golub (2012) suggested that the abuse of various compounds pass through several phases analogous to those seen in epidemics of infectious diseases: (1) *Incubation:* The abuse of a certain compound is infrequent within society, although it might be more popular with certain subgroups. Examples might be found in how marijuana was mainly limited to small segments of society (rebels, nonconformists, some musicians, and others.) before the 1960s when it entered the second stage: (2) *Expansion:* The abuse of that compound is more tolerated and a growing number of people try it at least once. Some of these users will continue to abuse that compound on an irregular basis, or go on to abuse that compound on a regular basis. During Stage 3, the abuse of that compound reaches a *plateau,* with many former users choosing to discontinue the use of that compound at about the same rate that others initiate the use of that compound. Finally (4), the cycle reaches the stage of *decline,* in which the number of people initiating or continuing the abuse of that compound declines. This is not to say that the abuse of the compound in question disappears entirely: There is always a small number of abusers who continue to use that compound, bringing the abuse cycle back to stage one—incubation. This pattern has been seen with virtually every drug of abuse.

The Continuum of Chemical Use

Not surprisingly, people often confuse the terms *substance use, abuse,* and *addiction.* Unfortunately these terms are often used synonymously even in clinical research studies (Minkoff, 1997). In reality, substance use is considered a normal learned behavior that falls on a continuum ranging from abstinence through limited use to excessive use and dependence (Budney et al., 2003, p. 249). Willenbring (2010) suggested that alcohol users fell into one of three categories, which formed a continuum: (a) normal drinkers (who never exceed the guidelines used to define normal drinking), (b) "at-risk" drinkers (persons who exceed the guidelines but who currently do not have symptoms of alcoholism and have never met the diagnostic criteria for this condition), and (c) persons who meet the criteria for an alcohol use disorder (AUD). Although useful,

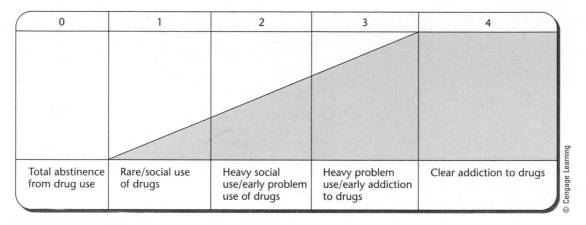

0	1	2	3	4
Total abstinence from drug use	Rare/social use of drugs	Heavy social use/early problem use of drugs	Heavy problem use/early addiction to drugs	Clear addiction to drugs

© Cengage Learning

FIGURE 2-2 The Continuum of Recreational Chemical Use.

this continuum fails to include those persons who never drink or use illicit drugs or whether a person might outgrow an SUD.

Substance use disorders are not static entities, but evolve over time. Movement up or down the spectrum is possible as the individual's substance use becomes more or less problematic. For this text, we will use the continuum shown in Figure 2-2, on which to examine substance use.

Admittedly this continuum is an artificial construct. There are few clear demarcations between one stage and the next, and it should not be assumed that a substance user will automatically move from one stage to the next (Brust, 2004; Washton & Zweben, 2006). Still, for the sake of this text, the various stages are defined as follows:

Level 0: ***Total abstinence*** from all recreational chemicals

Level 1: ***Rare to social use*** of recreational chemicals (Note: This might include the limited experimental use of a drug that is technically illegal, such as alcohol or tobacco for an adolescent or marijuana for a young adult.)

Level 2: ***Heavy social use/early problem use:*** Although the majority of substance abusers moderate or control their abuse of chemicals (Bennett & Golub, 2012), some users/abusers fall into a pattern of substance abuse that is clearly above the social norm. Such individuals might experience limited legal, social, vocational, or medical consequences caused by his/her substance abuse.[4]

Level 3: ***Late problem use/Early addiction:*** Individuals in this category may be physically dependent on a compound(s), and possibly also experience the classic withdrawal syndrome for the compound(s) being abused if they should abruptly stop using alcohol or drug(s) of choice.[5]

Level 4: ***Middle to Late Stage addiction:*** *Individuals whose substance* use would fall in this category demonstrate all of the classic signs of addiction: physical, medical, legal, occupational, and/or personal problems, as well as a possible physical dependency on alcohol/drugs.

One frequently encountered source of confusion when discussing SUDs is whether the individual is *actively* abusing a chemical, or if they have a *history* of abusing a chemical (Heyman, 2009). This dilemma is illustrated by the fact that up to 72% of those persons who develop alcohol dependence will remain dependent on it for 3–4 years then they discontinue, or at least significantly reduce, their alcohol use (Heyman, 2009; Tucker & Simpson, 2011; Willenbring, 2010). The individual's placement on the continuum outlined above will vary significantly whether you are discussing *lifetime* substance use patterns as opposed to *current* use patterns. The college student who at the age of 20 would meet established diagnostic criteria for an AUD might, a decade later, only be a rare social drinker now that they have work obligations, possibly

---

[4]This does not automatically mean that the individual is *addicted* to that compound, only that their substance use pattern is beyond the norm and is causing social problems.

[5]The claim "I can stop any time that I want to!" might be a motto for individuals whose substance use falls in this category.

a family, and most certainly, bills to pay.[6] This student could possibly fall into the self-limiting form of alcoholism identified by Willenbring (2010) rather than a more severe and chronic form of alcoholism. The element of *time* must be considered when assessing the individual's substance use pattern.

What Do We Mean When We Say That Somebody Is "Addicted" to a Chemical?

There is a wide discrepancy between how the average citizen defines *addiction* and what health care professionals mean when they use the same word (Szalavitz, 2010). Physical dependence on a substance is one of the traditionally accepted signs of addiction (O'Brien, 2011). However, beyond this there are no universally accepted definitions of the terms *problematic use, abuse,* or *addiction* (Wunsch, Boyd, & McMasters, 2009) and the definition of terms such as *substance abuse* or *addiction* are quite arbitrary (O'Brien, 2006). Medical professionals use a list of standardized diagnostic criteria, such as those outlined by the American Psychiatric Association's (2013) *Diagnostic and Statistical Manual of Mental Disorders*, 5th edition (or *DSM-5*) to assist them in making the determination whether a given individual does/does not have an SUD. The specific criteria identified in *DSM-5* can be grouped into four general categories (American Psychiatric Association, 2013):[7]

1. Impaired control over substance use
2. Multiple attempts to quit or desire to quit/reduce substance use
3. Most of individual's activities center around (a) obtaining the substance, (b) using the substance, or (c) recovering from the effects of the substance. This includes social, vocational, and legal consequences of substance use or using a substance(s) under "risky" (p. 483) conditions.
4. Pharmacological effects of the drug(s) on the individual, including "craving" for the substance when it is not actively being used.

---

[6]College loans leap to mind here, although other financial obligations might include a mortgage on a house, car loans, home remodeling costs, and so on.

[7]The reader is advised to consult the *DSM-5* for a full list of diagnostic criteria.

The reader referred to the *DSM-5* manual for more information about the specific diagnostic criteria for each drug of abuse. Shaffer's (2001) criteria for the diagnosis of an SUD offer an alternative to the *DSM-5* system, while the *International Statistical Classification of Diseases and Related Health Problems*, 10th edition (*ICD-10*) (World Health Organization, 1990) *offers an even more comprehensive diagnostic system than the DSM-5.* Both diagnostic systems share certain common elements: (1) the view that it is a primary disease, (2) that it has multiple manifestations in the person's life, including the social, psychological, spiritual, vocational, interpersonal, and economic spheres of their lives, (3) it is often progressive, (4) it is potentially fatal, (5) it is marked by the individual's inability to control (or, at least inconsistent control) of their substance use, (6) is marked by preoccupation with drug use, (7) the individual develops a distorted way of looking at the world so that it supports his/her continued use of that compound(s), (8) the individual becomes tolerant to the effects of that compound(s), and s/he either must go through "drug holidays" in which s/he loses some of the tolerance to that substance, or must use larger and larger amounts in a manner designed to overcome his/her tolerance, and finally, (9) that the individual will experience a characteristic withdrawal syndrome if s/he should discontinue the use of that compound(s).

Definitions of Terms Used in This Text

At this point it is necessary to establish a common language so that we are "all on the same page." Thus, for the sake of this text the following definitions will be used:

> ***Social Use:*** A point of confusion is that use of a substance is equated with an SUD, especially when the person is abusing illicit drugs. However, "being a substance user does not mean invariably that one has a substance use disorder" (Gonzalez, Vasisileva, & Scott, 2009, p. 456). The individual's culture defines what is the frequency with and conditions under which an individual might use a substance(s). Currently alcohol and tobacco are the only products that might legally be used in certain social settings,[8] although marijuana use is arguably also a "social" compound in certain social groups.

---

[8]An excellent example of how cultural norms are governing substance use.

Substance Abuse: is the term that is used when an individual uses a compound when there is no legitimate medical need to do so, or, when that compound is used in excess of the social standards (Schuckit, 2006a, 2006b). There is no physical dependence on the chemical(s) in question at this time, and it does not automatically progress to physical addiction of that compound (Swift, 2005).

Dependence: is said to exist when the individual meets the criteria for alcohol or drug dependence, as discussed in the *Diagnostic and Statistical Manual of Mental Disorders*, 5th edition.

Drug of Choice: Clinicians once spoke about the individual's *drug of choice* as an important component of the disease of addiction. Indeed, this was the reason on which Narcotics Anonymous was founded: Early drug addicts who attempted to join Alcoholics Anonymous (AA) in the 1950s and 1960s were told that they could only talk about their AUD at meetings because AA was not intended to address drug addiction, only alcoholism. With the growth of polydrug[9] disorders the concept of *drug of choice* has fallen into disfavor and few clinicians now place emphasis on this concept. Zuckerman (2012) suggested that the individual's search for novel sensations is the strongest predictor of the number of drugs a person abuses. However, the *availability* of alcohol and the various drugs of abuse also shape the individual's substance use pattern.

Loss of Control: is a poorly defined term. In essence the person cannot accurately predict in advance how much alcohol or drug(s) they will use on any given occasion might be said to have lost control over their substance use. An example might be the person who intended to have "just one or two drinks" with friends only to drink to the point of gross intoxication within hours could be said to have demonstrated a loss of control over his alcohol use.

Addiction/Dependence: These are poorly defined terms. Most clinicians now prefer the term *dependence* to a chemical, although a large number of health care professionals still use the older term *addiction* (Shaffer, 2001). Dependence is marked by the development of a characteristic *withdrawal syndrome* for compound(s) being abused that have not been prescribed. If the drug was prescribed by a physician for the treatment of a disease state the same process is called *neuroadaption*. This process will be discussed in more detail in the next chapter.

Tolerance: to a drug(s) of abuse is said to develop when the individual must use more of a compound(s) to achieve the effects once achieved at a lower dose. Some of the more significant subforms of tolerance will be discussed in more detail in the next chapter.

Withdrawal Syndrome: is a phenomenon experienced when the individual either stops, or significantly reduces, his or her intake of a specific compound(s). The withdrawal syndrome is usually the opposite of the compound's effects on the user's body. Thus, for example, alcohol acts like a chemical "brake" on the neurons of the brain. The neuron struggle to compensate, increasing the number of neurotransmitter receptor sites for excitatory neurotransmitters to overcome the inhibitory effects of the persistent alcohol use. When the alcohol-dependent individual stops drinking, this "brake" is removed, and neurons in the brain might become overactive. This is experienced by the heavy drinker as anxiety, withdrawal tremors, and in extreme cases the delirium tremens (DTs), all of which are discussed in more detail in Chapter 6.

The world of the addictions is replete with a range of other terms, which serve as a form of professional shorthand for individuals who work in the field, but the above terms should serve as a solid formation on which the reader can begin to understand the world of SUDs.

Behavioral "Addictions"

For the last quarter of the 20th century a fierce debate raged over the question of whether conditions such as sex, food, men, women, play, shopping, shoplifting, carbohydrates, unhappy relationships, french fries, compulsive use of lip balm, credit cards, and a range of other behaviors could be said to be an addiction (Barber, 2008; Jaffe & Anthony, 2005). There is little physical evidence at this time that non-drug-centered behaviors can result in a physical addiction, and clinicians are increasingly classifying these behaviors as "behavioral addictions" or compulsive behaviors as opposed to substance abuse or dependence (Fong, Reid, & Parhami, 2012). These behavioral addictions will not be discussed further in this text.

---

[9]Or "multi-substance" use issues.

Unanswered Questions

If you were a devotee of the television "talk" shows, or read a small sample of the self-help books that line the bookstore shelves, you would easily be left with the impression that researchers have discovered all that there is to be known about the cause(s) of and the treatment(s) for SUDs. Unfortunately, *nothing could be further from the truth!* Much of what is "known" about SUDs is based upon mistaken assumptions, distorted data, clinical myth, theory, or, in many cases, incomplete data. To illustrate one source of confusion few research studies identify the difference between the *lifetime* prevalence and the *period prevalence,* which is to say whether the individual has abused a compound in a specified period of time (Brook, Pahl, & Rubenstone, 2008). In many research studies both groups are lumped together as if they were a uniform group of substance abusers.

The difference between these two terms is seen in the fact that at some point in their adult lives 30–45% of all adults will demonstrate at least one sign of an AUD (alcohol-related "blackout," legal problem, and so on). This does not mean that 30–45% of the adult population of this country is or will become alcohol-dependent! Most people either use alcohol socially or, upon encountering a sign of a serious AUD, abstain from further use. Neither clinical researchers nor substance abuse rehabilitation professionals know how to identify the individual who will go on to develop an AUD[10] from the one who will experience a transient substance use problem in spite of their public displays of confidence.

An inconvenient truth is that there are serious questions that face researchers in the field of the addictions:

1. Are those individuals who seek treatment the same as those who do not?
2. Are those individuals who are "chippers" different in some poorly understood way from those individuals who go on to become physically dependent on a drug or alcohol?
3. Is research carried out on those individuals who seek treatment through the Veterans Administration Hospital system applicable to the general population?
4. How do men and women who have SUDs differ? Do the same treatment techniques work or each subgroup?
5. Are those substance abusers who hold full-time employment the same as, or different from those substance abusers who do not hold full-time jobs, and are individuals in either group the same as or different from those who are unemployed?
6. Are those persons who limit their substance use to alcohol the same as those who are poly-drug abusers or addicts?
7. It is known that the individual's motivation for substance abuse varies as a result of his or her age and past substance use history. How do these variables affect the processes of intervention and rehabilitation?
8. What is the contribution of the individual's genetic heritage to the development of an SUD, and how is this genetic heritage modified by environmental forces?

It is difficult to answer these or a host of other questions about SUDs because there is a dearth of appropriate research into SUDs. Much of the existing literature addresses only the AUDs, and thus is of limited value to clinicians in the field: For example, are the research findings from a study that focused on persons with only an AUD applicable to individuals with an AUD who also abuse narcotics or central nervous system stimulants? Are the same forces at work for men with an SUD the same as those for women with an SUD? For many years it was assumed that research data drawn from studies on men with an AUD automatically applied to women and adolescents, assumptions that are now being questioned.[11] The question of how age influences the trajectory of an SUD is only now being explored by researchers, leaving clinicians struggling to find appropriate treatment methods for older clients.

Unfortunately, we are learning that much of what we thought that we know about SUDs was not based on scientific research, but on assumptions, guesses, clinical myths, and limited data. However, it is on this foundation that an entire rehabilitation "industry" has been based. It is not this text to deny that SUDs

---

[10]The alcohol use disorders (AUDs) are a subset of SUDs. When the discussion is limited only to alcohol, the terms *alcohol use disorders* or *AUDs* will be used. When the topic is limited to cocaine abuse or addiction, the term *cocaine use disorders* will be used, and so on.

[11]See Chapter 18.

cause a terrible cost in individual suffering and to society, but hopefully the reader has started to understand how little is really known about SUDs.

Chapter Summary

In the end, the "nature of the beast" remains elusive and unclear. Only the foundations of understanding have been established, as reflected by the basic concepts used by researchers and clinicians who work in the field of substance abuse rehabilitation discussed in this chapter. Although many persons view SUDs in a black-and-white condition (either the person is addicted or not) the fact that a person's substance use behavior exists on a continuum and that their place on that continuum might change over time was discussed. This chapter also established the parameters of terms such as *substance use, abuse,* and *addiction, as* used in this text to establish a common language so rarely encountered in the clinical literature. The more pertinent elements of the American Psychiatric Association's (2013) *Diagnostic and Statistical Manual for Mental Disorders*, 5th edition, were reviewed, and the fact that it is barely compatible with the more widely used and comprehensive *International Statistical Classification of Diseases and Related Health Problems*, 10th edition (*ICD-10*) (World Health Organization, 1990) was discussed. Some of the pharmacological and social forces that contribute to the development of an SUD were introduced, and will be discussed in more detail in later chapters. Finally some of the unanswered questions facing mental health professionals in their quest to better understand SUDs were reviewed.

CHAPTER 3

A Brief Introduction to the Science of Pharmacology[1]

Introduction

It is virtually impossible to discuss the effects of the various drugs of abuse without touching on a number of basic pharmacological concepts. Although a complete understanding of the science of pharmacology can take years to attain, in this chapter we will discuss the impact that the different drugs of abuse might have on the user's body, and the pharmacological principles by which these effects take place.

A Basic Misconception

It is surprising how often people discuss the drugs of abuse as if they were somehow a special class of chemicals that are unique. In reality, most of the drugs of abuse were pharmaceutical agents in the past, and of those that were not actual pharmaceuticals, many were investigated as possible medications. Thus, they work in the same manner that the other pharmaceuticals do: by changing the biological function of target cells through chemical actions. As is true for most of the pharmaceuticals in use today, the drugs of abuse strengthen/weaken a potential that already exists within the body. In the case of the drugs of abuse, the target cells are usually in the central nervous system.

The Prime Effect and Side Effect of Chemicals

It is often surprising for students to learn that it is virtually impossible to develop a mind-altering drug without unwanted side effects. Because the brain is so highly integrated, it is not possible to circumscribe mental function without impairing a variety of other functions, typically causing generalized dysfunction of the brain and mind (Breggin, 2008, p. 2). Thus, in order to achieve the *prime effect*[2] of a compound, the user must endure the *side effects*[3] of that compound as well. Some of the side effects will be relatively minor, whereas others might be life threatening. This rule is true for both pharmaceutical agents prescribed by a physician for a patient, and for the drugs of abuse.

For example, a person might ingest a dose of aspirin to help them cope with the pain of a minor injury. However, aspirin also has an anticoagulant side effect, inhibiting the body's ability to form blood clots if necessary.[4] This anticoagulant effect increases the individual's risk for excessive bleeding either at the site of the original injury or at the site of a second injury in the unlucky victim. Another example of the difference

---

[1]This chapter is designed to provide the reader with a brief overview of some of the more important principles of pharmacology. It is not intended to serve as, nor should it be used for, a guide to patient care.

[2]See Glossary.

[3]See Glossary.

[4]This anticoagulant effect makes aspirin of value in preventing the formation of blood clots that might eventually cause a heart attack or stroke, and for breaking up blood clots that have already blocked key blood vessels in the heart.

between the primary and side effects of a medication is seen in a person who is prescribed an antibiotic such as amoxicillin, who has developed a bacterial infection in the middle ear (a condition known as *otitis media*). The desired effect is the elimination of the offending bacteria from the middle ear, but an unwanted side effect might also be the death of bacteria in the gastrointestinal tract where those bacterial strains assist in the process of digestion. Thus, for each chemical there are the desired *primary effects* and unwanted *side effects,* or what are also known as *secondary effects,* of every compound. The side effects can range in intensity from making the patient mildly uncomfortable, to life threatening.

The Method by Which a Compound Is Administered

One factor that influences the intensity of the drug's primary and side effects is the manner in which it is administered. The specific *form* in which a compound is administered will have a major impact on (a) the speed with which that compound begins to have an effect on the body, (b) the way that the compound is distributed throughout the body, (c) the intensity of its effects, and (d) the speed with which the individual will begin to experience any side effects from that compound. Kamienski and Keogy (2006) identified 13 different ways that a compound could be introduced into the body. Fortunately, drugs of abuse are administered either by the *enteral* or the *parenteral* route.

Enteral Forms of Drug Administration

Compounds administered by the enteral route enter the body by the gastrointestinal tract (Brody, 1994). Such compounds are usually administered in oral forms (Jenkins, 2007; Williams & Baer, 1994). The most common of enteral drug administration is in a tablet form, which is essentially a selected dose of a compound mixed with a binding agent that acts to give it shape and hold its form until it enters the gastrointestinal tract (GI). In most cases the tablet is designed to be ingested whole, although in some cases it might be broken up to allow the patient to ingest a smaller dose of that medication if desired. Once in the GI tract, the compound begins to break down and separate from the binding agent and is absorbed. A number of compounds are administered in enteral form,

including many pharmaceuticals, over-the-counter medications,[5] and some illicit drugs.

Another common method of oral medication administration is the capsule. This is a modified form of tablet, with the medication being suspended in a solution and surrounded by a gelatin capsule. The capsule is designed to be swallowed whole, and once it reaches the GI tract the gelatin capsule breaks down, allowing the absorption of the desired compound. Some compounds are simply administered as liquids, such as children's medication(s). This allows for the titration of the dose according to the child's weight. An excellent example of a drug of abuse that is administered in liquid form is alcohol.

A number of compounds might be absorbed through the blood-rich tissues found under the tongue. A chemical that is administered in this manner is said to be administered *sublingually,* which is a variation of the oral form of drug administration. Some of the compounds administered sublingually include nitroglycerin and buprenorphine. The sublingual method of drug administration avoids the danger of the "first-pass metabolism" effect (discussed later in this chapter) (Jenkins, 2007). However, in spite of this advantage, the sublingual form of drug administration is only rarely used.

Although many compounds are rapidly absorbed rectally, this method of drug administration is uncommon in medical practice and virtually unheard of by drug abusers (Jenkins, 2007). Methods of rectal drug administration will not be discussed further in this text.

Parenteral Forms of Drug Administration

The parenteral method of drug administration involves the injection of a compound directly into the body. There are several advantages to parenteral forms of drug administration: the drug(s) not being exposed to gastric juices; delays caused by the stomach-emptying process; the danger of being mixed with food in the GI tract, which might slow absorption by the body. But the parenteral method of drug administration also presents a number of dangers to the user. Depending on the substance being discussed, parenteral administration might be the preferred method of administration, especially when a rapid onset of effects is desired.

One form of parenteral drug administration is the *subcutaneous* administration of a drug administration

---

[5]See Glossary.

just under the skin. Compounds administered subcutaneously are only slowly absorbed. This is often a method by which illicit narcotics are first injected, and is referred to as "skin popping" by injection drug addicts. Although the onset of the drug's effects is slower than other forms of parenteral drug administration, subcutaneous drug administration methods allows for a reservoir of the drug to be just under the skin that is absorbed over time.

A second method of parenteral drug administration involves the injection of a compound(s) into muscle tissue (intra-muscular or IM injection). Muscle tissues have a good supply of blood, and many compounds injected into muscle tissue will be absorbed into the general circulation more rapidly than compounds injected just under the skin. This method of drug administration is used both for the administration of some pharmaceuticals in medical practice and sometimes by illicit drug abusers such as those who inject the anabolic steroid abusers. However, there are many compounds such as the benzodiazepine chlordiazepoxide that are poorly absorbed by muscle tissue and are rarely, if ever, administered by this route (DeVane, 2004).

A third method of parenteral drug administration is the intravenous (or IV) injection. In this process the compound(s) of choice are injected directly into a vein, thus being deposited directly into the general circulation (DeVane, 2004). This is a common method by which many pharmaceuticals, and many drugs of abuse, are administered. One serious disadvantage of the intravenous method of drug administration is that it does not allow the body very much time to adapt to the foreign chemical. Thus, the individual is at risk for a serious adverse reaction to that compound within seconds of when it was administered.

Parenterally administered compounds do not have an instantaneous effect. The speed at which any drug of drug(s) will begin to have an effect depends on a number of factors, which will be discussed in the section on drug distribution, later in this chapter.

Other Forms of Drug Administration

There are a number of additional forms of drug administration, which will only briefly be discussed in this text. The transdermal method of drug administration involves a compound being slowly absorbed through the skin. This has the advantage of allowing a low, but relatively steady, blood level of the compound(s) in question being established in the user's body. However, this method of drug administration does not allow for one to rapidly establish any significant blood level of a compound in the user's body. For example, transdermal nicotine patches might require up to 24 hours before a sufficient level of nicotine is established in the user's blood to block nicotine withdrawal symptoms.

Another method of drug administration, one that is used more frequently by drug abusers than in medical practice, is the intranasal method. In this method of drug administration, the compound is "snorted," depositing it on to the blood-rich tissues in the sinuses. Both cocaine and heroin powder are occasionally abused in this manner. This allows for a relatively rapid absorption of the drug(s) in question, but the rate of absorption is slower than the intravenous route of administration, and absorption is rather erratic.

The process of "snorting" is similar to the process of inhalation, which is used both in medical practice and with certain compounds by drug abusers. The process of inhalation takes advantage of the fact that the circulatory system is separated from direct exposure to the air only by a layer of tissue less than 1/100,000ths of an inch (0.64 micron) thick (Garrett, 1994). Many drug molecules are small enough to pass across this barrier relatively easily, rapidly entering the individual's circulation. An example of this would be surgical anesthetic gasses. When smoked, many of the drugs of abuse are also able to cross over this barrier, gaining access to the circulation. Some of these compounds include heroin and cocaine. Finally, in the case of some compounds, the process of inhalation is able to introduce small particles into the deep tissues of the lungs, where they are deposited. These particles are rapidly broken down into smaller and smaller form until they are small enough to pass though the tissue barrier of the lungs into the circulation (for example, when tobacco cigarettes are smoked).

Each sub-form of inhalation takes advantage of the fact that the lungs offer a blood-rich, extremely large surface area, allowing for the rapid absorption of many compounds (Jenkins, 2007). But the amount of a given compound that actually is absorbed into the general circulation is highly variable for a number of reasons: (1) The individual must inhale the compound(s) at exactly the right point in the respiratory cycle to allow the drug molecules to reach the desired point in the lungs. (2) some chemicals are able to pass through the tissues of the lung into the circulation comparatively slowly. Marijuana is a good example of this problem: The individual must hold his/her breath for as long as possible to allow the largest percentage of the molecules inhaled to cross into the circulation before the person must exhale.

Bioavailability

To have an effect, a compound must enter the body in sufficient strength to achieve the desired effect. This is referred to as the *bioavailability* of a compound. Essentially the bioavailability of a compound is the *concentration of unchanged chemical at the site of action* (Bennett & Brown, 2003). The bioavailability of a compound, in turn, is affected by the factors of (Bennett & Brown, 2003; Jenkins, 2007) absorption, distribution, biotransformation, and elimination. Each of these processes will be discussed in more detail in the following paragraphs.

Absorption

Except for topical agents that are deposited directly on the site of action, such as an antifungal cream, most compounds must be absorbed into the body to have any effect (Jenkins, 2007). This involves the drug molecules moving from the site of entry through various cell boundaries to the circulatory system, where it is transported to the site of action. Compounds that are weakly acidic are usually absorbed through the stomach lining, whereas compounds that are a weak base[6] are absorbed in the small intestine (DeVane, 2004; Jenkins, 2007).

The human body is composed of layers of specialized cells, organized into specific patterns that carry out designated functions. The cells of the circulatory system are organized to form tubes (gastrointestinal tract that are surrounded by blood vessels) that contain the cells and fluids collectively called *blood*. To reach the circulatory system a chemical molecule ingested orally must pass through the cell walls of the intestine and then the cell walls of the cells that form the blood vessels in order to reach the circulatory system, a process that will slow absorption. As noted earlier, the circulation is separated from the air in the lungs by a single layer of tissue (the cell wall of the individual alveoli). Compounds that are able to cross this one cell layer are able to reach the

general circulation in just a matter of seconds. In contrast to this, a compound that is ingested orally must go through the process outlined here to reach the circulation. Thus inhalation is a more rapid method of drug absorption than oral ingestion.

There are a number of specialized *cellular transport mechanisms* that the body uses to move necessary substances into/away from the circulatory system. Drug molecules can take advantage of these transport mechanisms to move from the site of administration to the site of action. Without going into too much detail, it is possible to classify these cellular transport mechanisms as being either *active* or *passive* means of transport (Jenkins, 2007). The most common method by which drug molecules move across cell membranes is called diffusion, a passive method of molecular transport. Active methods involve the drug molecule taking advantage of one of several natural molecular transport mechanisms that move essential molecules into various cells.

The process of drug absorption (Figure 3-1) is variable, depending on a number of factors, the most important of which is the *method of administration,* as discussed earlier in this chapter. Another major variable is the *rate of blood flow* at the site of entry. For example, an intramuscular injection into the deltoid muscle of a person suffering from hypothermia will result in poor absorption because the blood normally routed to this muscle has been routed to the interior of the body to conserve body heat. Under this condition, the muscle tissue will receive relatively little blood flow, and this will reduce the speed at which the drug molecules injected into muscle tissue(s) might be absorbed into the general circulation.

Yet another variable is the *molecular characteristics of the compound itself.* Some drug molecules are more easily absorbed than others. Yet another variable that influences drug absorption is whether it is ingested on an empty stomach or not (DeVane, 2004). Most compounds are better absorbed when ingested on an empty stomach, although some compounds are better absorbed if ingested right after a meal (DeVane, 2004). Still another factor that influences the absorption of a chemical ingested orally is if it does not have to compete with other drug molecules for admission into the body. All of these factors limit the absorption of some compounds into the circulation. The next section addresses the factor of *distribution* of a given compound is distributed in the body.

---

[6]See Glossary.

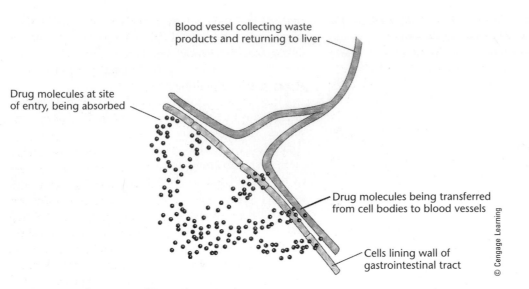

Blood vessel collecting waste
products and returning to liver

Drug molecules at site
of entry, being absorbed

Drug molecules being transferred
from cell bodies to blood vessels

Cells lining wall of
gastrointestinal tract

© Cengage Learning

FIGURE 3-1 The Process of Drug Absorption.

Distribution

The process of *distribution* refers to how the chemical molecules are transported within the body. This includes both the process of drug transport, and the pattern of drug accumulation within the body. As a general rule, very little is known about drug distribution patterns, especially in overdose situations (Jenkins, 2007). Although the process of distribution would seem relatively straight forward, in reality it is affected by factors such as the individual's age, sex, muscle/adipose tissue ratio, state of hydration, genetic heritage, and health. Because of such factors, there is significant inter-individual differences in the distribution pattern of the same compound at the same dosage level (DeVane, 2004; Jenkins & Cone, 1998).

Transport

Drug molecules are foreign substances, and their presence in the body is only tolerated by the body until its natural elimination/defense mechanisms are able to latch on to and remove them. Drug molecules must reach the general circulation, and be transported to the site of action before they are eliminated from the body. Some chemicals are able to mix freely with the blood plasma, and as such are often referred to as *water-soluble* compounds. Much of the human body is water so this provides a fine medium by which a water-soluble compound might be suspended and pumped around the body. Alcohol is a fine example of a water-soluble compound: After absorption the chemical molecules become intermixed with the blood plasma and pumped through the body by the circulatory system.

Other compounds must bind to one of the fat molecules that circulate through the body. Such compounds are called *lipid-soluble* or *lipophilic* compounds. Finally, a small percentage of chemicals are able to bind to protein molecules circulating in the blood. Lipids make up between 6 and 20% of the molecules in a cell and are found in the circulation as well. In the body lipid molecules in the circulation are used for a variety of purposes, including maintenance of cell walls. Any drug molecule that has attached itself to a lipid molecule will then be dragged along as the lipid molecule circulates and is ultimately absorbed into a cell for use in cellular maintenance.

However, molecular "binding" is usually not permanent. While the drug molecule is bound to the lipid molecule, it is safe from elimination from the body. However, it is also unable to achieve its desired effects while lipid bound. To become active again, a drug molecule must detach from the lipid molecule, enter the general circulation, and then be transported to the site of action. A compound that is 98% lipid soluble means that 98% of the drug molecules absorbed into the circulation are bound to blood lipids, leaving just 2% of the drug molecules to be biologically active. There are advantages and disadvantages to this characteristic of lipid binding. The process of lipid binding provides a drug reservoir within the body, allowing the newly detached drug molecules to replace those that have been eliminated from the body.

Depending upon the specific organ, between 6 and 20% of the tissue that organ is composed of is lipid molecules. An exception is the brain, which is

50% lipid molecules (Cooper, Bloom, & Roth, 2002). This allows compounds that are lipid soluble to become concentrated in the brain. The ultrashort and short-acting barbiturates[7] are excellent examples of this process. They are able to form bonds with blood lipids very rapidly, thus allowing them to take advantage of the brain's constant demand for lipid molecules to reach the brain rapidly and take effect. This is what makes these barbiturates useful as surgical anesthetics.

In contrast to the lipid-binding compounds, some drug molecules might bind to one of the protein molecules in the circulation.[8] Different drug molecules differ in their ability to bind with protein or lipid molecules. The antidepressant amitriptyline is 95% protein-bound, for example, whereas nicotine is only 5% protein-bound (Jenkins, 2007). The antianxiety agent diazepam is 99% protein-bound, and so its effects are induced by the 1% of the drug molecules that are unbound. As with the process of lipid binding, some drug molecules form stronger bonds with the protein molecule than others, and this is one factor that determines how long a given compound will remain in the body. As is true for lipid-bound molecules, protein-bound drug molecules are unable to have any biological effect as long as they remain bound to the protein molecule. Thus, there is a constant process of drug molecule replacement during the period of active dosing, as some molecules are eliminated from the body, and others break their bonds with the protein molecules and replace those that had been eliminated.

The number of binding sites on protein or lipid molecules is limited. If the individual were to take an unusually large dose of a drug, or if more the molecules of more than one compound were competing for the same binding sites on the protein or lipid molecule, those binding sites rapidly become saturated leaving a larger than normal percentage of drug molecules free in the blood to have a biological effect. This is one of the mechanisms through which pharmaceuticals might have a *synergistic*[9] effect: The effects of one compound reinforce the effects of a second compound, possibly with fatal results. Another form synergism effects is seen when different drug molecules bind at the same receptor site, increasing (or decreasing) the rate at which that neuron can "fire."

Biotransformation

The biotransformation mechanisms evolved over millions of years to help the body deal with potentially dangerous chemicals found in foods that have started to spoil (Wynn, Oesterheld, Cozza, & Armstrong, 2009). In humans these defensive detoxification systems are nonselective, eliminating poisons found in food with the same enthusiasm that they eliminate drug molecules. In some cases, the body is able to simply filter the drug from the blood unchanged. Penicillin is an excellent example of such a compound: Penicillin molecules are filtered from the blood and eliminated by the kidneys almost immediately. With the proper equipment it is possible to filter penicillin from the urine of a patient taking this compound, purify it, and reuse it.[10] There are other compounds that are removed from the body unchanged. However, in the majority of cases the chemical structure of the drug(s) must be modified before they can be eliminated from the body.

This is accomplished through a process that was once referred to as *detoxification,* or *drug metabolism.* However, because of the confusion over whether physicians were discussing the metabolic processes in the body, or the process of breaking down molecules of an illicit drug, The term *biotransformation* has gradually been gaining favor as the proper term for when a pharmaceutical agent is being discussed, whereas the older term *metabolism* is applied to the drugs of abuse. They both reflect the same process, which is labeled one way if it is a prescribed pharmaceutical and the other if it is an illicit drug. Biotransformation/detoxification is usually carried out in the liver, although on occasion other organ(s) might also be involved. The liver's *microsomal endoplasmic reticulum* produces a number of enzymes[11] that seek to transform toxic molecules into a form that might be eliminated from the body. There are essentially two forms of biotransformation: (a) the *zero-order biotransformation* process and (b) the *first-order biotransformation* process. In the zero-order biotransformation process the biotransformation

---

[7]Discussed in Chapter 9.

[8]The most common of which is *albumin.* Sometimes, compounds are referred to as albumin-bound, rather than protein bound. Technically, drugs that are more acidic tend to bind to albumin, whereas drug molecules that are more basic tend to bind to the alpha1-acid glycoprotein molecules in the blood.

[9]See Glossary.

---

[10]Actually, before methods of producing large quantities of penicillin were developed in the 1940s the patient's urine was collected and the penicillin was isolated, purified, and reused.

[11]The most common of which is the P-450 metabolic process, or the microsomal P-450 pathway.

mechanism(s) quickly become saturated if the person used a large amount of the compound ingested. In spite of the concentration of that chemical in the blood only a set amount of that compound can be biotransformed each hour (Bennett & Brown, 2003). Alcohol is an example of a compound that is biotransformed through a zero-order biotransformation process:[12] If the drinker ingests alcohol more rapidly than his or her body can metabolize it, he or she will become intoxicated.

In the first-order biotransformation process, a set percentage of the compound(s) in question is biotransformed each hour independent of the concentration of that substance in the blood. There are many compounds that are biotransformed through a first-order biotransformation process. Both the zero-order and the first-order biotransformation processes are carried out by the mechanisms of (Ciraulo, Shader, Greenblatt, & Creelman, 2006; Wynn et al., 2009): (1) oxidation, (2) reduction, (3) hydrolysis, and (4) conjugation. The chemistry of each form of biotransformation is quite complex, and are best reserved for those readers who wish to pick up a pharmacology textbook to review the biochemistry of the biotransformation process. It is enough for the reader to remember that there are two different forms and four different chemical mechanisms of biotransformation.

Both forms of biotransformation involve the drug molecules being chemically altered as rapidly as the enzymes involved in each step can accomplish. The goal of the biotransformation process is to alter the foreign chemical molecule until it becomes a compound that can be eliminated from the body. The process of biotransformation depends on the chemical characteristics of the drug(s) ingested, and this process might involve several steps. For example, compounds that are highly lipid soluble require extensive biotransformation before they become less lipid soluble, and are more easily eliminated from the body (Jenkins, 2007). The original substance is referred to as the *parent compound*. The compound that emerges at each step of the biotransformation process is referred to as a *metabolite* of the original compound. Metabolites may have their own psychoactive effect on the user, a factor that must

be considered by physicians when prescribing a pharmaceutical for a patient. If the parent compound had no or minimal biological effect, and its major effects are achieved by the metabolites of that compound, then the parent compound is referred to as a *prodrug*. Most compounds in use today are biologically active, and only a small number are prodrugs.

To add an element of confusion, sometimes the enzymes necessary for the biotransformation of one compound will increase the speed of the biotransformation of a second compound, reducing its effectiveness. Also, normal variations in the individual's biological heritage or various diseases can alter the speed at which some individuals biotransform a specific compound. Further the genetic inheritance dictates the speed at which the user's body is able to biotransform a given compound. Some individuals biotransform certain compounds more rapidly than others, making them *rapid metabolizers* of that compound. Genetic variations might also endow a person with a body that is slower at breaking down a given compound than is normal, making them a *slow metabolizer* of that compound. Disease states, such as alcohol-induced liver damage[13] can also alter the liver's ability to biotransform many compounds, in effect artificially making them slow metabolizers. In this situation the attending physician must also consider when prescribing a pharmaceutical to treat an ill patient. There is no way to identify these individuals other than clinical experience obtained by giving the patient a drug and observing their reaction, although there is an ongoing research in this area.

The First-Pass Metabolism Effect

The human digestive tract is designed not to let any chemical that is absorbed pass directly into the circulation, but to filter them first through the liver. This is called the first-pass metabolism effect (DeVane, 2004). By taking chemicals absorbed from the GI tract and passing them through the liver, any toxin in that food or drug might be isolated and the biotransformation process started, hopefully before that compound can do any damage to the body itself. One consequence of the first-pass metabolism process is that it interferes with the effectiveness of many orally administered compounds. For example, much of an orally administered dose of morphine is biotransformed by the first-pass metabolism effect before it reaches the site of action,

---

[12]Although, technically, alcohol's biotransformation at extremely high doses does not follow the zero order biotransformation cycle exactly. But alcohol's deviation(s) from the zero order biotransformation cycle is best reserved for toxicology texts.

[13]Discussed in Chapter 8.

limiting its effectiveness as an analgesic. Collectively, the first-pass metabolism process, and the various subforms of biotransformation work to prepare foreign chemicals for the last stage of pharmacokinetics:[14] *elimination.*

Elimination

The processes of biotransformation and elimination are so closely intertwined that some pharmacologists consider them to be a single process. The process of biotransformation changes the chemical structure of a compound so that the metabolites are more water soluble so it can then be removed from the circulation by the organs involved in filtering the blood. This usually is carried out by the kidneys, although the lungs, sweat glands, and biliary tract are sometimes also be involved in the process of drug elimination (Wilson, Shannon, Shields, & Stang, 2007). An example of this is the small percentage of alcohol that is eliminated through the sweat and breath when the person exhales, giving the intoxicated person a characteristic smell.

The process of drug elimination does not happen instantly. Rather, time is required for the enzymes involved in each step of the biotransformation process necessary to break down a specific compound. Depending on the exact compound under consideration this process might take hours, or in the case of long-acting compounds such as methadone, days. The goal of the biotransformation process is to allow the enzymes to transform the drug molecule(s) into a water-soluble metabolite that can be eliminated from the body. This brings us to another necessary concept to consider: the drug *half-life.*

Drug Half-life

The concept of a drug *half-life* provides a useful yardstick providing a *rough* estimate of a compound's effectiveness, duration of effect, and the length of time that it will remain in the body. There are several different forms of drug half-life, depending on different aspects of the compound's actions in the body. We will discuss some of the more important of these half-life forms in this section.

> ***Distribution Half-life:*** is the period of time that it takes a compound to work its way into the general circulation once it is administered (Reiman, 1997). This information is important to physicians in

overdose situations, where it is necessary to anticipate the long-term effects of compounds involved. It is also of importance in planning pharmacological interventions: If a patient is in acute pain, you would want to administer a compound that was able to rapidly reach the circulation rather than a compound that is slowly absorbed. A patient in chronic pain might benefit more from a compound that is more slowly absorbed but provides a steady level of analgesia to control their discomfort.

There are two subforms of distribution half-life (Cloos, 2010a): (a) the *alpha* half-life is the period following peak concentration of the drug in the blood and when it is redistributed to various body tissues and (b) the *beta* half-life is the decline in plasma concentration as the drug is biotransformed and eliminated from the body (Cloos, 2010a). This information is important to understanding the pharmacokinetics of a compound. For example, the beta half-life is often the criteria on which a benzodiazepine is classified as being a short-, intermediate-, or long-acting compound (Cloos, 2010a).

Therapeutic Half-life: is a rough measure of the compound's duration of effect. The therapeutic half-life is the time necessary for the body to inactivate 50% of a compound. This may be complicated by compounds where the metabolites also have a biological action on the body. The therapeutic half-life usually is a reference to a single dose of a compound, and regular dosing of that compound can alter the therapeutic half-life of a chemical.

Elimination Half-life: This is the time that the body requires to eliminate 50% of a single dose of a compound. In medical practice it is usually assumed that after the fifth dose, the individual will have achieved a *steady state* of a compound in his or her blood. Two factors that eliminate half-life are the individual's liver and kidney function. The elimination half-life of a compound might be extended in persons with impaired liver or kidney function, and the physician must make dosage adjustments for persons with such problems.

The various half-lives of a compound are not the same. A compound might have a therapeutic half-life of minutes but an elimination half-life of hours, such as is demonstrated by several of the ultra-short-acting barbiturates.[15] Further, all half-life

---

[14]See Glossary.

[15]Discussed in Chapter 9.

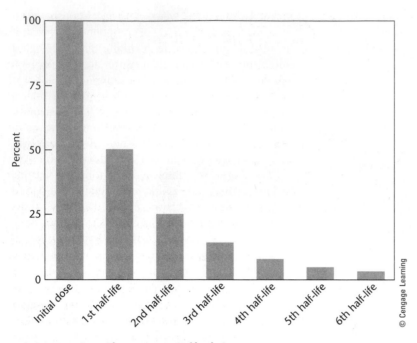

FIGURE 3-2 Drug Elimination in Half-Life Stages.

estimates are based on the assumption that the patient has only used one compound. If the patient is using multiple compounds, it becomes more difficult to estimate the drug half-lives, because multiple drugs might compete for the processes of absorption, distribution, biotransformation, and elimination.

One popular misconception is that it only takes two elimination half-life periods to remove a compound from the body. In reality, fully 25% of the initial dose remains after the end of the 2nd half-life period, and 12% of the body is still in the body after three half-life periods. Pharmacologists estimate that it will take five half-life periods before all of a single dose of a chemical is eliminated from the user's body, as illustrated in Figure 3-2.

Drug Interactions

In cases where a patient is receiving multiple medications, there is a very real danger of these compounds interacting in ways not anticipated by the user. Wynn et al. (2009) estimated that 5% of all hospitalizations in the United States were the result of adverse drug–drug interactions, with uncounted numerous less severe interactions causing the patient distress but do not require hospitalization. Serious drug–drug interactions result in an estimated 7,000 deaths in this country

alone, although this is only an estimate as many fatal drug–drug interactions probably are not reported, or the deaths attributed to other conditions according to the authors.

The Effective Dose

The concept of the *effective dose* (ED) is based on research that determines the approximate dose at which a given percentage of the population will respond to a designated dose of a compound. For example, the dose at which 10% of the general population is expected to have the desired response would be identified as the ED_{10}, whereas the dose at which 50% of the general population responds is the ED_{50}. Obviously, if you were a biochemist developing a new compound, you would want to find a dose level allowing a large a percentage of the general population to achieve the desired response. It would appear at this point that you could simply keep increasing the dose until *everybody* responded to the new drug. However as the dosage level increases, you are likely to (a) encounter the *ceiling dose effect* and (b) risk development of toxic reactions. The *ceiling dose effect* is just that: a dose above which additional drug molecules will not have any additional effect. Acetaminophen and ibuprofen are good examples of such compounds. If the individual were to ingest more than ceiling dose, s/he would only be more likely to experience a toxic reaction to that compound.

The Lethal Dose and Therapeutic Index

We will now discuss another useful concept: the *lethal dose*. Drugs are, by definition, foreign to the body, and although they might disrupt a body function(s) in a desired manner, they also present the risk of altering that body function so much that the user dies. A hypothetical compound that suppressed respiration at a certain dose might be a useful pharmaceutical for certain forms of surgery. However, too large a dose of that same medication might induce respiratory depression, hardly a desired response in most cases!

During the era in which the atomic bomb was being developed, scientists calculated the amount of radiation a person might be exposed to without becoming terminally ill. Such dose-response curves estimate what percentage of the population would die as a result of being exposed to a certain dose of a radiation, and these calculations were then applied to toxic chemicals. This figure is expressed as the *lethal dose* (LD) ratio. A dose of a drug that would cause 1% of the population to die would be abbreviated as the LD_{01} and the dose that in theory would kill 25% of the population would be abbreviated as the LD_{25}, and so on. For example, as will be discussed in the next chapter, 1% of patients with a blood alcohol concentration of 0.350 mg/mL would be expected to die without medical help. Thus, for alcohol the LD_{01} would be 0.350 mg/mL of blood.

By comparing the effective dose and lethal dose ratios, it is possible to obtain a raw estimate of the *therapeutic window* or the *therapeutic index* of a compound. If you had a hypothetical chemotherapy compound used to treat cancer that had an ED_{99} of 100 mg, and a LD_{01} of 1,000 mg, that compound would be said to have a wide therapeutic window. If in contrast this same hypothetical compound had an ED_{99} at 100 mg but had a LD_{30} at a dosage level of 150 mg it would be said to have a narrow therapeutic window. Unfortunately, as will be discussed in the next few chapters, many of the drugs of abuse have very narrow "therapeutic" windows, making it very easy to overdose on these compounds.

Therapeutic Threshold and Peak Effects

As the drug absorption process progresses following a single dose of a compound, the amount of a compound in the user's circulation will increase until it reaches the minimal level at which that compound might be effective. This is the *therapeutic threshold* for that compound. As the blood levels rise over time, the effects will continue to become stronger and stronger until the drug reaches its *peak effect dose*. Then as the process of biotransformation proceeds the effects of that compound will diminish until the blood levels of that compound fall below the therapeutic threshold. The period of peak effects varies from one compound to another. The peak effects of one of the ultra-short acting barbiturates might be achieved in a matter of seconds whereas a long-term barbiturate might take hours to achieve its peak effects. Further variables that affect absorption, distribution, biotransformation, and elimination will also impact a given compound when reaches its peak effects. Scientists have learned to calculate dose-response curves for many compounds in use today, including some of the drugs of abuse.

The Site of Action

Essentially, the site of action is where the compound(s) carry out their main effects. For most of the psychoactive pharmaceuticals, and the various drugs of abuse, specific regions of the central nervous system (CNS)[16] will be the site of action. The CNS is, without question, the most complex organ system found in the human body. At its most fundamental level, the CNS is comprised of approximately 100 billion neurons, each of which receives input from scores, hundreds, or perhaps thousands, of other neurons. Surprisingly although most of the CNS is squeezed into the confines of the skull, the individual neurons usually do not actually touch. Rather, they are separated by microscopic spaces called the *synapse*. To communicate across the synaptic void, or synaptic gap, one neuron will release a cloud of chemical molecules known as *neurotransmitters*. To date, more than 150 compounds that function as a

---

[16]Although the CNS is by itself worthy of a lifetime of study, for the purposes of this text the beauty and complexities of the CNS must be compressed into a few short paragraphs. Those who wish to learn more about the CNS are advised to seek a good neuroanatomy, neuropsychology, or neurology textbook.

neurotransmitter within the brain have been identified, but in this text we will limit our discussion to those few neurotransmitter molecules affected by the drugs of abuse.[17] The role that neurotransmitters play in the process of information transfer between neurons will be discussed later in this chapter.

The Receptor Site and the Process of Neurotransmission

At its most simplistic, the receptor site is the location on neuron "B" that receives information "A." This is accomplished through the process of neurotransmission. To understand the concept of a receptor, imagine the analogy of a key into a lock. The receptor site by way of analogy can be viewed as a lock, although on a molecular scale, and is usually a protein molecule located in the cell wall of the neuron. In normal neurotransmission the molecular "key" (neurotransmitter molecules) are released by neuron "A," some of which slide into the "lock" (receptor site) on neuron "B." If a sufficient number of receptor sites are occupied by neurotransmitter molecules at the same instant that neuron will "fire," passing the message on to the next neuron (Bennett & Brown, 2003; Olson, 2006). Each individual neuron has hundreds or even thousands of synaptic junctions and the total number of synaptic junctions in one individual's brain is larger than the total number of grains of sand on all the beaches on Earth combined (Stahl, 2008). Neurotransmitters: It was once believed that each neuron released just one type of neurotransmitter molecule. Things in the central nervous system are rarely so simple: Some neurons respond to multiple types of neurotransmitters or might itself generate more than one type of neurotransmitter for its own use.[18] In some cases a neuron might release a cloud of neurotransmitter molecules into the synapse to cause it to end the process of neurotransmission for a few moments. These "retrograde" neurotransmitters might be an entirely different compound than the one that the molecule uses to pass a message on to another neuron.

The strength of the attraction of the neurotransmitter molecule to the receptor site is called the *affinity* of that molecule to the receptor. Obviously, the neurotransmitter molecules have a high affinity for their intended receptor site. However, on occasion a compound might have a lower affinity level for an unintended receptor. This is seen most often with man-made chemicals and is one reason why a compound might induce side effects. To avoid the spurious generation of a message that will be passed from one neuron to the next a specific number of receptor sites on the postsynaptic neuron must be occupied by the appropriate neurotransmitter at the same instant. This can only be achieved if the presynaptic neuron released sufficient numbers of the appropriate neurotransmitter molecules at once to achieve the critical level necessary for neurotransmission to take place. When this critical level is reached a profound change is triggered in the postsynaptic neuron, and an electrochemical message flashes through the downstream neuron either causing it to "fire" (pass the message on to the next neuron by releasing its stores of neurotransmitter molecules to the next neuron in the network[19]) or inhibit the firing of the downstream neuron. In the human brain the main excitatory neurotransmitters that are of importance in substance abuse are glutamate and aspartate, whereas the main inhibitory neurotransmitter is GABA.

The response of the postsynaptic neuron falls into one of the two categories: the *fast* or *inotropic* response, which usually involve the downstream neuron altering the speed with which it can "fire" and pass the message on to the next neuron in that neural network. The presynaptic neurotransmitter molecules might also initiate a *metabotropic response* initiating long-term alterations in the postsynaptic neuron. These include (Stahl, 2008) making or destroying synaptic junctions, reinforcing neural networks, urging axons to sprout, the synthesis of proteins and enzymes, and neurotransmitter receptors that regulate the function of the postsynaptic neuron.

Neurotransmitter Reuptake/Destruction

After their release, one of three things can happen to the neurotransmitter molecules: (a) They can be retrieved by the upstream neuron through the use of molecular reuptake pumps for future use, (b) they can be destroyed by enzymes near the receptor sites produced by either the presynaptic or postsynaptic neuron, or (c) they can diffuse into the surrounding area and eventually be removed.

---

[17]I bet you thought that I was going to name them all, didn't you?
[18]A process known as cotransmission.

[19]In the process of which the neuron is transformed into the "upstream" neuron for the 3rd neuron, and so on.

The process of neurotransmitter reuptake is an interesting process through which molecular-sized "pumps" collect the neurotransmitter molecules from the synaptic junction for future use. This process requires less energy for the neuron than does generating new neurotransmitter molecules after it "fires." Since some neurons in the brain "fire" up to 200 times a second it becomes apparent how reusing as many neurotransmitter molecules as possible will save that neuron from having to expend a great deal of energy manufacturing new neurotransmitter molecules every time that it "fires."

Tolerance/Neuroadaption

Tolerance to a compound is defined as "a shortened duration and decreased intensity of drug effects after repeated administration" (Ghoneim, 2004b, p. 1279). When the compound is a pharmaceutical prescribed by a physician, this process is known as *neuroadaptation* also. When it involves an illicit compound the older term *tolerance* is used. Both terms identify the same process: A compound has a shortened duration of effect because the neurons have learned to compensate for the presence of that compound. On the behavioral level the individual might admit that it takes more of their drug of choice for them to achieve the desired effects. There are many subforms of tolerance/neuroadaptation, some of which are discussed in the following paragraphs.

Metabolic Tolerance

Through this process, the body becomes more proficient in the biotransformation of certain compounds, at least for a limited period. This is commonly seen in the early stages of alcohol dependence, for example, where the drinker will report that s/he must ingest more alcohol to achieve the same level of intoxication once achieved with a lower level of alcohol intake (Nelson, 2000). Unfortunately, the liver can only maintain this extra effort at alcohol biotransformation for a limited period before it starts to break down, resulting in the phenomenon of lower tolerance to alcohol often found later in the drinker's life.

Behavioral Tolerance

Behavioral tolerance reflects the behavioral outcome of the brain's efforts to maintain normal function in spite of the presence of foreign molecules. The individual's behavior appears almost normal in spite of the presence

of a compound in their body. Again, using alcohol as an example, even law enforcement or health care professionals are occasionally shocked to discover that the individual who appeared to only be mildly intoxicated was in reality significantly over the legal blood alcohol level. Their behavior did not reflect their true blood alcohol level in part because they had developed a degree of behavioral tolerance.

Cross Tolerance

Multiple compounds might affect the body through similar mechanisms such as when two or more compounds possess some affinity for the same receptor site. In this case the receptor site in question would react to the presence of either compound. As the neuron adapts to the constant presence of the first compound, these cellular changes (usually at the level of receptor sites) also influence the neuron's ability to react to the presence of molecules from the second compound. Alcohol and the benzodiazepines provide a good example of this process: The molecules of both compounds bind at a receptor site for the inhibitory neurotransmitter known as GABA. As the neuron adapts to the continual presence of alcohol by altering the number of GABA receptor sites it will also become less sensitive to the benzodiazepines, which use the same GABA receptors to achieve their effects.

Reverse Tolerance

Reverse tolerance or what is also called sensitization is a poorly understood phenomenon in which lower doses of a compound produces the same effect as higher doses did when the use of that substance was initiated (O'Brien, 2011). The possibility that the process of operant conditioning contributes to the individual's expectations of the compound's effects, making them more responsive to lower doses than were originally used (O'Brien, 2011).

Up/Down Regulation of Receptor Sites

The individual neurons attempt to maintain a relatively stable level of function. The molecules of any neuroactive compound, including the drugs of abuse, alter the normal function of the various neural networks, the individual members of which attempt to counteract the influence of that compound (Breggin, 2008; Cruz, Bajo, Schweitzer, & Roberto, 2008). One mechanism through which individual neurons attempt to maintain stable levels of activation is either the up-regulation[20] or down-regulation[21] of the number of receptor sites. If the neuron is constantly being subjected to high levels of a neurotransmitter it might *down-regulate* (which is to say reduce) the number of receptor sites for that specific neurotransmitter so that the molecules have fewer "targets." Some of the neurotransmitter receptor sites would be absorbed back into the neuron. The analogy of turning down the volume of a radio might not be inappropriate here: If the radio station was relatively close you would not need to turn the volume up very much to hear it. However, if the neuron was not being exposed to low levels of the neurotransmitter, it might increase (up-regulate) the number of receptor sites, making it easier for the neurotransmitter molecules to find a receptor site. To again use the analogy of the radio, if you were listening to a station that was far away, you would turn up the volume so that you could hear it. Up-regulation and down-regulation of receptor sites is one process through which tolerance to a compound develops.

Drug Agonists/Antagonists

Essentially, a drug *agonist* is a compound that activates a receptor site by being able to mimic or enhance the actions of a natural neurotransmitter (Wilson et al., 2007). For the drugs of abuse, the receptor sites are individual neurons in select regions of the brain. The more closely the molecule resembles that of the naturally occurring neurotransmitter, the greater is the affinity of that molecule for that receptor site and the stronger will be the drug's effect on the neurons in that region of the brain. The analogy of a "skeleton" key for a lock would not be out of place here: The narcotic analgesic family of compounds uses binding sites in the brain's pain perception system; however, the narcotics are not perfect matches for these receptor sites and only simulate the effects of naturally produced opioid-like molecules far less efficiently than their endogenous cousins.

However, some compounds are able to fit into the receptor site, *without* activating it. Such compounds are called *antagonists* (or antiagonists). The drug Narcan (used to treat narcotic overdoses) functions as an opioid antagonist, blocking the opioid receptor sites without activating them, thus preventing the narcotic molecules from reaching the receptor sites in the brain. The

analogy of a key that was broken off just beyond the handle might not be out of place, here. There are also compounds that are *partial agonists*. This means that the drug molecules are able to activate the receptor site very weakly if at all, while preventing other drug molecules the opportunity to bind at that receptor site. Again, using the lock-and-key analogy, imagine the night watchman who has a ring full of keys, who is forced to go through key after key to find the right one for a specific lock. Some of the keys might match some of the tumblers in the lock, but only one will match the specific combination necessary to open that lock.

Potency

The potency of a biologically active compound is the ratio between the size of a dose and the desired response (Ghoneim, 2004b). The difference between the effective dose of heroin and morphine illustrates this point. The standard conversion formula is that 4 milligrams of pharmaceutical[22] quality heroin provides the same degree of analgesia as 10 milligrams of morphine. Thus, heroin is said to be more potent than morphine. The pharmacology of both compounds will be discussed in Chapter 11.

The Blood–Brain Barrier

The human brain is an energy-intensive organ, receiving 10 times as much oxygen and nutrients as any other organ in the body. Twenty percent of the blood pumped with each heart beat is sent to the brain to supply it with needed nutrients and oxygen. However, the brain is also an especially vulnerable organ and direct contact with blood is toxic to neural tissue. To protect the brain from direct exposure to blood while still allowing necessary nutrients to reach neural tissues, nature has provided the brain with a circulatory system in which endothelial cells are tightly joined around the capillaries (Interlandi, 2013). The closely packed endothelial cells are part of the *blood–brain barrier* [23] (or, BBB), which is composed of the endothelial cells and a thin layer of cells known as

---

[20]See Glossary.

[21]See Glossary.

[22]Heroin is an accepted pharmaceutical in many countries. Obviously we are talking of pharmaceutical quality heroin, produced in facilities that meet the regulations of the appropriate regulatory agencies, and not the illicit heroin sold on the streets of the United States.

[23]To learn more about the blood–brain barrier, please review this subject in a good biological psychology or neurology textbook.

astrocytes[24] or pericytes, which collectively separate the brain from direct contact with the circulatory system.

Although it is referred to as a barrier, the BBB is better thought of as a selective screen. However, if it is intact the BBB will protect the brain from invasion from a range of micro-organisms and toxins in the environment. There are specialized cellular transport mechanisms between or in the endothelial cell walls, each one adapted to allowing one type of water-soluble molecule such as glucose, iron, and certain vitamins, to pass through the BBB into the neural tissues. Lipids are also able to pass through the endothelial cells, by first binding with, and slowly passing through the cell walls of the endothelial cells to eventually reach the brain. In the process, most compounds that are lipid soluble are also admitted into the brain. Although it is an imperfect system, the BBB does an exceptional job of protecting the brain from toxins or micro-organisms that would otherwise destroy it.

Chapter Summary

It is difficult to discuss the drugs of abuse without a grounding in those parts of the field of pharmacology and the sub-specialty of neuropharmacology. These fields are each worthy of a lifetime of study and it is not possible to do justice to either topic in this text. Some of the basic pharmacology concepts such as were the different methods by which a pharmaceuticals and their form of administration were discussed, as were the concepts of the prime effects and side effects. how the drugs of abuse are administered, absorbed, distributed, and biotransformed/eliminated from the body. The concepts of the drug agonist, the antiagonist (or, antagonist), and the mixed agonist/antagonist were introduced. A brief overview of the blood–brain barrier, and its function, was also provided, and the concepts of protein or lipid binding and the concepts of tolerance and cross-tolerance to a compound(s) were reviewed.

---

[24]See Glossary.

CHAPTER 4

An Introduction to Alcohol: Man's Oldest Recreational Chemical

… humans, as a species, like to drink. We consume wine, beer, cider, spirits … in fact the fermented product of almost anything we can turn to alcohol

(Dunn, 2013, p. 38).

Introduction

Ethyl alcohol[1] is occasionally found in the natural world, especially in various forms of fruit that ripen at specific times of the year. Various animal and insect species have learned to identify these fermented fruits by smell, in many cases apparently enjoying the effects of the alcohol produced by the process of fermentation (Dunn, 2013). Our hominid ancestors, who were quite familiar with the world around them, might have rushed to join these animals, although this is based only on historical speculation. Although speculative, archaeologists believe that the use of alcohol might predate the rise of "civilization" by 1–2 million years. By the time that modern humans emerged from Africa circa 100,000 B.C.E.[2] they knew which fruits and tubers would be ferment at certain times of the year to provide a naturally occurring cocktail or two (Tucker, 2011).

Arguably, the development of fixed settlements and the rise of agriculture circa 10,000 B.C.E. could be traced at least in part to the discovery that the surplus crops plants being cultivated could be allowed to ferment as a way of preserving it for use as a beverage. A liquid beverage is easier to store than grain, and is less likely to spoil. Unbeknownst to those early farmers the yeast involved in the fermentation process might even have contributed to the nutritional value of the beverage by adding various vitamins and amino acids to the mixture (Dunn, 2013). One could argue that "civilization"[3] itself could be traced to the need for semipermanent or permanent communities to house these early farmers (Dunn, 2013). The alcohol has continued to play a role lubricating social interactions throughout history, and given its role in society today it is important for the reader to have a working understanding of alcohol, how it is obtained, and the effects of social alcohol use.

---

[1]The designation *ethyl* alcohol is important to chemists, as there are at least 45 other compounds that might be classified as form of alcohol. Each of the other forms of alcohol is toxic to the body, although the length of time that is necessary for the toxic effects to manifest varies from compound to compound (Keany, 2011). *Ethyl alcohol* is the one most commonly consumed by humans, and these other forms of alcohol will not be discussed further.

[2]Which stands for "Before Common Era."

[3]Are we "civilized"? This is an arguable point.

Why Do People Consume Alcohol?

Theoretically, alcohol is but one of a rather extensive range of naturally occurring compounds ingested by humans for their psychoactive effects (McGovern, 2009). Mushrooms containing compounds with hallucinogenic potential are found in some parts of the world, but alcohol use is ubiquitous. Scientists exploring the ruins of various cities in what was once the ancient Sumerian empire and have found numerous clay tablets devoted to the process of brewing beer, especially a form of beer made from fermented honey known as mead (Cahill, 1998). Early alcohol-containing drinks (a) supplied at least some of the fluids necessary for the individual's daily survival, (b) were a valuable source of energy[4] (alcohol biotransformation results in the formation of glucose; Dunn, 2013; McGovern, 2009), and (c) had mild antibacterial properties that often made them safer to ingest than the local water (Johnson, 2006). From a reproductive perspective it is more advantageous for the individual to die of cirrhosis of the liver in his or her 40s than of a waterborne disease when the person was a child or adolescent (Johnson, 2006).

Currently individuals consume alcohol for a variety of reasons: In limited quantities it has some health benefits, and some people use it as a hypnotic.[5] Alcohol induces a sense of well-being or in some cases euphoria in the drinker, feelings that added to the allure of alcohol throughout history. Alcohol also facilitates social interactions, some of which unfortunately lead to countless thousands of unplanned children (Dunn, 2013). It is used in certain religious rituals and on very rare occasions by physicians for medicinal purposes. Folk medicine holds that a teaspoon of brandy helps to break up mucous in the lungs, allowing the patient to breathe more easily. Although this theory is attractive, alcohol is most commonly ingested for its ability to induce a sense of well-being and euphoria.

Daily consumption of *one* glass of wine a day appears to lower the individual's risk of developing cancer of the esophagus by approximately 56% (Kubo et al., 2009). Unfortunately, this effect is found only for wine drinkers, suggesting that it is a compound in the wine and not the alcohol itself that reduces the individual's risk for this form of cancer. As will be discussed in the next chapter, *heavy* alcohol use is a risk factor for the development of cancer of the esophagus, making the use of alcohol to avoid this form of cancer a dangerous practice (Kubo et al., 2009).

A Brief History of Alcohol

There is strong evidence that some insects and many animals are attuned to the smell of fruit and are drawn to it, a trait that early naturalists capitalized upon to capture specimens (McGovern, 2009). Because the seed pods, which are the fruits we consume, are also usually quite visually striking, the animal species that use visual cues to obtain food are drawn to these fruit pods. Some plants capitalize on the affinity of insects to them as a means of pollination, whereas animals that ingest the seed pods play a role in the distribution of that species by spreading seeds across their respective territories (thoughtfully complete with a little packet of fertilizer).

However, from time to time the outer skin of the fruit will crack or break open, allowing micro-organisms[6] entry to the lush interior of the fruit pod. In some of the fruit pods the process of fermentation will begin as yeast settles on the fruit and begins to consume it. From the perspective of the yeast, ethyl alcohol is not the goal of fermentation but only a waste product. In spite of its status as waste from the process of fermentation, alcohol is a concentrated source of energy. This, plus the intoxicating effects of the alcohol, apparently serves as incentives for many animal species to seek out and consume it if it was available. Researchers have observed tree shrews, distant biological cousins of human beings, selectively sipping nectar from certain palm flower clusters in which the process of fermentation has taken place ("A tree shrew's favorite tipple," 2008; McGovern, 2009). The liquid found in these palm flower clusters after fermentation has an alcohol content of 3.8%, approximately the same as modern beer. It is not unreasonable to assume that ancient hominids shared this preference for alcohol when it could be obtained.[7]

---

[4]One end product of alcohol metabolism is glucose, a blood sugar.

[5]See Glossary.

[6]Discussed in the section "How Alcoholic Beverages Are Produced Today," later in this chapter.

[7]This is only a theory as there is little evidence of intoxicated hominids in the geological strata in which these fossils are found. A *Homo habilis* skeleton from an intoxicated member of that species, when found by anthropologists, would look the same as any member of the *Homo habilis* genera, although one might argue that their intoxication might have contributed to their opportunity to become fossilized if it made them ignore predators in the area.

Mead, a form of beer made from fermented honey, appears to have been in widespread use during the latter part of the Paleolithic era,[8] whereas beer made from other ingredients might date back to 9,000 B.C.E. (Tucker, 2011). There is preliminary evidence suggesting that a form of beer was being manufactured in upper Egypt 18,000 years ago, although this evidence is still controversial (Tucker, 2011). These early forms of beer were quite thick and nutritious. By comparison, modern forms of beer are rather thin and anemic, contributing little to the drinker's dietary needs. Historically, the use of beer and wine as dietary agents are reflected in the fact that both are mentioned in Homer's epic stories the *Iliad* and the *Odyssey.*

The earliest written record of wine-making is found in an Egyptian tomb that dates back to 3,000 B.C.E., although scientists recently discovered a winery that dates to around 4,000 B.C.E. (Raw Data, 2011a). By the time of the Greek and Roman empires, wine was a central part of civilized life, in part because of its nutritional value (Walton, 2002). Alcohol is an extraordinary source of energy for the drinker,[9] providing as much energy as can be obtained from fat, and far more energy than from carbohydrates and proteins (Lieber, 1998). Ancient Greek prayers for slain warriors expressed the hope that they would enjoy a state of continuous intoxication in the afterlife. In pre-Christian Rome, intoxication was seen as a religious experience[10] (McGovern, 2009; Walton, 2002). The Holy Bible referred to alcohol as nothing less than a gift from God, and during the "Dark Ages" monks in various abbeys experimented with methods of wine production and discovered how to produce champagne (Woods, 2005) and various liquors. As early as the 8th century B.C.E., alchemists working in what is now modern Iraq had started to experiment with the process of distillation, allowing for the development of more concentrated alcoholic beverages (Blum, 2010; Tucker, 2011).

Beer and wine consumption continued through the Renaissance in Europe, the Age of Exploration, and into the early Colonial period when the first colonies in the "New World" were established.[11] Alcohol use was ubiquitous in the colonies and the early United States,[12] and the imposition of a federal tax on liquor to help repay loans from the French to help fund the Revolution led to the famous "Whiskey Rebellion" in the United States (Okrent, 2010). This tax was discontinued in 1802, but was resurrected to help pay for the War of 1812 and again allowed to expire in 1817. In 1862, a liquor tax was enacted yet a third time to help pay for the Civil War, after which the government found itself permanently dependent on the excise tax to help pay for its operating expenses (Okrent, 2010).

Alcohol use has been a contentious issue in Western society. By the start of the 19th century, public intoxication was viewed not as a sign of religious ecstasy but as a public disgrace, and in many communities during the later part of the 19th and early 20th centuries it was not uncommon for poorer people to "sell" their vote for credit slips at local bars (Okrent, 2010). In some communities in the United States there was a licensed drinking establishment for every 100 citizens, including women and children.[13] Widely disparate groups found a common ground in opposing the sale and use of alcohol in the United States and a decade after the end of World War I this country embarked on a social experiment known as Prohibition. During this period, alcohol use was in theory prohibited except when a physician prescribed it for the treatment of disease. Prohibition was openly flaunted even when this law was still in effect[14] and was repealed after approximately 13 years.[15]

---

[8]During what is commonly called the late "stone age."

[9]It has been estimated that the average adult in the United States obtains 99 calories/day from alcoholic beverages (Nielson, Kit, Fakhouri, & Ogden, 2012). However, this is an average, with non-drinkers obviously obtaining zero calories from alcohol while more studious drinkers will obtain more than 99 calories/day from alcohol.

[10]For example, a Roman proverb suggested "Bathing, wine and Venus exhaust the body, that is what life is about."

[11]When the Puritans set sail for the New World, for example, they stocked their ship with 14 tons of water, 10,000 gallons of wine, and 42 tons of beer (McPherson, Yudko, Murray-Bridges, Rodriguez, & Lindo-Moulds, 2009). Historians have suggested that the main reason why they elected to settle in Plymouth was because they had exhausted their supply of beer on the voyage across the Atlantic and needed to grow crops with which to produce more (McAnnelley, 1996).

[12]A little known fact is that John Chapman ("Johnny Appleseed") spread seeds that produced apples that tasted horrible, but which were ideal for fermenting into "hard" apple cider, which is to say apple cider containing alcohol (Okrent, 2010).

[13]There were also an unknown number of *unlicensed* drinking establishments in each community, although since by definition they were not licensed, the exact number remains unclear.

[14]To replace the tax monies lost with the onset of prohibition, when the exercise tax on alcohol ceased to exist, Prohibitionists suggested that another form of taxation be reinstituted: The income tax (Okrent, 2010).

[15]Prohibition started in 1920 and ended in 1933.

Alcohol Today

In the time since the process of distillation was developed, various fermented beverages made with a wide variety of flavors and in different concentrations of alcohol[16] have been developed. It is a common intoxicant, and at any given moment 0.7% of the world's population is intoxicated (Raw Data, 2009b). In the United States beer is the most common form of alcoholic beverage sold and has an alcohol content of 3.5 and 5%, although some special beers have an alcohol content of less than 3% or greater than 9% (Devour, 1999). It has been estimated that 6.3 *billion* gallons of beer are consumed each year in the United States, although there is significant interstate variation (Raw Data, 2013b). The state of New Hampshire has been awarded the dubious honor of consuming the most beer per person each year (43 gallons), whereas Utah has the lowest level of beer consumption (19.2 gallons per person/year) (Raw Data, 2013b).

Wine made in the United States is usually made from the fermentation of grapes or less often other fruits. In other countries, substances other than grapes, such as the famous "rice wine" of Japan known as *sake,* are used for the process of fermentation. In the United States, wine usually has an alcohol content of 8 and 17%. Although light wines might have as little as 7% alcohol and wine "coolers" only 5–7% by weight (Devourk, 1999). The process of distillation allows for some distilled spirits to be added back to wine, to form a beverage with a higher content. These are the "fortified" wines, which may have an alcohol content as high as 20–24% (Devour, 1999). "Hard" liquors usually contain 30–50% alcohol by content, although in some cases the alcohol content might be as high as 80% or more (Devour, 1999). Because high levels of alcohol ingestion can result in a sense of intoxication, scientists are attempting to identify ways in which this might be avoided, or ways in which the individual might recover from this intoxication more rapidly (Motluk, 2006).

How Alcoholic Beverages Are Produced Today

The production of wine had become relatively standardized in Europe and the Middle East by the time of the Greek and Roman empires. It was not until around the year A.D. 800, however, that an Arabian chemist experimented by boiling wine and collecting the steam that was produced by this process. Because alcohol boils at about 172° F and wine boils at 212° F, it is possible to heat a container of wine to the boiling point of alcohol and before it reaches the boiling point of water, the steam produced will contain a higher concentration of alcohol than the original wine. A cap placed over the container in which the wine was heated then directs the vapors to a metal coil that allows them to cool and form a liquid with a higher alcohol concentration than the original wine.[17] This is the process of *distillation,* which historical evidence suggests had reached Europe by around A.D. 1100 (el-Guebaly, 2008; Walton, 2002). Shortly afterwards, wine growers in Italy started using distillation to obtain these concentrated "spirits."

Over the years, they learned to mix these spirits with various herbs and spices to produce different flavored beverages. Physicians were quick to seize on the new beverages as a possible medicine in an era when little was known about disease or its treatment. Consumers were quick to recognize that the resulting drink was more potent than the original wine, allowing the drinker to more quickly achieve a state of intoxication. An additional advantage was that distilled spirits did not spoil as rapidly as did wine and for these reasons soon gained popularity for both medicinal and recreational use.[18]

Unfortunately, during the process of distillation many of the amino acids and vitamins found in the original wine are lost. Thus, although they are a rapid source of intoxication, the concentrated alcohol that results from the process of distillation is nutritionally empty. Reliance on this nutritionally neutral beverage can, if consumed to excess often, contributes to the condition known as *avitaminosis,* which will be discussed in the next chapter. However, alcohol is prized for its ability to produce a state of relaxation, and a state of altered consciousness that at its extreme is called *intoxication.* In a very real sense, we have come

---

[16]A standard by which alcoholic beverages are measured is that the drink must contain 12 grams of ethanol. This is the amount of alcohol found in one standard 12-ounce can of beer, 1.5 ounces of an 80 proof liquor or 4 ounces of regular wine.

[17]The alcohol concentration is measured in "proof" units. There are several competing theories about the origin of the term which, will not be discussed further here. The conversion formula is that a 10% alcohol concentration is 20 "proof" units, or a 1:2 ratio.

[18]A little known fact is that, after leaving the White House after his second term in office ended, Washington went into the distillation business, and was able to produce up to 11,000 gallons of whiskey per year on his plantation, much of which was sold for profit (Zax, 2008).

full circle, producing at will the same fluid so prized by insects and animals in the wild so that we might share the joys of intoxication with them.

A Working Definition of Rare or Social Drinking

It is difficult to define "social" drinking, in part because most research studies rely on retrospective analysis of the frequency of alcohol use and the amount consumed, each of which is subject to distortion (Lezak, Howieson, Bingler, & Tranel, 2012). In this text, social drinking is defined as *no more than* two standard "shots" (each 1.5 ounces) of liquor, two standard (12 ounce) cans of beer, or two standard glasses of wine in a 24-hour period (Lezak et al., 2012). Alcohol abuse or addiction is defined as somebody who will (a) possibly require the daily use of alcohol to function, (b) make attempts to limit his/her heavy alcohol use to a specific time (weekends, for example), with periods of abstinence in between the episodes of heavy alcohol use, (c) engage in continuous "binges"[19] that last for days, weeks, or months, interspaced with periods of abstinence, or who (d) engages in the daily use of alcohol in excess of what is prudent for health or social norms.

The person with an alcohol use disorder will experience any of a wide range of medical, social, legal, interpersonal, or vocational consequences associated with heavy alcohol use, and might possibly have engaged in multiple attempts to cut back, or control his/her alcohol use. Further, individuals with an alcohol use disorder are known to continue to use alcohol in spite of the fact that its use has caused or exacerbated a medical condition in their bodies.[20] In short, the rare or social drinker is the diametric opposite of the problem drinker, and it is important for the substance abuse

counselor to understand the difference between the rare or social drinker and the problem drinker.

Scope of Alcohol Use in the United States Today

It has been estimated that 80–90% of the adults in the United States have consumed alcohol at least once, 70% have done so in the past year, and that 51% of the population 12 years of age or older consume alcohol at least once per month (O'Brien, 2006; Sadock & Sadock, 2007; Schuckit, 2010a; Substance Abuse and Mental Health Services Administration, 2009). It has been estimated that there are 129 million active drinkers in the United States 12 years of age or older (Substance Abuse and Mental Health Services Administration, 2009). Another 12,000 people join this number each day as they take their first drink of an alcohol-containing beverage (Lemonick & Park, 2007).

Over the decades, there has been a marked fluctuation in the per capita amount of alcohol consumed in the United States. In the 1790s it was estimated that an average American consumed 5.8 gallons of pure ethyl alcohol each year, which by the 1830s had increased to 7.1 gallons (Brust, 2004). In 1920, alcohol consumption was outlawed in the United States, and remained illegal until 1933. This forced a reduction in the amount of alcohol consumed, although this is only a guess because so many people were making their own alcohol or buying it illegally. After the repeal of Prohibition, there was a gradual decline in the amount of alcohol consumed by each person in the United States annually, until the year 1996, when this trend reversed (Naimi et al., 2003). Currently, it is thought that the per capita level of alcohol consumption in the United States is equivalent to 23.6 liters of 80 proof vodka per adult in this country every year. This figure pales in comparison to the estimated equivalent 45.6 liters of 80 proof vodka per adult per year consumed in Moldova or the 39.4 liters of 80 proof vodka consumed per adult per year in Russia (Aldhous, 2013). Even in the normally staid United Kingdom the level of alcohol consumption is estimated to be the equivalent of 33.4 liters of 80 "proof" per adult per, year whereas in Canada it is estimated to be the equivalent of 24.4 liters of 80 proof vodka per adult per year.

These figures are *averages*, as there is a significant variation in the level of individual alcohol consumption.

---

[19]A "binge" is defined as when a man consumes five or more standard drinks, glasses of wine, or cans of beer in a 24-hour period, or when a woman consumes 3–4 or more standard drinks, glasses of wine, or cans of beer in a 24-hour period.

[20]Braithwaite and Bryant (2010) suggested, for example, that even nonproblematic alcohol use might interfere with the biotransformation of antiviral agents used to treat AIDS, or that the biotransformation process for antiviral agents used to treat AIDS might interfere with the biotransformation of alcohol, resulting in longer periods of intoxication for the drinker. Other examples of the adverse interaction between alcohol use and various disease states also exist.

It has been estimated that just 10% of those who drink alcohol consume 55–60% of the alcohol consumed in the United States each year, whereas the top 30% of drinkers consume 90% of all the alcohol consumed (Aldhous, 2013; Kilbourne, 2002). Beer is the most popular alcohol-containing drink in the United States (Naimi et al., 2003), although wine "coolers" and light wines are increasing in popularity.

The Pharmacology of Ethyl Alcohol

The alcohol molecule is a small, simple molecule, soluble in both lipids and water, although it shows a preference for the latter (Jones, 1996). It might be introduced into the body intravenously, rectally,[21] or as a vapor,[22] but the most common form of alcohol administration is as a liquid consumed orally. When used orally, small amounts of alcohol are absorbed through the mucous membranes of the mouth and esophagus, and 10–20% is absorbed in through the stomach (Sadock & Sadock, 2007; Swift, 2005; Zakhari, 2006). The majority of the alcohol is absorbed through the proximal portion of the small intestine (Schuckit, 2010a). Following absorption, the alcohol molecules are rapidly distributed throughout the body, especially to blood-rich organs such as the brain, where the concentration soon surpasses the concentration found in the blood (Kranzler & Ciraulo, 2005a). This is because alcohol is able to bind both to lipids and water, both of which are found in abundance in the brain. The alcohol molecule does diffuse into adipose[23] and muscle tissues but it does so with more difficulty than it does into the tissues of the CNS. Still, this characteristic of alcohol distribution means that a heavier person will have a slightly lower blood alcohol level than a lighter person after both consume the same amount of alcohol.

Following the ingestion of a single drink on an empty stomach, peak blood alcohol levels are achieved in 30 (Knapp, Ciraulo, & Kranzler, 2008) to 60 minutes (Sadock & Sadock, 2007). Some researchers believe that when alcohol is consumed with carbonated beverages the absorption of the alcohol is more rapid (Sadock & Sadock, 2007; Schuckit, 2008a, 2010a). When mixed with food, especially high-fat foods, the absorption of alcohol is slowed down to the point where peak alcohol levels might not be achieved until 1–6 hours after it was consumed (Baselt, 1996; Sher, Wood, Richardson, & Jackson, 2005). Thus, by mixing alcohol with food its absorption will be slower; however, eventually all the alcohol will be absorbed into the body.

The mechanism through which alcohol is able to induce a state of intoxication remains poorly understood. Different theories have been advanced to account for alcohol's intoxicating effects (Motluk, 2006). In the early 20th century, it was suggested that alcohol might be able to affect the molecular structure and function of lipids in the neural walls (Brust, 2004; Tabakoff & Hoffman, 2004). This was known as the *membrane fluidization theory,* or the *membrane hypothesis.* According to this theory, alcohol's ability to bind to lipids allowed it to bind to the lipids in the neural walls, making it more difficult for that neuron to maintain normal function. Although appealing, this theory is hampered by the facts that (a) very high concentrations of alcohol are necessary to achieve cellular membrane disruption and (b) that even small changes in body temperature produce more disruption on cellular membrane integrity than does alcohol (Woodward, 2009). For these reasons the membrane hypothesis has fallen into disfavor and there are few advocates of this theory at this time.

Another theory that attempted to explain the effects of alcohol was known as the *TIQ hypothesis.* Trachtenberg and Blum (1987) suggested that alcohol use significantly reduced the brain's production of natural opioid-like molecules known as *enkephalins* and the *dynorphins,* Further, during the process of alcohol biotransformation, an alcohol metabolite and naturally occurring neurotransmitters combined to form the toxic compound *tetrahydroisoquinoline* (TIQ) (Blum, 1988). TIQ was thought to bind to the opioid receptor sites within the brain's reward system, causing euphoria and a sense of well-being (Blum & Payne, 1991; Blum & Trachtenberg, 1988). However, TIQ's effects are short-lived, a characteristic that would force the individual to continue to drink to maintain the initial feeling of well-being achieved through alcohol use according to the authors.

---

[21]This is a rarely utilized method of alcohol administration. Alcohol is easily absorbed through the tissues of the rectum when used as an enema. However, it is exceptionally difficult to titrate the dose and there is a significant risk of serious, possibly fatal, overdose when administered in this manner (Northcutt, 2008). This method of alcohol administration is *not* recommended by the author or publisher of this text.

[22]Although devices have been introduced to take advantage of this characteristic of ethyl alcohol, many states have banned their use, and others are expected to do so, soon.

[23]See Glossary.

Over time, heavy habitual alcohol use was thought to cause the brain to reduce its productions of natural opioid-like molecules as the ever-present TIQ was substituted for these natural neurotransmitters (Blum & Payne, 1991; Blum & Trachtenberg, 1988). The individual's cessation of drinking would result in a lack of stimulation in the reward system, which the individual would experience as "craving" for further alcohol use. Although the TIQ theory had many proponents in the latter part of the 20th century and still is occasionally suggested as accounting for alcohol-induced feelings of euphoria experienced by drinkers, a number of research studies have failed to find evidence supporting the TIQ hypothesis and it has been found that changes in diet can also induce the same changes in TIQ as observed following alcohol ingestion (Woodward, 2009). There are few advocates of this theory now.

Scientists now believe that alcohol is a "dirty" compound. It does not seem to show a preference for a specific receptor sites, but alters the action of various neurotransmitters as well as interferes with the action of messenger molecules within the neuron itself (Knapp et al., 2008; Lovinger, 2008).[24] Some of the neurotransmitter systems altered by the ingestion of alcohol include (Cruz, Bajo, Schweitzer, & Roberto, 2008; Knapp et al., 2008) GABAa, glutamate, nicotinic, cannabinoid, opioid, and voltage-gated calcium ion channels. Alcohol enhances the effects of Gamma-Amino-Butyric Acid (GABA),[25] the main inhibitory neurotransmitter in the brain by binding at receptor sites utilized by GABA. When alcohol molecules bind at the GABAa-1 receptor, it enhances the influx of chloride atoms into the neuron, slowing the rate at which that neuron can "fire" (Tabakoff & Hoffman, 2004). When the alcohol molecules bind at the GABAa2s receptor site it induces a subjective sense of relaxation. When alcohol binds to the GABAa5s receptor site in sufficient quantities, it can induce memory loss, psychomotor impairment, and indirectly contribute to the experience of alcohol-induced euphoria (Mutluk, 2006).

Alcohol ingestion also alters the *N-methyl-D-aspartate* (NMDA) receptor sites in the CNS that are utilized by the neurotransmitter glutamate (Schuckit, 2008a). Glutamate is the main excitatory neurotransmitter found in the brain, increasing the firing rate of downstream neurons when it reaches the NMDA receptors (Pinel, 2003; Valenzuela & Harris, 1997). By blocking the action of glutamate at the receptor site alcohol might be said to be a glutamate antagonist. The subjective effect of alcohol is usually a feeling of gentle euphoria, in part because of alcohol's action on the endogenous opioid receptor system.[26] When the drinker drinks enough alcohol to achieve moderate to high blood levels, the alcohol molecules are known to promote the binding process at the mu opioid receptor site[27] (Cruz et al., 2008; Modesto-Lowe & Fritz, 2005; Stahl, 2008). The mu opioid receptor site appears to be associated with the experience of alcohol-induced euphoria, an observation supported by experimental research that suggests that the administration of opioid antagonists like Naltrexone reduce alcohol consumption by regular alcohol abusers. In contrast to this, the activation of the sigma opioid receptor site by high doses of alcohol appears associated with the aversive effects of alcohol (vomiting, etc.).

A competing theory suggests that alcohol-induced euphoria is caused by its ability to force neurons to empty their stores of dopamine back into the synaptic junction (Heinz et al., 1998). High levels of dopamine release in the nucleus accumbens region of the brain appears to be involved in the reward cascade. The disinhibitory actions of alcohol appear to reflect its ability to enhance the effects of the neurotransmitter *serotonin* at the 5HT3 receptor site (Tabakoff & Hoffman, 2004). This serotonin receptor subtype is involved in the process of inhibition of behavioral inhibition. Technically, alcohol intoxication is an acute confusional state reflecting cortical dysfunction (Filley, 2004; Schuckit, 2006a). At mild to moderate intensities, this cortical dysfunction can result in neuromuscular dysfunction, cognitive dysfunction, and speech problems. When consumed in sufficient quantities, alcohol is capable of interfering with the formation of memories in the drinker's brain. This condition is called *anterograde amnesia* (Ghoneim, 2004a; 2004b). At its extreme, it can be fatal through cardiopulmonary arrest. However, there is little evidence to suggest that social drinking is associated with the long-term neurocognitive changes

---

[24]To illustrate how little is known about alcohol and its effects, it was recently discovered that alcohol molecules alter the norepinephrine receptor sites in the brain, although the consequences of this process are yet to be identified.

[25]See Glossary.

[26]However, Cook (2010) observed that sufficient sleep deprivation magnifies alcohol's effects, so that the subjective experience of three standard drinks will have the same subjective effect as 6, although the individual's blood alcohol will only reflect the three drinks that were ingested.

[27]Discussed in Chapter 11.

found in persistent heavy drinkers (Rourke & Grant, 2009).

The Biotransformation of Alcohol

The liver is the primary organ that biotransforms alcohol, and the primary method of biotransformation is oxidation (Sadock & Sadock, 2003; Schuckit, 2010a; Zakhari, 2006). However, about 10% of the alcohol ingested is excreted unchanged or is broken down in other sites in the body (Edenberg, 2007). At extremely high blood levels, the percentage of alcohol that is excreted unchanged through the lungs, urine, and skin is increased, giving the intoxicated person the characteristic smell of intoxication (Sadock & Sadock, 2007; Schuckit, 2006a).

For the rare social drinker alcohol biotransformation begins in the stomach, which produces small amounts of an enzyme known as *alcohol dehydrogenase* (ADH) ("Alcoholism Metabolism: An Update," 2007; Sadock & Sadock, 2007). However, the stomach's ability to produce this enzyme is impaired by the concurrent use of aspirin (Schuckit, 2011). Alcohol dehydrogenase production is also dependent on the level of testosterone in the user's blood. Because women produce less testosterone than men, they produce less alcohol dehydrogenase, contributing to the tendency for the woman to become more intoxicated on a given amount of alcohol than a man (Sadock & Sadock, 2007; Swift, 2005). Women also usually have a lower muscle-to-body mass ratio, and about 10% less water volume then men (Zealberg & Brady, 1999), factors that also contribute to the tendency for women to become more intoxicated on a given amount of alcohol than does a man.

The liver is where the majority of alcohol is biotransformed. First, the liver produces large amounts of ADH, breaking alcohol down into a metabolite called *acetaldehyde*. It has been suggested that in prehistoric times the liver's ability to produce ADH evolved so that mammals could biotransform natural alcohol when fermented fruits were ingested, or, to help the body deal with the small amount of alcohol produced endogenously[28] (Jones, 1996). This metabolite, acetaldehyde, has been found to be extremely toxic to the human body (Melton, 2007). Normally, this is not a problem, because the body produces a family of enzymes[29] that are collectively known as *aldehyde dehydrogenase*. These enzymes, especially the form known as *aldehyde dehydrogenase #2*[30] rapidly break acetaldehyde down into acetic acid, which can be burned by the muscles as fuel (Melton, 2007). Ultimately, alcohol is biotransformed into carbon dioxide, water, and fatty acids (carbohydrates).

The Speed of Alcohol Biotransformation

There is some inter-individual variability in the speed at which alcohol is biotransformed and eliminated (Edenberg, 2007; Zakhari, 2006). An average person might biotransform one standard mixed drink of 80 proof alcohol, 4 ounces of wine, or one 12-ounce can of beer, every 60–90 minutes (Nace, 2005; Fleming, Mihic, & Harris, 2006; Schuckit, 2011), doing so through a zero-order biotransformation process. So the rate of alcohol biotransformation is relatively independent of the alcohol blood level, and if the person should consume alcohol at a rate faster than the speed of biotransformation, the blood alcohol level will increase. The outcome of this process will be discussed in the section devoted to the subjective effects of alcohol.

The Alcohol Flush Reaction

After drinking even a small amount of alcohol, 3 and 29% of persons of European descent and 47 and 85% of persons of Asian descent experience the *alcohol flush reaction* (Collins & McNair, 2002; Sher & Wood, 2005). The alcohol flush reaction is the result of a genetic mutation that prevents the liver from producing sufficient amounts of aldehyde dehydrogenase. This allows abnormally high levels of acetaldehyde to accumulate in the drinker's blood. As acetaldehyde levels climb to perhaps 20 times those seen in the normal person who had consumed a similar amount of alcohol the individual will experience symptoms such as facial flushing, heart palpitations, dizziness, and nausea. Persons from Asia are more likely to experience this effect, and this is thought to be why alcohol use disorders are less common in persons of Asia descent.

---

[28]Occasionally, a person arrested for driving while under the influence of alcohol will try to argue that it is because of this naturally occurring alcohol that s/he was intoxicated, and not because s/he had ingested alcohol-containing beverages. Unfortunately, the bacteria in the gastrointestinal tract produce about 1-2 teaspoons of ethyl alcohol in a 24-hour period, which is hardly sufficient to induce intoxication.

[29]Sometimes referred to as the *ALDHs*.

[30]Referred to in some of the literature as $ALDH_2$.

Weight (pounds)

Number of drinks in 1 hour	100	120	140	160	180	200	220
2	0.07	0.06	0.05	0.05*	0.04	0.04*	0.03
3	0.10	0.09	0.07	0.07*	0.06	0.05	0.05*
4	0.14	0.11	0.10	0.08	0.08*	0.07	0.06
5	0.18	0.14	0.12	0.11	0.10	0.08	0.08*
6	0.20	0.18	0.14	0.12	0.12*	0.10	0.09
7	0.25	0.20	0.18	0.16	0.12	0.12*	0.11
8	0.30	0.25	0.20	0.18	0.16	0.14	0.12

Level of legal intoxication with measured blood alcohol level of 0.08 mg/dl. Individuals at or above this level are legally too intoxicated to drive.

*Rounded off.

© Cengage Learning

FIGURE 4-1 Approximate Blood Alcohol Levels.

NOTE: The chart is provided only as an illustration and is not sufficiently accurate to be used as legal evidence or as a guide to "safe" drinking. Individual blood alcohol levels from the same dose of alcohol vary widely, and these figures provide an average blood alcohol level for an individual of a given body weight.

The Blood Alcohol Level (BAL)

Because it is not possible to measure the alcohol level in the drinker's brain, physicians have to settle for a measurement of the alcohol concentration in the drinker's blood, or exhaled breath, procedures that provide the *blood alcohol level* (BAL).[31] The BAL is reported in milligrams of alcohol per 100 milliliters of blood (mg/mL). A BAL of 0.10 would be 1/10th of a milligram of alcohol per 100 milliliters of blood. The BAL provides a *rough approximation* of the individual's level of intoxication and the behavioral effects of alcohol that should be expected from an individual with the measured BAL (Knapp et al., 2008).[32] The same individual might have different behaviors at different times with exactly the same BAL in response to different mood states and environmental factors (Stein & Rogers, 2009). Further, the drinker's subjective sense of intoxication appears to be stronger whereas the BAL is still rising, a phenomenon known as the *Mellanby effect* (Drummer & Odell, 2001; Greenberg, 2010; Sher et al., 2005). The Mellanby effect might reflect the individual's body as starting to become tolerant to the effects of alcohol even after just one drink, although this theory has not been proven.

The concentration of alcohol in the drinker's blood is proportional to the amount of alcohol in the breath exhaled, allowing for the rapid and minimally invasive measurement of the individual's BAL. Breath alcohol testing is preferred over blood tests because of its ease of measurement and accuracy, although blood tests are occasionally used to determine the individual's BAL.

As noted earlier, the BAL that will be achieved by two people who consume the same amount of alcohol will vary as a result of a number of factors, including whether they had recently had a meal, and body size. A hypothetical person who weighs 100 lbs and who consumed two regular drinks in an hour's time would have a BAL of 0.09 (just above the amount needed to be legally intoxicated). A second hypothetical person who also had consumed two regular drinks in an hour's time who weighed 200 lbs would have a BAL of only 0.04 mg/mL, however, as the alcohol would be distributed in a larger body volume in the latter case. Figure 4-1 provides a rough estimate of the BAL that might result if various hypothetical persons of different weights were to consume different amounts of alcohol.[33]

---

[31]Occasionally the term *Blood Alcohol Concentration* (BAC) is used.

[32]Persons who have been through gastric bypass surgery, for example, achieve higher blood alcohol levels than a person of the same weight who has not had such surgery, often resulting in the individual becoming intoxicated when he or she did not think that they had ingested enough alcohol to do so (Holt, 2011).

---

[33]This table is provided only to illustrate the process of intoxication at different levels of alcohol consumption, and is *not* intended to function as an aid to diagnosis or as a guide to safe drinking.

Subjective Effects of Alcohol on the Individual at Normal Doses in the Social Drinker

At high doses, alcohol is both a neurotoxin, and a psychoactive compound (Lezak et al., 2012). It also has very mild analgesic effect. However, most drinkers do not consume alcohol for its analgesic effect, but rather for its psychoactive properties. Surprisingly, at low to moderate BALs, the individual's *expectations* play a major role in how that person interprets the effects of alcohol and his/her drinking behavior (Sher et al., 2005). It has been found, for example, that alcohol users tend to have more positive expectations for the outcome of their drinking than do nondrinkers. These expectations begin to form early in life, perhaps as early as 3 years of age and become more entrenched between the ages of 3–7 years, well before the individual is old enough to legally consume alcohol (Jones & McMahon, 1998).

One effect that the individual does encounter after just 1–2 drinks is the *disinhibition effect*. It is believed that this is caused when alcohol interferes with the normal function of the cortex region responsible for inhibitions, as well as abstract thinking and speech. Neurocognitive changes are experienced when the individual's BAL is only 0.02 to 0.03 mg/ml of blood (1–2 drinks). This is the dosage range at which the individual also begins to "forget" social inhibitions (Julien, 2005), and might end up doing something that s/he might later regret. The consumption of too much alcohol could lead to the individual's death from respiratory arrest, an outcome that unfortunately is all too common among high school and college students. The effects of alcohol for the social or rare drinker are summarized in Table 4-1.

Medical Complications of Alcohol Use for the Social Drinker

A Note of Caution

There are many medical conditions such as diabetes or cardiovascular problems that can present as alcohol intoxication (Schuckit, 2011). Thus a physician should determine whether the individual is intoxicated or demonstrating a symptom of another medical condition.

A Speedy Recovery

Many different chemicals or combination of chemicals have been advanced over the years to reduce the period of time that it takes for a given person to recover from the acute effects of alcohol. What follows is a brief summary of the results of such research.

Caffeine

Although it was thought that caffeine counteracted alcohol's sedating effects, research has shown that the only benefit from drinking coffee when intoxicated is that the time necessary to drink the coffee provides the body with more time to biotransform the alcohol that the drinker had ingested.

TABLE 4-1
Effects of Alcohol on the Infrequent Drinker

BLOOD ALCOHOL LEVEL (BAL)	BEHAVIORAL AND PHYSICAL EFFECTS
0.02	Feeling of warmth, relaxation.
0.05–0.09	Skin becomes flushed. Drinker is more talkative, feels euphoria. At this level, psychomotor skills are slightly to moderately impaired, and ataxia develops. Loss of inhibitions, increased reaction time, and visual field disturbances.
0.10–0.19	Slurred speech, severe ataxia, mood instability, drowsiness, nausea and vomiting, staggering gait, confusion.
0.20–0.29	Lethargy, combativeness, stupor, severe ataxia, incoherent speech, amnesia, unconsciousness.
0.30–0.39	Coma, respiratory depression, anesthesia, respiratory failure.
Above 0.40	Death.

Sources: Based on Baselt (1996), T. M. Brown and Stoudemire (1998), Brust (2004).

CNS Stimulants

Compounds such as cocaine or the amphetamines were once thought to speed the recovery process. Research has shown that they simply *hide* the behavioral effects of the alcohol in the body, but do not speed up the biotransformation process (Woodward, 2009).

Narcan®

Based on the assumption that alcohol's euphoric effects are induced by activation of the reward cascade in the brain, it was hoped that Narcan®, a narcotic receptor site blocker used to treat opiate overdoses, might speed the process of recovery from alcohol ingestion. This theory has been found to be unfounded (Woodward, 2009). To date, the only known cure for acute alcohol intoxication is to allow the body to biotransform the alcohol ingested and eliminate it from the circulation.

The Hangover

Most people do not experience a hangover every time when they consume alcohol, but approximately 75% of drinkers will experience a hangover at some point in their life. Even small amounts of alcohol can cause headaches in migraine sufferers. Such headaches, although severe, are not *hangovers*. The hangover has been known to be an aftereffect to drinking for thousands of years. Physical manifestations of the hangover include fatigue, malaise, sensitivity to light, thirst, tremor, nausea, dizziness, depression, and anxiety (Schuckit, 2006a; Sher et al., 2005). There is evidence to suggest that some individuals are more prone to this alcohol withdrawal effect than others, possibly as a result of their genetic inheritance (Swift & Davidson, 1998).

Once the hangover develops, there is little that can be done to speed its resolution in spite of the wide variety of folk remedies purported to do this (Erickson, 2007). In spite of the individual's subjective discomfort, alcohol-induced hangovers usually resolve in 8–24 hours, and will require only conservative medical treatments such as antacids, bed rest, adequate fluids and over-the-counter analgesics. Researchers are still divided over the question of whether the hangover is caused by (a) the direct effects of alcohol on the drinker's brain, (b) the effects of a metabolite of alcohol biotransformation (such as acetaldehyde), (c) some of the flavoring agents mixed with liquors (called *congeners*), (d) an alcohol-induced state of dehydration that affects brain function, (e) reflects an early alcohol-withdrawal syndrome, or (f) the effects of an alcohol-induced reduction in brain ß-endorphin levels (Mosier, 1999; Swift, & Davidson, 1998). Some of the congeners contained within alcohol containing beverages include (Roshsenow et al., 2009) acetone, acetaldehyde, fusel oil, tannins, and furfural, although the proportion of these compounds varies from one compound to the next. Bourbon, for example, contains 37 times the concentration of congeners as does vodka (Roshsenow et al., 2009). However, the role of congeners in the development of the alcohol withdrawal is still only a theory and it is possible that another mechanism causes this unpleasant experience.

The Effects of Alcohol on the Cardiovascular System

The question whether rare social drinking brings with it a cardioprotective effect is controversial. The *moderate* use of alcohol, defined as the consumption of no more than two standard drinks per day for a man and half that for a woman, has been found to induce a 10–40% reduction in the drinker's risk of developing coronary heart disease (CHD) (Fleming et al., 2003). Early studies suggested that rare social drinking had a potential cardioprotective effect by increasing HDL levels of cholesterol (the "good" cholesterol) in the blood, making it more difficult for atherosclerotic plaque to build up on the walls of the drinker's arteries (O'Connor, Rusyniak, & Bruno, 2005). However, "rare social" drinking was defined as significantly lower than the recognized two standard glasses of wine or standard mixed drink per day each day of the week (Nichols, Scarborough, Allender, & Rayner, 2012). The authors suggested that the safe limit for social drinking was about one-half of a standard glass of wine, or mixed drink *per* day was the optimal level of alcohol intake. Even at this relatively conservative level of alcohol use the authors calculated that approximately 840 people would die each year in England alone from alcohol-related heart disease. However, the authors suggested that there would be 2,670 fewer deaths from cancer and 2,830 fewer deaths from liver disease in England each year at that level of alcohol use.

A possible solution to this dilemma was offered by Chiva-Blanch et al. (2012). The authors found that nonalcoholic red wine, which is to say wine with the alcohol removed but the other agents such as the polyphenols[34] left, appeared to provide the cardiovascular protection once attributed to wine. This research, if replicated, suggests a possible approach to the prevention or treatment of cardiovascular disease without exposing the individual to alcohol itself. The *moderate* use of alcohol is thought to be cardioprotective because of its functions as an anticoagulant and reduces fibrinogen levels (Klatsky, 2003). This apparent cardioprotective effect appears to be moderated by the individual's genetic heritage, lifestyle, and current health status with some drinkers obtaining more of a protective effect than others (Britton, Marmot, & Shipley, 2008; Hines et al., 2001; Karlamangla et al., 2009).[35] Unfortunately, this effect is achieved at a price, as there is a dose-dependent relationship between alcohol consumption and loss of brain volume that is seen even with just 1–2 drinks a day (Paula et al., 2008). This effect is stronger in women than in men, but does affect both women and men, according to the authors.

Many "binge" drinkers believe that they are immune to the cardiovascular dangers associated with heavy alcohol use[36] because they are only engaging in "binge" drinking. This belief is wrong: It has been determined that even "binge" drinking can speed up the formation of plaque in the coronary arteries of the drinker (Redmond, Morrow, Kunkiml, Miller-Graziano, & Cullen, 2008; Ruidavets et al., 2010). The causal mechanism appears to be that acetaldehyde, an intermediate step in the biotransformation of alcohol, can induce the binding of cells known as monocytes to artery walls contributing to the formation of plaque in the drinker's body (Redmond et al., 2008). The research team of Ruidavets, Ducimetiere. Evans et al. (2010) compared the incidence of coronary disease in 2,400 men in Belfast, Northern Ireland, where binge drinking was common against that of 7,340 men in France, where the use of alcoholic beverages was higher but was spread out evenly across the week. They found that middle-aged male binge drinkers in Belfast were 76% more likely to suffer a heart attack, or death from coronary artery disease than the French drinkers. This finding is concerning because younger drinkers

are more likely to engage in binge drinking. Binge drinking also can increase the risk of a cardiac arrhythmia known as *atrial fibrillation* by about 51% (Kodama et al., 2011).[37] A common complication of atrial fibrillation is the formation of blood clots, which break loose and might cause either a stroke or a heart attack when they lodge in an artery. The causal mechanism for this unexpected finding is not known at this time and little is known about the effects of binge drinking in persons at high risk for the development of atrial fibrillation because of pre-existing cardiovascular disease or diabetes (Liang et al., 2012). The social myth that moderate alcohol use is automatically protective against heart disease is thus not proven and might be false.

The Effects of Alcohol on Gastrointestinal Tract

At high blood alcohol levels, the stomach begins to excrete more mucus than normal and will close the pyloric valve between the stomach and the small intestine in an attempt to slow further alcohol absorption. The drinker will experience a sense of nausea and possibly might vomit as the body attempts to rid itself of the alcohol, which is after all a poison. Unfortunately, alcohol also interferes with the normal vomiting reflex, possibly to the point where the drinker's body might attempt regurgitation while the person was unconscious. This will expose the unconscious drinker to the danger of possible aspiration of the material being regurgitated, which can contribute to a condition known as *aspiration pneumonia*.[38] If the airway should become totally blocked, the unconscious drinker might very possibly die during this process.

The Effects of Alcohol on Sleep for the Social Drinker

Although alcohol, like other central nervous system depressants, might induce a form of sleep, it does not allow the drinker to follow a normal sleep cycle. Alcohol-induced sleep problems, although strongest in the chronic drinker,[39] can occur even in the social drinker especially after a "binge" drinking episode (Roshsenow et al., 2009). Even modest amount of alcohol consumed within 2 hours of when the initiation of

---

[34]See Glossary.

[35]While alcohol use advocates point to this fact as a reason why people should drink alcohol in moderation, they overlook the fact that the French, as a whole, have a higher incidence of alcohol-related liver disease (Walton, 2002).

[36]Discussed in Chapter 3.

---

[37]Sometimes called the *Holiday Heart Syndrome* since many people over-indulge by drinking too much on holidays.

[38]See Glossary.

[39]Discussed in Chapter 5.

sleep can contribute to both more frequent and longer episodes of sleep apnea.[40] Alcohol use prior to sleep has been shown to weaken pharyngeal muscle tone, increasing the tendency for the drinker to snore while asleep, and experience sleep breathing problems (Qureshi & Lee-Chiong, 2004). Even rare social drinkers with known sleep respiratory problems should consult a physician before using alcohol.

Social Drinking and Stroke

There is evidence that social or light alcohol use (defined as < 2 mixed drinks per 24 hours) will reduce the individual's risk for death from coronary artery disease. Paradoxically, consumption of < 1 standard drink per day was associated with an increased risk for death from a stroke (Ronksley, Brien, Turner, Mukamal, & Ghall, 2011). Earlier studies revealed contradictory evidence that social drinking might increase the individual's risk for a stroke; however, the study by Ronksley et al. (2011) would seem to provide a more comprehensive overview of the subject than earlier studies, strongly suggesting that even casual or social alcohol use will raise the individual's risk for a stroke. There was no observed relationship between level of alcohol use and functional outcome after the individual suffered a stroke, however, indicating that level of alcohol use was not a factor in poststroke recovery (Rist et al., 2010).

Alcohol Use and Neurocognitive Effects

There is a growing body of evidence that alcohol can start to induce brain damage even in social drinkers. The team of Biller, Bartsch, Homola, and Bendszus (2009) administered either three beers or two glasses of wine to research their subjects. The authors then examined the brains of their volunteers through a process known as magnetic resonance spectroscopy, and found that creatine, a chemical that helps to protect neurons, decreases as the individual's blood alcohol level increases. They postulated that this might be one of the mechanisms through which heavy drinking might cause brain damage. Acute intoxication has been identified as a factor in the disruption of the process of neurogenesis in the individual's brain (Crews, 2008). Even social drinking can induce some degree of depression on the drinker, possibly levels of depression

that will contribute to self-abusive behavior(s), as evidenced by the fact that as many as two-thirds of those individuals who commit self-injurious acts used alcohol prior to the commission of that act (McClosky & Berman, 2003).

The observed neurocognitive deficits appear to persist for hours after the individual's body has finished the process of biotransformation and elimination (Roshsenow et al., 2009). The authors found that binge drinkers in their study suffered longer reaction times in spite of the participants' subjective belief that they were capable of driving safely. This suggests that binge drinkers present a higher risk for motor vehicle accidents than do abstainers or those who choose not to drive the next day.

Other Consequences of Rare/Social Drinking

The most significant of the consequences of rare/social alcohol use is quite simply the death of the drinker. Alcohol is responsible for more deaths from chemical overdose than any other drug of abuse (Schuckit, 2006b). The amount of alcohol that must be ingested to induce intoxication is already a significant fraction of the lethal dose, and the higher that the individual's blood alcohol level becomes, the closer that she or he will be to death from an alcohol overdose. Alcohol also interferes with the body's ability to excrete uric acid from the body. This is a matter of some concern for individuals who suffer from high uric acid levels (such as those found in gout and certain forms of kidney stones). The team of Zhang et al. (2006) concluded that even occasional alcohol use would increase the individual's risk of an acute attack of gout if s/he were predisposed to this condition, with such attacks usually taking place within 24 hours of the individual's alcohol use.

Another relatively common consequence of social alcohol use is the dreaded "beer goggle" effect (Aldhous, 2008). In brief, alcohol consumption appears to make the drinker less selective in the choice of potential partner(s), resulting in a possible shock next day when the drinker awakens. Alcohol use by young adults has been found to alter the drinker's perception of the sexual attractiveness of both the drinker and that of potential sexual partners (Aldhous, 2008). Further, as noted above, the disinhibition effect of alcohol encourages the individual to engage in behavior(s)

---

[40]See Glossary.

that s/he would normally avoid. This would seem to account for the observation that in 80% of cases where a person was driving while under the influence of alcohol they had been binge drinking (Quinn & Fromme, 2012). Finally, there is a dose-related increase in the risk for breast cancer for the individual. Consumption of just 3–6 drinks per week results in a 15% increase in the risk for the development of breast cancer, although women who consume 30+ drinks per week experience a 50% increased risk for invasive breast cancer (Chen et al., 2011). Thus, even social alcohol use increases the risk of breast cancer for the woman drinker.

Drug Interactions Involving Social Alcohol Use[41]

There has been little research into the effects of social drinking (defined as 1–2 standard drinks a day) on the action of various pharmaceutical agents (Wethermon & Crabb, 1999). It is known that because alcohol functions as a central nervous system (CNS) depressant that it might potentiate the effects of other CNS depressants such as over-the-counter/prescribed antihistamines, benzodiazepines,[42] barbiturates,[43] opiates,[44] and various anesthetic agents used in medical practice (Weathermon & Crabb, 1999; Zernig & Battista, 2000). Patients who take nitroglycerine, used to treat certain heart conditions, should not use alcohol under any circumstances, as the combination of these compounds can cause a significant, potentially serious, drop in blood pressure (Zernig & Battista, 2000).

Patients taking the anticoagulant medication warfarin should not drink, as alcohol's anticoagulant effects will cause abnormal biotransformation patterns of the warfarin being used, with potentially dangerous results for the drinker. Because of its anticoagulant effects the danger of unwanted bleeding is increased when alcohol is ingested with aspirin. Although acetaminophen, a common alternative to aspirin, does not have an anticoagulant effect, the use of acetaminophen and alcohol increases the risk of acetaminophen-related hepatotoxicity[45] even if used at regular dosage levels (Ciraulo, Shader, Greenblatt, & Creelman, 2006; Woodward, 2009). Thus, the use of alcohol with over-the-counter analgesics should be avoided except under the advice of a physician.

Although there is evidence that the antidepressant amitriptyline might enhance the euphoric effects of alcohol, the concurrent use of both medications might cause rapid, potentially dangerous, blood pressure changes for the drinker (Weathermon & Crabb, 1999). Although the selective serotonin reuptake inhibitors (SSRIs) are antidepressants with fewer side effects or risks than the older antidepressant medications, the use of alcohol with the SSRIs increases the individual's risk for the development of the *Serotonin Syndrome*[46] (Brown & Stoudemire, 1998). Diabetic patients taking oral medications for their diabetes should not drink, as the alcohol ingested can interfere with the body's ability to biotransform alcohol, and can result in acute alcohol poisoning at even moderate BALs. Further, the anti-diabetic medication prevents the body from being able to break the alcohol down, extending the period of alcohol intoxication. Patients on monoamine oxidase inhibitors (MAO inhibitors or MAOIs) should not consume alcohol under *any* circumstances, to avoid the risk of intermixing their medication with the amino acid tyramine. This amino acid is produced during fermentation, and when mixed with a MAOI may cause dangerously high, perhaps fatal, blood pressure levels (Brown & Stoudemire, 1998).

Researchers have found that verapamil hydrochloride[47] inhibits the process of alcohol biotransformation, increasing the duration of intoxication (Brown & Stoudemire, 1998). Although early research suggested that the medications ranitidine and cimitidine (now sold as over-the-counter agents for control of stomach acid) should not be mixed with alcohol, later research failed to support this hypothesis. However, the mixture of these compounds should be avoided whenever possible. Also, alcohol use should be avoided in persons taking an antibiotic compound such as chloramphenicol, furazolidone, metronidazole, or the antimalarial

---

[41]The list of medications that might interact with alcohol is quite extensive. This is only a partial list of medications that might interact with alcohol. The reader is advised to consult a pharmacist and/or physician before mixing ethyl alcohol with any form of over-the-counter or prescription medication.

[42]Discussed in Chapter 10.

[43]Discussed in Chapter 9.

[44]Discussed in Chapter 14.

---

[45]See Glossary.

[46]See Glossary.

[47]A calcium channel blocker used for control of hypertension and sold under a variety of brand names.

medication quinacrine. When mixed with these medications, alcohol produces a flush reaction type of response that can be both uncomfortable, and potentially dangerous. Although the antibiotic erythromycin does not cause an alcohol flush reaction response, it does speed gastric emptying, causing abnormally high BALs (Zernig & Battista, 2000). Patients who are on the antibiotic doxycycline and who drink will find that the alcohol decreases the antibiotic blood levels, possibly to the point where it will no longer be effective (Brown & Stoudemire, 1998). Finally, the effectiveness of the anti-tubercular medication isoniazid (or "INH") will be reduced if the patient consumes alcohol and in extreme cases can induce hepatitis when mixed with alcohol.

Alcohol use can interfere with or enhance the effects of many of the drugs of abuse. For example, the concurrent use of alcohol and cocaine interferes with the pharmacokinetics of both compounds. Although there has been limited research into possible interactions between alcohol and marijuana, preliminary evidence suggests that alcohol's depressant effects might exacerbate the CNS depressant effects of marijuana (Garriott, 1996). As this list would suggest, alcohol is a very potent compound that has the potential to interact with a wide range of chemicals, and it should not be consumed by patients taking any over-the-counter or prescription medication.

Alcohol Ingestion and Injury

Pennock (2007) argues persuasively that following World War II what might collectively be called the "alcohol industry" had adopted several advertising strategies, all of which were designed to project an image of alcohol consumption as a mark of sophistication, a way to share a pleasant time, and a way to entertain guests. Missing from such advertisements were admissions that alcohol consumption also played a role in accidental injury, interpersonal violence, and death. Even if the drinker whose BAL is between 0.05 and 0.079, levels below that used to define legal intoxication, have a 546% higher risk of being in a motor vehicle accident if s/he were to drive, whereas a BAL of 0.08 increases the odds of that individual being in a motor vehicle accident by 1,500% (Movig et al., 2004). A recent research study found that 37% of drivers who died in single vehicle fatal accidents had blood alcohol levels above the legal limit of 0.08, and 25% tested

positive for at least one illicit drug[48] (Romano & Voas, 2011).

Alcohol use has also been found to be a factor in 51% of all boating fatalities (Copeland, 2011). Ethyl alcohol use has also been found to be a factor in 17–53% of all falls, and 40–67% of all fire-related fatalities (Lewis, 1997). Although bicycles are not usually thought of as a high risk activity, 32% of the adults who die in a bicycle accident were found to have alcohol in their systems at the time of their accident (Li, Baker, Smialek, & Soderstrom, 2001). This is consistent with the observation that 52% of patients treated at one major trauma center were found to have alcohol in their blood at the time of admission (Cornwell et al., 1998), because bike accidents are one potential form of major trauma. This list, although incomplete, does demonstrate that even casual alcohol use carries with it a significant risk of accidental injury or death.

There is a known association between alcohol use and interpersonal violence. It has been suggested that the alcohol-related disinhibition effect might explain, in part, the relationship between alcohol use and aggressive behavior. Alcohol was found to be involved in 38% of loud arguments, 57% of disputes that involve a threat being made, and 68% in which there is physical aggression of some kind (Giancola et al., 2009). In approximately 86% of homicides, 60% of sex offenses, 37% of physical assault, and 30% of child abuse, the perpetrator was under the influence of alcohol at the time of the offense (Greenfield, 2007; Parrott & Giancola, 2006). Further, an unknown percentage of victims in each category of crime identified above was also using alcohol. The association between alcohol use and injury is so strong that any patient who has been injured while under the influence of alcohol be assessed for a full alcohol use disorder (discussed in the next chapter).

As this information suggests, although alcohol is man's most popular recreational beverage, its use is not without significant danger. Alcohol is not as innocuous as many both in and outside of what might loosely be called the "liquor industry" would have us believe, it interacts with numerous pharmaceuticals, and its habitual use is responsible for death from various forms of organ failure as well as accidents.

---

[48]These two subgroups overlapped somewhat and were not mutually exclusive.

Alcohol Use and the *Diagnostic and Statistical Manual of Mental Disorders* (5th Edition)[49]

The *Diagnostic and Statistical Manual of Mental Disorders* (5th edition) (*DSM-5*) (American Psychiatric Association, 2013) identified five alcohol-related disorders, of which two are relevant in this chapter: (1) *alcohol intoxication* and (2) the *unspecified alcohol-related disorder*. If the premise that the post drinking "hangover" is a form of alcohol withdrawal then this category also applies to drinkers discussed in this chapter. The term *alcohol intoxication* reflects those individuals whose drinking has resulted in the state of intoxication discussed in this chapter. Unspecified alcohol-related disorders are clearly beyond that of social drinking, and identify individuals who are experiencing occupational, social, familial, psychological, or financial problems because of their drinking but who do not meet the criteria for alcohol dependence.[50]

Chapter Summary

People have long consumed ethyl alcohol as a relatively harmless recreational substance when used in moderation, research has shown that its use carries with it a significant potential for harm. It may be the first recreational chemical produced by humans, and over the years its production has become more sophisticated as its production moved through the use of fermented honey, to fermented fruits, on to distilled spirits. Distillation allowed manufacturers to increase the alcohol content in the beverage being produced above the 15% limit imposed by nature itself, allowing more concentrated beverages with higher alcohol contents to be developed. Alcohol's effects on the rare social drinker were reviewed, and some of the more significant interactions between alcohol and pharmaceutical agents were discussed. In the next chapter, the effects of chronic and heavy alcohol use will be explored.

---

[49]The material presented here is to illustrate the relationship between the alcohol use disorders and the *Diagnostic and Statistical Manual of Mental Disorders* (5th edition). This material should not be interpreted as, nor should it be used as, a diagnostic guide.

[50]This term is discussed in Chapter 5.

The Alcohol Use Disorders

Introduction

The focus of the last chapter was on the effects of ethyl alcohol on the rare social drinker, in which it was discovered that even limited alcohol use is associated with an increased risk of premature or accidental death. However, the spectrum of alcohol use does not stop with the rare or social use of alcohol and the continuum of alcohol use extends to include alcohol abuse and addiction. The neurological mechanisms that encourage excessive alcohol consumption are not known at this time although the release of endogenous opioids has long been accepted as a possible mechanism that promotes continued excessive alcohol use. However, new research suggests that the ingestion of even small amounts of alcohol by heavy drinkers initiates the release of larger amounts of the endogenous opioids than is true for rare or social drinkers (Mitchell et al., 2012). The implications of such discoveries are only now being explored by clinical researchers.

Psychosocial explanations for alcohol vary from individual to individual: Some persons enjoy its euphoric effects, consuming it so often that they become physically dependent on it. Other individuals abuse it because they believe that they need alcohol to cope with the pain of living. Many have abused alcohol for so long that they have now become physically addicted to it. There are many roads to alcohol abuse or dependence, which might be viewed as *a common end point*. The complications of heavy alcohol use makes it more harmful to the individual than cocaine or heroin (Nutt, King, & Phillips, 2010), and ranks among the leading causes of preventable death around the world (Mitchell et al., 2012). In this chapter we will examine the problem of heavy, regular alcohol use, and the consequences of its abuse.

A Working Definition of the Alcohol Use Disorders

At one point individuals with an alcohol use disorder (AUD) were said to (a) require the alcohol to function, (b) make attempts to limit their heavy alcohol use to a specific time (weekends, for example), with periods of abstinence in between the episodes of heavy alcohol use, (c) persons who engage in continuous "binges"[1] that last for days, weeks, or months, interspaced with periods of abstinence, or who (d) engage in the daily use of alcohol in excess of what is prudent for health, or social norms.

---

[1]A "binge" is defined as when a man consumes five or more standard drinks, glasses of wine, or cans of beer in a 24-hour period, or when a woman consumes four or more standard drinks, glasses of wine, or cans of beer in a 24-hour period.

This definition includes a wide range of drinking behaviors. Some persons will be weekend drinkers who abstain from alcohol during the work week to avoid problems at the job site. Others will abstain from alcohol during work hours, but will start to consume alcohol after the end of the work day, and possibly throughout the weekend. Yet other drinkers will intermix periods of alcohol heavy use with periods of lower use, or possibly even abstinence. Some drinkers will "hide" their drinking behavior(s) from significant others, whereas still others will openly consume alcohol abusively, demanding that family/friends accept their drinking as a price for their presence. The common element to all of these different drinking styles is the abusive use of alcohol to the point where they experience various psychosocial, vocational, or medical problems as a result of their alcohol use and possibly to the point where the drinker becomes physically dependent on it.

It is generally accepted by health care professionals that the consumption of 16 ounces of 80–100 "proof" liquor, or 11–15 12-ounce cans of beer, each day for 2–3 weeks will produce a physical dependency on alcohol (Perry, Alexander, Liskow, & DeVane, 2007). As a result of this level of alcohol intake the body will have attempted to compensate for the alcohol during, and upon cessation or significant reduction of alcohol intake, the compensatory mechanisms will then cause a characteristic alcohol withdrawal syndrome (AWS). The person with an AUD typically will experience any of a wide range of medical, social, legal, or vocational consequences associated with heavy alcohol use. The person with an AUD would possibly have engaged in multiple attempts to cut back, or control his or her alcohol use. Such individuals might have continued to use alcohol in spite of the awareness that its use caused or exacerbated a medical condition in their bodies. The formal diagnosis of alcohol abuse or dependence is made on the basis of the diagnostic criteria in the current edition of the *Diagnostic and Statistical Manual of Mental Disorders,* 5th edition (American Psychiatric Association, 2013).

Scope of the Problem

Each year an estimated 2.4 million persons around the world lose their lives to alcohol-related illness or injuries, a death toll that is approximately half of that wrought by tobacco-related illness ("First Shots in the War on Alcohol, 2009"). This makes alcohol use/abuse a factor in 3.8% of all deaths and 4.6% of all cases of disability around the world each year. Currently, Europeans have the dubious distinction of consuming the most alcohol in the world, with 5% of the men and 1% of the women meeting the diagnostic criteria for alcohol dependence ("Europeans heaviest drinkers in the world," 2006). In the United States 90% of all adults will consume alcohol at some point in their lives, and that 65% of adults are current alcohol users (Nace, 2005b; Schuckit, 2009). More than 60% of adults in the United States drank to the point of intoxication in the past year. Although these statistics would suggest that AUDs are widespread, in reality only a minority of these individuals have an AUD. Depending on the criteria used, perhaps 10–20% of the adults who consume alcohol[2] will ever meet the diagnostic criteria for an AUD,[3] although the team of Hasin, Stinson, Ogburn, and Grant (2007) suggested that the percentage of adults who will meet the diagnostic criteria for an AUD at some point in their lives might be as high as 30%. This figure should be considered a high-end estimate, and most clinicians estimate that the range of lifetime AUDs is more in the range of 10–20% of drinkers (Schuckit, 2011).

The individual's alcohol use pattern does not remain stable over the course of their life but will change as a result of internal and external forces. There is no single alcohol use "trajectory" but a number of different pathways that a person's alcohol use pattern might follow. Some daily abusive drinkers remain abusive drinkers, whereas others alternate between periods of abusive drinking interspaced with periods of abstinence or controlled drinking (Hasin et al., 2007). Some heavy drinkers "mature out" of their abusive drinking,[4] and learn either to be social drinkers, or to abstain from further alcohol use. Some drinkers who once met the diagnostic criteria for alcohol dependence based on their past drinking patterns might currently be abstinent from alcohol use. Some heavy drinkers might be abstinent

[2]Remember: since 90% of the adults are thought to drink at some point in their lives, in reality this is about 9–18% of the adults in this country.

[3]This figure includes those who *abuse* alcohol, and the smaller percentage of those who go on to become alcohol dependent at some point in their lives.

[4]As will be discussed in Chapters 23 and 24, this pattern is often seen in young adults and in college students who abuse alcohol for a period of time, then set it aside when they assume the duties and responsibilities of young adulthood.

because of situational stressors, such as being under Court supervision or at risk for losing their job, but without any desire to stop drinking once the external motivation for abstinence is removed.

A popular misconception of the heavy drinker is that of a person who is unemployed, and *who spends much of the day sitting on the curb drinking cheap whiskey from a bottle wrapped in* a brown paper bag. In reality, the majority of persons with an AUD live lives that appear on the surface to be successful and productive (Aldhous, 2010). This makes it difficult to identify the majority of heavy drinkers. Epidemiological studies suggest that 10.7 million people in the United States, or 7.7% of the population, are thought to have an active AUD at any given point in time (Lemonick & Park, 2007). The consequences of alcohol abuse or addiction become increasingly severe as the frequency and intensity of the individual's alcohol use increases. Statistically, alcohol-dependent persons lose about 15 years of potential life as a result of their AUD (Schuckit, 2006a). The economic impact of the AUDs in the United States is estimated to be $234 billion/year, with 13% of this amount being just for health care costs for persons injured or ill as a result of their AUD (Rehm et al., 2009).[5] The AUDs are also associated with problems in the interpersonal, educational, vocational, and legal and spheres of functioning, in addition to the alcohol-related medical problems alluded to earlier in this paragraph.

Who Is the Typical Person with an Alcohol Use Disorder?

This is a difficult question to answer, in part because AUDs take so many different forms. Alcohol abusers are predominately male, with 10–15% of male drinkers, but only 5–8% of female drinkers, will ever develop an addiction to alcohol (Schuckit, 2010a). Because so much attention has been focused on the daily drinker, binge drinking is an understudied aspect of the AUDs. The team of Naimi et al. (2003) focused on this subpopulation of abusive drinkers. They defined the "binge" drinker as a person who was not a daily drinker, but who consumed five or more cans of beer, or standard mixed drinks in a single episode of alcohol consumption. Using this definition, the authors concluded that 15% of the adults in the United States had engaged in at least one period of binge drinking in

the proceeding 30 days, and that 15% reported having done so on 12 or more days in the preceding year. An estimated 1.5 *billion* episodes of binge drinking take place each year just in the United States alone (Freiberg & Samet, 2005).

The typical alcohol-dependent person in the United States will experience their first psychosocial or medical problem as a result of their drinking in their 20s or 30s, and they will probably enter treatment for the first time when they are in their 40's (Schuckit, 2006a). When confronted, many persons with an AUD are able to offer a thousand and one reasons why they cannot possibly have an AUD. Such excuses may include the fact that they are nothing like the "skid row" daily drinker, how they hold a regular job, that they always go to work, that they can tell you the names of 10 people who drink 10 times as much as they do, that they never go to the bars, and so on. In reality persons with an AUD are viewed as being "masters of denial" (Knapp, 1996, p. 19). Only about 5% of heavy drinkers fit the image of the "skid row" derelict (Brust, 2004). Many of those who drink heavily are "high functioning" problem drinkers, with jobs, families, and a public image to protect (Aldhous, 2010; Benton, 2009). These individuals will often go to great lengths to hide their growing dependence on alcohol from others, and their personality defenses protect them from being aware of it themselves. It is only in moments of quiet introspection that the drinker might wonder why they do not drink like a "normal person."[6] As the disease progresses, these moments of introspection are thought to become increasingly infrequent. As these studies suggest, there is no "typical" person with an AUD. Table 5-1 provides an overview of the subtypes of persons with an AUD identified thus far.

Alcohol Dependence, Tolerance, and "Craving"[7]

There are many symptoms that, when present, suggest that the drinker has moved past simple social drinking, or even heavy alcohol use, to the point where s/he has developed a serious AUD. Perhaps the most important of these is the development of *tolerance*. As the drinker continues to consume alcohol over periods of time, the body begins to adapt to the continuous presence of

---

[5]Rehm et al. (2009) estimated that this is between 1 and 6% of the gross national product of the United States.

[6]Often referred to at 12-Step meetings as "Normies."

[7]The discussion of a "craving" for a substance is explored in more detail in Chapter 34.

TABLE 5-1
Subtypes of Alcoholism

SUBTYPE OF ALCOHOLISM	PERCENTAGE OF SAMPLE	AVERAGE AGE OF DEPENDENCE ONSET	SELECT CHARACTERISTICS
Young Adult	31.50%	20 years	Low rates of other drug abuse, low rates of mental illness, and about one-third still in higher education.
Young Antisocial	21.10%	21.1 years	Some familial history of AUDs, high rates of mental health problems and drug abuse.
Functional	19.40%	37 years	Well educated, usually with stable jobs and families. Limited history of AUDs in family of origin. Moderate rates of depression.
Intermediate familial	18.80%	32 years	Familial history of AUDs in many cases. High levels of depression and/or bi-polar affective disorders. Drug use disorders often present.
Chronic Severe	9.20%	29 years	Frequent history of familial AUDs. High rates of mental health issues and other substance use disorders (SUDs)

SOURCE: Based on Aldhous, 2010; Moss, Chen, and Yi (2007).

alcohol. S/he is said to demonstrate *tolerance* to alcohol. This process reflects the individual's (Swift, 2005) (1) drinking history and (2) genetic inheritance. For example, a person who consumed alcohol four times a week would be less likely to develop the same degree of tolerance to alcohol's effects than would a drinker who consumed the same amount of alcohol daily.

It is not unusual for physicians or drug counselors to have a client report that they needed to drink more to achieve a given level of intoxication than they required in the past, which is a reflection of the process of metabolic tolerance (Nelson, 2000). This is often interpreted

as a sign of increased tolerance to the effects of alcohol. Tolerance is very energy-intensive and the liver cannot maintain this higher-than-normal speed of alcohol biotransformation for extended periods of time. Eventually, the chronic drinker discovers that she or he does not require as much alcohol to achieve a given level of intoxication as they did when they were younger. At this point, the individual's tolerance to alcohol is said to be decreasing, and usually is a result of aging and the accumulated damage to the drinker's liver. The phenomenon of tolerance to alcohol is seen by comparing the effects of alcohol on the habitual drinker in Table 5-2.

TABLE 5-2
Effects of Alcohol on the Chronic Drinker

BLOOD ALCOHOL LEVEL (BAL)	BEHAVIORAL AND PHYSICAL EFFECTS
0.05–0.09	None to minimal effect observed.
0.10–0.19	Mild ataxia, euphoria.
0.20–0.29	Mild emotional changes.
	Ataxia is more severe.
0.30–0.39	Drowsiness, lethargy, stupor.
0.40–0.49	Coma. Death is possible.
0.50–0.60	Respiratory paralysis that may result in drinker's death.[a]

[a]Brust (2004) discussed how, on rare occasions, a patient with a measured BAL of up to 0.80 might be alert or conscious, although such exceptions are rare, and usually a BAL of 0.50 is fatal.

SOURCES: Based on information in Baselt (1996); Lehman, Pilich, and Andrews (1994); Morrison, Rogers, and Thomas (1995); Renner (2004a).

Many individuals with an AUD depend on alcohol for psychological support as well as a means to avoid physical withdrawal symptoms. Such individuals are said to be *psychologically dependent* on alcohol, believing that s/he needs alcohol in order to: relax, engage in intimate relations, sleep, cope with stress, and so on. In contrast to this, the phenomenon of *physical dependence* manifests when the individual suddenly stops drinking, and experiences the characteristic *AWS* (discussed later in this chapter). When deprived of alcohol many persons with an AUD begin to "crave" for it, seeking another source of alcohol to return to their previous level of intoxication. This craving has, on occasion, resulted in the drinker consuming mouth wash that contains alcohol and of late antiseptic hand gels that contain ethanol.

Complications of Chronic Alcohol Use

Alcohol is hardly a harmless recreational chemical. In the United States, alcohol is thought to be a factor in 85,000 to 90,000 deaths each year[8] (Coughlan, 2009; Danaei et al., 2009; Harris, Kivlahan, Bowe, & Humphreys, 2010; Myrick & Wright, 2008). Although used as an intoxicant, it is a mild toxin that after extended exposure may result in damage to one or more organs. This might be why habitual heavy drinkers lose up to 25 years of potential life compared with nondrinkers (Sullivan, 2007). Surprisingly, women with an AUD appear to have higher mortality rates from alcohol-related illness than do men (Roerecke & Rehm, 2013). Alcohol-related organ damage places a strain on the health care system in this country: There is a dose-dependent relationship between the amount of alcohol ingested by an individual, in both the frequency and the length of stay in hospitals (Hart & Smith, 2009).

The question of alcohol-induced organ damage has been proven beyond question. However, a variable that has rarely been considered is the effect of *age* on the drinker's body. The aging process will itself extract a toll on the individual's body independent of his or her alcohol consumption status. Unfortunately, it is impossible to determine the percentage of the damage observed in a given individual because of the aging process as opposed to the habitual use of alcohol. It is known, however, that habitual drinkers demonstrate a greater number, and more serious health problems, than nondrinkers of the same age.

The amount of physical damage that alcohol causes to the drinker's body is mitigated or enhanced by his or her genetic inheritance. For example, the individual's risk for developing Wernicke-Korsakoff's disorder[9] is mediated by genetically determined variations in the production of the enzyme transketolase (Rourke & Grant 2009). This should not be interpreted to mean that individuals who lack predisposing genetic histories are free from the risk of alcohol-induced organ damage. We do not know enough about human genetics to make such a statement. Rather, it should be assumed that like with other aspects of life the individual's genetic heritage is one factor that influences the potential development of alcohol-induced organ damage.

The Effects of Chronic Alcohol Use on the Digestive System

Alcohol has a profound impact on the digestive system. During the process of distillation many of the vitamins, minerals, and amino acids found in the original wine are lost, limiting the drinker's ability to find the vitamins and amino acids that he or she would have ingested before the alcohol was distilled.

To complicate matters, the body of the heavy drinker loses some of its ability to absorb needed nutrients from the food that is ingested, adding to the depletion of vitamin and mineral reserves in the body. Further, the end product of alcohol biotransformation results in the formation of carbohydrates, which makes the drinker feel satisfied, not hungry. These are called "empty calories" by nutritional experts since they contribute nothing to the individual's dietary requirements of protein, vitamins, and amino acids. In severe cases the daily drinker may obtain up to 50% of his/her daily caloric requirement from alcohol-derived calories rather than more traditional foods (Griffith & Schenker, 2006). Even if the heavy drinker should eat a balanced diet, their ability to absorb needed nutrients is often blocked by alcohol, because it interferes with the absorption of nutrients from the digestive system (Fleming, Mihic, & Harris, 2006; Sadock & Sadock,

---

[8]These figures include not only those deaths directly caused by alcohol, but also indirect alcohol-related deaths such as injuries, violence, cancer, and so on.

[9]Discussed later in this chapter.

2007). One mechanism that causes this is alcohol-induced diarrhea, which interferes with the body's ability to absorb necessary nutrients from food (Brunton, Parker, Blumenthal, & Baxton, 2008). Collectively, alcohol-induced diarrhea, anorexia, and the empty calories that result from alcohol biotransformation contribute to the development of malnutrition for the drinker. If the drinker's body should become vitamin-deficient, a common outcome of habitual heavy alcohol use, then s/he is said to have developed *avitaminosis*.[10]

Another possible gastrointestinal problem seen in heavy drinkers is the development of an inflammation of the pancreas, a condition known as *pancreatitis*. This condition can develop after a single episode of heavy drinking, but prolonged heavy drinking is the more common cause of alcohol-induced pancreatitis (Brunton et al., 2008). The causal mechanism for alcohol-induced pancreatitis seems to be the exposure of pancreatic cells to alcohol. Although there are other reasons why an individual might develop pancreatitis, about 10% of heavy drinkers eventually develop this disorder (Brunton et al., 2008; Schuckit, 2008a).

Daily alcohol use has been found to increase the individual's risk for developing various forms of cancer, and is thought to be the cause of 389,000 new cases of cancer each year (Druesne-Peccolo et al., 2009). Other regions of the body thought to be vulnerable to the development of cancer include in the oral cavity, pharynx, liver, stomach, colon, rectum, breast, and esophagus (Brunton et al., 2008; Chen, Rosner, Hankinson, Colditz, & Willett, 2011; Druesne-Peccolo et al., 2009). The observed relationship between alcohol ingestion and esophageal cancer is especially important since the long-term survival rate for patients with this form of cancer is quite low (Khushalani, 2008). The combination of cigarette smoking and heavy alcohol use is especially dangerous. Chronic drinkers experience almost a 6-fold increase in the risk of developing cancer of the mouth or pharynx (Pagano, Graham, Frost-Pineda, & Gold, 2005). Cigarette smoking by itself is associated with a seven-fold increase in such cancers; however, chronic drinkers who also smoke cigarettes have a *38-fold higher risk* of cancer of the mouth or pharynx (Pagano et al., 2005). On a positive note, the individual's risk of developing cancer of the

mouth or throat is reduced after 5 years of abstinence, and at the end of 20 years of abstinence is virtually the same as that of a person who never had an AUD (Rehm, Patra, & Popova, 2007).

The Effects of Chronic Alcohol Use on the Liver

The liver is a unique organ, which is sometimes classified as a part of the digestive system, and sometimes as an organ apart from the digestive tract. Because of its role in protecting us from the effects of many environmental toxins it is classified as a separate organ in this text. It is the organ where the process of alcohol biotransformation/elimination usually is carried out. This may be why the liver is the organ most heavily damaged by chronic alcohol use (Sadock & Sadock, 2007). One possible mechanism for alcohol-induced liver damage is by its ability to interfere with the production of the enzyme glutathione (Kershaw & Guidot, 2008). The liver produces this enzyme to protect itself from various toxin, and is also involved with the inflammatory response when tissues are damaged. Heavy drinkers demonstrate 80% lower glutathione levels compared with nondrinkers, suggesting that this is indeed one mechanism by which alcohol is able to damage the liver.

Between 80 and 90% of heavy drinkers[11] will develop an early manifestation of liver disease known as a "fatty liver," or steatosis. Individuals who have this condition have a liver that is enlarged and does not function normally (Bankole & Ait-Daoud, 2005). The "fatty liver" can develop after just a few days of heavy drinking (Khan, Morrow, & McCarron, 2009). Although there are few physical manifestations of this disorder that the drinker might detect, blood tests would reveal abnormalities in the drinker's liver enzymes that suggest liver damage (Schuckit, 2006a). Fortunately, in its early stages this condition will usually reverse itself with abstinence from alcohol (Khan et al., 2009). However, persons with active liver steatosis are at risk for premature death.

Persistent heavy drinkers who manifest liver steatosis and who continue to drink can experience a more severe form of liver damage: *alcoholic hepatitis*. This condition is essentially an extension of steatosis, with the additional symptoms of liver inflammation, pain, the death of liver cells, and development of collagen deposits in

---

[10]There are a number of causes for this condition, but the chronic use of alcohol is one of the most significant causes.

[11]Defined here as persons who drink 5+ drinks per day.

the liver (Schuckit, 2006a; Szabo & Mandreker, 2010). Approximately, 35–40% of heavy drinkers who have liver steatosis will eventually develop this alcohol-related complication unless they discontinue or significantly cut back on their consumption of alcohol (Szabo & Mandreker, 2010). The usual patient with alcohol-induced hepatitis will develop this condition after about 15–20 years of heavy drinking. When the liver is inflamed because of heavy alcohol use the person is diagnosed as having alcohol-related hepatitis. Such patients are considered poor surgical risks because of their hepatitis, especially if the surgeon was unaware of the individual's drinking history.

Of those individuals who develop alcohol-induced hepatitis, 10–35%[12] go on to develop a condition known as *cirrhosis* of the liver (Nace, 2005; Bankole & Ait-Daoud, 2005; Karsan, Rojter, & Saab, 2004). In cirrhosis, individual liver cells die, and are replaced by nonfunctional scar tissue. If the level of liver damage is great enough, the body becomes unable to cleanse itself and will eventually die. A physical examination of a patient with hepatitis will reveal a hard, nodular liver, an enlarged spleen, surface blood vessel changes producing "spider" angiomas, tremor, confusion, blood chemistry changes, and in some men testicular atrophy (Nace, 2005; Schuckit, 2010a). Although it would seem at first glance that alcoholic hepatitis would predate the development of cirrhosis, some heavy drinkers appear to manifest cirrhosis without previous signs of hepatitis ("Alcohol and the liver," 1993). Alcohol-induced cirrhosis has been documented in people who have consumed as little as 2–4 standard drinks a day for just 10 years (Karsan et al., 2004), which would seem to be somewhat counterintuitive in that one would expect that it would take a longer period of heavy drinking to cause this level of damage to the liver. This might reflect the effects of *free radicals*[13] generated during the process of alcohol biotransformation, which in theory can contribute to the death of individual liver cells and thus initiate the development of liver cirrhosis (Brust, 2004; Walsh & Alexander, 2000). Surprisingly, there is evidence that coffee consumption might reduce the individual's risk for developing alcohol-related cirrhosis (Klatsky, Morton, Udaltsova, & Friedman, 2006). The authors

suggested that the individual's risk of developing cirrhosis was reduced by 22% for each cup of coffee consumed in a day, although the exact mechanism for this effect is still not clear at this time.

At one point, it was thought that malnutrition was a factor in the development of alcohol-induced liver disease. However, subsequent research has failed to support that hypothesis. Scientists have discovered, however, that alcohol-dependent persons are at increased risk of contracting the Hepatitis "C" virus.[14] This, in turn, increases the drinker's risk for the eventual development of cirrhosis, and exacerbates the level of damage to the liver. Why alcohol-dependent persons would be at increased risk for Hepatitis "C" infection remains a mystery. It is known that there is a strong relationship between alcohol-induced cirrhosis and the development of liver cancer (Schuckit, 2006a; Bagnardi, Blangiardo, La Vecchia, & Corrao, 2001). However, Hepatitis "C" is also associated with an increased risk of liver cancer, and it is not clear whether this accounts for the association between heavy drinking and the development of liver cancer or not.

Other problems associated with alcohol-induced cirrhosis are sodium and water retention, problems that indirectly affect cardiac function (Nace, 2005b; Schuckit, 2006a). Further, as the liver becomes enlarged in response to inflammation and cellular damage, it compresses the blood vessels that pass through it. This causes an increase in blood pressure as the heart struggles to maintain circulation, a condition known as *portal hypertension*. The higher pressure levels can cause blood vessels in the esophagus to swell, and become weak, forming *esophageal varices*,[15] which may rupture with little warning. Ruptured esophageal *varices* are a medical emergency, with a 20–30% death rate even with the best of medical care (Hegab & Luketic, 2001). Between 50 and 60% of those who survive the initial episode of a bleeding esophageal varix will develop a second episode, which will carry with it an additional 20–30% death rate. Afdhal and Curry (2010) reported that in their research sample only 61% of patients who survived having one ruptured varix were still alive at the end of 1 year.

Scientists once thought that chronic alcohol use could reduce stomach's mucosal barrier, exposing it to its own digestive juices (Fleming et al., 2006). The

---

[12]Khan et al. (2009) reported that up to 70% of patients who develop alcohol-related hepatitis go on to develop cirrhosis of the liver. It is not known why these different authors provided such disparate estimates.

[13]See Glossary.

[14]Discussed in Chapter 36.

[15]The singular is an esophageal *varix*.

stomach itself might become inflamed, a painful condition known as alcohol-induced *gastritis.* Alcohol use can cause, or exacerbate, the formation of stomach ulcers. If the individual will develop a stomach ulcer over a major blood vessel in the stomach wall it may rupture, causing bleeding into the stomach. Such "bleeding" ulcers are known in extreme cases to require the surgical resection of the stomach. The individual need not be a heavy drinker to have a higher risk for gastrointestinal bleeding as it has been found that consuming just three or more standard drinks per day increases the individual's chance of a gastrointestinal "bleed" by 300%.

The chronic ingestion of alcohol also can induce damage to the endothelial cells lining the intestines, allowing certain toxins produced by gram-negative bacteria to enter the circulation more easily (Molina, Happel, Zhang, Kollsm, & Nelson, 2010; Szabo & Mandreker, 2010). Clinicians refer to this as a "leaky gut," which expresses through vitamin malabsorption syndromes as a result of the damaged intestinal lining, possibly exacerbating the effects of liver failure (Szabo & Mandreker, 2010). In reality, the term *vitamin malabsorption syndrome* is something of a misnomer, since habitual drinkers are known to have trouble absorbing not only vitamins such as Vitamin A, Vitamin D, and the "B" family of vitamins, but also the minerals such as calcium, sodium, phosphorus, and magnesium.

The alcohol abuser or addict will experience a change in the bacterial growth pattern in the mouth,[16] contributing to the condition known as *glossitis*[17] and to a possible stricture of the esophagus known as Barrett's esophagus (Fleming et al., 2006). This latter condition develops after the esophageal tissues have repeatedly been exposed to digestive juices during gastric reflux, as well as a possible traumatic rupture of the esophagus (Brunton et al., 2008). These conditions further contribute to the drinker's failure to ingest an adequate diet, adding to the possible alcohol-related dietary deficiencies. Finally, the abuse of alcohol contributes to a number of metabolic disorders, including the development of Type 2 Diabetes[18] (Wannamethee, Camargo, Manson, Willett, & Rimm, 2003). A significant percentage of drinkers with liver disease are either glucose-intolerant or diabetic, conditions that reflect alcohol-related interference with the body's normal glucose control mechanisms. Schuckit (2006b; 2008a) suggested that the diagnosis of true diabetes, as opposed to an alcohol-induced metabolic dysfunction, would require 2–4 weeks of abstinence for an accurate diagnosis to be possible.

Effects of Chronic Alcohol Use on the Circulatory System

Heavy alcohol abuse increases the individual's risk of coronary heart disease by as much as 600% (Schuckit, 2006a). It can also exacerbate hypertension and induce an increased risk of stroke (Chen, Smith, Harbord, & Lewis, 2008; O'Connor, Rusyniak, & Bruno, 2005). The team of Casolla et al. (2012) found that heavy alcohol users on average experienced a hemorrhagic stroke 14 years earlier than nondrinkers; however, the risk of stroke is not equal for both genders. Ikehara et al. (2008) examined the health histories of 34,776 men and 48,906 women in Japan, and found that heavy alcohol use was associated with an increased risk of death from strokes for men but not for women. However, frequent drinkers of either gender shared an increased risk for coronary artery heart disease according to the authors. This might reflect alcohol's ability to increase the blood levels of angiotensin II, a compound among other things that causes the blood vessels to constrict. This forces the heart to expend extra energy to pump the blood through the constricted blood vessels, contributing to the individual's possible hypertension (Kershaw & Guidot, 2008). Thus, where light to moderate drinkers have a 200% higher risk of stroke, heavy drinkers are thought to have a 300% chance of a stroke (Ordorica & Nace, 1998). These statistics suggest that the individual's increased risk of a stroke might outweigh any benefit that s/he might gain from using alcohol to reduce cardiovascular risk.

It has been found that the habitual use of alcohol can induce damage to the muscle tissues in the body, although the exact mechanism is still not clear (Lindsay, Bone, & Fuller, 2010). Virtually every heavy

---

[16]If, as Ackerman (2012) described, microorganisms contribute to the body's ability to cope with stress, extract nutrients from food, and possibly even contribute to our actions, then one must wonder what impact the abnormal bacterial growth patterns found in chronic alcohol abusers will ultimately have on the individual's behavior.

[17]See Glossary.

[18]Once referred to as "adult onset" or "noninsulin-dependent" diabetes.

drinker will demonstrate some degree of alcohol-induced muscle damage on special tests (Figueredo, 1997; Lee & Regan, 2002). It is for this reason that alcohol is said to be *cardiotoxic*. Alcohol inhibits the synthesis of proteins in the muscles, including proteins necessary for normal cardiac muscle function (Ponnappa & Rubin, 2000). Up to a quarter of chronic drinkers will develop early onset cardiovascular disease, and undetected clinical cardiomyopathy is thought to be present in 25–40% of chronic drinkers (Schuckit, 2006a). It does not take a huge amount of alcohol to induce damage to the muscles of the body, including those of the heart. It is thought that the ingestion of six cans of beer/day, or a pint of whiskey per day is enough to induce permanent damage to muscle tissues. If the cardiac muscle tissues are involved this will result in a general weakening of the heart muscle (O'Connor et al., 2005; Schuckit, 2005, 2006). Statistically, 40–50% of all cases of cardiomyopathy in the United States are alcohol related (Wadland & Ferenchick, 2004; Zakhari, 1997). If they continue to drink, between 40 and 80% of those individuals with alcohol-induced cardiomyopathy will die within 4 years of being diagnosed with this disorder (Brust, 2004; Stoschitzky, 2000; Figueredo, 1997).

The Effects of Chronic Alcohol Use on the Central Nervous System (CNS)

Although it is often assumed that the liver is the first organ to be damaged by the chronic use of alcohol, this is not always true. The CNS often is the first organ to demonstrate evidence of alcohol-related damage. The exact mechanism(s) by which heavy alcohol abuse causes CNS damage is not known at this time but may reflect such factors as (Rosenbloom & Pefferbaum, 2008): the amount of alcohol consumed over the lifespan, the individual's pattern of alcohol ingestion, the frequency and intensity of alcohol withdrawal episodes, and the individual's genetic heritage.

Research has demonstrated evidence of alcohol-induced memory deficits after as little as one drink. Fortunately, the drinker normally needs to consume more than five standard drinks in an hour's time, producing a blood alcohol level of 0.14 to 0.20 before alcohol is able to significantly interfere with the process of memory formation. This will cause "gaps" in the person's memories formed while s/he was drinking, a condition known as the *blackout*. (Schuckit, 2011). In an alcohol induced

blackout the individual might appear intoxicated but appears conscious, answers questions, is possibly able to carry on a coherent conversation, or carries out many complex tasks. However, the individual later is unable to recall part or all of the period of intoxication. The alcohol-induced blackout is a form of anterograde amnesia induced by alcohol's ability to disrupt the action of the gamma-aminobutyric acid (GABA) and N-methyl-D-aspartate (NMDA) in the brain (Nelson et al., 2004). Approximately two-thirds of alcohol-dependent persons will report having experienced at least one alcohol-induced blackout (Schuckit, 2008a). The individual's vulnerability to alcohol-related blackouts is influenced by their genetic heritage, with the result being that some individuals are more vulnerable to developing this condition than others (Nelson et al., 2004).

As a group, long-term alcohol abusers have been found to demonstrate evidence of impaired neurological testing up to 4 weeks after their last drink (Rourke & Grant, 2009). In 10% of the cases the level of neuropsychological impairment is found to be severe. This impairment in test function appears to reflect the physical damage to the brain of heavy drinkers found at the time of autopsy or through noninvasive imaging studies such as C-T scan or MRI studies. These neuroimaging studies have found, for example, that up to 50–70% of habitual drinkers demonstrate enlarged ventricles in the brain (Gilpin & Koob, 2008; Rosenbloom & Pefferbaum, 2008; Schuckit, 2006a, 2006b). With abstinence many heavy drinkers show evidence of subsequent neural growth on subsequent studies, suggesting that some degree of recovery from alcohol-related neurological damage is possible with long-term abstinence (Schuckit, 2005, 2006). However, it is not clear whether the former drinker can return to normal neurological functioning or not at this time.

Many habitual drinkers demonstrate evidence of damage to the prefrontal cortex[19] region of the brain (Brunton et al., 2008; Rourke & Grant 2009). Neuropsychological testing confirms the presence of prefrontal cortex damage in between one-half and two-thirds of chronic drinkers (Zahr & Sullivan, 2008). Another region of the brain that seems vulnerable to alcohol-induced damage is the *cerebellum*.[20] Approximately 50% of heavy drinkers show some signs of alcohol-related cerebellum damage (Schuckit, 2008a; Tomb,

---

[19]See Glossary.

[20]See Glossary.

2008). One percent of chronic heavy drinkers will develop the full *cerebellar atrophy* syndrome. Symptoms of this condition include a characteristic psychomotor dysfunction, gait disturbance, and problems coordinating muscle movements (Berger, 2000; Oehmichen, Auer, & Konig, 2005; Schuckit, 2009).

Chronic alcohol use has been proven to both directly and indirectly alter the function of the visual system. Through the depletion of vitamin stores in the body it is possible for the persistent drinker to develop *vitamin deficiency amblyopia*. Symptoms of this condition include blurred vision, a loss of visual perception in the center of the visual field,[21] and in extreme cases atrophy of the optic nerve, all of which may become permanent in spite of the most aggressive of medical care (Brust, 2004; Lee et al., 2010). These findings are consistent with the observation that alcohol is quite neurotoxic. This neurological damage is observed in both daily and heavy binge drinkers (Crews, 2008). Although suggestive, these studies cannot determine the exact relationship between habitual alcohol use and neurological damage, because researchers lack pre-drinking neuropsychological test data or radiographic imaging studies to allow them to compare pre/post-drinking test results (Crews, 2008).

Alcoholism is also a known cause of a form of dementia[22] although researchers disagree as to the causal mechanism for this condition. One theory holds that alcohol-induced dementia is the direct result of alcohol's toxic effects on the brain. A second theory is that alcohol induced vitamin deficiencies are the direct causal mechanism (Berent & Albert, 2005; Filley, 2004). A third theory is that alcohol-induced liver damage results in the brain being chronically exposed to toxins normally filtered from the blood, resulting in neuronal loss. Pfefferbaum, Rosenbloom, Serventi, and Sullivan (2004) suggested that all three of these factors contributed to alcohol–induced neurological damage.

A limited degree of cognitive function recovery is possible for *some* habitual drinkers who stop drinking; however, maximum recovery might take months (Filley, 2004; Gilpin & Koob, 2008) to years (Rourke & Grant 2009) of abstinence. However, the degree to which a given individual might recover from such neurological trauma is not known at this time.

Many heavy drinkers only demonstrate only a modest level of cognitive improvement after prolonged periods of abstinence and aggressive vitamin replacement therapies (Mancall, 2008; Schuckit, 2006a). In many cases the drinker must be institutionalized because of their memory problems, and 15–30% of all nursing home patients are there because of permanent alcohol-induced brain damage (Schuckit, 2006a). Scientists have identified a degree of brain size reduction in heavy drinkers on noninvasive imaging studies but after just 2 months of abstinence scientists have measured a 1.85% increase in brain volume[23] and a 20% improvement in communications efficiency in some heavy drinkers (Bartsch et al., 2007). Unfortunately, if the drinker should return to the use of alcohol, this recovery in brain function will be lost, and the progression of alcohol-induced brain damage will continue.

Wernicke-Korsakoff's Disease[24]

In 1881, the physician Carl Wernicke first described a neurological disorder seen in chronic drinkers that has since been called *Wernicke's encephalopathy* (Day, Bentham, Callagham, Kuruvilla, & George, 2004). It was thought that patients with Wernicke's encephalopathy demonstrated a distinctive triad of symptoms of (1) ataxia, (2) mental status changes, and, (3) nystagmus or ocular changes (Day et al., 2004; Mattingly & Groon, 2008; Schuckit, 2006a). Now it is known that only 10% of patients with Wernicke's disease demonstrate all three of these symptoms, and that 19% of patients do not demonstrate *any* of these traditionally accepted symptoms. Ninety six percent of patients with Wernicke's disease will demonstrate nystagmus, but only 87% will experience gait disturbance (Greenberg, 2010). Because some drinkers do not demonstrate all the traditional symptoms of Wernicke's disease it is frequently not diagnosed until postmortem examination of the body (Kinsella & Riley, 2007; Mattingly & Groon, 2008). In some patients with Wernicke's disease, the only symptoms are irritability and fatigue, or hyperthermia, chronic dyskinesias, and decreased muscle tone in the later stages of this disorder (Mancall, 2008; Mattingly & Groon, 2008; Tse & Koller, 2004).

---

[21]A condition known as *central scotomata.*

[22]Sometimes called *encephalopathy.*

[23]It is not known whether this increase in brain volume reflects neurogenesis, the development of new dendritic connections between existing neurons, or a combination of these two factors.

[24]Called *Alcohol-induced persisting amnestic disorder* in some texts.

It must be noted that there are other causes of Wernicke's disorder than long-term alcohol abuse or addiction. Such conditions as (Kinsella & Riley, 2007; Mattingly & Groon, 2008): Crohn's disease, anorexia nervosa, AIDS, cancer chemotherapy patients and patients who had gastric bypass surgery are also at risk for this disorder. The causal mechanism for alcohol-induced Wernicke's disease is thought to be the thiamine[25] depletion from the body. The body's thiamine reserves are limited and must constantly be replaced through the individual's dietary intake (Kinsella & Riley, 2007). The poor diet, vitamin malabsorption syndrome and tendency to rely on alcohol-based calories rather than to ingest a normal diet all interfere with the individual's ability to maintain adequate thiamine levels. The drinker's genetic heritage has also been suggested as a factor that might influence the development of thiamine depletion (Mancall, 2008). Vitamin depletion is quite rapid and can be detected after just 7–8 weeks of daily heavy alcohol use, although between 30 and 80% of these individuals will not demonstrate signs of Wernicke's disease (Ropper & Brown, 2005; Harper & Matsumoto, 2005).[26]

The signs of Wernicke's encephalopathy begin to manifest in the first few hours or days after the use of alcohol is discontinued by the heavy drinker (Fernandez, Eisenschenk, & Okun, 2010; Rourke & Grant, 2009). This is the period in which the individual is most likely to experience the AWS, making the diagnosis and treatment of Wernicke's difficult. Unfortunately, it is estimated that 20% of patients with untreated or inadequately treated Wernicke's encephalopathy will die, usually of cardiovascular collapse (Mattingley & Groon, 2008). It is thus imperative that the body's thiamine stores be replenished as soon as possible. Ropper and Brown (2005) recommended *automatic* intramuscular injections of thiamin even if the physician only *suspects* the possibility that the patient has Wernicke's encephalopathy. The current recommended protocol calls for intramuscular injections of 100 mg of thiamine for 3 days, followed by oral supplements of thiamine. However, Mattingley and Groon (2008) suggested that the standard protocol was too conservative and recommended intramuscular doses of 500 mg of thiamine three times daily, for a minimum of 3 days, with concurrent blood tests to determine the drinker's magnesium level once daily.

In the early 1900s, before aggressive thiamine replacement therapies were instituted, up to 80% of those patients who developed Wernicke's encephalopathy went on to develop *Korsakoff's syndrome* (Day et al., 2003; Rourke & Grant, 2009). Originally viewed as separate disorders it is now recognized that Wernicke's disease reflects the acute stage and Korsakoff's syndrome is the end stage of thiamine depletion-induced brain damage. These disorders are now often referred to as Wernicke-Korsakoff's disease or Wernicke-Korsakoff's syndrome. Unfortunately, even with the most aggressive of thiamine replacement therapies available today one in 500 heavy drinkers develop Wernicke-Korsakoff's disease (Schuckit, 2008a).

At least 10% of those individuals who develop Wernicke-Korsakoff's will be left with a permanent memory impairment (Fernandez et al., 2010; Rourke & Grant, 2009). It was long thought that one of the characteristic symptoms of Korsakoff's syndrome was the inability of the individual to acquire new information, or anterograde amnesia. Some degree of retrograde amnesia is also present in many cases, although long-term memory is relatively resistant to alcohol-induced memory loss (Lezak, Hannay, & Fischer, 2004; Mancall, 2008). The individual will be able to recall events from his or her distant past, although possibly with some degree of confusion, but will be unable to retain new information (Mancall, 2008). It is not unusual for alcohol-dependent patients with alcohol-related memory loss and/or organic brain damage show a marked indifference to their plight. When faced with evidence of a memory loss, they have been known to provide the assessor with "memories" of a past that never took place, a process known as *confabulation*[27] (Mancall, 2008; Ropper & Brown, 2005). In the past, confabulation was viewed as one of the diagnostic criteria for patients with Korsakoff's disorder. Mankcall (2008) suggested that confabulation reflects *suggestibility* by the patient: When the medical staff asks the patient a question(s) in a manner that s/he interprets as requiring an answer, the patient manufactures one to please the inquirer. Although dramatic, it should be noted that not every patient with Wernicke-Korsakoff's will confabulate (Brust, 2004; Ropper & Samuels, 2009), and when present it is usually seen in the earlier stages of Wernicke-Korsakoff's disease (Rourke & Grant, 2009).

---

[25]See Glossary.

[26]Another name for Wernicke's disease that is often used in clinical literature.

---

[27]See Glossary.

In extreme cases of Wernicke-Korsakoff's, the patient will appear almost to be "frozen" in time. The neurologist Oliver Sacks (1970) offered the example of man who was unable to recall anything that had transpired after the late 1940s. If asked, the patient would answer the question as if s/her were still living in the late 1940s, and was unable to assimilate information from after that point. The author of this text has interviewed several such individuals during the 1980s. These individuals expressed surprise upon being told that astronauts have visited the moon, that President John F. Kennedy was assassinated, and so on. These are extreme examples of this process, and most patients with alcohol-induced amnesia will be able to remember some of the past although being unable to recall other events from their past.

There is an emerging body of research data suggesting that the chronic use of alcohol does not directly destroy neurons so much as induce a *disconnection syndrome* in which the neural connections between neurons are destroyed (Harper & Matsumoto, 2005). Neurons are very energy intensive, and those neurons that are nonfunctional begin to wither and eventually die. This would account for the neural loss observed in the brains of chronic alcohol abusers.

The persistent, heavy use of alcohol has also been identified as a risk factor for the development of a movement disorder known as *tardive dyskinesia* (TD) (Lopez & Jeste, 1997). TD is a common complication seen in patients who were treated with neuroleptic drugs for the control of psychotic disorders for extended periods of time, but is occasionally found in chronic drinkers who have never been exposed to neuroleptic agents (Lopez & Jeste, 1997). The causal mechanism for this neurological condition as a result of chronic drinking is not known at this time, but when it does develop in a chronic drinker, it is usually only after 10–20 years of heavy alcohol consumption (Lopez & Jeste, 1997).

Alcohol's Effects on the Sleep Cycle

There is still a great deal to be discovered about the impact of alcohol on the normal sleep cycle, although it is known that the chronic use of alcohol interferes with the normal sleep cycle (Conroy, Arnedt, & Brower, 2008; Karam-Hage, 2004). Heavy drinkers report that they require more time to fall asleep, and that their sleep is both less sound and less restful than that of nondrinkers the same age (Karam-Hage, 2004).

Approximately 60% of persons with an AUD report symptoms of insomnia (Brower, Aldrich, Robinson, Zucker, & Greden, 2001; Conroy et al., 2008). This may reflect alcohol's ability to suppress the production of melatonin in the brain, a theory that makes sense because melatonin is involved with maintaining the normal sleep/wake cycle (Karem-Hage; Pettis, 2000). However, a second hypothesis to was offered by Milne (2007), who suggested that heavy drinkers are simply prone to overestimate the amount of time necessary to fall asleep, giving the impression of a sleep disorder being present.[28]

Alcohol use suppresses rapid eye movement (REM) sleep, which is important to memory formation and maintenance of several body systems. This effect is most pronounced in the chronic drinker (Hobson, 2005; Schuckit, 2008a). About 85% of our dream experiences take place during REM sleep and by suppressing the individual's REM sleep cycles alcohol will possibly interfere with the individual's cognitive function during his/her waking hours. Further, if REM sleep is suppressed by extended periods the individual will spend more time in the REM sleep stage when finally allowed to sleep. This phenomenon is known as *REM Rebound*. During REM Rebound, the individual will experience longer, more intense REM dreams. These dreams are often difficult for the newly abstinent drinker to separate from reality (Robber & Brown, 2005) and might be so intense and so frightening for the dreamer that they can serve as a relapse trigger for the former drinker. REM Rebound has been found to continue for up to 6 months after the individual's last drink (Schuckit & Tapert, 2004; Brower et al., 2001). Other forms of sleep disturbances can continue for up to 1–2 *years* after the individual's last alcohol use (Brower et al., 2001; Karam-Hage, 2004). Unfortunately, physicians will often treat persons who complain about sleep problems without the individual revealing that they have an AUD. This places the individual at risk for cross addiction because most of the traditional pharmaceutical agents that used to treat anxiety or insomnia also have a high abuse potential (Conroy et al., 2008). For example, the effects of the benzodiazepines have been called "alcohol in pill form" (Longo, 2005), or "freeze-dried alcohol" (McGuinness & Fogger, 2006, p. 25). Karam-Hage (2004) suggested that the anticonvulsant medication gabapentin (*Neurontin*®) is quite useful as a hypnotic agent in

---

[28]See "Sleep latency" in Glossary.

alcohol-dependent persons. The fact that it lacks the abuse potential found in other more traditional hypnotics makes it an especially alternative medication to use with persons with an AUD.

Although alcohol is a known neurotoxin, there is evidence that at some doses it might suppress some of the involuntary movements of Huntington's disease (Lopez & Jeste, 1997). Although this is not to suggest that alcohol is an accepted treatment for this disorder, it might account for the observation that patients with Huntington's disease tend to abuse alcohol more often than close relatives who do not have this condition (Lopez & Jeste, 1997). There is also evidence suggesting that chronic alcohol use can contribute to long-term psychomotor coordination problems (DeWilde, Dom, Hulstjn, & Sabbe, 2007). The authors found that recently-detoxified alcohol-dependent persons required longer to complete psychomotor tasks than what would normally be expected. There was some degree of improvement in the speed of psychomotor responses as the individual abstained from alcohol for longer and longer periods of time, but even persons who had been abstinent from alcohol for extended periods of time still required longer periods of time to complete assigned tasks than were required by their non-drinking peers.

The Effects of Habitual Alcohol Use on the Peripheral Nervous System

The human nervous system is usually viewed as two interconnected systems: the CNS and the peripheral nervous system (PNS). Unfortunately, alcohol-induced avitaminosis involves both subunits of the nervous system. One of the most common manifestations of alcohol-induced nervous system is *peripheral neuropathy*. This condition develops in 15% (Schuckit, 2005, 2008a; Tomb, 2008) of chronic drinkers. Symptoms of peripheral neuropathy include feelings of weakness, pain, and a burning sensation in the affected region of the body at the time of onset, followed by a loss of sensation in the peripheral regions of the body (Ropper & Brown, 2005).

The causal mechanism for alcohol-induced peripheral neuropathies is not known at this time although alcohol-induced depletion of the "B" family of vitamins is thought to be a major factor (Levin, 2002; Tomb, 2008). Another factor that might influence the development of a peripheral neuropathy is the individual's genetic predisposition.

The Effects of Alcohol Use Disorders on the Drinker's Emotions

The chronic use of alcohol can exacerbate pre-existing psychiatric disorders, whereas alcohol withdrawal can induce symptoms suggesting a previously undiagnosed mental illness. Depression, for example, is experienced by approximately 40% (Schuckit, 2008a) to 50% of persons with an AUD (Virani, Bezchlibnyk-Butler, Jeffries, & Procyshyn, 2012). The relationship between depression and the AUDs is bidirectional. In most cases the AUD appears to precede the development of a major depression, strongly suggesting that the individual's alcohol abuse induced the depression through an unknown mechanism (Fergusson, Boden, & Horwood, 2009). These findings are consistent with those of Hasin and Grant (2002), who examined the histories of 6,050 recovering heavy drinkers, and found that former drinkers had a 4-fold increased incidence of depression as compared to nondrinkers the same age.

Alcohol-induced depression usually resolves in 2–5 weeks, however there is a subgroup of drinkers with a pre-existing depression whose depression will not always resolve this quickly. There is some controversy whether antidepressant medications should immediately be initiated since such a large percentage of cases are alcohol-related depression. Charney (2004) recommended that every case of depression immediately be aggressively treated, and Gianoli and Petrakis (2013) observed that the various classes of antidepressants have all been found to be effective in treating depression. However, these medications do not appear to reduce the individual's alcohol intake significantly when their depression has been adequately treated (Gianoli & Petrakis, 2013).

Between 10 and 30% of persons with an AUD will report experiencing some form of anxiety (Schuckit, 2008a). This anxiety might take the form of a generalized anxiety disorder, or panic attacks (Schuckit, 2005, 2006). Some of these symptoms are secondary to the process of alcohol withdrawal, as evidenced by the fact that up to 80% of patients going through alcohol withdrawal report symptoms of anxiety (Schuckit, 2005, 2006). To cope, some drinkers turn either to further alcohol use, or anxiolytic[29] medications to help control what is perceived as a subjective sense of anxiety. Newly abstinent patients who report anxiety symptoms

---

[29]See Glossary.

Jefferson Community College
1220 Coffeen Street
Jules Center Watertown
NY, 13601
(315) 786-2260
1587mgr@fheg.follett.com
www.efollett.com

======================================

ITEM   FEE
====   ===
Concepts of Chemical Dependenc
    014918880 $0.00
817 01587 002 1021 8/14/19 3:26 PM
CHECKED IN

Concepts of Chemical Dependenc
    014918880 $0.00
817 01587 002 1021 8/14/19 3:26 PM
CHECKED IN

Patron ID: 11544263
Patron Name: jenae martinkovitch

Associate: Alicia
5088 1587   817   002   12/16/19 11:26 AM

Store Copy

may require as long as 2 weeks of complete sobriety before their need for antianxiety medications can be adequately assessed.

The relationship between the AUDs and anxiety is bidirectional: Between 10 and 20% of patients with an anxiety disorder will admit to an AUD (Cox & Taylor, 1999) whereas 10–40% of patients in treatment for an AUD report having an anxiety disorder of some kind (Cox & Taylor, 1999). The diagnostic dilemma for the clinician is complicated by the fact that withdrawal-related symptoms are virtually the same as those experienced by patients having anxiety attacks, or generalized anxiety disorder (GAD) (Schuckit, 2005). This determination is further complicated by the fact that chronic alcohol users might experience feelings of anxiety for months after their last drink (Schuckit, 2005, 2006, 2008a). Only a careful diagnostic history will reveal whether the patient's anxiety symptoms predated, or followed, the development of his/her AUD.

There is, unfortunately, a strong relationship between suicide and the AUDs. At least one-third of those persons who do end their lives are thought to have an AUDs (Connor et al., 2006). Research has suggested that alcohol-dependent persons are 58–85 times as likely to commit suicide as those who are not alcohol dependent (Frierson, Melikian, & Wadman, 2002). The lifetime risk of suicide for in chronic drinkers is as high as 5% (Preuss et al., 2003) to 7% (Conner, Li, Meldrum, Duberstein, & Conwell, 2003) to possibly as high as 18% (Preuss & Wong, 2000; Bongar, 1997), far above the statistical average for suicide in the general population.

Alcohol-related suicides are more likely to occur in late middle adulthood, when the effects of the drinker's extended alcohol abuse begin to manifest as physical organ damage (Nisbet, 2000). The team of Preuss et al. (2003) followed a cohort of 1,237 alcohol-dependent persons for 5 years, and discovered that during this period subjects were more than twice as likely to end their lives in suicide as were nonalcoholic individuals. The team of Dumais et al. (2005) concluded that alcohol's disinhibiting effect, combined with the impulsiveness demonstrated by many of those with a personality disorder, combined with the presence of a major depression, were all significant risk factors for suicide in heavy male drinkers. The topic of suicide, suicide prediction, and intervention, are far too complicated to discuss in detail in this text as entire books have been devoted to this subject. However, the reader should be aware of the inter-relationship between suicide and alcohol dependence.

One causal mechanism through which chronic alcohol use might contribute to the increase risk of depression in chronic drinkers (with the concurrent risk of suicide in those who are depressed, since this is the most common psychiatric diagnosis in completed suicides) is alcohol's ability to affect dopamine turnover in the brain. The constant alcohol-induced release of dopamine might cause a reduction in dopamine binding sites as the brain attempts to adapt to the constant presence of high levels of this compound (Heinz, 2006).

The Effects of Habitual Alcohol Use on the Respiratory System

The chronic use of alcohol has been found to both cause, and exacerbate, sleep apnea[30] both during the periods of active alcohol use, and for a number of weeks after the individual's last drink (Brust, 2004; Schuckit, 2008a). Sleep apnea itself has been identified as a cause of such problems as poor sleep hygiene, hypertension, depression, reduced concentration, daytime fatigue, and possibly falling asleep while driving. The association between heavy drinking and pneumonia has been recognized for centuries: Chronic alcohol abusers are at increased risk for aspiration pneumonia,[31] and various forms of respiratory failure (Kershaw & Guidot, 2008; Schuckit, 2006a). It has been demonstrated that the chronic use of alcohol alters the body's natural defense mechanisms from the mouth down to the alveolar spaces in the lungs, in part by reducing the effectiveness of the macrophages[32] guarding the lungs (Molina et al., 2010).

The Effects of Chronic Alcohol Use on Other Body Systems

The social image of alcohol is that it enhances sexual performance. In reality, heavy, regular drinkers have been known to suffer from a variety of sexual dysfunctions including decreased libido for both men and women as well as reduced vaginal lubrication and

---

[30]See Glossary.

[31]Discussed in Chapter 34.

[32]See Glossary.

menstrual cycle irregularities in women (Brunton et al., 2008; Schuckit, 2011). Male drinkers might experience decreased sperm production, count, and motility; decreased ejaculate volume; and possible impotence[33] (Schuckit, 2006a). As will be discussed in Chapter 20, alcohol use by a woman in pregnancy can have profound, devastating, effects for the developing fetus.

There is also evidence that suggests that heavy, regular, alcohol abuse will result in calcium loss for both men and women, weakening the drinker's bones (Jerslid, 2001). This will, in turn, increase the drinker's chances for injury and death due to accidental injury. Preliminary evidence does suggest that at least some bone loss will be regained with abstinence for male drinkers, however, providing yet another incentive for the individual to stop drinking alcohol (Malik, Gasser, Moncayo, Kemmier, & Fleischhacker, 2012). Traumatic brain injuries (TBI) are 2–4 times more common in drinkers as opposed to nondrinkers (Rourke & Grant, 2009). Traumatic brain injuries are unique: The majority of those individuals who die from a TBI do so within the first hour(s) of the injury, often before reaching the hospital. Of those TBI patients who *do* reach the hospital, 29–56% who live long enough to reach the hospital will test "positive" for alcohol at the time of admission (Kraus & Chu, 2005; Miller & Adams, 2006).[34] The individual's post injury use of alcohol can both mediate, and complicate, the patient's recovery from the TBI (Miller & Adams, 2006). Contrary to therapeutic expectation that the patient developed an AUD after the accident to self-medicate the pain and frustration of the aftereffects of the TBI, research data suggests that in most cases the AUD preceded the TBI (Miller & Adams, 2006).

The AUDs have also been identified as a causal factor in 40–50% of all motor vehicle deaths, up to 67% of home injuries (Miller, 1999). Statistically, the typical drinker is 10 times as likely to develop cancer as the nondrinker (Ordorica & Nace, 1998). It has been estimated that possibly as many as 4% of cancer deaths in men and 1% of all cancer related deaths in women are alcohol related. The role of the alcohol metabolite acetaldehyde is thought to play at least a limited role in the development of some of these forms of cancer (Melton, 2007). Habitual alcohol use appears to facilitate the spread of certain forms of cancer of the breast and colon (Forsyth et al., 2009). Chronic use of alcohol is also implicated as a causal agent in certain forms of gum disease (Schuckit, 2005, 2006). Further, the consumption of four–eight standard drinks/day has been found to interfere with normal immune system function, further increasing the drinker's risk for various infectious diseases such as pneumonia and TB (Jaffe & Anthony, 2005).

Chronic Alcohol Use and Medication Abuse

Individuals with an AUD are at higher risk for the abuse of prescription medications. The teams of McCabe, Cranford, and Boyd (2006), and McCabe, Cranford, Morales, and Young (2006) concluded that persons with an AUD are 18 times more likely to abuse prescription drugs as those individuals who do not have and AUD. The younger the individual was at the initiation of alcohol use, and amount of alcohol consumed per episode of alcohol use were found to be positively correlated with the concurrent abuse of prescription medications. Young adults are at highest risk for this problem as evidenced by the fact that 25–50% of alcohol-dependent persons also have a benzodiazepine addiction (Sattar & Bhatia, 2003). So similar are the effects of alcohol and the benzodiazepines that the benzodiazepines can be substituted for alcohol in situations where it would be unwise to use alcohol. The combination of two CNS depressants such as alcohol and a benzodiazepine also increases the individual's risk for an accidental, possibly fatal, overdose. Thus, the use of these medications by persons with an AUD is not without very real dangers. It was once thought that either alcohol alone, or the combination of alcohol with a benzodiazepine, might lower cortical inhibitions to the point where the individual would experience a *paradoxical rage reaction.*[35] However, the existence of this possible disorder has been challenged by some health care professionals, and it remains a hypothetical construct only at this time.

---

[33]Possibly as a manifestation of alcohol-induced peripheral neuropathy, discussed elsewhere in this chapter.

[34]Although rare/social drinkers might also suffer TBI, it is less likely to be as a result of their alcohol use, and thus this topic was reserved for this chapter.

---

[35]The rage reaction being paradoxical because it develops after the patient has ingested a CNS depressant, not a stimulant.

The Alcohol Withdrawal Syndrome

The AWS is split into two phases: the acute *and* extended phase. The acute phase begins 5–10 hours after the individual's last drink and is interpreted by health care professionals as proof that the individual has become physically dependent on alcohol. The intensity of the withdrawal syndrome depends on (a) the duration and severity of the individual's alcohol use (Perry et al., 2007), as well as (b) their overall state of health, and possible (c) concurrent SUDs. In severe cases the AWS can be life-threatening[36] (Fadem, 2009). The causal mechanism is the sudden reduction or cessation of alcohol intake after the brain has become tolerant to alcohol. When the alcohol level is markedly reduced, the neurons begin to work erratically because the delicate balance between excitatory and inhibitory neurotransmission processes has been disrupted in the absence of alcohol.

Clinically, the AWS is an acute brain syndrome that might be mistaken for such conditions as a subdural hematoma, pneumonia, meningitis, or infection involving the CNS unless the attending physician was aware of the individual's drinking history (Saitz, 1998).[37] Once it has been identified as AWS, the severity of the alcohol withdrawal is often assessed with the Clinical Institute Withdrawal Assessment for Alcohol Scale-Revised (CIWA-Ar) (Baron, Garbely, & Boyd, 2009; Maldonado, 2010). This noncopyrighted instrument measures 15 symptoms of alcohol withdrawal, with each symptom being rated in severity, for a maximum score of 67 points. A score of 0–4 is interpreted as minimal discomfort from the AWS, 5–12 points is interpreted as evidence of mild alcohol withdrawal. Patients whose score on the CIWA-Ar is between 13 and 19 points are thought to be in moderately severe withdrawal, whereas scores of 20+ points are interpreted as evidence of severe alcohol withdrawal. One advantage of the CIWA-Ar is that it might be administered repeatedly over time, providing a measure of the client's improvement or deterioration over time.

Unfortunately, co-existing conditions such as anxiety disorders might inflate the individual's score on the CIWA-Ar, giving the appearance that their alcohol withdrawal is worse than it appears on this instrument (Spiegel, Kumari, & Petri, 2012). Another defect in the CIWA-Ar is that it does not include the individual's vital signs as a criteria for determining the severity of the AWS for the individual although the vital signs could serve as an objective measure of the intensity of the AWS (Spiegel et al., 2012).

Mild alcohol withdrawal is marked by symptoms such as: agitation, anxiety, tremor,[38] diarrhea, abdominal discomfort, exaggerated reflexes, insomnia, vivid dreams or nightmares, nausea, vomiting, tachycardia, headache, memory impairment, problems in concentration, and possible withdrawal seizures (Kelley & Saucier, 2004; Messing, 2007; Perry et al., 2007). These symptoms begin about 16–24 hours after the individual's last drink, and in mild cases of the AWS usually subside within 48–72 hours after that time (Perry et al., 2007). Tremor, often one of the first withdrawal signs, is often self-medicated by the alcohol-dependent person through additional alcohol use It is not uncommon for many heavy alcohol users to keep a drink, or in some cases even a bottle, next to their bed so that they can have a drink even before getting up for the day. This is often done on the pretense of "helping steady my nerves," or the person needing an "eye opener." However, the reality is that this is one of the early stages of the AWS that the drinker self-medicates by drinking alcohol immediately upon awakening.

Severe AWS usually begins 8–12 hours after the individual's last drink. Although, if the patient has suffered significant levels of liver damage, the inset of AWS might get extended for up to 10 days after the individual's last drink (Baron et al., 2009; Maldonado, 2010). Symptoms of the severe AWS include all of those seen in mild to intermediate severity cases, but also can include perceptual distortions or frank hallucinations, hyperthermia, sepsis, and cardiac arrhythmias (Brunton et al., 2008). If the individual should experience actual hallucinations during withdrawal, the condition is said to have developed *alcoholic hallucinosis*. This condition develops in about 10% of the cases of AWS, and usually begins 1–2 days after the individual's last drink. The hallucinations are usually auditory, consisting of voices that are

---

[36]All real, or suspected, cases of alcohol withdrawal should be assessed by and treatment should be a carried out under the supervision of a physician.

[37]This is not to say that these, or any range of other life-threatening conditions might not also be present, complicating the task of the attending physician(s) working with a patient experiencing the AWS.

[38]Unfortunately, alcohol withdrawal can also exacerbate tremor caused by other conditions such as Parkinson's disease.

accusatory, threatening, or critical of the individual's past and current behavior (Ali et al., 2011). Normally, the hallucinations resolve in a few hours to days, although in rare cases they might persist for longer than this (Maldonado, 2010). Visual and tactile hallucinations during alcoholic hallucinosis are rare but still occur in rare cases (Kelley & Saucier, 2004; Olmedo & Hoffman, 2000; Ropper & Brown, 2005). Alcohol withdrawal hallucinations are often quite frightening for the individual who might not recognize the nature of the hallucinations (Tse & Koller, 2004). On occasion, individuals have been known to respond to the hallucinations as if they were actual experiences (Ropper & Brown, 2005), possibly attempting suicide or become violent in an attempt to escape from their hallucinations (Tekin & Cummings, 2003; Soyka, 2000).

There is a danger of seizures during the alcohol withdrawal process, especially in the more severe cases. The period of greatest risk for withdrawal-related seizures begins within 24 hours of the individual's last drink and peaks 48–96 hours after that time (Maldonado, 2010). Two to sixteen percent of heavy drinkers will experience a withdrawal seizure(s) (McRae, Brady, Sonne, 2001; Perry et al., 2007; Schuckit, 2010a), and in 60% of the cases where an individual does experience withdrawal seizures he or she will have multiple seizures (Aminoff, Greenbergh, & Simon, 2005; D'Onofrio, Rathlev, Ulrich, Fish, & Greedland, 1999). Anticonvulsant medications are rarely needed in uncomplicated withdrawal seizures (Sadock & Sadock, 2007; Schuckit, 2010a) and adequate dosing with benzodiazepines are thought to be the most effective immediate intervention for such seizures. However, in 2–4% of the cases the individual had a pre-existing seizure disorder. This seizure disorder may have been exacerbated by the alcohol withdrawal process. Medication compliance is often poor in heavy drinkers and it is possible that the drinker has discontinued taking their anticonvulsant medication(s). The prudent physician will order the appropriate blood tests to determine whether the individual has been taking their medication (Parent & Aminoff, 2008; Perry et al., 2007) and administer the appropriate anticonvulsant medications as indicated.

Approximately one-third of those individuals who experience a withdrawal seizure(s) will go on to develop the *delirium tremens* (DTs).[39] Persons who have engaged in heavy drinking for as little as 5 years have been known to develop the DTs upon cessation from drinking (Fadem, 2009). The DTs usually develop 1–5 days after alcohol cessation. Some of the symptoms of DTs include profound delirium, vivid visual hallucinations, agitation, delusional beliefs, terror, fever, hypotension, hyperthermia, peripheral vascular collapse, tachycardia, and possible death (Ali et al., 2011; Greenberg, 2010; Maldonado, 2010; Perry et al., 2007; Traub, 2009). Prior to the development of effective pharmacological interventions, 10–40% of persons experiencing the DTs would die, usually of cardiovascular collapse (Greenberg, 2010; Kinsella & Riley, 2007; Maldonado, 2010; Perry et al., 2007). Even today the DTs carry a 1–2% risk of death even with the most aggressive medical intervention[40] (Maldonado, 2010; Perry et al., 2007).

Current medical practice is carried out on the assumption that it is best to block the possible development of the DTs with appropriate doses of benzodiazepines during withdrawal. Drawing on the clinical history of 334 patients in Stockholm, Sweden, Palmstierna (2001) identified five markers that seemed to identify the patient at risk for the development of the DTs (1) existence of concurrent infections such as pneumonia during the withdrawal process, (2) tachycardia, (3) signs of autonomic nervous system over-activity in spite of an alcohol concentration at/above one gram per liter of body fluid, (4) history of previous epilepsy, and (5) a history of previously experienced the DTs.

Alcohol also inhibits the release of what has been called the *anti-diuretic hormone*[41] (ADH), altering the fluid balance in the drinker's body (Brunton et al., 2008). This results in the typical heavy drinker being in a state of fluid depletion while intoxicated, and with the onset of abstinence the drinker's body will often begin to retain fluids as the compensatory mechanisms for the constant presence of ADH break down. This will further increase the drinker's risk for cardiovascular and neurological damage. Such fluid retention, and cardiac arrhythmias, will require pharmacological intervention to increase the patient's chances of survival. The pharmacological treatment of the AWS will be discussed in Chapter 33. Patients going through the DTs are also at high risk for alcohol-related muscle

---

[39]Once called the "rum fits" (Maldonado, 2010; Ropper & Brown, 2005).

[40]Baron et al. (2009) gave a figure of 5–15% mortality rate from the DTs.

[41]Technically, vasopressin.

damage and the development of *rhabdomyolysis*[42] (Sauret, Marinides, & Wang, 2002; Richards, 2000). It is possible that there are other symptoms of the alcohol withdrawal process, but the information reviewed above does provide a fairly comprehensive overview of the dangers of the acute AWS.

Extended Alcohol Withdrawal

The period of extended withdrawal might last for 3–12 months after the person's last drink. During this time, some symptoms of the acute phase of the AWS, such as anxiety, sleep problems, and neuropathies might continue to be experienced (Schuckit, 2005, 2006, 2010a). Other symptoms reported during the extended withdrawal phase include depression, emotional excitability, fatigue, and emotional volatility. Further, during the phase of extended withdrawal the person will be exquisitely sensitive to alcohol use "cues" that might trigger a return to active drinking. Many of these cues will be found in the individual's environment, making it difficult for him or her to abstain from alcohol during those first critical months (Schuckit, 2010a). Part of this vulnerability to relapse is mediated by a subjective sense of craving for alcohol that continues long after s/he stopped drinking. This is often referred to as being "thirsty." During such times, the individual finds themselves preoccupied with drinking as a result of exposure to drinking-related cues. Such cues include events, times, and other stimuli associated with alcohol use. Surprisingly, the smell of cigarettes often serves as a relapse "cue," since cigarette smoking in bars is common. There is also evidence that repeated periods of alcohol use interspaced with alcohol withdrawal may enhance the negative effects of alcohol withdrawal, adding to the individual's motivation to continue drinking.

Alcohol Use and the *Diagnostic and Statistical Manual of Mental Disorders* (5th Edition)

The *Diagnostic and Statistical Manual of Mental Disorders,* 5th edition (*DSM-5*) (American Psychiatric Association, 2013) identified five subforms of the alcohol-related disorders:

- *Alcohol use disorder*
- *Alcohol intoxication*

- *Alcohol withdrawal*
- *Other alcohol-induced disorders*
- *Unspecified alcohol-related disorder*

Because there are no clear boundaries between alcohol use, abuse, and dependence, the categories *alcohol intoxication* and *unspecified alcohol-related disorder* were discussed in the last chapter. *Alcohol withdrawal* was discussed in the context of the rare or social drinker, but not in the context of the chronic drinker, which was done above. These terms will be reviewed from that perspective here. It is of interest to note that the *DSM-5* manual does not use the term "alcohol dependence." This term has been replaced, at least in the *DSM-5* manual, with the more ambiguous term *AUD*.[43] The diagnostic criteria for AUD has been modified slightly to include cultural and gender-specific issues that might influence an assessor's perspective of a drinker, but essentially are the same as the criteria used to diagnose alcohol dependence in past editions of the *Diagnostic and Statistical Manual of Mental Disorders,* including but not limited to[44] tolerance, failed attempts to quit, "craving" for alcohol, preoccupation with alcohol use, continued alcohol use in spite of physical or interpersonal risks, etc. (American Psychiatric Association, 2013).[45] Modifiers for the AUD include whether the individual is actively drinking, is remission (with modifiers for early or sustained remission), and whether the individual's drinking is curtailed because they are in a controlled environment.

The diagnostic criteria for a formal diagnosis of alcohol withdrawal are relatively unchanged from earlier editions of the *DSM* and will not be discussed further here. The *unspecified alcohol-related disorder* is a transitional category for those individuals whose drinking is clearly beyond that of social drinking, who are experiencing occupational, social, familial, or financial problems because of their drinking, but who not meet the full criteria for alcohol dependence at this time.

---

[42]See Glossary.

[43]This text uses the same term to denote *any* problematic alcohol use while the *Diagnostic and Statistical Manual of Mental Disorders,* (5th edition) (*DSM-5*) (American Psychiatric Association, 2013) apparently uses the term only for what would be called alcohol addiction in this text.

[44]The reader is referred to the *Diagnostic and Statistical Manual of Mental Disorders,* (5th edition) for a full list of the diagnostic criteria.

[45]The full list of the symptoms of an AUD, along with known cultural social and medical modifiers is discussed at length in the *DSM-5* manual and the reader is referred to the *DSM-5* manual for a more complete discussion of this topic.

The *other alcohol-induced disorder* category includes alcohol-induced conditions, which simulate other forms of psychopathology such as a psychotic reaction. These conditions usually resolve within a few days of the completion of the alcohol withdrawal process.

Chapter Summary

Ethyl alcohol is a toxin that affects virtually every organ system when consumed to excess. The brain appears to be especially vulnerable to the negative effects of heavy alcohol use, although the individual's genetic heritage does influence his or her risk for alcohol-related health problems. In spite of the widespread knowledge that alcohol can induce damage throughout the body the short-term reinforcement potential of alcohol entices a small percentage of those who consume it to drink to excess. Globally, 3.6% of the population is considered to have an AUD, accounting for 3.8% of all deaths worldwide (American Psychiatric Association, 2013). A combination of cultural, genetic, and interpersonal risk factors support or defend against the risk that any given individual will become physically dependent on alcohol. At this point the individual must go through the "detoxification" process to help their bodies return to normal functioning and minimize organ damage. The severity of the withdrawal symptoms is dependent on the individual's genetic heritage and their alcohol use history. In extreme cases the severity of the individual's alcohol withdrawal process will contribute to an organic brain syndrome known as the delirium tremens (DTs). A century ago this condition carried with it a 40% death rate. Today, even with the most aggressive of pharmacological interventions, the DTs still can result in the drinker's death in 1–2% of the cases, illustrating the neurotoxic effects of alcohol.

CHAPTER 6

Abuse and Addiction to Barbiturates and Barbiturate-Like Compounds

Introduction

In the United States today, the anxiety disorders are the most common identified form of mental illness, affecting approximately 14% of the general population (Getzfelt, 2006). Further, each year approximately one-third of the population will experience at least a period of transitory insomnia (Ghoneim, 2004b). Unfortunately, alcohol's effectiveness as an antianxiety[1] agent or a hypnotic is both limited and potentially lethal for the user. Then, at the start of the chemical revolution in the 19th century, chemists began to identify compounds that were able to reduce the individual's sense of dread and anxiety. Many of these same compounds could also induce a form of sleep at higher dosage levels, which was, if not normal, at least as close to a normal state of sleep as could be chemically induced. Unfortunately, many of these compounds had a narrow therapeutic window, making them rather dangerous even in the hands of a trained medical professional. Many of these compounds also became popular drugs of abuse in the 1950s and 1960s, and health care professionals occasionally still encounter a person who is abusing or is addicted to one of these compounds. In this chapter, we will discuss the barbiturates and similar medications, their role in history, the effects of these compounds, and their abuse potentials.

Early Medical Treatment of Anxiety and Insomnia

Many of the early anxiolytic/hypnotic agents introduced in the late 18th and early 19th centuries produced a dose-dependent effect on the user. Depending on the specific compound and the dose administered, the effects could range from sedation, to sleep, to a profound loss of consciousness, a state of surgical anesthesia, and, ultimately, to death, as illustrated in Figure 6-1 (Mihic & Harris, 2011). Chloral hydrate was introduced in 1870 and was marketed as a hypnotic[2] agent. Technically, chloral hydrate is a

prodrug, which is rapidly biotransformed into the biologically active metabolite *trichloroethanal* after oral administration. It was administered orally and a dose of 1–2 grams would cause the patient to fall asleep in less than an hour.

The effects lasted for 8–11 hours, making it appear to be ideal as a hypnotic agent. Unfortunately, physicians soon discovered that chloral hydrate had several problematic side effects. Chloral hydrate is quite irritating to the stomach, and that repeated use over a short period of time might result in significant levels of damage to the stomach lining. Also it was discovered that chloral hydrate is quite addictive, and that the therapeutic dose[3] is only 1/2 to 1/3 of the lethal dose (Virani,

---

[1]Technically an *anxiolytic* compound.

[2]See Glossary.

[3]Which is called a "narrow" therapeutic window, as discussed in Chapter 3.

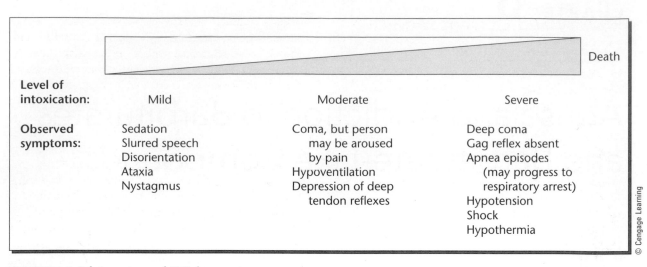

FIGURE 6-1 Relative potency of CNS depressants.

Bezchlibnyk-Butler, Jeffries, & Procyshyn, 2012). Finally, after it had been in clinical use for some time, physicians discovered that withdrawal from chloral hydrate could result in life-threatening seizures (Brown & Stoudemire, 1998). Chloral hydrate also interacts with commonly used anticoagulant drugs such as warfarin and can alter the biotransformation of numerous other compounds. Fortunately, this medication is only rarely used in helping elderly patients sleep, and its use is increasingly rare in the practice of medicine.

Paraldehyde was first isolated in 1829 and first used as a hypnotic in 1882. It proved to be an effective hypnotic, producing little cardiac or respiratory depression. However, it tends to produce a very noxious taste in the user's mouth, and users develop a strong, unpleasant, odor on their breath after ingestion. It is also irritating to the mucous membranes of the mouth and throat, and for these reasons is usually diluted in another liquid before use. Its therapeutic half-life ranges from 3.4 to 9.8 hours. Seventy to eighty percent of a single dose leaves the body unchanged, usually through exhalation, which accounts for the unpleasant odor on the user's breath. Paraldehyde has an abuse potential similar to that of alcohol, and paraldehyde intoxication resembles that of alcohol intoxication in many ways. After the barbiturates were introduced, paraldehyde gradually fell into disfavor, and is rarely, if ever, used at this time (Doble, Martin, & Nutt, 2004).

The *bromide salts* were introduced in the mid-1800s, and in an era before federal oversight of pharmaceuticals were enacted. These compounds were originally introduced as a treatment for epilepsy, and later as sedative and hypnotics (Bisaga, 2008). Soon after their introduction it was discovered that after a few days' continuous use, a reservoir of these compounds built up in the user's body, causing a drug-induced depression. The bromide salts also had a very narrow therapeutic window, and withdrawal from the bromide salts after extended use can induce such symptoms as: seizures, psychosis, and delirium (Bisaga, 2008). The bromide salts have been totally replaced by newer compounds and are no longer prescribed by health care professionals in the United States.

Diphenhydramine is an antihistamine with a strong sedative side effect. Because of this, it is often used as an over-the-counter sleep aid either by itself, or in combination with other compounds. However, its use in older persons can induce an anticholinergic-induced delirium, a complication also encountered in younger abusers ingesting higher than normal doses, or using it on a chronic basis (Perry, Alexander, Liskow, & DeVane, 2007). Chemically, the antihistamines are quite different from the compounds discussed so far, but in spite of differences in their chemical structures, all of these compounds are central nervous system (CNS) depressants.

Still, these compounds were the treatment(s) of choice for anxiety and insomnia until the barbiturates were introduced in the early 20th century.

History and Current Medical Uses of Barbiturates

In 1864, the German chemist Aldolph von Baeyer discovered barbituric acid, the parent compound from which the barbiturates are derived (Numeroff & Putnam, 2005). Barbituric acid is itself inactive, but derivatives of this parent compound yielded a large family of chemicals that could be used as sedatives, or (at higher doses) hypnotic agents. The first of these compounds, barbital, was introduced in 1903. In a short period of time, a flood of barbiturates were developed, so dominating the market that for the first half of the 20th century no nonbarbiturate sedative-hypnotic compounds were introduced (Nelson, 2000; Numeroff & Putnam, 2005). At their height of popularity, more than *1 million pounds* of barbiturate compounds were manufactured each year just in the United States (Brust, 2004). More than 2,500 different barbiturate compounds were developed, although most were never marketed and remained only laboratory curiosities. About 50 of these compounds were ever introduced into clinical use, of which perhaps 20 are still used by physicians (Nishino, Mishima, Mignot, & Dement, 2004). Table 6-1 provides a summary of the most commonly used barbiturates in the United States.

Originally thought to be nonaddictive, clinical experience with these compounds soon revealed the opposite

(Ivanov, Schulz, Palmero, & Newcorn, 2006). Legally, barbiturates are classified as Category II controlled compounds[4] and are available only by prescription. After the introduction of the benzodiazepines[5] in the 1960s, barbiturates slowly fell into disfavor with physicians, although their use is occasionally encountered (O'Brien, 2011). In addition there are still some areas of medicine where barbiturates remain the pharmaceutical of choice (Ciraulo et al., 2005). These include certain surgical procedures, treatment of some forms of migraine headache, and seizure control on both an emergency and long-term basis (Mihic & Harris, 2011; Nemeroff & Putnam, 2005; Ropper & Brown, 2005). Some physicians advocate the use of barbiturates to induce a coma to help control swelling of the brain following trauma, although this practice has been challenged (Brain Trauma Foundation, 2000; Nemeroff & Putnam, 2005). Questions have been raised about their use in inducing a coma in a terminally ill patient who is in extreme pain, and perhaps the most controversial application of the barbiturates is their role in the process of "lethal injection" of criminals sentenced to the death penalty.

The Abuse Potential of the Barbiturates

In light of all that has been discovered about their abuse potential, it is surprising to learn they have enjoyed a minor resurgence in popularity. Older generations, especially those above the age of 70, became addicted to these compounds decades ago, and often continue to abuse these compounds. Also, in the past decade a small number of physicians have attempted to avoid the extra paperwork imposed by some state regulatory agencies on benzodiazepine prescriptions by prescribing the older, less regulated barbiturates to their patients. Finally, this group of compounds has enjoyed an ongoing popularity with some illicit drug users (Ropper & Grown, 2005).

Pharmacology of the Barbiturates

As stated earlier, there are minor differences in the chemical structure between various members of the barbiturate family of compounds, differences that translate into variations in absorption, distribution, biotransformation, and elimination. However, they all have their main effects in the CNS, which is "exquisitely sensitive"

TABLE 6-1
Normal Dosage Levels of Commonly Used Barbiturates

BARBITURATE	SEDATIVE DOSE*	HYPNOTIC DOSE**
Amobarbital	50–150 mg/day	65–200 mg
Aprobarbital	120 mg/day	40–60 mg
Butabarbital	45–120 mg/day	50–100 mg
Mephobarbital	96–400 mg/day	Not used as hypnotic
Pentobarbital	60–80 mg/day	100 mg
Phenobarbital	30–120 mg/day	100–320 mg
Secobarbital	90–200 mg/day	50–200 mg
Talbutal	30–120 mg/day	120 mg

*Administered in divided doses.
**Administered as a single dose at bedtime.
SOURCE: Based on information provided in Uhde and Trancer (1995).

[4]See Appendix Four.
[5]Discussed in the next chapter.

TABLE 6-2
Clinical Applications of Barbiturates

DURATION OF EFFECT	APPLICATION
Ultra-short acting barbiturates	When injected, effects begin in seconds, and last for <30 minutes. Very lipid-soluble. Useful in dental surgical procedures.
Short-acting barbiturates	Usually administered orally. Effects begin in 10–20 minutes, and last for 3–4 hours. Elimination half-life may be longer than duration of effect. Lipid solubility falls between that of ultra-short acting and intermediate duration barbiturates.
Intermediate duration barbiturates	Usually administered orally. Effects begin in approximately one hour. Effects of a single dose last for 6–8 hours. Elimination half-life may be longer than duration of effect. Moderately lipid-soluble.
Long acting barbiturates	Usually administered orally. Effects of a single dose begin in about an hour, and last for 6–12 hours. Elimination half-life may be longer than duration of effect. Lipid solubility less than that of intermediate duration barbiturates.

SOURCES: Chart based on Brunton, Parker, Blumenthal, and Buxton (2008); Ciraulo and Knapp (2009); Meyer and Quenzer (2005); Mihic and Harris (2011); Zevin and Benowitz (1998).

(Brunton, Parker, Blumenthal, & Buxton, 2008, p, 270) to the effects of these drugs. Different barbiturate compounds have different degrees of lipid solubility. The barbiturates that have greater degrees of lipid solubility tend to be more potent and have a more rapid onset of action, although they also have a shorter duration of effect than barbiturates with less lipid solubility (Levin, 2002; Ropper & Brown 2005). This is clearly seen in the difference between the effects of pentobarbital as compared with phenobarbital. A single oral dose of pentobarbital, which is very lipid-soluble, will begin to have an effect in 10–15 minutes, whereas a single dose of phenobarbital, which is poorly lipid soluble, might require an hour or more to begin to act on the nervous system.

All the various barbiturates share the same mechanism of action: Inhibiting the closing of the GABAa channel in the wall of many neurons, thus slowing the rate at which it can establish the electrical differential necessary for it to "fire" (Brunton et al., 2008; Ciraulo & Sarid-Segal, 2005; Doble et al., 2004; Nemeroff & Putnam, 2005; Nishino et al., 2004). The barbiturates can cause this effect even in the absence of the GABA molecule itself (Parrott, Morinan, Moss, & Scholey, 2004; Doble et al., 2004).

Clinically, barbiturates are classified by their *duration of action,*[6] as reviewed, in Table 6-2.

[6]A number of different classification systems for barbiturates have been suggested over the years. This text will follow the system suggested by Zevin and Benowitz (1998).

In Chapter 3 it was noted that for some compounds the duration of effect is significantly different than the elimination half-life of that compound, a characteristic found in the barbiturates. This depends on the ability of that specific barbiturate to form chemical bonds with either lipid or protein molecules. Longer duration barbiturates have greater degrees of protein binding. Generally, shorter-term barbiturates require biotransformation by the liver before elimination, whereas long-acting barbiturates are eliminated from the body virtually unchanged. For example the barbiturate methohexital has a therapeutic half-life of 3–6 hours and is extensively biotransformed by the liver before elimination. In contrast phenobarbital has a half-life of 2–6 days and 25–50% of a single dose of phenobarbital will be excreted from the body unchanged (American Society of Health System Pharmacists, 2008). Because the barbiturates share the characteristic of being highly lipid or protein-bound, the drug molecules are redistributed throughout the body after ingestion, allowing a reservoir of potentially active medication to accumulate in the body tissues. When the person discontinues the medication, as he or she would do after using a single dose to help himself or herself sleep, the reservoir of barbiturate is released back into the circulation, causing a "hangover" effect for the user.

Barbiturates are usually administered orally, although many of the ultrashort-duration barbiturates are used intravenously to rapidly induce anesthesia for surgical procedures. On rare occasions, barbiturates may be administered through suppositories. Orally administered barbiturates are rapidly absorbed through the small intestine (Nemeroff & Putnam, 2005; Levin, 2002). Once in the general circulation, the barbiturate molecules are distributed throughout the body, and the highest concentrations are found in the liver and the brain (American Society of Health System Pharmacists, 2008). Behaviorally, the effects of barbiturates are very similar to those of alcohol (Ciraulo & Sarid-Segal, 2005; Nishino et al., 2004). The barbiturates will depress the level of neural activity, as is seen with alcohol ingestion, but they also have a minor impact on the heart, muscle tissues, and the respiration process (Ciraulo et al., 2005). In the brain, the barbiturate molecules tend to have their greatest effect on the cortex, the reticular activating system, and the medulla oblongata,[7] areas of the brain with higher concentrations of GABA receptors. By reducing the level of neural activity in the neurons in the cortex, at low doses the barbiturates are able to induce a sense of relaxation, and at slightly higher doses induce a form of sleep. However, the barbiturates have a very narrow therapeutic window. Depending on the exact barbiturate molecule involved, the therapeutic window might be only 1:3 to 1:10 (Brunton et al., 2008; Ciraulo et al., 2005; Meyer & Quenzer, 2005). In other words, the therapeutic dose is between one-third and one-tenth the lethal dose, a margin of safety that is significantly reduced or even totally negated if the individual had ingested another CNS depressant such as alcohol, a narcotic analgesic, an antihistamine, or a range of other compounds while taking a barbiturate.

The effects of barbiturate use are long lasting: Research suggests that using a barbiturate less than 18 times a year still elevates the individual's risk of death from all causes, a risk that increases as the number of doses used by the individual increases (Kripke, Langer, & Kline, 2012). Barbiturate-induced death can occur either as a result of a deliberate act or as a result of dosage miscalculation. It has been estimated that at the height of their popularity the annual death rate from prescribed barbiturates was 118 per 100,000 prescriptions (Drummer & Odell, 2001). Although they are not commonly prescribed today, the barbiturates continue to be used in suicide attempts.[8] This is one reason few physicians continue to prescribe these compounds (Perry et al., 2007).

Subjective Effects of Barbiturates at Normal Dosage Levels

At therapeutic doses, barbiturates cause the user to experience a sense of relaxation, or even a sense of euphoria (Ciraulo et al., 2005). Some users also report a sense of sedation or fatigue, drowsiness, ataxia, and an increase in reaction time similar to that seen in alcohol intoxication (Nishino et al., 2004; Filley, 2004). At slightly higher doses, the barbiturates induce a form of sleep. Since both the barbiturates and alcohol affect the same gated chloride ion channel in the neural wall normally controlled by GABAa, the pharmacological mechanism by which they achieve their effects is very similar, and thus the subjective experience is about the same. Indeed, patients who appear intoxicated but who have no sign of alcohol in their bodies should be tested for barbiturate ingestion.

Complications of Barbiturate Use at Normal Dosage Levels

Like alcohol, the barbiturates interfere with the normal function of cortical neurons and might potentially induce a *paradoxical rage reaction* (Ciraulo et al., 2005). Other side effects of barbiturates when used at normal dosage levels include feelings of nausea, dizziness, mental slowness. But anxious patients report that their sense of anxiety is reduced, if not eliminated, and patients with insomnia report that they can slip into a state of drug-induced sleep. Unfortunately, tolerance to the hypnotic effects of barbiturates will develop after a few days of continuous use (Drummer & Odell, 2001). In contrast, tolerance to the lethal threshold for these drugs remains unchanged. If the individual should increase the amount of the barbiturate being used or intermix barbiturates with other CNS depressants in an effort to regain the original anxiolytic or hypnotic effect, it is very possible for the individual to die from an overdose.

---

[7]See Glossary.

[8]*Any* known or suspected overdose of a barbiturate or other compound should *immediately* be evaluated by a physician.

Further, the sleep induced by barbiturates is not a normal form of sleep. Barbiturates interfere with the normal progression of sleep stages, and suppress the duration of the rapid eye movement (REM) sleep stage (Nemeroff & Punam, 2005; Nishino et al., 2004). Following the nightly use of barbiturates for as little as two weeks, REM sleep time has been reduced by as much as 50% (Brunton et al., 2008). Although reduced REM sleep time for one or two nights is not thought to be dangerous, long-term REM sleep impairment is thought to have long-term emotional and physical effects on the individual. When the barbiturates are discontinued after an extended period of use, the individual is at risk for the phenomenon of *REM rebound*.[9] The vivid and intense nature of dreams experienced during REM rebound borders on the experience of nightmares for the individual. These REM rebound dreams may serve as an incentive for the person to return to the use of barbiturates or similar compounds to "get a good night's sleep."

Barbiturates are able to cause the user to experience a drug-induced "hangover" the next day (Wilson, Shannon, & Shields, 2011). The subjective experience for the user is of "just not being able to get going," if not of continued intoxication by barbiturates. This drug-induced hangover effect is the result of the distribution and elimination characteristics of the barbiturate being used. As was discussed in Chapter 3, physicians estimate that it takes five elimination half-life periods to eliminate a single dose of a compound from the body. However, the extended elimination half-lives of many barbiturates results in significant amounts of the drug remaining in the user's body for hours or days after a single dose. For example, although the therapeutic effects of a single dose of secobarbital might last for 6–8 hours, the hangover effect might cause impaired motor coordination abilities for 10–20 hours that same dose was ingested (Mihic & Harris, 2011).Individuals with impaired liver function, such as the elderly or persons with advanced liver disease, are especially prone to barbiturate "hangover" effects.

For years, the primary application of the barbiturate phenobarbital was the control of epileptic seizures in certain patients. A number of alternative antiepileptic medications that have been introduced in the past 20 years and phenobarbital is increasingly being replaced by one or more of these newer compounds. This is perhaps a good thing because it has been discovered that persons who have taken phenobarbital for seizure control on a long term basis suffer an eight-point drop on IQ tests, although it is not clear whether this is an artifact, a drug-induced effect, or the seizure disorder (Breggin, 1998). It is also not known whether this measured loss of IQ is reversible. Other known complications of barbiturates when used at therapeutic doses include sexual performance problems and a loss of libido for both men and women (Finger, Lund, & Slagel, 1997). Hypersensitivity reactions have been reported in patients receiving a barbiturate, especially patients who suffer from asthma (Mihic & Harris, 2011). Other known complications include nausea, vomiting, diarrhea, skin rashes, and in some cases constipation. Finally, some patients develop an extreme sensitivity to sunlight known as *photosensitivity*, placing them at risk for sunburn after even short exposures to sunlight.

Persons who suffer from attention deficit hyperactivity disorder (ADHD), who also receive a barbiturate, usually experience a resurgence or intensification of the ADHD symptoms. This intensification of ADHD symptoms is possibly due to a weakening of cortical inhibitions, although some clinicians believe that this effect. Another theory is that this reflects the ability of barbiturates to suppress the action of the reticular activating system (RAS) in the brain. If, as is commonly believed, ADHD is caused by an under-active RAS, any medication that reduces the level of RAS activity such as the barbiturates will probably intensify the symptoms of ADHD.

Drug Interactions Involving Barbiturates

When used at therapeutic doses, barbiturates are able to potentiate the effects of other CNS depressants, including those of alcohol, narcotic analgesics, phenothiazines, benzodiazepines, and antihistamines. The interaction between the barbiturates and antihistamines is especially problematic because the latter class of chemicals blocks the action of histamine, a neurotransmitter that serves an excitatory function in the brain. Patients using monoamine oxidase inhibitor (MAO) medications should not take a barbiturate except under a physician's supervision. MAO inhibitors can block the biotransformation of barbiturates, placing the user at an unintended risk for a barbiturate overdose should they use medications from both categories simultaneously (Ciraulo, Shader, Greenblatt, & Creelman, 2006; Tatro, 2009). Barbiturates also reduce

---

[9]See Glossary.

the effectiveness of the antibiotic doxycycline, and speed up the biotransformation of the class of anti-depressant medications known as "tricyclic" anti-depressants (Ciraulo et al., 2006). They also speed up the biotransformation of oral contraceptives, corticos-teroids, the anticoagulant medication warfarin, and the antibiotic metronidazole. Barbiturates are biotrans-formed by the same region of the liver that biotrans-forms the anti-asthma medication theophylline, which may interfere with asthma control. Finally, patients using barbiturates and the over-the-counter analgesic acetaminophen are at increased risk for liver damage (Tatro, 2009). As this list would suggest, the barbitu-rates are exceptionally potent compounds, which should not be intermixed with other medications except under the supervision of a physician.

Effects of the Barbiturates at Above-Normal Dosage Levels

Individuals who ingest higher-than-normal levels of barbiturates demonstrate slurred speech and ataxia, as well as other behaviors similar to those seen in alcohol intoxication. Long-term users may, when they discon-tinue the intake of barbiturates, may experience a *delirium tremens* (DTs) like reaction (Ciraulo & Sarid-Segal, 2005). Barbiturates interfere with the normal cough reflex, placing the abuser at risk for conditions such as pneumonia and bronchitis. The barbiturates cause a dose-dependent reduction in respi-ration, which as noted earlier in this chapter can result in respiratory arrest. Hypothermia is also seen when the barbiturates are used at above-normal dosage levels (Ciraulo et al., 2005; Pagliaro & Pagliaro, 1998). Other symptoms seen when barbiturates are ingested at above-normal doses include a progressive loss of reflex activity, tachycardia, hypotension, coma, and possible death (Nemeroff & Putnam, 2005).

Although physicians have had access to a range of safer medications, even at the end of the 21st century intentional or unintentional barbiturate overdoses are not unheard of. Fortunately, barbiturates do not cause direct damage to the CNS. If the overdose victim reaches support before s/he develops shock or hypoxia, there is a good chance that s/he may fully recover from the overdose (Nishino et al., 2005). If only for this reason *any suspected barbitu-rate overdose should immediately be assessed and treated by a physician.*

Neuroadaptation, Tolerance, and Physical Dependence on Barbiturates

With periods of continuous use, the individual's body will begin the process of neuroadaptation[10] over a surprisingly short period of time. The process of barbiturate-induced neuroadaptation is not uniform, however. For example, when a barbiturate such as phe-nobarbital is used to control seizures, neuroadaptation does not appear to be a major problem, and after the patient adapts to the sedative effects of the medication, s/he might be maintained on the same dose for extended periods of time without fear of neuroadapta-tion. In contrast, a person using a barbiturate as a hyp-notic might become tolerant to this effect after just a couple of weeks (Nemeroff & Putnam, 2005). Both patients and drug abusers have been known to try to overcome their increasing tolerance to a given barbitu-rate by increasing their dose. As stated before, in spite of the process of neuroadaptation the lethal dose to a barbiturate remains relatively unchanged (Mihic & Harris, 2011; Meyer & Quenzer, 2005). By increasing the dose, the user runs the risk of a barbiturate over-dose, with possibly lethal consequences. Barbiturate abusers also develop tolerance to the euphoric effects of these drugs, which again might prompt many abu-sers to increase the dosage level, or intermix barbitu-rates with other CNS depressants. As stated earlier, the outcome of either process might be a fatal suppression of the respiratory reflex. Further, barbiturates have been documented to induce *cross-tolerance.*[11] Cross-tolerance between alcohol and the barbiturates is com-mon, as is cross-tolerance between barbiturates and narcotic analgesics, the benzodiazepines and the hallu-cinogenic PCP.

The barbiturates are able to induce a state of physi-cal dependence with a characteristic withdrawal syn-drome if the person should discontinue/drastically or reduce his/her barbiturate use. *Barbiturate withdrawal is potentially life-threatening and should be attempted only under the supervision of a physician* (Erickson, 2007; Meyer & Quenzer, 2005). Longer-acting barbitu-rates will tend to have longer withdrawal periods. The barbiturate withdrawal syndrome is similar to that of

---

[10]Or, if the drug is being abused, the same process is called "tolerance."

[11]See Glossary.

the alcohol withdrawal syndrome with symptoms including: confusion, seizures, muscle weakness, anorexia, muscle twitches, rebound anxiety, and trembling, agitation, a *delirium-tremens* like state, brain damage, and possible death. Barbiturate withdrawal seizures may begin on the 2nd or 3rd day of abstinence, and are rare after the 12th day of abstinence. The acute withdrawal syndrome normally lasts 3–14 days. Physicians may use any of a wide range of pharmaceuticals to help control the severity of the withdrawal process; however, patients should be warned that there is no symptom-free withdrawal.

The Barbiturate-Like Drugs

As physicians became aware of the many adverse side-effects of barbiturates, pharmaceutical companies began to look for substitutes that might be both effective, yet safe to use. This resulted in a number of compounds that were introduced in the 1950s to replace the barbiturates, including: *meprobamate, methaqualone, glutethimide, ethchlorvynol,* and *methyprylon.* The chemical structure of some of these compounds (such as gutethimide and methyprylon) is very similar to that of the barbiturates (Julien, 2005). Like the barbiturates, glutethimide and methyprylon are mainly biotransformed in the liver, and all of these compounds share the characteristic of being a global neural inhibitor rather than an anxiolytic or insomnia-specific compound. Although each of these compounds was introduced as "nonaddicting," subsequent clinical experience demonstrated that each had an abuse potential very similar to that of the barbiturates.

Gluethimide was initially quite popular; however, it soon became apparent that its effects were unpredictable. There are wide variations in this compound's absorption both among patients, and within the same patient over time, making it difficult to identify an effective dosage level for the user. Further, users were found to rapidly develop tolerance to its effects, and gluethimide was found not only to have a discontinuance syndrome but also a rather severe withdrawal process for this compound (Kranzler & Ciraulo, 2005b). Some of the symptoms experienced during the discontinuance syndrome include (but are not limited to): seizures, tremulousness nausea, tachycardia, fever, as well as catatonia-like symptoms (Kranzler & Ciraulo, 2005b).

The therapeutic dose of glutethimide is just a little below the toxic dosage range, placing the user at high risk for an overdose. The symptoms of a glutethimide overdose can take up to 120 hours to resolve (Kranzler & Ciraulo, 2005b). Detoxification with controlled doses of a long-term barbiturate such as phenobarbital was recommended at the rate of 60 mg of phenobarbital for each 500 mg of glutethimide ingested daily for stabilization, followed by a gradual reduction in each day's dose of phenobarbital until the patient was drug free (Kranzler & Ciraulo, 2005b). Because of the complications associated with its use, neither ethchlorvynol nor glutethimide is used by physicians except under special circumstances (Schuckit, 2006a). The prolonged use of ethchlorvynol can induce a loss of vision known as *amblyopia,* which will slowly clear after the drug is discontinued. When one reviews the side effects and effects of an overdose, one is hard-pressed to answer the question "why did people abuse this drug?" Apparently it was of interest to illicit drug abusers because when ingested with codeine it caused a sense of euphoria, although this has not been independently confirmed.

Meprobamate was first introduced in 1955 as a "non-barbiturate" compound that could be used in the daytime to treat anxiety and at higher dosage levels as a hypnotic agent at night. It was also marketed as a muscle relaxant, although its effects were on the CNS and not the muscles in the body (Lipman, 2010). Meprobamate rapidly gained wide acceptance within the medical community and in 1957 one-third of all prescriptions written in the United States were for this compound (Lipman, 2010). This compound's chemical structure is very similar to that of the barbiturate, but is just different enough so that the claim that it is not a barbiturate is justified.

Shortly after it was introduced, it was discovered that it could also induce a sense of euphoria when abused at high dosage levels (Bisaga, 2008). However, like its "non-addicting" counterparts it was soon discovered that there was a significant addiction potential associated with its use. Physical dependence on meprobamate is common when patients require 3,200 mg/day to achieve the desired effects (Cole & Yonkers, 1995). By current standards it is considered obsolete, and is very rarely prescribed today. Surprisingly, an over-the-counter prodrug, *carisoprodol* is biotransformed in part into meprobamate after ingestion, and there have been reports of physical dependence on carisoprodol (Bisaga, 2008; Gitlow, 2007).

Peak blood levels of meprobamate are seen in 1–3 hours after a single dose, and the half-life is between 6 and 17 hours, although when used on an extended basis the half-life might be extended to between 24 and 48 hours (Cole & Yonkers, 1995). The LD50 of meprobamate is estimated to be about 28,000 mg; however, some patients have expired after ingesting only 12,000 mg (Cole & Yonkers, 1995). When combined with other CNS depressants, the therapeutic window for meprobamate is reduced and fatal overdoses were not uncommon.

Methaqualone was introduced as a safe, nonaddicting barbiturate substitute in 1965, and it quickly gained a following among illicit drug abusers who discovered that if you resisted the hypnotic effects of this compound, you were able to induce a feeling of euphoria (Neubauer, 2005). Following oral administration methaqualone is rapidly absorbed from the gastrointestinal tract, and the effects begin in 15–20 minutes. Anxiolytic doses were usually about 75 mg, whereas hypnotic doses were between 150 and 300 mg. Tolerance to the sedative and hypnotic effects of methaqualone develops rapidly, usually after 2–4 weeks of continuous use (Virani et al., 2012). Unfortunately, after the development of tolerance many abusers would increase their dosage levels in an attempt to maintain the initial effect, ignoring the fact that methaqualone has a narrow therapeutic window and that the lethal dose remains the same in spite of possible tolerance to the drug's effects. In the United States, methaqualone is a Schedule I[12] compound and was withdrawn from the market. It is, however, still manufactured in other countries or in illicit markets, and so the alcohol and drug counselor should have at least a working knowledge of its effects.

Alcohol Use and the *Diagnostic and Statistical Manual of Mental Disorders* (5th Edition)

The classification of barbiturate abuse/addiction as presented in the *Diagnostic and Statistical Manual of Mental Disorders* (5th edition) (American Psychiatric Association, 2013) will be discussed in the next chapter. This is consistent with the inclusion of the barbiturates in the category of a sedative, hypnotic, or anxiolytic compound used in the *Diagnostic and Statistical Manual of Mental Disorders* (5th edition) (American Psychiatric Association, 2013).

Chapter Summary

The twin problems of anxiety and insomnia have plagued humans for thousands of years. For much of that time, alcohol was the only compound that was even marginally effective in relieving either disorder, although tolerance to the anxiolytic and hypnotic effects of alcohol develops rapidly when it is used on a continuous basis. The chemical revolution that began in the 1800s, which spawned the pharmacological revolution in its turn, resulted in the development of a number of compounds with anxiolytic and/or hypnotic effects, although each also had serious side-effects that limited its use. In the early 1900s, the first of a new family of compounds, the barbiturates, were introduced. These chemicals were in use for decades before it was discovered that they had a mechanism of action very similar to that of alcohol. It was, however, quickly discovered that cross-tolerance between alcohol and the barbiturates was possible, and that they had a high abuse potential.

Following World War II, a number of new compounds were introduced as safe, nonaddicting, replacements for the barbiturates. However, it was soon discovered that each of these compounds also had an abuse potential similar to that of the barbiturates. When the benzodiazepines[13] were introduced, compounds that are safer and more forgiving, the use of barbiturates and similar compounds virtually ceased. However, a small number of the barbiturates have a limited role in medicine even today, and the health care professional will occasionally encounter a patient who abuses these compounds.

---

[12]See Appendix 4.

[13]Discussed in the next chapter.

CHAPTER 7

Abuse and Addiction to the Benzodiazepines and Similar Agents

Introduction

In 1960, the first of a new class of antianxiety[1] compounds, chlordiazepoxide, was introduced in the United States. Chlordiazepoxide was the first of a family of drugs known as the benzodiazepines (BZs), which were identified as a result of the search for safe replacements for the barbiturates. With their introduction physicians now had a safer alternative to the more dangerous, potentially lethal, barbiturates and barbiturate-like chemicals (Cloos, 2010a; Mihic & Harris, 2011). Since the time of their introduction more than 3,000 different variations of the core benzodiazepine molecule have been identified. Approximately 50 BZs have been introduced around the world, and several are used as pharmaceuticals in the United States. The BZs have been found to be useful either as the primary or as an adjunct to the treatment of a wide range of disorders, including anxiety states, insomnia, muscle strains, and the emergency control of seizures (Bisaga, 2008). They are popular medications: Each year, between 10% and 15% of the adults in the Western world use a benzodiazepine[2] at least once (Dubovsky, 2005; Jenkins, 2007; Fenton, Keyes, Martins, & Hasin, 2010; Gitlow, 2007). These medications are also frequently abused either alone or in combination with other drugs of abuse. In this chapter we will review the history, current uses, pharmacology, and some of the ways that these medications are abused.

Medical Uses of the Benzodiazepines

The BZs were introduced with great fanfare as being both safe, and nonaddicting,[3] offering physicians an alternative to the more dangerous barbiturates then in use. Their relatively large therapeutic windows made

physicians feel more comfortable prescribing them for anxious patients. In the half century since the introduction of this class of medications, they have been supplemented as the "front line" anxiolytic medications (Shear, 2003). The selective serotonin reuptake inhibitors (SSRIs) have been found to provide long-term anxiety control without the risk of physical dependence inherent in the use of the BZs over extended periods of time. The BZs still have a limited role in medicine, being used to control *acute* anxiety (anxiety attacks, or short-term anxiety from a specific time limited stressor), and they continue to have a role in the treatment of such conditions as generalized anxiety disorder (GAD) (Stevens & Pollack, 2005).

---

[1]Technically these medications are known as *anxiolytic* compounds.

[2]These compounds are classified as Schedule II drugs. See Appendix four.

[3]However, even the pharmaceutical companies admitted that they were "habit forming," a term that was less likely to make the user anxious about their use than the more accurate term "addictive."

Some BZs currently in use in the United States, such as diazepam, have been found to be of value in such problems as seizure control, and helping muscles recover from strains. The benzodiazepine alprazolam is frequently used as an adjunct to the treatment of depression, and clonazepam has been found to be effective in long-term control of anxiety (Raj & Sheehan, 2004). In addition, in the latter part of the 20th century compounds such flurazepam, quazepam, triazolam, and temazepam were introduced as hypnotic[4] agents. However, because the introduction of a new class of medications known as *benzodiazepine receptor agonists* (alternately called *Z-compounds*, or *BRAs*,[5] discussed later in this chapter), the BZs have fallen into disfavor as hypnotics. The BRAs are more selective than the BZs, and are thought to have a lower abuse potential than the BZs ("Insomnia in Later Life," 2006). These medications will be discussed later in this chapter.

The Pharmacology of the Benzodiazepines

All the various BZs have only minor variations in chemical structure, variations mainly affecting their duration of action (Dubovsky, 2005). The relative potency and biological half-lives of some of the BZs currently in use in the United States are reviewed in Table 7-1.

Like many pharmaceuticals, it is possible to classify the BZs on the basis of their pharmacological characteristics (degree of lipid binding, etc.). After ingestion, those BZs that are most lipid-soluble will pass from the gastrointestinal tract into the circulation more rapidly than those that are not as lipid-soluble (Ciraulo et al., 2005; Raj & Sheehan, 2004). Another classification system for the BZs exists on the basis of their therapeutic half-lives:[6] (1) ultra-short acting (<4 hours), (2) short acting (<6 hours), (3) Intermediate duration (6–24 hours), and (4) Long lasting (24+ hours) (Mihic & Harris, 2011).

Once in the circulation, the benzodiazepine molecules bind to lipid molecules in the blood. Depending on the specific benzodiazepine being discussed between

---

[4]Sleep inducing.

[5]The term BRAs, or benzodiazepine receptor agonists, will be used in this text.

[6]Remember: There is the *therapeutic* half-life, the *distribution* half-life, and the *elimination* half-life. This table is based on the therapeutic half-life of the BZs being considered.

TABLE 7-1
Commonly Prescribed Benzodiazepines and Their Half-Lives

GENERIC NAME	EQUIPOTENT DOSE (mg)	ESTIMATED HALF-LIFE (hours)
Alprazolam	0.5	6–20
Chlordiazepoxide	25	30–100
Clonazepam	0.20	20–40
Clorazepate	7.5	30–100
Diazepam	5	50–100
Flurazepam	30	50–100
Halzepam	20	30–100
Lorazepam	1	10–20
Oxazepam	15	5–21
Prazepam	10	30–100
Temazepam	30	9.5–12.4
Triazolam	0.25	1.7–3.0

SOURCE: Based on Department of Medicine, Washington University School of Medicine (2001); Schuckit, 2006a; Brunton, Parker, Blumenthal, & Buxton (2008); Mihic & Harris (2011).

70% and 99% of the benzodiazepine molecules become lipid-bound. Diazepam, for example, is more than 99% lipid-bound, whereas only 80% of the benzodiazepine alprazolam molecules become lipid-bound (Mihic & Harris, 2011). Lipid binding and distribution pattern of that specific BZ are factors that influence the therapeutic effects of that compound on the body (Raj & Sheehan, 2004). Some of the BZs are sequestered in body tissues such as body fat, and are then slowly released back into the general circulation over extended periods of time, allowing that compound to have an extended half-life. This is often an advantage when a physician is trying to decide on a BZ to offer the patient for use as an anxiolytic or hypnotic. Age must also be considered when a benzodiazepine is prescribed. The body of older persons require longer periods to biotransform and eliminate a benzodiazepine. If a benzodiazepine is required for an older patient, the physician will often prescribe a compound with a shorter half-life, such as lorazepam, or oxazepam, compounds that do not require extensive biotransformation prior to elimination.

Lipid solubility determines how rapidly the unbound molecules of a specific benzodiazepine might pass through the blood brain barrier into the brain, where the primary site of action is the gamma aminobutryic acidA (GABAa) receptor site in various regions of the brain (Bisaga, 2008; Raj & Sheehan, 2004). However, researchers have identified more than 20 subtypes of the GABA receptor site, and the role of each in human behavior is still being explored. Thus, it is not clear whether the BZs must bind to GABAa receptors only in one part of the brain to induce their anxiolytic effect or if there are multiple sites of action within the brain. The chemical structure of many BZs makes the absorption of those compounds very erratic when they are injected into muscle tissue, and thus they are not usually used in intramuscular injections and are usually administered orally. One exception to this rule is when the patient is experiencing a seizure. In such cases intravenous injections of diazepam, or a similar benzodiazepine, can aid in seizure control.[7] Another exception to this rule is midazolam, which is sold under the brand name of Versed®, which is used as a pre-surgical anesthetic or for procedures that require "conscious sedation."

Many BZs require biotransformation before these compounds can be eliminated from the body. In the process of biotransformation some BZs produce metabolites that are themselves biologically active. Thus, the *duration of effect* for many BZs might be different from the elimination half-life of that compound (Dubovsky, 2005). An excellent example of this is the benzodiazepine flurazepam, which will produce five different metabolites during the process of biotransformation. Each of these metabolites has its own biological effect on the user. Because of normal variation in the speed at which a given individual's body can biotransform and eliminate flurazepam and its metabolites, a single dose might continue to have an effect on the user for *47–100 hours after a single dose*[8] (Mihic & Harris, 2011). Fortunately, there are BZs such as lorazepam and oxazepam that either are eliminated unchanged from the body, or produce metabolites that have minimal biological effect, making them ideal for some persons.

Although the BZs are often compared with the barbiturates, the mechanism of action of the BZs is more specific than that of the barbiturates, which is one factor that contributes to their large therapeutic index. The benzodiazepine molecules bind at the gated chloride channel activated by GABA but require that GABA molecules be present before they affect neural activity. In contrast, the barbiturates activate this ion channel even in the absence of GABA (Bisaca, 2008; Brunton, Parker, Blumenthal, & Buxton, 2008; Mihic & Harris, 2011). The BZs enhance the effects of GABA, forcing the chloride channel to remain open far longer than normal, thus reducing the "firing" rate of that neuron (Brust, 2004; Raj & Sheehan, 2004; Ramadan, Werder, & Preskorn, 2006).

Surprisingly, although the BZs have been used for more than half a century as anxiolytic medications, there is strong disagreement as to their long-term effectiveness as anxiolytics (Cloos, 2010b). Some researchers believe that the BZs are fully effective for only 1–2 months, after which they become less effective (Ayd, Janicak, Davis, & Preskor, 1996; Berry & Mugford, 2007; Fricchione, 2004; Whitaker, 2010). It is for this reason that many neuropharmacologists suggest that BZs be used concurrently with SSRIs for long term anxiolytic purposes, with the former class of drugs slowly being discontinued after 6–8 weeks (Fricchione, 2004; Raj & Sheehan, 2004). This treatment protocol avoids the danger of BZ-withdrawal "rebound" anxiety, or the "plateau effect" seen when the prescribed BZ becomes less effective as an anxiolytic over time. Other pharmacologists believe that the BZs are effective for the control of anxiety even over extended periods of time. They maintain that there is little evidence to suggest that persons become tolerant to the antianxiety effects of the BZs, although they do seem to reach a plateau after which the patient will often report that it "just doesn't work like it used to" (Ciraulo et al., 2005; Raj & Sheehan, 2004). In this case, a dosage adjustment might be called for, although Raj and Sheehan (2004) warn that the patient might be seeking that initial sense of relaxation achieved when the medication was first started. Thus, even within the medical community there is disagreement as to the optimal use of the BZs, and as we will discuss later in this chapter, their potential for abuse.

---

[7]Many BZs packaged for intravenous use are diluted in a compound known as propylene glycol which is toxic to the body. The toxicity of propylene glycol is additive and prolonged intravenous administration can result in such problems as cardiac arrhythmias, tissue necrosis, hypotension, seizures, and multiple organ failures (Maldoinado, 2010).

[8]Earlier editions reported an estimate of up to 280 hours, but researchers have revised that downward to 47–100 hours (Mihic & Harris, 2011).

Subjective Effects of Benzodiazepines at Normal Dosage Levels

When initially used as an anxiolytic at normal dosage levels, persons report a reduction in anxiety, and a sense of gentle relaxation. Some users report a disturbing sense of dissociation. Very few persons report a sense of euphoria at therapeutic dosage levels. When used as a hypnotic, the BZs initially reduce sleep latency,[9] and upon awakening the user reports having experienced a deep, restful period of sleep.

Benzodiazepines and Suicide Attempts

An ever-present danger when treating depressed persons is that the person will attempt to commit suicide. Because of their higher therapeutic index[10] the BZs have traditionally been viewed as being far safer to use with depressed persons than were the barbiturates. Although they do appear to be safer to use with persons who are potentially suicidal, this perception is not always accurate. Benzodiazepines are involved in one-third of prescription drug deaths (Webster, 2011). Alprazolam was found to be one of the compounds most commonly involved in causes of drug-induced death in Florida during the period 2003–2009 ("Drug Overdose Deaths—Florida, 2003–2009"). There have also been rare reports of benzodiazepine-induced suicidal thinking in persons who previously did not demonstrate such thoughts (Breggin, 2008).

When used in isolation the BZs are relatively nontoxic compounds, with a very large therapetuic window. However, when these compounds were simultaneously ingested with another CNS depressant (such as alcohol, narcotic analgesics) the benzodiazepine margin of safety was significantly reduced (Breggin, 2008; Cloos, 2010a). Jones, Mack, and Paulozzi (2013) reported, for example, that at least 77% of persons who died while taking BZs were also using either a prescribed narcotic analgesic or nonprescribed opiates.[11] If a person is suspected of having developed a drug overdose that person *should immediately be assessed and treated by medical professionals.*

Chemists have developed a benzodiazepine antagonist called flumazenil, which binds at and blocks the BZ receptor sites. Unfortunately, it is only effective for 20–45 minutes, and is specific to only BZs (Brust, 2007b; O'Brien, 2011). A greater problem is that the sudden blockade of the receptor sites normally occupied by benzodiazepine molecules can initiate sudden withdrawal if the individual were a long-term benzodiazepine abuser. As discussed elsewhere in this chapter, benzodiazepine withdrawal can induce seizures and is potentially life threatening (Traub, 2009). Thus, flumazenil is of value only in acute overdose situations, must be repeatedly administered at regular intervals, and should be used only under the supervision of a physician.

Side Effects of the Benzodiazepines When Used at Normal Dosage Levels

The BZs are usually prescribed as antianxiety agents; however, 4–9% of persons report a moderate to severe level of sedation when they first start taking a prescribed benzodiazepine. That effect will pass in a few days as the user's body becomes tolerant to the effects of these medications (Stevens & Pollack, 2005). When used as an anxiolytic or as a hypnotic the user might experience some degree of ataxia, as well as clouding of consciousness that has been described as a sense of floating, or detachment, from external reality.[12] These effects are compounded if the patient is using other central nervous system depressants, including over-the-counter medications such as antihistamines or alcohol.

Other side effects of the BZs when these medications are used at normal dosage levels include irritability, hostility, paradoxical rage, or aggression (Breggin, 2008; Brust, 2004; Drummer & Odell, 2001; Lipman, 2010; Virani, Bezchlibnyk-Butler, Jeffries, & Procyshyn, 2012). The aggression or rage response appears to reflect the benzodiazepine-induced cortical disinhibition effect,

---

[9]See Glossary

[10]Discussed in Chapter 3.

[11]Their study was based on an examination of the death certificates issued by county coroners in 2010. The authors noted that in 25% where a drug overdose was identified as the cause of death the specific drug(s) were not identified, so there is a chance that the proportion of drug overdose deaths involving benzodiazpines and narcotics could be higher than the 77% figure that the authors offered.

[12]Individuals who have been exposed to a traumatic stressor, and thus are at risk for the development of posttraumatic stress disorder (PTSD) have been found not to benefit from benzodiazepine intervention possibly because the dissociative effect of this class of medications contributes to feelings of not being in control, which is one of the factors that contributes to the development of PTSD (Cloos, 2010a; Shalev, 2009).

similar to that seen in alcohol abusers. Because both alcohol and the BZs affect the same calcium channel in the neural wall, cross-tolerance between alcohol and the BZs is common (O'Brien, 2006).

It has been found that even when used as prescribed the individual is 50% more likely to develop pneumonia. Risk of death is approximately 32% higher for the user as compared with nonusers. Since the time this class of medications was introduced, it has been discovered that at least some BZs increase the individual's vulnerability to infection and mortality from infection although the causal mechanism is not clear at this time (Oblora, Hubbard, Sanders, & Myles, 2012). In addition, the BZs have been found to interfere with normal sexual function in both men and women (Finger, Lund, & Slagel, 1997). The BZs have been found to interfere with normal sleep patterns even when used at normal dosage levels (Qureshi & Lee-Chiong, 2004). Further, when discontinued, the BZs have been found to sometimes cause a phenomenon called *rebound insomnia,* forcing the individual to endure episodes of insomnia until the body adapts to the absence of the BZs (Cloos, 2010a; Doghramji, 2003; Qureshi & Lee-Chiong, 2004). This may result in the patient starting to take the BZ again in an effort to sleep again (Gitlow, 2007).

Even when used at normal dosage levels, the BZs can interfere with normal memory function, a condition called *anterograde amnesia.* This condition, when is most commonly seen in older persons, still is so common that 10% of persons assessed for a memory problem are thought to experience benzodiazepine-induced memory impairment (Curran et al., 2003). The mechanism for the BZ-induced memory impairment appears to be similar to that of the alcohol-related "blackout," and it will last for the duration of the BZ's effects on the user (Drummer & Odell, 2001). The mechanism has been compared with that of Korsakoff's syndrome in which the same regions of the brain are involved in each condition (Ghoneim, 2004a).

Some BZs require extensive biotransformation before being eliminated from the body. If the patient were to ingest a second or third dose of the medication before the first dose was entirely biotransformed, s/he might begin to accumulate a reservoir of nonmetabolized medication in his/her body that will slowly return to the circulatory system and cause an extended effect on the user's body. Originally developed as a treatment for insomnia, flurazepam was found to produce a metabolite that itself remained biologically active for 40–280 hours[13] after just a single dose (Doghramji, 2003). If the patient should ingest a second dose the following night, s/he might develop significant levels of drug metabolites, causing extended periods of sedation for the patient. A single dose of the benzodiazepine diazepam might interfere with the individual's ability to drive for up to seven hours after the dose was ingested, and therapeutic doses of this compound have been shown to prolong the user's reaction time, increasing his/her risk of a motor vehicle accident by 500% (Gitlow, 2007). These medications have also been implicated in the development of a sense of emotional dulling, in which the user finds it difficult to express normal emotions such as grief following the death of a loved one (Breggin, 2008). It has been suggested that Xanax® (alprazolam), a benzodiazepine that has been marketed as an anxiolytic, might have a therapeutic half-life that is so short that the user might suffer early withdrawal symptoms before the next scheduled dose at least in some users (Bashir & Swartz, 2002; Breggin, 2008). This can result in a situation where the patient starts to take more medication to treat not anxiety, but the withdrawal symptoms from their last dose as it begins to wear off.

Neurocognitive Impairment

The BZs reduce the level of neural function in virtually every region of the brain to some degree (Breggin, 2008). In their exploration of benzodiazepine use and cognitive function, Gonalez, Vassileva, and Scott (2009) suggested that there was "compelling evidence" that long-term benzodiazepine use at therapeutic levels can induce "significant and widespread neuropsychological impairments that persist even after many months abstinence" (p. 436). These transient changes in cognition drug-induced changes may or may not resolve with abstinence (Stewart, 2005). Further, long-term use/abuse of a BZ might cause withdrawal-related seizures for up to two weeks after the individual's last use of the drug (O'Brien, 2011). More disturbing were the results of a research study conducted by Billoti de Gage et al. (2012), who found that the odds of developing dementia in persons 65 years or older was 60% higher for individuals taking a benzodiazepine(s) as opposed to persons not taking a BZ.

---

[13]This is a period of 12 *days.*

Neuroadaptation to, Abuse of, and Addiction to, the Benzodiazepines

O'Brien (2006, 2011) suggested that benzodiazepine abusers fall into one of two groups: Those individuals who abuse these compounds to achieve a sense of euphoria. This subgroup is rather small, as the majority of those who ingest a benzodiazepine do not report experiencing any significant sense of euphoria. However, *intravenous* BZ abusers report a greater sense of euphoria than do oral abusers (Bisaca, 2008; Brust, 2004). Abusers who wish to achieve a sense of euphoria are usually polydrug abusers, a fact which reinforces the injunction that these medications should rarely, if ever, be used to treat persons with substance use disorders (SUDs) (Jones, Knutson, & Haines, 2003; O'Brien, 2006). Polydrug abusers have been known to take a benzodiazepine(s) to supplement the effects of their drug(s) of choice, to minimize the effects of drug withdrawal, and only rarely as a source of euphoria.

The second subgroup suggested by O'Brien (2006, 2011) is composed of individuals who begin to abuse a prescribed BZ by taking more of it or for longer periods than was prescribed. These two groups are not mutually exclusive; however, for the most part the second group of BZ users was prescribed BZs by a physician and became tolerant to the anxiolytic effects of these medications over time. In their attempt to overcome their growing tolerance to the anxiolytic effect of the BZs, these persons might slowly increase their daily dose of the prescribed BZ to dangerous levels.[14] For example, although 5–10 mg of diazepam two or three times a day might initially cause sedation and relief from anxiety, there have been reports of abusers building their intake level to 1,000 mg/day as their tolerance to this compound develops over time, a dosage level that might prove fatal to the drug-naive user (O'Brien, 2006). Unfortunately, individuals who abuse BZs in this manner rarely are motivated to discontinue using BZs, in spite of their protests to the contrary (Work Group on Substance Use Disorders, 2007).

Fifty years after the introduction of the first benzodiazepine, data on the optimal duration of treatment with a BZ remains scarce (Cloos, 2010a). Most patients use these medications for less than one month, making it unlikely that they would experience a *discontinuation syndrome*[15] (Ciraulo & Knapp, 2009). The probability that the user will experience a discontinuation syndrome increases as a result of continual use of a BZ. Thirty percent of those individuals who take BZs at therapeutic doses for just eight weeks will experience a discontinuance process upon cessation of BZ use, for example (Virani et al., 2012). This process was confused with the development of tolerance seen in drug abusers, and many health care professionals have mistakenly interpreted this as a sign of benzodiazepine abuse or addiction.

The discontinuance syndrome reflects the ability of the BZs to initiate the process of *neuroadaptation*[16] to that compound (O'Brien, 2005; 2006). The neurons in the brain adapt to the continual presence of the inhibitory effects benzodiazepine molecules by making changes in the GABA receptor site responsiveness. If the patient abruptly discontinues the benzodiazepine, the delicate balance between excitatory and inhibitory neurotransmission is disrupted, inducing a "rebound" or discontinuance syndrome (O'Brien, 2005). Cloos (2010b) recommended that the BZs be used for only 1–3 months except in cases where more conventional treatments have failed to work to minimize the possibility that a discontinuance syndrome will develop. For similar reasons the Royal College of Psychiatrists in Great Britain recommends that BZs should not be used on a continual basis for more than four weeks (Gitlow, 2007).

The symptoms of the discontinuance process will vary as a result of the (a) duration that the person had received a BZ, (b) the dose used, (c) the half-life of the medication used, and (d) the individual's expectations. Approximately 44% of persons who took a low dose of a prescribed benzodiazepine over an extended periods report withdrawal symptoms, some of which were quite distressing to the user (Perry, Alexander, Liskow, & DeVane, 2007). Some of the more common symptoms of the benzodiazepine discontinuance syndrome are identified in Table 7-2.

The discontinuance syndrome in long-term BZ users is similar to that seen in the alcohol and barbiturate withdrawal syndromes, and range from mild to

---

[14]Usually by obtaining prescriptions from multiple doctors, different pharmacies, illicit suppliers, or by buying drugs from "Internet pharmacies."

[15]See Glossary.

[16]See Glossary.

TABLE 7-2
Benzodiazepine Discontinuance Syndrome Symptoms

Abdominal cramps
Agitation (possibly to the point of mania)
Anxiety (often called "rebound" anxiety)
Anorexia
Ataxia
Confusion
Delirium
Depersonalization/derealization
Depression
Dizziness/hypotension
Fatigue or muscle weakness
Formication
Irritability
Insomnia
Nausea/vomiting
Nightmares
Postural hypotension
Seizures (possibly leading to death)
Sweating
Withdrawal psychosis

SOURCE: Based on Bisaga (2008); Cloos, (2010a); Lipman (2010); Miller and Adams (2006); O'Brien (2011); Smith and Wesson (2004); Virani, Bezchlibnyk-Butler, Jeffries, and Procyshyn (2012).

severe in intensity. In extreme cases, the benzodiazepine discontinuance/withdrawal syndrome has the potential to be life-threatening[17] (Maldonado, 2010; Perry et al., 2007). In such cases, a gradual "taper" may be instituted over a period of 6–12 months to minimize the individual's discomfort and the risk to their life (Bisaga, 2008; Whitaker, 2010). When the individual's daily dosage level reaches 10–25% of their former dose, they might experience "rebound" anxiety, which could be more intense than the original anxiety for which they were placed on the BZ, at least for a few

weeks (Wesson & Smith, 2005). The use of mood stabilizers, or Seroquel® (quetiapine fumarate), has been suggested as an anxiolytic should the patient request help with his or her anxiety during the taper (Wesson & Smith, 2005). Further, anticipatory guidance might prove valuable for persons going through the discontinuance syndrome, so that the patient might understand the symptoms, their cause, and that this is a transitory phase.

Benzodiazepine Abuse

Fenton et al. (2010) defined the nonmedical use of a medication as (a) use without a prescription, (b) use of a benzodiazepine in doses higher than prescribed, or, (c) use of a medication for reasons other than that prescribed by the physician. Unfortunately, BZs lend themselves to each category of abuse. The fact that they *lower* dopamine levels in the mesolimbic system of the brain rather than increase dopamine levels (Bisaga, 2008) would suggest that they are unlikely drugs of abuse. Clinical experience has found that BZ abusers (1) use these compounds to enhance the effects of another drug of abuse, (2) control some of the unwanted side-effects of the primary drug of abuse, or (3) help control the effects of the withdrawal process from their primary drug of abuse (Longo, Parran, Johnson, & Kinsey, 2000). Research has found that 80% of benzodiazepine abusers are polydrug abusers and that the BZs are not usually their primary drug of abuse (Longo et al., 2000; Sattar & Bhatia, 2003). Benzodiazepines with shorter therapeutic half-lives such as diazepam, lorazepam, alprazolam, and triazolam have the highest abuse potentials (Ciraulo & Sarid-Segal, 2005); however, there is also emerging evidence that clonazepam is gaining favor with some drug abusers (Bubovsky, 2005; Longo & Johnson, 2000).

As noted above, one use of the BZs is to enhance the effects of other drugs of abuse, such as when a person on a methadone maintenance program will use one of the BZs to produce a sense of euphoria by mixing these compounds. The usual practice for the patient on a methadone maintenance program is to ingest a massive dose of a benzodiazepine (the equivalent of 100–300 mg of diazepam) between 30 and 120 minutes after ingesting their methadone to "boost"[18] its effects and induce euphoria (Lipman, 2010; O'Brien, 2005,

---

[17]It is for this reason that benzodiazepine withdrawal should *only* be attempted under the supervision of a physician.

[18]See Glossary.

2006). This effect might explain why 40–90% of persons in methadone maintenance programs also use BZs (Bisaca, 2008; Ciraulo & Knapp, 2009). It is not known how many of these individuals *need* a benzodiazepine as opposed to *want* them because of the interactive effect between these two medications. The exact mechanism for the euphoria reported when both compounds are used is not known but may reflect the suppression of cortical inhibitions (Ciraulo et al., 2005), or indirect activation of the Mu opioid receptor site (Bisaca, 2008).

An example of the second reason for BZ abuse is seen in persons who abuse a central nervous stimulant such as cocaine or the amphetamines who use BZs or alcohol to control the unwanted side effects of their primary drug of choice. Another category of benzodiazepine abuse is seen when alcohol-dependent persons who wish to avoid the smell of alcohol on their breath during the day use a BZ as a substitute. Benzodiazepine intoxication is very similar to alcohol intoxication, causing slurred speech and ataxia but without a residual alcohol smell in their breath. Another example of the third category of BZ abuse is seen in persons who are heroin-dependent, who are going through unsupervised heroin withdrawal. It is not unusual for these individuals to use large doses of a benzodiazepine to eliminate or mitigate their withdrawal distress.

Persons who are recovering from *any* SUD are "at risk" for a reactivation of their addiction if they should receive a prescription for a BZ. This is illustrated by the fact that approximately 25% of recovering alcoholics relapse after receiving a prescription for a benzodiazepine (Fricchione, 2004; Gitlow, 2007; Sattar & Bhatia, 2003). At best, there is only limited evidence that the BZs can be used safely with persons who have a SUD (Drake, 2007; Sattar & Bhatia, 2003). This is most clearly seen in the results of the study conducted by Clark, Xie, and Brunette (2004) who found that although the BZs are often used as an adjunct to the treatment of various forms of mental illness, their use did not improve clinical outcomes and that persons with a SUD were likely to try to abuse their BZs. It is for this reason that it is recommended that BZs be used *only* after alternative treatments have failed in persons with an SUD (Ciraulo & Nace, 2000; Seppalao, 2004; Sommer, 2005). Further, *if* benzodiazepine treatment is necessary, the prescribing physician should put special restrictions in place to limit the patient's access to large amounts of the medication, and that a BZ such as clonazepam should be used (Seppala, 2004).

Drug Interactions Involving Benzodiazepines

The most popular method of BZ administration is oral, a process that can be significantly slowed if the patient also takes a dose of an over-the-counter antacid (Raj & Sheehan, 2004). The concurrent use of cimetidine (Tagamet®) can result in increased benzodiazepine blood levels (Tatro, 2009), and thus the concurrent use of these medications should only be carried out under a physician's supervision. There have been a "few anecdotal case reports" (Ciraulo, Shader, Greenblatt, & Creelman, 2006, p. 267) of persons who had an adverse reaction while taking BZs and lithium. The authors reviewed a single case report of a patient who developed profound hypothermia, which was attributed to this combination of medications. Further, the authors suggested that the combination of lithium and the BZs diazepam or oxazepam may cause higher levels of depression for the patient due to an interaction effect from these compounds.

Persons who are taking disulfiram (Antabuse®) should use BZs with caution, because the combination of these medications can reduce the speed at which the liver can biotransform BZs such as diazepam and chlordiazepoxide (DeVane & Nemeroff, 2002; Tatro, 2009). Grapefruit juice has also been found to slow the P-450 metabolic pathway in the liver, slowing the rate at which the BZs might be biotransformed (Mihic & Harris, 2011). Further, benzodiazepine use can alter the blood levels of many antipsychotic medications such as haloperidol and fluphenazine by competing with the BZ molecules for access to the liver's biotransformation enzymes (Ciraulo et al., 2006).

There is limited evidence to suggest that BZs may enhance the respiratory depressant effect of buprenorphine if these medications are used concurrently, possibly with lethal results (Ciraulo et al., 2006). Benzodiazepine use has been shown to alter the blood levels of digoxin, and persons receiving both medications should have frequent blood level tests to avoid the danger of drug-induced digoxin toxicity. Persons receiving prescription medications such as phenytoin, mephenytoin, fluoxetine, propranolol, and metopropolol should be aware of the danger that these medications might interfere with the biotransformation of BZs such as diazepam (DeVane & Nemeroff, 2002).

There are also well-documented interactions between BZs and herbal medications: Persons using the anxiolytic medication alprazolam should not concurrently use St. John's Wort as the latter compound induces a more rapid biotransformation of the alprazolam, limiting its anxiolytic effects (DeVane & Nemeroff, 2002). Persons who use the herbal medicine Kava should not use any benzodiazepine, except under the supervision of a physician as the former compound will enhance the sedative effects of the benzodiazepine to potentially dangerous levels.

Because of the potential for a synergistic effect between the two medications, persons taking *any* form of CNS depressant medication should not take a BZ except under the supervision of their physician. There have been case reports indicating that the benzodiazepine blood levels in women using hormone-based birth control medications might be lower than normal because the birth control medication increases the speed of the benzodiazepine biotransformation (Tatro, 2009). In contrast to this, persons using propoxyphene[19] might experience higher than normal blood levels of BZs because the former medication inhibits the biotransformation of the BZs (Tatro, 2009).

It is important to note that persons taking valproic acid and lorazepam might become comatose because of the interaction between these two compounds (Wynn, Oesterheld, Cozza, & Armstrong, 2009). Although this list does not include every potential interaction between BZs and other compounds, it should alert the reader to the need for the patient to check with a pharmacist or physician before mixing BZs with other prescribed, over-the-counter, or herbal compounds.

Long-Term Consequences of Chronic Benzodiazepine Use

The BZs were originally introduced in the 1960s as safe and nonaddicting substitutes for the barbiturates, to be used both as anxiolytic and hypnotic agents. In the time since their introduction the BZs have been found to be neither safe, nor nonaddicting. Health care professionals have learned that they must weigh the potential benefits of the use of BZs against their potential dangers. Further, although frequently prescribed as anxiolytic agents, their use in the long-term treatment of anxiety has not been studied in detail (White, 2009). The BZs have been known to induce a form of psychological dependency as patients start to anticipate their next dose of a prescribed BZ to help them cope with what they view as insurmountable anxiety. Such persons may engage in "clock watching" as the time nears for their next anticipated dose, and then eagerly take the dose to avoid what might actually be "rebound" anxiety induced when the previous dose begins to wear off (Raj & Sheehan, 2004). This process is most commonly seen when the person is taking a benzodiazepine with a shorter half-life, such as alprazolam (Breggin, 2008). To minimize this danger the use of BZs with longer half-lives such as clonazepam has become increasingly more common. The longer half-life of this compound means that the blood levels will drop more slowly between doses, controlling "rebound" anxiety.

Although once widely used as a hypnotic, evidence suggests that the process of neuroadaptation to the hypnotic effects of the BZs causes them to lose effectiveness after perhaps a week or two of nightly use (Carvey, 1998). It is for this reason that the BZs are recommended only for the *short-term* treatment of insomnia, and only after other potential treatments of insomnia are ruled out (Conrow, Arnedt, & Brower, 2008; Taylor, McCracken, Wilson, & Copeland, 1998). Surprisingly, persons report having used a BZ as a hypnotic for weeks, months, or even years, suggesting that the process of taking these medications has become part of the psychological ritual that the individual follows to insure proper sleep more than a pharmacological effect of the BZs (Carvey, 1998).

The BZs do induce a form of sleep although they interfere with the normal sleep cycle, and suppress rapid eye movement (REM) sleep. If used for extended periods of time the REM suppression might cause the sleeper to experience *REM rebound*.[20] The patient should be warned that this is a possible reaction to the discontinuance of the benzodiazepine. It has been suggested that therapeutic doses of melatonin[21] might also prove useful in promoting normal sleep in the former benzodiazepine user (Garfinkel, Zisapel, Wainstein, & Laundon, 1999; Peles et al., 2007; Pettit, 2000).

---

[19]The manufacture of which is now prohibited in the United States.

[20]See Glossary.

[21]See Glossary.

Section Summary

As should be evident by this point, the BZs offer the user a double-edged sword. Although they have a number of potent applications, they also have many side effects that make their use problematic at best, if not life threatening. These compounds may be abused in a number of ways, and drug abusers may both seek them out for their primary effects. More commonly, the BZs are abused to control/mitigate the effects of the individual's primary drug(s) of choice, to control the symptoms of withdrawal from other compounds, or, as a substitute for other compounds that may not be available to the drug abuser at that time. Because of these drawbacks, pharmaceutical companies have continued the search for compounds that may offer a safer alternative to the BZs, many of which will be discussed in the next section of this chapter.

The Benzodiazepine Receptor Antagonists (Z-Compounds or BRAs)

Buspirone

BuSpar (buspirone) was discovered as a result of a search for an antipsychotic compound that lacked the harsh side effects of the existing agents; however, its anti-psychotic potential was found to be limited. However, researchers were impressed by its ability to reduce the individual's anxiety level, and initially thought that it would be as effective as the BZs as an anxiolytic (Drummer & Odell, 2001). It was introduced as an anxiolytic agent in 1986. Chemically, buspirone is a member of the *azapirones*[22] family of compounds, which differ from the BZs and unlike the latter group of pharmaceuticals does not appear to potentiate the effects of alcohol.

Indications for Use of Buspirone

Buspirone is most effective in controlling GAD, but does not seem to mitigate the discomfort of panic attacks that so often accompany GAD (Hudziak & Waterman, 2005). In some cases it does seem to help augment the effects of the selective serotonin reuptake inhibitor class of antidepressants (Egger &

Hebert, 2011). It was originally thought to function as an antidepressant in its own right, although there is little research evidence to support this theory (Egger & Hebert, 2011). It is not of value in treating the alcohol or benzodiazepine withdrawal syndromes (Hudziak & Wateran, 2005). There is limited evidence that it might assist persons who wish to discontinue the use of cigarettes who experience a degree of anxiety in this process (Egger & Hebert, 2011). However, it has no significant anticonvulsant potential and its use by persons who have a seizure disorder is not recommended (Virani et al., 2012).

The Pharmacology of Buspirone

Buspirone's mechanism of action is not well understood at this time. Presynaptically, it functions as a full agonist at the serotonin[23] 5-HT1A receptor site in the dorsal midbrain raphe, inhibiting the synthesis of serotonin in this region of the brain (Perry et al., 2007). It also appears to function as a partial agonist of the 5-HT1A receptor sites in the limbic region and cortex of the brain (Perry et al., 2007; Ramadan et al., 2006). The combined effects of these mechanisms of action appear to balance serotonin levels, stimulating the production if it is low, and reducing its production if it is high.

Depending on the individual's biochemistry, the peak blood levels of buspirone are achieved in 60–90 minutes following a single oral dose, although the absorption might be doubled if it is taken with food (Perry et al., 2007). It is extensively biotransformed during the "first pass metabolism" process (Hudziak & Waterman, 2005), and during biotransformation at least seven major and five minor metabolites are produced. Only one of the intermediate metabolites is thought to be biologically active[24] and it is hypothesized that this metabolite is the cause of buspirone's adverse effects. In the body 99% of the buspirone becomes lipid-bound, and its elimination half-life is approximately 2.5 hours. This requires to the need for the patient to take a dose 3–4 times a day, as opposed to just once or twice a day for the long half-life BZs like clonazepam or diazepam. There is no evidence of cross-tolerance between buspirone and alcohol or the BZs. However, persons taking a BZ might have to be "tapered" off of the original compound before being started on

---

[22]The team of Perry, Alexander, Liskow, and DeVane (2007) suggested that it was a member of the *azaspriodecanedione* family of chemicals.

[23]See Glossary.

[24]Which, if you must know, is 1-pryrimidinylpiperazine.

buspirone (Perry et al., 2007). The abuse potential of buspirone is limited (Smith & Wesson, 2004). There is no evidence of a discontinuation process similar to that seen in BZs, and no evidence of buspirone-related memory impairment or tolerance to its effects.

Adverse Effects of Buspirone Use

The most serious adverse effect of buspirone use is the development of the *serotonin syndrome*.[25] The development of the serotonin syndrome is more common when buspirone is used concurrently with the antidepressant medications bloxetine or fluvox-amine, but can develop under other conditions (Sternbach, 2003). There have been no reported deaths from buspirone overdoses. However, the potential exists that the individual has ingested multiple agents in an overdose and thus *any known or suspected drug overdose must immediately be assessed by a physician* to reduce risk to the individual's life (Perry et al., 2007).

Side Effects

Some of the reported side effects of buspirone include headaches, dizziness, drowsiness, nervousness, a sense of disquiet, dysphoria, a degree of psychomotor impairment, nervousness, excitement, fatigue, pria-pism,[26] nasal congestion, and gastrointestinal upset (Hudziak & Waterman, 2005; Perry et al., 2007; Virani et al., 2012). Buspirone has been determined to either induce a condition known as *pseudo*-Parkinsonism, and there have been reports that exacerbate the symptoms of Parkinson's disease (Perry et al., 2007). The safety of this compound during pregnancy has not been determined as of this time.

Drug Interactions Involving Buspirone

Buspirone is known to interact with the antidepressant medications known as monoamine oxidase inhibitors (MAO inhibitors, or MAOIs). It is recommended that persons taking these antidepressant medications discontinue them for two weeks or more before starting buspirone to avoid drug-induced hypertensive episodes (Ramadan et al., 2006). Persons taking the medications diltiazem, verapamil, erythromycin or intraconazole, or

clarithromycline should not take buspirone, as they block its biotransformation and cause buspirone blood levels to rise beyond the recommended level (Rakadan, Werder, & Preskorn, 2006; Venkatakrishnan, Shader, & Greenblatt, 2006; Virani et al., 2012). Persons taking this medication should avoid large amounts of grapefruit juice (Monthly Prescribing Reference, 2008). Although this list is not all inclusive, it does demonstrate the need for the patient to consult a psychiatrist before taking buspirone concurrently with any other mediation.

Zolpedem

Zolpidem, another member of the BRA class of medications, was introduced in 1993 and in the United States is sold under the name of Ambien®. This compound belongs to the *imidazopryidine* family of compounds, and is more selective than the BZs because it binds at a subset of the benzodi-azepine receptors in the brain. Zolpidem has only a minor anticonvulsant effect, and that is usually seen only above normal at dosage levels (Doble, Martin, & Nutt, 2004). Unlike the BZs, zolpidem causes only a minor reduction in REM sleep when used at normal dosage levels, and it does not interfere with the normal progression through the stages of sleep, allowing for a more restful night's sleep (Doble et al., 2004; Schuckit, 2006a).

Zolpidem is administered orally, and after a single dose peak blood levels are achieved in 2–3 hours (Dubovsky, 2005; Schuckit, 2006a). The elimination half-life is between 2 and 3 hours in the normal adult, and slightly longer in the geriatric adult (Doble et al., 2004; Dubovsky, 2005; Mihic & Harris, 2011). The majority of a single dose of zolpidem is biotransformed in the liver into inactive metabolites, which are then excreted by the kidneys. Both Folks and Burke (1998) and Holm and Goa (2000) suggested that there is little evidence of neuroadaptation to zolpidem's hypnotic effects even after as long as one year of regular use at therapeutic doses. However, Schuckit (2006) disagreed with this assessment, noting that a limited degree of neuoradaptation can develop after zolpidem has been used each night for as little as two weeks. There have also been rare reports of persons becoming tolerant to its hypnotic effects after using it at very high dosage levels for a number of years (Holm & Goa, 2000).

---

[25]See Glossary.
[26]See Glossary.

Adverse Effects of Zolpidem at Normal Dosage Levels

Some of the side effects reported to date include nightmares, headache, gastrointestinal upset, agitation, some degree of residual drowsiness, isolated reports of zolpidem-induced hallucinations or psychotic reactions, "hangover" effects, and rebound insomnia when the medication is discontinued (Breggin, 2008; Schuckit, 2006a). Like the BZs, zolpidem can induce states of anterograde amnesia, although zolpidem is less likely to induce memory impairment than BZs. There is evidence that the user will experience some cognitive performance problems, and there have been reports of people engaging in "sleep walking" like behaviors in which they eat meals, or drive motor vehicles after taking zolpidem without later recalling that they engaged in these activities (Breggin, 2008). There have also been reports of users experiencing suicidal thoughts while taking this medication as prescribed for unknown reasons (Breggin, 2008; Ciraulo & Knapp, 2009). The adverse effects of zolpidem appear to be dose-related and it is recommended that the patient be maintained on as low a dose as possible.

There is also a risk of the user falling. In hospital settings up to 3% of patients who received a dose of zolpidem experienced a fall as opposed to less than 1% of those patients who did not take it (Kolla, Lovely, Mansukhani, & Morgenthaler, 2012). Such falls increase the individual's risk of injury and can potentially be fatal. Unfortunately, there is little evidence that other hypnotic medications are substantially safer, thus posing a dilemma for the physician faced with a patient with insomnia (Kolla et al., 2012). Zolpidem is also contraindicated in persons with sleep apnea, as it increases the duration and frequency of apnea episodes (Holm & Goa, 2000).

Effects of Zolpidem at Above-Normal Dosage Levels

At dosage levels above 20 mg/day, zolpidem has been found to reduce REM sleep time, and there are reports of persons experiencing REM "rebound" when they discontinue the medication (Ciraulo et al., 2005). Volunteers who ingested 50-mg doses reported such symptoms as visual perceptual disturbances, ataxia, dizziness, nausea, or vomiting. Persons who ingested up to 40 times the maximum recommended dosage have recovered without ill effects. Although safe when taken by itself, there are numerous reports of fatal and near-fatal overdoses involving zolpidem and other CNS depressants taken simultaneously. *For this reason any known or suspected overdose must immediately be evaluated and treated by a physician.*

The Abuse Potential of Zolpidem

Since the time of its introduction, evidence has emerged suggesting that its abuse potential might be far higher than was originally thought. Currently its abuse potential is about the same as that of the BZs (Mihic & Harris, 2011), and tolerance to its effects does appear possible. Ciraulo and Sarid-Segal (2005) presented a case summary of an individual who increased their daily dose from 5–10 mg/day to over 800 mg/day over time. Like the BZs zolpidem use might trigger thoughts of returning to active drug use (Jones et al., 2003). On a positive note, the abuse potential of zolpidem appears to be highest only in persons with a prior history of a SUD (Ciraulo & Knapp, 2009; Gitlow, 2007; Holm & Goa, 2000).

In the late 1960s and early 1970s, there were reports of drug abusers who would ingest the medication methaqualone,[27] and then resist its effects to achieve a sense of euphoria. Surprisingly, there are rare reports of persons who will do the same with zolpidem, which means that after 50 years of dedicated research, we are right back to where we were in the middle of the 20th century: Sedating agents that are being abused for their euphoric effects.

Zaleplon

The compound zaleplon, sold in the United States under the brand name *Sonata®*, is a member of the *pryazolpyrimidine* class of pharmaceuticals and functions as a BRA ("Insomnia in Later Life," 2006). Animal research suggests that zaleplon has some sedative and anticonvulsant effects, but in the United States it is only approved for use as a hypnotic (Danjou et al., 1999). Zaleplon is administered orally, in capsules containing 5 mg, 10 mg, or 20 mg. In most cases the 10-mg dose is thought to be the most effective, although in persons with low body weight the 5-mg dose might be more appropriate (Danjou et al., 1999).

---

[27]Legal production of this medication in the United States was discontinued in the 1970s.

The strongest effects are observed in the first four hours after ingestion, and although it seems to improve sleep latency, there is little evidence that it affects total sleep time at therapeutic doses (Perry et al., 2007). This is consistent with the observed half-life of one hour (Doble, Martin, & Nutt, 2006).[28] The liver is the site of zaleplon biotransformation, with about 30% of the dose biotransformed through the "first pass" metabolism process, and less than 1% of the dose eliminated from the body unchanged. The majority of a dose is biotransformed by the liver into less active metabolites, which are eliminated in the feces and urine (Mihic & Harris, 2011). Zaleplon molecules bind at the same benzodiazepine subtype receptor site used by zolepidem (Mihic & Harris, 2011; Walsh, Pollak, Scharf, Schweitzer, & Vogel, 2000). There is little evidence of a drug "hangover" effect, but the patient is still advised not to attempt to operate machinery for four hours after taking the last dose (Danjou et al., 1999; Doble, Martin, & Nutt, 2003; Walsh et al., 2000).

Adverse Effects of Zaleplon

Some of the side effects observed at therapeutic doses include headache, rhinitis, nausea, myalgia, anterograde amnesia, dizziness, depersonalization, drug-induced hangover effects, constipation, dry mouth, gout, bronchitis, asthma attacks, nervousness, depression, ataxia, and paradoxical insomnia. Tolerance to the hypnotic effects of zaleplon develop rapidly, and for this reason this compound is intended only for the *short-term* treatment of insomnia. When used at therapeutic doses for more than two weeks, zaleplon has been implicated as the cause of problems such as muscle cramps, tremor, vomiting, and on rare occasions withdrawal seizures.

Persons have reported rebound insomnia after discontinuation, although this is more common when the patient was using higher dosage levels (Dubovsky, 2005). The abuse potential is similar to that of the BZs, especially triazolam (Smith & Wesson, 2004). Because of its potential to trigger addictive thinking, Jones et al. (2003) do not recommend it be used in persons with an SUD.

Lunesta®

Lunesta® (eszopiclone) is not a member of the benzodiazepine family of compounds, but functions as a hypnotic intended for the short-term treatment of insomnia, especially in persons who have trouble falling asleep. There is some dispute about the effectiveness of this compound as a hypnotic; however, it does have an abuse potential and should be used with caution in persons with a known history of an SUD. Eszopiclone is sold in 1 mg, 2 mg, or 3 mg strength tablets, and the usual dose is 2–3 mg shortly before bedtime. This compound is scheduled to become available as a generic equivalent to the brand name in 2014.

Reported side effects of eszopiclone when used at therapeutic dosage levels include "hangover" effect (daytime drowsiness), dizziness, poor concentration the day after it was used, anxiety, depression, nausea, stomach pain or loss of appetite the day after it was used, constipation, dry mouth, unusual taste, aggression, agitation, thoughts of self-harm or suicide, skin rash, headache, and both auditory and visual hallucinations. Some users have reported experiencing a headache or enhanced feelings of pain following the use of eszopiclone, and some users have reported a loss of sexual desire while taking this medication. There have also been isolated reports of breast enlargement in men[29] who have used this medication. There have also been rare reports of anaphylaxis[30] in persons taking this medication.

Like the BZs and BRAs, eszopiclone has been implicated as the cause of amnesia. The risk of this anterograde amnesia increases as the dosage level increases. There have been reports of persons engaging in driving automobiles or other complex tasks with no conscious memory of having done so the next day.[31] Because older persons or individuals with liver damage are sensitive to the effects of eszopiclone, it is recommended that the attending physician use the lowest possible effective dose to reduce the possibility of a drug-induced "hangover" effect the next day. This medication should be used with caution in persons with a history of sedative abuse or addiction. There are reports that when abused, eszopiclone can induce subjective effects similar to diazepam. The potential of eszopiclone to induce physical dependence is still not clear but the potential exists for it to be habit forming.

---

[28]Remember: It is generally accepted that it takes five half-life periods to eliminate almost all of a compound from the body, so after five hours, virtually all of the drug would have been eliminated from the patient's body, allowing the patient to awaken naturally.

[29]A condition known as *gynecomastia*.

[30]See Glossary.

[31]If this should happen, the prescribing physician should be notified *immediately*.

The person who is using eszopiclone should not mix it with other central nervous system depressants such as alcohol, BZs, or the antihistamines to avoid a synergistic effect between the substances being used. Patients should not use eszopiclone with psychotropic medications except under the supervision of a physician to avoid possible interaction problems. There has not been any research into the interactional effects between eszopiclone and any of the drugs of abuse.

Ramelteon

Ramelteon is sold in the United States under the brand name of Rozerem®. It is a novel hypnotic agent that binds at the melatonin receptor (Conroy, Arnedt, & Brower, 2008; Winkelman, 2006). By enhancing the effects of melatonin, ramelteon is thought to be able to facilitate the sleep cycle, an advantage with persons with alcohol use disorders because their melatonin levels are usually depleted when they stop drinking and enter the early stages of abstinence.

Ramelteon is administered orally, and is rapidly absorbed through the gastrointestinal tract, and peak blood levels following a single dose are found approximately 45 minutes after the medication was ingested (Neubauer, 2005; Winkelman, 2006). But the drug is extensively biotransformed in the "first pass" metabolism process, with less than 2% of the dose ingested reaching the brain (Neubauer, 2005; Winkelman, 2006). About 85% of the metabolites are found in the urine (Neubauer, 2005). There is no apparent potentiation effect between ramelteon and the BZs, and the compound has an elimination half-life of between 1.0 and 2.6 hours (Neubauer, 2005). It does not seem to exacerbate sleep breathing problems or chronic obstructive pulmonary disease (COPD). There is a minor potentiation effect between ramelteon and alcohol (Neubauer, 2006). Although it would appear to be safe to use in persons with a SUD, the possibility that it will trigger a relapse has not been ruled out as yet.

Rohypnol

Flunitrazepam, sold in other countries under the brand name of Rohypnol®, is a benzodiazepine that is not legally sold in the United States and for this reason is not discussed with the legal BZs discussed above. It is a Schedule IV compound under the controlled substances act of 1970[32] and possession of or

---

[32]See Appendix Three.

trafficking in flunitrazepam might be punished by up to 20 years in prison in the United States. However, flunitrazepam is used by physicians in other countries as a pre-surgical medication, muscle relaxant, and as a hypnotic (Gahlinger, 2004; Gwinnell & Adamec, 2006; Palmer & Edmunds, 2003). Some persons who travel abroad might receive a prescription for this medication when they are outside of the United States, and illicit drug traffickers have an unknown quantity of flunitrazepam smuggled into this country. It is for these reasons that substance abuse rehabilitation professionals should have at least some information about this compound.

Flunitrazepam abuse in the United States first came to the attention of the public during the mid-1990s, when it gained a reputation as a "date rape" drug (Gahlinger, 2004). Its pharmacological characteristics, especially when mixed with alcohol, could induce a state of anterograde amnesia that could last for 8–24 hours, a characteristic that many men are reputed to have taken advantage of to facilitate a date rape. To combat this, the manufacturer added a harmless compound that would turn the drink a dark blue if it were to be added to alcohol, thus alerting the drinker that it had been tampered with (Klein & Kramer, 2004; Virani et al., 2012).

Flunitrazepam is estimated to be 10 times as potent as diazepam, and this makes it hard to be detected with standard urine toxicology tests (Klein & Kramer, 2004; Gahlinger, 2004). The manufacturer has provided a free urine drug testing kit to law enforcement officials who suspect that the drinker was the victim of a "date rape" (Palmer & Edmunds, 2003). However, in addition to its reputation as a "date rape" drug, illicit drug abusers often mix flunitrazepam with other compounds (such as marijuana and alcohol) to enhance their effects. The combination of marijuana and flunitrazepam is said to produce a "floating" sensation. Adolescents have been reported to use flunitrazepam to remain intoxicated in class, while avoiding detection with standard drug urine toxicology test kids (Greydanus & Patel, 2003; Wesson & Smith, 2005).

When used in medical practice, physicians usually prescribe 0.5 to 2 mg of flunitrazepam. Peak blood levels are achieved in 30–120 minutes following a single oral dose (Saum & Inciardi, 1997). Flurintrzepam has an elimination half-life that is significantly longer than its duration of effect because it is rapidly sequestered in body tissues following absorption. This results in the compound having a therapeutic half-life of 8–10 hours but an elimination half-life of 15–66 hours (Klein & Kramer, 2004; Woods & Winger, 1997). Less than 1% of a dose of flunitrazepam is excreted unchanged. Drug abusers usually take double the recommended dose, which begins to produce sedation in 20–30 minutes with the desired results lasting 8–12 hours. Because it is a member of the benzodiazepine family of drugs, the effects are similar to those seen with other BZs in use in this country (Klein & Kramer, 2004). It is capable of causing dependence, and when discontinued will cause the characteristic benzodiazepine withdrawal syndrome. Withdrawal after extended periods of use is potentially dangerous, and like other BZs, flunitrazepam can induce withdrawal seizures. For this reason, *flunitrazepam withdrawal should be carried out only under the supervision of a physician.* Although it is a potent compound, it is unlikely to ever be legalized in this country.

Sedative, Hypnotic, or Anxiolytic Use Disorders and the *Diagnostic and Statistical Manual of Mental Disorders,* 5th Edition[33]

The *Diagnostic and Statistical Manual of Mental Disorders,* 5th edition (American Psychiatric Association, 2013) identified five subforms of the sedative, hypnotic, or anxiolytic-related disorders:

- *Sedative, hypnotic, or anxiolytic use disorder*
- *Sedative, hypnotic, or anxiolytic intoxication*
- *Sedative, hypnotic, or anxiolytic withdrawal*
- *Other sedative, hypnotic, or anxiolytic-induced disorders*
- *Unspecified Sedative, hypnotic, or anxiolytic-related disorders*

The *sedative, hypnotic, or anxiolytic use disorder* category in *DSM-5* essentially is an addiction to one or more medications in this category. Such medications include (but are not limited to) the barbiturates, BZs, and benzodiazepine-receptor agonists such as zaleplon. The *DSM-5* manual identifies 11 symptoms suggestive

of a *sedative, hypnotic, or anxiolytic use disorder,* and specifies that the individual must have at least two of the identified symptoms in a 12-month period.[34] Tolerance and withdrawal symptoms are accepted as evidence of a sedative, hypnotic, or anxiolytic use disorder, except in such cases where the person was taking the medication as prescribed under a physician's supervision. Modifiers such as "in early remission" or "in sustained remission" as well as "in a controlled environment" are suggested for use as indicated. A significant level of comorbidity between the use of these agents and the use of tobacco products, illicit drugs, and alcohol is suggested in the *Diagnostic and Statistical Manual of Mental Disorders,* 5th edition (American Psychiatric Association, 2013), which at times can make the differential diagnosis for the patient's condition difficult. Finally, substance withdrawal symptoms such as "rebound anxiety" could further cloud the diagnostic picture according to the *DSM-5.*

The *intoxication* to a sedative, hypnotic, or anxiolytic appears very similar to alcohol intoxication, except that the individual has not ingested alcohol and the observed symptoms are not attributable to another medical condition (hypoglycemia, for example). The *withdrawal* syndrome induced by the sudden cessation or major dosage reduction for these medications are discussed in the text of this, or in the case of the barbiturates and older drugs the preceding, chapters. Apparently, the *DSM-5* manual did not differentiate between the *discontinuance syndrome* seen when a patient discontinues his or her use of these medications. Illicit drug abusers experience a withdrawal syndrome when they discontinue taking any of these medications and the intensity of these withdrawal symptoms might be life-threatening, making medical supervision of the withdrawal process imperative.

Individuals who warrant a diagnosis of *other sedative, hypnotic, or anxiolytic-induced disorder* demonstrate symptoms of other psychiatric syndromes, the expression of which is either caused, or at least exacerbated by, the abuse of these medications. Such conditions include the various psychotic conditions, and states of depression, bipolarness, and anxiety. The

---

[33]The material presented here is to illustrate the relationship between the sedative use disorders and the *Diagnostic and Statistical Manual of Mental Disorders,* 5th edition. This material should not be interpreted as, nor should it be used as, a diagnostic manual.

[34]The *Diagnostic and Statistical Manual of Mental Disorders,* 5th edition (*DSM-5*) (American Psychiatric Association, 2013) has been referred to the reader for the full list of diagnostic criteria suggested by the American Psychiatric Association as signs of a sedative, hypnotic, or anxiolytic use disorder use disorder.

Unspecified Sedative, hypnotic, or anxiolytic-related disorder category is reserved for those individuals who demonstrate early signs of a *sedative, hypnotic, or anxiolytic use disorder* but who do not meet the full criteria for this diagnosis.

Chapter Summary

In the middle of the 20th century, pharmaceutical companies began to search for compounds that might be used as anxiolytics and hypnotics, but with a larger therapeutic index than was possible with the barbiturates. In the 1960s, a class of compounds known as the *benzodiazepines* was introduced that rapidly became the treatment of choice for anxiety control and to help the individual fall asleep. Unfortunately, although they were introduced as "nonaddicting" and "safe" compounds that might be substituted for barbiturates, it is now accepted that they have an abuse potential similar to that of the barbiturates, and they have become a part of the drug abuse problem in the United States.

Pharmaceutical companies have continued the search for safe, nonaddicting, compounds that might be used in the control of anxiety and induce sleep. The first of these nonbenzodiazepine compounds was buspirone, introduced in the United States as an anxiolytic and zolpidem, introduced as a hypnotic compound. Zolpidem is often referred to as a benzodiazepine receptor agonist, or BRA (also called a "Z" compound after its chemical structure). The former compound has found only limited applications in the medical field, whereas the latter has been found to be an effective hypnotic with an abuse potential similar to that of the BZs. Zaleplon, a BRA, was also introduced as a hypnotic shortly after zolpidem, and also has been found to have an abuse potential similar to the BZs. Pharmaceutical companies are searching for a replacement for these compounds, which are safer to use and which lack the abuse potential of the compounds discussed in this chapter.

CHAPTER 8

Abuse and Addiction to Central Nervous System Stimulants[1]

Introduction

Humans have long sought out compounds that would allow them to work harder, work for longer periods of time, fight with more vigor, and act as a medication to salve the many ills to which we are all heir. This search might have met with at least partial success 60,000 years ago as evidenced by the fact that scientists have found ephedra plants at Neanderthal burial sites in Europe that are thought to date from that era (Karch, 2009). Historical evidence suggests that Chinese physicians used the ephedra plant as a medicinal herb to treat respiratory disorders thousands of years before European chemists isolated the active agent in the ephedra plant in 1887 (King & Ellinwood, 2005). This compound was subsequently named ephedrine after the plant from which it was derived (Rasmussen, 2008), and over the past two centuries ephedrine has been the center of a long like of central nervous system (CNS) stimulants that have been isolated or developed. All of these compounds are rather controversial, and are the source of much confusion both in the medical community and among the lay public. For this reason, this chapter will be divided into two sections: In the first section the medical uses of the CNS stimulants, including their effects, side effects, and complications from their use, will be discussed. In the second section, the complications of CNS stimulant abuse will be reviewed.

CNS Stimulants as Used in Medical Practice

The Amphetamine-like Drugs

Ephedrine

Scientists have found ephedra plants at Neanderthal burial sites in Europe that are thought to be 60,000 years old (Karch, 2009). It is not known whether the plants were used for medical purposes, or were placed in the grave sites for decorative or religious purposes, but the fact that they were placed in the grave site is suggestive of the possibility that Neanderthal man was aware of the plant's CNS stimulatory effects. It is known that Chinese physicians were using the ephedra plant for medicinal purposes 5,000 years ago (King & Ellinwood, 2005). The main active agent in the ephedra plant, called ephedrine was first isolated by chemists in 1897, but remained nothing more than a laboratory curiosity until 1930 when a medical report appeared suggesting that ephedrine might be of value in treating asthma (Karch, 2009). Soon a large demand for ephedrine developed, and fears began to develop that the demand might exhaust the available supply. This spurred efforts to find

---

[1]Because there are no medical applications for "Khat," the discussion of this compound has been moved to the chapter "Drugs and Crime."

a substitute compound(s) that might be as effective as ephedra, but without the danger of demand exceeding supplies of this compound (discussed in "History of the Amphetamines,").

Medical Uses of Ephedrine

In the past, the medical uses of ephedrine included the treatment of asthma and respiratory problems associated with bronchitis, emphysema, and chronic obstructive pulmonary disease (COPD) (Westfall & Westfall, 2006). It was once considered a treatment for nasal congestion, but is no longer used for this purpose. In hospitals, ephedrine is used to treat symptoms of shock and in some surgical procedures where low blood pressure is a problem, because it is such a potent vasoconstrictor (Karch, 2009; Westfall & Westfall, 2006). Because it is a potent vasoconstrictor, it will limit blood loss when delicate tissues such as those found in the sinuses are injured. It was once used to treat some cardiac conditions, but the advent of newer, more effective medications have made its use in this arena rare (Westfall & Westfall, 2006). However, ephedrine is still used as an adjunct to the treatment of myasthenia gravis (Wilson, Shannon, & Shields, 2011).

Pharmacology of Ephedrine

In the human body, ephedrine's primary effects are in the peripheral regions of the body rather than the CNS, with an effect very similar to that of adrenaline (King & Ellinwood, 2005; Westfall & Westfall, 2006). The ephedrine molecule binds at the acetylcholine receptor sites[2] responsible for modulating the constriction of peripheral blood vessels (Rothman et al., 2003). When the capillaries constrict, the heart compensates by increasing the force with which it pumps, increasing blood pressure. This makes clinical sense because ephedrine blocks the reuptake of norepinephrine[3] (NE) as the receptor sites used by NE in the regulation of the individual's state of arousal and cardiac response, while causing the smooth muscles surrounding the bronchial passages to relax, improving air flow in and out of the lungs (Westfall & Westfall, 2008).

Depending on the patient's condition, ephedrine might be administered orally although it is well absorbed if injected via intramuscular or subcutaneous methods (Karch, 2009; Westfall & Westfall, 2006). Peak blood levels after a single oral dose are achieved in about 1 hour (Drummer & Odell, 2001). Surprisingly, little is known about the distribution pattern of ephedrine in the body. The half-life is estimated to be approximately 2.7–3.6 hours (Samenuk et al., 2002). Virtually all of the single dose is eliminated unchanged; however, the amount that is eliminated unchanged depends on the level of acidity in the urine (Westfall & Westfall, 2006).

Tolerance to the bronchodilation effect of ephedrine develops rapidly, and because of this ephedrine's effectiveness as a treatment for asthma is limited to short periods of time. Further, the chronic use of ephedrine can cause or exacerbate cardiac or respiratory problems for the user, again limiting its use to short periods of time. Although marketed as an over-the-counter diet aid, in reality ephedrine appears to have only a modest anorexic effect. Shekelle et al. (2003) found in their meta-analysis of the medical literature that ephedrine can help the patient lose 0.9 kilograms over a short period of time, but there is no data on its long-term effectiveness nor is there evidence that it will enhance athletic ability as is commonly believed (Shekelle et al., 2003).

Side Effects of Ephedrine at Normal Dosage Levels

Because the therapeutic index of ephedrine is rather small, it is possible to have toxic effects from even low dosage levels. Even at therapeutic doses, ephedrine users are 200–300% more likely to experience autonomic nervous system problems, upper gastrointestinal tract problems, and heart palpitations, as nonusers (Shekelle et al., 2003). Although some patients have reported experiencing a sense of euphoria when ephedrine is used at normal dosage levels, patients have also problems such as urinary retention, anxiety or feelings of apprehension, insomnia, headache, hallucinations, tremor, and seizures (American Society of Health System Pharmacists, 2008; Samenuk et al., 2002; Zevin & Benowitz, 2007). It was once thought that ephedrine could induce potentially fatal cardiac arrhythmias when used at normal dosage levels, but there is little evidence to support this belief (Hallas, Bjerrum, Støvring, & Andersen, 2008).

Medication Interactions Involving Ephedrine

It is recommended that patients taking one of the "tricyclic" antidepressants avoid the use of ephedrine, as these medications will enhance the stimulant effect of ephedrine possibly making the individual quite uncomfortable (DeVane & Nemeroff, 2002). Numerous other potential interactions between medications have been identified,

---

[2]Technically, the alpha-2 receptor sites, which control the degree of constriction in the muscles which surround these blood vessels.

[3]A stimulatory neurotransmitter. See Glossary.

and a pharmacist should be consulted before using ephedrine simultaneously with another compound.

The Amphetamine Compounds

History of the Amphetamines

The history of the amphetamine compounds is filled with twists and turns worthy of a movie plot. The first amphetamine compound was discovered in 1887, which remained little more than laboratory curiosity until 1927. The growing reliance on ephedrine to treat respiratory ailments started to raise concern over the possible danger of depleting the world's supply of ephedra plants. Chemists began to search for an artificial substitute for ephedrine to avoid this danger and because the amphetamine compounds were *analogs*[4] of ephedrine, they seemed to be the perfect solution to the problem.

The amphetamine compound Benzedrine® was found to have many of the medicinal effects as ephedrine and was soon introduced as a substitute for it (Jaffe & Martin, 2005). Benzedrine® was sold in a small glass vial with a cap on one end, surrounded by several layers of cloth. This vial initially contained approximately 325 mg of Benzedrine®. When needed, the patient would twist the ampule, breaking the glass and releasing the amphetamine compound into the surrounding layers of cloth. Then the patient would inhale the fumes, counteracting the effects of the asthma attack. It was not long, however, before the first reports of amphetamine abuse began to surface (Karch, 2009; Kind & Ellinwood, 2007; Rasmussen, 2008). Drug abusers of the era quickly discovered that you could carefully unwrap the glass containing the amphetamine compound, take out the ampule of concentrated Benzedrine®, carefully unscrew the cap or break it open at one end and obtain the concentrated amphetamine contained within for illicit use. It is not clear when the first illicit intravenous injection of Benzedrine® took place; however, this practice quickly gained widespread acceptance. By the early 1940s the amount of Benzedrine® in each ampule had been reduced by approximately 25% to 250 mg in part because of the practice of Benzedrine® injection. This dose still was the equivalent of fifty of the 5-mg tablets prescribed for oral use (Rasmussen, 2008). At these dosage levels the effects were found to be very similar to those of cocaine, which at the time was known to be a dangerous drug of abuse.

In World War II, both sides exploited the CNS stimulatory effects of the amphetamines to counteract the effects of fatigue and allow military personnel to work or fight longer. This was done in spite of the limited evidence that it was effective for these purposes, or that it was about as effective as caffeine, for this purpose. Its use by the military continued in spite of the knowledge that extended periods of use resulted in addiction and visual hallucinations (Rasmussen, 2008). Historical evidence strongly suggests that Adolf Hitler himself was addicted to amphetamines as part of a cocktail of compounds injected into him on a daily basis by his personal physician. Whether this addiction contributed to his ultimate breakdown and the defeat of Germany is open to debate. However, when military stores of amphetamine compounds became available there were epidemics of amphetamine abuse in Japan and in northern Europe in the years after World War II.

Medical historians now believe that it was the arrival of large amounts of amphetamine compounds, especially methamphetamine, which contributed to the outbreak of drug related violence that ended the "Summer of Love" in 1967 (Smith, 1997, 2001). By that time amphetamine abusers had discovered that high doses of amphetamines could cause agitation and death from cardiovascular collapse. It has also been discovered that following periods of intense amphetamine abuse, the user would enter a depressive state that might last for days or weeks after their last use, which might reach suicidal proportions. Although originally believed to be CNS stimulants that lacked the dangers associated with cocaine use, by the mid-1970s abusers had coined the phrase "speed kills" as a warning about the dangers of amphetamine abuse (Smith, 1997, 2001). Because of their identified abuse potential and the discovery that the amphetamines were not effective pharmaceuticals for any known disease, they were classified as Schedule II[5] compounds in the Controlled Substances Act of 1970.

Current Medical Uses of the Amphetamines

The amphetamines might be viewed as compounds in search for a disease that they might treat (Rasmussen, 2008). Because the amphetamines improve the action of smooth muscles in the body, many athletes came to believe that they could improve athletic performance. Subsequent research revealed that the amphetamines have an unpredictable effect muscle performance, possibly resulting in a *decrease* in athletic performance

---

[4]See Glossary.

[5]See Appendix Four.

rather than the desired improvement. Still, because of the myth that they can improve athletic performance, sports regulatory agencies routinely test for amphetamine compounds, which is one reason why their use by athletes is rather rare.

The amphetamines were found to have an *anorexic*[6] side-effect, and were extensively prescribed by physicians in the 1960s and 1970s for patients who wanted to lose weight. However, research soon demonstrated that tolerance to the anorexic effects of the amphetamines develops rapidly, and that it is not uncommon for patients to then regain the weight that they had initially lost. Simple dieting and exercise, behavioral modifications that do not rely on chemicals, was found to result in the same degree of weight loss and the amphetamines soon lost favor as anorexic agents. However, by this time the amphetamines were being touted as antidepressants by pharmaceutical companies. Research has since demonstrated that the antidepressant effects of the amphetamines currently in use are short-lived at best. They are still occasionally used as an *adjunct* to the treatment of depression because they augment the effects of many antidepressant medications. Physicians will occasionally exploit the euphoric effect of the amphetamines to counteract depression in the terminally ill, or to counteract the respiratory depression induced by other compounds (Brunton, Parker, Blumenthal, & Buxton, 2007; Fadem, 2009).

Currently the Food and Drug Administration only approves of the use of amphetamine compounds in the treatment of narcolepsy "off label" uses of these compounds include the treatment of some of the effects of AIDS,[7] dysthymia, chronic fatigue syndrome, Parkinson's disease, the control of anger/aggression in persons with traumatic brain injuries, and lethargy (Sadock & Sadock, 2007; Virani, Bezchlibnyk-Butler, Jeffries, & Procyshyn, 2012).

Narcolepsy is thought to be the result of a deficit in dopamine levels in certain regions of the brain. Because the amphetamines force neurons to release stores of dopamine, it would appear to be an ideal treatment for narcolepsy. In 1938 it was discovered that the amphetamines had a paradoxical calming effect on patients with attention deficit/hyperactivity disorder (ADHD). Subsequent research has revealed that the amphetamines are about as effective in controlling the symptoms of ADHD as is methylphenidate,[8] calming

about 50% of the patients with this disorder, and that an addition 25% will experience some degree of improvement when they take prescribed amphetamine compounds (Spencer et al., 2001). This effect is thought to reflect the amphetamine's ability to enhance the function of the neurons in the reticular activating system (RAS).[9] However, as is true with methylphenidate, the use of the amphetamines to treat ADHD is controversial, and there is little research into the long-term benefits or consequences of amphetamine use for this purpose. There are those who believe that these compounds may do more harm than good for patients who take them for the control of ADHD (Breggin, 2008; Spencer et al., 2001).

Pharmacology of the Amphetamines

The amphetamines have been in clinical use for almost a century and yet the pharmacokinetics of these compounds have not been studied in detail (Payer & London, 2009). The most common forms of amphetamine are dextroamphetamine (*d*-amphetamine sulfate), methamphetamine, and a combination of dextroamphetamine and pure amphetamine salts (Sadock & Sadock, 2007). Because of its longer half-life, and its ability to rapidly cross the blood brain barrier, drug abusers seem to prefer methamphetamine over dextroamphetamine; however, both compounds are abused (Albertson, Derlet, & Van Hoozen, 1999). The various amphetamines in use only have minor variations in chemical structure, which affect the potency and pharmacological characteristics of that compound. The chemical structure of the basic amphetamine molecule is similar to that of the NE and dopamine molecules, and technically the amphetamines might be classified as an agonist of both compounds (King & Ellinwood, 2007).

When ingested orally, the amphetamine molecule is easily absorbed through the lining of the small intestine, and the usual route of administration in medical practice is orally administered tablets or capsules. On rare occasions physicians will administer an amphetamine through intramuscular or intravenous injection. In the brain the effects of any amphetamine are region-specific, causing an increase in neurotransmitter activity in one region while inducing a simultaneous decrease in the release of other neurotransmitters in other regions of the brain (Hanson & Fleckenstein, 2009). At therapeutic dosage levels the main effects of

---

[6]See Glossary.

[7]Discussed in Chapter 35.

[8]Discussed later in this chapter.

[9]See Glossary.

the amphetamines appears to be its ability to alter the dopamine neurotransmission system (Fadem, 2009; King and Ellinwood, 2007). The amphetamine molecule causes the release of catecholamine molecules, especially dopamine, into the synaptic junction (Fadem, 2009; King & Ellinwood, 2007; Sadock & Sadock, 2007). Then the amphetamine blocks the action of the molecular reuptake pumps, allowing the dopamine to remain in the synaptic junction longer, thus enhancing its effects on the downstream neurons. However, they also induce the release, and block the reuptake of glutamate,[10] and it is possible that the amphetamine compounds also influence the effects of the acetylcholine neurotransmission system although this has not been studied in detail (Hansen & Fleckenstein, 2009).

The effects of a single oral dose of an amphetamine begin in about 20–30 minutes, and peak blood levels are achieved in 1–3 hours (Drummer & Odell, 2001). Dextroamphetamine sulfate is an excellent example of this dose-response process with rapid rate of absorption reaching peak effects 1–5 hours after ingestion, and a half-life of between 10–30 hours (Wilson et al., 2011). The biological half-life of methamphetamine is longer and is estimated to be 12.2 hours (Karch, 2002). The various forms of amphetamine in clinical use are lipid-soluble; however, because of the limited research into the pharmacokinetics of the amphetamines, it is not known whether one form of amphetamine is more lipid-soluble than any other. The peripheral effects of the amphetamine compounds are the result of their ability to stimulate the release of NE (Hanley, 2004). There is significant inter-individual variability to the effects of the amphetamines. Under normal conditions, 45–70% of a single dose of an amphetamine compound will be excreted unchanged in the urine within 24 hours (Karch, 2009). The exact percentage of the amphetamine that is excreted unchanged depends in large part on the acidity level of the user's blood. The more acidic the individual's blood, the greater the percentage of a given dose that will be excreted unchanged. However, if the blood is more alkaline, the kidneys tend to reabsorb the amphetamine molecules and return them to the circulatory system. The amphetamine molecules are biotransformed by the liver prior to elimination. Depending on the specific amphetamine ingested, the number of metabolites produced during the

biotransformation process will vary. For example, during the process of methamphetamine biotransformation, seven different metabolites are formed before the drug molecules are finally eliminated.

At one point it was thought that making the patient's blood more acidic would speed up the elimination of amphetamine molecules from the circulation, especially in situations where the patient had ingested an overdose (King & Ellinwood, 2005). However, some clinicians believe that this process also increases the patient's chance(s) of developing a cardiac arrhythmia, and/or seizures, placing the patient's life at risk (Venkatakrishnan, Shader, & Greenblatt, 2006). Thus, it is not clear which course of action the attending physician should follow if the patient should take an overdose of an amphetamine. To complicate matters there is also a great deal of inter-individual variability for toxic reactions to the amphetamines. Some persons have tolerated exceptionally large doses of amphetamines, such as in overdose attempts, without apparent ill effect. Other individuals have been unable to tolerate even low therapeutic doses without experiencing a range of potentially fatal side effects (discussed next). Although classified as CNS stimulants, almost 6% of patients taking an amphetamine compound in a clinical trial reported that they felt drowsy and less alert while taking one of these substances. Just under 4% reported feeling confused, and 8.7% reported feeling that they were depressed. Over 17% reported feeling irritable, agitated, and restless, adverse effects that the mainstream media often ignores (Breggin, 2008). These findings illustrate the fact that these compounds are neither perfect, nor is their use without risk.

Neuroadaptation to Amphetamine Compounds

The steady use of an amphetamine at therapeutic dosage levels will result in an incomplete state of neuroadaptation. When used to treat narcolepsy, the patient might remain on the same dose of the amphetamine for years without any loss of efficacy (Jaffe, Ling, & Rawson, 2005). In contrast to this, patients soon develop tolerance to the anorexic effect of amphetamines after only a few weeks, and the drug-induced sense of euphoria does not last beyond the first few doses when amphetamines are used at therapeutic dosage levels.

Medication Interactions Involving the Amphetamine Compounds

Patients who are taking any medication, even if it is an over-the-counter medication, should consult with a physician or pharmacist before starting to take an

---

[10]As discussed in the Glossary, glutamate is an inhibitory neurotransmitter.

amphetamine, to avoid the danger of potentially dangerous drug interactions. For example, there is limited evidence that individuals taking any of the momoamine
oxidase inhibitors[11] (MAO inhibitors or MAO-Is) should
not take an amphetamine compound for several days
after they discontinue the MAO-I to avoid potentially
lethal hypertensive episodes (Ciraulo et al., 2006).
Although the potential for these compounds to cause
such a hypertensive episode remains unproven, the danger has not been ruled out, and to avoid this possibility
patients should not take these compounds until s/he has
completed a MAO-I "wash out" period of 72 hours or
longer.

There is evidence to suggest that amphetamine
compounds may interact with at least some of the
antipsychotic medications currently in use in the
United States at this time (Ciraulo et al., 2006).
Although this list is hardly exhaustive, it does illustrate that the amphetamines have the potential to
interact with other pharmaceuticals in use. A physician or pharmacist should always be consulted about
the possible interaction between two different medications if used concurrently.

Subjective Experience of Amphetamine Use in Medical Practice

The subjective effects of an amphetamine administered
under a physician's supervision will depend on a number of factors, including the individual's mental state,
the manner in which the drug is administered, the relative potency of the dose administered, and the individual's substance use history. For example, a
hypothetical soldier, who has gone without sleep for
48 hours, ingests a 5-mg tablet of an amphetamine
will have a different reaction than that same soldier
would if well rested. The reaction of the hypothetical
soldier mentioned in the last sentence would be far
different still if s/he were to have a 5-mg dose of the
amphetamine injected into a vein rather than orally.

Amphetamine compounds do have a very small, virtually insignificant analgesic property of their own,
although they may multiply the analgesic effect of a
given dose of a narcotic analgesic (King & Ellinwood,
2005). However, amphetamine compounds are rarely,
if ever, used for their analgesic effects and this property
of amphetamine compounds will not be discussed further in this chapter. When used in medical practice, the

amphetamines are usually administered orally, in doses
of 5–60 mg/day (Jenkins, 2007). At such dosage levels,
the user will experience enhanced mood, less mental
fatigue, an improved ability to concentrate, and perhaps a mild euphoria especially when the medication
is first started (Sadock & Sadock, 2003). The user may
also notice that s/he is not hungry as often, and may
not feel the need to eat as much as before. As noted
earlier, the amphetamines do have an anorexic effect,
especially before the development of neuroadaptation
to these compounds (King & Ellinwood, 2005).

About 10% of patients started on an amphetamine
compound will experience drug-induced tachycardia
(Fuller & Sajatovic, 1999; Breggin, 1998). It is for
this reason that the physician should conduct tests
to rule out pre-existing cardiac problems in the
patient before starting the medication. Rarely, patients
taking an amphetamine compound at therapeutic
doses will develop a drug-induced psychosis (Ciraulo
et al., 2006). More commonly encountered are stereotypical, repetitive behaviors, which are especially common when these medications are used at high dosage
levels.

Patients with *Tourette's disorder*[12] often find that
amphetamine use exacerbates the symptoms of their
Tourette's disorder. Some patients begin to engage in
the characteristic vocalizations and movements of
Tourette's disorder when they begin to take a prescribed amphetamine. Further, although the amphetamines are CNS stimulants, about 40% of patients
taking them at therapeutic doses experience a drug-
induced feeling of depression that might become so
profound as to reach suicidal proportions (Breggin,
1998). When the patients discontinue a prescribed
amphetamine, they also are prone to experience a
depressive reaction, as well as fatigue and lethargy, lasting a few hours, or days. These compounds have also
been known to interfere with normal growth in children. As this information suggests, the amphetamines
are quite potent compounds, which even at therapeutic
doses have the potential to harm the user.

Methylphenidate

Methylphenidate has become a rather controversial
compound. It was originally introduced in the late
1950s as a safe alternative to the amphetamines,
which were then in use as antidepressants. Like the

---

[11]See Glossary.

[12]See Glossary.

amphetamines, Methylphenidate was a drug in search of a disease for many years, being used as an agent to promote weight loss and finally to control the symptoms of ADHD (Breggin, 2008; Sinha, 2001). An astounding 80% of the world's total annual production of methylphenidate is consumed in the United States and research has shown that consumption of CNS stimulants such as methylphenidate has increased 12% per year for each of the years between 2000 and 2005 (Breggin, 2008; Diller, quoted in Marsa, 2005; Horstman, 2010) in spite of the fact that methylphenidate does not seem to be the most effective treatment for attention deficit disorder and that about half of the prescriptions for this medication are never renewed (Breggin, 1998). There have been strident arguments both for and against the use of methylphenidate in the treatment of ADHD, and it is certain to remain a most controversial compound for many years to come.

Pharmacology of Methylphenidate

This compound has a chemical structure similar to that of the amphetamines, and that of cocaine (Horstman, 2010), and functions as a CNS stimulant. It was originally developed as a possible nonaddicting substitute for the amphetamines (discussed next) (Diller, 1998). The "habit forming" potential of the amphetamines had been identified by then, and so it was hoped that methylphenidate could serve as a safer substitute. Some neuropharmacologists classify it as a member of the amphetamine family of drugs. In this text it will be classified as an amphetamine-like compound.

When used in the treatment of ADHD, patients are prescribed daily doses of between 15 and 90 mg. Orally administered doses are rapidly absorbed through the gastrointestinal tract (Greenhill, 2006). Peak blood levels are usually achieved in around two hours following a single dose, although with extended release forms of methylphenidate this might not occur until 4–7 hours after the medication was ingested (Wilson et al., 2011). The estimated therapeutic window of methylphenidate is 1:100, which is to say that the effective dose is approximately 1/100th the estimated lethal dose (Greenhill, 2006). The half-life is between 1 and 3 hours, with the effects lasting 3–6 hours following a single oral dose. These figures are extended in situations where the patient has ingested an extended release form of methylphenidate, and might last for up to eight hours. About 80% of a single dose is biotransformed into titanic acid in the

intestinal tract, which is then excreted by the kidneys (Karch, 2009).

Within the brain, methylphenidate blocks the action of approximately 50–70% of the molecular dopamine reuptake pumps[13] in the neural wall, allowing the dopamine molecules to remain in the synaptic junction longer thus enhancing their effect (Jaffe et al., 2005; Volkow & Swanson, 2003; Whitaker, 2010). One region of the brain that benefits from this effect is the RAS, a region of the brain involved in the process of focusing attention. The RAS neurons are very sensitive to dopamine, and thus there is a dose-related response to methylphenidate with higher doses having a stronger effect on the neural reuptake pumps.

Medical Uses of Methylphenidate

Methylphenidate functions as a CNS stimulant, and is of value in the treatment of a rare neurological condition known as *narcolepsy,* ADHD, and is occasionally used as an adjunct in the treatment of depression. On occasion, it is used as an adjunct to the treatment of Parkinson's disease, control of anger/aggression in brain-damaged persons or AIDS-related neurological problems. There are few, if any, other medical applications of methylphenidate at this time.

Side Effects of Methylphenidate

Methylphenidate's long-term effects have not been studied because most follow-up studies involving methylphenidate are discontinued after a few weeks. Even studies involving the administration of methylphenidate to animals are usually discontinued after a few weeks to months, in part because of the cost of maintaining the animals over extended periods of time. Although it is reportedly safe at prescribed doses, there is emerging evidence that casts some doubt on this claim (Higgins, 2009). This is a matter of some concern because there is a growing trend for patients to be told that they must continue taking methylphenidate through childhood into adulthood (Higgins, 2009).

It was once thought that methylphenidate caused, or at least exacerbated, cardiac problems in users, even at therapeutic doses. In a retrospective study in which the clinical records of 1.2 million children and young adults ages 2–24 who had been placed on methylphenidate or similar compounds for treatment of ADHD

---

[13]See Glossary.

symptoms, Cooper et al. (2011) failed to find evidence of increased risk of methylphenidate-related cardiac problems. It is possible that children who die while taking methylphenidate as directed had pre-existing heart problems that coincidentally caused them to die while taking this medication.

Unfortunately, up to 5% of the children who receive therapeutic doses of methylphenidate will experience visual hallucinations and possibly a medically induced psychosis (Aldhous, 2006; Halevy & Shuper, 2009; Higgens, 2009). Children prescribed methylphenidate have been noted to demonstrate behaviors suggestive of the obsessive-compulsive disorder, symptoms that were not present prior to the initiation of this medication (Breggin, 2008). Other identified side effects of therapeutic doses of methylphenidate include anorexia, insomnia, weight loss or failure to gain weight, dry mouth, heart palpitations, angina, anxiety, liver dysfunctions, skin rashes, dizziness, headache, hypertension, and exacerbation of Tourette's syndrome, blurred vision, leukopenia, anemia, perseveration, and possible cerebral hemorrhage (Breggin, 2008; Higgins, 2009; Karch, 2009; Newcorn & Ivanov, 2007).

Because of its anorexic side effect, methylphenidate can interfere with normal physical growth (King & Ellinwood, 2005). Animal-based research has revealed that the CNS stimulants (including methylphenidate) can, by increasing the dopamine levels in the brain, interfere with the pituitary's[14] normal function, thus contributing to growth retardation (Higgins, 2009). Patients with a known seizure disorder should not be placed on methylphenidate, as this compound can exacerbate such disorders (Breggin, 1998). These seizures may be due to drug-induced changes in cerebral blood flow patterns, although this has not been proven.

Children who take prescribed doses of methylphenidate frequently report that the drug made them feel like a "zombie" and thus made them resistant to taking it (Breggin, 1998). This appears to be a common effect of methylphenidate (Diller, 1998). However, such reports are disputed. For example, Pliszka (1998) denied that this was not a drug-induced effect. Further, a small number of studies have suggested that there is a relationship between methylphenidate use in childhood, and possible affective disorders in adulthood (Higgins, 2009). On rare occasions therapeutic methylphenidate use can also induce a state of depression that may reach suicidal proportions (Breggin, 1998).

There is early research data suggesting a *possible* connection between the use of prescribed doses of methylphenidate, and the development of Parkinson's disease later in life (Rothenberger & Banaschewski, 2004). This obviously is a matter of some concern, and further research into possible mechanisms, treatment options, and alternatives is needed in this area. These studies suggest a need for further research into the benefits and long-term consequences of methylphenidate use even at therapeutic doses.

Medication Interactions Involving Methylphenidate

Patients who are using any of the "tricyclic" antidepressants should not use methylphenidate, as the interaction of these compounds can cause potentially toxic levels of the antidepressant medication to build up in the patient's blood (DeVane & Nemeroff, 2002). Patients using any of the MAO inhibitors should not use methylphenidate because of a potential toxic reaction between these compounds. Further, the use of methylphenidate with the selective serotonin reuptake inhibitor (SSRI) family of antidepressants can lower the seizure threshold, causing seizures (DeVane & Nemeroff, 2002). Finally, patients taking antihypertensive medications might find that their blood pressure control is inadequate, as methylphenidate interferes with the effectiveness of blood pressure medications (DeVane & Nemeroff, 2002). Although it is not possible to identify every potential drug interaction involving methylphenidate, this list should highlight the need for the patient to check with a physician or pharmacist before taking methylphenidate with any other medication.

Modafinil (Provigil®)

A recent entry into the field of CNS stimulants is modafinil, which is sold under the brand name of Provigil® (Baker, 2009). Provigil® was introduced in 1998 as a "wake-promoting agent" (Price, 2009, p. 3), a term that the author suggested was a carefully selected term to avoid the suspect term "stimulant."[15] This compound is recommended as a treatment of ADHD and narcolepsy (Thompson PDR, 2011). One "off label"[16] use of modafinil is to enhance cognitive endurance for persons suffering from fatigue (Baker, 2009). Like the other CNS stimulants, modafinil stimulates the release of dopamine within the

---

[14]See Glossary.

[15]A term associated in the minds of many with drugs of abuse such as cocaine, and so on.

[16]See Glossary.

brain, and as such has a mild abuse potential (Price, 2009; Volkow et al., 2009). For example, it is often abused by those who wish to improve concentration although they do not have ADHD. In this capacity it is often abused by college students who wish to enhance concentration during "all night" study sessions.

Pharmacology of Modafinil

The pharmacokinetics of modafinil are not well understood at this time. At clinical doses it appears to block the dopamine transporter system in various regions of the brain, thus enhancing the effects of dopamine in the receptor site. This includes the dopamine receptors in the nucleus accumbens region of the brain increasing its abuse potential in a manner similar to that seen with the amphetamines (Volkow et al., 2009). It does not appear to bind at the NE, serotonin, GABA, adenosine, histamine, melatonin, or benzodiazepine receptor sites in the brain (Thompson PDR, 2011). Following the administration of 2–4 doses (one per day) to establish steady state plasma levels, the elimination half-life is approximately 15 hours (Thompson PDR, 2011).

Following oral ingestion, the peak blood plasma levels of modafinil are seen within 2–4 hours when ingested on an empty stomach. Although it may be ingested with food, absorption of modafinil will be delayed by approximately one hour. Approximately 60% of the drug molecules bind to protein molecules in the blood (mainly albumin). It is biotransformed in the liver, with only 10% of the modafinil being excreted unchanged by the kidneys (Thompson PDR, 2011). This medication is not to be used by patients with a known allergic. Further, the challenge has been made that parents "medicate our kids more, and for more trivial reasons, than any other culture. We'd rather give them a pill than discipline them" (Diller, quoted in Marsa, 2005, p. 164). Such children are being turned into chemical "zombies" through prescribed methylphenidate or similar agents in the name of behavioral control (Aldhous, 2006; Breggin, 2008) to this compound (Thompson PDR, 2011).

Side Effects of Modafinil Use

This medication can induce shortness of breath, heart palpitations, chest pain, and transient changes in the electrocardiogram (Thompson PDR, 2011). Its use in patients who have suffered a recent myocardial infarction ("heart attack") has not been studied in detail and should be used in such patients only under a physician's supervision. One patient did develop symptoms of a drug-induced psychosis after taking exceptionally large doses of modafinil, but these symptoms did resolve after the medication was discontinued (Thompson PDR, 2011). Modafinil does not appear to induce the sense of CNS overstimulation seen when a patient receives methylphenidate or an amphetamine compound (Baker, 2009). It does, however, appear to have an addiction potential.

Medication Interactions Involving Modafinil

This medication is known to reduce the effectiveness of oral contraceptives. Possible interactions with alcohol have not been studied. It is recommended that the patient consult with a pharmacist before taking another medication (including over-the-counter compounds) with modafinil.

Strattera® (atomoxetine hydrochloride)

Technically, atomoxetine hydrochloride is not classified as a CNS stimulant by the manufacturer but has been classified as such by the *Physician's Desk Reference* (Thompson PDR, 2011). It will be classified as such in this text because, like the other compounds reviewed in this chapter, it is recommended for the treatment of ADHD.

Pharmacokinetics

Atomoxetine hydrochloride is administered orally, and following absorption approximately 98% becomes protein-bound *Physician's Desk Reference* (Thompson PDR, 2011). The exact mechanism of action remains unclear, but it is assumed to be a result of the drug's ability to alter NE release patterns in the neurons. The half-life of this compound is estimated to be approximately five hours in the typical patient.

Side Effects

Identified side effects include a mild increase in heart rate (approximately six beats per minute). Breggin (2008) noted that other reported side effects include irritability, mood swings, and aggressive behaviors by the child receiving this medication. Other reported side-effects include grandiosity, hyperactivity, insomnia, and in overdose situations seizures. The Food and Drug Administration has also required the manufacturer to include a "black box" warning about this compound apparently causing suicidal thinking or suicidal acts in children receiving it (Breggin, 2008).

Medication Interactions

Numerous medication interactions are identified in the 2007 edition of the *Physician's Desk Reference* and a pharmacist should be consulted before intermixing atomoxetine hydrochloride with other compounds.

Challenges to the Use of CNS Stimulants to Treat Identified Disorders

It has been suggested that the amphetamines are "orphan" drugs in search of a disease to treat. Touted first as a treatment for asthma in the 1930s and 1940s, they were then sold reputed antidepressants in the 1950s, and then in the 1960s as anorexic compounds that could be used to assist in weight loss programs (Breggin, 2008; Rasmussen, 2008). Currently, they are recommended as a pharmacological treatment for the attention deficit disorders and narcolepsy. At the peak of their popularity as pharmaceutical agents in the mid-1960s, fully 5% of the adults in the United States were taking a prescribed amphetamine compound. About half of these patients were abusing amphetamines for their euphoric effects, which underscores the abuse potential of this class of drugs (King & Ellinwood, 2005; Rasmussen, 2008).

Surprisingly, in spite of their use as agents to treat ADHD for more than a generation, there is little evidence of the long-term effectiveness of these compounds for treating such disorders, and a mounting body of evidence suggesting that psychosocial interventions are far more superior (Breggin, 2008; McDonagh & Peterson, 2006). In spite of this, pharmacological interventions are recommended by physicians and pharmaceutical companies, the latter being more than happy to learn that the diagnosed rate of ADHD might be as high as 9.5% (Visser, Bitsko, Danielson, Perou, & Blumburg, 2010).[17] Obviously, because psychosocial interventions cannot be patented by pharmaceutical companies, they are not mentioned in advertisements for CNS stimulants as treatments for ADHD. Unfortunately, as noted earlier in this chapter, the amphetamine-like drugs have also been identified as possibly causing neural damage even when used as prescribed (Breggin, 2008), raising questions whether the cure might be worse than the disease states that they are supposed to control.

CNS Stimulant Abuse

Scope of the Problem

The Amphetamines

Shortly after the time of their introduction, the first reports of amphetamine addiction began to appear in the clinical literature. In response the pharmaceuticals industry quickly began to describe the amphetamines as *habit forming* to avoid the charge that they were addictive and that users were not being informed of this potential danger (Rasmussen, 2008). Discussion of the problem of amphetamine abuse is complicated by the fact that different researchers define the term "amphetamine" in different ways: Some researchers limit the term to only the compound methamphetamine, whereas other researchers discuss the abuse of the amphetamine family of compounds (methamphetamine dextroamphetamine, etc.) (Rutkowski & Maxwell, 2009). Some researchers apply the term "amphetamine" only to diverted pharmaceuticals, whereas others include both diverted and amphetamine compounds produced in illicit "labs" under the rubric of "amphetamine" (Rutkowski & Maxwell, 2009). Some researchers classify methylphenidate as an amphetamine but this is not a universal practice. Finally, some researchers include the hallucinogen MDMA ("Ecstasy") as an "amphetamine," whereas others classify it as a hallucinogenic[18] compound.

In the United States the amphetamines, especially methamphetamine, are the second most popular class of illicit drugs of abuse, exceeded in popularity only by marijuana. The abuse of prescribed amphetamine compounds is widespread, as evidenced by the fact that 25% of the students at some colleges have used the amphetamine sold under the brand name of Adderall® to help them study for examinations or stay up all night to finish assigned projects (Owen, 2008). Arguably the main source of CNS stimulants found in the illicit job market is not the stereotypical "pusher"[19] but the health care professional in a white lab coat and a prescription pad (Owen, 2008; Rasmussen, 2008).

Globally, the abuse of the amphetamines or amphetamine-like compounds is thought to be a $65 billion/year industry (United Nations, 2011). The total number of people who abuse just methamphetamine around the globe is estimated to outnumber

---

[17]In their defense it should be noted that the authors of this study spoke about 22% of the children in the survey apparently outgrowing the disorder.

[18]The practice that is followed in this book is to classify MDMA, or "Ecstasy," as a hallucinogenic, not an amphetamine compound.

[19]One who sells illicit drugs.

the number of heroin and cocaine abusers *combined* (BBC News, 2006). The mass media in the United States has often spoken about a "meth crisis" in this country, although three-quarters of methamphetamine abusers live in Asia or Southeast Asia (Ling, Rawson, & Shoptaw, 2006). To put the problem of methamphetamine abuse in the United States into perspective, consider the following facts: Just less than 73 million people have used a cigarette, 125 million people have used alcohol, 2.4 million people have abused cocaine, and 7 million people were thought to have abused prescription narcotic analgesics in the past year (Fadem, 2009). In contrast, only about 583,000 people are thought to be regular methamphetamine abusers in the United States, and 257,000 people are estimated to be addicted to it (Acosta, Haller, & Schnoll, 2005; Miller, 2005; Owen, 2007). Although this is not to downplay the dangers associated with methamphetamine abuse or addiction, it does underscore how the media helps to shape our perception of substance use disorders on a day to day basis.

Young adults, or those who are about to become young adults, represent a special risk group for methamphetamine abuse. In a recent survey 11.4% of high school seniors admitted to having used an amphetamine compound, and 3.0 percent admitted to the use of methamphetamine at least once (Johnston, O'Malley, Backman, & Schulenberg, 2008a). As these figures demonstrate, the abuse of amphetamine compounds in the United States is both common and widespread. However, there is still much to be discovered about the epidemiology of amphetamine abuse both in the United States and around the world.

Ephedrine

Because it was once sold over the counter as a diet aid, and as a treatment for asthma, the true scope of ephedrine abuse is simply not known (Karch, 2009). Most certainly *some* of the ephedrine sold in the United States a decade ago was being used for medicinal purposes. However, illicit drug dealers often sell ephedrine under the guise of other, more potent, compounds. Ephedrine is also a precursor of the amphetamines, especially methamphetamine, and an unknown quantity of the ephedrine sold in the United States each year was being used to manufacture methamphetamine in small illicit laboratories. In 2004 the United States government attempted to forbid sale of ephedrine in this country, at which point illegal drug laboratories switched to pseudoephedrine in their efforts to manufacture illicit methamphetamine. The ban on the sale of ephedrine was overturned by the courts a year later ("Utah Judge Strikes Down FAD Ban on Ephedra," 2005). The legal status of ephedrine thus remains to be settled in this country.

Methylphenidate

There simply is no way to estimate the percentage of methylphenidate pills that are diverted to the illicit drug market, although it is known that they are popular drugs of abuse. There are multiple causes for methylphenidate abuse: Some abusers want to engage in tasks such as driving delivery trucks, or study for exams, for extended periods of time (Vedantam, 2006). Other abusers wish to stay awake at parties longer, or counteract the sedating effects of alcohol so that they can drink longer, whereas others seek a drug-induced feeling of euphoria (Aldhous, 2006; Arria & Wish, 2006). Such abuse is stimulated by the mistaken belief that this medication is not addicting. A conversion formula suggests that 15 mg of methylphenidate is about as potent as 5 mg of dextroamphetamine (Rasmussen, 2008).

Modafinil

The abuse potential of modafinil remains poorly defined, although it is acknowledged that a small percentage of users take the medication to help them remain cognitively alert for longer than normal. It is also increasingly being diverted into the hands of those for whom the drug was not prescribed (Price, 2009). Given the report that it was pharmacologically different than the amphetamine compounds when it was introduced, health care professionals have become complacent about the potential risks associated with modafinil abuse, which is rather frightening because of its growing popularity as a drug of abuse.

Atomoxetine Hydrochloride

No identified pattern of abuse for this medication has been reported as of this time.

Methods of CNS Stimulant Abuse and Their Effects

Ephedrine

Methods of Ephedrine Abuse

The most common method of ephedrine abuse is for the individual to ingest over-the-counter ephedrine tablets. On rare occasions, the pills might be crushed and the resulting power "snorted." On even more rare occasions, the pills are crushed, mixed with water, and then injected into a vein.

Effects of Ephedrine When Abused

The effects of ephedrine abuse are dose-dependent and essentially are an exaggeration of the adverse effects of ephedrine when used at normal doses.[20] Ephedrine can induce a feeling of euphoria when used at very high doses, providing an incentive for some people to abuse it. This sense of euphoria is less intense than that seen in amphetamine abusers and requires that the abuser ingest high levels of ephedrine (Erickson, 2007). Further, it is often touted as being a "safer" alternative to synthetic or semi-synthetic compounds such as the amphetamines (Gorelick, 2009).

Complications of Ephedrine Abuse

The therapeutic window for ephedrine is quite small, and as indicated above it can induce toxic effects even at therapeutic doses. Ephedrine abuse can result in impaired judgment, agitation, necrosis[21] of the lining of the gastrointestinal tract, nausea, vomiting, stroke, irritation of cardiac tissues (especially in abusers who have damaged their hearts), potentially fatal heart arrhythmias, and heart attacks. The causal mechanism for ephedrine-induced heart attacks appears to be a drug-induced increase of the cardiac muscle contractions, increasing the oxygen demand by those tissues. This is potentially dangerous if the person should have some form of coronary artery disease that independently limits the blood flow to the heart muscle.

When abused at high doses for an extended period of time, ephedrine abuse can also result in the formation of ephedrine-based kidney stones. Because ephedrine does not require biotransformation before excretion, these kidney stones are found to be almost entirely ephedrine when examined by physicians, and are quite painful when they move down the urinary tract of the abuser to the bladder.

The Amphetamine Compounds

Effects of Amphetamine Abuse

The amphetamine compounds, especially methamphetamine, might be ingested orally, used intranasally (i.e., "snorted"), smoked, or injected intravenously. Depending on the individual's tolerance to the effects of the amphetamines, the individual might experience a state

of heightened alertness, confidence, and euphoria. When smoked or injected, methamphetamine abusers report a sensation of a "whole body orgasm." The effects of the amphetamines depend on factors such as (a) dose, (b) method of administration, (c) possible concurrent use of other compounds, (d) the individual's state of health, and (e) the individual's past substance use history.

Orally administered amphetamine compounds begin to take effect in 20 minutes, whereas a "snorted" (intranasal) dose will begin to take effect in about 5 minutes. When injected or smoked, an amphetamine compound will take effect on the abuser in a matter of seconds (Gorelick, 2009; Rawson & Ling, 2008). The amphetamines and related compounds are popular drugs of abuse on the college campus, especially as students prepare for examinations (Azar, 2008). Surprisingly, there is no evidence to suggest that these compounds actually improve the individual's performance in the examination(s). Students still abuse them around exam time in the hope that they will give them an "edge" as they study. Then, having discovered that these compounds allow them to remain awake for longer periods of time than is normal, students often use the amphetamines so that they might party longer (Azar, 2008).

Until the 1990s, much of the methamphetamine abused in the United States came from small "laboratories" that would produce relatively small amounts of methamphetamine using various easily obtained chemicals for local consumption.[22] These "kitchen labs" proliferated in the 1990s when methamphetamine again became a popular drug of abuse. However, the process of making methamphetamine is dangerous and even legitimate pharmaceutical companies will suffer the occasional explosion in the production facility. Illicit laboratories are much more likely to experience an explosion during the manufacture process. So common were the explosions of "labs" that local police departments often wait for the explosion to help them identify a methamphetamine production site.

Unfortunately, methods and the necessary materials for methamphetamine production are available on the Internet. "Nazi meth" is one such preparation of illicit methamphetamine. The name is obtained from the

---

[20]This assumes that the abuser is taking *only* ephedrine.

[21]See Glossary.

[22]It has been estimated that for every pound of methamphetamine produced, 5–7 *pounds* of toxic waste are also produced, which then becomes an expensive hazardous waste problem for the community where the "lab" was located (Rollo, Sane, & Ewen, 2007).

Nazi symbols that decorated the paper on which the formula was originally written ("Nazi Meth on the Rise," 2003). Unlike some of the other formulas for methamphetamine manufacture, this method does not rely on the use of red phosphorus,[23] but rather uses lithium (obtained from batteries), and ammonia ("Nazi Meth on the Rise," 2003). The use of these compounds for the production of illicit methamphetamine exposes the abuser to various contaminants[24] (Graber, 2007). To combat the production of illicit methamphetamine, precursor compounds such as ephedrine and pseudoephedrine were placed under strict control in the United States. Persons are now only able to purchase a small amount of pseudoephedrine each month for self-medication of colds or allergies. The impact of this restriction has been minimal at best (Cunningham, Liu, & Callaghan, 2009), and illicit methamphetamine remains rampant.

There is a financial incentive for producing illicit methamphetamine. An investment of $200 in the chemicals used for illicit production of methamphetamine might produce enough to sell for $2,500 in the illegal market. This financial incentive attracted the attention of organized crime cartels, which set up large-scale production facilities (known as "super labs") in Mexico, and then the methamphetamine is smuggled across the border (Graber, 2007). These "super labs" have essentially replaced the smaller production facilities once commonly found in the United States, although on occasion such "mom and pop" laboratories are still discovered by police.

Methods of Amphetamine Abuse

There are multiple methods of amphetamine abuse. The amphetamine molecule is easily absorbed through the gastrointestinal tract, and thus oral administration is one common method by which the amphetamines are abused. The amphetamines are also well absorbed from intramuscular injections, the nasal mucosa, through the lungs if it is smoked, and from the general circulation if it is injected into a vein. When smoked, the amphetamine molecule is able to cross into the circulation easily, where it is then transported to the brain in just a matter of seconds. When injected into a vein, the amphetamine molecule is also able to reach the brain in just a matter of a few seconds. Amphetamine smoking and intravenous injection are the most common methods of amphetamine abuse in the United

States (Rollo et al., 2007). The amphetamine molecules are also easily absorbed through the tissues of the nasopharynx, allowing them to be "snorted" (Rollo et al., 2007). Although it might be absorbed through the tissues of the rectum, this is not a popular method of amphetamine administration among abusers and will not be discussed again in this chapter.

Subjective Effects of Amphetamines When Abused

The subjective effects of amphetamine abuse depend on several factors, including (a) possible concurrent substance use, (b) whether the individual has developed any degree of tolerance to the amphetamines, (c) the method by which s/he abuses the compound, (d) the purity of the compound being abused, (e) the method of administration, (f) the dose administered, (g) the duration of the amphetamine abuse, (h) the individual's expectations for the substance, and (i) the individual's state of health. All of these factors interact with the individual's expectations for the drug, to produce the subjective drug experience. Intravenous amphetamine abusers frequently report a period of intense, almost orgasmic feeling at first, followed by a gentle state of euphoria following the drug administration. Persons who take amphetamines orally or who "snort" it reported just the sense of gentle euphoria, which may last for a number of hours. In the case of methamphetamine, this "high" might last for 8–24 hours, a feature of this compound that makes it more addictive than cocaine[25] (Castro, Barrington, Walton, & Rawson, 2000; Rawson, Sodano, & Hillhouse, 2005). Abusers also report feeling less need for sleep, and, a reduced appetite. These are the effects that make amphetamine abuse desirable to the individual. The consequences of amphetamine abuse will be discussed later in the next section.

Amphetamine abusers quickly become tolerant to the euphoric effects of these compounds (Hanley, 2004). In an attempt to recapture the initial sense of euphoria, many amphetamine abusers engage in binge amphetamine use using the drug-free periods to allow the tolerance to dissipate (Gorelick, 2009). Other amphetamine abusers "graduate" from the oral use of these compounds to intranasal use, amphetamine smoking, or even injection. When the amphetamine injector becomes tolerant to the effects of the amphetamine being abused, s/he might embark on a "speed run" injecting more amphetamine every few minutes. In many cases, the cumulative

---

[23]Usually obtained from matches.

[24]The exact contaminants in illicit methamphetamine varies from one "batch" to another.

[25]Discussed in Chapter 9.

dose injected within a 24-hour span of time might be enough to kill a drug-naive person, and are well within the range of neurotoxicity found in animal studies (Haney, 2008). Such "speed runs" might last for a number of hours, or even days, after which time the abuser will usually fall into a state of deep sleep and/or depression that might reach suicidal proportions.

Consequences of Amphetamine Abuse

Because the amphetamines have a reputation for enhancing normal body functions (increased alertness, concentration, etc.), they are mistakenly viewed by some abusers as being less dangerous than other illicit compounds (United Nations, 2011). Unfortunately, there is a significant inter-individual variability for the development of amphetamine toxicity, with some individuals demonstrating evidence of toxic reactions at therapeutic dosage levels (Breggin, 2008). We will look at the toxic effects of amphetamine abuse on the major body organs in the following sections:

Brain Damage

Researchers have found that the abuse of any amphetamine can cause damage to the brain on both a regional and a cellular level, although it is not clear whether some of the amphetamine compounds are more likely to cause this effect than others (Yudko, Hall, & McPherson, 2009). Fatovich et al. (2010) found that at least one in five methamphetamine abusers had a lesion in the brain when examined by magnetic resonance imaging (MRI), although the significance of these findings were not clear, the authors admitted.

At the neural level, even at low dosage levels the amphetamines have been found to damage or destroy up to 50% of the dopamine-producing neurons (Rawson, Sodano, & Hillhouse, 2005). The danger of neurotoxicity from methamphetamine appears to be dose-related and is greater at higher doses of this compound (Hanson & Fleckenstein, 2009). At high doses the amphetamine compounds, especially methamphetamine, also appear to be highly toxic to both the dopaminergic and the serotonergic neural networks (Yudko et al., 2009). Animal research has found that dopamine and NE neurotransmitter levels might not return to normal for at least six months of abstinence from further amphetamine abuse (King & Ellinwood, 2005).

The causal mechanism(s) for this neurotoxicity is not clear, and there are at least two competing theories to account for this observed effect. One theory suggests that at high dosage levels methamphetamine and similar compounds will induce the release of peroxide and hydroxyquinone family of compounds, both of which function as "free radicals" at the synaptic junction (Ling et al., 2006). In theory, these toxins might then poison the neurons (especially those in the serotonergic neurotransmission system), inducing neural death (Jaffe et al., 2005; King & Ellinwood, 2005). A competing theory is that high doses of an amphetamine compound force the release of large amounts of glutamate, which in large amounts is also known to be neurotoxic.

Methamphetamine addicts have been found to have a significant reduction in the "gray" matter in the brains[26] on high-resolution MRI tests when compared with age-matched control subjects. The amphetamines have been implicated as the cause of temporary and permanent changes in cerebral blood flow patterns (Buffenstein, Heaster, & Ko, 1999; Payer & London, 2009) as well as cerebral vasculitis and cerebral vasospasm. There is also a known relationship between amphetamine abuse and strokes (Lezak, Howieson, Bingler, & Tranel, 2012) with abusers being at 200% higher risk for a stroke than nonabusers. High doses of methamphetamine might break down the blood–brain barrier,[27] increasing the risk of neurotoxicity and possible cerebral infections. Further, there is evidence of specific alterations in brain function, with some regions of the brain increasing in size during periods of active amphetamine abuse. This is thought to reflect localized trauma to regions of the brain such as the parietal cortex and caudate nucleus induced by long-term amphetamine abuse (Jernigan et al., 2005).

Hart, Marvin, and Smith (2012) found statistically significant[28] impairment on only a small number of cognitive functions in amphetamine abusers as compared with a control sample. The authors noted that the observed differences still fell within the normal range based on normative data for the measure(s) being used. Finally, the authors raised the possibility that researchers have a preconceived belief that *any* observed differences between methamphetamine abusers and control subjects on the measure(s) being used in that study

---

[26]See Glossary.

[27]See Glossary.

[28]*Statistically significant* differences are not always *clinically significant* differences if both scores fall in the normal range. An IQ of 110 and an IQ of 115 are statistically significant, but in real life is that difference of any real importance?

must be due to the methamphetamine abuse, a preconception that might have clouded the researchers to the implications of their findings. Thus, the issue of whether methamphetamine abuse causes cognitive decline has yet to be definitively settled. It has been demonstrated that methamphetamine can induce agitation, delirium, and seizures (Graber, 2007; Virani et al., 2009). Following methamphetamine cessation, many former abusers report having trouble concentrating for variable periods of time (Salo et al., 2009).

Also, there are rare reports of amphetamine-induced episodes of the serotonin syndrome,[29] which is potentially life threatening. Amphetamine abusers appear to be at increased risk for the development of Parkinson's disease (Lezak et al., 2012). Further, long-term amphetamine abuse can induce sleep disturbances that can persist for a number of months after their last use of such drugs.

Consequences of Amphetamine Abuse on the Emotions

Amphetamine abusers will often experience periods of deep depression between periods of active amphetamine use (Rawson et al., 2005). These depressive episodes can reach suicidal proportions. Further, the abuse of amphetamines can cause the user to experience significant levels of anxiety, and possibly panic attacks (Ballas, Evans, & Dinges, 2004; Breggin, 1998). Amphetamine-induced anxiety episodes may persist for weeks or even years after the individual's last use of an amphetamine, possibly because of drug-induced sensitization of those regions of the brain involved in the anxiety response (London et al., 2004). Often, the amphetamine abuser will attempt to control drug-induced anxiety through anxiolytics, marijuana, or alcohol.

During periods of active amphetamine use, the abuser might experience periods of drug-induced confusion, irritability, fear, suspicion or outright paranoia, hallucinations, or delusional thinking (Gorelick, 2009; Julien, 2005; King & Ellinwood, 2005; Miller, 2005). Other consequences of amphetamine abuse include agitation, assaultiveness, tremor, headache, irritability, weakness, and suicidal and homicidal tendencies (Albertson et al., 1999; Bella, Evans, & Dinges, 2004; Rawson et al., 2005). All the amphetamine compounds have the potential to induce a psychotic state that in its early stages is often indistinguishable from

paranoid schizophrenia. The risk of an amphetamine-induced psychosis appears to be strongest in methamphetamine abusers but also can be induced by the abuse of other amphetamine compounds (Ballas et al., 2004; Batki, 2001; Kosten & Sofuoglu, 2004). McKetin, Lubman, Baker, Dawe, and Ali (2013) concluded on the basis of their data that methamphetamine abusers were 5.3 times more likely to develop psychotic symptoms during periods of active methamphetamine abuse as compared with nonabusers. The authors also noted that there was a dose-related risk for the development of a methamphetamine psychosis.

Symptoms of an amphetamine-induced psychosis can result in symptoms as confusion, suspiciousness, paranoia, auditory and/or visual hallucinations, delusional thinking, anxiety, and possibly aggressive behavior (Haney, 2008; Iverson, Ivensen, Bloom, & Roth, 2009; King & Ellinwood, 2005; United Nations, 2011). Less common symptoms of an amphetamine-related psychosis include psychomotor retardation, incoherent speech, inappropriate or flattened affect, and depression (Srisurapanont, Marsden, Sunga, Wada, & Monterio, 2003). Chronic abuse of any amphetamine compound can induce a condition known as *formication*[30] (Fadem, 2009; Tekin & Cummings, 2003). Individuals with this condition have the subjective sensation of having bugs crawling on or just under their skin, and have been known to scratch or burn their skin in an attempt to rid themselves of these unseen creatures. The experience of formication appears to reflect the drug-induced over-stimulation of the nervous system.

The amphetamine psychosis usually clears within a few days to a few weeks after the cessation of drug use, although in 28% of the cases this condition might last longer than six months and might become permanent (Haney, 2004; Rawson & Ling, 2008; Rawson et al., 2005). There was an epidemic of amphetamine abuse in Japan following the end of World War II, and during this time researchers noted that the amphetamine psychosis required up to five years to clear in 15% of the cases (Flaum & Schultz, 1996). Using positron emission tomography (PET) scans, Sekine et al. (2001) were able to document long-lasting reductions in the number of dopamine transporter molecules in the brains of methamphetamine abusers. The authors suggested that this might be one mechanism through

---

[29]See Glossary.

[30]See Glossary.

which methamphetamine abuse is able to induce a psychotic state in the abuser. Although it was once thought that intravenous diazepam and haloperidol were the most effective in treating the toxic reaction to an amphetamine (Brust, 2004). However, recent evidence suggests that haloperidol might be neurotoxic to the cells of the substantia nigra region of the brain when used to treat amphetamine-induced psychotic states (Hatziperos, Raudensky, Soghomonian, & Wamamoto, 2007). Thus the optimal treatment of amphetamine-induced psychosis remains to be identified.

It was once thought that amphetamine-induced psychotic symptoms were rare. But, researchers have found that two-thirds of persons with a methamphetamine use disorder (MUD) will report at least some symptoms of a psychotic reaction upon detailed inquiry (Rawson et al., 2005). Again, it is not known whether other members of the amphetamines family of compounds share this characteristic. There is also evidence that the methamphetamine-related aggression may appear both during periods of acute intoxication, especially during the toxic psychosis, and during the withdrawal stage (Sekine et al., 2001; Sekine et al., 2006). There is an interesting body of research suggesting that high doses of methamphetamine are less likely to induce an aggressive response than are lower doses (Yudko et al., 2009). Amphetamine-related aggression is thought to reflect reductions in the serotonin transporter system in the brain, and that such changes in the serotonin transporter system seem to continue for at least a year after the individual's last amphetamine dose (Sekine et al., 2006). Further research is needed to determine the causes and clinical course of amphetamine-induced aggression.

The Digestive System

The amphetamines have a long history of being prescribed as anorexic agents to aid in weight loss programs, but their abuse can also result in such problems as diarrhea, constipation, nausea, vomiting, and ischemic colitis (Rawson et al., 2005; Sadock & Sadock, 2003). Further, because of their anorexic side-effect, individuals who abuse these compounds tend to neglect their daily dietary requirements, developing various dietary deficiencies as the body's stores of protein, various vitamins, and amino acids are depleted (Mooney, Glasner-Edwards, Rawson, & Ling, 2009).

Methamphetamine abuse is associated with acute abdominal pain, and gastroduodenal ulcers that sometimes can reach impressive size (Mooney et al., 2009). A poorly understood consequence of long-term methamphetamine abuse is a condition known as "meth mouth" (Davey, 2005; Fraber, 2007; Rawson et al., 2005). Individuals who suffer from this condition rapidly develop extensive tooth decay or damage and extensive dental repairs/extractions are often necessary. There are several competing theories about the cause of "meth mouth." First, methamphetamine abuse reduces saliva production to about 1/4th its normal level.[31] This interferes with saliva's role as a defense against dental decay. A second theory is that because methamphetamine abusers substitute sugar-sweetened soda/candy for food this increases their risk for dental decay (Rawson et al., 2005). A third possibility is that the compounds used to manufacture illicit methamphetamine cause or exacerbate dental decay, sometimes to the point where it becomes necessary to remove the individual's teeth and insert dental prosthetics (Davey, 2005; Rollo et al., 2007). This might reflect the fact that the first dental care that the methamphetamine abuser receives for many years is when s/he is first incarcerated.

The Cardiovascular System

There is strong evidence that amphetamine abusers are at higher risk for a myocardial infarction[32] than are nonabusers. The team of Westover, Nakonezny, and Haley (2008) examined the records of three million 18- to 44-year-old adults from the state of Texas, and concluded that amphetamine abusers were 61% more likely to suffer a myocardial infarction as nonusers the same age. One possible causal mechanism is the ability of compounds like methamphetamine to join sugar molecules to those of protein molecules (Treweek, Wee, Kopob, Dickerson, & Janda, 2007). This then alters the function of those protein molecules, possibly causing them to become toxic to the muscle cells of the heart. This hypothesis would seem to be supported by the work of Turdi et al. (2009), who found that methamphetamine alters biochemical processes necessary for proper cardiac muscle contraction, including the role of many proteins. This may also be one mechanism through which the abuse of methamphetamine can

---

[31]A condition known as *xerostomia*.

[32]Commonly called a "heart attack."

induce cardiac arrhythmias. Another phenomenon seen in some methamphetamine abusers is sudden cardiac death. Faith, Jiin-Cherng, Chan, and Chang (2012) offered hypothesis that this phenomenon is the result not of damage to the heart itself, although such is often found in amphetamine abusers, but to the failure of brain stem cardiovascular regulation.[33]

Long-term amphetamine abuse, especially the abuse of methamphetamine, has been implicated in the acceleration of plaque development in the coronary arteries of the user, contributing to coronary artery disease for the abuser (Karch, 2009). Amphetamine abuse can also result in hypertensive episodes, tachycardia, arrhythmias, and sudden cardiac death, when abused at high doses (Brust, 2004; Fadem, 2009; Fallas, Evans, & Dinges, 2004; Gitlow, 2007; Karch, 2009; Rawson et al., 2005). Other suspected cardiac complications from amphetamine abuse include cardiac ischemia, myocardial ischemia, angina, acute aortic dissection, and possible congestive heart failure (Acosta et al., 2005; Diercks et al., 2008; Oehmichen, Auer, & Konig, 2005; Wadland & Ferenchick, 2004). Methamphetamine abusers have been found to frequently suffer from "small vessel disease," which is to say micro-infarcts that individually do not seem significant but that collectively reduce the heart's effectiveness. This is why methamphetamine abusers have a 350% higher incidence of cardiomyopathy[34] than nonabusers of the same age (Yeo et al., 2007).

Amphetamine-induced hypertensive episodes are associated with an increased risk of stroke for the user. The amphetamine-related hypertension place stress on the walls of cerebral blood vessels, and if they are weakened by a birth defect, there is a danger of a hemorrhagic stroke as the weakened artery wall ruptures (Johnston & Elkins, 2008). Methamphetamine-related strokes are predominantly (but not exclusively) seen in the frontal lobes of the brain of the abuser (Mooney et al., 2009). Rare cases of methamphetamine-related cortical blindness have also been identified, as well as rare reports of subarachnoid hemorrhages (Mooney et al., 2009).

---

[33]The rostral ventrolateral medulla region of the brain stem is responsible for blood pressure regulation and control of the sympathetic nervous system. If this region of the brain stem is damaged, cardiac arrest can not be reversed, and the rest of the body then dies from what appears to be cardiac arrest.

[34]See Glossary.

Effects of Amphetamine Abuse on the Pulmonary System

Amphetamine abuse has been identified as the cause of such respiratory problems as sinusitis, pulmonary infiltrates, pulmonary edema, exacerbation of asthma in patients with this condition, pulmonary hypertension, and possible pulmonary hemorrhage or infarct (Acosta et al., 2005; Rawson et al., 2005). Methamphetamine smoking has been identified as the cause of shortness of breath, some forms of pneumonia and emphysema, possibly as a consequence of crushing tablets for smoking, thus admitting talc and other foreign agents into the lungs (Mooney et al., 2009).

Other Consequences of Amphetamine Abuse

The abuse of the amphetamines has been identified as a possible cause of ahabdomyloysis in some individuals, although the causal mechanism remains unclear at this time (Mooney et al., 2009). Amphetamine abuse has also been implicated as the cause of sexual performance problems for both men and women (Albertson et al., 1999; Finger, Lund, & Slage, 1997; Sadock & Sadock, 2007). In men, the chronic use of high doses of amphetamine compounds can cause an inhibition of orgasm for both sexes, and an inhibition of ejaculation in men. Individuals who abuse the amphetamines at high doses are at high risk for episodes of potentially fatal body hyperthermia (Ballas et al., 2004; King & Ellinwood, 2005; Rawson & Ling, 2008; Winslow, Voorhees, & Pehl, 2007).

There is evidence suggesting that methamphetamine abuse is the cause of liver damage (Karch, 2009; Rawson & Ling, 2008). Researchers have found that a "fatty liver" was present in 15.4% of methamphetamine abusers examined. Nine percent of methamphetamine abusers demonstrated frank cirrhosis of the liver (Karch, 2009). However, most methamphetamine abusers are polydrug abusers, and it is hard to determine whether methamphetamine itself is the cause of the observed liver damage, or just one of a range of compounds that induces the observed liver damage. Other identified consequences of amphetamine abuse include agitation, muscle twitching (Graber, 2007), and rarely hemorrhagic pancreatitis (Mooney et al., 2009).

The Addiction Potential of Amphetamines

There is no test by which a person might assess their potential to become addicted to these compounds, and if only for this reason even the experimental use of amphetamines is not recommended. There is evidence, however, that the amphetamines might induce an addiction in less time than cocaine (Payer & London, 2009). When abused, these compounds stimulate the brain's reward system (Haney, 2004), which is one of the reasons why they are such popular drugs of abuse. This effect, plus the brain's natural tendency to form strong memories of things that triggered the reward system, helps to sensitize the abuser to drug use "cues." Brust (2004) suggested that some individuals progress from their initial amphetamine abuse on through to full amphetamine addiction in just a few months, underscoring the addictive potential of these compounds.

Amphetamine Abstinence Syndrome

Following extended periods of amphetamine abuse at high doses, abusers or those who are addicted to amphetamines will experience a withdrawal syndrome including, anhedonia,[35] irritability, depression (which might reach the level of suicidal proportions), fatigue, increased need for sleep, sleep disturbance, REM "Rebound" and poor concentration (Brust, 2004; Miller, 2005). Post-amphetamine abuse anhedonia might last for months after the individual's last amphetamine use (Miller, 2005; Schuckit, 2006a). Other symptoms noted in the first few days following extended periods of amphetamine abuse include musculoskeletal pain, anorexia, "craving" for amphetamines, and impaired social function. These symptoms wax and wane in intensity over the first few weeks of abstinence (Brust, 2004). The amphetamine abstinence syndrome is noted for all cases where the individual was abusing an amphetamine at high doses for extended periods of time, although it is strongest in those individuals who abuse or are addicted to methamphetamine.

"Ice"

"Ice" is a form of methamphetamine prepared for smoking. The chemical properties of methamphetamine allow for it to be concentrated in a crystal that resembles a chip of ice (thus the name) or a piece of clear rock candy. The chip of concentrated methamphetamine is smoked, allowing the fumes to gain rapid access to the lungs and thus the general circulation, where it is transported to the brain in a matter of seconds. The practice of smoking Ice apparently began in Japan following

World War II, and knowledge of the practice was carried back to Hawaii by army troops involved in the post-war occupation of Japan. The practice became popular in Hawaii, and eventually spread to the continental United States where it has become popular in some parts of this country (Karch, 2009).

In the United States, the wave of Ice abuse went through three different phases: (1) In the earliest stages it was manufactured in Mexico and California, then shipped to various parts of the country (Rutkowski & Maxwell, 2009). (2) As the demand increased, local "meth labs" developed to meet local demand. The government has placed restrictions on precursor chemicals used in the production of methamphetamine such as pseudoephedrine, reducing local production to a limited degree. However, in spite of these restrictions about 35% of illicit methamphetamine used in the United States is produced through small, clandestine, operations using precursor chemicals such as pseudoephedrine and as few as two pieces of equipment. (3) The major sources of methamphetamine have moved to Mexico, and large amounts of the drug is then smuggled into the United States for consumption through a variety of routes.

How "Ice" Is Abused

Ice is a colorless, odorless, concentrated form of crystal methamphetamine. It is usually smoked, allowing the abuser to titer effects to suit his/her perceived needs. "Ice" is usually less expensive than cocaine on a dose-per-dose basis because it will last longer than cocaine when smoked (Rawson et al., 2005). Because of its duration of effect, it is *perceived* to be more potent than crack cocaine by the abuser in many cases. It does not require the elaborate equipment necessary for cocaine smoking, and does not produce a smell to alert others that it is being abused. Finally, if the individual should decide to stop smoking that "chip," it will reform as a crystal as it cools, allowing for the remainder to be used at another time. As will be discussed in the next chapter, when smoked, cocaine will burn off almost immediately, forcing the abuser to use it all at once.

Thus, the preferred method of methamphetamine abuse is smoking, although it may also be injected. On occasion, the chip of methamphetamine is melted down into a liquid and injected by intravenous methamphetamine abusers. This is usually seen if other forms of methamphetamine are not available to the user.

---

[35]See Glossary.

Subjective Effects of "Ice"

In contrast to cocaine-induced euphoria, which will last only 20 minutes, the euphoria induced by methamphetamine smoking is reported to last for hours. This is consistent with the pharmacological differences between cocaine and the amphetamines. The stimulant effect of cocaine lasts for a short period of time whereas that of an amphetamine compound might last for a period of hours.

The complications of methamphetamine smoking are essentially extensions of those seen with other forms of amphetamine abuse, because "Ice" is simply a form of methamphetamine, and that as such it shares the same side-effect and overdose profiles of other forms of amphetamine. Some abusers have reported experiencing a myocardial infarction up to 36 hours after their last use of "Ice," although the causal mechanism is not clear at this time (Tominga, Carcia, Dzierba, & Wong, 2004). Thus, "Ice" shares the potential for incredible physical, social, and emotional damage seen with the abuse or addiction to other forms of the amphetamines.

Methylphenidate

Effects of Methylphenidate When Abused

Methylphenidate is a favorite stimulate for students who wish to "cram" before an examination, although on occasion it is abused for other reasons (Vendantam, 2006). Serious methylphenidate abusers will crush the pills into a fine powder and then either inhale the power or inject it into a vein (Karch, 2009; Stahl, 2008; Volkow & Swanson, 2003). The strongest effects are achieved when the compound is injected into a vein. When injected, methylphenidate can induce a 50% blockade of the dopamine transport system within seconds, inducing a feeling of euphoria for the user (Volkow & Swanson, 2003; Volkow et al., 1998). For many abusers, this drug-induced sense of euphoria becomes desirable, and serves as a source of motivation for further methylphenidate abuse.

Consequences of Methylphenidate Abuse

One unanticipated consequence of methylphenidate abuse is physical addiction to this compound. Kim et al. (2009) administered methylphenidate to mice and found at the end of their trial period that the mice that received the methylphenidate had developed a greater number of spiny neurons in the nucleus accumbens than did the control mice. This is a region of the brain known to be associated with addiction to chemicals. However, the impact of this compound on the brain varies with the individual's motivation to use it: Patients who receive this medication for the control of ADHD usually do not develop signs of addiction to methylphenidate, whereas recreational abusers are prone to do so. This might reflect the timing or dosage of methylphenidate used by abusers as opposed to patients on this compound, or it might reflect another, as yet unidentified, process.

The physical consequences of methylphenidate abuse are essentially an extension of those seen when this compound is used medically. Even when used under a doctor's supervision, at recommended dosage levels, methylphenidate can occasionally trigger a toxic psychosis, with symptoms similar to those seen in paranoid schizophrenia (Aldhous, 2006; Karch, 2009). Most certainly large doses, such as those seen when this compound is abused, can trigger a toxic psychosis as well (Weiss, 2007). A small percentage of abusers will experience a methylphenidate-induced stroke, or cardiac problems (Karch, 2009). When methylphenidate abusers crush a table to use intravenously, they will inject not only the active agent of the compound, but also various "fillers"[36] designed to give the tablet shape and form (Volkow et al., 1998). The fillers may then form a thrombosis, causing damage to body tissues that depend on the now blocked artery for oxygenated blood and food. Sometimes, such damage occurs to the retina, causing visual field disturbance and possible blindness (Karch, 2009).

As this information would suggest, methylphenidate is not a safe compound, and the abuser takes on a very real risk of potential harm and addiction when s/he abuses this compound.

CNS Stimulant Abuse and the *Diagnostic and Statistical Manual of Mental Disorders,* 5th Edition[37]

The *Diagnostic and Statistical Manual of Mental Disorders,* 5th edition *(DSM-5)* (American Psychiatric Association, 2013) classified the (CNS) stimulants as

---

[36]See Glossary.

[37]The material presented here is to illustrate the relationship between the alcohol use disorders and the *Diagnostic and Statistical Manual of Mental Disorders* (5th edition). This material should not be interpreted as, nor should it be used as, a diagnostic manual.

including amphetamines or amphetamine-like compounds, as well as cocaine. The *DSM-5* identified five patterns of CNS stimulant abuse:

- *Stimulant (CNS) use disorder*
- *Stimulant intoxication*
- *Stimulant withdrawal*
- *Other stimulant-induced disorders*
- *Unspecified stimulant-related disorder*

Of these five categories of CNS stimulant abuse the *Stimulant use disorder* refers to what was earlier identified as an addiction to a CNS stimulant.[38] Some of the symptoms of which include the development of tolerance over time, recurrent use of the stimulant in situations where its use is known to be hazardous, a characteristic withdrawal syndrome, and continued use in spite of awareness of the drug's negative effects on the individual's vocational, academic, social, occupational or familial duties, to name a few of the criteria that must be met. Of the eleven criteria suggested by the American Psychiatric Association (2013) the individual would need to meet two within a 12-month period for a diagnosis of a stimulant use disorder. Modifiers to the diagnosis include whether the individual is in early or sustained remission, and if the individual was in a controlled environment where access to these compounds was difficult.

The *DSM-5* manual then identifies whether the individual's addiction to the stimulant was mild, moderate, or severe, further breaking down the list for the abuse of an amphetamine compound, cocaine, or an unspecified compound with appropriate ICD-10 classification numbers for each condition. In rare cases, physical dependence on a CNS stimulant has developed after just one week of continuous use (American Psychiatric Association, 2013), and so the length of time that a person has abused a stimulant should not be used as a yardstick to assess whether they are potentially addicted to one of these compounds or not. The development of tolerance and of a withdrawal syndrome are more reliable markers of a *stimulant use disorder* in the opinion of the author of your text.

The *DSM-5* manual does warn that the stimulant use disorders often mimic the manifestations of primary psychiatric disorders such as major depression or schizophrenia, making the differential diagnosis of

a stimulant use disorder difficult. As noted above, initially abusers experiencing *stimulant intoxication* will report feelings of increased energy and well-being. The signs of stimulant intoxication are discussed in this chapter as well as in the *DSM-5* manual. The physical manifestations of CNS stimulant abuse and potential dangers associated with the abuse of these compounds are as identified in this chapter or the Chapter Eight if the compound is cocaine. The *DSM-5* manual does identify a required modifier (whether the individual was addicted to amphetamines, an amphetamine-like compound, or cocaine), and suggested that if perceptual disturbances are present in the absence of medical conditions that might also cause such problems that this be noted as well.

Stimulant withdrawal develops within a few hours of the individual's last use of a CNS stimulant and the symptoms reviewed in this chapter should be interpreted as a sign of stimulant withdrawal only if the individual does not suffer from a medical condition that might induce such symptoms according to the *DSM-5* manual. *Other stimulant-induced disorders* are conditions that resemble symptoms of other psychiatric conditions that are caused by the abuse of stimulants. An excellent example would be the depressive symptoms that develop during stimulant withdrawal that normally resolve after the withdrawal process has ended. Finally, the *unspecified stimulant-related disorders* reflect cases where the individual's stimulant use causes impairment in their social, occupational, familial, or vocational lives but which do not meet the criteria for a *substance use disorder* diagnosis.

Chapter Summary

There are a number of compounds that function as CNS stimulants, including the natural substance ephedrine, which was isolated from the ephedra plant. This was found to be useful in the treatment of asthma, but fears developed that the demand for ephedrine might outstrip supply. Chemists examined compounds that had similar chemical structures in the hopes of finding substitutes. The analogs of ephedrine, known as the amphetamines, were isolated in the 1880s, but it was not until the early 1930s that they were introduced for the treatment of asthma. Later, these compounds were also found to have a paradoxical calming effect on some children who had what was then known as *hyperactivity*.

---

[38]The reader is referred to the *Diagnostic and Statistical Manual of Mental Disorders* (5th edition) (*DSM-5*) (American Psychiatric Association, 2013) for the full list of diagnostic criteria suggested by the American Psychiatric Association as signs of a stimulant use disorder.

Drug abusers also found that the effects of the amphetamines were similar to those of cocaine, which was known to be quite dangerous to abuse. The ampules of amphetamine-containing liquid could be carefully unwrapped, broken open, and the contents might be injected, providing a "high" similar to that seen with cocaine, but which lasted for a longer period of time. At the same time, physicians were prescribing amphetamines for their anorexic side effect, and as an aid to the treatment of depression. However, as physicians have come to better understand the abuse potential of amphetamines, they have come under increasingly strict controls.

Unfortunately, the amphetamines might also be easily manufactured in illicit laboratories, so when drug addicts were unable to gain access to pharmaceutical quality amphetamines, they switched to illicit sources of these compounds, and there was a thriving manufacture/distribution system for the amphetamines. The most commonly abused amphetamine is methamphetamine, although the other members of the amphetamine family may also be abused from time to time. In the process, the current generation of drug abusers has come to relearn the lesson that amphetamine abusers of the 1960s had discovered through grim experience: "Speed kills."

CHAPTER 9

Cocaine Abuse and Dependence

Introduction

Future historians will note that there have been at least three distinct cocaine use "epidemics" in the United States. In each epidemic cocaine abusers move through several steps in which (a) the warnings of earlier generations of cocaine abusers are ignored, (b) cocaine becomes a rare drug of abuse, (c) its abuse becomes more widespread, (d) the warnings of earlier generations are confirmed, (e) cocaine abuse is again deemed to be both dangerous, and not a panacea, and (f) its abuse becomes less and less common until it is again a rarely abused compound.

This cycle is clearly seen in the United States in the last century. Cocaine abuse was common in the first decade(s) of the 20th century and its dangers were well known to both drug abusers and physicians. In the 1930s the recently introduced amphetamine compounds became the stimulant of choice, in part because they were reputed to be a safe alternative to cocaine. As the dangers associated with amphetamine abuse became known, there was a resurgence of cocaine abuse in the early to mid 1980s. This wave of cocaine abuse peaked around the year 1986, and then gradually declined as drug abusers again returned to the abuse of the amphetamine compounds. However, the problem of cocaine abuse has never entirely disappeared, and there is evidence that cocaine abuse is again growing in popularity in the United States as reflected by the fact that the United States currently consumes 37% of the world's cocaine (Haney, 2008; Raw Data, 2013). Thus, the cycle appears to be starting again. In this chapter, we will discuss the use and abuse of cocaine.

A Brief History of Cocaine

Biologists believe that at some distant point in the past a member of the plant species *Erythroxylon coca* began to produce a toxin in its leaves to protect itself from predation by insects or animals (Breiter, 1999). This neurotoxin, cocaine, is quite effective in this role, allowing the plant to thrive in the relatively thin atmosphere of the high Andes mountains. Then, at least 5,000 years ago, it was discovered by early settlers of the region that by chewing the leaves of the coca plant, it was possible to ease feelings of fatigue, thirst, and hunger, allowing them to work for longer periods of time in the thin mountain air (Levis & Garmel, 2005).

By the time that the first European explorers arrived, they discovered the thriving Incan empire in what they called the "New World." The coca plant was used extensively by these people who believed it to be a gift from the sun god (Brust, 2004). The use of cocaine was generally reserved for the upper classes of the Inca society when the first European explorers arrived and eventually conquered the Inca Empire (Brust, 2004). The conquerors soon discovered that by giving native workers coca leaves to chew on, they would become more productive, and they encouraged its widespread use for that reason. Even today, the practice of chewing coca leaves, or drinking a form of "tea" brewed from coca leaves, is commonplace in South America. Natives will chew coca leaves mixed with lime obtained from sea shells, a practice that helps to negate the bitter taste of the coca leaf itself. The cocaine that is released by the practice of chewing is then absorbed into the chewer's system, providing a stimulatory effect that negates the fatigue normally felt when working at the high altitudes of the Andes. This practice may also allow the chewer to gain some small measure of nutritional benefit, although this has not been scientifically studied. European scientists took a passing interest in the coca plant, attempted to isolate the compound(s) that made it so effective in warding off hunger and fatigue and in 1855[1] a chemist by the name of Albert Neiman isolated a compound that was later named cocaine. This accomplishment allowed scientists of the era to obtain large amounts of relatively pure cocaine for research purposes. One experiment was the injection of concentrated cocaine into the bloodstream using another recent invention: the hypodermic needle. The world has not been the same since.

By the late 1800s extracts from the coca leaf were used to make a wide range of drinks and elixirs, one of which even won an endorsement from the Pope himself (Martensen, 1996). No less a figure than Sigmund Freud experimented with cocaine as a possible treatment for narcotic withdrawal symptoms. Freud later tried to warn others of his mistaken perception that cocaine was an effective treatment for these disorders, and that it was addictive but was ignored by scientists of the era (Gold & Jacobs, 2005; Markel, 2011). Cocaine had entered European society, and even today it remains stubbornly entrenched as a drug of abuse.

The natives of the high Andes continue to chew cocaine leaves to help them work in the rarified mountain air. Some researchers think that the fact that they are able to discontinue cocaine use when they descend to lower altitudes is evidence that it is not very addictive. However, this argument is undermined by the fact that chewing the coca leaf is not an effective method of administration. Much of the cocaine that is released during cocaine chewing is destroyed by digestive juices and the "first pass" metabolism process.[2] Still, the blood levels of cocaine obtained when cocaine leaves are chewed are in the lower end of the blood levels achieved when a cocaine abuser "snorts" cocaine powder, and although the amount of cocaine that reaches the brain is barely enough to have a psychoactive effect cocaine chewers are still thought to become addicted to it by some scientists (Karch, 2009). Thus, the question of whether coca chewing results in cocaine addiction has not been resolved.

Cocaine in U.S. History

The history of cocaine use in the United States is, surprisingly, intertwined with attempts to control alcohol use by the town fathers of Atlanta, Georgia. In response to the prohibition against alcohol use on Sundays John Stith-Pemberton developed a "temperance drink" (Martensen, 1996, p. 1615), which was alcohol-free but originally contained 60 mg of cocaine per 8 ounce serving (Gold, 1997). In time, the world would come to know Stith-Pemberton's product by the name of "Coke-Cola," and it has since become one of the most popular soft drinks sold.

The fact that Coke-cola once contained cocaine is surprising to modern readers. But it is important to keep in mind that at the turn of the 20th century consumer protection laws were virtually nonexistent, and compounds such as cocaine and morphine were available without a prescription and were often hidden ingredients in a range of "patent" medicines and other products. This practice contributed to a wave of cocaine abuse in Europe between the years 1886 and 1891, and in the United States between 1894 and 1899, and again between 1921 and 1929. These waves of cocaine abuse or addiction were fueled by the common practice of using cocaine as a "hidden" ingredient in so many products. Fears fueled by rumors that cocaine was corrupting Southern blacks prompted both the passage of the pure food and drug act of 1906 and the classification of cocaine as a "narcotic" in 1914 (Martensen, 1996). The pure food and drug act of 1906 did not prohibit the use of cocaine in products, but it did require that the ingredients be identified on the label, allowing consumers to avoid products that contained compounds such as cocaine. This prompted many manufacturers to entirely remove it from their products. When the Harrison narcotics act of 1914 was passed, the nonmedical use of cocaine in the United States became illegal.

These regulations, combined with the geographical isolation of the United States in World War I prior to

[1]Schuckit (2006) reported that cocaine was first isolated in 1857, not 1855.

[2]Discussed in Chapter 3.

the entry of this country into the conflict, and the introduction of the amphetamines in the 1930s virtually eliminated cocaine abuse in the United States. It did not resurface as a major drug of abuse until the late 1960s when it was viewed as the "champagne of drugs" (White, 1989, p. 34). As a new generation of drug abusers discovered its euphoric effects in the 1970s and 1980s it became increasingly popular as a drug of abuse. Reports of the physical damage induced by cocaine abuse at the turn of the 20th century or of its addiction potential were dismissed as exaggerations, or, given the primitive state of medicine in the era, as being a misdiagnosis of another condition (Peele, 2010; Walton, 2002).

A concurrent and possibly contributing factor to the rise of cocaine was the growing disillusionment with the amphetamines that started in the mid-1960s. As drugs of abuse, the amphetamines had gained the reputation as being both dangerous and potentially fatal, recreational substances. Drug users would warn each other "speed kills," a reference to the dangers associated with the use of "speed" (the slang term for the amphetamines). Cocaine had gained the reputation as being able to induce the same sense of euphoria as the amphetamines without its dangers. This, plus the emerging restrictions on amphetamine production and use, and its reputation as a "glamorous" drug, all helped to focus the attention of illicit drug abusers on cocaine in the late 1960s.

By the middle of the 1980s, the cocaine distribution and sales network in the United States had become the seventh largest industry of its time, generating an estimated $21 billion/year in profits. This in turn attracted the attention of what has come to loosely be called "organized crime." Cocaine distributors were looking for ways to increase sales and to open new markets for their "product" in the United States. The primary method of cocaine abuse during this era was intranasal inhalation of cocaine powder, although some abusers did smoke it after going through a long, dangerous, process of transforming the powder into a smokable form of cocaine. After a period of experimentation "crack" cocaine was developed. Essentially, crack is cocaine prepared for smoking before sale to the abuser, and its abuse now accounts for approximately 50% of the illicit cocaine market in the United States (Greydanus & Patel, 2005).

The wave of cocaine abuse that swept across the United States in the 1980s and early 1990s is a topic worthy of a book in its own right, and will be mentioned only in passing in this text. Just as the recently introduced amphetamines were adopted as a replacement for the known dangers of cocaine by drug abusers in the 1930s, cocaine was viewed by some as a safe alternative to amphetamine abuse in the 1970s and 1980s. The wave of cocaine abuse peaked in the mid-1980s, and the numbers of cocaine abusers in this country have slowly declined in the years since then. However, it has not disappeared entirely, and there is evidence that it might again be growing in popularity in some parts of the country (Acosta, Haller, & Schnoll, 2005; Gold & Jacobs, 2005).

Current Medical Uses of Cocaine

Cocaine was once a respected pharmaceutical compound used in the treatment of a variety of conditions. It was found to function as a local anesthetic by blocking the movement of sodium ions into the neuron, thus slowing the rate at which the neuron is able to transmit pain messages to the brain (Drummer & Odell, 2001). It was once used by physicians in surgical procedures in the ear, nose, throat, rectum, and vagina. As a topical anesthetic its effects would begin in about one minute, and would last for up to two hours (Wilson, Shannon, & Shields, 2011). No less a figure than Sigmund Freud exploited this characteristic of cocaine toward the end of his life when he struggled with cancer of the tongue (Stahl, 2008). Cocaine is still occasionally used by otolaryngologists today,[3] especially because of its vasoconstrictive and analgesic effects, but for the most part it has been supplemented by newer, safer, compounds.

Scope of the Problem of the Cocaine Use Disorders

The amount of land dedicated to the cultivation of cocaine around the world decreased by approximately one-third in the first decade of the 21st century although there are signs that this figure is stabilizing (United Nations, 2011). Globally, an estimated 0.3% to 0.5% of the world's population (or 14 to 20.5 million persons) is thought to have abused cocaine in the past year (United Nations, 2011). The vast majority of the world's production of cocaine was intended for the illicit drug market. Authorities have been able to interdict a significant

---

[3]Ear, nose, and throat specialists.

proportion of the total amount of cocaine produced, forcing distributors to resort to even more ingenuous methods to transport their product.[4]

The United States is the largest consumer of cocaine in the world, although collectively Europe consumes approximately the same amount of cocaine as does the United States (United Nations, 2011). Each day in the United States an estimated 2,000 persons use cocaine for the first time (McCord et al., 2008). Nationally 5–10% of the population, or about 30 million people, have abused cocaine at least once (Hahn & Hoffman, 2001; O'Connor, Rusyniak, & Bruno, 2005). Many of those who have abused cocaine have done so out of curiosity, and the number of regular cocaine abusers in this country is estimated to only be between 1.7 and 2 million people (Acosta et al., 2005; Carroll & Ball, 2005).

In spite of mass media campaigns to the contrary, cocaine is not automatically addictive. Perhaps 15% of those who begin to use cocaine will ultimately become addicted to it (Budney, Roffman, Stephens, & Walker, 2007), whereas 28% become regular users[5] (Leamon, Wright, & Myrick, 2008). There are wide variations in the popularity of cocaine abuse around the United States. It has been estimated that the per capita cocaine abuse in New York City is 172 grams per person, 73 grams per person per year in Washington, D.C. and 40 grams per year in San Francisco ("New York Remains Cocaine Capital of the World," 2007). As these figures suggest, cocaine remains a significant part of the illicit drug problem in the United States at this time.

Pharmacology of Cocaine

Cocaine is best absorbed into the body when administered as the water-soluble compound cocaine hydrochloride. After entering the circulation, it is quickly transported to the brain and other blood-rich organs of the body. The level of cocaine in the brain is usually higher than the blood plasma levels, especially in the first two hours following the drug administration ("Cocaine and the Brain," 1994; Karch, 2009). Cocaine's effects on the user appear

to be stronger when the levels are rising, with the same blood concentration that causes euphoria when the blood levels are rising causing dysphoria[6] when the blood levels are falling (Karch, 2009; O'Brien, 2006).

The pharmacological effects of cocaine are quite short-lived. The effects of "snorted" cocaine begin in 3–5 minutes, peak in about 10–20 minutes and last about an hour (Mendelson & Mello, 2010). Cocaine smoked and cocaine injected result in an almost instantaneous "rush" experience as the drug begins to work, and the half-life of injected or "snorted" cocaine is estimated to be between 30 and 90 minutes (Jaffe, Rawson, & Ling, 2005; Leamon et al., 2008). Mendelson and Mello (2008, 2010) offered a more conservative estimate of cocaine's half-life as between 40 and 60 minutes. The difference between these two estimates might reflect the significant inter-individual variability in the speed with which the body of different users is able to biotransform and eliminate cocaine. During the process of cocaine biotransformation, the liver will produce about a dozen metabolites of cocaine (Karch, 2009). About 80% of a single dose of intravenously administered cocaine is biotransformed into either *benzoylecgonine* (BEG) or *ecgonine methyl ester* (Levis & Garmel, 2005). Between 5% and 10% of a single dose is eliminated from the body unchanged, and about 10% is biotransformed into other compounds that are of minor importance and will not be mentioned again. Neither of the primary metabolites of cocaine has any known psychoactive effect. BEG has a half-life of about 7.5 hours and might be detected in urine samples for 48–72 hours. Thus urine toxicology tests usually attempt to isolate this cocaine metabolite rather than cocaine itself as evidence of cocaine use.

At the neural level, cocaine forces the release of dopamine stores from the presynaptic[7] neurons involved in the reward network of the brain, establishing strong drug-centered memories (Brust, 2004). This makes clinical sense: In the natural world it would be advantageous for sources of positive reinforcers such as food, water, or sex to produce a strong memory trace in the individual's brain so that s/he could find that positive reinforcer again when s/he wanted to. Unfortunately, cocaine abuse "short circuits" this reward system, causing a reward cascade

---

[4]Such as semi-submersible and submersible submarines.

[5]Regular cocaine use is a stepping stone to addiction. Some of these regular abusers will become addicted, and others will step back from the brink of addiction. Thus, about half of those who become regular users will become addicted to it.

[6]See Glossary.

[7]See Glossary.

stronger than that produced by natural reinforcers (Hanley, 2004). Animal based research suggests that cocaine suppresses the action of gene 9A, which in effect locks the "pleasure center" of the brain into the "on" position (Maze et al., 2010). It is not known whether this same process is found in humans, but their findings are suggestive of one mechanism through which cocaine is able to induce craving for additional cocaine use in abusers.[8]

Cocaine's reinforcing effects appear to involve those neurons that use dopamine as their primary neurotransmitter. There are at least five subtypes of dopamine receptors in the brain, and cocaine's reinforcing effects appear to involve the dopamine D1 receptor subtype (Romach et al., 1999). The authors administered an experimental Dopamine D1 blocking compound to cocaine abusing volunteers, and discovered that they failed to experience any major euphoria when they received cocaine. Not surprisingly, the Dopamine D1 receptor sites are located in the limbic system of the brain, where the brain's reward system is thought to be located. Research evidence suggests that cocaine also activates the opioid *mu* and *kappa* receptor sites, possibly as an indirect result of its ability to activate the dopamine D1 receptors.

Habitual cocaine abuse is thought to cause long-term changes in the activity of compounds in the brain such as ΔFosB[9] (Nestler, 2005) as well as the serotonin and norepinephrine neurotransmitter systems, although the significance of this effect is not known at this time (Acosta et al., 2005; Reynolds and Bada, 2003). Cocaine also alters the function of a protein known as *Postsynaptic density-95* (Sanna & Koob, 2004). Long-term changes in this protein, which is involved in the process of helping the synaptic junction between neurons adjust to changes in neurotransmitter density, are also thought to be involved in the process of learning and memory formation. This is thought to be one reason why cocaine abusers form such intense memories of their cocaine use, and why the relapse rate among newly abstinent cocaine abusers is so high (Acosta et al., 2005; Sanna & Koob, 2004).

Although abused for its euphoric effects, tolerance to cocaine-induced euphoria develops very rapidly (Schuckit, 2006a). To counteract the tolerance, the abuser may (a) increase the amount of cocaine abused to the point where it may be lethal to the drug-naive abuser or (b) inject small amounts of additional cocaine 2–3 times an hour after the initial euphoria begins to wear off. The ever-increasing dosage level of cocaine interferes with the normal function of the region of the brain known as the diencephalon, which helps to regulate body temperature. At the same time, the cocaine will cause the surface blood vessels to constrict, making it harder for the body to cool itself. These effects can result in cocaine-induced hyperthermia,[10] which is potentially life threatening as the abuser's body attempts to retain body heat at the very time that it will need to release it (Gold & Jacobs, 2005; Jaffe et al., 2005; Mendelson & Mello, 2008).

Drug Interactions Involving Cocaine

There has been remarkably little research into cocaine-pharmaceutical interactions (Karch, 2009). It is known that cocaine abusers often turn to other chemicals as a way to control the unwanted side effects of their cocaine use (Mendelson & Mello, 2008). For example, more than 62–90% of cocaine abusers have a concurrent alcohol use disorder (Gold & Jacobs, 2005). The use of cocaine during alcohol intoxication can alter the pharmacokinetics of both compounds. Scientists have observed a 30% increase in the blood plasma levels of cocaine in persons who abuse both alcohol and cocaine simultaneously, as the alcohol interferes with the ability of the liver to biotransform the cocaine. Further, a small amount (<10%) of the cocaine in the abuser's body will be transformed into *cocaethylene* (Karch, 2009; Repetto & Gold, 2005). Cocaethylene is a toxic compound that is thought to be 25–30 times as likely to induce death as cocaine (Karan, Haller, & Schnoll, 1998). Cocaethylene is thought to function as a calcium channel blocking agent in the heart, and has a biological half-life that is five times longer than that of cocaine alone, factors that are thought to increase the user's risk of sudden cardiac death 18 fold as compared to

---

[8]It is interesting to note, however, that Sukel (2012) discussed research suggesting that research has found more activity in the nucleus accumbens of female rat mothers ("dams") in response to exposure to their pups than to cocaine. When the female rats were lactating, it appeared as though the reward system was suppressed even when the female rats were exposed to cocaine. Such research suggests that there is still much to learn about cocaine-mediated activation of the brain's reward system.

[9]See Glossary.

[10]See Glossary.

that of the nondrinking cocaine abuser (Acosta et al., 2005; Hahn & Hoffman, 2001; Repetto & Gold, 2005). The concurrent use of alcohol and cocaine has also been identified as an element in the development of a potentially fatal pulmonary edema (Ciraulo, Shader, Greenblatt, & Creelman, 2006). Unfortunately, cocaethylene may extend the period of cocaine-induced euphoria, possibly by blocking dopamine reuptake, which acts as an incentive for the individual to continue to coadminister these compounds in spite of these dangers.

It is not uncommon for cocaine abusers to use both cocaine and a narcotic analgesic[11] simultaneously. For reasons that are not well understood, cocaine appears to enhance the respiratory depressive effects of the narcotic analgesics, possibly contributing to potentially fatal respiratory arrest. Further, as will be discussed later in this chapter, cocaine can induce feelings of irritation or anxiety, feelings that the abuser often attempts to control through alcohol, sedating agents and/or marijuana. There is evidence that patients taking disulfiram as part of a treatment program for alcoholism achieve higher blood levels when they take cocaine, and this combination appears to cause a higher heart rate than when the person abuses just cocaine (Karch, 2009). There is also evidence that persons taking antiviral medications may achieve higher blood concentrations of cocaine as the two compounds compete for biotransformation through the same metabolic pathway in the liver. Although this list is not comprehensive, it does illustrate the fact that cocaine can interact with many other drugs of abuse or medications.

How Illicit Cocaine Is Produced

The production of illicit cocaine has changed little over the past decades. First, the cocaine leaves are harvested; a procedure that in some parts of South America might be done as often as once every 3–4 months. The collected leaves are dried in the open sunlight for a few hours to a few days. Although this is technically illegal, the local authorities are quite tolerant and do little to interfere with this process for the most part. Then the dried leaves are placed in a pit lined with plastic then mixed with water and sulfuric acid (White, 1989). The leaves are then crushed by workers who wade into the

pit in their bare feet, stomping the mixture and from time to time draining off the liquids. Lime is mixed with the residue, which then forms a paste, which is called "cocaine base." It takes 500 kilograms of leaves to produce just one kilogram of cocaine base (White, 1989).

Next, compounds like water, gasoline, acid, potassium permanganate, and ammonia are added to the cocaine paste. This forms a reddish-brown liquid that is then mixed with a few drops of ammonia. This produces a milky solid which is dried, and then dissolved in a solution of hydrochloric acid and acetone, forming small particles that settle to the bottom of the tank. This is cocaine hydrochloride, which is filtered and dried under heating lights, and is then packed and shipped, usually in kilogram packages. As the cocaine moves through the distribution network, it is usually repeatedly adulterated, increasing its bulk and thus the profits for the dealer at each level of the distribution process.

Methods of Cocaine Abuse

Cocaine is abused in a number of ways. First, cocaine hydrochloride powder might be inhaled through the nose ("intranasal" use, or "snorting," technically known as "insufflation"). It may also be injected directly into a vein. Cocaine hydrochloride is a water-soluble compound, and thus is well adapted to both intranasal and intravenous use. Cocaine "base" might be smoked, and the fumes then rapidly gain access to the circulation for transport to the brain. Finally, cocaine might be administered sublingually (under the tongue), where the blood-rich tissues under the tongue allow it to gain access to the circulation as it is absorbed. Each method of administration, although offering advantages to the abuser, also exposes the user to potentially toxic levels of cocaine in spite of the assertion of drug dealers that they are "safe" (Repetto & Gold, 2005).

Insufflation

In 1903, the first case reports of cocaine-induced septal perforation began to appear in medical journals, suggesting that the practice of "snorting" cocaine is at least a century old (Karch, 2009). Those who "snort" cocaine arrange the powder on a piece of glass (such as a mirror), usually in thin lines of 1/2 to 2 inches long and about 1/8th of an inch wide (Acosta et al., 2005). One gram of

---

[11]A practice known as "speedballing."

cocaine will usually yield around 30 such "lines" of cocaine (Acosta et al., 2005). The powder is diced up, usually with a razor blade to enhance absorption. The powder is then inhaled through a tube such as a drinking straw, or rolled up paper depositing the powder on the blood-rich tissues of the sinus membranes. About 60% of the cocaine deposited in the nasal passages is rapidly absorbed, with the first cocaine reaching the general circulation in 30–90 seconds and it is then rapidly transported to the brain. The physical sensations peak intensity about 15–30 minutes after insufflation and begin to wear off in about 45–60 minutes following a single dose (Kosten & Sofuoglu, 2004). With repeated administrations, the peak effects might last twice as long as this (Hoffman & Hollander, 1997).

Because cocaine is a potent vasoconstrictor, it limits its own absorption through the nasal mucosa, with the result being that only 60% of the cocaine deposited into the nasal passages is absorbed (Gold & Jacobs, 2005). Then 70–80% of the cocaine absorbed through the nasal passages is biotransformed by the liver *before* it is able to reach the brain, limiting the intensity of cocaine-induced euphoria experienced by the abuser. These limiting factors make the inhalation of cocaine an ineffective means of cocaine abuse, and it is usually only seen in casual or inexperienced abusers.

Intravenous Cocaine Administration

It is possible to mix cocaine hydrochloride power with water, and then inject it directly into a vein. Intravenously administered cocaine will reach the brain in less than 30 seconds (Kosten & Sofuoglu, 2004), with virtually all of the injected cocaine being absorbed into the user's body (Acosta et al., 2005). Although this allows for the rapid introduction of cocaine into the user's body, it does not allow the abuser to titrate the dose for optimal effects, and this may cause unwanted agitation to the cocaine abuser. However, it is an effective way to achieve the "rush" or "flash" experience so desired by intravenous cocaine abusers (discussed later in this chapter).

Sublingual Cocaine Abuse

Cocaine hydrochloride powder is well adapted for absorption through the blood-rich tissues of the mouth, where it is rapidly absorbed and then transported to the brain in a manner similar to that seen with intranasal cocaine use. This method of cocaine

abuse has not been studied in detail although theoretically an unknown percentage of the cocaine that is absorbed will be subjected to the "first pass metabolism" effect. It is not known what percentage of the cocaine that is absorbed will ultimately reach the brain.

Rectal Cocaine Abuse

This practice is popular among certain groups, such as male homosexuals (Karch, 2009). Cocaine's local anesthetic properties provide some degree of relief from what would otherwise be painful forms of sexual activity. Unfortunately, the anesthetic properties of cocaine might also mask the pain signals that would warn the individual of physical trauma to the tissues of the rectal area, increasing the individual's risk for infection and possible death (Karch, 2009).

Cocaine Smoking

Historical evidence would suggest that the practice of burning or smoking, different parts of the coca plant dates back to at least 3,000 B.C.E. when the Incas would burn leaves at religious festivals (Hahn & Hoffman, 2001). The practice of smoking cocaine resurfaced in the late 1800s, when coca cigarettes were used to treat hay fever and opiate addiction. By the year 1890, cocaine smoke was being used in the United States for the treatment of whooping cough, bronchitis, asthma, and a range of other conditions. Although the practice of cocaine smoking for medicinal reasons dates back for more than a century, *recreational* cocaine smoking did not become popular until the mid-1980s.

Although cocaine hydrochloride was a popular drug of abuse in the 1970s and 1980s, abusers discovered that it could not be easily smoked. It had to be transformed back into the cocaine base ("freebase" or "base") through a complex, labor-intensive process that involved the use of potentially explosive compounds. The obtained mixture was then passed through a filter in an attempt to remove as many impurities as possible then smoked, inducing a sense of intense pleasure. Seventy to ninety percent of the cocaine enters the circulation from the lungs when it is smoked, reaching the brain in as little as seven seconds (Hahn & Hoffman, 2001; Mendelson & Mello, 2008). However, the risk of fire and/or explosion inherent in transforming cocaine back into coca base limited its popularity in the United States. To solve this problem, illicit distributors introduced a form of cocaine base that was already prepared for smoking: crack. This form of cocaine is called crack, because of the sound that it makes when smoked (Schuckit, 2006a).

Crack is essentially a solid chunk of cocaine base designed to be smoked before sale at the local level. This was done in illicit "factories" or "laboratories" that produce small, ready-to-use pellets that allow one or two inhalations. This form of cocaine for smoking has almost entirely replaced "freebase" cocaine in the United States (Karch, 2009). Although it would appear to be less expensive than cocaine prepared for intravenous injection, in reality crack is about as expensive on a gram-per-gram basis (Karch, 2009). Further, in spite of its reputation in some quarters as being safer than intravenously administered cocaine, it shares the same dangers as those found in cocaine injection.

On rare occasions, intravenous cocaine abusers have been known to attempt to dissolve pellets of crack in alcohol, lemon juice, vinegar, or water and inject the resulting mixture (Acosta et al., 2005). This is usually done by intravenous cocaine addicts who are unable to obtain cocaine hydrochloride for injection.

Gastrointestinal Absorption

It is possible to absorb cocaine through the gastrointestinal tract. If the person were to be a body packer[12] and one of the packets were to rupture, the individual will absorb a massive cocaine overdose resulting in the death of the individual (Karch, 2009). Coca-tea (commonly used in South America) will also allow the individual to absorb significant amounts of cocaine if too much is consumed. This can cause the abuser to test "positive" for cocaine and its metabolites on urine toxicology testing, and thus the use of tea made from coca leaves should be avoided by those persons subject to urine toxicology testing (Karch, 2009).

Subjective Effects of Abused Cocaine

There are several factors that influence the individual's subjective experience of cocaine abuse. First are the individual's *expectations* for the compound's effects. Memories of past episodes of cocaine abuse both help to shape the individual's expectations for the drug's effects, and, trigger memories of past cocaine abuse

that then contributes to the urge for the individual to engage in its abuse, again (Gold & Jacobs, 2005). The actual *dose being abused* is also a factor, although this is often difficult to estimate because of differences in the purity of cocaine sold in different locations. Finally, the *physiological effects* of the chemical help to shape how it is abused. For example, cocaine smokers are able to stop smoking it when the side effects become uncomfortable.

Low blood levels of cocaine tend to cause an increase in the individual's libido, a feeling of increased energy, and a generalized feeling of arousal. At higher blood levels, such as those achieved through smoked or intravenously administered cocaine, will induce a sense of intense euphoria known as the "flash" or the "rush" within seconds of the time that the drug was introduced into the body (Jaffe et al., 2005; Stahl, 2008). This experience has been compared to the sexual orgasm in intensity, and some male cocaine abusers have reported spontaneous ejaculation without direct genital stimulation as a result of cocaine injection or smoking. Within a few seconds the "rush" fades into a feeling of excitation or euphoria that lasts for 10–20 minutes.

Tolerance to the euphoric effects of cocaine develops rapidly. Abusers have developed several methods to overcome this tolerance. Some abusers switch from cocaine "snorting" to smoking or injection. Other abusers attempt to overpower cocaine-induced tolerance by engaging in extended periods of continuous cocaine abuse known as the "coke run." Cocaine "runs" last between 12 hours and 7 days, during which the abuser injects additional cocaine perhaps as often as 2–3 times an hour until the cumulative dose reaches levels that would kill the cocaine-naive individual (Mendelson & Mello, 2008). At the end of the coke "run" the individual may fall into a prolonged sleep that may last for hours, or even days, and might experience a profound, possibly suicidal level of depression that slowly resolves as the brain's dopamine levels return to normal.

Complications of Cocaine Abuse/Addiction

Death

Cocaine abuse is a factor in 40–50% of all deaths associated with illicit drug use (Karch, 2009). One possible explanation for this fact is that its abuse can exacerbate medical conditions that were present, even if only in

---

[12]See Glossary.

subclinical forms (Mendelson & Mello, 2008). In some cases, the abuser's death occurs so rapidly that s/he does not have a chance to reach a hospital, and the coroner is the only physician who will see the victim. In addition to simply killing the abuser, cocaine abuse can induce a wide range of other complications, including:

Addiction

It was believed in the 1960s and 1970s that cocaine was not physically addictive, a misperception brought on by the fact that cocaine was so expensive and so difficult to find during that era that few abusers could afford to use it long enough to become addicted. With the availability of cheaper, more potent[13] cocaine, it has been discovered that cocaine addiction is not only possible, but that it also develops more rapidly than addiction to other compounds such as alcohol or marijuana. The addiction potential of cocaine might best be illustrated by the observation that a monkey would spend hours pushing a lever until he or she had pushed it 6,000 times, just to get a shot of cocaine (Rasmussen, 2008).

Cocaine is often portrayed as a universally addictive substance, in reality only about 6% of those who begin to abuse cocaine will be physically addicted to it within the first year (Carroll & Ball, 2005).[14] If the individual continues to abuse cocaine, the percentage who become physically addicted on it increases until eventually 15% of those who initiated the use of cocaine will end up becoming addicted to it (Carroll & Ball, 2005; Jaffe et al., 2005).

Respiratory System Problems

Cocaine smokers experience side effects such as chest pain, cough, and damage to the bronchioles of the lungs (Gold & Jacobs, 2005; Jones & Weir, 2005). Approximately one-third of habitual crack abusers develop wheezing sounds when they breathe, and many experience an asthma-like condition known as chronic bronchiolitis ("crack lung"). It has been suggested that this might be due, at least in part, to contaminants in the cocaine that is smoked (Mendelson & Mello, 2008). Other cocaine smokers risk the development

of hemorrhage, pneumonia, and a chronic inflammation of the throat. On occasion, the smoker will experience a situation where the alveoli of the lungs will rupture, allowing the escape of air (and bacteria) into the surrounding tissues, known as a "pneumothorax," establishing the potential for an infection to develop as well as compromising the ability of the smoker's lungs to function properly. There is evidence suggesting that cocaine-induced lung damage may be permanent.

Cocaine smoking appears to be associated with an observed increase in the number of fatal asthma cases ("Asthma Deaths Blamed on Cocaine Use," 2007). Chronic cocaine "snorters" experience sore throats, inflamed sinuses, bleeding from the sinuses, hoarseness, and on occasion a breakdown in the cartilage in the nose, which can develop after just a few weeks of intranasal cocaine use (Karch, 2009). It is also common for intranasal cocaine abusers to experience the development of ulcers in the nasal passages, as cocaine-induced vasoconstriction and the impurities in illicit cocaine contribute to bacterial infections in these tissues.

Cardiovascular System Damage

The first report of a cocaine-related heart attack in the clinical literature was in 1886 (Gorelick, 2009). Cocaine abuse injures the heart through a variety of mechanisms. Cocaine abuse appears to be a major risk factor contributing to the buildup of plaque in the coronary arteries of abusers between the ages of 18 and 45 (Karch, 2009; Lai et al., 2005; Levis & Garmel, 2005; McCord et al., 2008). If the abuser is also infected with HIV-1 infection,[15] the process of plaque buildup is accelerated (Lai et al., 2005). Repeated episodes of cocaine abuse seems to trigger the "complement cascade" normally seen when the body is invaded by foreign microorganisms. The complement cascade allows the buildup of protein molecules on the cell walls of invading organisms, thus alerting the body's macrophages[16] to attack those cells. This would explain the theory that atherosclerotic plaque is formed when the macrophage cells mistakenly attack cholesterol molecules circulating in the blood and then attach these molecules to the endothelial cells of the coronary arteries. Over time,

---

[13] As compared to what it cost in the 1960s and early 1970s.

[14] If only because it is not possible to predict which individual is in danger of becoming addicted to cocaine, and which person is unlikely to become addicted to it, the experimentation with cocaine is not recommended.

---

[15] Discussed in Chapter 34.

[16] See Glossary.

significant amounts of cholesterol accumulate reducing the flow of blood through that vessel, contributing to the development of coronary artery disease. The factors that were the strongest predictors of coronary artery disease were: being male, and having an alcohol and cigarette abuse problems.

For years, physicians were taught that cocaine-induced coronary artery spasms were the cause heart attacks were so often seen in cocaine abusers. Although such spasms do take place, they seem to play only a minor role in cocaine-induced heart attacks. Rather, cocaine abuse appears to first cause the buildup of coronary artery plaque where the endothelium has already been damaged, and then cause the coronary artery to constrict at these specific points during subsequent periods of abuse, reducing blood flow to heart muscle. This process is also seen in cigarette smokers, although it does occasionally occur in nonsmokers as well (Jones & Weir, 2005). Patrizi et al. (2006) concluded that cocaine-induced coronary artery disease was the most common cause of myocardial infarctions in cocaine abusers as evidenced by their finding that cocaine abusers had significantly higher levels of atherosclerosis in their coronary arteries than nonabusers. It has been estimated that 25% of heart attack patients between the ages of 18 and 45 suffer at least once a cocaine-related heart attack (Jones & Weir, 2005). So strong is the association between cocaine abuse and heart attacks that Tomb (2008) recommended that physicians assume that cocaine abuse was involved when a young adult experiences a heart attack until proven otherwise.

Fifty percent of cocaine abusers who present at the hospital emergency room with heart pain have no evidence of atherosclerotic plaque buildup in their coronary arteries (Leamon et al., 2008). This does not negate the fact that cocaine is cardiotoxic, and in addition to causing a heart attack its abuse can result in severe hypertension, sudden dissection of the coronary arteries, cardiac ischemia, tachycardia, micro-infarcts myocarditis, cardiomyopathy, and sudden cardiac death (Greenberg & Bernard, 2005; Jaffe et al., 2005; Karch, 2009; Mendelson & Mello, 2008; Stahl, 2008). Cocaine also potentially can disrupt the normal electrical flow pattern in the heart, inducing potentially fatal cardiac arrhythmias such as atrial fibrillation, sinus tachycardia, ventricular tachycardia,

as the *torsade de pointes*[17] (Gold & Jacobs, 2005; Karch, 2009; Khan, Morrow, & McCarron, 2009; O'Connor et al., 2005). Preliminary evidence suggested that the compound dexmedetomidine might counteract many of cocaine's cardiovascular effects, offering the promise that physicians might soon have a new tool to protect the hearts of those foolish enough to abuse cocaine.

Some scientists believe that cocaine abuse causes "micro-infarcts"[18] in the cardiac muscle (Aquaro et al., 2011; Gold & Jacobs, 2005). Each micro-infarct slightly reduces the heart's ability to carry out its role as the circulatory system pump, and cumulatively may cause the abuser's heart to fail. This theory is supported by the observation that cocaine abusers frequently have abnormal electrocardiograms (EKG), even if they are not actively abusing cocaine at the time of the test. These abnormal EKG tracings may reflect sub-clinical drug-induced heart damage, which will be exacerbated if the individual should continue to abuse cocaine. It is not known whether these micro-infarcts are the cause of the chest pain reported by some cocaine abusers, but it is known that cocaine abuse can induce areas of ischemia in body organs, especially the heart and brain.

There does not appear to be a specific pattern to cocaine-induced cardiac problems, and both first-time abusers and those with a long history of prior cocaine abuse may both present with symptoms of a heart attack. Unfortunately, illicit drug dealers have been known to tell their clients that if the cocaine causes chest pain it is a sign that the cocaine is very potent and not a sign of a possible cocaine-induced heart problem. If the abuser should be hospitalized in the middle of an attack and fails to tell the physician that s/he was a cocaine abuser, the physician might attempt to treat the suspected heart attack with medications such as the beta-adrenergic antagonists, which can exacerbate the cocaine-induced vasoconstriction and possibly kill the patient (Thompson, 2004).

A rare, but potentially fatal complication seen with cocaine abuse is the *acute aortic dissection*, which might be caused by cocaine-induced episodes of hypertension (Karch, 2009; O'Brien, 2006; Westover & Nakonezny, 2010). Westover and Nakonezny (2010)

---

[17]See Glossary.

[18]Microscopic areas where the blood supply to cardiac tissue was disrupted, resulting in damage to the tissue supplied by those blood vessels.

suggested that 1.9% of the cases of aortic dissection reviewed were the result of cocaine abuse. This condition is a medical emergency and carries a high mortality rate even with surgical intervention. As the above information demonstrates, cocaine abuse carries with it a significant cardiovascular risk.

Cocaine Abuse as a Cause of Digestive System Damage

There is evidence that some of the metabolites of cocaine, especially cocaethylene, are quite toxic to the liver (Brust, 2004). However, the theory that cocaine abuse can directly cause/contribute to liver disease remains controversial (Karch, 2009). Still, some individuals have a genetic defect that prevents their bodies from producing an enzyme that plays a crucial role in cocaine biotransformation. This condition is the *pseudocholinesterase deficiency,* and persons with this condition are at risk for potentially fatal reactions to even small amounts of cocaine (Brust, 2004; Schuckit, 2006a).

On rare occasions cocaine abuse can induce hemorrhage within the gastrointestinal tract that might become so extensive that the abuser expires in a short period of time from acute blood loss (Lingamfelter & Knight, 2010). Cocaine abuse has also been identified as a cause of bruxism, decreased gastric motility, perforation of the bowel, gangrene of the bowel, necrosis of the tissues of the esophagus,[19] and ischemia to different regions of the intestinal tract. These later complications of cocaine abuse might become so severe that surgical intervention is necessary to remove the damaged portions of the intestinal tract.

Cocaine Abuse as a Cause of Central Nervous System Damage

Like the amphetamines, cocaine abuse causes a reduction in cerebral blood flow in at least 50% of those who abuse it (Balamuthusamy & Desai, 2006; Brust, 2004). Neuroimaging studies have found evidence of cerebral atrophy and enlarged ventricles within the brain, both indicators of the death of neural tissue (Bolla & Cadet, 2007). The observed changes in both the vasculature and structure of the brain might contribute to the lower cognitive functions

seen in cocaine abusers. Researchers have found deficits in the areas of verbal learning, memory, and attention of chronic cocaine abusers on neuropsychological test batteries (Kosten & Sofuoglu, 2004; Kosten, Sofuoglu, & Gardner, 2008). These neurocognitive deficits appear to continue for months after the individual's last cocaine use and it is not known at this time whether they will resolve with extended abstinence or not (Gonzalez, Vasisileva, & Scott, 2009).

Cocaine abuse is associated with an increased risk for either obstructive or hemorrhagic strokes (Bolla & Cadet, 2007; Khan et al., 2009; Mendelson, Mello, Schuckit, & Segal, 2006; Westover, McBride, & Haley, 2007). These cocaine-induced strokes might be microscopic in size ("micro-strokes") or may involve major regions of the central nervous system. Kaufman et al. (1998) suggested that cocaine abusers were twice as likely as nonabusers the same age to suffer a stroke, whereas Johnson, Devous, Ruiz, and Alt-Daud (2001) suggested that the risk might be as much as 14 times higher. There are no cocaine-specific areas of damage noted: Cocaine-related strokes have been identified in various regions of the brain, retina, and the spinal cord (Brust, 1997, 2004; Jaffe et al., 2005; Martin-Schild et al., 2010). The risk of suffering a cocaine-related stroke is apparently cumulative, with long-term abusers being at higher risk than new abusers, although both groups are at risk for a cocaine-induced stroke. Cocaine abusers suffer a worse prognosis than nonabusers the same age, and tend to have larger areas of brain damage than nonabusers (Chang et al., 2013; Martin-Schild et al., 2010).

The causal mechanism for cocaine-induced strokes is thought to be the cycle of drug-induced vasospasm during periods of active drug abuse and the reperfusion[20] that occurs in between these periods of cocaine use (Bolla & Cadet, 2007; Johnson et al., 2001; Karch, 2009). This can lead to damage to the blood vessel walls of the cerebral vasculature, facilitating the development of a stroke. Cocaine abusers are also at higher risk for *transient ischemic attacks* (TIAs) brought on as a result of their cocaine abuse, possibly because of cocaine-induced vasoconstriction (Kaufman et al., 1998).

Cocaine abuser are at higher than normal risk for the development of seizures, although the mechanism for this remains unknown (Fadem, 2009; Gold & Jacobs, 2005;

---

[19]Clinically known as "black esophagus."

[20]See Glossary.

Mendelson & Mello, 2010). Although the theory is not proven, these seizures may be the result of cocaine-induced interruptions in cerebral blood flow. There is also strong evidence that cocaine might initiate a neurological process known as *kindling*[21] with the individual's cocaine abuse both causing, and exacerbating, seizures disorders in abusers (Gold & Jacobs, 2005; Karch, 2009). Even first-time abusers have been known to suffer a cocaine-induced seizure, and there is no evidence to suggest that they are dose-related (Gold & Jacobs, 2005). One region of the brain thought to be involved in the kindling process is the amygdala, although other regions of the brain might also be sensitive to cocaine-use related kindling.

Cocaine abuse is thought to interfere with the process of body temperature regulation, causing periods of *malignant hyperthermia* (Karch, 2009; Mendelson & Mello, 2010). The brain can only operate within a very narrow temperature range, and if the body temperature exceeds these limits, there is a very real danger of damage to the brain, if not even the death of the patient. There is also an emerging body of evidence that suggests that cocaine abusers are at high risk for alterations of the brain at the level of the individual neuron (Tannu, Mash, & Hemby, 2006). The authors compared samples of brain tissue from 10 cocaine overdose victims with those of persons who had died from noncocaine-related causes. They found alterations in the expression of 50 different proteins involved in the process of forming and/or maintaining neural connections in neurons in the nucleus accumbens of abusers.

Habitual cocaine abuse has been implicated in the death of neurons, possibly because cocaine abuse alters the normal function of the *synuclein* family of proteins in the brain. Under normal conditions these proteins help to regulate dopamine transport within the neuron. Recent evidence suggests that chronic cocaine abuse can alter the process of synuclein production within the neuron, ultimately causing or contributing to the death of these neurons (Mash et al., 2003). Finally, there is also evidence suggesting that cocaine abuse may alter the blood–brain barrier,[22] facilitating the entry of the human immunodeficiency virus type 1 into the brain. Further, because of the various bacterial, fungal, or viral contaminants in some samples of illicit cocaine the abuser is being exposed to a number of potentially fatal infectious agents (Acosta et al., 2005). For example, the intranasal use of cocaine induces a state of intense vasoconstriction in the tissues of the sinuses. This might cause tissue death in the affected areas, establishing focal colonization points for bacteria resulting in sinusitis, loss of a sense of smell, nose bleeds, or even a potentially fatal brain abscess if the bacteria are able to access the brain through the nasal cavity (Roldan & Patel, 2008).

Cocaine's Effects on the Abuser's Emotions and Perceptions

It is not uncommon for cocaine abusers to report experiencing periods of depression or anxiety (Gorelick, 2009). Up to 64 percent of cocaine abusers surveyed had experienced some degree of anxiety as a result of their cocaine abuse (Louie, 1990). Cocaine abusers frequently attempt to control this anxiety by concurrently abusing sedating agents such as marijuana, benzodiazepines, alcohol, narcotic analgesics, and, on occasion, barbiturates. Cocaine-related anxiety attacks might persist for months after the individual's last cocaine use (Gold & Jacobs, 2005; Schuckit, 2006a). Further, there is evidence that cocaine abuse might lower the threshold at which the individual will experience an anxiety attack (Gold & Jacobs, 2005).

Statistically, cocaine abusers are also at increased risk for premature death from suicide and homicide (Oehmichen, Auer, & Konig, 2005). The authors found that suicide accounted for 10% of cocaine abuser deaths, whereas homicide accounted for another 20%.[23] There is a known relationship between cocaine withdrawal and depression, which is an independent risk factor for suicide. Further, cocaine abuse can exacerbate symptoms of both Tourette's syndrome and tardive dyskinesia (Lopez & Jeste, 1997). After extended periods of abuse, some cocaine abusers develop the sensation of having bugs crawling on, or just under, their skin. These hallucinations are known as *formication*[24] and cocaine abusers have been known to scratch, burn, or cut themselves in an attempt to relieve themselves of the torment of these nonexistent insects (Gold & Jacobs, 2005).

---

[21]See Glossary.

[22]Discussed in Chapter 6.

[23]Cocaine-induced heart disease, infections (including HIV-1), strokes, and accidents accounted for the other 70% of those cocaine abusers who died.

[24]See Glossary.

Cocaine abuse has also been identified as the cause of a drug-induced psychosis (Schuckit, 2006a). A significant percentage of chronic cocaine abusers will exhibit symptoms of a psychosis that are very similar to those seen in paranoid schizophrenia. This condition, known as "coke paranoia" by abusers, usually clears within a few hours or days of the individual's last cocaine use (Hanley, 2004; Karch, 2009; Schuckit, 2006a; Stahl, 2008). The mechanism through which extended periods of cocaine abuse is able to cause a drug-induced psychosis is not known and there is little research being conducted into this phenomenon.

Other Problems Associated with Cocaine Abuse

Men who abuse cocaine run the risk of developing erectile dysfunctions, including a painful, potentially dangerous, condition known as *priapism*[25] (Karch, 2009). Further, as noted earlier in this chapter, the rectal use of cocaine may, although it reduces the individual's awareness of pain, contributes to tissue damage, development of infection, and possible death. Cocaine has been implicated as a cause of death through the potentially fatal condition known as rhabdomyolysis[26] (Khan et al., 2009; Schuckit, 2006a). Rhabdomyolysis is thought to be the result of cocaine-induced vasoconstriction, causing ischemia in the muscle tissue (Karch, 2009; Repetto & Gold, 2005; Richards, 2000).

Cocaine Withdrawal

A few hours after the individual last "snorted" cocaine, or within 15 minutes of the last intravenous or smoked dose, the individual will slide into a state of deep depression that could reach suicidal proportions (Gold & Jacobs, 2005). Roy (2001) found that *one-fifth* of all suicides of adults under the age of 60 in New York City were cocaine-related. This depressive effect is thought to reflect the cocaine-induced depletion of the neurotransmitters dopamine and norepinephrine in the brain. After a period of abstinence, the neurotransmitter levels slowly return to normal. But, there is a possibility that the individual's cocaine abuse masked a pre-existing depressive disorder that will only become apparent after the individual discontinues the abuse of cocaine. In such

[25]See Glossary.
[26]See Glossary.

cases compounds such as desipramine or bupropion might be the best choices for antidepressant medications (Rounsaville, 2004).

Other symptoms frequently seen during cocaine withdrawal include fatigue, vivid intense dreams, sleep disorders (both insomnia and hypersomnia), anorexia, and psychomotor agitation or retardation (Carroll & Ball, 2005). Many cocaine abusers report experiencing cognitive problems upon cessation, which may continue for six months or longer (Morgan et al., 2006). There is evidence to suggest that cocaine abusers are less likely than the abusers of other compounds to report insomnia when they discontinue the use of cocaine, and that there is a positive relationship between the abuser's post-cessation insomnia and the possibility of relapse (Morgan et al., 2006).

CNS Stimulant Abuse and the *Diagnostic and Statistical Manual of Mental Disorders,* 5th Edition

The discussion of cocaine-related disorders under the *Diagnostic and Statistical Manual of Mental Disorders,* 5th edition (American Psychiatric Association, 2013) was discussed under one topic heading: The *stimulant use disorders,* which was presented in the last chapter. To follow the same outline used by the American Psychiatric Association, this discussion is found at the end of Chapter 8.

Chapter Summary

It is often surprising for students to learn that cocaine is nothing more than a natural pesticide produced by the coca plant, in an attempt to ward off insects or animals that might otherwise consume the leaves of the plant. By coincidence, this compound also has a strong impact on the central nervous system (CNS). Early settlers in the high Andes mountain regions found that by chewing the cocaine leaf, they could enhance their endurance while working at these high altitudes. It soon became a valued part of the culture prior to the arrival of European explorers.

With the development of the methods to chemically extract cocaine from the leaf and concentrate it, and the almost simultaneous development of the hypodermic needle, the world entered a new era of cocaine abuse. It was found that if concentrated cocaine were to be smoked or injected that it could induce a powerful sense of euphoria that is, at least in the opinion of some abusers, "better than sex." This soon made cocaine the stimulant of choice for many. Over time, it was discovered that although cocaine might indeed make the abuser feel good, it also contributed to a wide range of potentially lethal problems, and abusers drifted away from cocaine abuse to the supposedly safer pleasures of the amphetamines in the 1930s. By the 1960s or 1970s they had discovered that these compounds were dangerous, but the lessons so painfully learned by cocaine abusers at the turn of the 20th century had been forgotten. Cocaine again became a major drug of abuse, and the dangers associated with its use were rediscovered. It remains a significant component of the drug abuse problem in the United States in spite of the known dangers associated with its use.

CHAPTER 10

Marijuana Abuse and Addiction

Introduction

Although the exact age of this Chinese manuscript is disputed, current evidence would suggest that the earliest written reference to marijuana as a medicine dates back to 2727 B.C.E.,[1] (Grinspoon, Bakalar, & Russo, 2005). The fact that the exact age of this manuscript is disputed is in a symbolic way quite appropriate, for even back then marijuana was controversial. It remains the subject of controversy, sparks fierce debate, and has been the source of many "urban myths," not the least of which is that marijuana itself is a drug rather than a plant. It is a member of the *Cannabis sativa* family, which has long been known and used by humans. Indeed, the very name *Cannabis sativa* is Latin for "cultivated hemp" (Green, 2002). Historical evidence suggests that some varieties of the cannabis plant have been cultivated for hemp fiber that for over 12,000 years (Welch, 2009). The hemp fibers are then used to manufacture a variety of products,[2] the range of which often surprise the student.

In the United States the topic of marijuana has reached such a point of hysteria that *any* member of the *Cannabis sativa* family of plants is automatically assumed to have a major abuse potential (Williams, 2000). This is hardly the truth, for some varieties produce hemp *fiber*, which has little or no abuse potential, whereas others are bred to produce large amounts of those compounds that give marijuana a psychoactive effect. To differentiate between these two plant varieties, Williams (2000) suggested that the term *hemp* be applied to those plants grown for their ability to produce fiber, whereas the term *marijuana* be reserved for just those members of the *Cannabis sativa* family grown for their ability to produce compounds with a psychoactive effect. This is the convention that will be followed in this text as we explore the problem of marijuana use and abuse.

A History of Marijuana Use/Abuse

Almost 3,000 years ago, physicians in China were using marijuana as a treatment for malaria and constipation, to ease the pain of childbirth, and, when mixed with wine, a surgical anesthetic (Robson, 2001). In the United States historical evidence suggests that the settlers in Jamestown, Virginia, began to harvest cannabis for its ability to produce hemp fibers in 1611, fibers that, among other uses, were used to produce rope for the sailing ships of the era (Grinspoon et al., 2005). Its intoxicating effects have been known at least since the 1800s, although there is evidence that in Central and South America people may have used marijuana for its intoxicating effects even before this time (Grinspoon et al., 2005). Physicians in Asia, Europe, and the New World viewed cannabis/marijuana as a treatment for a wide variety of disorders. In the United States, for example, physicians were trained to prescribe

---

[1]"before common era."

[2]For example: Clothing has been made from hemp for thousands of years. The King James translation of the Bible was printed on paper manufactured from hemp. Both Rembrandt and van Gough painted on "canvas" made from hemp (Williams, 2000). Although George Washington cultivated cannabis to obtain hemp, which was used to manufacture rope and other products during the era, there is no direct evidence that he ever smoked marijuana.

marijuana as a sedative, hypnotic, a treatment for migraine headaches, and as an anticonvulsant. By the turn of the 20th century, no less a company than Sears, Roebuck and Company sold marijuana as a cure for the then prevalent morphine addiction (Brust, 2004).

By the 1930s, law enforcement officials and physicians had come to view marijuana use with some degree of suspicion (Walton, 2002). This suspicion was fueled by Henry Anslinger, who was the U.S. Commissioner of Narcotics in the 1920s. Anslinger appears to have been jealous of J. Edgar Hoover and the power that he wielded as the director of the Federal Bureau of Investigation and began to search for a substance that would justify an expansion of his department's powers. Marijuana was the ideal candidate. Although, in 1931, he testified before Congress that marijuana abuse was not a major problem, by 1935 he was telling members of Congress that it had become as much of a problem as heroin (McPherson, Yudko, Murray-Bridges, Rodriguez, & Lindo-Moulds, 2009). Lurid stories of marijuana-related axe murders and other criminal acts were used to justify the criminalization of marijuana (although there is evidence suggesting that at least some of these supposed criminal acts were entirely fictitious). Anslinger also suggested the now famous "gateway" theory that marijuana abuse leads to the abuse of hard drugs (McPherson et al., 2009). During this era its use was associated with socially unpopular minority groups and it was occasionally prescribed for a patient by a physician. By the mid-1930s marijuana was found to be less effective than, or at best only as effective as, many of the new pharmaceuticals being introduced at that time and was removed from the physician's pharmacopoeia. In 1937, the Marijuana Tax Act[3] was passed and marijuana was officially classified as an illegal substance.

The practice of recreational marijuana smoking for its psychoactive effects was introduced into the United States by immigrant and itinerant workers from Mexico who had come north to find work (Nicoll & Alger,

2004; Mann, 2000). With the start of Prohibition in 1920 the common man in this country was left without a recreational substance to use, and it is thought that many members of the working class turned to marijuana as a substitute. A minority of the population continued to smoke marijuana following the end of Prohibition, a fact seized upon by some politicians to further their political careers as they railed against the marijuana abuse "problem."[4] However, the "problem" of illicit marijuana use usually involved only a small minority of the population even during the time when Henry Anslinger was busy attempting to convince Congress of the contrary. By the 1960s it had slowly evolved into a popular drug of abuse in this country, in part not only because users saw its use as a form of rebellion but also because of its mild psychoactive effect. A measure of its popularity might be seen in the fact that more than 50% of the entire population has used it at least once (Gold, Frost-Pineda, & Jacobs, 2004; Gruber & Pope, 2002).

A Medico-Legal Conundrum

As a substance of abuse, marijuana is illegal. In spite of this technicality, physicians have offered antidotal evidence for more than a half of a century suggesting that marijuana, or at least a compound(s) in marijuana, be useful in treating one or more diseases that continues to plague mankind. Case reports surfaced in the 1970s that cancer chemotherapy patients reported having less nausea after smoking marijuana (Robson, 2001). These case reports resulted in the development of a synthetic drug Marinol® (dronabinol), which is concentrated Δ-9-tetrahydro-cannabinol (THC).[5] This compound met with only limited success in controlling chemotherapy-related nausea, possibly because the antinausea effects were induced by another compound than THC (Smith, 1997).

Patients with multiple sclerosis (MS) also reported improved functioning after smoking marijuana.[6] This

---

[3]The Marijuana Tax Act of 1937 did not make the *possession* of marijuana illegal. The Stamp Act imposed a small tax on marijuana that a person could pay. The person would receive a stamp to signify that the tax had been paid. Obviously, the act of buying the stamp would alert authorities to the possibility that this person either had marijuana, or was planning to buy it. So it was rather unusual for abusers to pay the tax and receive the stamp. However, the stamp did become popular among for stamp collectors, many of whom did pay the necessary tax to receive the stamp. In 1992, the United States Supreme Court ruled the Act unconstitutional ("Stamp Out Drugs," 2003).

[4]Whether marijuana use is itself a problem is an issue that has been debated for many decades without clear resolution. The reader is left to draw his/her own conclusions.

[5]The compound thought to be the primary psychoactive agent in marijuana.

[6]However, Papathanasopoulous, Messinis, Epameinondas, Kastellakis, and Panagis (2008) did question whether cannabinoids might also induce changes in brain function that would contribute to cognitive decline in patients with MS, and the final answer to the question of whether cannabis should play a role in the treatment of MS remains open to debate.

was consistent with the results of the research by Zajicek et al. (2012), who found that concentrated THC appears to reduce muscle stiffness in a subgroup of patients with MS. Such reports support the use of the compound Sativex®, a pharmaceutical introduced in Canada.[7] This compound is made from cannabis and designed to be sprayed under the tongue as an aid to the treatment of MS (Wilson, 2005). In the Netherlands, early research suggested that marijuana use could ease the symptoms of neurological disorders, pain, and help reverse the "wasting syndrome" so often seen in cancer and AIDS patients (Gorter, Butorac, Coblan, & van der Sluis, 2005; Villarreal, 2011).

Other researchers found evidence that suggested that at least one of the compounds in marijuana smoke might be of possible value in treating Alzheimer's disease (Eubanks et al., 2006; Horstman, 2010). There is also limited evidence suggesting that a compound in marijuana might have at least a short term beneficial effect for patients with amyotrophic lateral sclerosis (ALS) (Amtmann, Weydt, Johnson, Jensen, & Carter, 2004). Further, there is a growing body of evidence that one or more of the compounds in marijuana might reduce neuropathic pain, such as that associated with HIV-1 infection (Villarreal, 2011).

Using animal research, other scientists found that a compound(s) in marijuana seemed to function as a potent antioxidant, and thus it might prove of value in limiting the amount of damage caused by a stroke or neurological trauma[8] (Hampson et al., 2002; Papathanasopoulous et al., 2008). Early research studies suggested that smoking marijuana might help control certain forms of otherwise unmanageable glaucoma; however, follow-up studies failed to replicate these findings and this claim is now disputed (Green, 2002; Watson, Benson, & Joy, 2000). Physicians have reason to believe that a compound in marijuana might prove to be useful in treating asthma, Crohn's disease, anorexia, emphysema, epilepsy, and possibly hypertension (Green, 2002; Seppa, 2010). There is also strong evidence that a compound

in marijuana might inhibit tumor growth, including gliomas[9] (Salazar et al., 2009; Seppa, 2010). As a result of such reports, the Institute of Medicine concluded that there was enough evidence to warrant an in-depth study of possible medicinal uses for marijuana in the United States.

However, in 2006 the Food and Drug Administration (FDA) dismissed this conclusion in 2006, using as a justification for this action their conclusion that (a) because there are no well-designed scientific research studies documenting possible medical applications for any variety of the cannabis plant and (b) there is no need to look for possible medical applications for any member of this plant family ("No Dope on Dope," 2006). Because of this line of reasoning, it is quite unlikely that legitimate medical research into possible medical applications of any compound found in marijuana will ever be conducted in this country. The federal government's monopoly on legal marijuana production for research allows it to refuse to provide marijuana for research studies that might reveal a possible medical application for marijuana (Doblin, quoted in Frood, 2008). In response to citizen initiatives, a number of different states have legalized the medical use of marijuana after contentious debates and political initiatives that often place the laws of various states at odds with federal law. The ultimate status of marijuana is still uncertain although it is safe to say that marijuana abuse will remain controversial substance for many years to come.

A Question of Potency

Since the 1960s, marijuana abusers have sought ways to enhance its effects either by intermixing the marijuana with other compounds or by developing strains of marijuana with the highest possible concentration of those compounds thought to give marijuana its psychoactive effects. One such compound is THC[10] (Coghlan, 2009). In 1992, the average concentration of THC in marijuana seized by police was 3.08%, which had increased to 5.11% by the year 2002 (Comptom et al., 2009) and 9.6% by 2004 (Munsey, 2010; Office of National Drug Control Policy, 2006). There is evidence that the THC content of some strains

---

[7]This compound is not available in the United States at this time.

[8]Other evidence suggests that marijuana use by middle aged or older persons might *increase* the risk of that person suffering a stroke by 230% or more, raising questions whether marijuana would be of value in treating neurological trauma. Obviously there is a need for more research on this topic.

[9]See Glossary.

[10]Discussed elsewhere in this chapter.

of marijuana being sold today might be as high as 20% (Stratton & Hill, 2010) to 32% (Munsey, 2010). Unfortunately, much of the research data on marijuana, its potential uses, abuses and dangers was carried out 25 years ago when less potent strains were commonly abused, and thus there are questions as to its applicability at this time ("Potent Pot," 2008). Further, scientists are only now learning more about the endocannabinoid system, and how THC alters the function of this system in the brain, research that will take years to be completed. Thus, the conclusions of much of the early research into the safety of marijuana are no longer applicable, and the consequences of using the higher potency strains of marijuana are not known at this time.

A Technical Point

Marijuana is not a drug. It is a *plant*, a member of the cannabis family of plants. The strain *Cannabis sativa* is the plant most commonly abused and contains at least 400 different compounds, of which 61 or more are psychoactive (Gold et al., 2004; Mendelson & Mello, 2008; Sadock & Sadock, 2007). In the 1960s researchers discovered that the majority of marijuana's effects are caused by a compound commonly known as THC.[11] THC is found throughout the marijuana plant, but the highest concentrations are found in the small upper leaves and the flowering tops of the plant (Hall & Solowij, 1998). Historically, the term *marijuana* is applied to preparations of the plant used for smoking or eating. *Hashish* is used to identify the thick resin that is obtained from the flowers of the cannabis plant. When dried it provides a brown or black substance that has a high concentration of THC. The resin is then either ingested orally (often mixed with a sweet substance to mask its flavor) or smoked. *Hash oil* is a liquid extract from the plant, usually containing 25–60% THC, which is added to marijuana or hashish to enhance its effect. In this chapter, the generic term *marijuana* will be used for any part of the plant that is to be smoked or ingested, except when the term *hashish* is specifically used.

Scope of the Problem

Marijuana is the most commonly abused illicit substance on this planet (Coghlan, 2009; United Nations, 2011). The United Nations (2011) reported that marijuana is the most commonly abused illicit substance on this planet, with 125–203 million persons having used it at least once in the past year. In North America,[12] 32.5 million persons are thought to use cannabis annually. In Asia, the number of annual cannabis users is thought to be between 31.4 and 67.9 million persons. In Europe, the number of annual marijuana abusers is thought to be between 28.7 and 29.5 million persons (United Nations, 2011).

The estimated value of the annual marijuana plant harvest each year in the United States makes it *the* biggest cash crop raised in this country, generating more income than corn and wheat combined ("Grass is Greener," 2007; Stratton & Hill, 2010). The number of past and current marijuana abusers in the United States has been estimated to be just under 43% of persons over the age of 18 years. Each day approximately 6,000 more people in the United States use marijuana for the first time (Danovitch & Gorelick, 2012; Sadock & Sadock, 2007). The average age at which individuals begin to smoke marijuana in the United States is around 18–19 years of age (Ellickson, Martino, & Collins, 2004). In earlier age cohorts marijuana use peaks in the early adult years and then becomes less common during the individual's 20s and 30s. For the current generation of young adults, marijuana use has been viewed as a normal recreational activity for all of their lives (United Nations, 2011) and it is not clear whether this pattern of use will continue or if younger generations will establish different behavioral norms for marijuana use. It is known that marijuana makes up the greater part of the "illicit drug use problem" in the United States.

There are parallels between marijuana abuse patterns and those of alcohol: Fourteen percent of those who smoke marijuana do so daily, consuming 95% of the marijuana sold in the illicit market in this country (United Nations, 2011). The other marijuana abusers engage in rare marijuana use, and only a small percentage of abusers use more than 10 grams a month (enough for about 25–35 cigarettes) (MacCoun & Reuter, 2001). However given its legal status it is classified as an illicit substance, although its abuse does distort the drug use 'problem' since many abusers use only marijuana and other substances. The proportion of the drug abusers who use marijuana compared with the total number of drug abusers is illustrated in Figure 10-1. In spite of its reputation as not being addictive, some abusers do develop a psychological dependency on it, and 10–20% of marijuana abusers will become physically addicted to it (Sadock & Sadock, 2007).

---

[11]The chemical name of which is: Δ-9-tetrahydro-cannabinol.

[12]The United Nations includes data for Canada, Mexico, and the United States together.

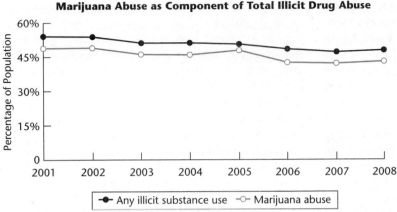

FIGURE 10-1 Exploring the Future data.

Source: Johnston, L.D., O'Malley, P.M., Backman, J.G., and Schulenberg, J.E. (2010). Monitoring the Future: National Results on Adolescent Drug Use. Bethesda, MD: National Institute on Drug Abuse.

Because of its popularity as a substance of abuse, the legal and social sanctions against marijuana use have repeatedly changed over the past half century, and are expected to continue to change in the years to come. In some states, possession of small amounts of marijuana for personal use is only subject to a fine, whereas in other states the possession of the same amount of marijuana would result in major legal sanctions. It has been decriminalized in some states, only to be prohibited just a few years later.

The Pharmacology of Marijuana

In spite of its long history as a popular substance of abuse, and its even longer history as a folk medicine, the pharmacokinetics of marijuana are still not completely understood (Grinspoon et al., 2005). It is known that the *Cannabis sativa* plant contains at least 400 different compounds, of which 61 or more are psychoactive (Gold, 2005; Sadock & Sadock, 2007; Mendelson & Mello, 2008; Welch, 2009). Of the 400 known compounds found in marijuana, at least 21 are under investigation as potential pharmaceuticals at this time (Welch, 2009). The majority of marijuana's effects are thought to be caused by a compound known as Δ9-tetrahydro-cannabinol (THC),[13] although the possibility that some of the other psychoactive compounds in marijuana might contribute to its effects through an unknown mechanism has not been ruled out. For example, a compound known as *cannabidiol* (CBD) is also inhaled when marijuana is smoked, and clinical research would suggest that although it does not bind at known THC receptor sites, it does appear to modify the effects of THC through an unknown mechanism[14] (Borgwardt, Allen, Bhattacharyya, & Fusar-Poli, 2008).

Because the potency of marijuana varies between samples significantly, there is no "standard" dose of marijuana. Further, if it is smoked, intra-individual and inter-individual variability in the smoking process can influence the amount of marijuana smoke reaching the lungs. Factors such as the number of "puffs," time interval between puffs, the depth of inhalation with each "puff," and time that the individual holds their breath after inhaling marijuana smoke, all influence the amount of THC that reaches the circulation. Once it reaches the circulation, THC is rapidly distributed to blood-rich organs such as the heart, lungs, and the brain. Then, over time it slowly works its way into less blood-rich tissues such as the body's fat reserves, where THC is stored. For the casual user this is not a matter of significant concern because the THC will be released back into the circulation and eliminated from the body within a few hours of the time that marijuana was smoked or ingested. Chronic abuse results in significant amounts of THC being stored in the body's fat cells, and upon cessation it slowly is released back into the blood (McDowell, 2005).

---

[13]"Δ" is the Greek letter for "Delta."

[14]There is also significant evidence suggesting that CBD might be useful in the treatment of seizure disorders, have an anti-inflammatory effect, and might even be useful in the treatment of schizophrenia. But, as discussed in Chapter 37, the Drug Enforcement Administration (DEA) will not allow research into possible medical applications for marijuana, or any compound found in the cannabis plant, for reasons discussed in Chapter 37.

In spite of strident claims to the contrary, rare marijuana abusers will usually only have marijuana metabolites in their urine for about 72–96 hours after their last use of this substance.[15] About 65% of a single dose of marijuana is excreted in the feces and only 20% in the urine (Huestis, 2009). Chronic marijuana abusers might test "positive" for THC in their urine for up to 30 days, but this happens only with exceptionally heavy levels of marijuana abuse (Stephens & Roffman, 2005). In the body THC is biotransformed into a compound known as 11-hydroxy-Δ9-THC, and this metabolite is thought to cause marijuana's psychoactive effects (Sadock & Sadock, 2007). Between 97% and 99% of the THC that reaches the blood is protein-bound, so its immediate psychoactive effects are caused by the 1–3% that remains unbound (Huestis, 2009; Jenkins, 2007). When it is smoked, the peak blood levels are seen within 10 minutes, and THC blood levels drop to 10% of the peak level within one hour (Gonzalez, Vassileva, & Scott, 2009; Hall & Degenhardt, 2005). The absorption, distribution, biotransformation, and elimination of marijuana is slower when it is ingested orally, but after absorption from the gastrointestinal tract the THC is still protein-bound in the same pattern as noted above.

THC mimics the action of two and possibly more naturally occurring neurotransmitters in the brain collectively called endocannabinoids[16] (Kraft, 2006; Lovinger, 2008; Villarreal, 2011). Receptor sites for the endocannabinoids have been found throughout the brain, including the hippocampus, cerebral cortex, basal ganglia, the cerebellum, and the dorsal horns of the spinal cord (Cruz, Bajo, Schweitzer, & Robeto, 2008; Gonzalez et al., 2009; Martin, 2004; Nicoll & Alger, 2004; Welch, 2009; Zajicek et al., 2003). There are virtually no known receptor sites for any of the endocannabinoids in the brain stem, which is consistent with the clinical observation that THC has no apparent effect on respiration. (Sadock & Sadock, 2007). THC is thought to be between 4 and 20 times as potent as the endocannabinoids and thus more likely to gain access to these receptor sites (Lovinger, 2008; Martin, 2004). Surprisingly, the endocannabinoid receptor site network matures during adolescence, a discovery that might have implications for substance abuse

rehabilitation workers who specialize in treating adolescents (Lewis, 2011).

The principal endocannabinoids that have been identified to date are the compounds anandamide and sn-2 arachidonoylglycerol (or, simply, 2-AG) (Cruz et al., 2008). Both of these compounds are synthesized in the body from lipid molecules, and in the time since their discovery they have emerged from obscurity to be recognized as essential components in normal bodily function. Anandamide appears to bind at what is called the CB1 receptor site and which is involved in such activities as the regulation of mood, memory, cognition, perception, muscle coordination, the regulation of sleep, body temperature regulation, appetite, pain perception, and possibly regulation of the immune system (Gruber & Pope, 2002; Parrott, Morinan, Moss, & Scholey, 2004; Martin, 2004; Nowak, 2004; Reynolds & Bada, 2003; Welch, 2009). Animal research suggests that anandamide also helps to guide the specification of what are known as pyramidal cells in the brain and the pattern of axon growth in new neurons[17] (Berghuis et al., 2007; Fields, 2009; Lovinger, 2008).

It would appear that CB1 is also involved in cellular necrosis, marking diseased cells for destruction and absorption by the body. Anandamide also functions as a retrograde neurotransmitter molecule, which modulates the release of many neurotransmitters from one neuron to the next (Lovinger, 2008). This reduces the firing rate of those neurons, which subjectively is experienced as a calming effect. Normally, this neurotransmitter inhibition continues for as long as the endocannabinoid molecules are present at the synaptic junction. Experimental research suggests that by blocking the endocannabinoid receptors, it is possible to reduce drug-seeking behaviors not only for marijuana, but also for food, nicotine, and possibly other drugs of abuse. These findings suggest new avenues of possible treatment for individuals with SUDs and possibly the eating disorders (Kraft, 2006; Le Foll & Goldberg, 2005; Mone, 2012).

The compound 2-AG is thought to be manufactured in the hippocampus region of the brain and it appears to bind at the CB2 receptor site (Parrott et al., 2004). It was once thought that CB2 receptor site was found exclusively in immune system, although emerging evidence suggests that there are at least a limited number

---

[15] Some abusers will claim that their urine toxicology test was "positive" for THC claiming that they had consumed a form of beer made from hemp. Although creative, this claim has not been supported by research evidence.

[16] A contraction of the term endogenous cannabinoids.

[17] A process known as corticogenesis, which is discussed in the Glossary.

of CB2 receptor sites in the hippocampus (Mone, 2012; Villarreal, 2011). This would appear to account for marijuana's ability to influence immune system activity. There is strong evidence that the endocannabinoids influence the development of cancer including carcinoma of the lung, gliomas,[18] some forms of thyroid cancer, leukemia, cancer of the skin, cancer of the uterus, breast cancer, prostate cancer, bowel, and neuroblastoma (Seppa, 2010). This is not to imply that 2-AG *causes* these forms of cancer, and there is evidence that at least one form of cancer, bowel cancer, develops only when 2-AG is absent or its action is suppressed by the evolving cancer.

All of these forms of cancer have a protein complex on the cancer cell's walls that form the CB2 receptor site. When activated, this receptor site induces a chemical cascade within the cell causing it to produce ceramide, a fatty molecule that induces cellular death (Seppa, 2010). At least some forms of cancer have learned to suppress or totally inactivate the action of 2-AG at these CB2 receptor sites, allowing the cancer to escape detection by the immune system. Another function of 2-AG appears to be helping to eliminate aversive memories (Cruz et al., 2008; Marsicano et al., 2002; Martin, 2004; Robbe et al., 2006). The available evidence would suggest that under normal conditions, 2-AG interferes with the firing sequence of subunits of the hippocampus involved in normal memory formation, a finding that is consistent with clinical experience with marijuana abusers who report having some memory problems.

Marijuana has also been found to affect the synthesis of acetylcholine[19] in the limbic system and the cerebellum regions of the brain (Fortgang, 1999). This might be the mechanism by which marijuana causes the user to feel sedated and relaxed. Marijuana has also been found to have a mild analgesic effect, and is known to potentiate the analgesic effects of narcotic analgesics (Anand et al., 2008; Martin, 2004; Welch, 2009). Because the cannabinoids are involved in peripheral pain perception, it may be possible to develop drugs that will target this pain perception system from a cannabinoid(s) without the intoxicating effects of marijuana (Anand et al., 2008). This effect appears to reflect marijuana-induced inhibition of the enzyme *adenylate cyclase*, which is involved in the process of transmission of pain messages in the CNS. Marijuana is also able to inhibit the production of cyclooxygenase,[20] which is possibly another mechanism through which it is able to inhibit pain perception, without the sedation seen when narcotic analgesics are used (Carvey, 1998; Whitten, 2008b). The analgesic effects of marijuana appear to peak about five hours after it was used (Welch, 2009). Scientists are not sure of the analgesic potential of marijuana, which was once thought to be about that of codeine, but are exploring the possibility of adapting a compound found in marijuana as an analgesic (Welch, 2009).

The mechanism through which marijuana is able to induce a sense of mild euphoria is not understood. Like other drugs of abuse, marijuana's euphoric effects appear to reflect its effects on the brain's endogenous opioid neurotransmitter system (Welch, 2009). The primary site of THC biotransformation is in the liver, and more than 100 metabolites are produced during this process (Hart, 1997). The half-life of THC appears to depend on whether metabolic tolerance to its effects has developed or not. Even under the best of conditions, the body is not able to biotransform THC quickly, and in chronic abusers the half-life might vary from 24 to 96 hours (Oehmichen, Auer, & Konig, 2005). About 65% of THC metabolites are excreted in the feces, and the remainder is eliminated from the body in the urine (Hubbard, Franco, & Onaivi, 1999). Tolerance to the effects of THC develops rapidly (O'Brien, 2006; Welch, 2009). After the development of tolerance, the abuser must either wait a few days before using marijuana again until the body begins to lose its tolerance to marijuana or change the method by which s/he uses marijuana to overcome their tolerance to marijuana. For example, oral abusers might switch to smoking marijuana, or marijuana smokers might switch to more potent varieties for smoking.

Interactions between Marijuana and Other Chemicals

There has been relatively little research into potential interactions between marijuana and other compounds. Thus, there is a significant possibility that there are undiscovered interactions between marijuana and various pharmaceuticals or drugs of abuse, and if only for this reason this list is not all-inclusive. Clinical

---

[18]See Glossary.

[19]See Glossary.

[20]See Glossary.

evidence would suggest that marijuana use by patients on lithium can cause the lithium levels in the blood to increase, possibly to toxic levels (Ciraulo, Shader, Greenblatt, & Creelman, 2006). Given the fact that lithium has only a very narrow "therapeutic window" and if too high may be fatal, the possible interaction between these compounds is thus potentially life-threatening. There is a single case report of a patient who abused marijuana while taking the antidepressant medication fluoxetine who developed a possible drug-induced psychotic reaction; however, there are no details about this case (Brust, 2004).

Cocaine abusers often will abuse marijuana in an attempt to counteract the agitation and excessive stimulation induced by high levels of cocaine abuse. It is known that marijuana abuse will cause an increase in the heart rate between 20% and 50%, and it is known that cocaine can cause a wide variety of cardiac problems (Hall & Degenhardt, 2005). Unfortunately, there has been no research into possible interactional effects as to the effects of concurrent cocaine and marijuana abuse either on previously healthy patients, or on those with unsuspected or known cardiac disease. Many alcohol abusers will also abuse marijuana while drinking, a practice that is potentially dangerous because marijuana inhibits nausea and vomiting. One of the body's natural defenses against poisons is to eject the poison from the body by vomiting. In theory individuals who have ingested too much alcohol are at increased risk of a potentially fatal alcohol overdose if they were also using marijuana since this will block the vomiting reflex (Craig, 2004). However, as this rather short list demonstrates, there is a dire need for further research into potential interactional effects between marijuana and both pharmaceuticals as well as the drugs of abuse.

Methods of Marijuana Abuse

Although it is possible to inject THC into the body, this is a very difficult process. The preferred methods of marijuana abuse are oral ingestion or by smoking (Brust, 2004; Erickson, 2007). Oral abusers used to be limited to baking marijuana into brownies or cookies; however, there are a range of products such as chocolate laced with THC, a peanut brittle laced with THC, honey mixed with THC, and capsules that look like over-the-counter Omega-3 fish oil capsules with the exception that they contain THC and not Omega-3

fish oils. Orally administered marijuana is slowly absorbed, with the results being that the abuser does not feel the first effects of THC until 30–120 minutes after ingesting it. A large amount of the THC ingested orally will be destroyed in the gastrointestinal tract by digestive juices with the result being that only about 4–12% of the available THC will reach the abuser's circulation (Drummer & Odell, 2001; Gold et al., 2004; Stimmel, 1997a).

The oral user must thus ingest approximately three times as much marijuana as a smoker will use to achieve the same effect (Sadock & Sadock, 2007). After oral ingestion, the peak THC levels are usually seen in one to five hours, and the effects last from 5 to possibly as long as 24 hours after ingestion (Brust; 2004; Drummer & Odell, 2001; Gruber & Pope, 2002). Oral ingestion does avoid the tell-tale smell of marijuana smoke that would alert employers, law enforcement, or school officials that the individual has been abusing marijuana, but makes it difficult, if not impossible, to titrate the individual's dose. This is more easily accomplished when marijuana is smoked, a practice that can be traced back for at least 5,000 years (Gruber & Pope, 2002; Walton, 2002). Neuropharmacologists disagree as to the amount of THC that reaches the circulation when marijuana is smoked. Stephens and Roffman (2005) suggested that 30–80% of the available THC is destroyed or is lost in "side stream" smoke in the process of smoking. Only 5–24% of the remaining THC was absorbed into the smoker's body according to Stephens and Roffman (2005). In contrast to this, Gold et al. (2004) suggested that almost 60% of the available THC was absorbed into the body when it was smoked. These two estimates of the amount of THC absorbed into the smoker's body might reflect the fact that there is significant intra-individual variability in THC absorption rates when it is smoked. However, as these discrepant estimates suggest, there is much to be learned about the process of marijuana smoking and the absorption of THC when it is smoked.

Although it might be intermixed with other compounds, marijuana is usually smoked alone in cigarettes commonly called "joints." The typical marijuana cigarette is estimated to contain between 500 and 750 mg of marijuana, providing an effective dose of 2.5–20 mg of THC to the smoker, depending on the potency of the marijuana being smoked. The average marijuana "joint" contains about 0.02 ounces of marijuana ("Raw Data," 2008). A variation on the marijuana cigarette is the "blunt," made by removing some of the outer leaves of a cigar, unrolling it, filling the core with high-potency marijuana mixed with chopped cigar tobacco, then re-rolling the cigar (Gruber & Pope, 2002). When smoked in this manner, abusers often report some degree of stimulation, possibly from the nicotine in the tobacco in addition to marijuana's sedating effects.

The process of smoking a "joint" is somewhat different than that used to smoke normal tobacco cigarettes. The user must inhale the smoke deeply into his/her lungs, then hold his/her breath for as long as possible (ideally 20–30 seconds) in an attempt to allow as much THC as possible to cross over from the lungs into the general circulation. Because THC passes across into the circulation very slowly, only about 25–50% of the THC in the smoke actually will be absorbed into the smoker's circulation (McDowell, 2005). But the effects of the THC that does enter the circulation are felt within seconds to perhaps a few minutes (Brust, 2004).

When smoked, the effects of marijuana reach peak intensity in 20–30 minutes, and begin to decline in about an hour (McDowell, 2005; Sadock & Sadock, 2007). THC is relatively potent, and the smoker must inhale only 25–50 micro-grams of THC for every kilogram of body weight, whereas the oral user must ingest 50–200 micrograms of THC per kilogram of body weight, to achieve a marijuana "high" (Mann, 2000). Exceptionally high blood levels of THC have been reported to have an hallucinatory effect (Lezak, Howieson, Bingler, & Tranel, 2012), although Mann (2000) suggested that this would require a dose five times higher than those usually used in the United States. Thus, hallucinations are only rarely reported in the United States in spite of its official classification as a hallucinogenic compound.

Subjective Effects of Marijuana Abuse

Marijuana smokers achieve the strongest effects, producing a mild sense of euphoria, relaxation, and some sensory distortions that alter the individual's perception of ordinary activities such as eating, watching television or movies, and having sex (Hall & Degenhardt, 2005). Some abusers report enhanced perception of sounds and colors as well (Earlywine, 2005; Zevin & Benowitz, 2007). In social settings, marijuana smokers are prone to infectious laughter, excessive talkativeness, and a feeling of relaxation. Individuals who smoke high-potency marijuana report a synesthesia[21]-like experience, in which the sensations of one sensory modality slip over into another (Earlywine, 2005). Over half of marijuana abusers report enhanced tactile sensations, and although the sense of taste is not improved, abusers speak of enjoying taste sensations more (Earlywine, 2005). Some abusers also report that marijuana's effects contribute to enhanced sexual pleasure (Earlywine, 2005). These claims have not been verified by scientific research and, as will be discussed later in this chapter, male users have discovered a host of marijuana-related sexual dysfunctions that appear to negate its potential to enhance sexual pleasure.

The effects of marijuana progress through two phases, which are influenced, in part, by the abuser's expectations for it (Brust, 2004). In the first phase, which begins shortly after THC enters the circulation, the individual experiences some mild anxiety, and decreased salivation. This phase is thought to last from two to four hours (Grinspoon et al., 2005; O'Brien, 2006; Sadock & Sadock, 2007; Zevin & Benowitz, 2007). The inexperienced user's reaction to these effects, the selective activation of the amygdala and cingulate cortex regions of the brain by THC, combined with the unexpected increase in cardiac rate, and marijuana-induced periods of depersonalization may be reasons why many inexperienced abusers experience some degree of anxiety after smoking marijuana.

However, more experienced abusers report a positive experience from marijuana use, including mild euphoria, a sense of relaxation, and reduction in subjective anxiety levels (Grinspoon et al., 2005; Hall & Degenhardt, 2005; O'Brien, 2011). These effects of marijuana appear to be caused by the THC isomer CBD, which appears to selectively suppress function of those regions of the brain involved in the fear response[22] (Fusar-Poli et al., 2009). These effects blend into the second phase of marijuana intoxication, in which the abuser will experience residual psychomotor problems, mood swings, and possible depression. These feelings last for at least 5–12 hours after a single dose, suggesting that marijuana's effects on the abuser should be classified as falling into either the period of acute, or extended,

---

[21]See Glossary.

[22]In this case.

effects (Freimuth, 2005; O'Brien, 2006; Sadock & Sadock, 2007; Tomb, 2008).

Clinicians often hear depressed patients claim that they abuse marijuana because it helps their depression. Research has demonstrated that very low doses of marijuana does seem to stimulate the release of serotonin in the brain, and thus might have an antidepressant effect in much the same manner that the selective serotonin reuptake inhibitors (SSRIs). However, there is only a very narrow dosing "window" for this effect, and if the individual uses more marijuana than necessary, it can contribute to feelings of depression (Bambico, Katz, Debonnel, & Govvi, 2007; Washton, & Zweben, 2006). Thus, marijuana's antidepressant effects are too limited to be of clinical significance.

After using marijuana abusers often report a sense of being on the threshold of a significant personal insight, but that they are unable to put this insight into words. Such drug-induced insights are rarely recalled after the period of acute intoxication ends. Further, marijuana-related creative efforts are usually found somewhat less than inspirational when the individual recovers from the period of acute intoxication. In such cases, the individual's subjective sense of insight and creativity appears to reflect the drug's effects on the brain rather than actual new perception of the self or the world around the abuser.

Adverse Effects of Marijuana Abuse

Dangers of Marijuana Abuse: An Ongoing Debate

Marijuana is viewed by many people as being relatively harmless, a perception that is supported by observations that the effective dose is estimated to be between 1/20,000th and 1/40,000th the lethal dose (Grinspoon et al., 2005). To express this safety margin in other terms, it has been estimated that a 160-pound person would have to smoke 900 marijuana cigarettes simultaneously to reach the lethal level (Cloud, 2002). An even higher estimate was offered by Schlossen (2003), who suggested that the average person would need to smoke 100 pounds of marijuana every minute for 15 minutes to achieve a lethal overdose.[23]

---

[23]It should be noted that some abusers have made commendable efforts to reach this level of marijuana intoxication, although apparently with little success.

In contrast to the estimated 200,000 deaths caused by the other forms of illicit drug use around the world each year, there are only two documented cases of a lethal marijuana overdose, although Coghlan (2009) did not provide specific information about these alleged marijuana overdose deaths. Although this information would suggest that marijuana has an impressive safety margin, it is not totally without risk.

Known and Suspected Adverse Effects of Short-Term Abuse

In the last decades of the 20th century scientists began to identify adverse effects of marijuana abuse (Aharonovich et al., 2005). However, with 400 known compounds and more than 2,000 known metabolites of these compounds being produced during the metabolism process, there is much to be discovered about marijuana's short-term and long-term adverse effects. Some of these metabolites might remain in the individual's body for weeks after a single period of marijuana use. In spite of this fact, research into the physical effects of marijuana on the brain of the abuser has been "surprisingly scarce" (Aharonovich et al., 2005, p. 1057).

There have been rare reports of anaphylactic reactions in marijuana abusers, although it is not clear whether these reactions were triggered by the marijuana itself or contaminants, or adulterants found in illicit marijuana samples (Brust, 2004). It is not uncommon for illicit marijuana to be adulterated, and these compounds add to the flood of chemicals introduced into the body when an individual abuses marijuana. To further cloud the issue, illicit marijuana is often exposed to herbicides sprayed on it by law enforcement officials in an attempt to destroy the plant(s) before they are harvested and sold. If the plants are harvested and sold, those herbicides are still on the plant, and will also be introduced into the body by the abuser.

A more common reaction for rare abusers is the development of "bloodshot" eyes (Mendelson & Mello, 2010; Mendelson, Mello, Schuckit, & Segal, 2006). This effect is relatively harmless, and is caused by marijuana-induced dilation of the blood vessels in the conjunctiva of the eyes. It can be quite striking to see for the first time. However, 40–60% of abusers will report at least one other adverse effect beyond "bloodshot" eyes (Hubbard et al., 1999). Further, marijuana intoxication impairs the motor skills necessary to safely drive a motor vehicle on about the same level as does a blood alcohol level of between 0.07% and 0.1% (Hall & Degenhardt, 2005) possibly in part because of its ability to interfere with normal depth perception. Even occasional episodes of marijuana abuse increase the individual's risk of being in a motor vehicle accident by 300–700%, possibly because of marijuana-induced loss of depth perception (Brust, 2004; Lamon et al., 2005).

Marijuana can induce a splitting of consciousness or even periods of depersonalization for the abuser (Earlywine, 2005; Johns, 2001). This might be one reason why 50–60% of marijuana abusers report experiencing at least one episode of marijuana-induced anxiety (O'Brien, 2006). Such episodes of anxiety are seen most often in novice abusers (Grinspook, Bakalar, & Russo, 2005; Gruber & Pope, 2002). Because marijuana smokers are able to titrate their dose more easily than those who ingest it orally, there is a tendency for oral abusers to experience anxiety more than marijuana smokers because the latter group can simply stop smoking it if they find its effects uncomfortable (Brust, 2004; Gold et al., 2004). Usually, the only treatment that is necessary is a gentle reassurance that it will soon pass (Brust, 2004; Sadock & Sadock, 2007).

Marijuana use has been identified as a cause of increased heart rate and cardiac arrhythmias. There have also been rare reports of myocardial infarction and atrial fibrillation in persons who have just used marijuana, although the causal mechanism still remains to be identified (Khan, Morrow, & McCarron, 2009). There are reports of abusers experiencing angina,[24] especially if they have pre-existing coronary insufficiency. Persons with known or suspected cardiac problems are advised not to use marijuana (Mendelson & Mello, 2010; Mendelson et al., 2006). Further, the particulates generated by smoking marijuana cause a dose-related reduction in pulmonary function. Unlike tobacco smoking, which produces microscopic particles that block the lung passages in the lowest levels of the lungs, marijuana smoking produces larger particles that block the larger air passages of the respiratory system (Aldington et al., 2007). This results in a conundrum: THC itself does not reduce the effectiveness of the respiratory system, but the method of delivery seems to block the air passages in the lungs.

There is one case report of a child suffering an episode of transient global amnesia after the child was accidentally exposed to marijuana, which resolved after a period of several hours (Prem & Uzoma, 2004). Although often believed to be an aphrodisiac, even limited marijuana use is known to reduce sexual desire, and for male abusers may result in erectile dysfunction, reduced sperm count, and delayed ejaculation (Greydanus & Patel, 2005; Hall & Degenhardt, 2005).

"Second Hand" Marijuana Smoke[25]

One topic that has rarely been explored until recently is the possibility that toxic compounds might be intermixed with the "side stream" or second hand smoke produced by marijuana smoking. Moir et al. (2007) examined this very topic. The authors utilized two "smoking machines" to "smoke" marijuana "blunts" under controlled conditions, and found that the side-stream marijuana smoke had 20 times as much ammonia as was found in regular cigarette smoke. Marijuana smoke also contains other toxic compounds such as hydrogen cyanide and nitric oxide in the second hand smoke at three to five times the concentration found in side stream smoke from tobacco cigarettes. Further, the authors detected known carcinogenic compounds in side stream smoke produced by the marijuana "blunts," possibly as a result of the tobacco found in the cigar also smoked at this time.

Consequences of Chronic Marijuana Abuse

The endocannabinoid molecules occupy their respective receptor sites for very short periods of time and then are reabsorbed into the body. In contrast to this, THC occupies these very same receptor sites for comparatively longer periods of time and researchers are not sure of the consequences of this prolonged endocannabinoid receptor binding. What follows is a summary of the current research and theories about the long-term effects of marijuana use.

Psychotic Reactions

Researchers have long been aware that marijuana abusers are at increased risk for psychotic reactions

---

[24]See Glossary.

[25]The claim that a urine toxicology test is "positive" for THC for a person in a legal or employment setting is discussed in Chapter 34.

(Welch, 2009). Most marijuana-induced psychotic reactions are short-lived, and clear up in a few hours, or days (Johns, 2001). There is debate over whether an ongoing psychosis reflected a predisposition toward a psychosis that was possibly unmasked by marijuana abuse (Compton et al., 2009; Hall & Degenhardt, 2005), or was induced by the individual's marijuana abuse. This latter theory is supported by the findings of McGrath et. al. (2010), who found an increased risk of psychosis in young adulthood for individuals who engaged in marijuana use earlier in life as compared to nonabusing siblings.

If this theory is true, then what initially presented as a marijuana-related psychotic reaction might activate the potential psychosis within the abuser and it will potentially become permanent. The age at which the individual begins to abuse marijuana is one apparent critical variable in the development of a later psychotic reaction. Research evidence suggests that individuals who had abused marijuana during adolescence, especially before the age of 15, have a higher incidence of schizophrenia later in life (Lezak et al., 2012; Raby, 2009). Another critical variable affecting the potential emergence of a marijuana-related psychosis is the intensity of use. Those individuals who smoke marijuana more often appear to have a higher risk of developing schizophrenia later in life. One study conducted in Sweden found, for example, that army recruits who had abused marijuana more than 50 times had a 670% higher incidence of becoming psychotic later in life than nonabusers (Iverson, 2005).

There is an emerging body of evidence suggesting that the body's endocannabinoids can produce transient schizophrenia-like symptoms. Because THC binds at the cannabinoid receptor site 40 times as strongly as do the natural endocannabinoids, this theory appears to make sense, although there is a need for further research. The regions of the brain known as the striatum and the cingulate, each have a high number of cannabinoid receptor sites (Bhattacharyya et al., 2009). These regions of the brain are also thought to be involved in the development of the symptoms of schizophrenia. An alternative theory is that marijuana can interfere with the normal function of the endocannabinoid 2-arachidonoyl-glycerol in the cortex and hippocampus of the brain with the same result. Yet a third hypothetical explanation for the apparent relationship between marijuana use and the development of psychosis was offered by Feilding and Morrison (2010). The authors, drawing upon recent research into the role of the compound CBD, noted that as strains of marijuana have been developed with higher levels of THC, CBD levels have dropped almost proportionally. Recent evidence suggests that CBD has an antipsychotic effect, theoretically counteracting the potential for THC to induce a psychosis. If this theory is true, an unintended side effect of development of new strains of marijuana with higher levels of THC has been reduced levels of CBD, a compound that might protect the user from psychosis. As these three competing theories suggest, there is still a great deal to be discovered about the effects of the various chemicals found in marijuana on the brain.

Metabolic Effects

In the brain the endocannabinoids are known to be involved in many diverse body regulatory functions including energy metabolism and appetite regulation. For this reason Muniyappa et al. (2013) attempted to determine the impact of marijuana use on the body's metabolism. Surprisingly, although marijuana use did cause some transient metabolic changes, the authors found little, if any, evidence suggesting long-term metabolic system changes in chronic marijuana smokers.

Neurological Changes

Using new high-resolution structural magnetic resonance imaging (MRI) technology (Yucel et al., 2008) found that chronic marijuana smokers had an approximate 12% reduction in volume of the hippocampus, and a 6% reduction in the size of the amygdala regions of the brain. These regions of the brain have a high density of cannabinoid receptors, and there was a clear relationship between duration of marijuana use and the degree of shrinkage in these regions of the brain, although it is not clear at this time whether this reduction in regional brain volume is permanent or not. It also is not known whether the observed changes in regional brain size contributes to the report that persons who have abused a hallucinogenic such as LSD often experience marijuana-triggered "flashbacks" (Hall & Degenhardt, 2005; Sadock & Sadock, 2007). Such flashbacks are usually limited to a six-month period following the individual's last use of marijuana, and usually will stop on their own.

A small but growing body of evidence suggests that chronic marijuana abuse can cause cognitive deficits in the abuser's brain (Khamsi, 2013; Vik, Cellucci, Jarchow, & Hedt, 2004). These cognitive deficits are often detectable on neuropsychological tests for up to 7–14 days after habitual marijuana abusers last used marijuana (Pope et al., 2001; Vik et al., 2004. Memory deficits appear to be progressive worse in heavy marijuana abusers who started to smoke marijuana heavily in their teen years (Meier et al., 2012). Long-term marijuana abusers have demonstrated evidence of neurocognitive impairment for up to two years after their last use of marijuana and their measured IQ is approximately eight points lower than that of nonusers (Gonzalez et al., 2009; Kahn et al., 2009; Khamsi, 2013).

Many chronic marijuana abusers have abnormal patterns of electrical activity on electroencephalographic (EEG) studies. It is possible that these EEG changes predate the individual's marijuana or other chemical abuse, although there is little evidence to support this hypothesis. Repeated, heavy episodes of marijuana use are associated with dose-dependent changes in the brain's internal electrical activity (Herning, Better, & Cadet, 2008). The authors speculated that the observed EEG changes might reflect altered brain perfusion (blood flow in the brain). Sneider et al. (2006) suggested that the altered changes in regional blood flow patterns in the abuser's brain might persist for at least the first few weeks after the individual stopped abusing marijuana.

Under normal conditions, the occasional activation of the endogenous cannabinoid CB1 receptor might have a neuroprotective effect (Freedman, 2008). However, the persistent activation of this receptor site appears to make the CB1 receptor less responsive thus negating this neuroprotective function. The affected neurons are no longer protected against the increased levels of excitation and neural death produced by such conditions as schizophrenia or continual marijuana abuse. This might account for the findings of Matochik, Eldreth, Cadet, and Bolla (2005), who found evidence of significant levels of neural tissue loss in the right para-hippocampal gyrus, and in the left parietal lobe in the brains of 11 marijuana abusers in neuroimaging studies. This loss of neural tissue was strongly correlated with the duration of marijuana use, according to the authors. Paradoxically, Jacobus et al. (2009) found evidence that adolescent marijuana abusers appear to have less

damage to the "white matter"[26] of the brain after episodes of binge drinking as compared with adolescents who engage in binge drinking but who do not smoke marijuana. The mechanism through which marijuana might provide a neuroprotective effect in such circumstances is not known at this time, and the findings of this study must be replicated in future research to confirm that this process does indeed take place.

Research studies exploring the potential use of marijuana in treating MS have produced conflicting results. Lakhan and Rowland (2009) concluded that a combination of THC and CBD reduced patient distress induced by MS-associated spasticity, and there was mixed evidence of a physical reduction in MS related-spasticity. Other researchers have suggested that at least one compound(s) in marijuana might speed up the cognitive decline seen in patients with MS (Ghaffar & Feinstein, 2008; Villarreal, 2011). Thus, the potential value of marijuana as an adjunct to the treatment of MS is not clear at this time.

Effects of Habitual Marijuana Use on Sleep

The habitual use of marijuana suppresses REM sleep, although it is not clear whether isolated episodes of marijuana abuse have any significant impact on REM sleep (McDowell, 2005). The consequences of short-term REM sleep suppression on the individual's health is probably minimal, although some research has suggested that long-term REM sleep suppression might negatively affect the individual's health.

Effects of Habitual Marijuana Use on the Pulmonary System

Marijuana smokers tend to smoke fewer "joints" than tobacco smokers who smoke cigarettes. Marijuana smokers also smoke unfiltered joints, increasing their exposure to microscopic contaminants in marijuana. This does not appear to result in damage to the pulmonary system in rare marijuana smokers (Pletcher et al., 2012). However, researchers have found pre-cancerous changes in the cells of the respiratory tract similar to those seen in tobacco smokers in chronic marijuana smokers (Gold et al., 2004; Taskin, 2005; Tetrault et al., 2007). Preliminary evidence would suggest that smoking of one marijuana "joint" a day might increase the individual's risk for lung cancer that was as much as if s/he were to smoke a pack of cigarettes per day

---

[26]See Glossary.

(Brambilla & Colonna, 2008). The authors went on to state that marijuana smokers who had smoked just one "joint" per day for 10 years had a 570% higher risk of lung cancer as nonabusers in spite of whether they smoked tobacco cigarettes or not.

Marijuana smokers were also found to have an increased incidence of cough and wheezing in a manner similar to that seen in cigarette smokers (Khan et al., 2009; Tetrault et al., 2007). Marijuana abuse by cigarette smokers appears to increase the individual's risk for the development of chronic obstructive pulmonary disease (COPD) later in life (Tan et al., 2009). This is perhaps understandable: Marijuana smokers are exposed to virtually all the toxic compounds found in tobacco cigarettes except nicotine. If they were to smoke a "blunt," the marijuana smoker is exposed to *all* of the toxins found in tobacco, plus other toxins found in the marijuana (Gruber & Pope, 2002). For example the typical marijuana cigarette has 10–20 times as much "tar" as tobacco cigarettes (Nelson, 2000). Marijuana smokers are also exposed to higher levels of carbon monoxide than tobacco smokers, although the exact mechanism of this finding is not clear because most marijuana abusers also smoke cigarettes.

Immunosuppressant Effects

Animal research also confirms that heavy marijuana abuse appears to suppress the immune system's effectiveness (Abrams et al., 2003; Gold et al., 2004). However, this finding is of potential significance to those persons who struggle with viral infections such as the hepatitis viruses or HIV[27] viral infection because it might interfere with the body's ability to fight off the invading organism.

Marijuana as a Possible Causal Agent for the Development of Cancer

It has long been known that marijuana smoking reduces the effectiveness of the respiratory system to resist infection (Gruber & Pope, 2002; Hall & Degenhardt, 2005). It has been hypothesized that the body's "scavenger" cells are on constant patrol for cells that are genetically different from those of the body, which would include external pathogens and cells in the body whose genetic structure has been disrupted. This is understandable because marijuana smoke has been found to contain many of the same carcinogens found in tobacco cigarettes, often in higher amounts than those found in regular tobacco cigarettes, Marijuana-induced suppression of the body's natural defenses combined with the exposure to these carcinogenic compounds might explain why marijuana smokers are at increased risk for cancer of the mouth, tongue, throat, and lungs (Gruber & Pope, 2002; Hall & Degenhardt, 2005; Han, Gofoerer, & Colliver, 2010).

There also is an emerging body of evidence suggesting that marijuana use increases the male abuser's risk for cancer of the testicles, especially the more aggressive nonseminomatouss form of testicular cancer (Daling et al., 2009; Lacson et al., 2012). Lacson et al. (2012) found that the risk of cancer of the testicles increased by almost 100% if the individual had ever engaged in marijuana use, whereas Daling et al. (2009) suggested on the basis of their research that the risk of marijuana-associated testicular cancer was influenced by factors such as the duration of use, frequency of use, and the time when the individual first began to abuse marijuana. These findings appear to justify the decision by the State of California to require medical marijuana dispensaries to label marijuana as a potential carcinogen (Dembosky, 2009).

Reproduction System Dysfunctions

Chronic marijuana abuse has been implicated as the cause of a number of reproductive system dysfunctions such as reduced sperm count, lower testosterone levels, and smaller testicular size in male abusers (Hubbard, et al., 1999; Schuckit, 2006a). Habitual female abusers have been found to experience menstrual abnormalities including possible failure to ovulate (Gold et al., 2004; Hubbard et al., 1999). These problems are so severe that women who wish to conceive are advised to abstain from marijuana use prior to attempting to become pregnant.

The Circulatory System

Heavy marijuana abuse has been identified as a cause of cardiac arrhythmias, although the heavy abuser can develop some tolerance to this effect (Khan et al., 2009). Older marijuana smokers who suffer an acute myocardial infarction (heart attack) were less likely to

---

[27]Discussed in Chapter 34.

survive than were nonsmokers of the same age who had suffered a similar cardiac event (Mukamal, Maclure, Muller, & Mittleman, 2008). The authors also found that heart attack survivors who continued to use marijuana were at higher risk of death than were nonsmokers who survived. It was not clear whether these findings were a direct result of the individual's marijuana use, or whether there were other causes (e.g., cigarette smoking) that contributed to the findings of this study.

Marijuana abuse, for example, is associated with a 30–50% increase in cardiac rate that might last for as long as three hours after the initiation of an episode of marijuana abuse (Craig, 2004; Hall & Degenhardt, 2005). This is potentially harmful for individuals who have a cardiac condition. Marijuana abuse is also associated with a reduction in the strength of cardiac muscle contractions and the amount of oxygen reaching cardiac tissues, which again are of importance to patients with cardiac disease. This also might be one mechanism by which marijuana abuse causes an increased risk of heart attacks in older abusers during the first few hours following the initiation of an episode of abuse ("Marijuana-related Deaths?," 2002; Mittleman, Lewis, Maclure, Sherwood, & Muller, 2001; Mukama et al., 2008; Schuckit, 2006a).

Other Conditions Associated with Marijuana Abuse

There is also an emerging body of evidence that suggests that long-term marijuana abuse might contribute to periodontal disease (Thomson et al., 2008). The authors, after examinations of 903 young adults, found evidence of periodontal disease in 32% of those who used marijuana at least once a week, in 12% who used marijuana less frequently than once a week, and in only 4% of nonusers in their research sample. This was independent of the individual's tobacco use, which itself increased the individual's risk for potential periodontal disease by a small margin, the authors suggested.

A more disturbing finding is that marijuana abuse seems to be associated with a more rapid progression of liver damage in patients infected with the hepatitis C virus[28] (Ishida et al., 2008). The authors speculated that at least some of the abusers identified in their research

---

[28]Discussed in Chapter 36.

sample had switched from alcohol to marijuana because of their fear that their alcohol use might accelerate the damage being done to their liver by the viral infection. However, marijuana abuse might also be associated with an acceleration in liver damage in hepatitis "C" patients the authors observed.

Daily marijuana use is also associated with a little known condition known as the *cannabis hyperemesis syndrome* (Chen & McCarron, 2013). This condition is encountered in marijuana abusers with a history of daily marijuana use predating the onset of the disorder by an average of 9.8 years, and is marked by such symptoms as food aversion, recurrent severe nausea, vomiting, abdominal pain/cramps, the development of compulsive showering or bathing that seems to bring about short-term relief from these symptoms, and the resolution of all symptoms when the individual discontinues the use of marijuana (Chen & McCarron, 2013). These symptoms are often attributed to another rare condition known as *cyclic vomiting syndrome*. Researchers have discovered that 50% of patients with *cyclic vomiting syndrome* will admit to daily marijuana use if questioned (Chen & McCarron, 2013). Symptom relief rapidly follows the discontinuance of marijuana use, but this condition might reappear should the individual return to the daily use of this substance (Chen & McCarron, 2013).

The "Amotivational Syndrome"

Scientists have found conflicting evidence that chronic marijuana abuse might cause the so-called "amotivational syndrome." This hypothetical condition is marked by short attention span, decreased drive and ambition, easy distractibility, and a tendency not to make plans beyond the present day (Hall & Degenhardt, 2005). Indirect evidence that such a condition might exist was provided by Gruber, Pope, Hudson, and Yurgelun-Todd (2003). The authors compared the psychological and demographic measures of 108 individuals who had smoked marijuana more than 5,000 times against 72 age-matched control subjects who reported having abused marijuana 50 times or less. The authors found that those individuals with the greatest level of marijuana use had significantly lower income levels and educational achievement levels than did the control group. Although suggestive, this study does not answer the question of whether these findings reflect the effects of marijuana, or if individuals prone to heavy marijuana abuse tend to have less drive and initiative prior to their marijuana abuse.

Many researchers have challenged the very existence of the "amotivational syndrome" in part because even heavy marijuana abusers demonstrate remarkable energy in the pursuit of their (marijuana-centered) goals. It has been suggested that the amotivational syndrome reflects nothing more than the acute effects of marijuana intoxication on the abuser (Johns, 2001) or the abuser's personality style rather than a drug-induced effect (Sadock & Sadock, 2007). Thus, the question of whether there is a specific amotivational syndrome that might be attributed to marijuana abuse has not been determined as of this time (Brunton, Parker, Blumenthal, & Buston, 2008).

The Myth of Marijuana-Induced Violence

In the 1930s and 1940s, it was widely believed that marijuana abuse would trigger episodes of violence. This belief was reinforced by politicians who wished to further political agenda by using it as a justification to outlaw marijuana. But researchers have never found evidence that supports this belief. Indeed, "only the unsophisticated continue to believe that cannabis [abuse] leads to violence and crime" (Grinspoon et al., 2005, p. 267). It is believed by clinicians that the sedating and euphoric effects of marijuana actually *reduce* the tendency toward violent behavior on the part of abusers (Grinspoon et al., 2005; Husak, 2004). However, the chronic abuser will be more tolerant to the sedating effects of marijuana, and thus capable of reacting violently if they have such a predisposition (Walton, 2002).

Addiction to Marijuana[29]

In spite of the belief of many abusers, marijuana is indeed addictive. There is some degree of controversy as to the danger of marijuana addiction. Zevin and Benowitz (2007) suggested that 8–20% of long-term marijuana abusers will become dependent on it (Budney, Roffman, Stephens, & Walker, 2007; Lynskey & Lukas, 2005; Zevin & Benowitz, 2007). Danovitch and Gorelick (2012) offered a more conservative estimate of 9.8% of marijuana abusers becoming addicted to it. The risk of marijuana-dependence might

be increased if the abuser is using a form of marijuana that has been bred to have a high THC content (Khamsi, 2013). However, the phenomenon of marijuana dependence is poorly understood and further research into this phenomenon is necessary.

Marijuana Withdrawal Syndrome

Marijuana does not induce the same dramatic withdrawal symptoms seen in alcohol or narcotic-dependent persons who discontinue the abuse of their desired drug(s). For this reason, people have long underestimated the addiction potential of marijuana. However tolerance, one of the hallmarks of physical addiction to a substance, does rapidly develop to marijuana (Stephens & Roffman, 2005; Welch, 2009). Approximately one-half of persons in treatment for marijuana addiction report experiencing some withdrawal symptoms upon cessation of marijuana use.

Upon cessation of marijuana use, chronic marijuana abusers experience acute withdrawal symptoms such as irritability, aggression, anxiety, depression, insomnia, irritability, sweating nausea, tachycardia, anorexia, a "craving" for marijuana, and vomiting (Brunton et al., 2008; Budney et al., 2007; Danovitch & Gorelick, 2012; Leamon, Wright, & Myrick, 2008; Raby, 2009; Welch, 2009). These withdrawal symptoms are experienced during the acute phase of withdrawal, usually beginning 1–3 days after the individual's last use of marijuana. The acute withdrawal symptoms peak between the 2nd and 10th days. In some abusers the intensity of the withdrawal symptoms might approach the intensity of nicotine withdrawal (Budney et al., 2007; Vandry, Budney, & Ligouori, 2008). Following the completion of the acute stage of withdrawal the individual enters the extended stage of the marijuana withdrawal syndrome, which lasts between 12 and 115 days depending on the duration and intensity with which the individual was abusing marijuana (Budney, Moore, Bandrey, & Hughes, 2003; Leamon et al., 2008; Sussman & Westreich, 2003). The symptoms that the individual will experience during the extended withdrawal phase are similar to those of the acute stage of withdrawal, but they will over time become less intense and less frequent for the individual. There is no specific treatment for marijuana withdrawal other than complete abstinence from all drugs of abuse (Danovitch & Gorelick, 2012). However, the marijuana withdrawal syndrome can serve as a "trigger" for further marijuana use, starting the abuser back down the road toward marijuana

---

[29]Unfortunately, it is not possible to determine *who* will become addicted to marijuana, and so its use is not recommended if only for this reason.

addiction (Crowley, 2007). As this evidence suggests, marijuana does meet the established criteria for an addictive compound.

Marijuana Use and the *Diagnostic and Statistical Manual of Mental Disorders,* 5th Edition[30]

The *Diagnostic and Statistical Manual of Mental Disorders,* 5th edition (American Psychiatric Association, 2013) identified five subforms of the marijuana-related disorders:

- *Cannabis intoxication*
- *Cannabis use disorder*
- *Cannabis withdrawal*
- *Other cannabis-induced disorders*
- *Unspecified cannabis-related disorder*

For unknown reasons, the authors of the *Diagnostic and Statistical Manual of Mental Disorders,* 5th edition (American Psychiatric Association, 2013) elected not to use the term *marijuana dependence* but instead used the more ambiguous term *cannabis use disorder.* The diagnostic criteria for cannabis-dependence are outlined in *DSM-5* but essentially are unchanged from the 4th edition of the *Diagnostic and Statistical Manual.* The only known "biological marker" for cannabis use is the detection of marijuana metabolites in the person's blood or urine according to the American Psychiatric Association (2013). The *DSM-5* does acknowledge that the nonproblematic use of cannabis is possible, and notes that the differentiation between nonproblematic use and problematic use often is complicated by denial or polydrug abuse. Some of the associated life problems associated with the use of marijuana include (but are not limited to): anxiety, a drug-induced persistent depression, a delusional disorder, and a lack of motivation according to the *DSM-5.*

The diagnostic signs of cannabis intoxication are essentially the same as those outlined in this chapter, although the *DSM-5* accepts the possibility that the individual might experience what it terms "perceptual disturbances" (p. 516), which is to say hallucinations.

---

[30]The material presented here is to illustrate the relationship between the marijuana use disorders and the *Diagnostic and Statistical Manual of Mental Disorders,* 5th edition. This material should not be interpreted as, nor should it be used as, a diagnostic manual.

The signs of marijuana withdrawal identified by the *DSM-5* are essentially the same as those outlined in this chapter, and are thought to develop 24–72 hours after the person's last marijuana use. As was discussed in this chapter, marijuana use is associated with the development of various conditions such as a sleep cycle disturbance or delirium, which fall under the rubric of *Other Cannabis Induced* Disorders in the *DSM-5.* The classification of *Unspecified Cannabis-Related Disorders* identifies those individuals whose marijuana use has resulted in significant impairment in their social, occupational, or social spheres of their lives but whose marijuana use does not fully meet the identified criteria for marijuana a marijuana use disorder.

Chapter Summary

Cannabis sativa has been cultivated for its fiber for thousands of years and at one point no less a person than George Washington cultivated it as a commercial crop for hemp fibers, which have been used for a variety of purposes over the course of history. However, at some unknown point it was discovered that some varieties of cannabis produced a substance, later to be called THC, which produced a sense of euphoria if smoked. Cannabis was thus transformed from a useful plant to a substance of abuse. Its abuse smoldered through the 1930s and 1940s, emerging as a substance of abuse for certain segments of the population in the 1950s. During the 1960s it emerged as a popular drug of abuse in the United States, and a large demand for it developed. Suppliers sought to develop strains of marijuana with ever increasing levels of THC for its enhanced effects to claim a larger share of the marijuana "market" during a time when its use became a mark of rebellion against the established authorities. These forces interacted to make its use so common that by the start of the 21st century more than 50% of the adults in the United States are thought to have used it at least once.

In spite of evidence to the contrary, the federal government continues to maintain that there is no medicinal value in any compound found in marijuana, and that for this reason research into possible industrial or medical applications of any compound found in marijuana is not necessary. In spite of this circular reasoning, physicians have started to accept the possibility that there are indeed possible benefits of marijuana use for some patients with certain conditions and "medical" marijuana is now legal in many states. The use of "medical marijuana" has been approved in a number of states, although it is noted that federal law overrides state law. Although proponents of the lifting of marijuana-use restrictions point to its relative safety, there is an emerging body of evidence suggesting that the chronic use of marijuana for recreational purposes is not without certain dangers. Further, it has been found to be an addictive substance, capable of producing a characteristic withdrawal syndrome. This information is certain to become part of the controversy surrounding the use, and possible abuse, of marijuana in the 21st century.

CHAPTER 11

Opioid Use, Abuse, and Addiction

Introduction

The experience of pain is something of an enigma to modern science: It is the oldest problem known to medicine, and can be experienced either as acute pain or chronic pain (Meldrum, 2003). Each year in the United States alone more than 70% of adults experience at least one episode of acute pain and approximately 30% of adults experience a period of chronic pain (defined as lasting 6 months or longer) (Johannes, Le, Zhou, Johnston, & Dworkin, 2010; Meldrum, 2003; Williams, 2004). However, in spite of much research the experience and treatment of pain remains elusive and there is no objective way to measure the intensity of pain (Chapman & Okifuji, 2004; Johannes et al., 2010).

Throughout much of history the treatment of pain was virtually synonymous with the use of opium; however, with the advent of the chemical revolution in the late 19th century, morphine and codeine were isolated from opium. In the time since then, pharmaceutical companies have churned out a plethora of new synthetic or semisynthetic narcotics. Because of their ability to induce sleep, these compounds are classified as *narcotics,* or *narcotic analgesics.* As a class the narcotic analgesics have an addictive potential that is not well understood by clinicians. However, because of this potential for abuse both physicians and the general public tend to view these medications with distrust in spite of their potential to relieve moderate to severe levels of acute pain. Myths about narcotic[1] analgesics have been repeated so often that many have been incorporated into professional journals and textbooks as clinical "fact," further complicating pain control (Vourakis, 1998). For example many physicians *underprescribe* narcotic analgesics to persons in pain and then interpret requests for additional analgesics by the patient as evidence of drug-seeking behavior(s) (Carvey, 1998; Kuhl, 2002).[2] It has been estimated that as many as 73% of persons in moderate to severe levels of pain receive less than adequate doses of narcotic analgesics because of the physician's fear of inducing an iatrogenic[3] substance use disorder (SUD) (Gunderson & Stimmel, 2004; Stimmel, 1997a).

As was noted earlier, a small but significant part of the population suffers from chronic pain, for which about 3% of the general population have been prescribed a narcotic analgesic for long-term pain control (Dunn et al., 2010).[4] Unfortunately some of these medications are diverted to the illicit drug market, further adding to the general public's distrust of this class of medications. For example, the

---

[1]Unfortunately, the legal definition of "narcotic" is different than the pharmacological definition. Legally, cocaine is classified as a "narcotic" but does not have a chemical structure similar to the opioids. In this chapter, the term "narcotic" will be used for compounds which produce effects similar to those of morphine or which are derived from opium.

[2]As opposed to a person who simply has not received an adequate dose for analgesia.

[3]See Glossary.

[4]Narcotic analgesics are increasingly being used to treat chronic pain as well, although this practice is still controversial and has not been challenged by some researchers.

pharmaceutical OxyContin® was introduced to control moderate to severe levels of pain, but in the time since its introduction it has emerged as a significant part of the drug abuse problem in the United States (Meier, 2003).[5] Statistics such as a 74.6% increase in the number of prescription analgesics between 2002 and 2010, especially in the 18–49 year age bracket (Jones, 2012). Unfortunately narcotic analgesics are also involved in more than 40% of overdose deaths[6] in the past few years (Franklin, 2012). Thus, it is of benefit for drug abuse professionals to have a working understanding of the narcotic analgesics, their potential benefits, and the consequences of their abuse. To assist in this process, this chapter will be split into two sections: In the first section, the use of narcotic analgesics within the medical setting will be discussed. In the second half of this chapter, the opioid use disorders (OUDs) will be discussed.

A Short History of the Natural and Synthetic Opioids

At some unknown point it was discovered that if you made an incision on the top of the *Papaver somniferum* plant during a brief period in its life cycle, the plant would extrude a thick resin that had medicinal value. Anthropologists now believe that opium has been in use as an analgesic for at least 3,500 years. There is evidence that the opium poppy was cultivated as a crop 10,000 years ago (Jaffe & Strain, 2005; Walton, 2002) suggesting that this early cultivation of opium does hint at the possibility that its analgesic properties were known at least then. For the greater part of history, opium was the mainstay in the treatment of pain[7] as evidenced by the fact that the English word *opium* can be traced to the Greek word *opion* which means "poppy juice" (Stimmel, 1997a). In many cultures opium was viewed as a gift from the gods because of its many uses: It could be used to control pain, as well as severe diarrhea from conditions such as dysentery,[8] for example, had some anxiolytic properties and just plain made the user feel good.

During the chemical revolution that began in the 19th century, this resin was found to contain:

an elaborate cocktail containing sugars, proteins, ammonia, latex, gums, plant wax, tars, sulphuric

acid and lactic acids, water, meconic acid, and a wide range of alkaloids (Booth, 1996, p. 4).

In 1806 a chemist by the name of Friedrich W.A. Serturner isolated a compound in opium that would later be determined to be its most active ingredient (Gutstein & Akil, 2006). Because it could make the user feel tired, this alkaloid base was named *morphine* after the Greek god of dreams, Morpheus. This potent analgesic compound is actually a waste product produced by the opium poppy. Morphine is one of 20 distinct alkaloid compounds produced by the opium poppy and is about 10 times as potent as opium (Gutstein & Akil, 2006; Heyman, 2009). Another of these alkaloid compounds was codeine, which was first isolated in 1832 and which will be discussed in more detail, later in this chapter (Gutstein & Akil, 2006; Jaffe & Strain, 2005).

In 1857, about a half century after morphine was isolated, Alexander Wood invented the hypodermic needle. This device made it possible to rapidly and relatively painlessly introduce compounds such as morphine directly into the body. By the time of the Civil War in the United States, both the hypodermic needle and morphine were freely available without prescription for a modest price. Morphine was widely used for medicinal purposes on the battlefields and after the end of the Civil War it was often added in many "patent" medicines[9] sold without prescription in the United States as a hidden ingredient. These compounds were often sold under brand names that, to the unsophisticated person at least, gave them an aura of authenticity as a medicinal compound (Rasmussen, 2008). Surprisingly, research has

---

[5]It is of interest to note that the International Narcotics Control Board (2008), an agency funded by and a part of the United Nations, stated that: "[the] diversion of narcotic drugs from the licit to the illicit market are virtually non-existent" (p. iii).

[6]Either alone, or in combination with other compounds.

[7]As will be discussed in Chapter 15, once aspirin was introduced the use of narcotic analgesics for mild pain fell into disfavor.

[8]See Glossary.

[9]The phenomenon of "patent" medicines in the 19th century is a topic worthy of a book in its own right, but must be mentioned only in passing here.

found that the vast majority of physicians recommended their use at least on occasion (Rasmussen, 2008). The unregulated use of morphine as a hidden ingredient in various elixirs, plus the extensive use of morphine in the battlefield and military hospitals, combined with the recently invented intravenous needle all contributed to an epidemic of narcotics addiction in the late 19th and early 20th centuries. A complicating social phenomenon was the practice of opium smoking, which had been introduced into the United States on a large scale by Chinese immigrants. These disparate forces combined, with the result being that by the year 1900 *more than 4% of the entire population of the United States was addicted to opium or other narcotics* (Brust, 2004).

Faced with this growing epidemic of unrestrained narcotic abuse, the U.S. Congress passed the Pure Food and Drug Act of 1906. This law required that manufacturers list the ingredients of their product on the label. Suddenly many members of the general public could see that many of their most trusted home remedies contained a narcotic compound(s), a discovery that helped contribute to the demise of the "patent" medicine movement. A decade later, the Harrison Narcotics Act of 1914 became law after which point only a licensed physician or dentist could prescribe a narcotic analgesic. Historians attribute the reduction in recreational opioid abuse seen after the passage of this act to the new law, although in reality the wave of opioid addiction had peaked approximately a decade earlier and the problem of illicit narcotics abuse was already on the decline. In spite of the best efforts of society the problem of narcotics abuse never fully disappeared. The popularity of these compounds as drugs of abuse has waxed and waned in popularity during the last century but never entirely disappeared (Heyman, 2009). Opioids, thus, present society with an enigma: They are popular illicit recreational compounds, and effective analgesics. In the next section we will start to explore the medical applications of the narcotic analgesics.

I. The Medical Applications of Narcotic Analgesics

The Classification of Narcotic Analgesics

Since the time morphine was first isolated, chemists have developed a wide variety of compounds that have similar pharmacological effects. These compounds are classified as falling into three groups: (1) natural opiates, which are obtained directly from the opium poppy (morphine and codeine are examples of this category); (2) semisynthetic opiates, which are chemically altered derivatives of natural opiates (dihydromorphine and heroin are examples of this category); and (3) synthetic opioids, which are synthesized in laboratories and not derived from natural opiates (methadone and propoxyphene are examples of this category of compounds). Although there are significant differences in the chemical structure of the different compounds in each category, for the sake of this text they will all be called: *opioids, opiates,* or *narcotic analgesics* because they have very similar analgesic effects.

The Problem of Pain

The word *pain* comes from the Latin word *poena,* which means a punishment or penalty, which effectively explains why most of us try to avoid it (Cheatle & Gallagher, 2006; Stimmel, 1997a). However the word "pain" is too simplistic. In reality there are several subforms of pain: (a) acute pain, (b) noncancer chronic (or persistent) pain, and (c) cancer-induced or related pain (Gunderson & Stimmel, 2004; Holleran, 2002). *Acute pain* is short, intense, and resolves when the cause (incision, broken bone, etc.) heals. *Persistent pain* that is not associated with cancer results from pathological conditions in the body (neuropathic pain, for example), whereas *cancer-related* pain is the result of a tumor's growth or expansion.

There are three different classes of compounds used to treat pain. The first class are the general anesthetic agents used to induce a loss of consciousness so that the person (hopefully) is unable to feel pain. Local anesthetic agents, the second category of analgesics, are used to block the nerve transmission of pain from the source of an injury to the brain. Cocaine was once extensively used in this capacity, but in the majority of cases has since been replaced by other, safer, compounds. The third group of compounds reduce/block the individual's awareness of pain within the central nervous system (CNS) without causing a loss of consciousness. There are several subforms in this category First are the narcotic analgesics, which are "unsurpassed analgesic agents" (Bailey & Connor, 2005, p. 60). A second class of analgesics are the new peripheral *mu* opioid receptor antagonists, a class of medications that do not work in the CNS. A third subgroup of such compounds are the over-the-counter (OTC) analgesics, which will be discussed in Chapter 15.

TABLE 11-1
Some Common Narcotic Analgesics*

GENERIC NAME	BRAND NAME	APPROXIMATE EQUIANALGESIC PARENTERAL DOSE
Morphine	—	10 mg every 3–4 hours
Hydromorphone	Dilaudid	1.5 mg every 3–4 hours
Meperidine	Demerol	100 mg every 3 hours
Methadone	Dolophine	10 mg every 6–8 hours
Oxymorphone	Numorphan	1 mg every 3–4 hours
Fentanyl	Sublimaze	0.1 mg every 1–2 hours
Pentazocine	Talwin	60 mg every 3–4 hours
Buprenorphine	Buprenex	0.3–0.4 mg every 6–8 hours
Codeine	—	75–130 mg every 3–4 hours**
Oxycodone	Tylox	Not available in parenteral dosage forms

*This chart is for comparison purposes only. It is not intended to serve as, nor should it be used as, a guide to patient care.

**It is not recommended that doses of codeine above 65 mg be used because doses above this level do not produce significantly increased analgesia and may result in increased risk of unwanted side effects.

Source: Based on information contained in Thomson PDR (2007) and Cherny and Foley (1996).

Where Opium Is Produced

As was noted earlier, natural and semisynthetic opioids are derived from raw opium, which is obtained from the resin of the opium poppy. The world's need for medicinal opium can be met by the opium fields of India. However, there are vast fields of opium poppies being grown in other countries, usually producing opium for the illicit market. It has been estimated that Afghanistan alone produces 63% of the opium produced on this planet, all intended for the illicit narcotics trade (United Nations, 2011). Painfully, the total amount of land devoted to growing opium poppies around the world increased by 5% in 2010 to a record 195,700 hectares[10] (United Nations, 2011).

Current Medical Uses of Narcotic Analgesics

For thousands of years, opium was one of the few compounds available to treat pain (Gutstein & Akil, 2006). When morphine was first isolated in 1806, the main agent for pain control gradually switched from opium to morphine, which provided more predictable analgesia. With the advent of the chemical revolution in the 20th century, a large number of narcotic analgesics

have been introduced, although they all work through the same general mechanism(s) and for the most part have only minor variations in potency, absorption characteristics, and duration of effect. The generic and brand names of some of the more commonly used narcotic analgesics are provided in Table 11-1.

Narcotic analgesics are used to control moderate to severe levels of pain, as well as to suppress the cough reflex and on occasion to treat severe diarrhea. Nationally, it has been estimated that approximately 5% of the adult population in the United States used a narcotic in the past 12 months (Kelly, Cook Kaufman, Anderson, Rosenberg, & Mitchell, 2008). The vast majority of these people used a narcotic analgesic under the supervision of a physician for short-term pain control. However, nearly half of narcotic analgesic users had been using one or more of these medications for more than 2 years, and one-fifth had been doing so for at least 5 years (Kelly et al., 2008). It would also appear that persons who use narcotic analgesics are more likely to have multiple prescriptions for various medications. Approximately one-third of those persons using a prescribed narcotic analgesic were simultaneously taking five or more other nonopioid medications on a regular basis as compared to the one-tenth of persons not prescribed a narcotic analgesic (Kelly et al., 2008). The reason(s) for or the implications of this disparity are not known at this time.

---

[10]See Glossary.

Pharmacology of the Narcotic Analgesics

Morphine remains the gold standard against which the effects of any narcotic analgesic are measured. Narcotic analgesics achieve their pain suppressant effects through one or more mechanisms: (a) inhibition of pain signals from the spinal cord to the brain, whereas (b) simultaneously activating pain-suppression systems in the brain and spinal cord, and (c) altering the person's perception and emotional response to their perceived pain (Savage, Kirsh, & Passik, 2008). Narcotic analgesics achieve these effects by their ability to mimic the effects of endogenous opioid peptides known as *enkephalins, endorphins,* and *dynorphins* (Gutstein & Akil, 2006; Schuckit, 2010b). These natural opioid peptides function as neurotransmitters in the brain and spinal cord, especially the hypothalamus.

Each family of opioid peptides is found mainly in a specific region of the brain, although there is a degree of overlap (Jaffe & Strain).[11] These endogenous opioids are involved in such activities in the CNS as moderation of the emotions, anxiety, sedation, appetite suppression, and the reward cascade, and they seem to have an anticonvulsant effect. Endogenous opioids are also involved in the process of smooth muscle motility and regulation of various body functions such as temperature, cardiac rate, respiration, and blood pressure. The opioid peptides (and narcotic analgesics) affect the activity of a wide range of primary and secondary neurotransmitters such as norepinephrine, serotonin, acetylcholine, adenosine, glutamate, the endogenous cannabinoid receptors, nitric oxide receptor sites, thyrotropin-releasing hormone (TRH), and histamine. As this list would suggest, the endogenous opioids are quite powerful compounds. For example, the endogenous opioid peptide beta endorphin (ß-endorphin) is, on a milligram-per-milligram basis, estimated to be 200 times as potent as morphine.

Narcotic analgesics function as opioid peptide agonists, occupying the endogenous opioid receptor site(s) to simulate or enhance the effects of these naturally occurring compounds (Vanderah, 2006). A number of these receptor sites have been identified in the brain, and their distribution patterns have been mapped. Researchers have used Greek letters such as *mu,* *kappa,* and *delta* to identify different endogenous opioid receptor sites. Many of these receptor sites in turn have subtypes: There are two known *mu* receptor subtypes, three known *kappa* receptor subtypes, and two known subtypes of the *delta* receptor subtype, for example (Jenkins, 2007). The primary function of the known endogenous opioid receptor types and their function are reviewed in Table 11-2.

There is much to be discovered about the impact of narcotic analgesics on normal brain function. There is strong evidence that when used in therapeutic doses, the narcotic analgesics alter the blood flow pattern within the brain, as evidenced by the results of the process of the single photon emission computed tomography (SPECT) scan studies (Schlaepfer et al., 1998; Schuckit, 2006a).

The effects of drug-induced *mu* opioid receptor activation are dose related and include respiratory depression, cognitive blurring, constriction of the pupils, urinary retention, and at high doses can result in the activation of the brain's reward system (Savage et al., 2008; Stahl, 2008). Activation of the kappa receptor site appears to induce less analgesia than is seen when the *mu* receptor site is activated, and medications that bind to this receptor site thus are effective only for mild to moderate levels of pain (Savage et al., 2008). For reasons that are not clear, the kappa endogenous opioid system seems to function as an antagonist to the *mu* receptor system: Activation of the kappa receptor site negates any analgesia achieved by activation of the *mu* receptor site (Savage et al., 2008).

The subjective effects of a single dose of a narcotic analgesic are different for persons experiencing pain as opposed to those who are not experiencing significant levels of pain. Volunteers who are not in pain and who have received therapeutic doses of narcotic analgesics usually report experiencing a feeling of *dysphoria*[12] and rarely report any degree of euphoria (Schuckit, 2006a). This would appear to reflect the activation of the sigma and kappa receptors when the pain recognition system is not active. Any sense of euphoria is thought to be caused by the effects of these compounds on the ventral tegmental region in the brain (Schuckit, 2006a). This region of the brain is rich in dopamine receptor sites, and is connected with the limbic system, with both regions of the brain thought to be involved in the reward cascade. Narcotic analgesics bind to what are known as interneurons, which inhibit dopamine

---

[11]The specific pattern of neurotransmitter distribution in the brain, and those regions where these endogenous opioid receptor sites overlap, is beyond the scope of this text. The reader is referred to a good neuropharmacology text, if she or he is interested in learning more about this phenomenon.

---

[12]See Glossary.

TABLE 11-2
Opioid Brain Receptors and Their Function

RECEPTOR SUBTYPE	FUNCTION IN CENTRAL NERVOUS SYSTEM
mu (subtype 1)	Analgesia
mu (subtype 2)	Gastrointestinal motility, bradycardia, respiratory depression
delta	Analgesia (at level of spinal cord), constriction of pupils, sedation, minor changes in psychomotor function
kappa	Analgesia (at level of spinal cord), sedation, respiration suppression, psychotic symptoms, reduced GI motility, dysphoria, gag reflex
sigma	dysphoria, hallucinations, decreased respiration, some increase in psychomotor activity levels
epsilon	function remains unknown at this time
lambda	function remains unknown at this time
orphan opioid-like receptor-1 (ORL-1)	function remains unknown at this time

SOURCES: Based on information provided in Barnett (2001); Jaffe and Jaffe (2004); Katz (2000); Knapp, Ciraulo, and Jaffe (2005); Stout (2009); Schuckit (2006a, 2010b).

production in the CNS through the production and release of the inhibitory neurotransmitter GABA[13] especially in the limbic reward system (Savage et al., 2008). Without GABA neuron inhibition, the limbic reward system produces large amounts of dopamine, triggering the reward system in the brain (Savage et al., 2008). The chronic administration of morphine or similar pharmaceuticals causes the dopamine-utilizing neurons to shrink in volume by about 25% (Sklair-Tavron et al., 1996). This appears to parallel reports of a reduced sense of euphoria over time from persons taking a narcotic analgesic.

The amygdalae (singular: amygdala[14]) regions of the brain have a large number of opioid receptor sites. Currently, it is thought that the amygdalae release endogenous opioids in response to sensory data, which influence the formation of emotionally laden memories (Jaffe & Strain, 2005). The sense of joy and accomplishment that one feels when she or he finally solves a complex math problem, for example, is the result of the amygdala's release of endogenous opioid neuropeptide molecules This in turn makes it more likely that the student will remember the solution to that problem if she or he should encounter it again. The amygdala is also involved in the initiation of the "fight or flight" response, and thus it is not surprising to learn that the endogenous opioids also play a role in dampening the fear response (Motluk, 2008).

On the basis of their research involving genetically engineered mice that did not produce any of the neurotransmitter serotonin, Zhao et al. (2007) concluded that there was no apparent analgesic effect from the narcotic analgesics administered to the mice, suggesting that the serotonin neurotransmitter system is somehow involved in analgesia through an unknown mechanism. As the information just discussed demonstrates, there is still a great deal to be learned about how narcotic analgesics impact the normal function of the human brain. In the next section, we will look at some of the pharmacological properties of the more commonly prescribed narcotic analgesics. We will now look at the pharmacokinetics of specific narcotic analgesics in use at this time.

[13]See Glossary.

[14]See Glossary.

Buprenorphine

This is a synthetic opioid introduced into clinical use in the 1960s. As an analgesic, it is well absorbed through intramuscular and intravenous injections, and is estimated to be 25–50 times as potent as morphine (Fudala & O'Brien, 2005; Karch, 2009). A standard conversion formula is that 0.3 mg of intravenously administered buprenorphine is approximately as powerful as 10 mg of morphine. However, the analgesic potential of this medication is limited and it has a slow onset of action. These characteristics, plus its long elimination half-life (up to 37 hours), are all reasons why it is a rarely used pain medication (Baron, Garbely, & Boyd, 2009; United States Department of Health and Human Services, 2004).

Approximately 95% of the buprenorphine in the blood is protein bound. It is extensively biotransformed in the liver, and 79% is excreted in the feces and only 3.9% being excreted in the urine. Surprisingly, animal research suggests that various buprenorphine metabolites are unable to cross the blood–brain barrier, suggesting that the analgesic effects of buprenorphine are induced by the molecules of the parent compound. Once in the brain, buprenorphine functions as a partial *mu* receptor agonist, but with some interesting properties. Rather than disconnecting from the receptor site after the initial activation the molecule remains locked into the receptor site, preventing other opioid molecules from reaching the receptor site until the buprenorphine molecule finally disconnects from that receptor. At high dosage levels buprenorphine acts as an opioid antagonist through this process, limiting not only its own effects but that of other narcotic analgesics as well (United States Department of Health and Human Services, 2004). Buprenorphine molecules also bind at the kappa receptor sites, and bind only weakly with the sigma receptor site, although the significance of these observations is not known at the present time (Fudala & O'Brien, 2005). Between 40 and 70% of persons who receive buprenorphine will experience sedation, constipation, urinary retention, and 5–40% experience dizziness (Donaher & Welsh, 2006). In rare cases (<1%) persons will experience drug-induced anxiety, euphoria, hallucinations, and possibly depression (Brown & Stoudemire, 1998). It is a power narcotic analgesic, which unfortunately is gaining popularity as a drug of abuse.

Carfentanil

This is a chemical cousin to fentanyl (discussed later). It is estimated that this compound is 10,000 times as potent as morphine. It is sold under the brand name of Wildnil®. This medication is normally used in veterinary practice to immobilize large animals (Karch, 2009). It is not intended for human use, and there is no data about the pharmacokinetics of this compound in humans. Fortunately it is also apparently not a common drug of abuse.

Codeine

This is an alkaloid compound found in the milky sap of the *Papaver somniferum* plant bulb, which was first isolated in 1832 (Gutstein & Akil, 2006). Codeine is a prodrug: About 10% of the codeine administered is biotransformed into morphine as an intermediate stage of the biotransformation process (Brunton, Parker, Blumenthal, & Buston, 2008; Gutstein & Akil, 2006). The analgesic potential of codeine is estimated as being about one-fifth that of morphine, but is unpredictable due to individual variations in absorption and biotransformation (MacDonald & MacLeod, 2010). Codeine is usually administered orally. It is used to control mild to moderate levels of pain, severe cough, severe diarrhea, and on rare occasions is used as an anxiolytic.

Although it has been used to control mild to moderate levels of pain for more than 200 years, scientists are only now starting to study the pharmacokinetics of codeine. Following a single dose the peak blood levels are seen in 1–2 hours, and the half-life is thought to be between 2.4 and 3.6 hours (Gutstein & Akil, 2006; Karch, 2009; Stout, 2009). It has been found that the analgesic potential of codeine is enhanced when it is mixed with OTC analgesics such as aspirin or acetaminophen; it is commonly mixed with such compounds in tablet form (Gutstein & Akil, 2006).

Codeine is biotransformed in the liver. Unfortunately, a genetic mutation, found in 7–10% of Caucasians, 5% of persons of Asian descent, and 1% of persons of Middle Eastern descent, prevents their bodies from biotransforming codeine into morphine. As a result of this genetic mutation these individuals obtain little, if any analgesia, from codeine, and require longer than normal time to biotransform and eliminate it (Brunton et al., 2008; Goldstein, 2005; Stout, 2009; Zevin & Benowitz, 2007). In addition the selective serotonin reuptake inhibitors paroxetine and fluoxetine, the antidepressant bupropion, and the antihistamine diphenhydramine all compete for the same metabolic pathway through which codeine is biotransformed, blocking the conversion of codeine into morphine, and thus codeine's effectiveness as an analgesic.

Known side effects include possible itching, nausea, vomiting, dry mouth, miosis, urinary retention, diminished libido, and possible allergic reactions. There have also been reports of life-threatening respiratory depression in adults and in two children prescribed codeine (MacDonald & MacLeod, 2010). Unfortunately, there is much to learn about this compound, and whether it still has a role in modern medicine is being debated.

Fentanyl

This is a synthetic opioid, introduced into the United States in 1968. It offers several advantages over traditional narcotic analgesics, and is especially popular during, and immediately after, surgery (Wilson, Shannon, & Shields, 2011). It is well absorbed from muscle tissues, and is also well absorbed following intravenous injection. Unlike morphine, it does not stimulate the release of large amounts of histamine, an important consideration in some cases (Brunton et al., 2008; Gutstein & Akil, 2006). Fentanyl is quite lipid soluble, and is slowly absorbed into the body through the skin. This makes transdermal fentanyl patches useful controlling chronic pain. Unfortunately, therapeutic levels of fentanyl will not build up for 12 hours after a transdermal patch is applied, a characteristic that requires the use of more traditional narcotic analgesics in the first 12 hours following application of the transdermal patch.

Pharmacology and Subjective Effects of Fentanyl

Fentanyl is quite potent, although there remains some controversy as to the relative potency of this compound as compared with morphine. Various researchers have estimated that fentanyl is about 10 times (Greydanus & Patel, 2005) to perhaps 50–100 times (Gutstein & Akil, 2006; Karch, 2009; Zevin & Benowitz, 2007) as potent as morphine. A typical intravenous dose is 1 microgram.[15] It is highly lipid soluble, with 80% binding to lipid molecules in the blood after intravenous administration, and it reaches the brain rapidly after intravenous administration, providing analgesia in a matter of minutes after intravenous administration. The biological half-life of a single intravenous dose of fentanyl is 1–6 hours, depending on the individual's biochemistry.[16] Most physicians use the average figure of 3 hours when planning for the person's analgesia. When it is administered intravenously, the analgesic effects of fentanyl peak in 5 minutes, last

for 30–120 minutes, both important considerations when planning the person's postsurgical analgesia (Brunton et al., 2008). It is rapidly biotransformed in the liver and excreted by the body in the urine (Karch, 2009). Unfortunately, fentanyl suppresses respiration for a longer duration than it induces analgesia, a characteristic of this compound that physicians must keep in mind when planning for postsurgical analgesia (Wilson et al., 2011).

Between 3 and 10% of persons who receive a therapeutic dose of fentanyl will experience some degree of somnolence and/or confusion, drug-induced anxiety, hallucinations, and/or feelings of depression (Brown & Stoudemire, 1998). Approximately 1% will experience some degree of paranoia, agitation and/or drug-induced amnesia. Other identified side effects include blurred vision, euphoria, nausea, vomiting, dizziness, delirium, and constipation (Wilson et al., 2011). Fentanyl can cause a 20% drop in the person's blood pressure, and it can also induce up to a 25% reduction in cardiac rate. Thus the attending physician must weigh the potential benefits of fentanyl use against its possible dangers.

Heroin

Chemically heroin is just two morphine molecules joined by an oxygen molecule, thus yielding its chemical name: diacetylmorphine (Brunton et al., 2008). As an analgesic, it is thought to be approximately twice as potent as morphine, and a standard conversion formula is that 10 mg of morphine has the same analgesic potential as 3 mg of diacetylmorphine (Brust, 2004). Its major first-stage metabolite[17] is 6-monoacetylmorphine (6-MAM), which is then broken down into morphine. The importance of this metabolite is that it crosses over the blood–brain barrier much more quickly than morphine (Gutstein & Akil, 2006). In the United States, heroin has no recognized medical use and is classified as a Schedule I substance[18] under the Controlled Substances Act of 1970 (Jenkins, 2007). It remains a recognized pharmaceutical in some other countries, and is used by physicians to treat severe pain.[19] There is an emerging body of evidence that suggests that heroin might have a

---

[15]Which is about 1/60,000th the weight of a postage stamp.

[16]Some individuals will be "fast" metabolizers, while others will be "slow" metabolizers. See Glossary.

[17]As with many compounds, heroin biotransformation goes through a number of stages.

[18]See Appendix Three.

[19]Obviously, the heroin used for medicinal purposes in medical centers overseas is produced by pharmaceutical companies under controlled conditions, producing a medication of known potency and purity. The only thing that this heroin has in common with illicit heroin is its name.

cardioprotective potential during periods of cardiac ischemia, although the exact mechanism for this is not clear at this time (Gutstein & Akil, 2006; Peart & Gross, 2004; Mamer, Penn, Wildmer, Levin, & Maslansky, 2003). This effect, if proven in future research, may make diacetylmorphine of value in treating heart attack; however, there is a need for further clinical research to identify the mechanism which causes this effect. Heroin as a drug of abuse in the United States will be discussed later in this chapter.

Hydrocodone/Hydromorphone

Hydrocodone is a semisynthetic narcotic derived from codeine, although it is more toxic than the parent compound. It is used to control coughs, and mild to moderate levels of pain. Technically it is a prodrug[20] and most of its analgesic effects are thought to reflect the action of a metabolite, hydromorphone. Orally administered doses of hydromorphone are thought to be five to seven times as potent as orally administered morphine, although in opioid abusers its potency might be reduced to approximately half of this figure due to the development of tolerance (Stout, 2009). Intravenously administered doses of hydromorphone have a rapid onset of analgesia (5 minutes), and provide 3–4 hours analgesia. The elimination half-life is thought to be approximately 2–3 hours (Stout, 2009). Orally administered doses are subject to the "first pass" metabolism effect. Side effects can include dizziness, sedation, mental confusion, anxiety, fear, nausea and/or vomiting, dysphoria, and respiratory depression (Alattar & Scharf, 2008). Persons receiving exceptionally large doses also experience allodynia and possible seizures (Stout, 2009). A controlled-release preparation of hydromorphone is available in Canada, but has not been approved for use in the United States as of this time.

Meperidine

Meperidine was once recommended for the treatment of persistent pain. Because many of the metabolites of this compound are toxic, its use in a medical setting is limited to 48 hours or less (Gutstein & Akil, 2006). The pharmacokinetics of meperidine are similar to those of morphine and will not be discussed further here.

Methadone

Methadone is a synthetic opioid developed in the years prior to World War II and was extensively used by German physicians during World War II as a substitute for morphine in treating battlefield injuries (Traub, 2009). Although it is a useful pharmacological agent, there is a great deal of confusion surrounding this compound. Today it is used as an analgesic, especially in cases where the person has persistent pain that requires long-term pain control (Toombs & Kral, 2005). However, because of its utilization in *methadone maintenance programs*,[21] many persons object to its use, saying, "I'm not an addict!" To ease some of the person's reservations about being placed on a compound that in their minds is associated with opioid addiction, the brand name form of methadone known as Dolophine® is often prescribed (Lipman, 2008; Schuckit, 2006a).

The methadone molecule is structurally similar to the morphine molecule, and as an analgesic it is about as potent as morphine (Stout, 2009). It is well absorbed from the gastrointestinal tract, when administered orally, with about 80% of a single oral dose being absorbed into the person's body (Lipman, 2008). It is also well absorbed from muscle tissue when administered in an intramuscular injection, and can also be injected subcutaneously as well as administered intravenously (Toombs & Kral, 2005). Because of its long therapeutic half-life, it can provide extended periods of analgesia and reduce "breakthrough" pain episodes that can cause distress in the person. In the opiate-naive person, analgesia is usually achieved with small oral doses of methadone (5–20 mg[22] two to four times a day).

Methadone is highly lipophilic, and once in the circulatory system is rapidly distributed to blood-rich organs such as the brain, liver, lungs, and kidneys. The analgesic effects of oral doses of methadone begin within 30–60 minutes, peak about 2–4 hours after the dose was administered, and continue to be effective for 4–6 hours depending on the individual's biochemistry (Lipman, 2008). Repeated doses of methadone provide a reservoir of methadone to build up in the body, which is then slowly released back in the circulation over time, providing a relatively steady level in the person's blood. However, methadone provides a prime example of how the therapeutic half-life might be shorter than the elimination half-life. In contrast to the therapeutic half-life, the elimination half-life of methadone is between 13 and 58 hours, and

---

[20]See Glossary.

[21]Which will be discussed in Chapter 33.

[22]A common abbreviation for "milligrams," which is a unit of measure.

depending on the individual's biochemistry, might possibly be as long as 128 hours in methadone-naive users who have not developed tolerance to this compound (Schottenfeld, 2008).

Toxicity to methadone varies from individual to individual, with doses of 50 mg or less proving to be fatal in nontolerant adults in some cases, whereas doses of 180 mg/day are often used in methadone maintenance programs. The potential for a lethal overdose is higher for children who accidentally obtain this medication, with doses as low as 5–10 mg having been fatal to children in some cases (Scottenfeld, 2008). The speed at which methadone is eliminated from the body is dependent upon the individual's biochemistry and the acidity level of the individual's urine (Drummer & Odell, 2001; Karch, 2009). If the individual's urine is very acidic, the elimination half-life of a single dose of methadone is reduced by 50% (Drummer & Odel, 2001). When administered over extended periods of time to treat persistent pain, the methadone biotransformation period becomes shorter, reducing the elimination half-life to around 48 hours (Schottenfeld, 2008).

The major route of methadone biotransformation is through the liver, with nine different metabolites emerging at various points in the biotransformation process. None of the methadone metabolites appear to have any analgesic potential of their own (Lipman, 2008; Stout, 2009). The majority of these metabolites are excreted in the bile (Lipman, 2008). When used to treat noncancer pain, it is recommended that the person be started at very low doses to avoid respiratory distress, and then the dose can be slowly increased every 4–5 days to avoid inducing respiratory depression and possible death (Lipman, 2008). However, because of this it might take up to 12 days of dosage adjustments before the person achieves a stable blood level of methadone and thus optimal levels of analgesia (Chou et al., 2009).

As is true with its chemical cousin morphine, tolerance to the effects of methadone develops unevenly. The person might quickly become tolerant to the euphoric effects of methadone, whereas tolerance to the gastrointestinal effects (constipation) might develop slowly, if at all (Lipman, 2008). Tolerance to the respiratory depression effects of methadone is incomplete, and the long elimination half-life of methadone can place the person "at risk" for respiratory depression for extended periods of time after they discontinue the use of methadone (Baron et al., 2009).

Sensitivity to the respiratory depressant effect of methadone might be magnified by the concurrent use of other CNS depressants such as alcohol or other pharmaceuticals. Further, neuroadaptation to effects of methadone are rapidly reversed after abstinence, so that if the person should resume this medication after a period of abstinence, it will be necessary to slowly increase the daily dose until the patient achieves the desired degree of analgesia (Lipman, 2008).

This compound does present some unique dangers, however. Methadone can induce cardiac arrhythmias even when used in therapeutic doses (Chou et al., 2009; Wedam et al., 2008). It is thought that methadone can prolong the QT interval[23] of the normal heart rhythm and induce a potentially fatal arrhythmia known as *Torsade de Pointes* (Chugh et al., 2008; Schottenfeld, 2008; Webster et al., 2011). The causal mechanism appears to be methadone's ability to block the normal action of the potassium channels in the cardiac heart muscles, which are required for the rapid repolarization of the muscles for the next heartbeat (Malik & Stillman, 2009). Between 10 and 15% of those people on methadone who develop this arrhythmia are thought to have a subclinical form of ventricular tachycardia,[24] which is then exacerbated by methadone.[25] The exact percentage of persons on methadone who go on to develop *Torsade de Pointes* is thought to be <1%, but physicians are advised to assess the person for this possible drug complication through the use of serial electrocardiogram (EKG) studies, because the mortality rates of these cardiac problems are so high.

In recent years, the media has focused attention upon the "epidemic" of methadone-related deaths. Although this is not to ignore the dangers associated with methadone use, the concurrent use of CNS depressants, such as the benzodiazepines or even OTC compounds such as antihistamines, can increase the risk of an overdose (Lipman, 2008). Methadone overdoses can be treated by blocking agents such as Narcan®, but the extended half-life of methadone makes it imperative that the person continue to repeatedly receive the appropriate dose of this antidote over extended periods of time. Methadone overdose deaths

---

[23]Technically, the time required for the activation and then recovery from a single heartbeat on an electrocardiogram.

[24]See Glossary.

[25]It is important to keep in mind that ventricular tachycardia has a number of causes, not just the use of methadone.

have been known to occur up to 24 hours after the individual's overdose was ingested, or after the narcotic blocker was discontinued (Scottenfeld, 2008).

However, when used as prescribed, methadone has a very good safety profile. Even after years of prescribed use there is no evidence of drug-induced damage to the lungs, kidneys, liver, brain, stomach, or spleen. Unfortunately, methadone interacts with *at least* 100 different pharmaceuticals currently in use in the United States ("Taming Drug Interactions," 2003). Depending on the exact nature of the compound(s) involved, a methadone–drug interaction might range from inconvenient to life threatening.[26] Some of the medications that might interact with methadone include (but are not limited to) carbamazepine, phenytoin, risperidone, Ritonavir, and the herbal medication St. John's Wort, all of which may reduce the person's blood methadone levels. Other medications such as fluoxetine, fluvoxamine, saquinavir, cimetidine, erythromycin, and ciprofloxacin may slow the rate of methadone biotransformation, causing higher-than-normal (possibly fatal) blood levels of the latter compound (Drummer & Odel, 2001; "Methadone-Cipro interactions", 2002). Persons taking methadone should avoid the use of other CNS depressants such as alcohol or antihistamines to avoid a potentially fatal potentiation effect between the chemicals being abused. For example, the synergistic effect of the benzodiazepines combined with methadone potentially can prove to be fatal at safe dosage levels if these medications were taken separately. There is also evidence that methadone might interfere with the antithrombotic action of aspirin, thus allowing the blood to form clots more easily, possibly contributing to a heart attack, stroke, or other serious medical problems (Malinin, Callahan, & Serebruany, 2001). Although this list of potential drug interactions is far from being inclusive, it does illustrate the potential for potentially fatal drug interactions between methadone and a wide range of other compounds. The reader is advised to consult with a physician or pharmacist before taking two or more medications to avoid the danger of a potentially fatal drug interaction.

Morphine

The resin that is collected from *Papaver somniferum* when the poppy head is lanced at the proper time contains 10–17% morphine (Brust, 2004; Jenkins, 2007). Morphine was first isolated more than 150 years ago, but it still remains the gold standard against which other narcotic analgesics are measured (Gutstein & Akil, 2006; Traub, 2009).

Morphine can be administered orally and is rapidly absorbed through the gastrointestinal tract. However between 60 and 80% of an oral dose of morphine is biotransformed by the "first pass metabolism"[27] effect before it reaches the brain (Stout, 2009). This makes orally administered doses of morphine of limited value in treating severe pain. A standard conversion formula is that 10 mg of injected morphine induces the same level of analgesia as 60 mg of orally administered morphine (Cherny & Foley, 1996). This, plus the fact that it is well absorbed from both intramuscular and intravenous injection sites, results in the usual routes of administration being intramuscular or intravenous injections. A rare but effective route of administration is rectal suppositories. This takes advantage of the fact that morphine is easily absorbed through the mucous membranes of the body such as those found in the rectum. However, this method of morphine administration is so rare that it will not be discussed again in this text.

The peak blood levels of a single dose of morphine are achieved in about 60 minutes after an oral dose, and within 30–60 minutes following intravenous injection (Wilson et al., 2011). After absorption into the body, about one-third of the morphine becomes protein-bound, providing a reservoir of yet-to-be-metabolized morphine in the body for several hours. This is an advantage because the unbound morphine molecules will be rapidly distributed to every blood-rich organ, including the lungs, muscle tissues, kidneys, liver, spleen, and the brain. The analgesic effects of a single dose of morphine last approximately 4 hours (Gutstein & Akil, 2006). The biotransformation half-life of a single dose of morphine ranges from 1 to 8 hours, depending on the individual's biochemistry, with most textbooks offering an average figure of 2–3 hours (Drummer & Odel, 2001). Morphine crosses through the blood–brain barrier slowly, taking between 20 and 30 minutes to accomplish this task, and thus the analgesic effects of morphine might require as long as a half hour to reach full effect.

The majority of the morphine is broken down into the metabolite *morphine-3-glucuronide* (M3G). A smaller amount is biotransformed into *morphine-6-glucuronide* (M6G), and the remainder is biotransformed into one

---

[26]As always, persons on *any* prescribed medication should consult with a physician or pharmacist before taking either another prescribed medication, or an OTC product.

[27]Discussed in Chapter 6, and in Glossary.

of several additional metabolites that do not appear to have a biological effect and will not be discussed again in this text (Brunton et al., 2008; Karch, 2009). Interestingly, M6G has a stronger analgesic effect than its parent compound (Wynn, Oesterheld, Cozza, & Armstrong, 2009). When morphine is administered on a repeated basis, the analgesic effect of M6G has been estimated to reach between 2 and 20 times that of morphine itself, possibly accounting for morphine's analgesic effects in such cases (Gutstein & Akil, 2005; Wynn et al., 2009). The elimination half-life of morphine is thought to be between 2 and 3 hours, but is slightly longer in men than in women (Lipman, 2008).

OxyContin

OxyContin was introduced in 1995 as a time-released form of oxycodone, itself a synthetic opioid. It was designed for use in cases where the person was suffering moderate to severe long-term pain that could be controlled by oral medications. There are two forms of OxyContin: standard and controlled release forms. Peak blood levels are achieved in about 1 hour when the regular form is ingested or in about 3 hours when the extended release form is ingested by the patient. It is recommended that the patient be started on 10 mg of the controlled release form every 12 hours, a dosage level that may be adjusted by the physician to achieve optimal pain control.

The mechanism through which oxycodone produces analgesia is still in dispute. Some researchers have suggested that it is a kappa opioid receptor agonist although others dispute this claim on the grounds that its effects are so similar to that of other opioid *mu* receptor agonists. A relatively stable blood level of OxyContin can be reached after two to three doses, providing better pain control than could be achieved using short-acting narcotic analgesics. Unfortunately OxyContin has become a major drug of abuse, which will be discussed later in this chapter.

Propoxyphene

This is a synthetic narcotic analgesic that is almost as effective an analgesic as codeine (Graedon & Graedon, 1996). It was widely prescribed for mild to moderate levels of pain, often in combination with over-the-counter analgesics such as acetaminophen. It was introduced as having little abuse potential, but within a short time of its introduction, "dependence and abuse became a problem of epidemic proportions" (Breggin, 2008, p. 397). In February of 2009 an advisory panel to the Food and Drug Administration (FDA) recommended that production of this compound be discontinued and that it be removed from the market. The FDA initially rejected this recommendation. However the discovery that propoxyphene could induce cardiac arrhythmias at therapeutic dosage levels resulted in the FDA reversing its decision, and its manufacture in the United States was discontinued in 2010. Obviously, pharmaceutical companies in other countries might continue to produce it, and propoxyphene could be smuggled into the United States. Patients might also have unused prescriptions for this medication, and so it is likely to remain available in this country for some time.

Propoxyphene is a very mild *mu* receptor antagonist when taken at recommended doses, and for this reason was used for mild to moderate levels of pain. However, when taken concurrently with other CNS depressants such as alcohol, or in overdose situations, it can induce respiratory depression and possible death. This compound has a reputation as being popular for suicide gestures, attempts, and completed suicides ("Propoxyphene pharmacokinetics," 2009). Even when used in therapeutic doses, propoxyphene is not without its dangers. A metabolite produced during the biotransformation process, norpropoxyphene (NP), is able to induce 2.5 times the level of cardiac depression than the parent compound. As noted, it can also cause cardiac arrhythmias. Further, the elimination half-life of NP is approximately 36 hours, or three times that of propoxyphene itself. Thus, with repeated propoxyphene doses being administered for analgesia, significant levels of NP can accumulate in the user's body. Further, propoxyphene (or its metabolite NP) inhibits the ability of the liver to biotransform a wide range of other compounds, some of which are used to control seizures ("Propoxyphene pharmacokinetics," 2009).

Tramadol

Tramadol is a distant chemical cousin to codeine (discussed earlier). It is used to treat mild to moderate levels of pain. It is thought to be of value in controlling the pain of childbirth because it induces less neonatal respiratory depression following birth (Brunton et al., 2008). As an analgesic, it is thought to be about as potent as morphine (Brunton et al., 2008). Between 70 and 75% of a single oral dose reaches the circulation, and 20% of this becomes protein-bound. Peak plasma levels are reached in about 2.3 hours, and the half-life is 5.5 hours following a single oral dose (Brunton, Lazo, & Parker, 2006).

Although tramadol has long been viewed as a safe narcotic analgesic for use in mild to moderate pain, the team of Daubin et al. (2008) described at length the clinical course of a person who had ingested a drug overdose of various compounds, including tramadol. The authors concluded that the prescribing physician needed to be vigilant when prescribing this compound, which is possibly more toxic than originally thought.

Sufentanil

This is a chemical cousin to fentanyl, and is sold under the brand name of Sufenta®. It is a pharmaceutical commonly used in cardiac surgery, and is estimated to be 1,000 times as potent as morphine (Brunton et al., 2008; Karch, 2009). The pharmacokinetics of this compound are similar to that of fentanyl.

Nonopioid Analgesics

A new analgesic compound is ziconotide (Prialt®), a substance derived from the venom of the marine snail *Conus magus*. This compound blocks calcium channels in neurons responsible for pain transmission signals, reducing the sensitivity of neurons involved in the process of pain recognition. This compound is not effective as a primary analgesic for acute injuries, but is of value for persistent pain conditions. It is extremely potent, and is administered through an indwelling pump. Ziconotide is capable of inducing neurological side effects, including (but not limited to) blurred vision, nystagmus, ataxia, gait disturbance, sedation, drug-induced psychotic reactions, and depression that might result in suicide. Thus, close clinical monitoring is necessary to identify these consequences and immediately discontinue the medication. However, for those persons who are able to benefit from this medication, it offers the hope of relief from persistent pain without the use of narcotic analgesics.

Peripheral *Mu* Opioid Receptor Antagonists

These are a new class of compounds, two of which, methylnaltrexone and alvimopan, have recently been introduced in the United States. These compounds have poor lipid solubility, and possess an electrical charge that prevents them from crossing the blood–brain barrier. They, thus, do not reverse opioid-induced analgesia in the CNS, but do bind at *mu* opioid receptor sites in the intestines, blocking the opioid-induced constipation which so often limits the use of opioids in pain control (Moss & Rosow, 2008). These compounds are also first in the class of a new family of compounds that may limit, or reverse, many of the adverse effects of opioids, allowing the latter drugs to be used more effectively as analgesics.

Neuroadaptation to Narcotic Analgesics

Analgesia is not a static process, but is influenced by a host of factors such as (a) genetic heritage, (b) disease progression, (b) increase/decrease in level of physical activity, (c) medication compliance/noncompliance, (d) medication interaction effects, and (e) the process of neuroadaptation to the medications being used by that person. The first point, the individual's genetic heritage, is occasionally a source of some confusion in that a small percentage of the population possesses what is known as *innate tolerance* to a narcotic analgesic (Chang, Chen, & Mao, 2007). This is observed from the very first dose of a narcotic analgesic and reflects the fact that the individual's genetic heritage is such that the individual is less responsive to some narcotic analgesics than others.

In contrast to innate tolerance is what is known as *acquired tolerance,* which reflects adaptive changes within the neurons to the presence of narcotic molecules. Neuroadaptation to narcotic analgesics is rapid, but incomplete, and develops at an uneven pace (Jaffe & Jaffe, 2004). Animal research has demonstrated changes in neuronal responsiveness to an opioid after just a single dose, demonstrating the speed at which neuroadaptation begins (Bailey & Connor, 2005). There is wide inter-individual variation in the speed at which neuroadaptation develops, with some persons becoming tolerant to opioid-induced analgesia after just a few days of continuous use at a set dosage level (Ivanov, Schulz, Palmero, & Newcorn, 2006). That the process of neuroadaptation is often incomplete is evidenced by the fact that persons on narcotic analgesics might never fully adapt to narcotic-induced constriction of the pupils even after extended periods of narcotic use (Schuckit, 2006a).[28]

Unfortunately, neuroadaptation is occasionally misinterpreted as evidence of opiate use disorder (OUD), making the physician reluctant to increase the individual's medication dosage. This condition is now termed *pseudo-addiction* as opposed to a real OUD.

---

[28]This rule does not apply to persons who have suffered some degree of traumatic brain injury (Schuckit, 2006a). In such cases the individual's pupils might respond to light in a manner not seen in the normal individual.

The differentiation between these two conditions lies in the fact that once the person's pain is adequately controlled, he or she will not request additional narcotic analgesics. Physicians have discovered that the use of *dextromethorphan,*[29] an NMDA receptor antagonist used to suppress the cough reflex, will slow the development of neuroadaptation and improve analgesia without the need for a dosage increase. It has also been found that the concurrent use of OTC analgesics potentiate the effects of prescribed narcotic analgesics through an unknown mechanism (Gutstein & Akil, 2006). Thus, a dosage increase is not the only answer to the development of neuroadaptation to narcotic analgesics.

The Problem of Hyperalgesia

In rare cases the neural pain receptors become sensitized, responding to noxious stimuli more strongly than normal (Vanderah, 2006). This process is not a sign of tolerance to the effects of the narcotic analgesic being used, but rather a neurological over-response to what would normally be a less painful stimuli. Surprisingly, in even less common cases the pain recognition system neurons might respond to normal stimuli as if it were a sign of injury, sending pain messages to the brain without an injury. This condition is known as *allodynia,* and is exceptionally rare.

Withdrawal from Narcotic Analgesics When Used in Medical Practice

Most persons who receive narcotic analgesics are able to discontinue the use of these medications without significant distress. A small percentage of these persons develop a *discontinuance syndrome.* The discontinuance syndrome might develop in persons who receive as little as 15 mg of morphine three times a day for 3 days (Ropper & Brown, 2005). This discontinuance syndrome is usually mild and does not require treatment, although in some cases the person is advised to gradually "taper" from the medication rather than to just discontinue it, and in rare cases supportive pharmacotherapy helps relieve the person's distress during this time.

Subject Effects of Narcotic Analgesics When Used in Medical Practice

There are several factors that influence the effects that a narcotic analgesic will have on a person, including the (a) route of administration, (b) interval between doses,

[29]Used in cough control agents.

(c) the actual dose of the medication being used, (d) the half-life of the medication being used, (e) the individual's anxiety level, (f) their expectations of the medication, (g) the length of time that she or he has used a given narcotic analgesic, (h) the individual's expectations, and (i) the individual's biochemistry. The last point is illustrated by the earlier observation that a certain percentage of the population lacks the ability to manufacture an enzyme necessary to break down codeine, and thus are unable to receive any benefit from this medication.

When used as an analgesic, between 80 and 95% of persons who receive a dose of morphine report that their fear, anxiety, and/or tension levels are lower after the medication begins to work (Brown & Stoudemire, 1998). Other descriptions include less intense pain, less discomfort, that they become sleepy, and possibly that their pain might have disappeared entirely (Knapp, Ciraulo, & Jaffe, 2005). When used to control cough, persons report that their cough is less frequent, and that they are able to get more rest. In rare circumstances, narcotic analgesics are administered to control massive diarrhea, although with the introduction of newer medications, this use of opioids is rather rare.

Complications Caused by Narcotic Analgesics When Used in Medical Practice
General Vulnerability

There is strong evidence that the individual's risk for developing an adverse reaction ("side effect") to any of the narcotic analgesics is affected by their genetic heritage, and surprisingly by environmental factors (Angst, Lazzeroni, Phillips, Drover, Tingle, Amrita, Swan, & Clark, 2012). The authors found that approximately one-third of the variability in side effects such as sedation, pruritus, and dizziness appeared to reflect both genetic and environmental factors such as age, sex, race, level of education, and mood.

Constriction of the Pupils

When used in therapeutic doses, narcotic analgesics cause the pupils of the eyes to become constricted (mitosis). Some persons experience this effect, even in total darkness (Wilson et al., 2011). Some physicians interpret this as a sign of opiate addiction, although it is a normal side effect of narcotic analgesics and is occasionally seen in a person who is not taking/abusing these medications.

Respiratory Depression

At therapeutic doses, narcotic analgesics make the brainstem less responsive to blood carbon dioxide levels, potentially causing some degree of respiratory depression (Brunton et al., 2008; Brust, 2004). Age is also a factor, with older individuals experiencing a greater degree of respiratory depression after using a narcotic analgesic (Angst et al., 2012). Because of this, there is an ongoing debate concerning whether narcotic analgesics can safely be used by persons with breathing disorders. Webster et al. (2011) noted, for example, that breathing disorders such as sleep apnea exacerbate the risk of an opioid-related death, especially in middle-aged, more obese, clients. This danger is increased with the concurrent use of other CNS depressants such as benzodiazepines. In contrast, Estfan et al., (2007) suggested that if the attending physician were to increase the person's dose in a timely and appropriate manner, there is little danger, even for persons whose breathing has been compromised by disease (Estfan et al., 2007). It has been suggested that the danger of an narcotic analgesic overdose when used as prescribed is not so much the medication as it is the skill and knowledge of the prescribing physician (George & Regnard, 2007).

Gastrointestinal Side Effects

When used even at therapeutic levels, narcotic analgesics can induce nausea and vomiting, especially during the first 48 hours of treatment, or a major dose increase (Barnett, 2001; Dilts & Dilts, 2005). At therapeutic doses, 10–40% of ambulatory persons will experience some degree of nausea, and approximately 15% will actually vomit following the administration of their medication (Swegle & Logemann, 2006). This unwanted effect of narcotic analgesics appears to be most common in the ambulatory person, and persons are advised to rest after receiving a dose of medication to minimize this effect. Further, the individual's vulnerability to this effect is mediated, in part, by his or her genetic heritage, with some individuals demonstrating opioid-induced nausea or vomiting even at very low dosage levels (Brunton et al., 2008). To combat this side effect, some clinicians advocate the use of *ultra-low* doses of the narcotic blocker naloxone to block the opioid-induced nausea (Cepeda, Alvarez, Morales, & Carr, 2004).

Even at therapeutic doses, narcotic analgesics have been found to alter the normal functioning of the gastrointestinal tract in a number of ways. All narcotic analgesics decrease the secretion of hydrochloric acid in the stomach, and slow the muscle contractions of peristalsis[30] (Gutstein & Akil, 2006; Dilts & Dilts, 2005). This side effect is of great value in controlling the diarrhea caused by dysentery or similar disorders, but is also a bothersome, occasionally life-threatening problem, for persons receiving narcotic analgesics for pain control. The muscle contractions might slow to such a degree that persons develop constipation, or possibly even an intestinal blockage (Jaffe & Jaffe, 2004; Swegle & Logemann, 2006). Tolerance to this effect does not appear to develop even after periods of extended narcotics use (Swegle & Logemann, 2006). Mild cases might be controlled by OTC laxatives (Barnett, 2001), and experimental evidence suggests that the compound methylnaltrexone might relieve extreme opioid-induced constipation (Barnett, 2001; Moon, 2008b).

Blood Pressure Effects

Narcotic analgesics should be used with great caution immediately following head trauma. Edema[31] in such cases is common, and if the narcotic analgesic administered to the person should reduce respiration, the heart will pump even more blood to the brain to compensate for the increased carbon dioxide levels, exacerbating cerebral edema if present.

Other Side Effects

At therapeutic doses, narcotic analgesics stimulate the smooth muscles surrounding the bladder, although simultaneously reducing the voiding reflex, causing urinary retention (Brunton et al., 2008; Dilts & Dilts, 2005). Sedation, although a desired side effect in many settings, may interfere with the individual's ability to safely handle power tools or a motor vehicle, and contribute to an increase in accidental injuries (Blondell & Ashrafioun, 2008). The initial dose(s) of a narcotic analgesic can induce transitory changes in cognition (including memory loss and/or confusional states), compounding the effects of infection(s), dehydration, metabolic dysfunctions, or late-stage cancer (Swegle & Logemann, 2006). It has been demonstrated that between 4 and 35% of persons receiving a narcotic analgesic for the control of pain experience some degree of drug-induced irritability, and that 4–25% experience some degree of drug-induced depression. The initial doses of a narcotic analgesic can reduce blood testosterone levels (Schuckit, 2008b). Nightmares, although well documented, have not been studied

---

[30]See Glossary.

[31]See Glossary.

in detail. When used at high dosage levels, all narcotic analgesics can induce seizures, although this side effect is more commonly seen when these compounds are abused, because abusers are more likely to utilize the higher dosage levels generally necessary to induce seizures (Gutstein & Akil, 2006).

Narcotic analgesics can cause the person to become dizzy, lose their balance, and fall, possibly compounding the problem(s) for which they were taking these medications. Although advancing age is a risk factor for falls and injury, even young adults are not entirely safe from this side effect. Unfortunately, an ever-increasing number of older persons are being prescribed narcotic analgesics for pain (Fauber & Gabler, 2012), suggesting that these medications be used with caution with older individuals.

The Danger of Physician-Induced Addiction

Many health care workers will admit to an ongoing fear that they might cause a person to become addicted to narcotic analgesics.[32] In reality, unless the person has a prior history of SUD, only one in every 14,000 persons who receives a narcotic analgesic for the *short-term* control of acute pain is thought to be at risk for the development of an iatrogenic addiction. This risk is higher with persons who have a prior history of a SUD. Yet such persons are often injured or require surgery for one reason or other, sparking a treatment dilemma for the attending physician(s).

A New Approach to Pain

For the most part, neuroscientists have ignored the possibility that the immune system plays a role in pain perception. This area of research offers the potential for new avenues for the treatment of pain. Further, the team of Zylka et al. (2008) have uncovered a new approach to pain, one that does not use narcotic analgesics. On the basis of animal research, the authors suggested that a previously unknown protein molecule, known as prostatic acid phosphatase (PAP), helps neurons generate adenosine, a molecule known for its ability to suppress pain at the neural level. This process appears to generate a level of analgesia eight times as powerful as that achieved by morphine, and seems to be applicable to neurogenic pain as well as possibly acute pain, without the sedation seen with narcotic analgesics, for extended periods of time. Further research into this novel approach to

pain control is needed, but this does offer an exciting nonopioid approach that seems promising.

Section Summary

As is evident from the preceding information, narcotic analgesics are powerful compounds that have the potential to bring great benefit to the person, but only at significant risk. Narcotic analgesics, be they natural, semisynthetic, or synthetic compounds, have similar effects on the brain: They block the person's awareness of pain, bringing relief to the person at a time when she or he is in distress. However, they are not perfect compounds, forcing the person to experience any of a wide variety of side effects such as constipation, alterations in consciousness, respiratory depression, and so on. Although scientists have searched for a compound that might produce analgesia without the side effects brought on by narcotic analgesics, thus far they have been unable to do so.

II. Opiates as Drugs of Abuse

The popular image of a narcotics abuser is that of a heroin addict huddled in a corner of a building, with a belt around his or her arm, injecting heroin into a vein. In reality such persons make up only a small percentage of drug abusers, with 97% of narcotic abusers obtain their drug not from illicit drug dealers, but from a friend or relative who has a prescription for medications such as Vicodin® or OxyContin® ("Adult Use of Prescription Opioid Pain Medications—Utah, 2008," 2010). To clarify such misunderstandings about the abuse of narcotic analgesics, in this section we will examine opiate use disorders.

Why Do People Abuse Opiates?

At first glance it would appear that the answer to this question is simple: They make the abuser feel good.[33] The exact mechanism by which opioids might induce a sense of pleasure remains unknown but appears to reflect a drug-induced activation of the reward system (Gutstein & Akil, 2006; Schuckit, 2008b). Depending on the specific compound being abused, the method by which it is administered, the individual's drug use history, and the user's expectations of the drug(s) abused, the intensity of these feelings can vary from mild to such an intense feeling that it has been compared to sexual orgasm (Jaffe & Strain, 2005; O'Brien, 2011).

---

[32]Which would, technically, be an *iatrogenic addiction.*

[33]Does anybody *ever* abuse a drug because it makes them feel bad?

The Mystique of Heroin

Heroin abuse or addiction accounts for 75% of opioid-use problem around the world, with an estimated 11.7 million persons consuming some 375 metric tons of heroin in 2009 (United Nations, 2011). It has been estimated that 9.3 million heroin users live in Asia, 3.6 million in Europe, and 1.2 million live in the United States (United Nations, 2011).

A Short History of Heroin

Heroin was first developed by chemists at the Bayer pharmaceutical company with headquarters in Germany. The chemists who first developed this compound tried it on themselves, found that it made them feel "heroic" and so it was given the brand name *heroin* (Mann & Plummer, 1991, p. 26). It was introduced for commercial use in 1898. Like its chemical cousin morphine, heroin is obtained from raw opium, with 1 ton of raw opium yielding 100 kilograms of heroin after processing ("South American drug production increases" 1997).

During the 19th century, large numbers of soldiers became addicted to morphine when it was freely administered to treat battlefield wounds or illness. Following its introduction, heroin at low doses was found to stop morphine withdrawal, and because of this was initially thought to be a treatment for morphine addiction (Walton, 2002). Further, both morphine and heroin were found to suppress the coughs associated with conditions such as pneumonia and tuberculosis, both leading causes of death at that time, and were thought to be a treatment for both disorders. The addiction potential of heroin was not recognized until about 12 years after it was introduced. However, by that time, heroin abuse and addiction had become a fixture in the United States. By the 1920s the term "junkie" was coined for heroin addicts who supported their drug habit by collecting scrap metal from industrial dumps for resale to junk metal collectors (Scott, 1998). Although the procedure(s) by which heroin addicts obtain their money has changed over the years, the process has not: Heroin addicts must still feed their "habit" every day.

The Pharmacology of Heroin

Essentially heroin is a prodrug[34] (Jenkins & Cone, 1998): a pair of morphine molecules bonded together by an oxygen molecule. The result is an analgesic that is more potent than morphine, and a standard conversion formula is that 3 mg of heroin has the same analgesic potential as 10 mg of morphine (Brust, 2004). The half-life of heroin has been estimated as between 2 and 3 minutes (Drummer & Odel, 2001) to perhaps as long as 36 minutes (Karch, 2009). Eventually heroin is metabolized into morphine, but an intermediate metabolite of heroin breakdown, 6-MAM as been found to be exceptionally lipid soluble and is able to cross the blood–brain barrier up to 100 times more rapidly than morphine (Brunton et al., 2008). This metabolite is biologically active, and may have an analgesic potential in its own right. However, the current theory is that heroin's analgesic power is the result of its breakdown into morphine (Drummer & Odel, 2001; Karch, 2009). A second metabolite of heroin, 3-monoacetylmorphine, is thought to be biologically inactive and will not be discussed again in this chapter.

Subjective Effects of Heroin When Abused

There are a number of factors that influence the subjective effects of heroin, including (a) the individual's expectations of the drug, (b) the dosage, and (c) the method of heroin abuse. Intranasally administered heroin, for example, is poorly absorbed by the body, with only 25% of the "snorted" heroin reaching the general circulation. The absorption of intranasally administered heroin is slower than that of intramuscular or intravenous injections as well. In contrast with this is the virtual 100% absorption rate achieved when heroin is administered intravenously. Intranasal users report achieving a gentle sense of euphoria, which is in contrast to the "rush" or "flash" experience that is very similar to a sexual orgasm and which lasts for about one full minute (Stahl, 2008) reported by intravenous and heroin smokers. Other sensations reported by heroin abusers include a feeling of warmth under the skin, dry mouth, nausea, and a feeling of heaviness in the extremities. There is some degree of nasal congestion that develops as heroin stimulates the release of histamine in the body. Heroin abusers also report a sensation of floating, or light sleep ("nodding off"), that lasts for about 2 hours, accompanied by clouded mental function. In contrast to alcohol, heroin abusers do not experience slurred speech, ataxia, or emotional lability while under the influence of heroin (Gutstein & Akil, 2006).

Other Opioids of Abuse

There are various legitimate narcotic analgesics that have abuse potentials and are often abused by narcotics addicts for their euphoric effects. A significant

---

[34]See Glossary.

percentage of those persons with an opiate use disorder identify a physician(s) as their main source for drugs, resorting to illicit drugs only if they are unable to obtain a pharmaceutical opiate to use. We will next discuss some of the more commonly abused narcotic analgesics below.

Codeine

Codeine has emerged as a drug of abuse, accounting for 10% of all drug-related deaths (Karch, 2009). There is little information available about codeine abuse, as this compound was long thought to be too weak to be of interest to drug abusers. It is possible that heroin abusers miscalculate the amount of codeine necessary to block opioid withdrawal symptoms, thus contributing to their deaths. However, this is only a theory and the possibility of codeine being part of a fatal polydrug "cocktail" is always present.

OxyContin

OxyContin was released in 1995. At the time of its introduction it was heavily marketed as having a low abuse potential, and only later was it revealed that manufacturer was quite aware of its abuse potential, but did not release this information to physicians (Meier, 2003). As one would expect on the basis of this information it became a drug of abuse shortly after its introduction. A generic form was introduced in 2004. It has been estimated that 13.7 million persons in the United States have used OxyContin for nonmedical purposes in the year 2003 (the last year for which data was available) (Collins & Leak, 2008). The pharmacokinetics of this medication make it especially attractive to drug abusers, who might crush the time-release spheres in the capsule and inject the material into a vein. Other abusers simply chew the tablets, defeating the time-release coating on the spheres, or take larger-than-prescribed doses for the euphoric effects.[35] It has been estimated that OxyContin alone is involved in approximately half of the estimated 4 million episodes of nonprescribed narcotic analgesic abuse that takes place each year in the United States (Office of National Drug Control Policy, 2006).

---

[35]Sometimes a person abusing OxyContin will also have traces of codeine in their urine if they are subjected to urine toxicology testing (see Chapter 33). Many individuals attribute this to their use of prescribed oxycontin. This is a sign of possible drug abuse as OxyContin is never biotransformed into codeine. See: *Forensic Drug Abuse Advisor, 22* (4), 29, p. 29.

Buprenorphine

Buprenorphine has emerged as a drug of abuse. When administered sublingually, it is a valuable alternative to methadone maintenance as a treatment for opioid addiction. However *intravenously* administered buprenorphine has a significant abuse potential. This practice is not common in the United States at this time (Ling, Wesson, & Smith, 2005). It has been reported that this compound is abused either alone, or in combination with diazepam, cyclizine, or temazepam.

Fentanyl

Fentanyl has long been a popular drug of abuse because of its high potency. It is a prescription-only medication, which is often diverted to the illicit drug market. Abusers have been known to smoke it, use it intranasally, or take transdermal patches, heat them, and inhale the fumes (Karch, 2009). Some abusers also take transdermal patches, poke holes in them, and consume the medication reservoir by any of the methods just noted in addition to ingesting the liquid in the reservoir. Because of its high potency, it is easy to overdose on fentanyl, possibly with fatal results.

Hydromorphone

Hydromorphone was introduced under the brand name of Dilaudid®, although it has since been introduced in a generic form as well. It is a chemical derivative of morphine but is about 8–10 times as powerful and is more lipid soluble. This results in hydromorphone crossing the blood–brain barrier more rapidly than morphine, allowing for a more rapid onset of effects. Orally administered doses are poorly absorbed, and intravenous administration is the preferred route.. Occasionally, it is administered orally and is available in tablets that are in doses of 1–4 mg each. Peak blood levels following oral administration are achieved in 30–60 minutes after ingestion. The half-life of this compound is estimated to be around 2.3 hours.

Illicit drug abusers often crush hydromorphone tablets and inject them, although the manufacturers do attempt to block this method of abuse by adding compounds to make this process very difficult or impossible. This is one of the reasons why oral hydromorphone is usually abused by injection. The side effects and risks associated with hydromorphone use are similar to those seen with morphine and will not be discussed again here. Hydromorphone has a high abuse potential and remains a popular drug of abuse among persons with OUD.

Propoxyphene

Propoxyphene is a compound that was sold under a number of brand names in the last quarter of the 20th century. This compound has little potential to induce euphoria by itself, but it was often used concurrently with methadone, providing a feeling of euphoria from the combined effects of these compounds. This compound has a significant abuse potential (Breggin, 2008); however, manufacture and use of this compound in the United States is now illegal.

Although this list is not all inclusive, it does underscore the abuse potential inherent in the use of all prescription narcotic analgesics.

Methods of Opiate Abuse

When opiates are abused, the preferred method of abuse depends on the individual's experience with the compound. These compounds might be taken orally, injected under the skin ("skin popping"), administered intravenously, smoked, or used intranasally (technically "insufflation"). Historically, the practice of smoking opium has not been common in the United States in the past half century, although it does continue in some quarters. However, the practice of smoking opium wastes a great deal of potential opium, and if supplies are limited (as they are in the United States), it is not a popular method of abuse.

Heroin, almost in a class all its own, is abused in a variety of methods. The practices of insufflation and smoking heroin powder have become popular in the United States, fueled in part by the popular myth that you cannot become addicted to narcotics unless you *inject* drugs into your body (Drummer & Odel, 2001; Greydanus & Patel, 2005; Gwinnell & Adamec, 2006; Smith, 2001). When heroin is used intranasally, the method of administration is very similar to that seen when cocaine is used through insufflation. The abuser will place the powder on a glass, then use a razor blade or knife edge to "dice" up the powder until it is a fine, talcum-like powder which is arranged in a line on a glass and then inhaled through a straw. In contrast to injected heroin, where the effects are felt almost instantly, it takes 10–15 minutes before inhaled heroin powder begins to take effect. Injected heroin provides an intense "rush," followed by a gentle sense of euphoria, which is the desired effect, and frequently a severe itching of the skin, nausea, and vomiting[36] (Gwinnell & Adamec, 2006).

Heroin is well absorbed through the lungs when it is smoked, although the onset of its effects are slower than when it is injected. The effects of heroin when it is smoked begin in 10–15 minutes, in contrast to the estimated 8 seconds before injected heroin begins to work. Smoking heroin is an ineffective method of delivery, with up to 80% of the available heroin being destroyed by the heat produced by the smoking process (Drummer & Odel, 2001). Drummer and Odel (2001) reported that when heroin is smoked, blood levels are only about 50% as high as those seen when heroin is injected[37] (Drummer & Odel, 2001). The practice of "chasing the dragon" is a variation on the process of smoking heroin. In this procedure, the abuser heats some heroin powder on a piece of aluminum foil, using a cigarette lighter or match as the heat source. The resulting fumes are then inhaled, avoiding the exposure to intravenous needles that might be contaminated by earlier abusers (Karch, 2009). Another variation of the practice of smoking heroin is seen when abusers intermix heroin with "crack" cocaine pellets. This combination is said to enhance the "high" induced by these chemicals, although possibly at the cost of exacerbating the respiratory depression seen when narcotics are abused.

The most concentrated blood levels of heroin are achieved when the abuser injects the compound into a vein. Sometimes the heroin addict will mix: heroin in the spoon with water, or glucose and water, in order to dissolve it. Lemon juice, citric acid or vitamin C may be added to aid dissolving. This cocktail is heated until it boils, drawn into the syringe through a piece of cotton wool or cigarette filter to remove impurities, and injected whilst still warm (Booth, 1996, p. 14).

This method of abuse allows for the rapid introduction of concentrated heroin into the body, inducing an intense reaction, as noted elsewhere in this chapter. Although veins in the arm are often used, some abusers or addicts will use arteries in the groin, between the toes or the neck, on the theory that this will allow the heroin to reach the brain more rapidly.

Sources of Illicit Narcotics

Currently, the available evidence would suggest that the diversion of prescribed narcotics is more prevalent than

---

[36]Sometimes called "the good sick" by heroin addicts.

[37]Smokers will compensate for the lower absorption level by smoking more heroin; this is why the two figures (amount destroyed when smoked versus blood levels) do not appear to make sense at first.

the use of illicit opiates (Davis & Johnson, 2008). Methadone was the most commonly diverted substance, although other narcotic analgesics were also frequently diverted. The pharmaceuticals were obtained through a variety of channels. Sometimes the individual would "make a doctor"[38] or dentist for a prescription, or arrange for a person who receives medication for legitimate medical reasons to "divert" some of their medication. Some opioid abusers have been known to befriend a person with a terminal illness to steal narcotics from the person for their own use. Others have burglarized pharmacies or brazenly held up the pharmacy to demand narcotic analgesics. Pharmacies on the "Internet" have become a major source of "prescribed" medications that are used for illicit purposes.

But these sources cannot supply the drug abuser with heroin, which is illegal in the United States. An elaborate distribution network has evolved to smuggle heroin into the United States, distribute it across the country, and from there to the individual abuser. To avoid conflict over territory, upper-level distributors have agreed that the heroin abused west of the Mississippi River would be smuggled through Mexico, whereas the heroin abused east of the Mississippi would be smuggled into the United States from other sources. The heroin that is sold at the street level is usually adulterated[39] with one or more foreign compounds with the result being that the purity of heroin sold to individuals is around 47%, although occasionally one will find a sample that is up to 85% pure being sold on the street level (O'Brien, 2008).

Health care professionals have been known to divert pharmaceuticals for their own use, although the strict controls over access and the use of narcotic analgesics make this increasingly difficult. Health care professionals are very likely to have access to medication preparations designed for injection and to sterile needles, and usually follow appropriate injection procedures to avoid the infection(s)[40] often associated with illicit drug injection. In contrast, illicit narcotic abusers often attempt to inject a tablet or capsule originally intended for oral use. These oral administration vehicles contain compounds known as "fillers"[41] intended to give the capsule or tablet bulk, making it easier for the person to handle them. These compounds are not intended for intravenous injection,

and normally are either destroyed by gastric juices or pass harmlessly through the gastrointestinal tract. The fillers, or adulterants often mixed into illicit heroin, potentially can form an emboli, or damage the vessel lining and thus contribute to the formation of a blood clot at the site of injection. Repeated exposure to such compounds can cause extensive scarring at the site of injection, forming the famous "tracks" associated with illicit opioid abuse/addiction.[42]

The Development of Tolerance

The mechanism through which tolerance to a narcotic analgesic develops is poorly understood (Kreek, 2008). It is known that tolerance to a narcotic reflects the same biological process as neuroadaptation, but the former term is used when discussing drugs of abuse and the latter when discussing prescribed medications. Tolerance to the effects of the narcotics develops rapidly, often within days or weeks of continuous use. As is true for narcotic analgesics that are used as prescribed, tolerance does not develop to all of the drug's effects. The illicit opioid abuser can develop significant tolerance to the analgesic, respiratory, and sedating effects of opioids. They become tolerant to the "rush" or "flash" effect that is initially experienced when they begin intravenously administered opioids (Jaffe & Strain, 2005). However, they still experience the narcotic-induced sense of gentle euphoria that is by itself an incentive for continued opioid use (Jaffe & Strain, 2005).

In spite of their growing tolerance to opioids, illicit narcotics abusers never fully become tolerant to the meiotic and constipating effects induced by narcotic analgesics (Jaffe & Jaffe, 2004; Jaffe & Strain, 2005). Unfortunately, the chronic abuse of opioids may result in significant constipation problems for the abuser, possibly to the point where an intestinal blockage will form and require emergency surgery. Tolerance to the "rush" or "flash" develops rapidly, and abusers often attempt to compensate for this by either switching to a more effective delivery method (such as moving from intranasal to smoked forms of heroin abuse), or by increasing the amount of drug consumed (O'Brien, 2006). These doses would be fatal to an opiate-naive person, and it is not uncommon for opioid abusers/addicts to miscalculate their level of tolerance and accidentally overdose on narcotics. Approximately 50% of

---

[38]See Glossary.

[39]The topic of drug adulteration is discussed later in this text.

[40]Discussed in Chapter 34.

[41]See Glossary.

---

[42]Which IV drug abusers might attempt to hide through the use of strategically placed tattoos (Greydanus & Patel, 2005).

opioid abusers experience at least one drug overdose (Schuckit, 2008b, 2010b). Other abusers go through cycles of drug use until their tolerance is such that they can no longer afford the necessary drugs to induce the desired state of euphoria, and then go through a period of withdrawal (usually with support from other illicit drugs, such as illicit benzodiazepines). Upon completion of the withdrawal cycle, they restart the abuse of opiates again. Eventually, the individual reaches the point where she or he is no longer using drugs to achieve a "high," but "just to maintain" his or her intoxicated state.

Scope of the Problem of Narcotic Abuse and Addiction

Physical dependence on opioids can develop in a very short time, possibly after just a few days of continuous use (Ivanov et al., 2006; Stahl, 2008). The United Nations (2011) estimated that there were between 12 and 21 million opiate abusers worldwide in 2009. Of this number, 4 million are opium abusers, the vast majority of whom live in Asia (United Nations, 2011). The abuse of opium is most common in Asia, and globally heroin abuse or addiction is much more common. Heroin accounts for 75% of all illicit narcotic abuse, with an estimated 12–14 million heroin abusers around the world[43] (United Nations, 2011). According to the United Nations (2011) estimate, 3.8 million narcotics abusers are thought to live in Europe, 8.4 million in Asia, and approximately 1 million to live in Africa.

The abuse of prescription narcotics is a growing problem in North America, especially in the United States, where approximately 2.4 million persons 12 years or older abuse a prescription narcotic(s) each year for the first time (Lembke, 2012). Only a fraction of those who *briefly* abuse opiates, perhaps only one in three to one in four people, will go on to become addicted to a narcotic (O'Brien, 2006).[44] This is clearly seen in the subpopulation of opioid abusers known as "chippers," who abuse opioids in response to social cues, but have no trouble abstaining from narcotics when they wish to do so. Though very little is known about opioid "chippers," some of those who once were

classified as a "chipper" go on to become addicted, some discontinue the use of these compounds, whereas still others remain a "chipper."

Males tend to predominate the opioid addiction problem by a ratio of about 3 to 1 (Sadock & Sadock, 2007). Using the estimate suggested by Lembke (2012) of 2.4 million persons in the United States with narcotic use disorder, this would mean that approximately 1.8 million are male, and 600,000 are female.

Prescription narcotic analgesics have become a significant part of the narcotic use disorder problem in the United States. Approximately 76% of narcotic analgesics that are abused were prescribed for somebody other than the user, 20% were prescribed for the abuser, and the rest came from other sources (Miller & Frankowski, 2012). Admittedly, not all of those who begin to abuse prescription narcotics will become dependent on them, as evidenced by the fact that whereas an estimated 31.8 million people over the age of 12 have abused a narcotic analgesic at some point in their lives (National Survey on Drug Use and Health, 2006), only a small percentage have become addicted to them.[45]

When the term "opiate use disorders" is used, it is important to keep in mind that there are various subsets of narcotics abusers/addicts. Some abusers are simply curious about these compounds, use them for a limited time, and then abstain from further narcotics abuse. Some individuals with opiate use disorder are individuals who require prolonged use of narcotic analgesics as an aid to the treatment of injuries suffered in an accident or the effects of illness.[46] These individuals may attempt to avoid being identified as being dependent on narcotics through the continued sanctioned use of a prescribed medication. It is often difficult to separate drug-seeking persons from those with a legitimate need for pain relief, especially in a person who has a physical illness.

Finally, there are those individuals with OUD who fit the stereotypical picture of a narcotics addict. But these individuals intermix the abuse of illicit narcotics with prescribed medication(s). It is not uncommon for such persons to visit different physicians or hospital emergency rooms to obtain multiple prescriptions for a desired medication(s). Such abusers often study

---

[43]Remember: This number includes not only those who are addicted to heroin, but also individuals who are "chippers" and persons who might experiment with heroin use a few times and discontinue the practice for a variety of reasons.

[44]However, since it is not possible to identify *who* will become addicted, the abuse of narcotic analgesics is not recommended.

[45]Abuse of narcotic analgesics or other compounds is, of course, not recommended.

[46]Known as an *iatrogenic* addiction. As noted in the section devoted to the medical uses of narcotic analgesics, this is rare. Still, it does happen.

medical textbooks to be able to simulate symptoms of a disorder virtually guaranteed to provide them with a prescription for a narcotic analgesic. It has even been known for some individuals to have a tattoo that simulates the scar of a surgical procedure, especially a back surgery, to justify a prescription for narcotic analgesics from a new physician. If stopped by the police, they are able to produce a prescription bottle with their name on it, affirming that there is a legitimate need for them to use that medication. These factors make it difficult to estimate the scope of narcotics use disorders in the United States. Still, it has been suggested that currently, there are approximately 800,000 to 1 million people in the United States who are physically dependent on narcotics (Hasemyer, 2006; O'Brien, 2008; Tinsley, 2005).

Scope of Illicit Heroin Abuse in the United States

There are those who *abuse* heroin, some of whom *go on to become addicted* to this compound whereas others experiment briefly with opiates and then discontinue the use of these compounds. Heroin addiction does not develop instantly, but will usually require approximately 2 years between the initiation of heroin use and the time that the individual has become physically dependent on it. Each year in the United States, approximately 146,000 people try heroin for the first time (Jaffe & Anthony, 2005), joining the estimated 3 million people who are thought to have used heroin at least once. Between 600,000 and 800,000 people in the United States are addicted to heroin (Jaffe & Strain, 2005).

In the late 1990s, heroin use was viewed as a sign of rebellion, possibly reaching its pinnacle with the rise of the "heroin chic" culture during that era (Jonnes, 2002). This contributed to a change in heroin abuse patterns in that decade: In 1988 the average age of the individual at first heroin use was 27, but by the mid-1990s this had dropped to the age of 19 (Hopfer, Mikulich, & Crowley, 2000). Adolescents were found to make up just under 22% of those who admitted to heroin abuse, a trend fueled by the availability of low-price, high-potency heroin, and its status as a sign of rebellion (Hopfer et al., 2000).[47] Heroin abusers in the

United States are thought to consume between 13 and 18 metric *tons* of heroin each year (Office of National Drug Control Policy, 2006). As this data suggests, the abuse of heroin overlaps the problem of prescription drug abuse in the United States, and that while a small but significant percentage of the population has abused an opiate at least once, only a minority of the population is thought to be addicted to one or more drugs in this category.

Complications Induced by Opiate Abuse or Addiction

Collectively, the abuse of opioid analgesics is so widespread and so dangerous that in many states there are more fatal overdoses involving this class of medications than deaths from motor vehicle accidents ("Increase in Fatal Poisonings Involving...," 2009). The complications seen in chronic opiate abusers fall into two categories: (1) those that are exaggerations of the complications seen when these compounds are seen in medical practice and (2) those complications that are forced on the individual by the lifestyle of the opioid-dependent person.

Addiction to narcotics exposes the individual to a significant threat of premature death, the most common causes of which are accidental overdose and cardiopulmonary failure (Fiellin, 2008; Smyth, Hoffman, Fan, & Hser, 2007). The team of Smyth et al. (2007) found, for example, that 48.5% of the original sample pool had died. The leading causes of death were overdose (17% of those who had died), chronic liver disease (15% of the sample), cardiovascular disorders (12%), cancer (11%), accidents (8%), and homicide (7%). The typical heroin addict lost approximately 18.3 years[48] of potential life either directly or indirectly as a result of their addiction (Smyth et al., 2007; Tomb, 2008). Other potential causes of death for opiate abusers or addicts include cerebral infarction and the formation of a thrombosis that can result in a stroke (Ricaurte, Langston, & McCann, 2008). Occasionally narcotic abusers or addicts develop aspiration pneumonia because of drug-induced respiratory suppression (Schuckit, 2010b). This condition, like all forms of pneumonia, carries with it the risk of premature death.

---

[47]In contrast to the typical heroin sample of the 1960s, which was perhaps 4% heroin and the rest fillers and adulterants, O'Brien (2008) noted that currently a heroin addict can expect to find illicit heroin to be around 45% heroin, and noted that some samples have been up to 85% pure heroin.

[48]If you assume that the average addict would have lived 80 years if he or she were not addicted to heroin, this means that the typical heroin addict loses about 22% of his or her estimated life because of addiction to heroin.

Narcotic Withdrawal Syndrome

The narcotic withdrawal syndrome experienced by opiate abusers or addicts is simply the opioid discontinuance syndrome observed when persons use these medications under a physician's supervision. Narcotic withdrawal syndrome is possibly more intense in scale than the discontinuance syndrome seen in normal medical practice because abusers or addicts use higher doses of opiates for longer periods of time than is the norm in medical practice. It should be noted, however, that in spite of common claims by those who abuse opioids, narcotic withdrawal syndrome is only rarely a life-threatening condition[49] (Fadem, 2009; Maldonado, 2010). In reality withdrawal distress has been compared to a severe case of influenza (Kosten & O'Connor, 2003; Tomb, 2008). There are two stages to the opioid withdrawal syndrome: (a) the stage of *acute* withdrawal and (b) the stage of *extended* withdrawal. Both of these stages are influenced by such factors as (1) the specific compound(s) being abused,[50] (2) the length of time that these compounds have been abused, (3) the speed at which the withdrawal processes progresses, and (4) the individual's cognitive "set" (Jaffe & Jaffe, 2004; Kosten & O'Connor, 2003). Health care professionals could use the tool prepared by the Clinical Institute Narcotics Assessment (CINA) to obtain an objective assessment of the withdrawal process (Mee-Lee & Gastfriend, 2008).

Obviously, the specific compound being abused will influence the withdrawal process. Acute heroin withdrawal symptoms, for example, peak 36–72 hours after the individual's last dose, and last for 7–10 days. In contrast to this, the acute withdrawal symptoms from methadone peak 4–6 days after the last dose, and continue for 14–21 days (Collins & Kleber, 2004; Kosten & O'Connor, 2003; Kreek, 2008). The withdrawal patterns for other opioids are similar, although there might be some variation depending on the half-life of the compound(s) being abused. The speed of the opioid withdrawal process is another factor that influences the symptoms experienced, and their duration. An opioid-dependent person who is placed on a methadone "taper" will experience withdrawal symptoms over prolonged periods of time as his or her medication

is slowly reduced. However, these withdrawal symptoms will be less intense if the person just stopped abusing drugs ("cold turkey"). The individual's withdrawal distress would be of a shorter duration in the latter case. Thus, physicians must balance the individual's discomfort with the speed of the withdrawal process.

The individual's cognitive "set" also influences the withdrawal process and the individual's perception of it. This reflects such factors as the individual's knowledge, attention, motivation, and degree of suggestibility. The influence of the individual's cognitive "set" might be seen in extreme cases, such as when the individual develops an almost phobic-like fear of withdrawal (Collins & Kleber, 2004; Kenny et al., 2006). Such individuals might have no personal investment in the success of the withdrawal process and thus are motivated to respond to every symptom as if it were major trauma being inflicted on them. In contrast to this, the highly motivated client might be eased through the withdrawal process through hypnotic suggestion (Erlich, 2001).

A complicating factor during the opiate withdrawal process is that the individual becomes more sensitive to pain as a result of increased muscle activity and the stimulation of the sympathetic nervous system (Gunderson & Stimmel, 2004; Kreek, 2008).[51] Further, the opioid withdrawal process induces a sense of "craving" for additional opioids, as well as anxiety, both emotional states that lower the individual's pain threshold and increase his or her sensitivity to pain. In the section to follow, we will examine the acute withdrawal process more closely.

Acute Opioid Withdrawal for the Addicted Person

During the acute phase of opioid withdrawal the individual usually reports an intense "craving" for more narcotics. Other symptoms include tearing of the eyes, runny nose, repeated yawning,[52] sweating, restless sleep, dilated pupils, anxiety, anorexia, irritability, insomnia, weakness, abdominal pain, nausea, vomiting, gastrointestinal upset, chills, diarrhea, muscle spasms, and in males possible ejaculation (Brust, 2004; Collins &

---

[49]Usually life-threatening withdrawal is seen in persons with concurrent medical problems. All cases of drug withdrawal should be assessed and treated by a physician to ensure proper medical care during this process.

[50]Including the half-life of each compound being abused.

[51]A medical examination will reveal whether the reported withdrawal distress is caused or exacerbated by a concurrent medical condition that needs treatment (Gunderson & Stimmel, 2004).

[52]A process that, according to Newberg and Walkman (2009), reflects the brain's efforts to "reset" the cognitive pathways so that the person can adjust to the change in the neurotransmitter levels within the opioid neurotransmitter system.

Kleber, 2004; Gunderson & Stimmel, 2004; Kreek, 2008). It has been suggested that 600–800 mg of ibuprofen every 4–6 hours can provide significant relief from the muscle pain experienced by many persons during this phase of withdrawal (Collins & Kleber, 2004). However, the etiology of the pain must first be identified to avoid the danger of not treating a real medical problem because it was assumed to be a withdrawal manifestation (Gunderson & Stimmel, 2004).

Where constipation is a problem for the person taking narcotics, during the withdrawal process, the individual might experience diarrhea as the gastrointestinal tract returns to a normal self-regulating state. On very rare occasions the opioid withdrawal process can cause seizures, or exacerbate a pre-existing seizure disorder (Collins & Kleber, 2004; Gutstein & Akil, 2006; Kreek, 2008). One exception to this rule is when the person abuses the narcotic meperidine, which is known to lower the person's seizure threshold. Anxiety too is common during opioid withdrawal, and might be so intense as to serve as a relapse trigger (Collins & Kleber, 2004). It has been recommended that rather than benzodiazepine, the compound Seroquel® (quetiapine fumarate) be used to control withdrawal-induced anxiety (Winegarden, 2001).

A Cautionary Note

Many opiate-dependent persons will emphasize their physical distress during the withdrawal process, in the hopes of obtaining drugs to limit their distress, and possibly provide a substitute for the unavailable opioid. Such displays are often quite dramatic, but are hardly realistic for the most part. Mild to moderate opioid withdrawal is, although uncomfortable, rarely a medical emergency in the healthy adult[53] (Baron et al., 2009). The subjective experience has been compared to a bad case of influenza, and will abate in the healthy individual even without medical intervention.

Extended Opioid Withdrawal Symptoms

The phase of extended opiate withdrawal might last for several months in some individuals and include symptoms such as fatigue, heart palpitations, "urges" to return to opioid use, and a general feeling of restlessness (Jaffe &

---

[53]Assuming that the individual was abusing *only* narcotics, and that she or he has not overdosed on an opioid or combination of drugs. The latter situation is a medical emergency that requires immediate intervention by a trained medical team (Sadock & Sadock, 2003; Work Group on Substance Use Disorders, 2007; Zevin & Benowitz, 2007).

Strain, 2006). Some persons also report concentration problems that might last 3–6 months after their last use of narcotics. These feelings become less intense over time, and the individual's level of function returns to normal over a period of weeks to months.

Organ Damage

Some persons who experience extreme pain, such as that seen in some forms of cancer, for example, receive massive doses of narcotic analgesics for extended periods of time without any sign of drug-induced organ damage (Ricaurte et al. 2008). For example, the famed surgeon William Halsted was addicted to morphine for 50 years, without suffering apparent physical harm (Brust, 2004). However, these are cases where the person is using pharmaceutical quality narcotic analgesics, and not "street" drugs commonly abused by illicit drug abusers. These illicit compounds of questionable purity are usually intermixed with compounds not intended for injection. There is little data on the health consequences of the abuse of other opioids beyond heroin.

Common health complications seen in heroin abusers include strokes, cerebral vasospasm, infectious endocarditis, botulism, tetanus, peptic ulcer disease, liver failure, disorders of the body's ability to form blood clots, malignant hypertension, neuropathy, pulmonary edema, and uremia (Brust, 2004; Greydanus & Patel, 2005; Karch, 2009). Because heroin has been used as a pharmaceutical in many countries for more than a century without evidence of organ damage, it must be assumed that these complications of heroin abuse in the United States are either caused by adulterants mixed in with the heroin, or the conditions under which it is abused. The abuse of illicit narcotics has also been found to reduce the effectiveness of the immune system, although again the exact mechanism for this disorder is not understood at this time (Karch, 2009). Intravenous opioid addicts are at increased risk for rhabdomyolysis, but it is not clear whether this is because of the effects of the narcotics, or one or more adulterants mixed in with the illicit narcotics (Karch, 2009). Oxycodone abusers appear to be vulnerable to developing an autoimmune disorder that attacks the kidneys, although the causal mechanism is again unknown (Hill, Dwyer, Kay, & Murphy, 2002).

The recreational abuse of opioids appears to induce the shrinkage of the brain's reward system. This appears to reflect an adaptive response by the brain to the constant presence of an opioid such as heroin, and may reflect the biological basis for tolerance to the euphoric effects of such compounds. With extended abstinence, this effect appears to reverse itself. The practice of smoking heroin has been identified as causing progressive spongiform leukoencephalopathy[54] in rare cases (Zevin & Benowitz, 2007). It is not known whether this effect is induced by the heroin itself, or by one of the adulterants mixed into the illicit heroin before sale (Roper & Brown, 2005; Schuckit, 2008b). There was an outbreak of heroin-induced progressive spongiform leukoencephalopathy in the Netherlands in the 1990s, a condition that is rarely encountered in the United States but which has debilitating consequences for the victim. Intravenous opioid abuse also has been seen to induce damage to peripheral nerves, as the individual rests for extended periods of time in the same position, cutting off the blood flow to the affected nerves. Also, nerves near the injection site might be damaged by the adulterants mixed with the illicit drug being injected (Ropper & Brown, 2005).

Cotton Fever

As noted earlier, heroin addicts attempt to "purify" the heroin about to be injected by pouring it through wads of cotton or cigarette filters. During times of hardship, some abusers attempt to use the residual heroin found in these "filters," and in the process inject microscopic cotton particles as well as the impurities that had originally been filtered out. This induces a condition known as pulmonary arteritis[55] (which is called "cotton fever" by addicts).

Overdose of Illicit Narcotics[56]

Ropper and Brown (2005) identified four mechanisms through which the abuser might overdose: (1) a suicide attempt, (2) the use of substitute or contaminated illicit drugs, (3) an individual's unusual sensitivity to the drug(s) being abused, and (4) errors in calculating the proper dosage. It has been estimated that at least 50% of illicit heroin users will overdose at least once, possibly with fatal results. Indeed, death may result so quickly that the individual is found with the needle still in their arm. The current theory is that death is the result of respiratory depression (Gutstein & Akil, 2006). An unknown but significant number of persons overdose on prescription narcotic analgesics diverted to the illicit drug market as well (Dunn et al., 2010; Webster et al., 2011).

Some of the symptoms of an opioid overdose include reduced level of consciousness, pinpoint pupils, cerebral edema, and respiratory depression (Drummer & Odel, 2001; Schuckit, 2006a). Even if the individual should survive the overdose attempt, there might be residual effects such as partial paralysis or blindness, or peripheral neuropathies, induced by the overdose (Dilts & Dilts, 2005). The onset of specific overdose symptoms is dependent on the compound(s) ingested or injected. For example, if methadone were the compound ingested, the first symptoms might not manifest for up to 3.2 *hours* after the overdose, and respiratory depression might require up to 8 hours to manifest (LoVecciho et al., 2007). To further complicate matters, the practice of polydrug abuse with the potential additive effects of various adulterants in the compound(s) being abused often cloud the clinical presentation of an overdose. For example, there is evidence that the concurrent use of marijuana and heroin might increase the individual's risk of a narcotics overdose through an unknown mechanism (Drummer & Odel, 2001). The practice of using amphetamines or cocaine might hide the symptoms of the overdose until it is too late to seek medical attention, because the stimulants might mask the early symptoms of an opioid overdose.

Even in the best-equipped hospital, an opioid overdose can be fatal. The current treatment of choice for an opioid overdose is a combination of respiratory and cardiac support and the intravenous administration of *Narcan*® (naloxone hydrochloride) (Ropper & Brown, 2005). This compound binds at the opioid receptor sites, blocking the opioid molecules from reaching them. If administered in time, this will reverse the narcotics overdose. However, the therapeutic half-life of *Narcan*® is only 60–90 minutes, and several doses might be necessary before the person fully recovers from the overdose. In the case of long-acting narcotic analgesics such as methadone, the individual might require *Narcan*® infusions for days to avoid long-term overdose effects. There is the additional danger of side effects of naloxone hydrochloride. These side effects will need to be assessed by the attending physician, and if severe enough to warrant intervention will need to be addressed by the attending health care professionals as well.

---

[54]Similar to "mad cow" disease.

[55]See Glossary.

[56]*ANY* real or suspected case of a drug overdose should be assessed and treated by a physician.

Opioid Use or Abuse and the *Diagnostic and Statistical Manual of Mental Disorders (5th Edition)*[57]

The *Diagnostic and Statistical Manual of Mental Disorders* (5th edition) (*DSM-5*) (American Psychiatric Association, 2013) identified five subforms of opioid-related disorders:

- *Opioid use disorder*
- *Opioid intoxication*
- *Opioid withdrawal*
- *Other opioid-induced disorders*
- *Unspecified opioid-related disorders*

Opioid use disorder (OUD) as defined by the *DSM-5* is equivalent to addiction to narcotics, as discussed in this section.[58] The *DSM-5* definition of opioid use disorder identifies 11 criteria that might indicate OUD, including tolerance and opiate withdrawal. The presence of any two of the diagnostic criteria within a 12-month period is the evidence of an OUD except when the individual is taking a narcotic analgesic as prescribed according to the *DSM-5* manual. The *DSM-5* definition of OUD also allows for the use of four modifiers: (1) in early remission, (2) in sustained remission (although "craving" for opioid use is exempt from the criteria for remission), (3) on opioid maintenance therapy, and (4) in a controlled environment.

Opioid intoxication is defined in the *DSM-5* as reflecting the recent use of an opioid, inducing symptoms such as drowsiness or coma, slurred speech, or memory impairment, not attributable to another condition. It is noted that rarely does the individual experience "perceptual disturbances" (*DSM-5*, p. 546) which again cannot be attributable to another medical condition. The abuse of sedating drugs such as barbiturates or benzodiazepines can induce symptoms very similar to those seen in opioid intoxication and the

probable use of these compounds must be eliminated before an individual is diagnosed with an opioid intoxication (American Psychiatric Association, 2013).

The *DSM-5* classification of *opioid withdrawal* is essentially the same as identified in this text. There is, however, the warning that the apparent opioid withdrawal symptoms do not reflect withdrawal from another substance of abuse, or a medical condition capable of inducing withdrawal-like symptoms. The category of *other opioid-induced* disorders refers to conditions such as depression, which can be a consequence of opioid abuse or withdrawal. If the individual were to have a *pre-existing* depressive disorder that was exacerbated by the abuse of opioids or the withdrawal process, this would be classified as *Unspecified opioid-related disorders* in the *DSM-5* (American Psychiatric Association, 2013). In this text such co-existing disorders are discussed in Chapter 24.

Chapter Summary

Opioids have been used effectively for thousands of years to treat pain. After alcohol, one could argue that opium is the second-oldest drug used by humans, with a known history going back thousands of years prior to the invention of writing. With the onset of the chemical revolution of the 18th and 19th centuries, chemists began to isolate the active compounds found in opium, producing a family of compounds that were found to be useful in controlling severe pain, severe cough, and severe diarrhea. It was soon discovered that the compounds isolated from opium, and their chemical cousins, presented the user with a significant abuse potential, as well as the potential for addiction.

With the advent of semisynthetic and synthetic opioids, chemists attempted to find a compound that would retain the analgesic potential of morphine, which has emerged as the gold standard for analgesia. There is an ongoing search for an effective analgesic for severe pain without the negative effects associated with the use of opioids. Unfortunately, this search has failed to yield such a compound, although it has provided a wide range of narcotic analgesics that have the potential to be abused, and induce addiction. These compounds have become the subject of great controversy both in the field of medicine and between members of the general public.

---

[57]The material presented here is to illustrate the relationship between the alcohol use disorders and the *Diagnostic and Statistical Manual of Mental Disorders* (5th edition). This material should not be interpreted as, nor should it be used as, a diagnostic manual.

[58]The reader is referred to the *Diagnostic and Statistical Manual of Mental Disorders* (5th edition) (*DSM-5*) (American Psychiatric Association, 2013) for the full list of diagnostic criteria suggested by the American Psychiatric Association as signs of OUDs.

CHAPTER 12

Abuse and Addiction to Hallucinogens

Introduction

To older persons the term *hallucinogen* is associated with the "Summer of Love"[1] in San Francisco, when arguably the "psychedelic" era of the 1960s and the hallucinogenic compounds that fueled it reached its pinnacle (Traub, 2009). In the time since then, these compounds have waxed and waned in popularity as drugs of abuse. Although they are perhaps less commonly abused now than in past decades, hallucinogenic compounds are still occasionally sought out by illicit drug users. Other substance abusers are unwittingly exposed to a hallucinogen that was used to bolster the apparent effect of low-quality marijuana or sold under the guise of another compounds. As will be discussed in Chapter 36, in the world of illicit drugs it is a case of "let the buyer beware."

Scientists have concluded that there are hundreds of different species of plants that contain compounds that might alter the user's state of consciousness. Although it is rarely thought of in this light, the tobacco plant is one such plant.[2] Some of the hallucinogenic compounds are used in religious ceremonies, healing rituals, and for predicting the future (Metzner, 2002; Sessa, 2005; Traub, 2009). One example is peyote, which anthropologists believe has been used for its hallucinogenic effects for at least 4,000 years (Nichols, 2006; Traub, 2009). The advent of the chemical revolution that began in the late 19th century and which continues through to this day saw many of these natural hallucinogenic compounds being isolated, and a range of synthetic hallucinogenic compounds being developed.

In the United States, certain religious groups continue to use mushrooms that contain the hallucinogenic psilocybin. Scientists, who for the most part have long shunned research into the hallucinogens,[3] are now actively investigating whether at least some of the known hallucinogenic compounds might have medicinal value (Brown, 2007; Karch, 2009; Ross, 2012). Since the start of the "cold war" following World War II, various agencies in the U.S. government developed an interest in these compounds. The U.S. Army, for example, looked at lysergic acid diethylamide (LSD) (discussed later) as a possible chemical warfare agent, going so far as to administer doses of this compound to soldiers without their knowledge or consent (Talty, 2003). The Central Intelligence Agency (CIA) is known to have experimented with some of the hallucinogenics as possible agents to aid interrogation. Nor were these agencies alone: Starting in the middle of the 20th century, some individuals advocated their use as a way to explore alternative realities or gain self-knowledge, trends that have continued until the present

---

[1]1968 for those who are just a little too young to remember this year from personal experience.

[2]Discussed in Chapter 16.

[3]Aided in part by the classification of these compounds as Category I compounds as defined by the Comprehensive Drug Abuse Prevention and Control Act of 1970, a step that made even legitimate experimental use of these compounds illegal. See Appendix Three.

day (Metzner, 2002). The hallucinogenics were classified as Category I compounds by the Comprehensive Drug Abuse Prevention and Control Act of 1970, and overnight were transformed into illegal substances. In this chapter, some of the most popular hallucinogenic compounds will be discussed.[4]

A Short History of Hallucinogens

Over the years chemists have isolated and studied approximately 100 different hallucinogenic compounds that are found in various plants or mushrooms.[5] Psilocybin is an example of one such compound. Psilocybin is found in certain mushrooms indigenous to the southwestern United States and the northern Mexico. However, there are a large number of other natural hallucinogenic compounds that have never been isolated or studied by scientists and the possibility that a novel hallucinogenic compound being isolated remains a possibility (Glennon, 2004). Experimental pharmacologists have also developed synthetic compounds with hallucinogenic effects, one of which is phencyclidine (PCP),[6] which became a part of the drug abuse problem in the United States shortly after it was developed.

One family of compounds that has been subjected to intense scientific scrutiny are those chemicals produced by the ergot fungus, which grows on various forms of grain. Some compounds produced by the ergot fungus have been found to induce such severe vasoconstriction that the entire limb has been known to auto-amputate[7] or cause the individual to die of gangrene (Walton, 2002). Historians believe that ergot fungus induced a widespread illness in the Aquitaine region of France around the year 1000 C.E.,[8] causing the death of at least 40,000 people who consumed bread made from contaminated grain (Walton, 2002).

Because these compounds were so potent, scientists tried to isolate them to see whether they might have medicinal value. In 1943, during a clinical research project exploring the possible application of a compound obtained from the rye ergot fungus *Claviceps purpurea,* a scientist by the name of Albert Hoffman accidentally ingested a small amount of the fungus. The intention was to isolate a compound that might be used to treat headaches, but the scientist began to experience hallucinations and visual perceptual distortions, which he correctly attributed to a compound produced by the strain of *Claviceps purpurea* that he had been working on. The next day, after recovering from the effects of the first unintentional exposure, he ingested a small amount of the fungus and again experienced the same effects. His experiences sparked research to isolate the compound responsible for these effects, eventually yielding lysergic acid diethylamide-25 (LSD-25, or, simply, LSD) as the causal agent.

Following World War II, there was a great deal of scientific interest into the effects of various hallucinogenics, sparked in part by the similarities between their effects and the symptoms of schizophrenia. In the 1950s, scientists coined the term *psychedelic* or *hallucinogenics* to identify this class of compounds. They were both the focus of scientific investigation, because of their ability to induce hallucinations in a manner similar to those of schizophrenia, and the military, as possible weapons of war. The ethics of the latter investigations is clearly demonstrated by the army's administration of LSD to unsuspecting recruits in the 1960s to observe its effects on the soldiers (O'Meara, 2009). Such a potent compound also became the focus of informal experiments by drug abusers in the 1960s and early 1970s as a way to liberate the mind from the shackles of conventional thought. The most popular of these compounds, LSD and later PCP, were classified as Schedule I controlled substances in 1970 by the Drug Enforcement Administration.[9] However, this did not prevent these compounds from becoming popular drugs of abuse in the last four decades of the 20th century. As noted in the Introduction, the hallucinogenics are

---

[4]On rare occasions a person(s) who will use venom from the species of toad known as *Bofu gargarizans* to induce hallucinations. There is a very narrow margin of safety for this toxin and abusers find that it is easy to reach a lethal dose in their quest for a hallucinogenic dose. Because of its toxicity and the fact that it is rarely encountered in the United States, it will not be discussed again.

[5]Although at first glance this statement might seem at conflict with the statement in the introduction that "thousands" of plant species contain hallucinogenic compounds, it is important to keep in mind that the same compound might be found in a number of different plants.

[6]Discussed later in this chapter.

[7]See Glossary, under the term *Auto-amputation.*

[8]Or, *Common Era.* This term replaces the older term *A.D.*

[9]See Appendix Three.

often sold as other substances or intentionally abused by those seeking their effects.

Scope of the Problem

In the United States the abuse of hallucinogenics is limited, usually involving a small percentage of adolescents and young adults for the most part. It was estimated that approximately 23 million persons over the age of 12 years have ever used LSD, 6.6 million persons in the same age bracket have ever used PCP, and 12 million people had ever used MDMA (National Survey on Drug Use and Health, 2008). However, these figures reflect lifetime *prevalence*. Less than 700,000 were thought to have used LSD in the year preceding the study, fewer than 200,000 people were thought to have used PCP, and 2.1 million had used MDMA (National Survey on Drug Use and Health, 2008). For the greatest proportion of abusers, their use of these compounds reflects transient, possibly experimental, use of these compounds. This conclusion is supported by the observation that in contrast to the number of people who have used MDMA noted above, there are only an estimated 450,000 regular users of MDMA in the United States (Lawton, 2009).

It is important to keep in mind that there is a difference between *declining* and *eliminated*. It is estimated that 943,000 persons over the age of 12 abused a hallucinogenic compound for the first time in the year 2007 (National Survey on Drug Use and Health, 2008). This data are consistent with the observation that although the hallucinogens are less popular than in past generations, they are still abused. An exception to the general decline in hallucinogen abuse is *Salvia divinorum*, a compound that has exploded on to the drug scene in the United States. It is thought that 1.8 million persons over the age of 12 years had ever abused this substance, with 750,000 doing so in the year preceding the National Survey on Drug Use and Health (2008). Again, the data suggest that the greater proportion of these people tried this compound out of curiosity.

Pharmacology of the Hallucinogens

Surprisingly, the effects of these compounds have not been studied in depth (Glennon, 2008). It is believed that the effects of a hallucinogen are based on factors such as (a) dose administered, (b) the specific compound

used, and (c) the route of administration (Weiss, 2007). Hallucinogens are thought to alter the delicate balance of neurotransmitters in the brain, especially the serotonin 2a receptor site, thus producing their effects.[10] The dopamine neurotransmitter system is also affected by the hallucinogens. Although compounds such as dopamine and serotonin are viewed as neurotransmitters they might also be viewed as *neuromodulators,* shifting the activity of neurons from one state to another. Subjectively, the experience of these neural activity shifts is reflected in such activities as concentration on a specific task, the euphoria experienced in a new love relationship, or the amnesia of sleep (Hobson, 2001). Disorders of this neurological balance during waking would then cause various abnormal brain states, such as those induced by the hallucinogens (Hobson, 2001). By altering the balance of neurotransmitters in the brain, it is possible to change the individual's subjective experience of consciousness.

The commonly abused hallucinogens are divided into two major groups (Glennon, 2008; O'Brien, 2011; Ross, 2012): (1) the phenylalkylamines (mescaline and MDMA fall into this class of compounds), which have a core structure similar to that of the neurotransmitter norepinephrine and (2) the indolealkylamines (which include psilocybin and DMT), which have a core structure similar to the neurotransmitter serotonin. LSD belongs to a subgroup of the indolealkylamines known as the *lysergamides* (Glennon, 2008). There are also atypical hallucinogens, which includes Ibogaine, which are of minor interest to drug abusers and will not be discussed further in this text. The mechanism through which the hallucinogens alter the normal balance of neurotransmitters is still being explored. Research evidence, for example, would suggest that LSD, like most of the other hallucinogenic compounds, acts as an agonist to the 5-HT serotonin receptor site, and the effects of this compound are blocked by experimental 5-HT serotonin receptor site antagonists (Drummer & Odell, 2001; Glennon, 2004).

In spite of their classification as *hallucinogens,* these compounds do not produce frank hallucinations except at very high doses[11] (Jones, 2005; O'Brien, 2011). At the

---

[10]The truth of this statement is easily proven by the experience of persons who suffer from a high fever during illness, or diabetic patients whose blood sugar levels fall to dangerously low levels. Each group of patients report distorted perceptions of reality, and behave in abnormal ways.

[11]To avoid confusion, these compounds will continue to be referred to as *hallucinogens.*

doses normally used by drug abusers in the United States, these compounds induce perceptual distortions (Jones, 2005; Tacke & Ebert, 2005). Abusers adjust their intake of the compound being abused to produce just the effects that they desire, but as noted at the usual dosage level being abused frank hallucinations are rare and the abuser will usually experience perceptual distortions (Schuckit, 2006a). It is common for the hallucinogen abuser to believe that he or she has achieved a new insight into reality while under the influence of hallucinogenics. These perceptions do not usually prove to be of value and for the most part are recognized by the abuser as being drug induced. Because LSD is the prototypical hallucinogen, and has been best studied, this chapter will focus on LSD first, and focus on other compounds only as needed.

Methods of Abuse

Hallucinogens might be ingested orally, smoked, or injected, although the latter method of abuse is rather rare and will not be discussed again here (Mendelson & Mello, 2010; Weaver & Schnoll, 2008). The exact method of abuse depends on the specific compound being abused. For example, LSD is usually ingested orally, whereas PCP (discussed later in this chapter) can be ingested orally, injected, or smoked. MDMA is usually ingested orally, although it might also be injected or inhaled (Klein & Kramer, 2004; Takce & Ebert, 2005). The most common method of LSD administration is oral ingestion although it can be administered intravenously or by inhalation. The potency of current illicit LSD samples are usually lower than those sold in the 1960s and 1970s, possibly to make the effects less frightening and more acceptable to the first time abuser. Experienced users will thus use two or three typical doses to achieve the desired effects. Because the effects are so variable from one time to the next, Zuckerman (2012) suggested that opioid abusers tend to avoid its use.

The Pharmacology of LSD

LSD has been the subject to intense scientific scrutiny since it was first isolated; however, there is still a great deal to learn about how this compound affects the brain (Sadock & Sadock, 2007). It is classified as a Schedule I[12] drug and as such is not thought to have

medicinal value, although some researchers believe that it is a possible adjunct to the treatment of alcoholism (Johansen, 2012; Ross, 2012). It has been estimated that LSD is between 100 and 1,000 times as potent as natural hallucinogens such as psilocybin and peyote, and perhaps 3,000 times as potent as mescaline (O'Brien, 2011), but weaker than the synthetic hallucinogen DOM/STP (Schuckit, 2006a). The LSD molecule is water soluble, making it possible for it to be both rapidly and completely absorbed from the gastrointestinal tract when it is ingested (Tacke & Ebert, 2005). Once in the circulation, LSD is distributed to all blood-rich organs in the body and only a small percentage of the original dose is thought to reach the brain (Tacke & Ebert, 2005). In the brain, LSD appears to function as a serotonin agonist (Jenkins, 2007; Klein & Kramer, 2004), especially at the 5-HT2a receptor site, although other binding sites might be discovered in the future (Glennon, 2004).

The highest brain LSD concentrations are found in the regions associated with the vision, the limbic system, and the reticular activating system (RAS).[13] In retrospect this should not be surprising, because these regions of the brain are involved in the process of interpreting and the emotional response to perceptions of reality. LSD appears to alter the normal function of serotonin in the dorsal midbrain raphe region of the brain (Hobson, 2001; Jenkins, 2007). By binding at the 5-HT2a receptor sites in this region, LSD is able to indirectly activate acetylcholine[14]-based neurons that suppress rapid eye movement (REM) sleep during the waking state. This allows those neurons to then become active, allowing perceptional and emotionally charged images normally seen only during sleep to slip over into the waking state as well as inducing the perceptual distortions and emotions characteristic of the LSD experience (Hobson, 2001; Jenkins, 2007). Tolerance to LSD's effects develops rapidly, often after just 2–4 days of the continuous use (Commission on Adolescent Substance and Alcohol Abuse, 2005; Jones, 2005). After tolerance develops, the abuser must abstain from additional hallucinogen use for 2–4 days to allow the tolerance to abate before restarting using LSD (Jones, 2005). Cross-tolerance between hallucinogens is common so the abuser must abstain from all hallucinogen abuse during this time. There is no known withdrawal syndrome from LSD (Fadem, 2009). Scientists have yet to determine the lethal dose of LSD, making it perhaps the safest compound known to modern medicine (Erickson,

---

[12]See Appendix Three.

[13]See Glossary.
[14]See Glossary.

2007; Pechnick & Ungerlieder, 2004; Ross, 2013).[15] Death in LSD abusers is rare and usually is the result of the perceptual distortions induced by LSD (Drummer & Odell, 2001; Pechnick & Ungerleider, 2004). This is not to imply that LSD is entirely safe. There are reports suggesting that LSD-induced seizures might occur up to 60 days after the individual's last use of this compound, although the causal mechanism for such seizures remains unknown (Klein & Kramer, 2004).

The biological half-life of LSD is estimated to be approximately 2.5–3 hours (Jenkins, 2007; Oehmichen, Auer, & Konig, 2005). It is rapidly metabolized in the liver, with only 1–3% of a single dose of LSD being excreted from the body unchanged. The rest is eliminated in the bile (Drummer & Odell, 2001; Tacke & Ebert, 2005). The biotransformation/elimination process is so rapid that the major metabolite of LSD, 2-oxy-LSD, remains in the abuser's urine for only 12–36 hours after it was ingested. Although illicit drug abusers often claim that the LSD detected in their urine was a result of passive absorption through the skin, there is little evidence that this is possible. The subjective effects of LSD last far longer than its biological half-life, and for the typical abuser the perceptual distortions usually last for 12–18 hours after the drug was first ingested (Drummer & Odell, 2001; Weiss, 2007). The discrepancy between the drug's duration of effects and its elimination half-life might reflect the fact that some abusers ingest large doses, thus allowing residual LSD to remain in their bodies, or that the substance-induced equilibrium in the balance of neurotransmitters requires several days to be reestablished.

The Subjective Effects of LSD

The subjective effects of LSD begin about 5–10 minutes after the dose was ingested. The negative effects include such symptoms as: anxiety, gastric distress, increased blood pressure, tachycardia, increased body temperature, dilation of the pupils, nausea, muscle weakness, exaggerated muscle reflexes,[16] dizziness, and possible

muscle tremor (Tacke & Ebert, 2005). These effects are usually easily tolerated by the experienced abuser. LSD-induced hallucinations or perceptual distortions begin 30–60 minutes after the drug was ingested, last at full intensity for 2–4 hours, and gradually wane over the next 8–12 hours (O'Brien, 2006; Pechnick & Ungerleider, 2004).[17] The individual's subjective interpretation of LSD's effects is thought to reflect his or her (a) personality,[18] (b) expectations, (c) the environment in which the drug was used, and (d) the dose ingested (Tacke & Ebert, 2005; Weaver & Schnoll, 2008).

Abusers often refer to the LSD experience as a "trip," during which time the abuser might experience a sensation of not having psychological boundaries, enhanced insight, a heightened awareness of sensory perception(s), enhanced memory recall, a feeling of contentment, and a sense of being "at one" with the universe (Callaway & McKenna, 1998). The trip is made up of several distinct phases: The first phase, which begins within a few minutes, is experienced as a release of inner tension. During this phase, the LSD abuser might feel the need to laugh or cry, and experience a sense of euphoria (Tacke & Ebert, 2005). Stage two begins between 30 and 90 minutes after the drug was ingested, and will involve sensations such as perceptual distortions, synesthesia,[19] and visual illusions (Pechnick & Ungerleider, 2004; Sacks, 2008; Tacke & Ebert, 2005; Traub, 2009). The third phase of the LSD experience begins 3–4 hours after the drug was ingested, and during this phase the individual experiences a distortion of the sense of time. Some individuals report a sense of ego disintegration and anxiety/panic reactions that possibly could trigger a "bad trip" experience from LSD and contribute to even more anxiety on the part of the user. During this phase, the individual might express a belief that he or she has quasi-magical powers, or that they are somehow in control of events around them (Tacke & Ebert, 2005). Such beliefs are potentially fatal, as LSD abusers have been known to jump from windows, or operate motor vehicles, during this phase. On rare occasions LSD abusers might experience suicidal thoughts or even attempt

---

[15]Boese (2007) discussed an incident from the year 1962 in which a trio of scientists decided to investigate the effects of LSD on an elephant. They injected an elephant at the Denver zoo with a dose of LSD estimated to be 3,000 times the typical dose used by a human. The elephant died within 1 hour for unknown reasons. The results of this study do suggest that it is possible to die from an LSD overdose, however. Why the scientists decided to inject the elephant with LSD has never been revealed.

[16]Known as *hyperreflexia*.

[17]Weiss (2007) suggested that some abusers might simultaneously use cocaine or an amphetamine compound to prolong the effects of LSD.

[18]In this context there is some evidence suggesting that LSD reinforces preexisting mood states, which are a reflection of the person's core personality.

[19]See Glossary.

suicide during this phase (Shea, 2002; Tacke & Ebert, 2005). These reactions might reflect LSD's ability to induce feelings of depression on rare occasions (Weaver & Schnoll, 2008).

The effects of LSD normally start to wane 4–12 hours after ingestion (Pechnick & Ungerleider, 2004). As the individual begins to recover, he or she will experience periods of normal perception, interspaced with periods in which the individual continues to experience residual effects of LSD, until eventually he or she is again fully in touch with reality. Following the last phase of the LSD trip, the abuser might experience a residual sense of emotional numbness that might last for hours to days.

The "Bad Trip"

LSD abusers often experience anxiety or outright panic reactions, which they call the "bad trip." Although it was once thought that only inexperienced abusers were prone to such reactions, it is now known that even experienced LSD abusers are vulnerable to this experience. Several factors that seem to influence the probability and course of a "bad trip" are the following: (a) the individual's expectations for LSD, (b) the setting in which LSD is used, and (c) the psychological health of the user (Strassman, 2005). Feedback from others also influences how the individual interprets the drug's effects.[20] If the abuser does develop an LSD-related panic reaction, he or she will usually respond to calm, gentle reminders from others that the feelings are a reaction to the drug, and that they will pass. This is known as "talking down" the LSD abuser.

Pharmacological intervention is necessary only in the most extreme cases,[21] and there is evidence that the "atypical" antipsychotic medications, clozapine and risperidone, bind to the same receptor sites utilized by LSD, aborting the drug "trip" within 30 minutes of the time that either compound was administered (Walton, 2002). Although some physicians advocate

the use of diazepam as an anxiolytic for such reactions, diazepam might further distort the individual's perception of reality, contributing to even more anxiety for the LSD abuser. Normally benzodiazepine-induced sensory distortion is so slight as to be unnoticed by the typical patient, but when combined with the effects of LSD it might become quite substantial and contribute to the problem being treated.

Even without treatment, the LSD-related "bad trip" will last only 6–12 hours at most, and will resolve as the drug's effects wear off (Jones, 2005). On rare occasions, however, LSD seems to "activate" a latent psychosis within the abuser, compounding the problem of treatment for that person (Erickson, 2007; Tacke & Ebert, 2005). This does not appear to be a drug effect so much as the activation of a latent psychosis within the abuser. Research has revealed that Native American tribes who use mescaline as part of their religious practices do not have higher rates of psychoses than the general population (Carvey, 1998). However, the ultimate answer to this question remains unclear, because:

> LSD experience is so exceptional that there is a tendency for abusers to attribute *any* later psychiatric illness to the use of LSD
>
> (Henderson, 1994, p. 65, italics added for emphasis).

As the author points out, psychiatric disorders that manifest weeks, months, or even years after the individual's last use of LSD are often attributed to hallucinogen abuse, even if this took place months prior to the first expression of a psychiatric disorder.

It has been suggested that LSD functions as a selective neurotoxin, destroying the neurons that inhibit excessive stimulation of the visual cortex (Gitlow, 2007). There is a need for further research into this possibility. Symptoms seen in an LSD overdose include: convulsions and hyperthermia[22] as well as an exaggeration of the normal effects of LSD. As is true for *any* suspected drug overdose, immediate medical care is imperative.

The LSD "Flashback"

A "flashback" is period of perceptual distortion similar to those experienced during LSD use, but during a period when the individual has not used a hallucinogen. The first clinical reports of hallucinogenic-related "flashbacks" are more than 100 years old (Jones, 2005). These

---

[20]The individual who provides such feedback is often called "ground control," and is usually not abusing LSD at the time that he or she functions in this role.

[21]On rare occasions, physicians will encounter a patient who took LSD mixed with belladonna or other anticholinergic compounds. If the physician were to attempt to treat the patient's anxiety and agitation with a phenothiazine (an older class of antipsychotic medications) the combination of these compounds might induce a coma, or even death from cardiorespiratory failure. This is one reason why the attending physician should be alerted about what compound(s) have possibly been ingested by the patient, and if possible provide with a sample of the drug(s) ingested, so that he or she might avoid potentially dangerous chemical interactions.

---

[22]See Glossary.

cases involved persons who had used mescaline and who continued to experience sensitivity to light, shade, or sounds for extended periods after their last use of this compound. The symptoms of the LSD-related flash-back[23] fall into one of three categories: (a) perceptual, (b) somatic, or (c) emotional issues, as well as feelings of depersonalization. Depersonalization flashbacks may involve the individual reexperiencing distressing emotions first experienced when the individual abused LSD (Weiss & Millman, 1998). Reported symptoms include visual field distortions, hallucinations, "flashes" of light or color, halos surrounding objects in the visual field, and the perception that things are growing larger or smaller (Pechnick & Ungerleider, 2004). Between 15 and 77% of LSD abusers will experience at least one "flashback," which can be a source of anxiety for the inexperienced LSD abuser who is unprepared for this phenomenon. Experienced LSD abusers might not report flashbacks unless specifically questioned about these experiences, accepting them as a normal consequence of their LSD abuse (Batzer, Ditzer, & Brown, 1999).

The exact mechanism behind the LSD flashback experience remains unclear at this time, but it is recognized by the American Psychiatric Association (2013) as a real phenomenon in cases where the "flashbacks" continue for extended periods of time (Drummer & Odell, 2001; Pechnick & Ungerleider, 2004). Clinical evidence with past LSD abusers suggests that the LSD-related "flashback" experiences most commonly occurs in the first 6 months following the individual's last use of LSD, although they have been reported to occur up to 5 years after the individual's last episode of drug abuse (Jones, 2005). In rare cases, it remains a permanent aftereffect of the individual's LSD abuse (Gitlow, 2007). It was once thought that the flashback required repeated episodes of LSD use, but clinical experience has revealed that even first time abusers have experienced "flashback" experiences (Commission on Adolescent Substance and Alcohol Abuse, 2005; Pechnick & Ungerleider, 2004). Flashbacks might be triggered by such things as: stress, fatigue, marijuana abuse, emerging from a dark room into the light, infections, and the use of CNS stimulants (Jones, 2005; Weaver & Schnoll, 2008). Armed with this knowledge, some persons will intentionally try to experience a flashback to experience and enjoy the effects of this phenomenon. The use of sedating agents like alcohol can also trigger flashbacks for unknown reasons (Batzer et al., 1999).

Treatment for the LSD-related flashback is usually limited to simple reassurance that this experience will last for a short period of time (usually hours, but sometimes longer than this), and that it is a normal consequence of LSD abuse (Sadock & Sadock, 2007). In some cases, the use of anxiolytic[24] medications is useful for acute flashback-related anxiety, if reassurance is not sufficient.

Drug Interactions Involving LSD

Unfortunately, there has been little clinical research into the possible drug interactions between LSD and other compounds. There are case reports suggesting that the selective serotonin reuptake inhibitor (SSRI) antidepressants might trigger/exacerbate LSD-related "flashbacks" (Ciraulo, Shader, Greenblatt, & Creelman, 2007). There are reports of LSD/SSRI-induced grand mal seizures, although it was not known whether this was a drug-induced seizure or a seizure caused by another factor. LSD can interact with the antiviral agent Ritonavir, used in the treatment of HIV infection,[25] resulting in higher blood concentrations of LSD with unknown consequences (Weiss, 2007). There are other potential interactions between LSD and other compounds, but there has been little research into this area.

Section summary: LSD has long been viewed as the prototypical hallucinogen. It is a very potent compound that affects multiple neurotransmitter systems in the brain, although its primary effects are thought to be caused by its ability to influence the serotonin neurotransmitter system. Originally discovered by accident, it was briefly investigated by various governmental agencies as a possible chemical warfare agent. Its use became popular in the 1960s and its popularity has waxed and waned since then. In spite of many years of research into this compound, there is still a great deal to be discovered about LSD.

Phencyclidine

Phencyclidine (PCP) was first introduced in 1957 as an experimental surgical anesthetic designed for intravenous administration (Tacke & Ebert, 2005) and the first reports of PCP abuse began to appear in the clinical

---

[23]Although a common consequence of LSD abuse, similar experiences might occur in patients with cerebral lesions, infections, a form of epilepsy that causes visual field disturbances, or delirium. Thus, a physician should be consulted in cases of suspected LSD flashbacks to determine whether the patient might have another cause of what appears to be an LSD-related "flashback."

[24]See Glossary.

[25]Discussed in Chapter 34.

literature around 1965 (Javitt & Zukin, 2005). As a surgical anesthetic, PCP was found to induce problems such as agitation, a drug-induced delirium and/or a psychotic reaction that lasted up to 10 days. These reactions made recovery from surgery difficult and its use in humans was quickly discontinued (Javitt & Zukin, 2005; Jenkins, 2007; McDowell, 2004). It still was used as a veterinary anesthetic agent in the United States until 1978, when all legal production of PCP in the United States was discontinued. It has since been classified as a Schedule I compound.[26] It is still legally manufactured by pharmaceutical companies in other countries as it is used as a veterinary anesthetic compound in other parts of the world.

By the time that its use as a surgical anesthetic in the United States had been discontinued, illicit drug abusers had discovered PCP. It has never been a popular drug of abuse in this country and the level of its abuse has waxed and waned in the United States over the years (Javitt & Zukin, 2005). However, it is still occasionally abused by some persons, and is a common adulterant added to other drugs of abuse. For these reasons, we will review the effects of PCP.

Scope of Phencyclidine Abuse

Currently, PCP is not a popular drug of abuse and its use outside of this country is rare (Mozayani, 2009). Even in the United States, *intentional* PCP use is uncommon (Zukin, Sloboda, & Javitt, 2005). However, it is often found as an adulterant in other compounds or is sold as other drugs of abuse. Unintentional PCP exposure might cause significant anxiety for the unsuspecting drug abuser contributing to the distress that might be induced by other compounds simultaneously being abused by the individual (Zukin et al., 2005). Currently, it is thought that less than 0.5% of the total population of the United States has ever abused PCP.

Methods of PCP Administration

PCP might be used intranasally, ingested orally, injected into either muscle tissue or intravenously, and when mixed with other substances, it might be smoked (Karch, 2009). Smoking is the most popular method of PCP abuse, as it allows the individual to titrate their total PCP intake to a level suitable, after which time they can just discontinue further PCP smoking for a few minutes, hours, or days.

---

[26]See Appendix Three.

Subjective Experience of PCP

When abused, PCP's effects have been found to last for several days. During this time, the abuser will experience rapid fluctuations in his or her level of consciousness, a sense of dissociation in which reality appears to be distorted or distant, euphoria, decreased inhibitions, a feeling of immense power, analgesia, an altered sense of time, and a loss of sensation in or the feeling that body parts are no longer attached to the abuser's body (Brust, 2004; Weaver, Jarvis, & Schnoll, 1999). Some of these experiences can be rather frightening to the inexperienced abuser inducing a panic reaction. Other reported symptoms include disorientation, confusion, assaultiveness, irritability, depression (which might reach the level of suicidal thinking or acts), and paranoia. As the list of PCP-induced effects would suggest, many of these effects are not desired by the abuser, and many abusers attempt to control them through simultaneous use of other compounds. Unfortunately (from the abuser's perspective), tolerance to PCP's euphoric effects develops rapidly (Javitt & Zukin, 2005). To overcome this tolerance, some abusers will go on PCP-free "holidays" (avoiding the use of PCP for days or weeks) whereas others increase their dose to possibly dangerous levels.

The Pharmacology of PCP

Because PCP is an illicit compound in this country, the phenomena of PCP abuse or dependence have not been studied in detail (Zukin et al., 2005). Much of what is "known" about PCP and its effects is based on antidotal case reports involving PCP abusers, or with the limited experience with PCP as an experimental anesthetic agent. Virtually, nothing is known about PCP dependence or whether there is a withdrawal syndrome for this compound.

Chemically, PCP is a weak base, soluble in both water and blood lipids. Because it is a weak base, it will be absorbed through the small intestine when ingested, resulting in a slower onset of the drug's effects than when it is smoked (Zukin et al., 2005). Orally administered doses of PCP begin to manifest in 20–30 minutes after the drug was ingested, but there is a great deal of intraindividual variability both in the onset of the drug's effects in the oral abuser and the duration of its effects after ingestion. When smoked, the effects begin to manifest in 2–3 minutes (Schnoll & Weaver, 2004). The effects of a small dose of orally administered PCP usually last 3–4 hours, whereas the peak effects of smoked PCP are achieved in 15–30 minutes, and last for 4–6 hours after a single dose (Jenkins, 2007). Much of the PCP that is smoked is destroyed in the smoking process, with the result being that only 30–50% of the available PCP smoked actually reaches the circulation.

Because of its lipid solubility, PCP tends to accumulate in body tissues with a high concentration of lipids, such as the brain (Scholl & Weaver, 2004). Measured levels of PCP in the brain might be 10–113 times as high as the blood plasma levels (Zukin et al., 2005). Once in the blood, PCP interacts with a number of different neurotransmitter receptor sites, acting as an antagonist for N-methyl-D-aspartic acid (NMDA) (Jenkins, 2007; Zukin et al., 2005). PCP also functions as a sigma opioid receptor agonist, and because activation of this receptor site causes dysphoric effects, this seems to be the mechanism through which PCP causes such unpleasant effects (Brust, 2004; Drummer & Odell, 2001). It also binds at some of the endogenous cannabinoid receptor sites, and this is assumed to be the mechanism through which it can cause hallucinations (Glennon, 2004).

The effects of PCP on the user's brain vary, depending on such factors as the abuser's experience with the drug, expectations, and the drug concentration in the abuser's brain. Depending on the concentration of PCP in the brain, it might function as an anesthetic, a stimulant, depressant, or hallucinogenic compound. At about 10 times the minimal effective dose, PCP begins to function as a monoamine reuptake blocker, blocking the action of neurotransmitters such as dopamine, and norepinephrine and inducing euphoria for the user. Depending on the concentration of PCP in the brain, it also may alter the normal function of the NMDA/glutamate receptor[27] in the brain, which might account for the excitement and agitation seen in some PCP abusers (Traub, 2009).

The typical illicit drug dose is approximately 5 mg. However, product potency in illicit drugs is always a problem and so it is impossible to predict in advance how much PCP is in a designated tablet without special testing. Most of a single dose of PCP is biotransformed by the liver into a number of inactive metabolites that are then excreted by the kidneys, and only about 10% of a single dose is excreted unchanged (Karch, 2009). The PCP half-life is about 20 hours, although there is a great deal of intraindividual variability in this figure (Jones, 2005). This estimate is based on the assumption that the individual ingested just one 5-mg dose of PCP and if the

individual has used an exceptionally large dose of PCP, the half-life might be extended to as long as 72 hours. Following a PCP overdose, the half-life might be as long as several weeks. One reason for this is the affinity of the PCP molecule for lipid molecules, which allows for significant stores of PCP to accumulate in the body's fat tissues that slowly "leak" back into the general circulation over time.

Physicians once believed that it was possible to reduce the half-life of PCP by making the urine very acidic. This was accomplished by having the patient ingest large amounts of ascorbic acid or cranberry juice. However, it has since been discovered that this practice may cause myoglobinuria and possible kidney failure, and is no longer recommended as a treatment for PCP overdoses (Brust, 2004). Although PCP is biotransformed at a relatively steady pace, heavy exercise, diet, or major injury might cause significant amounts of PCP to be released back into the circulation of the heavy abuser, possibly inducing a PCP "flashback" experience (Schuckit, 2006a). In the next section, we will look at some of the known complications of PCP abuse.

Complications of PCP Abuse

Phencyclidine is a dangerous compound with a narrow therapeutic window. Some of the complications of PCP abuse are reviewed in Table 12-1.

PCP-related death might either be a direct or indirect outcome of the drug's abuse. Following even mild levels of PCP intoxication is a period of adjustment that may last 24–48 hours, which may be prolonged in cases where the person ingested an exceptionally large dose. During this adjustment period, the individual will gradually "come down," or return to a normal level of function. Chronic PCP abusers report social withdrawal and feelings of depression following their last episode of PCP abuse. A mild withdrawal syndrome following periods of prolonged PCP abuse has been reported. Many abusers report having memory problems that seem to resolve after they stop abusing this compound. This is consistent with the evidence that PCP can cause neural necrosis[28] in the hippocampus (Javitt & Zukin, 2005). It is not known at this time what degree of recovery, if any, is possible from PCP-related brain damage.

Another possible complication of PCP abuse is a drug-induced psychosis. In the case of PCP, this

---

[27]See Glossary.

[28]See Glossary.

TABLE 12-1
Known Complications of PCP Abuse Dose

DOSE OF: 1–5 mg	5–10 mg	10–25 mg OR HIGHER
Alcohol-like intoxication	Aggression	Analgesia/anesthesia
Aggression	Analgesia	Arrhythmias (possibly fatal)
Anxiety	Anxiety (may be severe)	Coma (possibly with the eyes open)
Ataxia	Depersonalization	Death
Body image distortion	Euphoria	Encopresis
Confusion	Hypersalivation	Hallucinations (both visual and tactile hallucinations reported)
Distorted sense of time	Increased muscle strength	
Euphoria	Lethargy	Hypertension (possibly causing strokes or other damage to user's body).
Hallucinations (usually visual, but other forms of hallucinations also reported)	Memory impairment	Paranoia
	Nystagmus	Reduced reaction time
Nystagmus	Paranoia	Respiratory depression/arrest
Periods of rage	Psychosis (drug induced)	Rhabdomyolysis
	Sweating	Seizures

SOURCE: Based on information in Javitt and Zukin (2005), Mozayani (2009), Sadock and Sadock (2007), and Tomb (2008).

psychosis appears to progress through three different stages. The first stage of the PCP-induced psychosis is the most severe, and includes symptoms such as paranoid delusions, anorexia, insomnia, and unpredictable assaultiveness. During this phase, the individual is exceptionally sensitive to external stimuli such as bright lights or loud sounds, and the "talking down" techniques so effective with LSD "bad trips" will not work with patients in a PCP-induced psychosis. Restraints are occasionally necessary to prevent the patient from harming self/others during this phase.

The second stage of the PCP psychosis is marked by continued paranoia and restlessness, but the individual is usually more calm, and in intermittent control of his or her behavior. This phase usually lasts around 5 days, and gradually blends into the final phase of the PCP psychosis. Although the PCP psychosis is usually time-limited, in some cases recovery might take months, or even years. The final phase usually lasts 7–14 days, during which time the individual gradually returns to a normal stage of mind. In many cases abusers experience an episode of depression.

PCP Abuse as an Indirect Cause of Death

The PCP-induced hypertensive episodes noted earlier might last for as long as 3 days after the individual's last use of PCP, placing stress on the cardiovascular system during that time (Brust, 2004). Also, PCP-related periods of aggression have been identified as a factor in drug-related homicides in which either the perpetrator or the victim is under the influence of PCP when the homicide was committed. PCP can induce seizures, exposing the abuser to the same potential for death as those found in typical seizures and indirectly cause the user's death through this process. Finally, the dissociative and anesthetic properties of PCP can cause or exacerbate traumatic injuries for the abuser, possibly contributing to his or her death. Given this litany of undesirable effects, it is a mystery why people might choose to abuse this compound. However, as noted earlier in this chapter, PCP continues to lurk in the shadows, and may again become a popular drug of abuse.

Ecstasy (MDMA)

Prevalence of PCP Abuse Compared to MDMA

The compound N, alpha-dimethyl-1,3-benzodioxole-ethanamine (MDMA) is a much more popular hallucinogenic than PCP among high school students as evidenced by the data summarized in Figure 12-1 (Johnston, O'Malley, Backman, & Schulenberg, 2012a).

A Short History of Ecstasy (MDMA)

MDMA was first isolated in 1912 and a patent on the compound was issued in 1914 (Schuckit, 2006a).

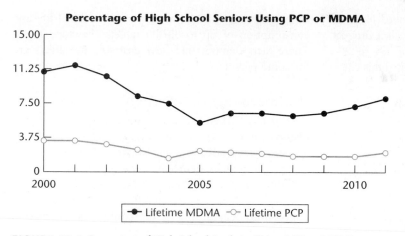

FIGURE 12-1 Percentage of High School Students Using PCP or MDMA.

SOURCE: Johnston, L. D., O'Malley, P. M., Backman, J. G., & Schulenberg, J. E. (2012a). End note crediting. *Monitoring the Future: National Survey Results on Drug Use, 1975–2011: Volume 1, Secondary School Students.* Ann Arbor, MI Institute for Social Research, University of Michigan.

Chemists had hoped that the compound would function as an appetite suppressant; however, subsequent research failed to support this theory and researchers quickly lost interest in MDMA. It remained only a laboratory curiosity until the early 1950s, when the U.S. Army asked the University of Michigan to determine its toxicity as part of a preliminary assessment as a possible chemical warfare agent (Karch, 2009). However, the decision was made not to pursue further research into this compound by the army, and it returned to chemical obscurity.[29]

In the mid-1960s, a small number of psychotherapists suggested that MDMA might be useful as an adjunct to psychotherapy. Research into this application of MDMA ended in 1985 when, in spite of testimony by physicians and the recommendation of an administration law judge, the Drug Enforcement Administration (DEA) classified MDMA as a Schedule I[30] compound rather than a Schedule III compound (Gahlinger, 2004; Mithoefer, 2011; Shulgin & Shulgin, 2007). Only a quarter of a century later, limited research into the possible application of MDMA as an adjunct to psychotherapy was again being conducted in both the United States and Europe (Mithoefer, 2011).

Unfortunately, in a pattern that eerily is similar to that seen with LSD MDMA escaped from the laboratory to become a drug of abuse. However, it was quickly overshadowed by LSD, which was both more potent and did not induce the nausea or vomiting experienced by many MDMA abusers. Illicit drug abusers began to become interested in MDMA in the mid-1970s in part because it was not then classified as an illegal substance. Drug suppliers began to market it as a commercial venture, engaging in premarketing discussions about possible product names much as an automotive company would for a new vehicle. The name "ecstasy" was eventually selected for this compound, a demand for the product was generated, and a supply/distribution network emerged to meet the demand (Karch, 2009; McDowell, 2004). The original samples of MDMA even contained a "package insert" (Karch, 2009) that was filled with psycho-babble, and which gave suggestions about the best ways to use MDMA. Within the span of a few years, MDMA became a popular drug of abuse in both Europe and the United States and was eventually classified as an illegal drug of abuse. In spite of this little inconvenience MDMA was a popular drug of abuse in the last decade of the 20th century.

Scope of MDMA Abuse

Worldwide production of MDMA is thought to exceed 8 metric *tons* per year and globally, 9 million persons between the ages of 15 and 64 years are thought to have used MDMA at least once in the preceding 12 months (United Nations, 2011). In the United States, 8 million people are thought to have used MDMA at least once, and 2.2 million people are thought to have done so in the past

---

[29]It has emerged, however, as a *possible* adjunct to the treatment of at least some forms of posttraumatic stress disorder (PTSD) (Mithoefer, Mithoefer, & Wagner, 2008). Further research into this possible medical application of MDMA is under way at this time.

[30]See Appendix Three.

12 months (Gwinnell & Adamec, 2006; United Nations, 2011). MDMA is the second most popular illicit drug in the young adult population, with 15% of 19- to 30-year-old adults in the United States having used this compound at least once (Kobeissy et al., 2007). In Europe, MDMA is also the second most popular illicit drug of abuse, exceeded only by marijuana (Morton, 2005).

It was originally thought that MDMA was harmless, a myth that helped it to find widespread acceptance by a subculture devoted to loud music and parties devoted to the use of MDMA, similar to LSD parties of the 1960s (Ramcharan et al., 1998). Such parties, called "raves" at the time,[31] first began in Spain, spread to England and across Europe, and then to the United States (McDowell, 2004; Rochester & Kirchner, 1999). Although these parties have become less common, MDMA has moved into mainstream nightclubs, especially those popular with older adolescents and young adults (Morton, 2005).

Patterns of MDMA Abuse

There is a great deal of interindividual variability in dosing levels because of: (a) the unknown potency of the tablet/powder being used and (b) the individual's tolerance for MDMA. Some tablets purporting to be MDMA have been found to contain no MDMA at all whereas others might contain 100 mg. This variability between tablets makes it very easy for the abuser to overdose, which will be discussed later in this section of the chapter. The typical MDMA abuser attempts to ingest 60–120 mg[32] at a time (Outslay, 2006). Ecstasy abusers usually engage in episodic MDMA abuse to allow themselves to recover from the drug's effects[33] (Commission on Adolescent Substance and Alcohol Abuse, 2005; Gouzoulis-Mayfrank et al., 2000). Ecstasy does appear to have a "ceiling effect," and beyond the ceiling dose the individual will not achieve more euphoria but will be vulnerable to the negative effects of this compound (Bravo, 2001). Although episodic use is the norm for MDMA, binge users have been known to take as many as 5–25 tablets[34] in a short period of

time and some MDMA abusers report a total lifetime consumption of up to 40,000 tablets (Lawton, 2009). These facts demonstrate how desirable its effects are for some persons.

Pharmacology of MDMA[35]

Technically, MDMA is classified as a member of the *phenethylamine*[36] family of compounds, but its chemical structure is also very similar to that of the amphetamines, and some neuropharmacologists classify it as a hallucinogenic amphetamine. For the sake of this chapter, it will be classified as a hallucinogenic compound, because this is the context in which it is most commonly abused. It is usually administered in tablet form, MDMA powder is gaining in popularity (Boyer, 2005). Because the potency of the powder is not known there is a significant potential for the user to die after suffering a lethal overdose (Lawton, 2009).

The pharmacokinetics of MDMA is rather complicated. There are two forms of the MDMA molecule,[37] known as the *left-handed* and the *right-handed isomer*[38] ("Pharmacokinetics of MDMA [Ecstasy] Studied," 2008). It is assumed that the pharmacokinetics of one isomer on the body are the same as its polar opposite, an assumption that might not be true. There has been limited research into the effects of MDMA on the human brain (Lawton, 2012a, 2012b), only limited research into its effects on the body and no research

---

[31]Welsh (2013) suggested that this term has been replaced by the phrase "dance-music festival."

[32]Although this is based on the theory that the MDMA ingested is pure and not adulterated.

[33]Although polydrug abusers might continue to abuse other compounds during these periods of abstinence.

[34]The potency of illicit MDMA tablets varies from one batch to the next, and so the actual dose of MDMA being ingested by these individuals is not known.

---

[35]This section is based on the assumption that the person ingested only one (1) dose of MDMA. Many individuals consume multiple doses over extended periods (8 to 12 hours), altering the pharmacokinetics of this compound. Higher doses result in higher plasma levels of MDMA for example, producing both stronger effects and greater exposure to contaminants in the compound ingested (Ricaurte, Langston, & McCann, 2008).

[36]Discussed in Chapter 36.

[37]Technically a *chiral* molecule. To learn more about this consult a good chemistry text book.

[38]Occasionally one encounters a drug where there are two forms of the molecule, each made up of the same atoms, but where one is the mirror image of the other. Pharmacologists refer to these mirror images as the *left handed* and the *right handed* isomer of the same compound. Pharmacologists engage in extensive clinical research to determine the pharmacokinetics of each isomer on the human body. Since MDMA is an illicit drug there is little to no funding for such research. The assumption is that the effects of the left handed isomer are the same as those of the right handed isomer, although this has not been proven in fact.

into the pharmacokinetics of each isomers on the body. So the information that follows is tentative, and may be revised as scientists discover more about the effects of MDMA on the body.

Ecstasy is well absorbed from the gastrointestinal tract, and thus the most common method of use is through oral administration. Some abusers, however, prefer to use MDMA powder by "snorting" it. The effects of an oral dose begin within 20–60 minutes of ingestion, and peak about 1–4 hours later (de la Torre et al., 2004; Gonzalez, Vassileva, & Scott, 2009; Karch 2009; McDowell, 2004, 2005; Virani et al., 2009). MDMA is extensively metabolized in the liver, and the elimination half-life has been estimated to be about 8 hours for the normal person (Karch, 2009; Tacke & Ebert, 2005; Virani et al., 2009). There is wide variation in the elimination half-life of MDMA, however. Some persons are "slow metabolizers" of MDMA and their bodies do not metabolize MDMA at the same speed than that of a normal person. In such persons the amount of MDMA necessary to induce toxicity is relatively low (Virani et al., 2009). There are two main metabolic pathways for MDMA. During the process of biotransformation about 9% of a single dose of MDMA is transformed into the metabolite MDA, which is itself hallucinogenic (de la Torre et al., 2004). One study using a single human volunteer revealed that three-quarters of the MDMA ingested was excreted unchanged in the urine within 72 hours. This raises a question: Was this individual "a slow" metabolizer of MDMA or is the belief that MDMA must be extensively metabolized[39] before excretion inaccurate? There is obviously a need for additional research into the pharmacokinetics of Ecstasy to answer this question.

Because MDMA is highly lipid soluble it is able to easily cross the blood–brain barrier and enter the brain without significant delay. In the brain, MDMA functions as an indirect serotonin agonist, first forcing the release and then blocking the reuptake of serotonin. To a lesser degree it also forces the release of the neurotransmitters norepinephrine and dopamine from their stores in the neurons (Gahlinger, 2004; McDowell, 2004, 2005; Mithoefer, 2011; Parrott, Morian, Moss, & Scholey, 2004). MDMA use also triggers the release of neurohormones such as oxytocin, prolactin, and

cortisol, all of which are involved in the process of pair bonding (Mithoefer, 2011). Its effects are strongest in the limbic system of the brain (Erickson, 2007). In cases where the MDMA abuser dies (which, as will be discussed later in this chapter, is a distinct possibility), the residual MDMA molecules in the abuser are extensively redistributed around the body. Thus, postmortem blood levels of MDMA may not be the same as the blood levels of this compound at the time of the abuser's death ("Pharmacokinetics of MDMA (Ecstasy) revealed," 2008). Although scientists have discovered a great deal about the pharmacokinetics of MDMA, there is much that remains to be discovered about the effects of this compound on the healthy individual (Lawton, 2012a, 2012b).

Subjective and Objective Effects of MDMA Abuse

Currently, there are at least six different identified methods for making MDMA and instructions on how to make MDMA are available on the "Internet" (Rochester & Kirchner, 1999). Specialized equipment and training in organic chemistry are both required to avoid the danger of contaminating the MDMA by a toxin(s) that inadvertently was included in the mixture as the result of a mistake in the manufacturing process. Beyond these requirements, MDMA is easily synthesized. Much of what is known about MDMA's effects are based on observations made of illicit drug users, and a limited number of research studies involving volunteer subjects receiving a measured dose of MDMA under controlled circumstances (Outslay, 2006).

The subjective effects of MDMA can be divided into three phases: (1) acute, (2) subacute, and (3) chronic (Outslay, 2006). The subjective effects of MDMA during the acute phase are dependent on such factors as the setting in which the drug is used, the dose ingested, and the individual's expectations for Ecstasy. At a dose of between 75 and 100 mg, abusers report experiencing a sense of euphoria, closeness to others, increased energy, mild perceptual disturbances such as enhanced color/sound perception, a sense of well-being, reduced defensiveness, and improved self-esteem (Bravo, 2001; de la Torre et al., 2004; Outslay, 2006). These effects begin to manifest about 30–60 minutes after MDMA is ingested, peak at about 75–120 minutes after it is first ingested, and last for 6–12 hours (Outslay, 2006). Some of the reported desirable effects of MDMA are

---

[39]Remember: The term *biotransformation* usually is limited to prescribed medications, and *metabolization* used to discuss illicit drugs, although they are the same process.

TABLE 12-2
Perceived Benefits of MDMA Use

Euphoria
Increased empathy toward others
Emotional openness
Increased empathy toward others
Increased psychomotor energy
Increased self-confidence
Enhanced mood
Increased sex drive
Feelings of intimacy
Increased feeling of personal desirability as sexual partner
Belief that individual has improved self-awareness/insight
Intense feelings
Different state of mind/perceptions

© Cengage Learning

TABLE 12-3
Possible Consequences of MDMA Abuse

Anxiety
Anorexia
Ataxia
Blurred vision
Bruxism (grinding of the teeth)
Central venous sinus thrombosis
Confusion
Dissociation
Headaches
Heart palpitations
Hydration abnormalities (over or under hydrated)
Hypertension
Hyperthermia
Hypothermia
Loss of consciousness (various causes)
Motor tics
Muscle tension
Nausea/vomiting
Seizures, possibly leading to status epileptics (potentially fatal)
Subarachnoid hemorrhage
Sudden cardiac death
Urinary incontinence

© Cengage Learning

identified in Table 12-2 (de la Torre et al., 2004; Kobeissy et al., 2007; Outslay, 2006; Passie, Hartman, Schneider, Emrich, & Kruger, 2005; Virani et al., 2009):

However, these effects are achieved at a cost, for MDMA can also induce many undesirable effects that are reviewed in Table 12-3 (Bravo, 2001; de la Torre et al., 2004; Grob & Poland, 2005; Kobeissy et al., 2007; McDowell, 2005; Virani et al., 2009).

The individual is more likely to experience one or more of these undesirable effects at higher dosage levels, although unpleasant effects are possible even at low doses (Grob & Poland, 2005). Bruxism is an excellent example of a side effect experienced at low dosage levels. Abusers attempt to control the drug-induced bruxism by using a baby pacifier or candy to suck on after ingesting MDMA (Gahlinger, 2004; Klein & Kramer, 2004).

Surprisingly, although MDMA induces enhanced feelings of sexual arousal and attractiveness, habitual MDMA abuse has also been implicated as the cause of decreased sexual desire, and for men inhibition of the ejaculatory reflux, as well as erectile dysfunction (Finger, Lund, & Slagel, 1997; McDowell, 2004). Research has also found that MDMA abusers are more than *eight times* as likely to experience episodes of sleep apnea as are nonabusers (McCann, Sgambati, Schwartz, & Ricaurte, 2009). The authors suggested that this increased incidence of sleep apnea might be because of MDMA's

ability to function as a selective serotonin neurotoxin, because serotonin is implicated in the maintenance of normal respiration during sleep.

Following the period of acute MDMA abuse, there is an extended withdrawal period. The subacute phase begins 6–12 hours after the individual ingested MDMA, and in most cases lasts 1–7 days, although in extreme cases it can last for up to a full month (Outslay, 2006). This phase is also called *coming down* or the *hangover phase* (Outslay, 2006). Some of the symptoms experienced during this phase include fatigue, dry mouth, anorexia, insomnia, irritability, drowsiness, difficulty concentrating, and headache (de la Torre et al., 2004; McDowell, 2005; Morton, 2005). It was once thought that the subacute phase of MDMA might also include feelings of depression, but Guillot and Greenway (2006) failed to find significant differences in the level of depression between a sample of MDMA abusers and MDMA-naive subjects. This would cast doubt on the belief that the subacute stage of MDMA includes depression.

As the subacute phase tapers into the post-withdrawal phase, the abuser will experience symptoms such as anxiety, depression, confusion, cognitive dysfunction, insomnia, irritability, low energy, and suspiciousness or outright paranoia (Outslay, 2006). These effects usually last for between 1 and 7 days, although in extreme cases they might continue for up to a month after the individual's last MDMA abuse.

Complications of MDMA Abuse

MDMA has a reputation on the streets as a "safe" drug, an illusion supported by the lack of obvious consequences of abuse such as those observed in persons who have abused methamphetamine, for example (Yudko & McPherson, 2009). The illusion of safety belies the fact that there is a significant overlap between the effective dose and the toxic dosage range of MDMA (Karch, 2009; Outslay, 2006; Ropper & Brown, 2005). For example, animal research suggests that the lethal level of MDMA in humans is approximately 6,000 mg (Rosenthal & Solhkhah, 2005), a dosage level that, given the potency of some illicit MDMA samples, might be achieved after ingesting only 20–30 tablets (Lawton, 2009). However, fatal reactions to MDMA have been noted at doses far lower than this and there is evidence that overdoses of MDMA are both increasing in frequency and are under-reported by health care providers (Centers for Disease Control and Prevention, 2010a; Lawton, 2009).

In addition to the symptoms of MDMA toxicity reviewed in Table 12-3, individuals who have ingested toxic doses of Ecstasy might possibly experience extreme (possibly fatal) elevations in body temperature, delirium, coma, hypotension, rhabdomyolysis,[40] and possible renal failure (de la Torre et al., 2004; Morton, 2005; Parrott, 2004; Rosenthal & Solhkhah, 2005; Zevin & Benowitz, 2007). As these symptoms clearly suggest, *any* real or suspected overdose of MDMA is a medical emergency that requires immediate medical intervention to avoid the danger of the patient's death. In the following section, we will examine some of the more specific dangers of MDMA abuse in detail.

MDMA-Related Cardiac Problems

It is now known that MDMA abuse can cause an increase in the heart rate, blood pressure, and an increase in the rate at which the heart muscle uses oxygen (Grob & Poland, 2005). MDMA abuse is a cause of cardiac arrhythmias such as the potentially fatal ventricular tachycardia (Gahlinger, 2004; Grob & Poland, 2005; Karch, 2009; Klein & Kramer, 2004). One study of the hospital records of 48 patients who had been admitted to a hospital Accident and Trauma Center following MDMA use found that two-thirds had heart rates above 100 beats per minute, or 38% higher than normal (Williams et al., 1998). It has been recommended that MDMA overdoses be treated with the same protocols used to treat amphetamine overdoses, with special emphasis placed on assessing and protecting cardiac function (Gahlinger, 2004; Rochester & Kirchner, 1999).

Animal research also suggests that MDMA functions as a cardiotoxin, causing inflammation of the heart muscle and damage to the left ventricle of the heart (Badon et al., 2002; Shenouda, Lord, McIlwain, Lucchesi, & Varner, 2008). In another study, the team of Patel et al. (2005) compared the heart muscle tissue samples of a group of deceased MDMA abusers (as confirmed by toxicology tests) with those of deceased nonabusers of a similar age and found that hearts of the MDMA abusers were on average 14% heavier than those of nonabusers. This would appear to reflect the development of fibrous tissue within the cardiac muscle, which could interfere with the transmission of electrical signals in the heart necessary for maintenance of a normal cardiac rhythm. The development of fibrous tissue within the cardiac tissues would appear to reflect the cardiotoxic effects of MDMA (Klein & Kramer, 2004).

There is also evidence that chronic MDMA use can result in heart valve damage (Setola et al., 2003). The authors examined the impact of MDMA abuse on tissue samples in laboratories, and found many of the same changes in heart valve tissue seen in the now-banned weight loss medication fenfluramine.[41] Given the widespread use of MDMA, these research findings suggest the possibility of a future epidemic of MDMA-induced heart problems in habitual abusers. Animal research does

---

[40]See Glossary.

[41]After it was introduced, scientists discovered that this medication induced degeneration of heart valve tissue, prompting the manufacturer to withdraw it from the market.

suggest that chronic MDMA abuse was associated with cardiac damage and potentially sudden cardiac death. The authors found that intracellular calcium levels were significantly higher in the hearts of MDMA-exposed rats than in MDMA-naive rats. The concentration of calcium within the heart muscle cell helps to determine the rate and force at which it can contract. This appears to be the mechanism by which MDMA abuse can induce sudden cardiac death, or at least damage the heart muscle, according to the authors.

MDMA-Related Neurological Problems

The question whether MDMA can cause or exacerbate neurological problems is rather controversial. Schilt et al. (2007) concluded that extended periods of MDMA abuse can result in cognitive decline. However, Krebs and Johansen (2008) challenged this conclusion on methodological grounds, pointing out that longitudinal research studies should answer this question more definitively than the retrospective studies, which are commonly used in research involving MDMA's effects on memory function.[42] Lawton (2009) observed that most MDMA abusers also abuse other compounds, making the isolation of MDMA's effects rather difficult. To address this problem, Halpern et al. (2010) examined the performance of 52 MDMA abusers with minimal exposure to other drugs of abuse with that of 59 non-users on a neuropsychological test battery. The authors found little evidence of neurocognitive deficits except in the area of impulse control, raising questions whether the findings of earlier studies might have reflected the effects of other drugs being abused rather than MDMA itself. There are, however, case reports suggesting that some abusers have suffered intracranial hemorrhage, whereas others have suffered occlusive strokes, both conditions that can also induce neurological damage.

A growing body of evidence suggests that MDMA use can cause a dose-dependent increase in cortical excitability (Bauernfeind et al., 2011). The cortical hyper excitability was strongest in those persons with a greater lifetime level of MDMA, which might be one mechanism by which MDMA can induce seizures. The authors also found that chronic MDMA use can cause lifelong alterations in the physiology of the visual system in human abusers, a finding that is of particular importance to abusers who have preexisting vision problems. This research is especially disturbing because the long-term implications of such cortical hyper excitability and visual system changes are not known at this time. They might become permanent, or, following illicit drug use cessation, resolve to an unknown degree.

Further, there is a growing body of literature from both animal and human studies that suggests that MDMA can cause memory problems that may persist for weeks, or even months, after the individual's last use of Ecstasy (McDowell, 2005; Morton, 2005; Yudko & McPherson, 2009). A rather frightening study conducted by Schilt et al. (2007) examined new (<2 months) MDMA abusers and found small, but measurable, cognitive deficits on the neuropsychological tests administered, and cognitive deficits are noted in patients who have ingested MDMA as infrequently as 20 times (Lawton, 2009). The cognitive deficits appear to be dose related, with abusers who report higher levels of abuse being found to have higher levels of cognitive dysfunction in such areas as memory and verbal learning, as well as increased distractibility and a general loss of efficiency (Lawton, 2009; Lungvist, 2005; Quednow et al., 2006).

MDMA abusers often report feeling insensitive to body temperature as they engage in heavy exercise such as prolonged dancing. In extreme cases, this can result in hyperthermia which might cause the individual's death. Hyperthermia is a symptom of the serotonin syndrome,[43] suggesting that this might be the mechanism through which MDMA is able to induce hyperthermia and dehydration in the abuser (Klein & Kramer, 2004). MDMA-related serotonin and dopamine release might also be a temperature-sensitive effect, with higher ambient temperatures being associated with higher levels of these neurotransmitters. Unfortunately, these neurotransmitters are involved in the euphoric sensations that many MDMA abusers seek, with the result being that being in an area with a high ambient temperature might increase MDMA-induced pleasure while simultaneously placing the abuser's life at greater risk (O'Shea et al., 2005).

For reasons that are not well understood, MDMA appears to be able to lower the seizure threshold[44]

---

[42]Asking a person who has been abusing MDMA for 3 years, for example, to estimate how often they have used this compound might yield less accurate results than a longitudinal research study that examined how often the person abused MDMA on a week-by-week or month-by-month basis carried out over a 3-year period of time.

---

[43]See Glossary.

[44]Seizures are potentially lethal through a variety of mechanisms, and thus MDMA-related seizures may indirectly add to the potential for the user's death.

(Henry & Rella, 2001; Karch, 2009). This might reflect genetic vulnerability on the part of the patient experiencing a MDMA-related seizure, as there is evidence that patients who have inherited two copies of what is known as the "short" serotonin transporter gene may be at greater risk for MDMA-related neurotoxicity (Roiser, Cook, Cooper, Rubinsztein, & Shakian, 2005). MDMA-related seizures also tend to be seen at higher dosage levels, although this is not a guarantee that lower doses will avoid the risk of seizures (Brust, 2004; Thompson, 2004).

As if all of this were not enough, there is strong evidence that MDMA functions as a selective neurotoxin that targets serotonergic neurons (Bauman, & Rothman, 2007; Brust, 2004; McDowell, 2005). Animal research suggests that this effect can be seen at dosage levels utilized by human abusers (Ricaurte, Yuan, Hatzidimitriou, Branden, & McCann, 2002). Although the MDMA-related brain damage is more likely in persons who have ingested large doses of this compound, it is possible even on the occasion of the first dose (McDowell, 2005). The mechanism through which MDMA might function as a serotonin-specific neurotoxin is still not known, but preliminary evidence suggests that fluoxetine might protect the serotonin-based neurons from damage if ingested within 24 hours of the time that MDMA was ingested (Walton, 2002).

Although it was once thought that MDMA would place the abuser at increased risk for Parkinson's disease later in life, this theory was later retracted (Brust, 2004; Yudko & McPherson, 2009). There is little evidence that supports earlier beliefs that there was a relationship between MDMA abuse and subsequent development of Parkinson's disease (Morton, 2005; Yudko & McPherson, 2009). However, there is research data suggesting that MDMA might weaken the blood–brain barrier[45] (BBB) for months, possibly years, after the last period of abuse (Vollmer, 2006). This would place the abuser at increased vulnerability to various toxins, and pathogenic organisms normally blocked by the BBB.

MDMA-Related Emotional Problems

There is evidence that MDMA abusers might experience "flashback" experiences similar to those seen after LSD abuse in the days following the MDMA use. MDMA abusers are also sometimes forced to relive past experiences that the individual might not wish to face. This is the effect that made psychiatrists consider MDMA as a possible adjunct to psychotherapy in the 1960s. However, when a MDMA abuser is forced to reexperience these memories, there is usually no therapist to provide guidance and support, possibly adding an additional layer of trauma on to the original pain, which is potentially detrimental to the abuser's mental health. MDMA abuse has also been linked with postabuse anxiety attacks, persistent insomnia, irritability, rage reactions, and a drug-induced psychosis (Commission on Adolescent Substance and Alcohol Abuse, 2005; Gahlinger, 2004; Karch, 2009; McDowell, 2005).

MDMA-Related Gastrointestinal Problems

In Europe, where MDMA abuse was common in the 1990s, there were reports of MDMA-related liver toxicity, and hepatitis. The exact relationship between MDMA abuse and the development of these liver problems is not known at this time. This might be the result of an idiosyncratic reaction on the part of a small number of persons, or a reaction to one or more contaminants mixed with the MDMA that was abused (Grob & Poland, 2002; Henry & Rolla, 2001).

Other MDMA-Related Problems

There are reports of MDMA-related rhabdomyolysis,[46] possibly induced by heavy MDMA-induced exercise such as prolonged dancing (Gahlinger, 2004; Grob & Poland, 2005; Karch, 2009; Klein & Kramer, 2004;). Although MDMA-related deaths are rare, they still occur. Some of the mechanisms of MDMA-related death include strokes associated with MDMA-induced hypertensive episodes, seizures, liver failure, or cardiac arrhythmias. The danger of MDMA-related death is increased if the abuser has ingested multiple compounds, or, high doses of MDMA. Kalantar-Zaden, Nguyen, Chang, and Kortz (2006) discussed a case in which an otherwise healthy 20-year-old female college student, who had a history of MDMA abuse, was transported to the hospital with abnormally low blood sodium levels. In spite of aggressive medical care, she died about 12 hours after her arrival at the hospital.

Medication Interactions Involving MDMA

In the past, physicians thought that beta adrenergic blockers (ß-blockers, or "beta" blockers) were helpful

---

[45]See Glossary.

[46]See Glossary.

in treating MDMA toxicity, but the team of Rochester and Kirchner (1999) challenged this clinical belief on the grounds that the alpha adrenergic system would remain unaffected, and this could impact on blood pressure in spite of the use of ß-blockers. The use of haloperidol was also not recommended, as the interaction between MDMA and haloperidol might interfere with body temperature regulation (Brust, 2004). The best treatment for MDMA toxicity is thought to be supportive treatment, with maintenance of normal body temperature, airway and cardiac support, as well as the judicious use of a benzodiazepine to control anxiety, if necessary (Schuckit, 2006a). There have been case reports of interactions between MDMA and the antiviral agent Ritonavir® (Harrington, Woodward, Hooton, & Horn, 1999). Each agent affects the serotonin level in the blood, and the combination of these two compounds can result in a threefold higher MDMA level in the blood. Some fatalities have been reported in abusers who have mixed these compounds.

Salvia Divinorum

Although *Salvia divinorum* has been used for generations in central Mexico and South America during religious and healing ceremonies, it is a relatively new arrival in the hallucinogenic market in this country. Media attention on the abuse of *Salvia divinorum* as the "next LSD" has helped fuel curiosity about this plant in the United States. It remains legal in most states, although both state and federal regulations against its cultivation, sale, and use are pending. Because it is a recent arrival on the drug abuse scene, the pharmacokinetics of *Salvina divinorum* remains unclear at this time. The active agent of this plant is *salvinorin A,* which functions in the brain as kappa opioid receptor agonist,[47] although there is evidence that it also functions as a partial dopamine D2 receptor agonist. It does not appear to have any effect on the serotonin 5-HT2a receptors, where compounds such as LSD or DMT bind. Users will chew the leaves, although abusers will also smoke the leaves or crush the leaves and drink the extract either alone or when mixed with soda.

The effects last between 30 seconds and 30 minutes, depending on the potency of the leaves and the individual's history of *Salvina divinorum* use. Abusers report experiencing dissociation and hallucinations or "visions." An unintended effect is reduced motility in the intestines, an effect consistent with its ability to bind at the kappa opioid receptor site. The primary method of abuse is oral ingestion of a form of "tea" made by brewing the leaves in water or by smoking. On rare occasions, the abuser will chew *Salvina divinorum* leaves. However, because *salvinorin A* is destroyed by gastric juices, the abuser usually will hold a "wad" of partially chewed leaves against the gum so that *it* can be absorbed through the oral mucosa. On exceptionally rare occasions, abusers will attempt to inhale vapors produced when *salvinorin A* is heated, although this exposes the user to possible lung damage from the high temperature involved in this process. When smoked the effects peak within 60 seconds and last for 1–5 minutes, after which the effects blend back into everyday reality within a half hour's time. The effects of this substance include laughter, revisiting memories, a sense of motion, visual disturbances, unusual thoughts, a sense of merging with objects in the environment, slurred speech, dizziness, mood swings, and dissociation. There has been a case report of a persistent psychotic reaction in a 21-year-old male who had abused *Saliva divinorum* (Przekop & Lee, 2009). Because it is a kappa opioid[48] agonist, its abuse potential is thought to be low and one is hard pressed to find a reason why it is abused beyond the fact that it is a novel substance of abuse.

Phencyclidine and Hallucinogen Use and the *Diagnostic and Statistical Manual of Mental Disorders* (5th Edition)[49]

The *Diagnostic and Statistical Manual of Mental Disorders* (5th edition) (American Psychiatric Association, 2013) elected to consider PCP separately from the other hallucinogens. The *DSM-5* reviewed the diagnostic categories that might result from the abuse of PCP or

---

[47]Discussed in Chapter 14.

[48]See Chapter 11.

[49]The material presented here is to illustrate the relationship between the alcohol use disorders and the *Diagnostic and Statistical Manual of Mental Disorders* (5th edition). This material should not be interpreted as, nor should it be used as, a diagnostic manual.

any of the other known hallucinogenics and identified nine subforms of the hallucinogen-related disorders:

- *Phencyclidine intoxication*
- *Phencyclidine withdrawal*
- *Phencyclidine use disorder*
- *Other phencyclidine-induced disorders*
- *Unspecified phencyclidine-related disorder*
- *Other hallucinogen use disorder*
- *Other hallucinogen intoxication*
- *Hallucinogen persisting perception disorder*
- *Unspecified hallucinogen-related disorder*

As is evident from the above list, PCP is considered independently and not with the other hallucinogens. The category *Phencyclidine Use Disorder* is approximately the same as PCP abuse or dependence discussed in this text. Some of the signs of a *phencyclidine use disorder* listed in the *DSM-5* include[50] (but are not limited to) (a) development of tolerance to its effects, (b) unsuccessful efforts to reduce or stop PCP use, (c) "craving" for this compound between periods of active use, (d) spending a great deal of time spent in activities either directly or indirectly associated with PCP abuse, and (e) use of PCP in situations where it is physically dangerous for the user to do so. The *DSM-5* allows the assessor to determine the intensity of the disorder and record the same through the use of the World Health Organization's *International Classification of Diseases* (9th edition) *(ICD)* coding system, again raising the question why the *Diagnostic and Statistical Manual of Mental Disorders* (5th edition) is necessary since eventually it all will be translated into the *International Classification of Diseases* 9th edition *(ICD)* coding system.

The symptoms of *phencyclidine intoxication* are the same as those discussed earlier in this chapter, as are the symptoms of the *phencyclidine withdrawal* syndrome. The category *Other phencyclidine use disorders* addresses the possibility that some of the observed symptoms are caused by the concurrent use of other drugs or preexisting psychiatric disorders. *Other hallucinogen intoxication* symptoms are the same as those discussed earlier in this chapter, and include (a) dilation of the pupils, (b) tachycardia, (c) sweating, (d) heart palpitations, (e) blurred vision, (f) tremor, and (g) loss of muscle coordination. These symptoms must develop in a person who has recently ingested a hallucinogen, in a person who is fully conscious, and are not symptoms of a co-existing medical disorder.

The *DSM-5* discussion of the hallucinogens is unique in that a withdrawal syndrome is not postulated for these compounds other than PCP. However, a *Hallucinogen persisting perceptual disorder* category was also suggested. These are the "flashback" phenomenon reported for compounds such as MDMA and LSD discussed in this text, which cannot be explained by the presence of a concurrent medical disorder. The signs of the *Other hallucinogen use disorders* as identified in the *DSM-5* essentially include experimental use of a hallucinogen or PCP The reader is referred to the *Diagnostic and Statistical Manual of Mental Disorders* (5th edition) (American Psychiatric Association, 2013) for a comparison of the similarities and differences between these PCP and other hallucinogen use categories.

Chapter Summary

The phenomenon of hallucinogen abuse has waxed and waned over the years, with abusers rushing to embrace first one compound, and then another. The compound LSD, the prototype hallucinogen, was popular in the 1960s, while PCP became popular in the 1970s and 1980s. Currently, MDMA is a popular hallucinogen of abuse. All of these compounds continue to be abused, although one or more is more common than the other. The phenomenon of hallucinogen abuse appears to reflect an inborn desire on the part of some people to alter their perception of reality, and possibly achieve euphoria from the drug's effects. As we stand on the brink of molecular pharmacology, it is logical to expect that the techniques used to develop more effective pharmaceuticals will eventually be used by illicit drug manufacturers to produce even more potent pharmaceuticals, insuring that the abuse of these compounds will remain a problem well into the 21st century.

---

[50]The reader is referred to the *Diagnostic and Statistical Manual of Mental Disorders* (5th edition) for a full list of the diagnostic criteria and an explanation of their meaning, should the reader be so motivated.

CHAPTER 13

Abuse and Addiction to Inhalants and Aerosols

Introduction

The term *inhalant* does not refer to a specific compound but to a *method of substance use* that introduces any of a wide variety of compounds into the user's body. Many such compounds are toxic, including various cleaning agents, herbicides, pesticides, gasoline, kerosene, certain forms of glue, lacquer thinner, and some of the chemicals used in certain felt-tipped pens. None of these compounds is intended to be introduced into the human body; however, when inhaled, each of these compounds alters normal brain function and may induce a sense of euphoria. Adolescents quickly discovered this fact, and younger individuals learned this by imitating their older siblings' behavior. Unfortunately, it is possible for children and adolescents to purchase dozens, perhaps hundreds of potential inhalants without parental permission.

Inhalant abuse is normally a time-limited phase for children and adolescents, and after a year or two they grow tired of this process and discontinue it. Many abuse an inhalant just a few times out of curiosity and then discontinue the practice. However, on occasion, the child or adolescent will continue to abuse inhalants, and it is not unheard of for an adult to enter treatment for inhalant abuse. Because these compounds are so readily available, widely abused, and have a terrible potential for harm to the abuser, this chapter will focus on the problem of inhalant abuse.

A Brief History of Inhalant Abuse

The use of inhaled compounds to alter the user's perception of reality might be traced back at least to ancient Greece. The Oracle at Delphi is thought to inhale fumes from a now dormant volcanic vent, and then while in a state of delirium, deliver prophetic statements that the recipient was then supposed to interpret (Hernandez-Avila, Pierucci, & Lagha, 2005). In the 19th century the use of the newly discovered nitrous oxide for recreation became popular, the medicinal potential of this compound not being recognized until after it became a popular recreational substance. The 20th century saw the introduction of gasoline and various industrial solvents, many of which quickly became compounds that were abused by inhalation (Commission on Adolescent Substance and Alcohol Abuse, 2005; Hernandez-Avila & Pierucci-Lagha, 2005; Sharp & Rosenberg, 2005).

The mainstream media paid little attention to the problem of inhalant abuse until the 1950s and 1960s, when the practice of "glue sniffing" became popular (Brust, 2004). The glue used to hold model ships, planes, and automobiles often contained the compound toluene,[1] which when inhaled can alter the individual's consciousness. It is not known why the practice of

---

[1]This compound has since been removed from model airplane glue.

"glue sniffing" began, but historical evidence suggests that it began in California. The first known reference to "glue sniffing" was in a Denver newspaper (Brust, 2004; Sharp & Rosenberg, 2005). Other newspapers began to cover the story of inhalant abuse, in the process explaining exactly how children or adolescents should use airplane glue to become intoxicated, and what effects they should expect. Although the media stories first appeared in the U.S. newspapers, the problem of inhalant abuse is now recognized as a worldwide one. In many "third world" countries, the abuse of inhalants helps to dull the individual's awareness of hunger while achieving a sense of euphoria (Weiss, 2007). Inhalant abuse is especially popular in Europe and Japan for recreational purposes and the problem has never entirely disappeared among young children and adolescents (Brust, 2004; Karch, 2009).

The Pharmacology of the Inhalants

The *inhalants* are not a specific drug, but a range of compounds that share a common method of abuse. Although cocaine or heroin may be snorted, this does not place them in the category of an inhalant because the goal of this process is to deposit the powder in the blood-rich tissues of the sinuses, not the lungs, for absorption. A true inhalant is absorbed through the lungs and passed into the general circulation from there. These compound(s) were never, however, intended to be used at the levels that inhalant abusers use, much less used for their intoxicating effects.

Inhalation is one of the most effective means to introduce a compound into the general circulation. Many molecules are able to cross over from the lungs into the circulation quickly and effectively, a trait that physicians often rely on to introduce anesthetic gasses into a patient's body to induce unconsciousness for major surgery. Inhalant abusers also rely on this rapid means of introducing a compound into the circulation to induce pleasure. Unfortunately, the abuse of inhalants is not very well understood and the limited research that is available leaves more questions than answers (McGuinness, 2006). A number of different classification systems of inhalants have been suggested, two of which are reviewed in Table 13-1.

Neither classification system is perfect. Children and adolescents will usually abuse compounds that fall into the first two categories, but will have limited access to

TABLE 13-1
Comparison of Two Inhalant Classification Systems

	BRUST (2004), CROWLEY AND SAKAI (2005)	ESPELAND (1997)
1	Solvents	Organic solvents
2	Propellants (used in spray cans)	Aerosols (used in spray cans)
3	Paint thinners	Volatile nitrites (Amyl nitrite or butyl nitrite)
4	Fuel fumes	General anesthetic gasses

© Cengage Learning

the third category of compounds in Espeland's (1997) classification system. The abuse of surgical anesthetics is usually limited to health care professionals, or medical school students, who have access to such compounds (Hernandez-Avila & Pierucci-Lagha, 2005).

The most common inhalants are simple, carbon-based molecules such as benzene, toluene, hexane, acetone, butane, and ethyl chloride (Ricaurte, Langston, & McCann, 2008). All of these compounds, plus gasoline fumes (another favorite inhalant in some regions of the world), are able to enter the bloodstream without their chemical structure being altered in any way (Bruckner & Warren, 2003). The compounds share the characteristic of being very lipid soluble, which allows those molecules to rapidly cross the blood–brain barrier (BBB) into the brain within seconds of their use (Commission on Adolescent Substance and Alcohol Abuse, 2005; Crowley & Sakai, 2004).

Parents will often ask why, if children are abusing various compounds through inhalation, the government does not just outlaw these products. The answer to this question is that this is impossible. There are hundreds to perhaps *over one thousand* common household or industrial products that might be abused as an inhalant (Howard, Bowen, Garland, Perron, & Baughn, 2011; McGuinness, 2006; Wolfe, 2009). Further, children and adolescents are adept at finding compounds around the house that might be abused as an inhalant. For example, the team of Feuillet, Mallet, and Sparad (2006) presented a case history in which twin sisters were discovered to be inhaling mothball fumes to become intoxicated.

The effects of an inhalant are dependent on (Wolfe, 2009): (a) the chemical(s) being abused, (b) the intensity of exposure, (c) the body size of the abuser, (d) the abuser's expectations for the effects of that compound, (e) the setting in which the inhalant abuse takes place, and (f) the abuser's general state of health. Given the interaction between these variables, and the wide variety of compounds that might be abused as an inhalant, it is impossible to speak of a class-specific "pharmacology" or "toxicology" of these compounds. The elimination half-life of different inhalants might range from hours to days, depending on the specific compound being abused (Brooks, Leung, & Shannon, 1996). The half-life of most solvents is also longer in obese abusers because these compounds bind to lipid molecules. Given the current epidemic of childhood obesity in the United States, this is a matter of some concern for health care professionals who work with inhalant abusers because it would be expected that the molecules of the inhalant(s) would bind to the adipose cells. This is, however, an assumption as here is virtually *no* information available as to the effects of these compounds on children or adolescents (Bruckner & Warren, 2003).

Many of the commonly abused inhalants do share some common toxicological characteristics, one of which is many of these compounds must be biotransformed by the liver before the process of elimination (usually by the kidneys) can begin (Bruckner & Warren, 2003). There are exceptions to this rule, however: The anesthetic gasses are exhaled without extensive, or in some cases any, biotransformation taking place (Crowley & Sakai, 2004). Because the pharmacokinetics of an inhalant varies from one compound to the next, virtually no information is available about the effects of that compounds at the cellular level (Haut, Moran, & Lonser, 2012; McGuinness, 2006). Even where such research has been conducted, abusers often use concentrations of the compound(s) of choice that are orders of magnitude beyond those achieved when that compound is used as directed (Bruckner & Warren, 2003). To illustrate this point, consider that the maximum permitted exposure level for toluene fumes in the workplace is 50–100 parts per million (ppm) (Crowley & Sakai, 2005). The concentration used by those who abuse this compound through inhalation is 50–100 times as high as the maximum permitted industrial exposure level. To further complicate matters, the abuser might use a compound in which the desired substance is a secondary ingredient, exposing themselves to the effects of the primary compound in that product as well as the desired substance (Hernandez-Avila & Pierucci-Lagha, 2005).

Scientists do not fully understand the mechanism(s) by which the inhalants alter the normal function of the brain (Commission on Adolescent Substance and Alcohol Abuse, 2005; McGuinness, 2006). As a group, the compounds abused by inhalation are thought to alter the normal function of the gamma-aminobutyric acid (GABA) and/or N-methyl-D-aspartate (NMDA) (Crowley & Sakai, 2004). Behavioral observations on animals exposed to an inhalant suggest that their effects are similar to those of alcohol, or the barbiturates, which is consistent with neurological data suggesting that all of these compounds bind at the same gated ion channel in the neural cell wall. It *has* been observed that some inhalants potentiate the effects of CNS depressants use such as alcohol and the benzodiazepines,[2] possibly with fatal results. As should be apparent by now, so little is known about the pharmacological effects of these compounds, and their effects can be influenced by so many different factors that there is no standard "pharmacology" of the inhalants.

Scope of the Problem of Inhalant Abuse

Inhalant abuse is a worldwide problem, a fact that is often overlooked by the mass media in this country. Approximately 9% of the population in the United States or approximately 22.5 million people have abused an inhalant at least once (Howard et al., 2011). This is consistent with the observation that 8.1% of high school seniors in 2011 admitted to the use of an inhalant at least once (Johnston, O'Malley, Backman, & Schulenberg, 2012a). It has been estimated that 2.4 million adolescents have abused an inhalant at least one time, 1 million have abused an inhalant in the past 12 months, and 44,000 children or adolescents abuse an inhalant each day ("Adolescent Inhalant Use and Selected Respiratory Conditions," 2010). Boys are more likely to abuse inhalants than girls although researchers are not sure of the ratio between male to female inhalant abusers. Brust (2004) suggested that boys were more likely to abuse inhalants than girls by a ratio of 10:1, whereas Spiller and Krenzoelok (1997) suggested that the ratio was only 3:1.

Many who abuse these compounds do not view this as a form of "drug" abuse (Wolfe, 2009). Fortunately inhalant abuse is usually limited to experimental use

---

[2]This list is hardly exhaustive, and the reader is reminded that any known or suspected overdose should *immediately* be assessed by a physician.

that occurs a few times and then is discontinued without the child/adolescent going on to develop other drug problems (Commission on Adolescent Substance and Alcohol Abuse, 2005; Crowley & Sakai, 2005; Howard et al., 2011; Marsolek, White, & Litovitz, 2010). The mean age at which abusers begin substance-centered inhalation is about 13 years, and the mean age of inhalant abusers is thought to be 16.6 years of age (Anderson & Loomis, 2003; Marsolek et al., 2010). There are reports of children as young as 3 years of age abusing inhalants, however, and so it is important to keep in mind the fact that children *do* abuse inhalants on occasion (Crowley & Sakai, 2005). Unfortunately individuals with an inhalant abuse problem are usually not referred to a rehabilitation facility until the individual is over the age of 18 years (Substance Abuse and Mental Health Services Administration, Center for Behavioral Health Statistics and Quality, 2011).

It has been estimated that only about 4% of inhalant abusers become addicted (Brust, 2004). Hernandez-Avila and Pierucci-Lagha (2005) identified four patterns of inhalant abuse:

1. *Transient social use*: This occurs for a brief period of time in response to social situations, usually involving individuals 10–16 years of age.
2. *Chronic social use*: The individual abuses an inhalant for 5 or more years with others, usually seen in individuals 20–30 years of age. These individuals demonstrate signs of brain damage and usually have minor legal problems in their histories.
3. *Transient isolated use*: A short history of solo inhalant abuse by individuals usually 10–16 years of age.
4. *Chronic isolated use*: A history of continuous solo abuse of inhalants lasting for 5+ years, with a history of serious legal problems, and possible evidence of brain damage.

There is a lively debate over whether inhalants serve as a "gateway" to further drug abuse or not. It has been found, for example, that 23% of cocaine abusers had a history of prior inhalant abuse (Worchester, 2006). People who admit to a history of inhalant abuse were found to be 45 times more likely to engage in the practice of self-injected drug abuse, whereas those individuals who admit to the use of inhalants *and* marijuana use were 89 times as likely to have used injected drugs as the general population (Crowley & Sakai, 2005). These figures, although disturbing, raise an interesting question: Does the inhalant abuse pave the way for further drug abuse, or are those persons who are more likely to abuse drugs begin with inhalant abuse, and then "graduate" on to other forms of substance use later in life? This debate has obviously not been resolved, and the debate over whether inhalants serve as a "gateway" to later drug abuse continues.

Methods of Inhalant Abuse

There are a number of ways that inhalants might be abused, and the specific method of abuse is dependent on the specific compound being abused (Anderson & Loomis, 2003; Wolfe, 2009). Some compounds may be inhaled directly from its container, a practice called *sniffing* or *snorting*. Helium-filled balloons are often abused in this manner (Northcutt, 2008). Other compounds are poured into a plastic bag, which is then placed over the abuser's mouth and nose so that the individual can inhale concentrated fumes, a practice called *bagging* (Anderson & Loomis, 2003; Nelson, 2000). Still other compounds are poured onto a rag, which is then placed over the individual's mouth and nose, called *huffing,* which allows the fumes to be inhaled along with air (Anderson & Loomis, 2003; Nelson, 2000).

Fumes from aerosol cans may be directly inhaled, or sprayed into the mouth. An example of those fumes that are directly inhaled are cigarette lighters. Abusers will activate the cigarette lighter without lighting it, allowing the fumes to escape the container for inhalation. Finally, there are those compounds that are heated, releasing the fumes that are then inhaled (Nelson, 2000). Obviously, if the compound being abused should be flammable, there is a significant risk of fire should the compound being heated be exposed to open flame or a spark, but this is a risk that inhalant abusers either are not aware of or dismiss as a cost of their abuse of inhalants.

Subjective Effects of Inhalants

The initial effects of an inhalant begin with seconds to, at most, minutes, and last for approximately 45 minutes per episode of abuse (Schuckit, 2006a; Zevin & Benowitz, 2007). The desired effects from inhalants include those listed in Table 13-2 (Anderson & Loomis, 2003; Brust, 2004; Sharp & Rosenberg, 2005; Wolfe, 2009; Zevin & Benowitz, 2007).

TABLE 13-2
Desired Effects of Inhalant Abuse

alcohol-like euphoria and sense of intoxicated or altered voice (when substances such as helium are abused)

altered state of awareness

hallucinations

fantasies (some vivid)

feelings of invincibility

loss of inhibitions

numbness

sense of spinning around

NOTE: Effects differ based on substance(s) abused.

© 2015 Cengage Learning

Complications Induced by Inhalant Abuse

When inhalant abuse first emerged in the 1950s and 1960s, most health care professionals did not think that there were any serious health consequences associated with this practice. This is no longer assumed to be true. In the last quarter of the 20th century, scientists concluded that depending on (a) the substance being abused, (b) the method of abuse, (c) the level of substance exposure, and (d) the frequency of abuse, the abuser might experience significant health problems and possible death (Worchester, 2006). The duration and intensity of exposure are important variables that cannot be quantified: In the industrial setting, a worker might be exposed to high levels of a compound(s) in an isolated incident, where an abuser might be exposed to far lower level each time that the same compound is abused. A partial list of potential consequences from inhalant abuse includes those listed in Table 13-3 (Anderson & Loomis, 2003; Brust, 2004; Crowley & Sakai, 2004, 2005; Han, Gofoerer, & Colliver, 2010; Haut et al., 2012; Howard et al., 2011; Karch, 2009; Lezak, Howieson, Bingler, & Tranel, 2012; Sharp & Rosenberg, 2005; Virani, Bezchlibnyk-Butler, Jeffries, & Procyshyn, 2012; Weiss, 2007; Wolfe, 2009; Worchester, 2006; Zevin & Benowitz, 2007).

Approximately 50% of deaths attributed to inhalant abuse are the result of inhalant-induced ventricular fibrillation,[3] or *sniffing death syndrome* (McGuinness, 2006). Such deaths can occur the first time that an

---

[3] A cardiac arrhythmia.

TABLE 13-3
Possible Health Consequences of Inhalant Abuse

CARDIOPULMONARY SYSTEM

anoxia and/or respiratory depression, possibly to point of death

aspiration of vomited material (may result in death, especially if abuser is unconscious)

bone marrow damage resulting in reduction in red blood cell production

cardiac arrhythmias such as ventricular fibrillation (may prove fatal)

cough/wheezing

erosion of nasal mucosa, formation of ulcers in nose, mouth, and throat

exacerbation of asthma or similar disorders

lung function changes, possible chronic lung disease/infections

sinusitis (irritation of sinus tissues—may become permanent)

tuberculosis (increased vulnerability toward development of)

CENTRAL NERVOUS SYSTEM

cerebellar ataxia

deafness or loss of hearing (may become permanent)

encephalopathy

nystagmus

organic brain damage (including possible drug-induced dementia)

peripheral neuropathies

Seizures

tremor (may become permanent)

visual impairment (may become permanent)

PSYCHIATRIC

anxiety

confusion

depression

psychological dependence on further inhalant (or drug) use

psychosis (drug induced) (possibly become permanent)

OTHER COMPLICATIONS

chemical burns to skin, especially around mouth/nose

kidney damage (might be permanent)

laryngitis

TABLE 13-3
(Continued)

light sensitivity

liver damage (possibly permanent)

muscle tissue damage secondary to rhabdomyolysis

vomiting, possibly leading to aspiration-induced death

© Cengage Learning

individual abuses an inhalant, or the 200th time ("Huffing can kill your child," 2004). Further, depending on the substance being abused, the individual might introduce various heavy metals such as copper or lead into their body, which will have lifelong consequences (Crowley & Sakai, 2005; Lezak et al., 2012). Lead was once an additive to gasoline and was found in many forms of paint in the United States, leading to it becoming a common cause of lead poisoning when its gasoline was abused as an inhalant. Lead has been removed from gasoline, and lead poisoning is rarely a problem now. If the compound being abused is a propellant-propelled substance (such as spray cans of paint, for example), the abuser runs the risk of coating the inside of the lungs with the compound itself, although the propellant was the desired substance to be abused. This may interfere with the normal function of the lungs, if not block it entirely, resulting in the abuser's death.

Although a standard neurological examination is often unable to detect solvent-induced organic brain damage until it is relatively advanced, sensitive neuropsychological tests often detect early signs of inhalant-induced brain damage even in industrial workers who are exposed to levels far lower than those utilized by inhalant abusers. Toluene is a prime example of this, and chronic toluene exposure can induce intellectual impairment, as well as leukoencephalopathy, and atrophy of the optic nerves (Crowley & Sakai, 2004, 2005; Ricaurte et al., 2008).

Upon the cessation of an episode of inhalant abuse, the abuser will go through a withdrawal syndrome, which at its extreme can be similar to alcohol-induced delirium tremens (DTs) (Hernandez-Avila & Pierucci-Lagha, 2005). The exact withdrawal syndrome will depend in large part on the exact compound(s) being abused, the length of exposure, the concentration of the compound(s) used, and possible concurrent substance abuse. Some of the withdrawal symptoms observed during severe inhalant withdrawal include muscle tremors, irritability, anxiety, insomnia, muscle

cramps, hallucinations, sweating, nausea, a foul odor on the abuser's breath, loss of vision, and possible seizures (Worchester, 2006).

Inhalant Abuse and Suicide

There is a strong correlation between inhalant abuse, depression, and suicidal behavior (McGuinness, 2006). Because depression is a risk factor for suicidal behavior, and depression is a common consequence of inhalant abuse, there is a potential for suicidal behavior following episodes of inhalant abuse. The more intense the frequency and duration of inhalant abuse, the greater the risk for suicidal behavior (Espeland, 1997; Freedenthala, Vaugh, Jensona, & Howard, 2007). Unfortunately, it is not always apparent whether the inhalant abuser intended to end their life unless they left a suicide note. Some of the methods of inhalant abuse lend themselves to ambiguity whether death was an intentional or accidental. For example, if the abuser inserts his or her head into a plastic bag after filling the bag with inhalant fumes and then closes the bag around the head and neck before beginning to inhale the fumes, it is difficult to determine whether the abuser's death was an actual suicide or just an accident unless the abuser left a suicide note behind. However, intentional and unintentional death is a very real danger when an individual abuses an inhalant.

Anesthetic Misuse

The first two anesthetics used, nitrous oxide and ether, were first recreational substances (Hernandez-Avila & Pierucci-Lagha, 2005). Their potential as surgical anesthetics were only recognized when Horace Wells attended a party in which people were indulging in nitrous oxide abuse and observed a person under its influence injure himself without apparent pain. Unfortunately, the first planned exhibition of nitrous oxide as a surgical anesthetic agent was something less than a success.[4] This did not prevent some intrepid explorers from examining the effectiveness of various compounds as potential surgical anesthetics with some success. The pharmacological effects of general anesthetics are similar to those induced by the barbiturates (Hernandez-Avila &

---

[4]At the time it was not recognized that nitrous oxide has a short duration of action when used as a surgical anesthetic. The patient woke up in the middle of the operation screaming in pain. The proper use of nitrous oxide as a surgical anesthetic was not discovered until several years after this inauspicious beginning.

Peirucci-Lagha, 2005). The general anesthetic gasses have a dose-dependent effect on the user's body, ranging from sedation at the lowest doses through analgesia and possible death if used to excess. Although medical school students will occasionally abuse compounds such as ether, chloroform, trichloroethylene, and halothane, the most commonly abused anesthetic gas is nitrous oxide, which we will examine in more detail in the following section.

Nitrous Oxide

The surgical anesthetic gasses are able to induce a loss of consciousness during which time the patient is less responsive to painful stimuli. It has been suggested that the person under the effects of an anesthetic might still be able to sense pain, a possibility supported by the observation that some patients can recall some thing said in the surgical theatre during their operation. This raises the question whether the surgical anesthetics block the individual's awareness of the pain or just make them less responsive to the pain that they experience, a topic that is being explored through research at this time.

Nitrous oxide is perhaps the prototypical surgical anesthetic and it is occasionally abused, so we will look at this compound's effects in more detail. Nitrous oxide blocks the glutamate neurotransmitter molecules from the NMDA receptor sites. Because glutamate is the main excitatory neurotransmitter in the brain, it becomes clear why it is able to function as an anesthetic gas. It also reduces the effectiveness of acetylcholine as a neurotransmitter, which contributes to the reduction in the individual's level of consciousness (Lewis, 2011). However, to prevent the risk of death by hypoxia,[5] the physician (or dentist, because it is often used as an esthetic during dental surgery) must supply oxygen at over pressure[6] during the procedure. Abusers often do not know about this characteristic of nitrous oxide, and very few have access to the equipment necessary to supply oxygen at over pressure. Thus, nitrous oxide abusers run a substantial risk of hypoxia-induced brain damage or even death while using this substance.[7]

In low doses, nitrous oxide abusers report feelings of euphoria, giddiness, hallucinations, and a loss of inhibitions. At higher doses, there is a loss of consciousness and possible death at extremely high doses. The volatile anesthetics are not extensively biotransformed by the body, but enter and leave the body virtually unchanged. Once the source of the anesthetic is removed, such as when the surgical procedure is completed, the concentration of the anesthetic in the brain will begin to drop, and eventually the patient is able to regain consciousness to begin the process of recovery.

The Abuse of Nitrites

There are different forms of nitrites commonly abused: (1) the pharmaceutical compound amyl nitrite, which is used in certain heart conditions, (2) butyl nitrite, and (3) isobutyl nitrite. Although inhaled, all of these compounds function as a coronary vasodilator, allowing more blood to flow to the heart. This is why amyl nitrite is used in the control of angina pectoris: When administered, it allows the coronary arteries to dilate for a short time, increasing the blood flow to the heart. Amyl nitrite is administered in small glass containers embedded in layers of cloth. When needed, the user will "snap" or "pop"[8] the container in his or her fingers, and inhale the fumes to achieve the desired effect.

With the introduction of nitroglycerine preparations, which are as effective as amyl nitrite but lack many of its disadvantages, amyl nitrite has fallen into disfavor, and is now only rarely utilized (Hernandez-Avila & Pierucci-Lagha, 2005). Still, it does have a limited role in medicine, such as in certain diagnostic procedures and the treatment of cyanide poisoning. Nitrite abusers prize these amyl nitrite capsules, using them in much the same manner that they abuse butyl nitrite or isobutyl nitrite. These latter compounds are available by mail order houses or specialty stores, depending on the state regulations for that specific area. In many areas, butyl nitrite is sold as a "room deodorizer," sold in small bottles that usually cost more than $10. Many abusers believe that butyl nitrite will induce a prolonged orgasm, if inhaled just before the abuser achieves this state.[9]

Because amyl nitrite is known to induce delayed orgasm and impotence in male users, it is not unreasonable to expect that its close chemical cousins would also induce these effects. The aftereffects of the use of

---

[5]See Glossary.

[6]See Glossary.

[7]This is a risk inherent in the use of many anesthetic gasses, but this lies outside of the scope of this textbook.

[8]Thus the name used by illicit users of "poppers" or "snappers."

[9]The author of this text has met butyl nitrite abusers who claim that rather than enhance sexual pleasure, butyl nitrite actually interfered with their enjoyment of the sexual encounter.

these compounds include an intense, sudden, headache, increased pressure in the fluid in the eyes (a danger for patients with glaucoma), possible weakness, nausea, retinal damage, and cerebral hemorrhage induced by nitrite-induced increased blood pressure (Audo, Sahel, & Paques, 2010; Karch, 2009). In addition, the nitrites appear to suppress the action of the body's immune system, especially the natural killer cells, possibly increasing the user's risk for an infection after using nitrites. Abusers are willing to run the risk of these adverse events, although most people wonder why a person would be willing to run these risks just for a few seconds of perceived pleasure.

Inhalant Abuse and the *Diagnostic and Statistical Manual of Mental Disorders* (5th Edition)[10]

The *Diagnostic and Statistical Manual of Mental Disorders* (5th edition) (*DSM-5*) (American Psychiatric Association, 2013) identified four subforms of the inhalant-related disorders:

- *Inhalant use disorder*
- *Inhalant intoxication*
- *Other inhalant-induced disorders*
- *Unspecified inhalant related disorder*

The *inhalant use disorder* is equivalent to inhalant addiction, a phenomenon that resembles alcohol intoxication. The *DSM-5* (American Psychiatric Association, 2013) warned that inhalant abusers often abuse several compounds simultaneously, making the differential diagnosis difficult. The *Diagnostic and Statistical Manual of Mental Disorders* (5th edition) (American Psychiatric Association, 2013) suggested that *Inhalant Intoxication* be considered when the individual demonstrates any of the criteria for intoxication outlined in this chapter,[11] without evidence of concurrent abuse of other compounds such as alcohol. One diagnostic sign of inhalant

intoxication is the smell of the compound(s) being abused on the individual's breath or the possession of compounds primarily used for intoxicating purposes.

Only about 10% of inhalant abusers develop *inhalant tolerance* to their compound of choice. Children with either a conduct disorder or an antisocial personality disorder appear to be at greater risk for inhalant abuse or addiction (American Psychiatric Association, 2013), although other personality types are also vulnerable to the lures of inhalant abuse. The condition *Other Inhalant-Induced Disorders* refers to psychiatric conditions caused or exacerbated by the abuse of inhalants in the *Diagnostic and Statistical Manual of Mental Disorders* (5th edition) (*DSM-5*) (American Psychiatric Association, 2013), whereas the *Unspecified inhalant-related disorder* refers to those cases in which the individual has developed social, occupational, familial, or other symptoms of an inhalant use disorder, but who do not meet the full criteria for this condition. For each of these conditions modifiers such as in early or in sustained remission as well as whether the individual is in a controlled environment where access to such compounds is limited may be applied as appropriate in the assessor's opinion.

Chapter Summary

Inhalant abuse appears to be a phase through which many children and adolescents pass. For the most part, the individual engages in a few episodes of inhalant abuse over a period of 1–2 years, and then discontinues the practice. However, a small percentage of individuals go on to abuse other compounds, and an even smaller percentage of abusers continue to use inhalants for extended periods. The effects of these compounds are short-lived, although this depends on the specific compound(s) being abused and the intensity with which the abuser inhales this compound(s). Because there are literally thousands of commercial products that may be abused as an inhalant, these compounds are easily available to children and adolescents and this fact may contribute to their attractiveness as a drug of abuse. However, inhalant abuse also exposes the abuser to compounds, the effects of which are unknown to toxicologists, or in dosage levels that have not been studied by toxicologists. Death or organic damage to various body organs is possible from inhalant abuse, making these compounds a dangerous "high" for children or adolescents.

---

[10]The material presented here is to illustrate the relationship between the alcohol use disorders and the *Diagnostic and Statistical Manual of Mental Disorders (5th edition)*. This material should not be interpreted as, nor should it be used as, a diagnostic manual.

[11]The reader is referred to the *Diagnostic and Statistical Manual of Mental Disorders* (5th edition) (*DSM-5*) (American Psychiatric Association, 2013) for the full list of diagnostic criteria suggested by the American Psychiatric Association as signs of inhalant intoxication.

CHAPTER 14

The Underrecognized Problem of Steroid Abuse and Addiction

Introduction

The term "performance-enhancing" compounds has frequently been in the news in the past year as blood or urine samples from one athlete or another have revealed evidence suggesting their use by athletes seeking a competitive edge. It often surprises the layperson to learn that ancient Greek warriors ingested deer muscle meat, or consumed special drinks and potions on the theory that this would increase their speed and endurance, and lion heart muscle on the theory that this would increase the athlete's bravery (Aschwanden, 2012; Stephens, 2008). The gladiators of ancient Rome used a wide variety of potions in the hopes of being able to gain a competitive edge over their opponents (Botre & Pavan, 2008). It is not known how effective these compounds were, but the user believed in them that may have enhanced their fighting or athletic ability if only through the placebo effect.

In the present era, there are a wide range of substances including the anabolic steroids that are abused by amateur and professional athletes either to enhance their own athletic performance or at least offset any advantage that their opponent might gain from using such compounds. The potential dangers associated with the use of such compounds are minimized or ignored by the abuser who seeks to either gain an advantage over the opposition or at least "level the playing field"[1] should their opponent be abusing such compounds. On rare occasions, abusers seek the sense of mild euphoria induced by performance-enhancing compounds. However, the major motivating factor is the desire to improve athletic performance both at the local and national levels.

In a sense, anabolic steroid abuse reflects two different social diseases. First is the emphasis on appearances. This is perhaps most clearly illustrated by the trend for advertisers to describe their product as being "on steroids," giving the impression of enhanced speed, durability, and attractiveness inherent in the use of such compounds (Pope & Brower, 2008; Rylkova, Bruijnzeel, & Gold, 2007). A small percentage of the population has come to believe that anabolic steroids will enhance their physical appearance as well. The second expression of this social disease is the belief that it is acceptable to "win at any cost," even if this involves the use of illegal and potentially lethal compounds. Many athletes will look for something—anything—that will give them a perceived "edge" over the competition. For example, Aschwanden (2012) spoke of a case where the U.S. Anti-Doping Agency suspended a teenaged

---

[1]Rylkova, Bruijnzeel, and Gold (2007) estimated that up to 95% of professional football players and 80–99% of other professional athletes use anabolic steroids to enhance performance.

in-line skater because performance-enhancing drugs had been detected in the athlete's urine. Subsequent investigation revealed that the father of the athlete in question had been injecting him with a combination of growth hormone and steroids since the skater was 12 years old, apparently to give his son an advantage over the competition.

At the end of the first decade of the 21st century, it would not be unreasonable to say that a "fierce competition" (Aschwanden, 2012, p. 56) has developed between those who use performance-enhancing compounds, a category that includes the anabolic steroids, and scientists who strive to develop tests that will detect the latest performance-enhancing compounds. An "arms race mentality" (Joyner, 2004, p. 81) has evolved in both amateur and professional athletics[2] in which individuals begin to use performance-enhancing compounds to overcome what they perceive as an unfair advantage that such compounds offer the opposition. To meet the demands of both those who wish to enhance athletic performance and those who wish to improve their appearance, an acquisition and distribution network has evolved. Because of the widespread abuse of these compounds, it can be assumed that some it is of value for the substance abuse counselor to have a working knowledge of these compounds and their effects.

An Introduction to the Anabolic-Androgenic Steroids

The term *anabolic* refers to the ability of these compounds to increase the speed of tissue growth or repair, possibly through the retention of nitrogen molecules within muscle tissue. The term *steroid* refers to the fact that these compounds are structurally similar to testosterone, the primary male sex hormone. Because of their chemical similarity to testosterone, steroids have a masculinizing (androgenic) effect on the user (Pope & Brower, 2008). This natural effect is seen when boys reach puberty and their bodies start to produce significant amounts of testosterone: Suddenly muscle growth and secondary sex characteristics emerge. Although the adolescent may have been exercising prior to the onset of puberty, it is only after puberty that their efforts result in significant muscle growth. It is for this reason that the anabolic steroids are sometimes referred to as the *anabolic-androgenic* steroids[3] (Lukas, 2009).

In humans, normal testosterone levels are associated with lower total cholesterol levels, lower levels of body fat, smaller waist circumference, and a reduction in the pro-inflammatory cytokines associated with atherosclerosis, the metabolic syndrome that often proceeds the development of diabetes and the onset of diabetes itself. The problems associated with excessive levels of anabolic steroids will be discussed later.

Medical Uses of Anabolic Steroids

Although the anabolic steroids have been in use since the 1950s, there are few approved uses for these compounds (Pope & Brower, 2005, 2008). Physicians will prescribe corticosteroids, close chemical cousins to the anabolic steroids to suppress the immune system as an adjunct to the treatment of various diseases. This is an important distinction for the reader to keep in mind. Anabolic steroids are occasionally used to treat delayed puberty in adolescents and as an adjunct to the treatment of certain forms of breast cancer (Lukas, 2009). They promote the growth of bone tissue following injuries in certain cases, and might be useful in the treatment of osteoporosis (Congeni & Miller, 2002). Evidence suggests that although the anabolic steroids might be of value in treating AIDS-related weight loss, there are few other legitimate applications for the anabolic steroids at this time. The corticosteroids have been found to be useful in treating a range of

---

[2]Aschwanden (2012) reported that the World Anti-Doping Agency tested about half of the 14,000 athletes participating in the 2012 summer Olympic games. All of the medal winners were tested as were a number of other athletes selected at random. Tests were also conducted on blood or urine samples collected from past Olympic games to determine whether there was evidence of abuse of performance-enhancing compounds that would not be identified by the technology of that era.

[3]For the sake of this chapter, the terms "steroids" or "anabolic steroids" will usually be used.

conditions. However, a discussion of this group of medications lies beyond the scope of this chapter and will not be mentioned again.

Why Steroids Are Abused

Athletes are often drawn to the anabolic steroids because these compounds can (1) increase lean muscle mass, (2) increase muscle strength, and (3) reduce the period of recovery time necessary between exercise periods (Karch, 2009; Pope & Brower, 2008). They also induce a sense of euphoria in some abusers (Eisenberg & Galloway, 2005; Hildebrandt, Langenbucher, Carr, Sanjuan, & Park, 2006). In contrast to alcohol or the other drugs of abuse where intense euphoria is the motivating factor for the substance use, anabolic steroid abusers most often seek improved athletic performance through these compounds especially if the steroid use is undetected by urine or blood toxicology testing.

Once the cycle of steroid abuse is initiated, many abusers continue because they develop a state of "reverse anorexia nervosa" (Kanayama, Barry, Hudson, & Harrison, 2006, p. 697; Lukas, 2009). Individuals with this condition, which is more descriptive than a diagnostic category, become obsessed with their body image and fear that they might look "small" to others. This body image disorder is usually seen after the individual has been abusing anabolic steroids for an extended time, and frequently functions as an incentive for further steroid abuse. Boys in the 12–18 year old age cohort who abuse anabolic steroids to help their muscle development for appearances are approximately two times as likely to abuse illicit drugs such as cocaine and methamphetamine as well as being at increased risk for binge drinking (Field, Sonneville, Crosby, Swanson, Eddy, Camargo, Horton, & Micali, 2013). Such body image disorders predate the abuse of anabolic steroids in many persons (Kanayama et al., 2006) and might explain why nonathlete steroid abusers believe that these compounds will help them look more attractive (Kanayama et al., 2006; Pope, 2010; Pope & Brower, 2008). This subgroup of steroid abusers includes a small percentage of adolescent girls who believe that these compounds will help them lose body fat and help them look more "toned" or attractive ("Girls are abusing steroids too," 2005).

Another subgroup of steroid abusers is composed of law enforcement and security officers, who believe that these compounds will increase their strength and aggressiveness (Eisenberg & Galloway, 2005; Galloway, 1997). These individuals hope that their use of steroids will give them an advantage when confronting a potential lawbreaker. However, the greatest proportion of steroid abusers are athletes who hope that these compounds will enhance their athletic performance. Thus, there is no "standard" steroid abuser, but various subgroups who share the characteristic of anabolic steroid abuse in common.

The Legal Status of Anabolic Steroids

In the United States, anabolic steroids have been classified as a Category III controlled substance[4] since 1990. At least 28 different compounds have been identified as anabolic steroids by law enforcement officials and their use for nonmedical purposes, or their sale by individuals not licensed to possess and distribute them, is a crime punishable by a prison term of up to 5 years (10 years if the steroids are sold to minors).

Scope of the Problem of Steroid Abuse

Anabolic steroid abuse is a silent epidemic, and the true scope of the abuse of these compounds is not known (Eisenberg & Galloway, 2005; Karch, 2009). There is little information about the use of performance-enhancing compounds (including anabolic steroids) by preadolescent athletes, although there have been isolated case reports in Europe (Laure & Binsinger, 2007). In the United States, urine toxicology testing for performance-enhancing drugs in athletes does not begin until high school, and so the abuse of such compounds in preadolescents is possibly more widespread than suspected (Laure & Binsinger, 2007).

Johnston, O'Malley, Backman, and Schulenberg (2012a) reported that 1.8% of high school seniors surveyed in 2011 reported having abused an anabolic steroid at least once. Although earlier studies suggested that adolescent girls might be abusing anabolic steroids in large numbers, Pope and Brower (2008) discounted this theory because these medications have an androgenic effect, which would be most unwelcome for the typical adolescent girl. In spite of this fact, there is preliminary evidence suggesting that the number of girls who are abusing an anabolic steroid is increasing ("Girls are abusing steroids too," 2005). Although anabolic

---

[4]See Appendix Three.

steroid abuse was seen most often in older adolescents, there is a disturbing trend for younger adolescent athletes to abuse these compounds, both to improve their appearance and to improve athletic ability (Calfee & Fadake, 2006; Rylkova et al., 2007).

The median age for anabolic steroid abusers is 18 (Karch, 2009), which is consistent with the observation that college-aged steroid abusers frequently report that they did not begin to use these compounds until just before or shortly after starting college (Dickensheets, 2001). Further, although the popular image of a steroid abuser is that of a professional athlete, Cohen, Collins, Darkes, and Gwartney (2007) found that the typical male steroid abuser in their research sample was a well-educated, Caucasian 30-year-old who held a "white collar" job.

Pharmacology of Anabolic-Androgenic Steroids

The anabolic steroids are members of a group of compounds that are similar to the testosterone molecule. The basic testosterone molecule, of which there are at least 1,000 known derivatives, lends itself to a variety of functions: Progesterone regulation in women, formation of adrenocortical hormones, bile acids, negating the effects of some poisons produced by various toads, and the development of some carcinogenic compounds. During gestation, testosterone plays a role in the differentiation of the sexes, especially during the third and fourth months of prenatal development, and is involved in the prenatal development of the hypothalamus in males. Following birth, especially after the onset of puberty, endogenous testosterone molecules reduce pain sensitivity and anxiety levels as well as motivate men to seek a sexual partner. These molecules are also involved in the formation of muscle mass following the onset of puberty, sperm production in adolescent boys, and bone maturation in both sexes.

A little known fact is that women's bodies produce small amounts of testosterone, and is involved in the regulation of sexual arousal in woman the pair-bonding process. For both sexes, endogenous testosterone is involved in a number of body system regulation activities.[5] It is thought that the steroids force the body

to increase cellular protein synthesis through the retention of nitrogen molecules in the cell wall. The anabolic steroids also inhibit the action of a group of chemicals known as the glucocorticoids, which cause tissue breakdown (Congeni & Miller, 2002; Casavant, Blake, Griffith, Yates, & Copley, 2007; Rylkova et al., 2007). The mechanism through which this is accomplished is not known, but appears to explain why anabolic steroids are able to counteract the effects of strenuous physical exercise, contribute to the development or retention of muscle tissue, and aid in developing physical endurance. It has been hypothesized that in the brain, the endogenous steroid molecules modulate the action of the GABAa receptor, altering the user's emotions since the GABAa receptor is found in the brain regions involved in the aggression response, anxiety, and reproduction (Rylkova et al., 2007).

The artificial anabolic steroids might be broken down into two subgroups: (1) those compounds that are active when administered orally and (2) those compounds that must be injected into muscle tissue to become active. The orally administered steroids are more easily administered but have a shorter half-life, are prone to biotransformation through the first-pass metabolism effect, and are more toxic to the liver than steroids administered parenterally. As will be discussed later in this chapter, anabolic steroid abusers have been found to experience a wide range of behavioral problems, suggesting that they cross the blood–brain barrier (BBB) and bind at some of the same endogenous steroid receptor sites used by endogenous testosterone molecules. However, the artificial anabolic steroid molecules are somewhat more powerful than the endogenous testosterone molecules, displacing the endogenous compounds from their receptor sites.

Sources and Methods of Steroid Abuse

Because anabolic steroids have few recognized medical uses, and strict controls are in place to limit the amount(s) prescribed by physicians, most anabolic steroids used in the United States are obtained from illicit sources (Eisenberg & Galloway, 2005). These sources include legitimate pharmaceuticals that are diverted to the illicit market, steroids intended for the veterinary market, semi-legal compounds manufactured by illicit drug producers, and compounds smuggled into the United States by a variety of means.

---

[5]Which lie outside of the scope of this text. If the reader is interested in learning more about the role that endogenous testosterone plays in body system regulation, he or she is referred to a good textbook on neurohormones and their role in the maturation and regulation of the body.

"Internet" pharmacies are an increasingly popular source of anabolic steroids abused in the United States, as the shipment of pharmaceuticals from the supplier to the "patient" is unlikely to be intercepted. Anabolic steroids might also be purchased in other countries and then smuggled into the United States. These compounds then move through an informal distribution network often involving patrons of health clubs or gyms (Eisenberg & Galloway, 2005; Karch, 2009; Mahoney, 2006).

A number of increasingly sophisticated "rogue chemists" (Piore, 2012, p. 39) have learned to search through professional research journals, legal databases, and copyright registries to find compounds that have been classified as a controlled substance by the Drug Enforcement Administration. Such rogue chemists exist both in the United States and in China where their skills are highly sought after. They seek to modify the chemical structure of existing compounds so that they technically become "new" and therefore noncontrolled chemicals. Unfortunately, the toxicology of these new steroid-like compounds has never been determined, and even simple mistakes in their production might potentially have devastating consequences for the abuser.

In the world of professional athletics, there is also a thriving market for what are known as "designer" steroids (Knight, 2003, p. 114). These substances are steroid compounds that are manufactured in secret and supposedly are undetectable by the current generation of urine or blood toxicology tests. One such example of a "designer" steroid is the compound tetrahydrogestrinone (THG). This compound was reported to have "all the hallmarks of an anabolic steroid, crafted to escape detection in urine analysis tests" (Kondro, 2003, p. 1466). THG was not detectable by urine toxicology tests until a new test was developed for it in 2003, at which time there was a "flurry" of reports that THG was found in the urine of a number of athletes ("Athletes Caught Using a New Steroid—THG," 2003; Knight, 2003). The development of tests to detect THG is only the latest round in an ongoing arms race between those who wish to abuse these compounds and those who wish to detect their abuse. Steroid abusers also have developed their own language for steroid abuse, which is summarized in Table 14-1.

Many of these practices are quite common among steroid abusers. For example, 61% of steroid-abusing weight lifters were found to have engaged in the practice of "stacking" their steroid dose (Pope & Brower,

TABLE 14-1
Terminology Used by Steroid Abusers

TERM	DEFINITION
Blending	Mixing different steroids for use at the same time. This might involve both oral and injected forms of steroids.
Bulking up	Increasing muscle mass through steroid use exercise. Steroids are self-administered on a fixed schedule, with the abuser also using a special diet along with anabolic steroids.
Cycling	Taking multiple doses of steroid(s) over time, with drug-free holidays intermixed with periods of active steroid abuse.
Doping	Using any of a range of compounds to improve athletic performance.
Injectables	Steroids designed for intramuscular injection(s)
Mega-dosing	Taking massive doses (possibly by *blending*)
Orals	Steroids designed for oral use.
Pyramiding	Process of slowly increasing the daily dose of anabolic steroids over time. When target dose is reached, the daily dose is then slowly reduced over time. Often done so that the individual will not test "positive" on urine or blood tests for steroids after competition.
Shotgunning	Taking steroids on an inconsistent basis.
Tapering	Slowly reducing one's daily dose of steroids over a period of time.

© Cengage Learning

2004, 2005; Porcerelli & Sandler, 1998). Some of those who "pyramid" steroid doses are, at the mid-point of their cycle, taking massive doses of one or more compounds, although it should be noted that many abusers who "pyramid" also interspace periods of active steroid use with periods of total abstinence, which might last weeks, months, or even as long as a year.[6] Unfortunately, these periods of abstinence might be marked by the loss of much of the steroid-induced muscle mass, resulting in the abuser returning to the abuse of anabolic steroids to recapture the lost muscle mass.

---

[6]This then makes the individual vulnerable to the "reverse anorexia nervosa" effect discussed earlier in this chapter, as the steroid-induced muscle mass is lost over time. The person becomes anxious about this process, and in many cases will restart the abuse of steroids counter this process.

The Unknown Hazards of Steroid Abuse

The long-term effects of anabolic steroid abuse have not been studied in detail and much of the clinical literature on their effects is based on their effects when used at therapeutic doses to treat disease (Pope & Brower, 2008). At therapeutic dosage levels, anabolic steroids can induce such side effects as sore throat, fever, vomiting (with or without blood being mixed with the material regurgitated), dark colored urine, bone pain, unusual weight gain, headache, and a host of other effects (Congeni & Miller, 2002). However, anabolic steroid abusers have been known to use dosage levels that are 40–100 to perhaps as much as 200 times (Congeni & Miller, 2002; Eisenberg & Galloway, 2005; Pope & Brower, 2008; Tomb, 2008), the maximum recommended dosage level for these compounds. There is virtually no systematic information available about the effects of such dosage levels, and what little is known is based on antidotal case reports of steroid abusers.

It is known that the effects of anabolic steroids on muscle tissue will last for several weeks after the drug(s) were last administered, a characteristic that athletes often rely on to avoid having a "positive" urine toxicology test for performance-enhancing compounds after competition (Knight, 2003). It is also known that the adverse effects of anabolic steroid abuse depend on (a) the route by which the compound was administered, (b) the specific compound utilized, (c) the dosage level(s) utilized, (d) the frequency of steroid use, (e) the general health of the abuser, and (f) the age of the steroid abuser. Many steroid abusers view themselves, arguably with justification, as being more knowledgeable about the adverse effects of these compounds than physicians,[7] and often seek to control these adverse effects without medical treatment (Hildebrandt et al., 2006; Pope & Brower, 2008). This is due, in part, to the steroid abuse fiasco of the 1970s in which physicians tried to discourage anabolic steroid abuse by attempting to convince athletes that they were ineffective as muscle growth agents. Based on their personal experience with these compounds, steroid abusers knew differently and thus the credibility of physicians as a source of information about anabolic steroid abuse and its consequences was destroyed (Pope & Brower, 2008; Stephens, 2008). An unintended side effect of this failed attempt at disinformation was that anabolic steroid abusers seek out information from their drug dealers about the effects of anabolic steroids rather than seek a physician's opinion (Pope & Brower, 2008).

Known Adverse Effects of Anabolic Steroids when Abused

On the Reproductive System

Male steroid abusers even at therapeutic dosage levels might experience an enlargement of the breasts[8] as the body converts the excess testosterone into estrogen (Botre & Pavan, 2008; Pope & Brower, 2009). This effect is more pronounced when the individual uses exceptionally high doses of steroids. Male steroid abusers might also experience an increased frequency of erections, or a continual erection (known as *priapism*, a medical emergency). Male steroid abusers might experience unnatural hair growth or loss, reduced sperm production, and an increased frequency of the urge to urinate, as well as degeneration of the testes, prostate gland enlargement, problems in urination, changes in libido, impotence, and sterility (Botre & Pavan, 2008; Eisenberg & Galloway, 2005; Pope & Brower, 2008; Schuckit, 2006a). Long-term steroid abuse might be a causal agent in the development of prostate cancer in some abusers (Pope & Brower, 2005).

Women who abuse anabolic steroids might become infertile, and remain so for months or possibly years after their last use of steroids (Casavant et al., 2007). They might also experience an abnormal growth of the clitoris, irregular menstrual periods, unnatural hair growth or loss, a deepening of the voice, atrophy of the uterus, and a possible reduction in breast size (Botre & Pavan, 2008; Casavant et al., 2007; Pope & Brower, 2004, 2008; Schuckit, 2006a; Volkow, 2006b). The menstrual irregularities seen in female steroid abusers may become permanent, as is true for many of the masculinizing effects induced in women who abuse steroids (Pope & Brower, 2005; Volkow, 2006b).

Effects of Anabolic Steroid Abuse on the Liver, Kidneys, and Digestive System

Steroid abusers may experience altered liver function that may be detected on blood tests such as the serum glutamic-oxaloacetic transaminase (SGOT) and the serum glutamic-pyruvic transaminase (SGPT) (Karch, 2009; Sturmi & Diorio, 1998). Elevations on these tests

---

[7]Often for good reason, since most physicians are not trained to detect, or treat, steroid abusers.

[8]Technically, this condition is known as *gynecomastia*.

are a sign of hepatoxicity.[9] There is evidence suggesting that, when abused for periods of time at high dosage levels, steroids might contribute to the formation of both cancerous and benign liver tumors (Eisenberg & Galloway, 2005; Karch, 2009; Pope & Brower, 2005, 2008; Sturmi & Diorio, 1998). Many steroid abusers discontinue the use of these compounds after learning that they have liver tumor. Unfortunately there is evidence that the form of liver tumor known as an adenoma may redevelop, or at least start to regrow, following steroid cessation even if successfully treated (Martin, Abu Dayyeh, & Chung, 2008). This strongly suggests that steroid use "holidays"[10] do not affect the growth of such liver tumors to a significant degree. Finally, anabolic steroid abuse might contribute to the retention of water in the body, increasing the work load on the heart (Botre & Pavan, 2008).

Anabolic Steroid Abuse and the Cardiovascular System

The heart is composed of muscle tissue and is strongly affected by the anabolic steroids ("Steroids and Growth Hormones Make Users 'Really Ripped,'" 2003; Weiner et al., 2009). Habitual steroid abusers have a four to six times higher incidence of sudden cardiac death than nonusers (Belhani et al., 2009). Steroid abusers are also more prone to heart disease than nonabusers, possibly because of a dose-related cardiotoxic effect of anabolic steroids (Casavant et al., 2007; Eisenberg & Galloway, 2005; Montisci et al., 2012). This cardiotoxic effect is demonstrated by the necrosis of cardiac muscle tissue found in all steroid abusers (Montisci et al., 2012). Other forms of steroid-related heart disease include hypertension, cardiomyopathy, and myocardial infarction. Ongoing steroid abuse induces a process known as "remodeling" of the heart, or changes in the physical structure of the heart that alters its normal size and function. The left ventricle is especially vulnerable to the effects of the steroids and the muscle tissue on the left ventricle is often found to be 25% thicker than it is in a healthy nonuser (Montisci et al., 2012).

Because of steroid-induced water retention, many anabolic steroid abusers develop edema in the hands and/or feet, which they often attempt to control by taking diuretic medication(s) (Eisenberg & Galloway, 2005;

Schuckit, 2006a). Steroid abusers have been known to experience a drug-induced reduction of high-density[11] lipoprotein in the blood, while simultaneously increasing the low-density lipoprotein levels by as much as 36%. This contributes to accelerated atherosclerosis of the heart and surrounding blood vessels (Kanayama et al., 2006; Pope & Brower, 2005).

Steroid Abuse and the Central Nervous System

It is now accepted that anabolic steroid abuse can induce behavioral changes in the abuser, although most abusers are reluctant to admit to neuropsychiatric problems induced by their steroid abuse (Pope & Brower, 2008; Pope, Kouri, & Hudson, 2000). There are no premorbid signs that would warn the abuser that he or she was at risk for steroid-induced neuropsychiatric problems (Pope et al., 2000). However, some regular anabolic steroid abusers experience a sense of dysphoria,[12] or even clinically significant depressive reactions especially during the withdrawal phase (Kilmer, Palmer, & Cronce, 2005; Pope & Brower, 2004, 2005, 2008; Schuckit, 2006a). Steroid withdrawal depression appears to respond well to psychotherapy and the use of selective serotonin reuptake inhibitors (SSRIs) (Pope & Brower, 2008). It is important to keep in mind that suicide is a frequent complication of depression, and approximately 4% of steroid abusers have made at least one serious suicide attempt (Pope & Brower, 2008).

Anabolic steroid abusers are at risk for a drug-induced psychosis and the development of a condition known as "[ster]roid rage" (Botre & Pavan, 2008; Eisenberg & Galloway, 2005; Pope & Brower, 2004, 2005). Steroid-related violence has been known to result in the death of the user or another person (Pope, Phillips, & Olivardia, 2000). So common is the relationship between steroid abuse and violence that it has been suggested that large, muscular, perpetrators of interpersonal violence be screened for steroid abuse upon arrest (Pope & Brower, 2004). These episodes of steroid-associated anger appear to be the outcome of drug-related changes in the GABAa, dopamine, and serotonin receptor sites in the mesolimbic region of the brain[13] and are consistent with reports of increased aggression by some steroid abusers.

---

[9]See Glossary.

[10]Periods of time in which the individual does not abuse a given compound.

[11]The so-called good cholesterol.

[12]See Glossary.

[13]Brain regions involved in the fight-or-flight response.

Although these reactions are attributed to steroid abuse, there is also the possibility that individuals who become violent while taking steroids might have a history of criminal thinking and antisocial behavior that predates their steroid abuse (Klotz, Garle, Granath, & Thiblin, 2006). Such individuals would be "at risk" for impulsive behaviors such as reacting with violence, which then would be attributed by researchers to their steroid use rather than their predisposing personality, according to the authors. Although this hypothesis is interesting, it has not been proven and thus is but one possibility for the apparent connection between steroid abuse and violent behavior. There is emerging evidence that some steroid abusers are also ingesting what are known as the 'atypical' antipsychotic medications to counter act some of these steroid-induced side effects.

Other Steroid-Related Disorders

Patients with medical conditions such as certain forms of breast cancer, diabetes mellitus, blood vessel disease, kidney, liver, or heart disease, and men with prostate disease should not use anabolic steroids except if directed to do so by a physician who is aware that the patient has these problems (Eisenberg & Galloway, 2005). There is evidence that anabolic steroid use contributes to, if not causes, cancer, and their use is not recommended for patients with either active tumors or a history of either benign or cancerous tumors, except if directed to do so by a physician who supervises the patient during the period of steroid use.

Other side effects caused by steroid abuse include severe acne, especially across the back ("steroid acne"), which some patients attempt to control by taking illicit antibiotics, and some develop oily skin (Botre & Pavan, 2008). The abuser might develop a foul odor on the breath (Casavant et al., 2007). There was one case report of unnatural bone degeneration that was attributed to the abuse of steroids. Further, animal research suggests that anabolic steroid abuse may contribute to tendon degeneration, possibly to the point where the tendon might rupture under stress (Casavant et al., 2007; Eisenberg & Galloway, 2005). Adolescents who abuse anabolic steroids are vulnerable to premature cessation of bone growth as the "growth plate" at the end of the bone prematurely fuses (Casavant et al., 2007). It has also been suggested that anabolic steroids might prove to be a "gateway" to other drug abuse as the abuser attempts to cope with muscle-related pain, acne, and other steroid-related problems (Kanayama, Cohane, Weiss, & Pope, 2003).

Finally, if the abuser should share needles with other abusers, an all too common practice, he or she is vulnerable to the acquisition of various blood-borne infections (Eisenberg & Galloway, 2005).

Drug Interactions between Anabolic Steroids and Pharmaceuticals

The anabolic steroids interact with a wide range of medications used to treat disease states and with many of the drugs of abuse. There is for example evidence of an interactional effect between acetaminophen[14] and anabolic steroids. Further, alcohol-dependent patients on Antabuse (disulfiram) should not take anabolic steroids, nor should patients who are taking the medication naltrexone, or the anticonvulsant medications such as phenytoin, valproic acid, or any of the phenothiazine class of antipsychotic medications. This is only a partial list of the possible steroid-medication interactions and a pharmacist should be consulted about such possible interactions.

Are Anabolic Steroids Addictive?

A quarter of a century ago, most physicians would have offered an unqualified answer of "no." Although the question is still being debated, evidence would suggest that this answer is wrong (Pope & Brower, 2008). Clinical evidence would suggest that anabolic steroid dependence rests on three pillars: (1) the individual's *psychological* reliance on steroids ("I need steroids to bulk up"), (2) the individual's perceived past benefit from past steroid abuse, and (3) ultimately the development of physical withdrawal symptoms. The psychological dependence on anabolic steroids rests upon the belief that the individual needs steroids to avoid the loss of muscle mass or maintain one's attractiveness to the opposite sex.

The second factor, perceived benefit, rests on a foundation of external feedback ("you look *great*" or "your endurance is improving"), functions to encourage continued steroid abuse as well as self-perception. Persons who are using high doses of anabolic steroids report a mild sense of euphoria from anabolic steroids, which serve as an additional incentive to continue abusing these compounds. The euphoric effects of anabolic steroids are assumed to be approximately the same as caffeine, nicotine, or possibly the benzodiazepines (Wood, 2004). Steroid-induced euphoria may reflect the impact

---

[14]Discussed in the next chapter.

of these compounds on the mesolimbic system, especially the dopamine neurotransmission system (Pope & Brower, 2005; Wood, 2004).

Chronic steroid abusers do experience a protracted withdrawal syndrome upon discontinuation of these compounds, with symptoms such as loss of muscle mass, and the development of a depressive reaction that might reach suicidal proportions (Lukas, 2005; Pope & Brower, 2005). Other symptoms experienced by the steroid abuser during withdrawal include insomnia, fatigue, dysphoria, restlessness, anorexia, headaches, and lowered libido (Kilmer et al., 2005; Lukas, 2009). Gradual detoxification from steroids and intensive psychiatric support limit the impact of these symptoms on the individual's life. Not surprisingly, the diagnostic signs of steroid addiction are virtually the same as those for other drugs of abuse, supporting the hypothesis that steroids indeed are addictive.

Anabolic Steroid Use or Abuse and the *Diagnostic and Statistical Manual of Mental Disorders* (5th Edition)

The *Diagnostic and Statistical Manual of Mental Disorders* (5th edition) (*DSM-5*) (American Psychiatric Association, 2013) does not directly address the problem of anabolic steroid abuse. By default, it falls within the domain of the "other substance use disorder" category, which it shares with the unknown substance use disorders. The *DSM-5* manual identified five subforms of the other substance use disorders:

- *Other (or unknown) substance use disorder*
- *Other (or unknown) substance intoxication*
- *Other (or unknown) substance withdrawal*
- *Other (or unknown) substance-induced disorders*
- *Unspecified other (or unknown) substance-related disorders*

The first requirement for a diagnosis of an *Other (unknown) substance use disorder* identified by the *DSM-5* is the "problematic pattern of use of an intoxicating substance" (p. 577) that does not fall within the other categories of substance use disorders. The anabolic steroids most certainly meet the latter part

of this requirement; however, as discussed earlier in this chapter, many steroid abusers use these compounds not for their intoxicating effects but for their ability to aid the development of muscle tissue. Thus, the steroids only partially meet the first half of this requirement since few steroid abusers seek a sense of intoxication from these compounds. The *DSM-5* manual identifies 11 criteria, including the development of tolerance and a withdrawal syndrome, with 2 of the 11 criteria within a 12-month period being sufficient to diagnose the individual with an *Other (or unknown) substance use disorder*.[15] Two of the criteria include a characteristic withdrawal syndrome and the development of tolerance, both of which are found in steroid abuse as noted in this chapter.

The category *Other (or unknown) substance intoxication* category is of dubious applicability to the steroid use disorders in that there is no characteristic pattern that would suggest steroid "intoxication." Although there is a steroid withdrawal process, it is not clear whether this meets the criteria for this diagnosis in the *DSM-5* manual. Most certainly, as outlined in this text anabolic steroid abuse contributes to the development of various medical and psychiatric conditions, thus meeting the criteria for the *Other (or unknown) substance induced disorders*. Finally, the ability of steroids to induce various pseudo-psychiatric disorders will allow the classification in *DSM-5* of such conditions as a steroid-related depression in the category of *Other (or unknown) substance-related disorder*.

Chapter Summary

The anabolic steroids emerged as drugs of abuse in the latter part of the 20th century, with several subgroups of abusers emerging over the years. But the dynamics of steroid abuse differ from those of other, more traditional, drugs of abuse. The primary reason why anabolic steroids are abused is not for their euphoric effects, although many abusers report that anabolic steroids do induce euphoria, but for their effects on muscle development. Some adolescents

---

[15]The reader is referred to the *Diagnostic and Statistical Manual of Mental Disorders* (5th edition) (*DSM-5*) (American Psychiatric Association, 2013) for the full list of diagnostic criteria suggested by the American Psychiatric Association as signs of an *Other (or unknown) substance use disorder*.

and young adults believe that the steroids will help them achieve a better physical appearance, whereas athletes believe that because the competition is using steroids they must do so to "level the playing field." Both groups continue to engage in anabolic steroid abuse in spite of the knowledge that these compounds alter the normal function of the central nervous system, and can cause premature termination of bone growth and cardiovascular damage that will be with them for the rest of their lives. The identification and treatment of steroid abusers is primarily a medical issue, although substance abuse rehabilitation professionals play an important adjunctive role in this process and thus should have a working knowledge of anabolic steroid abuse.

CHAPTER 15

Over-the-Counter[1] Analgesics: Unexpected Agents of Abuse and Danger

Introduction

At first glance, the reader might question why the over-the-counter (OTC) analgesics are included in a book on substance abuse. These compounds do not induce a sense of euphoria, and are not "recreational" drugs. Yet the OTC analgesics are ubiquitous: Seventy percent of adults over the age of 65 take an OTC analgesic at least once a week (Stillman & Stillman, 2007). Further, many drug abusers will also use an OTC analgesic either during the period of active drug abuse, or immediately after these periods of substance use. They often do so without any knowledge of possible interactions between the chemicals that they abuse and the OTC analgesics. The OTC analgesics are hardly innocuous compounds: Each year in the United States, an estimated 103,000 people are hospitalized because of OTC analgesic-induced medical problems and 16,500 people die from these OTC-induced reactions (Savage, Kirsh, & Passik, 2008; Stillman & Stillman, 2007). Even the OTC nonsteroidal anti-inflammatory (NSAID) compounds have been found to increase the risk of the myocardial infarction and stroke, each of which can result in death (Trell et al., 2011). Although the substance-abuse rehabilitation professional should not recommend the use of such medications, it is imperative that they have at least a working knowledge of the side effects of these compounds and their potential for harm.

A Short History of the OTC Analgesics

Folk healers have long used various plants or extracts from different plants to treat disease, especially pain and fever. One such plant extract is the bark of the willow tree, which contains *salicin* (from the Latin

word *salix*, which means willow) for relief from pain and fever for more than 2,000 years (Jeffreys, 2004; Stimmel, 1997a). Around the year 400 B.C.E., the Greek physician Hippocrates recommended that patients experiencing mild levels of pain, or fever, or women in labor, chew the bark of the willow tree. But the bitter taste, limited availability of the bark, and the inconsistent effect, forced physicians of the era to turn to opium as an alternative.

Then in the 1880s, the active agent of willow bark, salicin, was isolated. Scientists soon discovered that

---

[1]Over-the-counter medications are available without a prescription. Thus the term *over-the-counter* medications.

although it was an analgesic, salicin induced severe gastric distress. Chemists chanced upon salicylic acid that was easier to produce and had the same analgesic effects of its chemical cousin salicin. However, salicylic acid, like salicin, was found to cause a great deal of gastric distress when used. So chemists continued their search for a compound with the advantages of salicin, but without its harsh effects. In 1898, Bayer pharmaceuticals introduced the compound acetylsalicylic acid, which they sold under the brand name *Aspirin®*.[2] Like salicin, aspirin was found to be effective in controlling mild to moderate levels of pain, without the harsh gastrointestinal side effects seen when salicylic acid was used,[3] and it did not present the danger of addiction inherent in the use of narcotic analgesics.

Because of its multiple effects, aspirin[4] has become *the* most frequently used medicinal compound in the world. An estimated 50 billion doses of aspirin are consumed around the world each year, a quarter of which is consumed just in the United States each year (Page, 2001). However, these figures belie aspirin's potential for harm. Because of its often harsh side effects, pharmaceutical companies embarked on a search for compounds with the benefits of aspirin without its side effects. This resulted in the discovery of a class of compounds known as the *propionic acids* such as naproxen and ibuprofen.[5] Another compound that emerged as a result of this search was acetaminophen, which was introduced as an OTC analgesic in the 1950s. The term *acetaminophen* is a form of chemical shorthand for the compound *N-acetyl-para-aminophenol*. This compound was first isolated in 1878, and although it was recognized that it could lower fever, it was feared that acetaminophen had the same dangerous side effects as a close chemical cousin, para-aminophenol. So it remained a footnote in the chemistry textbooks until

the early 1950s (Mann & Plummer, 1991). By that time, sufficient evidence had accumulated to show that acetaminophen was much safer than para-aminophenol, and that it did not have the same potential for gastric distress found in aspirin. A massive advertising campaign followed the introduction of a brand name of acetaminophen, which placed emphasis on how this compound was not irritating to the stomach as was aspirin. This advertising campaign, combined with a growing awareness of aspirin's potential for gastric distress, made it the most commonly used compound for fever control on this planet at the start of the 21st century (Sharma, 2003). This is not to imply that acetaminophen has entirely replaced aspirin, as aspirin remains a popular OTC analgesic (Jeffreys, 2004). Indeed, more than a century after its discovery scientists continue to find new applications for aspirin, and it has been suggested that if it were to be discovered today, it would be classified as a prescription-only medication. However, aspirin does present the user with various potential side effects, some of which are potentially deadly to the user.

The Origins of the Term NSAID

As is true for the adrenocortical steroids, endogenous compounds produced by the body in response to stress, aspirin and the propionic acid derivatives have an anti-inflammatory effect. However, because these compounds have a different chemical structure than the adrenocortical steroids, they are classified as *nonsteroidal* anti-inflammatory drugs or NSAIDs. There are currently approximately 20 NSAIDs being sold in the United States, although most are available only by prescription. The exceptions to this rule are aspirin and propionic acid derivatives briefly discussed earlier. Other NSAIDs such as the COX-2 inhibitors, which were introduced in the 1990s, are available only by prescription, which will be discussed later in this chapter (Jackson, Jackson, & Hawkey, 2000).

Medical Uses of the OTC Analgesics

Aspirin

Aspirin was first introduced in 1897, and in spite of this fact, scientists are still discovering applications for this compound. Aspirin is able to reduce fever by causing the blood vessels in the peripheral regions of the body to dilate, and to encourage sweating. Although this effect

---

[2]Aspirin is a member of a family of closely related compounds, many of which have analgesic, anti-inflammatory, and antipyretic action. However, since all of these compounds are less powerful as aspirin, they will not be discussed further in this chapter.

[3]This does not mean that aspirin does *not* induce gastrointestinal distress, only that it is less likely to do so than its chemical cousin salicin.

[4]The word *aspirin* is a historical accident, discussed in detail in Mann and Plummer's 1991 text. It is far too complex to be discussed in this Chapter, but from this point the word *aspirin* with a small *a* will be used.

[5]Other compounds, such as ketoprofen, were also developed from the propionic acids but will not be discussed further in this chapter.

will reduce fever, it does not reduce the body temperature below normal. Aspirin has also been found to interfere with the production of a family of compounds known as the *prostaglandins*[6] (Wilson, Shannon, & Shields, 2011). In the closing decade of the 20th century, it was discovered that regular low-dose aspirin reduces the incidence of myocardial infarctions[7] in both men and women (Berger et al., 2006; Buring & Ferrari, 2006; Chan et al., 2007; Ogawa et al., 2008) and that it is of value *during* a myocardial infarction. Paradoxically, extended periods of aspirin use at high-dosage levels appear to *increase* the individual's risk for heart disease or strokes through what are known as *microbleeds* or microscopic strokes (D'Arcy, 2007; Vernooij et al., 2009). Thus, the physician must weigh the benefits against the potential risks associated with aspirin use before suggesting it to a patient (Xiong & Kenedi, 2010).

There are several mechanisms through which aspirin use can reduce the individual's risk for an initial, or subsequent, myocardial infarction. Aspirin is able to reduce the blood levels of the *C-reactive protein*, a compound that at high levels has been found to be associated with an increased risk of either a myocardial infarction, an occlusive stroke, or a blood clot that might block a vein (a venous thrombosis). However, for reasons that are not clear, this beneficial effect is noted only for individuals older than 50 years of age, and are strongest in persons with lower blood cholesterol levels. Another mechanism by which aspirin is thought to reduce the incidence of heart attack is through the inhibition of a form of prostaglandin known as *thromboxane A2,* which is found in blood. Thromboxane A2 is involved in the formation of blood clots (Hutchison, 2004; Jeffreys, 2004; Page, 2001). However, there is a great interindividual variation between the ability of low-dose aspirin to block thromboxane A2, and each individual's aspirin requirements should be assessed by a physician. Further, because blood platelets have a normal life span of 8–10 days, the body is constantly replacing old blood platelets with new ones, which have stores of thromboxane A2. Thus, it will be necessary for the individual to take aspirin at least every day, or possibly every second day, to provide the desired inhibition of blood clot formation.

Currently, there is an ongoing controversy in the medical field about whether some patients are resistant to the antithrombotic[8] effects of aspirin. Some physicians

argue that the "resistance" is because of medication noncompliance. Others argue that some individuals are indeed more resistant to aspirin's antithrombotic effects than are others for reasons such as concurrent diseases such as diabetes (Dalen, 2007; Halushka & Halushka, 2002; Krasopoulos, Brister, Beattie, & Bushanan, 2008). Yet, a third theory was offered by the team of Smith et al. (2011) who suggested that incomplete or delayed absorption of aspirin might reduce its effectiveness. Enteric coated aspirin, designed to reduce gastric distress for the user, might result in reduced aspirin absorption, a matter of critical importance for those persons who must take aspirin to prevent the formation of blood clots according to the authors. This debate about aspirin resistance continues in the clinical literature and there is no consensus within the medical community at this time.

Scientists have also found that low doses of aspirin are effective as an adjunctive treatment for a rare neurological disorder known as the *transient ischemic attack* (TIA). Regular use of aspirin in low doses has been found to slow the rate of cognitive decline in women who are at high risk for cardiovascular disease (Kern, Skoog, Ostling, Kern, & Borjesson-Hanson, 2012). There is also an impressive body of evidence suggesting that regular low-dose aspirin might reduce the incidence and spread of colorectal cancer (Rothwell et al., 2010; Rothwell et al., 2012). This appears to be true also for hormone receptor-positive breast cancer (Terry et al., 2004). There is also preliminary evidence suggesting that regular low-dose aspirin use is associated with a lower incidence of esophageal cancer, and ovarian cancer (Page, 2001), and possibly a form of skin cancer known as a melanoma. Aspirin has been found to improve the blood flow to capillaries that feed the retina, thus inhibiting the development of diabetic retinopathy (Adler & Underwood, 2002; Roberts et al., 2002). Further, there is evidence that regular low-dose aspirin use slows the process by which the eye forms cataracts, and might protect the sensitive structures of inner ear from damage during the normal aging process, or from certain medications (Coghlan, 2006a).

There is even evidence that salicylates, the family of compounds from which aspirin is derived, might be of value in treating Type 2 diabetes (Rumore & Kim, 2010). The authors point out that the ability of aspirin to inhibit the production of cyclooxygenase[9] appears to be partially responsible for aspirin's ability to inhibit insulin resistance and thus improve blood glucose control.

[6]See Glossary.

[7]Also known as a "heart attack."

[8]See *thrombosis* in Glossary.

[9]Discussed later in this chapter.

Unfortunately, to be effective in controlling Type 2 diabetes, aspirin would need to be used at levels far above those normally used, placing the patient at risk for a multitude of potentially serious consequences (Rumore & Kim, 2010). Still the early results of the research appeared promising. As this list of known and potential applications of aspirin suggest, this compound is far more potent than most people suspect.

Acetaminophen

There is some disagreement in the medical world whether acetaminophen should or should not be classified as an NSAID. Most researchers do not classify acetaminophen as an NSAID, although it is quite useful. It is as effective as aspirin in the control of fever (American Society of Health System Pharmacists, 2008). As an OTC analgesic, it is as potent as aspirin, and may be used to treat virtually every pain condition that aspirin does, except those induced by inflammation. Acetaminophen has no significant anti-inflammatory action.

The Propionic Acids

This class of NSAID compounds includes ibuprofen, naproxen, and ketoprofen,[10] all of which are available over the counter.[11] As a group, these compounds are about as effective as aspirin and can treat the same conditions. The anti-inflammatory action of these compounds makes them useful in treating rheumatoid arthritis, dysmenorrhea, gout, tendonitis, bursitis, as well as headaches, and the aches and discomfort of the common cold. When used with narcotic analgesics, scientists have found that the NSAIDs increase the analgesic potential of the latter compounds, allowing for a greater range of pain control without the need to increase the dosage of the narcotic. There is mixed evidence suggesting that the regular use of NSAIDs (including aspirin) may slow the progression of Alzheimer's disease and vascular dementia (Adler & Underwood, 2002; Veld et al., 2001; Vlad, Miller, Kowall, & Felson, 2008).

The NSAIDs all present the user with some risk of cardiovascular problems. This risk is thought to be lower when the patient uses ibuprofen or naproxen; however, the cardiovascular risks cannot be avoided when these compounds are used (D'Arcy, 2007). Further, the NSAIDs all function as nonselective cyclooxygenase[12] inhibitors, presenting the user with both benefits and the potential for harm. This will be discussed later in this chapter.

Normal Dosage Levels of the OTC Analgesics

Aspirin

Although some people easily dismiss aspirin as an analgesic, a standard dose of two 325 mg aspirin tablets provides an analgesic effect equal to that of 50 mg of the narcotic analgesic meperidine (Demerol), 32 mg of codeine, a 50 mg oral dose of pentazocine (Talwin), or 65 mg of propoxyphene (Darvon) (McGuire, 1990). However, the optimal analgesic dose of aspirin is still being debated. There is a "ceiling" effect that is encountered at doses of around 1,000 mg every 4 hours, after which larger doses do not bring about any more analgesia but do increase the possibility of an adverse reaction. The American Society of Health System Pharmacists (2008) recommends that the normal adult oral dose of aspirin should be 325–650 mg every 4 hours, as needed for pain. Furthermore, it is recommended that aspirin should not be used on a continuous basis for more than 10 days by adults, or 5 days by children, except under a physician's orders.

Acetaminophen

The usual adult dose of acetaminophen is 325–650 mg every 4 hours as needed for the control of pain (American Society of Health System Pharmacists, 2008). Acetaminophen's analgesic and antipyretic[13] effects are approximately the same as aspirin's. Like aspirin, acetaminophen has a "ceiling" effect of approximately 1,000 mg every 4 hours. It is recommended that the individual not use acetaminophen for longer than 10 days unless advised to do so by a physician.

Ibuprofen

In its OTC form, the recommended dose of ibuprofen is 200–400 mg every 4 hours for the control of pain. At these dosage levels, ibuprofen has an analgesic potential that is equal to that of aspirin or acetaminophen. As a prescription medication, dosage levels of 400–800 mg

---

[10]This compound will not be discussed in detail because it has only a small share of the over-the-counter analgesic market.

[11]These were all prescription-only medications at first, but were introduced as over-the-counter analgesics in modified dosage form from the prescription form of these compounds.

[12]See Glossary.

[13]See Glossary.

three or four times a day are usual (Wilson et al., 2011). Four hundred milligrams every 4–6 hours up to a maximum of 3,200 mg in a 24-hour period of time is recommended for the control of mild to moderate levels of pain (Wilson et al., 2011).

Naproxen

As an OTC analgesic, patients are advised to take one tablet every 12 hours. Prescription dosage levels are somewhat higher than the OTC analgesic dosage levels, but the patient is still advised to take the medication only twice daily.

Pharmacology of OTC Analgesics

Before these compounds are used, the *cause* of the fever, or pain, should be identified, lest the OTC analgesic being used mask the appearance of a serious medical condition that could be treated. Further, the patient is warned to follow dosing instructions for that specific OTC analgesic to minimize the risk to their life.

Aspirin

Aspirin is well absorbed from the gastrointestinal tract after oral ingestion either with food or on an empty stomach. If ingested with food, all the aspirin is still absorbed, but it will take 5–10 times longer than if the patient ingested the aspirin on an empty stomach. The food provides a "buffering" effect that might help protect the stomach lining from aspirin-related irritation, however, at the cost of slower absorption. To avoid aspirin-induced stomach irritation, it is often sold in combination with antacids, or enteric coating. However, these also result in erratic absorption rates, possibly contributing to the patient's pain (Wilson et al., 2011). Antacids also reduce the amount of aspirin that reaches the patient's circulation by 30–70%, a matter of some concern for patients who wish to control some form of pain.

When taken on an empty stomach, the absorption of aspirin depends on the speed with which the tablet(s) crumble, allowing individual aspirin molecules to pass through the gastrointestinal tract into the circulation. Peak blood levels of aspirin are achieved between 15 (Wilson et al., 2011) and 60–120 minutes (Stimmel, 1997a) after a single dose. Between 80–90% of single dose of aspirin is bound to plasma proteins providing a reservoir of aspirin that might slowly be released

back into the user's circulation over a period of time (Stimmel, 1997a). The therapeutic half-life of aspirin is 2–3 hours following a single dose, although this may be increased to 8–15 hours when aspirin is used on a regular basis. It is rapidly biotransformed into water-soluble metabolites, which are then removed from the circulation and excreted in the urine. Only about 1% of a single dose of aspirin is excreted unchanged. Tolerance to the analgesic effects of aspirin only rarely develops (Stimmel, 1997a).

Unlike narcotic analgesics, which work mainly within the brain itself, aspirin appears to work both at the site of injury and in the hypothalamus. There is also evidence that it works at still-to-be-identified sites in the spinal cord. To understand how aspirin works at the site of injury, it is necessary to investigate the body's response to injury. Every cell in the body contains a variety of chemicals, some of which alert the body to cellular injury and death. Some of these chemicals include *histamine, bradykinin,* and a group of chemicals known as the *prostaglandins.* Aspirin inhibits prostaglandin production, thus limiting the inflammation and pain that develops in response to cellular injury.

Unfortunately, prostaglandin production is necessary for the compound cyclooxygenase, which has two subtypes: COX-1 and COX-2. A third subtype, tentatively classified as COX-3, has been identified, although its role in the body is still unclear at this time. COX-1 is involved in normal cellular maintenance, especially in the stomach and kidneys. COX-2 is released only when body tissues are damaged, contributing to the inflammation response. Unfortunately, both forms share 60% of the same chemical structure, and it is through the shared elements of their chemistry that aspirin and the other NSAIDS act. Thus, the NSAIDs could be classified as nonselective COX inhibitors, which provides both a benefit (reducing COX-2 production) and a danger (reducing COX-1 production) for the patient (Stillman & Stillman, 2007). There is also evidence that COX-2 inhibition also reduces the body's ability to produce an enzyme[14] that has cardioprotective effects. This preliminary research has to be duplicated and verified, however.

The inhibition of COX-2 appears to be the mechanism through which aspirin appears to be able to limit the development of colorectal cancer (Baron et al., 2003; Kreeger, 2003). However, this only involves

---

[14]Prostacyclin or PGI-2.

those forms of colorectal cancer that over-express COX-2, and not all forms of colorectal cancer (Chan, Ogino, & Fuchs, 2007). The routine use of aspirin to protect against colorectal cancer was discouraged by Dube et al. (2007) who suggested that any potential benefit gained from the use of an NSAID such as aspirin is outweighed by the dangers associated in the use of these compounds.

Researchers believe that ingestion of just one 325 mg aspirin tablet a day for an extended period of time provides a modest degree of protection against prostate and breast cancer, but the operational mechanisms by which these effects are achieved, or the risk/benefit ratio for regular aspirin use as a protection against these conditions has not been calculated (Jacobs et al., 2007).

Acetaminophen

Acetaminophen is easily administered orally, in tablet, capsule and liquid forms. It may also be administered as a rectal suppository. After oral ingestion, virtually 100% of a single dose is absorbed through the gastrointestinal tract (Wilson et al., 2011). The peak effects are achieved in between 30–120 minutes, and acetaminophen is extensively biotransformed by the liver before excretion, although small amounts are possibly found in the breast milk of a lactating mother.

Acetaminophen is as potent as aspirin as an analgesic and antipyretic agent. However, acetaminophen is toxic to the liver, and doses greater than 4,000 mg/day or use for longer than 10 days are not recommended except under a physician's supervision. Also individuals who are alcohol dependent must not use acetaminophen except under the supervision of a physician to avoid the danger of liver damage brought on by the concurrent use of these two compounds. However, unlike the NSAIDs, acetaminophen does not interfere with the normal clotting mechanism of the blood, nor does it induce an allergic reaction as is possible with aspirin use. Scientists speculate that since acetaminophen is not an inhibitor of either COX-1 or COX-2, there must be another mechanism through which it functions as an analgesic. This has tentatively been identified as the "COX-3" enzyme, which if it exists is limited to the central nervous system (CNS). Thus, if acetaminophen does inhibit COX-3, it does so in a yet-to-be-discovered region of the brain. The mechanism by which acetaminophen is able to reduce fever is also unknown at this time.

Ibuprofen

Ibuprofen is usually administered orally and about 80% of a single dose of ibuprofen is absorbed from the gastrointestinal tract. Peak plasma levels are achieved after 30–90 minutes after ingestion of a single dose and the half-life is between 2–4 hours (Wilson et al., 2011). About 99% of ibuprofen molecules become protein bound after absorption, providing a reservoir of ibuprofen that is slowly released back into the circulation over time. Ibuprofen is extensively biotransformed prior to elimination and its metabolites are mainly eliminated through the kidneys. A small amount of a dose of ibuprofen is eliminated through the bile. Like aspirin, ibuprofen is a nonselective cyclooxygenase inhibitor. However, this is not to imply that it can be automatically substituted for aspirin in the control of inflammation. It requires 2–4 weeks of regular use before the full anti-inflammatory effects of ibuprofen are seen, and even then only if the individual is taking 2,400 mg/day or more. At this dosage level, it is about as effective an anti-inflammatory agent as aspirin. Unfortunately, one cannot take both aspirin and ibuprofen for control of inflammation, as the effects of one compound interfere with the anti-inflammatory effects of the other.

Ibuprofen is about one-fifth to one-half as irritating to the stomach as aspirin. Although this is an impressive improvement over aspirin, it still must be recalled that 4–14% of patients taking ibuprofen will experience drug-induced gastrointestinal irritation, and 3 of every 1,000 long-term users will experience ibuprofen-related gastrointestinal bleeding. Researchers have found that 27% of patients who had used ibuprofen on an extended basis had evidence of gastric ulcer formation, even if they had not experienced physical distress from this compound at the time. This risk is increased if the user also ingested alcohol on a regular basis.

Naproxen

Naproxen is another propionic acid compound. There is evidence suggesting that naproxen's anti-inflammatory action may be stronger than that of aspirin, and it also has an antipyretic effect, possibly by inhibition of prostaglandin inhibition in the hypothalamus region of the brain. But because naproxen only has a limited antiplatelet effect, it is of limited use in the treatment of cardiovascular disease or preventing heart attacks (Hutchison, 2004; Solomon, Glynn, Levin, & Avorn, 2002). When ingested orally, naproxen begins to work within 1 hour, and its analgesic effects last for 7–8 hours.

In the circulation, naproxen binds to blood proteins, which can absorb only so many naproxen molecules before they are saturated and the other molecules float in the circulation without binding to a protein. When prescribed by physicians, it was found that the steady-state blood level was achieved when the patient took 500 mg twice a day for 2–3 days (American Society of Health System Pharmacists, 2008). The elimination half-life of naproxen in the health adult is 10–20 hours. About 30% of a given dose is biotransformed by the liver into the inactive metabolite 6-desmethylnaproxen, and only 5–10% of a single dose is excreted unchanged.

Complications Caused by OTC Analgesic Use

The OTC analgesics are hardly "safe" medications, and they account for almost a quarter of the adverse drug reactions reported to the Food and Drug Administration (FDA). The OTC analgesics are responsible for 103,000 hospitalizations and 16,500 deaths each year in just the United States. In the section to follow, we will discuss some of the complications caused by each of the OTC analgesics.

Acetaminophen

There is little known about the phenomenon of cumulative dose toxicity induced by chronic acetaminophen use (Smith, 2007). Acetaminophen has a cumulative effects on the liver, and to avoid this, the patient is warned not to use this compound for more than 10 days unless directed to do so by a physician. Acetaminophen has also been implicated as the cause of anaphylactic reactions on rare occasions although the mechanism by which acetaminophen might trigger such a massive allergic response is not known at this time. It is also *nephrotoxic,* which is to say that its continued use at too high a dosage level might prove to be toxic to the cells of the kidneys. Its use was also once thought to be associated with the development of ESRD,[15] but this possibility has been ruled out (Fored et al., 2001; Rexrode et al., 2001). However, as with all medications, acetaminophen should be used only when the potential benefits outweigh the possible risk associated with its use.

Aspirin

Aspirin is the most commonly used compound in the United States, and each day 35,000 kilograms of aspirin are consumed in the United States, while an additional 6,000 kilograms are consumed each day in the United Kingdom (Halushka & Halushka, 2002). However, aspirin is hardly a safe compound. Research has shown that up to 5–15% of aspirin users will have one significant, potentially fatal, or adverse reaction. Aspirin induced hemorrhage is perhaps the most significant adverse reaction resulting in between 500 and 1,000 deaths each year in the United States alone. However, users often report other adverse reactions such as anorexia, nausea, and vomiting.

The daily use of aspirin increases the individual's risk for a major bleeding either in the brain or the gastrointestinal tract by 55% (DeBerardis et al., 2012). Even doses as low as 75 mg/day can significantly increase the user's risk for damage to the lining to the gastrointestinal tract. Aspirin users who ingest it with acidic compounds such as coffee, fruit juices, or alcohol increase their risk of gastrointestinal irritation, as the irritating effects of each compound enhances those of the other. Aspirin is thought to be a factor in 20–41% of "bleeding" stomach ulcers. These gastric ulcers are thought to reflect aspirin's ability to block the normal action of COX-1. For these reasons, aspirin is not recommended for patients who have a history of ulcers, bleeding disorder, or other gastrointestinal disorders (American Society of Health System Pharmacists, 2008).

Although aspirin allergy is rare in the general population (0.2%), approximately 20% of those individuals with *any* kind of an allergy will be allergic to aspirin. These patients are also likely to demonstrate cross-sensitivity to the other NSAIDs (Wilson et al., 2011). Those individuals with the "aspirin triad," that is to say nasal polyps, asthma, and chronic rhinitis, should not use aspirin or any other NSAID except under a physician's supervision (Wilson et al., 2011). Between 5 and 15% of asthma patients who use aspirin will experience a serious adverse reaction, and if the individual should also have a history of nasal polyps, this could increase to as high as 40%.

One would intuitively expect that aspirin would have little impact on the respiratory system. Unfortunately, this is not true. Approximately 33% of patients who use aspirin for an extended period of time develop a breathing problem(s), which seems to reflect the ability of aspirin to interfere with the normal actions of

---

[15]End Stage Renal Disease, briefly discussed earlier in this chapter.

COX-1. Between 4 and 11% of asthma patients who use aspirin on a regular basis will experience an aspirin-induced bronchial spasm at some point (Barr et al., 2007). Paradoxically, regular use of aspirin can have a mild protective effect against the development of asthma in later life. The mechanism for this apparent paradox is not known at this time. Unfortunately, aspirin (and the other COX inhibitors) can block the development of an immune response following an inoculation against various viral infections, such as the influenza inoculation offered each year (Ryan, Malboeuf, Bernard, Rose, & Phipps, 2006). Further research is necessary to support this finding, but it does seem to account for why older individuals, who frequently use COX-2 inhibitors for a variety of problems, do not seem to respond as well to inoculations as do younger patients. It also may account for the observation that aspirin use for symptomatic relief while the patient has a rhinovirus seems to extend the duration of the "cold" by a small degree.

Patients on anticoagulant therapy involving compounds such as heparin or warfarin should not use aspirin except if directed by a physician. The combined effects of aspirin and the anticoagulant medication might result in significant unintended blood loss if the patient were to have even a minor accident and might even contribute to a hemorrhagic stroke (He, Whelton, Vu, & Klag, 1998). Long-term aspirin use has also been found to increase the individual's risk of developing macular degeneration possibly by as much as 200%. Thus, the attending physician must weigh the potential benefits from the use of aspirin against the dangers in these individuals.

The combination of NSAIDs is dangerous, and should not be attempted except under a physician's supervision. All NSAIDs can induce *tinnitus*[16] in high doses or if used simultaneously. A very rare, but potentially deadly, side effect of aspirin is *hepatoxicity*, a condition in which the liver begins to fail to filter poisons from the blood. Also, aspirin has been known to induce clinical depression in rare users, and in the elderly has been known to induce or exacerbate anxiety states. Because of age-related changes in blood flow and liver function, elderly NSAID users are at higher risk for toxic reactions to any of the NSAIDs. These normal age-related changes make it more difficult for the body of an older NSAID user to biotransform and then excrete these compounds, adding to the danger

of toxicity from the NSAID being used. Further, because of its ability to interfere with COX-1 in the renal system, aspirin can both contribute to kidney failure and contribute to end-stage renal disease (ESRD) in rare cases (Fored et al., 2001).

In the last quarter of the 20th century, scientists discovered that the use of an NSAID such as aspirin to treat the symptoms of a viral infection was a two-edged sword. Although it might provide some symptom relief, aspirin might also contribute to the development of Reye's syndrome in children who have a viral infection (Jeffreys, 2004; Stimmel, 1997a). Acetaminophen is often suggested as an alternative to aspirin or other NSAIDs if the child should need symptomatic relief. The anti-inflammatory effect of the NSAIDs, especially aspirin, appears to interfere with the effectiveness of the intrauterine devices (IUDs) used to prevent pregnancy. Although aspirin reduces sperm motility by up to 50% when used at therapeutic doses, this is not to suggest that aspirin should be thought of as a form of birth control nor does the reduced motility outweigh the reduction in IUD effectiveness. However, aspirin use would seem to make it harder for a couple to have a child, should they wish to do so. Finally, it should be noted that an aspirin overdose can result in permanent organ damage, or the death of the individual who ingested the overdose.

Medication Interactions Involving Aspirin[17]

Individuals who are being treated for high levels of uric acid in the body should not use aspirin except as directed. Even at normal dosage levels, aspirin can interfere with the body's ability to excrete uric acid, and block the action of the medication probenecid, which is used to treat high blood uric acid levels. Acetaminophen is often suggested as an alternative to aspirin if the patient should require analgesia (Wilson et al., 2011).

Because of its ability to interfere with the normal function of COX-1, aspirin should not be used by patients with hypertension except as directed by a physician. Aspirin-induced COX-1 inhibition interferes with normal kidney function, and may contribute to fluid retention, increasing the work load on the heart. Also, patients using low-dose aspirin should not take

---

[16]See Glossary.

[17]It is not possible to list every possible interaction between aspirin and other compounds. A physician, or pharmacist, should be consulted before the simultaneous use of two or more compounds, even if one is only an OTC analgesic.

vitamin E, which also has an anticoagulant effect, to minimize the danger of excessive bleeding (Harkness & Bratman, 2003). Further, *any* of the NSAIDs can interfere with the body's ability to metabolize folate, resulting in higher than normal folate levels (Harkness & Bratman, 2003). High folate levels pose a health risk for the individual, thus making the concurrent use of these compounds a dangerous practice.

Patients taking the prescription medication valproic acid will experience higher than normal levels of this compound if they are simultaneously using aspirin, because the aspirin molecules will bind at the blood protein binding sites normally utilized by the valproic acid molecules (DeVane & Nemeroff, 2002). The patient should discuss his or her use of this compound, and aspirin use, with the attending physician to minimize the risk of an adverse outcome.

Individuals who plan to consume alcohol should not use aspirin immediately prior to, or during the period of active alcohol use. There is strong evidence to suggest that aspirin interferes with the activity of the enzyme gastric alcohol dehydrogenase, which starts to break down alcohol in the stomach, before it reaches the circulation. Finally, persons who are using aspirin should not use the herbal medicine ginkgo biloba, because the combination of these two compounds can result in excessive bleeding (Cupp, 1999). There is also evidence suggesting that aspirin attenuates if not blocks the effects of many selective serotonin reuptake inhibitors (SSRIs) such as citalopram.

Medication Interactions Involving Acetaminophen

Individuals who use acetaminophen for extended periods of time might find that this interferes with the anticonvulsant effects of lamotrigine, which is a matter of concern for those persons who rely on the latter compound for seizure control (Wilson et al., 2011). It is suggested that the individual consult a physician or pharmacist about the possibility of long-term interaction effects from these two compounds. There is also evidence suggesting that acetaminophen attenuates if not blocks the effects of many SSRIs such as citalopram. There is a need for further research into the mechanism(s) by which this occurs, and whether short-term use of acetaminophen is less likely to cause this effect as opposed to longer-term use (Warner-Schmidt et al., 2011). Although this list is not exhaustive, it does reflect the fact that this OTC medication has the potential to interact with prescription medications.

Ibuprofen

As an NSAID, ibuprofen shares most of the same complications caused by aspirin use. It also has a number of drug-specific complications, including (but not limited to) blurred vision in a small percentage of users. This condition usually clears up after the person stops taking ibuprofen. Patients who experience any change in their vision should contact their physician immediately. It has also been implicated in the formation of cataracts, and so patients with preexisting cataracts should use ibuprofen only if directed to do so by a physician. Ibuprofen has been identified as the cause of a skin rash in 3–9% of users, and can cause migraine headaches in both men and women. Other identified side effects include (but not limited to) heartburn, nausea, diarrhea, vomiting, nervousness, hearing loss, congestive heart failure in persons with marginal cardiac function, and like aspirin, it can elevate blood pressure (Thompson PDR, 2007). Acetaminophen has been suggested as an alternative to ibuprofen in patients with hypertension, unless directed otherwise by a physician.

Patients who suffer from an autoimmune disease such as systemic lupus erythematosus ("lupus" or SLE) should not use ibuprofen except under a physician's direction. Further, ibuprofen has been identified as a cause of *aseptic meningitis,* especially in patients with SLE (Rodriguez, Olguin, Miralles, & Viladrich, 2006). It is also possible for patients with no identified autoimmune disorder to develop aseptic meningitis after ibuprofen ingestion.

Drug Interactions Involving Ibuprofen

Patients with what is known as a bipolar affective disorder[18] are often prescribed lithium. When a patient taking lithium also ingests ibuprofen, the blood levels of lithium could increase as much as 25–60%, a matter of some concern in that lithium has only a very narrow therapeutic window (Pies, 2005). Ibuprofen related lithium toxicity is more pronounced in older patients, but is possible with younger patients who take these two compounds simultaneously. All patients on lithium should discuss their use of ibuprofen, or any OTC analgesic, with their physician, to avoid the danger of drug interactions.

---

[18]*Manic-depression* was an earlier term for this disorder.

Patients receiving the medication methotrexate should not take ibuprofen except under a physician's supervision, since this drug reduces the rate at which methotrexate is excreted by the body. This may contribute to toxic levels of methotrexate building up in the patient's body. Acetaminophen has been suggested as an alternative to the use of NSAIDs by patients on methotrexate. Further, ibuprofen has been found to block the actions of aspirin in controlling blood clot formation, a matter of concern for patients who use aspirin to avoid a heart attack, or blood clot formation. (Hutchison, 2004). The concurrent use of different NSAIDs should be avoided, unless ordered by a physician. There is also evidence suggesting that ibuprofen attenuates if not blocks the effects of many SSRIs such as citalopram. There is a need for further research into the mechanism(s) by which this occurs, and which antidepressants suffer from this interaction effect (Warner-Schmidt et al., 2011).

Naproxen

Much of the information that is available about naproxen and its effects is based on experience with the prescription strength form of this compound. Naproxen is an NSAID, and, like aspirin, should not be used in patients who have any of the symptoms discussed in the "aspirin triad" (discussed earlier) except under a physician's supervision. Because it is also a nonselective COX inhibitor, naproxen might interfere with the action of COX-1 in the body, resulting in the possible formation of gastric ulcers, and gastrointestinal bleeding. Because of its ability to inhibit the function of COX-1, which serves a protective function in the stomach, patients with a history of gastrointestinal bleeding are advised not to use naproxen except as ordered by a physician.

On occasion, male users have experienced naproxen-induced erectile problems, and the ability to ejaculate. As with any medication, the longer the patient uses the medication, the more likely he or she is to develop one or more complications induced by that compound. Other known side effects of naproxen include (but are not limited to) drowsiness, dizziness and/or vertigo, depression, diarrhea, heartburn, constipation, abdominal pain, and possible vomiting (Qureshi & Lee-Chiong, 2004). On rare occasions, patients taking naproxen have experienced side effects such as skin rash, headache, insomnia, loss of hearing, and/or tinnitus. All NSAIDs have been implicated as a possible cause of ESRD, and

there have been rare reports of patients taking naproxen developing aseptic meningitis (Rodriguez et al., 2006). Although this list does not identify every possible consequence of naproxen use, it does serve to identify this compound as a potent one, with great potential for danger to the user.

Drug Interactions Involving Naproxen

Individuals taking another NSAID, such as aspirin, should not concurrently take naproxen except under a physician's direct orders, as the negative side effects of one compound can reinforce those of the other. There is also evidence suggesting that naproxen attenuates if not blocks the effects of many SSRIs such as citalopram. There is a need for further research into the mechanism(s) by which this occurs (Warner-Schmidt et al., 2011).

OTC Overdoses[19]

Acetaminophen

When used as directed, acetaminophen has been called "the safest of all analgesics" (Katz, 2000, p. 100). However, acetaminophen does have significant risks associated with its use. There are more than 100,000 cases of acetaminophen overdoses each year in just the United States, 57% of which are unintended (Fontana, 2008). It is surprisingly easy to ingest an acetaminophen overdose, as he or she would only need to ingest 4,000 mg (8 extra strength tables) at one time, or less if he or she were drinking, or on a "starvation" diet (La Crosse Tribune, 99 (153), A1, A8). Long-term ingestion of 4,000 mg/day can also be toxic in some cases, even if the medication is taken in divided doses according to instruction (Dave, Miceli, & Modha, 2008).

Unfortunately, 20% of the patients who suffer an unintentional acetaminophen overdose will die, usually from acute liver failure (Fontana, 2008). Although it might be possible to perform a liver transplant on an emergency basis, liver transplants are difficult, in part because the demand for new livers exceeds the supply. Even if an emergency liver transplant is performed fully, 30% of these patients die within a year of the procedure (Fontana, 2008; Russo, 2006). A second group of people who are at risk for unintentional acetaminophen overdoses are persons who ingest very

---

[19]Any known, *or suspected*, drug overdose should be assessed by a physician immediately.

large doses of vitamin C[20] while using acetaminophen (Harkness & Bratman, 2003). The high doses of vitamin C appear to interfere with acetaminophen biotransformation, possibly to the point where the individual becomes toxic on acetaminophen. Again, it is imperative for persons taking any herbal medicine or vitamin supplement to consult with a pharmacist or physician about the relative safety of the compounds that they are ingesting.

The standard antidote for an acetaminophen overdose is N-acetylcysteine (NAC). However, it must be administered in the first 48 hours following the ingestion of the overdose to be effective, and its full effectiveness is only seen if administered in the first 12 hours following the overdose (Smith, 2007). Because so many patients unknowingly overdose, they are unlikely to seek medical attention during the critical 48-hour period. By the time the cause of their symptoms is identified, it is far too late for anything but an emergency liver transplant.

Another group of acetaminophen overdose patients are those who have intentionally ingested an overdose as part of a suicide gesture, or suicide attempt. Acetaminophen is involved in approximately 94%[21] of all intentional drug overdoses. Adolescents who ingest an overdose of acetaminophen usually are making a suicide gesture, and since the first objective evidence of acetaminophen toxicity does not develop until 12–24 hours after the overdose was ingested, the adolescent is often initially assured that he or she did no harm in the suicide gesture. By the time the adolescent is brought in to the hospital, hours or even days after the overdose was ingested, it is far too late for NAC to be administered, since it must be administered *within 12 hours* of the overdose to be fully effective.

Under normal dosage levels, about 4–5% of the acetaminophen is biotransformed into a toxic metabolite known as N-acetyl-p-benzoquinoneimine (Peterson, 1997). Usually, this is not a problem as this metabolite itself is rapidly biotransformed into other safer metabolites by the enzyme glutathione. However, chronic alcohol abusers, persons who suffer from malnutrition, who already have liver damage, or those who ingest an acetaminophen overdose, rapidly deplete their livers of glutathione leaving it vulnerable to acetaminophen induced

liver damage. The untreated acetaminophen overdose will progress through four different stages (Dave et al., 2008): Phase 1 begins within 30 minutes to 24 hours depending on the size of the dose ingested, during which time the individual will experience vague symptoms of distress, including anorexia, nausea and/or vomiting, and diaphoresis[22] (Dave et al., 2008; Smith, 2007). Phase 2 starts 24–72 hours after the overdose, and is marked by symptoms such as abdominal pain, oliguria, and a swollen, painful liver. Blood tests will demonstrate abnormal liver function and the kidneys may show signs of dysfunction. (Dave et al., 2008; Smith, 2007). In Phase 3, which begins 72–96 hours after the overdose was ingested, the individual will demonstrate nausea, vomiting, jaundice, and overt symptoms of liver failure (Dave et al., 2008; Smith, 2007). Other possible symptoms include hemorrhage, hypoglycemia, renal failure, and hypotensive episodes. It is during this phase that acetaminophen overdoses prove fatal. If the individual survives Phase 3, he or she will begin the final phase, which starts between 2 days and 4 weeks after the overdose.[23] During this phase, the liver begins to repair itself, a process that can last for months, or years, after the overdose (Smith, 2007).

Aspirin

Aspirin is frequently ingested as part of a suicide gesture/attempt. The estimated toxic dose is about 10 grams for an adult, and about 150 mg/kg for children. Symptoms of an aspirin overdose include: headache, thirst, dizziness, tinnitus, confusion and/or delirium, hallucinations, diaphoresis, visual problems, and hearing impairment. Other symptoms include restlessness, excitement, apprehension, tremor, seizures, stupor, coma, hypotension, and possible death (Wilson et al., 2011). Aspirin overdoses are also associated with bleeding problems as a result of its ability to block the ability of the blood to clot.

Ibuprofen

Symptoms of an ibuprofen overdose include seizures, acute renal failure, abdominal pain, nausea and/or vomiting, drowsiness, and metabolic acidosis. There is no specific cure for an overdose of ibuprofen other than general supportive medical care at this time.

---

[20]A popular vitamin often taken in large doses for its apparent antioxidant effects.

[21]It is also imperative to keep in mind that multiple agents may have been ingested as part of the suicide attempt.

[22]See Glossary.

[23]The exact point at which Phase 4 starts is dependent in part on the amount of acetaminophen ingested.

Like aspirin, another NSAID, ibuprofen overdoses can result in a tendency for the patient to bleed excessively.

Naproxen

The lethal dose of naproxen in humans is not known at this time. Some of the symptoms of a naproxen overdose include (but are not limited to) lethargy, drowsiness, nausea and/or vomiting, epigastric pain, respiratory depression, coma, hypotension and/or hypertension, as well as convulsions. Like the other NSAIDs, naproxen overdoses can induce a tendency for excessive bleeding (Thompson PDR, 2007). Treatment is supportive, as there is no specific treatment for the naproxen overdose, however, all known or suspected naproxen overdoses should be assessed and treated by a physician.

Over-the-Counter Analgesic Use and the *Diagnostic and Statistical Manual of Mental Disorders* (5th Edition)

The *Diagnostic and Statistical Manual of Mental Disorders* (5th edition) (*DSM-5*) (American Psychiatric Association, 2013) does not directly address the possibility of OTC abuse, which is not surprising since these are compounds rarely abused for euphoria. They were included in this text only because of their potential for harm is so rarely recognized, and that substance abusers are especially at risk for harm from these compounds because of interactional effects with their current drug of abuse.

Chapter Summary

Over-the-counter (OTC) medications, especially the OTC analgesics, are often discounted as not being "real" medicine. In reality, they are potent compounds that are quite popular with the general population. In the United States alone more than 20,000 tons of aspirin are manufactured and consumed each year and aspirin accounts for only about 28% of the OTC analgesic market. The OTC analgesics are quite effective in the control of mild to moderate levels of pain, and it has been discovered that when added to the narcotic analgesics in certain circumstances, they might actually enhance the analgesic effects of these more potent compounds as well. Many of the OTC analgesics have been found to control inflammation associated with autoimmune disorders. Some members of the OTC analgesic family of compounds are thought to suppress certain forms of cancer, or lead to their early detection. Although aspirin, the oldest OTC analgesic, is more than a century old, researchers are still discovering new applications for this potent medication. In the latter half of the 20th century, acetaminophen and the propionic acid compounds were introduced as alternatives to aspirin and are sold as OTC analgesics. These compounds all share the potential to interact with prescribed medications, alcohol, and possibly with the more popular illicit drugs.

CHAPTER 16

Tobacco Products and Nicotine Addiction

Introduction

The first settlers in what would be called the "Americas" began to experiment with tobacco use, shortly after they arrived in the Southeastern region of North America, and by 6,000 B.C.E.,[1] the use of tobacco was widespread throughout the two continents. Evidence suggests that by the year 5,000 B.C.E., the people living in Peru and Ecuador were actively cultivating tobacco (Burns, 2007). It was used in religious and social ceremonies, and when the smoke of the tobacco plant was delivered rectally, it was thought to be a useful medicine (Burns, 2007). The first written reference to tobacco was found in a Mayan carving thought to have been made around 600 B.C.E (Schuckit, 2006a).

Then the first European explorers arrived, and for all concerned the world changed. The art of tobacco smoking was carried across the Atlantic by the early European explorers who had adopted the habit of smoking while in the New World. In Europe, this practice met with some skepticism, if not outright hostility. In Germany, public smoking was deemed a crime that could be punished by the death, whereas in Russia, castration was the sentence for same offense (Hymowitz, 2005).[2] In Asia, the use of or distribution of tobacco was a crime punishable by death, whereas smokers were executed as infidels in Turkey. In spite of these sanctions, the practice of smoking tobacco continued to spread across Europe and into Asia (Schuckit, 2006a).

Fifteenth-century European physicians believed tobacco had medicinal properties, in part because they had so few medications that worked. Further, the social use of tobacco products gained acceptance as a sign of sophistication and social status in Europe and the Americas. However, in the last half of the 20th century, scientists began to explore the chemical properties of nicotine and the theory arose that the tobacco plant had "learned" to manufacture nicotine as a natural insect repellant. It is quite effective in this role: Only one known species of insect will consume the tobacco leaf and humans are the only known mammals to willingly engage in tobacco use. Scientists also began to identify long-term consequences of tobacco smoking in the 20th century and a campaign against its use began. These efforts to curb tobacco use met with a less than enthusiastic response from the tobacco industry, which sought to disprove or discredit any claims of harm from its products. These efforts continue and currently tobacco use remains widespread, controversial, and the subject of much debate. In this chapter, the practice of using tobacco, and the complications associated with its use, will be reviewed.

---

[1]Which stands for *before common era.*

[2]The reader may decide for themselves which punishment was the greater incentive for smoking cessation.

A Very Short History of Tobacco Use in the United States

Anthropologists now believe that tobacco was actively being cultivated in South America as early as 8,000 years ago (Burns, 2007; Walton, 2002). However, this was not the same form of tobacco that we know today. The original strain(s) of tobacco were more potent, and possibly have contained hallucinatory compounds not found in today's tobacco (Schuckit, 2006a; Walton, 2002). European smokers preferred the milder *Nicotiana tabacum* over the more potent *Nicotiana rustica* commonly used by the natives of the New World, and this is the form of tobacco that was cultivated by the first settlers from Europe (Burns, 2007). Arguably, the establishment of the first European colonies in the New World was fueled, in part, by the demand for tobacco in Europe. Tobacco was so highly valued in colonial America that it actually functioned as a form of currency in certain colonies (Burns, 2007).

At the time, the preferred method of tobacco use was by smoking, although there were those who insisted on chewing the tobacco leaf, either spitting the expectorant out or, if they were from the upper classes, swallowing it. No less a person than John Hancock himself chewed tobacco, and he went on to prove that he was a nonconformist indeed by being the first person to sign the Declaration of Independence in 1776. Tobacco played an interesting role during the Civil War: Soldiers from both sides would arrange for an informal truce from time to time to barter tobacco for coffee and sugar. By the mid-19th century, several forces combined to change the shape of tobacco use. First, new varieties of the tobacco plant were developed that provided greater yields and new methods of curing tobacco leaves were developed, allowing for a more rapid transit from harvest to arrival at the manufacturer's. Machinery capable of manufacturing large numbers of cigarettes were introduced: Just one machine, invented by James A. Bonsack, could produce 120,000 cigarettes a day, far in excess of what could be made by hand.

The introduction of machinery to the manufacturing process allowed for the sale of cigarettes to members of lower social classes, as the cigarette was now affordable to virtually everybody. Simultaneously, it was discovered that the practice of chewing tobacco and spitting the expectorant into the ever-present cuspidor contributed to the spread of tuberculosis and other diseases. In a piece of historical irony, public health officials began to endorse cigarette smoking as a safer, sanitary, relatively inexpensive, substitute for tobacco chewing. Unlike pipe or cigar smokers, cigarette smokers discovered that the smoke from their cigarettes was so mild that it could be inhaled. The practice of cigarette smoking quickly became the preferred method of tobacco use in the United States, although there were (and remain) those who preferred to chew tobacco.

Scope of the Problem of Tobacco Use

Globally, cigarette smoking is a $400 billion/year industry with an estimated 1 billion men and approximately 250 million women smoking at least once each day (Levitz, Bradley, & Golden, 2004; Rose et al., 2003). It has been estimated that 10 million cigarettes are sold each minute around the world, one-third of which is sold in China alone ("China's Healthcare Woes," 2008; Raw Data, 2010c; Tobacco, 2009). So popular is the practice of cigarette smoking around the world that the global per capita consumption of cigarettes is estimated at 1,000 for every man, woman, and child on earth (Sundaram, Shulman, & Fein, 2004).[3]

In the United States, 387.6 billion cigarettes are consumed each year (Kaufman, 2006). In contrast to the 1950s, when approximately half of the adult population smoked cigarettes, only 20.6% of the population now smokes (Dube et al., 2009). While cigarette use decreased by 32.8% in the period from 2000 to 2011, the use of pipe tobacco increased by 5.8% and cigars increased by 3.33% (Tynan, McAfee, Promoff, & Pechacek, 2012), suggesting that at least some former cigarette smokers have switched to these alternative methods of tobacco abuse. The above estimates are for the population as a whole. It is not uncommon for the subpopulations of individuals to have different concordance rates than the general population. For example, it has been estimated that between 71 and 100% of persons with a substance use disorder (SUD) smoke cigarettes (el-Guebaly, et al., 2002) and that at least 90% of patients with schizophrenia also smoke cigarettes (Pankiewicz, 2008).

The scope of cigarette smoking thus demonstrates wide variance around the globe, a variance explained in part by how accepting is the culture of cigarette

---

[3]This figure is for *every* person on earth, not just those who smoke cigarettes.

smoking. In the United States, there is a tacit, if not vocal, disapproval of cigarette smoking except among members of certain subgroups such as active substance abusers. In contrast to this is the culture in China, which is more accepting of cigarette smoking especially by men. As will be discussed in the Chapter 20, a large percentage of children have taken at least one puff of a cigarette and have formed opinions that are more or less accepting of cigarette smoking, suggesting that the roots of the nicotine use disorders often lie in childhood, but only find full expression a decade or more later during the individual's adult years.

The Pharmacology of Cigarette Smoking

The primary method of tobacco use is through cigarette smoking,[4] although chewing tobacco and cigar smoking are both gaining popularity in some circles (Schuckit, 2006a). Chemically, cigar smoke is very similar to tobacco smoke, although it does contain a higher concentration of ammonia. It also is too alkaline for the smoker to comfortably inhale the tobacco smoke very deeply, and in contrast to the tobacco smoker the absorption of nicotine (and the various other compounds found in tobacco smoke) for the cigar smoker occurs mainly in the upper airway (Burns, 2008).

The main psychoactive compound in tobacco is nicotine. However, this is but one of thousands of chemicals found in tobacco smoke, the exact composition of which is influenced by a number of variables, including (Dani, Kosten, & Benowitz, 2009): (1) the exact composition of the tobacco being smoked, (2) how densely the tobacco is packed, (3) the length of the column of tobacco (for cigar and cigarettes), (4) the characteristics of the filter (if any), and (5) the temperature at which the tobacco is smoked. Many studies of the composition of cigarette smoke were conducted in the 1960s, and these data are still often referenced in professional journals. The observed changes in the composition of cigarettes over the last half century raise questions about the relevance of research studies conducted in the 1960s to the modern cigarette.

Up to 40% of today's average cigarette is composed of "leftover stems, scraps, and dust" (Hilts, 1996, p. 44),

some of which is swept off of the floor before being added to the tobacco. Where in 1955 it took 2.6 pounds of tobacco to produce a thousand cigarettes, the use of these fillers has made it possible to produce a thousand cigarettes with only 1.7 pounds of tobacco (Hilts, 1996). These manufacturing practices allow for a 44% profit margin per pack of cigarettes sold (Fonda, 2001). As will be discussed later in this chapter, there is strong evidence that nicotine is being added to the raw cigarette by the manufacturer making it more addictive than the cigarette of the 1950s.

Researchers have isolated some 4,700 chemicals from tobacco smoke, of which 2,550 come from the unprocessed tobacco itself (Fiore, 2006; Schmitz & Delaune, 2005; Stitzer, 2003). It is possible that up to 100,000 other compounds wait to be discovered in cigarette smoke, although research in this area is limited (Schmitz & Delaune, 2005). A partial list of the compounds known to be in tobacco smoke includes:

> *Acetaldehyde, acetone, acetonitrile, acrolein, acrylonitrile, ammonia, arsenic, benzene, butylamine, carbon monoxide, carbon dioxide, cresols, crotononitrile, DDT, dimethylamine, endrin, ethylamine, formaldehyde, furfural hydroquinone, hydrogen cyanide, hydrogen sulfide, lead, methacrolein, methyl alcohol, methylamine, nickel compounds, nicotine, nitric oxide, nitrogen dioxide, phenol, polonium-210 (radioactive), pyridine, "tar" (burned plant resins) (Shipley & Rose, 2003, p. 83, heavy print in original deleted)*

Cigarette smoke is also known to contain low levels of arsenic, a known poison. Further, cigarette smoke contains at least 1,000 times the level of radioactive gases such as radium and polonium than was contained in the fallout from the nuclear reactor in Chernobyl, Russia, when it exploded in the 1980s (Papastefanou, 2007). These compounds are found naturally in the soil, are concentrated in the tobacco plant as it grows, remain in the leaves when they are harvested, and when the smoker inhales are carried into the lungs. The tobacco industry was aware of this fact more than 50 years ago, but suppressed this research to avoid alarming the smoker about radioactive compounds in cigarette smoke (Muggli, Ebbert, Robertson, & Hurt, 2008). Because of this fact, it was recommended that the standard federally mandated warning labels on the side of cigarette packages be modified to carry a radiation exposure label (Muggli et al., 2008). However, this proposal was not enacted.

---

[4]For this reason the words *cigarette smoking, smoking,* and *tobacco use* will be used interchangeably in this chapter, unless designated otherwise.

Prior to harvest, various herbicides, fungicides, and rodenticides are sprayed on to the tobacco plant, exposing the smoker to these compounds when the tobacco is smoked. Then there are the compounds found in the burning cigarette wrapper or formed when the paper is burned, as well as the various machine lubricants that drip into the tobacco or wrapping paper as it moves along in the manufacturing process (Glantz, Slade, Bero, Hanauer, & Barnes, 1996). Finally, there are the various perfumes that are added to the tobacco to give it a characteristic aroma (Hilts, 1996). The smoker will inhale molecules of some or all of these products when he or she smokes; however, there has been virtually no research into the pharmacokinetic or toxicological effects of these compounds in the human body.

The tobacco industry has invested a great deal of time and energy to give the impression that they want to make cigarette smoking less dangerous and more enjoyable. One response to the complaint that cigarette smoke was harsh tobacco companies began to add menthol to some brand names of cigarettes (Carter, 2013). Menthol provides the smoker with a cooling or soothing sensation, while binding at sensory receptor sites in neurons responsible for the sensations of pain or irritation in the upper respiratory tract (Carter, 2013). Unfortunately Vozoris (2012) suggested that smokers who used a mentholated brand of cigarettes were at higher risk for a stroke than were smokers who did not use such cigarettes. Arguably the menthol makes the cigarette *seem* less harsh to the smoker while placing them at increased risk for a stroke. The menthol might also contribute to the addictive potential of the brand of cigarettes in question, as evidenced by the observation that adolescents who smoke mentholated cigarettes appear to be more addicted to smoking than adolescents who smoke non-mentholated cigarettes (Carter, 2013).

In the last half of the 20th century, various tobacco companies produced "light" or "filtered" cigarettes to give the illusion that these modified cigarettes were safer than older, more traditional, brands. In reality, these changes did little to reduce the individual's level of exposure to the toxins found in cigarette smoke (Hilts, 1994; Pennock, 2007). Smokers of "light" cigarettes have the same coronary artery problems as smokers who used regular brands, and the addictive potential of these modified cigarettes were the same as regular cigarettes (Light cigarettes just as addictive as 'full flavored', 2006; Gullu et al., 2007; Hymowitz, 2005).

Nicotine

This compound was first isolated by chemists in 1828, and in 1889, nicotine's effects on nervous system tissue were first identified. A century later, scientists are still attempting to understand all of nicotine's effects on the central nervous system (Stitzer, 2003). Such research is important since nicotine is the primary reinforcing agent in tobacco. What might loosely be called "Big Tobacco"[5] knew for decades that nicotine was the major psychoactive compound in cigarettes, and that cigarettes were viewed as little more than single-dose administration systems for nicotine (Glantz et al., 1996; Hilts, 1994, 1996). Unfortunately tobacco companies are still using this knowledge against the smoker, as evidenced by the fact that cigarette manufacturers have increased the nicotine content of most major brands of cigarettes by 10% between 1998 and 2004 (Brown, 2006).

Because it avoids the risk of the first pass metabolism process, cigarette smoking is viewed as the ideal method by which to introduce nicotine into the body. Each "puff" of a cigarette introduces a small dose of nicotine, which then reaches the brain in a matter of seconds (Gwinnell & Adamec, 2006; Stahl, 2008). The typical one-pack-a-day smoker self-administers approximately 85,000 puffs on cigarettes each year, consuming 7,000 cigarettes while doing so (Shadel & Scharf, 2012),[6] with each "puff" initiating a small reward cascade for the smoker. In the brain, nicotine breaks down the levels of an enzyme known as monoamine oxidase ß in the brain. This enzyme normally helps to break down dopamine after its release into the synapse. By reducing brain monoamine oxidase ß levels, dopamine will have a stronger effect at receptor sites where it binds indirectly activating the brain's reward system. Further, nicotine stimulates the release of small amounts of nitric oxide in the brain, which again has the effect of slowing down the process of dopamine reuptake. This combined action results in the neurotransmitter dopamine that is released having a stronger and more prolonged effect on the smoker (Fogarty, 2003). Nicotine also binds at the acetylcholine receptors in the brain. This induces the release of vasopressin, GABA, glutamate, beta endorphin (ß endorphin), and epinephrine[7] when the smoker inhales (Bacher, Rabin, Woznica, Sacco, & George, 2010; Fogarty, 2003; Gwinnell & Adamec, 2006; Hymowitz, 2005; Schmitz & Delaune, 2005).

---

[5]Major cigarette producers.
[6]Through sheer repetition this becomes a habitual behavior through the process of "overlearning."
[7]Also known as *adrenaline*.

Nicotine-induced epinephrine release contributes to the smoker's sensation of alertness and reduced fatigue, whereas many of the other compounds released when the individual smokes are involved in the sensation of relaxation or pleasure. This might be why many smokers have believed that smoking helps them calm down during times of stress. The team of Gehricke et al. (2009) examined the mechanics of nicotine-induced relaxation through PET scans,[8] and found that individuals who had nicotine in their systems demonstrated a change in brain metabolism in such a way that it interfered with the cortical and subcortical regions of the brain responsible with the integration and expression of emotions with perceptions. This would appear to contribute to the smoker's sense of relaxation under stress. However, it should be noted that for some unknown reason the clinical effects of nicotine are different for those persons who struggle with a psychiatric disorder as compared with normal individuals (Bacher et al., 2010).

It has been found that nicotine induces a total saturation of one of the 12 known subtypes of the acetylcholine receptor in the brain (Brody et al., 2006; Stahl, 2008). Long-term binding at this acetylcholine receptor site subtype[9] induces desensitization, a process that by coincidence takes about as long as it takes to smoke just one cigarette (Stahl, 2008). Resensitization begins almost immediately, resulting in a state where the receptor sites not occupied by nicotine molecules cause or exacerbate withdrawal symptoms experienced between cigarettes, restarting the cycle as the smoker lights another cigarette (Brody et al., 2006; Stahl, 2008). This cycle takes about 45 minutes, with the result being that a one-pack-a-day smoker can keep this acetylcholine receptor subtype desensitized throughout the day (Stahl, 2008). This helps the smoker feel relaxed as a result of smoking, and contributes to the experience of "craving" when the smoker quits.

Peak concentrations of nicotine are achieved in the first few minutes after smoking a cigarette, and then drops as the nicotine is redistributed to blood-rich body tissues. The biological half-life of nicotine is approximately 2 hours (Dani et al., 2009; Hughes, 2005). Because only 50% of the nicotine from one cigarette is biotransformed in the first half-life period, a reservoir of nicotine builds up in the body during the day. This reservoir is constantly renewed as the smoker continues to smoke and the nicotine is slowly released into the circulation after the individual's last cigarette. A limited degree of tolerance to nicotine does develop during the day, but is just as rapidly lost in the night hours when the average smoker abstains (Hughes, 2005). This is why many smokers report that the first cigarette in the morning has such a strong effect on them.

It was once thought that cigarette smokers were able to metabolize nicotine more rapidly than nonsmokers; however, recent research has failed to support this belief. The majority of the nicotine absorbed into the body is metabolized in the liver before elimination, and only 5–10% is excreted unchanged (Dani et al., 2009; Hymowitz, 2005). The major metabolite of nicotine is *cotinine,* a compound that in recent years has been found to have a psychoactive action of its own (Schmitz & Delaune, 2005). Another metabolite of nicotine is *nicotine-n-oxide,* about which little is known. Both metabolites of nicotine are excreted in the urine.

Acetaldehyde

Tobacco smoke also contains a very small amount of acetaldehyde. This is the first metabolite of ethyl alcohol that is produced when it goes through the biotransformation process. Research has demonstrated that acetaldehyde that is absorbed will bond with the saliva. This in turn allows the toxin to remain in contact with oral tissues longer, increasing the individual's risk of oral cancers (Melton, 2007).

Drug Interactions between Nicotine and Prescribed Medications

Nicotine is metabolized through the cytochrome P-450 metabolic pathway in the liver. This alters the pharmacokinetics of numerous other compounds that must compete with nicotine for access to this metabolic pathway. One such compound is morphine and it has long been known that cigarette smokers will require more morphine for pain control than nonsmokers. Cigarette smokers will also have lower blood plasma concentrations of such compounds as propranolol, haloperidol, and doxepin at a given dosage level than will nonsmokers (Dani et al., 2009; Hughes, 2005). Tobacco smokers may experience less sedation from a given dose of a benzodiazepine than nonsmokers but paradoxically appear to be able to metabolize marijuana more rapidly than nonsmokers (Nelson, 2000). Tobacco also interacts with many anticoagulants such as Warfarin® (Ellingrod, 2013),

---

[8]See Glossary.
[9]Known as the a4ß2 nicotinic acetylcholine receptor subtype, in case you wondered.

making it difficult to achieve adequate coagulation control. Women who use oral contraceptives and who smoke are at significantly higher risk for stroke, myocardial infarction, and thromboembolism in comparison with women of the same age who are nonsmokers (Dani et al., 2009). When smokers who use theophylline quit smoking, they experience a significant rise in theophylline levels in the first week of abstinence. Further, the blood levels of caffeine might increase by as much as 250% following smoking cessation, possibly causing caffeine-induced anxiety symptoms for the individual. Anxiety is also an early symptom of nicotine withdrawal, which the smoker quickly learns to self-medicate by smoking another cigarette and stopping the withdrawal symptoms before they develop further.

Nicotine appears to decrease the blood levels of clozapine and haloperidol by as much as 30–50% as a result of its ability to induce the biotransformation of these compounds, reducing their effectiveness (Ellingrod, 2013; Kavanagh, McGrath, Saunders, Dore, & Clark, 2002). At the same time, it blocks the biotransformation of the antidepressant medications desipramine, doxepin, and nortriptyline, raising blood levels of these compounds possibly to dangerous levels. It has been discovered that 70–95% of heavy drinkers also smoke, possibly because nicotine is more reinforcing for the drinker than it is for the nondrinker.[10] This may reflect the fact that nicotine addiction is mediated by many of the same genes that are thought to trigger alcohol dependence (Le et al., 2006). Further, the stimulant effects of the nicotine appear to counteract some of the sedation induced by the individual's alcohol use, allowing that person to drink more, or drink longer. Because of the vasoconstrictive effect of cigarette smoke, it takes longer for an insulin-dependent diabetic to absorb transdermal injections of insulin, making blood glucose control more difficult (Dani et al., 2009). Although this list of possible interactions between cigarette smoke and medications does not discuss every possible interaction effect, it does demonstrate that nicotine is a very potent compound with the ability to influence the pharmacokinetics of many pharmaceuticals currently in use. A physician or pharmacist should be consulted before a smoker starts to take a new medication(s) to minimize the danger of an interaction between their cigarette smoking and the medication.

The Effects of Nicotine on the Smoker's Body

Nicotine is quite toxic (Hymowitz, 2005). The estimated lethal dose for an adult is 40–60 mg. Orally administered nicotine in adults is subjected to the "first pass metabolism" effect, limiting its effect on the individual. However it is possible to reach toxic levels of nicotine either by oral ingestion or by smoking an extraordinary number of cigarettes at once. Symptoms of nicotine toxicity include nausea, vomiting, diarrhea, abdominal pain, headache, sweating, and pallor (Hymowitz, 2005).[11] The bodies of children are able to absorb nicotine from the gastrointestinal tract more effectively than the body of an adult, thus making a tobacco overdose especially dangerous in children. Oral overdoses can also demonstrate symptoms such as dizziness, weakness, confusion, coma, and possible death from respiratory paralysis. These symptoms are very similar to those reported by first time smokers, suggesting that they are demonstrating nicotine toxicity as a result of their cigarette smoking. The degree of discomfort experienced by the individual who begins to smoke appears to be mediated, in part, by his or her genetic heritage (Whitten, 2011). As the smoker persists in his or her efforts to continue to smoke, the stimulation of the neurotransmitter systems involved in the reward cascade will help the new smoker learn to associate the practice of smoking with pleasure and relaxation.

In the body, nicotine stimulates the release of acetylcholine, which controls many body functions. This may account, at least in part, for nicotine's known effects on the cardiovascular system such as the increase in heart rate, increased blood pressure, and increased strength of heart contractions observed in the time after a person smokes a cigarette. Nicotine also induces a reduced rate and strength of muscle contractions in the stomach and causes the blood vessels in the peripheral regions of the body to constrict (Schuckit, 2006a). The process of smoking deposits many potentially harmful chemicals in the lungs, possibly contributing to the decreased action of the cilia[12] in the lungs. These nicotine-induced effects seem to account for at least some of the pulmonary problems seen in chronic smokers.

---

[10]Some drinkers have reported that they smoke *only* when they are drinking, and that they can abstain from cigarettes between periods of alcohol use.

[11]Any real, *or suspected*, overdose should always be assessed by a physician *immediately*.

[12]See Glossary.

Nicotine Addiction

Researchers for various tobacco companies have known that nicotine was highly addictive since the early 1960s, although this information was promptly suppressed by the tobacco industry (Hurt & Robertson, 1998; Slade, Breo, Hanauer, Barnes, & Glantz, 1995). Indeed, one industry memo from 1963 released by court order was cited by Slade et al. (1995) as an illustration of how the tobacco industry knew that it was "in the business of selling nicotine, an addictive drug" (p. 228). However, it was not until 1997 that a single major tobacco company in the United States admitted in court that tobacco was addictive (Solomon, Rogers, Kate, & Lach, 1997). Like the other drugs of abuse, nicotine alters the firing pattern of neurons in the nucleus accumbens region of the brain. Surprisingly, the compound that is closest to producing the same pattern of altered neural function is the opioid family of compounds (Britt & McGehee, 2008). This makes clinical sense because smokers report a sense of pleasure when they smoke, suggesting that nicotine stimulates the release of endogenous opioids in the brain. The addictive potential of nicotine would seem to be higher than that of cocaine, as illustrated by the fact that although 3–20% of those who try cocaine become addicted to it, at least 33–50% of those who experiment with cigarette smoking become addicted[13] to this practice (Oncken & George, 2005). Further, like the other drugs of abuse, the greater the individual's exposure to nicotine, the higher the chance that she or he will become addicted to this compound.

Scientists have documented physical changes in the brain's nerve pathways after just a few cigarettes, suggesting that even a limited exposure to nicotine may initiate the process of neuroplasticity in support of an addictive process (Mansvelder, Keath, & McGehee, 2002). This might explain why 94% of those children who smoke just four cigarettes go on to become regular smokers. Still, 5–10% of smokers are not addicted and just smoke occasionally. These people are classified as "chippers," but unfortunately very little is known about this subgroup of cigarette smokers. Given the chipper's genetic heritage, he or she might be more, or less, vulnerable to the addictive effects of nicotine (Whitten, 2011), and it is possible that some persons identified as "chippers" are in the transitional phase between recreational use and full addiction to nicotine.

Possibly as many as 90–95% of smokers are addicted to nicotine and demonstrate the characteristic symptoms of drug addiction: (1) tolerance, (2) a characteristic withdrawal syndrome, and (3) drug-seeking behaviors. Cigarette smokers titrate their smoking to maintain a fairly constant level of nicotine in their blood (Oncken & George, 2005). When given cigarettes with a higher nicotine content, smokers will smoke less, whereas they increase the frequency of their cigarette use when given cigarettes with a lower nicotine content. Smokers of low "tar" cigarettes have also been observed to inhale more deeply, and hold their breath longer, than do smokers of high tar cigarettes. Smokers also develop individualized smoking rituals, which seem to both provide them with a sense of security and contribute to the urge to smoke when the individual is anxious.

Nicotine Withdrawal

Withdrawal symptoms from nicotine typically begin within 2 hours of the smoker's last cigarette, peak within 24 hours (Oncken & George, 2005), and then gradually decline in intensity over the next 10 days. The exact nature of nicotine withdrawal vary from individual to individual, and in spite of the horror stories often told about nicotine withdrawal, approximately a quarter of those who smoke report no significant withdrawal distress when they do quit. The reported symptoms of nicotine withdrawal include sleep problems, irritability, impatience, difficulties in concentration, lightheadedness, restlessness, fatigue, drowsiness, strong "craving" for tobacco, hunger, gastrointestinal upset, constipation, headache, and increased coughing. Extended withdrawal symptoms appear to continue for as long as 6 months after the individual's last cigarette, although they vary in intensity from one person to another. Although many smokers report that smoking helps them to calm down, there is strong evidence that cigarette smoking can induce or exacerbate anxiety symptoms in those individuals with a panic disorder (Isensee, Hans-Ulrich, Stein, Hofler, & Lieb, 2003).

Complications of Long-Term Use of Tobacco Products

Cigar and pipe smokers or people who chew tobacco reflect only a small percentage of tobacco users. Although chewing tobacco, pipe or cigar smoking carry many of

---

[13]Leamon, Wright, & Myrick (2008) suggested that one-third of those persons who smoke just one cigarette will go on to become addicted to nicotine.

the same health risks associated with cigarette smoking (Rodriguez et al., 2010), cigarette smoking itself is considered the "most lethal delivery system" (Erickson, 2007, p. 133) possible. Although many cigarette smokers acknowledge this fact, they also maintain an illusion of personal immunity from smoking-related problems, at least until they develop a smoking-related medical disorder (Rogers, 2008). Outwardly the body of a cigarette smoker appears to be 5–10 years older than their chronological age (Woloshin, Schwartz, & Welch, 2008). The typical male smoker in the United States will lose 13.2 years of potential life to smoking-related illness, while the average female smoker is thought to lose 14.5 years of potential life to the same range of smoking-related disorders (Carmona, 2004; Sundaram et al., 2004).

These data are significant because the cost of smoking-related health care problems in the United States alone is estimated to be $400 billion/year (George & Weingerger, 2008). To put this into a different perspective, the cost of cigarette smoking in this country is approximately $3,000 for every man, woman, and child in the United States (Centers for Disease Control and Prevention, 2004). Smoking is thought to cause approximately 443,000 deaths each year in just the United States ("Cigarette smoking among adults—United States," 2007). This number includes the estimated 15,000 nonsmokers who are estimated to die each year as a result of "passive" or "secondhand" smoking (discussed later in this chapter). The exact distribution of smoking-related deaths each year in the United States is reviewed in Table 16-1 (based on Bacher et al., 2010).

Globally, smoking is thought to cause 5 million cancer-related deaths each year (Coghlan, 2009). However, there are regional differences in the proportion of deaths that are thought to be smoking related around the world, in part because the level of some compounds known or suspected to cause cancer are higher in cigarettes made in the United States than cigarettes made in other countries (Ashley et al., 2010). In the United States, smoking-related cancers account for 74% of all cancer deaths each year (Leistikow, Kabit, Connolly, Clancy, & Alpert, 2008). Cigarette smoking is also thought to cause 17–30% of all deaths of cardiovascular disease, 24% of all deaths from pneumonia/influenza, and 10% of infant deaths each year (Burns, 2008; Hughes, 2005; Miller, 1999).

Smoking-related cancers are not limited to the lungs, and the proportion of other forms of cancer that are thought to be smoking related are reviewed in Table 16-2.

Cigarette smokers are more prone to have a higher incidence of kidney cancer as compared with nonsmokers (Carmona, 2004). Although the relationship between cigarette smoking and cancer has been well documented, the causal mechanism has not been isolated. There are known carcinogenic chemicals in cigarette smoke and abnormalities in the bronchial cells have been found in 98% of current smokers as opposed to just 26% of nonsmokers (Wadland & Ferenchick, 2004). It has been suggested that a compound(s) in cigarette smoke is capable of causing damage to cellular DNA in the lungs, as evidenced by the results of a study by the team of Lee et al. (2010) who uncovered

TABLE 16-1
Causes of Annual Smoking-Related Deaths in the United States

CAUSE OF DEATH	PERCENTAGE OF DEATHS FROM THIS DISEASE RELATED TO SMOKING	TOTAL NUMBER OF ANNUAL DEATHS FROM THIS CONDITION INDUCED BY SMOKING
Lung cancer	28% of total	120,000/year
Coronary artery disease	23% of total	98,990/year
Chronic lung disease other than cancer	17% of total	73,100/year
Other forms of cancer	7% of total	30,100/year
Strokes	6% of total	25,800/year
All other forms of illness	19% of total	81,700/year

SOURCE: Based on Bacher et al. (2010) and Schuckit, 2006a

TABLE 16-2
Proportions of Cancer Cases Associated
with Smoking

Lung cancer	87%
Esophageal cancer	75%
Bladder cancer	30–50%
Pancreatic cancer	30%

SOURCE: Bacher et al. (2010); Freedman, Silverman, Hollenbeck, Schatzkin, and Abnet (2011); Hymowitz (2005); World Health Organization (2006).

evidence of *fifty thousand* genetic mutations in the body of a 51-year-old smoker with a history of smoking one and a quarter packs of cigarettes per day[14] for the preceding 15 years. In the next section, we will look at the effects of long-term smoking use on specific organ systems in the brain.

The Mouth, Throat, and Pulmonary System

Cigarette smokers are at increased risk for respiratory disorders during sleep, such as snoring and obstructive sleep apnea. The smoker is also 10–15 times as likely to develop lung cancer as the nonsmoker (Kuper, Boffetta, & Adami, 2002). Smokers are also thought to be 27 times more likely to develop laryngeal cancer than non-smokers, and the risk for these forms of cancer is dose related (World Health Organization, 2006). Cigarette smokers are also at increased risk for chronic bronchitis, pneumonia, and chronic obstructive pulmonary disease (COPD) (Brust, 2004). Surprisingly, only about one-third of patients tested were aware that they had COPD, a condition found in about 20% of cigarette smokers (Hill et al., 2010). It has been estimated that 80–90% of the deaths from COPD might be traced to the cigarette smoking (Anczak & Nogler, 2003).

The individual's vulnerability for developing COPD is based on part to their genetic heritage; however, once it develops, it is potentially fatal complication for smokers who continue to smoke (Sadeghejad et al., 2009). Ten percent of those individuals over the age of 65 who manifest COPD symptoms continue to smoke (Gwinnell & Adamec, 2006). It is not uncommon for these persons to rationalize their continued smoking because since the damage has already been done, there is no sense in quitting cigarettes. In reality, there are benefits to quitting, even for the elderly. For example,

[14]Often abbreviated as *ppd.*

3 months after quitting cigarettes, lung function will have improved by about one-third, which is a matter of importance for patients with COPD (Gwinnell & Adamec, 2006).

The Digestive System

Cigarette smoking is the cause of approximately half of all cases of gum disease and tooth loss (Centers for Disease Control, 2004). As noted earlier, smokers are also at increased risk of developing cancer of the mouth or throat. This effect is multiplied if the smoker is also a heavy drinker. Where heavy smokers have been found to have a sevenfold higher incidence of cancer of the mouth and pharynx as nonsmokers, and heavy drinkers have a sixfold higher incidence of these forms of cancer, the heavy smoker who is also a heavy drinker has a *38-fold* higher incidence of cancer of mouth and pharynx ("Alcohol and Tobacco," 1998).

Cigarette smoking contributes to the formation of gastric ulcers, especially peptic ulcers, cancer of the stomach, and is a factor in the development of some forms of cancer of the pancreas (Carmona, 2004). For reasons that are not understood, cigarette smokers are also at increased risk for the development of type 2 diabetes (Willi, Bodenmann, Ghali, Faris, & Cornuz, 2007; Yeh, Duncan, Schmidt, Wang, & Brancati, 2010). The reason for this association is not known, although lifestyle factors such as a lack of exercise and poor diet are possibilities, and the increased risk for type 2 diabetes does not appear to decrease with smoking cessation (Yeh et al., 2010). Again, the reason for this is not known.

The Cardiovascular System

Cigarette smoking has been identified as the leading risk factor for heart disease, and smoking-related heart disease causes a death every minute in the United States (Committee on secondhand smoke exposure and acute coronary events, 2009). The mechanisms by which cigarette smoking contribute to deaths from cardiovascular disease are varied. Smoking even a single cigarette has been shown to alter the cardiac rhythm and reduce elasticity of cardiac muscle tissues (McClain, 2006). In addition, the coronary arteries of the heart briefly constrict when a person smokes. Because the coronary arteries are the main source of oxygen and nutrients to the heart, anything that causes even a transitory constriction of the coronary arteries is a matter of concern. If the artery is also partially blocked by atherosclerotic plaque, the reduction in blood flow might be so severe that parts of the heart muscle begin to die for want of oxygen and nutrients. Heart attack survivors who continue to smoke are at increased risk for a second heart attack, bringing with it the risk of premature death from heart disease. This risk can be reduced by a reduction in cigarette use: If the smoker were to cut back just five cigarettes per day, they would reduce their chances of premature mortality by 18% (Gerber et al., 2009). If the smoker should quit after having the first heart attack, their risk of experiencing a second heart attack begins to drop within 6–12 months of his or her last cigarette.

Cigarette smokers have been found to be at increased risk for hypertension,[15] the development of aortic aneurysms, and atherosclerotic peripheral vascular disease. Smokers are also at increased risk for strokes, contributing to the 26,000 fatal strokes each year in the United States (Carpenter, 2001). Further, cigarette smoking introduces large amounts of carbon monoxide into the blood, blocking its ability to carry oxygen to the body tissues. The blood of a cigarette smoker might lose as much as 15% of its oxygen-carrying potential as smoking-induced carbon monoxide binds to the hemoglobin in the blood (Parrott, Morinan, Moss, & Scholey, 2004; Tresch & Aronow, 1996).

The Skin

Smoking has long been associated with a skin condition known as "premature aging" (Parrott et al., 2004). Drawing on the data obtained from a research sample of 82 subjects aged 22–91 years of age, the team of Hefrich et al. (2007) attempted to develop an objective scale to assess adult skin aging. They found that cigarette smoking was associated with a dose-related premature aging of the skin of the face as expected, but also found that this premature aging process involved the entire skin, not just the skin of the face, as had long been believed.

The Central Nervous System

There is an emerging body of evidence that a compound known as NNK,[16] a carcinogen found only in tobacco, appears to cause the release of proteins that contribute to inflammation as well as damage to the neurons of the brain (Ghosh et al., 2009). The possibility that a similar process might cause brain damage in human cigarette smokers has not been confirmed or ruled out. There is, however, strong evidence that smoking might speed up the progression of damage seen in multiple sclerosis, although this is still uncertain because of conflicting research findings (Healy et al., 2009). After periods of debate and contradictory research findings, cigarette smoking has been accepted as a risk factor for at least some forms of amyotrophic lateral sclerosis (ALS) (Armon, 2009).

Cigarette smokers are twice as likely to have suicidal thoughts as are nonsmokers (Bronisch, Hofler, & Lieb, 2008). This may, or may not, be associated with the altered brain function in former smokers that continues for an extended period of time after the smoker's last cigarette. Many former smokers will report that they "never felt quite right" after they gave up cigarettes. There is evidence suggesting that there is a decline in cognitive abilities in middle-aged smokers that might linger for many years after the smoker's last cigarette (Moon, 2008a). On the basis of their research, Dregan, Stewart, and Guillford (2012) concluded that smoking contributed more to cognitive decline than does hypertension. Although the authors stopped short of stating that cigarette smoking could lead to outright dementia, persons with multiple risk factors such as hypertension, diabetes plus smoking were at higher risk to experience a cognitive decline.

The Reproductive System

The impact of cigarette smoking on the women's health is discussed in detail in Chapter 21. It is sufficient to point out here that cigarette smoking interferes with the normal function of the women's reproductive system. Male smokers are at increased risk for various reproductive system problems, including smoking-related erectile dysfunction. The causal mechanism for this might be cigarette-related vascular damage to the blood vessels involved in the erectile response. Surprisingly, cigarette smoking does not appear to raise the individual's risk for cancer of the prostate. However, for unknown reasons, men who smoke and who have prostate cancer appear to have a higher *mortality rate* from prostate cancer (Carmona, 2004).

Other Complications Associated with Cigarette Smoking

For reasons that remain unclear, cigarette smoking is thought to either cause or at least exacerbate psoriasis. There is also strong evidence that cigarette smoking

---

[15]Itself a known risk factor for stroke.

[16]If you must know: 4-methylnitrosamino-1(3-pyridyl)-1-butanone.

might exacerbate rheumatoid arthritis in persons with the genetic predisposition for this disorder (Lundstrom et al., 2009). There is also an apparent relationship between cigarette smoking and bone density loss in postmenopausal women (Carmona, 2004). There is an association between cigarette smoking and breast cancer although the mechanism for this relationship is not clear. Guo et al. (2008) postulated that nicotine, even the reduced levels of nicotine found in secondhand smoke,[17] interacted with receptors in breast tissue cells, signaling the cells to begin uncontrolled replication and migration. In addition, there is preliminary evidence suggesting that cigarette smoking can speed up the progression of HIV infection[18] (Lezak, Howieson, Bingler, & Tranel, 2012). Smoking appears to be related to a higher incidence of cataract formation, although the causal mechanism is not clear at this time (Centers for Disease Control, 2004). Cigarette smokers also appear to be at higher risk for the development of macular degeneration (Tan et al., 2008).

A surprising complication of cigarette smoking is what Cutler-Triggs, Fryer, Miyoshi, and Weitzman (2008) termed "food insecurity," or concerns about obtaining sufficient food. In some families, up to 20% of the family income is spent on tobacco rather than on other more healthy products such as food, according to the authors. This drain on the familial income then contributes to a reduction in food availability if not a reduction in actual caloric intake, which then can contribute to nutrition-based developmental problems for the child. This is the environment in which an estimated 13 million children in the United States grow up. Cutler-Triggs et al. (2008) found that 17% of children who had at least one smoking parent could be classified as living in such a home, as opposed to just 9% of those children who were living in a home where the parents did not smoke. This drain on the familial income then contributes to a potential reduction in food availability, which then can contribute to nutrition-based developmental problems for the child.

Early studies suggested that cigarette smoking might provide some protection against the later development of Alzheimer's disease. This exciting research finding sparked a number of follow-up studies, which unfortunately did not reach the same conclusions of

the initial study. Subsequent research has suggested that cigarette smokers might be at *increased risk* for the development of Alzheimer's disease, vascular dementia, and general cognitive decline later in life (Lezak et al., 2012; Sundaram et al., 2004). Surprisingly, there is statistical evidence that cigarette smokers have a 59% *lower* risk for a rare type of brain tumor known as an acoustic neuroma (Palmisano et al., 2012). The authors hypothesized that the reduced blood flow caused by cigarette smoking might be a factor in this lower risk for such tumors. However, such tumors are so rare that the risks of smoking-related disease far outweigh any benefit in treating acoustic neuromas.

Smoking also results in indirect economic loss in the United States each year. For example, cigarette smoking is suspected of being a factor in the estimated 187,000 residential fires each year and $93 billion in lost productivity each year. These figures are not inclusive but even the limited data that is available suggests the economic drain brought on by tobacco use is significant.

Additives

It should be noted that the information about the adverse effects of tobacco use thus far involves *just* tobacco. Recent revelations based on classified documents released as part of litigation against a major tobacco company (Philip Morris) revealed evidence that their research into the safety of some 333 additives such as menthol was subjected to post-study changes in research protocols or the statistical analysis after to avoid the possibility that the study's findings would put cigarette additives in a negative light (Wertz, Kyriss, Paranjape, & Glantz, 2011). Vozoris (2012) suggested that smokers who used a mentholated brand of cigarettes were at higher risk for a stroke than were smokers who did not use such cigarettes.

Degrees of Risk

There is no such thing as a "safe" cigarette. Although the tobacco industry claims that it is attempting to find or develop a safer cigarette, "the search for a safer cigarette is akin to alchemists seeking to turn lead into gold" (Blum, 2008, p. 1646). Even smoking just a few cigarettes a day carries with it an increased risk for smoking-related medical problems and smoking cessation is the only known way to reduce these risks (Carcoma, 2004).

---

[17]Discussed later in this chapter.
[18]Discussed in Chapter 36.

"Low tar" or "light" cigarettes appear to offer the same degree of risk as regular cigarettes (Carcoma, 2004). Smoking as few as three cigarettes a day has been found to increase the individual's risk of cardiovascular disease by 65% (Pope et al., 2009). Further, the concurrent use of cigarettes, smokeless tobacco, and snuff increases the individual's risk for smoking-related illness even further (Thorne, McClave, Rock, Asman, & Malarcher, 2010).

Chewing Tobacco

There are three types of "smokeless" tobacco in use today: (1) moist "snuff," (2), dry snuff, and (3) chewing tobacco (often called "spit tobacco"). In the United States, only an estimated 3.5% of tobacco users (or, 8.7 million people) use "smokeless" tobacco products (Substance Abuse and Mental Health Services Administration, 2009). Generally, the chewing tobacco user starts between the ages of 13 and 17, although established cigarette smokers who are trying to quit might substitute the use of chewing tobacco for their cigarettes. These individuals represent a subpopulation of smokeless tobacco users and they tend to be older at age of initiation than the typical user of chewing tobacco.

The use of chewing tobacco is predominantly by men, although a small percentage of women (0.4%) do use chewing tobacco (Maldonado, 2010). Many of these people use chewing tobacco on the assumption that it is safer and it exposes them to lower levels of nicotine than smoked tobacco. Unfortunately, research has demonstrated that using chewing tobacco 8–10 times a day will result in blood levels of nicotine similar to those seen in a 1 1/2 to 2 pack per day cigarette smoker (Shipley & Rose, 2003). Further, some of the compounds found in chewing tobacco have been linked to hypertension, and there are at least 16 carcinogenic compounds in the typical sample of chewing tobacco (Hecht & Hatsukami, 2005). This places those who use chewing tobacco at higher risk for increased risk of cancer of the mouth and throat as nonusers (Hecht & Hatsukami, 2005). Indeed, the team of Hecht et al. (2007) found *higher* levels of one known carcinogen[19] in the urine of those who used chewing tobacco than was found in the urine of cigarette smokers.

Further, recent research shows that tobacco chewers are at *higher* risk for a fatal myocardial infarction and/or stroke than are cigarette smokers, and that it is of questionable value in smoking cessation programs (Boffeta & Straif, 2009; Piano et al., 2010). This might reflect smokeless tobacco's ability to increase heart rate and blood pressure (Boffeta & Straif, 2009). This is consistent with the known greater incidence of coronary artery disease in smokers as compared to nonsmokers. Those who use "chewing" tobacco also have a higher risk of cancer of the pancreas as well as a higher risk of oral and throat cancers (Boffetta et al., 2008). Those who chew tobacco often experience problems controlling their blood pressure, as well. Thus, although chewing tobacco is often viewed as the "lesser of two evils" by those who use it, this product is certainly not without its risks.

Secondhand Smoke[20]

The definition of "secondhand" or "environmental" smoke is exposure to the cigarette smoke of a cigarette smoker. Such smoke is potentially dangerous: It has been estimated that fully 1% of all deaths around the world can be attributed to the individual's exposure to secondhand smoke (Oberg, Jaakkola, Woodward, Peruga, & Pruss-Ustun, 2010). Clinically, this appears to make sense: Nonsmokers who associate with smokers are exposed to many of the same toxins found in cigarette smoke. Research has found, for example, that almost *88% of nonsmokers* demonstrated cotinine, a metabolite of nicotine, in their blood.

There is also strong evidence that the tobacco industry tried to discredit research that associated exposure to "secondhand" or environment tobacco smoke to heart diseases (Tong & Glantz, 2007). In spite of such denials, research has demonstrated that the coronary arteries of those exposed to secondhand smoke experience short-term coronary artery disease constriction after their exposure to cigarette smoke just as do cigarette smokers (Gullu et al., 2007; Otsuka et al., 2001). Exposure to environmental tobacco smoke also is thought to speed up the formation of atherosclerotic plaque by 20% in the person exposed to environmental tobacco smoke. While this is lower than the 50% faster for the active smoker, it is still significantly higher than

---

[19]Which was the compound 4-(methylnitrosamino)-1-(3-pyridyl)-1-butanol, and its metabolites.

[20]Also called *passive smoking* or *environmental tobacco smoke*. All three terms will be used in this chapter.

for the nonsmoker. The association between environmental tobacco smoke and heart disease is so strong that Hurt et al. (2012) advised that persons with known coronary artery disease avoid *all* exposure to secondhand smoke if possible.

There is a growing body of research evidence that extended exposure to environmental tobacco smoke increases the individual's risk of an initial, and if the individual survives subsequent myocardial infarctions. When the team of Pell et al. (2008) examined the hospital admission records of nine hospitals in Scotland after a law was passed banning cigarette smoking in bars, restaurants, and other public places, they discovered that the number of admissions to these hospitals for acute coronary syndrome dropped 17% in the first year following the start of this ban. This is a significant and not isolated measure of the contribution of second hand smoke to heart disease. The team of Meyers, Neuberger, and He (2009) also concluded that the risk of acute myocardial infarction drops by 17% in the first year of a public smoking ban, and in the city of Pueblo, Colorado, hospital admissions for acute myocardial infarctions dropped by 41% after implementation of smoking ban in public places ("Reduced hospitalizations for acute myocardial infarction ...," 2008). Finally, the team of Hurt et al. (2012) found a 33% reduction in hospital admissions for myocardial infarction as well as a 17% decrease in sudden cardiac deaths following the implementation of a ban on smoking in restaurants and the work place in Olmstead County, Minnesota.

Nonsmokers who are exposed to significant amounts of environmental tobacco smoke are at higher risk for developing pulmonary disorders such as lung cancer or tuberculosis (Leung et al., 2010). Between 3,000 and 8,000 nonsmokers die each year from cancer induced by environmental tobacco smoke just in the United States (Fiore, 2006). An interesting test of the theory that environmental tobacco smoke exposure could cause disease for nonsmokers was carried out by Stark et al. (2007). The authors compared data from a sample of 52 nonsmoking restaurant workers from bars where smoking was permitted against 32 bars where smoking was prohibited. They found that the former group had six times the level of the compound NNAL[21] in their urine than did those bar workers

from bars where smoking was not permitted. The importance of this study is in the fact that both sample groups were nonsmokers, and NNAL is a smoking-specific carcinogenic compound, thus suggesting that those bar workers in smoking-permitted bars were receiving significant exposure to toxic environmental tobacco smoke.

Adults who are exposed to secondhand smoke are also at higher risk for cognitive impairment than are those who are not exposed to cigarette smoke (Llewellyn, Lang, Langa, Naughton, & Matthews, 2009). The authors found that those adults with the highest level of exposure to environmental tobacco smoke were more likely to fall in the lowest 10% of cognitive testing, as compared with adults with lighter levels of exposure to environmental tobacco smoke. Further, children are also vulnerable to environmental tobacco smoke. Further, there is preliminary evidence that exposure to environmental tobacco smoke is associated with higher levels of mental health problems than for those not exposed to secondhand smoke, although the causal mechanism for this association is not known at the present time (Hamer, Stamatakis, & Batty, 2010).

Researchers believe that secondhand smoke causes approximately 6,100 deaths in children each year in the United States. For example, children exposed to environmental tobacco smoke are at increased risk for developing asthma, which may be fatal if medical assistance does not arrive in time (Guilbert & Krawiec, 2003). The team of Kwok et al. (2008) concluded that for infants the exposure to secondhand smoke in the first 3 months of life were twice as likely to develop an infectious disease(s), some of which were severe enough to require hospitalization, during the first 8 years of their lives. Another measure of the vulnerability of children to environmental tobacco smoke was provided by Kerrigan (2008), who utilized data from the State of Wisconsin infant follow-up studies; it was suggested that 56% of those infants who died after discharge from the hospital following birth had been exposed to environmental tobacco smoke.

Childhood exposure to secondhand smoke is, surprisingly, an apparent risk factor in the later development of pulmonary diseases such as emphysema (Lovasi et al., 2010) or lung cancer (Oliva-Marston et al., 2009) for that individual later in life. Lovasi et al. (2010) hypothesized that early damage to the alveolar walls might increase that child's chances of developing emphysema in middle to late adulthood. However,

---

[21]Chemical shorthand for: 4-(methylnitrosamino)-1-(3-pyridyl)-1-butanol.

although the results of these studies are suggestive, they are not proof that such relationships exists, and there is a need for further research into childhood exposure to secondhand smoke and adult pulmonary disease. As these studies, and those cited in earlier paragraphs suggest, environmental tobacco smoke is a serious health risk for those who are around the smoker, and a factor in premature illness or death for a significant number of infants or children who were in effect involuntary smokers.

It has even been suggested that exposure to tertiary or "third-hand" tobacco smoke could be harmful, although this claim is controversial (Robson, 2009). Tertiary tobacco smoke exposure occurs then the non-smoker is exposed to the residue of cigarette smoking found on the individual's clothing and on environmental surfaces. However, the scientific validity of such claims has been challenged not from the tobacco industry, but from a small group of independent scientists (Robson, 2009). For example, antismoking groups have seized on a research study that concluded that breathing secondhand smoke for 30 minutes increased your risk of a heart attack to that of an active smoker. However, the research data supporting this claim have been limited, and most physicians believe that such exposure will only result in a heart attack if the nonsmoker was on the brink of a coronary event.

Recent research has suggested that in the past "Big Tobacco" paid scientists to write articles contradicting the research suggesting that smoking was dangerous.[22] They remain mute about the fact that many scientists conducting research into the dangers of cigarette smoking receive funding from companies that make nicotine replacement products (Robson, 2009). This is not to imply that cigarette smoking, or environmental tobacco smoke, are not dangerous. It does, however, underscore the need for a careful, *unbiased,* examination of the evidence before claims of dangers of or the extent of such dangers from either direct or indirect exposure to cigarette smoke, are made.

---

[22]An interesting phenomenon is the so-called Tobacco Research Institute, which purports to conduct unbiased research into tobacco and its uses. It is funded by "donations" from each tobacco company, which are assessed on the basis of total market share that company holds (Pennock, 2007). However, fully 50% of the budget for this organization is devoted to public relations activities, a most curious application of research funds. Further, it continues to devote much of its activities to debunking research that suggests that tobacco smoking is dangerous.

Smoking Cessation

The most effective for nicotine addiction is for the individual to never begin smoking. To this end some nations now require graphic warning labels on the side of the cigarette package illustrating the potential danger(s) of smoking. It has been found that clear, graphic images of the dangers inherent in tobacco use prominently displayed for the smoker to see increases the percentage of smokers who contemplate smoking cessation, and their motivation to complete this task ("Cigarette Package Health Warnings and Interest in Quitting Smoking—14 Countries, 2008–2010," 2011).

Admittedly, the individual's risk for developing a smoking-related illness never disappears even with smoking cessation. Drawing on the data from an ongoing study of one million women in the United Kingdom, Pirie, Peto, Reeves, Green, and Beral (2012) found that former smokers were at one-third increased risk for premature death from smoking-related illness. This was especially true for those former smokers who quit at the age of 50, suggesting that younger former smokers might be at lower risk for death from smoking-related illness. Although the fact that women in the study who quit smoking still had a 33% higher risk of mortality from smoking-related illness might be used by some smokers to justify continued cigarette use, smoking cessation by the age of 50 still reduced the individual's risk of premature death from smoking-related illness by two-thirds, which is hardly insignificant.

Admittedly, it is difficult to quit smoking and only 4–7% of smokers are able to quit without assistance (Sepe, Kay, & Stober, 2012), which might explain why only 35% of cigarette smokers try to quit in any given year (O'Brien, 2011). The success rate for smoking cessation programs, even with pharmacological support, remains quite low. Between 70 and 80% of those who attempt to quit will relapse in the first 6 months, and typically will require 5–10 serious attempts to quit smoking before he or she achieves success. However, success is possible, as evidenced by the fact that there are more former smokers in the United States today than current smokers (Fiore, Hatsukami, & Baker, 2002; Hays et al., 2011; Hughes, 2005). Light smokers, defined as individuals who smoke 20 cigarettes a day or less, appear to be more capable of stopping on their own, whereas heavy smokers are more likely to require professional assistance.

There is a nicotine withdrawal syndrome that causes the individual to experience a degree of discomfort. The degree of discomfort that the individual will experience during the earlier phases of abstinence are to some degree genetically mediated (Uhl et al., 2008; Whitten, 2011). Uhl et al. (2008) observed that the genes that they identified as supporting smoking were similar, but not identical, to those suspected of being involved in other addictive behaviors. However, the authors found much less of an overlap between these two sets of genes than they had anticipated, suggesting that different genetic mechanisms might be at work between cigarette smoking and the other addictive behaviors.

Yet, the majority of smokers make determined efforts to quit. Hughes (2005) found that only 19% of cigarette smokers had *never* tried to quit smoking, which means that more than 80% of smokers have tried to quit at least once. The individual's *expectations* for nicotine withdrawal and smoking cessation influence their success rate. Those persons who expect the most withdrawal distress or a higher number of problems when they attempted to quit are more likely either to not attempt to quit, or to fail in their efforts to quit smoking.

In spite of public media advertisements suggesting that smokers require pharmacological support to quit, between two-thirds and three-quarters of former smokers were able to quit without pharmacological support, and found that quitting was easier than they had anticipated (Chapman & MacKenzie, 2010). However, little is understood about the smoking cessation process. There is strong evidence, for example, suggesting that the smoker's dietary choices might influence his or her success in quitting. The team of McClemon, Westma, Rose, and Lutz (2007) found that smokers who consumed meat, coffee, and alcohol experienced greater pleasure from cigarette use, whereas products such as dairy products, celery, and other vegetables reduced the smoker's sense of pleasure from smoking. Thus, those who wish to quit smoking must review their dietary habits, and change their diet to give themselves the best possible chance of quitting.

The most common, and possibly least effective, method of smoking cessation is the "cold turkey" method in which the smoker just quits smoking (Patkar, Vergare, Bakra, Weinstein, & Leone, 2003). The sudden discontinuation of cigarettes tends to result in high relapse rates, as opposed to those methods of smoking cessation that utilize a nicotine replacement component and psychosocial support (Patkar et al., 2003). The various pharmacological supports for smoking cessation are reviewed in Chapter 33.

Former smokers are vulnerable to "relapse triggers" that they encounter in the environment, the most important of which is being around people who are still smoking. Watching others smoke cigarettes, and smelling tobacco smoke from a distance, will trigger thoughts of returning to active smoking for the individual. Another relapse trigger is living in a home with more than one cigarette smoker. These relapse triggers are a factor in more than 50% of the cases where the former smoker relapses (Ciraulo, Piechniczek-Buczek, & Iscan, 2003). Thus, like other forms of drug addiction, the recovering person must change their friendships, and avoid "high risk" situations, and be aware that environmental triggers will make them think about smoking.

There is a poorly understood relationship between depression and cigarette smoking. Evidence suggests that depressed smokers experience more reinforcement from cigarettes than do those who are not depressed, and are vulnerable to possible relapse because of this (Patkar et al., 2003). This is not to say that cigarette smoking caused the depression. Rather, depression and cigarette smoking appear to be two separate conditions that appear to overlap, with depression possibly serving as a relapse trigger for recovering smokers. Other emotional states such as boredom, or anxiety, also can serve as relapse triggers, as many smokers have learned to cope with these emotions through smoking.

Cigarette Cessation and Weight Gain

Many smokers cite their fear of gaining weight as an obstacle to smoking cessation. Admittedly about 80% of former smokers will gain *some* weight in the early stages of recovery (Centers for Disease Control, 2004). However, this statistic is misleading: 57% of those who continue to smoke also gain weight during the same period of life suggesting that some of the weight gain might be falsely attributed to smoking cessation rather than just a tendency on the part of the smoker to gain weight as he or she ages. Still, individuals in the early stage of smoking cessation do need to watch their diets. The average smoker increases his or her caloric intake by about 200 calories a day, or the equivalent of about one sandwich per day (Stitzer, 2003). Over the course of a week, the extra accumulated caloric intake would amount to 1,400 calories, which means that the former smoker would be ingesting 8 days worth of calories every 7 days. This obviously will expose the former smoker to the danger of weight gain, at least in the short term.

Another factor that contributes to weight gain in the former smoker is that nicotine stimulates the body's metabolism by about 10%, forcing the body to "burn" calories faster than normal (Stitzer, 2003). Finally, many cigarette smokers are underweight because of nicotine-induced anorexia. When they stop smoking, their bodies will attempt to "catch up" and add weight to achieve the individual's appropriate weight level for his or her body frame. Finally, smokers are often fluid deficient, and when they stop smoking the body will add ingest extra fluids to achieve the appropriate fluid levels. These factors may contribute to cessation-related weight gain in the former smoker, which in a sense is true.

It has been found that clinicians underestimated the amount of weight gained by a cigarette smoker following cessation (Aubin, Farley, Lycett, Lahmek, & Aveyard, 2012). The approximate amount of weight gained by the average cigarette smoker is reviewed in Table 16-3 (Aubin et al., 2012).

Surprisingly, there is evidence suggesting that those individuals who gain more weight are also more likely to abstain from cigarettes. Further, although this weight gain is often distressing to the former smoker, there is evidence that after 6 months or so the average individual's body weight will return to precessation levels. Thus, cessation-related weight gain may be a transitional step in the former smoker's adjustment to life without cigarettes.

Although obesity is a known risk factor for cardiovascular disease, the health benefits that accrue following smoking cessation usually far outweigh the potential risks from smoking cessation–related weight gain (Clair et al., 2013). A former smoker would need to gain 50–100 pounds to place the same stress on her or his cardiovascular system as they did by smoking one to two packs a day. Thus, the postcessation weight gain is not as dangerous as continued cigarette smoking. Table 16-4 lists some of the benefits of smoking cessation.

Tobacco Use and the *Diagnostic and Statistical Manual of Mental Disorders* (5th Edition)[23]

The *Diagnostic and Statistical Manual of Mental Disorders* (5th edition) (*DSM-5*) (American Psychiatric Association, 2013) identified four subforms of the tobacco-related disorders:

1. Tobacco use disorder
2. Tobacco withdrawal
3. Other tobacco-induced disorders
4. Unspecified tobacco-related disorder

The *tobacco use disorder* appears to be a different, and confusing, term for nicotine abuse. The *DSM-5* (American Psychiatric Association, 2013) identified 11 criteria by which a tobacco use disorder might be identified, with individuals who demonstrate any two of these criteria in a 12-month period meeting the criteria for a diagnosis for a tobacco use disorder.[24] The identified criteria include (but are not limited to) (American Psychiatric Association, 2013): "Craving" for tobacco when not being used, recurrent tobacco use in situations where its use is dangerous (smoking in bed what the example provided in the *DSM-5*), continued tobacco use despite knowledge of physical and psychological dangers associated with its use, development of tolerance and a characteristic withdrawal syndrome. As with other substance use disorders classified in the *DSM-5*, manual modifiers such as in early or in sustained remission are suggested where appropriate.

TABLE 16-3
Weight Gain following Smoking Cessation

TIME SINCE QUITTING	WEIGHT GAIN
1 month	2.46 pounds
2 months	4.97 pounds
3 months	6.27 pounds
6 months	9.3 pounds
12 months	10.27 pounds

© 2015 Cengage Learning

---

[23]The material presented here is to illustrate the relationship between the alcohol use disorders and the *Diagnostic and Statistical Manual of Mental Disorders* (5th edition). This material should not be interpreted as, nor should it be used as, a diagnostic manual.

[24]The reader is referred to the *Diagnostic and Statistical Manual of Mental Disorders* (5th edition) (*DSM-5*) (American Psychiatric Association, 2013) for the full list of diagnostic criteria suggested by the American Psychiatric Association as signs of tobacco use disorder.

TABLE 16-4
Summary of Benefits of Smoking Cessation

CONDITION	BENEFIT
Stroke	Within 5–15 years, the former smoker's risk of stroke will be about the same as that of a person who never smoked
Cancer of the mouth, throat, and the esophagus	After 5 years of abstinence, the former smoker's risk of developing one of these cancers drops by 50%
Coronary artery disease	After 1 year of abstinence, the former smoker's risk of coronary artery disease drops by 50%. After 15 years of abstinence, it will be virtually the same as a nonsmoker
Lung cancer	The risk of lung cancer will drop by 50% in first 10 years of smoking abstinence
Hypertension	Drops as arterial walls become more flexible in first 10 years of abstinence from smoking.
Life expectancy	Former smoker adds between 2.5 and 4.5 years to their life expectancy
Neurosurgery patients	Lower risk of complications or mortality during and after neurosurgical procedure
Recovering cardiac patients	Former smokers are less likely to suffer a second heart attack compared with current smokers

SOURCES: Centers for Disease Control (2004); Grover, Gray-Donald Joseph, Abrahamowicz, and Coupal (1994); Lau, Berger, Khullar, and Maa (2013).

Other modifiers include whether the individual was in a nicotine maintenance program, in which the nicotine withdrawal syndrome is blocked by the pharmaceuticals being used, or if the individual was in a controlled environment with limited or no access to tobacco products.

It is noted in the *DSM-5* manual that smoking is related with a number of physical problems, most of which are discussed earlier in this chapter. Between 22 and 32% of smokers have another substance use or psychiatric disorder according to the *DSM-5* manual. It is also noted that there are cultural and educational factors that might predispose an individual to smoking cigarettes according to the *DSM-5* manual.

Within 24 hours of the individual's last cigarette use, he or she will begin the phase of *tobacco withdrawal,* the symptoms of which are reviewed in this chapter. The *DSM-5* manual warns that the symptoms being observed must not be caused by another condition such as the withdrawal from another compound being abused, and requires that the withdrawal process requires "clinically significant distress or impairment" (p. 575) for the individual, although as noted in this chapter a significant percentage of smokers report minimal to no distress during cigarette cessation. This would suggest a need for another category for persons going through nicotine withdrawal: "With minor distress only" in the opinion of the author of your text.

The category *Other tobacco-induced disorders* is applied to cases where the individual's tobacco use has contributed to another medical disorder (such as a sleep disorder, for example). Finally the *Unspecified tobacco-related disorder* category refers to individuals whose tobacco use has caused significant impairment in their physical health, occupational functioning, or familial life, but who do not meet the full criteria for a diagnosis of a *Tobacco use disorder.*

Chapter Summary

Tobacco use, which was once limited to what European explorers would come to call the "New World," was first introduced into Europe by explorers who learned the practice of smoking during their travels. Once the practice of smoking tobacco reached Europe, it spread rapidly in spite of rather draconian measures by authorities to try and stop its spread. By the end of the 19th century, tobacco chewing had become a common practice, although the concurrent development of machines that allowed for the rapid production of cigarettes allowed health providers to suggest cigarette smoking as a less offensive, and more sanitary, substitute for chewing tobacco.

In the time since its introduction into society, nicotine, the main psychoactive agent in tobacco, has been found to have an addiction potential similar to that of narcotics or cocaine. Significant numbers of people have become addicted to cigarettes, and each year 34% of current smokers attempt to quit. Unfortunately, only 2.5% of smokers are able to discontinue the use of cigarettes each time that they attempt to quit in spite of the best of pharmacological support (McRae, Brady, & Sonne, 2001). This fact is a testament to the addictive potential of nicotine, but also reflects the sad fact that the majority of those who smoke will continue to expose themselves to the dangers associated with tobacco use.

CHAPTER 17

Chemicals and the Neonate:[1] The Potential Consequences of Drug Abuse during Pregnancy[2]

> Despite information received by the general public on the adverse effects of substance abuse in pregnancy, there is still significant substance abuse among pregnant women in the U.S.
>
> —*Goler, Armstrong, Taillac, and Osejo (2008, pp. 3–4)*

Introduction

Maternal substance use, even the use of some prescribed medications, may have dire consequences for both a pregnant woman and her unborn child. The use of many prescription and over-the-counter medications might disrupt normal fetal growth and development or even be toxic to the fetus and/or the mother. Unfortunately, recreational drug abuse is most prevalent in the age cohort most actively involved in reproduction (Bolnick & Rayburn, 2003). Substance abuse treatment as an integrated component of prenatal care has been found to reduce the number and severity of drug-induced consequences during pregnancy (Armstrong et al., 2008). Unfortunately, health care providers are often hesitant to discuss substance use disorders with pregnant women (Chang et al., 2008). This might explain in many cases that the pregnancy in a woman with an substance use disorder (SUD) had a negative outcome even if they did receive prenatal care (Chang et al., 2008; Goler Armstrong, Taillac, Osejo 2008). In this chapter, the effects of maternal substance use during pregnancy will be explored.

Scope of the Problem

Maternal substance use during pregnancy is a common problem, with nicotine and alcohol arguably being the two substances most frequently used during this critical phase of fetal development. To illustrate this fact, consider the study by Behnke, Smith, Committee on Substance Abuse, & Committee on Fetus and Newborn (2013) who found that 16.3% of pregnant women smoked cigarettes and 10.8% of women consumed alcohol on a regular basis during pregnancy. Pregnant women will sometimes abuse other compounds as well: An estimated 4.4% of pregnant women will abuse an illicit drug(s) during their pregnancy, with the rate of illicit drug use being highest in the 15- to 17-year-old age bracket. It has been estimated that

---

[1] It is the author's belief that *all* recreational substance use during pregnancy is a danger to the fetus, and thus to be avoided.

[2] Technically, the study of how chemical compounds affect neonatal development is the field of *teratogenicity*. A compound that can harm the fetus is called *teratogenic*.

almost 10% of the women of childbearing age meet the criteria for admission to a substance use rehabilitation facility, although 85% of these women did not perceive the need or are never referred to a treatment program (Zilberman, 2009).

Until recently, physicians usually had to rely on maternal self-report to identify babies who were exposed to alcohol or drugs *in utero*. If meconium[3] testing was conducted, the results were usually not available for many days, in part because the physician might be forced to wait that time for the meconium to be expelled following birth. However, Montgomery et al. (2008) have suggested that the umbilical cord can be tested for fetal exposure to many compounds commonly abused. The authors found that of 498 umbilical cord tissue samples tested, 32% were "positive" for compounds such as methamphetamine, cocaine, marijuana, and phencyclidine.[4] The authors suggested that umbilical cord tissue testing might provide a rapid identification of infants who might require special care following prenatal exposure to these compounds. This would also avoid the problem of maternal dissimulation.[5]

A Period of Special Vulnerability

Compounds that have a negative influence on neonatal growth and development are referred to as *teratogenic* chemicals. The range of teratogenic compounds is vast and includes many prescribed medications, environmental forces,[6] and many of the drugs of abuse. The effects of the drugs of abuse will vary, depending on when during the pregnancy the woman abused the compound(s) in question, the compound(s) abused, the frequency, duration, and intensity of that substance use. For example, early in pregnancy nicotine, alcohol, marijuana, opiates, cocaine, and methamphetamine all have teratogenic effects (Behnke et al., 2013).

Researchers believe that approximately 5.1% of women use an illicit drug at least once during their pregnancy, a percentage that has been relatively stable since 2007 (Behnke et al., 2013). Women who abuse alcohol or an illicit drug during pregnancy should automatically be classified as having a "high risk" pregnancy (Finnegan & Kandall, 2008). The first trimester is especially important

to subsequent growth and development: Organ differentiation, for example, takes place during the third to eighth week of pregnancy, often before the mother-to-be is even aware that she is pregnant. Many women with substance use disorders do not even attempt to alter their substance use patterns until after their pregnancy has been confirmed (Bolnick & Rayburn, 2003). Maternal alcohol use can induce epigenetic[7] changes induced into fetal DNA, possibly with lifelong effects (Stelovich, 2011).[8] Not surprisingly many women who knowingly continue to abuse alcohol or drugs during pregnancy were raised by parents who also had substance use problems (Gwinnell & Adamec, 2006).

It was long thought that the placenta protected the fetus from foreign chemicals, a belief that has since been disproven (Minnes, Lang, & Singer, 2011). This, plus the limited fetal ability to break down drug molecules, raises the risk of prenatal damage from chemical exposure during pregnancy. For example, only 60% of the blood that the fetus receives from the placenta is processed by the immature fetal liver. The other 40% of the blood and any toxins in that blood directly enters the general circulation of the fetus. In addition, compounds that *are* routed to the liver are not always biotransformed at the same rate as would be found in the mother's body. This can both allow the toxins more time in the body of the fetus and allow the buildup of potentially fatal levels of some compounds in the fetal circulation. Also the fetal blood–brain barrier (BBB) is still developing, allowing many compounds easy access to the developing fetal nervous system (Barki, Kravitz, & Berki, 1998). Finally, the circulatory system of the fetus has lower blood protein levels than the adult, providing fewer binding sites for chemicals that are protein bound, in effect of increasing the concentration of those compounds in the fetal circulation. All of these factors combine to magnify the effects of a toxin(s) in the fetus.

In this era of polydrug abuse, it can be difficult to isolate the effect of one specific compound of the fetus (Chen & Maier, 2011; Mendelson, Mello, Schuckit, & Segal, 2006; Minnes et al., 2011). Additional factors such as the quality of prenatal medical care and maternal malnutrition influence neonatal growth. Following birth, factors such as being raised in an adverse social environment, or poor postnatal caregiving, also influence

---

[3]See Glossary.

[4]Each of which is discussed in the appropriate chapter of this text.

[5]See Glossary.

[6]Maternal radiation exposure, her stress level during pregnancy, or maternal diet are all excellent examples of environmental forces that might influence prenatal growth.

---

[7]Discussed in Chapter 25.

[8]A body of evidence suggesting that epigenetic changes introduced into the *mother's* body can also be passed on to the fetus, although this lies outside of the scope of this text (Stelovich, 2011).

the baby's growth and development. Maternal preoccupation with drug use, the effects of poverty, the impact of maternal depression on the parent–child relationship, the need to compete with siblings for parental attention, maternal anxiety, the intense needs of the drug-exposed infant for nurturance and care, all can combine to cause a poor developmental outcome in for the infant, child, and adolescent. It is not surprising that researchers have generally found lasting, but usually subtle, aftereffects of prenatal drug exposure (Malanga, 2009). However, because there are so many variables involved, scientists have for the most part failed to find a specific pattern to warn health care providers that the infant or child was exposed to the drugs of abuse during gestation.[9]

Although technically postpartum depression is not a known complication of fetal exposure to maternal substance abuse, there is a relationship between maternal substance use, depression, and attempted suicide following birth. The team of Comtois, Schiff, and Grossman (2008) examined the hospital records of women who gave birth in Washington State between the years 1992 and 2001. The authors found that substance abusing mothers who developed postpartum depression were six times as likely to attempt suicide in the first year following the child's birth than were nonabusing women. Given the central role of the mother as the primary caregiver in the first years of the infant's life, it is clear that maternal behavior certainly influences the growth and development of the child.

The discussion that follows must be interpreted as the current understanding of how maternal substance use affects the infant's growth and development. There is still much to learn in this area, and new information is being added to the existing database on a daily basis. In the following sections, we will examine the latest information on the effects of many compounds of abuse on fetal growth and development.

Alcohol

Approximately 10.8% of pregnant women use alcohol at some point during pregnancy (Behnke et al., 2013), a figure that has remained relatively unchanged since 1991 (Centers for Disease Control and Prevention, 2009b). Unfortunately alcohol (a) easily passes across the placenta into the fetal circulation, (b) with the result that the fetal blood alcohol levels reach those of the mother's in just 15 minutes. Also (c) alcohol and its primary metabolite, acetaldehyde are both teratogenic[10] compounds, and (d) the primary metabolite of alcohol, acetaldehyde, is also teratogenic (Fryer et al., 2009; Rose, 1988). So close is the relationship between the effects of maternal alcohol use and its impact on the fetus that if the mother were alcohol dependent and had been drinking before giving birth, the infant will be at risk for the alcohol withdrawal syndrome starting 3–12 hours after delivery (American Academy of Pediatrics, 1998).

In the early 1973, maternal alcohol use during pregnancy was identified as a major causal agent for birth defects in this country (Sokol, Delaney-Black, & Nordstrom, 2003). The pattern of developmental problems identified in infants born of alcohol abusing mothers was called the *fetal alcohol syndrome (FAS)*, which is now recognized as both the third most common cause of birth defects in developed countries and as the most preventable (Glasser, 2002; Getzfeld, 2006; Kruelwitch, 2005; Sadock & Sadock, 2007; Swift, 2005; Thomas, Waren, & Hewitt, 2010). For each alcoholic beverage consumed per day, the risk for damage to the developing fetus increases (Feldman et al., 2012). Prenatal exposure to alcohol does not automatically cause the fetal alcohol syndrome: Many children who were exposed to alcohol *in utero* will have some, but not all, of the symptoms of FAS (Cunniff, 2003; Rourke & Grant, 2009). These children were said to have *fetal alcohol effects (FAE)*. Although the terms *FAS* and *FAE* are still used in the clinical literature, physicians are increasingly using the term *fetal alcohol spectrum disorder (FASD)* for such children (Sokol et al., 2003). However, it is important to point out that FASD is not a recognized diagnostic category, and it remains a theoretical construct (Brown, 2006; Coles, 2011).

Scope of the Problem

Maternal self-report is a notoriously unreliable source of data about alcohol use during pregnancy. Many women do not report the frequency or amount of their alcohol use during pregnancy whereas others are left to having to rely on their memory to determine their level of alcohol use during the previous 9 months

---

[9]Some might argue that the fetal alcohol syndrome, discussed later in this chapter, is an exception to this rule. However, how many infants are exposed to alcohol in gestation who do not develop this condition because they lack the genetic heritage necessary to produce FAS? The answer to this question is not known.

[10]See Glossary.

(Chang, 2006; Coles, 2011). Unfortunately, there is no reliable biomarker available to physicians or researchers to help them identify infants exposed to alcohol prior to birth (Bailey & Sokol, 2011). To complicate matters, there are many confounding variables that influence the impact of maternal alcohol use during pregnancy: The stage of fetal development when the alcohol use occurred, amount of alcohol consumed, age of the woman, her stress level, diet, concurrent abuse of illicit drugs or use of prescribed medications, and cigarette smoking all complicate the problem of early identification of children with FAS or FASD (Bailey & Sokol, 2011). The problem of maternal cigarette smoking is hardly insignificant: Fifty-five percent of pregnant women who drink are cigarette smokers and cigarette smoking has itself been identified as a negative influence on fetal growth and development.

There is no safe level of alcohol use during pregnancy.[11] The possibility that the infant will develop FASD is dependent, in part, upon the level of maternal alcohol intake. Consumption of just four to six drinks per day, an amount that most women with an alcohol use disorder (AUD) would consider significant, will result in two-thirds of the children developing FASD. Kelly, et. al., (2013) suggested however that the consumption of up to *two* standard units of alcohol *per week* did not have a negative effect on fetal growth and development. However, further research is necessary to confirm these findings and until confirmed it would appear best for the pregnant woman to abstain from alcohol use.

Consequences of Maternal Alcohol Use

The fetal brain is vulnerable to alcohol exposure, especially in the first trimester. There are multiple mechanisms by which maternal alcohol use can disrupt normal fetal development during this critical phase (Fryer et al., 2009). One mechanism is the maternal use of alcohol inhibiting the production (biosynthesis) of a family of compounds known as *gangliosides* in the developing fetal brain. These enzymes are most active during the first trimester of pregnancy, playing a role in fetal brain development. By blocking the biosynthesis of the gangliosides during the first trimester of pregnancy, maternal alcohol use can prove especially destructive to the growing fetal central nervous system (CNS). This might, in turn, negatively influence the development of the prostaglandin system in the body and protein synthesis and result in periods of hypoxia due to decreased maternal blood flow to the placenta (Behnke et al., 2013).

To test the impact of maternal alcohol use on fetal neurological development, the team of Humphriss, Hall, May, Zuccolo, and Macleod (2013) examined the ability of almost 7,000 children in England who had been exposed to moderate levels of alcohol during pregnancy. The authors defined "moderate" alcohol use as no more than seven standard drinks in a week's time and found that at the age of 10 years the children who were exposed to alcohol *in utero* demonstrated any deficit in ability to maintain their balance, an indirect measure of possible neurological damage. The authors concluded that these results reflected chance variation in participant selection or their lack of participants who engaged in high levels of alcohol consumption during pregnancy. The authors of the study emphasized that the results did not indicate that maternal alcohol use during pregnancy was harmless.

It has been accepted by researchers that maternal alcohol use during pregnancy can increase oxidative stress and inhibit neural adhesion within the developing brain of the fetus. Further, the period of prenatal development is a high risk period for alteration of gene expression (epigenesis) by an environmental factor such as alcohol, leading to long-term (if not lifelong) changes in gene expression for the infant. This might be one reason why different structural components of the developing brain are especially vulnerable to alcohol's effects at different points in gestation (Thomas et al., 2010). Radiographic studies of the brains of infants born to alcohol-abusing mothers have found structural damage to the corpus callosum, if not the absence of this vital brain structure (known as *agenesis*[12] of the corpus callosum). Damage to such structures in the brain often results in the development of seizure disorders, and might account for the findings of Bell et al. (2010), who found a significantly higher

---

[11]Some women, having been told that they should ingest *no more* than one standard drink in 24 hours, believe that they can "save up" each day's acceptable level of alcohol intake, so that they can go on a "binge" later. Unfortunately, research has found that even one such "binge" will place the fetus at risk for FAS/FASD and other developmental problems (Brown, 2006).

---

[12]See Glossary.

incidence of seizure disorders in children exposed to alcohol *in utero*.

In 1973, maternal alcohol use during pregnancy was identified as a major cause of birth defects. This later was termed the *fetal alcohol syndrome*. As scientists learned more about FAS, it was discovered that 17% of FAS infants are either stillborn or die shortly after birth (Bailey & Sokol, 2011; Fryer et al., 2009; Renner, 2004a). It was also discovered that FAS is the most severe expression of what is now called the *fetal alcohol spectrum disorder* (FASD). Children with FASD will demonstrate a number of symptoms of FAS, but fail to meet the full criteria for a diagnosis of FAS. It is important to keep in mind that FAS and FASD are not recognized diagnostic categories, but only theoretical constructs (Brown, 2006). The annual cost to society for providing remedial services to children with FAS/FASD in the United States is estimated to be approximately $700 million per year (Bhuvaneswar & Chang, 2009).

Children with FAS, the most severe expression of FASD, will have a characteristic pattern of facial abnormalities, and one in five infants with FASD will have a major birth defect and approximately half will have an IQ that falls below 70[13] (Coles, 2011). A large percentage of the remaining children will have an IQ in the borderline range of intellectual function, placing them at risk for academic, vocational, and social adaption problems later in life. Infants who are born with severe FASD usually have a lower-than-normal birth weight and microcephaly[14] at birth. Noninvasive neurodiagnostic imaging studies of the brains of children exposed to alcohol *in utero* often reveal damage to the cortex, cerebellum, basal ganglia, hippocampus, caudate nucleus, and the corpus callosum of their brains (Carter et al., 2012; Cunniff, 2003; Fryer et al., 2009). These findings are important because the corpus callosum is the region of the brain that transfers information from one hemisphere to the other, whereas the caudate nucleus and the cerebellum are involved in the coordination of muscle movements.

In later life, these children experience behavioral problems such as attention deficit hyperactivity disorders (ADHD) (Greenbaum et al., 2009; Peters, 2007) as well as weaker emotional processing and social

cognition skills than normal children. Although behaviorally children with FASD appear similar to children with ADHD, it has been hypothesized that there are different neurological mechanisms between the two disorders (Greenbaum et al., 2009). The authors suggested that their behavior might reflect damage to the orbitofrontal region of the brain rather than those regions of the brain traditionally thought to be involved in ADHD. Children with FASD also experience short attention span, anger control issues, impulsiveness,[15] self-abusive behaviors, poor coordination, cardiac, renal and visual system disturbances, learning disabilities, and a variety of other developmental delays (Bhuvaneswar & Chang, 2009; Gwinnell & Adamec, 2006; Peters, 2007). It is important to remember that the intensity and number of symptoms that a child with FASD will demonstrate depends on a number of factors, including maternal tobacco use, which is itself a confounding factor as we struggle to better understand FASD.

The low–birth weight characteristic of FAS children at birth appears to at least partially resolve itself by adolescence, and children with FASD usually fall within the normal height and weight range for adolescents and adults their age (Peters, 2007). This does not negate the fact that these children often need lifelong social service support(s). There is also strong evidence that children exposed to alcohol *in utero* are at increased risk for developing an AUD of their own later in life[16] (Gilman, Bjork, & Hommer, 2007).

Other Consequences of Maternal Alcohol Use

There is also a mounting body of evidence that suggests that maternal alcohol use during pregnancy will increase the child's risk of developing acute lymphoid leukemia later in life (Menegaux et al., 2006). Infants who were exposed to alcohol *in utero* are at increased risk for premature birth and sudden infant death syndrome (SIDS) (Bailey & Sokol, 2011). Neonates who were exposed to significant levels of alcohol *in utero* were also at higher risk for anemia at birth, although this appears to have resolved by the age of 5 years

---

[13]An IQ of 70 or below is often used as the criteria for determination of eligibility for special education or social support services.

[14]See Glossary.

[15]Making them vulnerable to legal problems when the individual impulsively breaks the law.

[16]Raising an interesting question: Is the child's later increased risk for an (AUD) caused by the exposure to alcohol in utero, their genetic heritage, environmental forces, or an interactional effect between all three forces?

(Carter et al., 2012). Finally, there is evidence that maternal alcohol use during pregnancy increases the chances that the child will grow up to have an AUD in later life (Alati et al., 2006). It should be noted that all of these problems might develop in the infant exposed to alcohol *in utero* even if she or he does not develop a clinical FASD.

Breast Feeding and Alcohol Use

Mennella and Pepino (2010) found that women who have a familial history of alcoholism have a blunted response to prolactin if they were breast feeding. Such women tend to produce less breast milk and producing it for a shorter period of time per feeding episode. In such women, the authors observed a tendency for the women to breast feed the baby more frequently, but found little evidence to support the myth that alcohol use during breast feeding enhances milk production.

Alcohol in the mother's circulatory system passes freely into her breast milk and will shortly reach 90–95% of that found in the mother's general circulation. Fortunately, even if the infant were to nurse while the mother was quite intoxicated, the amount of alcohol ingested by the infant along with the mother's milk would be diluted throughout the baby's system, resulting in a lower blood alcohol level for the infant than was true for the mother (Heil & Subramanian, 1998). Even this limited alcohol exposure is associated with abnormal gross motor development for the infant, with a dose-dependent relationship between the mother's alcohol use and infant psychomotor problems. Further, it theoretically is possible that maternal alcohol use during nursing might interfere with the development of the infant's immune system, just as it interferes with the normal function of the immune system in the adult. For these reasons, maternal alcohol use during the time when she is breast feeding is not suggested (Behnke et al., 2013; Sadock & Sadock, 2007).

Disulfiram Use during Pregnancy

Disulfiram is often used as an adjunct to the treatment of alcohol addiction. It has been discovered that during gestation, a metabolite of disulfiram, diethyldithiocarbamate, can bind to lead and might bring that lead across the placental barrier. Fetal exposure to lead is known to disrupt normal neurological growth and development for the fetus, and so the use of disulfiram during pregnancy is not recommended.

Abuse and Addiction to Amphetamines and Amphetamine-Like Compounds during Pregnancy

In spite of the media emphasis on the methamphetamine "epidemic" in this country, there is surprisingly little research into the specific effects of maternal amphetamine use on fetal growth and development (Finnegan & Kandall, 2005; Minnes et al., 2011). It is assumed that the effects of maternal amphetamine abuse are similar to those of maternal cocaine abuse; however, this is an unproven assumption (Finnegan & Kandall, 2005). It *is* known, however, that unlike babies born to mothers who are actively drinking, or abusing opioids, babies born to a mother who is abusing an amphetamine compound are *not* born "addicted" to the amphetamine[17] (Erickson, 2007).

There is evidence that women who abuse methamphetamine during pregnancy are more likely to be younger, live alone, have a lower income, a lower educational level, and receive less prenatal care than their nonabusing counterparts (Winslow, Voorhees, & Pehl, 2007). Once they learn that they are pregnant the majority of women attempt to decrease their frequency and level of methamphetamine abuse or stop it entirely (Terplan, Smith, Kozloski, & Pollack, 2009). They remain reluctant to seek prenatal care because of their fear of legal sanctions or the stigma associated with methamphetamine abuse or addiction.

Preliminary evidence suggests that infants exposed to amphetamine compounds *in utero* are more likely to experience premature birth, suffer from congenital brain lesions, and a visual cortex dysfunction (Brust, 2004; Cloak et al., 2009; Rawson & Ling, 2008). Infants born to methamphetamine-abusing mothers are 3.5 times as likely as control infants to be small for their gestational age (Minnes et al., 2011), which is an indirect measure of neurological growth and maturity on the baby at birth. Infants exposed to methamphetamine *in utero* were significantly more likely to demonstrate higher levels of emotional reactivity at ages 3 and 5, as well as higher levels of anxiety and depression than infants who were not exposed to this compound *in utero* (LaGasse et al.,

---

[17]However, because of the problem of polydrug abuse, it is still possible for the infant to be addicted to another compound(s) that the mother was abusing.

2012). There is also evidence that infants exposed to methamphetamine *in utero* have altered neurological function in the frontal striatal and limbic regions of the brain[18] (Sowell et al., 2010). The infant's risk of neurological harm appears to be dose related, with those infants with a greater degree of exposure having the highest degree of risk for neurological damage (Behnke et al., 2013; Erickson, 2007). However, further research is needed to confirm these initial findings. Indirect evidence suggests long-term (possibly lifelong) changes in DNA expression for the mother and the infant, leaving the infant vulnerable to diabetes or cancer later in life ("Hunger leaves its mark on fetal DNA," 2008). Animal research would also suggest that prenatal exposure to methamphetamine might predispose the infant to the neurotoxic effects of this compound later in life (Heller, Bubula, Lew, Heller, & Won, 2001). It is not known whether this occurs in humans or not at this time, but is suggestive of a vulnerability to methamphetamine neurotoxicity later in life. Again, further research is necessary both to confirm these theories and to trace the implications of these findings across the lifespan for both the mother and the infant.

There is a strong body of evidence suggesting that maternal use of methamphetamine is associated with such problems as anemia, premature birth, and a tendency for the placenta to separate from the wall of the uterus (Winslow et al., 2007). Other possible consequences of maternal methamphetamine abuse might include meconium aspiration, infection of the amniotic cavity, placental hemorrhage, and neonatal anemia. Following birth, there is evidence suggesting that the infant is vulnerable to psychosocial development problems, and frontal lobe dysfunction, as well as sleep abnormalities and birth defects such as a cleft lip (Brust, 2004). It is not known what percentage of methamphetamine-exposed infants will experience these (or other) problems. Erickson (2007) suggested that the majority of infants exposed to methamphetamine *in utero* will reach most normal developmental milestones on time.

The amphetamines induce a state of anorexia for the user, and maternal malnutrition potentially contributes to epigenetic[19] changes for the infant. These epigenetic changes appear to leave the infant vulnerable to diabetes or cancer later in life ("Hunger leaves its mark on

fetal DNA," 2008) and might leave the individual more vulnerable to the neurotoxic effects of alcohol later in life. Further research is necessary to confirm and explore the implications of these findings, which contradict research suggesting a low potential for long-term damage to the fetus if they (a) receive proper postdelivery medical care, (b) receive adequate parenting, and (c) are allowed appropriate social interactions with other children[20] (Erickson, 2007). Although it appears evident that amphetamine abuse does result in damage to the fetal brain, the issue of whether there are methamphetamine-specific consequences to the fetus remains unclear at this time.

Amphetamine Abuse and Breast Feeding

The problem of maternal amphetamine use during breast feeding has not been studied in detail. It is known that some amphetamine ingested by the mother will be found in the breast milk and can induce neonatal irritability and poor sleep.

Barbiturate and Barbiturate-Like Drug Abuse during Pregnancy

Fortunately compounds such as the barbiturates, glutethimide, meprobamate, and ethchlorvynol are only rarely prescribed, and because of this their abuse is thankfully now uncommon. All of these compounds cross the placenta into the fetal circulation (Mihic & Harris, 2011). If abused in high doses by the mother for a sufficient period of time, following birth, the infant will experience a neonatal withdrawal syndrome similar to that induced by alcohol. This infant neonatal withdrawal syndrome might require up to 4 days to develop after birth, depending on the exact compound(s) being abused and the total dose ingested by the mother. If the physician was unaware of the mother's substance use disorder, the neonatal withdrawal syndrome could be mistaken for hypoglycemia, sepsis, a range of cardiovascular disorders, or meningitis. Physicians have found that phenobarbital, a barbiturate with a long therapeutic half-life, will allow for the gradual withdrawal from these compounds for the infant *after* the health care provider becomes aware of the cause of the infant's distress.

---

[18]Regions where methamphetamine is known to have a neurotoxic effect in adults.

[19]Discussed in Chapter 25.

[20]Unfortunately, if the mother continues to abuse methamphetamine, her ability to provide these things would be compromised, leaving the child to suffer.

Benzodiazepine Use during Pregnancy

Research has shown that small amounts of the benzodiazepine ingested by the mother will cross the placenta and enter the fetal circulation, although the exact amount varies depending on the exact benzodiazepine being used. For example, fetal blood levels of diazepam will reach 10% of the maternal blood level, whereas lorazepam only reaches 7%. There are numerous antidotal case reports suggesting that benzodiazepine use during pregnancy can result in facial abnormalities such as cleft palate, congenital heart defects, hernias, and pyloric stenosis. However, the research has failed to support the theory that benzodiazepine use is the cause of these problems (Iqbal, Sobhan, & Ryals, 2002), and the teratogenic potential of benzodiazepines remains unclear at this time. It is recommended that when used during pregnancy the prescribing physician use the lowest possible dose for the shortest period of time (Iqbal et al., 2002; Raj & Sheehan, 2004). As with any medication, they should be used only when the potential benefits are thought to outweigh the possible risks of their use in the opinion of the attending physician.

Maternal benzodiazepine addiction, following birth, will force the infant to go through benzodiazepine withdrawal (Hudak, Tan, The Committee on Drugs, & The Committee on Fetus and Newborn, 2012). This withdrawal process is potentially life threatening for the infant, and the attending physician should be made aware of the mother's dependency on benzodiazepines to enable him or her to prescribe appropriate medications to avoid or control the poorly understood benzodiazepine neonatal withdrawal process.

Benzodiazepine Use during Breast Feeding

The known benzodiazepines will cross over from the maternal circulation into breast milk. However, the amount that crosses over into the infant's circulation at therapeutic doses is so small that these compounds were deemed safe for the nursing mother to use (Ciraulo & Knapp, 2009). However, maternal diazepam use has been identified as a possible cause of neonatal sedation and lethargy (Iqbal et al., 2002). The benzodiazepines are biotransformed in the liver, an organ that is not fully developed in the neonate, and so the prescribing physician must weigh the potential benefits of the benzodiazepine to the mother against the risks to the infant.

Buspirone Use during Pregnancy

It is not recommended that the expectant mother use buspirone unless a physician determines that the anticipated benefits outweigh the potential risks to the fetus. Animal research has suggested that there is an increased risk of stillbirth, but little evidence of long-term cognitive deficits in rats exposed to buspirone *in utero*.

Cigarette Smoking during Pregnancy

Each year in the United States approximately 4 million women give birth. Of this number, between 16.3% (Behnke et al., 2013) and 28.6% (Chang, 2010) smoked cigarettes while pregnant. The number of women who discontinue the use of cigarettes at least on a temporary basis when they discover that they are pregnant is not known (Substance Abuse and Mental Health Services Administration, 2009). Unfortunately, many women who do so expose the fetus to the large number of compounds found in cigarette smoke that are able to cross the placenta into the fetal circulation (Buka, Shenassa, & Niaura, 2003). Surprisingly pregnant women who smoke make up approximately 23% of the age cohort most likely to engage in reproductive activities (Behnke et al., 2013).

Some of the consequences of maternal smoking during pregnancy include low birth weight, premature rupture of the membranes, premature labor, abruptio placentae, myocardial infarction,[21] venal and arterial thrombosis, vitamin and mineral absorption problems, placenta previa, and SIDS (Bhuvaneswar & Chang, 2009; Brust, 2004; Burns, 2008; Chang, 2010; Minnes et al., 2011). Maternal cigarette use is thought to account for 20% of low–birth weight children, 8% of the cases of premature labor, and 5% of the cases of perinatal death each year in the United States. The causal mechanism for premature labor and for underweight infants is thought to be nicotine-induced constriction of the blood vessels in the placenta, reducing the flow of blood to the fetus. Emerging evidence does suggest that if the woman stops smoking in the early stages

---

[21]Admittedly a rare complication of pregnancy, being seen in only 1 in every 35,000 pregnancies.

of pregnancy, the fetus become less likely to be an underweight child at birth (McGowan et al., 2009).

There is a possible relationship between maternal cigarette smoking and the failure of the limbs to develop properly (*congenital limb deficiency*). There also is evidence suggesting that infants born to mothers who smoke have reduced lung capacity, although the causal mechanism(s) for this are not known. The team of Weitzman, Govil, Liu, and Lalwani (2013) uncovered evidence that adolescents whose mothers smoked during pregnancy were nearly three times as likely to experience a low frequency unilateral hearing loss during adolescence. Maternal smoking during pregnancy can induce epigenetic[22] changes on ten different genes in the genome of the fetus, including some involved in the metabolism of tobacco products (Joubrt et al., 2012).

Unexpectedly, there appears to be a relationship between maternal smoking during pregnancy and the child's weight during adolescence: Adolescents whose mother smoked during pregnancy have a higher risk of obesity (Haghigi et al., 2012). The authors speculate that this might reflect subtle changes in the reward system in the fetus that are not expressed until adolescence, but this weight condition might also reflect the epigenetic changes initiated by the mother's smoking before birth.

There has been some controversy about whether maternal cigarette smoking during pregnancy might be associated with behavioral problems (especially substance abuse such as cigarette smoking) during the child's adolescence (Buka et al., 2003; Guilbert & Krawiec, 2003; Keyes, Legrand, Iacono, & McGue, 2008; Minnes et al., 2011). However, it is not clear whether maternal cigarette smoking is a causal agent in the development of these problems or just a confounding variable. To explore this possibility the team of D'Onofrio et al. (2012) examined data from two large cohort studies, one in Sweden and the other in the United States, and concluded that the apparent association between maternal cigarette smoking and subsequent adolescent substance use problems were due to shared familial factors. In contrast, the team of Gaysina et al. (2013) found that children whose mothers reported having smoked during pregnancy were more likely to have conduct problems than children born of nonsmoking mothers. This was true even if the child was raised by an adopted parent. The

authors also found a correlation between the number of cigarettes smoked per day by the mother and the probability that the child would develop a conduct disorder later in life. This would suggest that maternal cigarette smoking was indeed related to later behavioral problems by the child/adolescent.

Prenatal Exposure to Environmental Tobacco Smoke

Women who are exposed to "secondhand smoke" while pregnant are at risk for vaginal bleeding (Centers for Disease Control and Prevention, 2004). Further, maternal cigarette use appears to increase the odds that the infant will develop asthma and a conduct disorder later in life. Fetal exposure to secondhand tobacco smoke was associated with an increased incidence of hearing loss later in life, although the mechanism through which exposure to environmental tobacco smoke is able to cause this outcome is still not known at this time (Weitzman et al., 2013).

An often overlooked venue for infant exposure to cigarette smoke is parental smoking in the motor vehicle (Nabi-Burza et al., 2012). The authors found that less than one-third of parents had a "no smoking in the car" policy that they enforced both upon themselves and upon passengers in the motor vehicle. Exposure to cigarette smoke in a small, confined, space such as a motor vehicle exposes the infant or child to significant levels of smoking-produced microscopic particles that remain in the air even if a window is open, according to the authors, who pointed out that exposure to these microscopic pollutants increase the infant/child's possibility of developing a respiratory tract infection, SIDS, ear infections, or asthma.

Smoking and Breast Feeding

It is recommended that the mother abstain from cigarette smoking if she plans to breast feed her infant. Nicotine tends to be concentrated in breast milk and has a half-life in breast milk of about 1.5 hours. The total nicotine concentration in the breast milk depends on the number of cigarettes that the mother smokes and the time between her last cigarette and the time that she breast-feeds the infant. Because nicotine is a stimulant, and stimulants tend to have an anorexic side effect, it is not surprising to learn that infants born to smoking mothers who breast-feed tend to gain weight more slowly than other infants.

[22]Discussed in Chapter 25.

Nicotine Replacement Therapy during Pregnancy

Intuitively one might expect that a nicotine replacement therapy for a pregnant woman would be contraindicated. However, in reality this is helpful to the fetus, because there are over 4,000 known compounds in cigarette smoke, many of which hold the potential to interfere with normal fetal growth and development. The nicotine replacement therapy will thus reduce fetal exposure to chemicals from over 4,000 to just 1, and thus the benefits outweigh the potential hazards to the fetus.

Bupropion Use during Pregnancy

Bupropion is often used as an aid to smoking cessation. Its safety during pregnancy has not been established, however, and the effects of this compound on fetal growth and development have not been studied in detail.

Cocaine Abuse during Pregnancy

During the peak of the last wave of cocaine abuse in the United States, it was estimated that 100,000 infants who were exposed to cocaine *in utero* were born each year (Minnes et al., 2011). The implications of such maternal cocaine abuse on fetal growth and development remain unclear as there is no cocaine-specific pattern of symptoms or organ damage that might identify the child exposed to cocaine *in utero*. During the peak years of the last wave of cocaine abuse in this country, newspapers made dire predictions of an epidemic of "Crack" (cocaine) babies about to descend on society. These children would bring with them a need for huge expenditures for special education and social service support according to the media (Malanga, 2009). Although an estimated 2 million people in this country were exposed to cocaine prior to birth (Minnes et al., 2011), there is little evidence that such an epidemic ever developed.

This is not to say that maternal cocaine abuse during pregnancy is safe. The research data on the effects of maternal cocaine use on the fetus are very limited. The research does suggest that the infant will experience "lasting, albeit subtle, effects of prenatal drug exposure on brain structure" (Malanga, 2009, p. 2062). Stanwood and Levitt (2007) found, for example, evidence of permanent structural changes in the brains

of animals exposed to cocaine *in utero*. It has been found that the abuse of cocaine during pregnancy alters the normal pattern of development of the monoaminergic transmitters.[23] Such studies do suggest that maternal cocaine use has a strong negative impact on fetal growth. Unfortunately, every effect once attributed to prenatal cocaine exposure has subsequently been found to be caused by such factors as instability within the family unit, poor maternal nutrition, maternal depression, concurrent abuse of other compounds, lack of prenatal care, etc. (Ackerman, Riggins, & Black, 2010; Mendelson & Mello, 2010; Minnes et al., 2011). For example, it was once believed that maternal cocaine abuse induced a condition of placenta previa.[24] However, most cocaine abusers also smoke cigarettes, and cigarette smokers have a 2.3-fold higher incidence of placenta previa than nonsmokers. Further, most cocaine-abusing mothers engage in polydrug abuse and that half of pregnant cocaine abusers also consumed alcohol, a known toxin.

In the 1980s, many states enacted laws that mandated incarceration for the expectant mother who abused cocaine to protect the fetus. Such laws had an unintended effect. Many pregnant cocaine-abusing women stopped seeking prenatal health care to avoid the danger of prosecution. Other women feared that stigma associated with prenatal cocaine abuse, and did not admit to the abuse of cocaine when asked (Zilberman, 2009). Another unintended consequence of such protect-the-fetus laws is that the first medical care that many women receive during pregnancy is when they arrived at the hospital in labor. This lack of prenatal medical care contributes to the problem isolating cocaine's effects on the developing fetus.

Known and Suspected Effects of Maternal Cocaine Abuse

As the information reviewed above suggests, there is much to be discovered about the effects of prenatal cocaine exposure on fetal development. It is known that cocaine interferes with the normal transfer of amino acids in the placenta, but the significance on the fetus remains unknown (Karch, 2009). Because of the developmental immaturity of the infant's body

---

[23]A family of neurotransmitters that share chemical similarities. Dopamine is a member of this class of neurotransmitters.

[24]A condition involving the placement of the placenta in the uterus that can cause very severe bleeding during labor and delivery.

however, the cocaine that is absorbed will remain in the infant's blood for days after birth because the infant lacks the ability to rapidly biotransform cocaine (Karch, 2009). The impact of this cocaine exposure on the fetal growth remains unknown.

The team of Myers et al. (2003) attempted to identify a fetal cocaine-exposure syndrome by using the Brazelton Neonatal Behavioral Assessment Scale to compare infants who were and were not exposed to cocaine in utero. The authors failed to find any significant differences between these two groups of infants. Where researchers have identified differences between infants who were and were not exposed to cocaine in utero, these differences have been small in magnitude. For example, the team of Butz et al. (2005) measured the head circumference of infants exposed to cocaine and heroin in utero and at selected ages following birth. At age 3, the authors administered a standardized IQ test to the infants. The 204 infants who had been exposed to heroin and/or cocaine had smaller head circumference(s) at birth, but by the age of 3 years this difference had disappeared. Further, the authors found that both groups of children had similar IQs. These findings were similar to those of Ackerman et al. (2010), who found that observed differences between infants who were and were not exposed to cocaine in utero were both small and strongly influenced by environmental factors. Although the authors identified a pattern of the 6-year-old children studied having trouble focusing attention on problems and behavioral self-control problems, it remains to be proven that such problems result in permanent behavioral or cognitive problems according to the authors.

There is limited data that does suggest that children exposed to cocaine in utero might suffer developmental delays in such areas as psychomotor skills, language use, and overall mental development (Finnegan & Kandall, 2004; Lewis et al., 2004). There is also evidence that pre-birth cocaine exposure might be associated with: spontaneous abortion, abruptio placentae, low birth weight, strokes in the fetus, disruption in normal uterine blood flow patterns (which may initiate premature labor in some cases), increased frequency of respiratory distress syndrome following birth, malformations of the genito-urinary tract, and infarction of the arteries providing blood to the bowels (Acosta, Haller, & Schnoll, 2005; Finnegan & Kandall, 2005; Gold & Jacobs, 2005; Johnson, 2003; Karch, 2009; Keller & Keller-Snyder, 2000; Moffett, 2006; Oehmichen, Auer, & Konig, 2005).

There is also mixed evidence suggesting that the infant exposed to cocaine in utero might be at increased risk for the subsequent development of SIDS (Finegan & Kandall, 2005). Karch (2009) reported that approximately 20% of infants exposed to cocaine in utero will grow up to develop attention deficit-hyperactivity disorder. The infant exposed to cocaine in utero was approximately twice as likely to meet the diagnostic criteria for a condition known as oppositional defiant disorder than those children not exposed to cocaine in utero (17% versus 9%).

Cocaine and Breast Feeding

The data on the effects of maternal cocaine use on the breast-feeding infant are very limited (Zilberman, 2009). The cocaine molecule is highly lipid soluble, and it may be stored in breast milk and then passed on to the infant by the mother during breast feeding. The cocaine concentration might be *eight times* as high in breast milk as it is in the mother's blood, and for this reason maternal cocaine abuse during the period when she is breast feeding is to be discouraged.

Hallucinogen Abuse during Pregnancy

There is only limited research into the effects of maternal hallucinogen abuse on fetal growth and development (Kandall, 1999). What will follow is a brief description of the effects of the most commonly abused hallucinogens on the fetus. It is important to keep in mind that other hallucinogens might also be abused, and it is impossible to list every possible hallucinogen, and every possible effect of each on fetal growth and development. However, because so little is known about the pharmacokinetics of the hallucinogens, the use of these compounds by the nursing mother is *not* recommended.

LSD Abuse during Pregnancy

Virtually nothing is known about the effects of LSD abuse on fetal growth and development. It is, however, not recommended that nursing mothers use this compound, if only because its effects remain unknown.

MDMA Abuse during Pregnancy

Preliminary research into the effects of MDMA on the fetus would suggest that congenital growth problems are five times more common in the infants of MDMA abusing mothers than is normal. The mechanism by which MDMA might cause or contribute to congenital birth defects is not known at this time, and there is a need for further research into the effects of MDMA on the developing fetus.

PCP Abuse during Pregnancy

At most, there is limited information on the effects of phencyclidine on the fetus. The available evidence would suggest that infants exposed to PCP *in utero* are at increased risk for conditions such as hydrocephalus, sleep respiratory problems, and abnormal development of different body organs such as the heart, lungs, urinary system, or the musculoskeletal system (Brust, 2004). Immediately following birth, infants born to PCP abusing mothers demonstrate abrupt changes in their level of consciousness, fine motor tremors, sweating, and irritability. There is a possibility that some or all of these effects are caused by polydrug abuse rather than the abuse of PCP alone.

Salvia Divinorum Use during Pregnancy

Virtually nothing is known about the pharmacokinetics of this compound and its use prior to or during pregnancy is *not* recommended.

Inhalant Abuse during Pregnancy

Each year in the United States, 12,000 pregnant women are thought to abuse an inhalant at least once (Brust, 2004). Surprisingly, there has been virtually no research into the effects of inhalants on fetal growth and development. Current evidence does suggest that inhalant abuse is a cause of growth retardation *in utero*, developmental abnormalities; fetal death, neurodevelopmental problems, tremor and ataxia following birth, as well as smaller birth weight and increased risk of SIDS (Sharp & Rosenberg, 2005). The effects of toluene, which is known to cross the placenta, are unknown because this topic has not been subjected to clinical research. However, liver of the fetus and newborn is still quite immature and unable to metabolize toluene. There is preliminary evidence to suggest that toluene exposure during pregnancy can cause a syndrome similar to the fetal alcohol spectrum disorder (discussed previously). Bowen, Batis, Mohammadi, and Hannigan (2005)

exposed pregnant rats to toluene fumes and found that the "pups" suffered from growth restriction as well as a range of physical abnormalities. These are only preliminary results, but until proven otherwise toluene exposure by pregnant women should be avoided.

Marijuana Use during Pregnancy

There is only limited research data on the effects of maternal marijuana use on fetal growth and development (Bhuvaneswar & Chang, 2009; Finnegan & Kandall, 2004). The placenta is able to provide the fetus with some degree of protection against marijuana, and fetal blood levels of THC[25] are estimated to only reach one-sixth those of the mother (Nelson, 2000). However, even these low levels of THC potentially can have dire consequences on the fetus.

There is evidence based on animal research that the endocannabinoid anandamide helps to guide both the specification of what are known as pyramidal cells and the pattern of axon growth in neurons as cortical neural networks are established. Marijuana abuse during pregnancy holds the potential to interfere with the normal endocannabinoid function in the fetal brain, possibly causing long-term (if not permanent) changes in the brain's physical structure (Gold & Dupont, 2008). This might be the mechanism through which the subtle neuropsychological deficits reported by Zilberman (2009) develop. Also, marijuana abuse by the mother during pregnancy might potentially alter the development of receptor site patterns within the fetal brain, again possibly with lifelong consequences for the unborn child (Behnke et al., 2013).

Admittedly, it is difficult to isolate the effects of maternal marijuana abuse from the effects of tobacco or other drugs of abuse. It is rare for a mother-to-be to abuse only marijuana, and concurrent cigarette smoking is a complicating factor. Other variables that must be considered include (a) the potency of the marijuana being smoked, (b) the frequency of maternal marijuana use, (c) how deeply the mother inhaled when she did smoke marijuana, and (d) what other compounds (pesticides, for example) intermixed with the marijuana smoked. Finally, although it is assumed that THC is the only compound that will impact fetal growth and development, marijuana smoke contains a number of

---

[25]See Chapter 10.

different compounds and their impact on fetal growth and development has not been studied.

In spite of these unknown variables, scientists have tentatively concluded that children whose mothers abused marijuana during pregnancy are at higher risk for maladaptive social behaviors, cognitive problems, and psychomotor skills following birth (Gold & Dupont, 2008). They were also found to have lower reading comprehension skills at age 10 years (Goldschmidt, Richardson, Cornelius, & Day, 2004). This finding must be interpreted with caution however, because there are numerous other variables that might also affect the child's reading comprehension skills at the age of 10 besides maternal marijuana use. There is also evidence that children exposed to marijuana smoke *in utero* demonstrate abnormal tremors, startle reflexes, and eye reflex problems. Women who have smoked marijuana at least once a month are also thought to be at higher risk for premature labor, having children with lower birth weights, who have a higher risk of ventricular septal defects, and children who were smaller than normal for their gestational age (Bhuvaneswar & Chang, 2009). However, again, the separation of the effects of possible maternal cigarette smoking from maternal marijuana use makes these conclusions quite tentative.

In Jamaica, where heavy maternal marijuana use is common, researchers have failed to find any major differences between a group of infants exposed to marijuana *in utero* and a group of infants who were not exposed to marijuana during gestation (Dreher, Nugent, & Hudgins, 1994). Where the authors did find differences between these two groups, it was noted that they could be attributed to the mother's social status, the number of adults living in the household, the number of other children competing for the mother's attention, or other environmental factors rather than maternal marijuana use.

It is not known whether the effects of maternal marijuana use will manifest shortly following birth or later in the child's life. Given the crucial role of anandamide in guiding neural growth and development during corticogenesis, it should not be surprising to discover that there is evidence of prefrontal lobe dysfunction in children exposed to marijuana *in utero* that did not manifest until the child was 6–9 years of age. But there is much to be discovered about the effects of marijuana use during pregnancy and the long-term outcome for the child exposed to marijuana *in utero*.

Marijuana and Breast Feeding

There is no data suggesting that maternal marijuana abuse during breast feeding has any effect on the infant. Before birth the placenta provides some degree of protection against THC absorption. However, this compound is concentrated in breast milk and research has revealed that the THC level in breast milk is six times higher than that found in the mother's blood level (Nelson, 2000). Given the small size of the infant and the higher concentration of THC in the breast milk, the possibility exists that the infant will be exposed to significant levels of THC at a time when corticogenesis is still progressing. Thus, maternal marijuana use both during pregnancy and following birth is to be avoided.

Narcotic Analgesic Abuse during Pregnancy

There are no reliable estimates of the scope of maternal opiate abuse/addiction during pregnancy, however, Patrick et al. (2012) estimated that 3.39 of every 1,000 infants are born to mothers who are addicted to narcotics. These infant(s) are unwitting participants in the problem of opiate dependence who will be forced to go through opiate withdrawal following birth. Attempts to estimate the scope of the problem of narcotics abuse during pregnancy are complicated because (1) it is standard practice to administer narcotic analgesics during labor and (2) it is not unusual for the pregnant opioid abuser to switch to fentanyl because its potency makes it hard to detect on standard urine toxicology tests (Bhuvaneswar & Chang, 2009). Their continued opioid abuse during pregnancy potentially can remain undetected unless a health care professional were to request a test specifically to detect fentanyl. In addition (3), a number of women are directed to use a narcotic analgesic by their physician at least once during the period of pregnancy.

Although limited exposure to opioids under a physician's supervision appears to present minimal danger to the fetus, long-term exposure to this class of drugs, interspaced with periods of abstinence when the mother was unable to obtain drugs to abuse, does appear to hold the potential to harm the fetus. Notice that the word "potential" was used in the last sentence: There is little research into the possible long-term consequences of maternal opioid use or during pregnancy (Bhuvaneswar & Chang, 2009).

Statement of the Problem

Estimates of prenatal narcotic exposure are difficult to obtain and vary from 1 to 21% of infants (Minnes et al., 2011). It is possible that much of this variability depends on whether prescribed narcotics are included as a source of prenatal opiate exposure or not. For opiate abusing women many of the early symptoms of pregnancy, the feelings of fatigue, nausea, vomiting, pelvic cramps, and hot sweats, might be interpreted as early withdrawal symptoms rather than early symptoms of pregnancy (Bhuvaneswar & Chang, 2009; Kieser, 2005; "Medication-Assisted Treatment (MAD) during pregnancy—part 1," 2009). Unless the woman were to confirm the possibility of pregnancy through one of the commercially available "in home" pregnancy tests or medical examination, there is a danger that the opiate-dependent woman will attempt to self-medicate what is perceived to be early withdrawal symptoms by taking even higher doses of narcotics. This results in higher levels of fetal exposure to both the compound(s) being abused and the adulterants that are often mixed in with illicit drugs, plus an increased risk for the various infections inherent in the practice of illicit drug abuse.[26]

If the woman were to request a medical examination to determine whether she is pregnancy, she will find that even physicians experienced in the treatment of narcotics addiction often find it difficult to diagnose early pregnancy in this subgroup of women. The decision to seek out a medical examination is fraught with danger, however, because in many communities the physician is required to report the woman's pregnancy to the authorities so that appropriate steps might be taken to protect the fetus during this all-important developmental period.

To complicate matters, even under the best of conditions pregnancy carries with it the potential for life-threatening complications for the woman. If she has a history of narcotics abuse, the potential for developing one or more of these complications is increased. Some of the medical problems that might develop during pregnancy in the narcotics-addicted woman include those listed in Table 17-1 (Bhuvaneswar & Chang, 2009; Finnegan & Kandall, 2004, 2005; Kieser, 2005).

If the mother should have or acquire an infection during pregnancy, there is the additional risk that she will pass the infection on to the fetus prior to birth.

TABLE 17-1 Potential Complications for Mother and/or Infant When Mother Is Opiate Dependent
Potential complications for mother and/or fetus
anemia
stillbirth
breach presentation during delivery
placental insufficiency
spontaneous abortions
premature delivery
neonatal meconium aspiration syndrome (which may be fatal to the infant)
amenorrhea
postpartum hemorrhage
neonatal infections acquired from mother
lower birth weight
neonatal narcotics addiction/withdrawal
maternal diabetes
increased risk of SIDS

© Cengage Learning

Such infections are potentially fatal to the fetus as well as to the mother. For example, approximately 30% of those women who abuse illicit opiates and are pregnant develop bacterial endocarditis, a potentially fatal infection. Approximately the same percentage of pregnancies in women who abuse or who are addicted to narcotics end in fetal death (Bhuvaneswar & Chang, 2009). A high percentage of women who have viral hepatitis or HIV pass the virus on to their infant either during gestation or during the process of giving birth, a process known as *vertical transmission*.

To limit the risk to both the mother and neonate, physicians now believe that the mother should *not* be withdrawn from opiates during pregnancy. It is recommended that the mother be stabilized on methadone or buprenorphine to normalize the intrauterine environment (Bhuvaneswar & Chang, 2009; Jones et al., 2010; Polydorou & Kleber, 2008). This reduces the incentive for the mother to abuse other drugs, and there is evidence that suggests that children whose mother had been stabilized on an opioid agonist experience longer gestation periods and are heavier at birth (Finnegan & Kandall, 2005). There is some evidence that infants

---

[26]Discussed in Chapter 34.

whose mothers were stabilized on methadone had some visual problems following birth; however, the role of methadone (as opposed to other drugs of abuse) in the development of such problems, and the time before such problems resolve, is still unknown (Hamilton et al., 2010). There is also an emerging body of evidence suggesting that the opioid agonist buprenorphine administered during pregnancy to stabilize the mother's opiate addiction might allow the infant to experience less distress during the neonatal opioid withdrawal process (Jones et al., 2010; Whitten, 2012a).

A little known fact is that the half-life of methadone is reduced by about one-third in the mother, possibly as a result of hormone-related changes in the mother's body during pregnancy (Stout, 2009). Thus, methadone stabilization should only be attempted by a physician experienced in this process. Following birth, the infant and mother can then safely be detoxified from opiates. In the case of the infant, morphine is the opioid of choice neonatal opiate withdrawal. Some physicians also like to use a barbiturate during the withdrawal process, to avoid possible withdrawal-related seizures (Kieser, 2005).

Maternal addiction to narcotics means that the infant will also be addicted to these compounds following birth. The infant will be forced to go through the neonatal opioid withdrawal syndrome. Prior to the development of effective treatment protocols for the neonatal opioid withdrawal syndrome this condition carried up to a 90% mortality rate for the infant unwillingly thrust into the opioid withdrawal process (Brust, 2004). The risk of premature death has dropped significantly since effective treatments were developed, but has not been eliminated entirely. The neonatal opioid withdrawal syndrome begins within 24–72 hours of birth (depending on the specific compounds being abused by the mother) and has both an acute and extended phase. The *acute* phase of neonatal opioid withdrawal will last as long as three to six weeks.[27] During this time, the infant will demonstrate such symptoms as (Finnegan & Kandall, 2008, 2005; Kieser, 2005): yawning, wakefulness, watery eyes, fever, shrill or high pitched cry, stuffy/runny nose, salivation, hiccups, vomiting, diarrhea, poor weight gain, apnea, sneezing, tremors, and seizures.

The second phase of neonatal withdrawal, the extended phase, might last for four to six months. During this phase the infant might demonstrate such symptoms as restlessness, agitation, tremors, and sleep disturbance. These behaviors will add stress to the mother, who might be in the early stages of recovery from a substance use disorder, thus serving as a relapse trigger for the mother. Such infant behaviors also might interfere with the "bonding" process between mother and infant at a time when it is of critical importance (Kerrigan, 2008). As the information reviewed above suggests maternal opiate abuse/addiction is quite dangerous for the infant.

Maternal Narcotics Abuse and Breast Feeding

The narcotics, including heroin, do pass into breast milk, and thus the infant is exposed to the mother's narcotics abuse if she should breast-feed her children. During this phase of life, the infant's liver is still rather immature, and not fully functioning, theoretically allowing narcotics to build up in the infant's body between periods of active feeding. Theoretically, prolonged periods of maternal narcotics abuse during the time that she is breast feeding might cause the infant to become sleepy, eat poorly, and possibly develop respiratory depression from the trace amounts of the opioids being abused found in maternal milk.

Research has demonstrated, however, that breast-feeding mothers who are using morphine under a physician's supervision can do so safely because only a minimal amount of morphine is concentrated in breast milk, and an even smaller proportion of the morphine ingested by the infant will actually reach the baby's circulation (Hale, 2003). The concentration of narcotic analgesics such as methadone in breast milk is less than 1% (Kieser, 2005) and 3% (Schottenfeld, 2008) of the mother's blood level, and there is evidence that suggests that breast feeding during the first days following birth may help the physical distress experienced by the infant going through the opiate withdrawal syndrome (Paradowski, 2008). However, it is recommended that mothers using meperidine not breast-feed, as this medication can cause the infant to become oversedated (Hale, 2003).

However, as researchers learn more about the pharmacokinetics of codeine, it is becoming more clearer that individual genetic variations in the infant might make the child exceptionally vulnerable to the CNS

---

[27]Depending on the opioids being abused by the mother, Bhuvaneswar & Chang (2009) suggested that the first phase of the neonatal opioid withdrawal syndrome might last as long as 10 weeks.

depressant effects of codeine (MacDonald & MacLeod, 2010). Age is an apparent factor in the vulnerability to codeine's toxic effects in part because the blood–brain barrier is still relatively immature in the infant, and there have been reports of toxic reactions to codeine in infants whose mother was prescribed this compound for mild pain. This is true in spite of the fact that the level of codeine in the breast milk is only 5% of the mother's blood level (Hale, 2003). Thus the use of codeine should be considered by the physician only when the potential benefit outweighs the potential risks.

Over-the-Counter Analgesic Use during Pregnancy

Aspirin

Aspirin has been found to cross the placenta and thus enter the fetal circulation. Because of this, women who are, or who suspect that they might be, pregnant should not use aspirin except under a physician's supervision (Black & Hill, 2003; Wilson, Shannon, Shields, & Stang, 2007). There is a body of evidence that suggests that aspirin use during pregnancy might be a cause of stillbirth and increased perinatal mortality. Further, aspirin use by the mother might be a factor in the development of fetal anemia, retarded intrauterine growth, and antepartum and/or postpartum bleeding, especially if the mother should ingest the aspirin the week prior to delivery. The risk of bleeding is not limited to the fetus, for aspirin will also interfere with the mother's ability to form blood clots, which may place her life at risk during labor and delivery.

Acetaminophen

Physicians have recommend acetaminophen as an alternative to the use of aspirin during pregnancy (Black & Hill, 2003). However, there is preliminary evidence suggesting that exposure to acetaminophen *in utero* might increase the infant's risk of developing asthma in childhood (Beasley et al., 2008). Obviously, it will be necessary to examine this issue in more detail, and for now it is recommended that acetaminophen only be used under a physician's supervision.

Although low levels of acetaminophen are found in breast milk, there is no evidence at this time suggesting that this exposure has an adverse effect on the fetus, as long as the acetaminophen is used in appropriate doses.

However, as always, the breast-feeding mother should contact her health care provider to discuss whether it is safe to use any medication while she is nursing.

Ibuprofen

There has been limited research into the effects of the propionic acids on fetal growth and development (Black & Hill, 2003). The authors recommended that ibuprofen or similar compounds be used during pregnancy only upon the advice of a physician, because there is some research data that suggests that these compounds may prolong labor and possibly cause other effects on the developing fetus.

There is little evidence suggesting that ibuprofen enters human breast milk in sufficient quantities to cause problems for the newborn, when used at appropriate dosage levels (Hale, 2003). However, as always, the breast-feeding mother should contact her health care provider to discuss whether it is safe to use any medication while she is nursing.

Chapter Summary

If a woman with a substance use disorder were to become pregnant, the fetus that she carries would become an unwilling participant in the mother's SUD because the majority of the drugs of abuse cross the placenta and enter the fetal circulation. These compounds are often teratogenic, thus holding the potential to harm the fetus during gestation. This is especially true in the first trimester of pregnancy, which is a period of special vulnerability for the fetus. It is during this trimester that organ differentiation and the process of corticogenesis are underway. Disruption of these processes would potentially have lifelong consequences for the infant following birth.

If the mother were physically addicted to a compound(s), the infant might very well be born with a physical addiction to the same compounds. Indeed, if the mother were to have been drinking alcohol immediately prior to birth, it may be possible to smell alcohol on the infant's breath following delivery. Each compound presents a special range of potential dangers to both the mother and the fetus, and even the over-the-counter analgesics have been found to have a significant teratogenic potential in some cases. The more significant of these risk factors, and the compounds that might cause these complications, are reviewed in this chapter.

CHAPTER 18

Gender and Substance Use Disorders

Until very recently, drug abuse has been viewed as a marginal issue for women and portrayed largely as a male problem.

—*Fox and Sinha (2009, p. 65)*

Introduction

The issue of substance use disorders in women has long been overlooked by society. This oversight was fueled, in part, by the fact that for many years women were less likely to use illicit drugs than men (Anthes, 2010). However, women are closing the gender gap in the addictions. Epidemiological data currently suggest that 13.8% of men and 7.1% of women will struggle with a substance use disorder (SUD) at some point in their lives. This gap is slowly growing smaller with each generation as the abuse of alcohol and illicit drugs has become more socially acceptable (Anthes, 2010). These facts suggest that the SUDs in women are hardly a "marginal" issue, and given the woman's role as primary caregiver for the child, it is of extreme importance. The goal of this chapter is to try to dispel some of these stereotypes and to examine the forces that help shape the growth of substance use disorders in women.

Gender and Addiction: The Lessons of History

It is unfortunately true that the lens of history distorts events from the distant past and only rarely allows us to identify the parallels between a past situation and an evolving problem in time to avoid re-creating the same mistake(s) that fill our history books. An example of how the lens of history distorts images from the past is the social belief that most of those who were addicted to "patent" medicines at the turn of the 19th century were women. In reality, one-third of the total number of those persons who had become addicted to a "patent" medicine before the year 1900 were men, a fact that is rarely mentioned in the history books. This omission illustrates the double standard for men and women with an SUD that existed up until recently. Women who abused,

or were addicted to, a drug of abuse were[1] subjected to a greater degree of social condemnation than men (Lynch, Potenza, Cosgrove, & Mazure, 2009). Paradoxically, their substance use disorder was viewed for many years as being less important than that of men (Cohen, 2000; Jerslid, 2001). The net result of this process is that information on the natural history, clinical presentation, physiology, and treatment of substance use disorders in women is limited (Work Group on Substance Use Disorders, 2007, p. 44).

In the face of this lack of research data, clinicians struggle to find effective treatments for the increasing number of women who are seeking substance abuse treatment. Only 40% of rehabilitation programs provide any form of gender-specific treatment for individuals

---

[1]And, some would argue, still are subjected to a greater degree of social condemnation because they have a substance use disorder.

with an SUD and many programs utilize a "one size fits all" approach to substance abuse rehabilitation. Regrettably, just as society is starting to develop an awareness of the scope of the substance use disorders in women, advertising companies have come to view women as an untapped market for alcohol use. Increasingly, advertising companies target women with gender-specific advertisements. Alcohol use is portrayed as a sophisticated way to enjoy the company of friends, and its use is encouraged. This weakens the social prohibition against alcohol use, increasing the possibility that some women will engage in heavier alcohol use. A concurrent historical coincidence is that the other drugs of abuse have become more easily available in spite of efforts to interdict them or suppress the illicit drug trade. These factors all contribute to a growing substance abuse problem for women.

Statement of the Problem

For generations, society has struggled to understand the relationship between women and substance use. For generations, society's response to the problem of substance abuse by women has been to hide the issue, protect the individual, or totally isolate her from social and/or family support (Blume & Zilberman, 2004, 2005b; Cohen, 2000). This attitude is slowly changing, which is a welcome change in social attitudes because it is estimated that 6.5 million women in the United States struggle with a substance use disorder (Tracy, Munson, Peterson, & Floersch, 2010). However, the change is not complete and a double standard still exists. In the eyes of many, a woman who orders an alcohol-containing beverage at a public event will be perceived by both men and women as being more sexually available than a man who orders the same beverage, for example (Carr & Szymanski, 2011).

Social support systems, including peers influence on the individual's substance use behaviors. If a woman has a close associate who drinks heavily, for example, she is herself more likely to both drink heavily and associate with those who drink heavily (Rosenquist, Murabito, Fowler, & Christakis, 2010). Age cohort membership is another factor that influences the individual's substance use decisions as reflected by the data in Table 18-1, which isolate substance use disorders in women by age cohort membership.

Physicians and even peers do not always recognize the woman who has developed an SUD (Brady, Tolliver, & Verduin, 2007). It is not known whether

TABLE 18-1 Age Cohort Distribution of Substance Use Disorders in Women	
AGE COHORT	**PERCENTAGE OF WOMEN ABUSING ALCOHOL OR DRUGS**
18–25 years	15.70%
26–34 years	8.90%
35–49 years	5%
50 years and above	1.50%

Source: Based on "Substance abuse and dependence among women" (2005).

this reflects the social denial that existed in earlier generations, a lack of recognition skills among physicians and friends, or possibly a combination of these two factors. This lack of recognition does leave the woman with untreated SUDs vulnerable to the direct and indirect negative effects of substance abuse. Women with an alcohol use disorder (AUD), for example, are thought to be 23 times more likely to commit suicide as their nondrinking counterparts (Markarian & Franklin, 2005), whereas women with a drug use problem are 50–100% more likely to die as a result of their SUD, when compared to women the same age who do not abuse chemicals (Fox & Sinha, 2009).

The addictions have never been a popular area for clinical research, and for much of the 20th century the limited research carried out in the field of the addictions focused exclusively on *male* subjects. The findings were then generalized to women with a substance use disorder. Only now is it being acknowledged that hormonal, pharmacokinetic, neurochemical, and social factors alter a woman's ability to biotransform a drug of abuse, and affect her vulnerability to and recovery from substance use disorders (Carr & Szymanski, 2011; Lynch et al., 2009). Although gender-specific treatment programs are of value in the rehabilitation of the substance abusing woman, there is limited access to such programs in many parts of the country (Sinha, 2000).

The "Convergence" Theory

The "convergence" theory holds that the percentage of women with an SUD is slowly approaching that of men. There are many reasons for this convergence in substance use disorder rates. This theory is based on the mistaken assumption that substance use disorders for women at the start of the 20th century were rare and only became more common during the last quarter of the past century. Yet as was discussed earlier in this text, the majority of those who were addicted to a "patent" medication at the start of the 20th century were women, suggesting that the substance use disorders in women of that era manifested in different ways than was true for men. Further, given that a woman with a substance use disorder is less likely to be identified than a man with a similar SUD, this raises questions about the accuracy of the data on which the convergence theory is based.

Current research data suggest that the time from period of first use to the development of physical dependence on that compound is *increasing* for women (Keyes, Martins, Blanco, & Hasin, 2010). Indirectly, the results of this study support the "convergence" theory: Like their male counterparts, substance abusing women are more accepting of recreational chemical use and trying more chemicals before potentially developing a substance use disorder. More evidence supporting the convergence theory might be found in research revealing that 8.1% of adolescent girls and 8.0% of adolescent boys will develop a substance use disorder at some point during adolescence (Upadhyaya & Gray, 2009). Further, the number of fatal car accidents involving 19- to 24-year-old women, an indirect measure of substance abuse, has increased in the past few years (Tsai, Anderson, & Vaca, 2010). Thus, there does appear to be evidence supporting the convergence theory that male and female substance abusers are starting to experience the negative consequences of their SUD at a similar age, especially for younger age cohorts.

Does Gender Affect the Rehabilitation Process?

For a variety of reasons the answer to this question is: Yes! Women who enter substance abuse rehabilitation are more likely to suffer from a psychiatric disorder that predates the development of their SUD (Brady & Back, 2008). Further, sexual dimorphism in brain development raises questions whether the assumption that the neurological mechanisms of substance-induced reward is the same for men and women. Current evidence suggests different brain activation patterns for each sex when exposed to the drugs of abuse (Pigott, Walker, Tietelbaum, & Lu, 2009). Women's brains

appear to be more receptive to the rewarding effects of alcohol and the drugs of abuse when blood estrogen levels are higher by making the reward system of the brain more responsive to stimulation (Anthes, 2010; Lynch et al., 2009). Such a monthly variation in reward sensitivity has not been noted in men with a SUD. The woman's body also appears to break down alcohol and illicit drugs in a slightly different manner than does the man's. The liver's P-450 metabolic pathway is involved in the biotransformation of approximately 80% of all drugs (DeVane, 2009). However, there are differences between sexes in how the P-450 pathway functions, as well as wide interindividual variability, all factors that influence the biotransformation of various compounds (DeVane, 2009).

There are neurological differences between how each sex responds to the various drugs of abuse, very few of which have been explored. It is known that the brain of a woman has a different pattern of dopamine transporter molecules in certain regions of the brain as compared to those of a man. This potentially alters the reinforcement potential of a given drug of abuse for women. Because of this process, it has been suggested that women might become addicted to a drug(s) of abuse after less exposure to that compound than would be true for a man (Lynch et al., 2009). This theory is supported by the observation that female rats learn to self-administer drugs more rapidly than do male rats (Whitten, 2012a).

Then there are the social factors that influence how a person of either sex would fare in a treatment program. Women are less likely than men to enter a substance abuse rehabilitation program, in part because of social barriers that prevent them from doing so (Gordon, 2007). Social stigmatization is another factor that affects how women and men view entry into drug rehabilitation treatment, although the stigma against SUDs in women is lower in younger age cohorts (Lynch et al., 2009). External barriers to treatment admission include having sole possession of children following divorce (or termination of a relationship), limited funding for treatment, or a spouse who also has an SUD, all of which might make recovery more difficult for the woman (Blume & Zilberman 2004, 2005a, 2005b; Gordon, 2007). Although it is recognized that single parenthood is the barrier to treatment, few treatment programs have provisions for a woman who has custody of children (Blume & Zilberman, 2004; Ringwald, 2002). The financial cost of substance abuse rehabilitation also serves as an external barrier to treatment for women who are divorced because they frequently lack access to health care insurance after their divorce.

Another barrier to treatment is that women who enter a rehabilitation program tend to have a smaller social support circle, often discovering that friends, family, employers, and society are less tolerant of a woman with an SUD than for a man with the same problem (Gordon, 2007). Intuitively, it would be expected that an important source of social support for the woman with an SUD would be the spouse or significant other. Consistent with this expectation is the finding that being divorced is a risk factor for SUDs for women between the ages of 30 and 40. Surprisingly, being *married* is a risk factor for women between the ages of 40 and 50! The reason for this discrepancy is not known, but it is hypothesized that this reflects age cohort differences. However, for both age groups, women with an SUD usually receive less support from their partner for efforts to recover than do men, increasing their potential for relapse (Green, 2006). It is for these reasons that marital therapy is often a useful adjunct to the woman's treatment program (Fals-Stewart, Lam, & Kelley, 2009).

Where men are most often introduced to drug(s) of abuse by peers, women commonly report that they were introduced to drug(s) of abuse by their partner who then serves as their main source of supply for the desired compound(s) (Blume & Zilberman, 2005a, 2005b; Small, Fast, Krusi, Wood, & Kerr, 2009). This pattern might extend to alcohol as well as the drugs of abuse because there is less social stigma attached to a man buying a large bottle of liquor than to a woman doing so. This is one mechanism through which a woman's substance use disorder might be rendered "invisible" to others. Another manner in which the SUDs in women are rendered invisible is the fact that many women obtain desired medications from physicians. Thus, they are not viewed by society as "addicts" but as "patients."

Also, men and women tend to follow different pathways into treatment. Women are more likely to use the resources of a health care, clergy, or mental health professional at first, and only if their SUD is identified are they referred to a rehabilitation program (Blume & Zilberman, 2005a; Friemuth, 2005; Green, 2006). This tendency for women with SUDs to seek assistance from mental health professionals might be explained, at least in part, by the tendency for women to suffer from depression and/or anxiety disorders more often than do men. These are conditions that frequently result in referrals to health care or mental health services (Blume & Zilberman, 2005a, 2005b; Dixit & Crum, 2000; Green, 2006). Women who have an AUD are seven times as likely to suffer from depression as are men with an AUD, for example (Brady & Back, 2008). Although these referrals to mental health professionals are useful, such "indirect" treatment of the SUD is rarely effective and the substance use disorder itself must be addressed (Green, 2006).

There are also gender-specific factors that aid, or inhibit, retention in treatment once the woman is admitted to a rehabilitation program. Greenfield (2010) identified some of these factors as (a) having a higher income, (b) being married, (c) being unemployed, (d) personal stability, (e) a more stable family, and (f) lower combined burden of health, mental health, and social problems. Although at first glance factors "a" and "c" might seem to be contradictory, the loss of employment (especially in a high status field of work) would serve as an incentive for the woman to successfully complete treatment or start a job search.

In contrast to women, men are more likely to enter treatment because of legal, marital, social, employment, or familial pressure. Like men, women who are referred to a rehabilitation program by the criminal justice system tend to have better treatment outcomes (Greenfield, 2010). After entering treatment, men and women relate to their SUD differently: Men tend to externalize responsibility for their SUD, whereas women tend to blame themselves. This is clearly seen in the observation that women with an AUD have lower self-esteem as compared to men with a similar SUD (Cohen, 2000; Sinha, 2000). Another excellent example of how the dynamics of substance use disorders differ between men and women is that for the woman, the symptoms of depression are likely to serve as a relapse trigger for continued further substance abuse. Depression in the substance abusing man often triggers a reduction in substance abuse levels in an attempt to reduce his level of depression. This is not to say that men with substance use disorders might not suffer from clinical depression. Rather, this illustrates the different dynamics that are at work for men and women with a concurrent SUD and depressive disorder.

Another gender difference is found in how the abuser supports their substance use. Male abusers or addicts commonly support their drug use through discretionary spending funds or by drawing on family savings, or by the sale of drugs to others. Women who work out of the home frequently have to resort to spending savings or to prostitution to support their addiction.

Work, Gender, and the Substance Use Disorders

There is a complex relationship between the individual's work status, and the SUDs. Women who are unhappy with their jobs or who work in male-dominated professions are more prone to use alcohol more heavily (Jerslid, 2001). The importance of this observation becomes apparent when one stops to consider the fact that most women in the workforce are working below their capacity, often in low-status, high-frustration positions. Although work potentially offers the woman increased social status, financial support, and improved self-esteem, all factors that help protect her against the development of an SUD, she might not feel challenged by the demands of her job.

When compared with male drinkers, women are unlikely to come to the attention of authorities (or employers) because of substance-related behavioral problems (Johnson, 2003). One reason for this is that because women tend to be underemployed, a woman's chemical abuse is less likely to result in underperformance or unacceptable job performance than is true for a male worker (Blume & Zilberman, 2004). Even if the woman's substance use is identified, the low-status jobs that women usually hold do not generally allow for easy access to Employee Assistance Program counselors who act as "gatekeepers" to treatment programs. Also, the threat of loss of employment for a woman in a low-status position is not as effective an incentive to enter treatment as it is for men. Women can simply quit their job if threatened with termination unless they should enter treatment. If the woman is the primary breadwinner in the family, then the referral to treatment is blocked by other barriers that stand between a woman and substance abuse rehabilitation programs (discussed earlier).

Differing Effects of Common Drugs of Abuse on Women

For decades, much of what was assumed to be true about the effects of the drugs of abuse on women was extrapolated from studies using exclusively men, usually men in Veterans Administration hospital settings. The applicability of such research to women is open to interpretation. Further, research has demonstrated gender-specific differences in alcohol and drug distribution and biotransformation. Although scientists have long been aware that there are sexual differences in brain structure and function between men and women, how these affect the woman's responses to the drugs of abuse has not been explored (Newman & Mello, 2009).[2] The hormonal changes involved in the woman's monthly menstrual cycle have also been found to alter the woman's sensitivity to the effects of many drugs of abuse (Newman & Mello, 2009; Reed & Evans, 2009). A related issue is that research suggests that 20–40% of women of childbearing age utilize hormone-based methods of contraception. However, there has been no research into how such methods of birth control might influence the woman's response to a drug(s) of abuse (Reed & Evans, 2009).

There is also a growing body of evidence that suggests that substance abuse by a woman might result in an earlier onset of menopause. The possibility that premenopausal women might react to a drug(s) of abuse in a different manner than postmenopausal women has for the most part not been explored. The issue of the differences between the factors that initiate, maintain, and help assist the rehabilitation from the drugs of abuse is thus quite complicated. In the next section, we will examine some of the known differences in the effects of various compounds on women, as compared to men.

Alcohol Use Disorders in Women

The discussion of the AUDs in women reflects a rather complex problem. Different age cohorts have different norms for alcohol use, and their peak period of alcohol ingestion varies from age cohort to age cohort. Women between the ages of 18 and 24 appear to develop an AUD earlier in life than do women in the 25- to 49-year age bracket, which might reflect the different norms for substance use between these two age groups. It is thus difficult to discuss the AUDs in women, because there are within gender differences in the development of the AUDs.

Statistics demonstrate that women are less likely to develop an AUD than are men (Erickson, 2007). However, in those cases where the woman *does* develop an

---

[2]Persons who wish to learn more about this topic might wish to begin with Munto et al. (2006). Sex differences in striatal dopamine release in health adults. *Biological Psychiatry, 59,* 966–974.

AUD, she is less likely to be identified as having this disorder. This is due in part because women tend to be solitary drinkers, and only rarely engage in the problematic behaviors that commonly is seen with male drinkers (Myrick, & Wright, 2008; Nichol, Krueger, & Iacono, 2007). Solitary drinking by women might reflect the different dynamics for alcohol abuse between men and women. Men who drink abusively do so more to achieve the euphoric effects of alcohol, whereas the majority of women who abuse alcohol tend to do so to self-medicate emotional pain (Grahm, Massak, Demers, & Rehm, 2007; Payne, Back, Wright, Hartwell, & Brady, 2009). Older women who live alone are at increased risk for alcohol abuse in part because of loneliness and depression, which makes this subpopulation more likely to plan and attempt suicide (Payne et al., 2009).

There is controversial evidence suggesting that *moderate* alcohol use has a neuroprotective effect for women. Strandberg et al. (2008) concluded that women with a low to moderate alcohol intake level (defined by the authors as one to seven standard drinks a week) seem to demonstrate a significantly slower rate of cognitive decline as they age than do men. The authors speculated that the causal mechanism for the observed findings might reflect the protective effects of estrogen rather than the level of alcohol intake. However, they also did not rule out the possibility that the use of alcohol *in moderation* might also be a contributing factor to the apparent protective effect of alcohol use in women.

Unfortunately, women are more vulnerable to the negative effects of alcohol because of (a) lower body mass, (b) different fluid content, and (c) lower levels of gastric alcohol dehydrogenase in the stomach and liver (Myrick & Wright, 2008; Payne et al., 2009). Women also have a lower muscle mass to body weight ratio. As a result of these factors, the average woman needs to ingest 40% less alcohol to achieve the same blood alcohol level as a man (Blume & Zilberman, 2005a; Collims & McNair, 2002; Reed & Evans, 2009). To further complicate matters, the normal variations in estrogen levels during the menstrual cycle affect the speed that alcohol is absorbed and its effects on the woman (Reynolds & Bada, 2003).

Physical Complications

It has been hypothesized that because of the process known as "telescoping" women begin to experience physical complications from abusive alcohol abuse earlier in life than do their male counterparts (Blume & Zilberman, 2005a, 2005b; Brady & Back, 2008; Myrick & Wright,

2008; Payne et al., 2009). Women are more sensitive to the toxic effects of alcohol on the striated muscle tissue than are men, for example (Blume & Zilberman, 2005a, 2005b). Such damage to the striated muscle tissue is seen after the average woman has ingested a lifetime total of about 60% the amount of alcohol necessary to produce the same degree of muscle damage in men (Kinsella & Riley, 2007). It has also been found that the consumption of just two standard drinks per day increases the risk that the woman will experience cardiac arrhythmias such as atrial fibrillation (Conen et al., 2008). The team of Qureshi, Dominguez, Choi, Jan, and Curhan (2010) followed a sample of 83,000 nurses and found that women who consume just two standard drinks a week appear to be at increased risk for developing psoriasis for unknown reasons. Further, this risk appears to be dose dependent, with those women who consumed larger amounts of alcohol reporting a higher incidence of psoriasis, again for unknown reasons.

Women with AUDs also appear to be at increased risk for central nervous system damage as compared with male drinkers, developing this damage after a shorter drinking history (Rourke & Grant, 2009). The pattern of brain damage is slightly different between the sexes, however. Hashimoto and Wiren (2007) discovered, for example, that female mice demonstrated a *higher* level of neuronal death during alcohol withdrawal than did male mice. It is not known whether this is true for humans as well, but these results were suggestive of a sex-specific pattern of neural death during the alcohol-withdrawal process.

The average woman with an AUD who enters treatment will typically have more severe medical problems than the typical male drinker (Green, 2006; Sinha, 2000). The woman with an AUD, for example, usually requires just half the time to develop cirrhosis of the liver as a male drinker, and the cirrhosis is more likely to prove fatal for the woman with an AUD after it develops (Myrick & Wright, 2008). Further, if the woman has a concurrent Hepatitis "C" infection, she typically will die 10 years earlier than a man with both conditions. Women with an AUD are vulnerable to reproductive system dysfunctions such as amenorrhea, uterine bleeding, dysmenorrhea, and abnormal menstrual cycles, as well as a reduction in ovarian size, reduced fertility, and an increased rate of spontaneous abortions or miscarriages if she should be pregnant (Myrick & Wright, 2008; Payne et al., 2009; Schuckit, 2008a). They are also at increased risk for osteoporosis and breast cancer (Babor & Rehm, 2005;

Kovalesky, 2004; Myrick & Wright, 2008; Sampson, 2002). It has been found that women taking birth control pills have a lower rate of alcohol biotransformation than women who do not use this method of contraception, extending the effects of alcohol in these women (Erickson, 2007). Finally, if the woman should suffer from a concurrent eating disorder, her alcohol use might exacerbate the electrolyte imbalances induced by the eating disorder, increasing the risk to her life (Benton, 2009).

Interpersonal Resources

Women with an AUD usually have a smaller social network than do men of the same age and substance abuse history and they report that they receive less support for their efforts to abstain from chemicals than is typical for a man (Tracy et al., 2010). Women with an AUD are *four times* as likely to be living with a substance-abusing partner than are men. This appears to reflect the increased possibility that the woman will be financially dependent on her partner and thus less likely to seek a divorce from an abusive partner with an SUD (Blume & Zilberman, 2005a). Women who are exposed to interpersonal violence are five times as likely to develop a substance use disorder compared to women who are never exposed to these life experiences (Rees et al., 2011). Depressed women also tend to consume more alcohol per episode of active drinking, exacerbating the risk of alcohol-induced physical problems.

Women with a substance use disorder tend to experience more social stigma, contributing to the problem of familial alienation from the substance abuser. Even if the woman should seek treatment, she is likely to encounter barriers to rehabilitation such as child care, child custody issues,[3] pregnancy-related issues, and having smaller social support systems. Many rehabilitation centers refuse to work with a woman who has children or who is pregnant, and few residential treatment programs have facilities for child care while the mother is in treatment.

A Positive Note

Although a great deal remains to be discovered about the impact of gender on the substance use disorders and their treatment, there are also hopeful signs emerging from the research data. Women, for example, appear to be more aware of their substance use disorders, and to respond more positively to intervention(s) aimed at treating these problems. Thus, the treatment outcome for women with an alcohol use disorder is at least as good as, if not better than, men with similar disorders who entered treatment (Greenfield, 2010; Payne et al., 2009). Women who successfully completed treatment were found to be nine times as likely to abstain from recreational drug use than those who failed to successfully complete the treatment (Green, 2006).

A Cautionary Note

Alcoholics Anonymous (AA) is often suggested as an adjunct to recovery. Within the framework of such a program, the woman is able to express her fears and concerns, or seek guidance from others or from her higher power, without having to fear repercussions, shame, or retribution (Hamilton-Mason & Melendez, 2011). Unfortunately, AA might also expose what is perceived as a sexist mentality in a program based on confronting the perceived false pride on which addictions rest. Such an approach might not "… be helpful to a woman who needs to build her self-esteem from the ground up" (Jerslid, 2001, p. 6), in part because as a group, women tend to feel higher levels of shame than do men. It is for this reason that women are more likely to be solitary drinkers than are men with AUDs. But the AA program places great emphasis on uncovering the sources of shame, a characteristic that may make women feel uncomfortable or unwanted at these meetings (Blume & Zilberman, 2004; Jerslid, 2001). Complicating matters is that women now start to drink at a younger age and to consume far greater quantities than did earlier generations (Greenfield, 2003; Grucza, Norberg, Bucholz, & Bierut, 2008; Sinha, 2000). Thus, the challenge to AA at this time is to both eliminate the sexism inherent in the 12-step program and make the program relevant to all age cohorts of women. Whether this self-help program can accomplish this during the process of remaking itself to meet the needs of a woman with an AUD in the 21st century remains to be seen.

Amphetamine Use Disorders in Women

Methamphetamine is one of the family of the amphetamine compounds, but it has received the most publicity as a stimulant of abuse and thus will be the focus

---

[3]The woman's AUD is often used against her in child custody disputes, for example.

of this section. The ratio of male to female methamphetamine abusers is nearly 1:1 (Rawson & Ling, 2008); however, the dynamics of the methamphetamine use disorders are not the same for men and women. Male methamphetamine abusers tend to be drawn to the drug for its euphoric effects, whereas women are most commonly drawn to methamphetamine because of its ability to induce anorexia and to self-medicate depression (Rutkowski & Maxwell, 2009). Research has found that women tend to find CNS stimulants such as methamphetamine more pleasurable during that phase of their menstrual cycle when estrogen levels are highest (Anthes, 2010). The differences in reproductive hormones also appear to make women more vulnerable to the addictive potential of central nervous system stimulants than men (Torregrossa & Kalivas, 2009).

Pleasure is not the only reason why some women might abuse stimulants such as methamphetamine. Some women are forced into the illicit sex trade to support their addiction, while other women begin to abuse methamphetamine because it allows them to work longer hours. (Rutkowski & Maxwell, 2009). Women who admitted to the use of cocaine or the amphetamines are more likely to become the victims of interpersonal sexual violence (Gilbert, El-Bassel, Chang, Wu, & Roy, 2011). Seventy percent of women who abuse methamphetamine report a history of physical and/or sexual abuse in their lives (Rawson & Ling, 2008). This establishes a vicious circle in which the woman becomes addicted to an amphetamine compound such as methamphetamine, and in many cases is ultimately forced to work in the illicit sex trade to obtain the funds to support her addiction. The mild antidepressant effect of methamphetamine helps to understand the lure of this compound for women who have been abused or forced to work in the illicit sex trade. This might account for the fact that when an adolescent girl or young woman is admitted to a substance abuse rehabilitation program for a methamphetamine use disorder she will usually report higher levels of use than is true for the average adolescent male.

Approximately one-third of women who abuse methamphetamine report having an anxiety disorder *before* they began to abuse methamphetamine abuse, and two-thirds report symptoms of an anxiety disorder after starting to abuse methamphetamine (Brady & Hartwell, 2009). This raises the question whether anxiety symptoms might not serve as a relapse trigger for the woman with a methamphetamine use disorder, however, research on this topic is lacking at this time. There is preliminary evidence, however, suggesting that women might be less vulnerable to the neurotoxic effects of methamphetamine because of the limited protective action of estrogen.

These gender-specific dangers are beyond the physical and emotional risks of amphetamine abuse discussed in Chapter 8. Although there is still a great deal to be discovered about the effects of the amphetamine compounds on women, it should be clear from the information reviewed in this section that the dynamics and consequences of methamphetamine use by women are different from those for men.

Benzodiazepine Abuse by Women

There is little research data on the problem of benzodiazepine abuse by women or the pharmacokinetics of benzodiazepines in women, which is surprising in that the majority of prescriptions for benzodiazepines (BZs) are for women. When introduced, the BZs were marketed as useful in helping women deal with anxiety in the various medical journals in which the pharmaceuticals company paid for advertising. The advertisement usually began with a photo of a woman who was visibly distressed (sometimes with children or a work scene in the background), whereas a second photo of the same woman smiling and interacting with her children and/or peers was provided, suggesting that the BZ caused this transition.

It is known that BZ blood levels in women using hormone-based birth control medications might be lower than normal because the birth control medication increased the speed of the BZ biotransformation (Tatro, 2009). For unknown reasons, BZs that require conjugation as part of the biotransformation process[4] such as temazepam and oxazepam have longer elimination half-lives in women as compared to men. However, as stated, there is little gender-specific research data on the problem of BZ abuse or addiction or the normal pharmacokinetics of the BZs in women.

---

[4]See Chapter 3.

Buspirone Use Disorders and Women

The abuse potential of buspirone has been debated, and at least a small group of drug abusers do look upon buspirone as preferred drug of abuse. It is not known whether women are more vulnerable to the addictive potential of this compound or what personality characteristics might make the woman vulnerable to buspirone abuse.

Cocaine Use Disorders in Women

The phenomenon of cocaine abuse is not the same between men and women. There is evidence that the woman's gonadal hormones might influence her subjective response to cocaine (Newman & Mello, 2009; Reed & Evans, 2009). Higher progesterone levels have been found to mute the woman's sense of euphoria after using cocaine (Elton & Kilts, 2009; Lukas, 2006). Unfortunately, progesterone is involved in the maintenance of pregnancy,[5] and this may add to the incentive for the pregnant woman to use *more* cocaine per episode of abuse increasing the risk both to the mother and the fetus. A second danger is that because progesterone is a component in many hormonal-based methods of birth control, there is a danger that women using such methods of birth control might feel tempted to use more cocaine in an attempt to achieve the desired level of euphoria, again increasing her risk of an adverse reaction to the cocaine.

It has been observed that female rats appear to be willing to work harder for cocaine than are male rates, although the applicability of this finding to humans remains unclear. Human female cocaine abusers appear to be at increased risk for developing the adverse effects of cocaine than is true for male cocaine abusers. Some of the adverse effects for cocaine abuse by a woman include not just those identified in Chapter 12, but also include such problems as galactorrhea,[6] amenorrhea, and infertility (Mendelson & Mello, 2008). However, clinical research does suggest that women who abuse cocaine develop a lower number of cerebral perfusion defects, and lower levels of damage to the frontal cortex than do male cocaine abusers (Brady & Back, 2008).

Women who abuse cocaine begin to do so at an earlier age than do male cocaine abusers, and there is evidence that they are also more vulnerable to the addiction potential of cocaine (Lynch et al., 2009). Women with cocaine use disorders usually enter treatment at a younger age than their male counterpart. One surprising route of exposure to low levels of cocaine for a woman is through the semen of a male partner who is a cocaine abuser (Karch, 2009). It is not clear at this time whether the exposure to the small amount of cocaine in the ejaculate could induce any form of physical reaction in the woman or serve as a relapse "trigger," although this is unlikely because the amount of cocaine in the semen would be quite small.

Hallucinogen Abuse in Women

Ecstasy (MDMA)

There is little research into possible gender differences in the individual's response to a hallucinogen such as MDMA. There is preliminary evidence suggesting that for unknown reasons women are more vulnerable to MDMA-related neurological damage than are men (Greenfield, 2003). However, the findings of a study by Medina, Price, Harper, Logan, and Shear (2008) would argue just the opposite. The authors attempted to examine the effects of MDMA on executive functioning,[7] and found that there was a dose-dependent relationship between the abuse of MDMA and lower-working memory ability scores. Although the authors found a significant gender effect, male MDMA abusers were found to be more likely to demonstrate impulsiveness and impaired memory function as compared to female MDMA abusers. Thus the issue of whether there are sex-related differences in the pattern of neurological damage remains unclear at this time.

Yudko and McPherson (2009) suggested that lower functioning males appear to be at increased risk for MDMA-induced neurological deficits in the areas of verbal and visual memory, but not in women or in higher functioning males, suggesting that premorbid level of function might be another variable besides gender that influences the impact of MDMA on neurological

---

[5]The use of progesterone in birth control pills acts on the principle that this compound, normally found in high concentrations when the woman is pregnant, forces the body to assume that the woman is already pregnant. A fertilized egg will then be blocked from implanting itself in the wall of the uterus.

[6]See Glossary.

[7]See Glossary.

function. As this information suggests, there is a great deal to be learned about how the effects of MDMA on both men and women; however, because this compound is illegal it is doubtful that such research will be forthcoming.

LSD and Phencyclidine

There has been virtually no research into how gender might affect the individual's response to these compounds or how these compounds might have differential effects on men and women. There has been virtually no research into the impact of LSD or phencyclidine use/abuse on the user's neurological function, or how these compounds might have different effects for men as opposed to women.

Marijuana Use Disorders in Women

Statistically, women are more likely to begin to abuse marijuana at an older age than are men, with the mean age of first marijuana use being 17.6 years for adolescent girls as compared with 16.4 years for adolescent boys (McRae-Clark & Price, 2009). Men are about three times as likely as women to use marijuana daily; however, there is limited evidence suggesting that women progress to marijuana dependence more rapidly than do men (McRae-Clark & Price, 2009). There has been virtually no research into the possible gender-based differences in the path to marijuana use or possible gender-specific differences in the user's physiological reaction to marijuana.

Preliminary evidence does suggest that women who suffer from social anxiety disorder are more likely to turn to marijuana to self-medicate some of their distress than men, but further research is needed to explore this topic (McRae-Clark & Price, 2009). Although marijuana abuse can induce anxiety, especially in inexperienced users, it does not appear to do so more often in women than it does in men (Brady & Hartwell, 2009). At first the assertion by McRae-Clark and Price (2009) to the effect that 32% of women but only 13% of men experience marijuana-induced panic at some point in their marijuana use careers would seem to contradict the assertion made by Brady and Hartwell (2009), but it is necessary to remember that there is a difference between the experience of *anxiety* and that of pure *panic* to see where both statements might be correct.

Marijuana abusers are at increased risk for depression, but the causal mechanism for this effect, or whether it is the same causal mechanism for men and women, has not been explored (McRae-Clark & Price, 2009). It has been demonstrated that the woman's reaction to alcohol ingestion will differ at various points in the menstrual cycle. Unfortunately, there has been virtually no research to determine whether hormonal-specific differences into the individual's physiological or subjective response to marijuana exist (McRae-Clark & Price, 2009). It is known that some women abuse marijuana to self-medicate premenstrual dysphoria; however, there is no research data demonstrating the prevalence of this practice (Newman & Mello, 2009). There is preliminary evidence suggesting that men might be more sensitive to the positive effects of marijuana smoking than are women, but further research is needed to confirm this finding (Reed & Evans, 2009). As was discussed in Chapter 13, the use of marijuana often predates the onset of schizophrenia (Compton & Ramsay, 2009). However, women who abused marijuana and then went on to develop schizophrenia did so about four years later than did men (Compton & Ramsay, 2009). Whether this is a reflection of some kind of marijuana-induced partial protection against psychosis or of another, undiscovered factor, remains unknown.

Narcotics Abuse and Women

To date only a handful of studies have examined the possibility that men and women will react differently to a narcotic analgesic. Neuropharmacologists have discovered that women appear to be slightly more sensitive to the analgesic effects of morphine as compared to men, but that they also seem to require more time before experiencing morphine-induced analgesia (Newman & Mello, 2009). Research based on animal studies suggests that female rats will self-administer more opiates when given the opportunity to do so than will male rats, although the applicability of this data to humans remains uncertain (Brady & Back, 2008).

The problem of prescription diversion is an ongoing issue, and the limited data that are available would suggest that where 1.4% of men and 1.1% of women 18–25 years of age have abused a prescription narcotic, have done so (Brady & Back, 2008). This difference in incidence is more pronounced in older age cohorts because illicit drug use was either less socially acceptable or at least less frequently reported in older generations. Further, the limited data available at this time suggest that approximately 57% of women who are addicted to opioids are addicted to prescribed medications as compared with 37% of men with a narcotics addiction (Back & Payne, 2009). There is strong evidence suggesting that the dynamics for prescription opioid abuse differs between the genders. Women who abuse prescription opioids tend to do so to cope with psychological distress, whereas men who abuse prescription opioids tend to have more legal and behavioral problems (possibly suggesting antisocial tendencies on their part) (Jamison, Butler, Budman, Edwards, & Wasan, 2010).

Women who abuse narcotics tend to begin to abuse these compounds at an older age than do men, but that the average woman will enter treatment for her SUD at about the same age as male opioid abusers (Hernandez-Avila, Rounsaville, & Kranzler, 2005). This suggests that their opioid use disorder is "telescoped" into a shorter period as compared with male abusers. Whereas men are more likely to inject narcotics, women tend to use inhalation as the preferred method of administration, although there are exceptions to this rule. Finally, it has been found that women opioid abusers were more likely to be involved in a sexual relationship with another drug abuser than were male opioid addicts. More than half report having received drugs as a present from their partner on occasion, a pattern rarely seen in male opioid addicts. There is also limited evidence that hormonal changes seen in the menstrual cycle might increase the woman's sensitivity to pain, which might then become a relapse risk for her during the early stages of recovery. However, as noted earlier, there is a paucity of data concerning the opioid use disorders and gender,[8] and much remains to be learned about how gender affects the rehabilitation of opioid abusers.

Nicotine Use Disorders in Women

The number of research studies investigating the effects of cigarette smoking on women is limited and often contaminated by methodological errors. One such

error is ignoring the woman's emotional status and victimization status (Blalock et al., 2011). The authors found that women who were physically or emotionally abused in childhood and who developed high levels of nicotine use found it more difficult to stop or reduce smoking when they became pregnant. Surprisingly, sexual abuse in childhood does not seem to influence time between awakening and first cigarette according to the authors. A relationship between childhood abuse and later cigarette smoking intensity by pregnant women was discovered by Blalock et al. (2011). The authors found that those women who had suffered the highest levels of abuse in childhood were the least likely to stop or reduce their smoking while pregnant.

Researchers have only recently started to explore how normal hormonal levels found during menstruation impact on the pharmacokinetics of most drugs of abuse. The hormonal levels that are seen at various points in the woman's menstrual cycle might alter the drug's effects over time, although most research studies assume that their effects are the same over the woman's monthly cycle. Another confounding variable in research into the pharmacokinetics of drugs in women is whether she is using hormonal-based birth control methods (Newman & Mello, 2009). However, in spite of the paltry database addressing the issue of cigarette smoking in women, researchers *have* found that for the first time in recorded history women who smoke are as likely to die from tobacco-related illness as do men who smoke (Jha et al., 2013).

There are sexual dimorphic differences in the neural activation pattern of smoking between men and women. The team of Fallon, Keator, Mbogori, Taylor, and Potkin (2005) examined the brains of men and women (smokers and nonsmokers) using positron emission tomography (PET) scan[9] technology. They found a *decrease* in brain metabolism of the women in their study who were using transdermal nicotine patches, whereas the men in the study experienced an *increase* in brain metabolism when using transdermal nicotine patches. The exact ramifications of these findings remain unclear at this time. Caspers, Amdt, Yucuis, McKirgan, and Spinks (2010) found middle-aged women who smoked demonstrated greater deficits in visuospatial abilities, cognitive processing speed, and executive function than did middle-aged men with a history of tobacco use or similarly aged women who never smoked cigarettes.

---

[8]If somebody is looking for a good master's degree thesis or doctoral dissertation topic, you are welcome to develop this idea further.

---

[9]See Glossary.

To identify nicotine's differing effects on men and women, Sofuoglu and Mooney (2009) administered intravenous doses of nicotine to volunteer subjects and found that the women in their study reported a stronger "rush" effect and were more likely to respond positively to a given dose of nicotine than were the men in the study. However, the women were also more sensitive to the negative effects of nicotine according to the authors. The authors called for further research into how men and women might have different subjective effects from nicotine. There also is strong evidence that nicotine metabolism is different for men and women. Women appear to metabolize[10] nicotine more rapidly than do men, but seem to be more sensitive to the rewarding effects of nicotine (Brady & Back, 2008; Reed & Evans, 2009). Men and women appear to also follow different pathways to nicotine use disorders. For example, adolescent girls are more likely to initiate tobacco use, and less likely to stop smoking, than are adolescent boys (Wunsch, 2007).

Cigarette smoking is known to cause health care problems specific to women. The average woman who smokes is thought to lose approximately 14 years of potential life because of health care problems either brought or at least exacerbated by cigarette smoking. An excellent example of this is found in the observation that chronic obstructive pulmonary disease (COPD) is more common in women who smoke as compared with men (Newman & Mello, 2009). Nonsmoking women tend to experience their first heart attack about 10 years later than do men, which is known as the "myocardial infarction gender gap." However, this decade of protection is lost if the woman should smoke cigarettes (Herzog et al., 2007). Women who smoked were twice as likely to present to a hospital with symptoms of a specific form of heart attack[11] than their nonsmoking counterparts (Herzog et al., 2007). However, the authors also found that if the female smoker were to stop smoking, her risk for cardiac disease dropped to that of her nonsmoking counterpart within six months, thus providing another incentive for a woman to quit smoking. In another study, the team of Sandhu et al. (2012) examined the records of 101,018 women in the Nurse's Health Study and found that even smoking less than 14 cigarettes per day increased the woman's risk of sudden cardiac death and that for every five years that the woman continued to smoke her risk of sudden cardiac death increased by 8%. The authors also found that with smoking cessation the woman's risk for sudden cardiac death dropped until 20 years after the last cigarette her risk was the same as those women her age who had never smoked.

Cigarette smoking is *the* most common cause of lung cancer in women (Newman & Mello, 2009) as well as a cause of reduced fertility in women, and as a causal factor in fetal death or stillbirth (Carmona, 2004). Cigarette smoking has also been identified as a risk factor for the development of various forms of cancer in women, including cervical cancer, cancer of the esophagus, pancreas, kidney, bladder, breast, and pharynx. If the woman who smokes should quit, her risk of cancer slowly declines over the next few years. There is even evidence that smoking cessation may result in a reduction in the size of some cancers for women after these tumors develop. Cigarette smoking has been identified as a cause of bone density loss in postmenopausal women (Carmona, 2004). Women who smoke cigarettes are at higher risk for developing rheumatoid arthritis, and as a group, women who smoke have been found to have less strength, and less psychomotor coordination, than nonsmoking women the same age. The causal mechanisms for these effects remain unknown.

Unfortunately, an emerging body of evidence suggests "Big Tobacco" has focused advertising efforts on women and young girls ("'Deadly in Pink' Report Targets Big Tobacco," 2009). At least two major cigarette companies, Philip Morris USA and R.J. Reynolds Tobacco, have devised advertising campaigns designed to convince women that cigarette smoking is both fashionable and a sign of femininity ("'Deadly in Pink' Report Targets Big Tobacco," 2009). Given the gender-specific dangers of cigarette smoking, one must question the morality of these apparent advertising campaigns.

Smoking Cessation

There are several factors that influence the success of smoking cessation efforts in women that are not found in men. It has been found, for example, that the gonadal sex hormones involved in the woman's monthly menstrual cycle influence the subjective level of distress that she experiences in the early stages of

---

[10]Because nicotine is not a prescribed substance, the term "metabolize," rather than "biotransformed," is being used.

[11]Technically, known as the *ST-segment elevated myocardial infarction*.

smoking cessation (Newman & Mellow, 2009). The possibility of postcessation weight gain often serves as a deterrent for smoking cessation efforts by women smokers (Williams et al., 2010). It is not known whether men anticipate the same degree of negative consequences associated with postcessation weight gain and the role of gender-specific interpretations of postcessation weight gain has not been explored. However, Williams et al. (2010) found that moderate physical exercise in their sample of women smokers who were attempting to quit appeared to reduce potential weight gain, appeared to provide at least temporary benefits by reducing withdrawal distress, weight gain, and increased possibility of success on the part of the would-be former smoker. The authors called for a larger study with a more diverse sample of women to determine whether this effect can be replicated.

The observed benefits of smoking cessation might differ for men and women. Admittedly, both groups benefit from smoking cessation, but the pattern of recovery follows a slightly different path for each sex. For example, there is evidence suggesting that women are less likely to benefit from the pharmacological effects of bupropion during smoking cessation (Lynch et al., 2009). Nicotine replacement therapies also appear less effective for women who smoke and attempt to quit with the assistance of this pharmacological support as compared to men. Finally, the factors that enhance the individual's risk for relapsing are different between men and women, in part because of the hormonal changes associated with menstruation.

As this information suggests, there is a great deal to be discovered about how nicotine affects women and whether smoking cessation treatment methods need to be altered to accommodate the woman's menstrual cycle status.

Other Compounds

Aspirin

Although aspirin is not a drug of abuse in the traditional sense, it is often used to provide a degree of protection against heart attacks and to treat a heart attack once it has started, as discussed in Chapter 19. However, there are gender-specific aspirin effects for aspirin (Steinhubl et al., 2009). Men who take aspirin to prevent cardiovascular events appear to have fewer heart attacks, whereas women who take aspirin appear

to have fewer strokes. The possibility that aspirin might reduce the woman's risk of a heart attack remains unclear at this time, although it is still recommended for the treatment of a heart attack once this program is initiated (Chan et al., 2007).

There has been virtually no research into how the woman's menstrual cycle might influence her response to aspirin or the other NSAIDs.[12]

Chapter Summary

The relationship between gender and the substance use disorders has moved through several stages in the 20th century. At first, it was hidden from polite society. If acknowledged at all, the victim was viewed as a "fallen" woman whose morals were suspect. As society moved into the middle of the 20th century, the face of SUDs changed, with physicians prescribing many drugs of abuse to women for various complaints such as anxiety or insomnia. This again rendered a large part of the problem of substance abuse among women hidden from society, and to a certain degree legitimized it because the woman in question was only taking a prescribed medication.

In the last quarter of the 20th century, there was a growing awareness that a large percentage of women suffered from substance use disorders, as was true for men. When treatment was attempted, the treatment methods utilized were those that had been developed for male addicts years earlier on the assumption that they would also work for women. This was a mistaken assumption, and by the last decade of the 20th-century researchers had started to understand that the course of the substance use disorders, the roads by which each sex traveled to develop their SUD, and the role that the substance use played in their lives, differed between men and women. In the last decade of the 20th century, researchers began to discover that there were subtle, and often significant, differences in how a given compound affected men and women. This chapter explored what is currently known about how gender changes the individual's response to various drugs of abuse, and the need for further research to help scientists better understand this phenomenon.

---

[12]Discussed in Chapter 15.

CHAPTER **19**

Hidden Faces of Substance Use Disorders

Introduction

It would be nice if substance use disorders (SUDs) were to present with a singular set of signature symptoms. This would make the identification of these SUDs ever so much easier. Many of the stereotypical images of a person with an SUD are familiar: The "skid row" alcoholic, drinking a bottle of cheap wine wrapped in a plain brown paper bag, the heroin addict, with a belt wrapped around his arm and a needle in hand, about to inject heroin into his or her arm, for example. Such stereotypes heighten our awareness of the problem while simultaneously blinding us to the fact the SUDs do not always follow these familiar pathways and often hide in the shadows of daily living. Who, for example, would recognize the white, middle-class, heroin addict at work in an office setting or the cocaine-dependent mother who stops to buy some Crack cocaine on the way home from a shopping trip? How many people would recognize the benzodiazepine (BZ) dependency behind the smiling face of a day-care worker? In this chapter, we will examine some of the many hidden faces of the SUDs.

Substance Use Disorders and the Homeless

Between two and three million people in the United States, or about 1% of the total population, are thought to be homeless (Joseph & Langrod, 2005). Single men make up 41% of this number; families (usually headed by women) comprise 41%; single women comprise 13%; and children or adolescents make up about 5% of this population. Approximately one-third of those who are homeless are veterans of the armed forces of the United States, a number that is far out of proportion with the percentage of veterans in this country[1] (Darwin & Reich, 2011). Surprisingly, it is not depression or schizophrenia

that is the most common psychiatric condition encountered among those who are homeless (Nielsen, Rygaard-Hjorthøj, Elangsen, & Nordentoft, 2011). However, contrary to expectations, the individual is not at higher risk for developing an SUD after he or she becomes homeless (Arehart-Treichel, 2004; Smith, Meyers, & Delaney, 1998). Indeed, the experience of losing one's home appears to act as an incentive for the individual to *stop* abusing chemicals, at least in many cases (Arehart-Treichel, 2004).

The role of the individual's substance use in the loss of one's home is complex, and there is not always a causal relationship. The causes of homelessness might be traced to (Joseph & Langrod, 2005) (1) high rates of poverty, (2) chronic unemployment, (3) underemployment, (4) low-paying jobs, (5) loss of benefits, and (6) lack of affordable housing. It should be noted that Joseph and Langrod (2005) do not identify the SUDs as

---

[1]One-tenth of adults in the United States are veterans of military service.

a major cause of homelessness, although substance abuse disorders does indirectly contribute to the problem of homelessness.

Alcohol is a common substance of abuse among the homeless, reflecting the general substance use pattern of this culture. Methamphetamine-use disorders are also a significant problem for the homeless (Rutkowski & Maxwell, 2009). However, it is not whether there is a causal relationship between the abuse of these chemicals and homelessness. If substance abuse rehabilitation is attempted, homeless individuals present special challenges to the treatment program staff. Issues such as medical problems (increased incidence of tuberculosis,[2] for example), keeping appointments, attending 12-Step group meetings, or obtaining prescribed medications, all become barriers to rehabilitation. If the homeless person also had a child, or children, these barriers to treatment are compounded by many orders of magnitude. These are all social problems that must be addressed, but there does not appear to be any easy solution, especially during these financially troubled times.

Substance Use Disorders and the Elderly[3]

It was once thought that the alcohol use disorders (AUDs) were self-limiting because the negative health consequences of substance abuse were thought to prevent the majority of older drinkers from achieving their normal anticipated life span (Brennen, Schutte, & Moos, 2010).[4] There also is a popular misconception that older persons do not abuse drugs and so health care professionals do not need to worry about SUDs in this subpopulation. A result of these misperceptions is that health care professionals, who normally would be thought as one of the first groups to identify SUDs in the elderly, generally do not screen for substance abuse in older patients (Ellison, 2012).

All too often they lack the training and skills to diagnose SUDs in older patients (Klimstra & Mahgoub, 2010; Zimberg, 2005), and there are no screening tools for drug abuse designed and validated for use with the elderly that health care workers can call upon for assistance in making such a diagnosis (Klimstra & Mahboub, 2010).

This problem has been diagnosed just as seventy-five million baby boomers are about to reach or have reached retirement age. Untold millions of these people began to abuse alcohol, prescribed and/or illicit drugs since young adulthood (Kluger, 2006). As this age cohort reaches retirement age, they encounter a medical system that is ill-prepared to deal with older persons with SUDs (Dowling, Weiss, & Condon, 2008). The warning signs have been there: The AUDs are the third most common psychiatric problem found in older people (Luggen, 2006). However, few health care professionals paid attention to these warning signs until faced with a generation of older adults with substance use problems.

The age cohort born between 1945 and 1965, the so-called baby boomers, came of age in the 1970s and 1980s when there was a more permissive social attitude that tolerated substance use (Colliver, Compton, Gfroerer, & Condon, 2006; Drew, Wilkins, & Trevisan, 2010; Ellison, 2012; Zimberg, 2005). As this age cohort has moved into middle adulthood and beyond, members of this age cohort have retained their permissive attitudes about recreational substance use. For example, where 4.5 million teenagers smoked marijuana in 2008,[5] it is thought that 4.42 million Americans over the age of 45 did as well (Raw Data, 2010b). Marijuana use was found to be more common than the abuse of prescription drugs for adults in the 50–54 age cohort ("Illicit Drug Use Among Older Adults," 2009). In the United Kingdom, researchers found that where just 1.7% of adults now aged 65 years and older admit to the use of marijuana at some point in their lives, 11.4% of those adults in the 50–64-year-old age group reported having used marijuana just in the past 12 months (Fahmy, Hatch, Hotopf, & Stewart, 2012; Shadel & Scharf, 2012). An additional 11% admit to the use of an illicit drug over the past 12 months (Shadel & Scharf, 2012).

The percentage of adults over the age of 50 who are thought to abuse prescribed medications is thought to have increased from 2.2% in 2002 to 3.9% in 2009 with prescription analgesics being the most common category of abused pharmaceuticals, followed by anxiolytics and hypnotics (Wu & Blazer, 2011). However,

---

[2]Discussed in the chapter "Substance Use Disorders and Infectious Disease."

[3]For the sake of this text, post-retirement age is defined after the age of 65, although some studies use a cut off age of 50. Thus, there is some confusion about how "elderly" might be defined between different researchers.

[4]Although research data *do* suggest that older drinkers consume less alcohol than their younger counterparts, this might be an illusion caused by the fact that because of age-related changes in their bodies they do not *need* to drink as much to achieve the same effect as they did when they were younger.

---

[5]The last year for which data are available at this time.

there is evidence suggesting that this pattern of substance use among older persons is changing: Horstman (2010) suggested, for example, that older individuals are abusing central nervous system stimulants such as methylphenidate or the amphetamine compounds more often than in the past to help them compete with younger, more energetic, and intellectually more creative coworkers.

Scope of the Problem

The elderly, defined in this text as those people above the age of 65 years, make up about 12% of the general population in the United States. Currently, almost half of men and slightly over one-third of the women over the age of 60 use alcohol (Barnes et al., 2010). It should be pointed out that not all of these individuals *abuse* alcohol, and the greater proportion of alcohol users are social drinkers. However, because of age-related physical changes, health problems, and the concurrent use of over-the-counter and prescribed medications, even moderate alcohol use[6] carries the potential for negative consequences in the older drinker (Barnes et al., 2010; Ellison, 2012; Kalapatapu, Paris, & Neugroschl, 2010; Klimstra & Mahboub, 2010). Because of age-related physical changes, the level of moderate alcohol consumption in the elderly is now defined as just one standard drink or can of beer in a 24-hour period, and hazardous alcohol use is now defined as more than three drinks in one sitting or more than seven drinks in a 7-day period (Drew et al., 2010).

The individual's entry into the earlier stages of older adulthood does not automatically mean that one will alter his or her earlier substance use pattern. Many bring an established SUD with them as they enter the earlier stages of older adulthood. Others will develop an SUD only after they reach the age of 65 years. Alcohol is the most commonly abused compound by the elderly; however, 15% of older drinkers also have a concurrent drug abuse disorder (Ellison, 2012; Greenfield, 2007). Collectively alcohol or substance misuse either is, or will be, a problem for at least 19% of those above the age of 65 years (Blow, Serras, & Barry, 2007; Glazer & Wu, 2009). Further, it is estimated that 4.4 million older persons will present with a drug addiction by the year 2020 (Kluger, 2006).

What Are the Consequences of an SUD in the Elderly Person?

As a group, the elderly population use one-third of prescription medications and one-half of all over-the-counter medications sold each year in the United States (Gross, 2008; "U.S. face of drug abuse grows older," 2006). Unfortunately, many of the more popular drugs of abuse, including alcohol, can interact with pharmaceuticals used to treat many diseases such as arthritis, and heart disease, increasing the potential for a harmful alcohol–medication interaction. It has been estimated that at least 19% of older individuals who drink alcohol will experience at least one adverse alcohol–drug interaction (Brust, 2004). If the individual were to abuse compounds other than alcohol, the risk of an adverse drug–drug interaction is multiplied, possibly with fatal results (Gwinnell & Adamec, 2006; Stevenson, 2005; Zimberg, 2005).

The abuse of alcohol or other illicit substances can also exacerbate many medical disorders, adding to overuse health care resources for the treatment of disorders induced or at least exacerbated by alcohol or drug abuse (Stevenson, 2005). For example, older people with an AUD have also been found to be at increased risk for depression, memory problems, liver disease, cardiovascular disorders, and sleep problems (Luggen, 2006; Zisserman & Oslin, 2004; Rigler, 2000). Because the age-related decline in reaction time is compounded by the effects of various compounds of abuse,[7] older people with an SUD are also at increased risk for motor vehicle accidents.

Older people with an SUD are known to be at increased risk either for dementia, or pseudo-dementia—conditions caused or exacerbated by vitamin absorption deficiencies often seen in people with a longstanding SUD. Other complications of AUDs in older people include myopathy, cerebrovascular disease, gastritis, diarrhea, pancreatitis, cardiomyopathy, cirrhosis, hypertension, diminished immune response to infections, peripheral muscle weakness, electrolyte and metabolic disturbances, depression, and hypotension. Confusion rather than a tremor might be the most prominent sign of alcohol withdrawal in older drinkers, and older drinkers' visual and/or tactile hallucinations during withdrawal might persist for weeks or months after they stop consuming alcohol (Klimstra & Mahboub, 2010).

---

[6]As you will recall, defined as one to two standard drinks for a man and one standard drink for a woman.

[7]This increased reaction time might also be caused by many prescribed medications.

The mortality rate for drinkers aged 60 years or older is 60% if the individual continues to drink (Ellison, 2012).

Depression is a common problem in older adults, in part because of the vitamin malabsorption syndromes that develop with age and which can be exacerbated by an AUD. Other possible reasons for depression in this age group include lack of income, housing, and living alone. Older persons are at increased risk for depression and suicidal behavior, especially when socially isolated or when facing serious illness. It has been estimated that 25–50% of all older people who attempt suicide have used alcohol before their attempt to take their own lives. If the individual's SUD is not recognized, then the depression cannot be appropriately treated, increasing the person's risk for a suicide attempt.

Even limited abuse of cocaine, opioids, or amphetamines carries with it an increased risk of premature death for the user from accidents, medication–drug interactions, depression, or possibly an overdose (Kertesz et al., 2012). Although intuitively one would expect that drug overdoses would be most commonly found in the young adult population, one study of 3,700 drug-related deaths in California found that only 51 involved victims under the age of 20, and that more than half were between the ages of 35 and 54 years and the remainder involved older adults (Sherer, 2006). There are several possible reasons for these overdoses: First age-related changes in the body make the individual more vulnerable to the negative effects of alcohol or other drugs of abuse (Drew et al., 2010; Klimstra & Mahboub, 2010; Stevenson, 2005). For example, by the age of 65 cerebral blood flow has decreased by 15–20% (Ellison, 2012). There is also an increase in total body fat levels while lean muscle mass decreases with the passage of time (Ellison, 2012). Thus, although researchers have identified the elderly as being at higher risk for suicide, the relationship between higher risk for suicide in this age group and substance abuse is more tenuous and should be interpreted with caution.

Why Is the Detection of SUDs in the Elderly So Difficult?

There are several reasons for this problem. Older adults tend to have more medical problems than do younger persons, and in the earlier stages SUDs often mimic the symptoms of other disorders, making the differential diagnosis very difficult for the physician (Drew et al., 2010). Also, older substance abusers tend to attribute physical complications caused by their SUD to the aging process, a form of denial aided by physicians who rarely inquire about possible substance abuse in older people (Drew et al., 2010; Stevenson, 2005). Physicians might also fail to look for an SUD in an older patient, based on the assumption that this person *deserves* to use alcohol (or, less often, illicit drugs) as a reward for a lifetime of hard work (Stevenson, 2005; Zimberg, 2005). Further, because some physicians believe that the older person with an SUD is unlikely to respond to treatment, they do not inquire about SUDs in their patients.

Social isolation might also make it difficult for such individuals to be identified as having an SUD, especially if the person lives alone. For socially active older drinkers, their friendship circle might contribute to the pressure to continue drinking well into their later adult years (Brennen et al., 2010). Further, older people with an SUD will rarely demonstrate the traditional warning signs of an addiction, such as substance-related legal, social, or occupational problems, found in younger substance-abusing adults (Drew et al., 2010; Klimstra & Mahboub, 2010). If an older person with an SUD who is in the workforce should miss work because of an SUD-related problem, it is easily explained away as age-related problems or the stress of taking care of a sick spouse. If family members should suspect that their older family member(s) have an SUD, familial shame might demand that the issue remains hidden.

Different Patterns of Alcohol or Drug Abuse in the Elderly

Kalapatapu et al. (2010) suggested that alcohol use in older adults falls on a continuum:

Abstainer: Drinks less than 1–2 drinks in the previous year.

Social drinker: Drinks no more than one drink per day and does not show symptoms of an AUD.

At-risk drinker: Drinks more than recommended amounts but with few health or social consequences.

Abusive drinker: Drinks above recommended amounts and has experienced medical, psychological, or social consequences from drinking.

Dependence: Preoccupation with alcohol, loss of control over alcohol use, continued use in spite of adverse social and physical consequences, as well as physical dependence on alcohol.

Of these five categories, Kalapatapu et al. (2010) suggest that the majority of older persons fall in the first category.

Another classification of older alcohol abusers was offered by Klimstra and Mahboub (2010). The first subgroup is composed of those individuals who had no evidence of an AUD in young or middle adulthood but who did develop an AUD in late adulthood. These individuals are said to have *late-onset* alcoholism (Klimstra & Mahboub, 2010; Rigler, 2000; Mundle, 2000). A second subgroup of older adults with AUDs includes those people who had intermittent problems with alcohol in young and middle adulthood but who developed a habitual pattern of alcohol abuse only in late adulthood. This subgroup is called the *late-onset exacerbation* subgroup (Klimstra & Mahboub, 2010; Zimberg, 1995, 1996). Finally, there are those individuals who had problems with alcohol in young adulthood, which continued through middle adulthood into the late adult years, a pattern known as *early onset* alcoholism (Mundle, 2000; Zimberg, 2005). This subgroup makes up two-thirds of the older population with AUDs (Stevenson, 2005).

In the first decade of the 21st century, the number of older persons seeking admission to treatment for SUDs more than doubled in the period from 1992 to 2008 (Treatment Episode Data Set, 2010). In 2008 some 231,200 older persons sought treatment for an SUD, as opposed to just 102,700 people in 1998 (Treatment Episode Data Set, 2010). Older persons seeking treatment admissions were more likely to be unemployed (31% in 2008), homeless (20% in 2008), without a significant source of income (29% in 2008), and as having never been married (30% in 2008). The problem of SUDs in the elderly is complicated by the issue of age. Older drinkers (defined in this study as people between the age of 50 and 74) are more likely to misjudge their level of impairment at low to moderate levels of intoxication than younger adults (Gilbertson, Ceballos, Prather, & Nixon, 2009). Whereas younger adults are more likely to be polydrug abusers, mixing alcohol with cocaine for example, older adults were more likely to have just an AUD (Gross, 2008), it is not known whether the baby boomer generation will follow this pattern or not, although the fact that 5% of

geriatric patients misuse illicit drugs at least occasionally (Drew et al., 2010).

Older individuals with early onset alcoholism were found to come from lower socioeconomic levels, have less formal education, smoke more, socialize with other alcohol abusers more often, come from families where alcohol use was tolerated or encouraged, be single or divorced, and to more often come from estranged families (Stevenson, 2005). In contrast, individuals with late-onset alcoholism tend to report more adverse life events such as retirement, illness or death of spouse, loss of lifelong friends, deterioration in health, and depression (Stevenson, 2005). Surprisingly, negative health status does not appear to motivate the drinker to reduce his or her level of alcohol consumption (Brennan et al., 2010).

Prescription Drug Abuse

Prescription drug misuse is often overlooked in older age groups by health care professionals, although research has revealed that 20% take medications that are not currently prescribed for them (Barclay, Wright, & Hinkin, 2010). Drug misuse in older age cohorts can take several forms, including (1) mixture of alcohol and prescribed medications, (2) intentional overuse of a prescribed compound, (3) intentional underuse of a prescribed medication, often to extend the duration between refills, (4) erratic use of a prescribed medication, or (5) the failure of the attending physician to obtain a complete drug history, including that of over-the-counter medications, resulting in dangerous combinations of various compounds. Surprisingly, *underutilization* of prescribed medications is the most common form of medication misuse, usually reflecting the patient's inability to afford the medication (Barclay et al., 2010; Piette, Heisler, & Wagner, 2004).

Twelve percent of persons over the age of 65 are taking at least one BZ (Ellison, 2012). However, this class of medications presents a special danger for older users: They increase the individual's risk of falling and suffering a fractured hip by 50% for example (Klimstra & Mahboub, 2010). The BZs also exacerbate the symptoms of dementia, and abrupt BZ withdrawal can result in disorientation and confusion for the patient. These are symptoms that frequently are interpreted as signs of dementia rather than effects of BZs on older patients by health care professionals (Klimstra & Mahboub, 2010). Benzodiazepines that require oxidation as part of the biotransformation/elimination process are not recommended for older individuals or with persons with liver disease, because the drug or its metabolites might accumulate in the bodies of the users causing extended problems (Schuckit, 2006a).

The Treatment of Older Patients with SUDs

There are few treatment outcome studies that focus on older patients with an SUD (Zimberg, 2005; Satre, Mertens, Arean, & Weisner, 2004). Even when the older patient with an SUD is referred to treatment, there are few specialized programs that can meet the unique needs of older substance abusers. These special needs can include (1) a *primary prevention* program to warn the individual of the potential dangers of alcohol or drug abuse, (2) an *outreach* component to identify and help serve older patients who might be overlooked by traditional social service agencies, (3) *detoxification* programs designed to meet the needs of the older patient with an SUD (who may require longer-than-normal periods to complete the detoxification process), (4) *protective environments* for older patients, including the treatment program setting, (5) *primary treatment* for those people whose status would allow them to benefit from such treatment programs, (6) *aftercare* programs for older individuals. Ancillary services might include employment services and social work support to help the individual find employment and housing. All of the above would be in addition to long-term residential care for people who have suffered medical or psychiatric damage from their SUDs.

Given the current era of "managed care,"[8] it is unlikely that such extended treatment programs might be developed. However, the need is there: The detoxification process, which in younger adults might be completed in 3–7 days, might require 28 days or more to complete for the older adult with an SUD (Stevenson, 2005; Gomberg, 2004; Mundle, 2004). Even if the older patient does complete the detoxification process, they will often present treatment staff with a range of sensory deficits not seen in young adult patients and often dislike the profanity commonly used by younger adults to express themselves. Unless these special needs are addressed, older patients with an SUD are unlikely to be motivated to remain in treatment or might resist a

referral to treatment following relapse (Zimberg, 2005). It is imperative for treatment program staff to be aware of the age-specific stressors that an older person will present when they are in a rehabilitation center setting, such as bereavement, loneliness, and the effects of physical illness (Zimberg, 2005, 1996). On a positive note, there is evidence that older adults with an SUD respond better to an age-specific treatment program than do younger substance abusers (Drew et al., 2010). Older patients were found to remain in primary treatment alone and to respond to psychosocial interventions such as Alcoholics Anonymous with more enthusiasm while presenting a lower risk of relapse than seen with other subgroups of drinkers (Satre et al., 2004).

Substance Use Disorders in the Military

The subject of substance abuse in the military community is, in a figurative sense, like the elephant in the living room. The military culture is one that essentially tolerates if not actively encourages alcohol use and abuse. However, in the middle of the 1970s substance abuse became a significant problem among active duty military personnel, especially those assigned to combat assignments. Some units openly tolerated the abuse of chemicals even in combat areas, whereas other units discouraged substance use in combat zones but were willing to encourage it when the unit was not in a combat zone. In the 1970s, efforts were made to address this problem through urine toxicology drug testing and peer substance abuse counselors. One "dirty" urine sample could result in a referral to treatment, and a second result in dishonorable discharge from the military. These measures, plus the end of the controversial conflict in Vietnam and the end of the "draft," contributed to a reduction in the level of substance abuse among active duty military personnel.

However, the problem has not been eliminated: A recent study did find that 20% of active duty military personnel engage in heavy alcohol use, and that 47% engage in binge drinking (Institute of Medicine of the National Academies, 2012; Schumm & Chard, 2012). The ratio of male and female members of the military who have an SUD is approximately 3:1. AUDs appear to be most common among low-ranking enlisted personnel, although there are some members in the officer's corps who also meet the diagnostic criteria for an AUD. As is true in general society, older adolescents

[8]Discussed in the chapter "Relapse and Other Problems Frequently Encountered in Substance Abuse Rehabilitation."

and younger adults, the age groups that are most likely to have recently enlisted in the military, are most likely to meet the criteria for an AUD. Eleven percent of active duty military personnel admitted to the misuse of a prescribed substance or an illicit drug. However, the implications of these findings are difficult to interpret for a number of reasons (Schumm & Chard, 2012): (1) There is a high correlation between combat assignments and traumatic brain injury (TBI). (2) There is also a high correlation between TBI and AUDs. (3) Individuals whose military duty placed them in direct contact with enemy combatants and thus were most likely to have killed another person(s) in combat tend to drink more heavily.[9] Finally, (4) there is a high degree of correlation between AUDs and combat-related posttraumatic stress disorder (PTSD). The interplay between these as well as other unidentified environmental and individual-specific genetic factors makes it difficult to identify the role of AUDs for those who have served in the military. For example, although the self-medication hypothesis would appear to account for the increased use of alcohol by persons who had suffered combat-related PTSD, there is also a possible increased vulnerability to PTSD in persons who had an AUD prior to their exposure to the combat-related trauma (Schumm & Chard, 2012). Alcohol use following combat-related trauma, while offering short-term relief from intrusive memories, heightened startle response, anxiety, social isolation, and hyper-vigilance associated with PTSD, and it might block progress toward resolution of the PTSD by providing such short-term relief, thus becoming an avoidance mechanism that individuals might employ as they see the need to deal with the symptoms of PTSD (Schumm & Chard, 2012). The problem of substance use in the military—especially alcohol, because random urine toxicology testing makes it difficult to abuse other substances—has become so serious that the Institute of Medicine of the National Academies (2012) called for the hiring of mental health/substance abuse treatment professionals with advanced training in the treatment of SUDs. These individuals should also have advanced training in working with people who have developed PTSD as a result of combat-related trauma. Although this section has not provided an exhaustive discussion of the problem of the SUDs in the military,[10] it does underscore the fact that this is a problem. Substance abuse rehabilitation professions working with this population should obtain special training to develop expertise necessary to be effective while working with military personnel.

Substance Use Disorders in the Gay, Lesbian, Bisexual, and Transgender Communities

The clinical literature that explores the impact of SUDs on gay, lesbian, or transgender populations has for the most part focused on the role of alcohol and drugs of abuse among men who desire sex with other men (Hughes et al., 2006). By contrast, the problem of alcohol or drug misuse among bisexual or transgender persons and women whose sexual preference is other women has received relatively little clinical attention (Hughes et al., 2006; Shelton, 2011; Trocki, Drabble, & Midanik, 2009). Regrettably, clinical evidence suggests that SUDs, including tobacco use disorders, are more prevalent in the gay/lesbian/bisexual/transgender (GLBT) population (Cabaj, 2005, 1997; King et al., 2003; Trocki, 2009). This lack of clinical research thus will place the health care professional at a disadvantage when working with a GLBT substance-abusing client.

This lack of clinical research is perhaps most clearly seen with the problem of methamphetamine abuse in the GLBT community. It has traditionally been thought that the level of methamphetamine abuse within the GLBT subpopulation is higher than in the general population (Ling, Rawson, & Shoptaw, 2006), although the database for this assumption is weak at best. However, methamphetamine or other substance abuse among persons who identify themselves as being GLBT places rehabilitation center staff at a disadvantage: There are also fewer resources for therapeutic intervention with members of the GLBT community, and most staff members are uncomfortable working with this subpopulation if only because they lack proper training to do so.

---

[9]It would be logical to assume that as women are integrated into combat arms units rather than support or logistics units that the proportion of male to female service personnel with drinking problems would change as more women are exposed to situations in which they are forced to defend themselves or are exposed to situations that predispose the individual into developing PTSD. This is only a hypothesis, however, and has not been subjected to methodological verification.

---

[10]To save space, we will not discuss the problem of SUDs among dependents of military personnel.

Statement of the Problem

It is estimated that sexual minority group members comprise between 2% and 9% of the general population (Trocki et al., 2009).[11] This subpopulation has been found to have higher rates of illicit drug and alcohol use than the general population. This is illustrated by the discrepancy between non-injection drug use rates for non-injection drug abuse among the general population (10–12%) compared with the 28–35% of the gay/lesbian population who report having engaged in non-injection drug abuse (Cabaj, 2005). This discrepancy has been viewed as reflecting an increased vulnerability to the SUDs in the GLBT community for a variety of reasons.

First, individuals who announce their sexual orientation at an earlier age tend to experience negative feedback from friends and family at a time when they are concurrently attempting to come to terms with their sexual identity. Alcohol or drugs offer the promise of temporary escape from this stress. Second, living on the fringes of a society that is, at best, only slowly coming to accept homosexuality as a possible variant of human relationships, offers few opportunities for socialization within the general community. It is for this reason that the "gay" bar comes to play such a central role in the GBLT community. It is a place where one might go to socialize without fear of ridicule, meet potential partners, or simply to relax. The gay bar also may play a major role in the process of learning about one's sexuality and its implications for daily life.

There are different substance use patterns within the GBLT community. Current research suggests that lesbian and bisexual women are more likely to develop alcohol and drug use disorders,[12] whereas homosexual and bisexual men are at higher risk for illicit drug use problems, although there are exceptions to this rule (Green & Feinstein, 2012).

Homosexual or bisexual males are thought to abuse methamphetamine both for its arousal and its disinhibition effects (Rutkowski & Maxwell, 2009). Further, in rare instances homosexual/bisexual men will use compounds such as amyl or butyl nitrite at the moment of orgasm in the belief that these chemicals enhance the intensity of the orgasm.[13] These are substance use patterns thought to be rare in lesbians, transgender, or bisexual women.

Research suggests that lesbians or bisexual women are more likely to drink and that when they drink they tend to engage in heavy drinking more often than their heterosexual counterparts. More than half of women with a same-sex orientation will have an AUD at some point in their lives, a rate that is five to seven times as high as the norm for heterosexual women. However, the methodology on which these estimates are based has been challenged (Cabaj, 2005). The early research studies used samples drawn from volunteers at local gay bars that may erroneously inflate the percentage of women with an apparent AUD (Cabaj, 2005). Statistically those people most likely to frequent gay bars are going to be those people with an SUD, especially an AUD, resulting in an overrepresentation of persons with an SUD in samples drawn from these establishments. Further, emerging evidence suggests that it is inappropriate to include data from bisexual men or women with persons who prefer a same-sex orientation because this appears to be a distinct subpopulation with different substance use patterns than those seen in persons with a same-sex orientation (Green & Feinstein, 2012). Preliminary evidence suggests that bisexual men and women are at increased risk for an SUD than persons with a same-sex orientation (Green & Feinstein, 2012); however, there is a need for more research into this topic.

There has also been little research into the health care needs of bisexual or lesbian women, and virtually no research into the treatment method(s) that may be most effective for persons in the GLBT community (Cabaj, 2005; Shelton, 2011). Evidence suggests that lesbian or bisexual women are more likely to seek treatment than are gay or bisexual men. There are few dedicated treatment programs for GBLT clients, and those few programs that do exist are usually

---

[11]The lower estimates reflect those individuals who *report* a sexual identity that would place them in a sexual minority, while higher estimates reflect the percentage of the population that has engaged in behaviors typically seen in people who belong to a sexual minority subgroup (Trocki et al., 2009). Within this context, recreational drug use might provide an excuse for the individual to engage in otherwise unacceptable behaviors, blaming his or her state of intoxication for their "deviant" behavior(s) (Cabaj, 2005).

[12]Which might also include misuse of prescribed medications.

---

[13]And significantly increase the abuser's risk of a stroke because the individual's blood pressure is already significantly elevated at the moment of orgasm. The additional increase in blood pressure levels achieved through this practice might over tax the cerebral circulatory system and induce a hemorrhagic stroke.

located in major cities where there is a significant GBLT population. This puts a geographic barrier in place for those gay, bisexual, or lesbian people who live in more rural areas or smaller communities who do not have access to these programs. There also has been a movement to establish special Alcoholics Anonymous (AA) group meetings oriented toward the specific needs of the GBLT population. It is not known whether such specialized groups are more effective for the individual than more traditional 12-Step meetings (Boschert, 2010). Unfortunately such specialized 12-Step group meetings are also usually only found in major cities. Further, because formal religions often persecute or reject homosexual men and women, 12-Step recovery programs can make members of GLBT community uncomfortable because of past negative experiences with spiritual communities (Boschert, 2010; Shelton, 2011).

There is much to be discovered about the treatment of substance abusing GLBT persons. Few substance abuse rehabilitation professionals take the time to consider how they feel about working with persons in the GLBT communities, which has the potential for a poor therapeutic alliance if not treatment failure. There is thus a very real need for substance abuse rehabilitation professionals to be trained in and comfortable working with GLBT individuals.

Substance Abuse and the Disabled

It has been estimated that 19% of the population, or just under one-fifth of the entire population of the United States, has a disability. The most common disabilities are reviewed in Table 19-1 (Pearson, 2009).

These data do not include every form of disability possible. For example, it does not include those people living with some degree of hearing impairment or many forms of developmental dysfunctions such as congenital limb malformation syndromes. However, it does illustrate the fact that a significant number of people in this country are living with a long-term disability. Unfortunately, there is at best a limited body of information about the relationship and form of the SUDs and various forms of disability. The available evidence would suggest that the SUDs are more common among people with a disability than the general population (Corrigan et al., 2005; Pearson, 2009). This is clearly seen in the fact

TABLE 19-1
People Affected by the Most Common Forms of Disability in the United States

FORM OF DISABILITY	NUMBER OF PEOPLE
Spinal cord injury	400 thousand
Cerebral palsy	500 thousand
Poststroke disability	3 million
Learning disabilities	3.5 million
Alzheimer's disease	4.0 million
Serious persistent mental illness	5 million
Traumatic brain injuries	5.3 million
Mental retardation	7.3 million

that 62% of those people who are disabled have an AUD (Heinemann & Rawal, 2005).

Unfortunately social attitudes and a lack of training for health care professionals make the identification of a person with a disability problematic. The number of physicians who are fluent in American Sign Language (ASL) is quite limited, for example, leaving the physician dependent on family or friends to translate their questions into ASL and the patient's response back into English. Because of time pressures the physician might not ask the appropriate questions about the individual's substance use, or the translator (if a family member or friend) might censor the patient's responses. Even if a disabled person is identified as having an SUD, treatment resources are very, very limited. For example, many treatment programs rely not on professional sign language interpreters, but on friends and family members to carry out translation functions (Heinemann & Rawal, 2005). Even if treatment programs have videotapes of lectures that are closed captioned, more traditional treatment methods such as group therapy rarely involve interpreters if only because of confidentiality issues. Individual therapy sessions are problematic if the therapist is not fluent in sign language, and those treatment centers that rely on family members or friends to interpret might cause the individual to censor his or her comments to avoid revealing embarrassing information to these people. The lack of staff who are fluent in ASL prevents the client from participation in informal give-and-take discussions outside of group or individual psychotherapy sessions and can make the client feel isolated.

In contrast to this lack of treatment, resources *drug dealers* are quite happy to offer their "services" to the disabled. Some drug dealers have gone so far as to learn sign language to communicate with hearing-impaired clients, providing a service lacking in many rehabilitation programs. To complicate efforts at rehabilitation, many family members believe that the hearing-impaired person (or people with other disabilities) are entitled to use recreational chemicals because of their disability. In this manner, significant others might overlook signs of an SUD that requires professional intervention. As discussed in this section, the physically disabled population forms a hidden subgroup in the United States, which is underserved, and often hidden from view.

Traumatic Brain Injuries

The number of people living with the aftereffects of a TBI in the United States is slightly higher than the number of people living with a serious and persistent form of mental illness (Pearson, 2009). This fact often surprises the student as he or she is generally unaware of this fact or that SUDs are a serious coexisting problem for persons who have suffered a TBI. Many of those who suffer a TBI did so while under the influence of one or more chemicals (usually alcohol) at the time of the injury. However, between 10% and 20% of those people who struggle to live with the impact of a TBI on their lives did not have an SUD at the time of their admission to a rehabilitation program (Pearson, 2009). These individuals apparently turned to alcohol or illicit drugs to self-medicate their frustration after reaching the point where hope for further recovery is unrealistic.

Individuals who suffer a TBI often resort to denial about the role that their substances played in causing the accident. Unfortunately, the TBI might make it difficult for the individual to *understand* the role that substances played in the accident that resulted in their TBI. Sometimes the individual will be reluctant to discuss what they believe are ways to cope with the aftereffects of the TBI because they do not wish to give up these "coping" mechanisms. Thus, one challenge that faces the substance abuse rehabilitation professional who works with post-TBI patients is the determination whether their SUD (a) *predates* their injury, (b) was involved in causing the injury, or (c) developed after the injury. The role that a chemical plays in the individual's life in each of these three cases might be far

different and influences the treatment goals.[14] A confounding factor is the (d) degree of residual impairment that the individual struggles to adjust after the TBI. Another confounding factor is that personality disordered individuals comprise a significant percentage of those who have suffered a TBI. This forces the rehabilitation professional to address the issues of the personality disorder while helping the person recover from and adjust to the aftereffects of the TBI, while simultaneously addressing the SUD. Very few substance abuse rehabilitation professionals have been trained to do all of these tasks (Corrigan et al., 2005).

Treatment guidelines for working with the patient with a TBI who has an SUD are lacking, although there is evidence suggesting that duration of treatment is one predictor of treatment success (Corrigan et al., 2005). Financial incentives or job placement assistance might help motivate the individual to stay in treatment longer and are especially helpful when working with personality disordered substance abusers who have suffered a TBI. Unfortunately, these individuals are perceived as a source of frustration for most treatment program staff, especially those programs that do not normally work with patients who have suffered a TBI, who express the opinion that the person's needs would best be met "elsewhere." Except in vary rare cases "elsewhere" does not exist, and the substance abusing person with a TBI is either ignored or referred to a suboptimal treatment center.

Ethnic Minorities and Substance Use Disorders

Society has slowly started to accept that the SUDs in ethnic minorities might not follow the same pattern or follow the same trajectory as seen in the typical Caucasian substance abuser (Chartier & Caetano, 2010). However substance abuse rehabilitation professionals who work with members of various ethnic minority groups are faced with a conundrum: Rehabilitation programs appear to be as effective for ethnic minority members as it is for the general population (Blume & de la Cruz, 2005). However, ethnic minorities have limited access to general health care or substance abuse rehabilitation programs,

---

[14]For example, a person who suffered a specified degree of injury while intoxicated would offer different treatment challenges than a second person who suffered the same degree of impairment and turned to chemicals as a way to cope with their anger and frustration over suddenly becoming disabled.

and there is a paucity of research into the best modalities of treatment for minority group members (Niv, Pham, & Hser, 2009).

The relationship between SUDs and ethnic minority status is quite complex. One variable is the process of acculturation for the individual (Collins & McNair, 2002; el-Guebaly, 2008). Each successive generation moves closer to the social norms of the dominant culture in the United States. Yet in so doing members of many ethnic groups become more vulnerable to SUDs as cultural prohibitions that once protected individuals are discarded (Collins & McNair, 2002; el-Guebaly, 2008). There are thus intergenerational differences in the development of SUDs in minority groups. There are also significant intergroup differences between various ethnic groups, preventing the development of a substance abuse rehabilitation model that might be applied to all ethnic minority groups in this country. What follows is a brief summary of the substance abuse patterns of some of the larger ethnic groups in the United States (Niv et al., 2009).

Native Americans

The Native American population in the United States is subject to numerous misperceptions. First, there is no standard definition of "Native American." Some researchers include Alaskan natives with Native Americans, as if these diverse groups might share similar cultural and social traditions ("Alcohol and minorities: an update," 2002). This lack of a standard definition only serves to cloud the issue of the impact of SUDs on the Native American population. Another source of misunderstanding is the fact that there is no single Native American subgroup. The Native American population is not a single, cohesive group but a heterogeneous population of approximately 2 million people belonging to between 200 (Franklin & Markarian, 2005) and 500 (Collins & McNair, 2002) different tribal units. Even within the population of Native Americans there are many differences. For example, only about one-third of the identified members of the various tribes live on "reservations" (Beauvais, 1998). Just the fact that the other two-thirds live outside of an identified reservation makes them slightly different than those who live on the reservation even if, technically, they are members of the same tribal unit.

The different tribes have an estimated 200 distinct languages, as well as different cultural and social histories. This makes generalizations from research conducted on one tribal group to the next difficult, if not impossible. For example, in some tribes in the Northeastern United States, 111 of every 1,000 people meet the criteria for a formal diagnosis of an AUD, while in some tribes of the Southwest, only 11 of every 1,000 members would qualify for the same diagnosis. Obviously there are different forces at work within these different tribes to cause such a discrepant rate of alcoholism. There are also marked intergenerational variation within tribal units, with younger members abusing alcohol and methamphetamine more often than their elders (Beauvais, 1998; Rutkowski & Maxwell, 2009).

Although all of these issues make research into the interrelationship between the SUDs and tribal membership difficult, there are a few facts that are known. For example, the alcohol-related death rate for Native Americans is estimated to be 440% higher than for the general population in the United States (Ringwald, 2002). There is also an apparent relationship between alcohol use and suicide within the Native American population (Crosby et al., 2009). Approximately 37% of Native Americans who committed suicide in the 2005–2006 period met the legal definition for intoxication at the time of their death, while an unknown percentage had ingested smaller amounts of alcohol before their suicide (Crosby et al., 2009).

Statistically, Native American males have AUDs twice as often as do women ("Alcohol and Minorities: An Update," 2002). There are exceptions to this rule, however, as evidenced by the fact that approximately equal percentages of men and women in the Sioux nation have AUDs (Collins & McNair, 2002). Nor can the abuse of a given compound such as alcohol be viewed in the same context in different Native American tribal units. There is also evidence that Native Americans might develop an SUD for reasons different from the people of the mainstream culture, although both groups might abuse the same chemical(s) (Schmidt, Greenfield, & Mulia, 2006).

There is virtually no research about which treatment modalities might work best in working with a Native American substance abuser. Preliminary data suggest that substance abusing Native Americans might have a better recovery rate if they are referred to a program that specializes in working with Native American clients (Schmidt et al., 2006). However, the number of such programs is quite limited, and a referral to such a specialized program is not always possible because of geographic and funding limitations. All too often the individual is referred to a treatment center that is poorly equipped to deal with Native American substance abusers. Only 20% of substance abuse rehabilitation programs offer specialized components for Native Americans (Schmidt et al., 2006). Unfortunately there has been little to no research into the relevance of the material contained in the "specialized component" to members of different tribal units. Further there has been little research into the specific treatment skills necessary to work with Native Americans. Markarian and Franklin (2005) suggested, for example, that Native Americans might withdraw into themselves if faced with high levels of confrontation, an observation that has implications for rehabilitation programs serving this population. Rehabilitation center staff working with this population must be sensitive to the cultural differences and beliefs of these clients both within a single tribe and between tribes.

One popular misconception that cuts across tribal boundaries is that Native Americans are more sensitive to the effects of alcohol than are members of other ethnic groups. There is little factual evidence to support this belief (Caetano, Clark, & Tam, 1998). Further, although it is widely believed that European explorers introduced alcohol to Native Americans, there is historical evidence suggesting that at least some tribes used alcohol in religious ceremonies, as a medicine, and as a way to prepare for warfare, before the arrival of European explorers (Collins & McNair, 2002). So at least some tribes were aware of alcohol and its effects before the arrival of European explorers, and much of what we thought we knew about the SUDs in this population has been proven to be inaccurate. There is so much to be discovered about the history of alcohol use within the Native American population, the treatment modalities that are most effective in the rehabilitation of substance abusing individuals, and what treatment methods might be counterproductive in the treatment of Native Americans with an SUD that arguably most health care professionals are ill trained at best to work with Native American substance abusers.

Hispanic (Latino) Clients

It is estimated that approximately 11% of the entire population of the United States is Hispanic. However, there is a problem in speaking of a single Hispanic or Latino population in that individuals normally classified as Hispanic in surveys might in reality come from any one of 20 different countries (el-Guebaly, 2008). About 60% of the Hispanic population traces their roots to Mexico, 15% came from Puerto Rico, 5% from Cuba,

and the rest from various other countries. Each of these social groups has different attitudes, different cultures, and different attitudes toward alcohol and drug use (Franklin & Markarian, 2005). To illustrate the differences between these subgroups, on occasion a word that holds one meaning in one Latino subgroup will carry a different, possibly socially offensive, meaning in another subgroup. Yet these different subpopulations are all lumped together under the rubric of Hispanic or Latino by researchers, a mistake that introduces many variables into treatment effectiveness research that are not controlled for at the time of the research study.

Traditionally, alcohol use, especially heavy alcohol use, is a male activity within the Hispanic cultures (Collins & McNair, 2002). However, there are significant differences in the prevalence of substance abuse between the various Hispanic subgroups noted above. Eighteen percent of Mexican Americans are considered heavy drinkers, for example, while only 5% of Cuban Americans engage in heavy alcohol use. In both subgroups, it is rare for a woman to use alcohol and an even smaller percentage engages in heavy alcohol use (Collins & McNair, 2002). The need for specialized treatment resources for the Hispanic population exceeds demand: Only about one-third of substance abuse rehabilitation programs offer specialized components for Hispanic clients (Schmidt et al., 2006). Even if the individual does have access to a program with a specialized component for the Hispanic cultures, there are many barriers to treatment: Language barriers, perceived stigma, childhood custody and legal concerns over immigration status, in addition to financial and geographic issues all limit access to treatment even if such resources are available (Conner, Le Fauve, & Wallace, 2009; Niv et al., 2009). If the substance abuser is the mother, provisions must be made for child care and education and supporting the family while she participates in treatment and adequate financial resources should be found for the treatment program; all these factors conspire to make participation in treatment virtually impossible for the mother. If the substance abuser is a family member other than the mother, then the financial burden might still prevent that person from entering treatment.

Hispanic people also often experience longer delays in receiving care for their SUD, receive less active treatment for their SUD, and are less likely to be referred to residential treatment programs for their SUD (Dunigan, 2009; Niv et al., 2009). These delays result in increased risk to life: For example, approximately 29% of Hispanic people who ended their lives were legally intoxicated at the time of their death (Crosby et al., 2009). This figure does not include people of Hispanic heritage who consumed some alcohol prior to their suicide attempt but who were not legally intoxicated at the time of their death. Thus, there is a need for substance abuse rehabilitation programs to develop not just a sensitivity for working with Hispanic clients but also an awareness of the differences between various Hispanic subgroups and equality in treatment services offered.

Asian Americans

This term is also misleading: Depending upon the researcher and the definitions used, this term might include Chinese Americans, Filipino Americans, Asian Indians, Korean Americans, Japanese Americans, and Vietnamese Americans, people from Hawaii, Micronesia, and Polynesia ("Alcohol and Minorities: An Update," 2002; Conner et al., 2009). Each of these subgroups has its own diverse culture, traditions, and in many cases languages, yet in many research studies these subgroups are lumped together as being Asian American (Franklin & Markarian, 2005).

Depending upon the Asian American subpopulation under discussion, women are more likely to abstain from alcohol or drink only on special occasions compared with their male partners. However even this rule must be tempered with the observation that women from various subgroups have widely disparate alcohol use patterns. For example, only 20% of Korean American women admitted to the use of alcohol on occasion, whereas more than 67% of Japanese American women admit to using alcohol at some point (Caetano et al., 1998). Little is known about the needs of these subgroups or the treatment methods that might be most effective when they are admitted to a rehabilitation facility.

African Americans

Until recently there has been a paucity of research addressing SUDs in African Americans. Even now the number of research articles addressing the problem of illicit drug use in the African American population is limited at best, although there is a slowly growing body of literature addressing the issue of AUDs in this subpopulation. Such research has found that African Americans males with AUDs were more likely to initiate heavy drinking later in life than Caucasian males but were more likely to experience physical complications from alcohol use earlier in life (Edlund, Booth, & Feldman, 2009; Franklin & Markarian, 2005). These data suggest

that alcohol use patterns differ between the African American and the Caucasian population in this country.

To complicate matters there is also evidence suggesting that intergenerational differences in substance use patterns within the African American exist. African American women in the 18–29-year age cohort are significantly more likely to have an AUD than their older peers, with 3.8% of the younger age cohort meeting diagnostic criteria for an AUD as opposed to only 2.1% for older age groups (Payne, Back, Wright, Hartwell, & Brady, 2009). African Americans frequently follow a different path into a rehabilitation program(s). For example, African American women are 10 times as likely to be involved with the court system for a substance-related problem as Caucasian women (Schmidt et al., 2006).

Regrettably, there is preliminary evidence to suggest that African Americans with an SUD will receive a different quality of treatment than Caucasians with an SUD (Schmidt et al., 2006). African Americans tend to remain in treatment for shorter periods of time as compared with Caucasian clients, for example, and are more likely to be discharged before successful completion of the rehabilitation program (Niv et al., 2009). The possibility exists that African Americans with an SUD are less likely to perceive a need for treatment than Caucasians (Edlund et al., 2009), possibly combined with a lower quality of treatment services. As these data suggest, there is much to be discovered about this subpopulation and the treatment methods that might be most effective in helping individuals from this subpopulation recover from SUDs.

Combat Veterans and Substance Use Disorders

Combat veterans are a unique subpopulation. The opportunity[15] to participate in combat cuts across racial lines, leaving the victims with a common experience of having been in combat. It has been well established that people exposed to combat are at increased risk for SUDs (Santiago et al., 2010). It has been hypothesized that many veterans turn to alcohol as a way of self-medicating their combat-related traumatic memories, although alcohol use can also complicate the treatment of combat-related PTSD as well as TBIs resulting from combat (Santiago et al., 2010). Surprisingly, when SUDs

---

[15]There is a note of sarcasm here in case the reader missed it.

are detected in returning veterans, referrals to treatment are rare (Santiago et al., 2010). Soldiers who might be aware of their problem perceive a number of barriers to appropriate treatment including the lack of confidentiality within the military organization. In many cases, individuals pay for mental health or substance abuse rehabilitation through private providers to avoid having their treatment for these disorders becoming common knowledge on base. Other barriers to care include schedule conflicts, necessary assumption of child care responsibilities upon return from active service, and the lack of transportation to mental health treatment centers (Kim, Thomas, Wilk, Castro, & Hoge, 2010).

There are many reasons why combat veterans are at risk for SUDs. First, during combat men draw strength from their fellows and build a support system to help them cope, especially while in combat. However, units are often broken up and men are reassigned to other duties upon return from combat duty, separating the soldier from his or her support system. Multiple deployments to combat zones can further stress not only the individual's coping mechanisms but also the ability of the family to adapt (Darwin & Reich, 2011). It is possible that veterans and their families might turn to alcohol or illicit drugs as coping mechanisms for combat-related stress conditions[16] (Santiago et al., 2010).

Further, the age cohort from which enlisted men are drawn (ages 18–24) is also the age cohort most at risk for SUDs. This might explain why individuals in the lower ranks were more likely to abuse alcohol than were non-commissioned and commissioned officers. The "culture of drinking" found in many military units also can contribute to a tendency for the individual to abuse alcohol rather than address their mental health problems. Finally, the military places emphasis on the individual being able to cope on their own and instills a desire within the soldier not to appear "weak." Unfortunately, untreated SUDs are associated with a higher tendency for the individual to be "separated" from the service under dishonorable circumstances, while untreated PTSD and anxiety disorders cause untold suffering not only for the veteran but also for families who live with this person.

Chapter Summary

Although this chapter does not discuss the relationship between every subgroup of substance abusers and chemical abuse, it has attempted to demonstrate there are many subpopulations within this country where very little is known about the factors that might initiate, maintain the SUD, or the treatment methods that might be most effective with each subpopulation. All too often research studies that have been conducted in this area have utilized exclusively male samples, with the result being that virtually nothing is known about the factors that might initiate and maintain the SUDs in subpopulations.

The stereotypical image of what a "typical" person with SUD is like often blinds us to the fact that there are many hidden subpopulations with their own unique cultures and histories. The substance use trajectories for persons from each subgroup might be significantly different from members of other subgroups. The avenues toward the initiation of, maintenance of, and recovery from SUDs also differ from one subgroup to the next. These subgroups are rarely recognized by treatment professionals as being different. Their needs in rehabilitation programs and the barriers to treatment that they encounter are often ignored while they are referred to a standardized "one size fits all" treatment program.

---

[16]It is not only the soldier who experiences stress during a deployment to a combat zone. Family members must struggle to find financial resources to pay ongoing bills and maintain internal cohesiveness during a time of uncertainty about the well-being of the person on active duty.

CHAPTER 20

Substance Use and Abuse by Children and Adolescents

Introduction

Developmental psychologists, neurologists, and pediatricians all agree that childhood and adolescence are periods of "rapid physical, cognitive, emotional, social and behavioral changes" (Upadhyaya & Gray, 2009, p. 421). At this point, agreement between various researchers breaks down. A consensus has yet to emerge about such basic issues as when childhood ends or adolescence begins. If one accepts the onset of puberty as the definition of the start of adolescence, as Windle et al. (2009) suggested, one is then faced with the exceptional inter-individual variability of the onset of puberty. Some children reach this developmental milestone as early as 10 years of age whereas others do not do so until several years later.

The onset of puberty itself is a stressor that can contribute to substance use disorders (SUDs). Children who start puberty early are often ill at ease around their contemporaries because their physical size changes dramatically with the onset of puberty, and they might start to associate with older adolescents who approximate their own physical stature but are emotionally more mature.[1] Children who start puberty later than their peers are vulnerable to feelings of inferiority as they (literally) look up to their physically more mature friends.

During this time, the individual moves from elementary school on to middle or junior high school, a process that brings with it stage-specific developmental demands. It is important to keep in mind the fact that although the developmental changes in childhood and adolescence are tied to the individual's age, they are not synonymous with the aging process (Masten, Fade, Zucker, & Spear, 2009). Children or adolescents of the same biological age might be working their way through different stages of psychosocial growth (Masten et al., 2009). Unfortunately one of the challenges that the child or adolescent will face is the question whether to use or abstain from alcohol and illicit drugs, as evidenced by the fact that the average age at which the typical person uses an illicit compound[2] for the first time is 18.8 years (Substance Abuse and Mental Health Services Administration, 2009).

---

[1] A relative term in the sense that a 13-year-old is hopefully cognitively and emotionally more mature than a 9-year-old.

[2] Alcohol would be classified as an illegal compound for individuals in this age bracket because possession or consumption of alcohol by a minor is usually illegal except under special circumstances.

To understand child or adolescent SUDs, it is necessary to place the individual's substance use behavior in the context of his or her level of cognitive and social maturity. These chemicals offer the promise of pleasure and a sense of belonging to the child or adolescent at a time when he or she is possibly ill-prepared to understand the hidden dangers associated with the use of these substances or believe that these consequences will never happen to him or her. Thus, substance abuse rehabilitation professionals need to be aware of the differing needs and potentials that children and adolescents possess and how substance abuse by children and adolescents is a complex problem that is influenced by a variety of factors. Although the topic of child and adolescent substance abuse is worthy of a book, in this chapter we will briefly examine the complex problem of child and adolescent SUDs.

The Problem of Substance Abuse in Childhood and Adolescence

SUDs in childhood and adolescence have been a social problem for generations. In the 19th century, alcohol dependence was rampant among children and young adolescents in England (Wheeler & Malmquist, 1987). This fact sparked a social reform movement to protect children and adolescents from the ravages of alcohol or illicit drug use. Underaged substance use became less common but it never really disappeared, as evidenced by the fact that the economic cost to society by underaged alcohol use alone is $62 billion/year (Spoth, Greenberg, & Turrisi, 2009). Research has repeatedly demonstrated that children begin to form personal attitudes toward alcohol and later drug use early in life. By preschool children have at least a rudimentary knowledge of alcohol, its effects, and social norms that govern its use (Zucker, Donovan, Masten, Mattson, & Moss, 2009). Arguably the early childhood years form the foundation on which subsequent substance use rests.

Whereas preliminary substance use expectations are formed in early childhood, substance use behaviors commonly develop during adolescence. Although there is anecdotal evidence of substance abuse by children, the age cohort where substance abuse most commonly associated with the SUDs is adolescence (Crowley, 2007; Substance Abuse and Mental Health Services Administration, 2005; Zucker et al., 2009).

A Complicating Factor

Students are often surprised to learn that "childhood" and "adolescence" are social constructs, the definition of which varies from one culture to another[3] (Epstein, 2013). A century and a half ago children were viewed as essentially being little adults in European society[4] who entered an apprenticeship to learn a trade during childhood and from which they would graduate years later as young adults. Other children entered the workforce at an early age.[5] They did not keep the money that they earned but would use it to help support their family. With the arrival of the industrial age and mass production, "hundreds of thousands" (Epstein, 2013, p. 18) of individuals in the age cohort that we now call "adolescents" were displaced from the workforce. In a beautiful example of social evolution, the concept of adolescence emerged. Children were no longer viewed as little adults. The adolescent was expected to work only for supplemental income and to use this phase of life for socialization, vocational training, and educational experiences.[6] The expected period of education was extended from 8 to 12 years. An unintended side effect was the emergence of an age cohort that had relatively few responsibilities, comparatively a great deal of free time, and large amounts of disposable income.

In the post–World War II era, for example, it was possible for the individual to enter the workforce upon

---

[3]The proof for this statement is found in the simple question: When does infancy end and childhood begin? The answer to this question varies from culture to culture.

[4]And in the eyes of the legal system often punished as if they were adults.

[5]There are memorable photographs of children working alongside their fathers in a coal mine or in a factory setting in the late 1800s and early 1900s, for example.

[6]The truth of this statement is found in the observation that in over 100 different cultures those we would classify as children and adolescents work alongside their elders, learn from them, and through their work contribute to the family's resources.

graduation from high school and assume the responsibilities of full adulthood (Furstenberg, 2010). The shift in economic emphasis from manufacturing to skills and technology during the last half of the 20th century brought with it a reduced need for persons who seek to enter the workforce with only a high school diploma (Furstenberg, 2010). Concurrently, the educational qualifications necessary for entry-level positions in most professions were raised to a vocational-technical school or college graduate[7] or even a person with an advanced degree. Even with a college degree many young adults are finding it difficult to find a full-time position. To survive financially, many young adults are forced to work multiple part-time jobs. Again in an example of social evolution, Masten et al. (2009, p. 5) suggested that a new phase of life, "emerging adulthood," be accepted as the norm for these individuals.

Having established that "childhood" and "adolescence" are social fictions, or paradigms, which evolved to better understand the behaviors of these younger members of the parent society, we are forced to integrate the ongoing problem of SUDs into these socially defined phases of life. This is not an easy task. It is recognized that prolonged substance abuse in either childhood or adolescence can influence, or even block, growth and development that society defines as the norm for each stage of growth. This prevents individuals from moving on to the next developmental stage, in effect holding them back. Epstein (2013) argued that by holding people back from adulthood, society contributes to the depression, defiance, and anger typically associated with adolescence. With prolonged use, alcohol and the various drugs of abuse also inhibit the individual's emotional growth, possibly exacerbating the problems mentioned by Epstein (2013). The impact of alcohol or illicit drugs on socially defined growth norms are influenced by such factors as (a) the age at which the substance abuse is initiated, (b) the intensity with which a chemical(s) is abused, (c) the duration of substance abuse, and (d) whether such substance abuse has resulted in unanticipated physical injury (such as involvement in an alcohol-related accident, for example). The implications of SUDs are still being explored and then introduced into the gestalt of these social constructs—an exciting process in which we are participating even as you read these words.

Lamentably much of the research conducted on adolescents in the past 60 years is of limited value in understanding the current childhood and adolescent age cohorts.[8] The age at which children enter puberty in the 21st century is markedly lower than it was a century ago (Masten et al., 2009; Spear, 2010). Early puberty has been identified as a stressor for the individual, even if this is becoming the developmental norm in society. Those individuals who enter adolescence at an earlier age are more vulnerable to the development of an SUD than their peers who reach puberty at a more appropriate age (Brown et al., 2009; Wagner, 2009; Gunn & Smith, 2010).

Scope of the Problem of Substance Abuse in Childhood and Adolescence

Childhood Chemical Abuse Patterns

The database on the scope of child substance abuse behaviors is exceptionally limited at best (Gunn & Smith, 2010; Millar, 2009; Parekh, 2006; Zucker et al., 2009). Minkoff (2008) suggested that for many children, the initial substance use was well before the age of 9, possibly as early as 6 years; however, it is not clear whether these were isolated cases. These figures appear rather daunting but are also based on the assumption that *any* alcohol use by children is illegal. This assumption is false: In 31 states, parents can legally give alcohol to their children under the age of 21[9] (Hingson, 2010). Sometimes parents or other adults will allow the child to sip an alcohol to satisfy the child's curiosity about its effects. In some states, it is legal to allow alcohol to be served to a child under 18 years of age if a parent or responsible adult is present. It is not known whether the child might interpret survey questions about drinking as being applicable because of the

---

[7]A significant percentage of the jobs available today did not even exist 40 years ago. The professions of "information technology specialist" or "web page designer" spring to mind here.

[8]Each generation grows up in a separate technological and social matrix. Imagine, if you will, a world without cellular telephones, text mail messaging, or the Internet, for example. This is the world that your parents grew up in. We will not even begin to talk about the world that your grandparents grew up in!

[9]It is up to the reader to consult with an attorney to determine what law(s) apply to the geographical area where the student lives.

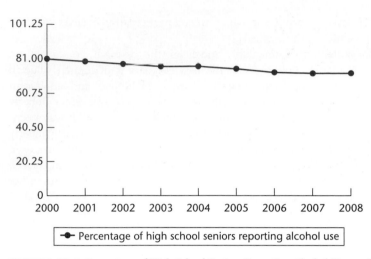

FIGURE 20-1 Percentage of High School Seniors Reporting Alcohol Use at Any Point in Their Lives.
SOURCE: Based on Johnston, OMalley, Backman, and Schulenberg, 2012a.

controlled use of alcohol under adult supervision. If a child admits to the limited use of alcohol at the age of 12 years, is this evidence of an alcohol use problem or of parental permission for that child to drink under carefully controlled conditions? The conclusions by Zucker et al. (2009), who reported that few children below the age of 9 consume alcohol without their parents being aware of this fact, would suggest the latter. If this is true, then the question of parental complicity in their children's alcohol use is raised.[10] With these problems in mind, Johnston, O'Malley, Backman, and Schulenberg (2012a) reported that their survey of high school seniors in 2011[11] revealed that 77.4% of high school seniors reported having abused alcohol at least once. There has been a gradual downward trend in the number of high school seniors reporting alcohol use in the past decade, as reflected in Figure 20-1 (based on Johnston et al., 2012a).

As a group, adolescents are estimated to make up 12–20% of the entire alcohol market in the United States, with 4.3 million adolescents consuming alcohol each year (Windle & Zucker, 2010; Wu & Ringwalt, 2006; Rosenbloom, 2005; Pumariga & Kilgus, 2005). There is evidence that alcohol advertisements are broadcast at times when children or adolescents are most likely to be watching television, an observation that, if proven, raises disturbing questions about the role of advertising in the development of alcohol use disorders AUDs in these age groups (Chung et al., 2009). Beer is the most commonly consumed form of alcoholic, although there is growing evidence that liquor is becoming increasingly popular with adolescents because it is more easily hidden from adults by mixing it with soft drinks (Centers for Disease Control and Prevention, 2007). There has been a very slight, gradual, downward trend in the level of alcohol use among high school students. However, as these data demonstrate, alcohol use is prevalent among students by the time of graduation from high school.

Whether it is sanctioned by a parent or not, the percentage of children or adolescents who report alcohol use at some point in their lives increases between the 8th and 12th grades, as evidenced by the conclusions of the Department of Health and Human Services (2010), which estimated that each day 508,000 adolescents between the age of 12 and 17 consume alcohol. There is a marked age gradient for alcohol use as evidenced by the findings of Johnston et al. (2012a). The authors found that 33% of the 8th-grade students surveyed reported having used alcohol at least once as opposed to 70% of 12th-grade students. Adolescent curiosity might account for some of this reported alcohol use, although a high percentage of the reported alcohol use reflected recreational drinking. Alcohol

[10]Which in some states might be interpreted as a form of child abuse. Again, see Footnote 9.

[11]The most current data available at this time.

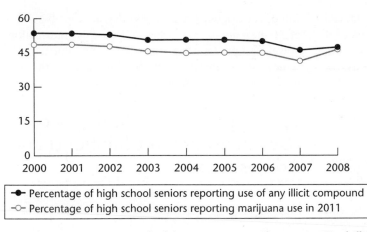

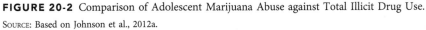

FIGURE 20-2 Comparison of Adolescent Marijuana Abuse against Total Illicit Drug Use.

Source: Based on Johnson et al., 2012a.

abuse is certainly the most common form of substance abuse for adolescents and contributes to traumatic injuries in this age group. One in ten adolescents who drink will drive after consuming alcohol, placing the adolescent, pedestrians, passengers, and other drivers at potential risk.

One-third of drug-related visits to the local hospital emergency room for persons in the 12–20-year-old age cohort involved alcohol, with males being the most likely to require such treatment ("Emergency Department Visits Involving Underaged Alcohol Use" 2008). Seventy percent of such visits involved alcohol alone, whereas 30% involved alcohol and/or drugs, according to the aforementioned report. The danger of adolescent drinking and driving is seen in the fact that teenaged drivers who have a blood alcohol level (BAL) of 0.08%[12] or higher are 17 times more likely to die in an alcohol-related motor vehicle accident than if they were sober.

Adolescent Substance Abuse Patterns

The database for adolescent substance use behaviors is marginally better than that for childhood alcohol and drug abuse. In one of the few realistic surveys of adolescent substance use, the Substance Abuse and Mental Health Services Administration (2009) estimated that in 2008:

- *9.3% of 12–17-year olds were current illicit drug abusers*

- *6.7% of 12–17-year olds had abused marijuana in the past 30 days*
- *2.9% had abused prescription drugs in the past 30 days*
- *1.1% had abused some kind of inhalant in the past 30 days*
- *1.0% had abused a hallucinogenic in the 30 days preceding the survey*
- *0.4% had abused cocaine in the 30 days preceding the survey*

A useful data source about adolescent substance use is surveys conducted on student populations from various schools. However, many high-risk students do not attend classes or at the very most do so on an inconsistent basis. For example, Hispanic students who are frequent alcohol abusers are more likely to drop out of school (Windle & Zucker, 2010). Adolescent substance use patterns reflect geographic location, regional availability of certain substances, peer group pressure(s), parental guidance (or lack thereof), current substance use "trends," and so on. Thus, the information that follows should be accepted as conservative estimates of the scope of the problem of illicit drug abuse by children and adolescents.

In a survey of the senior class of 2011, marijuana was the most commonly abused illicit compound, making up the greatest portion of the illicit drug use by this research sample as demonstrated in Figure 20-2 (based on Johnson et al., 2012a).

A growing problem for adolescents is the diversion of prescription medications for illicit use (Millar, 2009). When asked which prohibited substance was easiest

---

[12]The blood level of alcohol used by most states to define intoxicated driving.

for them to obtain, 15% of the students surveyed said beer, and 23% said marijuana, although the abuse of diverted prescription medications, especially opioids, has become more common (Johnson, O'Malley, Bachman, & Schulenberg, 2012; Madras, 2010; Wunsch, 2007). Approximately 25% of high school students report having used a medication prescribed for somebody else, usually sharing that medication with a member of the same gender (Eaton et al., 2010; Miller, 2007).

This switch in substance abuse patterns might reflect the fact that adolescent abusers often do not realize that these compounds can be both addictive and carry with it a high potential for overdose and possible death (Heymann, 2008; Madras, 2010). Adolescents often believe the myth that you can become addicted to narcotic analgesics only if you inject them. Thus, they believe that it is safe to use intranasal methods of administration, and then as their abuse evolves into an addiction they are forced to turn to injected narcotics to achieve the same results once achieved with lower doses or less intense methods of abuse (Collins & Leak, 2008; Marsch et al., 2005).

The diversion of central nervous system (CNS) stimulants such as methylphenidate or one of the amphetamine compounds is also of growing concern, with 23% of adolescents referred to a substance abuse rehabilitation program admitting to the abuse of such compounds (Croft, 2006). As the number of prescriptions for CNS stimulants aimed at controlling the symptoms of ADHD increases, there is evidence of an increasing problem of stimulant abuse and diversion as well (Setlik, Gond, & Ho, 2009). The usual method of abuse is by oral ingestion or intranasal use. In contrast to this information are those compounds that might be administered intravenously. The intravenous use of any compound is so rare during adolescence that it should automatically be seen as a sign of a serious SUD.

Although adolescent substance use, if only on an experimental basis, is the normal rather than the exception, the distinctions between substance *use, abuse,* and *dependence* are very indistinct. Because alcohol and illicit drugs are illegal by definition, many clinicians believe that *any* substance use during childhood or adolescence is a sign of a serious problem. Other clinicians maintain that *experimental* substance use, especially of alcohol and marijuana, is just one aspect of adolescence (Greydanus & Patel, 2005; Kaminer & Tarter, 2004). The essential questions, Greydanus and Patel (2005) suggested, "is not whether most teenagers

will use drugs, but which one(s) they try" (p. 392), how often they do so, and when. Given this information, how does a parent determine what is experimental substance use as opposed to problematic use? In the next section, we will examine this question in more detail.

Why Worry about Substance Use Disorders in Childhood and Adolescence?

There are many reasons why the abuse of alcohol or drugs by children or adolescents is of special importance. First, there is good evidence that adolescent cigarette smokers are 50% more likely to develop an alcohol use disorder later in life (Grucza & Bierut, 2006). Further, the SUDs are the leading cause of mortality for older adolescents, contributing to accidental death, suicidal thoughts and attempts, interpersonal violence, motor vehicle accidents, and the problem of individuals having unprotected sex (Kaminer & Buckstein, 2005; Miller, Levy, Spicer, & Taylor, 2006; Shepard, Sutherland, & Newcombe, 2006; Windle et al., 2009). Cumulatively, the estimated financial cost of alcohol-related rape, homicide, assault, larceny, burglary, motor vehicle theft, loss of employment, and medical care for underaged drinkers to society is $3 per mixed drink, a cost that far outweighs the estimated ¢10 in taxes generated by that drink.

Adolescent substance abuse is a significant part of the health care problem facing the United States at this time. Complaints of chest pain are the third most common reason why adolescents seek health care, for example. Research has demonstrated that 17% of adolescents in a hospital setting for assessment of their chest pain had ephedrine in their urine in spite of often strident denials that they had not abused this compound (James et al., 1998). The cost of the medical evaluation for a possible cardiac condition in the adolescent is both labor- and resource-intensive. If the adolescent's chest pain is found to reflect not a cardiac disorder but unsuspected drug use, then these health care resources become part of the health care problem in the United States.

The Neurological Factor

Since the turn of the century neuroscientists have determined that childhood and adolescence are periods of dynamic growth in the CNS (Hopson, 2013; Jorgensen, 2008; Parekh, 2006; Wetherill & Tapert,

2013).[13] Some of the neurological changes initiated in adolescence do not reach fruition until well into early adulthood. Because of this ongoing development process in the CNS and an innate drive for novelty and to learn, children and adolescents assess risk differently than do adults—a process that causes them to underestimate the dangers associated with unknown situations (Szalavitz, 2012). Children and adolescents also have different biological responses than adults to alcohol or the drugs of abuse (McVoy & Findling, 2009; Zimmer, 2011). All of these differences suggest that child or adolescent substance abusers are not miniature adults for whom the same treatment protocols will work, but a distinct subpopulation for whom new treatment paradigms must be developed.

The effects of the various drugs of abuse on childhood or adolescent neurological maturation are dependent on such variables as (a) begins to abuse the compound(s) in question, (b) duration of use, (c) intensity of abuse,[14] (d) frequency of abuse, and (e) emotional maturity level among other factors. Adolescence is a time of rapid neurological growth: The development of what is known as the "gray matter" in the human brain normally peaks at about the age of 11 in girls and approximately a year later for boys (Windle et al., 2009). After that point there is a gradual reduction in the volume of gray matter within the brain as the brain eliminates neural pathways[15] that are unused or redundant (Meyers & Dick, 2010; Windle et al., 2009). Binge drinking in adolescents results in altered fiber coherence in the "white matter"[16] of the brain (McQueeny et al., 2009). Even moderately heavy alcohol use during adolescence, such as that necessary to produce a hangover in the drinker, may effect neurological growth (Squeglia, Spandoni, Infante, Myers, & Tapert, 2009). To date, a similar process among adult drinkers has not been identified suggesting that this sign of neurological injury might be stage specific to adolescence, although the implications of this alteration in gray matter fiber coherence are not known at this time.

The hormonal changes that begin during puberty initiate neural changes in the brain's reward system, which achieve full expression during adulthood (Zimmer, 2011). However, this is an uneven process, and the cognitive assessment/control systems of the brain lag behind the growth in the brain's reward system during adolescence (Dobbs, 2011; Hopson, 2013). This might be why the adolescent brain is more sensitive to the rewarding effects of alcohol (and possibly the illicit drugs), while being less sensitive to the negative effects of these compounds than the adult brain (Rutherford, Mayes, & Potenza, 2010; Spear, 2010). A region of the brain known as the ventral striatum,[17] which is strongly interconnected with the limbic system, appears to amplify the rewarding effects of environmental stimuli for adolescents (Zimmer, 2011). In contrast to how adults attend to and interpret novel stimuli through the prefrontal regions of the cortex, adolescents appear to attend to the same stimuli through the activation of the amygdala[18] region of the brain, which is involved in emotional information processing (Thatcher & Clark, 2008). Thus adolescents process information differently than do adults, reacting emotionally when an adult would be more rational.[19] Because memories associated with strong emotions are stronger and are more deeply entrenched in the mind, substance abuse during adolescence exposes the user to the risk of establishing very strong positive memories of the effects of a compound(s) of abuse and positive associations between substance use and specific locations, making it more likely that she or he will want to repeat that experience later (Brenhouse & Anderson, 2008). There is also evidence that adolescents tend to interpret the very act of responding to a substance use cue as a rewarding experience in itself (Rutherford, 2010).

When compared with adult drinkers, adolescents appear to experience less sedation from a given dose of alcohol (Upadhyaya & Gray, 2009; Varlinskaya & Spear, 2006; Strauch, 2003). This lack of equal sedation can contribute to adolescent overuse of alcohol, overwhelming constraints against high-risk behavior(s)

---

[13]The topic of developmental neurology is rather fascinating. However, it lies outside of the scope of this chapter and must be referenced only in passing. The reader is referred to any of a wide range of textbooks on the subject if she or he is interested in learning more about this subject.

[14]Taking one puff off of a marijuana cigarette once a month as opposed to smoking an entire marijuana cigarette each day, for example.

[15]A process called "synaptic pruning" by neurologists.

[16]See Glossary.

[17]See Glossary.

[18]See Glossary.

[19]As any parent of a teenager could tell you.

such as driving while intoxicated or engaging in unprotected sex. This seems to explain why substance abuse in adolescence, especially early adolescence, raises the individual's lifetime risk for an SUD (Madras, 2010; Rosenbloom, 2005). The risk of developing an alcohol use disorder is four to six times higher for the adolescent who begins to drink before the age of 15 as compared with the individual who begins to drink at the age of 21 (Madras, 2010; Meyers & Dick, 2010). This increased risk level is reflected in the finding that almost half of those persons who become alcohol dependent do so before they are legal adults and entitled to buy alcohol (Nelson, 2007). In contrast to this, only about 20% of those individuals who develop an alcohol use disorder at some point in their lives do so after the age of 30 (Nelson, 2007). These figures illustrate one reason why adolescence is a period of special vulnerability for the later development of an SUD.

Unfortunately, the brain of the child or adolescent is also four to five times more vulnerable to alcohol-induced brain damage as is the adult brain (Wuethrich, 2001; Tappert, Caldwell, & Burke, 2004/2005). During adolescence, the *hippocampus*[20] appears to be especially vulnerable to alcohol-related damage (De Bellis et al., 2000; Tappert et al., 2004/2005). This might account for the small (7–10%) but still significant decline in psychological test performance in adolescent alcohol abusers as compared with nondrinkers (Strauch, 2003). This decline in measured cognitive abilities appears to be enhanced by concurrent use of marijuana and appears to be permanent (Spear, 2010; Wagner, 2009). In theory, this reduction in cognitive abilities might reflect alcohol-induced damage to the hippocampus and possibly other regions of the brain.

The Gateway Theory

This controversial theory was espoused by Henry Anslinger, the then U.S. Commissioner of Narcotics, to justify making marijuana illegal after the end of Prohibition, thus providing a rationale for the continued existence of the Bureau of Narcotics (McPherson, Yudko, Murray-Bridges, Rodriguez, & Lindo-Moulds, 2009). Anslinger provided Congress with lurid tales of depraved behavior by marijuana abusers, many of which were fabrications, to justify making marijuana illegal. As part of this campaign, Anslinger also

proposed (with remarkably little evidence) that marijuana abuse would prove to be a "gateway" to the abuse of more serious compounds. Since then, the gateway theory has become part of clinical lore (McPherson et al., 2009).

This theory has generated controversy for more than 70 years now. The team of Walker, Venner, Hill, Myers, and Miller (2004) found that there appeared to be a progression in adolescent substance abuse starting with alcohol to tobacco, then the inhalants, marijuana, and then other drugs of abuse. In another test, the gateway theory, the team of Ellgren, Spano, and Hurd (2006) administered cannabis to adolescent rats and then offered the rats the opportunity to use heroin. The authors found that the marijuana-exposed rats were more likely to self-administer heroin than were marijuana-naive rats. The authors interpreted this as evidence of the gateway theory.

In contrast to this conclusion, Rosenbloom (2005) suggested that the gateway theory is just an illusion and that the progression from one compound to another is not automatic. Several groups of researchers have concluded that personality characteristics such as conduct disorder during childhood or adolescence might be more predictive of subsequent SUDs than simple marijuana abuse in adolescence (Clark, Vanyukrov, & Cornelius, 2002; Watson, Benson, & Joy, 2000). More doubt on the gateway theory was generated by the study conducted by Tarter, Vanyukov, Kirisci, Reynolds, and Clark (2006). The authors reported that about 25% of the 200 male subjects who admitted to the use of marijuana did abuse this compound *before* using alcohol or tobacco products but that the majority of those who abused marijuana did not progress to the abuse of other drugs.

Another challenge to the gateway theory of substance abuse came from Kandel and Chen (2000) who examined the marijuana use patterns of a community-based sample of 708 marijuana abusers (364 male and 304 female abusers) and found that the early abuse of marijuana was not found to predict later problems with chemicals or a progression to later substance abuse (Kandel & Chen, 2000). This study was supported in part by the study conducted by Perkonigg et al. (2008). The authors followed a sample of 3021 adolescents over a 10-year period, with interviews at 4 years and 10 years after the initial survey. The authors found that 7% of their sample reported that they had used cannabis only once, that 11% of their sample reported using it two to four times, and

---

[20]See Glossary.

that only a minority of their sample (approximately 13%) met the criteria for a diagnosis of cannabis dependence at the start of their study, at the 4-year follow-up interview and at the end of the study. They also concluded that those adolescents who reported five or more episodes of marijuana use were the most likely to continue to use marijuana during the early years of adulthood but that the majority of their subjects did not continue to abuse marijuana.

One class of compounds that is frequently overlooked in the debate over the gateway theory of marijuana abuse is the inhalant. These compounds are often the first mood-altering chemical that children or young adolescents experiment with (Hogan, 2000). For most children or adolescents, inhalant abuse is usually a transient phase and so the individual's risk for inhalant-induced brain damage is limited. Such abusers usually engage in episodic inhalant abuse for 1–2 years, after which time they gradually discontinue it. A very small minority of children or adolescents become long-term, possibly lifelong, inhalant abusers, and an unknown percentage of childhood or adolescent inhalant abusers go on to abuse other compounds. The role of inhalant abuse by these children or adolescents is open to debate: Were these individuals unwittingly ensnared by the effects of the inhalants and then turn to the abuse of other compounds, or were those children or adolescents who abused inhalants the most likely to develop other SUDs? At this point there is no clear answer to these questions, and debate surrounding the very concept of the gateway theory of the SUDs continues.

Tobacco Abuse by Children and Adolescents

Cigarettes and other tobacco products occupy a unique place in society: They are known to be addictive, destructive, yet be legally purchased by adults. In contrast to this, children and adolescents are forbidden by law to purchase or use tobacco products. In spite of the legal restrictions against child or adolescent tobacco use, there are an estimated 3 million cigarette smokers in the United States under the age of 18 (Rosen & Maurer, 2008). The total number of adolescents who smoke cigarettes has been slowly declining since 1991, and the percentage of 12th graders who reported ever smoking a cigarette from 2001 to 2011 as opposed to having smoked in the past 30 days is reviewed in Figure 20-3 (based on Johnston et al., 2012a).

These data reveal two different trends: First, there is a downward trend for adolescent cigarette smoking in the United States during the past decade. The data suggest that about half of adolescents who smoke cigarettes are apparently not addicted to tobacco because they were able to abstain from smoking entirely for the past 30 days, according to Johnston et al. (2012a). Arguably these data might be interpreted as supporting the hypothesis that a large percentage of reported adolescent smoking reflects experimental cigarette use rather than addiction. Still, each day in the United States approximately 4,400 children or adolescents smoke their first cigarette (Centers for Disease Control and Prevention, 2010c; Rosen & Maurer, 2008). It is not known what percentage of these adolescents will

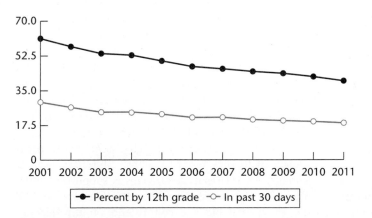

FIGURE 20-3 Percentage of High School Seniors Reporting Having Smoked.
Source: Based on Johnston et al., 2012a.

become addicted to tobacco products, although this is a very real danger for those who even experiment with cigarette smoking.

A small percentage of adolescents (about 5%) use "smokeless" tobacco. When asked, many adolescents will offer the explanation that this is a safer method of tobacco use and that they are attempting to quit. Unfortunately chewing tobacco usually does not replace the adolescent's cigarette smoking but becomes a supplement to it (Agalu et al., 2013). When used in this manner chewing tobacco allows the adolescent to continue to use tobacco products without smoking in class, for example.

The only assured way to avoid the possibility of addiction to nicotine, the primary addictive ingredient in cigarettes, is never to smoke. If an adolescent does begin to smoke and becomes addicted to nicotine, there are at best only limited resources to help that smoker quit (Blum, 2006). What might be termed "big tobacco" most certainly has an investment in reinforcing the incentive to smoke among children and adolescents. One major tobacco company has conducted research into the phases of cigarette smoking in adolescents (Hilts, 1996), and another tobacco company referred to adolescents in an internal memo as an "up and coming new generation of smokers" (Phelps, 1996, p. 1A). The R.J. Reynolds Tobacco Company, most certainly a major cigarette producer, went so far as to refer to 12-year-olds as a "younger adult" generation of smokers ("Big Tobacco's Secret Kiddie Campaign," 1991).

The neurological and behavioral immaturity of adolescents will make it difficult for them to accurately assess the risks associated with various behaviors, including cigarette smoking (Pumariga & Kilgus, 2005; Strauch, 2003). Indeed, there is evidence that for adolescents who smoke to help build their self-esteem, the warnings on the side of cigarette packages serve as an enticement to continue to smoke to prove their courage (Hansen, Winzeler, & Topolinski, 2010). Thus, the traditional method(s) of providing adolescents with information about the dangers of cigarette smoking might prove to have the opposite effect.

The tobacco and alcohol industries are spending $25 billion/year to advertise their products, usually in a format likely to be accepted by adolescents. Having peers who smoked cigarettes was an even stronger influence on individual smoking behavior than exposure to advertising according to the authors. Another influence on adolescent smoking behavior is whether the individual's parents smoke. This is supported by the observation that the majority of adolescent smokers have parents who also smoke cigarettes.

Stages of Childhood/Adolescent Smoking

The child or adolescent's transition from a nonsmoker to active cigarette smoking passes through four phases (Holland & Fitzsimons, 1991): (1) *Preparatory phase:* during which time the individual forms attitudes accepting of cigarette smoking, (2) *initiation phase:* when the individual smokes for the first time, (3) *experimentation phase:* when the smoker learns how to smoke after the first tentative smoking efforts, and (4) the *transition phase* to regular smoking. It is thought that proper intervention during any of these stages will reduce the chances that the individual will develop a long-term smoking use disorder.

Why Do Children and Adolescents Abuse Chemicals?

SUDs in childhood and adolescence do not arise in isolation, but are influenced by the individual's (a) constitutional predisposition (genetic heritage), (b) environmental factors (lack of parental supervision, exposure to substance-abusing parents, peer groups, etc.), and (c) life events (child abuse, victimization, etc.) (Upadhyaya & Gray, 2009). Further, there are the ongoing processes of physical, emotional, and neurological development during childhood and adolescence. Children, and most certainly adolescents, normally are becoming more independent, and as any parent will attest they are more than willing to tell you that they do not need to be told what to do! Unfortunately, a consequence of the process of neurological maturation for children and adolescents is that the individual is unable to adequately assess inherent risks in behaviors such as substance abuse because those regions of the brain responsible for this task do not fully mature until young adulthood. As a result of this developmental delay, children and adolescents tend to underestimate the negative consequences of high-risk behaviors, occasionally with dire results (Dobbs, 2011; Pamariga & Klingus, 2005; Hogan, 2000). This is supported by the observation that risky alcohol use behaviors peak in the 16–20-year-old age cohort and rapidly declines in frequency after that age (Chartier, Hesselbrock, & Hesselbrock, 2010).

Hogan (2000) offered five basic reasons why children and adolescent abusers use chemicals (Hogan, 2000; Millar, 2009): (1) to feel grown up, (2) to take risks or rebel against authority, (3) to fit into a specific peer group, (4) to relax and feel good, and (5) to satisfy curiosity about the effects of that compound(s). Drawing upon their survey data, the team of Johnston et al. (2012a) agreed that the majority of those who admitted to ever abusing an illicit substance did so on an experimental basis and did not abuse that compound more than a few times, supporting the curiosity hypothesis.

As noted previously, children and adolescents often engage in alcohol use because it helps make them feel older. This might also account for the growing trend for older children and adolescents to abuse narcotic analgesics that they find in the medicine cabinet of family or friends' homes. Unfortunately, they do not understand the risk of an overdose because of their small body size as contrasted to the medication dose, which is usually calculated for an adult. Some adolescents view various chemicals as an acceptable way to self-medicate negative feelings such as depression or perceived levels of stress (Spear, 2010; Wills, Sandy, Yaeger, Cleary, & Shinar, 2001), or demonstrate sexual prowess (Barr, 1999). As this list indicates, there is really no simple answer to why children and adolescents abuse chemicals. There are also other factors that will influence childhood and adolescent substance use patterns, which will be discussed further in this chapter.

Racial/Ethnic Group Membership

The research team of Johnston et al. (2012a) found that African American adolescents reported significantly lower rates of alcohol and drug use than Hispanic or Caucasian children. This is consistent with the observation that SUDs are most commonly found in Caucasian, middle-class adolescents. These are the individuals who are most likely to have money for discretionary spending and possibly experience lower levels of parental supervision because both parents have to work to maintain their established lifestyle.

The ethnic heritage of the adolescent has been found to influence that individual's substance use behaviors (Shih et al., 2010). Asian American children were less likely to smoke cigarettes or use alcohol, for example, especially if they perceived that such behaviors were unacceptable to siblings or to parents. Whereas Hispanic students frequently lack the "life skills" to reject offers of substance use, the authors found that Caucasian children might view substance use as a way to become more popular. According to the authors, educators needed to focus on the appropriate intervention for the ethnic composition of the student population rather than apply a generic approach to the task of teaching students about drug use.

Gender Differences

Adolescent males tend to be more likely to abuse illicit drugs by a factor of 2:1 as opposed to adolescent females by the time of high school graduation (Johnston et al., 2012a). Males were also more likely to be heavy abusers of illicit drugs than were adolescent females according to the authors. One exception to this was the abuse of amphetamine compounds, which were most commonly abused by adolescent girls, a difference that was possibly motivated by a desire for weight loss/control purposes by the adolescent girls in their sample. Finally the authors noted that the observed difference in prevalence rates between males and female adolescents appears in middle to late adolescence, which other research has demonstrated is when adolescent males are most likely to engage in impulsive, risky behavior.

Parental-Adolescent Relationship Patterns

Parents often forget that children (and adolescents) learn by interacting with and observing their parents, especially the behavior of the same-sex parent (Patock-Peckham & Morgan-Lopez, 2006). Later, they also begin to observe other adults as well, as they begin a lifelong process of social observation and learning. These early learning experiences are so important that research suggests that the pattern of parental interactions, especially how they resolve conflict, might affect the child's mental health as much as 30 years later ("Deteriorating Home Life Puts Kids at Risk," 2009). Unfortunately, parents often dismiss their influence on the developing child or adolescent especially during the latter period of life, when in reality they still retain a strong influence on fundamental issues such as behavioral morality, religion, and perceived importance of education for their adolescent children (Windle et al., 2009).

Although many parents believe to the contrary, parent–child relationship influences are generally stronger than those of adolescent peer groups, especially when the parents monitor their child's peer group membership. It is within the context of the parental–child relationship that children begin the social learning process referenced in the last paragraph, internalizing lessons provided by the parents, siblings, and parental substitutes[21] through passive observation. Watching an older sibling being punished for unacceptable behavior (such as throwing something across the room while angry, for example) offers the child the opportunity to engage in the process of passive learning. If the child should emulate his or her older sibling and meet a similar punishment, he or she starts the process of active learning. In this manner, behavioral rules are transmitted to the young child, thus playing a role in future behavioral choices (Hill, Steinhauer, Locke-Wellman, & Ulrich, 2009).

Consider, if you will, two hypothetical families on the day after Thanksgiving. In one family, the maternal uncle became grossly intoxicated during Thanksgiving dinner and started a fight with the child's father. The next day when the 3-year-old son inquires why his uncle became so angry and aggressive the day before, his mother simply replies, "Oh, that's the way your Uncle is when he drinks too much." In the second family, a maternal uncle also becomes grossly intoxicated and starts a fight with the child's father. The next day when the 3-year-old son inquires why his uncle became so angry and aggressive his mother replies, "That was disgusting behavior on your Uncle's part. He drank far too much and embarrassed everybody by his behavior! It was sickening! I don't ever want to see you act that way!"

Children often learn about the negative effects of alcohol and parental attitudes toward other forms of drug abuse through passive observation (Donovan, Molina, & Kelly, 2009; Thatcher & Clark, 2008). The quality of the parental supervision, openness to communication between the parent and the child, and enforcement of parental rules also plays a role in helping the child develop expectations for recreational substances. It is within the context of their family that behavioral decisions including substance use initiation are made (Winters et al., 2012). Although many parents view themselves as being powerless by the time their child reaches adolescence, in reality they retain a large degree of leverage over the adolescent's (a) cash flow, (b) credit card use, (c) access to a car, (d) curfew,

(e) cell phone use/access, and (f) computer use/access. In many states, adolescents under a designated age must have parental consent to hold a part-time job, which provides another element of leverage for the parent. The parent also retains some degree of control over those people that the adolescent associates with, although this power is not as strong as it was during the individual's childhood. These can provide powerful tools for the parent(s) attempting to control or modify unacceptable behaviors including substance abuse by their child or adolescent.

The social-learning process that begins in childhood and continues through adolescence is a two-edged sword: There is a strong relationship between *parental* substance use patterns during the childhood years and the subsequent substance use behavior of the adolescent (Brown et al., 2009; Chassin, Flora, & King, 2004; Donovan et al., 2009; Griffin & Botvin, 2010). This is a fact that is especially disturbing because by the age of seventeen 51% of adolescents would have seen one or both parents intoxicated on at least one occasion (National Center on Addiction and Substance Abuse at Columbia University, 2009b). Two percent of women with children[22] living at home meet diagnostic criteria for an illicit drug use or medication use disorder (Simmons, Havens, Whiting, Holz, & Bada, 2009). The experience of viewing parental intoxication in the face of parental admonitions against drinking or illicit substance use provides conflicting information to the child or adolescent[23] (Donovan et al., 2009; National Center on Addiction and Substance Abuse at Columbia University, 2009b) and might be one reason why children whose parents have an alcohol use disorder also tend to have higher rates of alcohol abuse and an earlier onset of social medical problems later in life (Tildesley & Andrews, 2008).

One frequently overlooked element of the child's relationship with his or her parents is the quality of the *attachment bonds* that develop with the parents in childhood (Hogan, 2000). Children with positive attachment bonds tend to be resistant to the urge to engage in substance use, have more positive peer relationships, are more socially competent, and demonstrate better coping skills than adolescents who have a more troubled relationship with their parents. Such strong attachment bonds are expressed by such

---

[21]Such as a respected teacher to cite one example among many.

[22]Defined as under the age of 18 years.

[23]"Don't do as I do, but do as I say!" A behavioral stance that adolescents are quick to dismiss as parental hypocrisy.

parental behaviors as consistently spending time with their children, positive parental substance use modeling behavior, and the degree of parental emotional involvement in the lives of their children (Kaminer & Buckstein, 2005). Children whose parents spend more time with them[24] and who make a greater effort to communicate with them report lower rates of alcohol and tobacco use.

An overlapping factor that influences adolescents' substance use patterns is parental *control* or supervision (Griffin & Botvin, 2010; Patock-Peckham & Morgan-Lopez, 2006; Windle & Zucker, 2010). Adolescents who report the highest levels of parental monitoring[25] and enforcement of rules have lower levels of misconduct, delinquency, and substance abuse[26] (Bahr & Hoffmann, 2010; Kaminer, 2008; Patock-Peckham & Morgan-Lopez, 2006; Tildesley & Andrews, 2008). This degree of parental supervision allows for intervention should the adolescent start to "stray" into dangerous territory. The adolescent has learned that his or her parents will intervene should they become uncomfortable with their behavior and thus parental intervention will not be viewed as harsh or excessive[27] (Griffin & Botvin, 2010). A related factor is the child's ability to *communicate* with the parents, to ask questions and express concerns about his or her exposure to individuals who abuse alcohol or drugs. Not surprisingly there is evidence that adolescents who associated with friends whose parents were warm and open to communication but who also set and enforced limits were themselves less likely to engage in behaviors such as cigarette smoking or alcohol abuse (Shakya, Christakis, & Fowler, 2012).

A reflection of parental control or supervision is their awareness of the substance use pattern by their child or adolescent: One percent of parents expressed a belief that their child had used a CNS stimulant to help them study, for example, whereas 10% of high school seniors say that they have engaged in this practice ("By the Numbers," 2013). They are less aware of the issues such as adolescent marijuana abuse or dependence as evidenced by the observation that 80% of parents expressed a belief that recreational chemicals were not at parties that their children attended where 50% of adolescents who reported that both alcohol and drugs were freely available at these parties (Sheff, Warren, Ketcham, & Evan, 2007). Drawing on a sample of 432 adolescents and at least one of their parents, Delaney-Black et al. (2010) found that parents were eight times as likely to under-report personal use of cocaine and opiates when asked, whereas adolescents were 52 times as likely to do so. This study not only illustrates how parental modeling behaviors helps to shape the adolescent's substance use but also illustrates how often adolescents deny the use of drugs even in the face of evidence to the contrary.

As a group, parents underestimated teenaged alcohol consumption by a factor of 4:1, inhalant abuse by a factor of 4:1, and illicit drug abuse by a factor of at least 2:1 (Center for Substance Abuse Research, 2006). However, this lack of parental awareness appears to be strongest during early adolescence (McGillicuddy, Rychtarik, Morsheimer, & Burke-Storer, 2007). The reason for this observed discrepancy is not known but might reflect a tendency for the parent to underestimate the possibility that their child is engaging in substance use behavior (McGillicuddy et al., 2007). Parents who struggle with psychosocial adjustment issues of their own are also less likely to be aware of their child's substance abuse pattern according to the authors.

Siblings

Feedback from siblings is an important, but rarely studied, component of SUDs in adolescents (Griffin & Botvin, 2010). A drug-abusing, despised, older sibling might set a negative example for a younger brother or an older sister's feedback might discourage her younger sister from initiating alcohol use in early adolescence, for example. However, as noted, this area has not been explored in detail, and there is much to learn about the role that feedback from siblings plays in the

---

[24]Such as having a common hobby, for example.

[25]Such as parental monitoring of (a) who their child is with, (b) where the child is, (c) the child's report of their activities and its congruence with feedback from other adults, (d) when the child will return, and (e) whether they actually do the things that they told the parents that they wanted to do.

[26]This is not to say that strict parental rules will *prevent* adolescent substance abuse. But high levels of parental monitoring and enforcement of established rules are generally associated with lower levels of deviant behavior(s), including alcohol or illicit drug abuse.

[27]In contrast to situations where the parent belatedly starts to assert parental authority. The sudden attempt by the parent to assert such authority will likely be met with levels of resentment and resistance far beyond that seen in healthy parent–child relationships. As the battle for control rages, many inadequate parents will retreat, leaving the adolescent to set their own boundaries.

development of or resilience against subsequent substance use behaviors.

Vocational/Occupational Choices

There is strong evidence of an association[28] between time spent working and tobacco or alcohol use for adolescents in school. Those students who spent more time at work than they did on study were more likely to engage in alcohol and tobacco use (Wagner, 2009). They were also more likely to seek part-time jobs consistent with their vocational interests and spend more time working on a part-time basis than their more academically minded counterparts (Mortimer, 2010). The individual's initial occupational choice(s) following graduation also is associated with substance use behaviors. Adolescents who enlist in the military, for example, both sever traditional sources of support such as peers and parents and simultaneously enter a subculture in which heavy alcohol use is accepted (Ames, Duke, Moore, & Cunradi, 2009; Benton, 2009; Zucker et al., 2009). In both the military and other occupations, heavy-drinking subgroups develop which provide a sense of belonging (Benton, 2009). It is within these subcultures that the adolescent completes the transition from adolescence into the first stages of adulthood. Behavioral choices made during this transitional period often are continued into adulthood.

Adolescent Mood States

It is rather simplistic to say that negative feelings can contribute to the impulse to abuse alcohol or illicit chemicals. What is a "negative feeling"? Are there universal negative feelings or does each person rate the intensity of their feelings differently? How intense does a feeling of depression have to become, for example, before it can be classified as a negative feeling as opposed to a normal mood swing? If a given adolescent who suffers from a major depression should also be abusing alcohol or illicit drugs, does this imply a causal relationship? There is mixed evidence, for example, suggesting that disorders of affect in adolescence might play a role in the development of an SUD in this age group (Rutherford et al., 2010). The authors suggested that disorders of emotional control increases the risk for the subsequent development of

an SUD for girls and that behavioral dyscontrol problems appear to be of greater importance for the development of an SUD in boys. Thus, the issue of gender-specific impact of negative mood states is raised: Are boys affected the same way as girls by a specific negative feeling?

Depression is frequently identified as a risk factor for adolescent substance abuse (Kaminer, 2008; Kricechbaum & Zernig, 2000). Unfortunately, the correlation between these two conditions is a modest one at best and is strongest for girls as opposed to boys (Fleming, Mason, Mazza, Abbott, & Catalano, 2008). The authors found that depression in early adolescence was positively correlated with alcohol, marijuana, and cigarette use for adolescent girls, but only for marijuana use for boys. This might reflect the fact that few adolescent boys, like their adult counterparts, recognize the existence of their depression or other negative emotional states (Mayeda & Sanders, 2007). Adolescent girls tend to be more in touch with feelings such as depression or anxiety, and it is for this reason that the affective disorders on substance use behaviors differs between adolescent boys and girls.

One interesting study was conducted by Rao, Hammen, and Poland (2009) in which the authors measured cortisol[29] levels in 151 adolescents (a process that required the collection of urine for 24 hours from each individual for testing). The authors found that adolescents who had higher levels of cortisol in their urine (an indication of stress, often a precipitant of depression in adolescents) were more vulnerable to the development of SUDs. Whereas an adult might require 2–7 years of habitual substance abuse before he or she becomes addicted to that substance, adolescents might become addicted to the same compound in as little as 12–18 months (Freimuth, 2005). The results of this study confirm the relationship between depression and subsequent SUDs in adolescents.

It is often surprising for parents to learn that behavioral extremes often signal problems for the adolescent (Lundeen, 2002). Total abstinence from any substance use during adolescence has been identified as a signal of impending problems. The critical issue is not whether the adolescent abuses alcohol or illicit drugs so much as *which compounds, how often, and in what quantities.* The adolescent who frequently

---

[28]As before, associational relationships are not the same as *causal* relationships.

[29]See Glossary.

abuses alcohol or drugs tends to have poor impulse control, be socially alienated, and experience high levels of emotional distress—all warning signs that the individual may lack social skills necessary to cope effectively. In contrast to this, the adolescent who is totally abstinent from alcohol and illicit drugs may be anxious, emotionally constricted, lack self-confidence, and may lack the social skills necessary to cope with life's demands. Thus, the adolescent's substance use pattern must be viewed within the context of his or her emotional adjustment.

Conduct Disorder/Oppositional Defiant Disorder

There is a known relationship between behavioral control disorders in childhood and the subsequent development of SUDs. These behavioral control disorders include the conduct disorder (CD) and the oppositional defiant disorder (ODD). Both these disorders share the common traits of impulsiveness and limited behavioral control, increasing the individual's risk for the development of an SUD (Clark et al., 2002). Behavioral problems usually proceed with the development of adolescent SUDs, possibly reflecting a common neurological basis for these conditions (Clark et al., 2002; Newcorn & Ivanov, 2007). This theory is supported by the observation that 50–80% of adolescents with a diagnosis of CD will develop an SUD at some point in their lives (Kaminer & Buckstein, 2005). However, the relationship between impulsiveness and substance abuse is not entirely clear and for some adolescents substance abuse might *precede* impulsive behavior(s) (Rutherford et al., 2010). There is thus a need for further research to determine the exact relationship between impulsiveness and substance abuse in adolescence.

The prefrontal cortex of the brain is actively involved in the process of assessing potential risks and behavioral control. Preliminary evidence suggests that individuals with CD and ODD, as well as adults with antisocial personality disorder, have altered neurological function in this region of the brain, possibly contributing to the behavioral problems central to either disorder. In order for a rehabilitation program to be effective, it is necessary to develop a program that addresses the issues of behavioral control into the SUD rehabilitation program (Clark et al., 2002). Such programs should not, however, be based on describing the negative consequences of substance use, as adolescents often view substance abuse in the face of these warnings as an expression of willingness to take risks and thus of gaining social status.

Peer Group Influences

Parents often overestimate the influence of peer groups on the behavior of their child or adolescent. Research findings suggest that peer groups *do* influence the individual's behavioral decisions; however, peer group influences peak between the ages of 11 and 13 (Cleveland, Feinberg, & Jones, 2012). In a manner that parallels the neurological maturation process, the adolescent's substance abuse in late adolescence is more frequently a *planned* activity and less likely to be in response to social opportunities to engage in substance use (Cleveland et al., 2012). Adolescent abstinence from alcohol or illicit chemicals is also more likely to be a planned behavior rather than a response to external constraints (Cleveland et al., 2012). Peer group influences are not always negative: Peer approval (or disapproval) might prove to be more important to the individual than the pharmacological reward potential of a compound(s) that might be abused. In this manner, the behavioral choices encouraged by the adolescent's peer groups may serve as either a protective or a negative influence on adolescent substance use behaviors (Brook, Pahl, & Rubenstone, 2008; Chartier et al., 2010; Ross, 2002; Simkin, 2002). Further, in spite of parental beliefs to the contrary, they still retain a strong influence on fundamental issues such as morality, religion, and perceived importance of education in adolescents (Windle et al., 2009).

The results of peer association studies must be interpreted with some degree of caution because of the individual's choices of his or her peers. Further peer group membership is not automatically, mutually exclusive: Any individual might associate with members of different peer groups should they wish to do so. However, peer influences are important determinants of the marijuana use patterns of the adolescent(s) (Mir, Amialchuk, & Dwyer, 2011). The study of adolescent obesity carried out by the team of Gessel, Tesdahl, and Ruchman (2012) provided partial support for this hypothesis: The authors concluded that those children and adolescents who associated with physically active peers were themselves more likely to be physically active. However, there is a self-selection process through which adolescents who are unwilling to be physically active drift away from their more active peers toward those who are less physically active.

The role of peers in SUDs is also limited by the pharmacology of the substance being abused. Peers might strongly influence the *initiation* of substance use, but their role in supporting its continued use is not as important as the pharmacological reward potential of the compound(s) being abused. As a result of this process, adolescents tend to gravitate towards peer groups with similar views toward substance abuse, values, expectations, and behavioral demands as their own (Mir et al., 2001; Pumariga & Kilgus, 2005; Simkin, 2002; Valente, Gallaher, & Mouttapa, 2004). This gravitational process would suggest that peer group selection is the *last* step in the chain of events that results in the adolescent joining a subgroup in which substance use is tolerated if not encouraged.

Telecommunications

The adolescent peer group affiliation is compounded by the telecommunications era.[30] The typical adolescent spends 6–7 hours a day listening to or watching some form of mass media, which in a sense would make it a "superpeer" (Hogan, 2000, p. 937) for this age group (Windle et al., 2009). The development of personal telecommunications devices, such as a cellular telephone and e-mail and text messaging devices, allows the adolescent to maintain a tenuous relationship with persons who they might never meet in person. The average teen sends approximately 100 text mail messages a day, often texting comments or photos that they would never share in person. These electronic adolescent interactions can be carried out from a distance, often in a clandestine manner that potentially circumnavigates parental supervision.[31] The telecommunications era is still evolving; however, it is clearly a potential contributing factor to unhealthy adolescent behaviors.

Religious Affiliation

Surprisingly, affiliation with and participation in religious activities in childhood appears to influence alcohol use patterns throughout adolescence and into adulthood. Those individuals who were members of more structured faiths that provided a firm identity[32] and which had an established moral code were able to use these resources to help them delay the initiation of alcohol use in adolescence (Koenig, Haber, & Jacob, 2011; Latimer & Zur, 2010). African American youth are more likely to be religious than their Caucasian peers, possibly because religion plays such a large role in African American culture, which would seem to explain why this subpopulation is less likely to engage in alcohol use as children and adolescents (Vaughan, de Dios, Steinfeldt, & Kratz, 2011). Thus, an emerging body of evidence suggests that membership in a structured religion in childhood and adolescence reduces the odds that the individual will engage in alcohol use during these periods of life (Mason & Spoth, 2011).

Music Selection

The typical adolescent spends approximately 2 hours each day listening to music, often on a personal music system controlled by a microchip system. The team of Primack, Dalton, Carroll, Agerwal, and Fine (2008) examined the content of the music that adolescents listen to and found either implicit or explicit references to substance use in a significant percentage of songs examined. The authors found that alcohol was the most commonly referenced substance followed by marijuana. They also found that Rap music contained the greatest percentage of references to substance abuse (more than three-quarters of the songs sampled) whereas pop music contained the least (10% of songs sampled). This disturbing finding is made even more frightening by the content of the references to alcohol or substance use: They glorified the use of the compound(s) in the content of that song, associating the use of these compounds with sexual, emotional, and/or financial gains for the user (Miller, 2008). It is not clear at this time whether the adolescent's choice of music is a response to his or her abuse of chemicals, is just a phase through which the adolescent must pass,[33] or whether the individual's alcohol or drug abuse might predate the abuse of chemicals. However, these findings are disturbing.

---

[30]This is especially true in the current era of telecommunications: Any individual might exchange text mail messages, photos transmitted over the Internet, or simple e-mail messages with members of a wide range of social groups.

[31]How many parents *really* take time to check to see who their teen has been sending messages to or receiving messages from on a consistent basis?

[32]Examples include the Catholic church, more conservative Jewish denominations, etc.

[33]In the sense that the adolescent finds such music exciting for a period of time and then discards this form of entertainment in favor of another form of music.

Personal Values

An often overlooked aspect of SUDs is the individual's values, which reflect his or her emerging personality. The child's parents help to establish the personal values that will grow over time. These may carry out a protective function against substance abuse or may facilitate the development of adolescent SUDs. There is a negative correlation between substance use and such factors as (van den Bree & Pickworth, 2005) academic achievement, church attendance, the individual's beliefs about the importance of academic achievement, and participation in organized sports (Latimer & Zur, 2010). However, it is not clear whether these factors help to protect the adolescent from SUDs or not as the correlation does not imply causality.

Rebellion

A factor that is closely intertwined with personal values is the adolescent's attempts to rebel against perceived parental authority. The natural rebelliousness of adolescents makes them vulnerable to the image of cigarette smoking as a way to rebel against parental authority (Greydanus & Patel, 2005; Dickinson, 2000), for example. This image is encouraged by tobacco companies, especially through advertising. Morgenstern, Sargent, Isensee, and Hanewinkel (2013) found, for example, that for every 10 cigarette advertisements seen by the adolescent the risk that the individual may smoke went up 38%. The abuse of other chemicals also appears to many adolescents to be an avenue through which they can express their rebellion and independence (Griffin & Botvin, 2010). However, there is a difference between isolated acts of rebellion and delinquency or conduct disorders. Periods of heavy drug abuse appear to serve as a catalyst for subsequent criminal activity in the latter groups (Heyman, 2009). Parental authority appears to hold such acts of rebellion in check, or at least limits their expression, whereas the lack of appropriate parental authority encourages the development of the latter problems.

Insomnia

An interesting theory was recently introduced suggesting that those adolescents who suffer from insomnia are at higher risk for later depression and SUDs ("Adolescents with Insomnia Are at Risk for Future Substance Abuse and Depression," 2008). The average adolescent requires between 8.5 and 9.25 hours of sleep per night, although at first the adolescent's sleep pattern shifts to one in which he or she goes to sleep later and wakes up later than do their older peers (Brown et al., 2009). Adolescents who sleep for shorter periods force sleep deprivation states on themselves in spite of catch-up opportunities for extra sleep on the weekends (Brown et al., 2009).

Although one might expect that sleep deprivation would be the result of substance abuse, an emerging body of evidence suggests just the opposite: Adolescents who habitually are sleep deprived may learn their sleep habits from friends, with the greater the number of sleep-deprived friends being positively correlated with cannabis abuse by the adolescent (Roane & Taylor, 2008; "Social Networks Show Drug Use Follows Lack of Sleep," 2010). Further, a surprising problem, once thought to be seen only in adults, is the possibility that the adolescent might suffer from obstructive sleep apnea,[34] a medical condition that causes sleep disruption and which appears to raise the adolescent's risk for an SUD, in part through its ability to induce depression.

Abuse History or Victimization

There is a body of evidence suggesting that physical, sexual, and emotional abuse during childhood and adolescence might be associated with the development of SUDs later in life (Clay, Allen, & Parran, 2008; Oshri, Rogoscu, Burnette, & Ciccette, 2011). Thirty to sixty percent of women in primary substance abuse rehabilitation programs report having experienced such severe levels of abuse that they meet the diagnostic criteria for posttraumatic stress disorder (PTSD). Although the exact causal mechanism(s) for this association have yet to be identified, it is thought that severe abuse could cause a dysregulation of the normal stress-response mechanisms in the body, which in turn could block normal maturation of the brain in adolescence and early adulthood, especially in the frontal and prefrontal cortex, those regions that govern behavior and anticipate the consequences of our behavior. More research is necessary to confirm whether this theory is accurate or not, but it does seem to be a mechanism through which physical, emotional, and sexual abuse might be associated with later SUDs.

---

[34]See Glossary.

Employment

Research has demonstrated that many persons begin to work on an informal basis (mowing lawns, babysitting, etc.) at around the age of 12, although by the age of 16 the individual is more likely to have graduated to a more formal part-time job (Mortimer, 2010). Part-time employment during adolescence provides the individual with a source of income that might be used for various items deemed important by the adolescent, including alcohol and drugs (Mortimer, 2010).

Section Summary

It is tempting to blame a single factor, such as peer group influences, for childhood or adolescent substance abuse. In reality, such a belief is too simplistic; identified risk and protective factors in childhood or adolescence are not destiny. At most they hint at the possibility that the child or adolescent *might* develop an SUD later in life (Winters et al., 2012). Unfortunately, adolescence substance abuse takes place during a period of social and neurological vulnerability, and the adolescent brain appears to be "hard wired" to put emphasis on environmental experiences that bring pleasure. This, plus the still-evolving frontal regions of the brain, combined with lax parental supervision and a permissive social environment are forces that help increase the individual's risk for developing an SUD in adulthood (Fiellin, 2008).

Substance Abuse: How Much and When Does It Become Too Much?

Prevention

Treatment of adolescent SUDs is difficult to arrange and its efficacy is unproven. Ultimately modifications to these early intervention programs are going to be necessary to make them more effective. However, society has finally started to recognize that *preventing* the development of the SUDs in children and adolescents is more cost effective than treatment after the disorder develops. Griffin and Botvin (2010) suggested that these early prevention programs might fall into one of three categories: (a) universal, (b) selective, and (c) targeted. Universal level prevention programs focus on the population of the age cohort for which that program is designed, with the goal of delaying or preventing the onset of substance use. Selective prevention programs focus on those children or adolescents who are at increased risk for the development of an SUD because of environmental conditions or life circumstances. Targeted prevention programs are specifically aimed at those individuals who demonstrate the early warning signs of being vulnerable to the development of an SUD. If such prevention programs fail, then the child or adolescent is "at risk" for the development of an SUD.

Childhood

The issue of childhood substance abuse is both more clear, and more difficult, for clinicians. Substance use or abuse by children is usually hidden, and few parents or health care professionals ask the specific questions necessary to identify the problem. The dangers of experimental substance use by children are self-evident: any use of alcohol, or illicit compounds, is potentially dangerous. The regular abuse of such compounds is certainly a sign of a serious problem. However, even if the child has been appropriately identified as having an SUD, treatment resources for these children are virtually nonexistent (Millar, 2009).

It has been hypothesized that early onset alcohol use by children (defined as before the age of 13) might reflect a genetic predisposition toward alcohol dependence (Agrawal et al., 2009). This conclusion is partially supported by the work of Hingson, Heeren, and Winter (2006), who found in their study of 43,000 adults in the United States that 47% of persons with an alcohol use disorder began to drink before the age of 14 years as opposed to just 9% of those who began to drink after the age of 21 years. Further, the younger the individual is at the time of drinking initiation, the more likely he or she will experience more severe alcoholism (Windle & Zucker, 2010). Similar information addressing the abuse of other chemicals by children is not available at this time.

Adolescents

Adolescence is a time of exploration as the individual establishes the foundation for a personal identity. Experimental substance use, especially of alcohol and marijuana, is potentially a part of this process of exploration. *Total* abstinence from alcohol and the drugs of abuse during adolescence is rare: Only 11% of adolescents abstain from all chemicals throughout adolescence (Chassin et al., 2004). For the majority of adolescents, *experimental* abuse of alcohol and marijuana appears to

TABLE 20-1

Comparison of Two Models of Adolescent Substance Abuse

PAREKH (2006)	GREYDANUS & PATEL (2005)
(1) Initiation: first use of a mood-altering chemical (either alone or with peers)	Stage 0: No substance abuse but is very interested in learning more about them, suffers low self-esteem, and is vulnerable to peer pressure
(2) Learning the mood swing: Adolescent is taught (by experience or by others) what to look for in the abuse of a chemical(s)	Stage 1: Experimentation. No real negative consequences encountered yet
(3) Regular use/seeking the mood: Continued abuse to maintain substance-induced pleasure	Stage 2: Adolescent actively seeks drug's effects, centers life more and more around use of chemicals
(4) Abuse/harmful consequences: Adolescent begins to encounter academic performance problems, and so on but continues to abuse chemicals	Stage 3: Preoccupation with substance use by adolescent. Mood swings and acting out behaviors noted in this stage. First negative consequences of substance abuse encountered
(5) Adolescent is now physically addicted to a chemical(s) and is trapped in a cycle of compulsive use to avoid withdrawal	Stage 4: Continued consequences. Substance use continues so that abuser can feel "normal" again

© Cengage Learning

be the norm. Unfortunately, there are no firm boundaries between experimental use, substance abuse, and substance addiction. Experimental use is a risk factor for the development of an SUD because you cannot become addicted to a substance that you have never used (Meyers & Dick, 2010; Kaminer, 2008).

Contrary to popular belief, substance *abuse* in adolescence is not always a prodrome to substance *addiction* later in life (Heyman, 2009; Kaminer, 2008). Admittedly some adolescent substance abusers do go on to become addicted to alcohol or drugs. The majority do not. This is supported by the study conducted by Knight et al. (2007) who found that although 44% of the 12–18-year-olds screened were identified as having either a past or current history of alcohol or drug abuse, the majority of these individuals did not progress to substance dependence later in life. Unfortunately, there are no methods to identify who is at high risk for the development of an SUD in adolescence and who is at a lower level of risk.

Stages of Adolescent Substance Abuse

There are a number of paths that an adolescent might follow once she or he begins to abuse chemicals. Two examples are the models suggested by Greydanus and Patel (2005) and Parekh (2006). Each suggests that adolescent substance abuse proceeds through five stages, which are contrasted in Table 20-1:

As has been stated before, the adolescent's progression from one stage to the next in either model is *not* automatic. Social forces and the normal developmental process during adolescence can either facilitate or block the progression from one stage of substance abuse to another. For reasons that appear to reflect genetic vulnerability and social forces, progression of substance abuse appears to be both accelerated and is more intense for a small percentage of adolescents. In such cases, the time between entering Stage 0 and the start of Stage 4 on the Greydanus & Patel (2005) model can be just a matter of a few months following initiation of substance use (Greydanus & Patel, 2005; Rutherford et al., 2010).

Adolescent Addiction to Chemicals

The question of whether the adolescent substance abuser might become physically addicted to a compound(s) is quite controversial (Commission on Adolescent Substance and Alcohol Abuse, 2005). The diagnostic symptoms of addiction normally found in adults who are dependent on a substance are not always found in the adolescent substance abuser (Evans & Sullivan, 2001; Pumariga & Kilgus, 2005). They rarely develop substance withdrawal syndromes seen in older patients (Johnson, 2012b),[35] and adolescent substance abusers rarely develop characteristic patterns of organ damage seen in adults addicted to chemicals. However, *tolerance* to the effects of

---

[35]*Rarely* is different from *never*. Some adolescent substance abusers *do* develop a substance withdrawal syndrome, and the probability that they will do so increases in proportion to the period of time that they have abused a substance.

their drug of choice can develop as rapidly (if not more rapidly) than that of the adult abuser of the same chemical(s) (Spear, 2010).

Problems in Diagnosis and Treatment of Adolescent SUDs

The first problem is that clinicians lack definitive criteria to identify adolescents for whom substance use has become a problem. Diagnostic standards are derived from those used with adult substance abusers, although there is strong evidence that these criteria do not automatically apply to children or adolescent substance abusers (Kaminer & Buckstein, 2005; Myrick & Wright, 2008; Wagner, 2009). The standards for assessment, diagnosis, or treatment decisions are still in their infancy at best, although progress is being made in this area (Kaminer & Goodley 2010; Wagner, 2009).

Having identified a specific child or adolescent who has an SUD places the typical health care professional in two conundrums: First, they lack the tools necessary to separate those adolescents who *abuse* a chemical from those who are *addicted* to that substance.[36] Second, current diagnostic systems do not take into account the fact that a person's substance use behavior changes over time. The adolescent who appears to be alcohol dependent at the age of 14, for example, might not meet the criteria for a current SUD when he or she is 17 years of age.

Whereas *loss of control over substance abuse* is one factor that clinicians look for when working with adult substance abusers, *loss of control over substance use* expresses itself differently for adolescents.[37] Individuals in this age group who have an SUD usually express loss of control through a violation of personal rules ("I will only drink on weekends," or "I did not *want to* use marijuana last night, but I couldn't help myself," for example). SUDs rarely interfere with job performance for adolescents because the adolescent's job is usually only a part-time position, and the adolescent can usually hide substance use from supervisors. However, their substance use might interfere with their ability to achieve grades that they would normally be expected to achieve.

Clinicians also usually lack tools to accurately assess the maturity level of the adolescent, the individual's motivation to participate in a treatment program, age-appropriate rehabilitation techniques, or the effectiveness of the rehabilitation program (Knight, 2000; Wagner, 2009). The problem of *access* to a rehabilitation program should not be underestimated: Over 1.1 million adolescents appear to meet the criteria for admission to a substance abuse rehabilitation program but less than 1 in 10 is ever admitted to treatment (Griswold, Arnoff, Kernan, & Khan, 2008; Wagner, 2009). There are many reasons for this. For example, each state varies as to the legal requirements under which an assessment of adolescent SUDs might be carried out. Parental consent might be required in some states, whereas it is not required in a neighboring state. Parental denial[38] that their child has an SUD is also a problem for the assessor. Many parents and their children view substance abuse as a sign of moral weakness making it difficult for them to admit that their child has been abusing chemicals (Corrigan et al., 2005).

Adolescent self-report of substance use is unreliable, as evidenced by the fact that many adolescents admitted to hospital emergency rooms for chest pain vehemently deny the abuse of cocaine in spite of having cocaine metabolites in their urine. Even in situations where the adolescent is promised confidentiality, he or she still might under-report substance abuse (Stein & Rogers, 2008). To complicate matters, the diagnostic criteria used for adolescents are based on standards used for adults, which are not automatically applicable to adolescents. Adolescent substance abusers are less likely to report having developed tolerance to their drug(s) of abuse—signposts of a possible SUD in the adult, for example (Myrick & Wright, 2008).

Less than a quarter of pediatricians surveyed reported that they felt comfortable assessing an adolescent for an SUD or in making a referral to a treatment program, and so this issue is often not discussed with the adolescent during a visit to the physician ("Doctors Often Skip Health Behavior Conversations with Teens," 2008). This is unfortunate because research has found that up to 65% of adolescents would like to discuss their substance use with their physician. This might be one reason why less than half of the pediatricians surveyed said that they routinely screen

---

[36]A differentiation that is important because intervention for substance abusers differs from intervention methods employed in the treatment of substance-dependent persons.

[37]The CAGE questions, for example, are ill-suited for use with adolescents. The CAGE is discussed in more detail in Chapter 27.

[38]"If we do not allow the assessment to be done, we will not have to face the possibility that our child is abusing alcohol or drugs."

adolescent patients for tobacco, alcohol, or drug use disorders (Winters & Kaminer, 2008). The team of van Hook et al. (2007) identified what they called the "Six T's" that block physician identification and referral of adolescent substance abusers: (1) lack of time, (2) lack of training, (3) presence of competing medical problems that require treatment, (4) lack of treatment resources, (5) tendency for parents to remain in the exam room (making the adolescent less likely to reveal substance abuse), and (6) tendency for physicians to have an awareness of screening tools available to the physician.

The physician, or other health care professional who works with adolescents should review the individual's (Griffin & Botvin, 2010; Myrick & Wright, 2008) (a) educational status (including school attendance, academic performance, and disciplinary actions within the school setting (if any), (b) the possibility of loss of control over the substance(s) being abuse, (c) familial relationships (including possible conflict within the family), (d) peer relationship patterns (substance abusing peers or non-using peers, for example), (e) legal status (including history of underaged drinking citations, arrests for possession of marijuana, etc.), (f) how the adolescent uses his or her free time, and (g) history of physical or sexual abuse. Unfortunately, few health care professionals address these issues when they meet with the child or adolescent.

Screening/Assessment Tools[39]

There is a difference between a *screening* instrument and an *assessment* tool. There are some fairly accurate screening instruments available as well as a number of well-designed substance use assessment tools for use with children and adolescents. Neither group is perfect and there is always room for improvement. In this section, we will look at some of the instruments that have been developed or adapted for use with this population. The gold standard against which both screening as well as assessment tools are measured is the clinical interview, especially if the assessor establishes an extensive database about the individual (Evans & Sullivan, 2001; Juhnke, 2002). It is necessary to interview each separately lest the presence of the parents, child, or adolescent prevents the interviewee from being completely

honest. Thus, inquiries about possible substance abuse should be made when the parents are not in the consultation room.

Assessment Instruments

One of the more popular instruments is the *CRAFFT*, which is a series of questions that the adolescent responds to. This includes questions about whether the adolescent has ever been a passenger in a vehicle where the driver was under the influence of chemicals. Other issues addressed are whether the adolescent has used chemicals to help him or her relax, forget problems, or if their substance use has ever resulted in psychosocial problems (including family, academic, and legal issues) for the individual or used chemicals when alone. The assessor should also inquire whether the child or adolescent has tried to hide their substance use from their parents.

A rapidly administered verbal screening instrument is the *TWEAK*, which asks the adolescent about *T*olerance, whether or not others have ever been *W*orried about their substance use, whether the adolescent has ever used an *E*ye opener in the morning, *A*mnesia during periods of substance use, and *K* (cut) attempts to cut down on substance use (Johnson, 2003). This instrument may also be used with adults and is a useful nemonic[40] device for the assessor to use with both adolescents and adults. For cigarette smoking, Doubeni, Li, Fouayzi, and DiFranza (2008) suggested two simple questions: (1) Would it be easy for you to obtain a cigarette? (2) Do you have friends who smoke? A "yes" answer to either question identified a child who was at high risk for cigarette smoking, and intervention procedures should be initiated, the authors suggested.

The *Drug Use Screening Inventory-Revised (DUSI-R)* (Kirisci, Mezzich, & Tarter, 1995) is a 159-item instrument (protected by copyright) that was designed for adolescents (or adults) who are suspected of having an SUD. The DUSI-R only requires about 10 minutes for the individual to complete, and it assesses such potential problem areas as the individual's (a) substance use behavior, (b) general behavior patterns, (c) health status, (d) psychiatric health status, (e) social skills level, (f) peer relationships, (g) and leisure/recreational habits. The DUSI-R is not diagnostic in itself but does identify problem areas that might be addressed in a clinical interview.

---

[39]It is not possible to review every screening or assessment instrument available. This summary is limited to some of the more popular or better designed instruments in the opinion of this author.

[40]See Glossary.

The Drug and Alcohol Problem (DAP) Quick Screen (Schwartz & Wirth, 1990) was designed for use by physicians in the office setting to be completed in approximately 10 minutes. One advantage of this instrument is that it attempts to identify adolescent suicidal thinking, an area of growing concern because adolescent suicide is a growing problem in society. Another instrument that is in the "public domain" is the *Problem Oriented Screening Instrument for Teenagers* (POSIT), developed by the National Institute on Drug Abuse (NIDA) and the National Institutes of Health (NIH). This instrument is composed of 139 questions that are answered either "yes" or "no" by respondents who are 12–19 years of age. The individual's response pattern provided information on his/her (a) substance abuse patterns, (b) physical health, (c) mental health, (d) family relations, (e) peer relations, (f) educational status, (g) social skills, and (h) aggressive behavior or delinquency tendencies by the respondent. Identified problem areas are then examined in more detail through clinical interviews with the client.

One of the more popular instruments used when assessing an adolescent is the adolescent version of the *Substance Abuse Subtle Screening Inventory-3 (SASSI-3)* (Juhnke, 2002). This instrument is used with adolescents who are 16 years of age or older and who have at least a 4th-grade reading level. The SASSI-3 is discussed in more detail in Chapter 27, but the reader should be aware that an adolescent version of this instrument does exist and might be used to help assess the adolescent client.

The *Adolescent Drinking Index (ADI)* is occasionally used by assessors, although there is limited data on its effectiveness, especially with adolescents who attempt to minimize their alcohol use (Stein & Rogers, 2008). Another instrument that is occasionally used when assessing adolescents for possible SUDs is the *Adolescent Drug Abuse Diagnosis (ADAD)* test. It attempts to measure nine different areas of the adolescent's life and then rate the degree of distress caused by substance abuse in each of these domains. This instrument can also be used to assess pretreatment and post-treatment changes for the adolescent (Johnson, 2003).

Finally, the *Teen Addiction Severity Index (TASI)* is occasionally used by assessors attempting to interpret the adolescent's substance use pattern. However, the normative samples for this instrument were small, and generalizability to the general adolescent population is open to question (Stein & Rogers, 2008). Although it is not possible to discuss every screening instrument, there are a number of instruments available to the assessor.

Each of these instruments has serious flaws or limitations, and the data provided by each test should be interpreted with caution. However, each also provides information that might be of value in identifying the child or adolescent substance abuser.

Possible Diagnostic Criteria for Children or Adolescents with Suspected SUDs

To aid the assessor during the clinical interview portion of the assessment process, the following are offered as possible indicators of a potential SUD in either a child or adolescent:

Children

Zucker et al. (2009) warned that the "predictors" of possible SUDs in children or adolescents must be viewed as probabilities rather than firm indications of the existence of an SUD in either age group. With this warning in mind, some of the identified risk factors for childhood alcohol use include (Millar, 2009; Meyers & Dick, 2010; Zucker et al., 2009):

- *Having a friend or close sibling who uses alcohol or drugs.*
- *Internalizing feelings instead of expressing them*
- *Externalization of feelings*
- *Social problems*
- *Poor impulse control*
- *Engaging in risk-taking behavior(s)*
- *Poor parental supervision and/or inconsistent discipline*
- *Trauma (including parental divorce)*
- *Victimization*
- *Poor academic performance*
- *Problems controlling the child's temper outbursts*
- *Parental alcoholism*
- *Caucasian heritage*

The issue of internalization versus externalization as predictors of a possible SUD by children would initially appear to be contradictory. However, each identifies a different pattern of risk factors that applies to different subpopulations of children (Zucker et al., 2009). Externalizers tend to demonstrate poor emotional and behavioral self-control, possibly finding full expression in those children diagnosed as having a conduct disorder (Zucker et al., 2009). In contrast, children who are internalizers tend to experience anxiety, depression, shyness, and excessive inhibition, according to Zucker et al. (2009). It should be noted however that the indicators of children with an SUD are limited, in part because of a lack of research in this area.

Adolescents

There is no single characteristic profile to warn parents that their adolescent child is at high risk for abusing alcohol and/or drugs. Every adolescent is unique and, thus, will present the assessor with a unique combination of strengths, weaknesses, and needs (Weiner, Abraham, & Lyons, 2001; Johnson, 2003; Thatcher & Clark, 2008). Although not definitive, the following are characteristics that hint at an increased risk of an SUD for adolescents (Clark et al., 2002; Crowley, 2007; Evans & Sullivan, 2001; Johnson, 2003; Kaminer, 2008; Kricechbaum & Zernig, 2000; Kirisci et al., 2005; Meyers & Dick, 2010; Miller, Davies, & Greenwald, 2000; Parekh, 2006; Wills et al., 2001; Zuckerman, 2012):

1. Familial history of SUDs
2. Affective illness
3. History of suicide attempts
4. Loss of loved one(s)
5. Low self esteem
6. High levels of stress
7. Poor social skills or maladaptive coping skills, social isolation
8. Troubled relationship with parents (either 9 or 10 of this list)
9. Parental permissive attitudes toward deviant behavior
10. Overly strict parental behaviors toward deviant behaviors
11. Adolescent coming from a single parent or blended family
12. Feelings of alienation or running away from home
13. Low commitment or low expectations for school
14. Early use of cigarettes
15. High levels of involvement with drug-using peers
16. Antisocial behavior (or conduct disorder)
17. Poor impulse control
18. Early sexual experience, including high-risk sexual activities
19. Early experimental substance use
20. Legal problems during adolescence
21. Absence of strong religious beliefs
22. Unsuccessful attempts to stop or cut back on substance use
23. History of substance withdrawal
24. Having experienced one or more alcohol-induced "blackouts"
25. Continued substance abuse in spite of consequences
26. Use of chemicals prior to or during school

The greater the number of the above criteria that apply to a given individual the higher the odds are that he or she has an SUD. However, adolescent substance use patterns are highly variable. Suris, Akre, Berchtold, Jeannin, and Michaud (2007) found that there were different subgroups of adolescent marijuana abusers. The authors found that some adolescent marijuana abusers did not use tobacco products at all. Such adolescents were (a) more likely to be involved with sports activities, (b) be in an academic tract, and (c) have higher academic achievement levels, as compared with adolescents who abused both marijuana and tobacco products.

It should be apparent by now that there is little consensus on the diagnostic criteria to apply to possible substance-abusing children or adolescents. Identified risk factors are vague, and many children or adolescents who have several identified risk factors will never abuse alcohol or drugs. However, in the next section we will review the possible health and psychosocial consequences of an SUD in a child or adolescent.

Consequences of a Substance Use Disorder in a Child or Adolescent

It is not possible to identify every negative consequence that a child or adolescent substance abuser might experience. What follows is a brief overview of the specific consequences that might result from the abuse of a specific substance in childhood or adolescence. Little is known about the effects of polydrug abuse in children or adolescents, although this is a common practice among certain groups.

Alcohol

Adolescents under the age of 21 are thought to consume 17–20% of all the alcohol sold in the United States each year (Commission on Adolescent Substance and Alcohol Abuse, 2005; Kaminer, 2006). Unfortunately, in abusing alcohol the child or adolescent becomes vulnerable to most of the undesired effects of alcohol use discussed in Chapter 4. Admittedly, it is unlikely that the child or adolescent will develop conditions such as cirrhosis of the liver frequently found in older, more chronic, drinkers; however, acute alcohol poisoning is a real possibility.[41] Although adolescents are unlikely to develop esophageal varices because of their drinking, it is possible that their alcohol abuse will interfere with academic performance or cause accidental injury. Alcohol-related high-risk decision making is also a problem, resulting in unplanned pregnancies and possible exposure to sexually transmitted diseases.

There is a lack of objective data on how child/adolescent alcohol use might affect the physical or emotional growth of the individual. However, antidotal evidence suggests that the abuse of or addiction to alcohol interferes with the individual's emotional growth: The individual is thought to stop growing emotionally at the age when he or she begins the heavy abuse of alcohol. This is a potential relapse trigger later in life: Imagine a 22-year-old newly abstinent adult facing life's problems using the emotional resources of a 13-year old! The individual who is in such a situation might be tempted to return to the oblivion promised by alcohol.

Although it is known that alcohol is a neurotoxin, the effects of alcohol abuse or addiction on the neurological maturation of a child or adolescent is not known. Preliminary evidence does suggest that adolescent girls are more vulnerable to the neurotoxic effects of alcohol than boys because of neurological differences between the two sexes (Rutherford et al., 2010). There is a need for more research in this area.

Benzodiazepines

There is virtually no research into the effects of intentional benzodiazepine abuse on childhood or adolescent neurological or psychosocial development.

Cocaine

Children and adolescents who abuse cocaine run the risk of the potential dangers of cocaine, which are discussed in Chapter 9. Unfortunately, many children and adolescents mistakenly believe that you cannot become addicted to intranasal cocaine, a misperception often

aided by those who sell the cocaine to the user. Cocaine abusers are at increased risk of contracting Hepatitis Type C as discussed in Chapter 35. If the user should be an intravenous cocaine abuser who shares needles, he or she also is vulnerable not only to the infectious diseases discussed in Chapter 35 but also to a host of other blood-borne pathogens. Unfortunately there has been little age-specific research into possible damage of cocaine abuse on the child or adolescent's neurological or psychosocial development. It is known whether individuals who do abuse cocaine in childhood or adolescence are still vulnerable to cocaine-induced strokes or cardiac dysfunctions discussed in Chapter 9 as well as other complications that can result from the abuse of this substance.

Hallucinogens

There has been limited objective research into the effects of the various hallucinogenic compounds on the growth and development of children or adolescents, which is surprising because hallucinogen abuse is most common in the <25-year-old age cohort. Children and adolescents who abuse these compounds do put themselves at risk for any of the negative consequences associated with the abuse of these compounds.

Inhalants

Although children and young adolescents are the age cohorts that most commonly abuse inhalants, there has been little systematic research into how the abuse of these compounds might influence neural growth and development in these age groups. Many of these compounds are neurotoxic, have the potential to trigger cardiac arrhythmias or both, making their abuse at any time potentially dangerous. Specific dangers associated with the abuse of hallucinogenics are outlined in Chapter 12.

Marijuana

Researchers believe that 4.5 million teenagers used marijuana in 2008,[42] exposing them to the endocannabinoid-like chemical THC. One function of the endocannabinoids[43] is to guide neural growth during the development of the cortex. This region of the brain is still in development during childhood and adolescence, and thus adolescent marijuana abuse

---

[41]Every year there are at least two reports about a high school or college student who died from an acute alcohol overdose after drinking at a school party.

[42]Last year for which data are available as of this time.

[43]See Glossary.

holds the potential to interfere with normal neurocognitive development (Gold & Dupont, 2008). The long-term implications of adolescent marijuana abuse are still being explored, but animal-based research suggests that marijuana abuse during adolescence might permanently alter serotonin and norepinephrine levels in the adult brain (Bambico, Nguyen, Katz, & Gobbi, 2009). Theoretically, this could lead to increased anxiety and depression in adults who engaged in daily marijuana abuse in adolescence; however, this has not been proven. Further, between 33% and 40% of adolescents who smoke marijuana daily will become addicted to it (Crowley, 2007; Gruber & Pope, 2002). Many of these individuals continue to use marijuana in part to avoid withdrawal symptoms,[44] a fact that may have lifelong consequences for that individual's cortical development during this critical period of life.

The adolescent brain is still developing and will continue to do so until early adulthood. This developmental process contributes to the fact that a marijuana use disorder (MUD) in the 15-year-old manifests itself differently, follows a different path, and might have different neurobehavioral consequences than an MUD in a young adult (Ellickson, Martino, & Collins, 2004). One characteristic that might identify adolescents with marijuana addiction is that they started to use it prior to the age of 16 and that they report having positive experiences when they first used it (Fergusson, Horwood, Lunskey, & Madden, 2003). However, criteria to help identify the adolescent or young adult with an MUD are still in the early stages of development, and the assessor must rely on more traditional criteria outlined earlier in this chapter.

Methamphetamine

The consequences of methamphetamine abuse in childhood or adolescence have not been explored in depth. The child or adolescent who abuses these compounds risks any of the adverse consequences inherent in the abuse of methamphetamine (discussed in Chapter 8), which may be permanent. Antidotal evidence would suggest that adolescents often begin to use methamphetamine intranasally and dismiss the addictive potential of methamphetamine on the mistaken belief that it is not addictive if you snort it. Children or adolescents who share needles are also vulnerable to the various blood-borne infections inherent in this practice, some of which are discussed in Chapter 35.

---

[44]Discussed in Chapter 13.

Tobacco

It is illegal in many states for persons under the age of 21, which belies the fact that more than 600,000 middle school and 3 million high school students smoke cigarettes (United States Department of Health and Human Services, 2012). Each day in the United States over 3,800 persons under the age of 18 smoke their first cigarette, of whom 1,000 will become regular smokers before the age of 18 (United States Department of Health and Human Services, 2012). In Russia, children as young as 10 years of age are often cigarette smokers (Tobacco, 2009).

These statistics are made more frightening in light of an emerging and quite impressive, body of evidence that supports the argument that the tobacco industry is actively manipulating the menthol levels in cigarettes with the intention of enticing adolescents and younger adults to begin smoking. Menthol levels used to cover the harsh taste of cigarette smoke were found to be more attractive to adolescents than non-menthol brands, and thus the authors suggested that it could act as an incentive for the adolescent or young adult to begin smoking (Kreslake, Wayne, Alkpert, Hoh, & Connolly, 2008). There is also evidence that adolescents tend to be unaware of the signs of an emerging nicotine dependence problem, increasing their risk for an addiction to nicotine as they continue to smoke (Doubeni, Reed, & DiFranza, 2010).

Opioids

The diversion of prescribed narcotic analgesics has become a major problem for adolescents in the past two decades—a problem fueled by the myth that narcotic analgesics are not addictive if ingested orally or if you are taking pharmaceuticals. The age of peak risk for the initiation of nonprescribed narcotic use is 16 years, although there are smaller peaks in the incidence of nonprescribed narcotic analgesic abuse at the 12–14-year and again at the 19–21-year age brackets (Meier, Troost, & Anthony, 2012). It would not be unreasonable to assume that individuals have formed their core belief about narcotic abuse before they first abuse one of these compounds. This would suggest that psychoeducational education programs that focus on the 12–14-year age cohort might be attempting to intervene *after* the adolescent has started to abuse narcotic analgesics (Meier et al., 2012). Further, Zhang et al. (2008) examined the rate of oxycodone self-administration by adolescent and adult mice and a significantly higher rate of self-administration in adolescent mice. This would suggest that the adolescent mice in this study seemed to be more vulnerable to the reinforcing effects of oxycodone than are adults. This study has not been replicated using human subjects but does have implications for therapists working with adolescent opiate abusers.

In cases of adolescent opioid addiction, the standard treatment has been a 2-week taper from opioids using an opioid agonist such as buprenorphine combined with psychosocial counseling (Woody, Poole, Subramaniam, Dugosh et al., 2008). The authors examined the use of longer-term (12 week) use of buprenorphine-naloxone followed by detoxification using the number of opioid-free urine toxicology tests and patient retention in treatment as measures and concluded that this approach was more effective than the standard 2-week detoxification sequence combined with substance abuse rehabilitation counseling. However, the authors also found that by the end of 12 weeks the number of adolescents who remained in treatment following the extended treatment was approximately the same as those who received the standard treatment. Thus it would appear that there are no treatment methods that offer superior results for this population.

Other CNS stimulants

There is an impressive body of evidence suggesting that methcathinone, which has virtually disappeared in the United States, has been resurrected as a drug of abuse in England. The core methcathinone molecule is often modified, forming a variety of methcathinone-like compounds. The effects of these compounds on childhood or adolescent growth and development are not known at this time.

Other Compounds Abused by Children/ Adolescents

There are clinical examples of children mixing nail polish remover with soda, and then drinking the obtained mixture to induce a state of euphoria (Brust, 2004). The extent of and long-term consequences of this practice are not known as of this time.

Adolescent Rehabilitation Programs

Having identified an adolescent with an SUD serious enough to warrant admission to a rehabilitation program, the assessor must choose a treatment setting.

This in itself is a difficult task because there is a shocking (Trivedi, 2010, p. xiii) dearth of treatment programs to which an adolescent might be referred. Combined with the lack of training for health care professionals who wish to work with this specialized population, only 10–15% of adolescents in need of professional assistance for an SUD receive such help (Kaminer, 2010). Fewer than one-third of rehabilitation programs surveyed offered treatment for adolescent substance abusers, and the quality of such programs is on average only fair (Knudson, 2009). Approximately 80% of these adolescent rehabilitation programs are outpatient programs (Kaminer & Goodley, 2010), and there is a decided lack of residential treatment programs for adolescents with an SUD (Kaminer, 2008). To complicate matters, few adolescent treatment programs for SUDs or behavioral issues seem to be effective (Dobbs, 2011). The assessor is thus often forced to accept a less-than-desirable treatment setting for the adolescent substance abuser because of a lack of access to better programs.

Even if the assessor is able to arrange for a given child or adolescent to enter a substance abuse rehabilitation program, there are many factors that can interfere with the effectiveness of treatment. Some of these factors include (a) unrealistic parental expectations, (b) hidden agendas for treatment by both the adolescent and parents, (c) parental psychopathology, and (d) parental substance use. Although it is useful to include the parents and family members in the treatment program, often they refuse to participate in the rehabilitation efforts. An example of parental psychopathology and parental substance use is found in the observation that even parental smoking has been found to influence the substance use patterns of the adolescent, suggesting that parents lose credibility when they try to prevent adolescent SUDs if they are themselves engaging in the use of a substance, even if it is "just" cigarette use (Keyes, Legrand, Iacono, & McGue, 2008). Fletcher (2013) also noted that parental attitudes about having an adolescent in treatment vary but might be a source of shame for the parent.

The Special Needs of Adolescent Substance Abuse Rehabilitation Programs

In contrast to more traditional rehabilitation programs that work with adult clients, the adolescent's cognitive abilities, strengths, weaknesses, and defensive style will evolve over the course of treatment as the individual matures. Further, treatment must address ancillary issues such as sexually transmitted diseases, birth control, and vocational needs—issues that might make the parents uncomfortable. The adolescent's cultural heritage should be a consideration in any rehabilitation program. A diverse treatment program staff or enlistment of ancillary staff from that individual's culture will enable the adolescent to find at least one person to identify with during his or her participation in a rehabilitation program.

It is also necessary to match the individual with a treatment approach based on the adolescent's personality. Conrad et al. (2013) trained a number of teachers, school counselors, and other educational professionals in selected schools in both cognitive-behavioral and motivational-interviewing techniques and found that when the educators were able to match the interventional approach to a specific student based on his or her personality they were able to achieve a 29% reduction in drinking as compared with the control group over the 2 years that the students were followed. This would suggest the possibility that one reason why adolescent rehabilitation programs are so often ineffective is that there is a conflict between the child's personality and the treatment approach.

A potential source of treatment failure and parent–child conflict is the common mistake of viewing the adolescent's physical size as an indicator of emotional or intellectual maturity. During the rehabilitation process, treatment center staff need to consider the individual's level of cognitive maturity when working with the adolescent. Adolescents and adults process environmental stimuli differently: Adolescents benefit from a here-and-now focus rather than on possible long-term consequences of their behavior(s) (Brook, 2008). Adolescents underestimate risk and over-anticipate rewards for substance use (Hopson, 2013; Rutherford et al., 2010). Thus, those regions of the brain responsible for top-down behavioral inhibition are still maturing while those regions of the brain involved in the reward cascade are fully functional (bottom-up control).

Group therapies designed to work with adults with an SUD, long a mainstay in most rehabilitation programs, are not always appropriate for adolescents. The group therapy format must be modified to work with adolescents and might best be discarded entirely because adolescents are not simply small adults (Fletcher, 2013). Further, adolescents should not be referred to mixed-gender therapy groups because of the differing developmental issues for either sex during this phase of life (Brook, 2008). A given adolescent might be reluctant to discuss personal problems if there are members of the opposite sex in the same group and might prefer to discuss these matters in individual psychotherapy with a properly trained mental health professional.

Group therapies with adolescents are more challenging than are such therapies with adult substance abusers. Confrontation and feedback is often more readily accepted if offered by a peer rather than a staff person, underscoring the difference between adolescent and adult substance abuse rehabilitation therapy groups. The group leader must assume a more active role in a limited setting with adolescents in a treatment group (Brook, 2008). Unfortunately, members of adolescent therapy groups often become enamored with the "war stories" that other group members tell of their drug experiences ("Does Teen Drug Rehab Cure Addiction or Create It?," 2010). It is the counselor's job to steer the group away from such discussions. Adolescents should not be involved in therapy groups for adult substance abusers (Fletcher, 2013). The information processing systems of adolescents differ from that of adults, providing ample grounds for misunderstanding and disruption in groups, and there is a danger that the older group members might try to take advantage of the adolescent group member. Further, the adolescent's need for problem-solving training usually differs from that of an adult who abuses the same compound. Finally, the family therapy format must be modified to address each adolescent's unique place in the family constellation as well as potential problems such as parental substance use problems.

Adolescent involvement in the juvenile criminal justice or child protection systems are unique, and treatment staff should include these agencies in the individual's rehabilitation program.[45] Finally, the adolescent's social support system must be examined and if necessary modified. Adolescents who had at least one non-using peer, and who remained in treatment or aftercare for approximately a year, were found to be less likely to relapse (Latimer, Newcomb, Winters, & Stinchfield, 2000). Adolescents who did relapse often did so as a result of social pressure. If there are 12-Step programs available for adolescent substance abusers, such groups might provide a useful adjunct to an individual's rehabilitation program. The rehabilitation

---

[45]The reader is advised to consult with an attorney familiar with the laws in his or her state to determine the child or adolescent's rights if referred to such a program prior to making the referral.

process should be sufficiently long and intense enough to adequately address identified problems during the adolescent's time in a treatment program.

Further, like their adult counterparts, adolescents who do abuse alcohol or illicit drugs may minimize their substance abuse, especially if they believe that this information might be used against them. They might admit to the use of "one or two beers," for example, without revealing that the beer cans are 40 ounce cans[46] and not the more traditional 12 ounce cans (Rosenbloom, 2005). This underscores the need for a multidisciplinary assessment of the individual to allow for an accurate identification of the client's strengths, weaknesses, the stage of substance abuse at which the individual is at, and her or his level of maturity and adaptive style, so that the staff might better understand how to work with the client. Finally, the rehabilitation center staff should be aware of the unique effects of the drugs of abuse on the adolescent.

Referral Sources

Referrals for substance abuse treatment come from many different sources. The juvenile court system, and especially the emerging "Drug Court" program, will often refer an offender for evaluation with the stipulation that the adolescent also follow treatment recommendations. School officials will often refer a suspected substance abuser for assessment, and it is not unusual for parents to make such referrals, especially in strict homes where even the first hint of substance abuse is not tolerated. The phenomenon of home urine drug tests has contributed to this process, although possibly at the cost of damaging parent–child trust. Parents rarely understand that a "positive" urine toxicology test does not automatically indicate illicit substance use or that "false positive" results might be possible.[47] Even if the test does accurately identify illicit drug use, this does not in itself prove that the child or adolescent is *addicted* as opposed to having abused a given compound or that there is then a need for rehabilitation, although this might indicate the need for an assessment of the adolescent's substance use pattern by a properly trained addictions counselor (Winters & Kaminer, 2008).

---

[46]Sometimes referred to as "silos" or "tall boys" by the drinker.

[47]The topic of urine toxicology testing is discussed in more detail in Chapter 33.

Adolescent Substance Abuse Treatment: A Cause for Optimism?

There is strong evidence suggesting that for every year that adolescents delay the initiation alcohol or prescription drug abuse the risk for developing a future SUD drops 5% (McCabe, West, Morales, Cranford, & Boyd, 2009). Further, adolescents with alcohol use disorders who are referred to a rehabilitation program appear to benefit more than adults who are referred to a similar program (Kricechbaum & Zernig, 2000). Behavioral therapies, including Motivational Interviewing (MI), appear to be at least moderately effective with adolescent substance abusing adolescents, although the program must be modified to meet the adolescent's needs (Macgowan & Engle, 2010). Further in many cases, psychological trauma that motivates an adolescent to abuse chemicals is easier to assess through psychosocial interventions than in adults (Jorgensen, 2001). Finally, although many parents fear the worst, the heavy abuse of alcohol or illicit drugs is often limited to just adolescence (Kaminer, 2008). Only a minority of those adolescents who briefly abuse a chemical continue on to develop an SUD later in life (Kricechbaum & Zernig, 2000).

Is There a Financial Incentive for Over-Diagnosis?

Many treatment programs for substance abusing adolescents are "for profit." To maximize profits, many admissions officers blur the line between adolescent substance use, abuse, and addiction. It is not unheard of for an adolescent treatment program to offer a one-size-fits-all diagnostic assessment and a similar style of treatment (Weiner et al., 2001). Many adolescent substance abuse rehabilitation professionals maintain that the treatment for the adolescent is automatically a positive, growth-enhancing experience, a belief that is untrue: An unknown percentage of adolescents are *harmed* by intervention or treatment programs (Fletcher, 2013; Szalavitz, 2006). The analogy of surgery might not be out of place here. If a surgeon were to advocate abdominal surgery stating that it is automatically a healthy thing for people to do, she or he would be charged with criminal intent and malpractice in short order.

There are adolescent treatment programs where the staff attempt to convince the parents that the adolescent will be permanently impaired because of the assumed SUD and that the adolescent or their families can never be emotionally "whole" without treatment. Lamentably, there is no research to support this philosophy, just as there is no evidence that telling the adolescent that he or she is a lifelong addict is either true or healthy for the adolescent. Indeed there is antidotal evidence that being told by staff that the adolescent is a drug addict or alcoholic cements the individual's identity as such ("Does Teen Drug Rehab Cure Addiction or Create It?," 2010). Such programs ignore research evidence that suggests that the majority of adolescents identified as having an SUD do not continue down the path to chemical addiction (Kaminer & Buckstein, 2005). Thus, when making a referral to a substance abuse rehabilitation program that works with children or adolescents with an SUD, let the buyer beware.

The legal framework within which the parents and the assessor must work varies from state to state. In some states, the adolescent can refuse to enter treatment if he or she is above a certain age. In other states, the adolescents can be forced into a rehabilitation program by the parents without their consent (Evans & Sullivan, 2001). Some states allow adolescents to refuse to let their parents see their treatment chart whereas in other states the child or adolescent has no such privilege. The assessor should consult with an attorney to discuss the legal requirements and restrictions for a rehabilitation counselor working with children or adolescents.

The Danger of Under-diagnosis

There is strong evidence that the majority of substance-abusing adolescents are never identified as such (Evans & Sullivan, 2001; Lee, Garnick, Miller, & Horgan, 2004). The implications of this failure are staggering: For example, SUDs are a significant part of the problem of adolescent suicide (Miller et al., 2006; Simkin, 2002; Weiner et al., 2001). Some of the other risk factors for adolescent suicide include[48] (a) adolescent affective disorders, (b) thoughts of suicide by the adolescent, (c) a family history of depression or suicide, (d) impending Court or legal problems, (e) thoughts about joining a deceased loved one, and (f) having easy access to a handgun (Simkin, 2002; Sorter, 2010). Adolescent substance abuse contributes to disinhibition and high-risk behavior(s), which are in turn a major factor for

adolescent accidental injuries (Miller et al., 2006). Approximately 40% of adolescents treated in one hospital emergency room had evidence of drugs or alcohol in their urine (Erlich, Brown, & Drongowski, 2006). It has been hypothesized that these behaviors reflect the belief by adolescents that they are invulnerable or that bad things do not happen to them. Another complication is that about 15% of adolescents believe that they will die at an early age. The authors found that almost 11% of their sample thought that they had only a 50% chance of living to the age of 35.[49] However, while this information was used to guide medical treatment for the injured adolescent, it was found to rarely result in a referral for assessment and possible treatment. However, an accidental injury or other high-risk behaviors for the adolescent might be one of the first signs that the adolescent might have an SUD.

The substance abuse rehabilitation professional must find a middle ground between over-diagnosis, and under-diagnosis, a process that is difficult at best, and possibly impossible. However, this dilemma does underscore the need for accurate diagnostic criteria to identify adolescent substance abusers.

Chapter Summary

Although society has reawakened to the problem of child and adolescent substance abuse or addiction, there remains a lack of serious research into the problem or its solution(s). It is known that peer pressure, the media's portrayal of substance use, parental substance use, and self-esteem are all intertwined and play a role in the adolescent's decision to begin and continue substance abuse, the exact role of these forces is not known. Yet child or adolescent substance abuse can have lifelong consequences. A cocaine-induced stroke at the age of 17 does not resolve when the adolescent turns 18 or 21, for example. Injuries sustained in an alcohol-related motor vehicle accident, even if the adolescent was only a passenger, will have lifelong implications for the individual's health and potential for advancement.

---

[48]This list is hardly comprehensive. The topic of adolescent suicide is the subject of many books, and the reader is referred to one of the many books, or research papers, on this subject.

[49]The examiner should take time to explore *why* the adolescent believes this. For many gangs, for example, early death is the norm and not the exception. Another example might be seen in the hypothetical adolescent. If the adolescent is from a family where many members died before the age of 35 from cancer, their belief that they might die at an early age might not be unreasonable.

In the face of a dearth of clinical research to guide the treatment professional, it is necessary to steer a cautious path between over-diagnosis, and under-diagnosis of an SUD. Just as is true for surgery, the treatment professional must weigh the potential benefits against the possible harm from this process, and there is indeed a potential for harm from an intervention effort that is poorly executed or forced on an adolescent who has engaged only in experimental substance use. Many adolescents mature out of their substance abuse as they reach young adulthood (Szalavitz, 2006). Others continue to abuse chemicals in a problematic way. The diagnostic criteria to identify those who are more likely to continue to develop an SUD are still lacking. Thus, the treatment professionals have no established principle to guide them in their efforts to identify, assess, or treat children or adolescents with SUDs. This is an evolving area of pediatric medicine, and health care professionals must attempt to assess and treat child and adolescent substance abusers while the guidelines for assessment and treatment are still being developed. This remains a daunting challenge.

Although childhood is not often viewed as part of the problem of cigarette smoking, researchers have found that the individual's pro-smoking attitudes are often formed during the childhood years and that children begin to experiment with cigarettes either in late childhood or early adolescence as evidenced by the fact that one-third of 9-year-old children in the United States have taken at least one experimental puff on a cigarette (Hymowitz, 2005). The median age at which individuals begin to experiment with regular cigarette use is around 15 years (Patkar, Fergare, Batka, Weinstein, & Leone, 2003). These facts have not been lost on the tobacco industry, which has experimented with such things as "flavored" cigarettes that might be attractive to smokers in their childhood years. Unfortunately, there is evidence that suggests that the physical addiction to nicotine develops within just a few days of the initiation of cigarette use, something that younger smokers might not understand when they begin to smoke (DiFranza et al., 2007).

CHAPTER 21

Substance Use Disorders in College Students[1]

Introduction

The college experience presents a divergence point in the life path of transitional adolescents: Some choose to pursue higher education, whereas others do not. However, it is increasingly difficult for a high school graduate to move directly into the workforce, and an ever growing percentage of high school graduates are choosing to pursue some form of higher education. This is clearly seen in college admissions statistics.[2] In 1970, 37% of persons in the 18–19-year-old cohort entered college, whereas in the year 2008, 49% did so. In spite of this increase in enrollment, only 20–24% of adults over the age of 25 will graduate from college. These data underscore the fact that behavioral observations of young adults who do pursue higher education do not automatically apply to the subgroup that do not, making them worthy of study as a special subgroup of transitional older adolescents. In this chapter, we will examine the problem of substance use disorders in the college population.

A Special Environment

The college experience provides transitional adolescents[3] or young adults[4] a unique environment: It is to some degree protected from the larger society within which it exists. Within the sheltered environment of a post-secondary educational facility, a sense of community membership evolves in both students who reside on-campus[5] and those who reside off-campus.[6] The institution provides an isolated environment in which there is minimal parental supervision for the most part, but in which the student is faced with unique academic, behavioral, interpersonal, developmental, and financial demands (Winters et al., 2012). Their ability to adapt is both tested and often rewarded with opportunities that do not exist outside of the post-secondary environment.

The college experience forces the high school graduate to attempt multiple tasks simultaneously: (a) learning to function independently in a challenging academic environment, (b) developing supportive social networks, and (c) possibly dealing with the feelings that follow separation from home for extended periods. During this phase

---

[1]In the original editions of this text, this topic was included as a subsection of the chapter on adolescence. However, given the relatively importance of this topic, the decision was made to review this material in a separate chapter.

[2]For the sake of brevity, "college" will be used to refer to any form of post secondary education, including vocational-technical school, community colleges, and four-year institutions.

[3]A term that, in this text, refers to the 18–20-year age cohort.

[4]For the sake of this chapter, young adult is defined as between 20 and 23 years of age.

[5]A term that includes those who live in fraternities or sororities ("Greek") houses, as well as college dormitory units.

[6]Apartments shared with others, or living with parents or relatives and commuting to classes, etc.

of life, the individual's relationship with his or her parents will also evolve, and often areas of conflict are outgrown as parents assume the new role of mentors in the young adult's life (Brown et al., 2009). As the college student makes this transition, his or her relationship with alcohol and illicit drugs also changes. This is not a static process but continues throughout the college years and overlaps with the other tasks outlined previously.

Peer Relationships

For the majority of college students, their high school peer relationships will either dissolve or assume new forms. College students begin the process of building a peer relationship support system consistent with their expectations and goals for college. Those students with the strongest motives for attending college are typically more likely to reach out to others with similar values and least likely to abuse alcohol or recreational drugs because this would interfere with their academic goals. This is seen in the fact that although 17.6% of young adults have abused an opioid, only 1.9% of college students report doing so (Schuckit, 2010b). There is, however, a subpopulation of undergraduates who turn to alcohol or other drugs as a means of dealing with the pressure to meet academic expectations (Vaughan, Corbin, & Fromme, 2009). Alcohol or recreational drugs offer the illusion of relief from some of the stress and anxiety associated with college. Substance abuse also can contribute to a vicious cycle of substance-related poor academic performance, increased stress, increased use of chemicals to address that stress, and then further deterioration in academic performance. Johnson (2010) reported, for example, that one-quarter of college students admitted that their alcohol use had caused drinking-related academic problems such as missing classes, poor grades, or failing to keep up with assigned materials.

In contrast to the student population with strong academic goals, some undergraduates find that heavy alcohol use facilitates the establishment of social relationships with other heavy alcohol users and is a strong motivating factor for continued heavy alcohol use. Unfortunately, there is an inverse relationship between the individual's level of alcohol use and academic performance, as many students discover to their dismay[7] (Vaughan et al., 2009). In the next section, we will look at the changing relationship between the student, alcohol, and the illicit drugs of abuse.

An Evolving Relationship

The individual's relationship with alcohol during the college experience does not remain static. Over the course of their academic careers, some students who were initially most heavily invested in alcohol use have been known to turn their attention to academic studies.[8] This change in priorities might be motivated by the discovery that the student is moving closer to graduation and soon will attempt to enter the workforce and seek a position in his or her chosen field (Vaughan et al., 2009). Also, students frequently find that upon reaching the status of legal adulthood the thrill of drinking is lost: It is no longer a prohibited activity for them. Some students, discovering a passion for another academic pursuit, find that their initial choice of a field of study no longer holds their interest. This change in academic focus[9] forces the student to develop new social networks, possibly establishing social networks with students who are more heavily invested in academic performance rather than alcohol or drug use.

While in college, students discover that there are rewards for their efforts and that life can be unfair, as the whims of fortune dictate. The distinctive demands of post-secondary education may conspire to prevent the individual from completing his or her chosen program of study for a variety of social or financial reasons. Some students, faced with overwhelming financial demands, drop out of school, transfer to institutions where the tuition is more affordable, or elect to pursue part-time studies intermixed with employment to pay for their educational careers. Some students fail to graduate because of illness, accidents, disease, or the unplanned demands of parenthood.[10] Each course of action forces the student to establish new social network systems with similar, or different, social relationships and to reexamine his or her substance use pattern.

---

[7]It is not unusual to discover that those freshmen who were most heavily invested in the "party" scene in the fall semester are either on academic probation during the spring semester or have been dismissed from college for their poor academic performance in the preceding semester. Unfortunately, this phenomenon is not limited to first-year college students.

[8]Well, it *has* been known to happen, on occasion.

[9]Also known as "switching 'majors'."

[10]Which itself might be a result of the disinhibition effects of alcohol abuse and high-risk sexual activity encouraged by alcohol's disinhibition effects.

One factor that influences the student's relationship with alcohol is his or her ethnic heritage. Many Latino and African American students are the first members of their family to attend college, thus introducing the possibility of familial pressures to perform well in the college environment and advance socially following graduation. These are strong factors that might inhibit the use of alcohol by these students (Vaughan et al., 2009). Asian American students often enter college with strong social and familial pressure to succeed in their studies even if they are not the first members of their family to attend college (Vaughan et al., 2009). In contrast, Caucasian students often bring their expectation that heavy alcohol use is an integral part of the college experience, contributing to alcohol abuse by this population of students (Vaughan et al., 2009). Women in all subgroups tend to be more academically oriented, especially during the early stages of the college experience, which tends to protect them from alcohol abuse problems in college (Vaughan et al., 2009).

Although it has not been proven, hypothetically the protected college environment might be one reason why college students are more likely to engage in binge drinking as opposed to their non-college peers. College enrollees were less likely to be binge drinkers in high school than their non-college peers, a pattern that reverses itself after they enter college. Forty-five percent of college students surveyed indicated that they had engaged in binge drinking compared with 35% of their non-college peers (Brown et al., 2009; Hingson, 2010; Lambert, Fincham, Marks, & Stillman, 2010). These results were significant because college students view beer differently from other forms of alcohol, consuming a greater amount of beer per binge than they would if they were consuming hard liquor (Bonar et al., 2012; Quinn & Fromme, 2012). This places them at higher risk for adverse consequences from a binge because of higher blood alcohol level.[11] Male college students reported that a binge required the consumption of a higher number of drinks than did female students, suggesting that studies on this topic should be gender specific (Bonar et al., 2012). College students are more

likely to drink with the goal of intoxication as opposed to their non-college peers. Persons who did not enter the college environment report more frequent alcohol use and are more likely to be daily drinkers than their non-college peers but tend to drink less per occasion as well. This fact underscores the differences between these two subgroups of transitional adolescents or young adults.

During the college experience, dating relationships continue to evolve and the student confronts the possibility of finding a future life partner. Courting rituals might be initiated to immediately progress to their anticipated goal, or the goal is acknowledged but, by agreement, is postponed until after graduation. Experimental relationships (heterosexual or homosexual) also evolve during the college years, often to slowly dissolve during or shortly after the college years. However, some relationships that began in college do continue and couples who marry after college graduation appear to experience a lower divorce rate (Furstenberg, 2010).

Scope of the Problem

Substance use by college students is hardly a new phenomenon. In 1354, for example, there was a drunken brawl between students of Oxford University in England and the local townspeople that left 63 students dead (Boyd, McCabe, & Morales, 2005). Currently, alcohol use remains ubiquitous in the college environment. The start of the "chemical revolution" eventually presented society with a growing number of new compounds that potentially could be abused, a fact that many students in post-secondary institutions have. For example, medical and dental school students have on occasion been known to abuse surgical anesthetic agents such as ether for recreational purposes. The use of stimulants to help the student cram for final examinations is pervasive, involving up to 25% of the student body at some colleges (Horstman, 2010). A number of students experiment with marijuana, hallucinogens, or other drugs of abuse out of curiosity, and some go on to make the use of such compounds an informal program of study. Unfortunately, for some students what started out as experimental substance abuse morphs into a substance use disorder over time.

Although it is illegal for students under the age of 21 years to drink, just under 90% of college students view alcohol as a central component to their social

---

[11]The team of Goslawski et al. (2013) found evidence of microvascular changes in young adult binge drinkers, for example, that they surmised might presage later cardiovascular risk. The study was based on a small number of subjects and this study should be replicated using a larger number of young adult binge drinkers to confirm these findings.

lives and consume alcohol. Approximately 40% of college undergraduates "engage in heavy episodic drinking at least once every two weeks" (Leeman, Toll, Taylor, & Volpicelli, 2009, p. 553). At many colleges, certain nights are identified as "party nights," with alcohol use being more common, if not expected, on these nights[12] (Benton, 2009). Student alcohol use also is very common during special events such as holidays and spring break (Lee, Lewis, & Neighbors, 2009), and certain colleges, in spite of their academic credentials, are also known as "party" schools. Students who live in dormitories were less likely to drive after drinking, possibly because they are less likely to have a car on campus or they have access to a greater number of social activities that do not involve alcohol (Quinn & Fromme, 2012).

Each year the team of Johnston, O'Malley, Backman, and Schulenberg (2009) conducts a survey of substance use among students, and they found that the prevalence of alcohol use by college students during the first eight years of the 21st century has remained relatively steady at around 80%.

As Figure 21-1 demonstrates, the percentage of college students reporting the use of alcohol at some point in their lives has remained relatively stable. However, certain environments on campus appear to encourage the use of alcohol more than others. The college fraternity offers one notorious environment for alcohol use, although this varies from fraternity (or sorority) to fraternity. Benton (2009) found that 86% of fraternity members binge drink, a figure that is approximately 35% higher than for college students who are not fraternity members. On a similar note, 80% of sorority members who live in a sorority house binge drink, a figure that is approximately twice that for women who are not sorority members (Benton, 2009). Students often self-select to gain admission to "Greek" houses with alcohol use patterns more consistent with their desired level of alcohol intake (Park, Sher, & Krull, 2009). There are many possible explanations for these findings. As noted earlier, the fraternity and sorority system might attract persons more likely to engage in abusive drinking, and in certain fraternities (or to a lesser degree sororities) alcohol (or other substance) use might be viewed as a rite of passage for the new member.

The Substance Abuse and Mental Health Services Administration (2009) reported that 61% of college

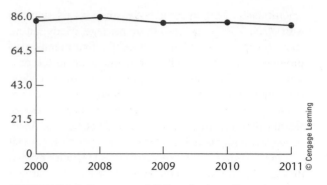

FIGURE 21-1 Percentage of College Students Reporting Lifetime Alcohol Use in the Years 2007–2011.[13]

students were current alcohol users, 40.5% were binge drinkers,[14] and 16.3% were identified as being heavy drinkers. Although there has been a slight increase in the percentage of college students who engage in binge drinking in the past decade, this increase was found in the 21–24 years age bracket[15] rather than the 18–21 years age group (Hingson, Zha, & Weigzman, 2009). Such binge drinking is, at least in theory, supported by the tradition of "happy hour(s)" at bars near the college campus, and there is an initiative by some institutions of higher learning to stop specialized events at local bars that encourage heavy drinking. It has been found, however, that even if such intervention efforts were successful, college drinkers simply turn to other sources of cheap alcohol and that the frequency of intoxication remains relatively unchanged in this age group (Wells, Graham, & Purcell, 2009).

Certain colleges have reputations as being "party" schools, and the rate of alcohol use by students at these institutions tends to be higher than at other colleges in the United States. Nelson, Xuan, Lee, Weitzman, & Wechsler (2009) found that 85–88% of students at these colleges engaged in alcohol use, with 53–58% engaging in heavy, episodic alcohol use—percentages that are significantly higher than the national averages for college alcohol use. To combat this problem, there has been an intense effort to curb alcohol use at the 18 colleges with the highest rate of alcohol use, but researchers have found that in the period from 1993 to 2005 the amount of alcohol use on each campus has been virtually the same each year (Nelson et al., 2009). Further, within the college

---

[13]Last year for which data were available at the time of revision.

[14]Defined as consumption of five 12-ounce cans of beer or standard mixed drinks in a period of drinking.

[15]Student age group for returning students or graduate school students.

---

[12]Which for some college students begins on Thursday night, depending on their class schedule.

environment there is a self-selection process through which students seek admission to specialized micro-environments (smoking-permitted versus smoking-prohibited dormitory units, for example) or off-campus drinking establishments. The "know" relationship between cigarette smoking and alcohol use would suggest that smoking-permitted dormitory units are more attractive to smokers and drinkers, encouraging the incoming student to seek admission to these housing units.

An estimated 20.2% of college students abuse illicit drugs (usually marijuana), a rate that was similar to that found in their non-college bound peers. An estimated 2.1% of college students are thought to have abused a hallucinogenic in the past year, with 1.2% abusing MDMA and 0.6% abusing LSD at some point during their month preceding the survey conducted by the Substance Abuse and Mental Health Services Administration (2009). The percentage of college students who report the abuse of any illicit drug, as opposed to marijuana use alone, is reviewed in Figure 21-2.[16]

As these data demonstrate the percentage of college students who report the abuse of any illicit drug as opposed to the abuse of marijuana has remained relatively steady over the past five years and that marijuana is the most commonly abused drug on campus.

One frequently overlooked aspect of college students with substance use disorders is the students' use of a performance-enhancing compound such as anabolic steroids, CNS stimulants, and nutritional supplements. The team of Buckman, Yusko, White, and Pandina (2009) examined this student subpopulation and found that students who used performance-enhancing compounds tend to demonstrate more problematic alcohol use patterns, are more likely to engage in tobacco abuse, are more likely to use cocaine, marijuana, hallucinogens, and more likely to abuse prescription drugs. The authors also found that this subpopulation of students was more likely to engage in risk taking and sensation-seeking behaviors. Surprisingly, many of the compounds being abused, such as tobacco products or alcohol, detract from athletic performance. This raises the question whether the abuse of performance-enhancing compounds by this subgroup of college students might reflect a more general tendency to abuse chemicals rather than a desire on their part to improve athletic performance. There is a need for further research into the substance use patterns of this group of college students to resolve this question (Buckman et al., 2009).

---

[16]2011 was last year that data were available at the time of revision.

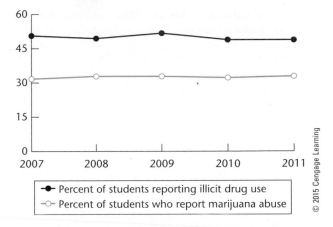

FIGURE 21-2 Degree to Which Marijuana Use Contributes to the Problem of Illicit Drug Use on Campus.

If It Is Statistically Normal Why Worry about College Substance Abuse?

The answer to this question is relatively straight-forward:

- *Forty percent of college students have been a passenger in a motor vehicle where the driver was known to be under the influence of alcohol in just the past month.*
- *Over seventy thousand college students are the victims of alcohol-related sexual assault or date rape experiences each year. In over 90% of these rapes, the victim knew the perpetrator.*
- *Over 599,000 college students suffered an alcohol-related accidental injury in 2001 (Mundt & Zaletskalia, 2012).*
- *An estimated 600,000 college students are involved in an alcohol-related fight each year, with the injuries sustained often becoming badges of honor or the source of bragging rights.*
- *Fifty-nine percent of off-campus fires involve alcohol, with approximately 10 students per year losing their life in these fires.*
- *Approximately 25% of students admit that their alcohol use has negatively affected their academic performance.*
- *One thousand eight hundred twenty-five college students died from unintentional*

alcohol-related injuries in 2005[17] (Mundt & Zakletskaia, 2012).

The relationship between substance use and accidental injury is quite complex. Mundt, Zakletskala, Brown, and Fleming (2011) found that 18% of the college students in their sample who never experienced a blackout suffered a traumatic injury in the two years before the survey. However, 49% of college students who reported experiencing six or more alcohol-induced blackouts in the same time frame reported experiencing a serious injury while intoxicated. It has been estimated that male college students were 19% more likely to suffer an injury for each day that they consumed more than eight drinks, whereas female college students were 10% more likely to suffer an injury for each day that they consumed five or more drinks (Mundt et al., 2011). This is only a short summary of the damage done each year by alcohol or drugs to the college student population. Unfortunately, alcohol use is often viewed as a rite of passage within the college community, a fact that might contribute to the observation that alcohol abuse and dependence is *three times that of the general population.* Transitional adolescents or young adults who do not go on to college tend to drink slightly more often than their college peers (Benton, 2009) and abuse illicit drugs more often (Latimer & Zur, 2010). The relative proportions of college and non-college drinkers in young adulthood are reviewed in Figure 21-3.

Although at first glance it would appear that they have similar drinking patterns, college students are less likely to drink on a regular basis than their non-college bound peers but are more likely to engage in heavy alcohol use when they do drink. The relationship between heavy drinking in young adulthood is shown in Figure 21-4.

There are many reasons for this disparity between the heavy use of alcohol by college students as opposed to their non-college peers. First, college students tend to overestimate their peers' acceptance of drunken behavior and second they overestimate the number of their peers who are engaging in heavy alcohol use (Hingson, 2010; Park et al., 2009; White & Jackson, 2004/2005). College students also both overestimate the frequency with which their peers suffer negative consequences from their drinking and come to believe that such negative consequences are not a sign of

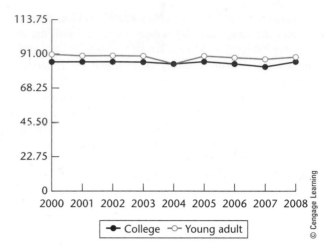

FIGURE 21-3 Relative Percentage of Lifetime Alcohol Use in Young Adults: Alcohol versus Non-College Adults.

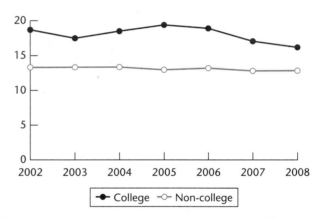

FIGURE 21-4 Heavy Drinking in Young Adulthood.[18]

Source: Based on data contained within the report by the Substance Abuse and Mental Health Services Administration (2009).

unhealthy alcohol use but as being the norm for their age cohort (Lee, Geisner, Patrick, & Neighbors, 2010). Unfortunately, because college students place great emphasis on peer group acceptance, these misperceptions become one of the strongest factors in shaping their alcohol use patterns as a student (Marlatt et al., 1998). Alcohol-related adverse consequences become the expected norm rather than an outcome to be avoided for many college students and thus lose their power to inhibit further alcohol use. Further, there is a relationship between the student's living

---

[17]Most recent year for which data are available.

[18]Figure based on data contained within the report by the Substance Abuse and Mental Health Services Administration (2009).

environment and their alcohol use level. College students experience a closed environment or what is known as "group insulation" (Neighbors et al., 2009, p. 14). As a result of this process, they are protected against all but the most severe repercussions of their alcohol use (Neighbors et al., 2009). This process tends to isolate college students from external influences on their behavior, especially alcohol use. External norms are often ignored, classified as irrelevant or discounted in favor of continued alcohol use (Neighbors et al., 2009). In the next section, we will examine some of the more common problems encountered by the transitional adolescent drinker.

Consequences of Substance Use Disorders in the College Age Population

The college student who abuses alcohol or any of the drugs of abuse has the potential to develop any of the adverse consequences for alcohol or the drugs of abuse identified earlier in this text. Research has suggested that the adolescent brain is four to five times more vulnerable to alcohol-induced brain damage than the fully mature adult brain (Tappert, Caldwell, & Burke, 2004/2005; Wuethrich, 2001). The implications of this are noteworthy because researchers have found a small (7–10%) but marked decline in psychological test performance in adolescent drinkers (Strauch, 2003). This decline in measured cognitive abilities appears to be permanent, suggesting that the alcohol abuse that college students engage in might have lifelong consequences. For example, alcohol-induced damage to the *hippocampus*,[19] potentially will have lifelong consequences for the college drinker. The frontal lobes have not become fully integrated into the brain's structure and assume their duty in assessing and planning behaviors, to cite another example (De Bellis et al., 2000; Tappert, 2004/2005). Unfortunately, the developmental immaturity of the student's brain during the early college years might *predispose* individuals in this age group to alcohol's reinforcing effects in spite of its potential for harm (Spear, 2002). To complicate matters, the individual's response to drug(s) of abuse will be influenced in part by their individual neural maturational stage, making it impossible to determine how a specific individual will respond to a given drug(s) (Jorgensen, 2008).

Heavy alcohol abuse has been identified as one factor that appears to facilitate the development of a compound known as *C-reactive protein*[20] in the body. This compound is thought to be associated with the development of heart disease (Gupta, 2007). If this theory is correct, then the individual's abuse of alcohol during the college years might have lifelong consequences for the drinker. Fortunately, only a minority of college students appear to continue to drink abusively after graduation, which would limit the alcohol-induced production of C-reactive protein following graduation. Alcohol abuse by college students carries with it other risks as well: Each year in the United States alcohol use is a factor in the death of 1,800 college students, 599,000 nonfatal injuries, 696,000 physical assaults, and 97,000 sexual assaults (Hingson et al., 2009; Hingson, 2010).

Binge Drinking

As was indicated earlier in this chapter, college students engage in more binge drinking than their noncollege peers. Lamentably, even binge drinking is not without its dangers. An emerging body of evidence suggests that binge drinking can contribute to neurological dysfunction. The team of Crego et al. (2009) identified a sample of college students who engaged in binge drinking and administered a battery of neuropsychological tests. The authors found that although the binge drinkers were able to complete the subtest tasks, they required higher levels of attentional effort needed to do so as compared with their nondrinking peers. The authors interpreted this as evidence that even binge drinking might result in subtle neurological deficits. An emerging body of evidence suggests that binge drinking in the early adult years is potentially a risk factor for cardiovascular disease later in life (Goslawski et al., 2013). The authors found evidence of systemic and microvascular blood flow changes in binge drinkers that were similar to those noted in adults with known cardiovascular disease they indicated.

It is the abuse of illicit substances that carries the most significant list of potential legal consequences for college students: The acquisition and possession of illegal substances are grounds for legal sanctions, which might include incarceration and loss of access to

---

[19]See Glossary.

[20]See Glossary.

financial assistance programs for the student. One area of special concern is the tradition in which the college student celebrates his or her 21st birthday with the consumption of alcohol. Between 80% and 90% of college students consume alcohol to help them celebrate upon achieving this milestone (Day-Cameron et al., 2009). This landmark is often marked by drinking rituals, many of which are sponsored or at least encouraged by the peer expectations and the drinking establishments near the campus. Many drinking establishments provide the birthday celebrant with free alcohol or alcohol at a markedly reduced rate (Brister, Sher, & Fromme, 2011).

The consumption of 21 drinks by the student on his or her 21st birthday is fortunately uncommon (2% of cases reviewed). The expectation that they do so within an hour's time is not uncommon among students who did consume 21 drinks to celebrate their 21st birthday. Students who engage in this practice often feel the need to prove that they are able to accomplish this task in spite of potential consequences or the fact that by following this practice the student plays a "chemical equivalent of Russian roulette" (Neighbors et al., 2009, p. 14). The outcome is often the need for emergency hospitalization for acute alcohol poisoning or even the student's death.

Indirectly the practice of celebrating one's 21st birthday with alcohol can lower inhibitions, which in turn can contribute to the individual's decision to engage in high-risk behaviors such as unprotected sex or driving while under the influence of an intoxicant (Brister et al., 2011). Undergraduate women who drank to the point of intoxication at an earlier age, and who engaged in heavier alcohol use in the 3 months before they officially turned 21 were all predictors of birthday drinking according to the authors. Peer group influences were an important part of the student's decision to drink to celebrate their 21st birthday, as were the individual's expectations for both the alcohol and the celebration. Peer pressure to drive after drinking also contributes to an increased risk for arrest for driving while under the influence of an intoxicant (Quinn & Fromme, 2012).

Energy Drinks

Approximately one-quarter of college student drinkers believe the myth that they can mitigate the effects of their alcohol use by interspacing periods of drinking with the ingestion of energy drinks (Spear, 2010). To explore whether this belief was true or not the team of Thombs et al. (2010) obtained blood alcohol levels from 802 college students who were selected at random when they exited a bar at the end of the night. They found that those students who had consumed energy drinks were 300% more likely to leave the bar highly intoxicated and 400% more likely to plan to drive home than were those students who did not consume energy drinks that evening. Thus, rather than mitigating the effects of the alcohol consumed, such behavior appears to encourage the overuse of alcohol with the concomitant dangers associated with excessive alcohol use.

CNS Stimulants

The abuse of central nervous system stimulants such as the amphetamines or Provigil® (generic name: modafinil) is rampant at some colleges, with as many as 30% of the students using a CNS stimulant(s) to help them cram for examinations (Frances, 2013). This is in contrast to the 1% of adults in the 19–20-year-old age cohort in the general population admitting to methamphetamine abuse over the course of their lifetimes and 0.4% of adults in the designated age bracket who admit to the unauthorized use of modafinil at some point in their lives (Johnston, O'Malley, Backman, & Schulenberg, 2012b). The earlier statement that college is a unique environment is underscored by the drastic differences in CNS abuse prevalence rates between college students and non-college adults the same age, and these figures illustrate how CNS stimulant abuse is a very real problem at many institutions of higher learning.

Tobacco Use

There is an interesting relationship between educational levels and use of tobacco products. An estimated 34% of young adults who did not graduate from high school smoke cigarettes, as opposed to 26.6% of individuals with some college experience and 14.0% of college graduates (Substance Abuse and Mental Health Services Administration, 2009). Surprisingly many college students begin to abuse tobacco products while in college, either for the stimulant effect of the nicotine to help them stay up to study longer, drink more alcohol, or for its anorexic effect to help them control their weight. These students risk any of the adverse consequences of tobacco abuse or addiction outlined in Chapter 16.

Graduate School

Graduate studies are a prerequisite for entry into some professions, such as the law, psychology, and medicine.[21] For some, graduate school is simply a way to escape from the responsibilities of adulthood for a few more years (Benton, 2009). For all graduate school students, substance use and abuse are potential problems. Some individuals continue the substance use pattern(s) established in their undergraduate program. However, the majority of graduate students begin to mature out of the substance use patterns established in their undergraduate years. Unfortunately for some professionals-in-training heavy alcohol use in social settings allows for professional "networking" in which both opportunities for clerkships or summer study programs might be discussed and the foundation for later professional relationships might be established. Alcohol use during these competitive graduate programs also provides students with a chance to "decompress," often with surprising results. A survey of medical school students found, for example, that 11% were excessive drinkers, whereas 18% met the criteria for a diagnosis of alcohol abuse (Benton, 2009). Surprisingly, these students appeared to perform better academically than their non-drinking peers (Benton, 2009).

Following graduation, students discover two inconvenient realities already discovered by their undergraduate friends: First, the sheltered environment of college does little to prepare the individual for the hustle and demands of the work environment. The department supervisor does not care whether you had competing deadlines for different projects: He or she will want assigned projects completed on time and within budget. Students might receive an extension for a term paper that was not quite finished, for example, but that same individual would be quite unlikely to get an extension on the work assigned. Second, students often discover with some degree of shock that the career that they prepared for, in which they invested a significant portion of their life and financial resources might not be the panacea that they had hoped for (Benton, 2009).

To help them face the demands of their work career in the face of these discoveries, most former students either modify or discontinue their abuse of chemicals. Personal expectations are adjusted, and career goals are either modified or possibly dropped entirely. For a minority of graduate school students, alcohol or the other drugs abused during college and graduate school might serve as an anchor during this transition period (Benton, 2009). Alcohol consumed during graduate school will have the same effect as alcohol consumed while in the workplace, providing a familiarity and predictability, not to mention escape from bruised emotions, that provides a strong incentive for the person to continue to abuse alcohol or other chemicals. Further, if heavy alcohol or drug use was the expectation during the "decompression" and networking periods after the week's studies, the former student might carry these expectations with them into the work environment with potential psychosocial, vocational, and legal problems resulting from their chemical use. Unfortunately, there is evidence suggesting that upscale men's clothing stores are using alcohol as a possible way to entice customers (Dokoupil, 2009), adding to the allure of alcohol during what is for many young adults a difficult transition.

Are There Forces That Help Protect the Student from Substance Use Disorders?

The answer to this question is an unqualified "yes." College students share the same risk factors and protective mechanisms that are found in the general population. Active religious involvement, for example, has been found to reduce the student's risk for developing an alcohol use disorder by 40% (Lambert et al., 2010). Peer group affiliation and personal goals and aspirations both might be viewed as protective factors. Strong interpersonal ties provide assistance in maintaining resilience in the face of adversity (Southwick & Charney, 2013). Parental influence, although not as strong as during the childhood and adolescent years, still can help to shape the student's substance use pattern. Role models also help to shape the student's substance use behaviors and finally an often overlooked factor that occasionally helps to protect the student from developing a substance use disorder is plain old common sense. This list is not all-encompassing (sibling feedback was not mentioned as a protective factor, for example), but it does illustrate that there are individual-specific protective forces that assist the transitional adolescent in avoiding the pitfalls of a substance use disorder.

---

[21]Which might be viewed as a form of graduate school.

Chapter Summary

The period of late adolescence or young adulthood presents a conundrum: Is the individual an adolescent or young adult? To solve this question, it is suggested that the individual be viewed as a *transitional adolescent*, a person who is legally defined as an adult and who presents both personality traits normally seen in young adults and other traits more traditionally seen in adolescents. During this phase of transition, the individual is faced with a number of choices that will influence the rest of his or her lives. One such decision is whether to pursue a college degree in the hopes of enhanced earning potential later in life or to enter the workforce immediately. Slightly under half of persons in the 18–19-year-old age cohort do enter an institution of higher learning. In many cases, the individual does not complete more than a semester or two before dropping out of school because of financial, social, or familial factors that prohibit further participation in higher education. The individual's relationship with alcohol and the illicit drugs is transformed now that they are in the earliest stages of adulthood, with different implications for those who choose to enter an institution of higher education as opposed to those transitional adolescents who do not follow this path. In this chapter, some of these differences were discussed.

CHAPTER 22

Codependency and Enabling

Introduction

Health care professionals who specialize in the behavioral sciences are often faced with a bewildering array of behaviors that they must both categorize and try to understand. To help them in this task, behavioral scientists use *constructs* or a form of professional shorthand that allows one professional to rapidly share complex information with another. A weather front is an excellent example of a construct. In reality, there are no lines that connect different weather cells, or firm boundaries between different bodies of air. By using the analogy of the battle lines of World War I, it was possible for meteorologists to develop a system that allowed them to portray complex data about the changing weather patterns in a visual media that other meteorologists could understand.

As mental health professionals began to explore the interpersonal dynamics within the family of a substance abuser, they developed a number of new constructs to help them both understand and explain the impact of substance use disorders (SUDs) both to family members and to others. Two of these constructs were *Codependency* and *enabling,* both of which were quite popular in the 1980s and early 1990s. They have become less popular in the early years of the 21st century, but because the terms were so popular, mental health professionals will occasionally use one or both of these terms to summarize the complex dynamics within the family of a substance abuser. In this chapter, these constructs will be examined in more detail.

Enabling

To *enable* a person with an SUD is to *knowingly* behave in such a manner as to make it possible for a person to continue to abuse chemicals, or in a manner that protects the substance abuser from having to pay the natural consequences for her or his behavior. The paradigm of "enabling" rests on the unproven assumption that within some families there is almost an unspoken conspiracy in which family members support the addicted person's continued substance abuse through these behaviors. Various theoretical reasons for these enabling behaviors have been suggested. Some family members feel threatened by a family member's substance abuse and they enter a stage of *denial* to avoid recognizing the problem. This denial might be motivated by a desire to avoid perceived blame for the dysfunctional member's behavior (Sadock & Sadock, 2007). In other cases, family members come to enjoy the power and responsibility given up by the dysfunctional family member and are hesitant to give that power up when the substance abuser attempts to reassert his or her role in the family.

Some persons affected by the individual's SUD are thought to become *overly protective*, confusing this protectiveness as an expression of love (Beattie, 2009; Ruben, 2001). Another example of enabling behavior is seen when a substance abuser is unable or unwilling to go to work because of intoxication or postintoxication recovery: A hypothetical parent or partner might call to report the substance abuser as being "sick" and thus unable to go to work that day. In doing so, they hide the true nature of the dysfunctional family member's problem and help them avoid consequences for their behavior. Enabling behaviors might be motivated by a variety of other factors, including social pressure to be a "good" spouse, to avoid the loss of income should the dysfunctional family member's behavior result in loss of employment, to fulfill the needs of the caregiver, or by pathological interdependency (Beattie, 2009; Sadock & Sadock, 2007). These behaviors are found not only within the context of a family unit. An "enabler" might be a parent, sibling, coworker, neighbor, supervisor, friend, neighbor, or even a health care professional. Many health care professionals, for example, will not add a diagnosis of alcohol or drug dependence to a patient's file, for a variety of reasons. Some physicians rationalize this as being a way to protect the individual from the condemnation of society, or possible denial of insurance benefits at a future date. Others might wish to protect the family of the substance abuser from the shame of having to acknowledge that such a problem existed in their home.

The essential point here is that the *enabler* is any person who acts to protect the substance abuser from the full consequences of her or his behavior. Enabling behaviors are not limited to those who are in the dysfunctional family member's immediate environment. The witness who refuses to testify against a criminal because he or she does not wish to become involved, because of the inconvenience or fear of reprisal, might be said to have enabled that person's criminal behavior. Unfortunately this concept has been applied to a range of social behaviors ("I'm enabling her over-eating by not saying anything when she orders dessert when we go out to eat," for example), making the term vague and ambiguous.

Codependency

The concept of *Codependency* emerged in the latter quarter of the 20th century, and it remains both a popular construct used in "pop" psychology and one of the cornerstones of rehabilitation programs. In spite of the fervor with which some rehabilitation professionals preach that many of us are Codependent, it is important to keep in mind that this is a *construct*, not reality.

Indeed, this is seen in the fact that there is no standard definition of Codependency, and various rehabilitation professionals argue over whether it should be spelled as one word (*Codependency*) or is possibly hyphenated (*Co-dependency*), although the former spelling appears to slowly be winning out (Jaffe & Anthony, 2005; Sadock & Sadock, 2007). Another controversy is whether it should be spelled with a capital "C" ("*Codependency*"[1]) or a lower case "c" (*codependency*). As will be discussed later in this chapter, there has even been strong disagreement between professionals about the validity of this construct (Blume, 2005).

Codependency Defined

For decades, family members have been quietly discussing how they had suffered, and often continued to suffer, from ongoing relationships with a dysfunctional (often substance-abusing) person. Gwinnell and Adamec (2006) defined *Codependency* as an "unhealthy relationship in which a person who is closely involved with an alcoholic or addicted person ... [and] *acts in such a way as to allow the addict to continue the addicted behavior*" (p. 68, italics added for emphasis). The concepts of Codependency and enabling are thus often intertwined, as indicated by the part of the above quote in italics. This relationship pattern usually is seen in a familial unit although it might also exist between close friends, between an employer and an employee, or even between a police officer and a person driving home under the influence of chemicals![2]

Beattie (2009) observed that *caretaking* is at the heart of Codependency, with the Codependent person placing the needs of others above their own. This is often done with the goal of giving the Codependent person a purpose for living and a reason to fill the sense of emptiness that they feel within themselves. This behavior also allows the Codependent person to appear that the dysfunctional person desperately needs them when in reality the exact opposite is true. The Codependent person in such a relationship is using their partner's behavioral problem to help define their own personality. This is similar to Blume's (2005) definition of Codependency

---

[1] The upper case "C" will be used throughout this text in the word "*Codependency*."

[2] In some communities, the police will simply escort the driver home, with the warning that the individual should not drive again until he or she is sober. This could be interpreted as a form of systemic or professional enabling that prevents the intoxicated driver from facing the full consequences for his or her behavior.

as "loosely an emotional dependence upon the person with a drug problem" (p. 168).

Various core components of the theoretical concept of Codependency have been advanced over the years, including (a) over-involvement of family members with a dysfunctional member, (b) obsessive attempts on the part of the Codependent person to control the dysfunctional person's behavior, (c) a tendency to base self-esteem on external sources of feedback, and (d) the tendency to make personal sacrifices in an attempt to "cure" (or at least limit) the dysfunctional member's problem behavior. These behaviors are all externally focused, which is to say that the focus is only on the dysfunctional member and not on the Codependent person.

The Relationship Between Enabling and Codependency

The reader will note that this chapter started with a discussion of "enabling" and not Codependency because these two constricts are deeply intertwined. To confuse matters, they both might be found in the same person, although this is not always the case. *Enabling refers to specific behaviors* whereas *Codependency refers to a relationship pattern.* Giving money to a beggar on the street might enable that person to buy more alcohol or drugs. The donor might suspect that the recipient will use the money for this purpose (enabled the recipient of the money), but does not need an ongoing relationship with that individual. A diagram of the relationship between the two might look something like that shown in Figure 22-1.

The Dynamics of Codependency

Beattie (2009) spoke of Codependency as being a process where the individual's life has become unmanageable because he or she is involved in a committed caretaking relationship with a dysfunctional person. This commitment is interpreted as prohibiting the Codependent person from leaving the dysfunctional member, or even confronting him or her about their behavior. Further, because of a blurring of boundaries within the familial unit, the Codependent person begins to believe that the behavior of the dysfunctional member is somehow a reflection on themselves. This process of extreme involvement in the life of another person illustrates the boundary violations often seen in Codependency known as *enmeshment.*

Enmeshment, or its polar opposite *fusion,* is based on the individual's unconscious fear of abandonment (Dayton, 2005). The Codependent person's self-esteem is threatened by the dysfunctional person's behavior, especially the threat of abandonment. To avoid this risk, the Codependent person often places personal aspirations and desires aside and devote all of their energy to the caretaking process (Beattie, 2009; Johnson, 2003). An extreme example of this might be seen when the Codependent person assumes responsibility for the dysfunctional person's recreational substance use, blaming themselves for the other person's substance abuse. Therapists and friends of the Codependent person are used to hearing phrases such as "I made (insert name here) so upset that (insert name here) started drinking again!," reflecting their belief that "It is all my fault."

An extreme example of caretaking is the attempt to control the dysfunctional person and their environment. For example, consider a hypothetical case in which a prison psychologist receives a telephone call from the elderly mother of an inmate. She asked that the psychologist "make sure that the man who shares my son's cell is [going to be] a good influence on my son," because "there are many bad men in prison and I don't want him falling in with a bad crowd." This request ignores the grim reality that her son was not in prison for singing off key in choir practice and in this example that he had a history of multiple prior convictions. The mother in this case might be said to be in serious denial about her son's behavior, as well as so involved in her son's life that she was still trying to control and "cure" him in spite of the thick prison walls and the armed guards.

In this hypothetical example, the mother might become quite disturbed when it was gently suggested to her that she needed to *detach* from her son and his dysfunctional behavior. *Detachment* is one of the cornerstones of recovery from Codependency (Brown & Lewis, 1995). Through this process the Codependent person

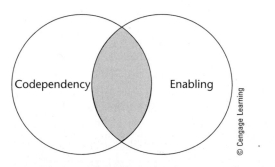

FIGURE 22-1 The Relationship between Codependency and Enabling Behaviors.

learns to "let go" and stop attempting to control the dysfunctional person's life. However, it is a difficult lesson to learn for many who have invested so much of their lives to the process of caretaking. Perhaps, in the example provided above, the mother's intentions were good, but her efforts reflected an overinvolvement with her son's life.

Another core element to Codependency is *control.* Through various adaptive behaviors, the Codependent person is viewed as attempting to achieve a sense of control over their own inner turmoil and over the dysfunctional person (Craig, 2002). Sometimes, the Codependent person sets the goal of "fixing" the dysfunctional person, so that he or she will no longer engage in inappropriate behaviors. Perhaps, they reason, the dysfunctional person will then come to appreciate the Codependent's efforts and possibly come to love them (Knauer, 2002; Ruben, 2001). However, this attempt at control often results in criticism of the Codependent by the dysfunctional person who does not understand (or appreciate) the sacrifices made by the Codependent person. A variation of this approach is seen when the Codependent person adopts a self-pitying approach. Guilt becomes the weapon here ("If you really loved me, you would stop") (Johnson, 2003); however, this attempt at control becomes meaningless if the substance abuser does not feel guilty. Other individuals adopt a rigid, controlling approach, seeking to stabilize the home through rules and repetition, to limit (if not eliminate) the dysfunctional behavior(s) by the other (Johnson, 2003).

The Rules of Codependency

Although Codependent persons often report that they feel as if they were going crazy, an unbiased outside observer will carefully note that there are certain unspoken rules within the family unit. Beattie (1989) identified several of these rules:

1. It is not OK for me to have personal feelings.
2. It is not OK for me to have problems of my own.
3. It is not OK for me to have fun, or a life of my own.
4. I'm not lovable and should feel grateful for the affection I receive.
5. I'm never good enough.
6. If people act crazy, I am responsible.

These rules are actively transmitted within the family, setting the foundation for Codependency: "If you did what I told you, I would not have gone out drinking last night!" is an example of rule number 6. "College! Don't even waste your time by applying, you'll never make it!" is

an example of rules 2, 3, 5 and possibly 4. Through the transmission of these rules, the Codependent person's will is shaped within the familial environment until in extreme cases she or he becomes unable to identify their own feelings when asked. They will be able to tell you what they have been *told* by significant others, but have little or no self-awareness of their own feelings.

There is an inherent power struggle between dysfunctional family member and a Codependent: The Codependent person wants to control the behavior of the dysfunctional person to keep peace within the family and avoid conflict. The dysfunctional family member wants to shape the Codependent so that he or she will not challenge their inappropriate behavior(s). An all-too-common experience for family and marriage therapists is for one partner to set up an appointment to ask that the therapist "fix" the other person. Whether the second person wants to be "fixed" is another matter. A hypothetical example might be the situation in which the cocaine-abusing husband and his wife enter marital therapy. The husband makes the demand that the therapist "make her stop nagging me" without revealing his cocaine abuse. The wife also avoids mentioning her husband's cocaine use disorder (remember: appearances are everything). In time continued marital therapy might reveal that her "nagging" reflects an attempt to control her husband's substance abuse problem. To protect the disclosure of the husband's cocaine use disorder, this hypothetical couple might even resort to the extreme of dropping out of marital therapy.

Are Codependents Born or Made?

Proponents of Codependency suggest that it is a *learned relationship pattern,* possibly the result of physical, sexual, or extreme emotional abuse during childhood (Knauer, 2002). The child experiences a boundary violation with each episode of abuse. If the child is not rescued by a protector, he or she learns to tolerate boundary violations because they are helpless to prevent them. Through this process the young Codependent individual is taught that he or she is "less than" others and not worthy of ordinary levels of respect or independence (Knauer, 2002). The child also might wrongfully assume responsibility for familial problems beyond their control, especially if they are blamed for these issues by significant others.[3] Over time the child learns to accept the dysfunction as the norm, and is

---

[3] A hypothetical example: "Your father and I never argued before you came along!"

socialized into accepting the role of a Codependent (Zelvin, 1997).

Communications between family members becomes limited to "safe" topics that will avoid giving the dysfunctional person another reason to have another temper outburst, engage in substance use, or other unhealthy behaviors. The children quickly learn that *nobody* mentions the inappropriate behavior by the dysfunctional person. "Don't say anything about (insert the inappropriate behavior), or else (the dysfunctional person) will become upset!"[4] is a common message to the child in such unhealthy homes. In cases of physical, emotional, or sexual abuse, the child is taught not to discuss it with others to maintain an uneasy facade of family cohesion and peace. Frequently the child learns to avoid facing intense negative feelings within themselves brought on by the abuse,[5] and learn to live a rigid, compulsive lifestyle focused on meeting the needs of the other person (Craig, 2004).

Codependency and Self-Esteem

In an attempt to maintain peace within the family, the Codependent person learns their emotional pain is subservient to maintaining peace within the family, a process known as *emotional constriction*. They are taught that they do not deserve to express their own emotional pain as it is unimportant when compared with the goal of familial peace. The Codependent's self-esteem might be damaged, or shattered, but as long as *the secret* is maintained this is unimportant from the perspective of the family unit. To protect the family secret, the young Codependent might watch as others engage in *denial* ("Your uncle is *not* an alcoholic, and I never want to hear you mention his drinking again," for example) and *minimization* ("Oh, it's not so bad."). The family might not foster feelings of independence and competence within the family unit because these things would potentially shatter the wall of denial surrounding the problem. This leaves the family member, especially children, vulnerable to feelings of low self-esteem: They are not rewarded for positive accomplishments, but for

not asserting themselves and for caretaking activities. Frequently the young Codependent person learns to measure self-worth by external standards (often set by the Codependent family member) rather than by their own achievements.

Although external observers will quickly identify the unhealthy expectations and goals of the Codependent person, the young Codependent frequently cannot envision another way of living. They often take pride in how much they have suffered, a behavior learned in childhood, and interpret their suffering at the hands of another as a form of moral victory or an affirmation of love. Because they are unable to envision any other way of living, these trials become almost a badge of honor and a defense against the feelings of worthlessness sensed within.

The Cycle of Codependency

Once the cycle of Codependency has started, it takes on a life of its own. A graphic representation of the cycle of Codependency might appear something like that in Figure 22-2.

In Figure 22-2, there are two essential elements. First, the Codependent person must suffer from fragile or low self-esteem. If the person has adequate self-esteem, then she or he would be able to affirm "self" without external validation, and thus not be vulnerable to the dysfunctional member's threats to withdraw affection or support. The self-affirming person would draw away from the dysfunctional member, thus blocking the unhealthy relationship from evolving in the first place. Equally important is that the significant other be dysfunctional in a manner that either consciously or unconsciously reminds the young Codependent of their home environment. This similarity serves as an unconscious lure that attracts a potentially Codependent person into a relationship.

A central tenet of psychoanalytic theory is that we recreate unresolved childhood conflictual relationships in later life in an attempt to find closure. A common experience for substance abuse rehabilitation professionals is to see where the Codependent spouse has replaced the dysfunctional family member from childhood with the same type of person as a marital partner. Freud called this the "repetition compulsion," a construct that suggests that individuals continue to struggle with unresolved issues from childhood, until they are resolved. To the believer in the Codependency model, this same relationship pattern is interpreted as

---

[4]Or, "Don't say anything to make your father upset and go out drinking," which implies that if the father *does* go out to drink that it was the fault of the person who said something to upset him. This pattern of behavior within the family serves to protect the father's drinking while responsibility for his drinking is placed on other family members.

[5]It is not uncommon for the victim of childhood physical, sexual, or emotional abuse to blame themselves for having been victimized.

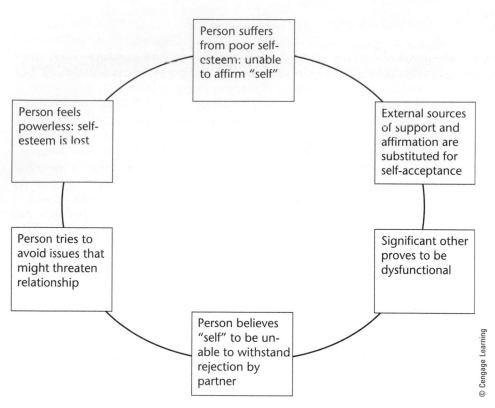

FIGURE 22-2 The Cycle of Codependency.

the Codependent being "addicted" to the dysfunctional style of the partner.

Patterns of Codependency

In the last quarter of the 20th century, substance abuse professionals attempted to group common coping styles used by Codependent persons. A number of such adjustment styles have been suggested, including those listed in Table 22-1 (Capretto, 2007; Craig, 2004; Ellis, McInerney, DiGiuseppe, & Yeager, 1988; Johnson, 2003).

The Codependency model maintains that family members of a dysfunctional person will adopt one or more of the coping mechanisms outlined above to deal with the stress that the substance abuser places on the family unit. An example of the "coconspirator" might best be seen in the hypothetical spouse of a cocaine addict who wanted marital counseling because the addicted partner would not limit her or his cocaine use to the $100 per week that was budgeted for their cocaine use. Other examples of this coping style might

be seen in the partner who goes to the bar with the dysfunctional partner to "try and show (him or her) how to drink in a responsible manner." These efforts to change the dysfunctional family member's behavior from within the family unit are usually doomed to failure.

A very good example of the messiah is the hypothetical father of an opiate-dependent young adult who is in a therapy group for family members. The father tearfully discussed the litany of problems that the addicted child had caused, and how the parents repeatedly had to take out personal loans to pay off their child's drug debts. Another group member suggested that the parents just force the wayward child to pay his or her bills, and be responsible for themselves. The father thought for a long moment and then said that if he did this, their child, now an adult, "might leave us." When several family group members suggested that this would not automatically be bad, because it would allow their child to "hit bottom" and see the need to address the addiction, the father quickly replied "Oh, I couldn't do that, (child's name) is not

TABLE 22-1
Common Coping Styles Demonstrated by Codependent Persons

COPING STYLE	GOAL OF COPING STYLE
Apathetic partner	(might also be called "silent sufferer") The partner simply stopped caring (emotional shutdown often seen with this pattern of coping)
Approval seeker	Constantly seeks the approval/acceptance of the dysfunctional partner (for external validation)
Caretaker	Devotes his or her life to taking care of their dysfunctional partner
Coconspirator	Consciously or unconsciously joins with the dysfunctional member to maintain pseudo-stability within the family unit (also called the "joiner")
Controller	Engages in manipulative behaviors in an attempt to control every aspect of the life of the entire family, as they feel (often with some justification) that their own life is out of control
Family mascot/clown	Family members who try to deflect attention from the substance-abusing family member to themselves, thus reducing the risk of conflict in family
Martyr	Self-righteous partner who receives support for being the "good" partner, substituting affirmation for lack of self-esteem
Messiah	Fights against the dysfunctional behavior(s) in such a way that the individual is never forced to face consequences of their behavior (also called *chief enabler*)
Protector	Seeks to maintain familial peace at any cost, even if it allows dysfunctional behaviors to continue
Persecutor	Blames everybody *but* the dysfunctional member for familial problems (may be called *get even* pattern of relationships)
Separator	Over time spends less and less time at home, avoiding conflict that might otherwise exist in family unit

© Cengage Learning

ready to assume responsibility for (his or her self) yet!" Thus, the parents continued to support their child's addiction, to avoid the short-term consequences of having the child become "angry" at them.[6]

The Relationship between Codependency and Mental Health

Although this model of the interactional pattern within the home where there is a substance abuser appears to make sense, there is a very real tendency for rehabilitation professionals to overidentify with the Codependency model. Even if the individual were to be Codependent, there are degrees of Codependency, just as there are degrees of heart failure or obesity. It is not (as some would have us believe) an all-or-nothing condition. Because of these degrees of Codependency "anyone is Codependent" (Beattie, quoted in Tavris, 1992, p. 194). The Codependency

model does not address the fact that many of the same behaviors that were outlined above are also found in healthy family relationships. Codependency, according to Wegscheder-Cruse and Cruse (1990) "is an exaggeration of normal personality traits" (p. 28). Only a few "saints and hermits" (Tavris, 1990, p. 21A) fail to demonstrate at least some of these behaviors on occasion. It is a matter of the individual's ability to adapt to life circumstances. If the Codependent person is consistently using one of the coping styles mentioned earlier to the exclusion of other, healthier behaviors, the individual's adaptive potentials are limited and he or she will potentially be trapped in an unhealthy relationship pattern.

As noted above, many of the behaviors used to define Codependency are exaggerations of normal behaviors. An example of this is the overlap between love and Codependency because of how love relationships are viewed within this society (Zelvin, 1997). Love is viewed as allowing for the blending of identities and the weakening or loss of ego boundaries. This is perhaps a strength of love, but it also allows for Codependency to develop if it is taken to an extreme.

[6]One might interpret the child's "anger" as a manipulative ploy to control the parents; however, such an interpretation must be made on a case-by-case basis because the adult child might lose control over their temper for a variety of reasons.

Between the extremes of total independence (the "hermit" noted earlier) and total dependence on the other (the Codependent) is an *interdependency*, which is the hallmark of healthy relationships. Each partner has the freedom to hold their own opinions, have their own hobbies, and so on, which bring variety to the healthy relationship without threatening it. Disagreements are resolved through discussion of the problem in the healthy relationship with compromise and tolerance and not threats or physical violence as so often seen in unhealthy relationships.

Although members of the substance abuse rehabilitation community embraced the concept of Codependency with great enthusiasm, as we will see in the next section, there have been a number of objections to the concept of Codependency, and to a lesser degree enabling.

Reactions to the Concept of Codependency

It is important to remember that Codependency is a *construct*, which might be attributed to M.L. Lewis's (1937) theory that the spouse of a person with an alcohol use disorder (AUD) (usually the wife) had a disturbed personality and was trying to resolve her own inner conflicts through the marriage to a person with an AUD. Suddenly, the partner was classified as being dysfunctional, although in a different way than the spouse with the SUD. From this point on, mental health professionals have struggled to determine whether Codependency is a legitimate form of psychopathology, a struggle that has not been helped by the fact that Codependency has been characterized as "an addiction, a personality disorder, a psychosocial condition, and an interpersonal style" (Hurcom, Copello, & Orford, 2000, p. 487).

As this last comment would suggest, Codependency is not a useful diagnostic category because it is too vague and there is little evidence that Codependency as a clinical entity even exists (Blume, 2005; Lilienfeld, Lunn, Ruscio, & Beyerstein, 2010). These doubts rest on the vague, ill-defined, nature of Codependency, because virtually every person will have at least one of the defining characteristics. At what point, for example, does a mother's natural protectiveness for her child become "overprotective"? How do you define "just protective enough" without going over that hypothetical line?

It is the opinion of many professionals that Codependency is a pseudo-problem more than a legitimate form of psychopathology. This is supported by the fact that research into Codependency and enabling both have failed to garner much research evidence supporting these concepts, and references to these construct have all but disappeared from the professional literature. If it were to be a legitimate problem, such as coronary artery disease, for example, why has it virtually disappeared from the professional literature? Most certainly the issue of coronary artery disease is a common topic in medical journals. In addition to these objections, many health care professionals are uncomfortable with the Codependency model because it transforms a relationship style, even if it is an unhealthy one, into a medical problem (Hurcom et al., 2000).

Further, the application of the label of "Codependent" to a marital partner *disempowers* the individual by expecting him or her to then accept the label and seek help from the appropriate professional. The paradigm of Codependency is based on traditional 12-step programs for SUDs that suggest that the "disease" of Codependency is progressive and can only be addressed by attending the appropriate self-help group (Randle, Estes, & Cone, 1999). This position rests on the flawed assumption that "a knife wound to the chest will heal but an injury to the mind will never repair itself" (Sherwood, 2009, p. 286). Clinical research would suggest that this is not true for the majority of persons. There is also a small but important body of research that fails to support the tenet that Codependent persons have similar life experiences and personality traits. The purported uniformity in patient histories and presenting symptoms might be an artifact of the therapeutic relationship. The therapist, expecting certain characteristics in the patient, selectively attends only to those characteristics that conform to the preconceived construct of Codependency. Further, the counselor or group will "reward" the individual for using the terminology of Codependency, praising them for their courage to reveal things about their past.

Another challenge to the validity of the Codependency construct is the observation that up to 99% of the adults in this country could be said to have been raised in a "dysfunctional" home.[7] The majority of parents provide a "good enough" home environment. Admittedly, there is always room for improvement in parenting styles; however, only a small minority of persons grow up in an

---

[7]The concept of Codependency has been extended to include entire communities, states, and countries (Hurcom et al., 2000).

extremely unhealthy home environment. Further, in many cases even when a child is raised in an unhealthy environment, the possibility of resiliency within the child is all too often discounted in spite of evidence demonstrating that this is the norm and not the exception. Adversity often serves as a stimulus for personality growth and not automatically an experience that blocks adaptive growth (Sherwood, 2009). Children have been raised in incredibly unhealthy environments for thousands of generations, yet the species continues to thrive. It would not thrive if the majority of its members were hobbled with major psychological trauma from childhood. Admittedly, not every member of society is happy and content. However, there is little evidence suggesting that the individual must be happy and content to function in society. Indeed, some of society's greatest leaps forward were initiated by those persons who were least content with the status quo.[8] This observation is also supported by the fact that the family is not (as is often suggested) an "incubator of [psychological] disease" (Kaminer, 1992, p. 12).

It has been suggested that self-help groups for Codependency misrepresent the promise of recovery while fostering dependence on the self-help group. In group meetings, the individual is expected to recover memories of parental behaviors consistent with the group's expectations, which is to say to continue to recall material and behave in a "Codependent" manner (Randle et al., 1999). Individuals who fail to follow the group's expectations are said to be in "denial." If the individual rejects the insights offered by various books on Codependency, she or he is also said to be in "denial." Further, no matter how serious or slight the parental misbehavior, there is just one model for recovery: the Codependency model. All emotional trauma is viewed within this model as being equally destructive.

Critics of the model of Codependency point out that this construct seems to excuse the individual from responsibility for his or her behavior. The individual just cannot help themselves because they are "Codependent." Further, through the "disease" of Codependency, blame is shifted from the substance-abusing individual to the significant other, who is automatically said to "enable" the partner's dysfunctional behaviors. The Codependent's behaviors are automatically deemed pathological, overlooking the

fact that their behavior might be healthy, role-specific response to the partner's SUD (Hurcom et al., 2000).

Further, the Codependency model reflects the *family disease model*. This therapeutic model suggests "the solution is for each family member to recognize that he or she has a disease" (Fals-Stewart, O'Farrell, & Birchler, 2003, p. 148). The family member who either has a SUD or the disease of Codependency is judged not on their own accomplishments but on whether the family member with the SUD is able to abstain from chemicals. Family members are guilty by familial bonds with a substance-abusing member, and the "problem" becomes not that of substance abuse, or sexual misbehavior, or physical violence on the part of the dysfunctional person, but on *family* members who suffer from the disease of Codependency!

The Lewis (1937) model was advanced almost a century ago and was resurrected in the 1950s as a popular theory that the spouse was a coalcoholic (Sadock & Sadock, 2007; Sher, 1991). This theory assumed that the spouse was as much in need of professional treatment as was the substance-abusing partner, because he or she (a) helped to cause the other's alcoholism, (b) continues to support it, and (c) thus obviously must be disturbed. These beliefs reflect the fact that throughout history the spouse of the alcoholic has "been blamed and pathologized for their partner's drinking" (Hurcom et al., 2000, p. 473). The fact that there has been little clinical evidence presented to support this theory, or to suggest that the spouse of an alcoholic has any consistent form of psychopathology, but this does not prevent the theory of coalcoholism from being resurrected under the name of "Codependency."

Another challenge to the Codependency concept was offered by Jaffe and Anthony (2005). The authors observed that this construct has been so watered down, and misused, that it has lost any possible hint of diagnostic specificity. This is seen in the definition of Codependency offered by Peck (1997a) in which Codependency is viewed as "a relationship in which partners cater to—and thereby encourage—each other's weaknesses" (p. 180). This definition could be applied to virtually every relationship, because we all make provisions for the other person's quirks and idiosyncratic behaviors on occasion! A spouse who knows that her or his partner is always a half hour late and makes plans accordingly could be said to be Codependent Peck's (1997a) definition.

Many critics of the Codependency construct point out that it rests on little more than "new age"

---

[8]John Adams as a moving force behind the ratification of the Declaration of Independence leaps to mind, although there is a plethora of other examples throughout history.

rhetoric. For example, the husband and wife team of Wegscheider-Cruse and Cruse (1990) speak knowingly about how Codependency results from the "interactions between one's own manufactured 'brain chemicals' (having to do with our reinforcement center) and one's behavior that stimulates the brain to establish compulsive and addictive behavior processes" (p. 12). The authors go on to conclude that Codependency is a brain disease on the assumption that "we have a brain that gives us an excessive rush, [and] we get into self-defeating behaviors that keep the rush coming (Codependency)" (pp. 12–13).

Admittedly, the human brain is evolved in such a way as to help us cope in a social environment (Gazzaniga, 2008). Further interpersonal relationships affect the neurochemical balance within each individual's brain (Gazzaniga, 2008). Any life experience changes the brain's neurochemistry. However, there is no evidence that a relationship can cause an "excessive rush."[9] Nor has science found evidence that we get into "self-defeating behaviors that keep the rush coming." This is not to dismiss the fact that there are many people who have suffered terrible psychological, and on occasion physical, injury from their involvement with an addicted partner. To automatically classify them as Codependent without an investigation into the dynamics of the relationship is unfair. Further, the Codependency model expects the Codependent person to come to terms with their pain and achieve emotional healing without blaming the addicted partner for virtually anything that he or she has done. In other words:

> According to adherents of [the theory of Codependency], families of alcoholics can not … hold them [the addicted person] responsible for the abuse. Somehow the victim must get well by dint of pure self-analysis, meditation and prayer, without reference to the social, economic, legal and psychological forces that create[d] [the] dysfunctional families. ("Codependency," 1990, p. 7).

For many people this is an impossible task, not because of a failure on their part but because the tools that exist for them to address these problems are often flawed.

Chapter Summary

Every 20–30 years, the theory is advanced suggesting that the spouse or family member with a SUD supports that person's SUD through their own behavior. This was first suggested by Lewis (1937) and this theory was resurrected in the 1950s as a popular theory that the spouse was a "coalcoholic" who was as dysfunctional as the substance abuser and who required professional assistance for this reason (Sadock & Sadock, 2007; Sher, 1991). This theory was eventually dismissed. Then in the 1970s the constructs of *enabling* and *Codependency* were introduced to help health care professionals view the addicted person and his or her support system in a different light. The construct of enabling was introduced to explain how others might behave in a manner that supported the continued dysfunctional behavior of a person with a behavioral disorder. The family member who maintains silence with full knowledge of an incestuous relationship within their home might be said to be engaging in enabling, for example. Through Codependency, family members, friends, employers, and others might be said to enter into a relationship that supported the continued abuse of chemicals by the identified patient. Proponents seized upon these constructs as proof that the disease of alcoholism (and, by extension, the other drugs of abuse) included not just the alcohol-dependent person but others who also needed "treatment." Self-help groups also evolved to meet the perceived need for rehabilitation by those who "suffered" from Codependency.

After a spell of initial enthusiasm, support for these constructs has faded. Indeed, in the first decade of the 21st century, a battle has raged over whether these are real entities, just as constructs that characterize certain behaviors, or pseudo-issues that cloud the problem of substance abuse rehabilitation.

---

[9]Which begs the question: What would be a sufficient "rush"? If something exists in excess, does this not imply that it also exists in a form where there is a sufficient supply, without being present in excess?

CHAPTER 23

Addiction and the Family

Outside of residence in a concentration camp, there are very few sustained human experiences that make one the recipient of as much sadism as does being the close member of an alcoholic.

—*Vaillant (1995, p. 22)*

Introduction

A conservative estimate suggests that one in every five adults has a close relative who has a substance use disorder and that four to five people are hurt by the behavior of every person with a substance use disorder (SUD) (Capretto, 2007). The most common source of such pain is through parental alcoholism. Yet in spite of this fact there has been little research into the issue of how parental alcoholism might alter familial dynamics or the interaction pattern within that family (Green, 2006). Further, in spite of the awareness of the widespread problem of adolescent SUDs,[1] there has been virtually no research into how the SUD of a child influences the family dynamics in the child's residence. There are many theories and personal beliefs but little hard data on which to view the impact of the SUDs on the family unit or to guide intervention efforts. In this chapter, the current theories about addiction's impact upon the family and the supporting evidence about addiction's impact on the family unit will be reviewed.

Scope of the Problem

Researchers currently believe that approximately 9.6 million children in the United States currently are living in a home where at least one parent has an active SUD (Capretto, 2007). This figure underestimates the full scope of the problem because, as was discussed elsewhere in this text, many individuals tend to alternate between periods of more and less abusive drinking perhaps twice this number of children are living in a home where one or both parents have abused a chemical in the past year (Capretto, 2007). By the time that they reach

adulthood, more than one-half of the adults in the United States will have lived in a family where one member has, or at least had, an active alcohol use disorder (AUD)[2] (Grant et al., 2006).

Addiction and the Family Unit

D. J. Siegel (2013) postulated that relationships are defined by the energy and information flow patterns between the members of that dyad. Open lines of energy and information flow reflect healthy relationships whereas closed lines of energy and information flow patterns reflect the opposite. Further, he suggested that within the family "one can see the *intergenerational transfer* of patterns of communication that are reinforced by the repeated experiences of energy and information flow exchange patterns" (pp. 2–3, italics in original). This overview might explain why marriage

---

[1]Discussed in Chapter 20.

[2]The differences between these two estimates reflect, in part, how "family" is defined in either study. For example, would a second cousin with an alcohol use disorder who lived 1,000 miles away be defined as a "family" member in both studies, or only in one study?

can serve as a protective factor against AUDs for most men and women: There is another person to communicate with us, provide feedback to us, and who knows us far more intimately than most other people in our lives. Unfortunately, 11% of married men and 5% of married women still will meet the criteria for an AUD at some point in their lives (Lau-Barraco, Braitman, Leonard, & Padilla, 2012), raising questions about the energy and information flow pattern within those relationships.[3] The fact that most families with a parental SUD also suffer from a wide variety of other issues such as mental health problems, underemployment, and financial issues (all conditions that would limit the flow of information and energy within the family) would potentially make it impossible to isolate the impact of just the parental SUD on the family unit.

It has been discovered that in marriages where there is a wide discrepancy in the alcohol use pattern of the partners, there are usually lower levels of intimacy than in marriages where the alcohol use pattern of the partners is more similar. There are two possible explanations for this pattern: First, this might be a side effect of the individual's AUD because it is known that alcohol can reduce the individual's perceived need for emotional or sexual intimacy. Heavy alcohol use might induce sexual dysfunctions in both men and women. A second possibility, however, is that those individuals who are drawn to heavy alcohol use have fewer intimacy skills to begin with.

Alcohol is the substance most commonly abused in this society. Clinicians are often asked by the spouse of a substance abuser how their partner has developed an AUD when he or she seemed so normal during courtship. The answer is that during the courtship phase and the first year of marriage, alcohol abusers commonly reduce their level of alcohol intake (Leonard & Mudar, 2003). There is also a shift in relationship patterns following marriage: The individual typically spends less time in non-marriage-centered social activities (or spend more time with their partners, depending on how you look at it) (Leonard & Mudar, 2003). Research into how one person's substance use influences that of their partner has yielded mixed results. Some studies have suggested that the person with an AUD selects a partner whose alcohol use pattern is very similar to their own (Grant et al., 2007). However, this similarity in substance use patterns might be an illusion because it has been discovered that both partners might adjust their alcohol use pattern until it is more consistent with that of their partner during courtship and the first few years of marriage. However, in such cases it is not unusual for the substance use patterns of the partners to slowly diverge after the relationship was established and maintained for a period of months or years. A third pattern of adjustment is for the partner who does not have an AUD to engage in "secondary denial" either in courtship or the first years of marriage (Benton, 2009, p. 109). This allows one partner to avoid conscious awareness of their partner's AUD, possibly facilitating their entry into a codependent relationship with the heavy drinker, or possibly the relationship might be terminated either during courtship or after marriage. The latter course of action requires that the individual have sufficient ego strength to end the relationship.

The Family System's Perspective

This theory holds that when we are born that the infant does not have a sense of "self," but that this sense of individual identity emerges as the infant becomes a child and then the child grows into an adolescent. The degree to which the individual is able to separate from the family system to establish a separate identity and be emotionally self-sufficient is labeled the process of *differentiation* by family systems theorists. This process of differentiation can be facilitated or inhibited by the family: Healthy family systems tend to facilitate the child's ability to learn healthy coping mechanisms and to separate from the family system in a slow but progressive manner. Unhealthy family systems tend to inhibit this process, leaving the child with poor coping skills and unmet needs. Family systems therapists also postulate that people tend to select partners who have achieved similar levels of "differentiation of self" (Bowen, 1985, p. 263). From this perspective each partner has achieved a similar level of emotional growth or maturity, although each partner might follow a separate path in their quest to accomplish this developmental task. There is no single path to growth: Some paths are more adaptive and healthy, and others just the reverse, but the process of growth continues, or at least tries to continue throughout the stages of ego growth. In healthy families the emotional attachments to the parents that evolved in childhood change as the child matures (Cozolino, 2002; Ross & Fuertes, 2010). In the healthy family, the child gradually learns to

---

[3]A possible Ph.D. dissertation topic if anybody is in need of one.

identify the needs of the self and those of others, while growing in her or his ability to self-regulate one's own emotions, make healthy decisions, and be available to nurture others (Cozolino, 2002).

Following birth the child's ego growth is facilitated through behaviors such as independent play, spending time with friends, appropriate punishment for transgressions to help the child learn socially appropriate behavior, and so on. In the healthy family, the parents recognize the child's emotional growth and gradually withdraw control as the child becomes more capable of independent living and self-nurturance.[4] However, in the dysfunctional home parental conflict interferes with this process. In normal families, the child's attachment bonds to the mother enhance the growth of conflict resolution skills and relationship competence, while the attachment bonds to the father enhance the growth of social skills, relational competence, and emotional adjustment (Ross & Fuertes, 2010). These attachment bonds are not interchangeable but are complimentary.

Frequent parental conflict, such as that between a drinking and nondrinking spouse, weakens the child's attachment process to either parent. In the dysfunctional home, parental conflict is quelled through the establishment of a pseudo-stability in which certain issues are avoided and certain behaviors not discussed. The child's emotional attachment to one parent is often discouraged or punished by the other. Emotional "power blocks" develop as conflict erupts within the family. The nonabusing partner, or children, might assume roles in the family system (provider, primary disciplinarian or primary decision maker, and others) that the substance-abusing partner does not feel capable of filling. In some cases, the unhealthy partner willingly relinquishes these roles because of personal psychopathology such as a substance use disorder. As a result of this change in familial roles, marital partners or family members may find themselves holding powerful positions within the family normally occupied by the dysfunctional family member's[5] substance abuse, which they are unwilling to give up later in life. The redistribution of power and roles within the family establishes a form of pseudo-stability that permits that family to survive and function.

However the child's growing emotional independence threatens the familial pseudo-stability. Where healthy families adjust to the child's growing emotional independence, unhealthy families become rigid and seek to block the emotional growth of the child. There is a loss of independent identity for the child in many cases and the rigidity between family members grows to support familial pseudo-stability. In response to the perceived threat of differentiation and separation by the child, the parents might respond with increased efforts at control and attempt to force the child to identify with the rules of the family system (Cozolino, 2002). The pseudo-stability must be protected at all costs!

The primary means by which parents attempt to maintain control and discourage emotional independence are *anxiety, guilt, shame,* and *threats of abandonment* (Cozolino, 2002). Abandonment can be both on a conscious and unconscious level. Consider, for example, the hypothetical case in which a father selectively spends more time with a compliant son than with a more vocal, defiant, daughter, even if that defiance is age appropriate and the daughter's behavior is reasonable.[6] The unspoken message is that if the daughter should desire more attention from her father that she must comply with the family's rules. Guilt is another powerful weapon employed in this process of enforcing parental control in the name of pseudo-stability. For example, at the funeral of a hypothetical 18-year-old boy who died in a motor vehicle accident, the mother might turn to his older sister who was in college far from home and say: "This would never have happened if you were here to keep an eye on him." The sister's decision to attend college threatens the familial pseudo-stability in this example because the parents have no control over what their daughter learns while she was away at school. However, this use of parental guilt might force the wayward daughter back into the familial environment following the death of her brother, allowing the family to attempt to reestablish a sense of pseudo-stability. Yet another example of manipulative guilt is the "silent treatment," where one or both parents simply stop talking to the child or adolescent until he or she apologizes, agrees with the parent's decisions, and so on.

On occasion, the child might be shamed for any deviation from parental expectations. Shame is a powerful emotion. If it is experienced for too long, or too

---

[4]There is a difference between the gradual transition between parental control to self-control as the child matures and a lack of parental *supervision.*

[5]The dysfunctional family member might demonstrate any of a very large number of forms of psychopathology. Because this is a text on substance abuse, we will focus only on those forms of parental distress that involve the substance use disorders.

[6]With the exception that he or she does not agree with the father, mother, or both.

intensely, the victim of the shame attack becomes motivated to escape, often by (a) compliance with parental expectations, or (b) detachment from their own emotions to survive. In this manner, the child learns to follow the family's rules to escape from the layers of shame and guilt that they are taught is rightfully theirs if they should deviate from the familial rules. Whether these rules are healthy or unhealthy is never discussed because to do so threatens the familial pseudo-stability. Mixed messages[7] are another way many parents use to control their child. The child or adolescent is locked into two mutually exclusive choices. Then the parents confront the child or adolescent for making the "wrong" decision, a process that usually involves guilt ("If you had listened to me …").

Parental Rules

In many dysfunctional families, three "rules" evolve to maintain the pseudo-stability within the family: (a) don't acknowledge the problem, or talk about it (b) don't have your own thoughts or feelings about the problem, and (c) don't trust anybody (Capretto, 2007). Within the framework of these rules, the child is forced to only rely on the parents for guidance and support. If the child does not recognize that his or her parents are dysfunctional in early childhood he or she will internalize the parent's opinions and beliefs without question, using these rules as a guide to help them form an identity and learn decision-making skills. That child will in turn transmit their parents' problems to the next generation when they become parents years in the future.

If the child should fail to receive positive feedback and parental support for their quest for emotional independence, the growing child might come to view themselves as being weak, incompetent, and incapable of standing alone. The family, especially the parents, might reinforce this assessment of the "self," discouraging further moves toward autonomy. The child begins to believe "I am not worthy … I am damaged … unable to stand on my own" (Juliana & Goodman, 2005; Sheff,

Warren, Ketcham, & Eban, 2007). It is upon this shattered self-image that the child or adolescent will seek to build their adult identity. Such beliefs do not encourage the child to learn to nurture the "self," which is one reason why the child will seek out external sources of feedback: All too often from the very dysfunctional people who raised the child.

Having been raised by a dysfunctional parent(s) often places the child in a difficult position years later, when the parents begin to experience the diseases associated with aging (Gore, 2013). Having possibly struggled to separate themselves from their parents' influence and the lessons learned in the family of origin as they entered adulthood, the now adult children are often thrust into the role of being a caregiver to parents who caused their deep emotional pain while they were growing up.[8] This forces those individuals to ask themselves what their obligations are to their parents (Gore, 2013). There is no single answer to this question, and unfortunately most solutions fall short of the ideal, leaving ample room for criticism from the parent(s) and self-criticism from the adult child who carries the emotional scars from their childhood.

The Marriage with a Partner with an SUD

There are three common forces found in families where there is a SUD: (a) the desire for stability, (b) the threat to the family stability, and (c) how the marital partners cope with issues (a) and (b). Unfortunately the individual with the SUD does not have the same priorities as the partner: His or her priorities revolve around the continued use of the chemical(s) in question, not the marital or familial unit. The SUD becomes a "silent partner" first of the marriage, and then of the entire family. However, to maintain a sense of stability the family often adopts a "no talk" rule in which even acknowledgment of the parental alcoholism is forbidden. Those who threaten to break the "no talk/no trust" rules identified earlier face possible emotional expulsion from the family (Dayton, 2005). This familial relationship style is then passed from one generation to the next. Children are taught not to trust their own perception(s) but to turn to others for guidance and

---

[7]For example, a hypothetical mother whose daughter is about to leave for a distant college might say: "Your father and I want you to do the very best that you can while at college," and later say "It is breaking our heart that you will be living so far away." This mixed message contributes to a potential conflict in the daughter's mind: If I go away to college (a) I will hurt my parents emotionally. If I stay here (b) I won't be able to attend the college of my choice. No matter which solution the individual makes, she loses.

---

[8]We *all* suffer some degree of emotional pain during the voyage to adulthood. It is not a question of whether we suffer some emotional pain in childhood or adolescence but the degree, form, and intensity of the pain that separates psychological trauma from the everyday emotional bumps and bruises that we all suffer in life.

support, even if these individuals are dysfunctional and do not have the child's best interests at heart.

The addiction of one parent to alcohol places a financial burden on the entire family (Salize, Jackie, Kief, Franz, & Mann, 2012). The authors found that the direct costs for alcohol and related items consumed up to 20% of the budget of the typical family with an alcohol-dependent member, a cost that fell to just 4% of the family budget if the addicted family member were to go to treatment. This is a contributing factor to the food insecurity problem briefly discussed in Chapter 20, and might contribute to a state of chronic stress for the child. In theory this chronic stress might cause higher levels of illness on the child's part (Wyman et al., 2007). It is not known whether this familial stress induces epigenetic changes in the child's genetic heritage; however, the potential for such changes does apparently exist.

Although viewed universally as a negative influence on the marital unit, on rare occasions the SUDs serve a *stabilizing influence* in some long-term relationships. It is thus imperative that the assessor determine the role of the substance use disorder plays when conducting a substance use evaluation (discussed in Chapter 27). If the individual's substance use *is* a stabilizing influence in a long-term relationship then taking this coping mechanism away from the couple requires replacing it with another, more effective coping mechanism for that couple.

As was stated earlier, codependent relationships are about control. As control issues to surface in the marital unit family members begin to work at cross purposes: each side trying to change the other. *Conditional love* becomes a weapon used by one or both sides to impose their will on the other. This conditional love threatens the other with a withdrawal of affection and support unless he or she adheres to the demands of the other. It also becomes a justification for continued substance use by the partner with the SUD, because they are obviously misunderstood, mistreated, and not loved (at least in their eyes) by the partner who is using conditional love as a weapon.

It is important to remember that at all times the family will seek to establish at least a pretense of stability if not actual stability. This is true in spite of boundary violations, psychosocial problems, and continued substance abuse by important members of the family unit. One way that this pseudo-stability is protected is the unhealthy behavior(s) by the dysfunctional partner are exempted from scrutiny. "We came here for *marital* counseling,"

the couple screams, "not to discuss (insert name here)'s drinking problems!!!" The parent who brings their child in for the treatment of depression might stomp out of the session in anger if a parent's incestuous behavior is revealed, and the parent might refuse to pay for services rendered because this was not why they brought the child in to see a mental health professional![9]

Because the SUD in the family is except from discussion, the family is forced to choose between (a) breaking the injunction against confronting the problem directly or (b) finding an alternative, less threatening, way to adjust. Silence[10] may be viewed as a safe alternative than confronting the problem. This is the foundation of the "no talk rule," which holds that no matter how obvious or obnoxious the individual's behavior might be, *nobody* will talk about it. This reduces the level of conflict within the family unit, and as such can be viewed as a short-term form of control over the issue. Another weapon often used in the quest for control by the non-abusing spouse is *emotional withdrawal.* Hurcom, Copello, and Orford (2000) discovered that almost 50% of the spouses without a substance use disorder admitted to using this tactic at least on occasion. Although the goal is that this will help the partner with the SUD reduce or stop the substance abuse, more often than not it has the opposite effect: because "a bottle" as is often repeated at Alcoholics Anonymous meetings "will never reject you."

All of the conflict discussed thus far takes place during a time when the child's neural networks are still in a stage of growth and development (Sheff et al., 2007; Teicher, 2002). It is known that constant stress can contribute to epigenetic changes to the individual's genome, possibly with lifelong consequences for the child. Parental conflict about a partner's SUD occurs when the child is developing "core beliefs about security and safety" (Sheff et al., 2007, p. 7). The inability to trust their parents because of *their* ongoing conflict might encourage the child to develop a pathological self-sufficiency. The child assumes a caretaker role, staying awake while the parent is out drinking, checking on the safety of sleeping siblings, cooking meals for their siblings, and develop elaborate coping plans in case of emergencies because the parent is emotionally if not physically unavailable. These are all responsibilities of the parent in a healthy home, but in the unhealthy home the adolescent might

---

[9]Mandatory reporting laws in most states will also result in the parent being reported to the authorities, possibly eliciting threats against the therapist from the parent.

[10]Expressed as *avoidance, rationalization,* or *denial.*

be forced to spend so much time and energy meeting basic survival needs that they are unlikely to have time to establish a strong self-concept or attend to other developmental issues of adolescence (Juliana & Goodman, 2005; Sheff et al., 2007). Extremes of abuse and neglect fostered by parental substance abuse, pre-occupation with parental substance use, parental arguments about further substance use, or possible divorce might also predispose the child to depression, anxiety states, suicidal thoughts or attempts at self-harm, impulse control disorders and their own substance abuse problem later in life[11] (Anda et al., 2002; Dube et al., 2001; Ross & Fuertes, 2010; Teicher, 2002). Unfortunately, children raised in such unhealthy environments frequently give off an aura of being mature, serious, and well-organized behaviors that unfortunately mask the true nature of their internal distress and are seen by others as signs of emotional maturity (Dayton, 2005; Ruben, 2001).

The home environment where one parent has a substance use disorder is often marked by intra-familial conflict. This, it has been suggested, contributes to children who seem to be "addicted" to excitement as adolescents and (Ruben, 2001). According to this theory, the constant exposure to stress in the home leaves the child with the impression that anything less than the level of conflict experienced at home as abnormal and so they engage in dysfunctional behaviors such as fire setting, and later in life seek out partners who are likely to provide the desired level of excitement and allow them to feel "normal." This then contributes to the tendency for the child to grow up and become involved in a dysfunctional relationship when they do achieve adulthood, as noted in the last chapter. Thus, the familial environment contributes later in life to the problem of Codependency.

Surprisingly, growing up in a home where there is a substance-abusing parent does not *automatically* result in problems for the growing child. There are a number of factors that influence the impact of parental SUDs on the child's emotional growth, including (a) the sex of the substance-abusing parent, (b) the duration of time the parent abused chemicals, and (c) the availability of parental substitutes. The effects of a parent's SUD that was active for "only" 3 years will be different that seen when a parent has been physically dependent on a chemical for

the child's entire life, for example. An uncle, neighbor, teacher, older sibling, or even a media star offers the child a surrogate parent whose behavior might model more appropriate behaviors than the substance-abusing parent.

In order to adjust to a home where there is a substance-abusing parent, adolescent children and the spouse sometimes spontaneously learn to *detach* from the unhealthy parent. Many therapeutic interventions seek to guide the family members to this same point, which is paradoxically a reflection of *unconditional love* by family members. Through detachment the child or spouse learns "your behavior is *not* a reflection on me" and that "I love you enough to let you be independent, even if this means that you choose a path of destruction." As part of this process, the individual learns to establish and maintain interpersonal boundaries (Black, 2003). This growth process can take many years, but in the end it blocks the unnatural enmeshment that had existed between family members, and makes the dysfunctional member responsible for his or her behavior(s).

The Cost of Adolescent SUDs

Until now, the discussion has focused on parental SUDs. However, the substance-abusing family member might also be a child or adolescent. Surprisingly, there has been virtually no research into how adolescent SUDs impact familial life or the mental health of their siblings. Families with an adolescent substance abuser do evidence (a) a lack of trust in the substance-abusing adolescent, (b) a history of threats, abuse, and violence, (c) siblings who are often angry with the substance-abusing adolescent for disturbing the familial tranquility, (d) a tendency for family members to isolate the substance-abusing adolescent, and (e) a tendency for parents to be blamed for the adolescent's substance's abuse. It is interesting to note that the causes of substance abuse in children or adolescents have been conclusively identified, but the parents are still blamed for this problem. This "finger pointing," however justified, often serves to reduce the parent's commitment toward change, reinforcing familial rigidity.

Interventions

The family in which there is a substance abuser or addict often is often left to find a way to adjust to the problem on their own. However, there are a number of potentially helpful therapeutic interventions for the

---

[11]After all, who is going to help the child learn to control internal impulses, or develop healthy attitudes about substance use in a family such as this?

family. The most effective of these interventions is known as *coping skills training*. Coping skills training (CST) does not attempt to identify why a certain family member has a SUD, and might not even include that person in the training sessions. The focus on CST is to help the family members learn how to cope with the afflicted member's behaviors. For example, if the identified patient has routinely asked for "loans" that were used to pay for alcohol or drugs, the CST program might focus on helping family members learn refusal skills. If the identified client should have a history of violence, and between one-third and one-half of male substance abusers have been violent toward their partner in the past year, the focus of the CST sessions might be on helping the spouse identify available resources and explore legal options to deal with this violence. Although the focus of CST is not to force the afflicted person into treatment, one common result of such training programs is that the alterations in the client's family prove to be an incentive for them to enter a rehabilitation program. Further, CST training helps family members make the transition from being victims of the afflicted person's addiction to actively taking protective steps to cope with the individual's SUD.

The Adult Children of Alcoholics (ACOA) Movement

In the latter part of the 20th century, a number of adults stepped forward claiming that they had been permanently scarred by parental substance abuse. Because parental alcoholism is more prevalent than the abuse of other chemicals, these individuals started to call themselves "adult children of alcoholics" (ACOAs). Although the therapeutic focus has shifted away from the ACOA model, health care professionals will still occasionally hear from patients who do espouse this theory. Surprisingly, there has never been a single, accepted, definition of the "adult child" of an alcoholic parent. Ruben (2001) suggested that the term "carries a double meaning: an adult who is trapped in the fears and reactions of a child, and the child who was forced to be an adult without going through the natural stages that result in a healthy adult" (p. 8).

Proponents of the ACOA model hold that children raised in a home with parental alcoholism are emotionally scarred for life (Ruben, 2001). It is postulated that because of parental alcohol dependence, the children

would (Ruben, 2001; Woititz, 1983) (a) have to guess at what normal behavior was in social situations, (b) have trouble forming intimate relationships, (c) have difficulty following a project through from start to finish (d) tend to lie in situations where it was just as easy to tell the truth, (e) not feel comfortable with the "self" but to constantly seek affirmation from others, (f) have trouble relaxing and having fun, (g) judge themselves harshly, (h) handle conflict situations poorly, avoiding conflict if possible, and (i) be loyal to others, even if that loyalty is misplaced (such as when they are physically or sexually abused, or when their partner has failed to respect their loyalty).

It has been suggested that other characteristics of the "adult child" might include a tendency to self-sabotage (Ruben, 2001), express internal distress through conduct disorder or SUDs in childhood or adolescence (Fals-Stewart, O'Farrell, & Birchler, 2003, 2004). There is a danger that they will not allow themselves to exceed their parents' level of competence or achievement in life lest they seem disloyal to their parents (Ruben, 2001). It has also been suggested that the traditional view of ACOA's is too narrow, and that some "adult children" develop the opposite traits of those expected of a child raised in a dysfunctional home. Thus, whereas some "adult children" have trouble following through with activities, others become overly responsible, compulsive workaholics, and possibly overachievers (Ruben, 2001). Within the ACOA paradigm a wide range of behaviors are interpreted as evidence that the individual had an alcoholic parent(s).

The team of Hart and Fiissel (2003) explored the impact of growing up in a home where there was an alcohol-dependent parent on the later adjustment on the children in that home and found that the children of alcohol-dependent parents might be vulnerable to later physical illness as an adult, although the exact reason for the relationship was not clear. It has also been suggested that being raised in a home where there was an alcohol-dependent parent might predispose the individual to problems such as depression, phobias, and many of the anxiety disorders.

The Growth of ACOA Support Groups

It is not possible to examine the self-help ACOA movement in detail. Historians will note, however, that the ACOA support groups emerged and grew more numerous at a phenomenal rate. At one point it was estimated that 40% of the adults in the United States were a member of some kind of 12-step support group, of which the ACOA groups were the most numerous (Garry, 1995). This phenomenal growth was fueled by many different factors, such as the large number of adults who thought that they had been hurt by parental AUDs, and the desire of many people to find peace and resolution by working through their feelings about their childhood experience(s) growing up with a parent with an AUD.

Criticism of the ACOA Movement

Perhaps the most revealing fact about the ACOA movement is how short-lived it was. There has been a significant reduction both in the number of ACOA groups and the number of participants in these groups. In some areas of the country there has been a 90% decline in the membership of ACOA groups, and once-thriving groups now struggle to muster 10–20 members (Gillham, 2005). There are number of possible reasons for this phenomenon. First, it has never been proven that growing up in a home with a parent with an AUD is *in itself* is sufficient to cause psychosocial problems for the children in that home when they reach adulthood (Bijttebier, Boethals, & Ansoms, 2006). Further, the philosophical grounds on which the ACOA movement is based has been challenged because it is essentially:

an enterprise wherein people holding the thinnest of credentials diagnose in basically normal people symptoms of inflated or invented maladies, so that they may then implement remedies that have never been shown to work. (Salerno, 2005, p. 2)

Perhaps the ACOA movement is a natural reflection of the American culture at the end of the 20th century. In the last half of the 20th century a "popular assumption that … without professional help most people are incapable of dealing with adversity" (Sommers & Satel, 2005, p. 6) emerged. This assumption called "therapism" (Sommers & Satel, 2005, p. 6), and the belief that a person needs professional assistance to deal with every form of emotional trauma is patently false. The proof of this is self-evident: People have been finding ways to deal with traumatic events for thousands of generations before the disciplines of psychiatry, psychology, social work, pastoral counseling, or mental health counselors emerged. Still, the belief that one needs professional help to deal with emotional trauma has spawned an entire industry that negates the possibility of personal resilience or

acknowledges that people might find a way to come to terms with adversity without professional intervention. The "therapism" industry maintained that to cope with trauma it was first necessary for the individual to express his or her feelings (with the assistance of a trained helper, who is often paid for this assistance), and then banish those feelings and memories from consciousness. Such techniques are supported by antidotal evidence rather than scientific research, raising the possibility that any "cures" achieved through this practice may just be "placebo" cures.

This is perhaps epitomized by a radio talk show conversation overheard by the author of this text: A woman called in to a talk show that was hosting the author of a book on rape trauma. The caller reported that she had been raped when she was a certain age, and the rape trauma counselor immediately interrupted the caller to say something to the effect of "You are a victim, and don't let anybody tell you otherwise!" Imagine this process being repeated a thousand times, and suddenly you have a demand for a new self-help book or therapeutic intervention, by consumers who have been lead to believe that they can only cope with even if the consumer does not need such "assistance." Another example of "therapism" can be seen in those school districts that threaten to file criminal-neglect charges against parents who refuse psychoactive medications for children identified as having attention deficit hyperactivity disorder, although most states also have laws stating that patients (or their representatives) can refuse any medication that they do not wish to take.

In the last half century "therapism" has become a big business. In retrospect it would appear that the greater part of the "research" conducted into the AODA phenomenon was carried out by publishing companies in an attempt to identify and anticipate emerging market trends (Salerno, 2005). Such "self-help" books offered to help the reader relive traumatic events (possibly long forgotten) under the guise of being a therapeutic intervention, while informing them of their victimhood status thus weakening the individual's coping abilities rather than assist them in further growth (Salerno, 2005; Zur, 2005). Salerno (2005) supported this argument with the observation that self-help books have been on the market since the 1950s, if not longer, and there is little evidence that the rate of psychopathology in the United States has appreciably declined in that time.

It has even been suggested that the ACOA movement reflects the "baby boomer" generation's attempt to hold on to a portion of their childhood by repeatedly recalling or generating resentments from their own childhood while blaming the previous generation for perceived misdeeds. It is "fashionable to be a victim" (Zur, 2005, p. 49). Based on this theory we can feel justified in failing to accomplish everything that we wanted when we were young adults while blaming our parents. Some individuals hold to this position so tenaciously that it is almost as if they were "addicted" to being in an ACOA or similar recovery group (Salerno, 2005).

The ACOA movement is based on what clinicians call the *damage model*. Proponents of this position hold that "all children are affected" by parental alcoholism, for example (Black, 1982, p. 27, 2003). Yet in spite of strident, vocal, advocates, the damage model has not been supported in the clinical literature. Most people find ways to adjust with trauma, and in some cases the traumatic event serves as an impetus for emotional growth (Bijttebier et al., 2006). To examine whether the "damage model" did indeed exist, Bijttebier et al. (2006) compared clinical data from a community sample of 10- to 14-year-old children from the Netherlands and Belgium who had a parent with an AUD and compared the results with a control sample of children who did not have a parent with an AUD. The authors found that the children from homes where there was parental alcoholism did not demonstrate higher levels of anxiety or depression when compared with a control group of children. These children did report lower levels of familial cohesion, which could contribute to the lower feelings of self-worth reported by the children, although it was not clear whether the lower levels of familial cohesion contributed to lower self-esteem or just the reverse. Further, it was discovered by the authors that parental support by the nondrinking parent, peer group relationships, and parental surrogates helped to mediate the impact of parental alcoholism in the family.

Admittedly, some children are raised in terrible, abusive environments. However, the assumption that growing up in such an environment *automatically* results in lifelong psychological trauma for everybody remains unproven. Indeed the "healthy" conflict-free family is a myth. There has been little research into what constitutes a "normal" family, or the limits of unhealthy behavior(s)[12] that a family might tolerate

and still provide a healthy environment for the children. Yet it is on this weak foundation that proponents of the ACOA model claim that 96% of the population was raised in a "dysfunctional" home (Salerno, 2005). This 96% figure has never been proven, but proponents of the ACOA model quote it as if it were an established fact.

People have been coping with what we would now call unhealthy environments for generations, and yet the species has survived. This possibly reflects individual resilience, which is overlooked by the ACOA construct, and informal social support for a child being raised in a dysfunctional home. There is evidence that resilience involves a gene that is involved in the synthesis of serotonin ("Resilience," 2006). This raises the possibility that the "damage" done by parental AUDs is caused by a genetic predisposition for depression and anxiety inherited by the child. Resilience does not mean that the individual is invulnerable to trauma, but that there is a natural development of the adaptive systems in childhood that may help the child resist the damaging effects of the environment (Blum, 1998; Masten, 2001). It is only when these protective mechanisms are overwhelmed by extreme events that the individual's normal growth is disrupted. However, resilient children are adept at finding ways to adjust with parental AUDs through the use of parental surrogates or peer group support(s), and a focus on future goals rather than current familial disruptions.

It has also been suggested that the ACOA construct reflects an oversimplification of the developmental process (Zweig & Wolf, 1997). Simply naming a process does not imply that one understands it. An excellent example of this is cancer. Calling it "cancer" does not mean that its causes, controls, developmental process, or suppression is understood. Further, it has been suggested that the ACOA model often leaves the reconstructive process unfinished, having failed to reach the deepest levels of the individual's psyche necessary for complete healing (Zweig & Wolf, 1997). Other detractors of the ACOA construct point to the emphasis of this model on what is called the "inner child," a phrase that has found its way into popular culture. The inner child is not a part of any established clinical theory, but reflects a complex blend of "[Carl] Jung, New Age mysticism, holy child mythology, pop psychology, and psychoanalytic theories about narcissism and the creation of a false self" (Kaminer, 1992, p. 17).

---

[12]If the truth be told, we all have some unhealthy behaviors.

ACOA proponents focus on the problems encountered by their "inner child," a concept that remains unproven in the clinical literature. By keeping the individual's focus on trauma suffered in childhood rather than those of adulthood the individual's ability to cope with current problems is compromised. Even if this elusive creature existed, the "inner child" reflects a phase of life when the individual was emotionally, developmentally, cognitively, and socially immature. Although individuals with emotional and social problems do exist, the causal relationship between parental alcoholism and the development of these problems in their children has not been proven. Finally, it has been suggested that the ACOA model is a white, middle-class invention. There has been virtually no application of this construct to inner-city children, for example, nor has this model been applied to substances other than alcohol. Yet there are children who have been raised in homes where the parents abused compounds such as cocaine or narcotic analgesics, and the literature that explores how being raised in such a home is quite limited. Given these challenges to the ACOA model, one must wonder whether the personality characteristics identified as having been caused by being raised in a home where there was an alcoholic parent reflect not psychopathology but every day problems in living. However now, thanks to an overabundance of self-help books, we have a language through which we might blame earlier generations for the problems in life that we might encounter rather than take steps to address them.

Chapter Summary

This chapter addressed the impact of parental SUDs on the family. Although this topic is a popular one for general discussion, there are few clinical studies that explore this subject in detail. Further, it has been revealed that much of what is true about the impact of parental alcoholism on the family is based on theory or personal beliefs, not established fact. On the surface, it would appear that parental SUDs result in the child being "trained" to become dependent on external feedback, which then contributes to the development of Codependency.

Arguably, proponents of the dysfunctional family model see only those individuals who have suffered as a result of parental alcoholism. Those individuals who have found a way to adjust to their past are hardly likely to call attention to themselves as being dysfunctional because of their past. Parental alcoholism as the cause of psychopathology in family members has been met with skepticism and the "adult child" concept has met with considerable criticism. Both topics have almost disappeared from research journals. Health care professionals point out that the damage model dismisses the possibility of individual resilience. This model automatically assumes that the experience of growing up in a home with a parent who has an SUD will result in trauma, theory that has not been proven. Health care professionals also suggest that the paradigm of the "adult children" places too much emphasis on perceived past slights during childhood, at the expense of current life problems for the adult.

CHAPTER 24

The Dual-Diagnosis Client: Substance Use Disorders and Mental Illness

Introduction

Three generations ago many psychiatric textbooks suggested that substance use disorders (SUDs) in patients with mental illness were rare. This claim, based on clinical lore and a lack of research data, was found to be wrong. When epidemiological studies on the SUDs among those with mental illness were conducted, health care professionals were surprised to discover that not only do the two conditions often exist in the same individual but that the majority of psychiatric patients also have a co-occurring SUD (Buckley, 2006; Minkoff, 2008; Seppala, 2004). This knowledge was only the first step, as health care professionals still struggle to understand the complex relationship between the SUDs and mental illness. Their confusion is perhaps best epitomized by the fact that clinicians have yet to even agree on whether to call these individuals dual-diagnosis clients, mentally ill substance abusers, or mentally ill/chemically dependent (MI/CD) patients.[1,2]

Although health care professionals now accept that dual-diagnosis patients are the norm rather than the exception, they still tend to view these patients as a single diagnostic category (e.g., "mentally ill substance abusers") as opposed to a heterogeneous population with multiple pathways to both SUDs and expressions of their mental illness (Hesselbrock & Hesselbrock, 2007). Thus, clinicians lack knowledge of such factors as those that initiate or maintain an SUD in those persons who have a mental illness (Drake, Mueser, Brunette, & McHugo, 2004; Petrakis, Gonzalez, Rosenheck, & Krystal, 2002). Research into effective treatment methods might be most effective when working with the dual-diagnosis patient is in its infancy, and the research into how the effects of the drugs of abuse might help to suppress (or exacerbate) psychiatric symptoms is lacking. Substance abuse can simulate the symptoms of virtually all forms of mental illness, making a differential diagnosis difficult. In this chapter, the unfolding issue of how to identify and treat dual-diagnosis patients will briefly be reviewed.[3]

---

[1] A term that ignores the possibility that the mentally ill individual might only be a substance *abuser* and not be physically dependent on it.

[2] For the purposes of this text, the term *dual-diagnosis* or *MI/CD* will be used. It is recognized that each term is limited in scope, but we have to begin somewhere, do we not?

[3] This topic, like so many other topics in the addictions field, is worthy of a book in its own right. This chapter will attempt to review the more important issues in working with the dual-diagnosis client.

Definitions

Dual-diagnosis patients are said to suffer from a concurrent form of mental illness, and a SUD. Coexisting disorders are not difficult to understand. Medical patients often have more than one disorder: A patient might suffer from hypertension and obesity, conditions that may be interrelated and which may interact (if you lose weight, your blood pressure will probably go down in this hypothetical example). When discussing dual-diagnosis clients, it is important to keep in mind that the SUD did not *cause* the psychiatric disorder, although it might be intertwined with it. This is an important point because for decades it was believed that if you addressed the psychiatric disorder that the SUD would resolve itself.

Unfortunately, there is little consensus about the forms of "mental illness" that should be used to define the dual-diagnosis client. It has been suggested that coexisting conditions such as the SUDs and (a) anorexia, (b) bulimia, (c) gambling, (d) spousal abuse, (e) compulsive shopping, (f) compulsive sexual behaviors, (g) AIDS, and even (h) other physical disorders qualify as dual-diagnosis clients (Minkoff, 2008). This text will limit this term *coexisting* to psychiatric disorders as defined by the American Psychiatric Association (2013) and an SUD. It is important to keep in mind that active substance abuse or the withdrawal from many drugs of abuse can magnify or simulate symptoms of psychiatric disorders (Buckley, 2006; Ross, 2008; Schuckit & Tapert, 2004). An excellent example of this is the anxiety often experienced by alcohol- or benzodiazepine-dependent persons during the withdrawal process. This anxiety is usually drug withdrawal-induced that will usually diminish or disappear entirely, when the individual recovers from the withdrawal process or the effects of acute substance abuse and thus do not qualify for the term "dual-diagnosis" (Minkoff, 2008). An example of the dual-diagnosis patient is a hypothetical patient with a bipolar disorder who also abuses alcohol. Each disorder can influence the progression of the other, a fact that complicates the treatment of both conditions (Drake et al., 2001). This is clearly seen in the increased risk for suicidal behavior in bipolar affective disorder patients who also have an alcohol use disorder (AUD) (Oquendo et al., 2010). Either group has an increased risk of suicide, which is increased even further if the person has both a psychiatric and SUD (Geppert & Minkoff, 2004; Mueser, Noordsy, Drake, & Fox, 2003; Ross, 2008).

Coexisting Substance Use and Medical Disorders

The example of a patient with hypertension and obesity offered as an example earlier in this section serves as an excellent example of how medical conditions can be intertwined. Sterling, Chi, and Hinman (2011) suggested that medical conditions and SUDs can also be intertwined, forming a distinct category of dual-diagnosis clients. The individual's SUD could (a) cause a medical condition such as cirrhosis of the liver, (b) exacerbate a medical disorder such as heart failure, or (c) increase the individual's risk of exposure to certain diseases (Sterling et al., 2011). The hypothetical individual in each of the above categories might become depressed, complicating the clinical picture even further by introducing a mental disorder into this case. Although this is an interesting perspective on coexisting medical and substance use issues, the main focus of this chapter will be on coexisting SUDs and mental illness.

Theoretical Models

Ross (2008) suggested four possible models for dual-diagnosis conditions. In the first model it was suggested that the SUDs and mental illness both reflect a common undiscovered factor. At best there is limited research evidence suggesting this possibility. A second theory is that substance use by persons with a mental illness reflects an attempt at self-medication. There is also limited evidence suggesting that persons with mental illness might use chemicals to self-medicate the dysphoria[4] commonly experienced in mental illness. There is little evidence of condition-specific substance abuse. The third model postulates that substance abuse is secondary to another form of psychopathology and thus should resolve when the "primary" condition is the third theoretical model. As noted above, although this theory was popular in the latter half of the 20th century, there is limited research evidence supporting this perspective. The final model suggested by Ross (2008) was that individuals with mental illness might be exceptionally sensitive to the effects of the drugs of abuse, increasing their attractiveness to the abuser. This "supersensitivity" model has some research evidence supporting it. However, it should be pointed out that no single model explains the problem of substance abuse by persons with mental illness.

---

[4]See Glossary.

Dual-Diagnosis Clients: A Diagnostic Challenge

Dual-diagnosis clients, or at least a client who possibly is a dual-diagnosis patient, offer a challenge to health care professionals. The assessor must have:

> the ability to distinguish the signs and symptoms of the primary psychiatric illness from those caused or exacerbated by a primary SUD [substance use disorder]. (Geppert & Minkoff, 2004, p. 105)

This is a daunting task. The majority of patients admitted to a substance abuse treatment program will have symptoms of a psychiatric disorder at the time of admission. Many of these symptoms are substance induced or withdrawal induced, and will subside after a period of abstinence. The assessor might have to wait for as long as 2–8 weeks for the diagnostic picture to clear (Jones, Knutson, & Haines, 2004; Ross, 2008; Work Group on Substance Use Disorders, 2007). A careful clinical history might help differentiate substance-induced from actual psychiatric problems (Minkoff, 2008). For example, if an individual (and family members) attest that the depressive symptoms appeared months or even years before the individual started drinking heavily, it would be safe to assume that the observed symptoms of depression reflect a preexisting disorder that now coexists with the SUD. The depression is not substance induced in spite of the apparent causal relationship. An accurate clinical history is thus of critical importance in the determination of actual dual-diagnosis clients as opposed to substance-induced psychiatric problems (Washton & Zweben, 2006). In cases where the individual's psychiatric symptoms are severe, the attending physician should immediately institute appropriate pharmacological treatment even if those symptoms are later determined to have been caused by a substance withdrawal syndrome (Busch, Weiss, & Najavits, 2005; Watkins, Burnam, Kung, & Paddock, 2001; Work Group on Substance Use Disorders, 2007). However, it should also be recognized that the diagnosis of a dual-diagnosis client is an ongoing process, and might need to be modified as the patient recovers from the acute substance withdrawal.

Unfortunately, it is not uncommon for individuals who have the label of being a dual-diagnosis patient to report that a careful clinical history was not carried out when they were admitted to a hospital or treatment center. More than one patient has reported having been diagnosed as having a "transient psychosis" and started on antipsychotic medication without any health care professional inquiring about the individual's possibly engaging in substance abuse. If the treating physician reaches for the prescription pad rather than to spend a few more minutes to carry out a complete assessment the person could potentially be exposed to potent medications without need. The diagnosis of a "transient psychosis" on his or her medical record is also a problem for the individual: Once a certain diagnosis is entered into a medical file, it is extremely difficult to have that diagnosis purged from the record even if it was a mistake.

The accurate diagnosis of either an SUD or any form of mental illness is complicated by the fact that each condition is often viewed as a stigma (Pies, 2003). Where a hypothetical person with one condition or the other might be motivated to use the defense mechanisms of denial and minimization, persons with a dual diagnosis frequently call upon these defenses to protect to *both* their SUD and their mental illness (Minkoff, 2008; Shivani, Goldsmith, & Anthenelli, 2002). Forceful questioning about either the possibility that he or she has an SUD or a mental health problem may cause the person to (a) experience significant levels of shame or (b) awaken fears in the patient that by their admission to having an SUD that they might lose entitlements (Social Security disability payments, and health insurance benefits, for example). Some dual-diagnosis clients fear that (c) their admission that they have an SUD could result in a refusal for access to psychiatric care, a fear that is not always unfounded. Finally (d) because many dual-diagnosis clients feel hopeless they have little motivation to stop abusing the chemicals that bring them some degree of relief from their emotional pain.

As the material reviewed so far suggests, the diagnosis of a psychiatric disorder in a substance abuser or the diagnosis of a substance abuse problem in a psychiatric patient can be extremely complicated. This raises the question that the next section attempts to answer.

Why Worry about Dual-Diagnosis Clients?

Perhaps the most eloquent answer to this question was provided by Geppert and Minkoff (2004), who suggested that:

> As a whole this population has worse treatment outcomes, higher health care utilization; increased risk

of violence, trauma, suicide, child abuse and neglect, and involvement in the criminal justice system; more medical comorbidity, particularly of infectious diseases; and higher health care costs than people with a single disorder. (p. 103)

The increased risk of suicide in dual-diagnosis clients has been estimated 60- to 120-fold higher than for the general population (Nielson et al., 1998). Further, dual-diagnosis clients are at increased risk for incarceration, less able to handle personal finances, have a weaker support system, and are more prone to depression and feelings of hopelessness.

Although a person with both a SUD and mental illness might not see the connection, dual-diagnosis clients run the risk of exacerbating their psychiatric disorder through their abuse of recreational chemicals. This "sensitization" effect to the drugs of abuse is especially noticeable in patients with schizophrenia (Ross, 2008). Even social use of alcohol, for example, can destabilize the dual-diagnosis client and result in a greater need for hospitalization (Mueser et al., 2003; Patrick, 2003; Prochaska, Gill, Hall, & Hall, 2005). Further, untreated psychiatric symptoms can serve as a "relapse trigger" for renewed substance abuse (Jones et al., 2004; Washton & Zweben, 2006). Dual-diagnosis clients are also at increased risk of being assaulted and homelessness (Brekke, Prindle, Woo Bae, & Long, 2001; Pankiewicz, 2008; Ross, 2008). They place an increased financial burden on society and often on their families by the individual's need for repeated hospitalizations. Persons with a dual diagnosis are at increased risk for infections: They face a 300% higher chance of contracting the virus that causes AIDS,[5] a 170% higher risk for contracting the Hepatitis B virus, and a 250% higher chance of contracting the Hepatitis C virus,[6] for example. The treatment of all three conditions is often carried out at public expense, placing a hidden drain on social support and health care resources. Finally, persons with PTSD have higher rates of SUDs and are at increased risk for re-traumatization (Mueser et al., 2003). Thus, there are significant social and personal financial losses either caused or exacerbated by substance use by psychiatric patients (Pankiewicz, 2008). All of these issues make the need to address dual-diagnosis issues undeniable.

Scope of the Problem

Currently 4 million individuals in the United States are thought to have a concurrent substance abuse and mental illness problem (Ross, 2008). Unfortunately, with the introduction of the first generation of antipsychotic medications in the late 1950s, society began to call for the "deinstitutionalization" of patients formerly hospitalized in private and state facilities.[7] It was rationalized that agencies such as community mental health centers would provide appropriate treatment for these individuals. However, as the "deinstitutionalization" movement gained momentum support services in the community were either overwhelmed or as was found in many areas simply did not exist. A complicating factor was that many formerly hospitalized individuals refused to take prescribed medications following their release from the hospital because of their harsh side effects. This often resulted in a "revolving door" at psychiatric facilities where a person would be admitted for stabilization, discharged with a prescription(s) for their psychiatric disorder, would stop taking these medications for any of a wide range of reasons including their side effects or financial reasons, decompensate and require rehospitalization for stabilization.

However, the "deinstitutionalization" movement has achieved one of its goals: Many state psychiatric hospitals were closed and in many cases the land was sold to private investors. An unforeseen side effect of this process is that at the start of the 21st century, many persons who would have been sent to state hospitals in earlier generations are now homeless or incarcerated (Ross, 2008). Indeed, so many persons with mental illness are now incarcerated that some authorities view the prison system to be the new state hospital system for the mentally ill.

Unfortunately, physicians are rarely trained to detect and treat SUDs in dual-diagnosis patients. It has been found, for example, that emergency room physicians will, when confronted with a dual-diagnosis client, commonly attribute the observed symptoms to the patients'

---

[5]These viral infections are discussed in the chapter "Substance Use Disorders and Infectious Disease."

[6]Often at public expense through Medicare and similar programs.

[7]Whitaker (2010) argues convincingly that changes in federal reimbursement policies that shifted reimbursement for the mentally ill from state hospitals to nursing homes started the process of "deinstitutionalization," and that the pharmaceuticals industry took credit for this process.

psychiatric disorder to the exclusion of a possible SUD[8] (Schanzer, First, Dominguez, Hasin, & Caton, 2006). In one study, only 24% of depressed patients were even assessed for an alcohol use disorder by the attending physician (McDowell, Lineberry, & Bostwick, 2011). These facts underscore the need for training for health care professionals to better understand and properly diagnose dual-diagnosis patients so that appropriate treatment referrals might be made. This would help correct the current situation in which only 8% of MI/CD clients received treatment for both disorders in the past year, and 72% have never had both issues addressed in a treatment setting (Prochaska et al., 2005). Where treatment is offered, it is most often for either the mental illness problem or the SUD, but not both disorders (Buckley, 2006). In the correctional system, "treatment" is usually limited to pharmacological control of the mental illness problem alone and it is a rare correctional system that provides pharmacological support for substance withdrawal.

If a patient has any form of mental illness, she or he is 270% more likely to have an SUD than the average person (Volpicelli, 2005). Various estimates suggest that between 30 and 80% of patients with a form of mental illness also have an SUD (Minkoff, 2008; Patrick, 2003; Roberts, 2004; Watkins et al., 2001). Table 24-1 summarizes the estimated concordance rate between the SUDs and various psychiatric disorders.

The relationship between a mental illness and a concurrent SUD is quite complex. There is evidence, for example, suggesting that the more serious the form of psychopathology, the more difficult it might be for the individual to abstain from drug abuse (Ritsher, Moos, & Finney, 2000). This is consistent with the findings of the team of Chambers et al. (2007), who concluded that rats that suffered damage to the amygdala region of the brain were both more responsive to novel stimuli, less responsive to dangerous stimuli, and more prone to cocaine addiction. Although suggestive, the assessment of amygdala function in the human brain is difficult, making it virtually impossible to determine whether this is a factor in human SUDs.

---

[8]In defense of the attending physician, in many cases the emergency room doctor has limited historical data on the patient, who may be unable or unwilling to provide a history. This makes it difficult to differentiate between psychiatric dysfunction and substance-induced problems. However, it should also be noted that a misdiagnosis can have lifelong implications for the client (Schanzer et al., 2006).

TABLE 24-1
Estimated Concordance Rate between Select Forms of Psychopathology and SUDs

CONDITION	ESTIMATED LIFETIME SUD PREVALENCE RATE
Depression	17–32%
Bipolar affective disorder	56–64%
Anxiety disorder	15–36%
Antisocial personality disorder	84%
Attention deficit hyperactivity disorder (ADHD)	23%
Eating disorders: Anorexia	17%
Bulimia	46%
Posttraumatic stress disorder (PTSD)	30–75%
Schizophrenia	50%
Somatoform disorders	Unknown

SOURCE: Chart based on Hartwell, Tolliver, and Brady (2009); Ross (2008); Ziedonis and Brady (1997).

Psychopathology and Drug of Choice

For many years, clinicians believed that there was a relationship between a patient's psychiatric disorder and his or her drug of choice. This hypothesis, although it continues to echo through the academic halls where health care professionals are trained, has not been supported by the clinical literature (Drake, 2007; Drake & Mueser, 2002). Part of the confusion might be traced to the fact that much of the clinical data is drawn from research studies that perhaps unknowingly intermixed substance *abusers* and individuals who are *addicted* to a chemical(s) in the same subject pool. It has been assumed that both abusers and addicted persons with mental illness engage in substance abuse for the same reasons, an unproven assumption at best. It is possible that a substance abuser might engage in chemical use (possibly to self-medicate emotional distress), whereas a mentally ill person with a physical addiction to a drug continues to abuse chemicals for other reasons (avoidance of withdrawal effects, association with a peer group, etc.)

(Weiss, 2005). By intermixing substance abusers with addicted persons with psychiatric conditions, the results might have failed to support what is a very defendable hypothesis: That substance abusers seek to self-medicate their emotional pain by abusing alcohol and drugs.

Proponents of the self-medication hypothesis often point to the apparent tendency for people who have developed PTSD to engage in substance abuse (Cross & Ashley, 2007; Khantzian, 2003b; Preuss & Wong, 2000). This is a complicated matter, for the course of PTSD varies over time.[9] The individual's goal in self-medication is also thought to vary over the course of time, depending on whether he or she was facing the intrusive memories of the trauma or the emptiness of emotional numbing (Khantzian, 2003b). The self-medication hypothesis has significant appeal to clinicians because it seems to have face value; however, there is little clinical research supporting this theory (Mueser et al., 2003; Ross, 2008). Perhaps some persons with a mental illness are drawn to substance use for the same reason as do other people: It is "cool" and a sign of rebellion (Sharp & Getz, 1998, p. 642). At the same time, substance abuse may offer the abuser an identity of sorts and on some level aid in the development of a social network (Busch et al., 2005; Drake & Mueser, 2002). Finally, in the minds of many dual-diagnosis clients the stigma associated with substance abuse is less severe than is that associated with mental illness, motivating many dual-diagnosis clients to substitute the less severe stigma of having an SUD for that of mental illness (Sharp & Getz, 1998).

Substance abusers, including those with a form of mental illness, tend to be more impulsive and interested in new sensations (Dervaux et al., 2001). This would suggest that mentally ill substance abusers might not be engaging in self-medication so much as seeking new sensory sensations for entertainment. This might also help to explain why cigarette smoking is two to three times more prevalent in persons with mental illness as it is in the general population (Kerr, Woods, Watson, & Hunter, 2013). A rarely considered variable is that the availability of alcohol or drug(s) influences on individual's substance use pattern (Drake, 2007). This hypothesis is supported by the study completed by Swartz et al. (2006) who concluded that the pattern

of substance abuse by schizophrenic patients studied were similar to those found in the general community. A similar finding was reported by Lybrand and Caroff (2009) who observed that cocaine abuse by persons with schizophrenia was rare in rural areas of the country, but more common in urban areas where it is more easily obtained.

The factor of drug availability may have confounded early studies that attempted to find a correlation between the form of mental illness and the substance (s) being abused. Most certainly there is little evidence to support a condition-specific pattern for substance abuse by those with mental illness who also have an SUD, although Miles et al. (2003) did find a positive relationship between CNS stimulant abuse and violence. It is not clear whether the observed violence was the result of CNS stimulant abuse, which in itself can contribute to violent behavior by the abuser, or it was the result of the individual's mental illness. Still, because the self-medication hypothesis has so many supporters, we will examine the relationship between various forms of mental illness and SUDs.

Attention Deficit Hyperactivity Disorder (ADHD)

In the final years of the 20th century, ADHD emerged from the depths of controversy to become an accepted diagnostic entity. Currently, it is thought that ADHD is about as prevalent as asthma, affecting 4–5% of the population (Khurana & Schubiner, 2007).

A relationship between ADHD and the SUDs was first suggested approximately a decade ago (Diller, 1998; Smith, Molina, & Pelham, 2002). For example, 21% of adults with ADHD are thought to have a concurrent cocaine use disorder (Acosta, Haller, & Schnoll, 2005). Both conditions are thought to reflect a dysfunction of the dopamine neurotransmission system of the medial forebrain region of the brain. There was a popular myth in the 1990s and early part of the 21st century that adolescents with ADHD were at increased risk for CNS stimulant abuse. The truth is just the opposite: If the adolescent's ADHD is adequately controlled, the individual appears to be at lower risk for the development of a SUD later in life (Work Group on Substance Use Disorders, 2007). However, it is still recommended that parents control access to the medication(s) being used to treat the ADHD to minimize potential abuse problems (Biederman et al., 2008; Knight, 2005).

---

[9]The issue of PTSD and its manifestations are discussed in more depth in "Break Out Discussion" number 1 for this chapter, available on the Internet.

The exception to this rule are those children who suffer from one of the conduct disorders[10] such as the oppositional defiant disorder.[11] These children do appear to be at increased risk for the later development of a SUD (August et al., 2006; Lynskey & Hall, 2001). This apparent association between children with a conduct disorder and subsequent substance abuse might reflect the fact that between 35 and 50% of children diagnosed with ADHD also have a conduct disorder and thus these findings are an artifact rather than a real clinical issue (Smucker & Hedayat, 2001).

There has been a great deal of research on childhood ADHD, and it has been discovered that in about 85% of the cases this condition does carry over into adulthood[12] (Khurana & Schubiner, 2007; Wilens, 2006). Between 15 and 25% of adults with ADHD will also have an SUD at some point in their lives, and active substance abuse can make the diagnosis of ADHD difficult (Wilens, 2006). In cases of proven adolescent ADHD, CNS stimulants such as methylphenidate or the amphetamines should *not* be the treatment of choice (Riggs, 2003). Rather, compounds such as bupropion, pemoline, and atomoxetine have been found to be both safe and effective in treating adolescent ADHD without the high abuse potential of the CNS stimulants.[13]

There is preliminary evidence suggesting that individuals with ADHD are more vulnerable to the disinhibiting effects of alcohol than persons without ADHD (Weafer, Fillmore, & Milich, 2009). Adults with ADHD demonstrated less behavioral control in response to a given amount of alcohol than did the control subjects, and that there was a dose-dependent loss of inhibition in both groups that was most pronounced in the ADHD group of subjects. The authors of this study call for further research into this area, which hints that adolescents and adults with ADHD might not respond to alcohol in the same manner as normal people will, possibly making them more vulnerable to AUDs although this has yet to be proven.

---

[10]See Glossary.

[11]See Glossary.

[12]Most substance abuse rehabilitation professionals are not trained in the diagnosis of ADHD. Suspected cases should be assessed by a psychologist or physician who specializes in the diagnosis of such cases.

[13]The clinician's suspicion that the patient might also have a concurrent SUD should be raised if the patient suggests that the *only* compounds that have worked for him or her are the CNS stimulants with higher abuse potentials.

The issue of ADHD has been controversial, and the construct has even been challenged in the clinical literature. However, cutting-edge research using functional magnetic resonance imaging (fMRI) hints at abnormal regional brain activation patterns in adolescents or adults with ADHD as compared with age-matched normal clients, suggesting that accurate tests to identify such patients can be developed in time. If such tests are developed, the client should be substance free at the time of assessment because these compounds can also cause abnormal regional brain activation patterns.

Schizophrenia

The relationship between schizophrenia and the SUDs is rather complicated. For example Jones, Lichtenstein, Grann, Långstrom, and Fazel (2011) suggested that individuals who have a preexisting AUD and who then go on to develop schizophrenia might not present with the same risk factors as do those individuals who develop an AUD after developing schizophrenia. Further research in this area is clearly needed especially because there is a clear relationship between the SUDs and schizophrenia. Research has shown that patients with schizophrenia have a 460% higher probability of developing an SUD as the average person (Weiss, 2010). Expressed in other terms between 40 and 50% of patients with schizophrenia have a concurrent SUD (Lybrand & Caroff, 2009; Roberts, 2004; Pankiewicz, 2008). Statistically, the most commonly abused substance was nicotine, with at least 90% of patients with schizophrenia also being cigarette smokers (Pankiewicz, 2008). The second most commonly abused substance is alcohol, which is used by 34% of persons with schizophrenia (Jones et al., 2011). About 13% of persons with schizophrenia will develop an SUD involving a compound(s) other than alcohol (Ross, 2008).

Illicit substance abuse by patients with schizophrenia is associated with an earlier onset of schizophrenia, a poorer response to psychiatric treatment, higher rates of rehospitalization due to a resurgence of psychiatric symptoms, greater likelihood of being noncompliant with medications prescribed for their psychiatric disorder, greater likelihood of suicidal behavior, increased violence, greater likelihood of being victimized, increased homelessness, and greater likelihood of being incarcerated than schizophrenic patients who do not abuse recreational chemicals (Jones et al., 2011; Lybrand & Caroff, 2009; Pankiewicz, 2008;

Weiss, 2010). A history of violent behaviors in persons with a diagnosis of schizophrenia was found to be highly predictive of the later development of an AUD, often by a period of several years (Jones et al., 2011).

Higher functioning patients with schizophrenia are more likely to have a concurrent SUD. Upon reflection this becomes apparent: Because of their higher level of function they have the interpersonal skills necessary to access alcohol or illicit drugs (Swartz et al., 2006). Although there is no apparent relationship between schizophrenia and the individual's substance of choice, it should be pointed out that availability is a significant factor in the patient's substance use behaviors. Surprisingly, many patients with schizophrenia will seek out hallucinogenic compounds to use. Given that hallucinations are a primary symptom of schizophrenia, intuitively one would expect that patients with schizophrenia would avoid these compounds. However, many of these patients defend their abuse of hallucinogens because these compounds at least give them some degree of control over *when* they experience hallucinations, which provides an insight into their motivation to abuse these compounds and the magnitude of emotional discomfort experienced by many patients with schizophrenia.

There is a significant interactional effect between schizophrenia and nicotine dependence. As noted above at least 90% of patients with schizophrenia smoke cigarettes and many are heavy cigarette smokers (Pankiewicz, 2008). Fully 44% of all cigarettes consumed in the United States are consumed by persons with a mental illness, which exposes them to the dangers associated with cigarette smoking[14] ("Why do the Mentally Ill Die Younger?," 2008). In the case of schizophrenia, it is thought that the nicotine in cigarettes helps to reverse many of the cognitive deficits associated with that disorder or the medications used to treat it (Pankiewicz, 2008). Persons who have both schizophrenia and a nicotine use disorder have twice the risk of heart disease and three times the risk of respiratory disease as nonsmokers (Kalman, 2010). Thus, the health risks associated with tobacco use mitigate any possible benefit from cigarette smoking in this population, and smoking cessation in this population is recommended (Hitsman, Moss, Montoya, & George, 2009).

It is interesting to observe that the cocaine withdrawal process is different for persons with schizophrenia than in normal cases (Carol, Smelson, Losonczy, &

Ziedonis, 2001). Further, individuals who suffer from schizophrenia and who habitually abuse cocaine are at higher risk for developing tardive dyskinesia[15] than those persons with schizophrenia who do not abuse this compound (Lybrand & Caroff, 2009). These disorders reflect a dysfunction of the dopamine neurotransmission system, and this might be the reason why schizophrenic patients appear to experience more intense craving for cocaine than did nonschizophrenic patients during cocaine withdrawal. This suggests that there is a need for intensive intervention, including possible modification of medications to help these individuals cope with the symptoms of cocaine withdrawal.

There has been little formal research into the issue of which medications might be most effective in treating substance-abusing clients with schizophrenia (San, Arranz, & Martinez-Rega, 2007). Antidotal reports suggest that the "second generation" or "atypical" antipsychotic medications are more effective in controlling the symptoms of schizophrenia in such patients than the older medications used to treat this condition, but there has been little formal research into this area (San et al., 2007).

Anxiety Disorders

The relationship between the SUDs and the anxiety disorders is quite complicated (Maremmani et al., 2010). Many of the drugs of abuse can induce anxiety either as a side effect of their use or during the withdrawal process. The amphetamines and marijuana are examples of the former whereas alcohol is a prototypical example of the latter. Thus, it is imperative that the health care professional(s) working with the individual determine whether he or she is experiencing substance-related (or substance withdrawal) anxiety, or if they have a concurrent anxiety disorder, to assist in the proper treatment of the patient. The team of Kushner, Specker, and Maurer (2011) observed that the term "anxiety" is too inclusive, as different forms of anxiety disorders have different risk levels for SUDs. Approximately 10.4% of persons with a generalized anxiety disorder (GAD) were found to have abused a drug in the preceding 12 months for example, but only 3.8% of persons with a specific phobia had done so.

One point that assists in the differentiation between substance-induced versus anxiety is that the anxiety disorders are thought to predate the development of

---

[14]Discussed in Chapter 19.

[15]See Glossary.

the SUD (Cheng, Gau, Chen, Chang, & Chang, 2004). However, Kushner et al. (2011) challenged this belief by noting that in approximately half of the cases where a person has a concurrent SUD and an anxiety disorder that the latter developed after the SUD. The authors supported this claim with the observation that pathological substance use exacerbated preexisting anxiety symptoms. These observations do underscore the need for a case-by-case evaluation to determine the exact relationship between the individual's anxiety disorder and her or his SUD.

The anxiety disorders, at least in theory, provide an example of the self-medication hypothesis advanced by psychoanalytic theorists (Khantzian, 2003b). Hypothetically, the individual would be drawn to the abuse of alcohol, opioids, or benzodiazepines, all compounds with an anxiolytic effect, to self-medicate their anxiety. This theory is supported by the research finding that up to 50% of those persons with a GAD will also have some form of an SUD (Alegria et al., 2010).[16] These individuals will present a more severe clinical GAD syndrome and their treatment is more challenging (Alegria et al., 2010).

The use of recreational chemicals by persons with a coexisting mental illness has been implicated as a cause of "telescoping" the development of the dependence on a drug(s) (Kushner et al., 2011).[17] There are a number of effective medications as well as psychotherapies for persons who suffer from some form of anxiety. Certain medications that at first glance would appear to be a good choice for addressing the problem of a substance use disorder in a person with a concurrent anxiety disorder should be avoided. For example, although the monoamine oxidase inhibitors (MAOIs) have been found to be very effective in treatment social anxiety disorder, these medications are contraindicated for patients with an AUD. Beer, wine, and liquor all contain compounds that might interact with the MAOI being used, inducing a potentially fatal hypertensive crisis (Book & Randall, 2002). Although benzodiazepines have been found to be useful for the short-term relief of anxiety, their abuse potential prohibits their use in treating patients with an anxiety disorder and a concurrent SUD (Jones et al., 2004; Riggs, 2003). The

selective serotonin reuptake inhibitors (SSRIs) are now viewed as the most appropriate treatment for these individuals (Book & Randall, 2002; Jones et al., 2004; Ross, 2008). Buspirone has also been found to be helpful in many cases where the person suffers from GAD, whereas "beta blockers" have been found useful in specific cases. Kushner et al. (2011) also observed that pharmacotherapy should not be the only treatment utilized, but that an integrated team approach would be most effective.

The Dissociative Disorders[18]

The dissociative disorders represent a series of related conditions in which the individual essentially is able to "detach" from reality for periods of time to escape from extreme psychological stress. One man, upon being told of the death of his spouse, recalls the sensation of watching himself from across the room as he lost consciousness and hit his head against a concrete wall and a cement floor before coming to a rest. While still looking at himself as if he were a separate person he thought "that's gonna hurt." This short period of dissociation illustrates how dissociation can help the person escape from psychological stress, although the man in this case was the first to admit that the emotional numbing did not last long enough.

It should be noted that dissociation does not involve the use of psychoactive chemicals. This state is achieved by the mind itself. In its most extreme form, the individual might manifest more than one personality[19]. This was once called the "multiple personality disorder" and is now called the *dissociative identity disorder* (DID). Approximately one-third of patients with DID have a coexisting SUD (Putnam, 1989). CNS depressants such as alcohol or the benzodiazepines are the most commonly abused substances by patients with DID, although on rare occasions the CNS stimulants are also abused. Hallucinogens do not seem to be a popular class of drugs to be abused for this subpopulation for unknown reasons (Putnam, 1989). Substance abuse by

---

[16]This study refers to *lifetime* prevalence rate, where Kushner et al. (2011) only spoke of anxiety disordered persons who had abused a drug in the previous 12 months. This accounts for the discrepancy between the figures used by each set of authors.

[17]See Glossary.

---

[18]Discussed in more detail in Break Out Discussion # 2.

[19]Although controversial, there are well-documented cases where the refraction of the eye changes between personalities: One personality might require eyeglasses and another personality not require glasses, or might require a different prescription for the lenses. There are also documented cases where one personality is anesthetized for surgery and suddenly a second, totally unexpectedly personality sits up in the middle of the operation and demands to know what the doctors and nurses are doing to them.

patients with DID does tentatively appear to fit the self-medication hypothesis discussed elsewhere in this text (Putnam, 1989). It does appear that there are differences between the "normal" patient with an SUD and a patient with a coexisting DID and SUD. The latter group of patients usually do not report reduced discomfort at the end of detoxification, but may report continued distress or even higher levels of distress following detoxification. The reason(s) for this are not known at the present time.

Obsessive-Compulsive Disorder (OCD)

This is the fourth most common psychiatric disorder found in the United States. Researchers disagree about the percentage of patients with OCD who have a concurrent SUD. Encrenaz et al. (2009) offered an estimate of 11.5% of men and 5.5% of women with OCD having a concurrent SUD. Drawing on another example, Goldsmith and Garlapati (2004) estimated that up to 36% of those persons with OCD will have a concurrent SUD. There does not appear to be a specific compound favored by individuals with OCD, although theoretically patients with OCD might be drawn to the CNS depressants with anxiolytic properties such as alcohol or the benzodiazepines.

Bipolar Affective Disorders

The bipolar affective disorders, or what was once called *manic-depression,* represent a complicated set of interlocking conditions that are still not clearly understood by clinicians. Problem drinking by persons with a bipolar disorder is associated with poor medication compliance, increased functional impairment, and possibly increased risk of suicide (Goulding & Fleming, 2011). The manifestations of this disorder can be exacerbated by the abuse of compounds such as the amphetamines, alcohol, and cannabis (Maremmani et al., 2010). Further, the process of withdrawing from the various drugs of abuse can induce either mania or depression even in the normal person and for the individual with a bipolar disorder the process of withdrawal can exacerbate the individual's preexisting psychiatric distress (Sonne & Brady, 2002; Suppes & Keck, 2005).

It has been estimated that between 40 and 70% of patients with a bipolar disorder will also demonstrate symptoms of an SUD at some point in their lives (Brown, 2005; Nery & Soares, 2011; Ostacher & Sachs, 2006; Tolliver, 2010). Substance abuse by these

dual-diagnosis patients appears to be a factor in the need for more frequent hospitalizations, less effective symptom control, and in an increased failure rate for therapeutic intervention for either condition (Maremmani et al., 2010; Nery & Soares, 2011; Sadock & Sadock, 2007; Tolliver, 2010). One reason for the increased rate of treatment failures is the possibility that the sense of confidence and enthusiasm often seen during the manic stage is often interpreted by rehabilitation center staff as treatment progress rather than a symptom of mania (Maremmani et al., 2010).

Clinical research suggests that substance abusers with a bipolar disorder tend to use more drugs of abuse during the manic phase of their condition, although an exception to this rule is the alcoholic with a bipolar affective disorder (Maremmani et al., 2010). It has been hypothesized that some patients might use CNS stimulants such as cocaine to simulate the manic phase of a bipolar disorder to prolong the sense of power and invulnerability experienced during the earlier phases of mania. In contrast, alcohol-dependent persons who are in the depressed phase of a bipolar disorder drink more than they do at other times, possibly in an attempt to "numb" themselves to their emotional pain (Maremmani et al., 2010).

Persons with concurrent bipolar and SUDs are also at high risk for other psychiatric problems such as GAD, panic disorder, and PTSD. For reasons that are not known persons with a concurrent bipolar affective disorder and a substance use disorder are also five times as likely to contract the hepatitis C virus[20] as persons who do not suffer from a bipolar disorder (Tolliver, 2010). One possible explanation is that persons in the manic phase are more likely to engage in high risk behaviors such as unprotected sex, exposing themselves to the virus more often than the average person.

In the bipolar-substance-abusing person, the depression that is often induced by the withdrawal process might serve as a relapse "trigger"[21] (Weiss, 2005). To complicate matters, persons with a concurrent bipolar disorder and an SUD are likely to deny their illness, making accurate diagnosis impossible (Tolliver, 2010). It is imperative that the clinician have an *accurate* clinical history to help determine whether the observed symptoms predate or emerged after the patient started to abuse chemicals (Minkoff, 2008). Collateral information

---

[20]Discussed in Chapter 26.

[21]Discussed in Chapter 34.

is often of value during the formulation of a differential diagnosis and formulation of treatment approaches (Minkoff, 2008; Ostacher & Sachs, 2006). Pharmacological treatment often involves the use of mood stabilizing medications, which have been proven to be safe and effective in the treatment of bipolar disorders (Maremmani et al., 2010). Unfortunately, there are few treatment guidelines for working with the person with a concurrent bipolar affective disorder and SUD. Pharmacotherapy[22] must be carefully initiated and monitored to ensure optimal response to the pharmaceuticals being used to treat both disorders.

Depression

The experience of depression, especially major depression, affects approximately 15 million people in this country (Horstman, 2010). The subjective experience is one of profound sorrow, pain, hopelessness, and despair. Research has shown that depressed individuals are at increased risk for the development of an SUD: 21% of those who have experienced depression in the last year also have an AUD, and 9% met the diagnostic criteria for a drug use disorder (Wells, Paddock, Zhang, & Wells, 2006). Over the course of their lifetime, 27% of patients with a major depression, and 31–43% of patients with dysthymia, will have an active SUD at some point in their lives (Evans & Sullivan, 2001; Goldsmith & Garlapati, 2004; McIlveen, Mullaney, Weiner, Diaz, & Horton, 2007). There is a marked gender gap between men and women with depression. Fourteen percent of men who are depressed also have an SUD, as opposed to just 5.8% of depressed women (Encrenaz et al., 2009). This discrepancy might reflect the tendency for women to seek professional help with depression more often than do men.

There is a strong financial incentive to identify and effectively treat patients with concurrent depression and SUDs. The amount of money spent treating patients with comorbid dysthymia and an SUD was five times higher than that necessary to treat a patient with only a SUD (Westermeyer, Eames, & Nugent, 1998). Further, untreated depression is a possible "relapse trigger" following detoxification for patients with comorbid depression and SUDs (McIlveen et al., 2007; Nunes & Levin, 2006). Although clinical lore holds that persons with an AUD are more prone to major depression, a more common pattern is that

individuals with major depression are at increased risk for the development of an AUD (Fergusson, Boden, & Horwood, 2009). Unfortunately, the treatment of concurrent depression and substance abuse is rather complicated in that the abuse of chemicals within this patient population can either exacerbate their depression or negate the effects of prescribed medications that are designed to help treat their depression. The reverse is also true: Untreated depression complicates the treatment of the SUDs (Wells et al., 2006).

To identify individuals with a primary depression,[23] it is necessary to obtain a detailed, comprehensive, psychiatric history (Minkoff, 2008; Nunes & Levin, 2006). This history will reveal whether the depression predated the SUD or developed after the individual began to abuse chemicals. However, in cases where the individual has a long-standing SUD, this differentiation might not be possible. In all cases the SUD should be addressed immediately, although the health care professional(s) continuously monitor the patient's status against the possibility that she or he has a primary depression that might have been masked by the SUD (Minkoff, 2008).

Eating Disorders

Although eating disorders are predominantly found in girls, adolescent girls, or women, there is a small subgroup of men who also have one form of an eating disorder or another.[24] There is a known relationship between the eating disorders and the AUDs, and each complicates the treatment of the other (Cohen & Gordon, 2009). The relationship between the eating disorders and the other forms of drug abuse is not clear at this time. It is known that persons with an eating disorder often use alcohol to suppress their appetite, avoid or suppress food "urges" (Cohen & Gordon, 2009). Because many of the other drugs of abuse suppress appetite or make the user "numb" to the sensation of hunger, it is not unreasonable to expect that some persons with an eating disorder use these compounds for the same reasons.

It has been suggested that the eating disorders are a form of self-medication of emotional distress, although

---

[22]Discussed in Chapter 33.

[23]As opposed to a substance-induced depression.

[24]There are several subtypes of eating disorders. The topic of eating disorders and the recognition of each subtype is beyond the scope of this text. The reader is referred to any of a growing number of books on the topic of eating disorders for more information.

this theory has not met with universal acceptance (Cohen & Gordon, 2009). It has also been suggested that the AUDs and eating disorders are different manifestations of a self-regulatory mechanism(s), although the exact causal mechanisms for either condition remains uncertain. It has been found that less than 20% of publicly funded substance abuse rehabilitation programs screen for eating disorders, and that only a small percentage of treatment programs have the ability to treat persons with co-occurring eating disorders and SUDs (Cohen & Gordon, 2009). As should be obvious by now, there is much to be discovered about the relationship between the eating disorders and SUDs, as well as the treatment of these conditions when they are both found in the same person.

Compulsive Gambling

Compulsive gambling was long viewed as a "behavioral addiction", which in moderation is not itself a sign of psychopathology. However, since compulsive gambling initiates the reward cascade in much the same way that the drugs of abuse do, it is now classified as an addictive disorder. The vast majority of the population will gamble at one time or another, even if the stakes are as small as the cost of a can of soda. However, about 2–7% of those who gamble do so compulsively, placing them at risk for a wide range of psychosocial and possibly legal problems (Grant, Kushner, & Kim, 2002; Nordstrom & Williams, 2012; Potenza, Fiellin, Heninger, Rounsaville, & Mazure, 2002). Further, there is a significant overlap between the SUDs and compulsive gambling. Compulsive gamblers are thought to be two to four times as likely to have an AUD as the average person (Grant et al., 2002), and 44% of compulsive gamblers will admit to an AUD at some point in their lives (Grant et al., 2002). Both disorders can initiate the reward cascade in the brain. Once initiated, the reward cascade potentially can become a relapse trigger for the other disorder.

A popular belief is that the negative experiences (financial losses) incurred while gambling entices the individual to use chemicals to make themselves "numb" to the emotional pain of their financial distress. Surprisingly, there is little correlation between the amount of money lost and the intensity of the individual's depression (Unwin, Davis, & De Leeuw, 2000). If the individual has lost a significant amount of money, then there is a danger of suicidal thinking, if not suicide attempts by the client. Long-term rehabilitation involves

confronting the individual's irrational beliefs about both substance use and gambling, and helping the gambler develop a coping style to address both problems. Self-help groups such as Gamblers Anonymous (GA), modeled after similar groups for alcohol and other drugs are often of value in this effort. However, clinicians must keep in mind that the compulsive gambling disorders frequently coexist with the SUDs, and that each condition can complicate the treatment of the other.

Personality-Disordered Clients

It has been estimated that 50–60% of clients with an SUD have a concurrent personality disorder[25] (Work Group on Substance Use Disorders, 2007). Individuals with a personality disorder and an SUD are overrepresented in the population of patients with SUDs, as evidenced by the study by Echeburua, de Medina, and Aizpiri (2005). The authors concluded that 40% of individuals with an AUD also met the diagnostic criteria for a personality disorder, but only 6% of the control sample were found to have a personality disorder (Echeburua et al., 2005). The most common subgroup were those individuals with a dependent personality disorder (13% of their research sample), followed by the paranoid personality disorder and the compulsive personality disorder (10% each), according to the authors.

Antisocial Personality Disorder and SUDs[26]

Over the course of their lives, just under 6% of the men and 1.2% of the women will meet the diagnostic criteria for ASPD (Daghestani, Dinwiddie, & Hardy, 2001). There is a great deal of overlap between ASPD and the SUDs. This single personality disorder accounts for 23% of the overlap between personality disordered clients and substance-abusing clients (Grekin, Sher &

---

[25]To learn more about the concept of personality disorders, the reader is referred to the *DSM-5* (American Psychiatric Association, 2013) or a good psychopathology textbook.

[26]MacKenzie (2012) observed that 25% of the population has evidence of exposure to *Toxoplasma,* a parasite that usually infects cats and mice. In humans this parasite can cause increased recklessness and reduced conscientious both of which are characteristic of persons with the antisocial personality disorder. Flegr (quoted in Walters, 2013) provided preliminary evidence that infection with this parasite can influence human behavior. This raises questions in the mind of the author about the possibility of a relationship between the toxoplasma infection and ASPD, as well as a possible relationship between toxoplasma infection and the SUDs. These observations are speculative on the part of the author but are worthy of consideration.

TABLE 24-2
Subgroups of Antisocial Disordered Clients

SUBGROUP	PERCENTAGE OF TOTAL SAMPLE	CONDUCT DISORDER IN CHILDHOOD?	CHARACTERISTICS
Early onset, strong ASPD features	10%	Yes	Meets *DSM-IV-TR* criteria for diagnosis of ASPD
Late onset, strong ASPD features	12%	Yes, but not as often as the above group	Antisocial personality disorder symptoms do not appear until adulthood. Individual will have only minor childhood behavioral problems.
Emotionally unstable ASPD subgroup	18%	Moderate history of childhood conduct disorder	Hostility, guilt, dependent behaviors, avoidant features all begin to manifest in adulthood
Non-ASPD/substance-induced features	17%	Rarely	Substance-induced ASPD features
Moderate substance abuse/ moderate ASPD features	15%	Rarely	ASPD features intermixed with low levels of guilt or depression and some substance-induced distress
Low ASPD	28%	Rarely	Rare reports of antisocial behaviors in adulthood

SOURCE: Based on Alterman et al. (1998).

Wood, 2006). Persons with ASPD who experiment with alcohol or illicit drugs have been found to engage in substance abuse at an earlier age, and are 21 times as likely to have an AUD than the average person (Moeller & Dougherty, 2001; Mueser et al., 2003). Nor is the overlap limited to the AUDs: Up to 48% of those individuals with a cocaine use disorder, 48% of those with an opiate use disorder, and up to 62% of polydrug abusers have ASPD (Vaglum, 2003). Alterman et al. (1998) examined the relationship between ASPD and opioid use disorders and found that in their sample of 252 individuals in a methadone maintenance program diagnosed with ASPD, there were six subgroups of patients as shown in Table 24-2.

As was noted in Table 24-2, for at least some persons the observed ASPD features may be a reflection of a substance-induced condition rather than a true personality disorder (Alterman et al., 1998; Evans & Sullivan, 2001). The lifestyle imposed on the individual by substance abuse may induce what at first glance appears to be an ASPD. Such individuals might be viewed as having an "acquired" personality disorder. Unlike persons with true ASPD, these individuals experience psychiatric distress such as anxiety and/or depression and might be able to benefit from substance

abuse rehabilitation programs (Evans & Sullivan, 2001; Modesto-Lowe & Kranzler, 1999).

Borderline Personality Disorder and SUDs

The borderline personality disorder (BPD) is often an enigma both to the mental health professional and the layperson. Clinically, individuals with BPD alternate between over-idealization of significant others and total rejection and distrust of the same person after a perceived slight or rejection.[27] They do, however, share the characteristic of impulsiveness and overemphasis on their own perceived "rights," as does the antisocial personality-disordered client, and are often misdiagnosed as having ASPD. Perhaps 30–50% of persons with an SUD will also have BPD (Work Group on Substance Use Disorders, 2007). The role of the chemical(s) varies from person to person with BPD, but for many alcohol or drugs of abuse help to make them calm the emotional fires within or distract them from their emotional pain. Substance abuse rehabilitation for persons with this disorder is often difficult and labor

[27]A therapist arriving 5 minutes late for a session might serve as sufficient provocation for a person with BPD to become angry and mistrust the therapist for an extended time afterwards for example.

intensive, requiring a commitment on the part of the therapist to continue to work with the client possibly for as long as a decade or more.[28]

Mixed Personality Disorders

Very few individuals present a "pure" personality disorder in which their personality type meets the diagnostic criteria for only one of the many personality disorders. Most personality disordered individuals present symptoms from two or more personality subtypes, although primarily from one personality type. Top date the most common diagnosis is that of a mixed personality disorder. A hypothetical person with histrionic personality disorder might have some ASPD traits and possibly some compulsive personality traits to cite one possible pattern. Experienced clinicians usually have seen many different combinations of personality traits intermixed in substance-abusing client.

Dual Diagnosis/Victimization Issues

There is a significant overlap between SUDs and a history of past or current victimization[29] (Carr & Szymanski, 2011; Smith, Homish, Leonard, & Cornelius, 2012). Such patients present a therapeutic dilemma to substance abuse rehabilitation professionals. Although it is thought to be necessary for individuals to come to terms with their abuse history as part of their recovery program (Cohen, 2000; Sinha, 2000), most substance abuse rehabilitation programs lack the resources, time, or treatment staff with sufficient training to help the individual address this issue (Blume, 2005; Cohen & Hien, 2006).

It is a mistake to assume that the victimization caused the SUD. Such a viewpoint reflects *post hoc, ergo propter hoc* ("after this, therefore because of this") reasoning (Lilienfeld, Lunn, Ruscio, & Beyerstein, 2010). This is not to deny that sexual abuse does not cause emotional

suffering, but the theory that childhood sexual abuse causes personality changes or SUDs later in life is not supported by the clinical literature.[30] In some cases, the SUD preceded the individual's victimization (Brook, Pahl, & Rubenstone, 2008). Because there are many factors that can cause or exacerbate an SUD, rehabilitation center staff must carefully access the relationship between the individual's SUD and victimization. This further underscores the need for gender-specific treatment programs. Women who have been victimized by a male might feel inhibited in a mixed group setting (McCrady, 2001). Further, the language used by many men in treatment is often offensive, if not demeaning, to women, contributing to a higher dropout rate for women in mixed group settings as opposed to gender-specific programs. Further, traditional substance abuse rehabilitation programs, following the example set by 12-step programs such as Alcoholics Anonymous,[31] place great emphasis on surrender and submission. Women with victimization issues find this to be difficult, if not impossible, to accept.

Posttraumatic Stress Disorder

Although not all forms of physical or sexual abuse result in the development of posttraumatic stress disorder (PTSD),[32] there does appear to be a relationship between the SUDs and exposure to situations that can induce PTSD. As is true for many forms of psychological distress, there is a marked discrepancy between the percentage of men and of women who develop this disorder. Women appear to develop PTSD about twice as often as men (Najavits, 2010). Whereas 20% of substance-abusing men report having experienced some form of serious sexual, physical, or emotional trauma, between 30 and 60% of substance-abusing women report having suffered through such life experiences (Finnegan & Kandall, 2008; Ross, 2008).

The individual who suffers from PTSD presents a difficult challenge to the treatment team. The adaptive mechanisms seen in PTSD often are interpreted by the individual as evidence that they are losing their mind and often make others uncomfortable. For example, the exaggerated startle reaction often seen in persons with PTSD is not a sign that they are losing their mind, but a common reaction to traumatic experiences. Clients

---

[28]The author has found that the *Addiction Treatment Planner* by Robert R. Personson and Arthur E. Jongsma provides many useful treatment goals for the counselor with a client with BPD.

[29]The reader should keep in mind that men are occasionally the *victim* of abuse and *not* the perpetrator. Male victims of abusive relationships are often reluctant to step forward because this is not consistent with social role expectations that the man be able to defend himself, especially from a female aggressor.

[30]This theory is commonly repeated in "pop" psychology and self-help books, and appears to survive because (a) it has been repeated so often that people come to believe it must be true (or why would people still be saying it?) and (b) it is a simplistic answer to a social problem.

[31]Discussed in Chapter 35.

[32]The topic of posttraumatic stress disorder (PTSD) is very complex and lies outside of the scope of this text. The reader is referred to Sadock and Sadock (2007) for more information about PTSD.

who have been exposed to interpersonal violence (IPV) frequently have postassault distrust of others, presenting an additional challenge to rehabilitation professionals. Victims of PTSD often turn to alcohol or illicit drugs to self-medicate their intrusive thoughts about the traumatic event, emotional "numbing," nightmares, and mood swings.[33] Unfortunately, the individual's SUD might predate the development of PTSD or even be a precipitating factor in the traumatic event that forms the core of PTSD.[34]

Systematic research into the percentage of patients with PTSD who attempt self-medication through the use of alcohol and illicit drugs is lacking. However, the team of Simpson, Stappenbeck, Varra, Moore, and Kaysen (2012) did find a relationship between the individual's experience of PTSD symptoms and alcohol use by their research subjects. The authors found that those subjects who experienced PTSD-induced exaggerated startle responses and increased anger/irritability were most likely to experience same-day craving for alcohol, whereas persons who experienced PTSD-related nightmares, emotional numbing, and PTSD-related hypervigilance were more likely to "crave" alcohol the next day.

Pharmacotherapy with clients with PTSD is difficult. The benzodiazepines are thought to either have no effect on posttraumatic anxiety or possibly even contribute to the development of posttraumatic anxiety because of the dissociative effect induced by this class of medications (Shalev, 2009). Cognitive-behavioral therapies (CBT), possibly combined with relaxation training and coping skills training, have shown promise in assisting individuals with PTSD; however, the research evidence for the effectiveness of such interventions is mixed (Shalev, 2009). A treatment team approach such as the integrated treatment team model discussed above might offer some promise in working with these individuals, especially because research suggests that if therapists focus only on the SUD that it is unlikely that the patient will experience much relief from their PTSD symptoms (Najavits, 2010).

The loss of hope in PTSD is one of the more damaging aspects of this disorder, thus establishing one therapeutic goal for the client at the outset of therapy (Najavits, 2010). However, in spite of these insights into the nature of PTSD and possible treatment approaches to help the client come to terms with past trauma, these clients will continue to present unique challenges to health care professionals, and rehabilitation workers must keep abreast of the latest developments in PTSD treatment to be able to assist their clients.

Problems in Working with the Dual-Diagnosis Client

The dual-diagnosis client is often difficult to work with. Their motivation for substance abuse rehabilitation will vary from individual to individual, but as a group they tend to request substance abuse treatment only as a result of personal/family/legal problems (Goldsmith & Garlapati, 2004). Often, they present with combinations of problems. Unfortunately, treatment resources (such as dedicated treatment programs for dual-diagnosis clients, financial support for treatment, etc.) are woefully scarce (Pepper, 2004). Dual-diagnosis clients frequently have fragile support systems, and 12-step support groups frequently are intolerant of the special needs of this population of persons. For example, many 12-step support groups view the use of any prescribed mood-altering medications as an indication that the client is substituting one addiction for another (Evans & Sullivan, 2001). Further, dual-diagnosis clients often feel out of place in 12-step groups, especially in the earlier stages of rehabilitation (Petrakis et al., 2002). Thankfully, there is a move to establish "double trouble" or dual-diagnosis 12-step support groups in many communities.

Many dual-diagnosis clients demonstrate a special form of denial that can be (for want of a better term) called *free floating* or *interchangeable denial*. This form of denial involves the utilization of one problem to defend the other. Thus, if a health care professional should attempt to focus attention on their psychiatric condition, they will express a desire to talk about their SUD. If a substance abuse rehabilitation professional should attempt to address the client's SUD, they will talk about their mental illness issues. A variation of this process is when patients with a dissociative disorder attribute their loss of memory (experienced when

---

[33]The reader is referred to the current edition of the *Diagnostic and Statistical Manual of Mental Disorders* (5th edition) (American Psychiatric Association, 2013) for a full listing of the diagnostic criteria for this condition.

[34]The individual's abuse of alcohol and/or illicit drugs might make them more vulnerable toward being victimized or lower inhibitions sufficiently that the individual then engages in violent behaviors that are atypical for them.

one personality is forced out of the seat of consciousness so that another might take over) to chemicals rather than to the process of dissociation.

To complicate matters, many health care professionals view dual-diagnosis clients as being primarily substance-abusing patients who require substance abuse treatment. At the same time, many substance abuse treatment professionals view the same individuals as being psychiatric patients. The deplorable outcome of this professional blindness is that the patient might be bounced between chemical dependency and psychiatric treatment programs (Minkoff, 2008). This is a legacy of the federal drug treatment initiatives of the 1970s and 1980s, which established a number of different agencies focused on the identification and rehabilitation of substance abusers (Osher & Drake, 1996). Responsibility for supervision and development of psychiatric treatment programs was assigned to a different series of federal agencies, and for the most part interdepartmental communication and cooperation was virtually nonexistent.[35] As a result of this process, it is the rare staff psychiatrist in a treatment facility that understands that intense emotions generated by psychiatric distress can serve as relapse triggers for the dual-diagnosis patient (Goldsmith & Garlapati, 2004). Further, in their efforts to ease the client's distress, the attending physician might administer potentially addictive compounds to the client with the best of intentions, but with little insight into how these compounds might complicate the individual's recovery from their SUD.

Traumatic Brain Injury and SUDs[36]

The term *traumatic brain injury* (TBI) is a nebulous term often used synonymously with the terms *head trauma* or *head injury*. Currently the abbreviation "TBI" is used to identify all possible injuries to the brain possibly found in the person who has experienced injury to the brain. The term *head* trauma *is not synonymous* with traumatic brain injury. By definition TBIs are a subset of head injuries, specifically reserved for events that cause injury to the tissues of the brain. Such injuries exist on a continuum from very mild to life threatening. In addition what initially appeared to be a mild TBI could, with the passage of time, prove to be life threatening. The outcome of a TBI can range from complete recovery to permanent disability or the death of the victim.

Physicians often assess the severity of a traumatic brain injury using the Glasgow Coma Scale (GCS), which attempts to measure the individual's level of consciousness on a scale of 3 to 15. The individual's ability to respond to verbal commands ("Open your eyes!"), to engage in voluntary movement ("Move your left hand!"), and to provide information ("What is your name?") are rated. Lower scores reflect more severe traumatic brain injuries, because the individual would be unable to respond to the verbal commands. TBIs are then classified as mild (GCS scores of 13 to 15), moderate (GCS scores of 9 to 12), and severe (GCS scores of 3 to 8). In spite of its widespread use the GCS score has only a limited ability to predict ultimate outcome.

By about this point the student is starting to wonder why all of this information is of importance to a text on SUDs. The answer is simple: Persons with SUDs are at high risk for TBIs. Research suggests that 29–58% of patients admitted to hospitals with a TBI have alcohol in their systems at the time of admission (Miller & Werner, 2011). As a result of the disruption of protective mechanisms such as the blood–brain barrier, active alcohol use can enhance neural damage suffered by the individual who has a TBI (Miller & Werner, 2011). Few studies have specifically examined the role that the drugs of abuse play in causing or contributing to traumatic brain injury, but it should be assumed that they are also potentially causal agents in TBI.

The effects of the TBI vary from one individual to the next, depending on the (a) cause of the brain injury, (b) location of the injury, (c) extent of the injury, and the (d) individual's level of function before the injury. A patient with a mild concussion suffered while playing football will usually have different presenting symptoms than a patient who suffered a major TBI in a motor vehicle accident, for example. In addition, the degree of recovery will vary from one patient to the next, although the greater the damage to the brain the less likely it is that the individual will return to their preinjury level of function. A formerly high functioning student might, after suffering a serious TBI, struggle to perform simple mathematics problems or even to sign their name. This hypothetical student, whose life once held such promise, might now require lifelong psychosocial support. There are also often postinjury changes in personality that might push preinjury relationships beyond the breaking point. This hypothetical student might refuse to

---

[35]A trend that, unfortunately, appears quite prevalent in most large organizations.

[36]The subject of TBIs is worthy of a large book in its own right. The reader is referred to any of a large number of neurology or neuropsychology textbooks.

acknowledge the role that chemicals played in their injury and might conceivably not understand that he or she has suffered a TBI.

Denial is a difficult problem for persons who work with individuals who have suffered a TBI. Preinjury or postinjury cognitive deficits might not allow the individual to understand the relationship between these two disorders. The individual might have developed retrograde amnesia[37] to develop as a result of the TBI: The person might not remember consuming alcohol or illicit drugs before their injury. The individual might be reluctant to give up recreational chemicals, which they have come to accept as a way to adjust to their new lives. If they should continue to abuse chemicals they might discover that they have developed a medication (or chemical) sensitivity, experiencing stronger reactions to these chemicals than a person of the same age who had not experienced a TBI. Their apparent denial might be a reflection of the therapeutic relationship and their lack of trust in the therapist.

The self-medication hypothesis would appear at face value to have some validity with this subpopulation: It has been suggested that patients with TBIs might turn to alcohol or drugs as a way to self-medicate their frustration. Persons who have suffered a TBI might with justification feel that they are "different" from others. Alcohol and/or illicit drug abuse offers them one avenue through which they can associate with others. An unfortunate social attitude is that the person with a TBI is entitled to abuse alcohol or illicit drugs because of what they have endured as a result of their TBI. Substance abuse rehabilitation professionals who work with individuals with co-occurring SUDs and TBIs should be well versed in each condition. For example, medical staff must differentiate between legitimate medication requests by the individual to treat medical or psychiatric conditions and drug seeking by that person, often. A concurrent treatment approach, adjusted to the individual's level of function and possible altered mental abilities, is the best treatment approach.

Postconcussion Syndrome (PCS)

Persons who have suffered a concussion represent a subgroup of traumatic brain injury cases. For years physicians had been taught that the individual who had suffered a mild concussion returned to their baseline level of function within a few minutes to at most hours. In the last 15 years it has been discovered that the effects of even a mild concussion persisted for longer than this. Persons who had suffered a mild concussion often developed mild cognitive problems, fatigue, dizziness, headaches, and personality changes that generally resolve in the first weeks or months after the person suffered the concussion. In some cases the post injury changes might last a year or longer. The prognosis is worse if the person had suffered a loss of consciousness at the time of the injury. Often, especially in cases of mild postconcussion syndrome, the postinjury cognitive deficits are detectable only on neuropsychological testing. However, as the severity of the TBI resulting in a concussion increases the possibility of more severe cognitive damage and personality change increases.

PCS is influenced by a range of factors, some of which are generic to all cases of TBI. Other factors include (but are not limited to) the individual's preinjury personality, secondary gain from the injury (being excused from work or school assignments, or attempts to avoid pending legal charges, for example), and litigation possibly is pending as a result of the injury. All cases of known or suspected PCS should be referred to a neuropsychologist or neurologist for assessment and treatment recommendations, and substance abuse rehabilitation professionals who work with persons with PCS should be trained in this specialty before attempting to work with these individuals.

Dual-Diagnosis Clients and Medication Compliance

As will be discussed in Chapter 33, medication compliance is a problem for all medical patients. This topic is discussed separately in this chapter because of the special nature of dual-diagnosis persons. As a group, dual-diagnosis clients are 8.1 times more likely to be noncompliant with their medication(s) as are traditional psychiatric clients (Drake, 2007). This complicates the treatment of both their psychiatric and SUDs. Medication noncompliance might be expressed in a variety of ways, such as (a) refusing to take prescribed medications, (b) continuing to use alcohol and/or illicit drugs, or (c) selectively taking only those medications that will provide the desired effects.[38] To avoid potentially dangerous

---

[37]See Glossary.

[38]Another issue, discussed in Chapter 33, is the inability to afford prescribed medications. Because this does not reflect willful noncompliance it will not be discussed further in this chapter.

interactions, some dual-diagnosis clients will discontinue psychiatric medications in anticipation of recreational drug use. The most common reason for these behaviors is not to self-medicate psychiatric distress or avoid unpleasant side effects, but simply to enjoy the "high" experienced through recreational chemical abuse.

It was noted in the last paragraph that sometimes dual-diagnosis clients will selectively refuse certain medications: Many psychiatric medications have a significant abuse potential of their own. For example, occasionally an individual will hoard anticholinergic capsules or pills[39] and then ingest them all at once for their psychoactive effects (Buhrich, Weller, & Kevans, 2000). These medications may also potentiate the effects of the amphetamine compound and might be abused for this reason. Dual-diagnosis clients may abuse psychiatric medications when they are unable to access more desired drugs of abuse. Urine toxicology testing[40] is useful in the identification of persons who fail to have prescribed medications in their urine or who have metabolites of recreational drugs in their urine.

Treatment Approaches with Dual-Diagnosis Clients[41]

Dual-diagnosis patients have long been shunned by both the psychiatric and substance abuser rehabilitation communities. Now treatment approaches are starting to emerge to guide professionals in their work with these clients. However, it should be noted that many of these treatment approaches rest not on a foundation of clinical research, but on expert opinion (Watkins et al., 2001) and antidotal case studies. There is a "dearth of empirically sound interventions" for dual-diagnosis clients (Bellack, Bennett, Gearon, Brown, & Yang, 2006, p. 427). To complicate matters, there is strong evidence that access to psychiatric care for substance-abusing clients is becoming more difficult as many treatment centers cut staff to reduce program costs (Knudson, Roman, & Ducharme, 2004) and research funding is increasingly difficult to obtain.

It is believed that the ideal treatment setting for dual-diagnosis clients is an integrated treatment program, in which both the SUD and the individual's psychiatric problems might be addressed simultaneously by treatment professionals from various fields of training who work as a team to help the patient (Busch et al., 2005; Pankiewicz, 2008). Such treatment programs achieve long-term abstinence rates of about 15%, which approximates the abstinence rate achieved in normal clients who enter rehabilitation (Pankiewicz, 2008). Surprisingly, there is little research supporting the advantages of integrated treatment approaches (Weiss, Potter, & Iannucci, 2008). Even if such programs are shown to be effective by future research studies, less than 10% of substance abuse rehabilitation programs offer such combined or integrated treatment formats (Patrick, 2003; Renner, 2004b).

More commonly, dual-diagnosis clients are referred to treatment facilities that use the serial treatment approach (Goldsmith & Garlapati, 2004). In such a program, the most serious issue is addressed until that condition is stabilized and then the client is transferred to a different unit so that the other disorder might be addressed. This might be either a different unit within the same facility or at a different rehabilitation facility entirely. A serious weakness of this treatment approach is that clients rarely follow through and enter the second program (Busch et al., 2005; Mueser et al., 2003). To complicate matters, the "managed care" initiatives of the middle and late 1990s[42] have made admission to one treatment facility difficult at best and referrals from one facility to another almost impossible (Evans & Sullivan, 2001; Mueser et al., 2003; Patrick, 2003). Even if sequential admissions are accomplished, treatment stays allowed under the managed care programs are often inadequate for treatment of either condition. Pankiewicz (2008) estimated that only 5% of dual-diagnosis patients treated in such a series of programs will achieve long-term abstinence.

An alternative to the serial treatment model is the parallel treatment model, in which both conditions are addressed simultaneously, but in different sections of the same facility (Busch et al., 2005). Hypothetically, the client's SUD might be addressed on the second floor of the east wing of a hospital setting, whereas the psychiatric illness is addressed on the fourth floor of the west wing of the same facility. There are numerous drawbacks to this approach, including poor

---

[39]Often prescribed to help control the unpleasant side effects of psychotropic medications being used to treat the mental illness.

[40]Discussed in Chapter 33.

[41]This chapter was written before the details of the Affordable Care Act ("Obamacare") were revealed to the general public. How this new health care initiative will change treatment funding for mental health or substance abuse services is not known at this time.

---

[42]Discussed in the Chapter "Treatment Problems."

communications between treatment staff on each unit and the act of physically moving the patient from one floor to another (where she or he must adjust to the treatment setting again) at a time of special vulnerability. Yet another drawback is that this model interferes with the development of a firm therapeutic relationship between the therapist on one unit and the patient, who upon stabilization, will be transferred to another unit (Drake & Mueser, 2002). Obviously, this makes for an inefficient treatment process and this model is the least effective of the three programs discussed thus far (Drake et al., 2004; Ross, 2008).

The Stages of Treatment

Substance abuse rehabilitation with dual-diagnosis clients is more complicated than with substance-abusing/addicted patients without a concurrent mental illness. The first goal in working with the dual-diagnosis client is the establishment of a good therapeutic relationship (Drake & Mueser, 2002). This task might take a protracted period of time, and the therapist must make every effort to be nonconfrontational, optimistic, empathetic, avoid making moralistic judgments, and work on establishing a therapeutic relationship (Patrick, 2003).

The second phase of treatment is that of persuasion (Drake & Mueser, 2002), or engagement or motivational enhancement/engagement (Geppert & Minkoff, 2004). During this phase of rehabilitation, the rehabilitation staff works to help the client understand the relationship between her or his SUD and psychiatric problems. Issues such as medication noncompliance and its relationship to decompensation and rehospitalization are addressed during this phase. Breaking through the client's denial without causing increased psychiatric distress is also carried out during this phase so that the client might see that abstinence is worthwhile both in reduced hospitalization and because substance abuse is destructive in its own right (Geppert & Minkoff, 2004; Patrick, 2003).

The third phase of rehabilitation is that of active treatment, during which time the staff teach the client coping skills, help her or him find sources of support, and manage his or her illness (Drake & Mueser, 2002). This stage has also been called that of prolonged stabilization: active treatment/relapse prevention (Geppert & Minkoff, 2004). The client is at high risk for relapse during this stage, if only because the motivation inherent in a psychiatric emergency has eased (Drake, 2007).

The use of group therapy is often of value during this phase, although because of the perceived stigma associated with mental illness in the eyes of the clients, it is best that these therapy groups be held on the psychiatric ward of the treatment facility.

One of the advantages of therapy groups is that more experienced patients might share their experience(s) about how even limited alcohol or drug abuse contributed to their psychiatric decompensation, and the problems in living that they encountered the last time that they had finished rehabilitation and returned to independent living. Such groups may reduce rehospitalization rates, although research has demonstrated that dual-diagnosis clients tend to continue to abuse chemicals after discharge from treatment. During the third phase of treatment, relapse prevention becomes a major focus. The patient and treatment staff identify relapse "triggers" that contribute not only to renewed substance use but also to psychiatric decompensation. Another focus is on helping the client learn how to build a substance-free support system, as a failure to establish such a substance-free support system is a major factor contributing to relapse for this population (Swartz et al., 2006).

It should be pointed out that although many of the same techniques developed for use with the average substance abuse client will work with dual-diagnosis clients, there is no single treatment method or intervention that is equally effective with each individual client (Geppert & Minkoff, 2004). Thus, treatment methods and interventions should be individualized, taking into account where the patient is in the recovery process, her or his psychiatric status, and willingness to change (Geppert & Minkoff, 2004). It should be noted that confrontational techniques often used with substance-abusing clients are rarely effective with dual-diagnosis patients, and may even be counterproductive (Ross, 2008). When confrontation is needed, it should be less intense than with more traditional substance-abusing patients.

Once the individual's psychiatric problems have been brought under control, his or her substance-related defenses again begin to operate, and the client will then return to the position of protecting their substance use. Dual-diagnosis clients often believe that once their psychiatric problems are controlled, they are no longer in danger of becoming addicted to the chemical(s) being abused. The client might try to tell the counselor "what she or he wants to hear" rather than what they need to say to address their SUD, or to avoid confrontation that is viewed as being harsh, rejecting, and confrontational by the client. This is why group therapy is so useful during this phase of treatment: Patients are often more willing to listen to another patient who shares her or his experiences with substance abuse following an earlier hospitalization than they are to a counselor. Also, group members are able to problem-solve together, with one patient being able to share his or her wisdom with another as they discuss life's problems.

The Outcome of Treatment

One variable that has been found to affect treatment outcome was the home environment into which the patient was discharged (Stahler, Mennis, Cotlar, & Baron, 2009). Discharging a patient into the environment where they abused chemicals will activate location-triggered substance use cues, and the effects of this are compounded if the patient lives a great distance from 12-step support groups (Stahler et al., 2009). This topic has opened a new avenue for clinical research that might offer insights into improving treatment outcomes.

Although complete abstinence is the desired goal, the program staff must also accept that for most dual-diagnosis clients a major reduction in substance abuse levels might be a more realistic outcome, at least at first. This "harm reduction" approach will limit the amount of damage to the individual and his or her life until she or he can realize the need for abstinence. Progress is often slow, with frequent regressions to an earlier level of functioning. With continued patience, it is often possible for dual-diagnosis clients to discontinue recreational drug and alcohol use over time. But this is the end point of a long, difficult, process for both the client and treatment staff.

Ancillary Issue: Smoking

Statistically, cigarette smokers with mental illness are more likely to die from smoking-related illness than from any other cause (Kalman, 2010). Unfortunately, the already dismal smoking cessation rate for smokers is even worse for smokers with a major mental illness. Dual-diagnosis clients who smoke will, on average, die 20–30 years earlier than their nonsmoking counterparts. Research has demonstrated that smokers with mental illness are 50% less likely to quit smoking as normal patients.

Chapter Summary

The dual-diagnosis client presents a difficult challenge for health care professionals. Once thought to comprise only a small fraction of psychiatric patients, it is now accepted that dual-diagnosis clients are perhaps a majority of those seen in a psychiatric setting. However, diagnosis of concurrent psychiatric and substance problems is complicated by the fact that virtually every symptom of mental illness can be simulated by active substance use or the various withdrawal syndromes. A careful clinical history often is of value in identifying those patients who have a preexisting mental illness as opposed to those whose psychiatric symptoms are induced by the substance abuse or withdrawal.

Clinical evidence suggests that dual-diagnosis clients often use the problems induced by one disorder to protect the other, a process called free-floating denial. If the health care professional attempts to focus on the client's health or psychiatric problems, she or he will shift the focus on to their SUD. If the substance abuse rehabilitation professional attempts to focus on the client's SUD, he or she will try to discuss their health issues, thus blocking therapeutic inquiry into areas that might induce change. However, it is possible to work with dual-diagnosis clients, if the therapist is willing to endure extended periods of minimal progress on the part of the client, if not outright regression. But, over time, it is possible to assist many dual-diagnosis clients to commit to abstinence.

CHAPTER 25

The Biopsychosocial Model of the Addictions

Treat the person with the disease, not the disease in the person.

—*Sir William Osler (1910)*

Introduction

For many years the medical sciences have adhered to the biomedical model of disease, which is an outgrowth of the discovery in the late 1800s that many common disorders were the result of bacterial infections (Johnson, 2012a). Although the biomedical model was instrumental in increasing the life expectancy in the United States from 43 years in 1900 to approximately 77 years for an infant born in 2000, it failed to recognize the psychosocial components of illness. Arguably this could be a reflection of the mind-body dualism that has dominated research in the behavioral sciences and medicine for so many centuries (Shadel & Scharf, 2012).

An unintended consequence of the rigid application of the biomedical model of medicine was that the nature of the substance use disorders was distorted by the perspective of the viewer rather than the nature of the disorder itself. Health care professionals viewed the SUDs as a medical problem, mental health professionals viewed it as a mental health issue, and the substance abuse rehabilitation professionals viewed it as a problem best addressed by them. These territorial disputes serve to confuse the fact that categories of "biological" factors or "psychosocial" factors were artificial constructs to better help the student understand the complex phenomenon of human behavior. These constructs were not intended to be mutually exclusive. Finally, in the last quarter of the 20th century researchers also began to accept that no single factor alone is a reliable predictor of the individual's future substance use behaviors (Winters, Botzet, Fahnhorst, Arria, Dykstra, & Oliver, 2012). In recognition of these facts, the SUDs are now viewed as a common endpoint that reflects the influence of person-specific biological, psychological, and social factors. In this chapter the bio/psycho/social disorder of the addictions will be reviewed.

I. Biology: The "Bio" Part of the Bio/Psycho/Social Model

Definition

The biological components of the bio/psycho/social model are the anatomical, structural, and molecular substrates of a disease, such as the SUDs and the effects of that disorder on the biological functioning of the individual (Sadock & Sadock, 2007).

History

Proponents of the medical, or "disease," model often point out that Dr. Benjamin Rush first suggested that alcoholism was a disease more than 260 years ago.

When he made this observation, a "disease" was classified as something that caused an imbalance in the nervous system (Meyer, 1996). By this standard, SUDs would appear to meet the definition of a "disease" state, although one that is quite different than what Dr. Rush envisioned. The SUDs are now thought to be the result of a biological dysfunction, possibly one on the cellular or even a molecular level, which alters normal biological processes within the body such as the "reward" system.

Process

Nature has provided us with a reward system designed to reinforce behaviors that are to the benefit of the individual or the species: Eating when we are hungry, drinking water when we are thirsty, or taking advantage of opportunities for sex when possible. These are the clearest examples of the role that the reward system provides, however, it is also involved in the feeling of warmth and joy that we feel when reunited with a loved one after a short absence, as well as the pair-bonding process that occurs when a mother and infant gaze into each other's eyes. Once the reward system of the brain is activated, the individual is taught that whatever they just did is important and should be repeated when appropriate.

Unfortunately we do not live only in a "natural" world: We are exposed to various chemicals of our own making that now have the potential to overwhelm our natural neurotransmitter system. By accident certain compounds developed by chemists are capable of creating an intense but false signal in the brain's reward system, memory centers, and the higher cortical areas that control reward-seeking behavior(s). Collectively activation of these regions of the brain gives the false signal that what the individual just did (in this case use a substance of abuse) is really, really, important. This is part of the neurological basis of the pharmacological reward potential of that compound. Strong substance-use memories are formed, helping to shape behavioral decisions that hopefully will lead to further drug-induced rewards (D. Brown, 2006; Bruijnzeel, Repetto, & Gold, 2004; Gendel, 2006; Lewis, 2011). Essentially, a normal biological process that evolved to help early humans survive has been subverted by the reward potential of man-made compounds (Marcus, 2008).

Support for the biological model of the addictions is found in research suggesting under certain conditions the release of the neurotransmitter dopamine in select regions of the brain initiates a neurotransmitter cascade in the reward system that is subjectively experienced as a sense of pleasure. This neurotransmitter cascade also reinforces the effects of Δ FosB[1] especially in the nucleus accumbens region of the brain where Δ FosB is involved in the process of learning on a neural level. In the natural world it is to the individual's advantage to recall cues that identify natural rewards such as food, water, or sex memories that are aided by the action of Δ FosB in the nucleus accumbens. This system is perfectly designed to assist the individual survive in a harsh prehistoric environment where survival was problematic at best and life exceptionally short by our standards. In other words, our bodies are perfectly designed for the paleolithic era, which ended thousands of years ago. This system continued to flawlessly serve our needs until the late 19th and 20th centuries when compound after compound that had abuse potential were isolated or developed. Suddenly society was faced with widespread abuse of chemicals and scientists have struggled to develop a paradigm that would allow them to understand the etiology of this phenomenon and provide a framework within which to treat it. In the next sections we will discuss some of the more influential models that help to shape our understanding and treatment of the SUDs.

Biological Determinism

At its extreme, humans are viewed as biological robots whose behavior is predetermined at the beginning of time. From such a perspective it could be argued that with sufficient knowledge of the interactions of the atoms within the individual's body it would be possible to predict that individual's behavior. However, many of these same biological determinists also take the stance that the mind, which makes decisions about the rewards obtained from past behaviors or which plans future behaviors, is forever unknowable and as such cannot and should not be studied (D.J. Siegel, 2013). This places those biological determinist theorists in the position of affirming that our behavior is biologically predetermined as long as certain convenient truths such as the "mind." are ignored. This fundamental conflict has yet to be resolved by radical biological determinists and more moderate biological determinists do not adopt this interpretation of the human being. Rather the "individual" is usually viewed by moderate biological determinists as being the result of

---

[1]See Glossary.

their biological heritage, current internal environment, and their past and current interactions with the external environment, over which the individual has no control.

Jellinek's work[2]

Archaeologists now believe that by the time that modern humans emerged from Africa circa 100,000 years BCE[3] they knew which fruits and tubers would ferment at certain times of the year to provide a naturally occurring cocktail or two (Tucker, 2011). It is unlikely that alcohol use was problematic during this era because it was so difficult to obtain in even limited quantities. The production of alcohol containing beverages became more standardized by the bronze age, although there are no records to indicate whether the alcohol use disorders were a social problem during the bronze and iron ages. By the late 19th century however alcohol abuse/addiction was a recognized problem for society. Individuals who had an alcohol use disorder (AUD) were viewed as being morally weak, a perspective that will be discussed later in this chapter. In contrast to this belief, the physician E. M. Jellinek (1952, 1960) argued that alcoholism was a disease just like cancer or pneumonia rather than a moral weakness. He reasoned that like other disease states alcoholism presented a specific pattern of symptoms, which in the case of alcohol dependence included (a) a loss of control over one's drinking, (b) a progression of physical and psychosocial problems, and, (c) if left untreated, could cause the drinker's death. Further, Jellinek (1952) argued the addiction to alcohol progressed through four different stages:

1. The pre-alcoholic stage, marked by individual's use of alcohol to self-medicate social tension, frustration, and anxiety. The individual is no longer drinking on a purely social basis, but has started to engage in what is called "relief drinking."
2. If the individual continues to engage in "relief drinking," she or he slips closer to, and their AUD eventually evolves into the prodromal stage. During this phase, the individual begins to demonstrate such alcohol-related problems as "blackouts," guilt over one's behavior while intoxicated, and the urge to hide one's drinking from others.
3. With the continued use of alcohol, the individual eventually becomes physically dependent on alcohol. The individual's self-esteem suffers from his or her alcohol use, and social activities that do not involve the use of alcohol are shunned in favor of alcohol-centered activities. At times, the individual will make an effort to reassert control over alcohol, only to return to abusive drinking again after a period of time.
4. Finally, with continued alcohol use, the individual would enter the chronic stage of alcohol use. During this phase the individual will demonstrate symptoms such as deterioration in morals, the use of alcohol substitutes when ethyl alcohol is not available,[4] the development of psychomotor "tremors" after drinking, and possibly drinking with one's social inferiors.

Jellinek's (1960) model was strongly biased in the direction of biological determinism as evidenced by his belief that once an AUD developed, it was automatically progressive. In his (1960) revision of his earlier work, Jellinek suggested that there were different patterns of alcohol dependence rather than a single pattern of drinking.

This paradigm did offer physicians an alternative to the moral model that had been the generally accepted view of the AUDs for generations. His theory provided a framework within which physicians could (1) classify different patterns of alcohol abuse as opposed to the more restrictive dichotomous view that the person was either alcoholic or not, (2) make the AUDs worthy of study by science, and (3) allow the individual access to medical care. Finally, the Jellinek model attributed the individual's AUD not to a lack of willpower, but to a physical disease state over which he or she had no control (Fletcher, 2013). The Jellinek model is not without its critics, however, and these challenges to this model will be discussed later in this chapter.

The Genetic Inheritance Theories

The genetic inheritance theories are strongly deterministic,[5] although many of their variations accept that the environment also helps to shape behavior. For example, in his discussion of the evolution of homo sapiens, Ian Tattersall (2012) expressed a strong deterministic

---

[2]It is important to note that work only addressed the addiction to alcohol. It has been applied to other forms of chemical dependency as well as some of the behavioral addictions by some clinicians although Jellinek's work was limited only to alcohol.

[3]Which stands for "Before Common Era."

[4]Discussed in Chapter 5.

[5]According to this perspective, you *are* only your genetic heritage.

genetic inheritance stance as evidenced by the following quote:

> *Individual human beings are substantially though not entirely the products of their own particular genomes, coming into the world as broadly the kind of persons they will be as adults ... (Tattersall, 2012, p. 229).*[6]

From this perspective the potential of the environment and life experiences to shape behavior was markedly less decisive than their biological inheritance, an influence over which they had no control. One of the earliest of the research studies supporting the genetic inheritance theory was advanced by Cloninger, Bohman and Sigvardsson (1981, 1996). The authors drew on the extensive records of 3,000 boys adopted shortly after birth from families in which one of the birth parents had an AUD and compared these records against adoptees in which there was no parental AUD The authors found that those adoptees one of whose biological parents had an AUD were themselves more likely to develop an AUD later in life even if adopted within days of birth by parents who did not drink heavily. The adoptees who did develop an AUD in adulthood fell into one of two categories: Group one was comprised of individuals who engaged in the moderate use of alcohol in young adulthood, demonstrated minimal involvement in antisocial behaviors, frequently were depressed, sought social approval, avoided high risk or novel situations, and typically developed an AUD only in later adulthood (Hesselbrock & Hesselbrock, 2007). These individuals were classified as "Type I" (also known as "Late Onset" or "Type 'A'") drinkers.

The second group was composed of individuals who were risk takers, who tended to seek out novelty, engaged in violent behaviors, consumed alcohol for pleasure, and frequently demonstrated an AUD before the age of 25 years (Hesselbrock & Hesselbrock, 2007). These individuals were classified as "Type II" (also called "early onset" or "Type 'B'") alcohol dependence. Statistically the heritability for Type II alcoholism was somewhat higher than Type I alcoholism, suggesting at least some genetic vulnerability that was transmitted

from natural father to the son according to the authors. However, this genetic predisposition was apparently modified by unidentified environmental forces (Tomb, 2008). A similar study completed by Kendler, Sundquist, Ohlssom, Palmer, Maes, Winkleby, and Sundquist (2012) suggested that this pattern was also true for women adopted at birth. Again, the authors drew upon the extensive adoption records maintained in Scandinavia and concluded that drug abuse was significantly higher for adopted offspring of birth parents with an SUD. The authors also noted that various nonspecific social and environmental factors influenced the expression of the suspected genetic predisposition for the development of an SUD. These environmental factors often work through the process known as epigenetics.

Epigenetics

As scientists learned more about the human genome they began to find that the interaction between the individuals' genetic heritage and their environment is more complicated than originally thought. One process through which environmental forces can alter the expression of the individual's genes is known as epigenetics. This new field of study offers the potential for insights not only into the SUD but also a wide range of other neurobehavioral and neurological disorders[7] (Starkman, Sakharkar, & Pandey, 2012). Essentially epigenetics refers to:

> *stable, but potentially reversible, alterations in a cell's genetic information that result in changes in gene expression but do not involve changes in the underlying DNA sequence (i.e., mutations). (Kobor & Weinberg, 2011, p. 300)*

It has been known since the 1950s that DNA molecules form a double helix within the cell nucleus. However, DNA exists only within the nucleus of the cell, making it necessary for a mechanism to exist that would take the genetic information of the DNA through the nucleus wall into the intracellular environment to control the function of that cell. This substance is known as "messenger RNA"[8] (or mRNA), which encodes a portion of the DNA chain necessary to

---

[6]Admittedly the topic of Tattersall's (2012) rather interesting book was on the evolution of the species. However the author of this text submits that his observation about the effects of the individual's genome on their growth is still relevant to the topic of this text.

[7]Which might explain why, if one member of a pair of identical twins has an alcohol use disorder, the probability that the other twin will develop an alcohol use disorder is approximately 50–50, for example.

[8]See Glossary.

instruct the cell to carry out a desired function such as production of different proteins within the cell.

According to the theory of epigenetics molecules known as histones[9] attach to the DNA double helix at what are known as promoter regions, much as the rungs of a ladder are attached to the sides of the ladder at specific attachment points. There are three known families of histones: (a) methylation (which usually blocks expression of a gene), (b) acetylation molecules (which are usually involved in the activation of a gene), and (c) phosphoration molecules, the role of which is still being explored. To continue to use the analogy of a ladder, if a rung of a ladder was to be removed it would be difficult, if not impossible, for a person to climb the ladder beyond that point. In a similar manner, the histone molecules attach to the double helix of DNA, altering the expression of that gene in response to the exposure to the environment, including toxins or stress that the individual might encounter (Nasrallah, 2011; Starkman et al., 2012).

Preliminary evidence suggests that some these critical periods of development include the prenatal period, puberty, and possibly young adulthood. These are time periods when it is thought that alcohol, tobacco, and illicit drugs influence the development of methylation histones that in turn attach to the DNA double helix blocking the full expression of that gene (Starkman et al., 2012; Yi Wong, Mill, & Fernandes, 2010). The messenger RNA is then able to copy only that portion of the DNA molecule not blocked by an inhibitory histone, thus limiting the instructions that it can transmit from the DNA in the nucleus to the cell outside of the nucleus. Epigenetic changes in cellular DNA appear to explain how environmental forces can alter the expression of certain genes.

For reasons that are still unknown the influence of environmentally altered genetic expression does not appear to be limited to one generation. To some degree altered genetic expression can be passed from one generation to the next. For example, Nasrallah (2011) found that men who smoked before puberty ultimately had children with heavier body weights than did men who did not smoke. Further, the author noted, animals subjected to caloric restriction live about 30% longer than those who received normal diets, and their offsprings lived 20% longer on average

even if they were not subjected to caloric restriction. The field of epigenetics is a rapidly evolving field of study that appears to be both deterministic and reflecting environmental influences, and holds the potential to change our understanding of genetically influenced disease states, including the genetic influence on the evolution of the SUDs and whether epigenetic changes in gene expression can be reversed or treated pharmacologically.

Neurobehavioral Theories

Another biological theory that overlaps with biological determinists is the neurobehavioral school of thought. Proponents of these theories maintain that through interactions between the environment and the individual's neurological pathways are established. Neurons that fire together reinforce the neurochemical bonds between those neurons so that they might work as a functional unit more easily when next called upon.[10] Neural networks that are not used are eliminated[11] to reduce the metabolic demands of the brain on the body. According to this theory, drugs of abuse alter the normal neurochemical balance within the central nervous system, especially those involved in the reward system.[12] Theoretically with repeated use of a chemical(s) an association is made between the use of certain chemicals and the initiation of the reward cascade, thus contributing to further substance use.

With repeated activation of the reward cascade the process of over learning[13] is initiated, in this case resulting in reliance on a chemical(s) to achieve that desired state of mind again.[14] The individual also becomes very sensitive to environmental cues associated with substance-induced pleasure ("Addiction and the Problem of Relapse," 2007; Viamontes & Beitman, 2006). This learning process appears to involve the

---

[9]In the hippocampus these compounds appear to be involved in the processes of learning (which is a topic of study in both the fields of neurology and psychology).

[10]If the neurons fire in sequence in response to the same stimuli a neural network is formed.

[11]"Pruned" is the technical term.

[12]Discussed in Chapter 10.

[13]Again, this illustrates the inter-connectedness of the bio/psycho/social model since learning is both a biological process and a psychological process.

[14]Cigarette smoking provides an excellent example of this process: Each time that the smoker inhales, he or she reinforces the neural connections between smoking and pleasure, stress relief, etc. This process might be repeated hundreds of times each day allowing for its over learning.

regions of the brain known as amygdala[15] and hippocampus[16] regions of the brain involved with memory formation. Under normal circumstances, the individual needs to know when not to engage in a specific behavior such as going to obtain water from a nearby river if a predator is in the area. This illustrates how behavior is shaped by a delicate balance of activation and inhibition neural systems, both of which are influenced by memories in the brain. This process plays a role in the survival of the person and contributes to the ongoing process of learning. However, the drugs of abuse trigger a reward cascade that is far more intense than that generated by normal reinforcers and causes the regions of the brain associated with behavioral inhibition (especially the insula region of the brain) become less active, paving the way for repeated abuse of that chemical(s) (Bechara, 2006; Gendel, 2006; Volkow, 2006a).

The Biological Differences Theories

The biological differences theories overlap the neurobehavioral schools of thought. Researchers tried to identify and isolate a biological difference between those individuals who were alcohol-dependent and those who were not. These theories are moderately deterministic in nature and overlap the neurobehavioral theories discussed in the last section. The biological differences theories hold that there are differences either in the brain, or in the way body metabolizes the drugs of abuse, that increases the potential for developing an SUD in certain individuals. There is some evidence to support these theories: Research has shown that after one or two weeks of habitual daily drinking there is a short-term 30% increase in the speed of alcohol biotransformation, allowing the drinkers to consume more alcohol before reaching their desired state of intoxication (Schuckit, 2006b). Individuals whose genetic make-up allows them to produce more of the enzymes alcohol dehydrogenase and aldehyde dehydrogenase would in theory be able to biotransform alcohol more rapidly, encouraging the excessive use of alcohol to reach and maintain a desired state of intoxication (Foroud & Phillips, 2012). However, these findings are preliminary and there is a need for further research in this area.

Another example of the biological differences between substance abusers and nonusers was identified by Nurnberger and Bierut (2007). The authors found

that individuals who were connected to electrodes that measured brain wave activity and were then exposed to a standard stimulus (a strobe light), exhibited a short spike in electrical activity in the brain between 300 and 500 milliseconds after the stimulus began.[17] As a group, it was found that individuals with an AUD and their children had a weaker response to this stimulus than did nondrinkers. Other lines of research suggest that individuals who have been identified as being high risk-takers appear to have different levels of the enzyme monoamine oxidize than their more conservative cousins, and that some behaviors reflect biological predisposition to some degree.

The number of neurons in the brain is not static but is influenced by the processes of neural pruning and neurogenesis[18] suggesting another avenue through which such biological differences might be expressed. It was discovered by Noonan, Bulin, Fuller, and Eisch (2010) that cocaine appears to suppress the process of neurogenesis in the hippocampal region of the brain of adult rats, reducing the growth of new neurons in the hippocampus. This region of the brain is involved in memory formation. The authors postulated that this might be a mechanism through which drug "craving" is generated in former cocaine abusers in the early stages of recovery.[19] Unfortunately, it is not known whether these neurological changes are permanent, although the epigenetic process does suggest that modification if not complete resolution of these changes is possible.

Mark Schuckit's extensive work into the nature of alcoholism (2005, 2006b to cite two of many articles or book chapters on the subject) is often cited as evidence of biological vulnerability toward the SUD, especially the AUDs. This study identified 223 men who were found to have an abnormally low physical response to a standard dose of alcohol. The authors found that 40% of the men raised by a parent with an AUD, but only 10% of the control group, demonstrated this reduced response to a standard dose of alcohol. A decade later, the men were reexamined and it was found that 56% of the men who had an abnormally low response to alcohol at the time of the first test had developed an AUD. This finding was interpreted

---

[15]See Glossary.

[16]See Glossary.

[17]Technically, this is called the *P-300* response.

[18]See Glossary.

[19]It should be kept in mind that the original studies were conducted on rats and not human subjects, and extrapolating from animal studies to human behavior is not always possible.

as evidence that a low physical response to a standard dose of alcohol might serve as a biological "marker" for the later development of an AUD and was called the low level response theory.

Research support for the low level response theory has been mixed (King, deWit, McNamara, & Cao 2011). The authors found that for a subgroup of drinkers alcohol appeared to have a stimulant effect while blood alcohol levels are still rising, a characteristic that King et al. (2011) found to be predictive of future binge drinking. The frequency of binge drinking was in turn found to be predictive of future alcohol use problems according to the authors. The authors speculated that because the earlier studies by Schuckit (1994) did not specify whether the blood alcohol levels of the subjects were rising or falling that the results of this study had been compromised confounding,[20] if not negating the study outcomes (King et al., 2011).

The Dopamine D2 Hypothesis

The dopamine D2 hypothesis overlaps with the "biological differences" school of thought outlined in the last section. There are five known subtypes of dopamine receptors in the human brain (Ivanov, Scholz, Palmero, & Newcorn, 2006). Scientists are still exploring the distribution and function of these subtypes of dopamine receptors and there is evidence suggesting that each subtype of dopamine carries out a different function in specific regions of the brain. Interestingly, the dopamine D2 receptor site appears to serve a regulatory function, controlling the dopamine subtype levels in various other parts of the brain (Murphy, 2012).

There is a growing body of evidence that suggests that individuals with reduced levels of the dopamine D2 receptors might be less sensitive to normal reinforcers such as food, water, and sex (Ivanov et al., 2006; Murphy, 2012). Compound(s) that forces more dopamine into the dopamine D2 receptor sites would in theory increase the level of neural activation to a more normal level that would be experienced as rewarding by the individual. This theory is supported by the observation that cocaine administration increases the level of dopamine in such regions of the brain as the nucleus accumbens[21] by 400–500%, whereas dopamine levels drop below normal in the nucleus accumbens during cocaine withdrawal (Ivanov et al., 2006). Thus research is increasingly pointing to the importance of dopamine, especially the D2

subtype, as a common element in the evolution of the SUDs (Brown et al., 2012).

Neuroimaging Studies

In recent years, it has become possible to peer into the working brain through the use of neuroimaging equipment. One such study was carried out by Goldstein and Volkow (2002). The authors tried to identify a difference(s) between those with an SUD and those who do not have an SUD by measuring the levels of neural activity in the brain and found that the orbitofrontal cortex and the anterior cingulate gyrus, both of which are interconnected with the limbic system, become active when the individual abuses a compound. These regions of the brain are thought to be involved in the process of integration of goal-directed behavior and motivation. It was hypothesized that repeated exposure to drug-use cues would lead the individual to learn to expect certain effects from the use of a chemical, whereas she or he also becomes less and less responsive to normal reward experiences. The authors suggested that individuals with an SUD might over value the reinforcing effects of a substance(s), which when no longer present causes them to focus time and energy in an effort to reacquire these rewards. Although this theory is still in its formative stages, it does appear to account for many of the facets of the SUDs. Trafton and Gilford (2008) also found evidence of altered neural function in such regions of the brain as the amygdala, orbitofrontal cortex, the ventral tegmental area, and the locus ceruleus.[22] Although the authors suggest that these changes account for the behaviors seen in individuals with a physical addiction to a drug(s), it is possible that the observed differences predate the development of the addiction and are not the result of it. As will be discussed later in this chapter, the application of neuroimaging technologies to the study of the addictions has been challenged.

Digestive System

The possible interaction between the brain and the human gastrointestinal tract has long been ignored by mainstream medical researchers. However, the gastrointestinal tract is the only organ system in the body to possess its own neural network[23] (Carpenter, 2012;

---

[20]See Glossary.

[21]This region of the brain is involved in the reward cascade.

[22]Essentially regions of the human brain involved in executive functions, and the limbic system, which is involved in the reward process.

[23]Comprised of approximately 100 million neurons embedded in the wall of the gastrointestinal tract (Carpenter, 2012) known as the enteric nervous system (Young, 2012).

Young, 2012). The enteric nervous system is involved with unconscious perception of environmental threats, the individual's response to such perceived dangers, and the production of stress-induced hormones such as ghrelin[24] (Young, 2012). This raises the possibility that the enteric nervous system might be involved in the risk assessment of substance withdrawal and possibly transmit this information to the brain for evaluation and behavioral response. Clinically this makes sense because the gastrointestinal tract is affected by both alcohol and drug abuse as well as the process of detoxification from the drugs of abuse.[25]

It is now believed that the normal balance of bacteria within the gastrointestinal tract, in combination with the body itself, forms a "super-organism." Many species of bacteria in the gastrointestinal tract produce neurotransmitters such as serotonin,[26] acetylcholine, and melatonin (Carpenter, 2012), which in the brain are involved with the process of memory formation, mood, and learning (Ackerman, 2012; Carpenter, 2012; Young, 2012). Researchers have even discovered that intestinal flora[27] influence brain growth and development in mice. This finding again hints that the bacteria in our gastrointestinal tract influence biological functions elsewhere in the body. Conceivably there could be an interactional process between the intestinal flora and the SUDs.[28] Consider the following: Human beings share 99.9% of the estimated 20,000 to 25,000 genes found in the human genome, so there is relatively little genetic variation between individuals. Yet the genetic makeup of intestinal bacteria can vary by as much as 90% between healthy individuals. Under normal conditions combination of bacteria found in the gastrointestinal tract of any single healthy individual tends to be stable over the course of years if not decades (McGowan, 2012). There are significant differences in the intestinal bacterial growth patterns even between identical twins, which might explain the paradox why if one twin is alcohol-dependent, the odds that

the other twin will also be alcohol-dependent are only about 50-50.

If, as is generally accepted, "information" is encoded on DNA, how much more information might be encoded in the estimated 3.3 million genes found in the estimated 1,000 different species of microorganisms normally found in the human gastrointestinal tract and what is their effect on the enteric nervous system (Ackerman, 2012)? Many of these species of microorganisms have coevolved with humans over tens of thousands of generations and it is unrealistic to think that each evolved separately from the other. The impact of the SUDs on the body's normal balance of bacteria is also not well understood. It is known that heavy drinking alters the normal bacteria balance in the mouth, throat, and gastrointestinal tract, whereas methamphetamine abuse results in alterations in disruptions in the production of saliva and the body's ability to resist infectious diseases. Conceivably these alterations in patterns of bacterial growth in the body might cause or contribute to behavioral changes in the substance abuser, and raises the question whether these substance-related gastrointestinal bacteria growth patterns account for at least part of the user's experience of "craving" drugs or alcohol after achieving abstinence.

The theory that infectious disease might be associated with psychiatric disorders has been entertained by a small number of researchers in the past generation, although their research has yielded mixed results. At least some researchers are starting to explore the possibility that the bacterial growth patterns in the intestinal tract might influence the evolution of physical disease. The team of Scher, Sczesnak Longman, Segata, Ubeda, Bielski, Rostron, Cerundolo, Pamer, Abramson, Huttenhower, and Littman, (2013) found that 75% of those individuals with new onset, untreated, rheumatoid arthritis had evidence of a strain of bacteria known as Prevotella copri in their gastrointestinal tract as contrasted to only 11.5% of those persons with longstanding rheumatoid arthritis. The authors speculated that the presence of Prevotella copri, a strain of bacteria which appears to aid in the inflammatory process, in the gastrointestinal tract of patients with new onset of rheumatoid arthritis could trigger an autoimmune response that is so often a hallmark of this form of arthritis. Currently it is thought that at least some forms of psychiatric disease are also the result of an autoimmune response that is possibly triggered by exposure to an infectious disease (Hornig, 2013). The author speculated that the

---

[24]This in turn triggers the release of dopamine in the brain, which is part of the reward cascade.

[25]This is, however, a hypothesis on the part of the author of this text and has not been investigated by clinical researchers.

[26]Ninety-five percent of the serotonin in the body is found in the gastrointestinal tract.

[27]A term that incorporates all of the micro-organisms in the gastrointestinal tract.

[28]This theory is, however, only speculation on the part of the author.

inconsistent findings found in past research might reflect differing levels of exposure to the causal agent, different levels of exposure, differences in the timing of the host to the infectious disease, or differences in the immune response between individuals who were exposed to the same disease (Hornig, 2013). At this point in time it is not unreasonable to questions whether the individual's vulnerability to an SUD might reflect not only genetic and environmental forces but also exposure to an infectious agent(s) that trigger an autoimmune response targeting specific receptor sites in the brain as well. This is only a speculative hypothesis on the part of the author of your textbook, but one that does offer a novel treatment approach to the addictions if this theory is proven.

Applications of the Biological Component of the Bio/Psycho/Social Model

The central tenet of the biological model of disease states is that information generated by research is subsequently used to develop treatments to treat these conditions. The SUDs are disease states and are treated as such by proponents of the biological theory of addictions. Such treatment has taken four general routes. First there is the pharmacotherapy route, where physicians attempt to alleviate the distress associated with the withdrawal process.[29] A second approach has been to develop pharmaceuticals that might moderate or eliminate the individual's desire to abuse a chemical. Each avenue of treatment has at best met with limited success. A third approach has been to recruit the body's own defenses against drug(s) of abuse (Giles, 2008). Experimental vaccines that prime the immune system to attack cocaine and methamphetamine molecules in the circulation appear to offer promise. Such vaccines will recruit the immune system into attacking the cocaine or amphetamine molecules while they are still in the circulation before they reach the receptor sites in the brain. Theoretically this would eliminate the reward potential for further abuse and make the individual more receptive to psychosocial interventions that are the mainstay of substance abuse rehabilitation at this time.

The final approach being explored within the framework of the medical model is the sequencing of the individual's genome to identify individuals at high risk for the development of an SUD so that these individuals might be targeted for intervention. The exact form of such intervention remains unclear at this time. Some clinicians believe that it might be possible to alter the individual's genome to reduce their risk of developing an SUD. In theory genes that are identified as contributing to the development of an SUD might be replaced by more benign genes, or their expression possibly blocked by artificial epigenetic changes to that gene. An alternative approach would be the development of pharmaceutical agents that would block the expression of the identified genes, again theoretically reducing the individual's risk for developing an SUD. These "treatments" are on the far horizon and might not be realized for generations, although the rapid progress in genetic engineering also suggests that these interventions might become a reality in the next generation or two.

Reactions to the Biological Component of the Bio/Psycho/Social Model

Although the bio/psycho/social model would appear to be comprehensive in scope there are those clinicians who argue that it is the wrong paradigm within which to view psychiatric disorders (including the addictions). Tavakoli (2009) offered five reasons why the bio/psycho/social model is flawed: (1) The biopsychosocial model further dichotomizes the breech between biological models of the SUDs and the psychosocial models of the SUDs. (2) The biopsychosocial model reinforces the stigma associated with mental illness. (3) Poor behavior is not a "disease" as is implied by the bio/psycho/social model, as evidenced by the fact that many forms of poor behavior (such as those demonstrated by antisocial personality disordered persons) cannot be treated by medical science. (4) The term "psychosocial" is poorly defined, leaving the clinician confused about which aspects of the individual's life are relevant social or psychological factors that must be considered in the formulation of a treatment plan. (5) Finally, the author suggests that the model "antagonizes" (p. 27) medical professionals, who then dismiss possible psychological or social contributions to the individual's medical status.

---

[29]Many of the medications used in this process are intended for other conditions and it is only by coincidence that they help with the withdrawal from alcohol or illicit drugs. This is discussed in more detail in Chapter 32.

In spite of Tavakoli's (2009) reservations the bio/psycho/social model has become one of the, if not the, predominant models in the addictions field and as a whole is rarely challenged (Tavakoli, 2009, being an exception). Individual components of the bio/psycho/social model have been challenged in the professional literature, however, and we will examine some of these challenges now.

Philosophical

What do we mean when we say that something is a "disease"? The minister Robert Harris suggested that addictions were disease states in 1619, for example (Heyman, 2011). One must ask whether the meaning of the word "disease" has changed in the 500 years since Reverend Harris classified addictions as a "disease" state (Heyman, 2011). It a disorder classified as a "disease" in the early 17th century, the same as a "disease" in the 21st century?[30] Does the identification of an individual as having an SUD offer the clinician scientific or prognostic information of value in treating the substance abuser or are they just pseudo-scientific labels (Bentall, 2009; Frances, 2013)?

If we attribute the individuals' SUD only to their genetic heritage we absolve them of responsibility for behavioral choices that they make (Frances, 2013). The individual's genetic heritage helps shape what he or she finds rewarding. However, it is the individual's choice to indulge in these experiences or not (Greenstein, 2012). Another challenge to the medical model of the addictions is based on the often repeated statement that the SUDs are chronic, relapsing disorders. This is not true: The SUDs remit at double the rate of other psychiatric disorders (Heyman, 2009).[31] This difference raises questions about the comparison between persistent medical conditions and the SUDs although this fact is quietly ignored by proponents of the disease model as an inconvenient truth.

Methodological

Although initially embraced with great enthusiasm, animal-based research studies in the field of the

addictions have become suspect. Although useful, data drawn from research conducted on animals does not simulate the human condition, and it is difficult to generalize from animal research into much more complex behaviors such as an SUD in an individual (Koob, 2008). The animals in the research studies do not ingest the compounds under circumstances that simulate the normal human's daily environment: It is not uncommon to learn that the animals were either forced to ingest the compound being tested or have it injected into their bodies[32] or that they spend most if not all of their days in a cage.

Reactions to the Jellinek Model

Many researchers have come to question the Jellinek (1960) model. The methodology on which Jellinek (1960) based his theory would now be viewed as flawed for several reasons: First, he mailed out 1,600 surveys to members of Alcoholics Anonymous (AA). However, of these 1,600 surveys only 98 were returned (a response rate of just 6%). Few research studies today would be carried out on such a limited participation rate. Second, Jellinek (1960) assumed that AA members were the same as nonmembers. This is a dangerous assumption: The very fact that they attended AA meetings, participants had identified themselves as being different in at least one aspect from nonmembers. Third, Jellinek (1960) assumed that those participants who returned his surveys were the same as those who did not return his survey. However, in the very act of returning their survey, the 6% who did so marked themselves as being different from the 94% who did not return their survey.

Also the Jellinek (1960) model used a cross-sectional design. Although this does not violate any known research rule, cross-sectional studies might not yield the same results as a lifespan (longitudinal) research design. For example: Did 50-year-old men with an AUD begin to drink for the same reasons that 20-year-old men with an AUD began to drink? The Jellinek (1960) model has not been found to accurately predict alcohol use patterns over the course of an individual's lifetime (Vaillant, 1995). Further, the automatic progression in the severity of the individual's drinking has been challenged: The typical individual with an AUD alternates between periods of problematic alcohol

---

[30]For example, what might be "diagnosed" as demonic possession in the year 1620 might be diagnosed as Tourette's syndrome today.

[31]Heyman (2011) suggested that by 40 years of age, 50% of persons who once met the diagnostic criteria for alcohol dependence and 78% of those who once met the diagnostic criteria for another form of substance dependence no longer meet the diagnostic criteria for these conditions.

[32]Admittedly many substance abusers *do* inject a drug(s) into their bodies. However nobody asked the mouse or rat in the research study if they wanted to be injected, raising questions about the applicability of such research to persons with an SUD.

use interspaced with periods of less problematic use or total abstinence (Schuckit, 2006b; Willenbring, 2010; Vaillant, 1995). Individuals who abuse illicit drugs also tend to follow a variable course rather than an automatic downward spiral (Toneatto, Sobell, Sobell, & Rubel, 1999).

Another central tenet of the Jellinek (1960) model, that the individual will experience a loss of control over his or her alcohol use, has also been challenged (Heyman, 2009; Schaler, 2000). There has been no research suggesting that alcohol or the drugs abuse alter the voluntary motor control regions of the brain (Alquist & Baumeister, 2012). The individual's behavior is thus voluntary, as evidenced by the fact that individuals with an AUD drink in such a manner as to achieve and maintain a desired level of intoxication. Rather than speak of loss of control, clinicians now speak of inconsistent control over their level of alcohol intake (Vaillant, 1995; 1990). There is little if any evidence that alcohol dependence is automatically progressive (Willenbring, 2010), although this is repeated over and over again to clients in substance abuse rehabilitation programs.

Reactions to the Genetic Inheritance Theories

The average person in the United States has almost been "programmed to believe [that] genetics rule" (Lipton, 2008, p. 186) with the result being that the average person views his or her genetic heritage as inalterable fate (Watters, 2006). This is known as "neurogenetic determinism" (Begley, 2007, p. 252). An extreme interpretation of this position is that the persons are then absolved of responsibility for their behavior because they did not select their genetic inheritance! In reality, the individual's genetic inheritance influences but does not control behavior (Gelernter & Kranzler, 2008). Genetic influence is perhaps most clearly seen in the individual's height. Although the individuals' genetic inheritance accounts for approximately 80% of their height, other factors such as their nutrition in the first two years of life, and their individual's health status appear to account for the other 20% of the variability in height.

For decades researchers have cringed when people begin to speak of a hypothetical "alcohol gene." The folly of this line of reasoning is readily apparent. There is, after all, no "fast ball" pitching gene, or a "scuba diving" gene, so why should a disorder as complex as the alcohol dependence rest on a single gene (Heyman, 2009; Nurnberger & Bierut, 2007)? Current research suggests that like most behaviors the addictions are polygenetic in nature. The sequence in which these genes are activated or inhibited from expression alters the influence of that combination of genes (Foroud & Phillips, 2012; Tattersall, 2012). As a result of these discoveries many researchers believe that the individuals' genetic heritage might account for perhaps as little as 10% of their risk for developing an SUD (Rappaport, quoted in Hamzelou, 2011).

Consider the humble honey bee: All female honey bees develop from larvae that are genetically identical. However, only the larvae fed a special food known as the "royal jelly" will grow to become a queen bee whereas the others simply become sterile workers (Young, 2008). Although human beings are a bit more complex than honey bees, this example does illustrate how external forces (in this case diet) influence the expression of the individual's genetic heritage (becoming a queen bee or a sterile worker bee). Another example of the fallacy of genetic determinism was clearly demonstrated in an experiment discussed by Tabakoff and Hoffman (2004): A number of genetically identical rats were sent to researchers in different laboratories around the country. The rats then received carefully calibrated doses of alcohol under closely controlled conditions. To the surprise of the researchers the rats in the various laboratories demonstrated significantly different responses to the same alcohol dosing regimen.

The researchers began to investigate why and discovered significant differences in the environment in each laboratory where the rat was housed. In some laboratories the rats were housed in sterile individual cages, whereas other laboratories housed the rats in individual cages with access to toys (what is often referred to as an "enriched" environment). Some laboratory workers did not touch the rats in their care per the protocol for that laboratory, whereas other laboratories encouraged the staff to pick the rats up, pet them, and in some cases allow the rats to interact in a large communal cage. All of these genetically identical rats received carefully calculated doses of alcohol at predetermined times, and promptly failed to consistently respond to alcohol in the anticipated manner.

An additional complicating factor is that those genes involved in helping to initiate substance use might not be the same genes involved in the process of maintaining these behaviors ("Addiction and the problem of relapse," 2007). Does the individual's genetic heritage predispose them to begin to abuse chemicals, continue to abuse chemicals, both or neither? The influence of the genetic inheritance upon behavior is simply not known at this time and if only for this reason it is premature to point to genetics as a major factor in the evolution of an SUD. We simply do not know enough about the role of genetic inheritance to make such generalizations yet.

Reactions to the Epigenetics Model

We know so very little about epigenetics that statements that the addictions cause permanent changes in the brain are premature. It is possible that the SUDs do induce permanent changes in cellular DNA expression, however, it is also possible that these changes are potentially reversible. Scientists barely understand the process of epigenetics and although discoveries about of do offer potential insights into the SUDs and their treatment, it is considered far too soon to invoke epigenetic changes as evidence that the SUDs induce permanent changes in DNA expression.

Reactions to the Dopamine D2 Receptor Site Hypothesis

The dopamine D2 receptor site hypothesis seems to be the most promising of the medical models explaining both the addictions and impulsive behavior in humans. Animal research suggests for example that rats that are deficient in the dopamine D2 and D3 receptor sites appear to be at increased risk for cocaine abuse (Dalley, Fryer, Brichard, Robinson et al., 2007). However, much remains to be discovered about the distribution of the dopamine D2 and D3 receptor sites in the general population and the influence of a hypothetical deficiency of dopamine D2 and D3 receptor sites on behavior and how behavior influences dopamine D2 and D3 receptor site status. Surprisingly, social status influences the number of dopamine D2 receptor sites (Volkow & Li, 2009). There is clearly a need for further research into the role of the dopamine D2 and D3 receptor sites on behavior and the prevalence of dopamine D2 and D3 receptor site deficiency in the general population.

Reactions to the Biological Vulnerability Studies

Marc Schukit's (1994) study, on which the low level response theory is based, is frequently cited as evidence

that there is a biological predisposition toward an AUD. The results of this study are suggestive. However, it should be noted that only 91 men in the original research group of 227 men had the abnormally low response to alcohol in the 1994 study. Of this group, 56%, or just 62 men, had progressed to develop an AUD at the time of the follow-up study. Whereas this study does illustrate a possible biological predisposition for an AUD, it should be noted that many men with the same abnormally low response to the test dose of alcohol at the time of the initial testing did not have an AUD at the follow-up study.

Research support for the low level response theory has been mixed (King et al., 2011). For a subgroup of drinkers alcohol appears to have a stimulant effect when their blood alcohol levels are still rising, a characteristic that King et al., (2011) found to be predictive of future binge drinking and eventually of future alcohol use problems according to the authors. The authors speculated that low level responses observed by early researchers in this field might have reflected the individual's response to alcohol when their blood alcohol levels were dropping and not while they were increasing, raising doubts about the accuracy of the early researchers' study (King et al., 2011).

Challenges to the Neuroplasticity Aspects of the Disease Model

Advocates of the medical model are quick to point to neuroplasticity[33] as evidence that the addictions are biological disorders. Proponents of this position suggest that the repeated use of a recreational drug of abuse causes the neurons in different regions of the brain to permanently alter their structure and function to the point where the individual no longer can exercise free will (Geppert, 2008). A counter point is offered by Heyman (2009), who suggested that drug-induced brain change is not sufficient evidence that addiction is an involuntary disease state. Drugs change the brain, but this does not make addiction a disease (p. 97).

Neuroplasticity is an ongoing process within the brain seen on a moment-to-moment, minute-to-minute, and hour-to-hour basis (Horstman, 2010). Diet, exercise, and even learning to play a musical instrument all induce changes in the structure of neurons in the appropriate regions of brain, but this does not make them "diseases." Further, the process of

---

[33]See Glossary.

neuroplasticity might be active both in the development of and recovery from the SUDs (Torregrossa & Kalivas, 2009). We just do not know enough about this process to make definitive statements about the role of neuroplasticity in the SUDs.

Challenges to the Brain Imaging Studies

Proponents of the medical model will often point to dramatic brain scan pictures obtained from neuroimaging studies in which certain regions of the brains of persons with an SUD become very active when they are exposed to drug use cues as evidence that the addictions are brain disorders. Some rehabilitation centers use such brain imaging studies to purportedly demonstrate to the individual and his or her family that the individual is indeed addicted to chemicals and that changes in the individual's brain imaging studies over time reflect the positive impact of rehabilitation programs. This process ignores the fact that while neuroimaging studies are valuable research tools, they do not demonstrate the existence of a mental disorder,[34] or even diagnose them (Fletcher, 2013). No psychiatric disorder can be diagnosed solely by brain scans (Breggin, 2008). This is especially true for the SUDs: Nobody has ever been referred to a rehabilitation program because of an abnormal PET or fMRI scan (Peele, 2010).

However, the average person does not understand the process of neuroimaging, or that it is very easy to read too much into brain scans (Noe, 2009; Peele, 2010; Satel & Lillenfeld, 2013; Shermer, 2008). Because the data generated by the procedures currently in use are so very complex there are an estimated 7,000 ways of interpreting brain scan data (Chen, 2013). Another confounding problem is that the statistical analysis methods of the study might inflate the apparent level of neural activity in the target region of the brain, distorting the outcome of the study (Giles, 2009; Legrenzi & Umilta, 2011; Noe, 2009). Statements that fMRI or PET scan study results allow us to see the mind in action are "enthusiastic overstatements of the truth" (Siegel, 2013, p. xix). They do not allow you to see the mind in action: They just tell you that one part of the brain is marginally more active than others.

The average person does not understand that the images from brain scans are based on data obtained from individuals placed in an atypical environment: Being crammed in a neuroimaging machine for up to an hour and being exposed to photographs of drug use cues is hardly the same as being in a street environment where the individual might be exposed to drug-use cues (Shermer, 2008). Further, those who point to the results of PET scan for fMRI study results do not often reveal that there are some individuals who are known to be addicted to a chemical(s) but who do not demonstrate activation of the same regions of the brain seen in other studies (Volkow & Li, 2009). The reasons for these differences are not known at this time.

Several researchers have identified increased blood flow to regions of the brain indirectly thought to be involved in the development of SUDs. However, cerebral blood flow patterns are more complex than a simple "person-views-drug-use-cue-increased blood flow to certain regions of brain" paradigm (Sirotin & Das, 2009). For example changes in the cerebral blood flow patterns might take place in anticipation of expected visual stimuli, not in response to it (Sirotin & Das, 2009). This makes empirical sense: When we are on a diet we start to salivate a second or two before the expected time of arrival of a dessert that we ordered earlier while at a restaurant.

The layperson does not understand the process of neuroimaging. They are thus unaware that the dramatic colors seen in photographic summaries of neuroimaging studies are based on very small differences in the level of neural activity in different regions of the brain. The public also only rarely understands that while one certain region of the brain might appear very active on a fMRI study that this might be because the level of neural activity in adjacent regions of the brain was suppressed, not because the target region of the brain was more active (Lillenfeld, Lunn, Ruscio, & Beyerstein, 2010). The average person is also rarely aware of the fact that the dramatic color differences that supposedly reflect levels of neural activity in different regions of the brain seen in fMRI[35] images are artificially constructed by technicians based on the study data (Legrenzi & Umilta, 2011; Satel & Lillenfeld, 2013; Vul, Harris, Winkielman, & Pashler, 2009). Such images do not reveal the level of neural activity in

---

[34] It should be pointed out that a consensus about the nature of mental *health* acceptable to all disciplines that address issues pertaining to the "mind" has yet to be suggested (Siegel, 2013). Given this fact, how can we as mental health or substance use rehabilitation professionals diagnose "mental illness"?

[35] See Glossary

adjacent regions of the brain other than the one region under study.

There is also the rarely mentioned fact that neuroimaging studies are unable to determine what the individual is thinking (Horstman, 2010). Neuroimaging studies using the fMRI procedure have demonstrated that many of the same regions of the brain active in persons who relapse in response to a drug use "craving" are also active in the brains of persons with an SUD who are experiencing a drug-use "craving" but who do not give in to it. Yet another confounding factor is that procedures such as the fMRI do not provide "real time" measures of brain activity (Frances, 2013). The images require several seconds to build up enough data to produce an image. During this time the neurons in that region of the brain being studied have "fired" hundreds or even thousands of times in response to internal and external stimuli (Noe, 2009). Can we say with any degree of confidence that the measured level of neural activity was all in response to drug-use cues? To further complicate the application of neuroimaging procedures to the study of the SUDs is the fact that the images presented in textbooks and at public discussions are statistical compilations of a number of individual brains, not the representation of a single individual's brain activity (Horstman, 2010; Shermer, 2008). Thus, while brain imaging studies present researchers with powerful new tools into brain function, it is far too soon to draw conclusions about what the findings mean. Neuroimaging is barely out of its infancy (Satel & Lillenfeld, 2013). To start making such dramatic claims as have been made in the popular press would be similar to announcing that a child will be a world-class runner after he or she took their first tentative steps. In each situation it would be best to wait to see what develops.

Challenges to the Genetic Modification Treatment Approaches

At this time knowledge about the genes possibly associated with an SUD remains theoretical and is of little practical value to the clinician at present (Meyers & Dick, 2010). Before such attempts are made it is wise to consider the possibility that attempts to alter the expression of individual genes, or combinations of genes, though associated with an SUD are fraught with danger. Genes do not carry out one function. Depending on the sequence in which genes are activated or suppressed, the role of any given gene varies.

Do we know enough about the human genome to safely make such changes to the individual's genetic inheritance? Like Murphy's Law, the "law of unintended consequences"[36] is always at work. There are always unanticipated consequences.

The Medical Model and Individual Responsibility

A central tenet of the medical model is that an urge to use a chemical is a compulsive, uncontrollable desire to use drugs that must be satisfied. This is simply not true for two reasons (Alquist & Baumeister, 2012; Heyman, 2009; Satel & Lillenfeld, 2013). First, theories about the uncontrollable nature of an "urge" or drug use "cravings" are based on reports from people who did not successfully resist these desires to use chemicals. We rarely receive feedback from those who were able to resist the urge to return to chemical abuse.

Second, research has repeatedly failed to demonstrate that behavioral choices become irrelevant when a person develops an SUD (Alquist & Baumeister, 2012; Satel & Lillenfeld, 2013). Substance use "cravings" or "urges" are one of a number of factors that might trigger a relapse to active substance use, but they are "not an obligation" (Heyman, 2009, p. 111) to do so. Any person who has been on a diet can testify that although difficult, the urge to snack can be resisted. Many individuals addicted to a chemical(s) will admit that they can indeed resist the urge to use that compound if the reward for doing so is high enough.

This introduces an element of free choice into a biological model that holds that free will is not a part of the disease process. Consider the following hypothetical example of a heroin addict who upon waking must (a) perceive the need for the drug, (b) obtain the funds with which to buy the desired drug, (c) find a dealer, (d) complete the financial transaction to buy it, (e) find a safe place in which to prepare the heroin for injection, (f) mix the powder with water,[37] (g) heat the mixture in a tea spoon, (g) pour it into a syringe, (i) find a vein into which to inject the mixture, (j) prepare the vein for the injection and then, (k) inject the drug into his/her body. This is a rather complicated chain of events, each step of which involves the active participation of the individual. This hypothetical

---

[36]See Glossary.

[37]The assumption here is that the heroin is to be injected.

individual discussed passed through multiple decision points, each requiring active participation on his or her part to allow the substance use to proceed, but is said to be a "victim" of the disease process. If we all had to go through all of these steps to become ill, it is doubtful that anybody would ever have to be sick again!!

This places the medical model of the addictions in a quandary: What to do with free will? O'Brien (2011) attempted to reconcile this apparent conflict by suggesting that the individual initiates the substance abuse and thus at least the start of the addictive sequence is a conscious choice. However, at some point this theory holds that substance-induced biological changes negate free will and the individuals becomes a slave to their addiction. This attempt at reconciling two apparently diametrically opposed ideas overlooks the inconvenient reality that a significant percentage of those who are addicted to chemicals do eventually learn how to discontinue substance abuse. Third, it is now generally accepted that the individual's behavioral choices influence the course of the persistent disease state such as diabetes or the addictions. This fact underscores the interlocking aspect of the bio/psycho/social model. If a hypothetical patient with adult onset diabetes were to lose 10% of his or her body weight, join a health club to exercise on a regular basis with, and make certain changes in his or her diet (all social or behavioral choices), he or she would change the course of the disease. The same logic applies to the individuals who have an SUD: They remain responsible for the behavioral choices that they make in response to their awareness of their SUD and its possible treatment (Washton & Zweben, 2006).

Unfortunately, the blind application of the biological model of the addictions often results in a situation where the rehabilitation professional thinks:

> that diseases as entities that invade or take hold of people [and] tends to lead to the kind of medicine patients often complain about. They notice when a doctor is more interested in some abstraction he or she calls a "disease" than in them and their suffering. (Gunn, 2003, p. 33)

The medical model as practiced today prevents human contact by placing on person into the role of the physician and the other into the role of the patient (Frattaroli, 2001). This is rather disempowering and one must ask how an impersonal medical relationship can ever hope to assist in the very personal and often painful disease state known as the addictions. In other words, the admonition made by Sir William Osler

quoted at the beginning of this chapter is totally ignored. The health care professional now treats the disease entity (SUD, cancer, neurological disorder, and so on) and not the person.

Spontaneous Recovery

Another challenge to the biological model of the addictions is spontaneous recovery. The prevailing opinion among physicians is that persons with SUDs are:

> exempt addiction from our beliefs about change. In both popular and scientific models, addiction is seen as locking you into an inescapable pattern of behavior. (Peele, 2004a, p. 46)

However, in reality "quitting is the rule, not the exception" (Satel & Lillenfeld, 2013, p. 55). While the SUD does not spontaneously resolve in every case, it has been estimated that up to 75–95% of those with an SUD eventually do so[38] (Heyman, 2011; Marano, 2012; Satel & Lillenfeld, 2013; Willenbring, 2010). This spontaneous remission rate is many orders of magnitude higher than that of other psychiatric disorders and raises serious questions about the loss of control that is supposedly a hallmark of addiction.

II. The Psychological Components of the Bio/ Psycho/Social Model

Definition

The psychological component of the bio/psycho/social model explores the impact of psychodynamic forces, learning, motivation, interpersonal interactions and personality on how the individual's substance use behaviors (Sadock & Sadock, 2007). This perspective is deeply interconnected with the biological and sociological components of the bio/psycho/social model. The individual's personality, which is both shaped by individual-environment interactions and helps shape future interactions with the environment, rests on a foundation of biochemical interactions within the brain. There are various theories within the psychological perspective of the SUDs, many of which are intertwined with the other two components of this model. The

---

[38]The majority of those who recover from substance use disorders do so without going into treatment.

application of the psychological sciences to various forms of psychological/psychiatric disorders is discussed in more detail in the chapter on dual diagnosis; however, some of the more significant of the theoretical psychological models will be discussed in this chapter.

The Moral Model

One of the first psychosocial models proposed, one that still has many adherents among the general public, is the moral model (Brust, 2004). The moral model can trace its roots back at least to the "demon rum" philosophy of the temperance movement of the 1800s. Proponents of the moral model view the addictions as reflecting a weakness of character.[39] The individual then succumbs to the temptations of alcohol (or by extension the illicit drugs) because of this unidentified but pre-existing character flaw. There is a strong element of predestination inherent in this model: The person did not select his or her moral character and thus is not entirely responsible for their attraction to alcohol. This is clearly seen in the result of a recent study conducted by Schomerus, Matschinger, and Angermeyer (2006). The authors interviewed 1012 adults living in Germany by telephone and found that 85% of those who participated in the study thought that the addictions were a self-inflicted disorder, and only 30% thought that it could be effectively treated (Schomerus et al., 2006). Satel and Lillenfeld (2013) were more optimistic, noting that research data finding widespread support for the moral model has been mixed, but apparently the moral model of the SUDs has strong advocates in some segments of society.

Learning Theory

Learning theory suggests that the SUDs exist because the individual has learned to engage in the abuse of alcohol or illicit drugs. Learning takes place in a social environment, with social, biological, and psychological factors being involved in this process. The strength of the learning process is perhaps best seen in the language acquisition process. At birth the child does not possess a

language as we use the term and even by the first birthday it is the exceptional infant who is able to mutter a single word (Walter, 2013). By the age of 18 months the child is thought to learn a new word every other hour, and by adolescence the once wordless infant is learning 10–15 new words a day (Walter, 2013). The process of language acquisition begins at first in the parent–infant interactions that make college educated adults sound like babies ("say da-da" or, "say ma-ma") and gradually grows to include siblings, peers, social media, educational establishments, and the written word. Notice how all of this takes place in an interpersonal environment, often by listening to others and how they use a specific word in their everyday lives (Walter, 2013).

Cigarette smoking provides another excellent example of the social learning process. The new smoker must overcome his or her body's initial response to the chemicals in cigarette smoke. However, friends are there to help the new smoker learn why admitting so many poisons into your body is such a good thing and how to overcome their body's initial response to cigarette smoke. These friends also provide role models that the new smoker might emulate. Once the new smoker has passed through the phase of nausea and vomiting, he or she will discover that he or she needs to continue to smoke to avoid nicotine withdrawal. Each time the smoker takes a puff, he or she is reinforcing the original impetus to smoke as a way to relieve stress by forestalling nicotine withdrawal symptoms and inducing smoking related relaxation. The neural networks involved in the reward cascade are thus strengthened as the individuals relearn what they view as the rewards of cigarette smoking. This establishes a process of over learning, reinforcing the tendency for the individual to turn to cigarettes as a way to cope with adversity. Breaking the bonds of this learning cycle has proven to be difficult, and neither the psychological sciences nor the biological sciences have developed an effective intervention for cigarette smoking thus far.

In theory, the same mechanism is at work when the individual abuses alcohol and/or the illicit drugs: Substance-induced pleasure reinforces the learning process, forestalls withdrawal distress, both of which then encourage further substance use. From this perspective, the SUDs might be reviewed as reflecting maladaptive learning (Lewis, 2011). Under normal conditions the human brain might be viewed as a constantly seeking new knowledge and experiences (Walter, 2013). If this is true then it should not be surprising to learn that the reward potential of a substance is strongest when its

---

[39]The "moral model" was applied not just to the substance use disorders such as alcoholism but also to physical diseases. Bynum (2012) briefly discussed how it was assumed by many in the late 19th century that persons who contracted tuberculosis (TB) did so at least in part because of a vague, illdefined, moral failing on their part. The same reasoning is applied to sexually transmitted diseases (STD): The person who contracts a STD is often viewed as being morally weak.

effects are unpredictable (Fiorillo, Tobler, & Schultz, 2003). In retrospect, this is obvious: Imagine the enthusiasm with which you would play a slot machine in Las Vegas if you were to win a consistent amount of money every time that you played. You would quickly become bored and look for something else to entertain you. This is true for substance abusers: Very few engage in the use of only one compound used at the same dose. They often intermix chemicals, doses, or periods of time when they abuse one compound rather than their primary drug of choice to achieve variety in their drug use experience.[40] This phenomenon might also account to explain why illicit drug users keep abusing substances where the purity is not known: The effects of each substance abused cannot be predicted in advance, thus providing an element of the unknown for the abuser.

Coping Systems Theory

In theory, alcohol and the drug(s) of abuse might become a learned coping mechanism for persons who suffer from depression or who have a severe psychological disorder. Psychoanalytic theorists have suggested that afflicted individuals use alcohol or drugs to numb themselves to emotional pain (Frattaroli, 2001; Horney, 1964) or to self-medicate anxiety disorders (Encrenaz et al., 2009). Many persons with schizophrenia abuse alcohol or illicit drugs to provide relief from the side effects of the medications prescribed to treat their disorder. Other persons with schizophrenia abuse alcohol or drugs to allow themselves a degree of control over when their psychiatric symptoms become active. The relationship between schizophrenia and substance abuse is discussed in more detail in Chapter 24 and for the sake of brevity will not be discussed again here.

Personality Defense Theories of Substance Use Disorders

This theoretical construct draws upon both the psychoanalytic view of personality defenses and psychological personality theory. We are all thought to react to information about ourselves that we do not wish to face by using one or more defense mechanisms. These defense mechanisms protect the individual from a perceived threat to their ego, albeit at the expense of long-term

adjustment. Proponents of the psychoanalytic model have repeatedly asserted that persons with an SUD overuse characteristic defense mechanisms because they work for that person.

According to the characteristic defense mechanism theory the most prominent defense mechanisms used by individuals with an SUD are those of denial, rationalization, projection and/or minimization. Unfortunately the belief that a substance abuser will automatically lie about their substance use pattern has become enshrined in clinical lore, as evidenced by the following quotation: [the] "use and abuse of alcohol and illicit drugs has long been associated with denial and misrepresentation" (Vitacco, 2008, p. 44). One of the most deeply entrenched beliefs by clinicians and the average person is that the individual with an SUD hides behind a wall of denial (Croft, 2006). Essentially denial is a form of unconscious self-deception, which is classified as one of the more primitive, narcissistic defenses (Sadock & Sadock, 2007). The conscious mind simply refuses to acknowledge something that is threatening to the ego (Sadock & Sadock, 2007). The analogy of "tunnel vision" might not be inappropriate, here. The person allows the self to see only what supports their desire(s) while avoiding recognition of those things that do not support their desire(s). Threatening information is just dismissed. The individuals' use of denial might be illustrated by a hypothetical case in which a patient is informed by the physician, "The test results are back. I am afraid that the results were positive: You have cancer." The individual might reply "No, you're mistaken." The doctors are mistaken, they mixed up the blood test results, the test results were altered by the individual's ingestion of a herbal medicine, and so on. The process of denial might also be seen in a hypothetical alcohol-dependent person whose spouse asserts "You have a drinking problem!" to which the drinker responds "No I don't, I can control it. I can quit whenever I want to." In the abusers' mind the problem is solved: It just disappears (at least in their own mind) and evidence to the contrary is ignored or dismissed.

Another personality defense that is often seen in persons with an SUD according to clinicians is projection. As the name would suggest, projection is a defense mechanism in which material that is unacceptable to the "self" is projected on to others (Sadock & Sadock, 2007). The young child's cry of "See what you made me do!" is not a bad example of this defense mechanism in action. The child projects responsibility for his or her misbehavior on to others to avoid being held accountable for his or her misbehavior(s).

---

[40]Their choice of substances to abuse is affected in part by the *availability* of chemicals to abuse, which is discussed in greater detail in the chapter "Drugs and Crime."

In many cases, it is hypothesized, the substance abusers justify their abuse of a chemical(s) because they are the helpless victim of mistreatment at the hands of another leaving no choice but to resort to alcohol or the illicit substances,[41] that they are a helpless victim of their genetic heritage, and so on.

Often, individuals will attempt to justify otherwise unacceptable behaviors through cognitive justifications, or rationalization. For example, a hypothetical 73-year-old alcohol-dependent person might explain: "The reason that I drink today is that my grandmother used to rub vodka on my gums when I was an infant." Admittedly, physicians often did make this recommendation in the first quarter of the 20th century to help dull the infant's pain during the teething process: Ethyl alcohol can function as an analgesic. However, the typical mother would dip her finger into a glass filled with vodka and rub less than a quarter of a teaspoon on to the infant's gums every few hours. It is hard to believe that this medical treatment carried out 70 years ago caused the individual to have an AUD today! Another example of rationalization might be found in the case of a hypothetical person who has a severe AUD and who argues that moderate alcohol use is good for the cardiovascular system[42] while ignoring evidence suggesting that they are not moderate drinkers and research data that found that excessive alcohol use can cause significant damage to the drinker's body. Again this defense mechanism allows the individual to justify otherwise unacceptable behavior (at least to themselves). Another commonly encountered rationalization is that marijuana is not dangerous because it is a plant, and how naturally occurring plants can be addictive or harm[43] the smoker because it is natural.

The individual who uses minimization as a defense will either consciously or unconsciously reduce the incidence of a socially unacceptable behavior, or its effects on others. For example, one person might explain "I only drink on the weekends" but might not offer the additional information that they define the "weekend" as starting on Friday afternoon or evening, and continuing until late Sunday evening. Another person might admit to "experimental" use of cannabis, whereas the spouse reports that he or she smokes it three times a day, every day of the week. Further, the "I had only two beers" story that police officers often hear when they stop a suspected intoxicated driver might be viewed as an attempt at minimization.

Behavioral Psychology Theories[44]

There is no consensus about the definition of the "behavioral psychology" schools of thought. The question whether this is a philosophy, a paradigm in which to view human behavior, or a therapeutic approach has yet to be resolved. The behavioral psychology theories are quite deterministic in orientation, however, behavioral therapists range from rigid, staunch believers in this philosophy through moderate behaviorists who accept the existence of basic biological drives such as hunger, thirst, and sex. To such theorists, the behavior of the organism is motivated by the desire to reduce the tension induced by unfulfilled biological drives such as those noted earlier. However, all behavioral therapists maintain "personality" is simply an illusion, and avoid the "black box" of human thought and personality.

At the risk of a gross over simplification, the central tenet of behavioral theory is that humans, like all animals, work to either (a) increase personal pleasure or (b) decrease discomfort. These are called stimuli (singular: stimulus). The individual's behavior(s) in response to a stimulus is called a response. Behavioral therapists maintain that all behavior can be understood in terms of stimulus-response cycles. Behaviors like (a) increase pleasure or (b) decrease discomfort are said to be a positive reinforcer for that response. Behaviors that result in a (c) decrease in pleasure or (d) increase in discomfort are said to be a negative reinforcer for that response. The influence of various reinforcement schedules[45] on animal behavior in the research laboratory setting has been explored, and it has been observed

---

[41]On occasion, the drugs of abuse do serve this function and the differentiation between those persons who are using projection to defend their addiction from those who are using a chemical(s) to help them cope rests on the skill of the assessor(s).

[42]See Chapter 8.

[43]Two counter arguments present themselves: First, tobacco is also a plant, and as discussed in Chapter 16, smoking is a major cause of premature death around the world. So, even "natural" plants can be harmful to the user. Second, both the tobacco and marijuana plants have been subjected to selective breeding experiments over the generations, with the result being that the plant that emerged from such experiments is far more potent than the original plants found in this country generations ago and is hardly a "natural" plant.

---

[44]For the sake of this text, the behavioral theories are classified as a psychological school of thought.

[45]The topic of reinforcement schedules on behavior is far beyond the scope of this text. The reader is referred to any of a number of excellent books on behavioral psychology theory to learn more about this topic.

that behaviors that result in a positive response induce the development of a habit, the strength of which reflects in part the reinforcement schedule that contributed to the development of that habit. The repeated failure of a given stimulus to elicit positive reinforcement or reduce punishments may result in the extinction of the identified behavior. The speed with which an identified behavior becomes extinct is dependent in part on the reinforcement schedule that initiated the development of that habit.

A simplified application of this model to the SUDs would suggest that it accounts for the behavioral patterns seen in persons with an SUD. Within this model the SUDs are viewed as meeting either condition "a" or "b" (stated earlier). However, repeated exposure to the drugs of abuse result in the individual become physically dependent on the drug(s) being abused. At this time the motivating force behind further substance use is to avoid either the loss of what is perceived as pleasure or possibly even going into a withdrawal syndrome (conditions "c" and "d," stated earlier). Obviously the behavioral psychology reinforcement schedules appear to account for many of the phenomena observed in substance abusers; however, there are significant exceptions as well: The documented alcoholic decides that the time has come to stop abusing alcohol and chooses to go through alcohol withdrawal, for example. So while the behavioral psychology theories offer valuable insights into the motivation for substance use behaviors, it does not provide the "grand unifying theory" of the addictions.

Cognitive-Behavioral Theories (CBT)[46]

The CBT theories emerged in the last quarter of the 20th century and reflect a modified form of the "behavioral therapy" approaches to treatment. CBT therapists do not address the issue of predestination but keep the therapeutic focus on the "here and now." The individual's thoughts, feelings, and beliefs are accepted as possible stimuli that trigger dysfunctional thoughts or logic chains within him or her. An example of such thoughts might be a hypothetical individual's belief that "nobody likes me" because of a lack of telephone contact with anybody in over a week's time. The goal of cognitive

behavioral therapy is to: (a) help the individuals identify their thoughts in reaction to a specific event, (b) determine how these thoughts contribute to their emotional response to that event, (c) determine which thoughts are dysfunctional or counter productive, (d) learn how to replace these thoughts with more appropriate responses to the event, and (e) monitor their efforts to replace these self-defeating thoughts with more appropriate thoughts. To extend upon the stated example, the client's use of "black-and-white" thinking ("Nobody likes me!") would be targeted and appropriate treatment goals would be established to assist the client in addressing these maladaptive thoughts.

Psychoanalysis[47]

Psychoanalysis is strongly deterministic in orientation. The individual is being both consciously and unconsciously motivated to engage in certain behaviors by past interpersonal relationships and unresolved conflict. In brief, this form of treatment calls upon the therapeutic relationship as the tool for behavior change. It has been suggested that the therapeutic relationship fosters neural reorganization as the process of neuroplasticity is triggered by and encouraged to continue through a neutral but supportive client-therapist relationship. Within this therapeutic relationship learning occurs, altering existing neural networks (Feldstein-Ewing & Chung, 2013). For this reason the psychoanalytic school of thought is viewed as falling in all of the biological, psychological, and social realms of treatment, although for the sake of clarity it was discussed in this subsection of the chapter.

The Addictive Personality

The theory of the "addictive personality" is strongly deterministic, as evidenced by fact that the "very word addict [which] confers an identity that admits no other possibilities" (Peele, 2004a, p. 43) [italics in original]. Drawing upon clinical experience with persons who were addicted to alcohol or drugs, a number of writers suggested that personality traits such as impulsiveness, thrill seeking, rebelliousness, aggression, and nonconformity were "robust predictors of alcoholism" (Slutske et al., 2004, p. 124). Clinicians began to

---

[46]Like every other therapeutic model reviewed in this chapter, this school of thought is far too complex to review in just a few paragraphs. The reader is referred to any of a wide range of books on the subject, including those by Albert Ellis or Aaron Beck to cite but two of the many pioneers in this field.

[47]Psychoanalysis was initially envisioned as a medical specialty although many other professionals now engage in the practice of psychoanalysis after completing the appropriate training. For the purposes of this text this school of thought is reviewed in the "Psychological" section of the bio/psycho/social model of the addictions.

look for evidence that clients in their care possessed at least some of these personality characteristics and not surprisingly concluded that their clients did have at least some of the personality features outlined above. These therapist-based conclusions then reinforced the theory that there was an "addictive personality" in the minds of some therapists.

Applications of the Psychological Component of the Bio/Psycho/Social Model

Assessment

The psychologist is often in a unique position of being able to assess the individual's intellectual and personality resources and areas of vulnerability. Substance abuse rehabilitation with a hypothetical person who has a measured IQ of 80 would proceed down different paths than a rehabilitation program with a person who has a measured IQ of 115, for example. Personality assessment might reveal that a certain person is overly dependent on others, or suspicious of others, both characteristics that will influence the course of a rehabilitation program. A psychologist might detect signs of trauma in the individual's past which will then need to be discussed with the individual as part of their rehabilitation program.

Neuropsychological Assessment

This is a specialized application of the psychological assessment process. The neuropsychological assessment is carried out to determine whether certain life events such as involvement in a motor vehicle accident have influenced their ability to understand and adjust to their environment. The neuropsychological assessment will reveal the level of impairment, if any, the functions that are impaired (language recognition as opposed to ability to do math problems, for example), and provide an over view of remedial services required by the individual.

Individual or Group Psychotherapy

Persons who struggle with a wide range of mental health problems often benefit from concurrent individual or mental-health group psychotherapy sessions as part of their rehabilitation program. In many cases,

the individuals will discuss issues with their individual therapist that they would never reveal in a therapy group setting. Many of these sensitive issues contribute to or help sustain the individuals' substance abuse.

Marital and Family Therapy[48]

Many health care professionals are trained in the art of marital and family therapies. An adjunct to substance abuse rehabilitation programs might involve marital and/or family therapy to help family members learn how to deal with issues such as how anger is expressed within the family unit, abuse from significant others, child discipline, financial decision making, sexual relations within the marriage, and the anger that partners feel about their spouse's substance use behaviors.

Although clinical wisdom suggests that the person with a severe SUD has alienated himself or herself from family and peers who might have provided a source of support, this belief has not been empirically tested. The possibility exists that for an unknown percentage of substance abusers it might be possible to effect a reconciliation with the family members or peers who might eventually become sources of support for the recovering substance abuser. The possibility also exists that the family or the marital partner might prove detrimental to the individuals' efforts at recovering from their SUD. Although it is the goal of the marriage and family therapist to achieve the former goal, he or she must also constantly assess the progress of the therapeutic process and help the persons in the early stages of recovery distance themselves from those members of their family who are unsupportive for reasons of their own SUD, unresolved anger issues, or for other reasons that are intractable to therapy in the early stages of the individuals' recovery program.

Although the psychological theories of addictions offer valuable insights into the forces that initiate and maintain the SUDs, they do not provide a grand unifying theory of the addictions. Another perspective also offers valuable insights into the SUDs: the social theories, which are discussed later in this chapter.

---

[48]The author recognizes that marital and family therapies do not fall exclusively under the umbrella of the psychological sciences and that social workers and many addictions counselors also engage in this adjunctive therapy after receiving the special training for this difficult task. However, for the sake of this text marital and family therapies will be discussed in the psychological sphere of the bio/ psycho/social model.

Reactions to the Psychological Models of the Addictions

Reactions to the Moral Model of the SUDs

The scientific foundation for the moral model is weak at best; however, it still has strong adherents among the general public (Brust, 2004). One of the goals of Jellinek's (1960) work was to eliminate prejudicial judgment of persons with SUDs by demonstrating that they had a medical illness. It is hard to judge whether this goal has been met: More than a half century after Jellinek's work was published the team of Pescosolido, Martin, Long, Medina, Phelan, and Link, (2010) found staggering rates of prejudice against those persons with AUDs. However, it is not known whether the rates of prejudice uncovered by Pescosolido et al. (2010) were higher than, equal to, or lower than those that existed at the time that Jellinek (1960) conducted his research.

One of the strongest challenges to the moral model is that it is more than 200 years old and was advanced well before the process of neurotransmission or regional specialization centers on the brain had been discovered. To illustrate the influence of time consider that it was suspected that the person who contracted tuberculosis (TB) was thought to have done so because of a moral shortcoming until the science of infectious diseases revealed that this was a bacterial infection. The very age of the moral model does not make it responsive to new discoveries about human motivation, or how personality disorders might predispose the individual toward an SUD, for example. It is suggested that the moral model is an antique best relegated to the history books.

Reactions to the "Alcoholic" (or "Addictive") Personality Theories

Although long established in clinical lore, the theory of the "alcoholic personality" is nothing more than a clinical myth (Gendel, 2006; Stetter, 2000). According to this theory, clinicians are trained to expect certain personality characteristics in persons with an SUD, and then selectively recall only those cases that meet these expectations.[49] Clinicians continue to operate on the assumption that their clients are (a) developmentally immature, (b) motivated to hide certain personality defenses, such as denial, and (c) that they tend to be impulsive. Treatment is then geared to address these perceived personality flaws in the client, whether they exist or not. Further, as noted earlier, the personality profiles of persons with an AUD were based on research studies involving persons in treatment for their AUD. This raises the questions whether what was being measured was an "alcoholic personality" or a "treatment personality" (Pihl, 1999).

In the face of this lack of supporting evidence, one must ask how the myth of the "alcoholic personality" evolved. One theory is that clinicians and researchers in the mid-20th century became confused by the high rate of comorbidity between individuals with an SUD, and, individuals with an Antisocial Personality Disorder (ASPD). This is understandable, because between 84 and 90% of males with ASPD will also have an SUD at some point in their lives (Preuss & Wong, 2000; Ziedonis & Brady, 1997). This is not to imply that the ASPD caused the SUD or the reverse. Rather they are separate, co-existing conditions, with each interacting with and affecting the course of the other. Given that individuals with the ASPD demonstrate many of the personality traits attributed to the "addictive/ alcoholic personality," it is easy to understand how one came to be confused as being synonymous with the other.

Challenges to the "Characteristic Defenses" Theory

The assertion that persons with an SUD overuse certain defense mechanisms has been repeatedly challenged, Indeed there is evidence suggesting that the belief that individuals with an SUD will automatically rely on the defense mechanisms outlined earlier in this chapter might do more harm than good (Foote, 2006). Miller and Rollnick (2002) suggested for example that as a group persons with an AUD do not use denial more frequently than any other group. Fletcher (2013) noted that persons with an SUD are likely to be honest about their substance use patterns if they have little reason to fear that the information that they provide will be used against them later. If one assumes that this is true, then the myth of client denial of substance use problems might at least in part reflect client defensiveness about possible prosecution if they reveal too much about their past.

However, because of selective perception by the therapist(s), the myth that the substance abusing

---

[49]This same process is seen in cases where other drugs of abuse are involved as well.

patient will automatically use the defenses discussed earlier in this chapter was established. To support their thesis, Miller and Rollnick (2002) point to what is known as the "illusion of correlation." The illusion of correlation suggests that we tend to remember events that confirm our preconceptions and dismiss or forget information that fails to do so. According to this theory, substance abuse rehabilitation professionals are more likely to remember those clients who demonstrated the defenses of denial, rationalization, projection, and minimization. This selective perception overlooks the possibility that the client's stage of growth and the treatment approach being utilized do not match and not that the individual is in a state of denial (Miller & Rollnick, 2002).

Challenges to the Behavioral Psychology Theories of the SUDs

Detractors to the behavioral psychology theories of the SUDs have mounted a spirited assault on what is otherwise a well established motivational theory. For example, although Baker, Stockwell, Barnes, and Holroyd (2011) noted above that a subgroup of their research sample were resistant to learning because of their depression, the question arises whether their depression prevented them from learning from experience (thus increasing discomfort in the long term) or if their failure to learn from experience contributed to their depression. Either way the authors indirectly raise the question of how the individuals' state of mind influences their ability to learn, an issue that is apparently unique to the human species.

A strong criticism of the behavioral psychology theories is that much of the early behavioral psychology research involved animals placed in artificial environments such as a cage fitted only with a lever. Each time that the animal pushed the lever he or she would receive a small reward (a food pellet or a small dose of a drug like cocaine administered through an indwelling catheter, for example). Such research did indeed uncover the basic laws of behavioral psychology and the animals in these studies behaved in a predictable manner: They would push the lever to receive the reward associated with that action. Various reward schedules were identified (continuous or 1:1 reinforcement paradigms, intermittent reward paradigms or fixed ratio reward schedule paradigms, for example) through such animal-based studies. However, such studies ignored the fact that the animal was in an artificial environment. In the stated

example the cage offered nothing more beyond the lever in the wall. The environment was not "enriched". It has been discovered that the animal will forgo the drug reward at times if given the option to interact with other animals or play with toys. Given this fact one must wonder whether the animal's observed substance use was motivated by a desire to use chemicals as opposed to sheer boredom.

A further challenge to the behavioral psychology schools of thought can be found in the discovery that mood states, a personality trait, can influence learning (Baker et al., 2011). A subgroup of their research sample consisted of a number of depression-prone individuals who were more resistant to learning from mistakes and more likely to continue counterproductive behaviors such as substance abuse. This study raises interesting challenges to the behavioral psychology paradigm because mood states appear to be strictly a human attribute that could not be anticipated on the basis of research studies using animals in cages. Further, humans retain the ability to prioritize both potential rewards and punishments. Many substance abusers willingly choose to endure the discomfort of substance withdrawal rather than to continue to engage in continued substance use for a variety of reasons, for example. This indicates that the individual makes a conscious choice about importance of substance-induced rewards as compared to other potential rewards in their environment, reintroducing the issue of personality into behavioral theory. It spite of its ambiguities and avoidance of the question of personality, however, the behavioral psychology schools of thought do offer insights into what might motivate some people to continue substance abuse.

Reactions to the Learning Theories of the SUDs

There has been little criticism of the learning theories, possibly because these theories do appear to account for many of the phenomena demonstrated by persons with an SUD. The learning theories do overlap with the behavioral psychology and cognitive behavioral schools of thought, for example, which are reviewed elsewhere in this chapter.

Challenges to the Epigenetic Theories of the SUDs

The discovery that there is an interaction between the individuals' genetic heritage and their environment through the process of epigenetics is an exciting discovery that potentially could explain much about the addictions[50] (Starkman et al., 2012). Unfortunately the relevance of epigenetics to the SUD is not known at this time. The theory does appear to have face validity and researchers might very well discover that suspected epigenetic changes do influence substance use behaviors.

However, and this is the crux of this section, we just do not know enough about epigenetics to make definitive statements that epigenetic changes in genetic expression is involved in the SUDs. The "critical periods" of development are theoretical and not established fact, although, again, this theory has high face value in the opinion of the author of this text. There is a need for further research into the applications of epigenetic theory to the SUD. Such research should help delineate the exact role that epigenetic changes play in the initiation and maintenance of the SUDs, whether the same epigenetic changes contribute to the individual's decision to initiate substance use as opposed to maintaining them is still not known at this time.

Reactions to the Coping Skills Theories

There has been remarkably little criticism of the coping skills theories, possibly because they are rather eclectic and are drawn from a wide range of other theoretical models.

III. The Social Component[51] of the Bio/Psycho/Social Model

Definition

Substance use or abuse does not take place in a vacuum: Each person is a part of a specific culture and participates in social subgroups that collectively add up to the "... chaotic, astonishing, tumultuous stew we call human culture" (Walter, 2013, p. 152). To understand the role that cultural and social forces play in the possible development of the SUDs one must explore the role that social relationships played in the evolution of human beings. Indeed, if it were not for the evolution of social relationships we might not have survived (Walter, 2013): Early hominids were poorly equipped to survive in a world filled with

predators armed with speed, fangs, and claws. Early social bonds facilitated food gathering, protection,[52] sharing of resources and in time the transmission of complex ideas such as tool making (Walter, 2013). This would appear to account for the apparent biological predisposition in humans toward acceptance of social rules and demands (Suddendorf, 2013).

The sociological perspective of the SUDs attempts to identify and possibly correct systemic issues within society that might influence the individual's decisions about substance use, including the cultural, environmental, and familial elements of the individual's life (Sadock & Sadock, 2007). These forces can either facilitate the development of an SUD or contribute to individual resilience against the SUDs (Winters et al., 2012). It is thus to a culture's benefit to identify those forces that foster the development of resilience while understanding and correcting problems that contribute to the development of the SUDs. To this end the social sciences have much to offer society in its struggle against the SUDs.

The Role of Substance Use in a Culture

Virtually every known culture encourages the use of a select chemical(s) to alter the individual's perception of reality[53] (Glennon, 2008). Social factors that influence the individual's substance use decisions include (Pihl, 1999): (1) the general cultural environment, (2) the specific community in which the individual lives, (3) subcultures within the parent community, (4) family and/or peer influences, and (5) the context in which the compound is used. Further, the perceived availability of a given chemical(s) and the individual's age also influence substance use behavioral decisions, although these factors are often overlooked by researchers (Bennett & Golub, 2012; Latimer & Zur, 2010).

Engaging in the use of accepted substances under appropriate conditions serves several functions within a specific culture: It might facilitate social bonding, serve as a means of religious communion with the gods, function as a form of personal recreation or as a form of rebellion by members of a subgroup(s) within

---

[50]Such as why, if one member of a pair of identical twins has an alcohol use disorder, the probability that the other twin will develop an alcohol use disorder is approximately 50–50, for example.

[51]The author has taken the liberty to use the words "culture" and "social" interchangeably.

[52]Social groups influence the potential for individuals in that group to survive and reproduce, for example, and the mutual interdependency provides greater resources for the individual to draw upon than he or she would possess alone.

[53]Before you begin to argue against this statement, consider the case of caffeine: How many of us would like to begin the day without that first cup of coffee or two (or three ...) in your system? Remember: Caffeine is a chemical, too!

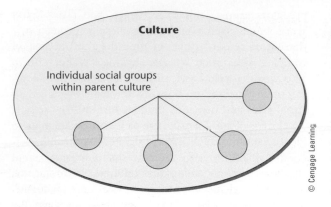

FIGURE 25-1 The Relationship between Different Subgroups and the Parent Culture.

the larger community, to cite but a few of the many roles that a substance might play in a given culture.

It has been suggested that art, rituals and the use of language are both unique to human beings and are found in every known culture (Froese, Woodward & Ikegami, 2012). The discovery that certain geometric designs are repeatedly found in prehistoric art from various cultures suggests that one commonality of these prehistoric cultures was the use of hallucinogenic substances that would activate the same neurological pathways in the brain (Froese, Woodward & Ikegami, 2012). The culture defines the meaning of the substance use, identifies behavioral rules by which its members are expected to abide the sanctions for violating these norms and the means by which those sanctions are enforced.[54] The relationship between subgroups and the parent culture is illustrated in Figure 25-1. Unfortunately, cultural norms are extremely slow to change, frequently leaving the individual without guidance when faced with misinformation and misperception about appropriate substance use behaviors.[55]

Individual substance use behaviors are in turn influenced by three factors: (a) drug (including the method of administration and pharmacological reward potential of that substance), (b) set (the individual's expectations for the use of that chemical, personality characteristics and current state of mind such as depression, suspiciousness, or feeling hopeless), and (c) setting (the context in which

the substance use takes place). Arguably "drug" might be said to fall in the purview of the biological sciences whereas "set" falls under the umbrella of the psychological sciences. "Setting" addresses the more salient social forces that help to shape the individual's substance use behavior. These categories are not mutually exclusive but interact to help shape the individual's substance use behaviors. An excellent example of this interaction effect was observed toward the end of the U.S. involvement in the Vietnam conflict. It was clear that victory was unlikely and large numbers of troops were being withdrawn from that country. Studies revealed that 45% of soldiers stationed in Vietnam were abusing heroin, which was of high purity, inexpensive, and plentiful. Follow-up research revealed that within a few months of their return to the United States only 5% of these individuals continued to abuse heroin.[56] These findings illustrate the strong influence of "drug" (high purity, low cost, readily available heroin) "set" (loss of hope for a victory) and "setting" (a military unit that was accepting of illicit drug use) interact to contribute to the individual's decision to use or not use a chemical(s).

Within the larger culture are various smaller social groups that reject at least some of the rules of the parent culture.[57] Those soldiers mentioned in the last paragraph who abused heroin while stationed in Vietnam illustrate the development of subgroup-specific values that were at odds with established military protocol, to cite one example. Some of the other forces that influence the individual's behavior include his or her perceived position within a social group (influential or peripheral member) and perceptions of the acceptable behavior(s) within that subgroup (Valente, Gallaher, & Mouttapa, 2004). It is possible that at least some of those soldiers who abused heroin while they were in Vietnam did so because they perceived that this was the behavioral norm for the unit to which they were assigned, not because of any internal desire to abuse opiates. This appears to explain why they were able to stop abusing heroin so easily upon their return to the United States.

Through the process of social learning or social modeling the individual participates in activities that define a subgroup (such as the abuse of certain

---

[54]This is clearly seen in how alcohol use by individuals in some Native American tribes is viewed as a sign of deviance and these individuals are shunned, while group drinking is viewed as the norm and at least tolerated by members of the community.

[55]Lest too many people become upset after reading this sentence it should be noted that *abstinence* is also a substance use behavior: The individual chooses to abstain from the use of alcohol, tobacco, or illicit drugs.

[56]It has been estimated that 31% of business travelers engage in illicit drug use away from home (Raw Data, 2012). One must question whether this substance abuse is motivated at least in part because the individuals were no longer in their home environment and thus felt less constrained by social mores that normally guide their behavior.

[57]The religious group known to historians as the "puritans" comes to mind here. They rejected the values of England to seek the right to practice their religion as they thought appropriate.

chemicals, style of dress, shared interests in certain forms of music, etc.) and reinforces the participant's identity as a member of a given subculture (Bennett & Golub, 2012). The social environment also can provide an awareness of the availability of drugs of abuse and their effects (Johnson, O'Malley, Bachman, & Schulenberg, 2012b). However, it is necessary to remember that membership in one subgroup does not exclude participation in other subgroups or the parent society (Bennett & Golub, 2012). Those soldiers who were abusing heroin while stationed in Vietnam, for example, were still members of the military, and subject to the rules and regulations that govern military life even if these rules and regulations were not rigorously enforced at the time.

Social Factors Influencing Individual Substance Use Decisions

There are a number of social factors that increase the individual's vulnerability for or help protect the individual from the SUDs. In this section we will briefly review some of the most important of these social factors:

Parenting

The topic of parental–child relationship patterns is discussed in more detail in Chapter 20. However, the reader must be reminded that the parent–child relationship that evolves over the course of the child's life is a potent social factor that can either constrain, give tacit approval to, or even encourage substance use by the growing individual. Parental influence on the child's behavior wanes over time but continues throughout the individual's life span.

Environmental Factors

Factors such as poverty, lack of social opportunities, lack of vocational opportunities, and familial structure either facilitate or help protect the individual from substance abuse (Dunlap, Johnson, Kotarba, & Fackler, 2010). For example: In certain levels of society the sale and distribution of drugs is viewed not with disdain but as legitimate ways for the individual to quickly acquire wealth and prestige where other opportunities to do so are limited at best. In their examination of adolescent alcohol use by inner-city youth, Epstein, Griffin & Botvin (2008) noted that the perceived benefits of drinking and social opportunities are the two most robust predictors of drinking by inner-city adolescents in their sample. It is not known whether these factors apply to the initiation of substance abuse although there is firm evidence to suggest that children

and adolescents tend to over estimate their peers' use of alcohol, tobacco, or other compounds, suggesting that they might over estimate the potential benefits of alcohol (and illicit drug) use, adding to their vulnerability toward development of an SUD.

Victimization[58]

Researchers have found a strong relationship between childhood abuse and neglect by the parents and subsequent substance abuse when the child grows up (Chaffin, Kelleher, & Hollenberg, 1996). There also is a relationship between victimization through interpersonal violence and the SUDs, as noted in Chapter 18. This is a bidirectional relationship, however, with some women who were victimized sexually turning to amphetamines or cocaine after the assault whereas in other cases the SUD might predate the assault(s) (Gilbert, El-Bassel, Chang, Wu, & Roy, 2011).

Hopelessness

Hopelessness overlaps the problem of victimization and is a robust predictor of substance abuse. This is demonstrated by the findings of the team of Zhang, Infante, Meit, English, Dunn, and Bowers, (2008) who concluded that the incidence of drug addiction and mental health problems are higher in the less affluent regions of Appalachia. This is an ill-defined region of the country that has long been economically disadvantaged, offering residents few opportunities for social advancement, especially those regions where the once predominant industry of coal mining has been curtailed and unemployment is higher. Hope for social and financial stability within this area is limited at best. The abuse of prescription drugs by teens and young adults has become rampant in Appalachia, although abuse of heroin and other illicit compounds is also not uncommon there. Alcohol as always plays a significant role in the substance abuse problem in this region if only because it is so accessible.[59] As this illustrates on a regional level the loss of hope contributes to vulnerability for the SUDs.

Music

Although often overlooked, music both helps to transmit social mores and provides behavioral models for the

---

[58]This topic is worthy of a book in its own right but we are forced to summarize the topic in just a few sentences.

[59]Arguably the long history of illegal alcohol distillation and sales in this region of the country could be said to have provided tacit approval of other forms of substance abuse

listener. The popular music of the 1950s frequently referred to marriage and lifelong commitment as appropriate goals. References to casual relationships was prohibited, or at least censored, as evidenced by the refusal of many ration stations to play the song "Kisses Sweeter than Wine" in the 1950s. The rationalization for this refusal was that the words were too provocative.[60] By the mid-1960s indirect, carefully worded references to illicit drug use were include in the lyrics of many popular songs, whereas by the late 1960s and throughout the 1970s popular music often expressed a casual "love 'em and leave 'em" (Epstein, 2012, p. 56) theme.[61]

The composition of music apparently is an unexplored element of its impact on the individual's social development. It is known that music stimulates the release of dopamine, and the nucleus accumbens becomes more active when the individual is listening to music, biological functions that parallel the individual's enjoyment of the music (Kalat, 2009). The majority of the popular songs in the 1960s were in a major key, which when combined with a fast tempo tends to elicit positive moods in the listener (Epstein, 2012). By the middle of the first decade of the 21st century, the majority of the popular songs were written in a minor key, which tends to elicit sadness and depression in the listener (Friedman, 2012). These are emotions that as discussed elsewhere in this text encourage substance abuse in an attempt at self-medication.

Social Mores

An interesting social experiment is currently taking place in Sweden. As the social restrictions against the use of tobacco products by women in that country relax, a greater and greater number of younger women are taking up the habit of smoking cigarettes (Kendler, Thornton, & Pederson, 2000). There is no evidence of a massive shift in the genetics of the population in that country, so it is logical to expect that cultural or social factors were acting as a balance to the desire by some women to smoke cigarettes. When these sanctions began to ease, the number of women in Sweden who smoked cigarettes began to increase. It is not unreasonable that social rules also strongly

influence other substance use behaviors beyond that of cigarette smoking.

Sex Ratio

Guttentag and Secord (1983) advanced a controversial theory that the male–female ratio helped to shape cultural norms. The authors suggested that when there is an excess of available men as opposed to women, social values tend to be more conservative and supportive of traditional marital values, strengthening the role of marriage as a stabilizing influence in that society. When the number of available women is equal to or exceeds that of available men, social values shift toward the liberal end of the spectrum according to the author. On this theoretical basis, Epstein (2012) suggested that the social values for the next 25 years will tend to be more conservative since the ratio of available men to available women will be approximately 1:1. This theory is quite provocative and obviously there is a need for more research in this area.

Legal Sanctions

Many of the legal sanctions imposed against those who break social rules governing substance use behaviors are well-known and need not be discussed further in this section. A new issue, however, is the move by some states to charge persons with metabolites of Tetrahydrocannabinol (THC) in their system to face criminal charges for "driving under the influence (of chemicals)" even if the persons were using "medicinal" marijuana. The judicial system has adopted the stance that any evidence of THC in the individual's blood or urine is ground for legal action.[62] Further, a number of states have legalized recreational marijuana use. The legal system in each state struggles with these issues.

Religious Affiliation

The individual's involvement with a formal religious group has been found to exert a mild to moderate deterrent effect on the individual's substance abuse and criminal behaviors. This deterrent effect begins to manifest during adolescence and continues through adulthood. Koenig, Haber, and Jacob (2011) identified several mechanisms through which religious affiliation might influence substance use behaviors and concluded that the (a) increased social support, (b) non-drinking norms, and (c) opportunity to gain relief from suffering

---

[60]It is ironic that the lyrics of this song refer to a lifelong commitment to a spouse, and is now broadcast without protest by many "easy listening" stations.

[61]Arguably this shift might be seen in the music of the band "The Beatles" over the years. A comparison of the content of their first songs compared with that of their final songs would arguably illustrate this shift in social values.

[62]As opposed to alcohol level in the person's blood: If the person's blood alcohol level falls below the defined level (usually 0.8 mg/dl of blood) he or she is not charged with driving under the influence of alcohol in most cases.

all appear to influence alcohol use decisions by members of that religious community. Unfortunately, the deterrent effect might reflect a self-selection process through which those individuals most likely engage in criminal behaviors or the abuse of illicit compounds avoid involvement with a formal religion. Still, there does appear to be a mild negative correlation between involvement in religion, especially active participation as opposed to simply attending services, and involvement in socially unacceptable behaviors.

Individual Life Goals

The individuals' identified life goals help to shape their substance use behavior(s) (Alquist & Baumeister, 2012). Again, the influence of individual life goals upon the person's behavior begins to manifest during adolescence and becomes stronger during late adolescence and young adulthood. At each point in life the individual must determine whether substance use or abuse is consistent with his or her long-term life goals. The more clearly defined the individuals' life goals and commitment toward achieving these goals, the less vulnerable they are to the development of a long-term SUD

(Alquist & Baumeister, 2012). However, the reverse is also true: If the individual's life goals are ill-defined, the greater the individual's vulnerability to the initial temptation of substance abuse and the possible development of a long-term SUD (Alquist & Baumeister, 2012).

Those individuals who constantly monitor their progress toward their life goals are less vulnerable to the temptations of substance abuse especially when such behavior is contrary to identified life goals. However, should the individuals become unsure about their priorities in life, they become more vulnerable to the dangers of substance abuse (Alquist & Baumeister, 2012). Commitment to life goals is rarely a problem for semi-socially approved compounds such as alcohol and tobacco. However, consider a low-level business executive who is being considered for a major promotion with another company, but who discovers that the potential new employer has a strict "no smoking" policy. The individuals then have a choice of either changing their smoking habits so that they could accept the new position, or, reject the new job because of the no-smoking policy. A flow chart of the decision-making process that the individual went through might look like the one in Figure 25-2.

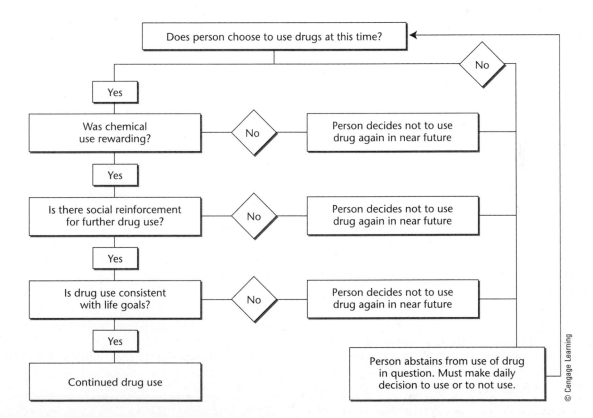

FIGURE 25-2 The Chemical Use Decision-Making Process.

Should this hypothetical individual have a clearly defined goal, say to be a mid-level or upper-level administrator in his or her chosen profession by the age of 40, he or she must reconcile continued substance abuse with the possibility of achieving this goal. Losing focus on this life goal might make the individual more vulnerable to the temptations of substance abuse (Alquist & Baumeister, 2012). Although the commitment to life goals will not entirely protect the individual from the dangers of developing an SUD, it is one factor that either lends impetus toward, or away from, such a problem.

Mass Media

A surprising social factor that apparently contributes to the SUDs is the media. The manner in which substance use, including that of alcohol and tobacco, is portrayed helps shape the individual's expectations for that compound's effects (Griffin & Botvin, 2010; Shadel & Scharf, 2012). After reviewing popular youth-rated movies released in the period from 1996 to 2009 the team of Bergamini, Demidenko, and Sargent (2013) concluded that only 22 movies each year portrayed cigarette smoking, a decline from earlier decades, which the authors attributed to the Master Settlement Agreement of 1998 that resolved claims against the tobacco industry by various states. However, in the same period portrayals of or references to alcohol use increased from 80 a year in 1996 to 145 a year in 2009.

Sports or entertainment celebrities are frequently viewed as role models by children, adolescents, and occasionally by adults. This is proven through the sales of replica football jerseys: The majority of jerseys sold have the name and number of a favorite player and only rarely is a second or third string player's name found on a jersey. The manner in which substance use is portrayed by the media, including music videos, also helps shape the individual's expectations about the degree to which the use of illicit drugs is acceptable (Griffin & Botvin, 2010). If a sports figure or media star were to be known to abuse a certain substance this would to some degree "legitimize" the use of that compound, especially for adolescents. However, there has been little systematic research into this topic and there is much to be discovered about the interaction between substance abuse by admired persons and the individual's substance use.

Advertising

Arguably one of the strongest influences on the use of those compounds that are legal to use, alcohol and tobacco products, is the advertising industry. This is demonstrated by the apparent correlation between the amount of money spent on tobacco product advertising and the number of children or adolescents who begin to smoke (Shadel & Scharf, 2012). The impact of advertising appears to be strongest prior to the initiation of cigarette smoking by children or adolescents, after which the addiction process appears to have more influence over the individual's smoking behavior than advertising (Shadel & Scharf, 2012). The influence of advertising on adult smoking behaviors, or that of alcohol use, is still not well understood at this time but there is no reason to suspect that advertising does not influence smoking or alcohol use behaviors by adults.

Expectancies

The development of the individual's expectancies for the effects of various compounds is shaped, in part, by how the abuse of those compounds is portrayed by the media. In medicine this would be called the "placebo effect": A compound works because the individual expects that it will work. When a pharmaceutical company applies for permission to market a new compound, it must (among other things) demonstrate that its product is more effective than a placebo. Unfortunately, the cognitive immaturity of children, adolescents,[63] as well as some adult substance abusers makes it difficult for the abuser to appropriately assess the benefits of or risks associated with substance use, contributing to a tendency for many to overvalue the perceived benefits of substance use while downplaying the risks associated with this practice.

Peer Groups/Social Support

Although the influence of peer groups on the individual's behavioral choices is strongest during childhood and adolescence, peers still retain some influence over the individual in the adult years. In adulthood, peers help to shape the individual's expectancies for alcohol and illicit drug abuse, possibly through the effects of social learning (Lau-Barraco, Braitman, Leonard, & Padilla, 2012). These relationships also indirectly reflect the individual's own drinking status: "[I]n young adults," Lau-Barraco et al. (2012) stated, "the proportion of heavy drinkers in one's social network predicts

---

[63]Discussed in chapter 20.

personal drinking" (p. 748). This effect appears to be strongest for men, although it applies to women as well (Lau-Barraco et al., 2012). These "drinking buddies" comprise a subset of the individual's social group whose primary shared interest is in the use of alcohol (Lau-Barraco et al., 2012). The alcohol use pattern of one's drinking buddies would be a strong predictor of an individual's own alcohol use.

The measurement of peer group influence is difficult, in part because the individual selects peer groups with substance use behaviors similar to his or her own. To avoid criticism from peers the individuals must choose to either change social groups to one more accepting of their substance use, hide their substance use from their peer group, or discontinue the abuse of those substances discouraged by their peers. Those individuals who perceive peers as being critical of their marijuana use tend to abstain from its use, whereas those who view their peers as being accepting of their marijuana use are more likely to engage in its use.

Surprisingly global levels of positive social support appear to have a stronger influence upon the individual's behavior than do recovery-specific non-supportive forces, possibly because the positive social support could enhance the individual's general feelings of competence and efficacy (Schmitt, 2003). Social support might fall into one of the following four different categories: (1) physical support (examples include financial assistance or assumption of child care responsibilities for limited periods of time[64]), (2) emotional support (unconditionally listening to the problems that the person in early recovery encounters, for example, or assisting the individual form non-substance centered friendships), (3) Information sharing (to help the individual in unbiased decision making), and (4) feedback from others to the individuals about their behavior (including possible early signs of a potential relapse as well as what others perceive the individuals are doing to help themselves). The positive form of any of these categories is supportive of abstinence from substance abuse while the negative form of any of these four categories might contribute to the individual's ultimate relapse to active substance use.

Cost

The economic investment in substance use often serves as a deterrent to alcohol use. The team of Zhao, Stockwell, Martin, Macdonald, Vallance, Treno, Ponicko, Tu, and Buxton (2013) examined the mortality statistics in British Columbia for the period from 2002 to 2009 and found that the government-mandated 10% increase in the minimum price of beer and distilled spirits resulted in a 32% drop in the number of deaths that were clearly alcohol-related such as alcohol poisoning and alcoholic cardiomyopathy. The authors speculated that one reason for the observed drop in alcohol-related mortality might be because even heavy drinkers reduced their daily alcohol intake in response to the increased cost of preferred beverages. This study is but the latest in a long series of research studies that discovered an inverse relationship between the cost of alcoholic beverages and the amount of alcohol consumed. It is not known whether this inverse ratio between cost and substance use applies to the illicit drugs, although this would appear to be fertile ground for clinical research studies.

Applications of the Social Component of the Bio/Psycho/Social Model

Griffin and Botvin (2010) suggested that the continuum of intervention into the SUDs involves three elements: (a) prevention, (b) treatment,[65] and (c) maintenance.[66] Prevention, according to the authors, is further subdivided into: (a) universal interventions, (b) selective interventions, and (c) indicated interventions. Universal forms of intervention focus on the general population with the goal of avoiding, or delaying, the initiation of substance abuse. Selective interventions target identified high-risk groups, while indicated interventions focus on those individuals who demonstrate early warning signs suggestive of a possible SUD developing. Indicated interventions might be viewed as falling under the umbrella of the psychological sciences, again underscoring the interrelatedness of the bio/psycho/social model of the addictions.

One selective intervention reviewed by Griffin and Botvin (2010) was the Community Trials Intervention to Reduce High-Risk Drinking (RHRD). This intervention model is based on five components, each designed to reduce potential high risk drinking: (1) reduced access to alcohol through application of community zoning ordinances, (2) training those who dispense

---

[64]Or, "babysitting."

[65]Discussed in Chapter 31.

[66]Discussed in Chapter 31.

TABLE 25-1
Factors That Support or Undermine Efforts to Abstain from Alcohol or Illicit Drugs

POSITIVE FACTORS (WHICH SUPPORT RECOVERY EFFORTS)	NEGATIVE FACTORS (WHICH UNDERMINE RECOVERY EFFORTS)
Emotional support	Preoccupation with problems others are experiencing (care taking)
Encouragement	Ties to past substance-centered support
Care and concern	("She used to babysit the kids when I went out to buy drugs," for example)
Communication (friends, family)	
Able to count on others for emotional support	Lack of support from social network (is made to feel guilty for past substance use, for example)
External support (checking up on person)	Lack of support from prior social network (former "using buddies" who now work to undermine the individual's efforts to abstain from drugs)
Praise and recognition for hard work ("You have worked so hard to stay clean," for example.)	
Positive social encounters	Identification with substance-abusing subgroup for sense of belonging
Tangible help (child care, place to live, etc.)	
Bringing personal items to person while in rehabilitation program (comb, shampoo-scented soap, etc.)	Members of social group who keep reminding person of past trauma ("Has your boyfriend beat you up since you stopped drinking?" for example)
Keeping lines of communications open (telephone calls, greeting cards, letters, etc.)	Living in proximity to drug dealers or substance-abusing "friends" visiting person attempting to abstain from alcohol or drug use
Involvement in social activities (going shopping with a friend, meeting for lunch, etc.)	Physically abusive or substance-using significant other
Providing information on and support for efforts to learn about effects of drugs	Lack of assertiveness skills
Social skills training	

SOURCE: Based on Tracy, Munson, Peterson, & Floersch (2010).

alcohol to recognize individuals whose alcohol use has put them at risk for driving after drinking, (3) application of law enforcement aimed at drinking activities such as sobriety checkpoints, (4) training retailers to recognize underage drinkers and refrain from selling alcohol to them, and (5) formation of community coalitions that will support and encourage the application of steps 1–4. One example of a community-wide or systemic intervention aimed at reducing high rates of alcohol abuse or alcohol use by minors was discussed by Zhao et al. (2013) who discovered that a state-mandated increase in taxes on alcoholic beverages apparently resulted in a 32% reduction in alcohol-related deaths.

Although the original intent of the paper by Tracy, Munson, Peterson, and Floersch (2010) was to identify social forces that might pressure a woman into or away from substance abuse, these factors could apply to either a male or female with a substance use problem. Development or emphasis on those positive social forces that impact the individual's recovery from an SUD offers the opportunity for increasing the individual's chances of success. Identification of negative social forces so that these issues might be addressed will reduce the possibility of the individual relapsing to, or continuing, the abuse of chemicals. Table 25-1 provides a summary of factors which both support or possibly undermine the individual's efforts at recovery.

Psycho-Educational Intervention Programs

The Drug Abuse Resistance Education (D.A.R.E.) and similar programs are examples of social interventions and are quite popular. Such programs are based on the theory that by teaching children about the harmful effects of alcohol or drugs while helping them build self-esteem would inoculate them against the desire to abuse chemicals in later life. The D.A.R.E. program is usually led by a local police officer, and is carried out in the classroom setting. Other programs utilize the services of various mental health or school guidance professionals. Although there is a great deal of anecdotal support for such programs, there is only limited clinical research data suggesting that they are effective and arguably such programs have not reached their full potential for curbing childhood or adolescent SUDs (Spoth, Greenberg, & Turrisi, 2009).

Critics of psycho-educational programs such as D.A.R.E. are growing increasingly vocal, challenging the need or effectiveness of such programs for a number of reasons. Although brief, individualized interventional programs tailored to the student's personality style have been found to be of value (Conrod, Castellanos-Ryan, & Strang, 2010), psycho-educational programs such as D.A.R.E. use a "one size fits all" approach that fails to take the student's individual needs into account. Further, the question of whether primary intervention for an SUD is an educational systems issue has been raised (Zunz, Ferguson, & Senter, 2005). Many school districts find that such programs impose significant demands upon the classroom instructors, detract them from already limited classwork instructional time, all apparently with limited benefit to the students. Lillenfeld (2012) even raised the disturbing possibility that psycho-educational programs such as D.A.R.E. have the potential to harm those who are essentially coerced into participating in the program sessions.

Other critics point out that these programs usually provide negative propaganda about the effects of alcohol or drugs, an approach that has never been demonstrated to work (Leavitt, 2003; Walton, 2002). At best, the critics of psycho-educational programs note that the:

> evidence suggests that, although knowledge can be increased, and expressed attitudes may be changed, affecting drinking behavior through school programs is a very difficult task. (Room, Babor, & Rehm, 2005, p. 525)

There is no reason to suspect that changing other forms of substance use behavior would be different. The vast amounts of information provided to the participants will, at best, provide a temporary modification of the individual's behavior (Reyna & Farley, 2006/ 2007). Indeed, there is evidence that programs such as D.A.R.E. are counter productive, increasing the student's curiosity about the drugs of abuse (McPherson, Yudko, Murray-Bridges, Rodriguez, & Lindo-Moulds, 2009). When the child or adolescent experiments with

a recreational substance (or knows of a friend who has done so) and finds that the dreaded consequences did not happen to him or her, the credibility of the information provided is lost.

There is a modest body of evidence suggesting a positive short-term effect from programs that use a format based on peer interaction, refusal skills training, and skills that helped the student change normative beliefs were more effective than classroom instructional programs facilitated by a teacher or law enforcement staff member (Windle & Zucker, 2010). Characteristics of such programs include smaller numbers of students (thus facilitating peer interactions), a greater number of contact hours per week, and focus on social changes outside of the school itself were found to be more effective than those programs that focused simply on classroom instruction about the dangers of drug abuse (Windle & Zucker, 2010).

Critics of psycho-educational programs suggest that such programs continue because they give the illusion of doing something about the growing problem of childhood and adolescent SUDs (Leavitt, 2003), but they little more than provide an illusion. This possibility is supported by the observation made earlier that students are not provided with the full continuum of care, and that those students most in need are not served by psycho-educational programs. Fortunately, many school districts are starting to fight back against such programs, citing their lack of proven success and the loss of classroom instruction time as reasons for rejecting such programs.

Chapter Summary

In spite of almost a century's effort, no "grand unifying theory" of the addictions has emerged. Some therapeutic theories appear to offer some insight(s) into various behaviors often noted in people who have SUDs. However, the degree to which these theoretical models explain the SUDs vary from one person to the next. Some substance abusers appear to use chemicals to cope with psychological distress, whereas others do so in response to social pressure and yet others appear to be biologically predisposed to abuse chemicals. In response to this lack of consensus, the American Society of Addiction Medicine has suggested a bio/psycho/ social model of the addictions, a model that at this time appears to provide clinicians from multiple disciplines' theoretical support for their efforts to understand and treat the SUDs.

CHAPTER 26

The Substance Use Disorders as a Disease of the Human Spirit

Introduction

It is possible to view a select individual from a range of perspectives: The individual is (or, is not) a taxpayer, is male or female, is in perfect health or suffering from an acute or chronic disease(s), and so on. People are also spiritual beings[1] a descriptor that is rarely used in today's world, who are either actively or passively involved in a relationship with a Higher Being.[2] The individual does not suddenly stop being a spiritual being when he or she consults with a physician, psychologist, social worker, or other health care professional (Pargament, 2007). The individual remains a spiritual being in every aspect of her or his life, whether this is acknowledged by the person or not.

Wade (2009) argued that "[t]here is no church of oneself" (p. 2). Arguably, in spite of this assertion, the substance use disorders (SUDs) might be viewed as an example of a church of oneself in that the service of the individual's addiction becomes the prime focus of that person's life. "I want what I want, when I want it!!!" is the litany of the addicted person, who then decries that "I deserve to feel the way that I want to feel (or not to feel the discomfort of withdrawal)!" Such self-centered thinking places the medical sciences in a conundrum: At its best, medical science is uncomfortable with the idea of spirituality, leaving physicians with the task of dealing with patients who are spiritual beings, although lacking the conceptual framework or training within which to do so (Pargament, 2007). This unfortunately robs that health care professional of a potentially insightful perspective into one of the forces that helps to shape the individual's response to illness. In this chapter the perspective that the addictions are a product of a spiritual disorder will be examined.

How the Soul Was Lost

Why am I here? What is the purpose of my life? These are questions that each individual must face, and possibly answer before he or she leaves this life. There are no firm answers: Just questions within questions, held together by doubt or answered by that increasingly rare commodity: faith. In the span of a few centuries the face of Western civilization changed in response to the Renaissance, and with it the spiritual lives of tens of millions of people in the Western world were altered forever. How did this happen?

The Renaissance was sustained by the rediscovery of ancient Greek and Roman literature, much of which had been recovered from the Islamic cultures in the Middle East as Europe awoke from the social and

---

[1]It should be noted that there is a difference between spirituality and religion.

[2]Arguably, the atheists could, by their very rejection of the concept of a Higher Being still could be said to be relating to that Being in a negative manner: "I do not believe that such a Being exists."

philosophical disaster collectively called the "dark ages." These writings offered a powerful new paradigm—the humanities—emerged. Proponents of the humanities quickly declared this new field of study to be superior to medicine, the law, and especially theology. Unfortunately the proponents of the humanities failed to realize that the paradigm that they were building, as powerful as it might seem to be, was only a theoretical model, a lens as it were through which to view and interpret that which is external to the viewer.

Proponents of the humanities loudly proclaimed the superiority of their new paradigm, and thorough process: "Science has replaced Religion as the ultimate arbiter of Truth in many people's minds" (Wilcock, 2011, p. 4). There is no "mind" or "soul" to the proponents of this humanistic perspective, just electrochemical laws that shape our view of ourselves and the universe around us. This perspective has proven itself to be very strong indeed, and many of the questions about how the universe works have apparently been answered. However, individual still struggles with the age-old questions: Who am I? and Why am I here? In seeking the answer to these questions, the individual returns to the world of spirituality, although often through a quasi-humanistic perspective that blinds the person to the true scope of his or her journey. In this manner, spirituality becomes a motivating force or a void within the individual's life. To seek the answer opens the door to a spiritual quest that lasts a lifetime.

The humanist urges the searcher to pass by the door, turning away from the spiritual and look to the physical world for the answers in the cold, hard, dead, reality that science offers. They are blinded by the reality that those who follow the spiritual path, the humanist, and the scientist all seek the same answer: Ultimate truth. The theologian and scientist just disagree as to the definition of ultimate Truth. Is all that is seen and unseen part of a divine plan,[3] which in turn implies that there is a Planner, or did it just happen?[4] Would the theologian or scientist be able to accept the other's ultimate Truth?

Scientists have now understood that the dichotomy between mind and body, which emerged during the Renaissance, is artificial, and unnecessary. Without the body, there is no "mind". Without the mind, the body exists only as a platform for biological functions such as reproduction to be carried out.[5] However, significant questions remain to be answered: Is what is called the "soul" a product of the mind, of self-awareness, or does it have a separate existence from the body? These questions remain unanswered in spite of the best efforts of generations of scientists and philosophers. Does the mind have a separate existence from the body? Is the "soul" limited to self-awareness or is it the expression of a larger, unseen force? The answers to these questions influence how the person views life?

Since ancient times, philosophers have suggested that there exists within each of us a spark of divine light, which was called spiritus by the ancient Romans. Once it is extinguished the light of that individual's life is lost forever (Doweiko, 1999; Milstein, 2008). Few scientists have attempted to define or measure spiritus; it has for the most part remained ignored, or viewed as an ill-defined relic from the past. Pragmatic scientists argue that because spiritus cannot be replicated in a laboratory it is unworthy of study, or that it is an illusion. At the same time mainstream society appears to be developing a growing sense of spirituality and one of the major treatment modalities for the SUDs is a program designed to facilitate spiritual growth.

Many now postulate that the "mind" reflects nothing more than the outcome of chemical interactions within and between neurons. The "mind" is nothing more than an illusion created by the brain, they argue, and as such should be subjected to the same methods of scientific study applied to other realms of existence. It is argued that in time the neurochemical foundation(s) of the entity called "mind" will be discovered through scientific inquiry.[6] However, scientific inquiry, even if it does reveal the neurochemical foundation(s) of the mind, does not explain why scientific inquiry itself came to exist or why the mind exists at all. It is ironic that at the same time that many neuroscientists deny the existence of the "mind" as a separate entity from the brain itself, pharmaceutical companies

---

[3]Which would imply that there is one who made the Plan.

[4]A position that then implies that existence is meaningless, unless the individual strives to give it meaning. Paradoxically this would require a decision on the part of the individual, who then assumes the role of a Planner, at least to a limited degree.

[5]For those who decry this statement remember that early hominids, like most members of the animal kingdom, live just long enough to produce the next generation and then quietly die off from accidents, predation, or disease. Early *Homo sapiens* for example had an average lifespan of 25–30 years.

[6]When this point is reached, will the era of mind-control be far behind?

are heavily invested in the search to find compounds that might heal, or at least calm, troubled minds.[7]

Still, in their search for a pharmacological treatment to emotional pain and suffering, the spiritual aspect of the individuals' existence is totally ignored (Pargament, 2007). The pharmacological treatments for "mental illness," itself a poorly defined term whose very existence has been challenged, seek to calm troubled minds. Thus, one group of scientists denies the existence of the human spirit, whereas other scientists seek pharmacological treatments to ease its suffering. This conundrum appears to reflect the fact that science has "driven a wedge between faith and reason" (p. 2). Is this wedge (for want of a better word) appropriate? Countless thousands of generations invested untold millions of man-hours in the exploration of spiritus and its implications for daily life. Further, they did so in an era when the intensity of work necessary for basic survival was far higher than it is today. Perhaps, it is argued here, one reason why these earlier generations invested so much time and effort into this search was because it was important to define the 'self' in an era where life seemed so uncertain. The wedge that science has forced between faith and reason might, in generations to come, be proven to have undermined the search for the very answers that it seeks to find.

Are science, faith, and reason natural enemies? Each provides the proponent of that perspective a source of stability on which to stand and to define the "self." Arguably this spiritual "grounding" has been lost in a process that began with Renaissance and gathered momentum from the 17th century to the present. The philosopher Roger Bacon[8] argued that only those facts that could be observed, measured, and/or replicated were worthy of belief (Cahill, 2006). This was a radical idea at a time when the Church was viewed as the ultimate authority about reality and the reason for human existence. These cultural rules have been eroded by the onslaught of scientific inquiry to the point where the current generation has become "probably the first major culture in human history with no shared picture of reality" (Primack & Abrams, 2006, p. 4). Traditional rituals used by earlier generations to help define "self" and provide a sense of being "grounded" for the individual have been abandoned (Pargament, 2007).

A reflection of this process is how the very concept of Spiritus is under attack by the "pervasive doctrine of scientific materialism" (Frattaroli, 2001, p. 20). Everything can be understood, it is argued, if you break things down to their most elemental units.[9] Scientific materialism offers empty references to the "mind," or the "brain," as if these things were synonymous with and replaced the word soul (Frattaroli, 2001). This contributes to a fundamental void on which the individual is expected to build his or her life. The whole of existence, including yourself, is a great cosmological accident, it is argued, and on that foundation you should build your life and find a reason for being. Alcohol and/or drugs appear to answer these fundamental questions: "I am here to seek pleasure by manipulating the chemical basis on which my sense of 'self' is based." From this perspective one might argue that the SUDs are a form of chemical narcissism in which the desires of the "self" are made central to one's view of the universe. Unfortunately in many cases the individual discovers that these chemicals offer not answers, but enslavement.

Human beings are a strange creature because we "are each ... able to conceptualize and characterize ourselves as objects distinct from the rest of nature—and from the rest of our species" (Tattersall, 2012, p. 62). To the philosopher William James there were two interconnected forms of self-awareness: the spiritual (internal psychological forces) and the social (knowledge of one's place in a larger group of unique individuals). The latter is at this point most important, for one cannot develop an internal sense of "them" without concurrently developing a sense of "I," as an individual (Tattersall, 2012). The journey toward becoming an individual begins in infancy when the mother fails to instantly respond to the infant's cries and over the course of the individual's life she or he becomes increasingly aware of a chasm that will never be crossed no matter how hard one might try. Spirituality, which is part of the shared view of reality shared by earlier generations, helped to provide security in the face of this ultimate isolation and to some the promise of crossing that chasm to join with a higher being.

Yet between scientific materialism and spirituality exists a conundrum: Although the ability of science to

---

[7]See Breakout Discussion # 3 for Chapter 26 for a discussion on this topic.

[8]Bacon, Roger: B. 1214(?)–D. 1294. English friar, scientist, and philosopher.

[9]A counterargument to this assertion might very well be: At what level of integration does the collected pool of chemical interactions between and within cells become self-aware, or, develop spiritual desires?

reproduce experimental findings and replicate these findings gives it a self-defined air of authority, it is not (as many assume should they stop to think about this issue at all) the ultimate authority on matters of the spirit. Issues of the soul, or the individual spirit, must be experienced, a process that does not lend itself to replication or external measurement (Frattaroli, 2001). Spirituality allows not for replication and measurement, but for the discovery of meaning in the face of the absurdity of life (Milstein, 2008). For, life is indeed absurd: Science might ultimately answer the question of how, however, its ability to answer the question of why remains very much in doubt. By definition, God[10] the creator, is outside of creation and is not subject to the methods of scientific verification that evolved within His creation (Cahill, 2006).[11] A logical conclusion (using the perspective of modern science) is that God must not exist. To the spiritual believer, this lack of objective verification is unimportant since the creator would stand outside of His creation and thus could not be measured from those within it.

Is it true that things unmeasured do not exist? A person's perceptions cannot be measured, although they certainly do exist. For example, Pargament (2007) suggested that spirituality is "a critical and distinctive dimension of human motivation" (p. 60). It is a search for personal identity, self-knowledge, and a defining purpose in the individual's life (Pargament & Sweeney, 2011). If, as Siegel (2008) suggested, relationships shape and direct energy flow both between and within individuals, and the individual believes in nothing outside of the "self," then there is no energy flow from that individual to another. Without the spiritual, there is nothing against which to measure the demands of the "self." Unfortunately, large segments of society have turned away from the spiritual perhaps accounting for why many report a sense of drifting through the experience of life without direction

or meaning. Technology[12] offers toys to entertain the masses, and science attempts to find and measure truth: Neither can provide a sense of purpose, or a direction in life. If the individual has a spirituality centered life, then he or she will:

> *begin to build their lives around the sacred [and] the sacred can begin to lend greater coherence to disparate thoughts, feelings, actions and goals by superseding all other values, integrating competing aspirations into a unified life plan, and [provide] direction and guidance from day to day. (Pargament, 2007, p. 72)*

The reverse is also true: If the individual lacks a spirituality component to his or her life, he or she is left with a void. It is into this void that alcohol and the drugs of abuse slip. Although they do not ultimately offer a direction in life, they do offer an illusion of a purpose, along with the illusion of control over one's feelings. Control, or at least the illusion of control, has been found to be one of the forces that helps to define happiness (Marcus, 2008; Pargament, 2007). For the self-absorbed narcissist, the drugs of abuse offer the individual a god-like power to feel not that which is experienced, but that which is desired.[13] This is a seductive power which ensnares many by its charms, at least until they discover that the desired control over their emotions is only an illusion, and that they are now physically addicted to a chemical(s).

The Ghost in the Machine

There are some philosophers who believe that the story of the Garden of Eden, as related in the Holy Bible, might not relate to the physical act of Eve taking a bite out of an apple from the Tree of Knowledge, but to the development of self-awareness (Fromm, 1956). Many animals have limited abilities to vocalize, using various calls to warn of predators, identify the location of other members of the clan or attract mates. The ability of humans to vocalize using an extensive vocabulary of words and gestures allows us to communicate, admittedly in an imperfect manner, an almost infinite range of ideas. Arguably language evolved to help the individual, however,

---

[10]The term here is used in the sense of a Higher Power, although the title He-Who-Has-No-Name might be better, since she or he would stand outside of creation and thus not be bound by its inherent limits.

[11]In reality, both science and spirituality seek the same thing: Truth. But many lose track of this fact, and see each as antagonistic to the other. Truth is not antagonistic to itself, nor can it ever be. The methods that Francis Bacon espoused might not be the same as those selected by those on a spiritual journey, but each seeks to answer the same question: Who am I, and, why am I here?

[12]Including the various chemicals of abuse that have emerged as a result of man's creativity.

[13]Which possibly helps to explain why adolescence is a "high-risk" period in life for the development of the substance use disorders. Adolescents are notoriously self-centered and rebellious at times, characteristics that make them vulnerable to the allure of the drugs of abuse.

imperfectly cross the chasm between "self" and "other." It is because of this sense of isolation that we strive to join or merge with something beyond the "self," be it another person, a Higher Power, or a chemical that holds the promise of existential anesthesia.

"The awareness of human separation," wrote Fromm (1956), "without reunion by love is the source of shame. It is at the same time the source of guilt and anxiety" (p. 8). The experience of ultimate isolation becomes an "unbearable prison" (Fromm, 1956, p. 7). The prison can be escaped though the offering of love to another. However, love is a risk: It is all too often an imperfect expression of our feelings and when offered to another there is the risk of rejection, forcing us to acknowledge our isolation and imperfections. Further, no matter how passionately we might love, or how deeply we might love, in the end we are powerless to fully cross the chasm between "self" and "other."

This reality proves both painful for the individual, and provides the drugs of abuse an opportunity to seduce the user through the promise of effortless joy and peace. Although this hypothesis cannot be proven, the fact that many of the drugs of abuse trigger the reward cascade through the same nerve pathways activated by a strong love relationship would seem to offer circumstantial support for this theory. It is our very isolation that allows the drug(s) of abuse into the lives of those who seek to escape, and to join with something greater than the "self," according to the spiritual model. Some adherents of this model go further and suggest that it is through the ability of drugs to enslave the individual that the Evil one[14] seeks to work his will upon humanity.

Self-awareness brings with it the right of self-determination, but also carries with it the responsibility for making choices. A bird does not choose to be a bird. A tree does not choose to be a tree. But the individual is able to choose how to behave. Fromm (1956, 1968) suggested that this ability to choose and responsibility for our choices is the ultimate price that we pay for individuality. It the individual were to choose to give of the "self" to another through love, she or he might transcend the ultimate isolation, but this is only attempted at the risk of failure.

The mid-20th century philosopher Thomas Merton (1978) took a similar view on the nature of human existence when he argued that the individual cannot achieve happiness through any form of compulsive behavior (Merton, 1961, 1978). Rather, the individual "self" is defined by the love that is shared openly and honestly with others (including a higher spirit). Martin Buber (1970) took an even more extreme view, stating that it is only through the relationships that the individual chooses to enter into that the "self" is defined. However, if the relationship that one enters into is not with others, but with a chemical(s) to provide pleasure to the "self," is there a relationship? Love, according to Pargament (2007), reflects the ability to shift focus from the "self" to others. What if one withdraws love from others, in order to invest that emotional energy and gratification into the "self"? Would this not, as the founders of Alcoholics Anonymous suggested, be a "disease" of that individual's spirit?

From this perspective, the individual with an SUD might be viewed as being on a form of a:

> spiritual search. They really are looking for something akin to the great hereafter, and they flirt with death to find it. Misguided, romantic, foolish, needful, they think that they can escape from the world by artificial means. And they shoot, snort, drink, pop or smoke those means as they have to leave their pain and find their refuge. At first it works. But, then it doesn't (Baber, 1998, p. 29).

Admittedly, we all experience pain and a sense of discontent or being incomplete in life. Further, the stress of daily living conspires to shatter the individual's spirit in a thousand different ways. To survive, some pull within the "self." Others seek the mindless illusion of safety offered by false gods such as possessions, or drugs of abuse. A minority choose to embark on a lifelong journey of spiritual growth.

The Pain of Life

To be alive, an ancient Hebrew proverb maintains, is to know pain. It is a necessary part of the human experience, and this same proverb states that not to know pain is not to be fully alive. We all begin life with "hope, faith and fortitude" (Fromm, 1968, p. 20). But in each era these traits are assaulted on a moment-to-moment basis by the trials and tribulations of life. The individual's sense of hope is shattered, and without a sense of groundedness, the individual is left with nothing but a sense of emptiness, or a painful void within (Tillich, 1957). It is at this point that some recoil

---

[14]Which is an interesting debate, although it is far beyond the scope of this text.

in horror, and become spiritual narcissists: self-centered, unwilling to see any reason to deny the "self" any desire or pleasure.

This is not to say that every individual with an SUD has faced an existential crisis of the kind described here. Even in cases where the person has faced such a crisis, it may have remained unconscious, hidden behind walls of self-deception and denial. In both the cases where the individual is, or is not, aware of the struggle within, he or she is still overwhelmed by the stressors of daily living, and that the various drugs of abuse offer at least the illusion of protecting the individual from the pain of isolation and existence.

Diseases of the Mind/Diseases of the Spirit: The Mind/Body Question

It is possible for a spiritual disorder to manifest as a physical disease? There are many answers to this question. The American humorist Samuel Clemens[15] once stated that since he was born when Halley's Comet was high in the sky in 1835, that he was destined to pass from this life when Halley's Comet was again high in the sky above the Earth. This prediction did indeed come true when he died in 1910. Did he "program" himself to pass from this life? It is indeed a point that could be debated at length without a clear answer. Most health care professionals can relate a similar story in which a seemingly healthy individual predicted the time of his or her death in advance. At what point do these spiritual issues become a physical disease? One person, having lost a deeply loved spouse, might "pine away" for their now deceased partner, and slowly fade from life. These are very real examples of how a spiritual[16] disease can manifest as a physical illness that are well known to any person involved in a patient care capacity.

The question of whether the SUDs are a brain disorder, as is suggested by proponents of the medical model, a result of a psychosocial process, as is suggested by proponents of the psychosocial models of the SUDs, or a spiritual disorder (the premise of this chapter) is one that may have implications for other disorders as well. Although many are uncomfortable in discussing spiritual matters, there is an emerging body of evidence that suggests that individuals with strong spiritual beliefs are less likely to become addicted to a chemical(s), to live longer, and, more likely to recover should they develop an SUD (Haber, 2008; Sterling et al., 2006).

Modern medicine struggles to adhere to an artificial mind-body dichotomy[17] that began to evolve in the 14th century. But the addictions do not fall into this neat dichotomy of mind/body. The SUDs are not totally a physical illness, nor are they exclusively a disease of the mind. Rather, they rest on a triad of supports: mind, body, and spirit, with the latter showing great potential to moderate the alcohol use disorders (AUDs) (and by implication the other SUDs as well) (Haber, 2008). This model, although it would seem to account for the observed phenomena of the SUDs, still makes many uncomfortable because of the inclusion of spirituality.

The Growth of Addictions: The Circle Narrows

The AUDs provide a very clear example of the relationship between the spirituality and the AUDs. The use of alcohol is a behavioral choice. In the case of heavy alcohol use, it can be viewed as being an axis (Brown, 1985; Hyman, 2005) around which the individual's life now revolves.[18] Alcohol (and, by implication, the other drugs of abuse) assumes a role of "central importance" (Brown, 1985, p. 78) around which the individual centers his or her life. It is often difficult for those who have never struggled with a SUD to understand this point. But, it is not uncommon for the addicted person to choose continued substance use over family, friends, their jobs, or even personal health.

Individuals with SUDs often present others with a level of self-centeredness that puzzles, if not offends, others. Whether this is a real, or pseudo-personality disorder has never been resolved. But the individual is

---

[15]Also known as Mark Twain.

[16]Some would argue that these are "psychological" disorders and not "spiritual" issues at all. Where the line falls between psychological and spiritual diseases is left to the reader to decide.

[17]Actually, the mind-body dichotomy is an artificial one, as each blends into the other.

[18]As will be discussed later in this text, there is evidence that many persons with an evolving SUD turn aside from this path.

viewed as having a form of "moral insanity" in which they:

> could not manage our own lives. We could not live and enjoy life as other people do. We have to have something different, and we thought that we found it in drugs. We placed their use ahead of the welfare of our families, our wives, husbands, and our children. We had to have drugs at all costs (Narcotics Anonymous 1982, p. 11, italics in original deleted).

There are persons whose all-consuming interest is limited only to themselves. Such persons are often presented as an object of ridicule in the popular media. They care about nothing beyond that little portion of the universe known as the "self." Their only love is of the "self," which they view as being worthy of adoration or as being superior to the average person. Just as this personality type epitomizes self-love, and as such is a perversion of love itself, so the SUDs might be viewed as another form of a perversion of self-love. The individual's initial choice to use a recreational chemical(s) might reflect curiosity or a desire to partake in a social activity. But it also could be viewed as an attempt on the part of the individual to impose his or her will on external reality, supporting the delusion that there is nothing as important as the "self." Unfortunately:

> pandering to delusions of self-importance weakens the true self, and diminishes our ability to distinguish desires from needs. (Norris, 1996, pp. 14-15)

This latter point is important, for individuals who abuse chemicals often confuse their wants with their needs, a confusion that the drug(s) of abuse reinforces through their ability to overstimulate the brain's reward system. Eventually, the individuals reach the point where they come to believe that continued substance use is a need on their part. This accounts for the tendency for the exaggerated concern of a person with an SUD to maintain an adequate supply of his or her drug(s) of choice. For example, consider the hypothetical alcohol-dependent person who, with six or seven cases of beer already in the basement, went to buy six more cases "just in case…you can never have too much of a good thing." This individual's emphasis on having 12 cases of beer as a "good thing" clearly reflects the manner in which they have centered their life around the continued use of alcohol. Other people are viewed as either an inconvenience to the individual's goal of continued substance use, or as an object to manipulate in order to sustain access to further substance(s).

However nothing is allowed to come between the individual and his or her drug(s) of choice, if at all possible.

The Circle of Addiction: Priorities

As the SUD comes to dominate the individual's life, the person finds that more and more effort must be expended just to maintain the SUD. For example, many heroin or cocaine addicts have reported that they had to engage in prostitution (either heterosexual or homosexual), as well as theft, in order to obtain the money necessary to buy the next day's supply of drugs. Possessions are sold, or traded, for chemicals, and over time the individual might even begin to deteriorate socially as more resources are directed to the maintenance of his or her SUD. The addicted persons, if they were not manipulative prior to the onset of their addiction, become manipulative in the service of their addiction.

Some of the Games of Addiction

Given that the individuals demands continued access to a desired substance(s) at the center of their life, it is only to be expected that the persons will attempt to build a support system that will enable them to continue to engage in the use of that chemical(s). Part of this support system is maintained through an intricate web of manipulative "games," the sole purpose of which is to protect the addiction. "I cannot risk offending Aunt Clara," one person with a SUD might think, "because she is old and ill, and I will lose any chance of an inheritance if I do offend her." Thus the individuals choose a path that will enable them to present themselves in the best possible light.

Having a real or feigned illness is a popular manipulative "game" utilized by those who either do not wish to face the consequences of their addiction, or, wish to obtain desired drugs from a physician. So, rather than going to work with the smell of alcohol still surrounding them because he or she had been out drinking the night before, the person calls in "sick." To block the effects of early alcohol withdrawal while at work, an alcohol-dependent person might visit a physician(s) for treatment of an "anxiety" disorder, although being careful to make no mention of his or her AUD. In each case, the individual's substance-related behavior is now made legitimate by the illusion of an illness, and friends/coworkers/physicians become unwitting elements of that person's substance use support system.

To protect their source of drugs, and to justify its continued use, patients must often go through elaborate ruses to keep their SUD hidden. They might study medical textbooks in order to learn exactly what symptoms they need to report to a physician in order to obtain a desired prescription, or even engage in "doctor shopping"[19] in order to find one willing to prescribe their desired drug(s).[20] Patients have been known to engage in feigned outrage, tears, threats of abandonment, threats to file a complaint with a regulatory board, pleading, promise to change, and even outright seduction, in order to obtain the drug(s) that they desire.

One favorite tactic is for the patient to visit the local hospital emergency room in order to obtain prescriptions for desired medication(s) through real or feigned displays of distress. Some individuals have even gone so far as to have false surgical scars tattooed onto their backs to support their claim of having back pain that was not corrected through surgical intervention. Experienced physicians are used to hearing stories about how (a) "nobody else has been able to help me (except you)," (b) "my dog/horse/cat/space aliens ate my prescription,"[21] (c) "my house/apartment was burglarized, and the only thing stolen was my prescription for _____," or the ever popular (d) "I lost my prescription and need it refilled or else I will go into withdrawal and it will be your fault!" The goal of each of these manipulative games is to obtain a prescription for a desired substance.

Some inventive patients have gone to the hospital with a report that they are passing a "kidney stone." When asked for a urine sample (which should have traces of blood it in from the damage that the kidney stone is doing to their body) have been found to prick their finger with a pin, and squeeze a drop of blood into the vial of urine to provide the necessary "bloody urine" sample to confirm their report. Others have inserted a foreign body into the urethra prior to going to the hospital, in order to irritate the urethral lining so that it will bleed when they are asked for a urine sample.[22] Finally, there are those patients who have actual injuries or illnesses, who go from hospital to hospital to obtain a prescription for a desired medication.

The point to keep in mind is that the person with an SUD will either consciously or unconsciously engage in various manipulative games to support their addiction. All of these behaviors are then viewed as a reflection of the individual's spiritual illness by those who espouse the Spiritual model of the addictions.

A Thought on Playing the Games of Addiction

It often surprises the non-abuser to learn the intensity with which individuals with an SUD will engage in interpersonal "games," and the indifference with which they often treat their victims. It is necessary to remind non-abusers that the addiction lifestyle is just that: a lifestyle. It is their whole life, and a part of that lifestyle is avoiding responsibility for one's SUD, or all too frequently other behaviors. Indeed, so pervasive is the tendency to be intentionally or unintentionally dishonest that an old joke from the earliest days of Alcoholics Anonymous went like this: "How you tell if an alcoholic is lying? (Pause before delivering the punch line.) Their lips are moving!"

The SUDs, especially when at their most extreme, involve both conscious and unconscious lifestyle adjustments that often shock the nonuser. There are many variations on these lifestyle adjustments, but they share the common characteristic of "a fundamental inability to be honest … with the self" (Knapp, 1996, p. 83, italics in original). Indeed, in speaking of her own AUD, Knapp (1996) compared her relationship to alcohol to that of a love relationship. When one is in love, one will do virtually anything for the beloved. A parent will defend his or her child to the death. All too often, the same is true for SUDs: One will do almost anything for the beloved.

It is only in fleeting moments of self-examination that the individual will ask themselves: "Could it be my drinking, or drug use?" But such moments of honest introspection are rare, and, as the SUD continues, become less and less frequent. Nor is the addicted

---

[19]See Glossary.

[20]This problem has become significantly more pronounced because of the "Internet."

[21]Why is it that the dog/cat/horse/space aliens *never* eat amoxicillin, or antidepressant medications, or blood pressure medications, and how do they manage to survive what would be many times the lethal dose for such a small creature without any medical intervention?

[22]This tactic involves the risk of poking a hole right through the lining of the urethra or of infection, but this is seen as an acceptable risk for those individuals who use this tactic.

person immune from the deceptive tactics. It is not unusual for the persons with the SUD to go "on the wagon" to prove to themselves (and others) that they can "still control it." Unfortunately, by trying to prove control, the persons actually demonstrate that their SUD is out of control. "But I can't be alcoholic," one individual might cry out when confronted with evidence to the contrary. "Why two years ago I went for six months without drinking!" Perhaps this was true … but that was six months ago, and why did this person return to the use of alcohol?

A common refrain heard from friends, family members, and medical professionals is that "they sounded so sincere." Yes, they may have sounded sincere. They might even have had an honest desire to stop abusing chemicals, at least at that instant. However, the fact remains that ultimately substance use becomes a lifestyle, not just an inconvenient aspect of one's life. It requires much effort to change that lifestyle, and many choose not to pay the price for a substance-free life that they might only barely remember.

There appears to be no limit to the manipulations that the person with an SUD will use to support/protect their SUD. The only way to avoid being caught up in such manipulations is to maintain an attitude of quiet watchfulness, and complete honesty with both the "self" and the "other."

Honesty: A Building Stone of Recovery

It is often shocking to those around the persons with an SUD how they could be so blind to the severity of their condition. "Well, everybody gets arrested for driving under the influence [of chemicals] three times," a hypothetical alcohol-dependent person might say to defend his or her AUD. Another might boast, "I've been completely clean for the last two months," ignoring the fact that he or she is awaiting trial and that substance use would be a violation of pre-trial restrictions and possibly grounds for incarceration. To make the lifestyle changes necessary to eliminate this degree of self-deception is not easy, and it requires total honesty with the "self."

An examination of the individual's motivation for remaining substance-free is often quite revealing. One person might abstain from substances because of a fear of incarceration, whereas another might fear a threatened divorce. Although such sources of external motivation are of value at times, they do not protect the individuals from responsibility for not making a choice to abstain. They are possibly "clean"; they are not "in recovery." There is still an element of deception at work if either presents as being "in recovery," although the individual with the SUD might not recognize it.

In a very real sense, many persons with an SUD might be said to have lost touch with external reality. Many a person with an AUD, for example, will take the "marijuana cure," switching their substance use from alcohol to marijuana in order to avoid the legal sanctions that would result should they continue to use alcohol while under the supervision of the Court. Some will even go so far as to claim extended periods of "recovery" to others, although not mentioning that they have been smoking marijuana on a regular basis (but not drinking), for example.

This is not to imply that every person with an SUD engages in conscious deception. Rather, the point being made here is that the layers of conscious and unconscious deception serve to isolate the individual from the reality of his or her SUD, in order to protect it. Persons with an SUD have been known to be shocked to learn that they were unsuccessful in their attempts to deceive others about their substance abuse, and even more shocked to learn that they have become addicted to the substance that they thought that they were using only on a recreational basis. In many cases, the only person deceived for any length of time is the person with the SUD. But along the way they will lie to family members, spouses, children, probation/parole officers, judges, therapists, friends, and physicians, and then wonder why these people hold such grudges against them.

Thus, one of the cornerstones of recovery is *honesty*. As the persons with the SUD come to understand that they were deceiving themselves along with others, they begin to question their perceptions and decisions. Where once they did not pay attention to feedback from others, the recovering person must learn to seek out such feedback, and to listen to it no matter how much it hurts them. Many fail to reach this point, and in all too many cases, their SUD claims their life.

False Pride

The Disease of the Spirit

As has been stated before, every addiction is, at its core, a disease of the spirit. The persons with the SUD feel entitled to their chemically induced feeling(s). The book

Twelve Steps and Twelve Traditions of Alcoholics Anonymous (1981) spoke of addiction as being a sickness of the soul. Not surprisingly, those individuals with a stronger involvement with the church tend to have a reduced risk of SUDs (Haber, 2008). Historical evidence beyond the scope of this text would suggest that a strong spiritual life, which is the antithesis to the false pride on which an addiction rests, helps to protect the individual from SUDs.

The individual whose spirit comes to be diseased does not begin life with a damaged spirit. We "all start out with hope, faith, and fortitude" (Fromm, 1968, p. 20). But for some the accumulated insults over a lifetime come to disease that person's inner world, and some turn to chemicals to fill the perceived void within or to ease their pain. Some believe that they are entitled to the chemically induced pleasure(s) of substances, whereas others find some measure of peace in the arms of a chemical lover that will ultimately betray them to the harsh reality of an addiction. This is not unique to those who have an SUD: We all face moments of supreme disappointment (Fromm, 1968). It is at this point in the individual's life that he or she is faced with the choice of either reducing his or her demands to that which is attainable, or, turning away from the harsh light of reality to the perceived safety of the chemical's embrace. This is the moment that existential therapists speak of as the time that the individual realizes the utter futility of existence, or of personal powerlessness. At this moment, the individual might either accept his or her place in the universe, or, continue to distort his or her perception(s) to maintain the illusion of self-importance through the continued use of chemicals. Spiritual growth involves the acceptance of the pain and suffering that life might have to offer, a task that many turn away from. Some become grandiose or demonstrate the pathological narcissism so often found in persons with an addiction (Nace, 2005a, 2005b).

The loss of false pride exposes the individual to despair (Merton, 1961). Through the spiritual the individual is enabled to establish "a sense of self-transcendence and a sense of meaning construction" (Milstein, 2008, p. 2440). The counter to this is humility: An honest, realistic, view of "self" worth. When one's distorted view of the "self" is forcefully ripped away, the individual experiences despair. Some turn away from this despair into the perceived warmth and comfort of a chemical. Brown (1985), for example, spoke of how alcohol provided the user with the illusion of being able to control his or her feelings. Others invest a greater and

greater amount of time and energy into maintaining the false image in spite of growing evidence to the contrary. This ego-centered personality is the antithesis of a healthy spirituality (Reading, 2007). A few choose to face their despair and their fears to learn and to grow. This honest acceptance of one's lot in life (which is humility) seems to be both the antithesis of the false pride on which the SUDs rest and the basis of psychological health.

To counter this false pride, 12-step programs such as Alcoholics Anonymous offer a chance for the individual to learn to be humble, a personality characteristic that might be sadly lacking in some persons. It takes humility to both profess and accept to being powerless over one's drug of choice, and through an honest exploration of the "self" the individual will come to learn how much of his or her life has been centered around and affected by his or her chemical use. Many people believe that humility involves a denial of one's strengths or skills. This is hardly the truth: Humility involves an honest understanding of the "self," or of the soul. This requires psychological strength, for it is an ongoing, lifelong process. In spite of the contention by many that the substance-abusing person might be involved in a spiritual journey through the use of chemicals (Chopra, 1997), this "short cut" comes to demand more and more of the individual's life resources, dominating his or her choices until he or she must center his or her life around the continued use of that chemical and abandon his or her search for something better. To turn aside from this path requires strength, courage, and an honest understanding of the "self."

A very real manifestation of the spiritual illness that surrounds the SUDs is found in the process of "euphoric recall." If you listen to persons with an SUD discussing their substance use experiences, you will be left with the impression that they are talking about a valued friend rather than a drug of abuse (Byington, 1997). Many persons with an SUD have spoken at length about the semi-sexual thrill that they achieved through the use of cocaine, the amphetamines, or heroin, without ever mentioning that this thrill was achieved at the cost of a spouse, family members who are estranged, and perhaps the loss of tens of thousands of dollars, not to mention the risk to the user's life, for example. There is a name for this distorted form of thinking: It is called the insanity of addiction. This form of moral insanity is supported by perceptual and cognitive distortions, and propped up by the individual's false pride.

One aspect of modern society that supports this false pride is the series of media-generated illusions that the latest trend will bring happiness to the individual. This mindless search for happiness is perhaps best seen in the mindless pursuit of happiness through the latest trend in cellular phones, cars, or clothing. "If only I had _____, then I would be happy (or would impress people, and so on)" is a thought that flashes through the minds of countless millions when the latest model is revealed to the public. Perhaps the apex of this process was seen in the early days of cellular telephone service, when it was both expensive, and service was limited. Some companies started to produce fake cell phones that the user could carry to try and impress others with the fact that he or she was both rich enough, and important enough, to warrant such a service.

But to seek gratification of the "self" through externals is dangerous, for the external world is always changing. Yesterday's cutting edge computer is now an antique, whereas the designer clothes of last week are copied and are now available in discount stores. The SUDs might be viewed as a prime example of this attempt to satisfy the "soul" without the need to compromise or work to achieve the spiritual insights necessary to attain these feelings. Just take the right combination of pills, and you will instantly be transported to nirvana (or so the drug dealers would have us believe). If the present combination of alcohol and pills does not help you to achieve your goal(s), well, let us try again. The goal is to keep you happy. Not content, but, happy.[23]

Surprisingly, meditation or other spiritual techniques, which will, if carried out correctly, force the individuals to confront their self-pride and activate the frontal lobes of the brain. This is a region that is often underactive in the substance abuser. Mediative practices have been shown, with practice, to bring about permanent changes in brain activity and structure (Newberg & Walkman, 2009). Thus, humility is one of the foundations of a good recovery program, although it can take years for a person to learn to be humble, utilize the proper techniques, and a lifetime of learning to bring it to perfection. A very real danger here is that the individuals will convince themselves that their spiritual beliefs are strong enough to help them face the trials and tribulations of life without the benefit of external feedback about their spiritual

growth. This might be why King et al. (2012) found that people who claimed to be spiritual but were not affiliated with an established religion were twice as likely to have abused illicit drugs at some point in their lives. Perhaps the illusion of self-directed spirituality without external feedback allows for a loss of focus and the development of a spiritual narcissism that leaves the individual vulnerable to SUDs.

The Role of Defense Mechanisms in the Spiritual Model

The traditional view of the spiritual model is that the individual with an SUD will utilize four characteristic defense mechanisms: denial, minimization, rationalization, and projection, all of which were discussed in the last chapter. These defenses are thought to operate on an unconscious level, to protect the individuals from an awareness of realities that might threaten their adjustment. Being forced to admit that what one thought was a harmless recreational drug has actually become an addiction is one of those harsh realities that the defenses strive to keep us from having to deal with. Although these defenses operate in situations other than situations where the individual has an SUD, they are a core component to the spiritual model.

Reactions to the Spiritual Model

Reactions to the spiritual model are becoming increasingly vocal. Some seek legal redress to what they view as a violation of their civil rights, with some success. Since 1996 various state and federal courts have ruled that individuals in a government-supported treatment program cannot be mandated to attend 12-step groups such as Alcoholics Anonymous on the grounds that they are part of a religious program. Further, treatment staff at a government-funded treatment program who require this of patients in treatment might be held personally liable for this violation of the patients' civil rights[24] (Horvath, 2007).

Foote (2006) challenged the concept that the failure of an individual to abstain from a drug(s) of abuse following treatment is the patient's fault. Rather, this therapeutic failure might be viewed as a mismatch between the patient and the program staff, in Foote's opinion. Further, the more confrontative the therapist

---

[23]The difference between these two concepts, "happiness" and "contentedness," makes for an interesting debate, does it not?

[24]The "Freedom of Religion" clause in the Bill of Rights also includes the freedom *from* religion, if the person should so choose.

becomes in attempting to overcome the client's "resistance," the less cooperative the client will be in the therapeutic process. Indeed, confrontation is a powerful predictor of a negative outcome, as the client is confronted over and over again about his or her lack of "progress" (Foote, 2006).

Chapter Summary

Proponents of the spiritual model of the addictions suggest that the SUDs rest in part upon a spiritual weakness within the individual. To understand the role that the SUD plays in individuals' life, it is first necessary to understand their spiritual beliefs and the reason why they hold these beliefs. Numerous courts at the state and federal levels have ruled that people with a substance use disorder cannot be required to attend a 12-step group such as Alcoholics Anonymous because this would violate their Constitutional right to freedom of speech. This ruling closes one avenue through which the individuals' spiritual beliefs might be reinforced, which in the opinion of those who believe that the addictions rest upon a spiritual weakness increases their vulnerability for addictive behaviors. In this chapter the role of spirituality in the process of recovery from an SUD is explored.

CHAPTER 27

The Assessment of Suspected Substance Use Disorders[1]

[The] successful treatment of substance use disorders depends on a careful, accurate assessment and diagnosis.

(Greenfield & Hennessy, 2008, p. 55)

Introduction

Almost two generations ago, Samuel Shem (1978) wrote a novel about a man's internship year at a fictional hospital in the Boston area titled *The House of God*. In this novel a wiser, more advanced resident set down various "laws" to help the interns survive, not the least of which was the rule that "If you don't take a temperature, you can't find a fever" (p. 420). This dictum applies to substance use disorders as well: Many health care professionals avoid discussing the patient's substance use or abuse to avoid having to deal with this uncomfortable issue. This might be why the majority of referrals to substance abuse rehabilitation programs do not come from a health care provider (Madras, 2010). Unfortunately, there is a consequence of this therapeutic myopia: The substance use disorders (SUDs) are all too often an unacknowledged causal factor in various disease states, as well as its contribution to the problems experienced by dual diagnosis clients,[2] not to mention the various legal, financial, interpersonal, vocational and personal problems either caused or at least exacerbated by SUDs. These problems make it imperative that the health care professional obtain an accurate history of the patient's substance use patterns (Johnson, 2003). Further, in this era of major changes in the health care insurance system in this country, where the health care professional must obtain "prior authorization" and justify each procedure in advance to ensure maximum return for each dollar spent on health care, the need for a referral to rehabilitation must be firmly established on a bedrock of clinical data.

This foundation is established, in large part, through the process of assessment. This process serves the roles of (a) helping identify those individuals who require professional assistance to help them come to terms with their SUD, (b) serving as a "gate keeper" providing justification for admission to the proper level of treatment, (c) the identifying of strengths and weaknesses on the part of the individual, and (d) identifies potential goals to be addressed in the rehabilitation program (Juhnke, 2002). In this chapter, the process of assessing an adult with a SUD, and how the assessment process relates to the process of rehabilitation, will be explored.

---

[1]The assessment of suspected child/adolescent substance use disorders and instruments used for this purpose is discussed in Chapter 23.

[2]Discussed in Chapter 24.

The Theory behind Substance Use Assessments

It is not uncommon for employers, parents or inexperienced health care professionals to cite evidence of a single episode of illicit drug use, or a single "dirty" urine toxicology test[3] as proof that the individual is addicted to chemicals (Winters & Kaminer, 2008; Washton & Zweben, 2006). This is patently false: You cannot make such a conclusion based on a single data point. The abuse of a substance, even if that substance is illegal, does not prove that the individual is addicted to that compound (Gitlow, 2007). These facts simply underscore the need for a complete substance use assessment to determine whether a given individual has a SUD. This assessment process is "more than a one-time paperwork procedure conducted at the onset of treatment to simply gather minimal facts and secure a … diagnosis" (Juhnke, 2002, p. vii). It is the first step in the rehabilitation process, if this is necessary, and it continues throughout treatment as the individual's needs and resources are continuously assessed and addressed (Daley & Marlatt, 2006).

Life would be much easier if there were a single, accurate, universally effective standard for the detection of SUDs (Fleming, Mihic, & Harris, 2006). That such an assessment process will emerge in the near future is unlikely: Scientists have yet to agree upon a standard definition of even the basic term addiction (Erlich, 2001; Fletcher, 2013). Thus the assessor must go into the assessment process with imperfect tools, and then is asked to make a diagnosis that might have lifelong implications for the patient. One hypothetical example might be the individual's ability to purchase affordable health care insurance at the age of 50 because of a diagnosis of an SUD made when he or she was only 20 years of age.

The assessment process is complicated and involves several steps. The process of screening a patient is carried out to identify those patients who might have a certain disease or condition (Knight, 2005). If all substance abusers were alike, then there would be no need for the assessment process to move beyond the determination of whether the individual does or does not have a chemical use problem. However, all substance abusers are not the same, and there is no "one size fits all" presentation of substance abusers. Clients vary as

to their age, gender, marital status, culture, ethnicity, degree of insight into their problem(s), legal status, medical condition, and willingness to change (Greenfield & Hennessy, 2008). Thus the assessor must consider a wide range of factors during the screening process, and if there is a reason to suspect a SUD is present, a complete assessment is carried out. This is done to confirm or rule out the presence of that disorder, assess its severity, identify individual strengths, and to help guide treatment (Blume, 2005; Knight, 2005). It is at this point that the assessment process enters its final phase: that of diagnosis. Each of these interrelated steps will be discussed in more detail, in the sections that follow.

Screening

The core of the screening process is the clinical interview with the client. This clinical interview must be long enough to allow for the assessor to build a complete overview of the client's substance use pattern (Greenfield & Hennessy, 2008). This is often based both on the client's responses during the clinical interview, collateral information, and a review of past records. The screening process might also involve the use of one or more paper-and-pencil instruments to help identify those individuals who might have an SUD. Although such information is valuable to the assessor, a test score by itself does not establish whether the individual does or does not have an SUD. The test score is but one perspective on the individual's substance use pattern. Such instruments might either be filled out by the client (known as self-report instruments) or by the assessor as he or she asks questions of the person being assessed.

An important point that must be assessed is whether the client has ever experienced withdrawal symptoms (or is currently going through a substance withdrawal syndrome) both at the time of the interview and in the past (Greenfield & Hennessy, 2008). This is not definitive proof that a person is addicted to a compound(s), although it is strong evidence that the individual is at least a heavy abuser of that substance(s) and underscores the need for an in-depth assessment of the individual's substance use patterns.

Verbal Screening Aids

A rapidly administered verbal tool that might be used with both adolescents and adults is the TWEAK.

---

[3]This is to say a urine toxicology test that reveals evidence of illicit drug use.

The letters serve as a useful mnemonic[4] device for the assessor to remember to ask the clients (a) whether they have developed Tolerance to alcohol or drugs, (b) whether or not others have ever been Worried about their substance use, (c) whether the client has ever used an Eye opener in the morning, (4) Amnesia during periods of substance use, and (5) made attempts to K (cut) down on substance use (Johnson, 2003). A negative answer to all of these questions does not rule out an SUD but does suggest that the patient probably is at low risk for such a problem. Alternatively, a "yes" answer to one or more of these items suggests a possible SUD.

Another popular screening instrument is the CAGE questionnaire (Ewing, 1984). The CAGE questions have been in use for more than a quarter of a century. CAGE is an acronym for the four questions used in this screening tool:

- *Have you ever felt that you should **cut down** on your drinking?*
- *Have people ever **annoyed** you by being critical of your drinking?*
- *Have you ever felt bad or **guilty** about your drinking?*
- *Have you ever needed to have a drink the first thing in the morning to steady your nerves or get rid of a hangover (**eye-opener**)?*

It was suggested that a "yes" response to one question suggested a need for a more thorough inquiry by the assessor, whereas "yes" response to two or more items suggests a high probability that the individual has an alcohol use disorder. This instrument has been estimated to have an accuracy of 80–90% when the client answers "yes" to two or more items. Unfortunately, the CAGE questionnaire has been found to have serious problems: First, it is not sensitive to "binge" drinking, It does not identify the frequency of the individual's alcohol use or the individual's level of consumption (Cooney, Kadden, & Steinberg, 2005). Alcohol-dependent persons who are abstinent will be identified as having a problem because of past alcohol use behavior(s) and not their present drinking status. Further, it also does not identify individuals who abuse substances other than alcohol. The test is also very vulnerable to deception (Stein & Rogers, 2008). Finally, it is of limited value as a screening instrument for adolescents (Knight, 2002), women or minority members who have an alcohol use disorder ("Screening for Alcohol Problems—an Update," 2002), or for persons in the earlier stages of an alcohol use disorder (Washton & Zweben, 2006). Because of these (and possibly other, yet to be identified) flaws, the CAGE is estimated to miss up to 50% of at-risk drinkers (Fleming, 1997).

To address this problem, the team of Brown, Leonard, Saunders, and Papasoulioutis (1997) suggested a simple, two-question screening instrument:

1. In the last year, have you ever drunk or used drugs more than you meant to?
2. Have you felt that you wanted or needed to cut down on your drinking or drug use in the past year?

The authors suggested that, in spite of its brevity, a "yes" answer to one question indicated a 45% chance that the individual had a SUD, whereas a "yes" response to both questions indicated that there was a 75% chance that the individual had an SUD. However, this instrument also can yield "false positive" results, warned the authors, and so the assessor should not rely too heavily on these (or other) verbal interview responses to rule out an SUD, but should consider their responses as one piece of information to be used in the development of a diagnosis.

The team of Smith, Schmidt, Allensworth-Davies, and Saitz (2010) suggested that a single question was able to identify a person with a drug use problem 100% of the time. The question was simply: "How many times in the past year have you used an illegal drug or used a prescription medication for nonmedical reasons?"However, this question is also rather obvious in its intent, and thus vulnerable to dissimulation should the individual be predisposed to this.

Paper-and-Pencil Screening Instruments

Self-report instruments offer the advantages of being inexpensive, and they may be less threatening to the client than face-to-face interviews because clients might experience feelings of shame, distrust, hopelessness, and discomfort during the face-to-face interview (Greenfield & Hennessy, 2008). This is one advantage that self-report instruments have over the clinical interview: The client does not need to feel shame or hopelessness while filling out a paper-and-pencil form. A disadvantage of self-report instruments is that they are more vulnerable to client attempts at deception, and are designed with the assumption that the client is reasonably literate. Such

---

[4]See Glossary.

instruments do not prove that a person has a SUD (Washton & Zweben, 2006). However, when used properly such instruments provide the assessor with an additional source of data that could be incorporated into the assessment process.

One way to minimize this danger is to administer different instruments that cover the same aspect of the client's behavior. A client who denies having alcohol-related blackouts on one instrument but admits to having blackouts on another instrument has presented contradictory information. In such cases the assessor should attempt to reconcile the two answers with each other. Another technique is for the same instrument to be administered at different times, perhaps a week apart for example, and then the client's responses compared with each other. Again, there might be significant discrepancies between the two response sets, which should be explored by the assessor.

Sometimes, the client will consent to have their significant other sit in the office while the assessor reviewed the results with the client. If the client had answered a test item on the Michigan Alcoholism Screening Test[5] addressing alcohol-related motor vehicle accidents negatively, the spouse might then ask "What about that time when you drove your car into a ditch, two years ago?" In this hypothetical example, the client might respond that the police had ruled the accident was a result of ice-covered roads, but the partner might then go on to say, "But you told me that you had been drinking earlier that night!" The assessor must then determine to the best degree possible whether that person's alcohol use was a factor in the accident.

For alcohol use disorders, one of the most popular instruments used for screening is the Michigan Alcoholism Screening Test (MAST) (Selzer, 1971). The MAST is composed of 24 questions that can be answered either "yes" or "no" by the respondent. Test scores are weighted with a value of 1, 2, or, in some cases, 5 points (Craig, 2004). A score of 7 or more points is interpreted as evidence that the individual has an alcohol use disorder (Craig, 2004). Although the MAST is a popular instrument even in the first decade of the 21st century, it does present some inherent problems. First, it can only be used in cases of alcohol dependence, and not alcohol abuse (Vanable, King, & deWit, 2000). Second, it provides only a crude

measure of the individual's possible alcohol use problem. Third, the intent of the items on the MAST are readily apparent, and thus subject to dissimulation if the test taker should be less than honest (Stein & Rogers, 2008). Next it is insensitive to "binge" drinking, and it does not address the use of compounds other than alcohol. Finally, it does not differentiate between the individual's current and past drinking history, with the result being that abstinent drinkers could be identified as having an ongoing alcohol use disorder on the basis of their response set (Schorling & Buchsbaum, 1997). Thus the MAST is best suited for the detection of individuals with a severe alcohol use disorder, and should be interpreted with caution.

A paper-and-pencil screening instrument developed by the World Health Organization (WHO) is the Alcohol Use Disorders Identification Test (AUDIT). The AUDIT was standardized on samples drawn from six different countries around the world, with the intent of developing a short, easily administered screening instrument that might be used in different countries in the identification of persons in the early stages of developing an alcohol use disorder (Babor, Higgins-Briddle, Saunders, & Monterio, 2001). The AUDIT is composed of 10 different questions,[6] which tap the domains of (a) hazardous alcohol use, (b) dependence symptoms, and (c) harmful alcohol use (Babor et al., 2001). To this end, it has been estimated that the AUDIT is over 90% effective in detecting persons with an alcohol use disorder (Bradley et al., 2003; Brown et al., 1997). Indeed, it has been identified as being superior in performance to the CAGE and the MAST in a variety of clinical settings, and appears to be valid for both male and female respondents (Babor et al., 2001). However, the AUDIT tends to miss active drinkers over the age of 65 (Isaacson & Schorling, 1999) and is not appropriate for use with adolescent drinkers (Knight, 2002). Another limitation of the AUDIT is that it is designed for use in detecting alcohol use disorders and not other forms of substance abuse. It cannot isolate current drinking patterns from past alcohol use patterns, and finally, the intent of the items on the AUDIT is easily discerned, and thus the test is subject to dissimulation if this is the intent of the individual (Stein & Rogers, 2008).

---

[5]Discussed in the next paragraph.

[6]There is an abbreviated version, known as the *AUDIT-C*, which is composed of only three questions, but available evidence suggests that the full AUDIT might be more effective than the abbreviated version (Holzel, Weiser, Berner, & Harter, 2008)

A popular screening instrument is the Substance Abuse Subtle Screening Inventory-3 (SASSI-3) (Juhnke, 2002). SASSI is a copyrighted instrument, which can either be computer- or hand-scored. It is administered to individuals who are at least 16 years of age, and who have at least a fourth-grade reading level. It takes about 15 minutes for the client to take the SASSI-3, and it provides measures on 10 different scales, including two "truth" scales. Some of the items are quite obvious in intent, whereas others are rather subtle. It can be hand-scored, although the computer-administered/scored version is becoming increasingly popular with the growing popularity of desktop computers. Although the SASSI does not provide data on which substance(s) the individual might abuse, it does provide a score that suggests that the individual is or is not likely to have a SUD.

Thus far, the discussion has focused on screening instruments useful for detecting possible alcohol use disorders. A screening tool that is useful for the identification of substance abuse is the Drug Abuse Screening Test (DAST). This instrument is rapidly administered, usually in five minutes or less, requires a sixth-grade reading level, and excludes alcohol use. The DAST was modeled after the MAST, but focuses on illicit drug use. It is composed of 20 questions that are answered either "yes" or "no." It was originally intended for use with adults, but a modified form has been developed for use with adolescents. Scoring is easy, as 18 of the 20 items are scored as "hits" if the individual responded "yes," and the other two are scored as "hits" if the individual responded "no." A score of 7+ points suggests a SUD. A disadvantage of the DAST is that the intent of the items is readily apparent, allowing the individual to lie about his or her substance abuse, if motivated to do so.

The utility of these instruments in the detection of alcohol or drug use disorders has been challenged ("California Judges Get Tougher on Science," 1997). However, they do provide one piece of data in a comprehensive assessment process that uses multiple data points to arrive at a diagnostic formulation. One such data point might be one of the semi-structured clinical interviews designed to allow the clinician to obtain the data necessary to adequately determine if there is a SUD or not.

An instrument often administered during the screening process is the Beck Depression Inventory (BDI). Although the BDI does not address substance use issues, it does provide an objective measure of the client's depression, which may both form the basis for a referral to a mental health professional for evaluation and treatment, and, because the drugs of abuse can often cause or contribute to depression, further inquiry into the reasons why the client is depressed. A hypothetical man with a high score on the BDI, which suggests high levels of depression, might reveal upon inquiry that his wife took the children and moved out because of his longstanding SUD. The BDI is a copyrighted instrument that must be purchased from the publisher, however, it does have the advantage of being easily administered and scored in just a few minutes.

One instrument that is often mistakenly considered to be a screening tool is the Minnesota Multiphasic Personality Inventory (MMPI).[7] The original MMPI was introduced almost 75 years ago, and the MacAndrew Alcoholism Scale[8] was introduced in the mid-1960s after an item analysis suggested that alcohol-dependent individuals had a tendency to answer 49 items of the 566 items differently than non-alcoholic persons. A cut off score of 24 items answered in the "scorable" direction correctly identified 82% of alcohol-dependent persons in a sample of 400 psychiatric patients (Graham, 1990). In 1989, the venerable MMPI was updated, and the Minnesota Multiphasic Personality Inventory-2 (MMPI-2) was introduced. The "Mac" scale was slightly modified, but essentially retained its original form. At this time, the modified "Mac" scale is thought to be about 85% accurate in the detection of SUDs (Craig, 2004).[9]

Following its introduction, it was suggested that the MMPI-2 "Mac" scale identified personality patterns more commonly associated with SUDs than the actual SUDs (Rouse, Butcher, & Miller, 1999). Clients who are extroverted, who experience a "blackout" for any reason,[10] who tend to be more assertive, or who enjoy risk-taking behaviors, tend to score higher on the "Mac" scale, even if they do not have an SUD (Graham, 1990). Further, in spite of the validity scales built into the MMPI-2, Otto, Lang, Megargee, and Rosenblatt (1989) discovered shortly after the revised MMPI was introduced that alcohol-dependent persons might be able to "conceal their drinking problems

---

[7]The MMPI and the MMPI-2 are both copyrighted instruments.

[8]Also known as the "Mac" scale.

[9]Because of the shortcomings of the "Mac" scale, it should be used as one piece of data, and by itself should not be interpreted as evidence of a substance use disorder.

[10]For example, a person who has a seizure disorder.

even when the relatively subtle special alcohol scales of the MMPI are applied" either through conscious or unconscious denial (p. 7). Finally, taking the MMPI is time-intensive, which does not make it a convenient test for screening purposes. The MMPI is, however, of use in the diagnosis stage of the assessment process.

Section Summary

The process of screening for a possible SUD can involve either a verbal, face-to-face interview, the use of various screening instruments, or ideally, a mixture of both. At the end of this process, the assessor should be able to determine whether or not there is evidence of a SUD. If there is no evidence of an SUD, then the screening processes ends at this point. However, if evidence of an SUD is detected, then the assessor moves on to the next stage, the Assessment.

Assessment

If the screening process suggests that a SUD is present, the assessor then attempts to measure the severity of the individual's SUD. Having identified the possible presence of an addictive disease the assessor then must explore says little about the quantity or frequency of that person's abuse of chemicals (Gitlow, 2011).[11] It is the duty of the assessor to strive to be as accurate as possible, always being cognizant of the process of "diagnostic inflation."[12] The assessor must also remember that the same disorder might have far different presentations as the disease progresses (Greenfield & Hennessy, 2008). The end-stage alcoholic, for example, will have a different clinical presentation than the young adult drinker who is in the earlier stages of alcoholism. Both qualify for a diagnosis of an alcohol use disorder although the manifestations of the disorder will be different. Further, both individuals will present a different clinical picture than the hypothetical person who was once an active drinker but who had not used alcohol in a decade but was cocaine dependent.

---

[11] An analogy might be an example of a person who had lung cancer that was treated with a combination of surgery and radiation therapy. Even if there was no sign of recurrent tumor(s), the diagnosis of "lung cancer" would stay on the patient's chart, although with the modifier "apparent surgical cure (and a specific date)."

[12] See Glossary.

There are three formats for the assessment process: (a) unstructured, (b) semi-structured, and (c) structured. The clinical interview is usually an unstructured assessment process although there are semi-structured and structured interview manuals in use that do not permit elaboration of atypical responses. Juhnke (2002) identified four benefits of the clinical interview: (1) flexibility, (2) establishment of rapport with the client, (3) reassurance to clients uncomfortable working with written tests or computers (if the test is administered on a computer), and (4) allows the therapist to watch the client's nonverbal behavior in response to question(s), to identify areas for subsequent exploration.

The first part of the interview process is the introduction by the assessor. The assessor will explain he or she will be asking questions about the client's possible substance use patterns, and that specific responses would be most helpful. At this time the assessor might want to explain that many of these questions might have been asked of the client by others in the past; however, this information is important and so the assessor will request this information from the client again. The client is provided with the opportunity to ask any questions that he or she might have, and then the interview process begins. It is not uncommon for the interview to take place within a framework provided by the *Diagnostic and Statistical Manual of Mental Disorders*, 5th edition (*DSM-5*) (American Psychiatric Association, 2013), although other formats, such as the one utilized by the American Society of Addiction Medicine (ASAM), might also be utilized. Each of these diagnostic manuals provides certain criteria within which the individual's SUD might be evaluated, and provides a common language that health care professionals understand.

The information that the client offers (or withholds) during the clinical interview is itself a valuable component of the assessment process. However, this data is also vulnerable to one of four different "response sets" that might distort the assessor's opinion of the client's SUD (Stein & Rogers, 2008): (1) Disacknowledgment: The individual repeatedly offers "I don't know" or "I can't remember" responses to questions that might reveal incriminating information. (2) Misappraisal: The individual simply might be confused about the amount of the substance being abused (client reports consuming 3–4 drinks a night where collateral information sources report that the client had ingested 8 mixed drinks on a given night, for example), or the frequency of use (individual reports using 2 times a week when spouse reports 4–5 times a week is closer to the truth). These same behaviors might be present not because of honest error on the individual's part but because of (3) Denial: Client might be motivated to avoid consequences of substance use behavior such as legal sanctions by not admitting to the use of certain chemicals. Finally there is (4) Exaggeration: The individual might intentionally inflate the frequency or amount of their substance use. The assessor must establish the motivation for this behavior: In adolescent substance abusers this behavior might serve as a "cry for help," where many individuals facing criminal charges might utilize this form of distortion to try to establish grounds for a claim of mitigating circumstances at the time of sentencing.

A conundrum that faces the assessor is the myth that substance abusers will automatically lie about their substance abuse. This is often repeated as clinical fact by many clinical substance abuse counselors. It is possible that people will be less than honest about their substance abuse, especially if they believe that the information that they reveal might be used against them later (Fletcher, 2013). This does not apply only to situations where a person is facing possible legal charges: As Frances (2013) pointed out that on occasion, the frequency or amount of a person's substance use might be wielded like a sword in family feuds, for example. It is for this reason that the assessor must consider the reason that the individual had been referred for an assessment. For example, if the client is being seen as part of a child custody evaluation or pre-employment evaluation, the individual might either consciously or unconsciously distort the information that he or she provides to the assessor. Collateral information (past treatment records, court documents, information from family members, etc.) often proves helpful in detecting such distortion should it exist.

It is useful for the assessor to ask different questions during the interview that are designed to explore the same client response from different perspectives. This is done to provide a form of internal validity to the data obtained during the clinical interview. For example, the client might be asked: "In the average week, how often would you estimate that you use alcohol or drugs?" At a later point in the interview, the assessor might ask: "In the average week, how much would you say that you spent on alcohol or drugs?" If there is a discrepancy, the assessor will want to explore it. Clients who report using alcohol just once a week, but who claim to spend

$100 a week on their alcohol use might upon inquiry, say that they always buy drinks for their friends when they go out to drink, or that they have a gambling or SUD other than alcoholism.

One point that the assessor will wish to consider is the estimated percentage of his/her income spent on alcohol or drugs of abuse. If the client is receiving unemployment compensation checks for $200 each week, for example, but is spending $50 a week on alcohol or drugs, then he or she is spending a significant percentage of his or her income on substances in spite of his or her employment status. In contrast to this is the client who makes $2000 a week, but who spends $15 each week on beer, for example, provides evidence of a far different pattern of drinking. The amount of their weekly income spent on alcohol or drugs does not in itself establish the diagnosis of an SUD, but serves as one data point that is potentially helpful in making such a diagnosis.

An indirect source of collateral information is medical test data, a topic that will be discussed later in this chapter. There are no current blood/urine tests specific for detecting an SUD, and even if a substance is detected in the individual's urine/blood at this time, it does not mean that the individual is a chronic user. It only means that the substance was in their blood/urine at the time of the blood or urine test. However, a series of "positive" blood or urine test results makes it far harder for the client to argue that he or she does not abuse chemicals. Further, urine toxicology tests can also determine whether prescribed drugs that should be in the client's system, such as antimanic or antipsychotic were present. Urine toxicology tests cannot determine the amount of a chemical in the client's body, although blood tests are usually able to provide such information. Finally, the appropriate blood or urine tests can help identify concurrent medical disorders that might complicate efforts at treating the SUD (e.g., an untreated infection, or heart problem) (Work Group on Substance Use Disorders, 2007).

Psychological Test Data

Psychological test data may directly or indirectly assist the assessment process. A number of instruments have been discussed elsewhere in this chapter that are of value in the screening and assessment process. A major disadvantage of paper-and-pencil tests is that they are subject to denial, distortion, and outright misrepresentation on the part of the client, and thus are better suited to situations where the client is unlikely to "positively dissimulate" (Evans & Sullivan, 2001).

Psychological test data might shed help identify client personality characteristics that might influence his/her substance use pattern. A depressed client, for example, might be using alcohol or drugs to self-medicate a depression, although the reverse is also possible: The observed depression might be substance induced. Psychological tests other than those directly developed for screening or assessment of SUDs can offer little direct evidence that these problems exist ("California Judges Get Tougher on Science," 1997).

The assessor must not make assumptions about the client's responses. If a client reported "only this one arrest" for a drug-possession charge, the assessor must not make assumptions. Rather, the assessor must ask questions such as "What about in other states or countries?" or "Were there any substance-related charges brought against you while you were in the military?" The client's responses may be revealing.

Standardized Tests[13,14]

Although the clinical interview forms the cornerstone of the assessment process, the assessor should also utilize standardized test results as an aid to the assessment process (Juhnke, 2002). The client's responses will become a part of the data base upon which the assessor draws upon for the final stage of the assessment process: the diagnosis (discussed later in this chapter). Such self-report instruments provide a comparison between the individual's characteristics and those of patients who have been identified as substance abusers and who have benefited from intervention(s) (Samet, Waxman, Hatzenbuehler, & Hasin, 2007).

One popular instrument used for individuals over the age of 16 is the Alcohol Use Inventory (AUI). This copyrighted[15] instrument is composed of 228 items, and it takes 30–60 minutes for the individual to finish. The test data is then interpreted across 24 domains to help the assessor better understand the client's alcohol use pattern. Unfortunately, the AUI is limited to alcohol

use disorders. Further, the normative data for the AUI make it inappropriate to use with certain subgroups.

The Addiction Severity Index (ASI) on the other hand is a "public domain" instrument that forms the core of a semi-structured interview with the client. There are 161 questions on the fifth edition of the ASI, each of which the interviewer will ask the client while recording his or her responses. The ASI is useful in the assessment of SUDs other than alcohol use disorders, and measures such areas as the client's interpersonal relationship patterns, possible medical problems, legal history, and so on (Samet et al., 2007). The client is asked to rate his or her level of distress on each domain from "0" (no distress) to "4" (extreme distress), whereas the assessor also notes areas that should be addressed through professional intervention. Although useful, the normative population for the ASI were patients in the Veteran's Administration hospital system, and this instrument has been found to have limited validity in working with special populations such as the homeless or clients with concurrent substance use and mental health problems[16] (Monti, Kadden, Rohsenow, Cooney, & Abrams, 2002; Samet et al., 2007; Stein & Rogers, 2008).

The Structured Clinical Interview (SCID) was based on the *Diagnostic and Statistical Manual OF Mental Disorders*-IV (SCID) (American Psychiatric Association, 2000). SCID is an instrument available in one form for researchers and another form for clinicians (Samet 2007). The clinical version of the SCID requires training as a therapist, and is a semi-structured instrument that will allow the assessor to explore client responses that might require clarification. It is applicable to both alcohol use and SUDs, but it can require up to several hours for the therapist to administer to the client, depending on his or her status and level of function. Fortunately, it is designed to be administered in a series of modules and the clinician might utilize only those modules that are of relevance to that client (Samet et al., 2007). It is not known at this time whether this instrument will be updated or revised following the publication of the *DSM-5* (American Psychiatric Association, 2013).

The Drug Use Screening Inventory-Revised (DUSI-R) assesses three domains: (1) personal history, (2) a drug use screening instrument portion, and (3) a demographic, medical, and possible prevention or treatment applications (Johnson, 2003). Although this instrument

---

[13]There are a number of assessment tools that have been devised for research studies, but which are not used in clinical practice. These tools will not be discussed in this text.

[14]The author is frequently asked to render an opinion as to the *best* test or instrument to use. There is no single test that is universally accepted, and each has certain strengths and weaknesses.

[15]An instrument protected by a "copyright" is privately owned, and the user must pay a royalty fee for using it.

[16]Discussed in Chapter 22.

provides a great deal of useful information, it is not popular at this time.

Section Summary

In this section, some of the more popular paper-and-pencil assessment instruments currently in use are reviewed. These instruments form part of the data base on which the assessor will base his or her conclusions. However, they do not take the place of a formal clinical interview and the clinician should not base his or her diagnosis only on the test results.

The Assessment Format

There is no standardized format for the assessment process. Rather, the format utilized for the assessment process will vary depending on the needs of the assessor and the facility for which he or she works. Assessments need to be sensitive to the cultural beliefs of the client, and be aware that different cultural groups might have different beliefs about substance use than the dominant culture (Greenfield & Hennessy, 2008). Frances (2013) offered a "STEPPED DIAGNOSIS" (p. 222, capital letters in original) approach to psychiatric assessments that he summarized in the following manner:

Step 1: Gather baseline data.
Step 2: Normalize problems. Take them seriously but consider the possibility that the behaviors in question were a predictable response to the stressors of everyday living.
Step 3: Watchful waiting: Continue the assessment process without having a preconceived diagnosis. Diagnostic impressions at this point should be tentative and considered in light of the data, and treatment efforts should be minimal and open to modification as events unfold.
Step 4: Minimal intervention: Structured interventions such as available computer-based self-help groups, assigned reading, and psycho-educational groups.
Step 5: Brief counseling.
Step 6: Formation of final diagnosis and initiation of appropriate treatment(s).

Admittedly, Frances's (2013) assessment recommendations were designed for work with psychiatric as opposed to substance-abusing patients, but there are lessons that the assessor might learn from this

model. For example, the person who is being assessed after being arrested for driving under the influence of intoxicants, whose substance abuse was apparently a reaction to the unexpected death of a spouse or child, and who did not demonstrate any sign of a SUD before this tragic life event is far different than a person with a long history of substance abuse or addiction (see Step 2). However, there are some common elements to the better assessments, which will be reviewed next.

Circumstances of Referral

Why is this client here, today? Individuals with an SUD will only rarely come in for help on a voluntary basis, and are usually forced into the assessment and subsequent rehabilitation program through external pressure (Craig, 2004). Thus, the manner in which the client answers the question "What brought you here, today?" will offer valuable information about his or her willingness to participate in the assessment process, evasiveness (or honesty), level of function, understanding of the problem(s) that he or she is facing, and so on.

Substance Use Patterns

The client's substance use patterns should have been identified in the assessment phase. However the assessor should also identify the grounds on which the client's self-report is/is not assumed to be accurate. For example, a person who claimed to have been alcohol- and drug-free for the past nine months (but who was incarcerated for that period of time) may not be demonstrating the internal motivation necessary for successful treatment. The assessor thus must determine the client's current living situation, whether he or she is under the supervision of the courts (probation, parole or incarcerated), and the client's beliefs about his or her substance use. It is not uncommon for clients to minimize the impact that their SUD has on their vocational life during an assessment ("he fired me, but I was about to quit, anyway") for example.

Past Treatment History

This is relevant for a number of reasons. Past research has shown that approximately half of those entering treatment for an alcohol use disorder (AUD) are entering treatment for the first time (LoCastro, Potter, Donovan, Couper, & Pope, 2008). First-time treatment participants for AUDs have significantly different alcohol use histories than do those being admitted to treatment for the second or third time. The social context of their alcohol use, needs, motivation for treatment, expectations, and health status will be significantly different than of the typical individual who has been admitted to treatment for an AUD more than once (LoCastro et al., 2008).

Individuals who are entering treatment for the first time tend to drink less per occasion of drinking, are probably less knowledgeable about the nature of SUDs, are less likely to acknowledge the severity of their SUD, and are less likely to accept total abstinence as a viable treatment goal (LoCastro et al., 2008). They are also more likely to be younger, male, and employed at the time of their admission to treatment (LoCastro et al., 2008).

Clients who have been in treatment programs in the past might be "treatment wise," an observation that is indirectly supported by LoCastro et al. (2008) that the treatment-naive group in their study appeared to have less motivation for change than did the treatment-experienced group. They were more likely to reduce their level of alcohol use prior to the admission to treatment (LoCastro et al., 2008). This suggests at least the possibility that the latter group knew the right words to say to impress staff with their willingness to "change," although it is possible that they were indeed motivated to make life changes supportive of abstinence.

The client's past treatment history also provides an indirect measure of the severity of the client's SUD. A client who claims not to have a serious SUD, but who has been in a rehabilitation program three different times, is providing both information that is quite contradictory, and might be signaling that he or she really will not be very cooperative with any efforts at rehabilitation. Thus a review of the client's past substance abuse treatment history is important.

Legal History

Increasingly, court conviction records are available through the "Internet." Such records, or records provided by the court, reveal (a) the nature of legal charges brought against the client in the past, and their disposition, and possibly (b) the nature of any current charges pending against the client. It is important to keep in mind that the original charges might be reduced through the process of plea negotiation(s). Thus, the client who had been arrested for possession of six ounces of marijuana might have been convicted of possession of less than an ounce by the court through plea negotiations. Also, a computer-based background check might reveal that a given client has charges pending in another state that have yet to be resolved, or a string of previous arrests that he or she failed to mention. Thus, the client's accuracy about his or her legal history provides information about the relative accuracy of his or her self-report.

Past Military Record

One very important, and frequently overlooked, source of information about a client is his or her past military history (if any). Some clients will only report legal convictions from their civilian record, ignoring charges/ convictions from their military service. It is important to keep in mind that "reprimands" in the military often function as a form of plea negotiation, avoiding formal legal charges as would be brought against the individual by a courts martial trial.

If the client should deny having ever been in the military, it might be of interest to determine why he or she never enlisted. A client who responded "I didn't want to enlist" is possibly far different than the client who responds "I couldn't enlist because I had a felony conviction on my record!" Finally, the client's discharge status should be discussed. A client who has a "general discharge under honorable conditions" might be far different than the client who received a "general discharge under dishonorable conditions" or just a "dishonorable" discharge from the military. Finally, the assessor should keep in mind that military discharges might result from medical disabilities or injuries, and thus are not automatically a sign that the individual's military service was marked by conflict with the authorities.

Educational/Vocational History

This information, based on the clients' self-report and available records, provides data on the clients' level of function, and whether their chemical use has interfered with their educational/vocational experiences to date. The client who reports that he or she "just barely graduated" because he or she had trouble with the classwork is far different than the client who reports that he or she "just barely graduated" because he or she was under the influence of alcohol or drugs so often. Both hypothetical clients also present a far different clinical picture than the client who holds a Bachelor of Science degree from a well-known university.

The degree to which the client's substance use might have interfered with his or her vocational history should also be explored. Many substance-abusing clients report that they are "self-employed," which for them might be a subtle way of saying that they cannot hold a regular job because of their SUD. Thus, the individual's success as a self-employed worker should also be discussed. For employed or self-employed clients, their employment history should be explored in detail. Why did the client leave each job? Did they leave a given job because their substance use made it impossible for them to continue to work there, or because they were offered a promotion with a different company?

Developmental/Family History

Discussion in this area is often a treasure trove of information about the client's early history and the environment that he or she grew up in. It also provides a chance for the assessor to explore how the client feels about his or her parents, whether they had a SUD of their own, how they addressed it (if they did), whether either parent had a handicap, or whether either parent died while the client was growing up. Clients who hesitate to say that their father was alcohol-dependent, but compromise to say that he was "a problem drinker," might also be hinting that they would hesitate to apply the same term to themselves, if asked. An exploration of the developmental history might reveal that several siblings also have SUDs, which is a significant piece of information. Parental alcohol/SUDs might hint at a genetic predisposition[17] toward an SUD as well as possible modeling behaviors on the part of the parent that might make the child more accepting of personal substance abuse. A discussion of the client's home environment would also suggest how permissive/strict his/her home was, whether the client has unresolved feelings of anger toward a parent who had an SUD, and even possibly hint at self-hatred issues now that the client has developed an SUD just as the disliked parent struggled with years earlier.

[17]It should be pointed out that a suspected genetic predisposition is not the same as a genetic *cause* of the person's substance use disorder.

Psychiatric History

It is amazing how often assessors overlook the client's past psychiatric history. Clients have been known to be hospitalized for such problems as a "brief reactive psychosis" or "atypical psychosis," only to later reveal that they had been abusing a hallucinogenic substance that caused a bad reaction. All too often, when asked, these clients admit that nobody ever asked them whether they had abused any drug(s), and that a urine toxicology test to detect possible drug use was never performed.

There is a known relationship between SUDs and suicidal thinking, and it is often productive to inquire about whether the "suicidal" client had been abusing alcohol or drug(s) prior to being admitted to the hospital for suicidal thinking or an attempted suicide. This does not imply that the client might not be a legitimate suicide risk!!! However, the client's motivation for making the suicide threat or attempt should be fully explored. If possible, the assessor should also obtain a copy of the client's discharge summary, if not the entire treatment records, from the facility where he or she received psychiatric treatment.

Medical History

This topic often overlaps with the client's psychiatric history. However, the assessor needs to explore the client's medical history (Gendel, 2006). A history of a past hospitalization for treatment of internal injuries sustained in a motor vehicle accident might hint at a possible alcohol/drug-related accident that the client failed to report earlier in the assessment process. A client might deny having any SUD, but admit that he or she had been shot twice by rival drug dealers in the past three years. If they did not have an SUD how did they happen to be shot twice by drug dealers in the past three years? These two pieces of information must be reconciled during the assessment by the assessor.

The assessor should inquire about any current or recent prescription medications to identify those clients who might have been "doctor shopping"[18] to obtain desired medications. The assessor should also note

[18]A term applied to the process of looking for a physician who will prescribe a desired medication. Sometimes, this might require that they see two, three, four, or even more physicians, before they fine one willing to diagnose them with a condition that makes their use of a desired medication legitimate. Substance abusing clients have been known to study what symptoms they need to report/demonstrate, in order to convince the physician to prescribe a desired medication(s).

how many different health care providers are involved in the patient's care, and whether these individuals are aware that the client had consulted the other(s) for care. Over-the-counter medication use should be discussed as well, because such medications can exacerbate problems caused by prescription medications, alter the pharmacokinetics of prescribed medications when used concurrently by a client, and some have an abuse potential of their own.

Finally the individual's expectations for their drug(s) of abuse should be reviewed. For example, Reich and Goldman (2005) found that high-risk and low-risk alcohol users appear to have different expectations for the outcome of alcohol use. As a group, high-risk drinkers tended to anticipate a more positive outcome to their use of alcohol, for example. Low-risk drinkers were more likely to expect more negative outcomes of their alcohol use, especially in terms of the level of sedation and alcohol's negative impact on their social skills. Thus the assessor should discuss the individual's expectations for their drug(s) of abuse to determine what role they play in the person's life.

In order to exist, the addictions require that the individual make certain personality adjustments to allow the SUD to continue to exist. The assessor must try to determine the client's core personality from those characteristics that evolved as a response to their SUD (Grekin, Sher, & Wood, 2006). For example, Vaglum (2003) suggested that between 20 and 40% of opiate addicts who were diagnosed as having an antisocial personality disorder actually engaged in antisocial behaviors because of their addiction, but that that they did not have an antisocial personality disorder prior to the development of their SUD. It is not uncommon, for example, to hear a client tell a therapist or a treatment group that "I never thought that I would reach the point where I would not _____, but, well, I did it." In this hypothetical case, the substance of choice forces the individual to engage in previously forbidden behaviors, to allow them to continue to abuse chemicals.[19]

Real versus Pseudo Personality Disorders

One point that often is overlooked by assessors is that long-term substance abuse requires that the individual's personality adapt to the continued abuse of that chemical. The behaviors noted during the clinical interview, or in the client's past while she or he was abusing chemicals, might not reflect the client's core personality. The possibility of a substance-induced pseudo personality disorder must be considered by the assessor.[20] Frequently a careful history will reveal that the individuals being assessed were forced into a pattern of antisocial behavior to support their SUD without having an ASPD. One determining factor is whether the personality pattern that the client presents predated the development of the SUD, or is a consequence of the SUD (Grekin et al., 2006). The differentiation between real and substance-induced personality disorders is of major significance because this has profound implications for the individual's rehabilitation potential.

Section Summary

On the basis of the information obtained through the clinical interview, collateral information, and test data the assessor will then be in a position to determine where, on the continuum of drug use disorders identified in Chapter 1, the client appears to fall, based on available evidence.

The Assessor and Data Privacy

The issue of confidentiality has always been a difficult issue, and recent changes in state and Federal data privacy laws have served to make matters even more complicated.[21] Many clients fear, for example, that their parents, spouse, employer, law enforcement agencies, or professional licensing boards will have access to the records, making them hesitant to discuss problems or concerns openly. The assessor will need to review the data privacy laws with the client, so that he or she knows in advance who will, and will not, have access to their records. It will also be necessary for the assessor to discuss the conditions under which information provided by the client might be released.

To further complicate matters, the data privacy rules addressing therapy or assessment sessions with a child or adolescent might differ from the laws that apply to sessions with an adult. In some areas, adolescents

---

[19]An interesting point to debate is whether the individual who is unwilling to make this adjustment (unwilling to "pay the cost" for his or her addiction) is characteristically protected against the development of an SUD.

[20]At this point, the reader is welcome to groan in frustration, or despair.

[21]It is recommended that the reader consult an attorney to discuss what data privacy regulations apply in that specific state, as well as the Federal guidelines that also must be kept in mind. One Federal law is the *Health Insurance Portability and Accountability Act* (HIPAA).

above a certain age might request professional services that, while the parent is obligated to pay for such sessions, are still protected information that cannot be discussed with the parent (Greenfield & Hennessy, 2008).Traditionally, information revealed by or about a patient is considered privileged and protected. There are exceptions to this rule, however. If a patient were to reveal that he or she were actively abusing a child, the therapist might be obligated to report this to the authorities under what are known as "duty to report" laws. Another exception to the privilege of confidentiality is cases where the individual reveals specific plans to kill themselves or another person. In such cases, proper steps must be taken to protect the client and the potential victim(s). There are states in which the court is permitted to order that certain information be released to the court, usually when that information is relevant to an ongoing legal investigation.

Clients will frequently reveal that they have been in a treatment program on previous occasions, and these treatment records are useful adjuncts to the assessor. To obtain copies of these treatment records it will be necessary for the assessor to obtain a Release of Information authorization from the client. This is a written form signed by the client that gives his or her permission for one facility to release information to another facility. The client also has the right to specify which information can be released by a facility. Finally, the client has the right to refuse to even talk to the assessor, if he or she should choose to do so. The privilege of confidentiality is always the client's, except under very specific circumstances, and is not breached lightly.

When the final evaluation report is composed, the assessor should identify the exact source(s) of information utilized in the formulation of the report. Collateral information sources should be notified in advance that the client, and/or the client's attorney, has a right to request a copy of the final draft of the report, and thus their contribution to the final draft of the report might become known to the client. Further, although it is rare, on occasion the client does request a copy of the final report, and technically has a right to do so after filling out the proper Release of Information authorization forms.

Diagnostic Rules

Many individuals will resist a diagnosis of a SUD, at least at first. Because of this, there are two diagnostic rules that the assessor should adhere to as much as possible: Always gather collateral information. As a group, alcohol-dependent persons will be reasonably accurate about their substance use, especially if sober, when they are asked about their substance use pattern. There are exceptions to this rule, however, such as when the individual is facing the threat of legal action (Gendel, 2006). A person facing the possibility of a long prison or jail sentence may exaggerate his or her self-report of having an SUD, not because it was true, but because this might serve as a mitigating factor that might reduce the severity of his or her sentence. In contrast to this, dual diagnosis clients often underreport the extent of problems caused by their SUD because they fear loss of entitlements (social security and so on).

One advantage of collateral information data is the determination of whether the client's reported behavior(s) when under the influence of a compound is consistent with the known characteristics of that compound. Collateral information sources might support the client's claim of atypical effects from a drug(s) of abuse, or deny that the client even abused alcohol or drug(s) at times when the client claims otherwise. Every assessor has experienced the scenario in which the client claims to use alcohol "just once a week, perhaps not even that often." When asked, the spouse admits that the person uses alcohol nightly, drinking to the point of intoxication every night after work. Obviously, time constraints limit the assessor's ability to contact collateral sources of information to some degree. If the report is due in 72 hours, it might not be possible to contact collateral information sources, but an attempt should be made after obtaining the proper Release of Information authorization. Collateral information sources might include:

1. the patient's family
2. friends of the patient
3. employer or coworkers
4. clergy members
5. local law enforcement officials (criminal convictions are public and might be accessed over the "Internet"
6. primary care physician
7. psychotherapist or family therapist (if any)

It will be of value to note whether the collateral information sources cooperate or if they refused to cooperate. It should also be noted whether the client was able to contact the collateral information source before the therapist to coach them on what to say. In more than one case the assessor has heard the client in the background, telling the collateral information source how to answer the questions asked during a telephone conversation. This information should also be noted in the assessment report.

Rule number two is always assume deception until proven otherwise. As noted it has been found that as a group, alcohol-dependent persons tend to be honest about their drinking pattern; however, there are exceptions to this rule. A recent study in England concluded, for example, that 40% of heavy drinkers lie to their physicians about the extent of their drinking ("Heavy Drinkers 'Lie to Doctors,'" 2008). Further, clients might consciously or unconsciously distort information provided to the assessor, possibly because of their distorted way of thinking (Ross, 2002). The client who claims to be an "infrequent" drinker, but who actually consumes 5–7 beers each evening with coworkers at the end of the day might be attempting to deceive the assessor, or might actually believe that this constitutes "infrequent" drinking. After all, it is expected that he or she join coworkers at the end of the day, and the individual might only consume alcohol on rare occasions other than at the end of the workday with coworkers.

Unconscious deception is a very real danger during the assessment process. A wise assessor will keep in mind that even "cooperative" clients might engage in such deception. One client might smugly report that she or he spends $20 a week on alcohol. When confronted with the reality that this amounts to $1,040 a year, that same client might become indigent and claim that she or he was spending only $20 a week for alcohol because his or denial system will not allow him or her to think otherwise. It is also common for the person to claim to drink "once or twice a week," until confronted with the fact that their medical problems are unlikely to have resulted from such a limited level of alcohol use.

It is important to ask not only about legal problems associated with the client's substance use in one's home state, but also in other states and while in the military. A client who admits to "one" arrest for driving under the influence of alcohol might, when pressed, admit to other charges in other states, and defend their response on the grounds that they thought that the assessor "only meant this state" or that the client did not think that those other convictions applied, because they happened while the client was enlisted in the military. Fortunately, the Internet allows access to court records from many other states, because a criminal conviction is a public document.

Other Sources of Information: Medical Test Data

There are no definitive blood or urine tests that will prove that a person is addicted to alcohol or drugs. As will be discussed later, a single "dirty"[22] urine toxicology test does not, in itself, prove that the client has a substance use problem. A series of three or four "dirty" urine samples is more definitive, and it is hard for clients to claim that the urine toxicology test was done right after their first experimental use of a chemical if they had three "dirty" urine samples over two months!

Breath analysis might identify the blood alcohol level in the client's system, but not how long that individual has been drinking. Abnormal blood test results should serve as a warning that a patient might be abusing alcohol or illicit drugs. However, there are other potential causes of abnormal blood test results. For example, elevated liver function tests might reflect alcohol-related damage, or they might be caused by other medical conditions. Medical tests can often:

1. confirm the presence of certain chemicals in the patient's body,
2. identify the specific compounds that are present,
3. possibly determine the level of that chemical in the patient's body, and
4. hint at how long the patient has been abusing chemicals.

Further, the appropriate medical tests can identify concurrent medical disorders that might complicate efforts at substance abuse rehabilitation, such as a cardiac problem (Work Group on Substance Use Disorders, 2007).

Diagnosis: The Outcome of the Assessment Process

At the end of the assessment, the assessor should be able to answer four interrelated questions: (a) whether the individual does/does not have a SUD, and the evidence on which that conclusion is based, (b) the severity of the individual's substance use problem, (c) the client's motivation to change, and (d) factors that contribute/support further substance use (Connors, Donovan, & DiClemente, 2001). In other words, the

---

[22]Meaning that metabolites of illicit drugs were apparently found in the urine.

assessor should be able to make a diagnosis at the end of the assessment process.

Many mental health professionals mistakenly believe that the American Psychiatric Association Diagnostic and Statistical Manual of Mental Disorders (*DSM-5*) (American Psychiatric Association, 2013) provides a tool for a comprehensive assessment of the SUDs. This is not true. Like its predecessors, the *DSM-5* does not identify the role that a substance might play in the person's life or how to proceed with treatment decisions. The *DSM-5* does suggest that some of the signs of an SUD include:

1. preoccupation with continued substance use,
2. using more of a substance than originally planned,
3. development of tolerance,
4. characteristic withdrawal syndrome,
5. continued use of the chemical to avoid symptoms of withdrawal,
6. intoxication at inappropriate times (at work, or school, for example),
7. situations when withdrawal interferes with normal activities,
8. reduction in social, occupational, or recreational activities in favor of using that time for additional substance use, and
9. continued use in spite of social, emotional, and physical or vocational problems caused by the substance use.

Surprisingly, the *DSM-5* criteria do not identify substance-related legal problems as one of the diagnostic criteria used to identify an active SUD. The *DSM-5* does attempt to assess the severity of the individual's SUD on the basis of the number of criteria that apply to a specific individual

If the client claims to be abstinent at the time of the assessment, it is necessary to determine the circumstances under which this abstinence was achieved. A client who claims to have abstained from all drugs of abuse for the past four months (while incarcerated for the last four months) presents a different clinical picture than the client who reports no alcohol or illicit drug use for the past four months while living independently. Clients who are under the supervision of the court system (or probation/parole officers) may abstain from alcohol and drugs because they are required to submit to urine toxicology testing on a random basis, for example. Thus, the assessor must determine why the client has abstained from chemicals, if she or he reports abstinence.

Although the diagnostic process is often viewed by clinicians as only a necessary step to ensure that an insurance company pays for the recommended treatment (and ensures the continued employment of the assessor!), in reality it is far more than this. It is an ongoing process against which the client's needs, strengths, and resources are measured on a day-to-day basis. Figure 27-1 depicts a flow chart of the assessment process.

In addition to an accurate diagnosis of the client's substance use pattern, the assessor should also be able to identify the individual's motivation for seeking the assessment. The client who is seen after being ordered to have the assessment by a probation officer offers a different level of motivation than does a person who seeks help because of substance-related life-threatening physical illness, and both individuals present the assessor with different forms of motivation than the person who is self-motivated to stop abusing alcohol or drugs.

It should be noted that some clients seek a substance use assessment and treatment recommendations not because they wish to come to terms with their SUD, but for impression management purposes (Wild, Cunningham, & Hobdon, 1998). The willingness to enter treatment for a SUD does not automatically translate into the willingness to change one's chemical use pattern (Connors et al., 2001). Individuals with pending court hearings on unresolved legal charges, especially drug-related legal issues, might seek admission to "treatment" without any desire to do more than "look good" before the judge ("I have been through treatment, your Honor!"). Imagine, for a moment, a person who has been arrested for the crime of selling drugs, but who does not actually abuse alcohol or drugs.[23] The question facing the assessor is whether to refer this individual to a substance abuse treatment program, when the client does not have such a disorder, or recommend that the client be referred elsewhere. Although the majority of clients referred to a rehabilitation facility are there because of external pressure (wife, employer, the court system, and so on), the person who enters treatment for the sole purpose of attempting to manipulate the court system wastes

---

[23]Yes, such people exist. Their motivation for drug sales is not to support their own substance use disorder, but to partake of the profits made through the sale of illicit drugs.

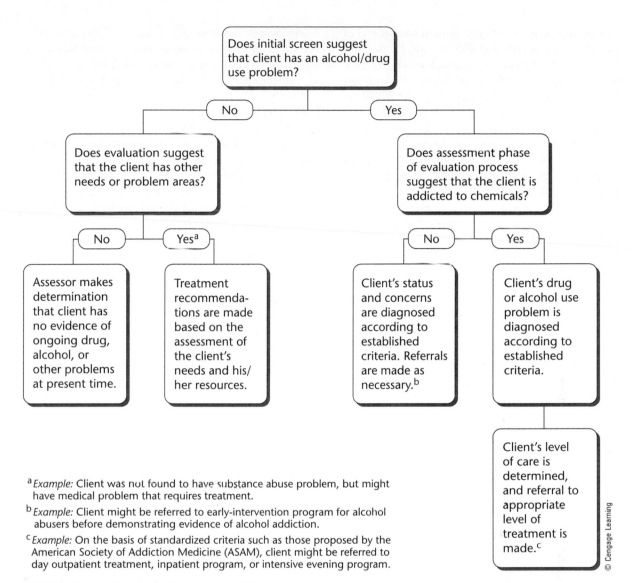

FIGURE 27-1 A Flowchart of the Assessment Process.

^a*Example:* Client was not found to have substance abuse problem, but might have medical problem that requires treatment.

^b*Example:* Client might be referred to early-intervention program for alcohol abusers before demonstrating evidence of alcohol addiction.

^c*Example:* On the basis of standardized criteria such as those proposed by the American Society of Addiction Medicine (ASAM), client might be referred to day outpatient treatment, inpatient program, or intensive evening program.

valuable treatment resources better used to treat others.

Treatment Referrals

Having established that the client does, or does not, have an SUD, the next step is the determination of the appropriate level of care. The Work Group on Substance Use Disorders (2007) suggested seven criteria that should be considered when making a decision about the appropriate level of care for the client: (1) the individual's ability and willingness to participate in treatment, (2) the individual's ability to carry out self-care activities,[24] (3) the individual's family and social environment, (4) the individual's need for structure to assist him or her in achieving abstinence, (5) need for ancillary treatment for concurrent medical or psychiatric problems, (6) the availability of treatment programs in a given area, and, (7) the client's preference for a specific form of treatment.[25]

---

[24]Often called *activities of daily living,* or *ADLs.*

[25]Although the client's wishes for a specific form of treatment should not dictate the level of treatment recommended, it should be taken into consideration by the assessor and if dismissed a rationale for why it was dismissed be included in the final report.

The criteria offered by the American Society of Addiction Medicine (ASAM) also provide an excellent guide to determining the appropriate level of care for a given client (American Society of Addiction Medicine, 2001). The ASAM patient placement guide is not, in spite of belief to the contrary, a comprehensive assessment tool. It is a guide to the appropriate level of patient care the diagnosis of a SUD has been established (Fletcher, 2013). This program guide has become the most commonly utilized system to determine client level of care needs (Gastfriend, 2004a, 2004b) and in some states its use is required by state law.[26] The most recent revision of the ASAM patient placement criteria identify six levels of care (eight levels for adolescents):

1. *Level 0.5: Early intervention*
2. *Level I: Outpatient treatment*
3. *Level II: Intensive outpatient treatment/partial hospitalization*
4. *Level III: Residential/inpatient treatment*
5. *Level IV: Medically managed intensive inpatient treatment*
6. *Level OMT: Methadone Maintenance Programs*

The ASAM patient placement criteria have been found to be effective by research studies designed to test whether they stand up to "managed care" demands for specific level of care decisions (Mee-Lee & Gastfriend, 2008). Some of the factors that the assessor must keep in mind are: (a) client strengths, (b) client weaknesses, (c) potential for withdrawal from alcohol or drugs of abuse, (d) potential for serious medical problems during withdrawal and while in treatment,[27] and (e) strength of the client's abstinence support system.

These factors influence the assessed client need for a specific level of care. Another factor that is rarely discussed is the client's legal status. The level of care decision might have been made by the court system, which will mandate a specific level of care for the client, and failure to complete treatment at that level will result in revocation of probation/parole.

There are other systems available that will guide the assessor in making this determination. All of these patient placement guides are governed by the principle of the least restrictive treatment alternative in which the client's strengths, needs, and his or her treatment history, potential for relapse, availability of a support system, and so on, are then reviewed to help determine the appropriate level of care (Work Group on Substance Use Disorders, 2007).

Chapter Summary

The evaluation process consists of three phases: (1) screening, (2) assessment, and, (3) diagnosis. Each of these phases rests on the one before it, and closely parallels the medical diagnosis process. If there is evidence that a condition might exist (screening), it is then assessed. During the assessment process, the parameters of the condition, its duration, intensity, factors that might reduce its severity and others that might exacerbate it, are explored. At the end of the assessment stage, the assessor is in a position to make a formal diagnosis and to make treatment recommendations. Included in the treatment recommendations is the level of care that would be most appropriate for the individual client. Some of the aids available to assessors for use in each stage of the assessment process were reviewed.

[26]Always consult with an attorney to determine in requirements in your state.
[27]As determined by qualified health care professional.

CHAPTER 28

Intervention[1]

> The most promising way—perhaps the only way—to put enough addicts into treatment long enough to make a difference entails a considerable measure of coercion.
>
> *(Satel & Farabee, 2005, p. 690)*

Introduction

There are many who would challenge the validity of the above quote. There are also those who would defend its validity, in part because many persons with substance use disorders (SUDs) do not perceive the need for rehabilitation (Edlund, Booth, & Feldman, 2009) or believe that there is a stigma attached to entering treatment for a SUD (Fletcher, 2013). The subject of intervention has become widely acknowledged as a result of often dramatic television programs in which a counselor joins a family in confronting a family member with an SUD while the camera(s) are recording every moment. Many of these televised programs show the eloquence and grace of a bar room brawl, and one must wonder how much having the television cameras present has changed the dynamics of the intervention session. However, these programs do illustrate different forms of intervention, which is the topic of this chapter.

Surprisingly, health care professionals still have no single definition of intervention. Admittedly, there are benefits to treating the SUDs, providing justification for clinical intervention with substance abusers. Researchers have found a 26% reduction in hospitalizations for general health problems, a 25% reduction in the length of hospitalization following admission, a 38% reduction in visits to hospital emergency rooms, and a 14% reduction in physician visits following the cessation of alcohol use, for example (Weiss, 2005). The average monthly medical cost for a drug abuser has been estimated at $750/month, which is reduced to $200/month following treatment, as compared to $100/month for a person the same age who has never abused alcohol or drugs (Rosenbloom, 2000). Further, researchers have found that successful completion of substance abuse treatment is associated with a significant reduction in suicide attempts or completed suicides (Ilgen, Jain, Lucas, & Moos, 2007).

In spite of these obvious advantages, individuals with alcohol use disorders rarely perceive the need for treatment (Flora, 2005; Wu & Ringwalt, 2005). It must be assumed that the same is true for individuals with other SUDs. Thus, some form of intervention is necessary, but the methods for intervention are still in development. In this chapter, the process of intervention will be reviewed.

---

[1]The material in this chapter is provided for illustrative purposes only. It is not intended for, and should not be used as, a guide to the intervention process.

A Definition of Intervention

Sadock and Sadock (2007) suggested that the patient with an alcohol use disorder (the prototypical addiction) must "be brought face-to-face with the reality of the disorder (intervention), be detoxified if necessary, and begin rehabilitation" (p. 403). The core concept of his intervention is making the individual with an SUD face the reality of his or her addiction and the harm that it has caused the individual, family, and friends. However, intervention takes many forms, not just the dramatic televised events seen on so many television programs. A spouse's comment that his or her partner is drinking too much is a form of intervention. The physician's warning that if the person continues to drink or abuse drugs she or he might die is another form of intervention. The supervisor's warning that the individual seems to have a problem and that he or she should consider going into treatment is yet another form of intervention.

But at what point does "feedback" from a friend, supervisor, spouse or the courts become a formal intervention project? All forms of intervention begin with the same starting point: Is it necessary for some form of intervention to be carried out? If the answer is "no," then obviously the process stops at this point. If it is agreed that some form of intervention is appropriate, then the decision must be made about the form of intervention, and, who is to participate in that intervention effort. For the sake of this text, intervention will be defined as being an (a) organized effort by a (b) person or persons who are part of the addicted person's environment, to (c) break through the walls of denial and rationalization that surround the addictive behavior(s), which is (d) often supervised by a trained professional, with the goal of obtaining an agreement from the addicted person to (e) immediately seek admission to a designated treatment center. In theory this process is relatively straight forward. The application of the intervention process is usually quite difficult.

A Brief History of Intervention

It was once thought that a person with an SUD would not be receptive to efforts to intervene until she or he had "hit bottom."[2] "Hitting bottom" was thought to be necessary for the addicted persons to understand that their SUD was harming them, and that they needed to stop abusing chemicals. An unfortunate side-effect of this process was that many substance abusers die before reaching their personal "bottom." Others find that they have a successive series of "bottoms" as they bounce from one situation to another, never accepting the need for them to address their SUD.

Then, Vernon Johnson (1980) suggested a different perspective: He did not believe that the person must "hit bottom" before being able to accept help with his or her addiction. Because of the physical, emotional, social, and vocational damage that uncontrolled alcohol use could cause, he advocated early intervention rather than waiting for the person to "hit bottom." He suggested that the alcohol-dependent person (with whom he had the most experience) might comprehend the reality of his or her alcohol use disorder if that information was presented in a language that the drinker could understand. Even low functioning persons (McCrady, 2001) or the individual who was "not in touch with reality" (Johnson, 1980, p. 49) because of his or her substance use was still capable of understanding some portion of the message expressed to them in Johnson's opinion. An all too common consequence of intervention efforts is that the person with the SUD will resist efforts from concerned others to guide them into a rehabilitation program. To help family and friends address this apparent misperception, a small industry emerged in the 1980s and 1990s in which trained, semi-trained, self-trained, and untrained individuals offered to guide an intervention project. Such intervention projects have even become the focus of prime-time television programs. The well-intentioned goal of these projects was to convince a person with an SUD to agree to immediately enter treatment. Having the person simply promise not to drink or use drugs again was not perceived as sufficient, as it was known that individuals with SUDs would often make such promises, only to break them the next day. The goal was for the individual to agree to and then enter treatment and such intervention projects have become enshrined in clinical lore as both useful, and, often necessary.

Characteristics of the Intervention Process

The characteristics of the intervention process depend, to a large degree, on the setting and the individual(s) involved.

---

[2]"Hitting bottom" is a term loosely defined as the point where the substance abuser has to admit to total, absolute, defeat in life because of his or her SUD.

Physician-based Brief Intervention

One form of intervention is the brief alcohol intervention approach used by many physicians. A physician in the consultation room who informs a patient that if he or she should continue to abuse chemicals he or she will probably not live another five years, and that the physician could recommend some good treatment programs, might be said to have attempted to intervene. A brief intervention discussion between a physician and a patient in the emergency room has been found to result in a significant reduction in later alcohol use (SBIRT Research Collaborative Group, 2007). Unfortunately the brief intervention interview with a physician failed to demonstrate a significantly higher reduction in harmful drinking as compared with simply handing the patient a leaflet about the dangers of drinking or a five-minute session about lifestyle changes (Kaner, Bland, Cassidy, Coiulton, Dale, Deluca, Gilvarry, Godfrey, Heather, Myles et al., 2013). This unexpected finding casts doubt on the effectiveness of brief physician intervention and further research into this topic is necessary.

Informal Intervention

The intervention process can take many forms. A spouse who says "if you don't stop using _____, I am leaving!" might be said to have attempted an intervention. A friend who expresses concern about his friend's substance use, how much it scares him to see his friend following the same road that he was once following, and how much he would like to see his friend enter treatment and stop abusing drugs, could also be said to have attempted an informal intervention project.

A supervisor or employer, if asked to participate in the intervention project, might assert that one stipulation of continued employment is that the designated individual take part in a random drug toxicology testing program, and that evidence of illicit drug use or failure to obtain a physician's excuse for taking time off from work for illness will result in the person losing his or her job. This is a semi-formal intervention project because specific sanctions for noncompliance are identified. Legal intervention projects, which will be discussed later in this chapter, also do exist; although, they are more formal.

The Mechanics of Intervention

The goal of the intervention project is to assist a given individual in making the decision to stop using alcohol or drugs. If the informal discussions outlined earlier in this chapter have failed to assist the designated individual in making the desired behavior change, a more formal intervention process, usually but not automatically involving family members, might be appropriate. When the decision is reached to attempt a formal intervention meeting, one or more practice sessions should be set up with the counselor who will be the chairperson for the meeting. This principle reflects a cornerstone of the intervention process: It is planned in advance. During the planning session(s) the most probable objections and the most appropriate response(s) are discussed. The hoped-for outcome of the intervention project should be discussed and participants agree on the specific outcome in advance.

The coordinator of the intervention meeting should emphasize that the purpose of the meeting is to allow participants to express their concern for the designated individual, their desire that the individual enter a rehabilitation program, and not to allow them to voice their anger about past transgressions (Flora, 2005). Decisions about the proper response to the probable objections and the identification of a specific agency to refer that individual to should be resolved before the start of the intervention project.

Paradoxically, by the time that intervention project(s) are being considered, addicted individuals will rarely deny the reality of their SUD; although, this might not be true if they believe that the information will not be used against them in criminal proceedings (Fletcher, 2013). People with an SUD are usually well aware of their substance use problem, even if they will allow this awareness into their conscious mind only on rare occasions. When confronted, however, many individuals attempt to deflect confrontation with the observation that their substance use is hurting only them, not other family members (Flora, 2005). To break through such rationalizations, the designated individual is confronted by persons (family members, coworkers, and so on) whose lives have been affected by the individual's SUD. Comments such as "I saw you taking OxyContin from your grandmother's medicine bottle a week before she died of cancer" both provide the specific data and demonstrate how the addict's behavior has affected others.

The intervention project is carried out with the goal of having the client agree to enter treatment immediately. If the client admits that perhaps his or her SUD has affected others, and agrees to enter treatment, he or she is then immediately escorted to the treatment center admissions office by family members. When intervention is attempted, the persons doing the intervention should have specific referrals in place. The identified patient has the right to refuse to enter treatment. In such case those who participate in the intervention project should have identified sanctions ready to put into place.

These sanctions are not to be viewed as empty threats but rather as the first steps in the process of detachment. Through this process the person imposing the sanction is saying that he or she will no longer be part of the individual's addiction support system. Thus, a sister might say "Although you have the right to keep abusing chemicals, you are no longer welcome at my home until you have successfully completed a treatment program." The parents in this hypothetical example might affirm the same decision.

Thus a physician might say "In this case, I can no longer in good conscience continue to prescribe [name of specific medication(s)] to you. The risk of a fatal interaction between the medications that I prescribe and the drugs that you take is too great." A family member might inform the person with the SUD: "You are no longer welcome in my home until you have completed treatment and remain abstinent for a full year." Then these sanctions need to be maintained.

Sometimes, the identified family member will offer vague assurances that he or she will seek assistance, which is used in the service of denial, protecting their SUD. "Yes, I know, you're right," the individual might say. "But it is late. I'll call the treatment center tomorrow." However, "tomorrow" never seems to arrive, and the individual offers a thousand and one reasons why he or she could not enter treatment today or at the specified treatment center. "I can't afford to enter treatment! I have bills to pay and need to go to work!" is a common objection offered by the addicted person as a reason why he or she cannot possibly enter a rehabilitation program at this time. Such objections might be sincere, but also deny the reality of the person's addiction. Bills might have been left unpaid, or only partially paid, but the person always found the money to pay for his or her alcohol or drugs.

On occasion, the intervention efforts will be countered with an effort on the clients' part to give the impression of compliance without acceptance of the need to fully enter the treatment process. The family intervention project had required that they enter treatment. Nobody said anything about the designated person finishing it, right? They offer a thousand reasons why they could not complete treatment: "I had to leave ... they kept stuffing this 'God' crap down my throat!!!"

is a common excuse. The reality may very well be that the designated family member heard the word "God" twice in one evening, but as rationalizations go you have to work with what you have, and this is a good one. Individuals have been known to drive to a treatment center, sit in the parking lot, then after a few hours' drive home to say to the family "I went there and they didn't admit me." By this subtle manipulation of the facts, the addicted person implies that she or he did not really need treatment. To avoid such manipulation, designated family members should accompany the addicted member to the treatment center and participate in the admissions interview so that the counselor has an honest overview of the identified patient's SUD and its impact on others.

The identified person will often exploit indecision in the service of his or her addiction possibly to avoid a referral to treatment entirely. Promises will be made, and later broken, but by then the unified front by those involved in the intervention project will have been shattered by the demands of each individual's life. Clients have been known to make promises for a lesser sanction, such as going to an outpatient treatment program rather than an inpatient rehabilitation facility, knowing that after time the family's resolve will weaken, and they can drop out of treatment.

Although the intervention process has been in use for more than a generation, there is little evidence to support its effectiveness (Flora, 2005). It is possible that some families will benefit more from intervention efforts, whereas others might suffer great harm from the same process. In a very real sense the intervention process might be said to be the clinical application of a theory that has not been tested to identify either the optimal or minimal conditions where it might be applicable.

The Ethics of Intervention[3]

The process of intervention is fraught with ethical dilemmas (Scott, 2000). For example, it is based on the assumption that, through treatment, the substance abusing person can be saved from the negative consequences of the SUD. However, the success rate of existing treatment modalities does not offer much of a

---

[3]Persons planning on an intervention process are advised to consult with an attorney as to the specific laws that apply in that geographic location, and what they can or cannot do to carry out the intervention process.

guarantee that this assumption will be met (Kleinig, 2004). Further, the judgment that a person constitutes a sufficiently significant danger to himself or others that some intervention is justified is often highly speculative (Kleinig, 2004, p. 381).

Thus, the need for an intervention must be firmly established and documented. The participant(s) need to carry out an honest, thoughtful, review of the benefits and possible consequences of the intervention process, documenting that such a review did take place, and what was assessed (Kleinig, 2004).

Another ethical concern is whether the designated individual wishes to participate in the intervention project. The person with the SUD must not be physically restrained, for example, except in cases where there is a danger to self or others.[4] However, if the designated individual should express a desire to leave, she or he should be allowed to do so. The designated person is free to leave the intervention program at any time, with the exception of when he or she presents a danger to self or others.

Another ethical concern is whether informed consent is a necessary component of the intervention project (Kleinig, 2004). Years ago, the simple authoritative assertion of a health care professional was sufficient for an intervention program to be deemed necessary. The courts now hold that the professional must offer informed consent (and document that this was offered) before the client is introduced to the intervention process (Kleinig, 2004). During the intervention process personal information about the client, or his or her behavior, might be revealed to other people who were unaware of these facts. Data privacy is of special importance in hospitals, where people might be exposed to information about the patient's SUD in spite of the individual's desire to keep such information private.

A point of law holds that a patient has the right to refuse any recommended treatment. However, there are exceptions to this rule.[5] Kleinig (2004) suggested that one such exception is when harm to one person will occur because of the SUD of another person. Because a mother's cocaine abuse might harm the fetus, the courts in many different states have remanded many pregnant women into treatment on the justification that the mother's continued substance use might harm the fetus (Kleinig, 2004).

The potential conflict of interest must be assessed, especially if the substance abuse rehabilitation professionals should refer the client only to themselves, or a facility where they work (Fals-Stewart, O'Farrell, & Birchler, 2003; Fletcher, 2013). Care must be taken by the substance abuse rehabilitation professional to insure that she or he has no economic vested interest in where the client goes to treatment. Ideally the client should be offered a number of treatment options; although, in reality economic and geographic realities might limit the options available to the client. Finally, the counselor's qualifications and his or her adherence to professional codes of ethics also need to be considered when planning an intervention project (Kleinig, 2004). Obviously, legal counsel is necessary to help the substance abuse rehabilitation professional through the quagmire that surrounds her or him, to avoid violating State or Federal laws (Scott, 2000).

Some Common Forms of Intervention

Family Intervention Projects

There are a number of family intervention project models, the most common of which is the format advocated by Johnson (1986). Collectively, these family intervention efforts are second only to legal pressure to force the individual into treatment (O'Farrell & Fals-Stewart, 2008). However, it should be recognized that the person who is the center of the intervention project is unlikely to be enthusiastic about this process, and there is a danger for serious damage to familial relationships as a result of family intervention programs (Blume, 2005; Flora, 2005). This danger is increased if the intervention project is poorly planned or executed. Although it is the goal that the intervention project be carried out without malice and in a nonjudgmental manner (Fals-Stewart et al., 2003; Sadock & Sadock, 2007), many family members will view the intervention project as a time to voice resentments about the individual's SUD or past behaviors, increasing the danger of a negative outcome. It must be recognized that family intervention sessions are "emotional powder kegs that can go horribly wrong" (Flora, 2005, p. 41). What follows is a brief summary

---

[4]In which case the police should be called to restrain the individual.

[5]Thus the recommendation that the substance abuse rehabilitation professional seek legal counsel as to the laws that apply in her or his State before attempting an intervention project.

of two of the more common family intervention models.

The Johnson Model

This is the model most often associated with the word *intervention*, and its original force was advanced by Johnson (1986). This form of intervention is often portrayed in many popular books, articles, and the occasional prime-time television program, usually in a positive light. Johnson model intervention projects usually involve three to four educational or rehearsal sessions before the actual intervention effort, to prepare family members, friends, or coworkers for the actual intervention session. Those persons who are either actively abusing alcohol or illicit drugs, or who refuse to participate in the intervention project, should not be invited (O'Farrell & Fals-Stewart, 2008).

During the pre-effort training sessions, participants are taught about the disease model of addictions, reducing the potential for anger or malice as the participants learn that the affected person suffers from a disease and is not intentionally being mean or unsupportive. Family members are encouraged to bring written notes to the intervention session with them. Such notes should be very specific as to dates, times, and the client's behaviors that resulted in that person's decision to be part of the intervention project. Statements such as "You often come home drunk" should be replaced with specific comments such as "Last week you came home intoxicated on Monday, Wednesday, Thursday, and Saturday night!"

Role-play simulations are also carried out to prepare family members for possible scenarios that might emerge during the actual intervention session. If, for example, the addicted person should claim not to have driven while under the influence after going to the bar because "Mark drove me," a family member should check with Mark (if he is not a participant) to see whether this excuse is valid or not. Other possible scenarios to be addressed include what to do if the affected family member should become angry, attempt to leave, or attempt to manipulate family members into disagreement. During these pre-effort sessions, family members will discuss the goal of the intervention project (usually to secure a commitment to immediately enter treatment). If successful, the participants will have prearranged admission to a treatment facility.

When all is ready, the affected family member is either invited or escorted to the intervention effort session. Such sessions often have all of the elegance and style of a hanging in the days of the Wild West, and as

noted there is the danger for lifelong damage to familial relationships even in the best of intervention efforts. Further, in spite of the intentions of participants, Johnson (1986) model intervention programs result in a commitment to enter treatment only in approximately 30% of the cases (O'Farrell & Fals-Stewart, 2008; Miller & White, 2007).

The ARISE Model[6]

This is a three-stage model of intervention in which the level of pressure applied by the family to encourage the affected member to enter treatment is gradually increased (Landau & Garret, 2006). This model is based on a graduated series of contact sessions with the patient over a period of time with the goal of securing the addicted person's entry into treatment. The first stage is usually telephone contact with the client, followed by a family therapy session to explore the problem and its ramifications. In stage two, the client is invited to attend a family therapy session, and the entire family discusses options that they see available to them at that time. In the third stage, if the individual does not enter treatment within a designated period of time a more confrontational intervention session comparable to the "Johnson model" in many ways is then carried out. Through this manner the client is only exposed to strong levels of confrontation if he or she should fail to respond to more gentle feedback from family members about how their SUD has affected the family members.

Intervention by the Legal System

Individuals who participate in court-mandated treatment arrive at this point through a variety of avenues. Some have been convicted of driving a motor vehicle while under the influence of alcohol or drugs (a DWI as it is called in some states[7]). Others may have been arrested for possession of illicit drugs, or for any of a wide range of substance-related legal offenses. In theory, the individual retains the right to choose incarceration over treatment (Leamon, Wright & Myrick, 2008). Essentially the individual is placed into an either/or situation: Either the client successfully completes treatment, or he or she will go to jail. This is

---

[6]Which stands for "A Relational Intervention Sequence for Engagement."

[7]In other states, it is called an OWI, or "operating a motor vehicle while under the influence of intoxicants."

called contingency management (Morgan, 2003). Individuals who enter a rehabilitation facility under such situations are said to demonstrate controlled motivation (Wild, Cunningham, & Hobdon, 1998). Unfortunately, court-mandated treatment is rarely viewed as an opportunity for growth, and is usually viewed as a punitive response by the legal system for past behavior(s) by the individual (Dill & Wells-Parker, 2006).

Court- mandated treatment reflects the theory that the individual might benefit from external motivation during the early stages of recovery from an SUD (Satel & Farabee, 2005; Satel, 2000; DiClemente, Bellino, & Neavins, 1999). It is hoped that eventually internal motivation might develop and the individuals will apply themselves to the treatment process. There is mixed evidence suggesting that court-mandated clients work harder on treatment goals than voluntary patients and are also less likely to prematurely leave treatment if they are there because of an agreement with the court. This process offers the additional advantage that the very nature of the circumstances surrounding admission makes it quite difficult for the clients to deny that they have a problem with chemicals!

Court-mandated clients have been found to have experienced fewer negative consequences to their substance use than clients without legal pressure (Kelly, Finney, & Moos, 2006). At first this would seem counterintuitive until one considers that the voluntary client is more likely to be older and to have experienced some of the adverse physical or social consequences of his or her SUD. The court-mandated client has also been found to be as likely to benefit from treatment as traditional patients (Kelly et al., 2005; Satel & Farabee, 2005). Further, there is evidence that those persons who seek treatment at the invitation of the court system may remain in treatment for a longer period of time than traditional clients, and are less likely to reoffend following discharge from treatment (Satel & Farabee, 2005).

In spite of the obvious benefits of court-mandated treatment, there are also some problems with this form of treatment. First, many insurance companies are, by law, able to refuse payment for court-mandated treatment (Dill & Wells-Parker, 2006). Court-mandated treatment is not a guarantee of long-term abstinence because long-term abstinence rates for those who complete treatment at the invitation of the courts appear at best to be the same as for voluntary patients (Leamon et al., 2008). Further, some clinicians view court-mandated treatment as being coercive and that the outcome of this process is coerced abstinence

(Jaffe & Anthony, 2005; Szasz, 2009). Treatment by court order places special requirements on the treatment center.[8] Such treatment also raises interesting questions about the relationship between the law and the rehabilitation industry: If, as the medical model asserts, alcoholism is a disease then how can the courts order it cured? Thus, there is some disagreement among treatment professionals as to the value of court-mandated treatment.

Drug Court

The Drug Court concept was first tried by the Miami, Dade County Florida, in 1989 (Speck, Connor, Hartig, Cunningham, & Fleming, 2008), and since then over 2,000 similar programs have been instituted in 1,100 counties across the United States (Speck et al., 2008). The "Drug Court" goal is to:

> *quickly identify substance abusing offenders and place them under strict court monitoring and community supervision, coupled with effective, long-term treatment services [during which] the drug court participant undergoes an intense regimen of substance abuse and mental health treatment, case management, drug testing, and probation supervision while reporting to regularly scheduled status hearings before a judge with specialized expertise in the drug court model.* (Huddleston, Freeman-Wilson, & Boone, 2004, p. 1)

Accountability is the core concept of the Drug Court (Speck et al., 2008). Such programs are most effective for first-time, non-violent offenders with the goal of avoiding the "revolving door" cycle of repeat offenses (Goldkamp, White, & Robinson, 2002). Drug Court programs should (Work Group on Substance Use Disorders, 2007):

1. assess the individual's need for treatment.
2. identify the proper level of treatment for the client,
3. identify the treatment facility best suited to the client,
4. monitor client adherence to treatment through therapist reports,
5. administer periodic urine toxicology tests,
6. provide for a reduction in legal charges if the client completes the program,
7. provide for "aftercare" groups, and so on.

---

[8]For example, the treatment center might be expected to *immediately* notify the authorities should a client leave treatment against staff advice.

The Drug Court program is composed of three stages (Speck et al., 2008): Stage I: Detoxification, which is usually completed within 14 days unless the individual was abusing drugs with longer half-life, or has relapsed during the detoxification period. During this phase there is an intensive schedule of individual and group therapy sessions, as well as regular court sessions, that the client must follow. Readiness to move on to stage II is dependent on staff assessment of the individual's progress and a history of seven consecutive "clean" urine toxicology tests (Speck et al., 2008). Once this transition is achieved, the client moves into Stage II: Stabilization. This stage can last 16–52 weeks, depending on the needs of the individual. The individual is expected to follow a very intense schedule of individual and group therapy sessions, community support group meetings, and maintain frequent contact with the court. Urine toxicology testing during this stage is expected to show no evidence of alcohol or drug use. If the individual should relapse, staff has the option of referring the client back to State I, or simply starting the client over at the start of Stage II.

When deemed ready, the client moves on to Stage III, Aftercare, which lasts 8–9 months. Clients continue the regimen of individual and group therapy appointments, but also start to prepare for self-directed recovery and living (Speck et al., 2008). This might require that the client participate in literacy training, earn long-neglected high school equivalency or GED diplomas, and start to train for employment in the client's chosen field. The client is still expected to abstain from alcohol or illicit drug use, and if they should relapse, the staff has the option of placing him or her in an earlier stage to relearn necessary skills from that stage.

There has been some dispute concerning the effectiveness of the Drug Court programs, which are both labor- and time-intensive. Reuter and Pollack (2006) suggested that these programs are cost-effective and lower recidivism. For example, it was estimated that New York State saved $250 million in one year through its Drug Court programs, whereas in St. Louis, Missouri, it was found that for every $1 invested in Drug Court, there was a savings of $6.32 in reduced welfare, medical, and law-enforcement expenses (Taylor, 2004). In contrast to these claims, Eckholm (2008) suggested that Drug Courts only reduce recidivism 8–10%, a figure that is only slightly higher than the figure of 13% offered by Rempel (2005).

Although such data is very promising, there have been few well-designed research studies into the effectiveness of Drug Court programs as the very nature of the population served would make such research difficult, if not impossible (Rempel, 2005). Those research studies that have been carried out have been classified as unreliable at best, because (a) the very people who design a local Drug Court program are the ones who also design and carry out tests of its effectiveness, (b) the Drug Courts "cherry-pick" (Drug Policy Alliance, 2011, p. 2; Justice Policy Institute, 2011) the clients admitted to the program, typically those convicted of petty crimes or low-level drug use law violations, (3) short-term periods of incarceration used for rules infractions often collectively add up to more time than if the individuals had served their original sentence, and (4) the financial costs of these programs are often underestimated (Drug Policy Alliance, 2011).

Nationally, various Drug Court programs report successful graduation rates of 30–70%, and in many programs there is a tendency for increased recidivism following discharge from the program for any reason (Drug Policy Alliance, 2011). Further, the core concept of the Drug Court program forces the judicial system to adopt a punitive stance toward addiction, which is the antithesis of the disease model. Although many participants are referred to either outpatient or inpatient rehabilitation programs, access to such programs is often limited, and their effectiveness must be questioned. Although there are many success stories, antidotal evidence does not equate to effectiveness. Those who have failed to successfully complete the program are not trotted out in front of the media by program staff as a testament to the program's effectiveness.

One problem with the Drug Court concept is that it is based on the theory that the substance abuse treatment programs that the clients are referred to are very effective. This is at best an unproven assumption at best because it has proven virtually impossible to measure the effectiveness of individual rehabilitation programs. Further, the Drug Courts will place an additional demand on the already limited number of treatment beds through mandated treatment requirements. Participation in a Drug Court program requires an admission of guilt on the part of the client, and whereas the charges are dropped should the individual successfully complete the program many potential participants opt for the possibility of being proven not guilty (McPherson, Yudo, Afsarifard, & Freitas, 2009).

Finally, the issue of the individual's motivation for participation in a Drug Court program must be considered. Some Drug Courts have admitted individuals who are not addicted to drugs but who wish to avoid prison for the sale of such compounds. Because these individuals were never addicted to the compounds that they sold, this would inflate the success rate of that Drug Court program[9] (Eckholm, 2008). Thus, the issue of the Drug Court movement, its effectiveness, and when the individual should not be referred to a Drug Court program is quite complicated.

Court-Mandated Involuntary Treatment

In more than 30 states it is possible for people to be committed to a treatment facility against their will. To do this one must prove to the courts that the individual is in imminent danger of harm to self or others (Gendel, 2006). The provisions under which a person might be remanded to treatment vary from state to state, but in essence this provision of the law provides for people to be sent to treatment against their will if there is reasonable evidence to believe that they are a danger to themselves or others. Although these laws are often utilized to send one person or another to a rehabilitation program, there is little evidence into the effectiveness of court-mandated involuntary treatment. There is a very real chance that the client will simply comply with treatment expectations to escape the court's supervision as rapidly as possible, without making any permanent changes in his or her substance use behaviors.

It is rare for an individual to request treatment, a phenomenon known as autonomous motivation (Wild et al., 1998). It is more common for the individuals to admit that they would continue to abuse chemicals, if they could do so. It is for this reason that external pressure in the form of familial, legal, or professional pressure is utilized to help the addicted person see the need for treatment.

Other Forms of Intervention

Morgan (2003) suggested that contingency management techniques are often very effective when working with individuals with an SUD. In a sense, contingency management situations are "either/or" forms of external pressure similar to sanctions often utilized by the courts to help a certain individual find the motivation to enter treatment. A spouse might confront his or her partner with the warning "If you don't stop abusing alcohol or drugs, I am filing for a divorce!" If the

individual should continue to abuse chemicals, then the partner should follow through with the sanction and file for divorce. A failure to do so means that warnings of further sanctions will be ignored by the addicted person, because his or her partner did not enforce the original sanction.

Thus, a friend who had expressed a desire not to have his or her friend drink before or while they are playing golf might, upon seeing that the friend was drinking a can of beer, could just turn around and leave. The plea from the drinker that it was "only beer" should be met with the comment, "I said that if you were drinking, or appeared to have been drinking, that I would not play golf with you!" The previously stated sanction is then enforced and should remain in place until the drinker does indeed enter treatment.

Employer-Mandated Treatment

With the advent of workplace urine toxicology testing to reduce employee accidental injuries and use of sick leave, it is not uncommon for people to seek admission to a substance abuse rehabilitation program because their employer threatened to fire them if they did not. Employers justify such behavior on the grounds that employee SUDs cost them money. A company with just 500 employees will typically spend $133,000 in health care costs for alcohol-related problems among employees each year (Brink, 2004). Further, individuals with an alcohol use disorder use more "sick" days, and are five times as likely to file a "workman's compensation" claim as nondrinkers (Brink, 2004). Thus, employers feel justified in guiding employees into treatment, or out the front door. Surprisingly, there is little research into whether such employer-mandated treatment is effective, or the conditions under which it is most useful. As discussed in Chapter 18, many women (or other workers in low-level jobs) often find it more convenient to just quit and look for alternative employment rather than to enter treatment as the original employer suggested.

Reactions to the Concept of Intervention

A common misperception of the intervention-treatment recommendation process is that the individual is sent away to get "fixed." In reality intervention is part of the assessment/intervention/treatment continuum and it involves both the individuals with the

---

[9]In the sense that this person was not abusing drugs and thus could not be counted as a "drug abuser" in that community.

SUD and their families. It is part of a growth process for all concerned.

Although the intervention process might obtain a commitment to enter rehabilitation from the substance abuser, it is also not uncommon for individuals who are referred to a rehabilitation program to object that "treatment does not work." This is a myth, although a popular one among those who seek to avoid admission to a substance abuse rehabilitation program. Research has demonstrated that rehabilitation programs are cost effective.[10] However, when does coercion for a person to enter treatment, even if that treatment is cost-effective? In his discussion of this topic, Bentall (2009) argued that paternalism and coercion could be justified only if doctors and other mental health professionals reliably knew what was in their patient's best interests. However, their track record is appalling (p. 273, italics added for emphasis).

This is supported by Marano (2012) who observed that confrontational methods such as the intervention process as practiced in the United States are unique to this country. Such intervention programs imply that those who confront the person with the addiction are somehow morally and psychologically superior to the subject of the intervention, an often dubious assumption. Further, although rehabilitation professionals are governed by the principle of first do no harm, coercion has become such an accepted tool used by mental health or medical professionals that it now does not raise ethical questions for those who wield these weapons against an individual who by social standards might have a "problem" (Bentall, 2009).

Chapter Summary

In rare cases, clients will demonstrate autonomous motivation for treatment. However, because of the pharmacological reward potential of the drugs of abuse, most drug abusers are not interested in abstinence or recovery. Thus contingency motivation has been viewed as an appropriate manner to guide the addicted person to rehabilitation. It is hoped that while in treatment, the individual will come to see how her or his life was out of control, and centered around continued chemical abuse, in spite of the damage being wrought to both themselves and significant others.

Intervention projects may be informal, as when a physician confronts a patient with the reality that continued substance use will result in a deterioration of health, and ultimately death. Another informal intervention might be seen when a friend sets a limit as to what he or she will tolerate in the relationship, and then when the individual with the SUD continues to engage in substance-related behaviors, enforce sanctions such as ending their friendship. An employer or supervisor might confront the employees with evidence that their continued substance use is harming productivity, and that if they do not enter treatment and maintain continued abstinence following the completion of rehabilitation, they will be fired. Formal intervention projects involve family members and friends meeting with the identified individuals, confronting them with evidence of how their SUD is hurting both themselves and others, and attempting to obtain a commitment from the identified individuals to immediately enter treatment. If the client agrees, then appointed family members will escort the individual to an identified treatment center, and participate in the admissions interview. If the client should refuse, then previously identified sanctions should be employed to help family members and friends detach from the person with the SUD and his or her behavior.

The rights of the individual who is the focus of the intervention process are discussed, as is the fact that the identified patient has the right to leave the intervention project should he or she wish to do so. Employer- and court-mandated interventions are discussed, as is the fact that the effectiveness of such incentives for treatment remains unproven.

---

[10]As discussed in Chapters 30 and 31.

CHAPTER 29

Treatment Settings

Introduction

In Chapter 27, we reviewed some of the many issues associated with the screening and assessment process. One question that is rarely asked: Is treatment necessary? After all, Willenbring (2010) suggested that three-fourths of the people with an alcohol use disorder reduce or stop drinking entirely without professional treatment or involvement in a 12-step support group. However, if the individual has failed in an attempt to "quit" the abuse of chemicals, or if his or her disorder is causing severe interpersonal or medical problems, a referral to a rehabilitation program is strongly indicated. Depending on the client's assessed need for a specific level of care, the treatment process might take place on either an outpatient or an inpatient basis. There is a great deal of debate within the professional community as to the relative merits of each treatment setting, but the emerging consensus is that each offers advantages and disadvantages for both the rehabilitation center staff and the client. The advantages of rehabilitation are clear: Individuals who were involved in a treatment program or 12-step program were more likely to be abstinent 16 years after they entered rehabilitation (Moos & Moos, 2006). In this chapter, we will briefly review the different settings where the client's substance abuse disorder might be addressed.

Detox Programs

A popular misconception is that "detoxification" ("detox") programs are a form of treatment. Detox programs are designed to help the individual safely withdraw from the drugs of abuse while keeping withdrawal-related distress at a minimum. At the completion of the detox cycle, the individual should be ready to move on to the rehabilitation program that best meets their needs. The first question that must be addressed by a medical professional is whether medically supervised detoxification is necessary. If detoxification is deemed necessary by a physician, the decision must be made whether this can be safely carried out on an outpatient basis or if it should be carried out within a medical facility. Withdrawal from some drugs of abuse, such as the barbiturates and benzodiazepines, can be life-threatening and probably should be carried out in a controlled medical setting, although with the proper social and outpatient medical support it is possible for detoxification to be carried out at home. One requirement for outpatient detoxification is that the substance abusing person have a strong-willed family member who will administer prescribed medications as per instructions and to contact the authorities if the person should demonstrate signs of medical distress.

An Introduction to Outpatient Treatment

Outpatient Treatment: A Working Definition

The outpatient substance abuse rehabilitation program might best be defined as (a) a formal treatment program involving one or more substance abuse rehabilitation professionals, (b) designed to help the person with an substance use disorder (SUD) develop and maintain a recovery program, (c) which will utilize a variety of treatment approaches (psycho-educational, family and marital therapies, individual and group therapy formats), which is (d) designed to do so on an outpatient basis. Such programs are quite popular: It has been estimated that 85% of all patients who participate in a substance abuse rehabilitation program will initially be treated on an outpatient basis (Tinsley, Finlayson, & Morse, 1998). Many individuals might come to terms with their SUD through outpatient treatment. However, such programs might also serve as a transitional, or step-down, stage for persons who originally were in an inpatient program and for whom a less intensive form of support is thought appropriate before they attempt self-directed recovery (Work Group on Substance Use Disorders, 2007).

Components of Outpatient Treatment

Outpatient treatment programs will often utilize both individual and group therapy formats to help the clients address their SUD, with ancillary treatment services such as assertiveness training, social skills training, marital and family therapy, vocational counseling, and so on. Most outpatient treatment programs follow a 12-step format. Program participants are expected to attend regular self-help group meetings on their own as part of their rehabilitation plan. The person who coordinates this program is a certified chemical dependency counselor or mental health professional who specializes in the treatment of the addictive disorders.

A formal treatment plan is established at the beginning of treatment, with review sessions being scheduled on a regular basis to monitor the client's progress toward mutually agreed-upon goals. Psycho-educational lectures and bibliotherapy[1] are also often utilized in outpatient rehabilitation programs to help the clients recognize the consequences of their SUD if it is not arrested. Many outpatient rehabilitation programs include a "family night" component held either once a week or once a month, where family members might ask questions or express concern about the client's progress, the nature of the addictions, and so on. Such "family nights" should not be interpreted as

"family therapy," which is a more intensive process (Fletcher, 2013).

There is some debate within the treatment community whether abstinence from alcohol and illicit drugs should not only expected, but be a prerequisite for participation in outpatient treatment. The analogy of requiring that the applicant to a weight loss program to lose the weight before applying to a weight loss program might not be out of place, here. Although total abstinence from alcohol and the drugs of abuse is the ultimate goal, many programs accept a reduction in the level and frequency of substance use as an intermediate step.

Appropriate pharmaceutical supports[2] prescribed by a physician are often called upon, and progress is confirmed through the client's self-report, collateral information, alcohol breath testing, and urine toxicology testing. If the client should relapse, this is also addressed on an outpatient basis unless it comes apparent that the client is unable or unwilling to abstain from chemicals while in an outpatient treatment program. In this case, a referral to a more intensive level of treatment would be indicated.

Although intuitively one would expect that individuals referred to outpatient rehabilitation programs would be unlikely to discontinue treatment because such programs are inherently less intrusive than residential programs, research has found just the opposite: Outpatient rehabilitation programs experience high dropout rates, and many of those who do enter outpatient rehabilitation programs eventually are referred to a residential treatment center.

Varieties of Outpatient Rehabilitation Programs

There are a number of different outpatient treatment formats, and client referral to one form of treatment or another is dependent on the available resources and the client's assessed needs for a specific level of care. Perhaps the least restrictive form of treatment is the DWI school.

DWI School[3]

These programs utilize a psycho-educational approach and are usually limited to the first-time offender who is

---

[1]Assigned readings of specified material to assist in the rehabilitation process.

[2]Discussed in Chapter 32.

[3]Which is short for "Driving While under the Influence of Mood Altering Chemicals." In some states, this is called an "OWI," or Operating a Motor Vehicle While under the Influence of Intoxicants.

assumed to have made a mistake by unintentionally driving a motor vehicle under the influence of alcohol or other mood-altering chemicals.[4] Individuals referred to a DWI school are not, in the opinion of the assessor, addicted to alcohol or drugs. The DWI school format involves 8–12 hours of psychoeducational lectures, individual and group therapy sessions to help the individual better understand the dangers associated with operating a motor vehicle while under the influence of chemicals.

Individual Rehabilitation Counseling

Depending on the individuals' needs and the severity of their SUD, they might be seen by an addictions counselor or mental health therapist[5] on a 1:1 basis. Such treatment approaches are usually restricted to motivated clients who are willing to engage in inter-session therapy-related projects (assigned reading, for example) and utilize existing support services (12-step groups, and so on). The treatment orientation of the addictions counselor will depend on her or his training and experience, but might include motivational interviewing, cognitive behavioral therapies, or 12-step oriented techniques.

Short-Term Outpatient Programs

These programs are usually time-limited, and are aimed at helping those persons with a mild to moderate SUD achieve abstinence. Short-term outpatient programs utilize a blend of individual and group therapy formats, with the client being seen one or two times a week. In addition, participants might be expected to attend at least one self-help group meeting a week, are assigned material to read before the next individual or group session, and are expected to meet with their case manager at least once a week for between 1 and 2 months. Surprisingly, such programs have not been found to be effective for clients who lack an extensive substance abuse problem, although the reason for this is not clear. One possibility is that the clients are unwilling to

accept the severity of their SUD, and thus dismissive of treatment efforts.

Intensive Short-Term Outpatient Programs

These programs are called by a variety of names, including "partial hospitalization," "evening," or "day treatment" programs (Work Group on Substance Use Disorders, 2007). These programs might serve either as a primary treatment intervention for the client, or as a step-down level of treatment for patients who have completed a more intensive treatment program (Weiss, Potter, & Iannucci, 2008; Work Group on Substance Use Disorders, 2007). Clients are usually seen four to five times a week. Treatment is carried out through a blend of individual and group therapy formats and such programs last for up to 6 months. Ancillary services such as family or marital counseling are utilized as necessary, and clients are expected to participate in a community support group[6] meeting at least once a week.

Intensive Long-Term Outpatient Treatment

These programs are usually open-ended, and are designed for individuals whose SUD has been assessed to be moderate to severe in intensity. Individuals referred to these programs have usually been unable to achieve lasting abstinence either on their own, or after completion of less intensive treatment programs. Clients are seen for a blend of individual and group therapy sessions, and are seen for 3–5 days or nights a week for between 12–18 months. Ancillary services such as vocational counseling, individual psychotherapy and marriage, and family therapy and are offered as needed. The participant is expected to attend at least one community support group meeting a week. Surprisingly, such programs have been found to be less effective than short-term rehabilitation programs (Shepard, Larson, & Hoffmann, 1999).

Advantages of Outpatient Rehabilitation

Outpatient treatment programs are quite popular. There are a number of reasons for such popularity, not the least of which is that they are far less expensive

---

[4]One fact that many people do not understand is that it is possible to be charged with Driving While under the Influence (DWI) while taking prescribed medications if those chemicals are mood-altering compounds.

[5]Depending on state regulations this might be a Master's degree level therapist or an earned doctorate in an approved field might be required to meet State licensure requirements. The reader is advised to check the local licensure requirements to determine what qualifications are necessary for substance abuse rehabilitation work in their geographic area.

[6]There was a time when Alcoholics Anonymous (AA) or Narcotics Anonymous (NA) was the only community support group available to the recovering person. In the past decade, there have been founded a number of faith-based and nontraditional community support groups have been founded, providing some alternatives to either AA or NA. These groups will be discussed in Chapter 34.

than residential treatment programs. It has been estimated that outpatient treatment programs cost $77 to $93 per week (Belenko, Patapis, & French, 2005) as opposed to $45,000 to $60,000 for a 30-day residential treatment program at a "high end" (Fletcher, 2013, p. 104) rehabilitation program. Outpatient treatment programs also minimize the need to remove the individual from his or her daily environment, allowing him or her full participation in normal family life, continued employment, and so on. Outpatient treatment programs are more flexible than residential programs, allowing individual and group therapy sessions to be scheduled in the daytime or evening hours depending on the individual's schedule. Such programs also avoid the need for a reorientation period after the individual graduates from the treatment program. Further, such programs offer some degree of flexibility: allowing alterations to accommodate the client's work schedule or family emergencies, as needed. A mixed blessing is that outpatient rehabilitation programs do not remove the individuals from their environment, forcing them to confront drug-use "cues" within the context where they are engaged in alcohol or drug abuse. This might allow the individual to practice recovery skills learned while in treatment using the outpatient program for support and help should they relapse while in treatment. If the individual is able to achieve abstinence while still living in their home, he or she might experience a sense of mystery over their environment. Outpatient treatment programs also allow the individual to establish a support system in their home environment where they have friends, family, and others.

Disadvantages of Outpatient Treatment Programs

The review of outpatient treatment programs is not to suggest that such programs are a panacea, nor are they the ultimate solution to the problem of substance abuse or addiction. "Graduates" of outpatient treatment programs are as likely to relapse as are those who successfully complete a residential treatment program. This is not to imply that these programs are equally effective (or ineffective) as residential treatment. Outpatient programs tend to work with a different client than do residential facilities. This fact makes comparison between the two types of programs difficult.

Although residential treatment programs are far more expensive than outpatient treatment, because of insurance company co-pay requirements it is possible

that residential treatment will actually cost the individuals less out of their own pocket for a residential rehabilitation program as opposed to an outpatient treatment facility (Fletcher, 2013). Indeed, depending on the provisions in the individual's health insurance policy, it is possible that the insurance company will not pay anything toward the individual's participation in outpatient treatment.[7]

Another disadvantage of outpatient treatment is that such programs do not offer the same degree of structure and support inherent in a residential treatment setting. Family members might be reluctant to report substance use relapses or inappropriate behaviors on the part of the client, and the individual might have a limited abstinence-based support system during the earlier stages of the rehabilitation program. Such problems indicate that outpatient treatment programs are of limited applicability for clients who require a great degree of support during the earliest stages of recovery. Clients are often left in the position of having to endure strong "craving" for chemicals in the very environment in which they were abusing them. Exposure to drug-use "cues" can contribute to the high relapse rate seen in graduates of such programs. If the client does relapse, she or he will need to be reassessed to determine the proper level of treatment. These problem areas are sufficient to suggest that outpatient is not the ultimate answer to SUDs and that residential treatment might be necessary.

Introduction to Residential Treatment Programs

Definition of Inpatient Treatment

Surprisingly, there is no standard definition of inpatient (or, as it is often called, "residential") treatment (Weiss et al., 2008). Residential treatment programs provide a 24-hour treatment milieu with staff members on duty 24 hours a day. However, staffing levels vary from one program to the next. Some residential treatment programs are poorly equipped to meet the needs of patients who require acute medical care and refer these individuals to other facilities. Other programs,

---

[7]The passage of insurance "parity" for mental health services, passed in 2005, may require that insurance companies reimburse the client for treatment expenses for outpatient treatment. The issue is not clear at this time.

usually based in a hospital setting, treat the person's medical problems in-house (Weiss et al., 2008). However, residential treatment programs all share the characteristic of offering a more intensive focus on the individual's recovery from the SUDs than outpatient treatment programs (Work Group on Substance Use Disorders, 2007). These programs are especially effective in working with the resistant, suicidal, or homicidal clients,[8] or clients who are unable to abstain in the less restrictive outpatient treatment programs (Work Group on Substance Use Disorders, 2007).

Most residential treatment programs have a strong 12-step group orientation, with clients being expected to attend multiple 12-step meetings during the week. Some programs utilize in-house 12-step programs while other programs utilize the resources of community based 12-step groups. Some residential programs carry out all treatment activities in a group setting, whereas other programs allow for ancillary appointments with psychologists, social workers, dietary therapists, and others as indicated (Fletcher, 2013). The client should meet with the case manager at least once a week. Barriers to recovery are identified, including an assessment of the client's support system, client's level of motivation, and past treatment history, with appropriate interventions being designed to help the individual address problem areas in his or her life.

Clients who are referred to a residential treatment program are those individuals:

> *whose lives and social interactions have come to focus exclusively on substance use and who ... lack sufficient motivation and/or substance free social supports to remain abstinent in an ambulatory setting (Work Group on Substance Use Disorders, 2007).*

The decision to utilize inpatient treatment as opposed to an outpatient treatment program is based on the assessed need for a specific level of care.[9] Such programs might be offered by a general hospital, a freestanding facility, or in a therapeutic community setting. We will look at many of the residential treatment formats in the sections that follow.

Hospital-Based Residential Treatment

Hospital based rehabilitation programs offer a range of services, including (but not limited to) medical stabilization for ongoing (often untreated) medical problems, group, individual, marital, and family therapy programs, as well as psycho-educational programs, and social service support as needed (Work Group on Substance Use Disorders, 2007). Clients will also have assigned "homework" projects, and bibliotherapy[10] while in treatment. Although many of these programs utilized the "Minnesota Model," and managed care initiatives have made extended stays for residential treatment this less common as insurance companies have demanded shorter stays for clients. There is usually a strong emphasis on 12-step group participation, and clients are expected to participate in 12-step group meetings held within the hospital, or, are escorted to community-based 12-step group meetings at least once a week (Fletcher, 2013).

There is no set duration for residential community treatment, although the goal is to help the client reach a point where she or he can abstain from alcohol or drugs with the support of less restrictive outpatient treatment programs. Funding is always a major consideration, and treatment center staff needs to balance the client's needs against available funding from the client's health care provider and the client. These topics will be discussed elsewhere in this text.

Therapeutic Communities

The Therapeutic Community (TC) concept originated in the 1960s as a self-help alternative to traditional treatment programs for drug addiction. The original TCs were marked by harsh ego-stripping confrontation techniques that included 24-hour "marathon" group sessions as well as a "hot seat" in the center of a group circle where a person was expected to sit while group members confronted him or her with perceived personality flaws. All staff positions were held by former residents, with minimal input from health or mental health professionals. Some TCs expected a lifetime commitment from the client, who was viewed as unable to live independently without substances and therefore the individual must remain within the therapeutic community.

The TC movement has moved away from these early techniques to become a more generic term for a

---

[8]This is not always true. Some residential treatment programs lack the resources to help suicidal or homicidal residents, and will refer the individual to a psychiatric treatment facility.

[9]Discussed in Chapter 27.

[10]See Glossary.

range of programs that include short-term residential, long-term residential, and day treatment forms of treatment. Some TCs also have made provisions to work with women who have children, or patients with HIV/AIDS[11] (DeLeon, 2008). However, all of these modifications of the original TC program concept retain the core belief that the SUDs reflect deviant behaviors that reflect an immature personality (DeLeon, 2008; Satel & Farabee, 2005). According to this theory, reflections of this immature personality might be seen in the mood disturbances, unrealistic thinking and educational, social, and moral deficits often seen in people addicted to drugs. In response to the arrested development of the addicted person, the TC attempts to assist the individual in making a global lifestyle change allowing life without the drugs of abuse (DeLeon, 2008). Unlike the original therapeutic communities, current TCs now prescreen applicants excluding those people from admission who have a history of attempted suicide or homicide, attempted arson, or severe uncontrolled psychiatric disorders (DeLeon, 2008). Another reason that a given applicant might be excluded from admission is the belief that she or he can "do it on my own," as this attitude reflects an unwillingness to accept the need for treatment (DeLeon, 2008). A final exclusionary criterion is the clients' unwillingness to make the commitment to remain in the entire program (DeLeon, 2008).

Therapeutic communities are usually free-standing[12] programs that, although initially quite resistant to the use of 12-step community support groups, have started to integrate these self-help groups into the program (Ringwald, 2002). TCs utilize a highly structured daily program that usually starts at 7 a.m. and continues until 11 p.m. This structure, plus the belief that it is the community that is the agent of change or healing, is thought to assist in the desired personality change. In a sense, the TC might be viewed as providing an extended family for the program participant. The TC program format has evolved to the point where it has been integrated into some penal institutions to work with convicted felons who have an SUD, and with persons who have addictions to multiple compounds (DeLeon, 2008).

Clients are viewed as passing through three different stages during treatment: (a) compliance, (b) conformity, and (c) making a personal commitment for change (Satel & Farabee, 2005). To assist the individual in moving through these stages, the TC retains a strong emphasis on self-examination as well as public confession of past misbehavior both in group and during individual counseling sessions. More advanced clients are presented as role models for initiates, and although there are a small number of professional staff in most modern TCs, it is the process of "supportive confrontation" (DeLeon, 2008, p. 465) from other residents that is viewed as the main vehicle of personality change. Participants are expected to carry out assigned work projects, first within the TC itself, and later in the outside community, which are considered a privilege that the program participants earn through their progress in the TC program.

DeLeon (2008) also suggested a three-stage model for long-term TC programs: (1) orientation/introduction, (b) primary treatment, and (c) reentry. During the first phase, orientation/introduction, which lasts for approximately the first 60 days, the person is confronted with the tasks of being oriented and assimilated into the program, while staff members continue to assess the individual to determine whether participation in the TC is appropriate. The second stage, primary treatment, lasts from the 2nd until the 12th month, during which time the individual learns to become more autonomous, accepts more desirable job assignments within the TC, and begins to teach others. The final stage, reentry, lasts from the 13th until the 24th month and focuses on helping the individual strengthen skills for maintaining abstinence, autonomous decision making, and vocational skills. During this phase, the individual might find a job outside of the TC to both earn a salary and begin the transition to independent living.

Some components of the TC program include encounter groups, which are peer-led, meet three times weekly, and which last approximately 2 hours each. Tutorial sessions include training and educational experiences for the clients. Individual therapy sessions are also held, and a small minority of TC's still hold encounter groups that are extended groups aimed at helping individuals resolve life experiences (a history of sexual or physical abuse, for example) that are thought to have contributed to the individual's substance abuse (DeLeon, 2008). Unannounced urine toxicology testing is also carried out on a random basis,

---

[11]Discussed in Chapter 34.

[12]Is not associated with a hospital program and is funded either through donations or monies earned by participants who work in various capacities in the community.

with decisions concerning the retention of the client, in-house job assignments, or whether to allow the client to progress from one level to the next being made in part on the basis of the results of these tests (DeLeon, 2008).

Whereas the original TCs would accept only self-referrals to the program, at this time approximately two-thirds of program participants are under the supervision of probation or parole agents (Hiller, Knight, Rao, & Simpson, 2002). This element of legal coercion is viewed as providing an additional incentive for the individual to remain in the TC until she or he has started to internalize the recovery philosophy and lifestyle (Satel & Farabee, 2005). Unfortunately, both self-referred and legally mandated clients often fail to successfully complete the treatment program, and such programs suffer from significant drop out rates (Satel & Farabee, 2005; Work Group on Substance Use Disorders, 2007). DeLeon (2008) suggested that 30–40% of those admitted to a TC will drop out of treatment in the first 30 days, and that only 10–15% will complete the typical two-year program. Many clients are asked to leave the TC because of accumulated rules infractions.

Therapeutic communities are not without their detractors. Over the years, lawsuits have been brought against various TCs alleging physical or emotional harm to the residents. Therapeutic communities are also viewed with suspicion by many who were trained in the more traditional substance abuse rehabilitation model. In spite of these facts, proponents of TCs point to studies that suggest that more than 90% of those who complete the program remain drug-free in the first year after discharge, and that five years after completion of the TC program 70% will still be abstinent.

However, this is an excellent example of how statistics can often mislead a person. Retention is a problem for therapeutic communities, just as it is for every other form of substance abuse rehabilitation. Between 30–40% of new residents drop out of the program in the first 30 days and are thus lost to follow-up (DeLeon, 2008). Such premature termination carries with it a risk of a relapse back to active substance use. Just 25% of those who drop out of the program in less than a year were found to be drug-free at the end of a two-year follow-up period, and 50% of those who drop out of treatment after remaining in the TC for a year were found to have relapsed in the first two years after they left the program (DeLeon, 2004). Although proponents of the TC concept point

out that 90% of program graduates might remain substance-free for the first year following graduation, only 10–15% of those who begin the program actually graduate (DeLeon, 2004). Only 10 of every 100 patients originally admitted are substance-free at the end of the first five years following graduation. These figures suggest that even TC graduates do relapse on occasion. The picture for those who drop out of the TC is even more bleak, with a significant percentage of those who drop out of a therapeutic community maintaining abstinence from alcohol and the drugs of abuse.

One follow-up study suggested that 3 years following successful completion from a TC half of those graduates who were still alive were either working full time, or in a training program to prepare them to begin full-time work (Berg, 2003). This would suggest that the TC concept is exceptionally useful in treating the substance abuser. However, detractors of the TC program movement point out that as these figures suggest, the TC movement is not a panacea for the treatment of SUDs.

Is There a Legitimate Need for Inpatient Treatment?

Unfortunately, the debate over whether inpatient or outpatient rehabilitation programs are most effective is often fueled by financial or political considerations, not by scientific research (Weiss et al., 2008). Some critics of residential treatment point to the Project MATCH Research Group findings in the mid-1990s, which concluded that inpatient treatment is not automatically superior to less intensive treatment methods. The purpose of Project MATCH was to isolate patient characteristics that might predict a better outcome in an outpatient or an inpatient treatment setting, but failed to accomplish this goal (Rychtarik et al., 2000). Indeed, research has failed to demonstrate a clear advantage of inpatient treatment over outpatient treatment, or the reverse (Mee-Lee & Gastfriend, 2008).

Although clear advantages over outpatient treatment have not been demonstrated by research studies, it has not been recommended that inpatient treatment programs be abolished. For example, although most patients start out with outpatient treatment, three quarters of patients with an AUD eventually require a residential treatment program. Clients with other forms of

SUDs might benefit more from residential treatment because of the intensity of their addiction. In both cases, one factor that appears to predict whether a given inpatient rehabilitation program will be effective is the client's willingness to participate in "follow-up" or "aftercare" programs. There is strong evidence suggesting that over time the benefits of residential treatment accrue for not only alcohol-dependent persons, but also for persons with other SUDs. Further, there is evidence of a "threshold effect," with those people who remain in residential treatment for longer than 14 days being more likely to benefit from residential treatment than those who remain in residential treatment for a period shorter than 14 days.

The Advantages of Inpatient Treatment

It is a mistake to compare those who enter an outpatient substance abuse rehabilitation program with those who are referred to a residential treatment program. These are two distinct subgroups of substance abusers. People referred to a residential program are assessed as needing a more comprehensive level of care than those who might be referred to an outpatient treatment. Weiss et al., (2008) observed that the combination of detoxification and residential treatment programs offers the additional advantage of taking people who support their addiction through violent crime off the streets. Hopefully, once their addiction has been addressed, the motivation to engage in violent behavior will also be minimized, if not eliminated.

Residential treatment programs also offer the advantage of allowing intensive focus on environmental issues that contributed to the maintenance of the SUD. The client might be taught "refusal skills," or learn alternative behaviors that will help them abstain from further substance abuse while building a substance-free support system. For example, research has shown that persons with an SUD tend to live alone or lack close interpersonal supports. The inpatient treatment "community" can function as a pseudo-family, guiding the person in acquiring those skills necessary to establish close, non-substance-centered, interpersonal supports.

Further, people referred to residential treatment programs tend to have more medical problems than those referred to outpatient treatment. Inpatient programs allow for proper treatment of these medical problems (untreated hypertension, or diabetes, for example). Malnutrition is a common problem among substance abusers, and inpatient residential treatment programs allow medical professionals to address the long-term effects of malnutrition. Further, the level of staff control over the client's environment helps to discourage continued substance use. A visitor who is a known drug dealer, for example, might not only be refused admission to the treatment facility, but might be informed that the police will be called should he or she attempt to "visit" former customers again.

If a client should attempt to utilize alcohol or drugs while in treatment, staff members in a residential facility are more likely to detect this than are those persons who work in an outpatient treatment program. Staff members are able to establish a routine of individual and group therapy sessions, combined with spiritual counseling, vocational counseling, and ancillary services, to counteract the chaotic lifestyle often seen in substance abusers. This external structure may be internalized by the recovering substance abuser, providing some degree of structure once she or he leaves treatment and begins to live on his or her own. Programs that require participation in community support groups might expose a client to these external support groups for the first time in the person's life, and serve as a bridge between the residential treatment program and the client's use of such community supports after discharge.

Disadvantages of Residential Treatment

First, there is mixed evidence about the effectiveness of residential treatment (Weiss et al., 2008). Some residential treatment programs become a "revolving door," admitting and discharging the same client(s) time after time. Also, residential treatment is quite expensive, with estimated average costs of $525–792 per week not being uncommon (Belenko et al., 2005). It is disruptive to the individual's established life routine to have to enter residential treatment, and this will interfere with the individual's ability to go to work and earn a living while the individual is in treatment (Polydorou & Kleber, 2008). Another disadvantage of residential treatment is that patients are usually not stratified as to intensity of need, with the result being that more severely disturbed individuals are often housed with those persons whose requirements are less intense (Larimer & Kilmer, 2000). Residential treatment has often been compared to a concentration camp, but given the client's level of dysfunction and substance-induced harm, this comparison is hardly fair. Finally, residential rehabilitation programs may be geographically isolated, preventing appropriate contact between the client and his or her family.

Aftercare Programs

Health care professionals view the SUDs as chronic, relapsing disorders, and the continuing care or aftercare program was introduced as an aid to abstinence. Such programs have been found to significantly reduce client relapses, and increase total days of abstinence (Ritsher, Moos, & Finney, 2000; Smith et al., 2006). The focus of such groups should be on such issues as (a) maintenance of gains made in treatment and (b) helping to prevent a relapse back to active substance abuse. Such groups provide the client with a safe environment in which to discuss "urges" to use chemicals again, thoughts triggered by environmental stimuli, and "using" dreams, all of which appear to contribute to relapse, and receive encouragement from other group members in their efforts to abstain.

As part of the last goal, irrational client beliefs (for example, "I can't cope without a drink!") should be identified and addressed, thus reducing the possibility of a relapse. Clients receiving pharmacological support for their efforts to abstain (discussed in Chapter 32) should be encouraged to take their medications as prescribed as well. Clients who report in group that they have not renewed their prescription for disulfiram[13] might be telegraphing an intention to return to active alcohol use, and group members should discuss this with the wayward individual. Client behaviors that might contribute to relapse, such as maintaining a supply of alcohol in one's home ("but it's just for friends when they come to visit!") or frequently a bar ("but everybody knows that the bars have the best pool tables!"[14]) or the places where one used to go to obtain chemicals, need to be identified and addressed.

Partial Hospitalization Options

The partial hospitalization option offers several advantages over traditional residential treatment programs, while addressing the costs of inpatient treatment. Partial hospitalization is one option. Such programs allow the client to live at home, but to report to the residential treatment center during the day. The advantage of partial hospitalization is that it allows for a greater intensive treatment than is possible through an outpatient treatment, while still avoiding the need for expensive residential treatment programs. It also allows the client to start to rebuild strained familial relationships while still having the benefit of the intensive support of the day hospitalization staff. For partial hospitalization programs to be effective, the client should have a stable, supportive, home environment. If the client's spouse, or other family member, should also have an SUD, or a serious, untreated psychiatric problem, then partial day hospitalization is not an option. If the client's home environment is indeed supportive, then partial day hospitalization may be a viable option to his or her recovery program.

The goal of the "aftercare" program is to provide support during the client's transition from intensive treatment to self-directed recovery. Such programs are usually conducted on an outpatient basis, and include individual and sometimes group therapy sessions as well as specialized adjunctive programs such as a continuation of marital therapy started while the patient was in a more intensive form of treatment for example.

Aftercare programs are part of the continuum treatment services (Work Group on Substance Use Disorders, 2007). These programs are often automatically offered to clients following treatment, but recent research evidence suggests that they should not be mandatory for persons following discharge from treatment. Berg (2003) identified a subgroup of former drug abusers who were (a) stable at the time of follow-up, but who (b) refused to participate in aftercare programs because they did not wish to reawaken memories of their behavior while actively abusing drugs. For this subgroup of patients, participation in an aftercare program, especially if it includes group therapy, might be counterproductive. Thus, careful screening of each client before making a referral to an aftercare program is necessary to determine which individuals would, and would not, benefit from an aftercare program.

Halfway Houses

The halfway house concept emerged in the 1950s, providing an intermediate step between inpatient treatment and independent living. If the client should lack a stable support system, a halfway house might bridge

---

[13]See Chapter 32.

[14]Although nobody has ever explained how having a 350-pound intoxicated person violently regurgitating on a pool table has ever helped the play on that specific table.

the gap between residential and independent living. Halfway houses share several characteristics: (1) small population (less than 25 residents), (2) short patient-stay (less than a few months), (3) emphasis on the use of community support groups, (4) minimal rules, (5) small number of professional staff members, and (6) expectation of total abstinence from alcohol or drugs of abuse. Clients are also expected to work, and are assigned tasks within the halfway (cleaning the dishes, housekeeping activities, and so on).

There is mixed evidence about the effectiveness of halfway houses. This might reflect the different treatment philosophies of different halfway houses. Some facilities place strong emphasis on continued abstinence, whereas others make little or no attempt to continue the treatment process. However, since research has repeatedly demonstrated that the longer that a person remains involved in treatment activities and community-based support groups, this would indirectly support the need for halfway houses (Moos, Moos, & Andrassy, 1999).

Sober Houses

The "sober house" is a variant of the halfway house. This is not a form of treatment (Fletcher, 2013) but a transitional step between more intensive forms of treatment and independent living. The sober house should be self-policing, with residents confronting others suspected of either breaking house rules or of abusing alcohol/drugs. As people demonstrate more responsibility and achieve longer recovery periods, they are granted increased privileges until they are ready to assume the task of living on their own without chemicals.

Chapter Summary

There is significant evidence that inpatient or residential treatment is not always required to help the person learn how to abstain from further substance abuse. A significant percentage of those persons with an SUD come to terms with that disorder without professional intervention or assistance. People who do require assistance often encounter the problem that most therapists or rehabilitation programs offer only one philosophical model to clients, a process that might not meet the client's needs (Mee-Lee & Gastfriend, 2008).

Treatment itself might be carried out either on an inpatient or outpatient basis, with outpatient treatment programs offering an alternative to residential treatment. Outpatient treatment is most effective with individuals who have a strong social support system, and for whom there is no coexisting psychiatric or medical illness that might complicate the individual's treatment. An advantage of outpatient treatment programs is that the individual might remain in his home environment, and possibly even continue to work on a full-time basis depending on when the rehabilitation program activities are carried out. This avoids the need for a reorientation program following residential treatment.

Outpatient treatment programs also offer the advantage of long-term therapeutic support, an option that is not always possible with a short-term residential rehabilitation program. Such therapeutic supports include individual and group therapies, ancillary services such as vocational counseling, spiritual counseling, urine toxicology testing to detect continued substance use, and so on. Outpatient treatment appears to be about as effective as residential treatment programs, but usually works with people who have not abused chemicals for as long those referred to residential facilities. However, outpatient treatment programs do suffer from high dropout rates, and a significant number of those people who are initially treated in an outpatient facility eventually require residential treatment.

Residential treatment facilities, in turn, offer advantages and disadvantages over outpatient treatment programs. It is viewed by many as a drastic step, yet for many people this is necessary if the individual is ever to regain control over his or her life. The inpatient rehabilitation program offers 24-hour support and referrals to ancillary treatment. Although questions have been raised concerning the need for residential treatment, these programs do seem to offer a glimmer of hope for those whose SUD is deeply entrenched. Further, evidence suggests that the length of time that the individual remains involved in treatment or aftercare counseling increases the odds of achieving lasting sobriety, which is the goal of both inpatient and outpatient treatment.

CHAPTER 30

The Treatment of Substance Use Disorders[1]

Introduction

There are many misperceptions about substance abuse treatment and its effectiveness. For example, some people question whether treatment is at all effective for people with a substance use disorder (SUD). When seen in this light, however, arguments that rehabilitation is not effective break down in the face of studies that have found that for every dollar invested in treatment the community saves from $4 to $12 (Breithaupt, 2001; Dobbs, 2007; Mee-Lee, 2002) to possibly as much as $50 (Garrett, 2000).[2] This is clearly illustrated by a study conducted in the 1990s in which the State of California found that an investment of $209 million for substance abuse rehabilitation resulted in a savings of $209 *billion* in reduced criminal activity and health care costs (Craig, 2004). As a group the cost of health care for alcohol-dependent persons are ten times that of non-dependent individuals, and health care costs for their families are five times higher than those for normal families (McLellan, 2001). Thus, while not universally effective, there are obvious benefits from outpatient or residential treatment programs for the SUDs.

A second misperception of substance abuse treatment is that treatment is a single entity such as an inoculation. In reality, substance abuse rehabilitation is a dynamic process that includes a variety of rehabilitation formats and intensities of therapy carried out over time (Mee-Lee & Gastfriend, 2008). Yet another misperception of substance abuse rehabilitation therapy, or "treatment," is that it is of a fixed duration rather than a process in which the patient's progress and needs help determine the duration and focus of the rehabilitation effort (Mee-Lee & Gastfriend, 2008). At the end of the residential or outpatient treatment program, persons with substance use disorders are offered a series of intermediate steps[3] to assist them in their transition to self-directed recovery. Treatment for the SUDs is admittedly not universally effective. The same might be said for surgical or radiological intervention for conditions such as heart disease or cancer.

---

[1] A story about a fictional residential treatment center in Maine that provided program participants with drugs until they found their own reason to stop abusing drugs was published by *Playboy* as the winner of its 2012 College Fiction writing competition (Peteroy, 2012). There is a danger that this work of fiction will become part of treatment lore and legend, with individuals in need of treatment requesting a referral to this fictional treatment center.

[2] These various estimates reflect, in part, different variables included from study to study. For example, one study might include long-term reductions in health care costs that another study does not include in its estimates of the savings that result from treatment.

[3] Discussed in this chapter.

The debate over whether the treatment of the SUDs is cost effective is not aided by the fact that many of the rehabilitation formats currently in use are not guided by scientific research but by tradition or what the counselor believes will be effective. Unfortunately many of the treatment methods that are least effective appear to be the most deeply entrenched in the rehabilitation system (Miller & Brown, 1997). Another fact that undermines the argument that treatment is effective is the observation that "most alcoholics who become abstinent do so *in spite of* treatment, not because of it" (Tomb, 2008, p. 151, italics added for emphasis). Detractors from substance abuse rehabilitation programs often point to the proper utilization of existing legal sanctions as a way to deal with the substance abuse problem in the United States. Unfortunately legal sanctions also do not appear to be the answer.[4] This places the substance abused rehabilitation counselor in a conundrum: He or she is being asked to help those with an alcohol or drug use problem work towards abstinence with tools that have not been proven to work, often hampered by institutional beliefs that some of the least effective interventions are to be used by the counselor in his or her struggle to help substance abusing clients. In this chapter, the benefits, advantages, and disadvantages of different forms of substance abuse treatment will be discussed.

Characteristics of the Substance Abuse Rehabilitation Professional

It is through the therapeutic relationship with an addictions counselor and treatment center staff that healing and recovery take place. Because of this critical importance, it has been suggested that the rehabilitation professionals share certain characteristics. Individuals who are dealing with substance use or serious psychological issues of their own should be discouraged from actively working with clients in treatment at least until they have resolved their own problems. This makes sense: If the counselor is preoccupied with personal problems, their ability to work effectively with the persons entrusted to their care will be reduced or possibly eliminaetd entirely.

The therapist who works with individuals with SUDs must possess many characteristics, some of which include genuineness, empathy, modeling of the desired behaviors, and an appropriately humorous outlook (Shea, 2006, p. 13). Further, the therapist should be adept at guiding the clients toward recovery rather than to tell them what to do. Most people have

the resources to solve their own problems, if they are assisted in finding that solution (Shea, 2006). Thus, the therapist's job is to assist and guide, not to demand or order the clients about their search for the answer(s). These skills are especially important during the early stages of treatment, when the client's commitment toward a major life change is still tentative and weak (Simpson, 2004).

It must be understood that clients who enter treatment do so with different levels of motivation and problem severity (Simpson, 2004). In many cases, clients who enter a rehabilitation program are admitting that they are unable to change their own lives through this very act. However, as was discussed in the last chapter, many individuals who enter treatment do so under external motivation. Therapists with strong interpersonal skills would be better equipped to help the client change. The client's acceptance of the therapist's efforts to assess him or her in making this change is one of the most essential characteristics of a successful therapeutic relationship. These relationships are based on mutual trust and openness, as well as the client's ability to accept external help. Miller (2003) identified several factors that seem to facilitate or inhibit recovery from substance use disorders as reviewed in Table 30-1.

One common misperception of substance abuse professionals is that they are "bleeding hearts" who

---

[4]Discussed in Chapter 35.

TABLE 30-1
Factors That Facilitate or Inhibit Recovery from SUDs

FACTORS THAT FACILITATE CHANGE	FACTORS THAT INHIBIT CHANGE
Empowerment	Disempowerment
Active interest in client as a person	Hostility, disinterest
Empathy	Confrontation
Making client feel need for change	Making client feel that she or he is not responsible for change
Advice on how to change	Ordering client to change
Involving client in the change process	Giving client a passive role
Environment supportive of recovery	Environment does not support recovery

will excuse virtually any misdeed by the client because of their SUD. Indeed, many therapists in the early stages of their careers attempt to "buy" client approval through such permissiveness. It is important to keep in mind the fact that caring for a client does *not* mean protecting him or her from the natural consequences of his or her behavior! It is through these consequences that the client will come to see the need for change.

Confrontation and Other Techniques

In the latter half of the 20th century, clinical theory, supported by antidotal evidence, made clinicians believe that heavy confrontation was necessary for the rehabilitation process to begin (Miller & White, 2007). This has proven to be a therapeutic myth that is enshrined in rehabilitation training programs. Unfortunately, there is little evidence that such confrontation helps the client to begin or make behavioral change (Miller & White, 2007; Miller & Rollnick, 2002). Research has shown that as the level of confrontation increases, so does the level of client resistance. This makes sense, because one factor that predicts successful treatment is the client's satisfaction with the rehabilitation process (Hser, Evans, Huang, & Anglin, 2004). However, there is also a danger that the health care professional will become too passive, failing to focus on the problems that the client has (or, possibly will) encounter if he or she continues to abuse chemicals (Washton & Zweben, 2006).

In contrast to confrontation, empathy for the client's struggle has been found to be more appropriate. Where confrontation is necessary, it should be infused with caring and concern for the client with a focus on

his or her current or anticipated problems (Ramsay & Newman, 2000). The client should not be "shamed" into conformity, but should be allowed to develop the skills necessary to abstain from substance abuse by utilizing the resources at hand. This is a slow process, to be sure, but it also empowers the client to then learn that she or he has the resources necessary to change, and how to apply them. The therapist serves as a guide and confidant, helping the client explore behavioral alternatives while achieving a sense of self-efficacy. Such a therapeutic style places emphasis on the client's ability to and responsibility for personal change, not heavy confrontation. The therapist advises, helps the client develop behavioral alternatives, and develop a sense of self-efficacy. In this manner, it is hoped that the therapist can guide the client to a substance-free lifestyle.

The Minnesota Model of Substance Abuse Treatment

George Vaillant (2000) identified four factors that were common to all substance abuse rehabilitation programs: (1) compulsory supervision, (2) introduction of and use of competing behavior to replace the SUD, (3) new love relationships (in the sense of a commitment to recovery rather than substance use), and (4) increased spirituality and religiosity. The "Minnesota Model" of substance abuse treatment met all four of these criteria, and dominated the therapeutic scene for the last half of the 20th century. It still remains a strong influence on both inpatient and outpatient rehabilitation programs (Foote, 2006; Ringwald, 2002).

The "Minnesota Model" was developed in the 1950s by Dr. Daniel Anderson. To earn money to finish his college program of study, Dr. Anderson worked as an attendant at the now defunct Willmar State Hospital, in Willmar, Minnesota. Following graduation, Dr. Anderson returned there to work as a recreational therapist. He was assigned the task of working with alcoholics, which was considered the least desirable position at the time. Anderson was himself influenced by the work of Mr. Ralph Rossen, who was to later become the Minnesota State Commissioner of Health. At the same time, the growing influence of Alcoholics Anonymous was viewed by Dr. Anderson and a staff psychologist at the State hospital by the name of Dr. Jean Rossi as a means of understanding and working with the alcohol-dependent people. They were supported in this new approach by the medical director of the hospital, Dr. Nelson Bradley (Larson, 1982).

These individuals joined together to better understand and treat the alcohol-dependent patients sent to the State hospital. Each person represented a different profession, and thus contributed a different perspective about the clients' needs, strengths, areas of weakness, and the issues that needed to be addressed to prepare the individuals for a life without alcohol. A spiritual advisor by the name of Rev. John Keller was also assigned to the treatment team. With his arrival, the staff had "knowledge of medicine, psychology, AA, and theology together under one roof to develop a new and innovative treatment program" (Larson, 1982, p. 35).

This new treatment model, the Minnesota model, was developed for work with alcohol-dependent people. It has since been applied to the treatment of all forms of substance abuse. The Minnesota model is centered around the treatment team approach in which the skills of a substance abuse rehabilitation counselor, psychologist, physicians, nurses, recreational therapists, and clergy were brought together to work with the client. Each professional was allowed to make recommendations for the areas to focus on, and the document that emerged from this process was identified as the treatment plan. Other interested parties, such as family members, probation/parole officers, and the clients, were also invited to participate in the process of building a treatment plan. The treatment team meeting was chaired by the individual who was ultimately responsible for the execution of the treatment plan, and who was thus identified as the patient's case manager.

The treatment plan that emerged was, in theory, multi-modal, offering a wide variety of individualized goals and treatment recommendations. It identified specific problem areas that needed to be addressed, and behavioral measurements by which each goal could be assessed. A target date for completion of that goal was also identified. The treatment plan itself will be discussed in more detail later in this chapter, but a flowchart of the treatment plan process might look like that in Figure 30-1.

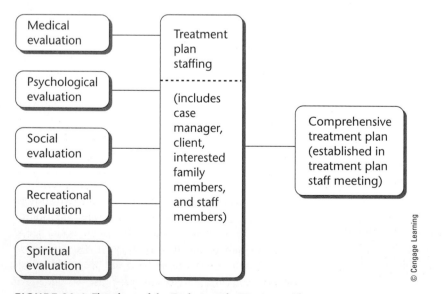

FIGURE 30-1 Flowchart of the Evolution of a Treatment Plan.

© Cengage Learning

One strength of the Minnesota model of rehabilitation was in its redundancy and the multiprofessional treatment team. The chemical dependency counselor did not need to be a "jack of all trades, master of none" but could make referrals to other members of the treatment team in response to the client's shifting needs. This feature helped to make the Minnesota model one of the treatment program models for more than 50 years, although under managed care initiatives it has been modified or replaced by other treatment formats.

Reaction to the Minnesota Model

The Minnesota model has not met with universal approval or acceptance. One early challenge was based on the fact that although it was designed for working with alcohol-dependent persons, it was rapidly applied for use with individuals with addictions to other compounds as well. There has been little research into whether the Minnesota model is equally effective with these other forms of drug addiction. However, it is still utilized in the treatment of other drug addictions in spite of clinical research such as the study by McPherson, Yudo, Afsarifard, and Freitas (2009) that found that this model has been ineffective in the treatment of CNS stimulant addiction.[5]

The Minnesota model draws heavily on the principles of Alcoholics Anonymous (AA),[6] and participation in AA is required as part of the program. Yet, AA is not in itself a form of treatment, and there is no clear evidence that AA is effective for individuals who were coerced into treatment. Surprisingly, even in cases where there is a wide discrepancy between the spiritual orientation of the rehabilitation program and the individual's own spiritual beliefs, there was no negative influence on the client's self-reported desire to drink (Sterling et al., 2006). Such discrepancies did not appear to increase premature termination from treatment, nor did it appear to slow progress in the rehabilitation process, according to the authors. Thus, the apparent contradiction in the Minnesota model in that participants are required to join an organization centered on spiritual growth does not appear to be a major issue at this time.

Another challenge to the Minnesota model was the arbitrary decision that treatment should last 28 days. There was little evidence to support a 28-day treatment program, although it did become something of an industry standard for a number of years and served as a guide for insurance company reimbursement policies. A grim, unintended effect of this process is that many individuals are admitted to a 28-day treatment program not based on his or her needs, but because the insurance companies would pay for only a treatment stay of 28 days! Where research suggests that those individuals who remain in treatment for 90+ days have a greater chance of abstaining from alcohol or drugs, it is not uncommon to read in a treatment program discharge summary that the individual was discharged from treatment after 7, 14, or perhaps 28 days not because of their progress toward meeting treatment goals but because their insurance benefits had expired.

Unfortunately, much of substance abuse rehabilitation is based not on scientific research, but on antidotal evidence or therapeutic myth, with the Minnesota model being a fine example of this. The Minnesota model was advanced at a time when there was little formal treatment for alcoholism, a factor that resulted in its widespread acceptance (Willenbring, 2010). In spite of the enthusiasm with which it was received and with which supporters defend this program paradigm, there is little evidence to suggest that the Minnesota model is effective (Hester & Squires, 2004; McCrady, 2001). Fortunately, it has become almost extinct, except in a few private treatment centers where the client is able to "self-pay" for extended substance abuse treatment (Monti, Kadden, Rohsenow, Cooney, & Abrams, 2002).

Other Treatment Formats for Substance Use Disorders

In the years since the Minnesota model was introduced, and especially since the managed care initiates of the 1990s, health care professionals have explored a number of alternative treatment formats to allow them to work with individuals with SUDs. Many of these alternative treatments have become incorporated in substance abuse rehabilitation programs as ancillary services. In the following section we will briefly examine

---

[5]This discontinuity between clinical practice and clinical research is an ongoing problem in the addictions treatment field. Many rehabilitation staff say that they used "evidence-based" treatments, but then they essentially go on to use the same treatment methods that were used when they went through treatment or that they have used in the past (Fletcher, 2013).

[6]Discussed in Chapter 34.

some of the more common treatment models that have emerged in the last four decades.

Acupuncture

This is a form of "alternative medicine" that has on occasion been utilized in the treatment of SUDs. Antidotal reports suggest that acupuncture has a calming effect on the client and reduces "craving" for alcohol or drugs. The theory behind this technique is beyond the scope of this text, but in practice, small, sterile needles are inserted into specific spots on the body in an attempt to liberate or block the body's energy. There is limited evidence supporting the effectiveness of acupuncture in the rehabilitation of substance abusers, and the current consensus is that it appears to be about as effective as placebos when used to treat substance abusers (Ernst, 2002; Hester & Squires, 2004; Margolin et al., 2002).

Computer Simulations

With the growing strength and speed of personal computers, a range of "virtual reality" simulations are emerging to help persons recover from their SUDs. In the computer-assisted treatment, an "avatar" for the individual is generated, which is either projected onto the computer screen, or, on to the screen of a special visor that the participant wears. The advantage of the latter approach is that the visor provides a wider field of view, thus simulating normal vision. Both methods of computer simulation are especially attractive to younger persons who grew up with desktop computers and computer simulation games.

One advantage of the virtual reality approach is that individualized scenarios can be set up to enable the client to practice situation-specific skills. For example, one program could be set up in which the client and his or her spouse argue, all seen from the client's perspective. Then the background might change to show what it would look like if the client were walking down the street and entering a favorite bar after the argument. Upon entering the bar, the bartender (a computer simulation) could be programmed to greet the participant by name, and ask what he or she would like to drink whereas other patrons (also computer simulations) also greet the participant by name and invite him or her to join them. The client then could practice refusal skills in a setting in which he or she once consumed alcohol following a marital dispute. After this skill is practiced then the goal might be for the clients to stop before

entering the bar following the argument with their spouse, and substitute other behaviors (also included in the simulation) such as calling a friend to meet them to talk over a cup of coffee about the argument and how the clients might deal with the problem, or going to a local 12-step support group meeting. Desktop computers also allow for "virtual" 12-step group meetings in which computer simulated "persons" (specifically built up to resemble the actual person) will walk into the meeting room, and interact with other participants in real-time meetings. Such virtual reality 12-step groups have the advantage of being available to persons who are geographically isolated, or who need group feedback on a real-time basis, using equipment now used by participants of virtual reality war game simulations, for example.

The application of virtual reality approaches to substance abuse rehabilitation has only started to be explored, and it is certain that in the years and decades to come computer-based assisted treatment approaches will become ever more important to the individual's rehabilitation program.

Detoxification

Technically, the term "detoxification" refers to the process of removing any toxin from the body. A second, related definition refers to the medical management of a person's withdrawal from alcohol or drugs (Haack, 1998). One common misperception is that the process of detoxification is a form of "treatment" in itself (Fletcher, 2013). Research has consistently demonstrated that the majority of those individuals who go through a "detox" program for their SUD will relapse without formal treatment (Craig, 2004). It is for this reason that "detox" is viewed as a prelude to the rehabilitation process (Fletcher, 2013; Gerada, 2005; Leshner, 2001a, 2001b; McPherson, et al., 2009). The goal of the detoxification process is to offer the individual a safe, humane withdrawal from alcohol or illicit drugs. The patient's safety is assured to the degree that is possible by having a physician who is both trained and experienced in this process supervise the detoxification process. Under the physician's supervision, the detoxification process will be carried out either on an outpatient basis if possible,[7] or on an inpatient basis if necessary. Traditionally "detox" from alcohol has been carried out in a hospital,

---

[7]A process that has also been called "ambulatory detoxification" or "social detoxification" (Blondel, 2005).

although currently it is believed that this is necessary for the 10–15% of alcohol dependent persons who are unable to complete an outpatient detoxification regimen (Anton, 2005; Blondel, 2005). The final decision whether to attempt inpatient or outpatient detoxification from alcohol rests upon the attending physician. Several of the factors on which this decision should rest include: (1) The individual is experiencing only mild to moderate withdrawal symptoms, (2) has no major coexisting medical or psychiatric problems, (3) has a responsible support person who can closely monitor their progress, (4) has not failed at home detox in the past, and (5) has a stable home environment supportive of recovery; it is possible that the withdrawal cycle for alcohol dependence might be carried out at home (Fletcher, 2013). People who are geographically isolated, have experienced serious withdrawal symptoms from past detoxification efforts, or who lack a stable home environment, should be referred to a residential detoxification program (Anton, 2005).

Part of the individual's support system should include a nurse who will stop by the patient's home once or twice a day to monitor the patient's blood pressure and monitor the patient's health status as necessary. If the patient should relapse or show signs of major medical or psychiatric complications, a referral to an inpatient detoxification center or hospital would then be made (Anton, 2005). Ambulatory detoxification from prescribed or illicit compounds is based on the individual's past drug use history and medical status. Some of the drugs of abuse, such as the barbiturates or benzodiazepines, can cause severe, life-threatening problems during detoxification. In some cases, the patients can be monitored at home by another responsible adult, and placed on a gradual "taper"[8] regimen to allow them to safely reduce and eventually stop their abuse of these compounds.

If the individual's environment does not permit ambulatory detoxification, or if the person should experience serious medical or psychiatric complications during the detoxification process, a referral to an inpatient "detox" program is automatically made. Nonprescribed substance use, often justified on the grounds that the person needed some additional assistance during the "detox" cycle, suggests that urine toxicology testing be carried out to both insure that the patient is taking recommended medications and to insure compliance with the regimen (Blondel, 2005). In spite of strident cries from individuals who are opiate-dependent, withdrawal from these compounds is rarely

life threatening,[9] but because of the tendency for such patients to relapse, inpatient "detox" is usually more successful than outpatient detoxification for this class of medications.

Many rehabilitation professionals believe that "detox" programs serve a gateway function, guiding patient into a rehabilitation program. Unfortunately, some treatment centers add a "detox" component to their rehabilitation program even if the person should not require this, whereas other programs will refer the individual only to one rehabilitation program exclusively (Fletcher, 2013). This is often justified because many patients fail to go on to enter a rehabilitation program after completing the detoxification process (Miller & Rollnick, 2002). The individual and their family should be provided with a list of available programs in the area and the decision which rehabilitation program the person should enter is made by the person and their family rather than forced upon them as the only option beyond "detox." The fact that the patient and family were provided with a list of possible rehabilitation programs that the individual might enter should be carefully noted in the chart to avoid possible conflict-of-interest charges at a later date.

Detoxification programs are subject to a number of abuses. Some individuals will "check into detox" to find a place to hide from drug debts, the media, or to escape from the police. Opiate-addicted persons have been known to enter a "detox" program to be cleansed of illicit drugs and allow their tolerance to opioids to drop, making it less expensive for them to return to opioid use upon discharge.[10] Thus, although detoxification programs provide a valuable service, they are also vulnerable to abuses.

Family/Marital Therapies

Although viewed with a measure of disdain in the middle of the 20th century, family and marital therapies have proven to be valuable components to substance abuse rehabilitation programs and are now considered an integral part of treatment (Fals-Stewart, Lam, & Kelley, 2009). Goal of such ancillary therapy is to help the spouse and family members learn how to support the patient's efforts to achieve and maintain abstinence (Work Group on Substance Use Disorders,

[8]See Glossary.

[9]This is based on the belief that the patient is abusing *only* opioids.
[10]Unfortunately, it is not uncommon in this situation for the patient to misjudge her or his drug dosage following detoxification, and overdose on opioids because of this (possibly with fatal results).

2007). Another goal is to identify marital conflict issues that might have contributed to the individual's SUD, that they might be addressed (Fals-Stewart et al., 2009).

The terms marital and family therapy are generic terms applied to a number of different therapeutic approaches including the psychodynamic, family systems, and structural and behavioral family therapy approaches. Within the field of substance abuse rehabilitation, the best-known and most common form of family therapy is the family disease model, which postulates that substance abuse in the family unit is an illness of the entire family and not just the substance abuser (Fals-Stewart, O'Farrell, & Birchler, 2003, 2004). Proponents of this model believe that every member of the family plays a role, and the therapist(s) works to identify the role that the SUD plays within the family. For example, some partners will use alcohol as a way to punish their partners, whereas others will use alcohol to make themselves "numb" to what they perceive as rejection by their partner.

In families where a member has an SUD, communications patterns tend to be confused, or unhealthy, supporting the individual's SUD (Alter, 2001). Boundaries within the family are fluid, or do not exist at all. Familial defenses often become interlocking, allowing the family to maintain a form of stability even in the face of rehabilitation efforts. Power roles within the family (such as parenting) are often assumed by other family members, who then resist efforts for them to relinquish these roles so that the now-recovering family member might resume those roles. All of these forces contribute to efforts to undermine or resist any effort to change by the addicted individual, including efforts at abstinence.

Given the impact that an individual's SUD has on the marriage and familial unit, marital or family therapy can be a valuable adjunct to treatment, and its importance has repeatedly been demonstrated in the clinical literature (Fals-Stewart et al., 2004). For example, the team of Neto, Labaz, Agular, and Chick, (2008) found that social support provided by an adult who is close to the recovering alcoholic (usually the spouse) resulted in significantly longer periods of abstinence in the first 180 days following treatment, with the mean time for relapse being approximately 150 days. But family/marital counseling is a specialized area of expertise that requires extensive training and supervision to be effective. It should not be attempted unless the therapist has the appropriate

training and experience in family or marital therapy. Unfortunately, many treatment centers offer what they classify as family or marital therapy that fails to be the intense, dynamic process of such therapies in which the marital partners or family members meet with the appropriately trained therapist on a frequent basis (Fletcher, 2013).

Individual Therapy Approaches[11]

One of the inconvenient truths on which addictions counseling rests is that research to date has not been able to isolate the mechanisms through which behavior change takes place (Morgenstern, Naqvi, Debellis, & Breiter, 2013). There are a wide variety of individual therapy techniques that might be applied during substance abuse rehabilitation, including psychodynamic, Motivational Interviewing (MI), cognitive-behavioral therapies, the various forms of Gestalt psychotherapy and psychodrama to cite many of the different in use in the field of mental heath at this time. Long viewed as being less effective than therapy groups, individual therapy session still offers the advantage of allowing the client to discuss issues too personal to discuss in a group format (victimization issues, sexual orientation, guilt over past behavior(s), etc.) with an individual therapist with whom the client has an established therapeutic relationship. Depending on the client's assessed level of care needs, individual counseling might be the most appropriate form of treatment for a given individual. Individual therapy should only be carried out by properly trained health care or substance abuse rehabilitation professionals who are well versed in the methodologies, advantages, and risks associated with this treatment format.

Many of the questions raised by Nasrallah (2010b) about individual psychotherapy apply to the substance rehabilitation program that claims to use an individual counseling/therapy component: (a) What is the optimal schedule for psychotherapy? (b) What is the primary indication for individual psychotherapy? (c) Are there conditions for which it is contraindicated? (d) Is there a "loading dose" for individual psychotherapy sessions after which the individual is most likely to

---

[11]Substance abuse rehabilitation professionals who are in training and who are using this text to learn more about substance abuse are encouraged to explore these various individual therapy approaches in more detail, and receive the appropriate training necessary to successfully apply each technique when working with an individual client.

benefit from additional treatment? (e) How long does a psychotherapy session need to be for maximum effectiveness? (f) Is there a best time of the day in which to conduct psychotherapy sessions? Ideally most rehabilitation and aftercare programs (discussed later in this chapter) utilize a mix of individual and group therapy formats. However, some programs do not provide the frequency of individual therapy sessions that would be appropriate for the individual (Fletcher, 2013).

Cognitive-Behavioral Therapies

The term "cognitive-behavioral therapy" has evolved over the past two decades to include cognitive therapy, cognitive-behavioral therapy, contingency management, self-monitoring, problem-solving, assertiveness training, behavioral rehearsal, and the social-learning therapies (Macgowan & Engle, 2010). The cognitive-behavioral therapist will often draw from a wide range of different therapeutic schools of thought, making the exact definition of a behavioral treatment approach very difficult (Macgowan & Engle, 2010). Traditionally, cognitive-behavioral approaches to rehabilitation of substance abusers involve 10–20 individual therapy sessions. Cognitive-behavioral approaches for SUD appear to be moderately effective for both adult and adolescent clients, although the clinical literature supporting the latter is more limited than is the pool of literature supporting the use of cognitive-behavioral therapies with adult substance abusers (Macgowan & Engle, 2010; Winerman, 2013).

Cognitive-behavioral therapies help the individual to learn inhibitory control techniques, in part by confronting irrational thoughts or beliefs that the client might have. One such irrational thought might be "I cannot endure the urge to use!" The therapist might help the individual look back to when they experienced similar episodes of drug-use "urges" when they did not resort to drug use, examine how they were able to endure that period without engaging in the abuse of chemicals, explore whether similar coping strategies might work under the present circumstances, and finally point out to the individuals how their past behavior proves that they can endure the urge to abuse chemicals without giving in to it.

Motivational Interviewing

The theoretical roots of the motivational interviewing (MI) approach to working with a substance abuser can be traced back to the social learning and cognitive-behavioral therapies (Macgowan & Engle, 2010). Over the years, the exact definition of motivational interviewing has become blurred as different therapeutic techniques have fallen under the umbrella of MI. MI is a therapeutic technique used in short-term interventional therapy that places great emphasis on helping the individuals identify how they are currently living and how they wish to be living in the future. This process involves a collaborative effort between the therapist and the client to (a) identify problem behaviors and (b) the client's view of effective behavior change (Macgowan & Engle, 2010). In MI sessions the individual is not required to admit having a SUD but only to consider the possibility that a lifestyle change is in his or her best interests. Open-ended questions, affirmation for signs of progress,[12] reflection of client's comments, and summarization of progress made to date all are part of the therapeutic approach used by the therapist who draws on MI techniques (Miller & Rollnick, 2002; Winerman, 2013).

The pool of clinical literature supporting the effectiveness of MI is mixed, with some researchers failing to find a significant difference in outcome between clients who were treated by a therapist who used MI and control groups. The effectiveness of MI interventions for adolescent substance abusers is very limited although MI does appear to work with adolescents who abuse chemicals. MI appears to hold promise as a brief interventional technique for clients who are seen for short term (1–5 sessions) therapeutic interventions (Macgowan & Engle, 2010).

Contingency Management

This therapeutic approach uses immediate rewards with tangible incentives for abstinence (Winerman, 2013). A person whose urine toxicology tests were "clean" for signs of illicit drug use might receive a point for each sober day that can be applied against the purchase of a desired item such as a personal radio that is available for 30 points. Sometimes local businesses will contribute items that the client can

---

[12]Miller and Rollnick (2002) advocated the technique of affirming the client for every sign of forward progress. If the individual reports that he or she drank to the point of intoxication only 5 nights out of 7 in the past week, as opposed to 6 out of 7 nights in the week before that, he or she would receive positive feedback from the therapist for this sign of progress.

work toward or offer employment opportunities in return for proven abstinence; cash incentives such as a pay increase are always welcome (Winerman, 2013). Paradoxically, although the value of the reward item would appear to be modest at best in comparison to the immediate reward of the drugs of abuse, many individuals place great emphasis on earning a desired reward item. When used appropriately, contingency management programs provide a powerful tool in the fight against the SUDs.

Psychoanalysis

This therapeutic school of thought has a long history of being tried with substance abusing individuals with at best limited success. A central tenet of the psychoanalytic theories is that the individual's emotional growth is blocked by unresolved emotional conflicts. It is believed by psychoanalytic therapists that awareness of these unresolved issues evokes anxiety. In the face of such unresolved issues, the individual is postulated to use characteristic behaviors and defenses to protect themselves from the immediate experience of anxiety. These defense mechanisms, including possible SUDs, provide some relief from the anxiety albeit at the expense of long-term adjustment. Many marijuana abusers for example speak of the brief periods of euphoria that they experience while using marijuana as a way to escape from their problems, for example. Another example is Khantzian's (2003b) theory that individuals with anxiety disorders might be drawn to the use of compounds such as alcohol, the benzodiazepines, narcotics, marijuana, and the increasingly rare barbiturates, because of their anxiolytic[13] effects.

The effectiveness of psychoanalysis in treating persons with a SUD has been debated. In theory, the therapeutic relationship provides the framework in which neural reorganization takes place, counter-acting the neural network changes induced by the drugs of abuse (Feldstein-Ewing & Chung, 2013). Many therapists from different schools of therapy will borrow selected psychoanalytic techniques to assist them in their work with individual clients; however, this is not psychoanalysis. The therapists are just borrowing certain techniques to help them with their work. True psychoanalysis is labor-intensive, the costs are often prohibitive, the technique does not lend itself to treating large numbers of substance abusers. However, in contrast to popular opinion, psychoanalysis is receptive to change as new information about the central nervous system is uncovered, allowing it to incorporate new techniques to increase its effectiveness. The therapeutic learning process initiated by psychoanalysis can be a valuable adjunct to treatment, and as scientists learn more about how psychoanalysis initiates neural-cognitive reorganization, it might become an even more effective tool for the addictions counselor.

Group Therapy Approaches[14]

Group therapy is the most common modality through which psychosocial change is attempted (Brooks, 2008). Unfortunately, the term "group therapy" is a generic term for a wide variety of therapeutic approaches carried out in a group setting, including cognitive-behavioral therapy, rational-emotive therapy, Gestalt therapy, psychodynamic group therapy, psychodrama, assertiveness training, and so on (Work Group on Substance Use Disorders, 2007). There is little evidence that the type of group counseling used in most treatment centers, a form of 12-step based discussion of superficial issues is effective (Tomb, 2008).

Theoretically the individual recreates his or her family of origin within the group setting, allowing interactional process between group members to help the individual resolve issues from their childhood (Brook, 2008). To achieve this goal, the group leader should have received extensive training in the theory and applications of group therapy, something that is often lacking in many treatment centers where abstinence is given more credence than formal education. Indeed, in some treatment centers the group leader might lack even a high school diploma (Fletcher, 2013). There is debate whether it is appropriate to intermix persons at different stages of the recovery process in the same group or if the rehabilitation center should offer different groups for persons at different stages of recovery (Fletcher, 2013). In the therapy group setting, substance abusers might learn how to form healthy, non-substance-centered relationships while enhancing self-esteem (Brook, 2008).

Cognitive-behavioral therapies can be used in a group therapy format if the group leader has received the proper training to call upon this treatment

---

[13]See Glossary.

[14]Substance abuse rehabilitation students who are in training are encouraged to explore the various forms of group therapy through appropriate training under the supervision of a properly trained professional.

modality. Group members learn to help each other identify self-defeating thoughts, the painful emotions that are caused by these thoughts, and ways to replace these unhealthy thoughts with more appropriate thoughts. Personality-disordered individuals, for example, often utilize a black-and-white interpretation of the world around them ("everybody is against me," or "I can't do anything right," for example), a cognitive pattern that enhances their frustration and tendency to abuse chemicals. A psychodynamic therapy group could allow a client to better understand the psychological forces that supported his or her addiction to continue, whereas a psychodrama group format might allow the clients to resolve conflicts that have blocked their recovery efforts to date through the appropriate simulations.

One very useful form of treatment group is the coping skills group. Many of those individuals with substance use problems began to abuse chemicals when they were children or adolescents, blocking the process of developing strong interpersonal coping skills (Monti et al., 2002). Social skills training might include substance use refusal skills training as well as helping the patient learn how to engage in non-substance-related pleasant activities (Morgan, 2003). Refusal skills training might take place within a group setting, where different group members participate in role-play simulations to help the individual learn how to refuse opportunities to abuse a chemical(s). Social skills training programs might help a client learn interpersonal skills to engage in non-substance-centered recreational activities, as well as to learn how to feel more confident when interacting with others.

Although group therapy formats are very useful in the rehabilitation of substance abusers, it is necessary to carefully screen potential group members. Acutely suicidal or homicidal clients should be referred to individual therapists, or hospitalized immediately for psychiatric treatment depending on the individual's needs (Brook, 2008). Persons who are unwilling or incapable to maintaining group confidentiality should not be admitted or retained in the group (Brook, 2008). Some persons feel threatened in the group environment and might do better with intensive individual psychotherapy (Fletcher, 2013). Individuals who are in the acute stage of a psychotic episode should be excluded from substance abuse therapy groups, as should group members who wish to utilize the group setting as a venue for selling drugs (Brook, 2008). These rules apply to community-based self-help groups as well as institutionally based therapy groups. However, when these rules are observed therapy groups might play a major role in the individual's rehabilitation from a substance use disorder.

Biofeedback Training

A number of studies have been carried out investigating the applicability of biofeedback programs to substance abuse rehabilitation. Biofeedback is a process where the individual is provided real-time information about internal body functions, such as brain wave or skin resistance patterns. With proper training and feedback from the appropriate device, the individual learns to modify body functions, such as muscle tension, skin tension, brain wave patterns, heart rate, and so on, without the use of alcohol or drugs. This discovery in itself often helps a client understand that it is possible to change body states, such as how to relax, without the use of chemicals. As a result of this process, biofeedback programs encourage the development of self-efficacy as she or he develops skills to change body states once thought to be alterable only through the use of chemicals. There is preliminary evidence that supports the use of such techniques in rehabilitation programs, although there is no standardization as to the modalities used or the methods by which these modalities might be modified.

Clinical research has suggested that persons with SUDs demonstrate different brain wave patterns, which possibly reflects a neurological predisposition to the development of SUDs. Neurofeedback, or brain wave biofeedback, is "less than mainstream treatment" (Trudeau, Sokhadze, & Cannon, 2009, p. 241) for the SUDs. However, it does appear to be a promising adjunctive treatment modality for the process of rehabilitation. Follow-up research conducted 3 years after participation in a substance use rehabilitation program that included neurofeedback found that 85% of the men in the study reported consistent reduction in or abstinence from alcohol (White & Richards, 2009).

Neurotransmission involves electrochemical signals being passed from one neuron to another. These signals can be amplified and recorded. The pattern of neurotransmission signals can then be grouped together by the wave frequency of these signals. "Theta" band patterns of brain activity have been found to accompany the process of "reprogramming" the brain, and is accompanied by subjective experiences such as serenity and relaxation combined with a breakdown in ego defenses[15] (White & Richards, 2009). By learning to achieve this state of mind without the use of alcohol or drugs, it is theorized that the individual's motivation for substance use will be reduced or eliminated and the individual's sense of ego mastery improved. Although this adjunctive treatment approach appears to offer promise in the rehabilitation of select substance abusers, large-scale studies into the applicability of neurofeedback are limited at this time (Trudeau et al., 2009).

Harm Reduction[16] (HR) Model

In contrast to the Minnesota model is the Harm Reduction (HR) model. The HR model does not attempt to help the individual abstain from chemicals, at least not at first. It is based on the assumption that it is possible to change the behavior(s) of individuals who have SUDs over time, reducing the immediate consequences of their continued substance abuse. Eventually, it is hoped, the individual will accept abstinence as a goal, but even if they do not, they are reducing the damage being done by their use of chemicals. Nicotine replacement therapy is one example of this process. Many individuals find it difficult to stop using the nicotine replacement therapy that they used in their smoking cessation program. However, their continued use of the nicotine in the spray, or inhaler, exposes the individual to just one chemical, nicotine and not to any of the other 4,500 compounds found in cigarette smoke.

Another good example of the HR model is opioid agonist replacement[17] programs using Methadone or buprenorphine. It is thought that by providing the opioid-dependent person medication in a controlled manner the individual will be less likely to share needles, inject illicit drugs, engage in criminal behavior(s), and so on. Noninfected intravenous opiate abusers who are placed on methadone maintenance programs have been found to cut their risk of contracting HIV infection[18] by 54%, which is an additional benefit of the methadone maintenance program concept (MacArthur et al., 2012). Other forms of HR include needle "exchange" programs. Because many infectious diseases

can be spread through the sharing of contaminated needles, needle exchange program helps to limit the spread of infectious disease among intravenous drug abusers. If a needle exchange program prevents just one or two new cases of an infection such as AIDS per year in a given community, the program will have paid for itself. Unfortunately, in spite of the obvious advantages of this process, there is strong resistance toward needle exchange programs in many regions of this country (Reuter, 2009).

Hypnosis

There has been little systematic research into the effectiveness of hypnosis in treating SUDs. The limited research that has been carried out usually involves the use of hypnosis to treat nicotine addiction, and there is little evidence to suggest that this treatment modality is viable in the long term (Work Group on Substance Use Disorders, 2007).

Videotape/Self-Confrontation

In the late 1980s and early 1990s, videotapes were made of the individual shortly upon his or her admission to a detoxification unit. This was viewed as a technique that would show the client what he or she looked like under the influence of chemicals, in the hope that it would provide a degree of motivation for the client to discontinue the use of alcohol or drugs or at least seek help for their SUD. There is little data to support this technique, and some data suggest that it might actually contribute to higher client dropout rates (Hester & Squires, 2004; Miller & White, 2007). A few programs still utilize this procedure, although for the most part it has been discontinued by treatment or rehabilitation programs.

Yoga or Meditation

As is true with hypnosis, there has been little systematic research into the possible application of yoga or similar relaxation procedures in the treatment of SUDs. There is, however, a rich body of research data supporting the use of yoga as a means to reduce stress, and it has been found to be a useful adjunct in the treatment of depression (Trandon, 2007). It is also potentially a method to enhance mindfulness, a measure of being grounded in one's environment that holds the potential to foster neuroadaptive change in the brain (Witkiewitz,

---

[15]Effects that sound suspicious like the reasons offered by drug abusers for their drug use.

[16]Also known as *harm minimization*.

[17]Discussed in Chapter 33.

[18]Discussed in Chapter 35.

Lustyk, & Bowen, 2013). Meditation was hypothesized to counteract the lack of self-awareness during periods of "craving" (in which the individual's focus is on externals such as obtaining a substance to use) (Witkiewitz et al., 2013). Thus, the use of medication in the treatment of SUDs would seem to make clinical sense at this time, especially because by definition the SUDs reflect an imbalance in the individual's life (Trandon, 2007).

The Treatment Plan

The substance abuse rehabilitation professional will have a wide range of techniques, many of which are briefly discussed in this chapter, to bring to bear on the problem of a substance abusing client. The therapist and client should together develop a treatment plan to guide the client during the rehabilitation process. The treatment plan is based on the information obtained during the assessment process discussed in the last chapter. It "serves as the plan of action for pursuing the identified goals of treatment" (Connors, Donovan, & DiClemente, 2001, p. 82). The exact format of the treatment plan varies from one rehabilitation center to another depending on the treatment methods being utilized and the certification requirements for that specific health care facility. However, the treatment plan should be a written document that in some states is a required part of a rehabilitation program and is viewed as a legal document.

All treatment plans share certain similarities. First, the treatment plan should provide a brief summary of the problem(s) that brought the client into treatment. An example of this might be that the "client is alcohol dependent." Some treatment plans include a brief summary of the client's physical and emotional health, sometimes in the client's own words. The generalized statements of goals and specific objectives[19] are identified. Using the previous example, the objective might be: "Client will successfully complete alcohol detoxification process as measured by staff assessments of patient status, within 5 days."

Next, there is a summary of the discharge criteria, listing the steps necessary for the client to accomplish in order for treatment to be successfully completed.

Using the previous example, the client's progress in ingesting an adequate diet, which may counteract some of the dietary deficiencies associated with alcohol dependence, could be stated as: "The client will consume 80% of meals provided 95% of the time for 3 days, as measured by staff report." Finally, there is a summary of those steps that are to be made a part of the client's aftercare program (discussed later in this chapter). Again, using the previous hypothetical example, this might be a statement such as "Client to identify a rehabilitation program that (she or he) wishes to enter by time (she or he) is deemed medically ready for discharge, and make arrangements to enter that treatment program."

Another example of a treatment plan goal for a hypothetical 24-year-old polydrug addict (cocaine, alcohol, marijuana, and occasionally benzodiazepines or opioids), who has a 3-year history of addiction to these compounds, might be as follows:

Problem: Client has been addicted to chemicals for the last 3 years, by self-report.

Long-term goal: Total abstinence from alcohol and drugs.

Methodology (1): Successful completion of detoxification program, as measured by staff and patient report.

Methodology (2): Successful completion of residential treatment program

Methodology (3): That patients take Naltrexone as prescribed 95% of the time.

Methodology (4): That patients have "clean" urine test results 100% of the time, for 180 days as measured by laboratory reports.

Methodology (5): That patients identify community support group(s)[20] and join same to begin to develop substance-free support system.

Methodology (6): That patients identify substance-free housing before discharge, or within 30 days of admission to treatment.

Each of the target goals might be modified, or additional goals added as needed. For example, a patient who indicates that she or he "just can't say 'no' to

---

[19]A *goal* is a generalized statement, such as "I want to lose weight." An objective is a measurable expression of that goal, such as "I want to lose 10 pounds."

[20]This does not automatically refer to 12-step program groups since church prayer groups, informal mutual support groups or any of the alternative groups that have emerged as a reaction against the 12-step program movement.

drug dealers" might have the additional objective added to the treatment plan:

Methodology (7): That patients demonstrate appropriate refusal skills in role play simulations 100% of the time, as measured by staff report and patients report of comfort level using these techniques.

The treatment plan is a dynamic document that is modified as additional client needs are identified. For example, if an individual were to lose a close sibling in a motor vehicle accident while in a rehabilitation facility, a new long-term goal of helping the client come to terms with his or her feelings of loss and grief without the use of illicit drugs might be an appropriate addition to the treatment plan. The methodologies might include:

Methodology (1): That patients participate in 5–10 grief counseling sessions with pastoral counselor prior to discharge from treatment.

Methodology (2): That patients write a memorial letter to lost sibling within 2 weeks and discuss same with their individual therapist at end of that time frame.

Methodology (3): That patients identify fitting memorial for their lost sibling within 30 days and implement same at time of their choosing.

Methodology (4): That patients join grief group of own choosing and attend three group meetings prior to discharge.

Methodology (5): That patients visit grave of lost sibling with staff person of their choice within 30 days to end this phase of their relationship with their sibling and start a new form of relationship with lost relative. Patients to discuss their feelings about and during this process with staff member of their choice on an individual basis for 1–5 hours at time of their own choosing.

In this manner, the treatment plan is modified to accommodate changes in the client's status while in a "rehab" program, reflecting the dynamic nature of the treatment plan and the rehabilitation program itself.

Aftercare Programs

Because the SUDs are viewed as chronic, relapsing disorders, treatment does not end with the individual's discharge from an inpatient or outpatient rehabilitation program. Rather, participation in a continuing care or aftercare program is recommended. Such programs have been found to significantly contribute to client abstinence rates (Ritsher, Moos, & Finney, 2000; Smith et al., 2006). Aftercare programs work on the assumption that rehabilitation does not end with discharge from intensive treatment, but that this is the first step that the client takes on the road to long-term recovery.

These aftercare programs usually are carried out in a group format, and focus on issues such as: (1) maintenance of goals made in treatment and (2) helping the individual avoid relapse back to active substance use. Individual therapy sessions with a professional rehabilitation counselor are utilized as an adjunct to the group therapy sessions. A major component of aftercare programs is helping the client identify mistaken beliefs that might contribute to relapse ("It is all right for me to drink beer, but I have to stay away from the hard stuff," or "Marijuana can't hurt you, it is natural, and natural things can't hurt you!"). Another goal of an aftercare program is to help the clients learn self-monitoring skills to help them take responsibility for their recovery program. Such self-monitoring skills are a crucial part of an aftercare program because it has been found that "the benefits of abstinence in the first year operate in part through building self-efficacy to abstain from alcohol use" (Maisto, Clifford, Stout, & Davis, 2008, p. 735). An important component in the development of such self-efficacy is the identification of "high-risk" situations in which the client is more likely to relapse[21] (being around those who are abusing alcohol or illicit drugs, as suggested in the hypothetical examples offered earlier in this paragraph) and the development of coping skills through which the client might deal with such "high-risk" situations.

Many aftercare programs require that participants attend community self-help group meetings on a regular basis.[22] Aftercare groups might help clients learn to address medical issues such as chronic pain without relapsing, and offer feedback, guidance, and support for clients addressing such needs as transitional housing, employment, guidance toward appropriate post-treatment family or marital counseling, and encouragement for the client to report "urges" or thoughts that might contribute to a relapse to the group. Should the clients relapse, the

---

[21]Relapse prevention is discussed in Chapter 32.

[22]Discussed in Chapter 35.

group should offer both encouragement as the clients struggle to rebuild their recovery program, and help them examine their previous recovery system to identify problem areas that may have contributed to the relapse.

The Treatment/Research Disconnect

Many treatment programs claim to use "evidence-based" treatments. In reality, clinicians in the substance abuse rehabilitation often pay little attention to the research literature and the treatment format for that rehabilitation center continues essentially unchanged for years. For example, clinical research has demonstrated that lectures are perhaps one of the least effective treatment modalities[23] to assist people take their first steps on the long road to recovery. However, a huge percentage of treatment programs continue to use group lectures on the pretense that this will impart knowledge that people will need in their recovery program. Another example of the research/therapy disconnect is how clinical research has suggested that disulfiram is not effective in helping people abstain from alcohol use. Yet, it is still frequently recommended by staff for the client in the early stages of recovery. In essence, an untold number of treatment professionals use the "What worked for me will work for you" approach, making little or no effort to review new clinical research much less integrate it into their practice (Fletcher, 2013; Winerman, 2013). To be fair, treatments that appear promising in the research setting do not work in the field, but the willingness to review the clinical literature and accept new, proven treatment approaches where appropriate is the hallmark of an effective therapist.

Chapter Summary

This chapter reviews some of the varieties of individual therapy applicable to both the Minnesota model of treatment, which long dominated the inpatient rehabilitation programs. Individual therapy sessions were viewed as ancillary to the residential process for the most part, although in reality such therapy might be the most appropriate level of care for the client. The need for the therapist to develop a formal treatment plan was discussed, as were various treatment modalities such as detoxification from chemicals, biofeedback, marital and or family therapies, group psychotherapy, and the role of blood and urine samples in the rehabilitation of the client were briefly explored.

---

[23]This is not surprising: How many students *really* pay attention to a classroom lecture? How many put their mind in "neutral," doze off, carry on side conversations with other students, or start to think about subjects other than the lecture topic? Why should substance abusers be expected to not follow this pattern?

CHAPTER 31

The Process of Treatment

Introduction

It is common for the average person on the street and many people in the health care field to speak of recovery from a substance use disorder (SUD) as if it were a single step. This reflects a gross misunderstanding of the nature of the addictions: They are not an acute condition like a broken leg or infection that can be fixed by brief episodes of treatment. Actually many acute medical disorders require multiple treatment exposures. A broken leg might require several operations for insertion of surgical screws and plates or the removal of these items after the bone has healed. A further complication to the problem is that even experts in the field of addictions have trouble defining what is, and is not, part of "treatment" (Fletcher, 2013). Different rehabilitation facilities utilize differing methodologies, although the majority of inpatient or outpatient treatment programs use the Alcoholics Anonymous (AA) 12-step model as a component of the program (Fletcher, 2013).

In the past decade, the concept of rehabilitation programs as a form of disease management for the SUDs has emerged. As is true for the treatment of chronic medical conditions such as heart disease and diabetes, the individual with an SUD will experience periods of relative stability interspaced with acute exacerbations of their disorder. Such acute exacerbations of the core illness will require innumerable visits with health care providers, or in the case of the SUDs various rehabilitation professionals. This process parallels the process of disease management for other chronic medical conditions. In this chapter, the mechanics of rehabilitation programs will be reviewed.

The Decision to Seek Treatment

Clients enter a substance abuse rehabilitation program for a number of reasons and vary in their motivation for a major life change such as abstinence from a desired substance (Cooney, Kadden, & Steinberg, 2005). The most important factor in recovery from any psychiatric disorder, including the addictions, appears to be readiness to change (Mintz, 2011). There is an emerging and exciting body of evidence suggesting that people who enter rehabilitation program on a voluntary basis begin to alter their substance use behaviors in the days or weeks prior to their entry

into treatment (Willenbring, 2010). This would suggest that the actual admission to treatment is the culmination of the decision to end or reduce one's alcohol or drug use in effect providing a behavioral measure of the individual's commitment to change for those individuals who enter treatment on a voluntary basis (Willenbring, 2010). People who enter a formal rehabilitation program tend to be more impaired, and have more severe life problems than those who are able to abstain without entering a formal treatment program (Moos, 2003). People who seek professional assistance with an SUD usually have been addicted for 5–8 years, or have engaged in heavy substance abuse for 10–19 years prior to seeking treatment (Kessler et. al., 2001). Substances that result in a greater level of immediate impairment (cocaine, for example) will seek treatment earlier than those individuals who are addicted to alcohol, which requires time before its negative effects begin to manifest (Kessler et al., 2001). Further, as Willenbring (2010) suggested, the alcohol use disorders (AUDs) might follow different trajectories in different individuals. This raises questions whether the treatment methods designed for people whose AUD is following one trajectory would be appropriate for those with another. This might explain why substance abuse rehabilitation so often ends in failure: The program is not able to adapt to the special requirements of the individual's form of alcoholism.

Methods of Treatment

There are different therapeutic methods utilized in the therapeutic process. Although most treatment centers will claim to use those methods that have been scientifically proven to be effective, this claim is often not supported by the facts since many rehabilitation counselors adapt a "This is what worked for me when I was in treatment, so that is the method that I will use" attitude (Fletcher, 2013). In this section, we will examine three evidence-based habilitation methodologies.

Motivational Interviewing

The core elements of Motivational Interviewing (MI) involve expressing empathy for the clients, helping them see that there are discrepancies between their goals and values and their behavior.[1] The counselor avoids resistance to change not through confrontation but by assisting the individuals conclude that they need to change the target behavior. For example, the individuals who wish to avoid further substance-related legal problems but who continue to drink heavily demonstrate a conflict between behavior and their goals. The counselor will support the individuals during the change process, praising even the smallest of signs of progress (Adamson & Sellman, 2008). The MI model views "resistance" as a therapeutic mismatch between the client's stage of growth, therapeutic goals, and the treatment approach being utilized (Miller & Rollnick,

2002). An example of this might be found in cases where the client's goal is to find a way to drink "socially," whereas the therapist's goal is total abstinence. The client's continued use of alcohol normally would be interpreted as a sign of resistance, not of a therapeutic mismatch between therapist's and client's goals. However, the therapist who is using the MI model reinforces the client's efforts to change, possibly going to the extreme of praising the individual for abstaining from alcohol for just one night of the week. The therapeutic model establishes a "no failure" approach to treatment.[2]

The initial research studies were quite supportive of MI and its application to the treatment of AUDs. However, long-term (5-year) follow-up studies have failed to demonstrate increased efficacy of MI approaches with non-directive therapy approaches or no counseling at all (Adamson & Sellman, 2008). There is a need for further research into the elements of MI that are effective, those that must be modified to enhance efficacy and the form(s) of alcoholism that would be most responsive to the MI model of treatment.

Cognitive-Behavioral Therapies

The term "cognitive-behavioral therapy" is an umbrella term that includes a number of therapeutic systems with many similar elements. One cornerstone of all cognitive-behavioral therapeutic systems is that the individual has developed a series of false or irrational assumptions on which their psychosocial problems, including their SUD rest. These core assumptions are expressed through the individual's thoughts, or "self-talk." These internal messages help shape the individuals' self-concept, how they view others and their behavior. An example of one such thought is that the person can not possibly cope with the demands of work, their marriage, and so on, without abusing a drug. Another irrational thought might be: "If my spouse becomes violent it is my fault. So I have to please my spouse to avoid (his or her) violent behavior. If I am successful in this endeavor, I will be able to feel good about myself."

Cognitive-behavioral therapy is usually carried out either through 8–16 individual therapy sessions or in a group therapy format designed to help the individual identify these irrational thoughts and correct them. The

---

[1]People who state that their goal is to own their own business but who spend most of their free time at a bar drinking, for example, is demonstrating such a discrepancy between goals and their behavior.

[2]An example of which might be the counselor praising the client for drinking only three drinks on a night when they would normally consume seven or eight, as a sign of possible progress.

individual is helped to learn the difference between a thought and feelings, and how the former contributes to the latter[3] is explored. The manner in which this basic misunderstanding contributes to their emotional distress is discussed. To illustrate this process consider the hypothetical person who states that "I feel like everybody is against me" during the session. The fact that " ... feel like everybody is against me" is a thought on which a feeling (in this case, dejection and depression) is established. Then the validity of the thought "everybody is against me" is explored and a more realistic form of feedback is suggested ("There are times when I think that everybody is against me. That makes me feel depressed," for example). Written homework assignments are commonly used by the therapist to help the clients work on their recovery between sessions. Black-and-white messages to the self such as " I have to win the approval of everybody that I know or I am a failure" are identified. The evidence supporting or failing to support this self-talk is reviewed, as is the manner in which the individual takes these irrational thoughts and then behaves as if it were true are reviewed. In the last phase the individual is taught to use more realistic self-feedback ("There are times when I think that everybody is against me, but I know that some people agree with me," for example).

In addition, the individual's use of "demand words,"[4] which reflect black-and-white thinking which makes the individual vulnerable to failure and potential relapse are explored. The differences between setting a goal ("I would like to be liked ... ") and the demand ("I have to be liked ... ") as well as the relationship of such perfection demands to the individual's SUD are explored. The individual is helped to see that it is more realistic to set goals ("I would like to ..." rather than demands ("I have to ... ") and how the latter reflects black-and-white thinking is discussed.

---

[3]An analogy that this author often uses is that the thoughts are the foundation, and the feelings are the house. If the foundation is flawed, it is suggested, then the house will probably also be flawed. This establishes the grounds for the clients to begin to explore how their thoughts are maladaptive and contribute to self-defeating behaviors or feelings.

[4]Examples of which include: "should," "have to," "got to," "must," and "ought to," or their negation such as "should not" and so on. In AA meetings members are often admonished not "to should all over yourself," illustrating how members of the group recognize the self-destructive nature of these behavioral demands.

Voucher-Based Reinforcement

The process of voucher-based treatment involves the distribution of vouchers worth a certain number of "points," or even credit at a local store, for periods of abstinence confirmed through urine toxicology testing. Such a program might award a voucher the client could use to buy a desired item (stereo, and the like), if he or she could accumulate the desired number of points (in this hypothetical example, perhaps 50 points). Such approaches are combined with more traditional forms of addictions counseling to reinforce the early stages of abstinence. If the individual fails to earn sufficient points to be able to obtain the desired item, staff help the individual identify the obstacles that prevented him or her from achieving this goal. The relationship of such obstacles to the individual's substance abuse is explored and new methods of dealing with the identified problem are devised. Actual money is not used, as this would be a relapse trigger for the client, but points that could only be traded in at a specified store would lack the potential to serve as a relapse trigger, and this process has been found to enhance abstinence in the early stages of recovery.

A number of different therapeutic schools of thought have been advanced over the years and it is not possible to do full justice to each of these schools of thought in this chapter. The efficacy of these different therapeutic systems in treating the SUDs remains unproven in most cases. The question of whether one therapeutic school is superior to another is often a meaningless question since therapeutic techniques advocated by one school of thought are often "borrowed" by a therapist working with a specific person to meet the needs of that specific therapeutic relationship. The reader is advised to explore different therapeutic systems by directed reading about that theoretical school to learn the strengths and disadvantages of a specific therapeutic system.

The Stages of Recovery

As hard as it is to believe, there is virtually no research into the natural history of the SUDs! This places the substance abuse rehabilitation counselor in the position of attempting to help the individual "recover" from a condition that very little is known about. Physicians can treat a person for coronary artery disease because they have a working knowledge of the normal blood flow level through the normal coronaries, and the level of blood flow through these arteries that are required to diagnose an abnormal blood flow pattern. They know what will happen when a certain level of blockage develops in each artery and are working to find the appropriate treatments for such problems

Substance abuse rehabilitation counselors are not so fortunate: They are called upon to help "rehabilitate" a person with an SUD without an understanding of the natural course of that disorder. If a person achieves abstinence, is this because of their participation in a rehabilitation program or just a coincidence? We do not know. Indeed, there is a chasm between strongly held clinical beliefs and the research data. The former postulates that the SUDs are chronic, progressive conditions, whereas clinical research suggests that a significant percentage of those people who meet the diagnostic criteria for an SUD in their late teens or early twenties will either have discontinued or at least greatly reduced their substance use by their late twenties (Heyman, 2009). Only a minority of those people who demonstrate one sign of an alcohol use disorder, for example, go on to develop an AUD. The majority will curtail or discontinue their use of alcohol to avoid further alcohol-related problems. This data is counterintuitive, especially in the face of clinical lore that maintains that the addictions are chronic and progressive, and this contrast illustrates the chasm between clinical research into the addictions and the belief system by people who work in the field of addictions rehabilitation.

To better understand the recovery process, a number of different stage recovery models have been proposed, thus illustrating that recovery from an SUD is a process. The challenge, however, has been to establish a theoretical system that could then be tested, accepted, and applied to clinical practice, to help the clinician. The most widely known stage recovery model was introduced by Prochaska and DiClemente in the waning years of the 20th century (Prochaska, 2002; Prochaska, DiClemente, & Norcross, 1992). This model was based on the work by the authors on smoking cessation and then applied to the other SUDs. Within the framework of this model it was postulated that the individual would move from one stage to the next on his or her road to recovery, and that the needs and characteristics of people in different stages of change differ (Connors, Donovan, & DiClemente, 2001; Sadock & Sadock, 2007).

The first stage in this model is that of precontemplation (Blume, 2005; Connors et al., 2001; Prochaska, 2002, 1998). The individual who is in this stage is still actively abusing chemicals, and has no thought of trying to abstain from alcohol or illicit drugs in the next 6 months (Prochaska, 2011). If the person has thought about abstinence, he or she views starting a recovery program as a long-term goal and not as one to be started within the next 6 months. The challenge for the substance abuse rehabilitation professional working with a client in this stage of the change process is to: (a) teach him or her the negative effects of his or her substance use, (b) the dangers of continued substance use, (c) address the client's ambivalence to change, (d) help the client envision an alternative lifestyle (e) help the client to identify barriers that might block this attempt at a lifestyle change, (f) help enhance the client's self-esteem so that she or he will believe that a lifestyle change is possible (Blume, 2005; Ramsay & Newman, 2000; Rose, 2001). In other words, to spark the readiness to change Mintz (2011) identified the readiness to change as the most important factor in psychiatric treatment and it is the counselor's goal when working with a person at this step to develop the readiness to make a lifestyle change. The stages of change are reviewed in Figure 31-1.

It is important for rehabilitation center staff to avoid focusing on behavioral change issues at this point, as the clients still do not view their SUD as being a major problem (Connors et al., 2001). The main emphasis of treatment at this stage should be to help clients think about an alternative (drug-free) lifestyle. It is during this stage that defense mechanisms such as denial and rationalization are most prominent (Ramsay & Newman, 2000). If the client is in treatment under external pressure, he or she might attempt to use compliance as a defense against actual lifestyle change (Blume, 2005), an issue that must be identified and addressed to prepare the ground for meaningful behavioral change to occur.

It is only during the next stage, contemplation that individual begin to entertain vague thoughts of stopping alcohol or drug use "one of these days." About 40% of substance abusers are in this stage. There is no firm date set for quitting, although the client is actively thinking about quitting at some point within the next 6 months. The individual remains ambivalent about change while simultaneously also experiencing a growing sense of dissatisfaction with his or her present lifestyle. It is during this stage that the efforts from the

Stage	Behaviors	Therapeutic challenge
Precontemplation	Individual is still actively using chemicals and has not thought of stopping the use of recreational chemicals. Individual might not see use of chemicals as a problem.	Teach client about effects of drugs of abuse and risks associated with their use. Help client build self-esteem. Help client identify barriers to recovery.
Contemplation	Individual is still actively using chemicals but has ambivalence about whether she or he wants to continue.	Teach client about effects of drugs of abuse and risks associated with their use. Enhance motivation for change.
Preparation/ Determination	Individual has decided to quit in the immediate future.	Enhance motivation for change. Help individual make behavioral plans to support impending change.
Action	Individual has started to try to avoid further chemical use.	Identify relapse triggers. Help individual recognize symptoms of impending relapse.
Maintenance	Individual has made behavior change and continues to work to learn behaviors that will support recovery from chemical use.	Ensure stability of change. Help individual identify and deal with any personal issues that might be a threat to his or her recovery program.

Relapse pathway

Termination stage: Patient has made cognitive changes that support abstinence.

FIGURE 31-1 The Stages of Recovery.
SOURCE: Based on Prochaska (1998) and Prochaska et al. (1992).

previous stage, to help the individual develop the willingness to change, bear fruit. In the contemplation stage the person might entertain doubts about the benefits of cessation. However, they are receptive to the possibility of change (Prochaska, 2011). The individual might remain in this stage for months or years. The client is not working toward recovery during this phase, although he or she might begin to engage in preliminary action that moves him or her closer to actively attempting to change. For example, the three packs a day cigarette smoker might slowly reduce his or her cigarette consumption to one pack a day in anticipation of eventually quitting.

For the therapist working with a client in the contemplative stage, the challenge is to (a) enhance motivation to change, (b) awaken within the client a desire for spiritual growth,[5] and (c) help the client make a firm decision to change. Sills (2013) observed that the person who makes a firm commitment to saying "no" when faced with temptation is helping to define who

they are as a person, an observation that certainly appears true for the addictions. "I am a former cigarette smoker" implies a state of commitment that is far different than "I hope to quit this year," for example, since in the former case the individual defines his or her "self" by being a former smoker.

It is not uncommon for a client during this stage to express amazement at how much his or her SUD has impacted the family, for example. An alcohol-dependent man might; after adding up the combined costs of medical treatment, court fines, lost employment, and the physical cost of the alcohol consumed; discover that his or her AUD has resulted in a financial loss that totals well into six digits. "My God, I drank [the equivalent of the purchase price of] a house," a hypothetical client might exclaim after adding up the accumulated costs induced by his or her AUD, for example. Another technique that often works is to develop a worksheet on which the pros of continued substance use are compared with the negative consequences of continued substance use.

The next stage is the stage of preparation. The client is now ready to change his or her attitude and behavior(s)

---

[5]See Chapter 26.

within a specific time frame, usually within the next month. The individual might even build upon the initial steps in the change process taken earlier (Connors et al., 2001). For example, the person who, in the contemplation stage, said to themselves "I should get some help" with their SUD might in the preparation stage obtain information about various local treatment centers that could help them. Unfortunately, very few individuals reach this or subsequent stage(s). The therapeutic goal during this stage is for the therapist to assist the client in making realistic decisions and to set realistic goals. Another therapeutic goal is for the therapist to address maladaptive thoughts that support continued substance use ("I can keep a bottle in my house for friends, as long as I do not actually use it myself," for example). A danger is that the client's unrealistic goals or maladaptive thoughts during this effort will undermine further efforts to change or convince them that change is impossible.

The next stage is the action phase in which the client takes concrete steps to modify the identified problem behavior. During this phase, the client implements his or her behavior change plan. It is to be expected that they will encounter problems during this step, and a therapeutic challenge is for the counselor to both reassure the individuals that change is possible while helping them identify the ways that the original change plan was flawed and take corrective action. Other therapeutic goals during this phase center around (a) optimizing opportunities for individual growth, (b) being alert for signs that the client is experiencing additional problems, (c) encouraging the client to begin the process of building a substance-free support system, (d) helping the client deal with the "emotional roller coaster" experienced during this period, (e) helping the client be realistic about the pace of his or her recovery ("I can handle being in a relationship, now," a hypothetical client might say after only 2 months of abstinence).

If the client is able to abstain from alcohol or drugs for at least 6 months, he or she will enter the maintenance stage of recovery. During this phase the individual develops behaviors supportive of recovery, addressing problem areas ignored during the period of active chemical abuse (employment or marital relationships, for example), and confronts personal issues that contributed to or exacerbated the SUD. Ultimately, only 20% of clients with an SUD reach this phase (Prochaska, 2002). During this phase the individuals learn how to cope with "using" thoughts or "urges" to return to chemical use, increasing their self-efficacy

and belief that they can succeed in maintaining behavior change. Increased self-efficacy at the end of the first year of abstinence, including a lower number of days in which alcohol was consumed, and lower amount of alcohol consumed per drinking day, appear to be a predictor of abstinence at the end of a 3-year period (Maisto, Clifford, Stout, & Davis, 2008). The therapeutic challenge during this stage is for the therapist to function as a parent-substitute, mentor, cheering section, and guide for the client to ensure the stability of change and identify issues that might undermine his or her recovery program.

Relapse[6] is an ever-present danger. In past, this was viewed as a "treatment failure" by many health care professionals. This view has been challenged on the grounds that the addictions are chronic, relapsing disorders similar to cancer, diabetes, or hypertension. Most certainly a patient whose blood pressure at best was under tenuous control after a trial of one hypertensive medication would not be classified as a "treatment failure." Some diabetic patients require repeated hospitalizations for stabilization and treatment, and yet they are called a "brittle" diabetic patient and not a "treatment failure." Arguably the same reasoning should apply to the treatment of the SUDs.

Recovery from the SUDs is a dynamic process that will often move through the various stages of change in a cyclical rather than a linear manner (Connors et al., 2001; Prochaska, 2002, 1998). The comparison to how patients work through the stages of grief might not be inappropriate here. In both cases the clients will be very vulnerable to internal and external "cues" that reawaken old thought patterns. The recovering smoker might, upon smelling cigarette smoke, start to think about how nice it was to sneak out of the office to have a cigarette. The recently bereaved person might, upon hearing a song once shared with a loved one, find herself or herself mired in the pain and misery of mourning their lost partner, again.

This is one of the more frustrating aspects of substance abuse rehabilitation. The client might make a step forward, then fall back two steps. Over time, she or he might again reach the point where she or he took the step forward, and this time progress to yet another step forward. A comparison with recovery from nicotine addiction is not out of place here. Periods of smoking abstinence are intermixed with periods of active smoking

---

[6]Discussed in more detail in Chapter 33.

that hopefully will become less frequent and shorter in duration as the person learns to live without cigarettes. This is not to say that rehabilitation professionals should accept continued substance abuse as being unavoidable. Rather, this is to say that the process of recovery from an SUD differs from one individual to the next, and that relapse is a constant danger against which both the client and the therapist must be on guard.

One motivational factor against relapse is the client's assessment of the alternatives to continued substance use (Heyman, 2009). Clients will reassess the benefits and consequences of abstinence differently at each stage of the recovery process (Cunningham, Sobell, Gavin, Sobell, & Breslin, 1997). If the client's assessment that the benefits of abstinence do not outweigh the perceived benefits of continued substance use, that person is unlikely to abstain from alcohol or illicit drugs. The treatment professional must thus continually discuss the client's perception of benefits and consequences of continued substance use throughout the rehabilitation process. Another goal of the rehabilitation professional is to enhance the individuals' belief in their ability to make major changes in their life[7] such as learning how to abstain from drugs or alcohol.

The model suggested by Prochaska et al. (1992) appears to apply both to those individuals who seek professional assistance in learning how to abstain from chemicals and to those who recover from an SUD without professional assistance. Upon reflection, this makes sense, because "natural" recovery from an SUD is the norm rather than the exception (Bennett & Golub, 2012; Heyman, 2009; Walters, Rotgers, Saunders, Wilkinson, & Towers, 2003). This should not be interpreted as meaning that every SUD will spontaneously remit and at this point in time it is impossible for mental health professionals to identify those people whose SUD will spontaneously remit and those who will be unable to quit without assistance. However, both "natural" and "assisted" recovery work toward the same goal—abstinence from substance abuse. It is only logical that they would follow the same process and similar steps to reach that common goal.

Nowinski (2003) suggested an alternative model of recovery to the model suggested by Prochaska. The first stage of the Nowinski (2003) model is that of acceptance. This might be achieved either by the individual reaching the decision that the consequences of further substance abuse outweigh the perceived benefits or through participation in a self-help group such as AA.[8] If professional assistance is utilized to help the individuals recover from their SUD, they have the option of utilizing either outpatient or inpatient rehabilitation programs. The goal of all of these programs during this stage is the same: to assist the client in accepting the reality of his or her SUD and the pain and harm caused by this disorder. It is also imperative that the client understand that willpower alone will not guarantee abstinence from alcohol or drugs. Indeed, this belief may be utilized to avoid actual acceptance of the individual's SUD. "I can deal with it on my own" is a common refrain heard by health care professionals, as is the claim that "I know that I can do it on my own, this time." It is not until the individual has reached the second stage of recovery in the Nowinski (2003) model, that of surrender, that he or she becomes willing to begin to make the lifestyle changes necessary to support recovery. This is often a difficult step for alcohol or drug abusers to achieve. Because of their denial, they tend to believe that they have an inordinate amount of control not only over themselves, but also over their SUD. Surrender does not come easily to one who strives to be in charge of one's life, and quitting involves a commitment to do so in spite of the discomfort involved in this process. During this stage, the substance abuse rehabilitation professional works to help the client both recognize the impact of the SUD on both self and others, and to learn how to accept powerlessness as a step toward recovery. This is not always an easy process, even if the client is well motivated. It is much more difficult to accomplish when the clients are unmotivated to recognize or accept the need to change unhealthy behaviors in their lives especially when they are involuntarily mandated into treatment.

Reactions to Stage Models of Recovery

The stage models of recovery discussed in this chapter have not met with universal acceptance. Few new theoretical constructs are accepted without criticism, review, modification, and possibly extensive revision.

---

[7]"Regulate" can also mean "abstain from the use of" as abstinence is a form of self-regulation. This does not mean that the confidence in one's ability to change is the only element of recovery from an SUD. However, such recovery is unlikely if the individual does not believe that it is possible.

[8]Discussed further in Chapter 34.

In the field of psychology, stage models tend to pass through several stages as follow before final acceptance:

1. A phase of uncritical acceptance following the introduction of the new model which after time gives way to
2. guarded criticism offered about possible problems with the new theoretical model. Over time,
3. the criticism increases in volume and frequency until the theoretical model is awash in a sea of hostility, which results in
4. The theoretical model being relegated to the archives or textbooks as an illustration of the process under consideration, since there are exceptions to the progression postulated by the theoretical model. Finally,
5. the model is accepted as a general outline of a process within which there is individual variation.

To use an analogy, compare the reaction to Albert Einstein's original paper on the theory of relativity in 1905. His theory was scorned because he was only a patent clerk in Switzerland who had the audacity to think that he could solve this vexing problem. Initially only a few people in the field of theoretical physics could understand his theory and the mathematical proof that supported it. However, with the passage of time it received greater acceptance and is now the theoretical solution to the problem of how matter and energy are related to each other.

In the field of substance abuse rehabilitation, stage models such as those discussed in this text are often viewed as holy gospel. In reality, such models are "at best descriptive rather than explanatory" (Davidson, 1998, p. 32). One person might remain in a given stage of recovery for months or even years. Another person might make rapid progress through that same stage in a matter of weeks. It is not that the model of change is incorrect, but rather it is a reflection of the average individual's progression down the path to recovery. Each individual differs in his or her level of motivation, history of past efforts to change, intrapersonal and interpersonal resources towards meaningful personality change.

Although the stages-of-change model suggested by Prochaska (Prochaska et al., 1992) has an elegant beauty suggesting that it is accurate and true, it has received only limited support from research scientists. Gossop, Steward, and Marsden (2007) found in their study of recovering heroin addicts, for example, that there was little correlation between their actual progress and the various measures of readiness to change. Indeed, Gossop et al. (2007)

found that the patients with the highest measured levels of readiness to change tended to be using the highest levels of heroin at the end of the 1-year follow-up period! This may reflect a greater measure of desperation on the part of heroin addicts who were unable to change, or it might indicate that the current stage models of change are not applicable to every form of SUD. There is obviously a need for further research in this area.

Then What Works in Predicting Recovery from SUDs?

One of the most frustrating tenets of substance abuse rehabilitation work is the expectation that the people in treatment for the abuse of a compound(s) are automatically the same as the people who are not in a rehabilitation program. This bias has distorted both clinical research and the development of rehabilitation models because it ignores the fact that many, perhaps a majority, of the people with a SUD, never seek professional assistance for their SUD (Heyman, 2009). Many persons with an SUD "mature out" of their chemical use disorder, as evidenced by the research findings that almost 50% of those people who met the diagnostic criteria for substance dependence in adolescence or young adulthood did not report even one sign of a current SUD in the past 12 months by the age of 24, and by the age of 37 this figure had increased to 75%!

This raises an interesting problem: We do not know what factors predict recovery from an SUD, mainly because only a minority of those people with a SUD actually are ever admitted to a treatment program. Those who are admitted to a rehabilitation program are possibly the least likely to be able to discontinue their substance use (Heyman, 2009). Generalizations from those people in a substance abuse rehabilitation program to all people with an SUD might be ill advised. We simply do not know how to answer the question posed at the start of this section. With that caveat in mind, it is possible to tentatively state that there are a multitude of factors that interact to support, or detract from, the individual's recovery efforts. It has been found, for example, that "ongoing environmental factors can augment or nullify the short-term influence of an intervention [program]" (Moos, 2003, p. 3). Many of these factors, such as a substance abusing spouse, simply lie outside of the counselor's control. Unfortunately, many substance abuse rehabilitation professionals overestimate the impact that their treatment program might have on a given client. It has been found that "relatively stable factors in people's lives, such as informal help and ongoing social resources, tend to play a more enduring role" (Moos, 2003, p. 3) in assisting the person's recovery efforts. Treatment might best be envisioned as the foundation for a recovery program, not that it will turn the client's life around and save her or him from utter destruction.

The foundation on which a client's recovery might be established appears to include:

Interpersonal Relationships: Individuals who drink more have been found to have few interpersonal resources to draw upon for support.

Cognitive Reappraisals: Many former drinkers report that their realization that alcohol was causing physical, emotional, and emotional damage to their lives was the point when they decided to stop drinking.

Demographic variables: Individuals who drink more tend to come from lower socioeconomic groups, which may provide fewer social supports necessary for recovery.

Severity of the SUD: Physical problems, health issues, or legal problems may serve as warning signs that the individual has started to reach problematic levels of substance use.

Involvement in AA or religious groups: This may help the individuals better understand the damage that their SUD has caused, while providing social support for recovery.

Individual expectations and self-valuation: This will help to shape the individual's perception of recovery, his or her perception of barriers to recovery, and self-concept issues that might assist or undermine recovery efforts.

A further factor that should be considered is the congruence between the individual's expectations and goals and those of the therapist. A client who wishes to attempt to be a "social drinker" might not participate in a rehabilitation program with a counselor who insists that abstinence is the only possible outcome for therapy. Individuals who do not view themselves as being capable of abstaining from a chemical(s), or who utilized a drug(s) to make themselves numb to feelings of low self-esteem, might have trouble in a recovery program until these issues are adequately addressed. There are so many variables that can influence a given individual's recovery program that only general statements about the "path to recovery" can be made.

Should Abstinence Be the Goal of Treatment?

This question is fiercely debated. The philosophy of the vast majority of substance abuse rehabilitation programs is that total abstinence from all drugs of abuse is the only acceptable goal. In contrast to this stance only a small percentage of those persons in treatment actually want or achieve total abstinence: Many will state that they wish to find a way to control their substance use without becoming addicted to a drug(s). Thus there is a conflict between the outcome expectations of the client and those of the rehabilitation program almost from the moment that the individual enters treatment. Admittedly full abstinence from alcohol or illicit drugs reduces the possibility of interpersonal conflict, health care problems, legal problems, and the financial strain inherent in purchasing a drug(s) of abuse. However, until the client accepts the goal of total abstinence from alcohol or the drugs of abuse, the potential for conflict over the goals of treatment exists. However, there are age differences in the willingness to accept abstinence as a treatment goal. The team of Rawson and Ring (2008) found, for example, that for people over the age of 25, abstinence appeared to be the superior goal and yielded the highest success rates. For people under the age of 25, abstinence-based goals did not appear to improve the success rate for treatment, for reasons that could not be determined from their data. This is consistent with the observations of George E. Vaillant (1995, 1996; Vaillant & Hiller-Sturmhofel, 1996) who, in his work with alcohol-dependent individuals found that rather than maintain abstinence the subjects in his studies tended to alternate between periods of abstinence and more or less problematic drinking.

The method(s) by which the success or failure of a rehabilitation program achieves this goal is evaluated in terms of client abstinence rates from alcohol or drugs at the end of a given period (usually 3, 6, or 12 months). However, usually such assessments reflect more the ideology of the assessor more than the results of sound scientific research (Muir, 2008). Thus, should the treatment center force its goal for total abstinence as a goal for a client who does not share this objective?

If so, how should this goal be introduced to the client in a manner that does not immediately cause resistance? The approach suggested by McLellan (2008) of accepting rehabilitation as a form of disease management, similar to how physicians attempt to control diabetes or hypertension, is more appropriate.

Specific Points to Address in Substance Abuse Rehabilitation

During the rehabilitation process, there are a wide range of issues that must be resolved to successfully work with the client with an SUD. The first, as noted above, is whether total abstinence should be the appropriate goal. Another issue is whether the initial substance abuse rehabilitation program should be carried out on an outpatient or inpatient basis. The answer to these questions varies, depending on the substance(s) being abused, the length of time that the individual had abused that substance, past health history, past treatment history, and his or her expectations for the rehabilitation program. In the next section we will review some of the more pertinent points to address when working with a person who abuses each of the following chemicals.

Alcohol

Substance abuse rehabilitation professionals need to work with the client to (1) identify consequences of their AUD, (2) assess its impact on not only themselves but also on their families and significant others, (3) determine whether they thought that abstinence was a worthy goal in light of this understanding, and (4) determine what factors motivated the individual's use of alcohol or might serve as a barrier to recovery. A client who says "I am here only to please my probation officer" has identified a significant barrier to recovery (no desire to do more than achieve a degree of impression management), for example. The therapist in this case must assist the client in building a desire to change for personal reasons, not because of external pressure.

A significant problem that asserts itself not only with alcohol but with all of the substances of abuse is the illusion of control. A client might go into a bar while on "pass," and drink only soda that evening interpreting this as evidence that he or she has achieved the ability to control desire to drink. This problem is discussed in more detail in Chapter 33, but in brief this

client is at high risk for a major relapse. The next time that this individual enters a bar, she or he might only have one or two beers without suffering any adverse consequences. On these grounds the individuals might dismiss everything that they learned while in treatment, setting the stage for an ultimate relapse.

Narcotic Analgesics

Simple detoxification from narcotics is not the answer: Ninety percent of those opioid-dependent people who only completed a "detox" program return to the abuse of chemicals within 6 months (Schuckit, 2006a). The goal of abstinence for a person addicted to a narcotic analgesic is one that depends on the length of time that the person has been addicted, personality characteristics, and their motivation for a drug-free lifestyle. A person who has only recently become addicted to a narcotic and who is highly motivated to abstain will present a different clinical picture than the person who has been addicted to narcotics for the past 10 years, and who is only interested in a methadone maintenance program.[9]

Although opiate abusers deny this fact, the opiate use disorders are a significant contributor to the problem of premature death in around the world (Hser, Hoffman, Grella & Anglin, 2001; Whiteford, Degenhardt, Rehm, Baxter, Ferrari, Erskine, Charlson, Norman, Flaxman, Johns, Burstein, Murray & Vos, 2013). In light of this grim reality, the substance abuse rehabilitation counselor has only a limited number of options: (a) help the client work towards total abstinence, (b) participate in an opiate replacement program, or (c) participate in a harm reduction program. While narcotic agonist replacement therapies[10] are not a perfect solution to the problem of narcotics addiction, such programs do at least offer the promise of helping the individuals to control their craving for opioids while they address other life issues. Further, as research has demonstrated, approximately one-third of opioid-dependent people will eventually become free of narcotics after an extended struggle with their SUD. Thus, the question that faces substance abuse rehabilitation counselors and their clients is whether to focus on achieving a substance-free lifestyle or enter into an opioid agonist treatment program. Unfortunately there are no known genetic markers to identify those individuals who are most likely to benefit from one of the

---

[9]Discussed in Chapter 32.

[10]Discussed in Chapter 32.

options outlined above or form of rehabilitation that would be best suited for a given individual.

CNS Stimulants

Unfortunately, there are no proven genetic markers to identify those individuals who are at high risk for the development of an addiction to a CNS stimulant(s). There is also virtually no research into the factors that might contribute to, or protect against, the development of a CNS stimulant use disorder. Traditionally, addiction to the CNS stimulants is not in itself grounds for admission to an inpatient "detox" facility. Exceptions to this rule include the possibility that the individual has a potentially life-threatening medical condition(s) caused or exacerbated by his or her abuse of CNS stimulants, suicidal depression, concurrent addiction to other compounds that might require inpatient detoxification. A qualified health care professional should assess each client, keeping in mind that the client's state of mind, past history of suicidal thinking or attempts, current medical status, support systems, and history of success or failure at past detoxification attempts, all help to determine the client's specific needs for a given level of care.

It is important to keep in mind that CNS stimulant withdrawal proceeds through both an acute and an extended withdrawal phase. Some of the emotional and physical problems experienced during both the acute and extended withdrawal phases may serve as relapse "triggers" for the client, and thus must be addressed by the attending health care staff. However, available evidence suggests that for those individuals who are able to remain abstinent from CNS stimulants such as cocaine for 12 weeks, up to 80% will remain drug-free for the first 6 months following treatment. But as will be discussed in Chapter 33, even people with extended periods of abstinence will find suddenly themselves experiencing periods of "craving" for CNS stimulants, usually in response to external stimuli associated with past substance abuse (songs, smells, physical appearance of a person seen in passing, and so on).

One very real problem for the counselor working with a CNS stimulant abuser is that the individual often has forgotten what a drug-free lifestyle is like. Also, addictive behaviors develop to help the individual come to terms with feelings of hopelessness (Dodes, 2013) and the person will need to learn new methods of addressing these feelings without falling back to the

use of CNS stimulants. These life experiences underscore the need for relapse prevention[11] training as well as a referral to social support groups, ancillary treatment service such as those discussed elsewhere in this text such as AA, Narcotics Anonymous, Cocaine Anonymous, or one of the emerging faith-based support groups.

Marijuana Abuse

Although it has been estimated that only 10% of those who abuse marijuana eventually become addicted to it, marijuana addiction is still a very real phenomenon. It is difficult to convince adolescents or young adult abusers of this danger and it is rare for a person with an SUD to abuse only marijuana. Further, it is rare for a person who is addicted to marijuana to present for treatment, unless there is some form of external coercion.

Total abstinence from all drugs of abuse is thought to be imperative when working with the marijuana abuser or addict (Smith, 2001). Compounds that cause any of the psychoactive effects of marijuana would reawaken memories of marijuana use, and thus serve as a relapse "trigger." Further, because many individuals use marijuana as a way to cope with negative feelings, rehabilitation professionals must help the client learn non-drug-centered coping mechanisms for these negative feelings. A complete assessment of the client's motivation for marijuana use and the development of alternative coping mechanisms for these problems are imperative. Ancillary support services such as community-based support groups are also of value.

Smoking Cessation

This topic is reviewed in Chapter 16. The task for the counselor working with the individual who is attempting to quit smoking is to provide sufficient support during the most critical phase of smoking cessation— the first 96 hours. The counselor should also monitor the client's progress and be ready to offer situationally specific interventions to help the individual cope with weak moments. The phases of smoking cessation are outlined in Chapter 16.

Anabolic Steroids

It is important to keep in mind that the individual's motivation to abuse anabolic steroids is rarely the

---

[11]Discussed in the chapter "Relapse and Other Problems Frequently Encountered in Substance Abuse Rehabilitation."

same as that seen in other drug abusers. The individual's motivation for abusing these compounds will need to be identified. For example, the anabolic steroid abuser who believes that these compounds will enhance her or his physical appearance will present with a different motivation than the steroid abuser who wishes to build muscle strength.

Medical supervision of the steroid abuser is mandatory. The physician can order blood and urine tests that, although they do not directly indicate anabolic steroid abuse, do strongly hint that the patient has continued to abuse these compounds. The physician is also in the best position to confront the anabolic steroid abuser, who might otherwise dismiss a substance abuse rehabilitation professional's attempts at intervention with a wall of denial and medical jargon that the counselor is ill prepared to refute. The physician on the other hand can identify specific test results that warn of cardiac, liver, or other organ damage induced by the abuse of these compounds, and dismiss the client's semi-informed rationalizations of harmlessness with the "facts."

A very real problem in working with anabolic steroid abusers is that many of the complications caused (or exacerbated) by these compounds do not appear until years after the individual started to abuse them. A high school football player, for example, will often dismiss warnings that the anabolic steroids can exacerbate the buildup of atherosclerotic plaque. These problems are decades away, at least in their opinion, and winning is everything, is it not? As was discussed in Chapter 20, adolescents (and young adults) do not process information about the dangers associated with substance abuse in the same manner that older adults do and the substance abuse rehabilitation professional needs to keep this in mind when working with a steroid abuser.

The client's motivation for abusing steroids should be identified, and the possibly of co-existing disorders (such as body image problems) should be explored and such issues addressed as necessary. Proper nutritional guidance will often prove to be a valuable adjunct to rehabilitation as the client learns that he or she can achieve many of the same desired effects without the use of steroids. Group therapy with other recovering anabolic steroid abusers may prove to be of value. Community-based support groups may also prove useful, but there are very few such support groups devoted only to individuals who have abused anabolic steroids.

Hallucinogen Abuse

Individuals who abuse hallucinogens rarely have the same motivation as do alcohol or narcotic abusers. Although many of the hallucinogenics may induce a sense of euphoria, abusers tend to point to their desire to induce sensory distortions as the main reason why they use these compounds. Some hallucinogenic abusers believe that they are more creative when under the influence of these compounds, a source of motivation that is virtually never seen in narcotic analgesic abusers, for example. Although the potential danger(s) of hallucinogen abuse is limited,[12] the use of these compounds does impact psychosocial functioning and is illegal, and these are factors that the rehabilitation center staff might wish to emphasize in working with clients who abuse these compounds.

Chapter Summary

In this chapter, two different stage models of the recovery process were identified and discussed. The most popular model was introduced by Prochaska et al. (1992). This model suggests that although progress is not linear, individuals who wish to make behavioral change(s) move from a pre-contemplation period, in which no behavioral change is being considered, into a phase where the individual is starting to consider the possibility of a behavioral change, known as contemplation. The individual may remain in this stage for a number of months, or even years, thinking about the possibility of attempting a major behavioral phase "one of these days," but without firm plans to do so starting on a specific date.

Individuals in the contemplation phase struggle with a vague sense of dissatisfaction with their present life circumstances. Fully 80% of people with an SUD are in the first two stages of this model, and only a small percentage of those with an SUD move to the action phase. It is during the action phase that the person attempts to make the behavioral change(s) being contemplated. After achieving a substance-free lifestyle for at least 6 months, the individual enters the maintenance phase, working to identify and develop behavior(s) that will assist in maintaining the behavioral change(s) achieved to date. The maintenance phase blends into the termination phase after about 5 years

[12]MDMA's effects on memory being an exception to this rule.

of abstinence. Only 20% of those who move beyond the contemplation phase ultimately reach this phase, underscoring the need for more research into the factors that motivate the person to move from one stage to the next.

Also discussed were some of the factors that might support the individual's attempt at abstinence and factors specific to each class of drugs of abuse that rehabilitation professionals must consider in working with clients abusing those compounds.

CHAPTER **32**

Pharmacological Interventions for Substance Use Disorders[1]

Introduction

Pharmacotherapy, or the utilization of select pharmaceuticals to treat a specific condition, often is employed in the treatment of the substance use disorders. Pharmaceutical companies, however, have not demonstrated any significant interest in developing agents specifically for treating persons with substance use disorders (SUDs) in part because they view this market as being too limited (Ciraulo, 2004; Nutt, Robbins, & Stimson, 2005). Further, there is significant evidence that suggests that the major pharmaceutical companies are reducing their efforts to develop new psychopharmaceuticals (Nierenberg, 2010). This is unfortunate as such treatments are often valuable adjuncts to the rehabilitation process (Lukas, 2006; Rounsaville, 2006), which when combined with traditional cognitive behavioral psychotherapy appears to increase the individual's potential for a successful treatment outcome (Koski-Jannes, et. al., 2013).

Most of the pharmaceutical agents currently in use to treat the SUDs are compounds originally developed to treat other conditions and were by chance found to be also useful as adjuncts to treating the SUDs (Ciraulo, 2004). The use of these compounds in substance abuse rehabilitation programs is often classified as "off label"[2] applications, which have not been adequately examined by the pharmaceuticals company and which leave the prescribing health care provider vulnerable to malpractice suits should there be an unfortunate outcome when such compounds are used. There is thus little evidence suggesting that new addictions-specific pharmaceuticals will soon be developed or introduced, and even less evidence that many of the compounds being used "off label" will be subjected to efficacy and safety studies for the treatment of addictions by the pharmaceuticals company that developed them for the treatment of mental illness. Thus, it is imperative that health care professionals have a working knowledge of some of the more common pharmacological interventions used to treat the SUDs, their original intended purpose, and how they are being used "off label" to help physicians treat persons with SUDs.

---

[1]The information provided in this chapter, like the information provided in the rest of this text, is intended to illustrate the manner in which certain medications are used by physicians to treat illicit drug use. It is neither intended nor should it be used as a guide for the treatment of any given individual(s).

[2]See Glossary.

The Theory behind Pharmacotherapy of SUDs

Lukas (2006) identified several subgroups of medications that might be utilized as adjunctive treatments for SUDs: (1) medications that control withdrawal symptoms, (2) medications that control the individual's "craving" for drugs, (3) aversive agents that cause dysphoria when certain compounds are used, (4) compounds used to treat concurrent psychiatric disorders, (5) agonist compounds used in certain "maintenance" programs, and (6) medications used to treat drug overdoses. Only minimal discussion of the 4th category of compounds, psychopharmaceuticals used to treat mental illness, will be included in this text.[3] All medications discussed in this chapter fall into one or more of the categories suggested by Lukas (2006). A very real danger in using pharmaceuticals to treat an SUD is that the patient will become "enamored" (Washton & Zweben, 2006, p. 103) with pills. Their use might thus be, for at least some substance abusers, an extension of their "addictive thinking" rather than an adjunct to treatment. Finally, not every patient will require pharmaceutical support for her or his recovery program, whereas others will reject such adjunctive aids (Harris, Kivlahan, Bowe, & Humphreys, 2010). So, although pharmacotherapy is often useful, it is not a panacea for the treatment of the SUDs. In the next sections we will examine the pharmacological treatments of various SUDs.

Pharmacological Treatment of Alcohol Use Disorders

There are two subcategories of medications used in the treatment of alcohol use disorders (AUDs): (1) the medications used to control the symptoms of the alcohol withdrawal syndrome, and (2) aversive agents that cause dysphoria when the individual ingests alcohol. An emerging category are those agents that will reduce or eliminate the individual's desire to drink. We will begin our discussion with the medications used to control the alcohol withdrawal syndrome.

Pharmaceutical Treatment of the Alcohol Withdrawal Syndrome (AWS)

Currently, the benzodiazepines are accepted as the treatment of choice for controlling the symptoms of the AWS (Bayard, McIntyre, Hill, & Woodside, 2004; Daeppen et al., 2002; Mariani & Levin, 2004; McKay, Koranda, & Axen, 2004). Physicians use these medications to first control the withdrawal symptoms and then to safely titer the dose down over a period of time so that the patient avoids most of the discomfort and risks associated with the AWS. The intermediate or long-acting benzodiazepines are the compounds of choice, as they avoid the danger of "rebound" withdrawal symptoms caused by between-dose variations in the blood benzodiazepine levels. Some physicians advocate the use of diazepam,[4] lorazepam, or chlordiazepoxide to control the AWS.

However, there is a minor controversy about how the benzodiazepines should be employed for the control of alcohol withdrawal symptoms. Some physicians advocate a fixed-dosing regimen in which a specified amount of the selected benzodiazepine is administered on a schedule, such as an oral dose of 50–100 mg of chlordiazepoxide every 6 hours, with an additional dose of 25–100 mg administered every hour until the withdrawal symptoms are controlled. Then, over a period of days the dosage level is reduced until the patient is medication free. If diazepam is used, the dosage level is usually between 5 and 20 mg every 6 hours until the symptoms are controlled, although in an extreme case a daily accumulated dose of 2,000 mg/day might be necessary to control the AWS (Bayard et al., 2004).

Most physicians now advocate a symptom-driven approach to the pharmacological treatment of the AWS (McKay et al., 2004). Symptom-driven withdrawal programs allow for the dose to be adjusted depending on the patient's observed symptoms, resulting in significantly lower daily total benzodiazepine dosage level (Bayard et al., 2004; Spiegel, Kumari, Petri, 2012). If the patient should experience higher levels of agitation or hallucinations, a low dose of an antipsychotic medication such as haloperidol can be added to the patient's regimen to further augment the pharmacological support being offered to the patient (Bayard et al., 2004). Unfortunately, benzodiazepine-induced disinhibition might be mistaken for alcohol-withdrawal

---

[3]There are a number of textbooks on psychiatry that provide excellent discussions of how these compounds are applied to the treatment of mental illness, and if interested in learning more about these compounds, the reader is advised to seek information through these sources.

[4]The benzodiazepines are discussed in more detail in Chapter 7.

disinhibition, resulting in larger benzodiazepines doses being administered to try and control the disinhibition mistakenly attributed to alcohol.

There is some research evidence suggesting that the anticonvulsant medication carbamazepine might be a safe alternative to use in treating mild to moderate intensity AWS. This medication has been used for this purpose in Europe with great success (Bayard et al., 2004). The initial dose utilized is 800 mg, and then this is reduced by 200 mg/day over the next five days (Bayard et al., 2004). An advantage of carbamazepine over the benzodiazepines is that it is not sedating, and like the benzodiazepines appears to reduce the individual's "craving" for alcohol during the withdrawal process.

The team of Addolorato et al. (2007) suggested that the compound baclofen might be useful both during the acute withdrawal phase as well as during the post-withdrawal phase. This compound functions as an agonist at the gamma-aminobutyric acid$_b$ (GABA$_b$) receptor site, which has the effect of lowering the individual's sense of "craving" for alcohol during the withdrawal and immediate post-withdrawal phases. The initial research study results look promising, but must be replicated.

Pharmacological Treatment of the Alcohol Use Disorders

In spite of the terrible damage wrought by the AUDs, it is surprising to learn that (a) only a minority of people with an identified AUD receive pharmacological support for their efforts to abstain from alcohol (Harris et al., 2010) and (b) there are only four medications specifically sanctioned for the treatment of the AUDs (Johnson, 2010; Sherman, 2008): (a) disulfiram, (b) oral naltrexone, (c) injected extended release naltrexone, and (d) acamprosate. Other compounds have either "off label" applications of medications used for other purposes to treat the AUDs, or are being investigated as possible agents to use in treating AUDs. Arguably these compounds have met with limited success, and there is research under way to identify new compounds that might be of value in treating the AUDs, it should be noted that to date there are no criteria to identify those people who would benefit most from pharmacological treatment(s) for the AUDs or which pharmacological agent(s) would be most appropriate for different individuals (Aldhous, 2010).

Disulfiram

At the 1949 annual meeting of the American Psychiatric Association, the team of Barrera, Osinski and Davidoff (1949/1994) presented a paper on using the medication Antabuse® (disulfiram[5]) as an antidipsotrophic[6] compound. The compound would cause "unpleasant effects" when mixed with alcohol the authors suggested, and as such seemed to show promise in the treatment of AUDs. These "unpleasant effects" were discovered quite by accident by workers in rubber factories who were experimenting with disulfiram as a possible way to vulcanize rubber. Many of these workers would stop off for a drink or two after work, only to become violently ill from an unsuspected interaction between the alcohol and the disulfiram ingested through their skin (Bohn, 2001).

A few years later, researchers searching for a way to treat worm infestations in animals administered disulfiram to the animals, and then went to have a few drinks with coworkers before going home. Like their counterparts in the rubber industry, they also experienced an unpleasant effect between the alcohol and the disulfiram that they had inadvertently absorbed through the skin. A veterinarian observed the interaction and suggested that perhaps disulfiram might be useful in treating alcoholism (Bohn, 2001). It was developed as such a medication and is the oldest antidipsotrophic medication in use (Sherman, 2008).

Clinically, disulfiram is a prodrug[7, 8] that must be biotransformed into another compound before it has the desired effect (Swift, 2010). The metabolite of disulfiram[9] interferes with the biotransformation of alcohol by destroying the enzyme aldehyde dehydrogenase. Aldehyde dehydrogenase is an enzyme that breaks down acetaldehyde, an intermediate metabolite produced during the alcohol biotransformation process. Normally, acetaldehyde is broken down very rapidly in the drinker's body. Without aldehyde

---

[5]This is the generic name.

[6]Literally, *anti-dipsomania*, a term popular in the 19th and early 20th centuries for alcoholism. Both terms are obsolete.

[7]See Chapter 3 and the Glossary.

[8]Few people actually are aware of this fact. The compound that it must be biotransformed into is S-Methyl N,N-diethyldithiocarbamate (MeDDC), which is a metabolite of disulfiram (Swift, 2010).

[9]For the rest of this chapter we will simply refer to this compound as disulfiram.

dehydrogenase, acetaldehyde, which is about 30 times as toxic to the body as alcohol, builds up in the body causing discomfort to the drinker (Moalem & Prince, 2007). As the acetaldehyde levels increase further into the toxic range, the drinker will experience facial flushing, heart palpitations, a rapid heart rate, difficulty in breathing, nausea, vomiting, and hypotension (Sofuoglu & Kosten, 2004; Schuckit, 2006). The disulfiram/alcohol reaction can be fatal, especially in cases where the individual has ingested large amounts of alcohol or is sensitive to the interaction effects of these compounds. Thus, immediate medical treatment is necessary to help ensure the drinker's survival.

Under normal conditions, it takes 3–12 hours after disulfiram was first ingested before it can block the alcohol biotransformation process. Thus, physicians usually prescribe a 3–5 day "loading dose" period in which the medication is administered daily, to establish a therapeutic blood level of disulfiram in the patient's blood. When a patient whose disulfiram level has reached a therapeutic level ingests alcohol they will usually experience the interaction within about 30 minutes of the time that they first began to drink. Because of its long half-life, disulfiram is usually administered only two, or three, times a week after the loading dose period. On rare occasions it is administered daily. Disulfiram remains fully effective for 24–48 hours, and in most cases there is no alcohol–disulfiram interaction after 6–7 days; although there are reports of such reactions taking place 14 days after the patient's last use of disulfiram in rare cases.

The alcohol–disulfiram interaction continues for 30–180 minutes, although there are isolated cases where this interaction has continued for longer than this. It must be stated again that the alcohol–disulfiram interaction effect can be fatal, and patients with this condition should be brought to a hospital emergency room for assessment and medical support, as needed. Factors that influence the strength of the alcohol–disulfiram interaction include: (a) the length of time that the person has been taking disulfiram, (b) the duration of time since the last dose of disulfiram was ingested, (c) the amount of alcohol ingested, and (d) the individual's biochemistry. As with any other medication, the biochemistry of some people is such that their bodies biotrans-form disulfiram more rapidly than the average person, weakening the alcohol–disulfiram effect.

Because it takes a number of days for disulfiram to be totally eliminated from the body, many clinicians believe that disulfiram will provide an additional source of support for the drinker in early abstinence. This allows the drinker time for "second thoughts," and a possible recommitment toward the goal of abstinence. To help patients understand the consequences of mixing alcohol with disulfiram, some treatment centers advocate a learning process in which the patient receives a "loading" dose of disulfiram over the course of several days, and then is allowed to ingest a small amount of alcohol. This will induce the alcohol-disulfiram interaction effect under controlled conditions, in the hopes that the drinkers will then be less likely to carry out this experiment on their own after discharge from treatment.

Disulfiram, like all pharmaceutical agents, has an extensive list of side effects. Before 1970, mega-doses of disulfiram[10] were used, causing such side-effects as delirium, depression, anxiety, mania, and psychotic reactions. The recommended dose of disulfiram has been drastically reduced to only 250–500 mg per dose since then; however, it is recommended that patients with diabetes, hypothyroidism, cerebral damage, epilepsy, nephritis, or women who are pregnant do not use disulfiram (Gitlow, 2007). At the dosage levels currently in use, identified side effects include skin rash, fatigue, halitosis, a rare and potentially deadly form of hepatitis, peripheral neuropathies, hallucinations, and potential damage to the optic nerve (Schuckit, 2006; Tekin & Cummings, 2003). There are also indications that it may exacerbate the symptoms of schizophrenia and may interfere with male sexual performance. Further, disulfiram is not recommended for elderly patients because it may contribute to cardiovascular problems for these patients (Drew, Wilkins, & Trevisan, 2010; Klimstra & Mahboub, 2010).

There are a number of potential disulfiram-medication interactions that need to be considered. It potentiates the effects of the anticonvulsant medication phenytoin,[11] and patients with a seizure disorder who take phenytoin should consult with a physician before taking disulfiram to avoid the danger of medication toxicity (Monthly Prescribing Reference, 2008). Disulfiram also potentiates the effects of oral anticoagulants, a matter of some concern for patients who are

---

[10]In case you wanted to know, these dosage levels were 1–2 grams per dose (or 1,000 to 2,000 mg per dose).

[11]Often sold under the brand name of Dilantin.

receiving anticoagulant therapy, as well as the antibiotic isoniazid. The use of alcohol is contraindicated in patients receiving (or have recently received) metronidazole, to avoid a disulfiram-like interactional effect. This is important because there are many "hidden" alcohol preparations such as elixirs, certain foods, or aftershave products that might inadvertently trigger a disulfiram-like interactional effect when used by the individual.

There are many other problems associated with disulfiram's use as an adjunct to treatment. Medication compliance is difficult: Only 20% of those prescribed disulfiram take it as prescribed (Myrick & Wright, 2008; Rounsaville, 2006). Researchers have attempted to develop disulfiram implants that would provide a long-term supply of medication that could be absorbed over extended periods of time; however, research has failed to demonstrate that these preparations result in any significant increase in abstinence rates over the traditional oral forms (Bohn, 2001). Because of its limited effectiveness, and the danger of disulfiram-induced side effects, its use is becoming increasingly rare (Standridge & DeFranco, 2006). It has been found that disulfiram is no more effective than a placebo as a support to abstinence (Bohn, 2001; Carroll, 2003; Mariani & Levin, 2004; Sofuoglu &Kosten, 2004). This lack of effectiveness may be due, in part, to the fact that disulfiram does not reduce the individual's "craving" for alcohol in the early stages of abstinence.

Naltrexone

It has been found that alcohol ingestion causes the release of endogenous opioids within the brain's "pleasure center," especially the mu opioid receptor. It is thus logical to assume that any compound that blocks the mu receptor will reduce the individual's incentive to drink. There is mixed evidence that naltrexone, a mu opioid agonist, achieves this effect (Mariani & Levin, 2004). Initial expectations for naltrexone as the "magic bullet" that would control urges to relapse have failed to be supported by subsequent research (Swift, 2010). One study found that 50% of patients on naltrexone relapsed within the first 12 weeks (Kiefer et al., 2003). A number of studies have failed to find any benefit from naltrexone in preventing relapse back to active alcohol abuse (Mariani & Levin, 2004). Further, there is evidence of a dose-dependent toxic effect on the liver, limiting its use for patients with some form of liver damage.

There is some evidence suggesting that naltrexone is of limited value in the treatment of a subform of alcohol dependence known as "reward" drinkers. Such individuals crave alcohol, and when they give in to these cravings and drink, they experience a profoundly rewarding experience. Naltrexone blocks the reward cascade, thus reducing the incentive for these individuals to consume alcohol (Myrick & Wright, 2008). This would explain why, although naltrexone does not prevent the initial "slip," it does appear to reduce the chance that the "slip" will become a full-blown "relapse" (Volpicelli, 2005). There is also evidence suggesting that individuals with a familial history of AUDs may be more likely to benefit from naltrexone than patients who do not have a familial history of an AUD, although the mechanism for this effect is not known at the present time (Gilman, Bjork, & Hommer, 2007).

Medication compliance with naltrexone is a problem. Forty percent of patients prescribed this medication discontinue taking it within 30 days, and 60% within 90 days (Carroll, 2003). To address this issue, a time-released form of naltrexone has been developed and marketed under the brand name Vivitro® (Prescribing Information, 2006). This form of naltrexone is injected once a month, but whereas it helps to control the "craving" for alcohol in the early stages of recovery, its high cost prohibits its use by many patients (Garbutt, Kranzler, O'Malley, Gastfriend et al. 2005).

Acamprosate[12]

Acamprosate (sold in the U.S. under the brand name Campral®) has been used by physicians as an aid to the treatment of AUDs since 1989 (Hunter & Ochoa, 2006). Acamprosate is derived from the amino acid taurine, which itself has effects similar to those of alcohol (Stahl, 2008). Like ethyl alcohol and taurine, acamprosate inhibits the glutamate receptors while enhancing GABA receptors. This compound appears to limit the release of glutamate both during and after the period of alcohol withdrawal. This appears to be accomplished through a drug-induced alteration of the calcium channels in neurons, slowing the responsiveness of those neurons to stimulation (Carroll, 2003; Hunter &

---

[12]The chemical name for this compound is *calcium acetylhomotaurinate*. We will use the term *acamprosate* as this is the name most commonly used in the United States for this compound.

Ochoa, 2006; Mariani & Levin, 2004; Overman, Teter, & Guthrie, 2003). This action both blocks some of the rewarding actions of alcohol and limits the "craving" for alcohol reported by many alcohol dependent people in the early stages of recovery (Stahl, 2008).

Acamprosate has a limited side effect profile, and there is no evidence of a "rebound" effect when it is discontinued (Hunter & Ochoa, 2006). There has not been evidence of acamprosate abuse. Its safety profile even allows it to be used during acute alcohol withdrawal (Gual & Lehert, 2005). There are no reports of drug interactions between acamprosate and other pharmaceuticals, including disulfiram (Overman, Teter, & Guthrie, 2003). Between 10 and 17% of patients started on this medication will experience transient diarrhea, which usually resolves within a few days (Hunter & Ochoa, 2006; Standridge & DeFranco, 2006). Other rare side effects include depression, nausea, drowsiness, dry mouth, and increased sexual desire (Hunter & Ochoa, 2006). It is excreted virtually unchanged by the kidneys (Overman, Teter, & Guthrie, 2003). There is some evidence suggesting that it might improve sleep during the early stages of recovery (Stanner et al., 2006). This is an advantage, because sleep disturbance is a common complaint in patients in the early stages of recovery.

Unfortunately, medication compliance is a problem because this medication must be taken three times a day. Further, the clinical evidence supporting the use of acamprosate is limited, with some studies finding no difference in abstinence rates between those patients who use this pharmacological support and those who do not (Anton et al., 2006; Gitlow, 2007; Swift, 2010). Thus, further research must be carried out to determine whether acamprosate has a role in the treatment of AUDs, and, if so, how it might most effectively be utilized.

The compounds just discussed are those that are approved for the treatment of AUDs. In the section that follows, we will examine some of the compounds that are thought to be of value, or that are being examined as a possible pharmaceutical aid to the recovery from AUDs.

Topiramate

This medication was originally introduced for the control of epilepsy. When used as an "off label" treatment for alcohol dependence it is thought that topiramate enhances the effects of GABA in the brain, blocking the rewarding effects of alcohol and thus the individual's incentive to drink (Johnson et al., 2008; Mariani & Levin, 2004; Sofuoglu & Kosten, 2004). Preliminary studies do support this theory (Paparrigopoulos, Tzavellas, Karaiskos, Kouriaba, & Llappas, 2011). The team of Baltieri, Daro, Ribeiro, and de Andrade (2008) found for example that 67% of their research sample had remained abstinent at the end of 4 weeks of treatment, 62% remained abstinent at the end of 8 weeks, and 46% were still abstinent at the end of 12 weeks of treatment. All three of these abstinence figures were significantly better than those achieved with naltrexone or a placebo, the authors reported.

It has also been found that patients on topiramate had a significantly lower level of those liver enzymes that are elevated when the liver is damaged as compared with those persons who did not receive this medication (Johnson et al., 2008; Rubio, Martinez-Gras, & Manzanares, 2009). These studies would suggest that topiramate might be a valuable asset in the pharmacological treatment of AUDs in younger adult drinkers. However, because topiramate can induce cognitive impairment in older drinkers and presents other side effects that might make the patients or their physician reluctant to use it (Drew et al., 2010; Shinn, & Greenfield, 2010).

Baclofen

Experimental research suggests possible value in alcohol dependence, because it is not hepatotoxic (Addolorato et al., 2007). It appears to reduce alcohol withdrawal distress at least as well as diazepam (Addolorato et al., 2007). However, the long-term effectiveness of this compound in treating alcohol dependence is still being explored. The team of Garbutt, Kapmov-Polevoy, Gallop, Kalka-Juhl, and Flannery (2010) failed to find any evidence of positive clinical effect from this compound on people with an AUD. However, the research sample was small, and further research into the possible application of baclofen in the treatment of persons with an AUD needs to be carried out.

Aripiprazole

Aripiprazole, an agent used to treat both psychotic disorders as well as the bipolar disorders. It has been considered as an "off label" compound for the treatment of the AUDs. However, this medication has been found to reduce alcohol's ability to induce euphoria through its ability to block dopamine receptors There is a need for further research into the possible role of aripiprazole in the treatment of the AUDs.

Nalmefene

This is an opioid antagonist similar to naltrexone in terms of its chemical structure (Mason, Salvato, Williams, Ritvo, & Cutler, 1999). However, nalmefene has a longer half-life than naltrexone, and it also binds more effectively at the mu, kappa, and sigma receptor sites, which are the neurotransmitter receptor sites that are thought to be involved in alcohol-induced euphoria. This would suggest that this compound is at least as effective as naltrexone as a pharmacological support for the treatment of the AUDs, but there has been little interest in exploring the application of this compound in this manner.

Buspirone

Initial research suggested that buspirone might have value as a pharmacological support of the treatment of AUDs. However, subsequent research has found that buspirone is only of value for individuals who had a pre-existing anxiety disorder and were abusing alcohol as a form of self-medication (Mariani & Levin, 2004).

Metronidazole

Metronidazole is an antibiotic compound that was considered as a possible adjunct to the treatment of the AUDs in the 1970s. This medication, when mixed with alcohol, will induce a disulfiram-like response. However, subsequent research has failed to suggest that metronidazole is effective as an antidipsotrophic[13] medication (Hester & Squires, 2004).

Lithium

In the last decades of the 20th century, there was a great deal of research into the possible use of lithium to treat the AUDs. Lithium is an element that has been found useful in the treatment of the bipolar affective disorders.[14] Early research was promising, but subsequent research failed to replicate the early research

evidence, and it is generally assumed that lithium is only of value for those individuals who have a concurrent AUD and a bipolar disorder.

Ondansetron

This compound has been used to treat early-onset alcoholism in Europe with some success (Johnson et al., 2000). It is based on the theory that early-onset alcoholism might be the result on a serotonergic system dysfunction. Ondansetron is an experimental 5-HT$_3$ blocker. The 5-HT$_3$ receptor site has been found to be involved in the subjective experience of alcohol-induced pleasure. So, by blocking this receptor subtype it would be possible to reduce the individual's incentive to use alcohol because the drinker would derive no pleasure from the alcohol use. A disadvantage of this compound is its relatively short half-life. The individual must take it twice a day, with the result that the drinker could discontinue its use a day or so before drinking, with minimal to no drug-induced blockage of the 5-HT$_3$ receptor. At this point, ondansetron remains an experimental compound.

Selective Serotonin Reuptake Inhibitors (SSRIs)

Given the theory behind the use of ondansetron as a 5-HT$_3$ blocker, one would assume that the SSRIs would also be useful in the treatment of the AUDs. Unfortunately, these compounds have proven to be ineffective in the treatment of the AUDs, unless the patient should have a concurrent depressive disorder (Bohn, 2001; Mariani & Levin, 2004).

Varenicline

There is preliminary evidence based on research studies in which this compound (sold under the brand name of Chantix® for smoking cessation) was found to also be useful as an aid to alcohol use cessation. The team of McKee, Harrison, O'Malley, Krishnan-Sarin et al. (2009) found that heavy drinking persons who also smoked were less likely to smoke when given varenicline than were those who received a placebo. They also reported having fewer periods of "craving" for alcohol. The authors found that 80% of their research sample did not drink during the study period, as compared with only 30% of those who received a placebo, suggesting that there is need for further study into varenicline as a possible aid to alcohol use cessation.

---

[13]See Glossary.

[14]Formerly known as *manic depression.*

Prazosin

There is some evidence supporting that prazosin, an alpha-1 adrenergic antagonist, might be useful in the treatment of alcohol dependence (Simpson et al., 2008). This compound is normally used to treat hypertension and is sold under a variety of brand names. A research study involving only 24 subjects did find that those people who received this medication reported drinking fewer days of the week as opposed to the control group, although there was no difference between the two groups as to the amount of alcohol consumed per session.

Antihypertensive Agents

Adjunctive treatment for the alcohol withdrawal syndrome often involves the use of medications more traditionally used as antihypertensives. Clonidine, one such compound, limits autonomic nervous system hyperactivity, which is often seen in the AWS. The various ß-blocker compounds also limit central nervous system overstimulation, and are thought to reduce the period of time required for benzodiazepine support during the AWS (Greenberg, 2010).

Phenobarbital

This medication is an alternative to the benzodiazepines, and like the benzodiazepines also has the additional advantage of reducing the possibility of withdrawal seizures during the AWS (Greenberg, 2010).

Section Summary

Although the search for pharmacological agents that might assist the alcohol-dependent person abstain from future alcohol use is limited, there is evidence that some current, and experimental, compounds might assist the individual in this task. Major pharmaceutical companies, however, are not committed to the search for such compounds, and if such a medication were to be found it probably will be as an incidental finding for a pharmaceutical introduced for another disease state. Further, there is a danger of "mission creep" (Aldhous, 2010, p. 43), which is to say that if a new medication were to be proven effective in the treatment of the AUDs, then physicians might be tempted to say to a patient "You show signs of possibly having an AUD, so let's put you on this medication as a precaution." Another form of "mission creep" is when the diagnostic criteria become less strict, allowing the number of potential patients who could legitimately be prescribed a new medication to increase.[15] Finally, there are no diagnostic criteria that can be used to identify those individuals who might best benefit from pharmacotherapy for an AUD (Aldhous, 2010).

Pharmacological Treatment of Amphetamine Use Disorders

At this point, there are no known, reliable, pharmacological treatments for the amphetamine use disorders (Haney, 2008; McLellan, 2008; Jayaram-Lindstrom, Hammarberg, Beck, & Franck, 2008). Scientists are exploring a number of lines of research in an attempt to identify such a compound(s) (Ling, Rawson, & Shoptaw, 2006; Winslow, Vorhees, & Pehl, 2007). Although the amphetamines and cocaine are both classified as CNS stimulants, it should be pointed out that medications under investigation for possible use in treating amphetamine addiction might not work for persons addicted to cocaine, nor would the reverse automatically be true (Haney, 2008).

Bupropion

Initial clinical trials have indicated that this compound might help to block the "craving" that many amphetamine abusers, especially methamphetamine abusers, experience in the early stages of recovery. Further research to confirm these initial research studies is ongoing at this time (Rawson & Ling, 2008).

Mirtazapine

The team of Colfax, Santos, Das, McDermott-Santos, Matheson, Gasper, Shoptaw, & Vittinghof, (2011) explored the use of mirtazapine as a possible adjunct to the treatment of methamphetamine addiction. The authors found a modest reduction in methamphetamine abuse levels in spite of poor medication adherence, suggesting a need for further research into the

---

[15]An excellent example of this process might be seen in the marketing and prescribing tactics used by pharmaceutical companies that produce medications prescribed for "erectile dysfunction." Over the past 20 years or so the suggested use of these medications went from men with pathological erectile dysfunction to all men who experience erectile dysfunction even if it is a normal part of aging. In receiving such a medication, those individuals with milder forms of this problem are also exposed to the dangers inherent in any medication use.

possible application of this compound to the treatment of methamphetamine addiction.

Modafinil

Modafinil, a compound sold to treat narcolepsy, appears to hold some promise in the treatment of methamphetamine abuse or addiction through its ability to activate some of the nerve pathways involved in attentiveness without initiating the reward cascade (Rawson, & Ling, 2008; Vocci & Elkashef, 2009). Further research into the utility of this compound in the treatment of the amphetamine use disorders is needed (Vocci & Elkashef, 2009).

Naltrexone

There is preliminary evidence suggesting that naltrexone can reduce the incentive to abuse amphetamines (Jayaram-Lindstrom et al., 2008). The causal mechanism for this effect is not clear; however, because naltrexone blocks the endogenous opiate receptors involved in the pleasure cascade, this might block the ability of the amphetamines to induce euphoria and thus the incentive for their use. The authors found that 62% of their research sample who were placed on naltrexone remained compliant with taking the medication, and that at week 12 of the study these subjects reported less subjective "craving" for amphetamines than did those who were not on naltrexone. Research into the possible utility of this compound in the pharmacological treatment of amphetamine addiction continues at this time (Vocci, & Elkashef, 2009).

Topiramate

As an anticonvulsant, this compound helps to normalize neural activity, especially in seizure focal points in the brain. This action suggests that it might also help to normalize neural functioning during the period of acute withdrawal from an amphetamine compound such as methamphetamine. Research into this possibility is in progress at this time (Rawson & Ling, 2008; Vocci, & Elkashef, 2009).

Gamma-Vinyl-GABA (Vigabatrin®)

This is an anticonvulsant medication approved for use in Europe, but not in the United States. It functions as a dopamine receptor antagonist in the nucleus accumbens, which is involved in the reward cascade. It is under investigation as a possible pharmacological treatment for the amphetamine use disorders at this time (Vocci, & Elkashef, 2009).

Immunological Therapies

There are also a number of studies under way attempting to use the immune system to "attack" amphetamine (especially methamphetamine) molecules in the circulation. This would prevent the amphetamine molecule from binding at the receptor site, thus preventing it from inducing any sense of pleasure (Vocci, & Elkashef, 2009; Knaresboro, 2011).

Pharmacological Interventions for Cocaine Use Disorders

At least 19 compounds have been considered as a possible pharmaceutical intervention(s) for cocaine abuse or addiction, without a single compound being found to be effective in this role (Payer & London, 2009). It is also important to point out that although both the amphetamines and cocaine are classified as CNS stimulants, there is little reason to suspect that a compound found to be useful in treating the addiction to amphetamines would automatically be effective in treating cocaine addiction (Haney, 2008).

At one point researchers thought that the antidepressant medication might help control post-cocaine "craving," but research did not support this expectation (Kosten & O'Connor, 2003).

Another medication that is being examined as a possible pharmacological support for the treatment of the cocaine use disorders is Baclofen, a muscle relaxant that is apparently able to reduce the individual's emotional responsiveness to conditioned cocaine use cues (Kampman, 2005). Finally, the anticonvulsant topiramate also appears to have a modest effect in helping to prevent a relapse back to active cocaine use following detoxification (Kampman 2005).

Experimental Pharmacological Interventions for the Cocaine Use Disorders

In an interesting approach to the treatment of cocaine abuse or addiction, researchers have explored the use of the antipsychotic medication aripiprazole to block cocaine craving in rats, and found that the experimental animals were less likely to resume self-administration of cocaine if they received aripiprazole

(Feltstein, Altar, & See, 2007). This effect was dose-dependent, with those rats receiving the highest doses having the lowest rates of apparent cocaine seeking behaviors. Because aripiprazole blocks the dopamine receptor sites in the brain, and cocaine affects these same receptor sites, the observed effects do make clinical sense. However, further research is needed to determine whether this medication would be effective in treating human subjects with the same results as those observed in the original experiment.

Buprenorphine

The initial research studies suggested that this compound might be useful in the treatment of cocaine abuse or dependence. However, subsequent research has failed to consistently replicate the original studies, suggesting that this medication probably is not effective in the treatment of cocaine use disorders (Kosten, Sofuoglu, & Gardner, 2008). Research into the possible utility of this medication in the pharmacological treatment for cocaine is ongoing.

Clonidine

Early experimental studies have suggested that this antihypertensive might be useful in curbing cocaine "craving" (Kosten et al., 2008). Further research is necessary to replicate the initial research findings.

Desipramine

There is mixed evidence that this antidepressant compound might reduce cocaine "craving," but it is useful in treating depression in cocaine abusers.

Disulfiram

The use of disulfiram in the treatment of cocaine addiction has received mixed results. Evidence suggesting that disulfiram[16] might reduce cocaine post-withdrawal "craving" by increasing norepinephrine levels in the brain has been suggested (Sofuoglu & Kosten, 2004). This compound also functions as an indirect dopamine agonist by inhibiting the action of the enzyme dopamine beta hydroxylase. In theory, when a patient on disulfiram abuses cocaine, she or he will experience an intense feeling of dysphoria (Kampman, 2005; Rounsaville, 2006). However, the team of Oliveto et al. (2010) failed to find evidence of a positive effect in cocaine abusing opiate-dependent

patients stabilized on methadone. The authors called for further research into the possible use of disulfiram in treatment of cocaine use disorders.

Gabitril®

This is an anti-convulsant medication known by the generic name tiagabine and sold under the brand name Gabitril®. Preliminary research suggests that this compound might be of use in controlling cocaine craving during the early stages of recovery. This compounds functions as a GABA reuptake blocker, thus enhancing the sedating effects of GABA[17] during the early stages of recovery (Heidbreder & Hagan, 2005).

Immunological Methods

Researchers are also attempting to teach the body's immune system to attack cocaine molecules (Sergio, 2008; Knaresboro, 2011). This is done by attaching a foreign molecule, such as a biological toxin known to trigger a strong immune system response, to the cocaine molecules. Over time, the immune system "learns" to attack the cocaine molecules before they reach the brain, and thus before they can initiate the reward cascade in the abuser (Sergio, 2008). This approach appears to have promise, although more work needs to be done on the vaccine. The initial vaccine was found to be only 38% effective in stimulating the addict's body into producing sufficient numbers of antibodies to suppress cocaine's effects, and that these effects only lasted for about 2 months, suggesting that while this approach is promising that more work needs to be done to develop a more effective vaccine (Martell et al., 2009). However, the development of such a vaccine raises profound ethical questions: Does society have the right to force a cocaine-dependent individual to accept the vaccine, for example (Horstman, 2010). If it is discovered after the vaccine has been in use for a period of time that it can induce debilitating side effects, does the individual forced to take the vaccine have right to legal redress against the state? Further research into this treatment approach is ongoing (Knaresboro, 2011) and the ethical implications of this vaccine must be addressed.

Methadone

Animal research suggests the possibility that methadone (discussed later) might prove of value in the

---

[16]Discussed earlier in this chapter.

[17]Or, counteracting the activating effects of NMDA, depending on how you want to look at it.

Pharmacological Interventions for Substance Use Disorders

treatment of cocaine addiction (Leri et al., 2008). The authors of this study concluded that steady-state Methadone elevated the mu opioid receptor mRNA[18] expression in the nucleus accumbens and basolateral amygdala regions of the rat brain, reducing the reinforcing effects of cocaine for the experimental animals. However, the applicability of this research to humans remains unproven.

Modafinil

This compound, which is normally used to control the symptoms of attention deficit hyperactivity disorder (ADHD), has been found in an initial study to also normalize sleep patterns in newly abstinent cocaine addicts experiencing sleep problems (Morgan, Pace-Schott, Pittman, Stickgold, & Malison, 2010). The authors found that the administration of a therapeutic dose of modafinil to a small research sample in the morning resulted in increased daytime sleep latency and reduction in the level of subjective daytime sleepiness, by improving night time sleep. Further research into the effects of this compound on cocaine withdrawal and stabilization of sleep patterns in the acute phase of cocaine withdrawal are needed.

Propranolol

There also is preliminary evidence that the ß-blocker (or "beta" blocker) propranolol might also prove useful during acute cocaine withdrawal (Kampman, 2005). This is accomplished by a ß-blocker-induced reduction in the individual's sensitivity to both adrenalin and noradrenalin,reducing his or her feelings of anxiety and agitation during this period (Kampman 2005). Further research into the possible use of this compound in the treatment of the cocaine use disorders is needed.

Tiagabine

This compound is a GABA reuptake inhibitor, and has been found to reduce the frequency of cocaine use and the amount of cocaine use in research subjects over a 10-week period of time (Kosten et al., 2008). Further research is necessary to explore possible applications of this compound to the treatment of cocaine abuse/addiction.

Topiramate

Originally introduced as an anticonvulsant, this compound appears to reduce the desire to abuse cocaine,

---

[18]See Glossary.

but the original studies must be replicated to insure that it is indeed effective when used to treat cocaine use disorders (Kosten et al., 2008).

Pharmacological Treatment of Inhalant Use Disorders

There are no known pharmacological treatments specifically for the inhalant use disorders (Brust, 2004). Depending on the presence of possible comorbid conditions or inhalant-induced medical complications, a wide range of compounds might be employed to assist the individual in recovering from the abuse of these compounds.

Pharmacological Treatment of Marijuana Use Disorders

At this time, there are no medications that specifically treat marijuana use disorders (Danovitch & Gorelick, 2012; Sheff, Warren, Ketcham, & Evan, 2007). An interesting study conducted by Levin, McDowell, Evans, Nunes et al. (2004) explored the possibility that the anticonvulsant medication divalproex sodium could be used to treat marijuana abuse. The subjects in this study reported lower levels of marijuana "craving" while taking divalproex sodium, but there was little evidence of sustained abstinence from marijuana use in this research sample. The compounds buspirone, and rimonabant have demonstrated some promise in controlling marijuana "craving," although it would appear that cognitive-behavioral psychotherapy and/or behavioral psychotherapy offers greater promise in marijuana dependence (Benyamina, Lccacheux, Blecha, Reynaud, & Lukasiewcz, 2008).

Pharmacological Treatment of Narcotic Use Disorders

There are three subcategories of medications used in the treatment of opioid use disorders (OUDs): (1) medications to treat opioid overdoses, (2) medications used to control the symptoms of the opioid withdrawal syndrome, and (3) opioid agonist agents to block the opioid withdrawal syndrome. Each of these subgroups of compounds will be discussed, in turn.

Medications to Treat Opioid Overdose

The mainstay treatment is Narcan® (naloxone hydrochloride), which is a pure opioid antagonist. It is available only in intravenous form (Thompson PDR, 2011. When injected, it reverses the sedation, respiratory depression, and hypotension induced by an opioid overdose usually starting to do so within 2 minutes. Unfortunately, it has a relatively short half-life (estimated at approximately 30–80 minutes) and so multiple doses might be necessary before the patient has completely recovered from the overdose. A second side effect of Narcan® is that it will induce the opioid withdrawal syndrome at the same time that it is reversing the opioid overdose.

Narcan® is metabolized in the liver, with 25–40% of the original dose being excreted in the urine within 6 hours (Thompson PDR, 2011). In the circulation there is limited amount of protein binding, and this compound will cross the placenta into the fetal circulation.[19] It is not known at the present time whether this compound will cross over into breast milk. Unfortunately the effects of Narcan® are specific only for narcotics, so the effects of other compounds possibly ingested or injected by the patient will remain unaffected. Any known or suspected narcotic overdose should immediately be assessed and treated by a physician.

Compounds to Treat Opioid Withdrawal

The opioid withdrawal syndrome can cause some degree of physical distress to the opiate abuser. This is true for the patient who has been receiving narcotic analgesics during an extended period of medical treatment, or to the person who is physically dependent on any of the legal or illegal opioids available for abuse. In this section, we will examine the medications most commonly utilized to help control the symptoms of the opioid withdrawal syndrome.

The opioid withdrawal syndrome does not automatically mean that the patient is an opioid abuser or addict. Patients who have suffered a severe injury that requires extended use of a narcotic analgesics will go through the process of neuroadaptation,[20] for example. This does not mean that the individual is opiate

dependent but simply that the brain has adapted to the constant presence of narcotic analgesic molecules and is thus less responsive to these compounds than it was originally. Physicians often interpret patient requests for more medication for analgesia as a sign of an iatrogenic addiction, the patient who has developed some degree of tolerance to the analgesic effects of a narcotic will stop requesting dosage increases once their pain has been adequately addressed.

To minimize the patient's distress while they are being withdrawn from their medication many physicians will often set up a gradual "taper" program. This allows the individual's body to gradually adapt to the lower doses of narcotic analgesics, minimizing their physical distress. A long-acting narcotic such as methadone is often selected for this process because the extended half-life of this compound helps to avoid rapid changes in blood levels.

Methadone

Methadone is often used by physicians for the "taper" process from prescribed narcotics described in the last paragraph. It is also used to help opiate-dependent drug abusers gradually be withdrawn from their narcotics, which is essentially the same process except that in the first case the individual's body had gone through a process of neuroadaptation while in the latter the individual was physically dependent on narcotics because of self-administration of illicit compounds. The extended half-life of methadone also makes it ideal for opioid agonist treatment programs. As an analgesic it is often used to treat both cancer-related and chronic pain. Unfortunately methadone has a significant abuse potential and it is easy to overdose on methadone. Such overdoses are potentially fatal and must immediately be assessed and treated by a physician (Breggin, 2008).

Although some physicians and many members of the general public share the belief that methadone withdrawal for the opioid addict is a waste of time. This stance appears to reflect preconceived prejudice against those addicted to narcotic analgesics rather than scientific data. Methadone-based withdrawal regimens are not by themselves a form of treatment. However the various forms of pharmacological support utilized during the opioid withdrawal process increase the chance that the individual will remain in an abstinence-centered rehabilitation program for a longer period of time following the completion of the withdrawal process (Dijkstra et al., 2008). Unfortunately illicit drug abusers who complete a medication-assisted

---

[19]This is a matter of some concern, because it means that the fetus will also immediately go into opioid withdrawal if the mother was an opioid addict, even if the fetus is in utero.

[20]See Glossary.

withdrawal from opiates has a high probability of returning to illicit drug use after the completion of the withdrawal regimen.

Although it is possible to carry out a methadone "taper" on an outpatient basis, most programs for illicit drug abusers do so on an inpatient basis. Successful completion rate for an outpatient opioid detoxification regimen is only 17%, as opposed to 80% of those who are detoxified on an inpatient unit (Polydorou & Kleber, 2008). Also, there is a danger that the patient has also been abusing other compounds besides narcotic analgesics, or that the individual will attempt to intermix different chemicals to avoid withdrawal discomfort or to find an alternative combination of drugs to bring about a desired state of euphoria. Such person-directed polypharmacy brings with it the danger of an inadvertent overdose and possible death. Polysubstance abuse or addiction reduces the patient's potential for successfully completing the withdrawal sequence and of accepting a referral to a rehabilitation program. Inpatient detoxification programs minimize these dangers and reduce the possibility of medication diversion since the patient receives the prescribed dose of methadone as administered by staff. Finally, inpatient detoxification allows for medical supervision of the patients in case of unreported concurrent medical problems.

When used to help minimize opiate withdrawal symptoms in illicit drug abusers, the patient is observed until the onset of withdrawal symptoms. Then oral doses of methadone are administered in increments of 10 mg/hour until the withdrawal symptoms are brought under control (Collins & Kleber, 2004; Polydorou & Kleber, 2008). This then becomes the starting dose for the withdrawal sequence on day two, when the patient receives this same dose all at once. Perhaps, in a hypothetical case, a patient required eight 10-mg doses before his or her withdrawal symptoms were initially brought under control. On day 2 this patient would receive a single 80-mg dose, usually in the morning. Then the patient's daily dose of methadone is reduced by 5–10 mg/day until she or he is completely withdrawn from all narcotics (Collins & Kleber, 2004). Sometimes the physician will order a slower taper when the daily dose reaches 10 mg/day, perhaps reducing the individual's daily methadone dose by only 2 mg/day, a process that remains unproven in terms of patient retention (Collins & Kleber, 2004).

Patients must be reminded that when their daily methadone reaches 30 mg (or in some cases less),

they will experience some degree of withdrawal distress. There is no symptom-free withdrawal, and it is at this point that patient retention becomes a problem. Extended withdrawal regimens, some lasting up to 180 days, have been used in the hopes of improving patient retention. This approach does not appear to be more effective than the traditional 5–21 day methadone withdrawal cycle (O'Connor, 2000). An interesting approach is the slow reduction of the patient's daily methadone requirements until the individual reaches a 30 mg/day dosage level. At this point the patient is switched to buprenorphine (discussed below), and then tapered from buprenorphine over the appropriate period of time (Polydorou & Kleber, 2008). There is a need for further research into the efficacy of this approach.

Buprenorphine

This compound, used in some opioid agonist programs, has also become a popular agent for control of the withdrawal symptoms from narcotics. When used in this capacity, the patient is observed until she or he demonstrates moderate level withdrawal symptoms, a process that usually requires 8–12 hours. At that point 2–4 mg of buprenorphine is administered in a sublingual dose (Polydorou & Kleber, 2008). If the withdrawal symptoms continue for another hour, another 2–4 mg of buprenorphine is administered in a sublingual dose. Yet a third sublingual dose of 2–4 mg of buprenorphine might be necessary to control the individual's withdrawal symptoms in extreme cases. Once the withdrawal symptoms are controlled, the individual's daily dose of buprenorphine is slowly reduced (usually at a rate of 1–2 mg/day) until the "taper" is completed. It should be noted, however, that elderly patients are likely to experience periods of respiratory depression when taking buprenorphine, and thus this medication should be used with caution in this age group to avoid exacerbation of respiratory problems (Klimstra & Mahboub, 2010). It should be noted, however, that persons taking the antibiotic Rifampin® for a tuberculosis infection when on buprenorphine will experience opioid withdrawal symptoms because of the ability of Rifampin® to induce liver enzymes that speed the buprenorphine biotransformation process.

Clonidine

Clonidine was originally developed as an antihypertensive agent. It also has a mild analgesic effect, although it is rarely if ever used in this capacity

(Polydorou & Kleber, 2008). As was discussed in Chapter 11, narcotic analgesics suppress the action of the locus ceruleus region of the brain. This region of the brain becomes hyperreactive during narcotics withdrawal, contributing to the individual's distress. clonidine, which is technically an alpha-2 adrenergic agonist, helps to suppress the activity of the locus ceruleus, reducing the individual's withdrawal discomfort and withdrawal distress. However, it has been found that clonidine-assisted withdrawal by itself results in significantly higher patient dropout rates than does a withdrawal regimen in which clonidine is used in combination with other compounds (Weiss, Potter, & Iannucci, 2008). This would seem to reflect the fact that clonidine does not completely control the individual's "craving" for opioids.

Another disadvantage of clonidine-assisted withdrawal is that this compound is an antihypertensive, and can cause abnormally low blood pressure levels (increasing the risk of patient falls) in many persons. Also, many patients have learned to combine clonidine with methadone, alcohol, benzodiazepines, or other compounds to induce a feeling of euphoria. Thus, health care professionals must closely monitor the patient to insure both patient safety and minimize the danger of non-prescribed drug use during the withdrawal process.

Experimental Methods of Opiate Withdrawal

Ultra Rapid Opiate Withdrawal

In the late 1990s, the concept of "ultra rapid" opiate withdrawal was introduced. Developed at the Center for Investigation and Treatment of Addiction (CITA) in Israel, the process of "ultra rapid" detoxification from opiates is carried out when the patient is in a chemically induced coma to minimize or totally avoid opiate withdrawal related discomfort (Kaye et al., 2003; Whitten, 2006). After the coma is induced, the patient receives both clonidine and opiate antagonists, and the entire withdrawal process is completed within a single day. Although there was a great deal of media attention when this procedure was first introduced, follow-up studies have revealed that it is only about as effective as traditional methods of opioid detoxification (Collins, Kleber, Whittington, & Heitler, 2005; Polydorou & Kleber, 2008; Whitten, 2006). There is little evidence to suggest that patients who go through

this process are more likely to abstain from further opioid abuse than those who are detoxified through traditional methods, raising questions as to the need for such a costly, and dangerous, process[21] (Brust, 2004; Collins & Kleber, 2004; Kosten & O'Connor, 2003; Whitten, 2006).

Opiate Agonist Agents

The use of opioid agonist agents is based on the theory that, by blocking some of the opioid receptor sites, it will be possible to control, if not avoid, the patient's withdrawal symptoms without inducing euphoria. In this section, we will look at the commonly used opioid agonist agents.

Methadone

In addition to its role as an adjunct to opiate withdrawal methadone is the commonly utilized compound used in medication based opiate maintenance programs (MMPs). Although methadone is a potentially lethal compound if abused, when used properly by medical personnel it is relatively safe.[22] The mortality associated with methadone maintenance programs is 1,500% lower than that of untreated opiate addiction, a fact that supports its use in the control of opioid withdrawal symptoms for those who are addicted to narcotics ("Methadone Overdose in MMT," 2007). The vast majority of deaths associated with methadone use are caused by overdoses of methadone obtained from illicit sources. However, the danger of drug-drug interactions between prescribed methadone and other prescription medications can also result in a fatal reaction ("Methadone Overdose in MMT," 2007). Further even therapeutic doses of methadone have the potential to cause cardiac arrhythmias, as discussed later in the section Complications of Prescribed Methadone Use, below.

There are approximately 1,200 methadone maintenance clinics in the United States at this time ("OTPs: Past, Current, Future—Part III," 2008). Four states have no methadone maintenance programs at all in spite of the significantly higher death rate for untreated opioid addicts ("Methadone Overdose in MMT," 2007). Although this number would seem impressive, in reality only about 20% of the estimated 810,000

---

[21]There is a risk every time that anesthesia, or a drug-induced coma, is utilized, even in a hospital setting.

[22]All medications carry a degree of risk, even when used as prescribed.

opioid-dependent persons in the United States are thought to be in a methadone maintenance program at any time (Lipman, 2008; O'Brien, 2008). Access to these programs is limited: The average waiting period between the time that an opiate-dependent person applies for admission to a methadone maintenance program and final admission is 10.6 weeks.

History

The use of methadone to control the "craving" for narcotics that so often disrupts efforts at rehabilitation was first explored by Dr Dole and Dr Nyswander in the mid-1960s (Dole, 1988; Dole & Nyswander, 1965). There was a wave of heroin addiction in the United States at the time, and the standard treatment[23] had proven inadequate to meet the need for rehabilitation at the time. Dole and Nyswander (1965) suggested that long-term opioid abuse caused permanent changes in the brain's structure on a cellular level, and that these changes contributed to the addicts' experience of "craving" for opioids if they could not obtain their drugs. This "craving" was hypothesized to continue for months, or even years, after the individual's last use of a narcotic, prompting her or him to start to abuse opioids to feel "normal" again (Dole & Nyswander, 1965). The authors hypothesized that if a compound could be found that would block the individual's craving for opioids, it would then be possible for the individual to participate in a psychosocial rehabilitation program (Dole & Nyswander, 1965).

Dole and Nyswander found that subanalgesic doses of oral methadone would block the individual's craving for opioids for at least 24 hours (Kreek, 2000). However, in an excellent example of how one department of the federal government does not know what another department is doing, the Drug Enforcement Administration (DEA) threatened to arrest Dole and Nyswanger (both federal employees working for another federal agency) for conducting this line of research ("After 40 Years the Basics of MMT are Still Valid," 2005). Eventually, the DEA relented, and Dole and Nyswander were allowed to continue their research.

Pharmacokinetics and Clinical Application

It has been found that to prevent withdrawal symptoms from opioids only 25–35% of the opioid receptor sites need to be occupied (Kreek, 2000; Schottenfeld, 2008). Further, the pharmacokinetics of methadone made it possible for once-daily administration for the control of opioid withdrawal symptoms. These factors made methadone "corrective but not curative" of opioid addiction (Dole, 1988, p. 3025). In spite of its potential in controlling withdrawal symptoms, methadone does not change the individual's personality, vocational skills, or support system (Gerada, 2005). Following stabilization on methadone, the individual will still require psychosocial counseling (Dole, 1988) and it might require a number of years before significant social or vocational progress is seen (Schottenfeld, 2008).

As noted in the last paragraph, to be effective the patient must receive a sufficient dose of methadone to block "craving" for narcotics, which research has found requires a minimal dosage level of 80 mg/day (Dole & Nyswander, 1965). Unfortunately, at least one-third of existing programs prescribe no more than 60 mg/day for the program participants (D'Aunno & Pollack, 2002),[24] in spite of the observation by Virani et al. (2009) that doses of 100 mg/day are usually sufficient to control the individual's symptoms. This can cause the patient to experience subclinical withdrawal symptoms, contributing to the risk of relapse to active drug abuse. Further, consumption of four or more alcoholic drinks a day will reduce the blood methadone levels as the alcohol increases the speed of the methadone biotransformation (Borg, Kravets, & Kreek, 2009). Thus in addition to the danger of mixing two central nervous system depressants and risking a synergistic effect, the person on a methadone maintenance program must abstain from alcohol to avoid inducing subclinical blood levels of methadone through concurrent alcohol use.

When utilized appropriately, methadone maintenance programs have been found to be cost-effective, with each dollar invested in such programs ultimately providing a return of $38 to society through reduced health care costs, criminal activity, and increased employment (Clausen, Anchersen, & Waal, 2008; Zarkin, Dunlap, Hicks, & Mamo, 2005). In spite of these apparent advantages, methadone maintenance is still extremely controversial (Khantzian, 2003a).

---

[23]There were just two treatment centers for narcotics addicts in the 1960s, both controlled by the federal government. These programs essentially provided just detoxification services for opioid addicts, who in most cases returned to narcotics use shortly after their discharge from the treatment center.

---

[24]Often this is because the state legislature in the state where that program is located prohibits the use of doses above 60 mg/day.

Complications of Prescribed Methadone Use

If patients on MMPs are injured and would require analgesia, MMP participants require more of a narcotic analgesic to achieve the same degree of pain relief as opioid non-abusers (Schottenfeld, 2008; Toombs & Kral, 2005). Methadone occupies less than 35% of mu opioid receptors to block "craving" for narcotics, a level far too low to achieve significant levels of analgesia (Schootenfeld, 2008). Unfortunately, many physicians continue to dismiss the need for additional analgesic medications because she or he "is on methadone, and shouldn't need any additional medications" following surgery or injury, causing many patients on MMPs to suffer needless often extreme, pain following an accident or injury.

A second, overlapping, concern is the potential for multiple health care providers to be working with the same individual (Walley, Farrar, Cheng, Alford, & Samet, 2009). Research has found that the primary health care provider was unaware of the patient's participation in a methadone maintenance program in 30% of the cases, and in part because of this fragmentation of care 69% of patients on a methadone maintenance program were receiving concurrent prescriptions for at least one medication that could interact with methadone with potentially fatal results (Walley et al., 2009). Another important patient safety consideration is that methadone has the potential to induce or exacerbate potentially fatal cardiac arrhythmias including Torsade de Pointes (Justo, Gal-Oz, Paran, & Seltser, 2006; Roden, 2004; Tatro, 2009).[25] Periodic reassessment of the patient's cardiac risk status, including serial electrocardiogram (EKG) studies, should be carried out by the prescribing physician (Schottenfeld, 2008).

Another, often unanticipated, problem with methadone maintenance programs is the potential for insurance liability when a patient on methadone is involved in a motor vehicle accident or other incident in which another person is injured ("OTP Liability and Insurance Claim Trends—An Interview with Richard J. Willetts," 2010). Although there is little evidence that persons stabilized on methadone present a risk for impaired driving because of their methadone, the court system does not share this perspective and the prescribing clinic assumes a financial liability should there be an accident ("OTP Liability and Insurance

Claim Trends—An Interview with Richard J. Willetts," 2010). If the person is visibly impaired, this liability level is increased. Liability insurance and proper patient supervision, as well as updated information about concurrent medication use by a person on a methadone maintenance program, are essential to limit potential liability.

Application of Methadone in Maintenance Programs

Following stabilization on methadone, the patient's medication is usually administered once a day, although some of the more progressive programs allow for "split dosing" to allow the patient to take part of the dose of methadone over a span of time. This medication is usually administered in liquid form to minimize the risk of drug diversion and is often mixed with fruit juice to make it easier to swallow. Patients who meet the federal and program guidelines may be permitted "take home" dosing privileges, receiving a designated number of doses to be taken at home as per their medication schedule.

It is recommended that the patients remain involved with the MMP for a minimum period of 1 year to allow the individual sufficient time to address problems in living, and for some patients the commitment to methadone is a lifelong, again reflecting that their addiction can be arrested, but not cured. Although psychosocial support services have been found to be useful adjuncts to the individual's rehabilitation, they are rarely offered. Kraft, Rothbard, Hadley, McLellan, & Asch (1997) concluded that three counseling sessions a week for each client was the most cost-effective in helping clients abstain from heroin use. Such counseling is labor-intensive, and unfortunately most programs have become little more than drug distribution centers, some providing subtherapeutic doses of methadone whereas making no effort to provide actual rehabilitation services (Kauffman, 2003a, 2003b).

Criticism of Methadone Maintenance Programs

Dole developed the model of methadone maintenance on the theory that opioid agonist treatment was similar to the role that insulin played in the control of diabetes (Kleber, 2002). This analogy, although useful in understanding the role that methadone might play in the pharmacological treatment of opioid dependence is not automatically true. It is just a conceptual model, and does not make opioid dependence a true disease

---

[25]Discussed in Chapter 11.

state just because the analogy is useful (Marlowe & DeMatteo, 2003).

Critics of the methadone maintenance program model also suggest that it is simply switching their addiction from the drug(s) obtained from illicit sources to an addiction on a drug obtained from a legal source (Joseph, 2004; Kauffman, 2003; Kleber, 2002). Many MMP patients also abuse alcohol, or cocaine, both compounds that speed the biotransformation of the methadone. In many cases, they then claim a need for a higher dose of methadone than was originally prescribed to avoid withdrawal symptoms (Karch, 2009; Mendelson & Mello, 2008). Other participants in MMPs use these compounds while on Methadone because they find that they enjoy the mixture of these chemicals. Further, many patients on methadone maintenance programs attempt to obtain prescriptions (or illegal sources) for propoxyphene,[26] which enhances the effects of methadone and causes the user to experience a sense of euphoria. Other patients attempt to obtain benzodiazepines through either legal or illegal sources in an attempt to enhance the methadone-induced euphoria ("Dangers of Benzodiazepine Abuse during MMT," 2009). Both medications are ingested simultaneously for this reason, exposing the individual to the risk of benzodiazepine addiction, and the potential for an overdose from the combined effects of these two medications.

At the very least these observations suggest that MMPs are not the ultimate answer to the problem of opioid dependence. Dole acknowledged as much when he observed that methadone is "highly specific for the treatment of opiate addiction" (1989, p. 1880), doing little to block the euphoric effects of other forms of substance abuse. Further, it was acknowledged that medication diversion was a problem (Dole, 1995). There is antidotal evidence that some opiate-dependent people will purchase illicit methadone to carry out a methadone "taper" at home, reducing their drug dosage requirements. Finally, there is a significant dropout rate for patients in MMPs. These observations support the observation that MMPs are not the ultimate answer to the problem of opioid dependence.

Buprenorphine

This compound is a chemical cousin to morphine, and is sold in the United States under the brand name of Suboxone®. When administered intravenously it is thought to be 25–50 times as potent as morphine. A standard conversion formula is that 0.3 mg of buprenorphine has the same analgesic potential as 10 mg of morphine (Fudala & O'Brien, 2005). It can be administered through intramuscular or intravenous injections, but is rapidly destroyed by gastric secretions and so oral dosing is impossible. It can, however, be administered sublingually. It is extensively biotransformed by the liver after being administered in this method limiting its effectiveness as an analgesic. However, this characteristic, in combination with the ability to bind to the mu opioid receptor site for periods of time far beyond the time that it activates these receptor sites, makes it of value as an oral opioid agonist that can be used in much the same manner as methadone. It also makes it virtually impossible to overdose on buprenorphine (Collins & Leak, 2008).

Unlike methadone, buprenorphine does not appear to cause any delay in psychomotor or cognitive performance (Weiss, 2007). It is highly lipid bound (96%), providing a reservoir of medication that can control opioid withdrawal symptoms for an extended time (Weiss, 2007). When administered sublingually, it is absorbed by the blood-rich tissues that line the mouth. The bioavailability of buprenorphine is only 30–50% that is achieved after an intravenous dose (Donaher & Welsh, 2006). The medication that is absorbed then blocks the opioid receptor sites, acting much as methadone does in blocking the opioid withdrawal symptoms, without inducing a significant degree of euphoria. Sublingual doses of 2–8 mg/day of buprenorphine are about as effective as 65 mg of methadone (Donaher & Welsh, 2006). There is some controversy about the maximum effective dose of buprenorphine when used as an opiate agonist. Donaher and Welsh (2006) suggested that doses up to 32 mg/day in divided doses might be necessary in extreme cases (Donaher & Welsh, 2006; Sofuoglu & Kosten, 2004). However, O'Brien (2011) recommended that if the individual has not been able to control his/her drug "craving" at doses of 16+ mg/day of buprenorphine, then he or she be switched to methadone agonist treatment.

A major advantage of buprenorphine is that the withdrawal syndromes experienced when a patient discontinues this medication are not as long, nor as intense, as those seen during the methadone withdrawal syndrome (Glasper, de Wet, Bearn, & Gossop, 2007; O'Connor, 2000). Antidotal evidence would

---

[26]The legal production of which has now been discontinued in the United States.

suggest that it is better suited for patients who do not have longstanding opioid- dependence problems, and at best it is only as effective as methadone in controlling opioid withdrawal symptoms (Donaher & Welsh, 2006). Further, there is a significant problem with drug diversion, as intravenously administered buprenorphine has some abuse potential (United States Dept. of Health and Human Services, 2004). For this reason, buprenorphine is often mixed with naloxone, which will precipitate opiate withdrawal if the tablet is crushed and injected (Leinwand, 2000). Further, some centers advocate that buprenorphine only be administered in a supervised setting, so that the patient is not sent home with tablets that might later be diverted.

A major disadvantage of buprenorphine is that opioid-dependent patients must be totally abstinent from opioids for a matter of several days to avoid a drug-induced withdrawal cycle when they start buprenorphine (United States Dept. of Health and Human Services, 2004). It has also been found to interact with a wide range of other compounds, including (but not limited to) benzodiazepines, alcohol or other CNS depressants that might cause a potentially fatal drug potentiation effect. Buprenorphine has also been found to interact with many antiviral agents used to treat HIV infection (Fiellin, Rosenheck, & Kosten, 2001; Tatro, 2009). Also its use with children or adolescents has not been approved by the Food and Drug Administration, which is a problem given the growing problem of adolescent opioid addiction (Fiellin, 2008).

An interesting experimental modification of buprenorphine was reported by Bai-Fang, Sobel, Sigmon, Walsh et al. (2004). The authors utilized an experimental polymer micro-encapsulated long-acting form of buprenorphine to be injected into the user's body. This allowed for the gradual release of buprenorphine over a 4- to 6-week period of time, blocking narcotic-induced euphoria and allowing the patient to gradually discontinue the use of narcotics without significant distress, according to the authors. This method did demonstrate some promise, but has not been more fully developed as of this time.

Naltrexone

Originally this compound was developed for the treatment of the AUDs, and is discussed in this context earlier in this chapter. It also has been found to be of limited value in the treatment of opioid use disorders. Naltrexone is an opioid antagonist blocking the mu opioid receptor site. Oral doses of naltrexone are well absorbed and peak blood levels are achieved in about an hour. The half-life of naltrexone has been estimated to be between 3.9 and 10.3 hours, and clinical research suggests that naltrexone blocks the euphoric effects of abused opiates for up to 72 hours after it was last ingested. When used as an adjunct to the treatment of the opioid use disorders, 100 mg of the medication is usually administered every other day, with the patient receiving 150 mg on Friday to block opioid craving over the weekend.

The theory behind the use of naltrexone is that by blocking the euphoric effects of the opioids, the individual would have little incentive to abuse this class of medications. It does, however, present the danger of inducing the opioid withdrawal if administered before the patient has been completely detoxified from the opioids. Ling, Mooney, and Wu (2012) recommended that the individual be opiate-free for several days before he is started on naltrexone. Some opioid abusers have tried to "shoot through" naltrexone by using exceptionally large doses of opiates, placing themselves at risk for a potentially fatal overdose (Ling, Mooney, & Wu, 2012).

Although in theory naltrexone would seem to be useful in the treatment of opiate abuse and addiction, it has proven to not be a "magic bullet" for the opioid use disorders (Kraly, 2009; Ling, Mooney, & Wu, 2012). Indeed there is no unequivocal benefit from the use of this compound in the treatment of opiate use disorders (Kraly 2009). It appears to be most effective for those patients who are motivated to follow treatment recommendations. Medication compliance is a problem: The vast majority of patients started on naltrexone discontinue the use of this medication within 6 months. One reason offered by opiate abusers for discontinuing the medication is it does not make them feel "high" (Ling, Mooney, & Wu, 2012). Further, there is no suppression of opiate "craving" while the patient is on naltrexone, which often comes as a nasty surprise to the individual on this medication and this is another reason why many individuals choose not to use this medication.

In 2006 a time-release, injected form of naltrexone was introduced under the brand name of Vivitrol (Prescribing Information, 2006). The applicability of this preparation in the treatment of opioid dependence has not been determined. However, its high price would prohibit its widespread use in the treatment of opioid use disorders even if it is found to be effective in the treatment of opioid use disorders. The danger of an individual switching from opioids to other drugs of abuse cannot be ignored. Ngo, Tait, & Hulse, 2008) found that patients who had received naltrexone implants were more likely to require hospitalization for treatment of nonopioid overdoses in the first 6 months of the study, and after a 3-year follow-up period it was found that those patients in the naltrexone-implant sample were then more likely to require hospitalization for (or die from) nonopiate overdoses. The authors called for further research into their observed findings to attempt to replicate these results. Thus, the applicability of naltrexone to the long-term treatment of opioid use disorders at best remains in doubt.

LAAM

Initial research suggested that LAAM[27] was useful as an opiate agonist agent that would function much like methadone maintenance. The extended half-life of LAAM (> 48 hours as compared with methadone's 24-hour half-life) added the additional advantage that the patient would only need to come in for dosing every second or third day rather than daily as in methadone maintenance programs. Unfortunately, shortly after it was introduced, it was discovered that LAAM could induce potentially fatal cardiac arrhythmias at therapeutic doses, and the production of this product in the United States was discontinued in 2004 (Ivanov, Schulz, Palmero, & Newcorn, 2006).

Experimental Compounds for Opiate Use Disorders

Ibogaine, an alkaloid obtained from the root bark of the shrub Tabernanthe iboga, has been considered as a possible agent for the treatment of opioid use disorders. This shrub grows in certain regions of Africa and has some hallucinogenic properties (Abrams, 2003). Either because of, or in spite of, this characteristic, ibogaine is reputed to eliminate the individuals' "craving" for opioids, especially in the earliest stages of recovery (Glick & Maisonneuve, 2000). Scientists are uncomfortable with the use of ibogaine itself as evidence suggests that at high doses it can cause neural damage and induce side effects that are intolerable for many users.

However, researchers have also discovered that the major metabolite of ibogaine, a compound called nor-ibogaine, might prove useful (Abrams, 2003). This compound has a half-life of several weeks and a chemical structure that lends itself to manipulation by scientists who hope to find a way to retain its reputed benefits while avoiding the harsh side effects (Glick & Maisonneuve, 2000). An experimental compound known as 18-MC appears to accomplish this goal, but there are still many misconceptions and governmental bureaucratic hurdles that stand in the way of the clinical application of this compound, if it is found to be effective in human subjects.

Immunological Therapies

The first research into the possibility of using the body's immune system to combat heroin addiction was started in the 1970s, but the success of opioid agonist treatments such as methadone and buprenorphine put a halt to further research in this area (Knaresboro, 2011). However, researchers are now starting to again look at the possibility that the immune system could be recruited into the fight against the opiate use disorders, turning their attention first to the problem of heroin abuse/addiction (Knaresboro, 2011).

Pharmacological Treatment of the Tobacco Use Disorders

Nicotine has been shown to be the most addictive of the vast number of compounds found in cigarette smoke, and thus has been the focus of a great deal of clinical research. Several pharmacological interventions for the tobacco use disorders center around nicotine replacement therapies. This both limits the individual's exposure to other chemicals and allows for a gradual reduction in nicotine dosage levels over an extended period. However, recent research has raised questions about the long-term effectiveness of such techniques in smoking cessation (Alpert, Connolly, & Biener, 2011). The authors pointed out that statistically individuals who used nicotine replacement aids as part of their smoking cessation program were just as likely to return to the use of tobacco as were those who did not use such pharmaceutical supports as part of their smoking cessation effort. We will briefly discuss some of the more common forms of pharmacological intervention for the nicotine use disorders, in the following sections.

---

[27]Or, *L-alpha-acetylmethadol.*

Nicotine Replacement Systems

Nicotine Gum

Nicotine-containing gum was first introduced as a prescription-only compound in 1984, but later became available without a prescription (Anczak & Nogler, 2003). It was hypothesized that this would provide a safe, convenient nicotine replacement mechanism for the smoker who wished to quit. The initial research suggested that 27% of patients who utilized nicotine-containing gum were smoke-free 6 months after the start of their abstinence program. However, subsequent research has shown that the true abstinence rate for smokers who utilize nicotine-containing gum is no higher than that achieved by a placebo (Okuyemi, Nollen, & Ahluwalia, 2006).

Smokers who elect to use nicotine-containing gum either as the primary tool or as an adjunct to their smoking cessation program must learn a new way to chew the gum to gain maximum effect. The individual must learn to chew the gum once or twice, and then "park" it between the gum and the cheek for a few moments, before repeating the procedure. When this procedure is followed, 90% of the nicotine in that piece of gum is released within the first 30 minutes. However, a 2 mg piece of nicotine-containing gum will allow the user to achieve a blood nicotine level that is only about one-third as that achieved by smoking a cigarette. Although the 4-mg preparation doubles this blood nicotine level, it still falls short of the amount of nicotine released into the blood by cigarette smoking. This may result in "craving" for additional nicotine on the part of the smoker, who then discontinues the attempt to quit.

Further, nicotine-containing gum has been found to have many side effects, such as sore gums, excessive salivation, nausea, anorexia, headache, and the formation of ulcers on the gums where the person "parked" the gum. Beverages with a high acid content, such as orange juice or coffee [28] also block the absorption of the nicotine from the gum. So the former-smoker-to-be must closely monitor the form of his or her beverage intake to avoid such compounds that might negate the benefits of the gum. A recently identified danger in such nicotine-containing gum is that the nicotine in the gum might up-regulate the FOX_{M1} gene in the tissues that come into contact with the gum, increasing the individuals risk for the development of oral cancer (Gemenetzidis, Bose, Riaz, Chaplin et al. (2009).

Transdermal Nicotine Patches

Transdermal nicotine patches have been found to be moderately effective. They have been found to reduce the insomnia so often reported by smokers who attempt to quit on their own, which is an advantage. It is generally assumed that only 3% of those who attempt to quit smoking on their own will be able to do so. The 10–16% success rate of smoking cessation for the first 6 months is thus a significant improvement, but this still means that 85% of smokers who attempt to quit fail to do so on this attempt at smoking cessation. This may reflect the fact that, in contrast to the nearly instantaneous delivery of nicotine to the circulation achieved with cigarette smoking, transdermal nicotine patches require approximately an hour for blood nicotine levels to reach their peak. This time delay is hardly appropriate for a behavioral modification program designed to extinguish an undesired behavior. Finally, the blood nicotine levels achieved through the use of the transdermal nicotine patch often are lower than those achieved by the process of smoking, inducing a "craving" for additional nicotine.

However, there is a very real danger should the smokers attempt to supplement their nicotine levels by smoking. Individuals who smoke either while still wearing the nicotine patch, or within an hour of removing the transdermal nicotine patch, are vulnerable to a nicotine toxicity that may potentially be fatal. It is recommended that if the individual should feel the need for additional nicotine that he or she use nicotine-containing gum, or in extreme cases (as in a three-to-four- pack- a day smoker) multiple skin patches might be used under the supervision of a physician. The transdermal nicotine patch can cause skin irritation, and so different sites around the body should be utilized on different days. Nicotine transdermal patch use has been associated with abnormal or disturbing dreams, insomnia, diarrhea, and a burning sensation where the patch is attached to the skin. Also, whereas it might seem obvious that the user would remove the last day's transdermal patch before attaching a new one, there have been cases where the patient has left the old skin patches in place.

The former smoker is vulnerable to smoking "cues" in the first weeks and months following smoking cessation, and some patients become either psychologically or physically dependent on the transdermal

---

[28]How many people smoke cigarettes but never drink coffee?

nicotine patch. From a harm-reduction viewpoint, this is an acceptable compromise because there are over 4,500 known compounds in cigarette smoke, and only one in the nicotine transdermal patch (Gitlow, 2007).

Nicotine Nasal Spray

A nicotine-based nasal spray has recently been introduced, which is available only by prescription (Sofulogly & Kosten, 2004). The user will administer one "puff" of the spray to each nostril where the nicotine will be absorbed by the blood-rich tissues of the sinuses. The spray can be used up to 40 times a day. Within 10 minutes of administration, the blood nicotine level will reach two-thirds of the level seen when a smoker smokes one cigarette (Anczak & Nogler, 2003). Initially, it was suggested that the patients use this product for less than 6 months, in part because of a concern that they might become addicted to the nicotine spray. However, there has been little evidence that such addictions have developed (Anczak & Nogler, 2003). A degree of sinus irritation is possible from this spray, but there has been little research into whether this degree of sinus irritation is the same as that seen when an individual smokes a cigarette. Smokers who used the nasal spray were less likely to gain weight during their cessation attempt and tended to gain less weight than those who did not use the spray. Just under one-third of those who attempt to quit using this method remained smoke-free 6 months after quitting, as opposed to just 14% of those who received a placebo (Okuyemi et al., 2006).

In the late part of the 1990s, McNeil Pharmaceuticals introduced a nicotine "inhaler" for use by those smokers who were attempting to quit. The inhaler was housed in a device similar to that of a cigarette or cigar filter. This device was to be used in place of cigarettes, although it was held in the hand in a manner similar to the way that cigarettes are held. Only 4 mg of the 10 mg of nicotine in the cartridge is absorbed, and this inhaler is designed only for short-term use. Twenty-three percent of those who used the inhaler remained cigarette-free for 6 months, as compared to just 11% of those who received a placebo (Okuyemi et al., 2006).

Combination Therapies

An interesting approach was utilized by Piper, Smith, Schlam, Fiore et al. (2009), who found that although the transdermal nicotine patch was somewhat effective in helping smokers quit, the combination of oral nicotine lozenges and transdermal nicotine patches produced significantly higher abstinence rates than approaches such as transdermal patches or bupropion alone. The study did not utilize nicotine lozenges plus varenicline, which was a shortcoming of the study, but did suggest that the combination of transdermal nicotine patches and oral nicotine lozenges offered greater effectiveness to the smokers if they complied with medication dosing schedules. The authors found that medication compliance was an issue, with a positive correlation between compliance with dosing and smoking cessation.

Non-nicotine Replacement Pharmaceuticals for Smoking Cessation

Although it might be argued that nicotine replacement therapies reflect a form of "pharmaceutical" intervention for smoking cessation, in this section we will discuss nonreplacement methods of smoking cessation intervention.

Bupropion

This antidepressant's primary effects are on the serotonin and dopamine neurotransmission systems, although it has a mild acetylcholine reuptake blocking effect. Often sold under the brand name of Wellbutrin® in the United States, the side effects of bupropion have been found to control the craving for cigarettes in some former smokers. This was discovered when some depressed smokers reported feeling less "craving" for nicotine while taking this medication. Subsequent research demonstrated that 21–30% of those individuals taking this medication as an aid to smoking cessation were able to remain smoke-free for 6 months, as opposed to only 10–19% of those receiving a placebo (Okuyemi et al., 2006).

Chantix® (Varenicline)[29]

Varenicline was introduced as an aid to smoking cessation in 2006 (Alfonso, 2008). In the time since it was introduced, Varenicline has been found to be the most effective pharmacological intervention for smoking cessation currently available. It is not perfect, and there is a need for research into other pharmacological agents that might assist smoking cessation (Ebbert, 2009). Varenicline functions as a partial agonist at selected

---

[29]The generic name for this compound.

nicotinic acetylcholine receptor sites,[30] partially stimulating these receptor sites without activating the dopamine cascade necessary to cause pleasure and blocking nicotine from these receptor sites when the individual smokes (Chantix Prescribing Information, 2006). Maximum blood levels are achieved 3–4 hours after a single dose and steady-state blood levels are achieved about 3–4 days of regular use at prescribed doses (Chantix Prescribing Information, 2006). Less than 20% of varenicline is protein- bound, and the elimination of half-life of this compound is about 24 hours with 92% of this drug being excreted in its original form (Chantix Prescribing Information, 2006).

The side effect profile for varenicline includes (but is not limited to) nausea, abdominal pain, flatulence, visual problems, depression, suicidal thoughts or attempts, mood swings, vivid (sometimes frightening) dreams[31] and rare reports of angina pectoris, myocardial infarction, and gingivitis (Chantix Prescribing Information, 2006; Rogers & Pies, 2008). The Food and Drug Administration (FDA) requires a special warning for prescribers to the effect that varenicline use is a possible cause of increased aggression and possible suicidal thinking (Moore, Glenmullen, & Furberg, 2010; Price, 2009). These unprovoked thoughts or acts of violence disappeared when the medication was discontinued, and in three cases they developed again when the medication was restarted (Moore, Glenmullen, & Furberg, 2010). It should also be noted that when people with a preexisting history of depression were placed on this medication, they tended to report feelings of tension or agitation, as well as irritability, anger, continued depression, confusion, and problems with concentration during the first 3 weeks of treatment (McClure et al., 2009).

Because patients with a preexisting psychiatric history were excluded from the original product safety and efficacy trials, the relationship between varenicline use and psychiatric symptoms remains unclear according to the authors McClure, Swan, Jack, Catz et al. (2009). The team of Moore, Furberg, Glenmullen, Maltsberger, and Singh (2011) went even further by examining the methodology used by the FDA and concluding that this underestimated the true risks associated with the use of this compound. The authors noted that the FDA limited its focus to persons taking varenicline who became hospitalized for depression or following a suicide attempt, a process that downplayed the true danger associated with this medication because it did not include those cases of suicidal thinking or depression that did not result in hospitalization. Because of this the authors recommended that it not be the first choice of clinicians for persons who wanted to stop smoking. This is consistent with the 2008 decision by the Federal Aviation Administration that pilots and air traffic controllers do not use this compound in part because of its side effect profile. Obviously, varenicline "is not a panacea for smoking cessation" (Klesges, Johnson, & Somes, 2006, p. 95). The benefits appear to last only about 12 weeks, possibly because of the process of neuroadaptation to the drug's effects (Smith, 2008), and there is a need for further research into pharmacological therapies for smoking cessation.

Although the above would suggest that varenicline is not a perfect pharmacological intervention for tobacco smoking, research evidence does suggest that persons who are placed on this medication are significantly more likely to remain smoke-free at the end of 6 months as compared with persons who were placed on bupropion or those who received only a placebo (58% vs. 46% vs. 26%), suggesting that it is a valuable, although imperfect, aid to smoking cessation (Cinciripini, Robinson, Karam-Hage, Minnix, Lam,, Versace, Brown, Englemann, & Wetter, 2013).

Experimental Compounds for Smoking Cessation

Buspirone

It was once thought that buspirone might counteract the anxiety and agitation often experienced by smokers in the early stages of smoking cessation. However, subsequent research failed to support this theory, and it is not utilized as an aid to smoking cessation unless the smoker experiences high levels of anxiety during the smoking cessation process (Covey et al., 2000).

Clonidine

A number of clinicians have attempted to utilize the antihypertensive drug clonidine to control the craving for nicotine often reported in the early stages of smoking cessation. Although the initial studies were promising, subsequent research suggested that the side effects were so severe for the average user that it was not useful as an initial approach to smoking cessation (Anczak

---

[30]Technically the $\delta 4\beta 2$ receptor site.

[31]Sometimes called "Chantix dreams."

& Nogler, 2003). However, it might prove useful in the subpopulation of smokers who experience high levels of agitation when they attempt to quit smoking (Covey et al., 2000).

Immunological Approaches

Researchers have started to explore the potential for recruiting the body's own immune system defenses against the nicotine molecule, with a number of experimental vaccines being developed at this time (Knaresboro, 2011). It is possible that a nicotine-specific vaccine will be introduced in the next decade, designed to prime the body's immune system to attack nicotine molecules in the blood before they reach the brain.

Inversine (Mecamylamine)

This is an antihypertensive compound that is an acetylcholine receptor antagonist, blocking the receptor sites in the brain. This compound would then block the individual's craving for cigarettes, and has been moderately successful in smoking cessation programs, although it has not found widespread use in this application.

iSmoke®

This is an experimental method of smoking cessation, sometimes referred to as "e-cigarettes," that is available over the Internet from the United Kingdom (Thomson, 2009). The "cigarette" is based on microprocessor technology in which a computer "chip" causes the end of the "cigarette" to glow red and releases a measured amount of vaporized nicotine for the smoker to inhale. This product is available in a number of different strengths offering different nicotine levels to different users. This feature makes iSmoke® useful in smoking cessation programs, according to the manufacturer, because the user can slowly reduce the amount of nicotine being administered until he or she is cigarette-free.

There are mixed claims about the effectiveness of this device, and its use is quite controversial. Advocates point out that it does not produce the "sidestream" smoke that results in environmental tobacco smoke. They also point to the fact that it does not expose the user to the wide variety of other compounds in tobacco smoke besides nicotine, thus making it safer to use than traditional cigarettes. Detractors point out that it is heavier than a traditional cigarette and does not produce the aroma found when a cigarette is smoked

(Thomson, 2009). It also produces limited amounts of the nitrosamines, which are carcinogenic compounds found in abundance in cigarette smoke, as well as acetaldehyde produced by the small amounts of ethyl alcohol used in the iSmoke® cartridge (Thomson, 2009). The amount of acetaldehyde produced by the iSmoke® cartridge is quite small, however, and is rapidly biotransformed into metabolites that are then eliminated from the body.

Its safety or effectiveness as a smoking cessation aid has not been demonstrated, and the World Health Organization does not support the use of this product. This product is not commercially available in the United States at this time, and might be classified as a prescription-only produce for those who wish to attempt to quit smoking (Thomson, 2009). Until proven effective, this product must be considered experimental, at best.

Nortriptyline

This antidepressant is viewed as a second-line smoking cessation agent, in part because of its toxicity and potential for a fatal overdose if taken in excess. However, it might be useful in working with depressed cigarette smokers, and there is a need for further research into the potential use of this compound in smoking cessation (George & Weinberger, 2008).

Silver Acetate

This is a compound used in Europe for many years as an aid to smoking cessation. It is available as a form of chewing gum and a lozenge. When a person who has used silver acetate-containing chewing gum or lozenge smokes, they will experience a noxious, metallic taste, providing an immediate punishment that will help the smoker extinguish the desire to smoke. This compound is also quite dangerous. Massive doses can result in a permanent discoloration of the skin and body organs. Still it is being examined as a possible aid to smoking cessation.

Clozapine

Clozapine is an "atypical" antipsychotic medication that has been shown in a small number of studies to not only reduce the symptoms of psychosis, but also of substance abuse in dual diagnosis patients (Lybrand & Caroff, 2009). The use of other "atypical" antipsychotic medications as an aid to the treatment of SUD, especially in those patients with a comorbid psychotic disorder, has yielded mixed results, but also suggests that there is a need to determine whether these compounds offer any promise of assisting the substance abuser (either with or without a psychotic condition) to abstain from alcohol or the other drugs of abuse.

Chapter Summary

The pharmacological treatment of the SUDs, like the treatment of all other disease states, involves the application of selected medications to either control the manifestations of that disease, or cure it. Pharmaceutical companies often invest significant amounts of money to develop a compound(s) for these purposes, but dismiss the need to search for compounds to treat the SUDs because the market is too limited to provide a reasonable financial return on their investment.

Thus most of the pharmacological compounds in use for the treatment of the SUDs are actually medications used to treat other conditions that have been found to be also useful as a pharmacological adjunct to the treatment of SUDs.

Several subgroups of medications utilized as adjunctive treatments for SUDs were reviewed: (1) medications that control withdrawal symptoms, (2) medications that control the individual's "craving" for drugs, (3) aversive agents that cause dysphoria when certain compounds are used, (4) compounds used to treat concurrent psychiatric disorders, (5) agonist compounds used in certain "maintenance" programs, and (6) medications used to treat drug overdoses. Also, experimental methods through which the body's immune system might be trained to attack specific drug molecules for both cocaine, and possibly the amphetamines, were reviewed.

CHAPTER 33

Relapse and Other Problems Frequently Encountered in Substance Abuse Rehabilitation

Introduction

Research has repeatedly demonstrated that treatment is more cost-effective than criminal justice sanctions as a way of dealing with substance use disorders (SUDs). But it also is not a panacea, either. There are numerous problems that might arise for the client both in an inpatient or the outpatient substance abuse rehabilitation program. In this chapter, we will look at some of the more common and potentially more serious problems encountered by rehabilitation professionals working with the substance abuser.

Limit Testing by Clients

Clients in therapeutic relationships, including those with SUDs, will often "test" therapeutic limits. This is done either consciously or unconsciously by the client to determine whether the therapist can be trusted or, in some cases, if it is possible to find a way to control the therapist. Limit testing takes many different forms. The client might repeatedly miss appointments, or call to cancel a previously scheduled appointment at the last moment. Other clients might abuse alcohol or drugs while in a rehabilitation program. Such situations present the therapist with opportunities to demonstrate that "dependability" and "consistency" are part of the foundation to rehabilitation. For example, treatment programs that warn clients that a certain number of "dirty" urine toxicology test results[1] will result in discharge from that program tend to have greater success than programs that fail to set such limits.

[1]Discussed later in this chapter.

The Counselor and Treatment "Secrets"

One common method of manipulation often attempted by clients is when they request an individual conference with a staff member and then confess to a rules infraction. Sometimes such confessions are made to a student, or intern, at the rehabilitation facility. The client then begs the staff member to keep this a secret, for fear of being discharged from the program, put into jail by a probation officer who learns of this chemical use, divorce by an angry spouse, and so on. The substance abuse rehabilitation professional who honors this request then enters into a state of collusion with the client. This becomes a relationship in which the staff person, who is attempting to help the client outgrow addictive thinking, becomes an enabler of that client. Further, the client can then use the counselor's silence as leverage for blackmail ("If you don't do [*fill in the blank*], I will tell them that you didn't report my relapse last week!"). In correctional facilities, inmates often try to convince a staff person to bring contraband into the jail or prison. This also can be used as leverage for blackmail ("If you don't bring in more contraband, I will report you!"). The proper response to this problem is for the staff person to properly document the discussion immediately, in writing and through proper channels, without acting on the client's request. This either can be a memo to the facilities administration or an entry into the client's progress notes. The staff person should also discuss the revelation with his or her immediate supervisor. This is all done without malice, both to ensure uniform enforcement of the rules and protect the staff person's reputation.

A Double Standard

To illustrate the double standard applied to the field of addictions rehabilitation, consider the contrast between oncology treatment programs and substance abuse treatment programs. Cancer programs do not insist that a hypothetical person be "in remission" before being admitted for treatment of pancreatic cancer. However, it is not uncommon for alcohol and drug rehabilitation programs to require abstinence before admitting a person for treatment (Blume, 2005).[2] A person with diabetes who is repeatedly admitted to the hospital for stabilization of their medical condition is called a "brittle" diabetic. The alcohol- or drug-dependent person who relapses is called a "treatment failure" and is all too often treated as such.

Treatment Noncompliance

In no other sphere of medicine is there a social stigma attached to a failure to comply with treatment protocols. Health care professionals find noncompliance to be a source of frustration; however, there is no social stigma associated with it. Social stigma is associated with the individual's failure to comply with substance abuse rehabilitation program protocols and is often cited as evidence that treatment is not effective. This social stigma is expressed through comments that the client "did not really want to get well," "lacked

TABLE 33-1
Medication Noncompliance

CONDITION	NON-COMPLIANCE RATE
Epilepsy	30–50%
High blood pressure	30–60%
Lipid-lowering agents	25–30%
Antidepressant medication	30–40%
Immunosuppressive agents	18%
Antidiabetic medication	30–50%
Anticoagulant medication	30%
Antiasthma medication	20–60%

© Cengage Learning

motivation," "was only going through the motions to make a good impression on the judge," and so on.

Treatment noncompliance is an ongoing problem in all fields of medicine. It has been found that people with a chronic illness take their medication as prescribed only 50–70% of the time (Pegler & Underhill, 2010). For example, older people who are prescribed digoxin for their heart condition were found to have their prescriptions filled so rarely that it was estimated that they were taking their medication only 111 days of the year (Shea, 2006). Table 33-1 provides a summary of different medical conditions and the rate of medication noncompliance for that disorder.

There are many reasons for medication noncompliance. Some individuals find that the practice of taking prescribed medications is a reminder that they have developed a chronic illness, and their treatment noncompliance reflects, in part, their individuals' denial and defensiveness surrounding their medical condition (Rogers, 2008). Other factors that contribute to treatment noncompliance include: (a) health care provider's failure to inquire about treatment compliance, (b) improper tone during the adherence interview, (c) lack of financial resources to purchase prescribed medications, (d) treatment professionals' attitudes toward the noncompliant individual, and (e) assignment of blame rather than reassessment and development of a new treatment approach to the problem (Weiden, 2011).[3] Surprisingly, whereas

[2]One exception to this rule is when the person applies for admission to a methadone maintenance program (MMP). To avoid the danger of an inadvertent overdose and possible death from respiratory arrest when the applicant starts taking methadone, he or she is asked to abstain from the use of alcohol or illicit drugs before admission.

[3]Admittedly, Weiden's (2011) article addressed noncompliance issues in the treatment of schizophrenia, but the principles appear to be equally applicable to treatment noncompliance in substance abuse rehabilitation.

treatment noncompliance[4] is of obvious importance in the treatment of various medical disorders, it is rarely emphasized in the training of most physicians (Shea, 2006).

Treatment noncompliance and medication noncompliance are often intertwined: Moderate-level drinkers are less likely to have prescriptions filled than are nondrinkers (Bryson et al., 2008). The authors found that only 58% of moderate and heavy alcohol users had their prescriptions for antihypertensive and lipid control agents filled, as opposed to 64% of non-drinkers.[5] Of those advised to enter a rehabilitation program by medical professionals, less than one-third follow through with this recommendation. Clients who request "detoxification" often fail to complete the detoxification cycle because of concurrent medical problems, unwillingness to experience the withdrawal process, "urges" to abuse drugs, encouragement from others to restart drug use, and so on (Franken & Hendriks, 1999). Although 90% of heavy drinkers could be detoxified through "social" or outpatient detoxification programs, only 70% complete the process (Myrick & Wright, 2008). Of this percentage, only half go on to substance abuse rehabilitation resulting in just 35% of those who enter outpatient detoxification programs being admitted to a rehabilitation program. Rehabilitation program professionals have attempted to identify personality traits that might help in the early identification of those people at risk for premature termination of treatment, to date this search has been unsuccessful (Miller, 2003). To complicate matters, a client's willingness to enter a rehabilitation program might not reflect his or her level of motivation to make a major lifestyle change, such as achieving abstinence, but the strength of such sources of external motivation as the courts or employer mandates (Connors, Donovan, & DiClemente, 2001).

Substance abuse rehabilitation programs do suffer from significant levels of attrition. In men some of the factors associated with premature termination from substance abuse treatment programs include: social isolation, solitary drinking, not being married, having no children, and being unemployed. There has been little research into the factors that might predict premature termination from treatment for women, which is discussed in Chapter 18.

---

[4]Also called *nonadherence*.

[5]Which still means that just over one-third of nondrinkers also failed to have their prescriptions for anti-hypertensive medications filled.

Lapse and Relapse

The problem of client relapsing, or experiencing a lapse, might reflect a conflict between programmatic goals and treatment outcomes: Whereas 99% of treatment programs aspire to the goal of total abstinence, only a minority of those who graduate from substance abuse rehabilitation treatment will completely abstain from further alcohol or drug use (Leavitt, 2003). Between 50 and 90% of those treated for an SUD relapse at least once during the first 90 days following completion of a treatment program. In the case of alcohol, 45–50% will have returned to their pretreatment level of alcohol consumption within a year of their discharge from treatment (Polivy & Herman, 2002). There is obviously a conflict between the abstinence-based treatment philosophy at most programs and treatment outcomes, as evidenced by these statistics.

Another contributing problem is that there is no firm boundary between a lapse and a relapse, making these terms a source of endless confusion both to the lay public and rehabilitation professions. For the sake of this text, a lapse will be defined as when the individual initially abuses a compound after a period of abstinence, such as the first puff of a marijuana cigarette or the first swallow of alcohol. This results in a state of abstinence violation and the individual reaches a decision point: Does she or he reaffirm her or his commitment to abstinence, or continue to abuse the chemical(s)? In the latter case, the individual is said to have relapsed.

The term relapse is drawn from the medical model, and reflects a state where the person falls back into an active disease state after a period of remission (Marlatt & Witkiewitz, 2005). However, adherents of the medical model do not extend the analogy further. Significant proportions of people with serious medical conditions experience a resurgence of the disorder after achieving a period of stability if not an apparent cure. Even with the best of medical care many patients who experience a return of their disease fail to survive the relapse. In contrast, eventually 40% of people with an SUD achieve complete abstinence from recreational chemicals either alone or with professional assistance (Gitlow, 2007). To put this figure into perspective, this rate of recovery from the SUDs is almost three times that is seen with lung cancer. An additional 20% of those treated for an SUD return to periods of episodic abuse, whereas the remaining 40% go on to develop a progressive SUD that might ultimately prove fatal (Gitlow, 2007). This latter group forms the basis of the saying that the addictions can be arrested, but can never be cured (Gitlow, 2007).

Relapse prevention is defined as a self-management program designed to assist the individual in arresting his or her addiction to the best degree possible (Marlatt & Donovan, 2005). Within this context, the individual's relapse is not a sign that treatment failed any more than would a diabetic person's re-hospitalization for stabilization of his or her medical condition would be a sign that his or her diabetes treatment regimen failed. However, just as there are many reasons why a treatment program for diabetes might fail, there are many reasons why the individual in a substance abuse rehabilitation program might relapse. The team of Witkiewitz and Masyn (2008) concluded after their analysis of 563 individuals, who had relapsed to active alcohol use, that there were three different paths following the initial lapse: Following the initial relapse, the first group engages in infrequent, moderate alcohol use. The second group were those individuals who initially engaged in heavy alcohol use, but whose frequency of alcohol use gradually became less and less frequent over time. The final group were those people who returned to a pattern of heavy alcohol use and continued to drink abusively. Surprisingly, the majority of their sample reported returning either to total abstinence or to infrequent and moderate alcohol use following their lapse back to drinking (Witkiewitz & Masyn, 2008). The authors also found that coping skills at the time of the individual's first lapse was positively related to less frequent and less intense alcohol use at the time of relapse.

It has been suggested that relapse is triggered by one or more of the following mechanisms: (1) drug exposure (either to the same or other compound), (2) stress exposure, or (3) cue re-exposure (environmental cues previously associated with substance use) (Boles, 2007; Clay, Allen, & Parran, 2008). Remember: Different neural circuits are involved in the initiation of substance use and those that contribute to a relapse (Leamon, Wright, & Myrick, 2008). Thus situations that contributed to the initiation of use (and thus activation of certain neural networks) are not the same as those neural networks that might contribute to the continuance of substance use after a relapse. These are problems that must be anticipated and addressed in the latter stages of treatment.

Drug exposure may be unintentional (such as a recovering smoker rounds a corner outside of work and encounters a cloud of cigarette smoke from coworkers).

It might be the result of a prescription from a physician (for example a former alcohol-dependent person who receives a prescription for a benzodiazepine, then relapses as a result of the similarity of effects between these two compounds). People used to using physicians for desired drugs might find the experience of being in a doctor's office for a necessary medical examination to be a relapse trigger (Washton & Zweben, 2006). Stress exposure is a frequent relapse trigger (Haney, 2008). It has been discovered that when exposed to significant levels of stress men and women will activate regions of the brain that control habit-based behaviors, not those regions of the brain involved in cognitive assessment and control (Elton & Kilts, 2009). From an evolutionary standpoint this makes sense: If the source of the stress is a predator about to attack, you might not have time to make a cognitive appraisal of the situation and thus falling back on your instincts might save your life.

Unfortunately, when faced with stress, the first response of many substance abusers might be to fall back on the habit of using chemicals to self-medicate stress. The individual might not adequately assess the situation and then select the most appropriate behavioral response, especially in the early stages of recovery. However, stress as a relapse trigger often takes unexpected forms. It is not the experience of stress that triggers a relapse but the individual's loss of hope, demoralization, and depression in the face of stress appears to activate the habit-based substance use response (Elton & Kilts, 2009; Miller & Harris, 2000). If the individual believes that she or he has the resources to deal with the demands being placed on them by life, they are less likely to break down under that stressor and relapse.

Social isolation[6] and other social factors such as living with substance abusers can function as a relapse triggers for the individual. Interpersonal problems such as marital conflict, divorce, or child custody issues[7] (Boles, 2007) might also serve as relapse triggers. Physical illness is a significant stressor, and often can induce thoughts of new chemical abuse as a way of coping with physical distress. For example, the physical sensations experienced when the person has a bad cold, or influenza, often are similar to those sensations of

---

[6]Which in part explains the need for participation in a substance-free support group.

[7]Such as when the state asserts that the parent is unfit to retain custody, for example.

unmedicated opiate withdrawal. Unfortunately, for individuals who have suffered a traumatic event, and especially those people who have developed Post Traumatic Stress Disorder (PTSD) intrusive, traumatic memories can serve as relapse triggers (Work Group on Substance Use Disorders, 2007).

Finally, through the process of associative learning, a large number of external cues are associated with substance use. One rarely recognized factor in relapse is the individual's sense of smell (Levin, 2008). Memories associated with smell have been found to have a stronger influence on memory retrieval than memories associated with the other senses (Konnikovam, 2012). Clinically, this makes sense because human evolution has resulted in a process through which the process of smelling something also activates memory centers. In ages past, being able to recognize the smell of a predator and then rapidly recognizing the smell as a source of danger would be advantageous. A side effect of this evolutionary adaptation in the present world is that smell might also trigger memories associated with substance use. For the alcohol-dependent person, for example, the smell of cigarette smoke might be associated with the experience of being in a bar, where cigarette smoking is pervasive. Surprisingly, few treatment centers even mention the possibility that smells can act as relapse triggers.

Marlatt and Wikiewitz (2005) identified a number of factors that influence the successes of the individual's recovery program:

- Self-efficacy: *The individual's confidence in his or her ability to cope with high-risk situations, thoughts, urges, and so on.*
- Outcome expectancies: *Individual expectations about the outcome of substance use, should the person relapse. Euphoric recall[8] often is activated by outcome expectancies.*
- Craving: *Although "craving" in itself is a poor predictor of relapse, it might be triggered by substance-use cues (sights, smells, sounds), that in turn trigger memories of past substance use. For example, a former smoker might see a cigarette that has been snubbed out in the bottom of an ashtray, initiating "craving" for a cigarette.*
- Motivation: *The individual's motivation for change, or commitment to change, plays an important role in whether she or he relapses or remains abstinent.*

- Coping style: *This poorly understood determinant of relapse reflects the individual's ability to call upon learned coping skills to deal with substance use cues.*
- Emotional states: *There is a strong association between substance use and relapse. Negative emotions are more often seen in cases of a full relapse, while positive states appear to be more often associated with behavioral lapses.*
- Interpersonal support: *The individual's access to a strong, substance-free, support system during times of craving contributes to continued abstinence if the individual calls upon this resource.*

For each of these forces, one must also consider the proximal [9] or distal[10] relationship of that factor to the individual's relapse (Donovan, 2005). The individual's genetic heritage might be viewed as a distal factor for relapse (Donovan, 2005; Westphal, Wasserman, Masson, & Sorenson, 2005). A hypothetical example of a more proximal relapse trigger might be the need to have blood drawn for medical testing where the feel of a needle entering the skin reawakens memories of past injected drug abuse for IV drug abusers.

Factor analysis has yielded three categories of proximal warning signs for potential relapse (Donovan, 2005): (a) cognitive factors, (b) emotional states, and (c) behavioral characteristics of the client. These factors interact within the individual, moving him or her either closer to or further from a potential relapse. Cognitive factors have also been called maladaptive thoughts[11] by the cognitive-behavioral therapies (Beck, 2004; Daley & Marlatt, 2005; Keller, 2003). Examples of such maladaptive thoughts include: "I can control it now," or "I have learned enough to avoid relapsing," or the ever-popular "I will stay out of trouble if I only bring $20 with me to the bar. I only leave when I have spent it all." Maladaptive thoughts might allow the individual to (a) convert normal sources of stress into excessive stress and justification for continued substance use

---

[8]See Glossary.

[9]Proximal forces are those in close temporal proximity to the event in question. For example, hitting a major pothole in the road might cause a driver to lose control of the motor vehicle, and thus is the proximal cause of the resulting accident.

[10]Distal forces are those that are more distant from the event in question. To use the example cited previously, the past winter's freeze-thaw cycles might have weakened the pavement, allowing the pothole to form, eventually causing the accident discussed in the last footnote.

[11]Often referred to in 12-step groups as "stinking thinking."

(example: "I cannot stand to feel this way!"),[12] (b) transform distress into craving (example: "I can't cope without using_____!"), or (c) rationalize a potential relapse as being acceptable (example: "Surely I can handle just one.") (Beck, 2004).

Another category of maladaptive thoughts reflect the individual's desire for indulgence (Blume, 2005). Many persons view substance use as a reward for past behavior(s), thus believing "I deserve a drink after all that I've done!" Other people may view substance use as a way to escape life's pressures, if only for a while. Planned or unplanned meetings with substance-abusing "friends" offer the individuals a sympathetic ear (while they indulge in substance use), and thus represent a high-risk situation for a potential relapse (Blume, 2005; Westphal et al., 2005). Such maladaptive thoughts must be identified and then the appropriate countermeasure(s) taken, to ensure that the individual can remain abstinent. The last example, for example, offers an illustration as to why a substance-free support group is so important.

Many people find that the anticipated rewards of abstinence are not as immediate as the pharmacological reward induced by the drugs of abuse. Others, faced with life's adversities without their usual substance-based coping mechanisms, become prone to relapse. A hypothetical client who has been abstinent for 6 months only to be informed that he has a serious, potentially life-threatening medical problem would be hard pressed not to at least think of returning to chemical use as a way of "coping" or of at least making himself "numb" to external reality. A second hypothetical client who, after 6 months of hard-won recovery returns home to be informed that her spouse has filed for a divorce might very well wonder where the rewards of abstinence are to be found if she is hit in the face with such realities.

Although clinical evidence has identified negative emotional states such as anger, fear, or confusion as possible relapse triggers, it is surprising to learn that positive emotional states might also serve as a relapse trigger as well. This surprising discovery reflects a process through which the individual seeks a way to ensure that the positive feelings experienced thus far will continue. Clients thus need to learn to experience life as it unfolds and not try to control or negate it by chemical abuse. Negative life events happen to us all, not just to those in the early stages of recovery, although the person in the earliest stages of recovery might not understand this fact, yet.

Another common cognitive error is when the client takes a short-term view of recovery. It has been discovered that if clients should remain abstinent for 6 years, they are unlikely to relapse. Treatment staff must thus work with the client to help them understand that they must remain on their guard until recovery becomes a lifestyle, which will take a number of years to accomplish. Like many post-surgical people, the clients in the early stages of recovery must learn not to attempt tasks that they are not ready to deal with. One possible coping technique for the individuals is to carry a card with the negative effects that they have experienced from their abuse of substances, and to review these consequences during a period of "craving" when such cognitive errors might occur. This cognitive reorientation technique will help the individual reframe a return to substance use into a negative rather than positive event.

Social pressure was found to play a significant role in the individual's return to alcohol or drug abuse by Zywiak et al. (2006). The authors based this conclusion on their analysis of data from 592 enrolled in a larger research study called "Project 'MATCH'" and found three classes of relapse: (a) negative affect or family influences, (b) craving cued relapses, and (c) social pressure. The latter category accounted for more than 58% of the identified relapse events according to the authors. The authors of this study also found that motivational interviewing procedures seemed to provide greater protection against social pressure-induced relapse events than other forms of intervention utilized in the Project MATCH study.

Spiritual issues have been found to both lead back to, or away from, continued substance abuse (Gitlow, 2007). Such issues might include the client's on-going feelings of shame, worthlessness, or not feeling "grounded," especially in the early stages of recovery. These spiritual issues often overlap with psychological stressors that can trigger a relapse. An often overlooked factor is that substance use often fills a need in the individual's life. The bar, for example, might offer social contacts for an otherwise socially isolated person

---

[12]A technique that the author of this text often calls upon when dealing with this maladaptive thought is to paint a graphic picture of $1 million in $20 bills. Then the clients are asked whether they could deal with the feeling of "craving" for 24 hours, at the end of which they would receive the $1 million dollars. If the clients say "yes," it is then pointed out to them that they have just demonstrated that they *can* deal with the stressor and how they are responding to the stressor with addictive thinking ("I can only cope with this problem by using!"). The next step is to develop a coping mechanism to cope with that form of urge to use chemicals.

who is hesitant to initiate social contact out of a fear of rejection. Thus the individual's core personality is a distal relapse trigger that may predispose some people to relapse (Donovan, 2005; Chiauzzi, 1990, 1991). Individuals who tend to have a compulsive component to their personality makeup are especially vulnerable to relapse because of psychological pressures. Such people do not react well to even minor changes in their daily routine. Dependent personalities[13] are thought to abuse alcohol or illicit drugs as a way to cope with their anxiety in social situations. Dependent people also may have difficulty refusing alcohol or drugs when confronted with people who offer chemicals to them.

People with passive-aggressive traits tend to be unwilling to accept personal responsibility for their behavior and blame others for mistakes. "He offered it to me" is a common cry after a relapse. "I did not want to be rude and not accept it!" In this manner, the responsibility is placed on the person who offered the compound in question, not on the person who relapsed. In contrast to this is the narcissistic personality. Narcissistic personalities tend to view themselves as being above the rules that govern everyday society. They are quite self-centered and have trouble admitting to weakness of any kind. These characteristics make it hard for them to ask for help if tempted to use alcohol or drugs. Finally, a number of personality subtypes struggle with impulsiveness, distrust of others, and rebellion. Many people view the traditional path to recovery as form of control being imposed on them, for example. These (and other) personality types must be viewed as distal relapse triggers that must be addressed if the client is to achieve long-term recovery.

Clients with a SUD often, when moving toward abstinence, turn to substitute addictions as a way to trigger the reward pathways once engaged by the chemical(s) of abuse. Examples of such substitute addicts include the use of other chemicals. The alcohol-dependent people might turn to beer rather than hard liquor, rationalizing this as being "safe" because of the comparatively low alcohol content of beer and the fact that they had trouble only after consuming hard liquor. People addicted to OxyContin,[14] for example, might be able to discontinue the use of opioids, but later admit that they have started to engage

in heavy marijuana abuse. There are endless ways that a person in the early stages of recovery might attempt to substitute one behavior for their SUD. The recovering alcoholic, for example, might turn to gambling, and about a quarter of recovering alcohol-dependent people eventually develop a compulsive gambling problem. Drug rehabilitation professionals must learn to inquire about such substitute addictions. Urine toxicology testing[15] is often of value in detecting unauthorized compounds in the individual's body, although the range of substances that might be detected is limited and might not detect the development of a substitute addiction.

Relapse is a process and not a single event. It is preceded by a series of subtle, often irrelevant choices known as "mini-decisions" that individually do not portend a relapse but which collectively move the individuals toward this step (Keller, 2003). Few clients are sensitive to these warning signs or the dangerous mini-decisions in the earlier stages of recovery (Daley & Marlatt, 2005). A client's decision not to have a prescription for Antabuse®[16] refilled is a decision that appears to be innocent by itself. However, in combination with other decisions (such as participation in company-sponsored softball games where beer is available), it might ultimately lead to the individual's relapse back to active drinking.

Individuals in the early stages of recovery often place themselves in high-risk situations, which expose them to both relapse cues and opportunities to use again. The client might, for example, go to a bar "to hear my brother's band play." The desire to hear a brother's band play is innocent enough. The setting where the band is working might present the person in recovery with a high-risk situation. One does not have to walk very far to obtain alcohol if that person is in a bar, and soon the soda that one is drinking pales as the person begins to remember past drinking experiences in that environment. Other high-risk situations involve interpersonal conflict (Daley & Marlatt, 2005; Keller, 2003). People who have just had a disagreement with a spouse, for example, may be in a high-risk situation if they were accustomed to using alcohol or drugs to cope with their angry feelings in the past. For some clients, the simple act of receiving a paycheck places them in a high-risk situation, as they now have money with which to buy alcohol or drugs.

One time of special vulnerability is the Thanksgiving/Christmas holiday season. For some people the stress of being around family members, their potential

---

[13]The issue of personality type is reviewed in the *DSM-IV-TR* (American Psychiatric Association, 2000), or in Sadock and Sadock, (2007), as well as in many books on psychopathology.

[14]Discussed in Chapter 11.

---

[15]Discussed later in this chapter.

[16]Discussed in Chapter 32.

TABLE 33-2
Most Common Causes of Relapse

CATEGORY	DESCRIPTION OF SITUATION	PERCENTAGE OF CASES
Negative emotional states	Patients experience feelings of frustration, anger, anxiety, depression, boredom, and so on.	35%
Peer pressure	Pressure comes from either a single person or a group of people (coworkers, for example) to resume the use of a chemical(s) (tobacco, for example).	20%
Interpersonal conflict	There is a conflict between client and a close friend, spouse, child, employer, employee, and so on.	16%
"Craving" for drugs or alcohol	Person becomes preoccupied with use of alcohol or drugs, especially in early abstinence	9%
Testing personal control	Patients expose themselves to a high-risk situation to see whether they can resist resulting urge to use alcohol or other chemicals.	5%
Negative physical states	Person is experiencing illness, post-surgical distress, or acute injury, for example.	3%

SOURCE: Based on Daley & Marlatt (2005) and Dimeff & Marlatt (1955).

alcohol use (even if on a social basis) and familial squabbles are all potential relapse triggers (Aldhous, 2009). For others, the pain of being alone over the holiday season is a potential relapse trigger. Thus, one must help the client develop coping mechanisms for dealing with the holidays without drinking by developing alternative coping plans and coping skills (such as leaving the room when others are drinking, or asking that they not consume alcohol when the individual is in the room, or going to support group meetings, for example) to help the client avoid relapsing back to active alcohol use during this time of stress.

Substance abuse rehabilitation professionals must help the client identify high-risk situations, and develop the appropriate coping skill(s) to deal with that problem. This increases the client's self-efficacy and self-confidence, although the individuals should also be warned that this does not mean that they are ready to place themselves in the high-risk situation again. A client who has been coached in alcohol-refusal skills still is not ready to go to a bar to hear a brother's band play, for example. Temptation is just around the corner, and those refusal skills might not be up to the task even if the client should call upon them. To help the client develop skills necessary for long-term recovery from alcohol, instruments such as the Inventory of Drinking Situations (IDS-100)[17] may help identify high-risk situations

for the alcohol-dependent person. Staff then can help the client learn how to cope with such problem areas. A recovering friend might be asked to attend the client to a sister's wedding, to ensure that the client does not ingest alcohol at the wedding reception. Other techniques might include having the client carry a reminder card(s) with step-by-step instructions on how to deal with the potential relapse situation, limiting the chance of a relapse. Although it is not possible to identify every high-risk situation, Table 33-2 identifies many of the more common antecedents to relapse:

It is possible to anticipate every problem area and help the client develop the appropriate behavioral coping skills for many situations, (Daley & Marlatt, 2005; Witkiewitz & Marlatt, 2004). Further, the research evidence supporting the concept of relapse prevention training has been mixed (Hester & Squires, 2004; Irvin, Bowers, Dunn, & Wang, 1999). Relapse prevention programs do seem to be of value in helping the individual cope with the sense of demoralization, anger, and depression (Miller & Harris, 2000). Further, continued involvement in "relapse prevention" programs involving both individual and/or group therapy sessions does seem to increase the individual's chances of achieving long-term abstinence (McKay, 2006). It is even possible to integrate relapse prevention work with community-based support group work,[18] to provide

---

[17]A 100-item questionnaire that will shed light on situations where the person is most likely to drink.

[18]Alcoholics Anonymous, Narcotics Anonymous, or any of the other emerging secular or faith-based support groups.

ongoing individual and group support for the individual during times of crisis.

However, these steps are not a guarantee, and even people involved in the most comprehensive relapse prevention programs will be at risk for slipping back into substance abuse, or active addiction. Unfortunately it is not uncommon for people who have relapsed to be referred to the same rehabilitation center where they were treated, and exposed to the same treatment methods used during their earlier rehabilitation program (Fletcher, 2013). If a person has proven unresponsive to a given treatment format once, there is little to be gained by exposing her or him to the same treatment process a second, third, or fourth time. In such cases "more of the same" might not be the most appropriate response to a relapse and individualized treatment programs should be established.

Acute Injury

People with SUDs are often at higher risk for acute injury than non-abusers. However, the substance-abusing person who presents with a traumatic injury presents the health care professional with many therapeutic dilemmas (Woods & Bartley, 2008). For example, if an opioid addict should present at a hospital emergency room with a broken arm, and even after the administration of a medication that would normally provide adequate analgesia requests additional pain medication, is this person drug seeking, or has the patient's pain been undertreated?[19]

All too often, pain is inadequately treated even in people with no history of a SUD. Health care accreditation agencies have recognized that pain is too frequently undertreated and have made this a priority for their attention. Thus, all patient reports of pain should be accepted, assessed, and appropriate attempts made to address the pain (Woods & Bartley, 2008). It would be immoral for the health care professional to dismiss the person's claims that she or he is still in pain simply because "she or he is only an addict," or in cases where the person is on an opioid agonist program, to dismiss the person's request for additional analgesic

medications as irrelevant because "he (or she) is already on methadone." This dismissal could prove rather embarrassing for the health care professional if the ever-so-casually dismissed pain was proven to be an indicator of a potentially treatable condition.

The client's substance abuse history will be one of the factors that will influence the person's perception of pain following an injury. Opioid-dependent people who present with a fractured arm, for example, might require more pain medication for adequate analgesia simply because of their acquired high tolerance to narcotic analgesics, a fact that is often forgotten or misunderstood by health care professionals attending to the person's needs (Woods & Bartley, 2008).

Another danger is that the use of analgesics, even if appropriate under normal conditions, may predispose that individual to a relapse if she or he were to be recovering from an SUD, especially an opiate use disorder. Thus, issues surrounding relapse prevention must be addressed immediately after the person's stabilization. Recovering alcohol-dependent people, for example, might find themselves re-experiencing some of the same sensations achieved by their abuse of alcohol if placed on a sedating agent such as a barbiturate or benzodiazepine, even if the use of this compound is medically warranted. The similarity of effects would then trigger strong urges to use alcohol again, potentially causing a major relapse on the part of the client.

Although this discussion is not exhaustive, it does illustrate how even substance-abusing people might present with legitimate complaints of pain in the acute-care setting. Unfortunately, such people have also been known to abuse health care facilities to obtain desired medications. The health care professional is thus forced to engage in a very thorough investigation to determine whether the person's complaints are real or unfounded, often in a setting where she or he has limited time to address the matter. Tests such as the Opioid Risk Tool, or the Screener and Opioid Assessment for Persons—Revised will help with this process (Jackman, Purvis, & Mallett, 2008). Even without the use of these instruments, the substance abuse rehabilitation professionals must address the issue of how the person's use of a prescribed substance for what was deemed to be a medically appropriate reason might impact his or her SUD or recovery program. This is a complicated matter, which varies from person to person and within the same person over time.

---

[19]To complicate matters, as if this author would ever do such a thing, people on an opioid agonist treatment program (methadone or suboxone) often require *more* medication to achieve a given degree of analgesia because some of the opioid receptor sites are blocked by the agonist used to control withdrawal symptoms.

The Problem of Chronic Pain in the Substance Abuser

Chronic Pain

More than 20% of the general population in the United States, or 65 million people, live with a non-cancer-related persistent (or chronic) pain disorder (CPD) (Porreca & Price, 2009; Smith, 2008). In about half of these cases, the CPD will resolve within a year. Individuals with a history of an SUD are not exempt from the problem of chronic pain. Unfortunately, there has been little research into the problem of treating CPD in persons with a history of substance abuse (Juska & Balon, 2013), making the appropriate treatment of either disorder in the person with a concurrent SUD and CPD difficult, if not impossible. About 37% of patients on a methadone maintenance program will report experiencing a CPD, whereas 60% will report some level of pain even while on methadone maintenance (Barry et al., 2009). There is virtually no clinical literature on how to assess or address these problems in the patient on methadone maintenance programs, although evidence would suggest that the treatment of coexisting psychiatric problems (depression, and the like.) will often reduce the patient's pain intensity (Barry et al., 2009).

It is imperative for health care professionals working with substance-abusing persistent pain-patients to understand that the lifestyle of the addicted people often makes them intolerant of incomplete solutions, or of lengthy treatments. "I want what I want, and I want it now!" is the mantra of a large percentage of persons with an SUD, forcing the medical staff to establish boundaries almost immediately and to rigidly enforce them. Treatment contracts outlining program rules and expectations should be a standard practice (Miller & Frankowski, 2012). Violation of this contract by a person who "only wanted some more pain relief" by taking nonprescribed medications should be considered grounds for termination of treatment. Once the word is spread that a given CPD program expects cooperation and will enforce program rules there will be fewer such cases to deal with.

A complicating problem is that people with a concurrent CPD and SUD may become pain-sensitive because of acquired partial tolerance to the pain medication(s) being administered (Chang, Chen, & Mao, 2007; Compton & Athanasos, 2003). To address this problem Miller and Frankowski (2012) identified several criteria that should suggest to the clinician that the individuals might be abusing their medication. These criteria include (1) deterioration in work performance, (2) involvement in illegal activities, (3) alteration of route of administration, (4) multiple episodes in which the individual reports "lost" or "stolen" prescriptions, (5) refusal to comply with toxicology testing, (6) concurrent abuse of other compounds, (7) use of multiple pharmacies or physicians, (8) requests for medication beyond which would normally be necessary for pain control with their condition, (9) unsanctioned dosage escalation, and (10) nonadherence to the entire pain treatment program (which might include physical therapy, and so on) but continued use of narcotic analgesics. If a person has been discharged from another pain management program for noncompliance this should raise the clinician's suspicion about similar behaviors by the client in her or his present setting. Finally, inquiries about what medications/dosages other patients are receiving, or justification for dosage increases because another person is receiving a higher dose of a certain medication, are also significant "red flags" suggesting possible medication seeking.

To assist the attending physician in making the determination as to the appropriate medication decisions, a treatment team that works together closely, is in constant contact, uses consultations with appropriate treatment professionals when needed, and the use of a treatment contract are of value. The treatment contract will specify that the person must use only one specified pharmacy and only one doctor (except in emergency situations). In the latter case, the patient-physician contact must be reported to the patient-care coordinator within 72 hours so that the treatment team can determine whether there was a legitimate need for the patient to see another doctor or not. The treatment contract should also specify that the patients will be required to submit to urine toxicology testing on a random basis at least once every 6 months,[20] and that they will be called back for "pill counts" to make sure that they are taking prescribed medications per instructions.[21]

Many physicians advocate the use of a long-term opioid agonist methadone for the treatment of CPD. The long therapeutic half-life of methadone reduces

---

[20]The urine toxicology test should utilize technology to detect synthetic and semi-synthetic narcotics often not detected by less sophisticated tests. This topic is discussed in more detail later in this chapter.

[21]Patients who should have 18 pills of a specified medication left when called back for a "pill count," but who have only 12 pills in the bottle should raise suspicion that either they are taking more than was prescribed, or are diverting medication.

the possibility that the individual will experience "breakthrough" pain, which is a common problem when other narcotic analgesics with shorter therapeutic half-lives are used. A fear among physicians treating pain-patients with narcotic analgesics is that the continued use of these medications will induce an addiction. It has been suggested that younger, male patients, those who have access to a larger supply of medication that they can take without medical supervision and those with a preexisting SUD are at highest risk for developing an opioid use disorder or of medication misuse (Edlund, Steffick, Hudson, Harris, & Sullivan, 2007). The authors recommended that those individuals at highest risk for the development of an addiction be issued smaller amounts of the necessary medications (one week's worth at a time, for example) and have frequent meetings with a health care professional familiar with the SUDs to monitor the individual's need for continued use of a narcotic analgesic.

Although narcotic analgesics are the mainstay of treatment of acute pain (<16 weeks), the effectiveness of such compounds for longer than 16 weeks is in dispute (Blondell & Ashrafioun, 2008). Researchers have isolated compounds that might potentially function as nonopioid medications to treat chronic pain on the distant horizon, however, until these compounds are proven to be effective and are available to the general physician for use with substance abusing patients with a CPD, medical professionals will have to struggle to find the right balance between use of narcotic analgesics and the individual's reported chronic pain disorder.

Controlled Drinking[22]

In England 75% of all alcohol rehabilitation programs offer assistance in helping their clients learn how to moderate their drinking. In the United States the concept of "controlled" drinking has met with skepticism. When preliminary research studies suggested that it might be possible for some alcohol-dependent people to learn to control their drinking, many people with a severe alcohol use disorder have seized these reports as justification for their continued alcohol use. Although the initial studies were promising, Miller, Walters, and Bennett (2001) found that after their discharge from

treatment 12 months earlier only 10% of test subjects were able to remain controlled drinkers. In contrast to this, other studies have found that the long-term success rate in achieving and maintaining long-term controlled drinking is less than 2% (Vaillant, & Hiller-Sturmhofel, 1996). Controlled drinking is perhaps a viable goal for individuals who are not physically addicted to alcohol, have a shorter drinking history, and who have not encountered significant psychosocial problems as a result of their alcohol use disorder. However, research has found that "stable moderate drinking [is] a rare outcome among treated alcoholics (Wallace, 2003, p. 19). People with more severe alcohol use disorders rarely remain moderate or controlled drinkers but rapidly return to their abusive drinking patterns according to the research data, and Morgan (2003) warned against a goal of controlled drinking for this subgroup of drinkers.

This conclusion is supported by the conclusions of the team of Adamson, Heather, Morton, & Raistrick, (2010), who found that the clients' stated goal of desiring to learn how to control their drinking as opposed to abstinence was a predictor of long-term success. People who worked toward abstinence were more likely to be abstinent than those who wanted to be "controlled" drinkers 3 months after treatment (22% were abstinent whereas only 13% were controlled drinkers, according to the authors). The authors also found that after 12 months 44% of those people who had stated that their goal was controlled drinking had achieved this goal, in contrast to the 71% of those people who had worked toward abstinence. However, many of those whose initial goal was controlled drinking shifted their goal toward total abstinence after encountering problems or losing control over their drinking.

However, allowing the person with an alcohol use disorder attempt to return to controlled drinking is often a useful goal in the person's ultimate rehabilitation. A failed attempt at returning to "controlled" drinking helps the client realize that abstinence is a more viable goal than attempting to return the social use of alcohol. However, the treatment professional needs to weigh the potential benefits of this experiment against the possible risks, and document in the clinical record that the clients were warned of the risks inherent in their attempt to return to "controlled" drinking, including the fact that only a minority (perhaps 1–2%) of those who attempt this are able to maintain long-term "controlled" drinking as opposed to relapsing back to abusive or addictive alcohol use.

---

[22]Obviously, because by definition illicit drugs are illegal, the concept of "controlled" use of an illegal substance is nonexistent.

Early Recovery and Sexual Activity

It is important for health care professionals to recognize that people with an SUD might have learned to associate the use of certain compounds (such as cocaine, for example) with sexual activity. Through associational learning they might have come to believe that "normal" sex involves the use of these chemicals, and find that intimacy is not as rewarding without the use of these chemicals (Gitlow, 2007). Other people might find interpersonal intimacy rather uncomfortable without using a chemical(s), possibly because of feelings of inadequacy or social anxiety. Still a third group of substance abusers have been the victims of sexual assault at some point in their lives, and they have learned to use the anxiolytic[23] effect of alcohol, marijuana, or other compounds to make themselves "numb" to the feelings reawakened by sexual contact.

For all three subgroups of people, interpersonal intimacy without the use of alcohol or illicit chemicals might prove to be frightening. Indeed, some people will have abused alcohol or illicit drugs for so long that they have no memories to guide them in a relationship without a chemical in their system. For example, a hypothetical 50-year-old father of three children might report that he has not been intimate with his wife for the last 15 years of their marriage without having some alcohol in his system, and that he is afraid of possibly being rejected by her. For all three subgroups of substance abusers, interpersonal intimacy might serve as a relapse "trigger." It is not unusual for the client to also keep these fears to themselves, in large part out of shame, or be unwilling to discuss them to an opposite-sex therapist. A referral to a therapist of the same sex who will then assess the role that alcohol or drugs have played in that person's sexual activity would be appropriate, and appropriate referrals to a licensed, experienced sex therapist, individual psychologist, social worker experienced in marital therapy, and so on should be made.

"Cravings" and "Urges"

It is interesting to note that in spite of the importance attached to the concepts of drug use "craving" or "urges" by substance abuse rehabilitation professionals, there is no standard definition of either term, nor is there an objective way to measure either construct (Anton, 1999; Ciraulo, Piechnczek-Buczek, & Iscan, 2003; Weiss et al., 2003). Different researchers use the same terms in different ways, contributing to confusion not only between professionals but also in the popular media about the experience of a drug use thought and a relapse.

A drug use thought is just that: a thought. A client who, at the end of a hard day's work, might think that "a cold one [beer] would be nice, now" has just experienced a drug use thought. The experience is transitory, as are all thoughts. Clients should be taught that such drug use thoughts are normal, especially in the early stages of recovery. These thoughts are the result of associational learning. In the hypothetical example cited previously, the client might very well have learned to associate a beer(s) with the end of the work day. In such a case, having such a thought is normal. Acting on that thought is inappropriate. We all have thoughts, and if the truth be told we all occasionally think about doing some inappropriate things ("I wonder what it would be like to rob a bank?" for example). Most of us do not act on those thoughts.

Drug craving is an intense, subjective, emotional and physical experience for the individual that varies in intensity between individuals. People might find that they are responding as they normally would if they were about to use a chemical(s), such as having sweaty palms, feeling anxious, increased heart beat, and possibly increased salivation, or the other physical sensations that they came to associate with substance use. They focus almost compulsively on drug use cues, and may view themselves as being overwhelmed by these feelings. Neurologically, this experience appears to parallel the reduction in glutamate receptor sites in the nucleus accumbens region of the brain in the early stages of recovery, as well as blood flow changes in the brain's reward system (Tapert et al., 2003; Weiss, 2005).

Thus, drug "cravings" are the subjective experience of the neurological changes taking place as the brain adapts to the absence of the drug(s) of abuse during the early stages of recovery. The craving might be triggered by an internal stimulus (a thought or physical sensation, for example) or an external drug use cue (seeing a used hypodermic needle in the gutter, for example). These drug use cues trigger a subjective experience of "craving" for the individual. Unfortunately, because of the process of neuroplasticity, urges become stronger if the individual should give in to

---

[23]See Glossary.

them even once because neural pathways (and associated receptor sites) increase when used (Schwartz & Beyette, 1996). The reverse process, extinction, will require that the brain rewire itself, a process that takes time. During this process, the individual will experience "craving" and urges to return to the use of chemicals.

Surprisingly, because craving for a chemical is a subjective experience, one individual might interpret the same symptoms of craving as intense by one person, as moderate by a second, and as quite weak by a third person (Weiss et al., 2003). The experience of craving waxes and wanes in intensity during the first 12 weeks of abstinence, and the client should be warned that their craving will be most intense during this period (Carol, Smelson, Losoczy, & Ziedonis, 2001). However, clinical experience suggests that after the first 90 days the individual's experience of craving will become less intense, and less frequent, feedback that might offer the client some hope to cling to during the early days of recovery.

It is important to keep in mind that there is a vast difference between a hard choice to abstain from chemicals, and no choice but to abuse those chemicals (Gendel, 2006). Urges and cravings are not the same as obligations to use alcohol or drugs (Heyman, 2009). Such cognitive experiences are just part of the early recovery phase. Clients should be warned both to expect them, and trained in how to respond to them.

The "Using" Dream

A common phenomenon that has not been well researched is the "using" dream. These dream experiences may be quite frightening to the person in the early stages of recovery. Lewis (2011) spoke about how "using" dreams contributed to a relapse back to opiate addiction on his part: The dream memories would cause him to ruminate about opiate use until he could not stand it any longer and had to fulfill that desire with actual drug(s). Other clients will report having awakened after having a dream in which they just used drugs or alcohol that was so intense and seemed so real that they had trouble separating reality from the dream experience for the first few seconds after awakening. Such dreams may make the client wonder about his or her commitment to recovery. As noted earlier they might also be a relapse trigger by themselves. It is thus important to warn the client

that these dreams are both common, and usually not a sign of impending relapse.

There are two types of dreams: (a) the Rapid Eye Movement (REM) dream, which accounts for about 85% of dream experiences, and (b) the Non-REM dream, which accounts for about 15% of dreams. Dreams that take place during REM sleep are noted for bizarre, intense, imagery that often makes no logical sense: A long-dead relative walks through the wall in the dream, and the dreamer simply asks "Would you like some tea?" (Doweiko, 2002). Non-REM dreams tend to be rather dull, and involve the dreamer carrying out routine tasks.

During both REM and Non-REM dreams, there is a neuromuscular blockade that prevents the body from acting on motor movement commands generated by the sensory motor region of the cortex during sleep. The brain's production of acetylcholine[24] drops significantly during dream sleep, which appears to be part of the psychomotor blockade that develops during REM sleep. If awakened, the dreamer will recall vague sensations of not being able to move normally, intense emotions, and confusing, often irrational, thoughts.

Another process that seems to take place during the REM dream is that the brain practices the "fight or flight" response. Dreaming is a safe time to do this, because the body is unlikely to act out on the motor movement commands involved in the "fight or flight" response. During REM dreams the amygdala[25] is exceptionally active, a fact that supports this theory. These fight or flight response emotional memories are intense sensations of fear and anxiety, feelings that might carry over into the dream's waking state for a few seconds.[26] In the normal waking brain it is the duty of the cortex to make sense of internal and external sensations, and if the dreamer is feeling fear, then there must be something in the dream experience that initiated that fear. Memories of substance abuse would certainly cause the dreamer to feel anxious, if they were committed to abstinence.

The outcome of these two processes is that (a) the dreamer has vague memories of not being able to move naturally in the dream, memories that closely simulate their experience(s) while under the influence of chemicals, and (b) the dreamer recalls feeling anxious, if not

---

[24]See Glossary.

[25]See Glossary.

[26]A process called *dream carryover*. Through this experience the dreamer continues to experience emotions generated during the dream during the first few seconds of consciousness.

very frightened during the dream state as the brain's neurochemical balance shifts from the dreaming state to the waking state. A relapse would be a situation that could trigger such intense emotions. Fortunately, anticipatory guidance[27] will help the client deal with such dreams. Further, as the associational memories between substance use and various substance use "cues" weaken over time, these "using" dreams will become less intense and less frequent over time. It seems rare for a client to report such dreams after the first 3 months of recovery, although on rare occasions clients will report such dreams and as having awakened with the thought on their minds "Why would I ever want to do that?"

Toxicology Testing

Urine[28]

The issue of urine toxicology testing is one of the more controversial issues in the field of substance abuse rehabilitation. Appropriate urine toxicology testing must balance the factors of (a) method of sample collection for analysis, (b) comprehensiveness (range of compounds being tested for), (c) speed at which test results are made available to assessor(s), (d) sensitivity of test procedures to detection of specific compounds, (e) possibility of "false positive" findings and (f) cost. The discussion of the method of sample collection must begin with urine toxicology testing. This procedure is relatively noninvasive, painless, allows for on-site urine sample collection. However, there are a variety of urine toxicology testing procedures, each of which offers benefits and liabilities to the assessor.

Most on-site urine toxicology tests utilize a variation of the Thin Layer Chromatography (TLC) procedure (Craig, 2004). This procedure allows for the testing of a large number of urine samples simultaneously at relatively low cost, and the results are often available in less than 2 hours. However, the results are reported only as either "positive" or "negative," and many commonly abused drugs are not detected by these tests (Craig, 2004; Franklin, 2012). This characteristic of

TLC test results might lead the assessor into a sense of false security because many assessors assume "negative" results mean that the individual did not engage in substance abuse. In reality a "negative" finding only suggests that there was no evidence of the abuse of those compounds that the test is designed to detect.

For example, although they are both classified as narcotic analgesics a TLC test designed to detect evidence of morphine abuse is unlikely to detect evidence of fentanyl[29] abuse because most such tests are designed for the detection of morphine-like compounds and fentanyl is potentially active at such small doses. Further, TLC tests require that the metabolites of the drug of abuse be present at specific concentrations[30] before the test is classified as "positive." Remember that the body is always actively attempting to eliminate all foreign molecules, and thus the concentration of the metabolites of a specific compound will change over time. If a TLC test requires that drug molecules for a hypothetical substance "A" be present at 50 mg/deciliter of urine for a "positive" result and the actual concentration is only 30 mg per deciliter of urine, the test will provide a "negative" result because the concentration is below the detection threshold.

Another urine toxicology test procedure that lends itself to rapid testing of large numbers of urine toxicology samples is one of the Immunoassay family of tests. Collins (2009) identified five different immunoassay procedures currently in use: (1) radioimmunoassay (rarely used now), (2) enzyme immunoassay, (3) fluoroimmunoassay, (4) kinetic micro-particle immunoassay, and (5) lateral flow immunoassay.[31] Immunoassay procedures use specifically designed antibodies to detect certain substances (Standbridge, Adams, & Zotos, 2010). Such tests offer the advantage of being rapid, and can be used to test large numbers of urine samples for the initial screening (Craig, 2004). However, structural similarities between certain compounds may result in "false positive" test results, a process known as cross-reactivity (Collins, 2009; Craig, 2004). As a result of cross-reactivity the reagent used to detect one class of illicit chemicals reacts to another, possibly unrelated compound. An excellent example of this is that on some tests the use of the cough suppressant dextromethorphan at

---

[27]A fancy term for helping the client anticipate that certain experiences might happen to them, so that they might mentally prepare for them.

[28]The information provided in this section is designed to illustrate the known strengths and weaknesses of toxicology tests. It is not intended for, and should not be used as, a guide for prosecution, treatment or employment sanctions.

---

[29]Discussed in Chapter 11.

[30]Called the detection threshold.

[31]The specific methodology for each procedure is rather complicated to discuss, and the reader is referred to Collins's (2009) text for more information if they are interested in this information.

therapeutic doses may result in that person being identified as a phencyclidine abuser (Mozayani, 2009; Traub, 2009).

"It is important to keep in mind," Collins (2009) observed, "that cross-reactivities and interferences may change with reagent lot changes, new formulations, and variable antibody specificity" (p. 31). Further, physical disease states such as proteinuria,[32] nitrites, ketones, or blood in the urine, as well as bacterial and fungal infections can cause nonspecific cross-reactivity between these compounds and the immunoassay procedure being used (Collins, 2009). Thus the process of cross-reactivity is not static and it is the responsibility of the laboratory to remain informed as to the variables that might affect the test outcome with each of the reagents utilized on an ongoing basis.

"False-positive" test results are a significant problem with the relatively unsophisticated "on-site" test kits used by many employers, parents, and law enforcement officials. Some of these tests have a false-positive rate of 30–35% (Schuckit, 2006b; "Why Confirmatory Testing is Always a Necessity," 1997). Because false-positive test results are possible, confirmatory testing always should be carried out. Methods such as Gas Liquid Chromatography (GC) are useful at this stage of the assessment process. Gas liquid chromatography is a more expensive, and labor-intensive, procedure that requires the use of expensive laboratory equipment operated by specially trained technicians. The GC procedures require time for completion and do not lend themselves to rapid screening of large numbers of urine samples. In spite of the disadvantage of being time intensive, GC tests have a lower risk for false-positive results and provide the assessor with quantitative levels of the chemical(s) detected in the individual's urine (Craig, 2004).

Other procedures such as the gas chromatography/mass spectrometry (GC/MS) test might also be called upon to confirm a "positive" urine sample from a less sensitive test procedure. GC/MS is very labor intensive, expensive, and limited to testing only a small number of urine samples at a time. One advantage of GC/MS procedures is that they can detect a wide range of individual substances, reducing the risk of false-positive results. In the example cited earlier, the hypothetical person who had used the cough suppressant dextromethorphan at therapeutic doses will have the dextromethorphan molecules in the urine sample identified as such and not as phencyclidine. Because of this specificity, GC/MS results may be introduced as legal evidence of illicit drug use in many states.

However, illicit drug abusers and companies attempting to produce appropriate testing procedures are involved in an "arms race" of sorts (Jones, 2009). Many companies sell products that can break down metabolites produced by illicit drugs over time. If too much time between the immunoassay test and the GC/MS test should pass, the initial test could suggest drug use, whereas the GC/MS test indicates no evidence of illicit drug use because the test-defying chemical finally had time to work (Jones, 2009). Even if the individual had not attempted to alter the test results, urine toxicology procedures will not detect signs of illicit drug use until at least 6 hours after the individual's use of a compound because the body needs time to begin the biotransformation and elimination processes before urine toxicology testing can detect evidence of substance use (Juhnke, 2002).

Urine toxicology testing is more complicated than obtaining a urine sample and submitting it for analysis. Most states require the client's written consent to the urine toxicology testing process, many states require that strict chain-of-evidence procedures be followed and that the results are only interpreted by a trained medical review officer (MRO). Such a review of test results should address the ongoing myth that a "positive" urine toxicology test indicates impairment (Stein & Rogers, 2008). Insurance companies and employers argue that even the smallest trace of a drug in a person's urine after an accident is evidence of impairment and thus grounds for job termination, legal action, and so on. Such a stance ignores the reality that substance-induced impairment cannot be inferred just because toxicology testing suggests that a given compound was present in the individual's body (Reisfield, Goldberger, Gold, & DuPont, 2012). It is impossible to determine substance-induced impairment solely on the basis of drug concentration levels in body fluids other than for alcohol for which there is an extensive research data base demonstrating levels of impairment at various blood alcohol levels (Jemionek, Copley, Smith, & Past, 2008; Reisfield et al., 2012; Stein & Rogers, 2008). The team of Reisfield et al. (2012) suggested that by the very nature of these substances such determinations remain only an illusion.[33]

---

[32]See Glossary.

[33]As was discussed in the chapter on CNS stimulants, there are cases where one individual has become toxic on a therapeutic dose of an amphetamine whereas another individual might be using a dosage level far above the therapeutic range without signs of amphetamine toxicity, for example.

As is evident in the material reviewed to date urine or blood toxicology testing is controversial and fraught with the potential for misinterpretation[34] even by medical professionals. In spite of these problems, urine toxicology testing provides the assessor with one source of data about the individual's possible substance abuse.

Clients Attempts at Deception

It is not uncommon for substance-abusing clients to attempt to manipulate the urine toxicology test to avoid having their recent illicit drug use detected. These attempts at detection avoidance generally fall into one of three categories: (a) in vitro adulteration, in which the test subject adds a prohibited chemical to the urine sample to hide evidence of recent drug use, (b) in vivo adulteration, in which the test subject ingests a compound prior to testing (including the simple ingestion of large amounts of water) to dilute or disguise signs of illicit drug use, and (c) urine substitution, in which the test subject substitutes a "clean" urine sample for one known to be "dirty" Another means of test manipulation is to simply not keep a scheduled appointment if the client has reason to anticipate being asked to submit to urine toxicology testing at a given time ("I have to work, honest!" or the ever popular "My car won't start!") (Gitlow, 2007).

In vitro urine toxicology, test deception methods rest on the assumption that it is possible to "hide" evidence of illicit drug use by adding a foreign chemical(s) to the urine sample. A partial list of adulterants used at one time or another to disguise urine samples tainted with illicit drug metabolites can be found in Table 33-3.

It should be noted that when Drano® or salt is added to the urine sample, there is a high probability of undissolved crystals being suspended in the sample, at least a first. This will assist in the detection of tampering, if the urine sample is closely examined as soon after collection as possible.

In vivo methods of urine toxicology test, deception includes compounds designed to bind with the drug metabolite, altering its chemical structure so that it does not register as an illicit substance. There are also a number of products that are propertied to remove

| TABLE 33-3 |
| Sample List of Agents Used in Attempts to Hide Drug Abuse |
| Ammonia |
| Bleach |
| Blood |
| Drano® |
| Ethanol |
| Gasoline |
| Kerosene |
| Lemon juice |
| Liquid soap |
| Peroxide |
| Vinegar |
| Table salt |
| Sodium bicarbonate |
| Vitamin C |

© Cengage Learning

"toxins" from the body, or correct electrolyte imbalances induced by the clients' attempts to "flush" their body with large amounts of fluids (Gwinnell & Adamec, 2006; Jaffe, 2010; Coleman & Balelt, 1997). Some people have been known to ingest large amounts of water in an attempt to flush drug metabolites from their body, or at least dilute the drug metabolites to a level that they will fall below the detection level, a process that exposes the individual to the risks inherent in water intoxication.[35]

On rare occasions, the addition of such compounds to a urine sample will actually hide evidence of recent illicit drug use, although they also alter the chemical characteristics of the "urine" sample submitted (Schuckit, 2006a). Some compounds will make the urine sample more alkaline than possible for human urine, for example (Jenkins, Tinsley, & Van Loon, 2001). Small amounts of the compound alum will hide metabolites of methamphetamine in a urine sample, but at the cost of changing the acidity of the sample that can be detected by treatment or laboratory staff when they check the sample's acidity level. If possible, the specific gravity, acidity level, and creatinine levels

---

[34]Reisfield et al. (2012) pointed out, for example, that a valid prescription for a controlled substance was an affirmative, but not absolute, defense against an impaired driving charge. *However,* should that individual demonstrate clinical signs of impairment he or she could be charged with driving while under the influence of mood-altering substances even though it was a prescribed medication according to the authors.

[35]Including, but not limited to, cardiac arrhythmias and cerebral edema.

of the urine sample submitted should be assessed to determine whether a given urine sample is appropriate for testing or has been altered through such methods (Coleman & Balelt, 1997). These adulteration methods do work under certain circumstances, and health care professionals might wish to consult with toxicology laboratories to determine which compounds might work with that specific method of drug testing, and how their use might be detected.

Another method by which illicit drug abusers might attempt to manipulate the urine toxicology test results is by urine substitution. This is a method of deception through which the person will substitute other compounds as their "urine." A partial list of compounds submitted as "urine" by various clients includes apple juice, citrus flavored sodas, dilute tea, ginger ale, lemonade, salt water, plain tap water, and white grape juice. Again, testing the sample's specific gravity and acidity level (as well as the amount of sugar in the sample!) will detect these attempts at substitution.

People have also been known to attempt to substitute a "clean" (i.e. drug-free) urine sample available, possibly hidden in a balloon or small bottle, that can be substituted for their own urine sample if nobody is watching them closely. This is easily done is most cases, because the majority of urine toxicology test samples are not collected under supervision (Sutheimer & Cody, 2009). Even if urine samples for toxicology testing are collected under supervision, there are companies that will also sell a rather realistic-looking artificial penis, so that the male client might submit a substituted urine sample while being observed. The urine is held in a storage container that is squeezed, forcing it through a tube and into the collection bottle, just as would occur if the man were to normally submit to urine toxicology testing. A similar device is sold for female drug abusers. If done properly, the results are very realistic. An extreme method of deception is a urine substitution method through which clients will void their bladder, then insert a catheter and fill their bladder with another person's urine to provide a urine sample for testing if asked[36] (Stein & Rogers, 2008).

Clients who have been asked to submit to urine toxicology testing have been known to claim to be unable to urinate when somebody is watching them in an attempt to avoid supervised urine collection, or to "accidentally" dip the urine sample collection bottle into the toilet water. The specific gravity and level of acidity of the "urine sample" will reveal this attempt at deception, because toilet bowl water has a different specific gravity and acidity level than does human urine. Some treatment centers add a coloring agent to the toilet water, to foil these attempts at substitution. Further, toilet water is usually rather cool when compared with the human body, and urine is always within 1–2 degrees of the core body temperature if the temperature of the urine sample were to be tested within 4 minutes of the time that it was collected (Katz & Fanciullo, 2002). This fact is embarrassing to those clients who attempt to simulate normal body temperature for the urine sample to be substituted by putting the sample into a microwave oven prior to reporting for toxicology testing. Temperature testing at the time of collection will thus help to identify urine samples that are unusually warm/cool, alerting staff to possible attempts at deception.

Urine toxicology testing should be carried out on a random basis (Juhnke, 2002). Some court-associated outpatient programs assign a "color" to each client, who must then call a central telephone number to see whether clients with that color will be called in for urine testing that morning. In residential programs, a client might be selected at random and told that he or she is to report for urine toxicology testing, and then escorted to the collection site so that the client does not sneak into their room and pick up a chemical or urine substitution sample. The information reviewed later provides an overview of the detection windows for various compounds commonly abused.[37]

Alcohol

Under normal conditions, clients will only show traces of alcohol in their urine for about the same time as it can be detected in their breath. Thus, breath analysis is the preferred method of detecting alcohol in a person's body, although later confirmatory testing in a certified laboratory might be carried out by law enforcement officials. Recently, a urine toxicology test for alcohol was introduced to detect a metabolite of ethyl alcohol known as ethyl glucuronide. This compound is specific to alcohol use, and remains in the individual's blood

---

[36]This process, however, exposes the individual to all of the risks inherent in using a catheter, and to potential infectious organisms in the urine of the person who supplied the urine sample to be substituted.

[37]This information is provided for illustrative purposes only, is not intended for, and should not be used as the basis for employment screening, legal, or other purposes.

for up to 5 days after the person's last drink. Unfortunately, there is a growing body of evidence that suggests that exposure to alcohol through such things as hand sanitizer[38] might also cause a "positive" test result (Kirn, 2006). Given the popularity of such products, the results of the ethyl glucuronide test must be interpreted with caution.

Amphetamine Compounds

In the casual user, amphetamine compounds might be detected for 24–48 hours (Bolnick & Rayburn, 2003; Greydanus & Patel, 2005; Schuckit, 2006a). However, high doses of ephedrine or pseudoephedrine might cause a "false positive" test result. For this reason, federal guidelines require that amphetamine molecules be identified through specific testing procedures such as the Gas Liquid Chromatography (GC) test (discussed earlier) to rule a urine sample "positive" for amphetamine compounds such as methamphetamine. In the case of methamphetamine, it is important to keep in mind that once ingested the body breaks methamphetamine down into amphetamine, but ephedrine or pseudoephedrine are not biotransformed into this compound. This allows the presence or absence of amphetamine or methamphetamine to be confirmed by the appropriate test procedures after the initial test results suggest amphetamine use.

Benzodiazepines

Depending on the specific benzodiazepine being used, urine toxicology tests might reveal evidence of benzodiazepine use for 1–4 weeks after their last use (Craig, 2004). Schuckit (2006a) suggested a shorter detection window of only 3 or more days. This discrepancy appears to reflect whether one is testing a rare abuser of a benzodiazepine, or a chronic user. The benzodiazepine Rohypnol (flunitrazepam) is technically a member of the benzodiazepine family of compounds, but is not legally available in the United States. Routine toxicology tests will not detect it, although special tests can detect it in a urine sample if the test is carried out within 60 hours of the time that it was ingested. These tests are usually available only to law enforcement agencies investigating date rape claims.

Cocaine

Depending on the route of administration, the frequency with which the individual abuses cocaine, and the amount of cocaine abused, it is possible to detect metabolites of cocaine in urine for 72–96 hours (Schuckit, 2006a). Heavy abusers might continue to test "positive" for cocaine metabolites for up to 10 days after their last use of this compound (Traub, 2009). Greydanus and Patel (2005) suggested that chronic cocaine abusers could test "positive" on urine toxicology screens for up to 2 weeks after their last use of this compound, whereas Schuckit (2006a) simply stated that chronic abusers would test positive for "several days" (p. 30) after their last cocaine use.

One of the exceptions to this rule is when the person is using a prescribed product with traces of cocaine in it, such as certain skin lotions. If the person were to be using one of these compounds, this would produce a false-positive test result. Fortunately, these skin lotions are available only by prescription, and thus it is rare for this situation to arise (Ahrendt & Miller, 2005). Passive absorption of cocaine is possible for a physician or dentist, if their practice brings them into frequent contact with this compound, in which case they will have metabolites of cocaine in their urine for 72–96 hours (Gitlow, 2007). Fortunately, it would be relatively easy to determine whether that health care professional's job duties did indeed bring them into frequent contact with cocaine.

LSD

LSD might be detected in a person's urine for up to 8 hours after it was last used, but the laboratory must use special testing procedures to detect this substance (Craig, 2004).

Marijuana

Although the cannabinoids have been the most commonly detected illicit substance in urine toxicology tests for more than 20 years, the detection of marijuana through urine toxicology testing remains rather complicated (Huestis, 2009). The excretion of marijuana metabolites from the body is variable, but it correlates well with the amount of marijuana used by the individual (Goodwin et al., 2008). The rare social user will have traces of THC in their urine for 3–5 days after they last used marijuana (Greydanus & Patel, 2005; Goodwin et al., 2008; Schuckit, 2006a). There is a persistent myth on the streets that a person who smokes marijuana will have traces of THC in their urine for 30 days after their last use of marijuana, and casual abusers will often repeat this myth as if it were gospel to try and avoid sanctions for illicit substance abuse.

---

[38]Many brands of hand sanitizer contain ethyl alcohol.

The unusually heavy, chronic marijuana smoker[39] will build up significant THC reserves in their bodies, which will leak back into the blood through osmosis for between 20 and 45 days depending on the frequency with which they used marijuana and the potency of the marijuana smoked (Greydanus & Patel, 2005; Jenkins et al., 2001). Exceptionally heavy marijuana smokers have been known to have measurable amounts of THC in their urine for up to 2 months after their last use ("Weight Loss and the Release of THC from Fat," 2009).[40] Katz and Fanciullo (2002) suggested that a habitual marijuana smoker might test "positive" for THC for up to 80 days, although this figure has not been supported by other researchers.

Many marijuana abusers test "positive" for marijuana for such extended periods because THC enters the body's adipose tissues and is slowly released back into the circulation after the abuser stops marijuana use. To avoid controversy, it has been suggested that the client submit to daily urine toxicology testing until his or her urine sample fails to show evidence of marijuana abuse for 3 straight days. The program staff must make sure that the person does not have a prescription for the compound Marinol, which is a form of synthetic THC used to treat chemotherapy-induced nausea, as this will register as marijuana on urine toxicology tests.[41]

Occasionally, clients will attempt to claim that they have THC in their system as a result of passive inhalation. Passive inhalation of marijuana smoke to allow the individual to absorb sufficient marijuana smoke to test "positive" on urine toxicology testing has been called "extraordinarily unlikely" (Ahrendt & Miller, 2005, p. 962). However, it is possible to passively inhale enough marijuana smoke to test "positive" for it on a urine toxicology test. To do so it is necessary to sit in an airtight chamber so filled with marijuana smoke that the person will need swimmer's goggles to protect her or his eyes from the irritating effects of the smoke ("Oral Fluid Drug Testing," 2005). The authors suggested that because most motor vehicles or houses are not airtight, and so the claim of passive inhalation is not supported by the evidence. The team of Rohrich, Schimmel, Zomtlein, Becker, Kaufmann, Kuntz, and Urban (2010), using a different methodology, reached essentially the same conclusion.

MDMA

Ecstasy can be detected for 24–48 hours after it was used, but special urine toxicology testing must be carried out to detect it (Craig. 2004).

PCP

In the casual abuser, phencyclidine can be detected for 48–72 hours after it was last used (Jenkins et al., 2001). Craig (2004) offered a detection window of 2–8 days for the casual abuser, and up to 21 days for the chronic abuser. Depending on the testing methodology utilized, some over-the-counter medications can cause false-positive reactions, and thus confirmatory testing should be carried out to confirm the initial test results (Ahrendt & Miller, 2005).

Hair Sample Testing

Whenever a person ingests a chemical, molecules of that substance are circulated throughout the body. In many cases molecules of that compound are then incorporated into the body's cells including the hair cell follicles and ultimately the hair. Scientists have developed the technology to detect drug metabolites of many illicit drugs in the hair of the abuser. It has been suggested that because this is true, that the collection of hair samples would be less intrusive than collecting urine samples, and much more difficult to falsify. Hair samples also offer a detection window of 7–100 days (Gwinnel & Adamec, 2006; Stein & Rogers, 2008; Sutheimer & Cody, 2009). This extended detection window foils the attempt of the drug abuser to avoid detection by abstaining from drug use for a few days before a toxicology test (Craig, 2004). Although some drug abusers think that they can foil this process if they shave their heads, any body hair can be used for such tests.

Advocates of hair follicle testing point out that this procedure is far less intrusive than urine toxicology testing. However, there have been several challenges to the use of hair tests for toxicology testing. The Food and

[39]Which is to say somebody who smokes marijuana daily or more often, and is not a reference to body size.

[40]It should be pointed out that "measurable amounts" is not the same as THC levels above the detection threshold utilized by the Department of Transportation to identify active marijuana abusers.

[41]One favorite trick of drug addicts is to obtain a blank prescription sheet, and have a friend fill out the form as if it were a standing order for Marinol®. If their marijuana use is then detected by a toxicology test, they can show the prescription sheet and claim that it was the prescription drug that was detected, not illicit marijuana. Thus, such prescriptions should be verified with the physician who supposedly prescribed the Marinol® if THC is detected in a urine toxicology test.

Drug Administration (FDA) has warned that several of the test kits sold might result in false-positive test results on occasion ("FDA Revised Guidelines, Label Warnings," 2004). Further, initial "positive" results should be confirmed by a second test that utilizes a different methodology (Sutheimer & Cody, 2009). One study found that where 60% of the tests indicated illicit substance use, confirmatory testing did not support this conclusion ("FDA Revised Guidelines, Label Warnings," 2004). Further, fully 50% of the preliminary "positive" results for amphetamine abuse, 10% of the preliminary "positive" results for marijuana abuse, and 2% of the preliminary "positive" results for cocaine abuse were found to be false-positive results upon confirmatory testing.

Marijuana abusers will often claim passive exposure to marijuana smoke as an explanation for the "positive" test results. Uhl and Sacks (2004) suggested that the test try to detect metabolites other than THC, such as 11-nor-delta-9-tetra-hydrocannabinol-9-carboxylic acid (THCA) to differentiate between actual marijuana use and passive exposure to marijuana. This metabolite is produced only when the person has abused marijuana, not through passive exposure, and for this reason hair samples from persons exposed to marijuana smoke failed to reveal evidence of THCA when tested (Uhl & Sacks, 2004). This discovery will allow actual marijuana abusers to be identified, and foil their claim of passive exposure to marijuana smoke.

Detractors to the process of hair testing point out that a number of hair strands must be removed. Craig (2004) suggested that as many as 40–60 hair strands be removed. Further, it is hard, if not impossible, to detect when the individual indulged in illicit drug use. In theory, hair grows at the rate of 1 centimeter (cm) per month, which if true would allow the tester to estimate the time since the user last used that compound. Questions have also been raised whether this estimate of the hair growth rate is the same for all ethnic groups (Gitlow, 2007; Sutheimer & Cody, 2009). Further, at any point 15% of hair follicles are either in a resting phase or ready to fall out at any given time, factors that can potentially influence the accuracy of hair toxicology testing. Hair toxicology tests cannot detect substance use in the 7 days prior to the collection of the hair samples, and do not detect alcohol use (Gwinnell & Adamec, 2006; Juhnke, 2002). Research has found that different laboratories often provide different results for the same hair sample (Sutheimer

& Cody, 2009), and there is no standardization in hair collection and preparation procedures between laboratories. These observations raise questions as to the validity of hair sample toxicology testing (Stein & Rogers, 2008; Sutheimer & Cody, 2009). For these, and other reasons, the federal government has discontinued the practice of testing hair samples to detect illicit drug use ("How Long Does Cocaine Remain in the Hair of Former Users?" 2009) for job sites where such testing is mandated.

Even if there is evidence of illicit drug use detected in hair strand testing, this does not provide information on the level of impairment caused by the individual's drug abuse (Juhnke, 2002; Stein & Rogers, 2008). The fact that hair toxicology testing requires the removal of hair from the body, as opposed to the collection of urine, a waste product expelled from the body, makes it of limited value in serial toxicology tests (Craig, 2004). Thus, there are strong objections to the use of hair toxicology testing, making its applicability uncertain at this time.

Saliva

Another emerging technology is the use of saliva to test for traces of alcohol or drug use. New techniques make this procedure attractive for workplace drug testing programs. There are a number of variables that must be resolved before the accuracy of saliva drug testing can be established because: saliva flow can ... be decreased because of menopausal hormone changes, stress, smoking, anti-cholinergic drugs that inhibit [the] parasympathetic nerve impulses, anticonvulsants, and tranquilizers (Moore, 2009, p. 206).

Saliva toxicology testing is also hampered by a smaller detection window than is possible with urine toxicology testing (Moore, 2009). The test results are available in approximately 20 minutes, and depending on the substance might offer a detection window of 1–36 hours (Dolan, Rouen, & Kimber, 2004; Stein & Rogers, 2008). As with any screening procedure, confirmatory testing is necessary to rule out false-positive results.

Sweat

A number of companies offer skin patches impregnated with compounds designed to react to and reveal evidence of illicit drug use. Such detection devices are useful for continuous monitoring of the individual over a 1–14 day period (Kadehjian & Crouch, 2009;

Stein & Rogers, 2008). The sweat drug detection patch is designed to allow passage of water molecules through, while stopping the larger drug molecules that had diffused into the sweat from the circulation (Kadehjian & Crouch, 2009). However, illicit drug use will not be detected for several hours after the individual abused that compound because it requires time for the drug molecules to diffuse into the sweat glands.

To avoid detection, some abusers will remove the skin patch the day that it was applied, and then reapply it 6 or 7 days later, when they report to their probation officer, employer, and the like, to have it removed. Such tampering is evident to the skilled patch user because the patch is designed to separate internal membranes from the outer shell if it is removed before being examined (Kadehjian & Crouch, 2009). Although some clients might claim that their skin naturally produces an oil(s) that will cause the patch to fall off, or, that it just fell off while they were taking a shower, these claims are extremely unlikely that the patch will just fall off on its own. Further, although clients might claim that the patch tested "positive" for one or more substances because of environmental contamination, research has shown that this is virtually impossible except under specialized laboratory conditions (Kadehjian & Crouch, 2009).

Funding

Imagine that you had a form of cancer: You call your insurance company representative to determine whether you have coverage for potentially life-saving surgery. When you speak to the customer service representative on the telephone you are informed that whereas your insurance policy does appear to include such surgery as a covered expense, this is not a guarantee of payment for the surgery. Or consider this second, equally hypothetical, scenario: You have been diagnosed as having the same form of cancer but when you check with the customer service representative at the insurance company's home office you are told that your policy will pay only for the first 10 days of a 30-day chemotherapy regimen, or perhaps not pay anything toward a chemotherapy regimen on the grounds that the pharmaceuticals involved are still classified as "experimental" by that insurance company. Or, consider a third hypothetical scenario: Your health care insurance provider informs you that they will pay for a portion (or all) of your treatment expenses only if

you enter a program at what they call a "preferred provider," the effectiveness of which is suspect.

The money that the insurance company must spend paying for health care for policy holders is considered a financial loss[42] for that company's shareholders. The insurance company thus attempts to maximize inflow of money, while limiting payments distributed. One way to do this is to exclude many people from receiving an insurance policy because she or he had a "preexisting condition." Another way to limit losses is to avoid identification of people with a disorder(s). To this end, only 34% of insurance companies required that the physician screen for substance use or mental health disorders when doing a physical examination (Horgan, Garnick, Merrick, & Hoyt, 2007). If the insurance company will not reimburse for a specific part of the examination the physician is less likely to carry it out, increasing the chance that the client's mental health or SUD will not be detected.

Mental Health Parity Laws

Funding dictates the form and duration of treatment. In an ideal world the level of care offered to an individual with an SUD would be determined solely by need. In reality, decisions about treatment are often shaped by funding. The middle class is caught between making too much money to qualify for public treatment funding and an inability to pay for extended treatment services "out of pocket" (Fletcher, 2013; Leamon, Wright, & Myrick, 2008). Striking a fair balance between the need for the treatment of SUDs and funding availability has proven difficult.

Students are thus surprised to learn that in spite of the widespread media attention paid to the passage of "mental health 'parity' laws," health care insurance providers are not required to provide funding for mental health or substance abuse treatment. The law requires that they pay for substance abuse treatment at the same level of reimbursement as other covered medical disorders *if* the insurance policy includes coverage for mental health and substance abuse rehabilitation programs.

Surprisingly, 77% of all substance abuse rehabilitation programs are paid for by public funds. These funds are drawn from state-funded programs that are a part of the criminal justice system in that state, the Medicare and Medicaid programs, or on the federal level the Veteran's Administration treatment system

---

[42]Or an operating expense.

(Stewart & Horgan, 2011). Services are paid for either by the fee-for-service or the fixed budget system (Stewart & Horgan, 2011). Neither system of payment is perfect. In the fee-for-service system reimbursement is based on units of service provided, such as the number of group or individual therapy hours provided to the individual in treatment. This can serve as an incentive for a for-profit rehabilitation program to offer a large number of more expensive, ancillary services to increase revenue (Stewart & Hogan, 2011).

In contrast to this, the fixed budget system involves a contractual agreement that is reached between the payer and the treatment provider(s) in which a fixed fee is paid to the provider independent of the number of referrals made or the intensity of treatment necessary. For example, a hypothetical county might pay an equally hypothetical treatment program $100,000 to provide substance abuse rehabilitation services for that county for 1 year. That fee is then paid to the rehabilitation program even if only two individuals are referred to that program in the fiscal year. Of course, if 1,000 individuals are referred to the rehabilitation program in a fiscal year, the county still only reimburses the program $100,000! Such programs thus have a financial incentive to eliminate ancillary services provided to maximize profits (Stewart & Hogan, 2011).

These forms of reimbursement are found in privately funded,[43] publicly funded and third-party payer[44] reimbursement situations. Health care insurance providers have attempted to hold down the cost of substance abuse rehabilitation through a variety of mechanisms, the most notorious of which is called managed care (MC). Managed care has essentially been called medical rationing by accountants, and it can be argued that the needs of the individual are subservient to the company's desire to save money. Frequently decisions about the services that will be reimbursed are governed not by client-centered risk-benefit calculations but by company-focused cost-benefit algorithms. The patient's quality of care becomes subservient to the company's desire to make money. In far too many cases, rapid, cheap, symptom reduction (not resolution of the problem) is the goal because this saves the company money. It also applies a system of "rigid protocols with a preset, algorithmic approach" (Nasrallah, 2010a, p. 14) to the treatment of human beings. In some cases funding for treatment is

so limited that further funding is cut off before the individuals have completed the detoxification cycle for their drug(s) of abuse (Fletcher, 2013)! This is especially true for older people with an alcohol use disorder who require longer period to withdraw from alcohol than do younger drinkers.

In the time since the managed care (MC) programs were introduced it has become clear that this is a system that rations health care access in all but name (Sanchez & Turner, 2003). Many health care providers have started to refer to "managed care" as "managed profits" because of the way that the system limits the amount of money distributed by insurance companies for designated services. As Nasrallah (2010a) observed: The not-so-hidden agenda of the business-oriented managed care systems is to lower costs, not to provide the best personalized medical care (p. 13–14).

Some MC programs utilize a preferred provider system in which the client's level of coverage for services provided is higher if they are seen exclusively by a provider who is part of their referral network. Often the preferred provider has signed an agreement with the insurance company to reduce charges for their services in anticipation that the higher volume of clients will offset any potential revenue loss. Another system by which MC companies attempt to control expenses is through a capitation payment system in which services for an individual are reimbursed up to a predetermined limit. If the provider is able to accomplish the desired treatment goals for less than this limit, the program will make money. If the expenditure to reach treatment goals exceeds this limit, the program will not show a profit. Obviously, if the program should wish to survive in today's economic climate they wish to make a profit, and so there is an incentive for the rehabilitation program to limit length of stay and intensity of treatment (Stewart & Hogan, 2011).

Unfortunately, in spite of research findings that indicate that the longer that a given individual is involved in treatment programs the more likely they will abstain from alcohol or drugs, authorization for treatment stays of 14 days or less have become the norm (Ceren, 2003; Daley & Marlatt, 2006; Olmstead, White, & Sindelar, 2004; Simpson, 2004). Finally, managed care programs aggressively push for pharmaceutical treatment(s) of identified conditions rather than for behavioral treatments (Breggin, 2008). Some health care insurance providers include a capitation provision in insurance policies sold limiting the number of admissions for "detox" or treatment admissions to a

[43]On rare occasions a person might pay for treatment out of pocket.
[44]Also known as treatment paid for by "health care insurance."

preset limit, possibly only one such admission in the person's lifetime. Such reimbursement programs have been found to cut the cost charged to the insurance company while doing little to change long-term health care risks for the clients (Nasrallah, 2010a). It is not known how mental health "parity" laws will change this practice, or even if it will change this practice.

Many MC companies demand that rehabilitation programs follow "evidence-based" treatment protocols. Unfortunately much of the research on which "evidence-based treatment" is based is of little value in the real world. One research study might specify only people who are male, in treatment for the first time, between the ages of 21and 34 and who have no concurrent physical or mental illness. Such practices are defended on the theory that these confounding variables would make interpretation of the study results meaningless. Unfortunately treatment rehabilitation center staff must work with clients who have glaucoma, diabetes, AIDS, a history of head trauma, multiple prior treatment admissions, and who might also be depressed or suffer from schizophrenia, not the pristine research samples on which "evidence-based" treatment is carried out. Even research carried out through the Veteran's Administration (VA) Hospital system is atypical because only those people who have successfully completed a tour of duty in the armed forces are entitled to use the VA system for health care.

Another way for insurance companies to limit financial loss is to limit treatment to symptom reduction. To accomplish this, the insurance company adopts a very liberal interpretation of what is considered "recovery." Is the person still having delirium tremens? Is their blood pressure still elevated? If not, she or he should be ready for discharge in the next 24 hours, right? If you wish additional time you will need to obtain prior authorization. Although research has demonstrated that older drinkers might require up to 30 days to completely detoxify from the effects of long-term alcohol abuse, insurance company benefits often are limited to 5–7 days for "detoxification" and treatment unless authorization is obtained for a longer stay in treatment. Such treatment extensions are then subject to review, usually every second or third day,

with the goal of ending further insurance funding once the client reaches a certain minimal set of criteria. Although such policies might be considered cost-effective by the insurance company, a sad consequence of this process is that many clients are referred to "aftercare" before they have finished detoxification.

As this text is going to press the debacle called the "Affordable Care Act" (ACA) is being unveiled. The impact of this law on substance abuse rehabilitation funding is not known at this time, but potentially can change how substance abuse treatment is funded for better or worse. Only time will tell whether the ACA will be a positive change in how substance abuse treatment is funded or not.

Chapter Summary

Even after a given client has been identified as being in need of either outpatient or inpatient substance abuse rehabilitation, the obstacles facing that substance abuse rehabilitation professions are often daunting. Some clients will challenge the accuracy of the diagnosis or the accuracy of urine toxicology test results. Some may come to treatment sessions under the influence of chemicals. Even if the clients consent to treatment, their health care insurance provider must be contacted, "prior authorization" must be obtained for the treatment program, and continual justifications for treatment beyond the limited number of days that the insurance company authorizes provided for extensions of the initial treatment period must be authorized.

Treatment noncompliance is an ongoing problem in a wide range of medical conditions, but if a substance-abusing person should be noncompliant, the medical profession often just labels the person as being a hopeless alcohol or drug addict, and turns away. Even if the client successfully completes treatment, there are the obstacles facing the client: relapse "cues" and "triggers," and prejudice by health care providers toward people with an SUD. Although treatment staff may recommend extended "aftercare" programs for the client, many resist such recommendations or fail to actively participate in such programs. There are also other obstacles facing the client, which are discussed in this chapter.

CHAPTER 34

Support Groups to Promote and Sustain Recovery

Introduction[1]

For many years, Alcoholics Anonymous (AA)[2] has had a "near exclusive dominance" (White & Nicolaus, 2005, p. 59) as a community-based support group for those who had an alcohol use disorder. It has been estimated that 95% of substance abuse rehabilitation programs utilize some kind of 12-step group model similar to that offered by AA and that recovering center staff are quite disinterested in treatment approaches that do not utilize such an approach (Brigham, 2003). Professional support is quite strong for 12-step-based approaches, as evidenced by the observation by McPherson, Yudo, Afsarifard, and Freitas (2009), who suggested that participation in 12-step groups is an essential element in recovery.

However, in the past two decades there have a growing number of secular support groups that reject many of the core elements of the AA program, offering alternatives for those who feel uncomfortable with the spiritual emphasis on the traditional 12-step group movement, for example. In this chapter we will briefly examine the role that self-help groups play in the recovery from a substance use disorder.[3]

---

[1]In earlier editions of this text, the 12 steps of the AA program were included as part of the chapter introduction. Permission to do so was kindly granted by the Alcoholics Anonymous World Services, Inc. For this edition, the 12 steps have been moved to Appendix 4.

[2]Over the years, the membership of AA has evolved from one in which the members exclusively abused alcohol to one where the member usually has a substance use disorder involving multiple substances. However, because the AA program was originally designed for persons with an alcohol use disorder, this focus will be retained when discussing Alcoholics Anonymous.

[3]A health care provider might assume a degree of liability when referring a specific individual to a self-help group. Salzer and Kundera's (2010) paper provides an excellent overview of this issue. Health care providers should consult an attorney for the state(s) in which they practice to become aware of the specific liabilities that they assume when making a referral to a self-help group.

The History of Alcoholics Anonymous

There were many diverse forces that were to blend over time to form the organization that was to become known as Alcoholics Anonymous (AA). First, there was the social atmosphere in the United States, which has traditionally placed great emphasis on public confession, contrition, and salvation through spirituality. These were elements of a nondenominational religious movement that was known as the Oxford Group, which also came to influence the evolving self-help group. Finally, there was the attempted psychoanalysis of an American alcoholic by Carl Jung. The former was especially influential, providing to the AA movement a strong belief in free will and personal responsibility (Committee on Addictions of the Group for the Advancement of Psychiatry, 2002).

Historically, AA is thought to have been founded on June 10, 1935, the day that an alcoholic physician had his last drink (Nace, 2005a). Shortly before this the physician, Dr. Robert Holbrook Smith ("Dr. Bob") had a meeting with a stock broker, William G. Wilson. William, or "Bill" Wilson,[4] was struggling to protect his newly established sobriety while on a business trip to a new city. After making several telephone calls to various people that he hoped might help him, somebody suggested that he talk to Dr. Smith, who was actively drinking. He did so, but rather than ask for support in his own struggle to abstain from alcohol he began to talk about why he wanted to abstain from alcohol. At the end of the meeting, he concluded that he now understood why he made the original decision to quit drinking and thanked Dr. Bob for listening. The self-help philosophy of AA was born from this moment.

At first, AA struggled to find itself, as evidenced by the fact that within the first 3 years there were only three AA groups and only a scattering of success stories. But the fledgling movement continued to grow slowly and by the fourth year of its existence there were about 100 members in isolated AA groups (Nace, 2005a). To guide the newcomers, those early members who had achieved abstinence decided to write of their struggle to abstain and to share their discoveries with others. These reports were then compiled into the first edition of the book *Alcoholics Anonymous*, published in 1939, now called the "Big Book" of AA. The organization continued to grow and there are now approximately 57,900 AA "clubs" in the United States and some 108,000 located in 150 different countries around the world (Fletcher, 2013). Perhaps 5 million people in the United States attend a self-help group because of alcohol or drug use disorders at least once each year ("New Nationwide Report Reveals that 5 Million People Participate in Self-Help Groups Each Year," 2008).[5]

---

[4]As a historical side note, Bill Wilson rejected the disease model of alcoholism.

[5]Although these statistics appear to be in conflict with each other, the former statistic discusses *active* members in AA, whereas the latter statistic addresses how many people attend a self-help group in a given year, including those who attend only one meeting that year.

Elements of AA

There are several elements that contribute to the effectiveness of a self-help group such as AA, not the least of which is that it is freely available to all (Ries, Galanter, & Tonigan, 2008). Further, such programs are widely available (the city of Seattle, Washington, alone has at least 1,200 meetings a week) (Ries et al., 2008). Further, meetings are "closed" to all people but those who have an honest desire to stop drinking. There are three types of "closed" meetings: (1) The first type of closed AA meeting is a discussion meeting. The group leader has identified a topic applicable to the recovery program of all members (getting along with others, for example), which is discussed at the meeting. (2)The second type is a general meeting in which members are encouraged to discuss their recovery programs, problems that they might have encountered, what is working for them, and so on. (3) The third type of closed meeting is a step meeting, in which one of the 12 steps is identified, and the whole focus of the meeting is on that step and how it applies to every member, their understanding of that step, and so on. Some AA groups rotate through the 12-steps every 3 months, whereas other groups devote an entire month to each of the steps. There is no established protocol how to carry out step meetings.

Another aspect of AA that enhances its effectiveness is that all people involved have shared the same problem. By definition a self-help group is just that: a self-help group, and as such should be self-governing. It does not attempt to provide formal psychotherapy, but through example and feedback offers an educational experience for the participant. Self-help groups place great emphasis on individual responsibility for one's problems in a person who has made a personal commitment to change (Committee on Addictions of the Group for the Advancement of Psychiatry, 2002). To this end, the individual must choose to participate in the group process. Self-help groups place great emphasis on anonymity, a factor that separates it from social groups. Finally, there is only a single purpose to the group, which again differentiates it from social groups. The early members of AA freely borrowed from the fields of religion and medicine to mold a program that worked for them, the famous "12 steps," which form the core of this self-help movement.

There are also "open" meetings. Any interested person can attend an open meeting and there is no expectation of active participation placed upon those who attend. One or two volunteers will speak about how the program helped them abstain from alcohol, and visitors are encouraged to ask questions about AA and how it works. For some people with an SUD, attending an open meeting is less threatening as a first step into recovery than going to a closed meeting. After attending one or two open meetings, the individual is then encouraged to begin to attend closed meetings for personal growth.

A Breakdown of the Twelve Steps

At the core of AA are the 12 steps.[6] These steps are not required for members, but are suggested as a guide to how a person might achieve lasting recovery (Beazley, 1998). A central tenet of AA is that individuals' resources alone are inadequate to help them abstain from alcohol. It is only through a commitment to a support group that the people are able to draw upon the strength of the entire group in their battle to abstain from alcohol (Davison, Pennebaker, & Dickerson, 2000; "How Alcoholics Anonymous Works," 2007). In this sense, AA might be viewed as functioning as a form of folk-psychotherapy that aids personal growth through a series of successive approximations toward a better life. The 12 steps might be viewed as these successive approximations.

New members are not encouraged to seek the cause of their alcohol use disorder (AUD). The problem is the individual's current drinking. "It is not so much how you came to AA, as what you are going to do now that you are here," one hypothetical member might say to a newcomer. New members are not admonished for relapsing. Members in AA know that this is an ever-present danger. However, it is the goal of the group to offer individuals a new lifestyle that they hopefully will adopt in place of their alcohol-centered former lives. The 12 steps are one guide to this transition.

In the process of following the 12-step program, the individual will encounter the first of many paradoxes: The first step is the only one that mentions alcohol by name. This step asks the individual to make a conscious choice to admit that she or he is powerless over alcohol on the deepest level of his or her being. This process requires a difficult choice, for it requires great humility, and an admission of defeat in the sense that people admit that they have been unable to deal with their AUD on their own. However, to accomplish

this, people also must make a choice to view their best "friend" (alcohol) not as a solution but as the problem. The 12 steps guide individuals through this process.

The 12 steps fall into three groups, the first of which includes steps 1–3. These steps focus on helping the individual make a profound choice: First to confront the social stigma associated with the addiction, second, accept that this disease does affect the individual, and third, admit that the individual is powerless over alcohol. Included in the first three steps is the act of surrendering and turning one's life over to a "Higher Power" of the individual's choice. Through the act of admission to powerlessness the individual opens the door to emotional support from other, more experienced members (Felices, 2012). The individuals are also asked to remove themselves from their self-appointed role as the center of the universe and accept that there is a Higher Power. The only requirement for a Higher Power is that this indeed be something greater than the person. Programs that suggest that a doorknob, for example, could be a Higher Power serve only to belittle the 12 steps and the individual. By turning one's life over to a Higher Power one moves alcohol from the center of one's mental arena, a place that normally should be occupied by one's Higher Power. The first goal of the new member in this phase is simply to abstain and to establish a relationship with the Higher Power of his or her choice.

Steps 4–9 are a series of change-oriented procedures designed to help the individual (a) identify, (b) confront, and (c) ultimately overcome the personal character shortcomings that are thought to support the individual's addiction. These steps allow the individual a mechanism through which he or she might work through the guilt that arises from past misdeeds and recognize the limits of personal responsibility. The individual is encouraged to develop a recovery-oriented support system, something that is often alien to the person in the early stages of recovery and also to the family of that person. The person learns the disease theory of alcoholism as AA uses the term, the mechanism by which to find help (sponsor, recovering friends, and forth) and the means to access help when needed (calling one's sponsor, a friend who is also in recovery, and the like). Guilt felt by the individual for past alcohol-centered behavior(s) is hopefully replaced by a sense of gratitude for assistance offered, and the learning of new ways of living. It is during this phase that individuals must identify and then face resentments for past harm that they have suffered,

---

[6]In Appendix 5.

and learn to "let go" of these resentments and forgive the person who caused this harm.

Finally, steps 10–12 challenge the individual to continue to build on the foundation established in earlier steps. Part of this process includes a continued search to identify additional personal shortcomings, which are then addressed by that person. The person has also hopefully learned to suspend judgment about others and to beware of the false pride that could lead back to a relapse. Spiritual growth continues to be encouraged, and finally, in step 12 the individual is encouraged to carry this message of hope to others.

Although the AA program is one designed to aid spiritual growth, this process is not rapid. Indeed, the foundation of spiritual defects on which alcoholism is said to rest is resistant to change, and the process of rebuilding the "self" can take many years. Beazley (1998) suggested that the individual must remain actively involved in AA for at least 5 years to allow the process of spiritual growth to proceed. However, once this process is started individuals begin to wonder how they could possibly have lived otherwise. This is the promise held forth by proponents of Alcoholics Anonymous. The 12 steps are not forced on any member. Rather, they are offered as a guide to assist the person in a program of spiritual growth, and there are those who insist that the 12 steps were instrumental in saving their lives.

The Relationship Between Alcoholics Anonymous and Religion

One complaint often heard by those people who are resistant to participate in AA is that they do not like the religious aspect of the program. For some people, this complaint is a convenient excuse not to participate in an AA group. For others, this hesitancy reflects individual confusion over the manner in which the words *faith*, *religion*, and *spirituality* are used interchangeably within this culture. There are very real differences between these words. Religion is an organized set of beliefs that are encoded in certain texts considered sacred by believers and are viewed as providing answers to life's questions by those who belong to that faith community (Ameling & Povilonis, 2001). Faith is viewed as the expression of belief in the face of ever-present doubt.

Although the following quote is quite old, it does illustrate that within the AA program, alcoholism is viewed as a "spiritual illness, and drinking as a symptom of that illness. The central spiritual defect of alcoholics [is] described as an excessive preoccupation with self … Treatment of the preoccupation with self is the core of AA's approach" (McCrady & Irvine, 1989, p. 153). Within this framework, compulsive alcohol use is viewed as the opposite of true spiritual growth, and it has been found that there is a strong relationship between spirituality and abstinence from alcohol (Nace, 2005a; Robinson, Cranford, Webb, & Brower, 2007). In contrast to the focus on alcohol as the person's answer to life's problems, true spirituality is a reflection of the individual's search for meaning in life and placing one's "self" into a relationship with a transcendent power. The difference between religion and spirituality is, unfortunately, a source of endless confusion by those who view AA from the outside, and those who are just starting the journey to recovery.

The difference between spirituality and religion was perhaps best summarized by McDargh (2000), who observed that "religion is for those who are afraid of going to hell … spirituality is for those who have already been here [as a result of their SUD]." Within this context, it is possible to view the person with an AUD as having found a Higher Power in alcohol (or, by extension the other drugs of abuse) (Ringwald, 2002). Twelve-step programs seek to assist the individual switch from the higher power of alcohol to a more benign one (Wallace, 2003). It is through this process that AA presents itself as a program for spiritual growth, but not as a religious movement (Vaillant, 2000; Wallace, 2003). To better understand this point, it is helpful to view religion as the form, whereas spirituality is the content of belief. The spiritual aspect of the AA program helps the new member to "let go," a concept that many newcomers find confusing. However, "having faith is not a question of clinging to a particular set of beliefs, a particular set of … practices or psychotherapeutic techniques. Having faith … requires that we let go of what we are clinging to" (Rosenbaum, 1999, p. xii).

This is, perhaps, most clearly seen in the inverse relationship between prayer and alcohol use, for, in prayer one reaches out to a Higher Power and with humility establishes a relationship with that Power (Lambert, Fincham, Marks, & Stillman, 2010). This in turn will assist the individuals in learning how to correct their distorted perception(s) of how to deal with conflict, relate to others, or have fun without the use of alcohol.

The AA program is not forced upon the individual, but the 12 steps are suggested as a road to recovery. Participation in AA requires that the individual at least be receptive to the possibility that there is another way, and have a true desire to quit drinking. In the early stages, it is sufficient that the person just be receptive to the possibility that there is another way, one that requires a conscious decision to take this alternative path. The first step on this alternative path is the decision to turn personal will over to God, as the individual should understand this Higher Power to be. The emphasis on spiritual growth in the AA program rests on the dual assumptions that (a) each person desires a relationship with a Higher Power and (b) that it is the individual's distorted perception of "self" as being the center of the universe that makes him or her vulnerable to alcoholism (Ringwald, 2002; McDargh, 2000).

As part of this ongoing dialogue with the Higher Power, the individual is encouraged to carry out a daily self-examination similar to that of the Examen or Conscious Examen proposed by Ignatius as one of the foundations of the Jesuit order of the Catholic Church. In the Examen, the people enter into an ongoing dialogue with their Higher Power, while they examine their thoughts, desires, and resentments. It is up to the individual to select his or her Higher Power, and then make a conscious choice to enter into a relationship with that Higher Power. The conscious choice then makes the individual an active participant in the recovery process, as opposed to "patients" who lie passively for treatment to be performed on them (Nowinski, 2003). In this manner AA offers a program of spiritual growth, without a religious dogma, which might offend some members.

One "A" Is for Anonymous

Anonymity is central to the AA program ("Understanding Anonymity," 1981), and when honored, it is a major advantage of 12-step groups (Ries et al., 2008). This is a major reason why most AA meetings are closed. However, in the time since its inception the concept of anonymity has been challenged, and sometimes violated in ways that the founders of AA would never have envisioned (Coleman, 2011). Many members have published memoirs, in which they identified themselves as members of AA or of similar groups, and although the authors only disclose their addiction to alcohol and then their involvement in this self-help

group, technically it is still a violation of the admonition for confidentiality (Coleman, 2011). However, the publication of photographs taken at AA meetings and then posted on the Internet is a more blatant and inclusive violation of the anonymity of the AA meeting: Everybody in the photograph is by definition a member of AA.

This trend disturbs many members of the self-help group movement in general, and of AA in specific. Anonymity is a cornerstone of the AA meeting. Who attends AA meetings, what is said at a meeting, and who said it is supposed to remain at the meeting. This presents a dilemma for AA groups that allow people who are court-mandated or employer-mandated to attend. To obtain confirmation that they did indeed attend the meeting, people must ask another AA member to sign some form of attendance verification, thus violating the anonymity of AA meetings. In this manner, the requirements of the court system and that of AA conflict. However, the attendee is still expected to have somebody sign an attendance confirmation form or else face the judge's wrath.

Another aspect of anonymity is that no single person might assume the role of speaking for the entire AA group ("Understanding Anonymity, 1981"). This allows each member of the group to strive for humility, which is a cornerstone of the AA group. Each member is equal to the others, and there is no "board of directors" for the local AA group. Rather, special service boards or committees are set up by the group as the need arises. These boards remain answerable to the group as a whole. The members of the service board or committee are "but trusted servants; they do not govern" (Twelve Steps and Twelve Traditions, 1981, p. 10).[7] Further, because of the equality of members, interpersonal conflict is hopefully avoided or minimized.

Alcoholics Anonymous and Outside Organizations

Each local AA group is both not-for-profit and is self-supporting. Each group is autonomous financially, supporting itself only through donations made by members. Further, each member is prohibited from contributing

---

[7]The *Twelve Steps and Twelve Traditions* of AA will not be reviewed in this text. Interested readers are invited to read a copy of the "12 by 12" as it is often called. This book might be purchased from the Alcoholics Anonymous World Services, Inc. Web site on the Internet.

more than $1,000 per year, and outside donations are discouraged, lest conflict develop within the group as to how the financial windfall should be used. Further, as stated in the Twelve Steps and Twelve Traditions (1981), AA groups will not "endorse, finance, or lend the AA name to any related facility or outside enterprise, lest problems of money, property and prestige divert us from our primary purpose" (p. 11).

Thus, many AA groups meet in churches, which donate the use of the room(s) for the meeting. Some AA groups, however, do purchase independent buildings in which to hold meetings. These structures are not called Alcoholics Anonymous buildings, as this would violate the sanction outlined earlier. In many cases the structures are called Alono buildings or by a similar name, but the name Alcoholics Anonymous is not used in the building's name.

The Primary Purpose of Alcoholics Anonymous

The AA group movement seeks to first provide a program for living to guide the newcomer during the transition stage between active alcohol use and recovery. This is accomplished not by preaching at the member, but by presenting a simple, realistic picture of the disease of alcoholism in the words of other members who have experienced the same (or similar) problems as a result of their own AUD. *Confrontation*, when used, takes a different form than this word normally suggests: In AA, members share their own life stories, making a public confession of sorts in which they give examples of the lies, deceptions, and rationalizations that they used to support their own AUD. In so doing, the speakers present a picture of themselves when they were at a stage similar to that of new members, hoping that they will see themselves and the need to join AA now rather than suffer all of the consequences that the speakers outlined in their history.

Service to others is also a central theme in AA, because:

Even the newest of newcomers finds undreamed rewards as he tries to help his brother alcoholic, the one who is even blinder than he … And then he discovers that by divine paradox of this kind of giving that he has found his own reward, whether his brother has yet received anything or not (Twelve Steps and Twelve Traditions, *1981, p. 109).*

In this statement one finds one of the paradoxical components of AA: By helping you, I find part of my own recovery from alcohol. If people were speakers at a meeting, their first step would be an admission that they were powerless over their alcohol use. This is not an admission of helplessness, but only that they were powerless (Wallace, 2003). By joining AA, and with the admission of powerlessness, the members seek the strength of the group as a whole. By admitting the reality of their own AUD, the speaker is reminded of "what my life was like, and by having shared it with you, I am reminded again of the reason why I will not return to drinking, again."

This is the method by which Bill Wilson, in his first meeting with Dr. Robert Smith,[8] was able to recommit himself to his own recovery. He did not preach but simply spoke about his own history, and then thanked Dr. Smith for listening to his story. In a sense, the speaker asserts that "I am a mirror of yourself, and just as you cannot look into a mirror without seeing your own reflection, so you cannot look at me without seeing a part of yourself." In so doing, the speaker benefits from sharing this message as well as the recipient (Zeymore, Kaskutas, & Ammon, 2004).

Three factors have been found to determine the success of AA: First is the frequency with which the individual attends meeting. The person who attends a meeting a month will receive less benefit from the group process than the person who attends two meetings a week, for example. Second is the individual's level of participation in the meeting. The client who sits quietly in the back of the hall and then slips quietly away at the end of the meeting will derive less benefit than the person who actively participates in meetings, asks questions, meets with members after the meeting to discuss points that they are confused about, and so on.

Active AA involvement appears to reflect some of the forces that predict successful efforts to change (Moos & Moos, 2005; Nace, 2003). Finally, there is the emphasis not on long-term recovery, but on simply keeping the focus on "one day at a time," which is the third factor that appears to predict success. Individual members are encouraged not to worry about distant problems, but to keep the focus on the problems that might undermine their recovery program today. They will have time to worry about tomorrow's problems when tomorrow arrives, or so it is believed.

---

[8]Often referred to as "Dr. Bob" in the AA group movement.

Outcome Studies: The Effectiveness of Alcoholics Anonymous

Since its inception in the middle 1930s, virtually every element of AA has been questioned, challenged, and defended. Still, in spite of almost a century of experience and research into the issue, the question remains: Is AA effective? Many substance abuse and health care workers view AA as being the single most important element of an individual's recovery program. However, AA is not a single entity, and the format of meetings varies from one AA group to the next (Arkowitz & Lilienfeld, 2011). This very variability makes research into the effectiveness of AA as either an adjunct to or a form of treatment meaningless. Thus we are left with the conundrum of referring individuals to a support system that is not definitively proven to be effective.

In spite of clinical lore, there has been relatively little research into (a) whether people referred to AA actually attend group meetings, (b) the degree of their involvement or participation in these meetings, and (c) the effectiveness of the 12-step group (Ferri, Amato, & Davoli, 2006). One study that did attempt to address some of these issues was conducted by the team of Kaskutas, Ammon, Delucchi, Room et al. (2005). This study examined the posttreatment AA participation of 349 people who had entered a formal treatment program for an AUD. The authors found that the posttreatment AA involvement of their research subjects fell into four subgroups:

- Low AA involvement: *These people attended AA just during the first year following treatment.*
- Medium AA involvement: *Individuals in this subgroup attended about 60 AA meetings in the first year following discharge from treatment, but had slightly increased their level of AA involvement by the fifth year following discharge.*
- High initial AA involvement: *Individuals in this subgroup attended 200 meetings in the first year following the discharge from treatment, with a slight decrease in their level of AA involvement by the end of their fifth year following discharge.*
- Declining AA involvement: *Individuals in this subgroup initially attended 200+ AA meetings in the first year following discharge from treatment, but by the end of the fifth year following discharge this had fallen to about 6 meetings a year.*

Further, the team of Kaskutas et al. (2005) found that there was a correlation between level of AA group involvement, with 79% of those people in group one were abstinent[9] from alcohol, and 73% of those people whose level of AA group involvement placed them in group two were still abstinent from alcohol at the end of the fifth year. Sixty-one percent of those individuals who fell into group three were still abstinent from alcohol at the end of the fifth year, whereas 43% of those individuals in group four were still abstinent at the time of the follow-up study. Brust (2007a) suggested that AA had a success rate of 34%, but did not elaborate as to the criteria utilized to reach this conclusion. Lemonick and Park (2007) suggested that AA was effective "about 20% of the time" (p. 42).

There is a growing body of evidence that suggests that 12-step oriented treatment programs have higher success rates and lower costs than programs without such a focus (Humphreys & Moos, 2007; Ries et al., 2008). Humphreys and Moos (2007) found that treatment programs that included 12-step group involvement was both 30% less expensive than cognitive-behavioral programs and that 30% more clients from the 12-step involvement group were alcohol-free at the end of 2 years. These findings suggest that 12-step programs can serve an important adjunctive role in substance abuse rehabilitation programs.

Data obtained from national surveys[10] have found that the average AA member has 84 months of sobriety, that 18% have been alcohol-free for more than 60 months, and that 30% have less than 12 months of recovery to their credit (Nace, 2003). Individuals who have been found to be less active in group meetings appear to be most likely to relapse (Chappel & DuPont, 1999; Gitlow, 2007; Zemore, Kaskutas, & Ammon, 2004). Unfortunately there is no objective way to measure participation. A given person might claim to have attended several 12-step group meetings recently, but he or she might have sat in the back of the room, arrived late, left early, never spoke with anyone, and didn't have a sponsor (Gitlow, 2007; p. 226–227).

The need for the individual to be actively involved in a 12-step group makes sense, because programs such

---

[9]Which the authors of this study defined as no alcohol use in the past 30 days.

[10]One problem with surveys is that those people who choose to participate in the study are, by definition, different than those who decline to do so.

as AA offer such things as (a) external supervision, (b) substitute dependency, (c) new abstinence-centered supportive relationships in place of alcohol-centered relationships, and (d) increased spirituality (Kelly & Yeterian, 2011; Vaillant, 2000, 2005). Having a sponsor, especially during the first year of the recovery effort, appears to be a helpful addition to the individual's AA program (Tonigan & Rice, 2010). Further, involvement in the process of helping newcomers to AA appears to also assist the helper in their struggle to maintain abstinence, an observation that reinforces the need for active participation in the AA program to assist the individuals in their recovery (Pagano, Friend, Tonigan, & Stout, 2004).

Although many 12-step-based rehabilitation programs or require 12-step group involvement while the person is in treatment, AA group involvement after discharge from treatment is positively correlated with sobriety (Arkowitz & Lilienfeld, 2011; Brigham, 2003; Moos & Moos, 2005, 2006; Nace, 2003). Moos and Moos (2006) found, for example, that individuals who remained active in AA following discharge from treatment had better outcomes than did those people who did not, and that people who participated in AA by attending at least 27 meetings in the first year following discharge were more likely to be abstinent both in the second year following discharge, and again 16 years later. Thus involvement in AA appears to mirror the individual's efforts to make meaningful changes in other areas of his or her life, such as developing non-chemical means to cope with stress.

Unfortunately, the very nature of AA or similar self-help groups virtually makes it impossible to design a study that would isolate those elements that might help make AA effective, and the patient characteristics of those who are most likely to benefit from a 12-step group such as AA (Gernstein, 2003). By definition, people who join AA are not representative of those people who have an AUD, if only because of their decision to join AA.[11] Those people who drop out of AA are, by the very fact that they dropped out of this self-help group movement, different than those who remain active in it. Given the fact that at the end of 3 months at least half of the new members who joined will have dropped out, and that at the end of 1 year 95% of new members will have stopped attending meetings (Nace,

2003), it must be asked how representative those who remain in this self-help group program are of alcohol-dependent individuals.

Although these studies are suggestive, there is still insufficient evidence at this time to answer the question whether AA is effective in the treatment of AUDs at this time.[12] One point of continuous confusion is the AA program's emphasis on spirituality, as opposed to religion. The available evidence does not suggest that the individual member's religious beliefs change while they participate in AA, although they do grow spiritually (Robinson et al., 2007). This spiritual growth is then associated with a higher abstinence rate (Kelly, Stout, Magill, Tonigan, & Pagano, 2010; Robinson et al., 2007). It is assumed that spirituality based recovery programs might be most effective for those people who had strong religious beliefs prior to the onset of their AUD (Cooney, Kadden, & Steinberg, 2005); however, this is only a theory.

Narcotics Anonymous[13]

In 1953, a new self-help group that followed the Alcoholics Model was founded that called itself Narcotics Anonymous (NA). Although this group honors its debt to AA, the members believed that:

We follow the same path with only a single exception. Our identification as addicts is all inclusive in respect to any mood-changing, mind-altering substance. "Alcoholism" is too limited a term for us; our problem is not a specific substance, it is a disease called "addiction." (Narcotics Anonymous, *1982, p. x*)

To the members of NA, the problem was the common disease of addiction. This self-help group emerged for those whose only "common denominator is that we failed to come to terms with our addiction" (Narcotics Anonymous, 1982, p. x). Many outsiders view the major difference between AA and NA as being one of emphasis: AA addresses only AUDs, whereas NA addresses addiction to chemicals including alcohol. Indeed, where in the first step of the AA's 12-step program

---

[11]Yet it was on a sample drawn from members of AA that Jellinek (1960) based his research on alcoholism, raising questions about the validity of his research.

[12]See "Breakout Discussion #2" for Chapter 35, on the Internet.

[13]Alcoholics Anonymous and Narcotics Anonymous are not affiliated with each other. There is an element of cooperation between the two organizations (M. Jordan, personal communication, 27 February, 1989).

the word "alcohol" is used, the first step of the NA program uses the word "addiction."

The growth of NA has been exceptional. Currently there are more than 25,000 chapters of NA, with more than a quarter of a million active members (Ringwald, 2002). Each self-help group offers a similar 12-step program offering the person with an addiction a day-by-day program for recovery. This is not surprising, because NA members based their program on AA. Some people are quite comfortable going to AA and believe that this group offers them all that they need to address their SUD. Other people believe that NA is a better group for them because it addresses substance use disorders other than just alcoholism. There appears to be no inherent advantage of one program over the other. It is more important to determine which group works best for which individual?

Al-Anon and Alateen

The book Al-Anon's Twelve Steps and Twelve Traditions provides a short history of this movement. In brief, while substance abusers were attending one of the early AA meetings, their partners would meet to talk about different topics, including their significant other. At some point the decision was made to adapt the same 12-steps that their partners found so helpful in their own recovery program, and the Al-Anon movement was born. At the start of the 21st century there are an estimated 30,000 Al-Anon groups in the United States with an estimated 390,000 members (Gwinnell & Adamec, 2006; White, 2005).

Although at first each group modified the 12-steps as they felt necessary, by 1948 the wife on one of the cofounders of AA became involved in the growing organization, and over time a uniform support group for members of AA members emerged. This was a self-help group movement that was in response to the fact that 86% of family members in which there was an alcohol-dependent person felt that their mental health had suffered by the AUD of the other person (Gwinnell & Adamec, 2006). The program that evolved from this phenomenon was known as the Al-Anon Family Support Group, which made minor modification to the Twelve Steps and Twelve Traditions of AA to make them applicable to the needs of family members.

Surprisingly, family members find it useful to attend Al-Anon meetings even if the substance abusing member continues to abuse chemicals. This not only allows family members to learn how to deal with the stress of a substance-abusing member, but in approximately 20% of the cases the substance-abusing individual eventually agrees to enter a treatment program (O'Farrell, & Fals-Stewart, 2008).

Alateen

By 1957, it was recognized that teenagers presented special needs and concerns, and the Al-Anon program was modified to provide a group for these individuals that came to be called Alateen. Currently, it is thought that there are 2,300 Alateen groups in the United States (Capretto, 2007; Gwinnell & Adamec, 2006). Alateen programs follow the same 12-step program outlined in the Al-Anon program, but provide an opportunity for teenagers to come together to share their experiences, their problems, and provide encouragement to each other. The group also provides information about the disease of alcoholism, how these teens did not "cause" the alcoholism in their families, how to detach from the alcoholism in their families, and how they can build a rewarding life in spite of the continued AUD in their family.

Support Groups Other Than 12-Step Groups

There has been a great deal of criticism aimed at 12-step groups such as AA or NA because of their emphasis on spirituality or failure to empower women, for example. In response to this criticism, several new support groups have emerged, many of which will be discussed next.

Rational Recovery[14]

The Rational Recovery (RR) movement attempted to apply the tenets of cognitive-behavioral psychology to the problem of substance use disorders. This movement discontinued group meetings in January 2000. This step was necessary because it was believed that group meetings impeded the individual's progress toward recovery (Horvath, 2005). In the place of group meetings, RR utilizes services available through books, videos, and Internet-based material designed to help the individual recognize, and then change, "addictive thoughts" that contribute to the individual's continued abuse of chemicals. This program uses different methodology than does AA, and suggests that the

---

[14]www.rational.org

"one-day-at-a-time" philosophy of AA is counterproductive rather than supportive of a recovery program (Rational Recovery Systems, Inc., 2008).

Self-Management and Recovery Training (SMART)[15]

This program was started in 1985, and maintains a Web page on the Internet. SMART was originally part of the Rational Recovery movement, but broke away from it in 1994 (Horvath, 2000, 2005). The SMART program draws heavily on cognitive-behavioral schools of therapy, and has four central goals for adults with SUDs: (a) to enhance and maintain the individual's attempt to abstain from alcohol or drugs, (b) to help the individual learn how to cope with thoughts or cravings about chemicals, (c) to help the individual resolve old conflicts and problem behaviors, and (d) to develop a lifestyle balance (Gernstein, 2003; Horvath, 2000). The SMART program maintains that the individual's abuse of alcohol or other chemicals is the result of self-defeating thoughts such as "I have a right to use _____!" or that their abuse of chemicals is not really the cause of all of their problems. Yet another category of dysfunctional thoughts are those that allow the individuals to rationalize their relapse back to active substance use ("You made me so angry that I went out and drank!").

SMART groups believe that virtually any approach to recovery will be of some value to the individual and thus encourages participation in traditional 12-step groups (Horvath, 2000). About 10% of SMART group members also participate in AA groups (Gernstein, 2003). Participants are taught how to view abstinence as a form of self-affirmation and how not to rely on substance use for good feelings about one's self. This program has been found to be moderately effective for clients with an internal locus of control.

Secular Organizations for Sobriety (SOS)[16]

This self-help group was founded in 1986, and by 2000 it was estimated that there were more than 2000 SOS groups in existence, although the program has been viewed as struggling by some (Gernstein, 2003). SOS groups are a response to what is perceived as a heavy emphasis on spirituality in traditional 12-step groups (Ringwald, 2002). The guiding philosophy is heavily influenced by the cognitive-behavioral psychotherapy principles, and stresses personal responsibility, the role of critical thinking in recovery, and the identification of each individual's "cycle of addiction" (Horvath, 2005).

The SOS model postulates that the addictions rest on three elements: (a) the physiological need for the chemical brought about by tolerance, (b) the learned habit of using a chemical(s) as a way to cope, and (c) the denial of (a) and (b) (Horvath, 2005). In contrast to traditional 12-step groups that suggest that the individual must rely on a Higher Power to abstain, SOS holds that the individual has the potential to learn how to live without chemicals within himself or herself (Ringwald, 2002). The program takes a neutral stance toward participation in traditional 12-step groups, and a significant portion of members are either currently attending a 12-step group or have done so in the past.

Women for Sobriety (WFS)[17]

This self-help group movement was started in 1976 by Jean Kirkpatrick, who passed away in June 2000 at the age of 77 (Horvath, 2000). This organization is specifically for women, in response to the belief that traditional 12-step groups have failed to address how recovery from the addictions requires different forms of support for men as opposed to women. There are 13 core statements or beliefs in WFS, which are designed to assist the member in building self-esteem and a new perspective of the self that is not based on the use of chemicals. Unlike more traditional 12-step groups, WFS members are encouraged to leave the group when they feel that they are ready to graduate from the program and assume responsibility for their own recovery program (Ringwald, 2002). Thus, the small number of active members actually does an injustice to the program, because only a fraction of the members are actively involved in the program at any time.

Moderation Management (MM)[18]

Moderation Management was founded in 1993 and has been quite controversial since its inception. The founder, Shirley Kishline, was frustrated with traditional 12-step group programs. She had been referred to 12-step based treatment programs over the years, but her own addiction to alcohol was never firmly established in her mind and she believed that she was only a "problem drinker" (Kishline, 1996, p. 53). Ms. Kishline defined a problem

---

[15]www.smartrecovery.org

[16]www.secularsobriety.org

[17]www.womenforsobriety.org

[18]www.moderation.org

drinker as a person who consumed only 35 drinks per week and who had experienced only mild to moderate alcohol-related problems. The MM core philosophy rests on the foundation that 9 out of 10 "problem drinkers" avoid more traditional 12-step groups and that they shun the traditional label of "alcoholic" (Horvath, 2005; Humphreys, 2003; "What is Moderation Management?" 2008). The alcohol-dependent person, in contrast, was the person who would experience severe withdrawal symptoms if he or she should discontinue the use of alcohol, in Ms. Kishline's opinion.

Moderation management maintains that moderation should be a more appropriate goal than abstinence for many people, especially those who are not physically dependent on alcohol (Kelly & Yeterian, 2011). Members of MM were encouraged to work on the goal of consuming no more than four standard drinks in any given 24-hour period (Horvath, 2005). Initially, the MM concept gained support and MM groups were established in approximately 25 states. Then the founder, Ms. Kishline, was involved in an alcohol-related motor vehicle accident in which her vehicle struck another on an interstate highway, killing a man and his son. Her measured blood alcohol level was 0.260, or more than three times the level defined as legally intoxication in that state resulting in legal charges and a conviction (Noxon, 2003). It is not clear how the arrest of the founder of Moderation Management or its low measured success rate[19] will affect the MM program movement. This is unfortunate because the teachings of MM are not totally contrary to those of more traditional 12-step groups and many individuals were members of both groups. Research has found that at best only about 18% of people once dependent on alcohol can learn to drink in moderation again (Lilienfeld, Lunn, Ruscio, & Beyerstein, 2010), a finding that raises questions about the legitimacy of the theory on which MM was based.

LifeRing[20]

This program is another alternative to traditional 12-step groups. It is based in Oakland, California, and still is a relatively small movement. LifeRing rejects more traditional 12-step groups in part because of what it views as the inflexible nature of such groups. LifeRing maintains grounds that there are multiple paths to recovery, as opposed to the single path suggested by traditional 12-step groups. Further, LifeRing maintains that the individual's spirituality is a private matter. However, members are not discouraged from attending more traditional 12-step groups, either.

Each individual is encouraged to develop a recovery program that will fit her or his needs, guided by the central philosophy of "whatever works" for that person. Currently there are meetings in about 20 states, and four foreign countries. Members tend to be white, middle-aged, college-educated individuals, with a slight preponderance of male members (58%) as opposed to female members (42%) (White & Nicolaus, 2005).

Faith-based Recovery Initiatives

There is a growing trend for recovery programs to be established to function within the religious doctrine(s) of different churches. Such programs range from well-established to fledgling programs, and there are too many to be discussed here. Collectively there is limited evidence that secular treatment approaches are more effective than more traditional 12-step programs (Leamon, Wright, & Myrick, 2008).

Minority Group-Oriented Recovery Programs

There are a small number of programs that attempt to address the special needs of members of a minority group who have a substance use disorder. Such programs tend to be local initiatives serving the needs of minority group members in a limited geographic area. One good example is the Healing Journey Program at the Minnesota Indian Women's Resource Center (Fletcher, 2013). Such programs attempt to integrate traditional beliefs of a specific minority group with more traditional recovery-oriented self-help groups such as AA.

Challenges to the Traditional 12-Step Movement

The traditional 12-step movement has established an almost irreproachable status in the addictions recovery community, and clinical researchers who suggest that total abstinence from alcohol or illicit drugs might not be the best goal are often accused of committing what

---

[19]In response to those critics who will scream that 18% is a significant success rate, would you want to undergo a surgical procedure that had an 82% failure rate (possibly leaving the patient with no benefit, possible significant medical sequelae, or even death)?

[20]www.unhooked.com

might be called "medical blasphemy" (Lilienfeld et al., 2010, p. 234). However, in spite of the privileged status that traditional 12-step groups hold within society, it is not without a small, vocal group of critics. In this section we will review some of the criticism of the AA program, which as the earliest program to be established has drawn the greatest level of criticism. However, each point discussed next could also be applied to the other 12-step group movements discussed earlier.

A charge often made by those who do not wish to attend meetings is that the traditional 12-step groups are "cults." This charge is false because cults have a defined hierarchy or leader(s) (Newsome, 2011). In spite of this, the charge has been made that public confession of past transgressions by members and testimonial speeches by those who attribute their recovery to a 12-step group appear "more like a Baptist tent revival than a recovery program"[21] (Newsome, 2011, p. 125). Further, it is often pointed out in traditional 12-step group meetings that whereas people might be recovering from an SUD, they have never recovered or been cured (Fletcher, 2003; Gilliam, 1998). They remain dependent on the group for continued assistance and support for the rest of their lives. Yet the AA "Big Book" repeatedly speaks of people having "recovered" from alcohol dependency and as no longer needing to attend meetings to maintain sobriety (Fletcher, 2003). This fact, critics of the movement point out, is quietly ignored by proponents of 12-step programs.

A major criticism of traditional 12-step groups is that they are based on a fundamentalist tradition of the 1840s known as the Washington Revival (Newsome, 2011; White & Nicolaus, 2005). This was essentially a white, conservative Protestant movement that replaced physicians and ministers who were providing temperance lectures with lay people who were "reformed" or "reforming" (White & Nicolaus, 2005, p. 58). The influence of this movement on the early AA movement might be seen in the emphasis on public confession of one's addiction to alcohol (White & Nicolaus, 2005). The leaders of the Washington Revival were later charged with "the sin of humanism" (White & Nicolaus, 2005, p. 59), which is to say placing their own will above that of God, and were subsequently discredited by the religious authorities of the time. However, the lessons of attempting to establish a secular recovery group were remembered, and eventually these lessons helped to form the foundation of the

Oxford Group, which immediately preceded the formation of AA.

These lessons were heeded by the founders of AA, who attempted to strike a middle ground between secularity of the Washington Revival and the religious orientation of the Oxford Group. However, state courts have ruled that AA is essentially a religious movement. This ruling is based in part on the program's heavy emphasis on an external, possibly supernatural Higher Power that the individual must "surrender" to as part of her or his recovery program (Wallace, 2003; Gernstein, 2003). The courts have repeatedly ruled in various states that forcing an individual to attend such a group violates the law (Peele, 2004b). This has not prevented other local courts from offering the person with an AUD the alternative of attending AA as an alternative to incarceration.[22] When the program is forced upon the individual, or if the group is very confrontational, the potential exists that it can be more harmful than helpful (Arkowitz & Lilienfeld, 2011; Szalavitz, 2006). This may be one reason why only 33% (Lillienfeld et al., 2010) to 50% (Nace, 2005a) of new members remain active in AA after 3 months of their initial meeting. To further complicate matters, there is research evidence suggesting that those people who are court-mandated to attend AA following an arrest for driving a motor vehicle while intoxicated have a higher recidivism rate and worse subsequent driving records (as evidenced by motor vehicle accidents, for example) than those people sentenced to incarceration by the courts (Bufe, 1998).

Another challenge to the 12-step group movement is based on the fact that there were only a limited number of people (100 individuals) who had achieved abstinence when the 12-steps were formulated. The world view of these early members was formed during the Great Depression of the 1930s and was designed to deflate the individual's ego during a time when many struggled to maintain self-esteem.[23] This is justified on the unproven assumption that grandiosity is a common characteristic of alcohol-dependent people. This core assumption is disempowering to individuals who join a 12-step group (Newsome, 2011), and the applicability of these assumptions to the person living in the second decade of the 21st century, almost 80 years later, has

---

[21]With apologies to readers who are Baptist.

[22]Technically, the individual "chooses" to attend the 12-step group meetings and is not being forced to do so.

[23]The unemployment rate was estimated to reach 25% or higher during the height of the Great Depression.

been questioned. "A vibrant society," Frances (2013) noted "depends on having responsible citizens who feel in control of their actions and own up to the consequences of their actions" (p. 191). This perspective is diametrically the opposite of the tenets of the 12-step movements.

Further, the AA program is a one-size-fits-all program, which demands conformity to a single approach to recovery and discourages individuality (Newsome, 2011). It has even been charged that 12-step groups follow a process of "indoctrination" (Bufe, 1998, p. 6) and fear. The individual is repeatedly warned that the disease of alcoholism will automatically progress, and that the individual must rely on the strength of the group to overcome individual weakness and avoid a relapse. These assertions that are not supported by the clinical research[24] that suggests that alcohol-dependent people rarely follow the downward spiral thought to be inescapable by AA but alternate between periods of more and less abusive drinking (Vaillant, 2000). Further, the 12-step program does not attempt to address the issue that AUDs can take many forms and that there is no single road to alcoholism. Rather, the individual is offered a single program as a road to recovery. Indeed, Szalavitz (2006) took this criticism even further noting that the 12-step program has been adopted virtually unchanged to address a wide range of maladaptive behaviors such as overeating, heroin addiction, compulsive shopping, and so on. Not only is it a "one-size-fits-all" program, but a "one treatment model fits all problems" approach as well!

It is a common belief that the spiritual experience by one of the original founders of AA, "Bill" Wilson, was a critical step in the evolution of the AA movement. A little known fact, however, is that this experience was possibly aided by a belladonna injection[25] administered by his physician to help him overcome the acute effects of alcohol withdrawal[26] (Bufe, 1998). Thus, the foundation stones on which AA was founded may have at the very least been a medication side effect if not the result of the combined effects of the alcohol withdrawal

process and the belladonna. Another criticism of the 12-step program is their emphasis on the waiting until the individual "hits bottom" and reaches a state of spiritual desperation. In any other field of psychological or psychiatric treatment, waiting for the individual to experience to "hit bottom" would be branded abusive by the mental health community (Fletcher, 2003). Although this belief is growing less and less common in AA, there are still those who espouse that it is necessary for the alcoholic to reach this step before attempting to intervene.

Other critics of the 12-step group movement point out that it is based not on a foundation of scientific research, but on testimonials by individuals who assert that it was indeed essential to their recovery. Anecdotal stories, though perhaps very moving, do not constitute scientific research data supporting claims that AA (or similar groups) is effective. However, just as individuals who were "recovered" or "recovering" replaced physicians or ministers as speakers at temperance meetings, in many 12-step meetings one person is a designated speaker who affirms how the group saved his or her life. Dissenting opinions from mental health professionals are often dismissed because they "do not understand" the disease of addiction, or because they have "not been there."[27] In contrast to this program participants are elevated to the role of "experts" because they were once actively addicted to chemicals (Szalavitz, 2006).

Finally, research has demonstrated that only about 20% of those who join AA will abstain from alcohol for the rest of their lives (Lilienfeld et al., 2010). As these various points of criticism suggest, although the 12-step group movement may have played a major role in the recovery, there are many points of contention suggesting that these programs are not a panacea for individuals with alcohol (or, by extension, other drug) use disorders.

Chapter Summary

Alcoholics Anonymous was one of the first, and has grown into the predominant, almost exclusive self-help group model for individuals with an AUD. The program emerged as the first 100 members of the fledgling AA group movement who achieved long-term

---

[24]This clinical research, however, is ignored on the grounds that researchers just do not understand the disease of addiction, as will be discussed later in this chapter.

[25]This was an acceptable treatment method for alcohol withdrawal symptoms at the time.

[26]Another obscure fact is that "Bill" Wilson advocated the use of LSD to help the individual overcome some of the obstacles that prevented the person from achieving lasting recovery (Newsome, 2011).

[27]So, when you are having a heart attack, will you demand that you be cared for only by a physician who has "been there" by having a prior heart attack?

abstinence met to discuss the common elements that contributed to their recovery. This consensus resulted in the famous 12 steps of the AA program.

The AA program is designed to place emphasis on spiritual growth, without addressing religious issues. It is confrontative, without using confrontation, relies on external support for advertising or financial resources, and is not required of members but simply offered as a road that members might find useful in their quest for recovery from alcoholism. There is no "board of directors," and members who serve in various capacities do so as being an equal among equals. The growth of AA was slow initially, but has become a worldwide movement, with chapters in virtually every nation around the world, and has a total membership in the millions.

Questions have been raised about the effectiveness of AA as an effective adjunct to treatment for people with an AUD. By extension, these same questions apply to self-help groups modeled after the AA program. There is preliminary evidence suggesting that AA is a useful adjunct to the treatment of some, but not all, people with an AUD. Variations of this program have been applied to other problems, such as being the spouse of a person with an AUD (Al-Anon), and being the child of a person with an AUD (Alateen).

The AA program was also modified and applied to other drugs of abuse, resulting in programs such as the Narcotics Anonymous program, which was reviewed in this chapter. It has also been applied to a variety of non-drug-related compulsive behaviors such as compulsive eating, compulsive shopping, and so on. Further, there are a number of emergent self-help programs that reject one or more of the tenets of the AA program, but that still attempt to help individuals find abstinence from alcohol and other drugs of abuse.

CHAPTER 35

Substance Use Disorders and Infectious Disease[1]

Introduction

As a group, alcohol and illicit drug users are significantly more likely than nonusers to use the services of a hospital emergency room to require hospitalization and tend to require longer hospital stays before being ready for discharge as well. A major reason for this fact is the increased risk for infectious disease found in people with an substance use disorder (SUD). The SUDs contribute to infectious disease(s) through a variety of mechanisms. Chronic alcohol use depletes the body of essential nutrients, reducing the effectiveness of the immune system, whereas aspiration of material regurgitated can contribute to pneumonia. Intravenous drug use, rarely carried out under antiseptic conditions, pushes bacteria normally found on the skin into the circulation, bypassing the body's normal defenses against such invasion. Shared compounds for smoking (such as marijuana, for example) allow infectious micro-organisms in the lungs to be passed from one person to the next. The general environment in which illicit drug abusers live also predisposes them to infections. Some of the infectious diseases more commonly encountered in illicit drug abusers include peripheral cellulitis, skin abscesses, pneumonias, lung abscesses, brain abscesses, various viral diseases, and tetanus. In this chapter, we will discuss some of the more common infections associated with the SUDs.

Why Is Infectious Disease Such a Common Complication for People with an SUD?

There are many answers to this question. The general state of malnutrition so often found in the person with an SUD can compromise the effectiveness of the body's immune system. For example the methamphetamine addict might subsist on a "diet" of soda and candy bars, which will quell the pangs of hunger but hardly constitute a healthy diet. The alcohol-dependent person might, if asked, assert that they did indeed have dinner last night. When the matter is pursued, however, the drinker might admit that he or she had two bags of peanuts, some pretzels from the bowl on the bar, half a hamburger, and almost a dozen bottles of beer, a diet that is hardly going to support a health immune system. Further, there is evidence that alcohol use by itself can impair the immune system, placing the drinker at increased risk for infectious disease.

Sterile Technique

The conditions under which illicit drug abusers inject their drug(s) of choice make some form of infection almost certain. This is because the injected drug abuser rarely uses the "sterile technique" used by health care professionals. If a compound must be injected into the

---

[1]The author would like to express his appreciation to John P. Doweiko, MD, for his review of this chapter for technical accuracy.

body, health care professionals will use a new, sterile, needle and prepare the injection site with either alcohol or an antiseptic solution before injecting a sterile compound into the patient's body. The needle is then discarded. In contrast to this process, intravenous drug addicts usually just find a vein and insert the needle without even attempting to wash the injection site with soap and water. In the process, the addicted person will also push micro-organisms found on the surface of the skin into the body, effectively bypassing the body's normal defenses. The needle itself is rarely a new, sterile, needle, exposing the current user to all of the blood-borne infections in the body of the most recent past user. Obviously these acts both increase the individual's risk of contracting an infection.

Contamination

Illicit drugs are often contaminated with various microscopic pathogens, which are then injected directly into the body if the drug is administered via intravenous injection. Surprisingly, although pharmaceutical preparations are highly prized among illicit drug abusers because of their purity and known potency, they also might become contaminated as the abuser prepares the capsule or tablet for injection. The tablet or contents of the capsule are crushed into a fine powder so that it might be prepared for injection. The flat surface that is selected for this process, however, might be contaminated, transferring micro-organisms to the compound about to be injected. If they are forced to share the same needle, some IV drug abusers do not even attempt to sterilize it. At best they might lick the needle to clear off residual blood, and in the process transfer bacteria such as *Neisseria sicca* and *Streptococcus viridans* to the needle surface. These are bacteria normally found in the human mouth where the body has developed defenses against them, but by injecting them directly into the body, these defenses are circumvented.

Some intravenous drug abusers do attempt to rinse the rig[2] in tap water. This process contaminates the needle with various micro-organisms normally found in tap water (which when swallowed are destroyed by the body's defenses). These micro-organisms are then injected directly into protein-rich muscle tissue or the general circulation depending on the method by which the compound is abused, again side-stepping the body's natural defenses against such microscopic invaders.

The stage is now set for either a localized or a systemic infection.

The list of infectious diseases that might be transferred from one IV drug abuser to the next through contaminated needles includes (but is not limited to): the various viral forms of hepatitis (discussed later in this chapter), HIV-1 (the virus that causes AIDS),[3] syphilis, and even malaria. Some of the more commonly encountered infections seen in substance abusers are discussed next.

Assorted Bacterial Infection Seen in Intravenous Drug Abusers

Endocarditis

This is a bacterial infection of the valves of the heart. Normally, only 1 in every 20,000 people develop this condition, which can be the result of such infections as community-acquired pneumonia (discussed later). But intravenous drug abusers are considered a "high risk" population, with 1 in every 500 intravenous drug abusers developing this disorder (Robinson, Lazo, Davis, & Kufera, 2000). One reason for this is the chronic exposure to the irritating chemicals often used as adulterants.[4] But another cause is the failure of intravenous drug abusers to follow sterile technique: Many of the strains of bacteria that are introduced into the body colonize the tissues of the heart valves upon reaching them, establishing ongoing endocarditis. Finally, shared needles may transfer bacteria from one person with endocarditis to another abuser, who then goes on to become addicted in turn.

Necrotizing Fasciitis

This is a bacterial infection in which subcutaneous tissues are attacked by strains of bacteria normally only found on the surface of the skin (Karch, 2009). Cocaine abusers might be especially vulnerable to this condition, possibly because of its vasoconstrictive effects. However, any intravenous drug abuser who fails to utilize proper sterile technique will push any bacteria at the injection site through the skin into the subcutaneous

---

[2]See Glossary.

[3]Also discussed later in this chapter.

[4]Discussed in Chapter 36.

tissues, where they might establish an active infection. As the bacteria destroy the tissues under the skin they might also be carried by the circulation to other organs of the body. The subcutaneous tissues are destroyed first and the surface of the skin can appear to be normal until late in the disease cycle, making diagnosis difficult. Necrotizing fasciitis is a life-threatening infection, which is frequently fatal.

Skin Abscesses

The intravenous, or subcutaneous, drug abuser is vulnerable to bacterial infections at the injection site. Some of the adulterants mixed with heroin or cocaine will either cause or at least exacerbate skin abscesses. These adulterants are usually not water soluble and when injected will irritate surrounding tissues. These abscesses may become life threatening, require prolonged treatment, and leave the abuser with scars at the infection site for the rest of their lives if they survive.

The Pneumonias

Technically, the term *pneumonia* refers to an acute infection of the lungs, usually caused by bacteria or fungi.[5] It is usually diagnosed by radiological examination[6] of the lungs. Although pneumonia can develop in nonabusers, conditions such as the alcohol use disorders, immune systems disorders, cigarette smoking, extreme age, vitamin malabsorption syndromes, and malnutrition, all can contribute to the development of a pneumonia in a patient. People with an alcohol use disorder, for example, are twice as likely to develop bacterial pneumonia than are nondrinkers.

Fungal Pneumonia

The development of a fungal pneumonia is a common complication of HIV infection (discussed later in this chapter) and of heroin use/abuse (Karch, 2009). Heroin abuse interferes with the normal function of the immune system, reducing the body's ability to defend itself against these pathogens. But many samples of illicit heroin are also contaminated with fungi, which when injected into the body are transported by the circulation to the lungs where they might establish an infection site. Fungal pneumonia frequently requires

surgical removal of the infected tissues and the use of antibiotic compounds for an extended period of time.

Aspiration Pneumonia

There is a strong relationship between the alcohol use disorders and aspiration pneumonia, although many of the other drugs of abuse also can cause this condition and on occasion it will develop in a person without a history of an SUD. The chronic use of alcohol places the drinker at risk for various forms of lung infection (Kershaw & Guidot, 2008). If the individual should aspirate while regurgitating, she or he would be vulnerable to two different potentially life-threatening dangers. First, the material being regurgitated might be aspirated into the lungs, blocking the air passages. If the drinker is unable to clear the airway in time, hypoxia and possible death may be the result (Johnson & Hirsch, 2003). A second problem is that even if this threat is avoided some of the material aspirated could possibly start to decompose in the lungs, establishing a growth medium for bacteria.

To further complicate matters, chronic alcohol use alters the normal pattern of bacterial growth in the mouth and throat, again allowing these pathogens access to the lungs if they are aspirated. The respiratory system has few defenses against these micro-organisms because they are normally found in other regions of the body. To make things more complicated, the body's defenses are ill equipped to deal with bacterial growth in the respiratory system of a person whose immune system is often strained by malnutrition and vitamin malabsorption syndromes (Karch, 2009; Marik, 2001). The true incidence of aspiration pneumonia in the community is not known, because many cases are misdiagnosed as either community-acquired or nosocomial forms of pneumonia (Johnson & Hirsch, 2003). It is known that this is a common problem amongst people with an SUD, that it is potentially fatal, and is always a medical emergency that should be assessed and treated by trained medical professionals.

Community-Acquired Pneumonia (CAP)

Intravenous drug abusers, cigarette smokers, and people with alcohol use disorders are all at increased risk for a condition known as community-acquired pneumonia (CAP) (Karch, 2009). Each year in the United States between 2 and 3 million people contract CAP. Infected individuals will pass the offending bacteria, usually *Streptococcus pneumoniae*, to others through

---

[5]Plural of the word *fungus*.

[6]A fancy term for X-rays.

aspiration or inhalation of droplets that form when the person coughs (Musher, 2008). People living in close, crowded, quarters (such as shelters for the homeless, day-care centers, etc.) are more likely to spread *S. pneumoniae* to those around them (Musher, 2008). People whose immune system was compromised by malnutrition, vitamin malabsorption syndromes, or conditions that reduce the effectiveness of the immune system such as HIV infection have a reduced resistance to the offending bacteria, making it more likely to contract CAP. Cigarette smokers are especially vulnerable to a form of CAP caused by the bacteria *Haemophilus influenzae.*

Mild cases of CAP might be treated on an outpatient basis, but eventually 20% of individuals with this condition will require hospitalization, and 45,000 people die each year from CAP in spite of medical care. Individuals with comorbid conditions, such as people with an SUD, are more likely to require hospitalization either for the infection itself or for infection-related complications such as meningitis, endocarditis, and so on. Fortunately, a vaccine was introduced in the early 1980s, which will provide a degree of protection against *S. pneumoniae*–induced CAP (Musher, 2008).

Tuberculosis

Tuberculosis (TB[7]) is one of the oldest diseases known to plague humans. Genetic analysis suggests that the bacteria that cause TB first began to evolve 3 million years ago (Lehrman, 2013) and anthropologists have found evidence of tuberculosis at least 500,000 years ago (Barry & Cheung, 2009; Bynum, 2012; Raviglione & O'Brien, 2008; Roth, 2009). Since then, it has been estimated that TB has killed approximately 1 billion people, a number that far surpasses the estimated 40 million deaths around the world caused by the influenza epidemic of 1918–1920, or the total estimated number of deaths caused by the bubonic plague (Roth, 2009). Between the years 1600 and 1900, one in every five deaths in Europe is thought to have been caused by tuberculosis (MacKenzie, 2007). Nor has the infection become less lethal: At the start of the 21st century evidence is emerging suggesting that *Mycobacterium tuberculosis* (bacterium that causes TB) is evolving into new, more virulent forms that are resistant to

the antibiotics used to treat this disease (Lehrman, 2013).

Globally, tuberculosis is widespread: Almost one-third of the world's population is thought to be infected with TB, an additional 9 million more people[8] contract the infection each year and 1.4 million people die from it (Bynum, 2012; Lehrman, 2013; Schurr, 2007). Each infected person passes the infection to 10–15 other people, maintaining the chain of infection from one generation to the next (Barry & Cheung, 2009). At the start of the 20th century approximately 50–65% of infected individuals died within 5 years of the initial infection. The introduction of effective antitubercular medications and the development of effective dietary support in the mid-20th century made death from tuberculosis in the United States very rare at the start of the 21st century (Barry & Cheung, 2009; Simon, 2007). Currently 98% of TB-related deaths occur in the Third World countries, where treatment is difficult or even impossible to obtain (Barry & Cheung, 2009; Raviglione & O'Brien, 2008). Even in the industrialized countries where access to appropriate medical care is more easily obtained tuberculosis remains a potential danger, and the number of people contracting this infection is increasing (Bynum, 2012).

What Is Tuberculosis?

TB is an infection caused by one of the seven known genetically similar bacterium *Mycobacterium tuberculosis* (Bynum, 2012, Hauck, Neese, Panchal, & El-Amin, 2009; Lehrman, 2013; Raviglione & O'Brien, 2008). Most strains of *M. tuberculosis* replicate very slowly, and to the consternation of physicians has a protein molecule pattern in the cell wall that leaves it virtually unaffected to many antibiotics used to treat other bacterial infections. *M. tuberculosis* seems to prefer oxygen-rich organs in the body such as the lungs, although cases have been found involving virtually every other organ system in the body (Bynum, 2012; Raviglione & O'Brien, 2008). There is even evidence that *M. tuberculosis* can live without oxygen (Barry & Cheung, 2009).

There are a number of factors that help to determine whether a given individual might develop TB. Environmental factors such as intensity of exposure and malnutrition, combined with the individual's genetic

---

[7]Technically shorthand for Tubercle bacillus, although TB is generally accepted as an abbreviation for tuberculosis.

[8]This number is estimated to reflect only 60% of the actual total, because many countries do not track and report TB-related deaths (Raviglione & O'Brien, 2008).

predisposition and poor health all interact to influence the possibility of a person developing TB (Raviglione & O'Brien, 2008; Schurr, 2007). The higher the number of risk factors that a person might have, the greater the possibility that he or she will contract TB. There is also preliminary evidence suggesting that dietary or metabolic factors that influence the individual's ability to absorb vitamin D also influence the individual's risk of contracting TB (Wilkinson et al., 2000). Given that individuals with an alcohol or other SUDs often have a poor diet, the vitamin D hypothesis might help to explain why this subgroup tends to be at high risk for TB infection. Paradoxically, obesity seems to offer some degree of protection against tuberculosis (Roth, 2009).

How Is Tuberculosis Transmitted, and How Does It Kill?

The usual mode of transmission is on microscopic droplets of liquid expelled whenever the host sings, talks, coughs, or sneezes. These droplets might remain suspended in midair for extended periods of time, allowing another person to inhale them into the deepest regions of the respiratory system (Bynum, 2012; Markel, 2004). In the healthy individual, the pulmonary defenses destroy or control more than 90% of the inhaled *M. tuberculosis* bacteria (Bynum, 2012; Raviglione & O'Brien, 2008). However, in cases where the person's pulmonary defenses are compromised by poor health, malnutrition, or concurrent infection, it becomes more difficult for the body to effectively eject *M. tuberculosis* before it becomes established in the lungs. In these cases the immune system attempts to mount a counterattack. The initial wave of the immune system response is when the body's macrophages engulf the invading bacteria, surround them, and wall them inside little pockets known as *granulomas*. In response, the *M. tuberculosis* enters a dormant state within the granulomas where it might remain for years if not decades.

However, if the individual's immune system should become compromised by another infection, or malnutrition, the body loses its ability to keep the *M. tuberculosis* bacteria in the granulomas.[9] It then becomes

possible for the bacteria to burst out and invade the surrounding tissue. This is known as reactivation TB, which accounts for a large percentage of all cases of TB in the United States at this time (Lehrman, 2013; Markel, 2004). It is at this point that the body attempts to use a different strategy to attack the invading bacteria: the lymphocytes are called upon to destroy the bacteria. Unfortunately, during this process the lymphocytes also release a toxin that destroys the surrounding tissue, usually the lung tissues. In the case of a TB infection in the lungs, less and less of the lung is able to function properly, and eventually the patient dies of pulmonary failure.

The Treatment of TB

Unfortunately, physicians and public health officials became complacent about TB, and in many cases treatment programs that were effective in essentially eliminating TB in this country in the 1950s and 1960s were rapidly scaled back or eliminated entirely. Then around the year 1984 health care professionals were stunned to find a growing number of "reactivation" cases of TB in patients whose infection was formerly latent and often unsuspected by health care professionals (Markel, 2004). Researchers soon discovered that between 10 and 15 million people in the United States had a latent TB infection providing a "pool" of infected people, each of whom had the potential to infect others should their infection become active again (Hauck et al., 2009).

Several antibiotics have been developed that are effective in treating tuberculosis. However, the bacteria is also evolving in ways that makes it resistant to these antibiotics (Bynum, 2012; Migliori, De Laco, Besozzi, & Cirillo, 2009). Currently, it is estimated that 5% of new cases of TB around the globe are resistant to at least one of the antibiotics traditionally used to treat it (World Health Organization, 2008). More alarmingly, about 9% of new cases of tuberculosis are resistant to the standard dosing schedule of every known medication used to treat this disorder (Barry & Cheung, 2009; Coghlan, 2012; Migliori et al., 2009).[10] However, in general, physicians still have a number of medications that they might call upon to treat the average person

---

[9]Bynum (2012) noted that the person who has been infected with tuberculosis has a 5–10% chance of developing an active infection at some point in their lives. The person with HIV infection has a 5–10% chance of developing an active TB infection per year because of their compromised immune system.

[10]Laboratory studies have suggested that the use of Vitamin C in combination with existing antitubercular medications increases their effectiveness, although this research has not been replicated and further research to determine whether this phenomenon will work in humans or remain just a laboratory curiosity must be carried out (Vilcheze, Hartman, Weinrick, & Jacobs, 2013).

who has tuberculosis. The second-line medications that they call upon when the more common treatments fail are not as effective as first-line antitubercular drugs and the treatment regimens might require that the patient take medications three to four times a day for up to 24 months (Cohen, 2004; Markel, 2004). However, if used as directed these medications can usually clear the infection from the person's body after 1–2 years. There are new drugs under development that will cut the treatment regimen to just a single week-long course of antibiotics, but these medications will require years before they are available for clinical use (Cohen, 2004). Further, it should be noted that the eradication of an active TB infection does not confer any degree of protection against possible reinfection should the person again be exposed to *M. tuberculosis.*

There are many reasons for the development of drug-resistant strains of tuberculosis. Patient noncompliance with taking prescribed medications is a major factor in the development of treatment-resistant tuberculosis (Barry & Cheung, 2009; Markel, 2004; Simon, 2007). Other factors that contribute to the development of treatment-resistant strains of tuberculosis include limited access to medical care or failure to follow through with recommended treatment(s). In the Third World countries, access to appropriate treatments is limited at best and the medications are often impossible to obtain except by those who can afford the medications in parts of the world where such treatments are hard to obtain. The untreated are simply left to live their lives as best as possible, spreading the infection to those around them. This is most clearly seen in the fact that globally the greatest proportion of treatment-resistant TB cases are found in countries where medical care is difficult or impossible to obtain (World Health Organization, 2008). Finally, the *M. tuberculosis* antibiotics are just another in a very long line of environmental challenges to be met through the mechanism of selective survival: Those strains of the bacteria that are best able to resist the antibiotics are most likely to reproduce, leaving an increasingly resistant pool of bacteria to infect new victims.

Substance abusers are not immune to tuberculosis infections. Oeltmann, Kammerer, Pevzner, and Moonan (2009) found that 18.7% of the 28,650 patients infected with TB examined also had an SUD, with alcohol being the most commonly abused substance. Given alcohol's ability to damage the liver, and the fact that many of the medications used to treat TB are metabolized in the liver, this finding has clinical significance for patients

currently being treated for this disorder. It might be necessary for the physician to extend the period of active treatment in such patients, according to the authors. Patients with a concurrent SUD were also found to be less likely to adhere to the medication program, and medication adherence often be monitored by a health care professional to ensure that the patient completes the entire course of treatment. Thus, the SUDs are a significant complicating factor for the treatment of tuberculosis, and threaten to reawaken a plague that once killed millions of people around the world each year in pandemics that have shaped the course of history.[11]

The Viral Infections

The viral infectious process often is confusing to the person who is not a health care professional. It is also confusing to scientists who are still debating whether the virus is a living organism in itself or not. Essentially, once a virus particle enters the target cell, it "reprograms" the cell's genetic instructions so that it now starts to produce thousands of copies of that virus rather than maintain normal intracellular function. When that cell ruptures, it releases those copies into the body, where they then infect other cells. Eventually, hundreds, millions, or even billions of cells are involved in the process of producing new viral particles. Normally there are two stages to the body's immune system response to a viral infection.

The first time that the body is exposed to a new pathogen, it must rely on generalized disease-fighting cells known as lymphocytes. These generalist immune system cells roam through the body, seeking out and attacking any cell with a foreign protein pattern in their cell walls. However, although the lymphocytes are staging the initial counterattack to the viral infection, another process is taking place: The body learns to manufacture specific antibodies for that virus so that the body might fight off the infection. Every species of bacteria, virus, or fungus has a characteristic pattern of protein molecules in the walls of its cells. The immune system learns to recognize the specific molecular pattern in these disease-causing micro-organisms and to attack them. This process may take hours, days, weeks, or in some cases years. After they are formed, however, these antibodies drift through the body,

---

[11]This topic lies outside of the scope of this chapter, although it is discussed in far more detail in infectious disease textbooks.

searching for the specific invading pathogens for which they were tailor made, and the person is said to be "immune" to that disease. However, this process is not perfect and there are several forms of viral infection commonly found in alcohol or drug abusers that can result in permanent infection, and massive damage to body organs if not recognized and treated. In this section we will look at some of the more common forms of such viral infection.

Acquired Immune Deficiency Syndrome (AIDS)

A Short History of AIDS

In 1981 scientists had collected data suggesting that a previously unknown disease was spreading through the United States. In afflicted people the immune system would fail, leaving the person vulnerable to a range of rare "opportunistic infections"[12] rarely seen except in those people whose immune system had been seriously compromised. Initially this disorder was found mainly in homosexual males, leading to the name gay-related immune deficiency, or GRID. Within a short time the infection began to appear in intravenous drug abusers and people who had received a blood transfusion, suggesting that it was a previously unknown blood-borne pathogen.

Researchers renamed this disorder the Acquired Immune Deficiency Syndrome, or AIDS, and subsequently discovered that it was caused by an infection with the human immunodeficiency virus, type 1 (HIV-1). Scientists now believe that the HIV-1 virus "jumped" from chimpanzees to humans in Africa in the period between the years 1884 and 1924, although it is possible that in isolated cases humans might have been infected with HIV earlier ("Scientists trace AIDS virus origin to 100 years ago," 2008). This virus is part of the human retrovirus family,[13] genetic cousins of the human retrovirus family infect sheep, goats, horses, cattle, cats and monkeys (Fauci & Lane, 2010). It was originally thought that there was just one virus that infected the human immune system, although it has since been recognized that there are two such viruses in this family: HIV-1 and HIV-2. The virus that causes AIDS in humans is usually referred to as "the AIDS virus" or "HIV" for the most part, although some centers utilize the more correct term *HIV-1* or *HIV-2* infection. HIV-2 infection is rare in the United States but is more common in Europe.

What Is AIDS?

Technically, AIDS is not a disease in its own right. Rather, it is a syndrome induced by the infection with HIV-1 or HIV-2 that ultimately causes the individual's immune system to break down. As the HIV infection progresses, the untreated patient develops and ultimately dies from a secondary infection, neoplasm, or other condition once easily controlled by the body's immune system.[14]

Where Did HIV Come From?

Current research evidence suggests that the HIV virus "jumped" from chimpanzees to humans approximately 100 years ago (Crawford, 2011). Other diseases that made the "jump" into humans include the West Nile Virus, hantavirus, and Elbola (David Baltimore, quoted in Svitil, 2003). This is known as a "trans-species jump"[15] and is one of the survival strategies for the virus: Individual host species might die out or build resistance to the virus, but by making the "jump" to another species the virus can continue to exist. There is little, if any, creditable evidence that the virus was intentionally released into the population to target homosexual males or other minority group members, or that it is divine retribution for past sins (Vaughn, 2006). Those who doubt that a virus can cause HIV infection either do not understand the viral infection process or doubt this theory for ideological reasons.

The Scope of HIV Infection

The human immunodeficiency virus is remarkable: In the span of a half of a century AIDS has been transformed from an obscure virus found only in isolated areas of Africa to the fourth most common cause of

---

[12]It is estimated, for example, that people with HIV infection have a sixfold higher risk for developing a methicillin-resistant *Staphylococcus aureus* infection (MRSA) than who do not have HIV infection (Popovich, Weinstein, Aroutcheva, Rice, & Hota, 2010).

[13]Subfamily lentiviruses if you are interested in such things.

[14]The antiviral agents currently in use can induce their own constellation of side effects (such as accelerated atherosclerotic changes in the circulatory system), which are technically not induced by the HIV infection itself.

[15]See Glossary.

death around the world (Lashley, 2006; Markel, 2004).[16] An estimated 34 million people around the world are infected with the AIDS virus, with about half of these people not being aware of this fact (United Nations, 2012). Globally, another 2.5 million people become infected with HIV each year, many in countries where antiviral treatments are difficult to obtain at best (United Nations, 2012). Each year between 56,000 and 66,000 people in the United States are infected with HIV (Harmon, 2010).

Most of those who have died from HIV infection or who are currently infected with this virus are in the Third World, especially the sub-Sahara region of Africa (Rhame, 2009). Although only 11% of the world's populations lives in the sub-Sahara region of Africa, 67% of the world's HIV infections, 70% of new infections each year, and 75% of HIV-related deaths each year are found there (Rhame, 2009). In the United States, 1 to 1.18 million people have been infected with HIV. Each year 50,000 new cases of HIV infection are identified in the United States. A quarter of these new cases are people in the 13- to 24-year age bracket. Fully 60% of those people who are infected with HIV in the United States do not know that they carry the infection (Centers for Disease Control and Prevention, 2012). HIV infection carries with it a significant degree of social stigma, which might express itself through a bidirectional distrust of and by the medical establishment by many of those who are infected (Earnshaw, Bogart, Dovidio, & Williams, 2013). Racial disparities in access to treatment resources also exist contributing to the spread of HIV infection of among previously uninfected populations.

Pediatric AIDS

An unexpected subgroup of persons infected with HIV are under the age of 18. The fact that most members of society ignore this fact is remarkable because HIV infection is the seventh most common cause of death for children and adolescents (Van Dyke & Chakraboety, 2013). In the United States, in 2010, 12,200 of the new cases of HIV were in children and adolescents, 59.5% of whom were initially unaware that they were infected (Van Dyke & Chakraboety, 2013). Vertical

transmission of the infection at birth, sexual contact with an infected partner,[17] and experimental intravenous drug use are three of the methods through which HIV infection is transmitted. These individuals are often ostracized and socially isolated after revealing that they have HIV, contributing to feelings of depression on their part.

The introduction of effective antiviral medications has resulted in a pool of individuals who were infected as children or adolescents living to adulthood. The therapeutic and social support needs for this population will depend on the individual's level of maturity, intelligence, and age, and will change as the individual matures. A support team comprised of physicians, social workers, and if the individual has an SUD a substance abuse rehabilitation counselor will help the individual make the transition from adolescence to young adulthood; however, this step will frequently be difficult for the individual even with this support system.

How Does AIDS Kill?

The AIDS virus differs from many of the traditional viral agents that infect the body. HIV infects the very cells sent out by the body to destroy it: The CD4 cells of the immune system (Bell, 2009). The CD4 cells, also known as the T-helper cells or lymphocytes, are generalists that roam the body looking for foreign invaders (Covington, 2005; Markel, 2004). It has been estimated that following infection between 93 and 99% of the total number of HIV viral particles in the person's body are found in the CD4 cells. Small concentrations of the virus particles are found in the cells of the retina, the brain, the testes, and other regions of the body (Pomerantz, 1998, 2003). These sites provide a reservoir of viral particles that might reinfect the person whose body had otherwise been cleansed of the virus (Pomerantz, 1998, 2003).

One of two protein molecules found in the CD4 cell wall is known as the chemokine receptors. Following the introduction of the virus into the body the virus particles join with the CD4 cells and inject its own genetic instructions into the latter cell. In the initial phase of the infection (1–4 weeks of the time of infection) between 50 and 90% persons will develop nonspecific symptoms of a viral infection (Chu & Selwin, 2010). These nonspecific symptoms of early stage HIV

---

[16]There is a divergence between the sexes in this area however, with AIDS being the most common cause of death for women around the world. In men heart disease is the most common cause of death around the world, with AIDS and traffic accidents tied for second place for men (Hamzelou, 2013).

[17]Many of whom, as noted, were initially unaware that they were infected with HIV.

infection usually resolve in 2–4 weeks, usually without raising suspicion of a possible new HIV infection. Thirty years ago, it was thought that HIV-1 infection went through a "latency" period. However, it is now recognized that the virus begins to replicate almost immediately after it gains admission to the human body. The so-called latency period was an illusion caused by the fact that early blood tests for HIV infection did not reveal signs of the infection for up to 56 days after the individual contracted the virus (Chu & Selwin, 2010). Currently, blood tests can reveal signs of HIV infection within 11–15 days of initial infection (Chu & Selwin, 2010). However, HIV-1 can remain asymptomatic in infected persons for up to 10 years before one of the opportunistic infections caused by the disorder develop, by which time the infection might have progressed to an advanced stage. Indeed, in about 20% of the cases, the development of an opportunistic infection(s) is the first sign outward that the person is infected with HIV (Silvestri, 2009).

The HIV-1 virus has developed methods to thwart the body's immune system. First, the HIV-1 virus has been found to have three protein clusters in the viral coat that render it invisible to the body's immune system after it infects a cell (Schaefer, Wonderlich, Roeth, Leonard, & Collins, 2008). One of these proteins also marks the infected cell so that it will not be attacked by the virus a second time according to the authors. Next, each time that the AIDS virus replicates in the victim's body it produces slightly different copies of itself. The specific mechanism for this is quite technical, and well beyond the scope of this text. However, in brief the HIV tends to be "sloppy" during the process of replication, allowing subtle mistakes to slip into the genetic code of each new generation of virus particles. These new "daughter" virus particles are also called "mutations" or "variants" (Forstein, 2002). These variants are released back into the general circulation, but because they do not have the exact molecular pattern of the original viral particle the body must learn to produce antibodies against these "new" invaders as well. At the end of the person's life, the body might literally have billions of slightly different viral particles in his or her body, each of which causes the body to respond to it as if it were a separate virus, overwhelming the immune system. As the immune system weakens, various "opportunistic" infections once easily controlled by the immune system develop. In many cases the individual's death is the result of one of the opportunistic infections.

There is also an emerging body of evidence suggesting that persons with HIV infection are at about a twofold higher risk for a heart attack (myocardial infarction) (Freiberg et al., 2013), and also at risk for sudden cardiac death (Tseng et al., 2012). The authors found that persons with HIV infection were 2.6 to 4.5 times as likely to suffer a sudden cardiac death even with low blood viral load counts, although the authors did admit that their study was retrospective in nature, and might overestimate the extent of sudden cardiac death because their sample had a higher percentage of subjects with preexisting heart disease. Still, this is an area that warrants further research to identify the causal mechanism and possible treatments. Another risk factor for HIV progression is whether the infected person smokes cigarettes, which appear to accelerate the progression of the AIDS virus in the infected person for unknown reasons.

The Chain of HIV Infection

In spite of its reputation, HIV is a rather fragile virus, and is not easily transmitted from one person to another (Oldstone, 2010). There are several methods of HIV transmission: Male-to-male sexual contact is the most common method of HIV transmission in the United States at this time, accounting for 57% of new cases of HIV (Smith et al., 2010). Receptive anal intercourse is an effective method of HIV transmission because the microscopic tears in rectal tissues provide the virus with access to the bloodstream of the receptive partner. It has been estimated that the odds of contracting HIV infection from receptive anal intercourse with an infected partner are as high as 1:10 (Mayer, Skeer, & Mimiaga, 2010). Unfortunately 60% of those who are infected with HIV are unaware of their infection, contributing to the continued transmission of HIV. Seventy-two percent of new cases of HIV infection in the United States were in men in the 13- to 24-year age bracket who engaged in same sex relations.

Unprotected heterosexual intercourse (where only one partner is infected with HIV) is the second most common method of HIV transmission, although vaginal intercourse is not a very effective method of HIV transmission. The odds of contracting HIV after a single unprotected coital act with an infected partner has been estimated to be approximately 1:2,000 (Mayer et al., 2010). Obviously, repeated sexual contact with an infected partner increases the odds of viral transmission to the uninfected partner. Seventy-five percent of women who have contracted HIV infection are thought to have done so as a result of unprotected sexual activity with an infected partner.

The sharing of intravenous needles by drug abusers or addicts is the third most common method of disease transmission in the United States at this time ("HIV Infection Among Injection Drug Users—34 States, 2004–2007," 2010). HIV infection among intravenous drug abusers has been reported in 120 countries around the world (Arasteh & des Jarlais, 2008) and it has been estimated that approximately 40% of intravenous drug abusers are infected with the HIV (MacArthur et al., 2012). In the United States there has been an 80% drop in the number of people who contract HIV through shared intravenous needles, which is a tribute to the effectiveness of harm reduction efforts (Centers for Disease Control and Prevention, 2009a). The development of appropriate blood screening tests has made HIV transmission via transfusion or use of blood products in medical procedures very rare.[18]

A less common method of HIV transmission is known as "vertical transmission." During this process an infected woman passes the virus on to her baby, usually during childbirth. The odds of vertical transmission is reduced to <1% if the mother is fully compliant with an aggressive antiviral medication regimen (Havens, 2009; Rhame, 2009). It is also possible for the mother to infect the infant through breast feeding (Fauci & Lane, 2008). The risk for a health care worker who suffers an accidental "needle stick" has been estimated as between 0.3 and 0.9% (Fauci & Lane, 2008; Longo & Fauci, 2008), and the possibility of HIV transmission through an accidental needle stick will not be discussed further in this text.

Research into HIV-1 has shown that there are multiple subtypes of the HIV virus each of which has a different distribution pattern around the world. Further, when two infected individuals share an intravenous needle or have sex, the virus particles in their blood intermix, conjointly infect cells in each individual, and within the cell swap genetic material so that the emerging virus daughter cells are unlike any of the earlier generations of virus particles. As a result of intermixing of different strains of the virus as well as the natural process of genetic mutation in the virus, at least 48 different strains of HIV have been identified by genetic coding techniques vastly altering the process of diagnosis and treatment of HIV infection in humans because it is now possible to avoid the use of medications proven ineffective for certain strains of HIV in favor of more effective compounds (Tebit & Arts, 2010).

Stages of HIV Infection

Sax (2003) identified six stages of the typical HIV infection:

1. Viral transmission: Point where a previously uninfected person first contracts HIV.

2. Acute HIV infection: Within 1–4 weeks of stage 1, 50–90% of newly infected people develop a mild, flu-like syndrome. This may be dismissed by the individual, and because the symptoms are vague and nonspecific this might be misdiagnosed by the physician, if consulted. If the physician is suspicious, she or he might order a HIV viral load test, but it might take 2–6 weeks between stage 1 (above) and the time that the viral load test will detect the first virus particles in the patient's blood (Sax, 2003; Yu & Daar, 2000).[19] It should be noted that during this time, although the individual's body has not started to produce an HIV-specific immune response, he or she remains capable of passing the infection on to others.

3. Seroconversion: This occurs within 6 months of the date of infection and marks the point where the individual's body has started to mount an HIV-specific immune response. It is at this point that HIV-specific antibodies are first found in the individual's blood. The individual is now said to be seropositive, or HIV positive. Those people who do not show signs of an HIV-specific immune response are said to be seronegative. There are two possible reasons why a person might be seronegative: (1) the person has never been exposed to HIV or (2) it is still too early for blood tests to detect an HIV-specific immune response. It is recommended that the individual be retested 3 months later, to rule out this possibility. Obviously, if the individual engages in a "high risk" behavior, he or she will have to wait 6 more months before having a blood test to detect a HIV-specific immune response, and then 3 more

---

[18]Rhame (2009) reported that this route of transmission in the United States has been "virtually eliminated" (p. 38) as a result of rigorous blood testing prior to transfusion.

[19]The current HIV viral load tests can detect as few as 20 virus particles per cubic milliliter of blood (Mylonakis, Pailou, & Rich, 2001; Work Group on HIV/AIDS, 2000). As long as the viral load in the patient's blood is less than the level of detection, the infection can slip under the "radar" of modern medicine.

months for confirmatory testing. If the individual should have a "positive" test, follow-up testing should be performed to rule out a "false positive" result on the initial test. Once the HIV-specific immune system response is detected physicians will usually order a viral load test, which provides a measure of the patient's status (Mylonakis et al., 2001).

4. Asymptomatic infection: At this point the HIV infection might only be detected through blood tests, although the virus is replicating in the patient's body and he or she can pass the virus on to others.

5. Symptomatic HIV infection: At this point the individual's immune system has started to break down, allowing "opportunistic infections" to begin to develop. Such infections include "thrush," cervical dysplasia or cancer, constant low-grade fever, unexplained weight loss, development of peripheral neuropathies, and so on (Sax, 2003).

6. Acquired immune deficiency syndrome (AIDS): The body produces special cells to fight off invading microbes that are known as the CD4+ T (sometimes called the T-helper cells). Normally there are between 1,000 and 1,200 CD4+ T cells per cubic milliliter of blood. When the number of CD4+ T cells falls below 200 per cubic milliliter of blood, the individual becomes vulnerable to various opportunistic infections that are the hallmark of AIDS. The most common opportunistic infection in the respiratory system is pneumocystis pneumonia (PCP), although tuberculosis and CAP[20] are often encountered as well.[21] Tuberculosis is 100 times more common in those people infected with HIV than in the general population (Bartlett, 1999). In many cases TB is the first outward sign that a person has AIDS, and the infection seems to progress more rapidly in HIV-infected people (Raviglione & O'Brien, 2008).

Life Expectancy for People with HIV-1 Infection

Before the development of effective antiviral medications for HIV, the mean survival time after the person contracted this viral infection was 10 years (Cooper, 2008).

About 10% of those people who were infected were "rapid progressers" who developed AIDS within 5 years of infection, whereas about 10% of those infected were "slow progressers" who took an exceptionally long time to progress to AIDS.[22] Although great strides have been made in developing medications that will slow the replication of the virus, even with the best antiviral treatments available the average HIV-infected person is thought to lose 10 potential years of life (Cooper, 2008).[23] The infected person who is also an active intravenous drug addict is thought to lose approximately 20 years of potential life span to the combined effects of HIV infection and their SUD (Cooper, 2008).

There is a very small subgroup (approximately one out of every three hundred infected persons) whose body seems to have fought the infection to a standstill (Walker, 2012). Their bodies still carry the virus. The body of these individuals appears to be able to hold the virus at bay, preventing it from progressing further (Walker, 2012). Scientists are trying to isolate the protective factor in their blood to determine whether it might be a potential treatment approach for this disease.

The Treatment of HIV Infection

There are ongoing efforts to develop a vaccine to prevent HIV infection, but to date these efforts have met with little success (Andersson, 2008). One of the most important factors in the treatment of HIV infection is early detection, so that antiviral therapies can be initiated. Unfortunately, HIV is spreading far more rapidly than people are being placed on antiviral therapy regimens (Coghlan & MacKenzie, 2011). One reflection of this fact is that it is not uncommon HIV infection to be detected only about 1–3 years before the onset of AIDS (Carr & Lynfield, 2009; Shouse et al., 2009). This reflects, in part, the complacency that has developed in the general public who have mistakenly come to believe that HIV/AIDS no longer presents a threat to the individual.[24]

---

[20]Discussed elsewhere in this chapter.

[21]It should also be noted that the Hepatitis C virus (discussed below) can also be transmitted through contaminated intravenous needles. At least 33% of HIV positive persons in the United States are also infected with the Hepatitis C virus.

[22]The introduction of effective antiviral treatments made it impossible to determine the median survival time for slow progressers.

[23]This figure assumes that the person has been infected with HIV just once. There is strong evidence that suggests that subsequent infection with HIV from other sources (infected sexual partner or intravenous drug use involving a shared IV needle with an infected person) might accelerate the progression of HIV to the stage of AIDS (Smith et al., 2004).

[24]It also reflects the average time between initial infection and when the first blood test for HIV infection is carried out, as few people suspect infection in the early stages of HIV infection.

Once infected, a very important component of HIV treatment is the patient's nutritional status (Hendricks & Gorbach, 2009). Intravenous drug abusers typically lack access to adequate food sources, and even when appropriate food is ingested illicit drugs can interfere with the absorption of many vitamins and minerals needed for adequate health (Hendricks & Gorbach, 2009). One such micronutrient is selenium. Individuals who took a selenium supplement as prescribed were found to have no increase in viral load levels, and an increase in the CD4 T cell count (Hurwitz et al., 2007). The authors concluded that the daily supplementation of the individual's diet with selenium was an inexpensive way to both suppress the virus replication process and increase the CD4 T cell count. Further research into the impact of dietary malabsorption syndromes on health status of HIV-infected patients is necessary.

Pharmaceutical companies have developed an ever-growing number of antiviral agents to assist in the fight against AIDS, turning what was once a virtual death sentence into a chronic but treatable infectious disease. Unfortunately: (1) these compounds slow but do not eliminate the replication of HIV and (2) the high cost of obtaining these medications prohibits some people from being treated (Craig, 2004). There are several classes of antiviral agents and a brief summary of the different classes of antiviral agents and their mechanism of action are found in Appendix Three. To combat the problem of viral resistance to the antiviral medication(s), physicians simultaneously prescribe medications from different classes of antivirals (Henry, Alozie & Bonham, 2009). Once termed HAART ("highly active antiretroviral therapy") this treatment format is often referred to as CART ("combination antiretroviral therapy").

Medication noncompliance is the main reason why CART is less than 100% effective. It has been estimated that the patient must take a minimum of 80–90% of the prescribed medication doses at the proper time to achieve maximum effect and limit the development of strains of HIV that are resistant to the medications (Scott & Marcotte, 2010). The team of Barclay, Wright, and Hinkin (2010) offered an even higher figure of 90–95% compliance being necessary to achieve the highest degree of viral suppression. Unfortunately, up to 40% of patients on HAART medication programs are not compliant with taking their medications as prescribed, in part because of their harsh side effects. Another reason for treatment noncompliance is the concurrent use/abuse of recreational chemicals.

Braithwaite and Bryant (2010), for example, stated that even "sub-hazardous" level of alcohol use is associated with a lower level of treatment compliance (p. 285) and increased mortality. Other reasons for treatment noncompliance include those persons who are depressed or who have unrealistic expectations for the treatment process.

Although antiviral medications might slow the replication of HIV in the human body, they do not eliminate the virus from the body. To date, the complete eradication of HIV from the body remains a goal that has not been achieved. To accomplish this, it would be necessary to eliminate every one of the estimated 1 trillion (1,000,000,000,000) of the virus particles found in the body, including those within infected cells, to achieve a total cure (J. Doweiko, personal communication, 2010). A few antidotal reports of HIV remission have been reported; however, the total cure for HIV infection remains an elusive goal at this time. In theory new treatment methods could prevent the spread of HIV and hint at the possibility of a cure in the distant future (Coghlan & MacKenzie, 2011).

AIDS and Suicide

There is a great deal of controversy about the relationship between HIV infection and suicide. It is currently thought that individuals infected with the AIDS virus who are receiving adequate antiviral therapy are three times as likely to commit suicide as an uninfected person the same age (Carrico, 2010). The period of greatest risk appears to be the period immediately after the individual learns that he or she has been infected with the virus. It is thus recommended that a suicide risk assessment be carried out with each patient with HIV, periodically after treatment has started, and that comorbid psychiatric conditions be addressed (Carrico, 2010).

AIDS and Kaposi's Sarcoma

When AIDS was first identified in the early 1980s, physicians thought that a rare form of cancer known as Kaposi's sarcoma was a manifestation of this disease. This misunderstanding was result of the fact that 40% of individuals infected with HIV also developed Kaposi's sarcoma (Antman & Chang, 2000). However, since then it has been discovered that Kaposi's sarcoma is caused by a virus from the herpes virus family (Antman & Chang, 2000), and thus is a separate disorder from HIV.

AIDS and Neurocognitive Dysfunction

Shortly after the individual is infected with the HIV virus, it enters the brain where the virus is able to cause inflammation and the accumulation of neurotoxic compounds such as the cytokines. This in turn will activate the brain's defensive immune response system, resulting in the destruction of both neurons and glial cells (Fauci & Lane, 2010; Scott & Marcotte, 2010). This appears to be the mechanism for neurocognitive problems that are found in at least 50% of those people infected with HIV (Scott & Marcotte, 2010). The degrees of neurocognitive deficit can range from very mild to severe, and were classified by Scott and Marcotte (2010) as follows:

Asymptomatic: Neuropsychological test performance at least two standard deviations below expectations in two of five areas assessed, but the patient retains ability to carry out activities of daily living (ADLs).[25]

Minor neurocognitive deficits: In addition to aforementioned criteria, the individual does have a mild impairment in his or her ability to carry out ADLs but does not meet the criteria for dementia.

HIV-associated dementia: Neuropsychological test scores that are at least two standard deviations below norms on two of the five areas assessed for that individual, and marked impairment in their ability to carry out ADLs.

Strict medication adherence has been found to reduce the probability that the individual will develop HIV-related neurocognitive problems, or at least the severity of such deficits if they develop (Scott & Marcotte, 2010).

HIV Infection and Employment

It has been estimated that HIV infection results in a $22,000 per year reduction in earning potential for the individual (Scott & Marcotte, 2010). Because many insurance companies are unwilling to pay for the high cost of programs such as HAART/CART, individuals who are infected with HIV often must stop working and turn to programs such as Social Security, so that their medications will be paid for by other agencies.

HIV and Mood Disorders

Depression is common among persons with HIV, but care should be taken to differentiate between the individual being demoralized because of their health status, bereavement over the loss of friends and loved ones to HIV, accidents, or other diseases, and actual depression (Cohen, 2013). Cohen (2013) also suggested that posttraumatic stress disorder is common among patients who carry the AIDS virus; however, there has been little other research suggesting that this is true.

Section Summary

AIDS has been identified as the end stage of a viral infection caused by the HIV, a blood-borne virus that is a member of a family of viruses that share certain common characteristics. Over time, different members of the HIV family of viruses have been identified, which are now identified by numbers (HIV-1, HIV-2, etc.). AIDS is now known to be the end stage of an infection by either HIV-1 or, more rarely, HIV-2 (Lashley, 2006). Initially, infection with either virus was a virtual death sentence, and prior to the introduction of effective antiviral medications the average survival period between initial infection and death from an opportunistic infection(s) was approximately 10 years. The new antiviral medications have transformed HIV infection from a virtual death sentence to that of a chronic disease that can be controlled such as diabetes or heart disease, and there is a glimmer of hope that it might be possible to cure an infected person of this disease although this remains a very distant goal.

Viral Hepatitis

The term *hepa* refers to the liver, whereas *titis* denotes an inflammation of the specified organ system. Thus, the term *hepatitis* is a general term that means inflammation of the liver, which then must be qualified by the causal agent such as "alcohol-induced hepatitis" or "toxin-induced hepatitis," and so on. Viral hepatitis refers to an inflammation of the liver, induced by any of a number of different viral agents (Orr, 2008). In this section, we will briefly discuss some of the forms of viral hepatitis commonly encountered in the treatment of people with an SUD. Scientists have labeled each of the viral agents that can induce hepatitis by a letter, to better classify them.

A Brief History of Viral Hepatitis

Physicians have long known that if a person were to be exposed to water or food contaminated by fecal matter that he or she might become ill with any of a wide

---

[25]See Glossary.

variety of diseases.[26] It was only in the 20th century that physicians began to understand that there were viral pathogens that might attack the liver. The first such virus to be identified was initially called just "viral hepatitis." But physicians also were aware that some patients developed hepatitis after receiving a blood transfusion, a condition that they began to call "serum hepatitis." In 1966 a virus that was classified as Hepatitis Type "B" (HVB) was isolated. Unfortunately, it was soon discovered that HVA and HVB could not explain every case of what appeared to be viral hepatitis. It was hypothesized that yet another, undiscovered, virus could also cause viral hepatitis in humans, and patients with hepatitis who did not appear to have either type "A" or Type "B" hepatitis were said to have "non-A/non-B" hepatitis. Then in 1988[27] an additional five viruses that could infect the human liver were identified, which are now classified as Hepatitis type C (HVC), Hepatitis type D (HVD), Hepatitis type E (HVE), Hepatitis type F (HVF), and Hepatitis type G (HVG). There is evidence to suggest that the virus that causes HVG is a distant genetic cousin to the virus that causes HVA, and that as a result of a process known as "genetic drift" has evolved into a distinct subtype of HVC.

Hepatitis "A" Virus

Method of Transmission

Viral hepatitis caused by the "A" virus (HVA) most commonly is transmitted by oral-fecal transmission[28] (Orr, 2008), although 5% of cases are thought to involve the sharing of a contaminated intravenous drug needle. A person might be exposed to the virus by changing a diaper that is contaminated by fecal matter, changing contaminated bed linens from a bed where an infected person was resting, and then failing to wash their hands. Other methods of transmission include swimming in contaminated water or having food products served that have not been properly cooked to ensure the death of pathogens, for example. Proper hand washing, appropriate food preparation, or not sharing intravenous needles are all ways to avoid exposure to the Hepatitis "A" virus.

Syndrome Induced by HVA

After exposure to HVA, the individual will usually experience a flu-like syndrome for about 4 weeks, although in 1% of the cases the individual develops acute liver failure (Fontana, 2008). This is usually seen in older adults who contract HVA, but can occur in younger patients as well (Dienstag, 2008). The individual remains contagious throughout the period in which he or she demonstrates symptoms of HVA infection, after which time she or he will have lifelong immunity to the virus (Orr, 2008).

Consequences of HVA Infection

HVA tends to be a time-limited disorder, although in very rare cases HVA infection can result in liver failure and the patient's death. In rare cases, the patient will developing relapsing hepatitis in the weeks to months after apparent recovery. This is rare, but if it does develop the patient will reexperience many of the symptoms of the original infection (Dienstag, 2008). This second episode is a manifestation of the original infection that has not fully resolved. The individual remains infectious during this period, and hepatitis "A" viral particles have been found in fecal matter of people experiencing relapsing HVA, suggesting that they remain infectious during this time. Once the patient recovers from the HVA infection, she or he will have lifelong immunity to this virus.

Hepatitis "B" Virus

Method of Transmission

The virus that causes Hepatitis type "B" (HVB) has six known subtypes, all of which are quite contagious. It has been estimated that this virus is 100 times as contagious as the virus that causes HIV infection.[29] Although the virus that causes AIDS will die within minutes after exposure to air, scientists believe that HVB can continue to live on contaminated surfaces such as counter tops, and so on, for up to 7 days after being deposited there by an infected person if the surface is not properly cleaned and can infect others.[30]

---

[26]Cholera is another example of a disease that might be contracted through contracted through contact with water contaminated with fecal material, for example.

[27]Pearlman (2004) suggested that the Hepatitis C virus was isolated in 1989, not 1988.

[28]Which is one reason why washing your hands after using the toilet is so important.

---

[29]Discussed elsewhere in this chapter.

[30]Such as toys in day care centers, counter tops in restaurants or homes, and so on.

The hepatitis B virus is a blood-borne disease, which requires exposure to the body fluids of an infected person. Known methods of hepatitis B viral transmission include sharing a toothbrush, or a razor, sexual contact with an infected partner, or even by simply kissing an infected person. The virus can be transmitted through blood transfusions, although blood donations are now screened for donors and the rate of infection is less than 1 case for every 250,000 units of blood administered. Because it can be contracted as a result of sexual intercourse, HVB is often classified as a sexually transmitted disease (STD) as well as a blood-borne pathogen.[31] Indeed, the transmission from an infected person to a noninfected partner during sexual intercourse is considered the most common method of HVB transmission in the United States at this time (Russo, 2004). Vertical transmission from an infected mother to the fetus during child birth is possible, resulting in a low-grade lifelong infection for the baby following birth. This is the result of the "immunologic tolerance" that the baby's body develops for the virus (Dienstag, 2008, p. 1938). In spite of this immunologic tolerance, HVB infection may culminate in liver failure decades later in life (Dienstag, 2008).

The second most common method of HVB transmission in the United States is the sharing of intravenous needles between drug abusers.[32] Globally, 22 million new cases of HVB develop each year because of the sharing or reuse of contaminated needles (White, 2011). Intravenous drug abusers in a prison setting often try to avoid this by making the "yellow guy"[33] use the needle last, ignoring the fact that virus particles still will remain in the needle when it is next used hours, or days later, thus passing the infection on to the next abuser. Research has shown that 45–90% of intravenous drug abusers will have been exposed to HVB within a year of the time that they start to share intravenous drugs.

Syndrome Induced by HVB Infection

Individuals who have been infected by HVB might not demonstrate outward symptoms of an infection

for 1–5 months after exposure, although blood tests will demonstrate an immune response to HVB within 1–12 weeks of the initial infection. The physical symptoms that eventually develop are similar to those seen with Hepatitis A infection, and will include such symptoms as anorexia, nausea, vomiting, fatigue, malaise, headache, photophobia, pharyngitis and cough, followed 1–2 weeks later by symptoms of jaundice as the virus attacks the liver (Dienstag, 2008). These symptoms usually continue for 4–6 weeks, but on rare occasions it can continue for as long as 4–12 months following infection. Once the individual has recovered from HVB infection, she or he is immune to the virus, and blood tests will reveal HVB-specific antibodies for the rest of the individual's life (Orr, 2008).

Consequences of HVB Infection

The prognosis for the healthy person who contracts HVB is quite favorable, and it has been suggested that 90–95% of previously healthy adults eventually recover completely (Dienstag, 2008). This figure was disputed by Pungpapong, Kim, and Poterucha (2007), who utilized DNA testing procedures and reported that they found traces of HVB in people who were thought to be virus-free up to a decade after the acute infection resolved. Thus, the question of whether healthy people infected with HVB fully recover or not has not been fully resolved.

One of the more dangerous consequences of HVB infection is acute liver failure. This complication from Hepatitis "B" infection has been estimated to develop in less than 1% of cases that occur in healthy adults (Fontana, 2008). However, the rate of fulminant liver failure for HVB patients is markedly increased if he or she should also have contracted the hepatitis "D" virus as well (Dienstag, 2008).[34]

The issue of whether the typical patient completely recovers from the acute HVB infection is unresolved, and physicians argue whether the virus is ever completely eliminated from the body of an infected individual. Five to ten percent of those individuals infected with HVB will develop a chronic HVB infection. One of the manifestations of this chronic infection with the hepatitis B virus is the slow destruction of the patient's liver (Ganem & Prince, 2004; Pungpapong et al., 2007; Russo, 2004). About 20% of patients with a long-term

---

[31]Which is to say that the virus is found in all body fluids.

[32]It is interesting to observe that in spite of this information only 68% of substance abuse rehabilitation programs offer either on-site blood testing or have contractual agreements with private health care providers who will perform these tests for persons who enter treatment (Bini et al., 2012).

[33]Which is to say the guy who has jaundice.

[34]It has been estimated that only 28% of substance abuse rehabilitation programs offered blood testing for HVB either on site or through contractual agreements with health care providers off site (Bini et al., 2012).

HVB infection will develop cirrhosis of the liver (Ganem & Prince, 2004). Each year in the United States, HVB-related cirrhosis causes the death of approximately 5,000 people.

It was once thought that the virus directly caused the death of liver cells, but recent evidence has suggested that it is the body's immune response to the HVB infection that causes the liver damage rather than the virus itself (Dienstag, 2008; Ganem & Prince, 2004). Long-term HVB infection also is an indirect cause of death, as evidenced by the fact that people who have contracted HVB are 10–390 times more likely to develop liver cancer as a noninfected person, for example (Ganem & Prince, 2004; Gordon, 2000; Orr, 2008). Liver cancer is difficult to detect, treat, and is usually fatal. It has been estimated that HVB-related cancer causes approximately 1,200 annual deaths in the United States alone.

As if that were not enough, there is evidence that suggests that even if the individual was to recover from HVB infection, he or she is two to four times as likely than normal to develop cancer of the pancreas (Hassan et al., 2008). The causal mechanism for this is not known. People who were diabetic and who had past exposure to HVB were found to be seven times as likely to develop cancer of the pancreas than people without either disorder, according to the authors.

Treatment of HVB Infection

Currently, the most effective "treatment" for HVB infection is prevention. Vaccines to prime the immune system against HVB infection have been developed and are recommended for people who might be exposed to this virus such as health care workers, spouse of an infected person, children, and adolescents. Some school districts require proof of vaccination before allowing the student to enter school for the academic year. Blood barrier precautions (gloves when handling blood products or other body fluids) are also helpful in preventing HVB transmission. A number of pharmaceuticals are being investigated as possible treatments for those who are already infected with HVB.

Hepatitis "C" Virus

Mode of Transmission

It has been estimated that 170 million people, or 3% of the world's population, have a chronic HVC infection (Wilkins, Malcolm, Raina, & Schade, 2010). Approximately 3 million people in the United States are infected

with HVC (Sostre & Tiu, 2013). Although we speak of HVC as if it were a single entity, the virus has nine known genetically distinct subtypes (Wilkins et al., 2010). The virus is thought to be about 10 times as infectious as the HIV virus[35] and is classified as a blood-borne pathogen (Mehta et al., 2011). HVC infections are thought to take more lives than does HIV in the United States each year, killing 15,106 people in the year 2007[36] alone (Ly et al., 2012). Intravenous drug abusers make up the largest proportion of new cases of HVC, although researchers disagree about the exact percentage of new cases found in this subpopulation. Williams, Bell, Kuhnert, and Alter (2011) offered an estimate of 45% of new cases being attributable to intravenous drug abuse, whereas Sostre and Tiu (2013) suggested that 65–70% of new cases of HVC infection occur in intravenous drug addicts. There has been a modest drop in the number of new cases of VC infection because of needle exchange programs in some communities.

Unfortunately, many middle age experimental drug abusers who shared an intravenous needle only once or twice in their late teens or early 20s are now discovering that this experiment had unanticipated long-term health consequences. Further, HVC can be transmitted through sexual contact with an infected partner, or through used tattoo needles (Davies, 2005; Wilkins et al., 2010). Other sources of HVC infection include organ transplants from infected donors or occupational exposure to blood products, such as hemodialysis workers who might contract the infection as a result of their exposure to blood products at work (Dienstag, 2008). Approximately 10% of HVC victims contracted the virus before the advent of effective blood screening methods for blood donors. Currently, the risk of contracting HVC through a blood transfusion has been estimated at 1:2,300,000 (Dienstag, 2008). The HVC virus can also remain on surfaces and still be infectious for up to 4 days unless the contaminated surface is disinfected.[37] Another possible route of infection might be the shared use of straws used by multiple people to inhale cocaine, although this is controversial and has not been proven to be a route of HVC transmission.

---

[35]Discussed elsewhere in this chapter.

[36]Last year that data was available to the researchers.

[37]A fact that makes you want to think twice about using public toilets, does it not?

Consequences of HVC Infection

The acute period of illness following infection with HVC is less severe than that seen with HVA or HVB (Dienstag, 2008). In approximately 20% of the cases where a person is infected with HCV, her or his body is able to overcome the infection, usually within the first 6 months (Davies, 2005; Hines, 2002; Sostre & Tiu, 2013; Woods & Herrera, 2002). In the remaining cases HVC establishes a smoldering infection that will slowly destroy the individual's liver over a period of 20–30 years. Such patients remain asymptomatic until the level of liver damage has reached severe levels. Research has shown that up to 70% of patients who develop acute liver failure during the initial stage of HVC infection will succumb to liver failure in the more advanced stages of the infection (Fontana, 2008).

Like many viral infections HVC does not produce a distinct syndrome during the earlier stages of the infection. Most patients remain asymptomatic until it has reached the advanced stages, although its effects can be detected in routine blood testing, which will alert the physician to the presence of the infection. HVC does not establish an ongoing viral infection in every person who contracts the virus: Approximately 20% of HVC-infected people will be able to fight off the infection, usually in the first 6 months after exposure to the virus (Davies, 2005; Hines, 2002; Sostre & Tiu, 2013; Woods & Herrera, 2002). Scientists believe that 1–5% of those infected will develop liver cancer each year. The causal mechanism for this association remains unknown (Orr, 2008).

If untreated, the victim might live for 20–30 years before the cumulative level of liver damage might result in acute liver failure, and at this point an emergency liver transplant is the only hope of saving the patient's life (Davies, 2005). Every day in the United States, three people die as a result of HVC infection, and HVC-induced liver damage is the most common reason for liver transplantation in the United States at this time (Orr, 2008). Individuals with an alcohol use disorder, or who abuse marijuana, seem to progress through the different stages of the disease more quickly than non-drinkers, and alcohol use is absolutely contraindicated for people with HVC infection (Karsan, Rojter, & Saab, 2004; Sylvestre, 2008; Wilkins et al., 2010).

Many persons infected with HVC infection continue to abuse of alcohol or illicit drugs (Sostre & Tiu, 2013). Persons with untreated HVC often report feeling fatigued, have trouble with their memories, trouble making decisions and concentration problems, all of which contribute to a lower quality of life. These symptoms appear to be independent of liver dysfunction.

Treatment of HVC Infection

There is no vaccine that will prevent HVC infection (Wilkins et al., 2010). The most effective "treatment" for HVC infection is the use of barrier precautions to prevent direct exposure to blood products and not to share intravenous needles with others. New pharmacological treatments for HVC infection are evolving to supplement the traditional combination of Interferon and ribavirin[38,39] such as the new HVC protease inhibitor Telaprevir® and similar compounds. Side effects of these pharmacological agents include fever, chills, headache, anxiety, mania, depression, anorexia, suicidal thinking, memory, and concentration problems, all of which make patient adherence to the treatment regimen difficult to maintain (Sostre & Tiu, 2013). Another complication of HVC infection is that even after apparent cures, low levels of the HVC virus might remain in the person's T-cells[40] for extended periods of time, allowing that person to infect others in spite of blood tests that fail to find evidence of active HVC infection (MacParland, Pham, Guy, & Michalak, 2009).

If it is not possible to cure the HVC infection, then the goal of treatment shifts to halting, or at least slowing, the progression of liver damage (Wilkins et al., 2010). There are a number of medications in various stages of development that offer the promise of either controlling the virus or possibly eliminating it from the body. One such medication is being developed under the brand name of Telaprevir® by Vertex pharmaceuticals. This medication is a protease inhibitor, and early studies suggest that the addition of this compound to existing treatments for HVC might improve the cure rate by 50% over standard treatments and will require a treatment protocol that is only half as long (Kapadia, 2008; Newman, Clay, Davis, McHutchison, & Liang, 2009). If this medication lives up to its initial promise, and is approved for use, it will be a significant advancement against HVC infection.

Hepatitis D

These viral infections are only rarely found in the United States. Of the estimated 15 million people

---

[38]This compound is a nucleoside analogue compound that is taken orally.

[39]It should be noted that there are a number of compounds being investigated by the pharmaceutical industry that show promise in treating HVC, and which might be introduced in the next decade.

[40]Component of the immune system.

with Hepatitis D (HVD) around the world, 70,000 are thought to live in the United States. There are an estimated 5,000 new cases of HVD each year in this country (Karsan et al., 2004). It is interesting to note that HVD is an "incomplete" virus, which requires a concurrent infection by the Hepatitis B virus to be able to infect the host. Because the largest proportion of people infected with HVB contracted that infection through contaminated intravenous needles, it should not be surprising to learn that many drug abusers with Hepatitis B have also been exposed to HVD at some point in their lives. Proper vaccination against HVB appears to have the added benefit of blocking HVD infection as well.

Hepatitis E

Hepatitis type E has received scant attention in the medical literature in spite of the fact that possibly a third of the world's population has been exposed to this virus (Zhu et al., 2010). The HVE virus can be transmitted through direct contact with body fluids. The most common method of transmission of HVE appears to be exposure to water contaminated by a person infected with HVE. If infected, the only treatment for the person is supportive medical care. However, a vaccine has been developed for HVE that is both effective and safe to administer prior to possible exposure to this virus, which is quite effective (Zhu et al., 2010).

Chapter Summary

Substance abusers are at high risk for a wide range of infectious diseases both as a direct result of their substance use and as an indirect consequence of their SUD. Individuals who share intravenous needles will spread pathogens from one person to the next, directly spreading pathogens from one person to the next. But the failure to follow "sterile technique" often results in the intravenous drug abuser "punching in" pathogens normally only found on the surface of the skin, where these bacteria and fungi then infect the abuser. This is an example of an indirect infectious disease consequence of injected drug abuse, for example. Malnutrition that is a side effect of drug use disorders also is an indirect cause of infectious diseases in injection drug abusers.

People with alcohol use disorders share the dangers of malnutrition as a possible risk factor for infections. However, they are also at risk for aspiration of material being regurgitated, setting the stage for aspiration pneumonia in these people. Injected drug use using contaminated needles also puts the person at risk for viral, fungal, and bacterial infections not normally found in the normal person. Some of these disorders include HIV infection and the various forms of infectious hepatitis. All of these disorders have the potential to kill the patient without (and sometimes even with) the best of medical care.

CHAPTER 36

The Debate Over Drugs: The Relationship Between Drugs and Crime

Introduction

In his science fiction classic *I Will Fear No Evil*, Robert A. Heinlein (1970) introduced the concept of the Abandoned Area. This is an urban area in which poverty, crime, the deterioration of the infrastructure, and drug use were so rampant that the government just gave up on them. Laws were ignored within these zones and illicit drug use was so rampant as to appear to be the norm rather than the exception. Virtually any drug, or service, could be obtained within an Abandoned Area for the right price. Amazingly, this science fiction portrayal of a fictional world appears to have presaged the state of affairs in much of the western world a half century later.[1] The direct cost of drug-related crime (exclusive of the cost of police services, criminal prosecution an incarceration) is the largest single cost of substance use disorders (SUDs) (Nordstrom & Williams, 2012). Social scientists have long been aware of the strong correlation between SUDs and criminal activity. However, as statistics instructors repeat to their classes, correlation does not imply causality. The individual's SUD might predate criminal activity, might develop after the individual has started to engage in criminal activity, or both might reflect the influence of a third unidentified factor shared by those who abuse chemicals and engage in criminal activity. The debate over which of these theories is the most accurate one has raged for decades (McCollister & French, 2002). However, adherents to all the three theories agree that there is a strong correlation between SUDs and criminal activity. In this chapter, we will review this relationship and discuss some of the controversies that rage over these issues.

Criminal Activity and Drug Abuse: Partners in a Dance?

The relationship between substance misuse and criminal behavior is hardly an insignificant one. Globally, 200 million people are thought to use an illegal drug(s) at least once each year, and 4 million farmers are thought to be economically dependent on the cultivation of illegal crops ("Losing tolerance with zero tolerance," 2005). In the United States, the cultivation and sale of domestically produced marijuana makes it the biggest cash crop raised in the country at this time despite its legal status ("Grass is Greener," 2007). In Mexico, "narco-terrorists" from various drug cartels engage in

---

[1]If you wish to challenge this assertion, please do so only after spending 24 hours living on the streets of the ghetto region of any number of cities in the United States.

gun battles on the streets, fighting for their share of the money spent by Americans for illicit drugs and leaving thousands dead in the process (English, 2011). These statistics suggest that the illicit drug trade is an established aspect of modern society not only in the United States but also around the world.

The response to this worldwide epidemic of substance abuse has been to attempt to interdict supplies of illicit drugs before they reach the level of being sold on the street to individual abusers. The effectiveness of these efforts might be seen in the fact that in the last decade of the 20th century, the supply and scope of drug abuse around the world increased rather than dropped ("Losing Tolerance with zero tolerance," 2005). Depending on the facts one chooses to embrace, and those that are ignored, it is possible to argue that the SUDs are, or are not, causal agents in criminal activity. However, an argument against the role of the SUDs as being a causal agent is that juvenile delinquency usually precedes the development of SUDs, in the adolescent, and that while the individual might outgrow delinquent behavior(s) with maturation, maturation from an SUD might take longer for the individual. This little detail makes it difficult to argue that SUDs cause an individual's criminal behavior(s).

Elliott (1992) offered a different perspective on the relationship between SUDs and criminal behavior. The author suggested that chemical abuse and criminal behavior are both a reflection of the "decline in the power of cultural restraints" (p. 599) that periodically takes place in this culture. The author supports his argument with the observation that Europe has suffered "Tidal waves of crime" (p. 599) every few decades since the 14th century. A similar pattern has emerged in the United States over the past 200 years, and in each cycle there is "an erosion of personal integrity, widespread dehumanization, a contempt for life, material greed, corruption in high places, sexual promiscuity, and an increased recourse to drugs and alcohol" (Elliott, 1992, p. 599, italics added for emphasis).

There are multiple pathways between SUDs and criminal activity, with substance abuse both arising from, and predicting, criminal behavior (Newcomb et al., 2001). Early substance abuse was found to predict later criminal activity in a community sample, according to the authors. Substance abuse was found to impair impulse control, contributing to the tendency for the abuser to engage in socially inappropriate behavior(s). The authors found evidence of a "proneness toward criminality" (p. 190) that was associated

with SUDs. As was discussed in Chapter 23, early substance abuse is a common complication of such childhood behavior problems as the conduct disorders, and the findings of this study are consistent with the involvement of conduct-disordered children with substances.

Alcohol, which is the most popular legal drug of abuse in this country, is also the substance most commonly involved in criminal activity (Husak, 2004). Twenty-one to 26% persons incarcerated for violent crimes report that they were under the influence of alcohol at the time of the offense, 3% reported having abused cocaine immediately prior to committing the offense, and just 1% were under the influence of heroin at the time of the criminal behavior (Husak, 2004; Nace, 2005b). Thus, the compound most commonly associated with criminal behavior is the one that is legally obtained, which casts doubt on the theory that illicit substance use causes criminal activity in the majority of cases.

Criminal Activity and Personal Responsibility

The relationship between SUDs and criminal behavior is quite complicated, and is bound to become more intricate. Advocates of the medical model often suggest that SUDs reflect damage to the structure of the brain itself, pointing to neuroimaging studies that indicate that persons with SUDs have variations in the anatomy of the brain than do those people who do not have an SUD. The question raised by such studies is whether, given these anatomical variations, the individual can be held responsible for his or her behavior (Horstman, 2010). The individual can hardly be held responsible for the anatomy of their brains, and the anatomy of the brain affects what the individual thinks, so to what degree can society hold an individual responsible for their behavior if they have abnormal brains?

This dilemma is seen in the fact that over 50% of opiate-dependent persons have been arrested for a criminal act(s) before their first use of narcotics (Jaffe & Strain, 2005). This would suggest that the predisposition toward crime was present prior to the use of illicit narcotics. Was their behavior prior to and after the development of the SUD a result of willful misconduct, or a reflection of an abnormal brain? Where between 51 and 76% of adult males and 39–85% of adult females arrested for criminal activity have evidence of at least one illicit chemical in their bodies at the time of arrest (Farabee, Prendedrgast, & Carier, 2002; Makki, 2003) this again raises a question: Is their criminal activity a reflection of their substance abuse, or, an extension of a pattern of antisocial behaviors that existed prior to their arrest?

If the person was under the influence of a chemical(s) at the time of the offense, what is his or her level of responsibility? Is it the same as it would be should he or she not have been under the influence of chemicals? To issue of personal responsibility is often sidestepped by the legal system through the assumption that drugs somehow interfere with the individual's ability to think coherently.[2] This position rests on the unproven assumption that substance use obliterates free will (Husak, 2004; Szasz, 2009). This is an extension of the "demon rum" claim often made in the 19th and early 20th centuries that postulates that:

> If intoxication is wrong, it is in large part these days because it is perceived to be guilty of inciting criminality and other antisocial activities in too many of those who regularly take intoxicants. (Walton, 2002, p. 75)

Note that it is the substance that is blamed for the criminal behavior, and not the individual. Proponents of this position believe that once the individual ingests alcohol or a drug that it overwhelms the individual's ability to make rational choices thus inciting criminal behavior. In some states, a "diminished capacity" defense might be used to mitigate against the full weight of the charges offense(s) committed under the influence of chemicals (Gendel, 2006; Husak, 2004). However, the legal system holds that the individual is still responsible for the decision to take the initial dose of alcohol or a drug.

The decision to bring the full weight of the legal system to bear on substance abusers demands that clear decisions be made about what is acceptable behavior for individuals in society. The:

> ... person to be blamed must have done something wrongful; no one can merit blame for conduct that is permissible. But whether and to what extent someone should be blamed is not simply a function of the wrongfulness of his conduct. We must also decide whether the wrongful act is fairly attributed to him,

> that is, whether he is responsible for it. (Husak, 2004, p. 405)

If the person with the SUD acts in a manner entirely consistent with that of a person with an SUD, should he or she be punished? This is a legal conundrum. To punish a person with an SUD simply because he or she has an SUD violates the 8th Amendment to the Constitution of the United States (Gendel, 2006). However, the Courts have interpreted the law to the effect that a given individual should not be punished for addictive behavior, but then the individual is still held accountable for behavior(s) that are clearly part of the addiction (Gendel, 2006). However, even this line of reasoning is not followed to the letter by those who prosecute drug offenders. Those persons most likely to experiment with new drugs of abuse are white, middle class, sub-urban males, who tend not to believe that they can be harmed by a drug(s) of abuse, and who have significant amounts of discretionary money at their command (Boyer, 2005). By the time that a new compound of abuse has reached the inner cities, it is already a well-established drug of abuse in other social circles (Boyer, 2005). However, the focus of antidrug criminal prosecutions tends to be on social groups other than white, middle class, suburban males.

Manufactured Criminals

The national prohibition against the use of certain compound(s) has resulted in a situation where these compounds are available to those who abuse or are addicted to them only through illicit channels.[3] Because access to these chemicals is under the control of suppliers willing to break the law in return for a rather large profit, the usual laws of a free market economy do not apply in the illicit drug world (Reuter, 2009). Those who supply illicit drugs demand money for their product, and justify the high cost that they charge on the grounds that they risk criminal prosecution by trafficking in those compounds. To obtain the money necessary to purchase the drug the individual must engage in both legal and illegal activities. Some persons exhaust personal finances, borrow money from family members, and engage in theft, sale of drugs to others for profit, or prostitution (heterosexual or homosexual).

---

[2]So, if the person tends to engage in antisocial behaviors in general, but is unable to think clearly at the time of the current arrest because he or she is under the influence of alcohol or drugs, does this exonerate him or her of responsibility for the current criminal act?

[3]An exception to this rule are those individuals who have prescriptions for controlled substances, such as patients who receive prescriptions for narcotic analgesics to control pain.

The person who engages in theft will engage only a fraction of that item's actual worth, forcing him or her to steal even more to obtain the desired funds. It has been estimated that the typical heroin addict must steal $200,000 worth of material each year to support their addiction (Kreek, 1997). It can thus be argued that the national prohibition against the use of heroin (or, because a similar process exists for the other compounds deemed illegal) has contributed to the wave of crime that swept across the country in the latter half of the 20th century.

Drug Use and Violence: The Unseen Connection

Violent crime is estimated to consume 11.9% of the Gross National Product of the United States each year (Schiffer et al., 2011).[4] Brust (2004) identified three categories of substance-related violence: (1) pharmacological violence, or drug-induced violent behavior, (2) economic compulsive violence, or violent crimes committed by a person to obtain money necessary to purchase illicit compound(s), and (3) systemic violence, or the violence that is associated with the illicit drug distribution/sales network. All these forms of violent behavior(s) have been demonstrated by various illicit drug abusers on a daily basis.

The most commonly abused chemical, alcohol, provides an excellent example of pharmacological violence. Approximately 50% of all sexual assaults, for example, are committed by men who have ingested alcohol (Abbey, Zawacki, Buck, Clinton, & McAuslan, 2001). Although one might argue that the disinhibition effects of alcohol might entice individuals to carry out a sexual assault, the use of such "date rape" compounds as GHB[5] and flunitrazepam[6] would argue that such an act was premeditated rather than spontaneous. Most certainly those who use such compounds as GHB or flunitrazepam engage in a degree of prior planning,

but at what point does an impulsive act become a premeditated act?

The effects of amphetamines and cocaine provide excellent examples of pharmacological violence, because both compounds predispose the user toward violence, both against others and against the "self." Cocaine abusers, for example, are more likely to die from homicide or suicide than are age-matched control subjects (Gold & Jacobs, 2005). There are many reasons for this: First, the lifestyle forced on those persons who abuse these compounds bring them into frequent contact with people who are more likely to respond with violence either because of their premorbid personality or because of pharmacologically enhanced violent tendencies. Also, the behavior of a person under the influence of cocaine or amphetamines might induce others to respond with violence, possibly resulting in a "victim-precipitated homicide." Also, women who admitted to the recent use of heroin were 2.7 times more likely to suffer a physical injury as a result of interpersonal violence in the next 6 months (Gilbert, El-Bassel, Chang, Wu, & Roy, 2011). In addition, women who were the victims of sexual interpersonal violence were more likely to resort to amphetamine or cocaine abuse after the assault (Gilbert et al., 2011). The authors suggested that the hospital emergency department setting provided a milieu for brief intervention and treatment referrals with victims of interpersonal violence, with the anticipated result of reduced morbidity and mortality for victims of interpersonal violence in the future.

Earlier in this chapter, it was noted that the disinhibition effect of alcohol contributes to many sexual assaults each year in this country. It is not unreasonable to assume that the same mechanism might be involved in many homicides that take place each year in the United States. This is not to say that the alcohol use caused the individual to commit the homicide in every case. Rather, a significant percentage of homicides were apparently planned in advance, and then the perpetrator(s) consumed alcohol to bolster their courage before committing the act. In other cases, the homicide was an unplanned act brought on during the heat of passion, in which the individual's self-control was reduced through his or her use of alcohol.

A common cause of substance-related death is criminal attack either by drug dealers, other addicted persons, or individuals looking for vulnerable persons to prey upon. Drug dealers have been known to attack customers, safe in the knowledge that the victim is

---

[4]For example, the lost productivity due to violent crime, medical treatment of those who survive their brush with violence, burial expenses for those who do not, fees for law enforcement personnel to apprehend and incarcerate violent offenders, the costs of the judicial system as the case slowly winds its way through the courts, and if convicted the costs associated with incarceration of a violent offender, plus parole supervision upon release.

[5]Discussed in the next chapter.

[6]Discussed in Chapter 10.

unlikely to go to the police to report a criminal attack when the victim was also been involved in criminal activity (drug use itself, or the various activities that the addicted person must engage in to support their addiction). Kleiman (2011) observed that: "In an illicit market, the level of violence and the share of the revenue available to those who use it, rises along with the level of [law] enforcement" (p. 124). This is consistent with the fact that drug dealers have been known to kill clients for unpaid drug debts and as a warning to others who might also owe the dealer money.[7] They also have been known to kill bothersome clients by selling them a bag of exceptionally potent drugs so that the client will die of an overdose. Drug addicts have also been known to kill drug dealers, although it is not known at this time the frequency with which such assaults are premeditated. Rival drug dealers have been known to engage in gun battles over "turf"[8] and drug dealers have been dumped in front of a hospital emergency room by a rival, who speeds off before the police arrive. Sometimes the victim will live, but it is unlikely that he or she will provide the police with any useful information to avoid self-incrimination.[9]

The team of Schiffer et al. (2011) utilized brain imaging technology to examine the brains of violent offenders as opposed to substance abusers and a sample of control subjects. The authors found that violent offenders tended to have a higher concentration of neurons (the "gray matter" of the brain) in the mesolimbic reward system of the brain, suggesting that for these persons the reward system is more easily activated.[10] Persons with SUDs demonstrated subtle anatomical differences in the form of reduced numbers of neurons in such areas of the brain as the orbitofrontal complex, suggesting that for this group violence might be a result of reduced inhibitions rather than increased pleasure in violent behaviors.

Partner-Associated Violence

There is a known relationship between SUDs and violence between relationship partners. However, violence at the hands of a relationship partner is often multifaceted (Smith, Homish, Leonard, & Cornelius, 2012). The reason for the violence varies from case to case and there has been little systematic research into this topic. Many of the drugs of abuse lower inhibitions, including those that supposedly help control anger, contributing to partner-associated violence. In other situations, both relationship partners might be under the influence of chemicals at the time of the violent outburst(s), possibly contributing to one or both individuals engaging in violence-precipitating behaviors that normally would be out of character for them.[11] The violence might ensue following verbal altercations between partners over the diversion of financial resources to fund substance use by one or both individuals, confrontation by one partner about how the other is not living up to financial, emotional, or parental duties, or over the allocation of substances to be abused.

Following the violence the victim, and often the perpetrator who might feel remorse for their behavior, turn to the drugs of abuse for solace. Smith et al. (2012) noted, for example, that women who were the victims of interpersonal violence often abused alcohol and narcotic analgesic medications, but only rarely engaged in the abuse of other compounds. Men who were the victims of interpersonal violence were found by the authors to abuse narcotic analgesics as well as other drugs of abuse but only rarely abused alcohol (Smith et al., 2012). This attempt at self-medication might then contribute to increased vulnerability on the part of the victim. There is a relationship between partner-associated violence and posttraumatic stress disorder,[12] a common consequence of partner-associated violence, which might further contribute to the abuse of chemicals by the victim who seeks escape from the painful symptoms of this condition.

---

[7]One popular method used by cocaine dealers who wish to kill a bothersome client is to sell the troublesome cocaine addict the powered residue of car battery acid that accumulates on the battery terminals, possibly mixed with cocaine, which then will kill the cocaine abuser when used. This is often referred to as a "hot shot."

[8]Usually a street corner on which to sell drugs, although on occasion the right to sell drugs in a certain part of the community.

[9]"Well officer, I was just standing on the street corner, minding my own business and selling the occasional bag of heroin, when this guy pulls up in a car and shoots me so that he can sell heroin from that street corner!" This is a discussion that is quite unlikely to take place, is it not?

[10]Which is consistent with the comment made by many sociopaths that they simply like to fight.

---

[11]Such as one partner slapping the face of the enraged partner who was holding a weapon, or verbally encouraging the enraged partner to use the weapon ("come on, you're too much a coward to use that!" for example, with unfortunate results).

[12]Discussed in Chapter 24.

The relationship between SUDs and interpersonal violence is extremely complex and it is not the purpose of this chapter to provide a comprehensive overview of this problem so much as to provide the reader with an awareness of the relationship between these two issues.

Adulterants

Unless the drug being sold is a pharmaceutical agent that was diverted to the illicit drug market, it is rare for drugs of abuse to be sold to the individual drug abuser in their pure form ("Deadly Drug Adulterants," 2008). More commonly, the compound sold to the individual drug abuser has been highly adulterated. Various estimates suggest that between 75 and 90% of the cost of cocaine or heroin at the street level is the result of adulteration after that product reaches this country (Kleiman, 2011). For example, the upper level drug dealer might buy a kilogram of cocaine, combine it with mannitol, and sell the two kilograms of resulting powder to a lower level drug dealer, doubling his or her profits ("Deadly Drug Adulterants," 2008). If the drug must pass through four or five levels of distributors, each of whom also adulterates the compound by 50% to increase profits, the final product might be one that is quite diluted.

The impact of adding an adulterant to an illicit drug is clearly demonstrated by the fact that:

> It costs approximately $300 to purchase enough coca leaves to produce a kilogram of cocaine, which retails for about $100,000 in the United States when sold in one-gram, two-thirds pure units [of cocaine]. (Reuter, 2009, p. 50)

The other one-third of the product sold are adulterants added to the cocaine at various stages in the production or distribution process to increase profits. Levamisole®, a compound once used by physicians in the United States to treat roundworm infection (and which is still used in veterinary medicine for that purpose) is one common adulterant (Zhu, LeGatt, & Turner, 2009). Approximately one-third of the cocaine samples tested were found to contain levamisole, which is capable of inducing the blood disorder known as agranulocytosis[13] in rare cases.

Another example of this process is found in the illicit narcotics production and distribution process: The opium farmer might be paid $90 for a kilogram of raw opium, which is then adulterated at each step of the distribution process, increasing profits by as much as 1,600 times when the drug reaches the level of the individual abuser (Schuckit, 2006a). Street samples of illicit heroin in the United States have been found to range from 18 to 71% pure heroin ("How they smack up," 2005), which means that adulterants make up the other 31–82% of the samples sold on the streets. This is consistent with the dictum that product reliability and safety are hardly priorities for those who traffic in illegal substances. Deception is also common, illustrating how in the world of illicit drugs "let the buyer beware!" Compounds are often misrepresented ("oh yes, it's pure!") or in some cases do not even contain the compound that it is reputed to be. For example, less than 50% of the MDMA tablets sold actually contained that compound, with compounds such as caffeine, aspirin, cocaine, phencyclidine (PCP). LSD, narcotics, GHB, ketamine, dextromethorphan, and paramethoxyamphetamine (PMA) being sold under the guise of MDMA (Grob & Poland, 2005).

One rarely considered aspect of drug adulteration is that these compounds have a potential to do damage to the abuser's body and the abuser's emotional state independent of the drug(s) of abuse. A person who unknowingly smokes low-grade marijuana that has been intermixed with PCP to make it seem more powerful might suffer significant psychiatric harm if they have little or no experience with the effects of phencyclidine, for example. If the illicit drug is abused intravenously, the adulterants are injected directly into the abuser's body, bypassing the defensive acids and enzymes of the digestive tract (Leavitt, 2003). Popular belief suggests that drug dealers will mix deadly compounds in with the drug(s) being sold, although this is rarely done because it would (a) kill off the dealer's customer base, (b) thus be bad for business, and (c) give that drug dealer a bad reputation in a market where word-of-mouth advertising is the only form of advertising that exists ("Deadly Drug Adulterants," 2008). This is not to deny that toxic compounds are not intermixed with illicit drugs, but that highly lethal compounds are rarely used to adulterate an illicit drug except on rare occasions. Still, either by accident or design, deadly adulterants are sometimes included in the mixture.

Identified categories of adulterants fall into one of five categories—(1) various forms of sugar, (2) stimulants,

---

[13]See Glossary. The nature of this disorder lies outside of the scope of this text, and interested readers are referred to the appropriate medical textbooks.

(3) local anesthetics, (4) toxins, and (5) any of a wide range of inert compounds—that can be added to give the product bulk. Some of the compounds found in samples of illicit "drugs" include (Gold & Jacobs, 2005) mannitol, lactose, glucose, caffeine, lidocaine, amphetamine compounds, quinine, and even on occasion heroin.[14] Marijuana is frequently adulterated, and it is not uncommon for up to half of the "marijuana" purchased to be seeds and woody stems that must be removed before it can be smoked. Low-potency marijuana has been known to be laced with other compounds such as Raid® insect spray, PCP, cocaine paste, dry cow manure,[15] alfalfa, apple leaves, catnip, cigarette tobacco, hay, licorice, mescaline, opium, wax, and wood shavings.

Samples of marijuana sold have been found to have been sprayed with a herbicide such as paraquat. Two compounds found in samples of marijuana recently purchased in Europe are homosildenafil (HS) and thio-homosildenafil (THS), compounds whose effects are very similar to that of the sildenafil family of compounds, which is sold in the United States as treatment for "erectile dysfunction" ("Cannabis booster," 2008). Authorities are not sure whether these compounds have been added to marijuana to enhance the absorption of the psychoactive compounds in the smoke, or to enhance the reputed aphrodisiac effect of marijuana. Unfortunately, scientists do not know how these compounds will affect the human body if smoked, because this is not the usual method of administration of sildenafil compounds ("Cannabis booster," 2008).

A partial list of the compounds found to be mixed with illicit cocaine samples can be found in Table 36-1. This is only a partial list, and new adulterants are being identified almost daily. As this list illustrates, however, when it comes to the world of illicit drugs, let the buyer beware!

Because of the problem of adulterants, drug abusers prize pharmaceutical agents. These compounds are of known potency, and are unlikely to be contaminated. However, they are mixed with "fillers" that help give the tablet or capsule shape and form. When a drug abuser takes a compound orally, the digestive juices help break down the inert compounds intermixed with pharmaceuticals to give them bulk and form. For example, methylphenidate tablets are mixed with talc, which helps give the tablet form. When crushed and injected, the talc in the methylphenidate tablet is injected into the body as well, forming microemboli in the circulation that might potentially damage organs such as the heart, eyes, lungs, and brain (Greenhill, 2006). The same phenomenon is found when an illicit drug is abused: The adulterants may be introduced into the body, with unknown consequences. In many cases, the adulterants cause local irritation to the tissue(s) into which they were injected, which then establishes the potential for an infection as the body's defenses break down at the site of injection.

The subject of adulterants is worthy of a book in its own right, for the various adulterants can damage virtually every organ in the body.

"Designer" Drugs

When a pharmaceutical company develops a new drug, it applies for a patent on that compound. This process requires, in part, that the chemists for that company identify the exact chemical structure of that drug molecule. After review by the Food and Drug Administration (FDA), the pharmaceutical company might be granted a patent of that specific drug molecule. It becomes a specific molecule protected by copyright. Unfortunately, because of the "Internet," production methods for illicit compounds are dissimulated virtually instantly, and "… legitimate chemical research can be hijacked by anyone with a hot plate and an Internet connection" (Piore, 2012, p. 43). The goal of this process is to find an "almost like" compound that has not been classified as a controlled substance by law enforcement agencies. That chemical might then be sold without fear of criminal prosecution, at least until law enforcement agencies are able to have that drug molecule banned.

Because drug molecules are complex structures involving hundreds of atoms, it might be possible to develop dozens, or scores, of variations on the "parent" drug. Many of these compounds are then sold, in the hope that one will become the latest craze and make the drug distributor rich. These compounds are called "designer" drugs, many of which are less potent than the original "parent" drug. Some designer drugs are equally potent, whereas some are even more potent than the parent drug molecule. All that it takes is for a chemist to alter the chemical structure parent drug molecule, possibly by as little as one atom.

---

[14]Which can be a problem if you did not know that the product that you had purchased contained heroin, since this could lead to a potentially fatal overdose.

[15]Which may expose the user to salmonella bacteria.

TABLE 36-1
Known Adulterants in Illicit Drugs

ILLICT COCAINE: KNOWN ADULTERANTS	ILLICIT PCP: KNOWN ADULTERANTS	ILLICIT HEROIN: KNOWN ADULTERANTS
Acetaminophen	Ammonium chloride	Acetaminophen
Aminopyrine	Benzocaine	Acetone
Ascorbic acid	Caffeine	Acetylcodeine
Aspirin	Ketamine™	Arsenic
Benzene	Magnesium sulfate	Caffeine
Benzocaine	Procaine	Diazepam
Boric acid	Toluene	Ethanol
Caffeine		Fentanyl
Corn starch		Lidocaine
Dextrose		Methaqualone
Diphenhydramine		Phenobarbital
Ephedrine		Quinine
Fentanyl		Strychnine
Heroin		Thebaine
Inositol		Toluene
Lactose		Vitamin C
Levamisole		
Lidocaine		
Mannitol		
Methaqualone		
Niacinamide		
Phenacetin		
Phentermine		
Phenylpropanolamine		
Procaine		
Quinine		
Sucrose		
Tetracaine		

SOURCE: Based on Karch (2009); Roth, Benowitz, and Olson (2007)

To illustrate this process, assume that the illustration in Figure 36-1 is that of an illicit drug "molecule" of a hallucinogenic compound. Admittedly, the "molecule" used to illustrate the process of making "designer" drugs has only four "atoms" as opposed to the thousands of atoms found in actual drug molecules, but it does serve to illustrate the process.

To create more demand, and possibly avoid criminal prosecution the chemical structure of the original parent compound might be altered, possibly by adding

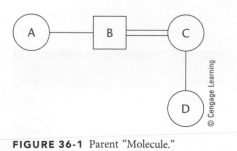

FIGURE 36-1 Parent "Molecule."

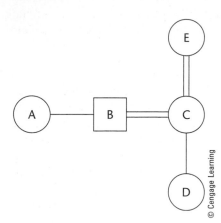

FIGURE 36-2 First Analog.

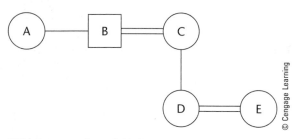

FIGURE 36-3 Second Analog.

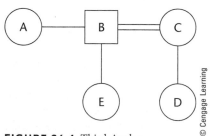

FIGURE 36-4 Third Analog.

just a single atom. Technically, this addition makes this a "different" drug, because the molecular structure is not exactly the same as that of the parent compound (Figure 36-2).

The new compound is called an analog of the parent compound. It might be less potent, as potent, or even more potent as the original compound. However, because of their altered chemical structure that compound might not have been deemed illegal, yet. The FDA does have the power to declare drug analogs a controlled substance until a formal law can be passed, but to do so it is necessary for their chemists to identify the exact chemical structure of the analog. When this happens, it would be a simple matter to alter the chemical structure of the analog to build a new "designer" drug, starting the process over again. For example, see Figure 36-3.

The change might be very subtle, and either to escape criminal prosecution or increase profits by creating a new product, which illicit drug distributors are willing to provide for a very high price, the chemical structure of the compound might be altered yet again, as in Figure 36-4.

Although the "drug" molecule used to illustrate this process is a very simple one, it does serve to illustrate how it is possible to produce analogs of an original compound. In the case of real drug molecules, there might be dozens, or even hundreds of possible analogs. Further, the speed with which illicit drug "chemists" carry out this process might be seen in the fact that by the time that the recreational substance mephedrone was classified as an illegal substance in England, new substitutes that had yet to be banned were being sold ("Ban later, ask questions first," 2010). In the next section, we will examine some of those drug analogs that have been identified by law enforcement agencies over the years.

Some Existing Drug Analogs

Amphetamine-Like Designer Drugs

The amphetamine molecule lends itself to experimentation, and several analogs of the parent amphetamine molecule have been identified to date. One is 2,5-dimethoxy-4-methyl-amphetamine, or the hallucinogen DOM, which is rarely used by illicit drug abusers. The compound MDMA ("Ecstasy") is considered an analog of the amphetamines by some pharmacologists, and there are 184 known analogs of the MDMA molecule, some of which are also known to have a psychoactive effect on the user. For example, the compound

3,4-methylenedioxyamphetamine, or MDEA has a chemical structure that is very similar to that of MDMA and has very similar effects on the user. This substance is often sold under the name of "Eve." There have been isolated reports of deaths associated with MDEA abuse, and the long-term effects of this compound on the user are not known at this time.

Another designer drug is known as "Ya ba" ("Crazy medicine"). It is most commonly used in Southeast Asia, especially in Thailand where up to 5% of the population admits to having used it at least once (Hilditch, 2000; Kurutz, 2003). Isolated cases of its use on the west coast of the United States have also been reported. This compound is a blend of ephedrine, caffeine, methamphetamine, lithium (obtained from batteries), and some other chemicals obtained from household cleaning agents. It reportedly provides an 8- to 12-hour "high." It can be inhaled, smoked, or used through a transdermal patch; however, the preferred method of abuse is orally. Long-term use appears to contribute to suicidal or homicidal thoughts[16] and most abusers follow a pattern of using the compound for 2–3 days followed by a day or two of deep sleep. Very little is known about the toxicology of Ya ba, which has not been subjected to clinical research studies by pharmacologists.

Khat

In the 1990s it was feared that methcathinone ("Kat," "Quat," or "Khat, also known as "miraa" in some areas) might become the next popular drug of abuse in the United States. However, by the start of the 21st century, methcathinone has virtually disappeared from the illicit drug market in the United States, and is rarely abused except for some immigrants from sub-Saharan Africa who continue the practice of chewing the leaves for their psychoactive effect (Karch, 2009; "Khat Calls," 2004). On the other hand, it is of growing concern in England, where the basic molecule has been modified by illicit drug dealers so that it then becomes a "legal" drug ("Concern at new 'legal high' drugs," 2008). These drugs are then sold to illicit drug abusers as a "safe" alternative to Ecstasy.[17] These variations on the methcathinone molecule were declared illegal in 2009 ("Concern at new 'legal-high' drugs," 2008).

Where Khat Is Obtained

Khat is naturally found in several parts of the world, including east Africa and southern Arabia (Haroz & Greenberg, 2005). In the natural world, the plant grows to between 10 and 20 feet in height, and the leaves produce the alkaloids cathinone and cathine. Illicit drug manufacturers began to produce an analog of cathinone[18] known as methcathinone, which has a chemical structure very similar to that of the compounds such as the amphetamines and ephedrine (Karch, 2009). It was then made available to drug abusers in the United States.

The Legal Status of Khat

Khat was classified as a Schedule I compound in 1992, and its manufacture or possession in the United States is illegal. However, cathinone is easily manufactured in illicit laboratories to chemically transform the ephedrine molecule by adding an oxygen atom to it using such products as drain cleaner, epsom salts, battery acid, acetone, toluene, and various dyes. The end product is a compound with the chemical structure (2-methylamino-1-pheylpropan-l-one) which is then sold to illicit drug users. By the year 2008, illicit laboratories had been found in at least 10 different states in the United States ("Parkinson-like symptoms linked to illicit Khat use," 2008).

In an attempt to circumvent the prohibition against cathinone, various products such as "bath salts" were introduced. These compounds contain cathinone as the primary ingredient, but because they were sold as "bath salts" and as such not intended for internal consumption their sale was technically legal. Such products are now being used by stimulant abusers to access the cathinone in the mixture and there are growing prohibitions against the sale of "bath salts."

Methods of Khat Administration and Effects of This Compound

Abusers typically smoke Khat, although it can be injected. On rare occasions, the leaves are also chewed. The effects of Khat are very similar to those of the amphetamines. This is understandable because the Khat plant contains norephedrine, and cathinone, which is biotransformed into norephedrine in the body following ingestion. Like the amphetamines, Khat can induce dopamine release, and a sense of

---

[16]Thus, this compound's name.

[17]Discussed in Chapter 15.

[18]Known in Europe by the name ephedrone.

euphoria, excitement, grandiosity, increased blood pressure, and flushing of the skin. There are reports that the effects last in excess of 24 hours, although more reputable sources suggest that the effects last 3–4 hours. However, methamphetamine is easier to manufacture, and so Khat never became a popular drug of abuse in the United States.

Adverse Effects of Khat

There has been little research into the actions of Khat on the body. What little is known is drawn from clinical data from physicians who have treated patient(s) who have abused this compound. Known adverse effects of Khat include vasoconstriction, hyperthermia, hypertension, insomnia, anorexia, constipation, a drug-induced psychosis, hallucinations, paranoia, aggressive episodes, anxiety, cardiac arrhythmias, mood swings, and depression (Haroz & Greenberg, 2005). Following extended periods of abuse, it is not uncommon for the abuser to fall into an extended period of sleep that might last for days.

There is preliminary evidence suggesting that Khat is capable of inducing a Parkinson's disease-like syndrome ("Parkinson-like symptoms linked to illicit Khat use," 2008). In one of the few studies to be published in this area, Stephens et al. (2008) drew on clinical evidence from of 23 adult intravenous Khat addicts from Latvia, where Khat abuse is common. The research subjects had an average period of injected Khat use of 6.7 years, and their average age was 37.5 years. It was noted that a gait disturbance predated the development of other symptoms, and there were no psychiatric problems noted in the research sample. Unfortunately, it was discovered that even if the patient discontinued the use of Khat, there was no improvement in their neuropsychiatric status, suggesting that the damage to the brain is permanent (Stephens et al., 2008).

Mephedrone

The compound is a synthetic analog of cathinone, and as such is thought to have the same central nervous system (CNS)-stimulant effects (Fleming, 2010). Although it was first synthesized in 1929, drug abusers did not discover it until around 2003. It was not a controlled substance at the time, and little is known about the effects of mephedrone and related compounds in the body. There has been a great deal of media attention devoted to mephedrone, much of it based on hearsay or secondhand knowledge (Owen, 2013).[19] As of this time, it has been classified as illegal in at least 13 countries (Fleming, 2010) including the United States, which classified it as an illegal substance in July of 2012.

There has been virtually no research into the pharmacokinetics of this compound, and what is known is based on case reports of persons who have abused these compounds. Peak effects following oral use of mephedrone peak after about 2 hours if taken on an empty stomach. Food will delay absorption of mephedrone, but eventually it is all absorbed by the body. When "snorted" it will begin to take effect in about 30 minutes. The effective dose for "snorted" mephedrone is lower than when ingested. Rectal insertion of the compound into the body[20] also requires a lower dose to achieve the desired effects. Mephedrone's desired effects appear to be very similar to those of MDMA: A sense of empathy and closeness with others, possible sexual arousal and CNS-stimulant effects such as those seen when a person has ingested MDMA. Some of the reported side effects of mephedrone include anxiety, tachycardia, hypertension, nose bleeds, sweating, piloerection, nausea, and vomiting. There have been case reports of death subsequent to mephedrone use in both the United States and Europe (Maskell, De Paoli, Seneviratne, & Pounder, 2011). There has also been one isolated case of mephedrone-induced delirium, in one case resulting in subsequent death from cardiac arrest (Lusthof et al., 2011).

MDPV (3,4-Methylenedioxypyrovalerone)

MDPV is a chemical relative of mephedrone and was also sold as "bath salts" either in isolation or mixed with mephedrone. The bags containing the "bath salts" were labeled "not for human consumption" and thus were not classified as an illegal compound at first. There has been little systematic research into the toxicology of this compound and much of what is known

---

[19]Owen (2013) offered as evidence the story that the "Miami Zombie," who was confronted by police after biting off a piece of another person's face and who was ultimately shot by the authorities. The news media reported that he was under the influence of "bath salts" and this story was repeated time after time. Unfortunately, extensive toxicology testing failed to detect any evidence of mephedrone or other components of "bath salts," although the results from these tests were not available when the initial news reports were issued.

[20]Sorry. You will have to use your imagination on this one!

about its effects is based on clinical case reviews. It first emerged as an abused compound around 2004 and has been increasing in popularity since then (Leo & Goel, 2012). MDPV powder can be "snorted," ingested orally, or inserted rectally, and will produce effects very similar to those induced by cocaine, methylphenidate, or dextroamphetamine (Leo & Goel, 2012). Abusers report feeling more alert, feeling less need for sleep, and a sense of euphoria. As the dose and duration of use increase the abuser is more likely to experience the negative effects of MDPV, which include increased blood pressure, tachycardia, peripheral vasoconstriction,[21] anxiety, irritability, agitation, panic, psychosis, and delirium (Leo & Goel, 2012). Although the desired effects seem to last 3–4 hours, MDPV's ability to cause tachycardia and hypertension seems to last about 6–8 hours after it was used. This compound was classified as an illegal compound by the Drug Enforcement Administration in July of 2012.

Kratom[22]

Kratom is derived from the plant *Mitragyna speciosa*, a plant species normally found in Southeast Asia where it has been used for its medicinal properties for generations (Troy, 2013). Kratom contains a number of alkaloids, some of which act as *mu* opioid agonists in the brain.[23] Kratom might be legally purchased in the United States, and when abused the leaves can be smoked, brewed into a form of tea, or ground up and mixed with another liquid for ingestion (Troy, 2013). The pharmacokinetics of kratom have not been studied in detail. It is known that the effects are dose dependent but surprisingly produce a stimulant effect at lower doses and an analgesic effect at higher doses. There are rare reports of seizures associated with kratom abuse. It does produce a withdrawal syndrome that is reported to be similar to but less intense and shorter than that seen when the individual experiences the traditional opiate withdrawal syndrome (Troy, 2013).

THC-Like Designer Drugs

In recent years, a compound sold as "synthetic marijuana" appeared on the market. Local names for this compound include (but are not limited to): "Spice." There are two compounds that have been included in Spice, each a tetrahydrocannabinol (THC) analog but with higher potency than THC itself. HU-210 is a compound first synthesized at the Hebrew University in 1988 as chemists there attempted to find a compound that would help treat depression (Barth, 2012). It was not long before illicit drug chemists discovered that the similarity between HU-210 and THC would allow the individual to become "high" off of the compound. Further, because it was packaged as a form of incense and the packets were marked "not for human consumption," it could be legally sold in the United States for many years.

The HU-210 molecules are about 100 times as potent as THC itself (Barth, 2012). This raised the possibility that the individual might inadvertently become toxic on HU-210, and a number of abusers were hospitalized after abusing this compound. Its use in the United States was banned in 2011. Illicit drug chemists then switched to a THC-like compound known as JWH-018. This compound is one of the easier THC analogs to produce (Barth, 2012). It was also banned by the Drug Enforcement Administration in 2011. Illicit drug chemists then switched to a chemically similar, but still legal, THC-like compound known as JWH-073 within a matter of weeks (Barth, 2012). In this manner, the "bath salts" side-stepped the laws until JWH-073 was banned in March of 2012 (Barth, 2012).

Research into the toxicology of these compounds is lacking, especially because producers had marked the packages "not for human consumption" and thus were not required to carry out toxicology testing prior to introducing the product. Early studies suggest that side effects can include elevated blood pressure and increased heart rate, nausea, paranoia, anxiety, insomnia, suicidal ideations, and hallucinations (Furek, 2011). Acute kidney disease requiring hemodialysis has also been reported in abusers of "synthetic marijuana" (Murphy et al., 2013). The possibility of a substance-induced heart attack has also been suggested, although the causal mechanism remains unclear (Mir, Obafemi, Young, & Kane, 2011). As is true for marijuana synthetic THC analogs can exacerbate the individual's chances of developing schizophrenia.

[21]See Glossary.

[22]The placement of kratom in this chapter placed the author in a conundrum because its effects at low doses are that of a stimulant while at higher doses an analgesic. The author made the decision to include it here based on its effects at low doses.

[23]At this point scientists believe that one alkaloid in Kratom, mitragynine, is 13 times as potent as morphine (Troy, 2013).

This compound and its chemical cousins have been declared a controlled substance by the Drug Enforcement Administration.

Hallucinogenic Designer Drugs

PCP is a popular drug molecule for illicit chemists to experiment with, and there have been at least 30 drug analogs of PCP identified to date. Some of these compounds are more potent than PCP is, such as the compound N-ethyl-1-1phenylcyclohexylamine (also known as PCE), or the compound (1-(1-1-thienylcyclohexyl) piperidine) (or, TCP). Another drug analog of PCP is (1-(-phenylcyclohexyl)-pyrrolidine) (PHP), and (1-piperidinocyclohexanecarbonitrile) (PCC). These complex chemical names provide some idea of how the PCP parent molecule might be manipulated by chemists to develop other compounds.

Ketamine[24]

Ketamine is a chemical relative to phencyclidine (PCP), which was discussed earlier in this text. It is used by physicians as a surgical anesthetic that does not cause the respiratory or cardiac depression caused by other anesthetics (McDowell, 2005; Schultz, 2002). Ketamine also has a role in veterinary medicine. There is experimental evidence suggesting that it is effective in the treatment of depression, often bringing about a remission in the symptoms of depression in just a few hours. Ketamine has been classified as a Schedule III compound.[25] It has a fairly wide therapeutic window, and thus is relatively safe when used as directed in a medical setting. It does have a shorter duration of action than PCP, with peak blood levels being seen approximately 20 minutes after it is ingested orally. When it is used as an anesthetic and is injected into a vein, its effects are seen within seconds (Sadock & Sadock, 2007).

In the brain, Ketamine binds at the N-methyl D-aspartate (NMDA)-receptor site, enhancing the effects of glutamate by forcing a calcium ion channel in the wall of the neuron to close (McDowell, 2004, 2005). This slows the rate at which that neuron can "fire." The elimination half-life of Ketamine is 3–4 hours, and it is extensively biotransformed by the liver before elimination. Only about 3% of a single dose is excreted unchanged in the urine. Standard toxicology tests will not detect Ketamine, and so if a "date rape" situation is suspected a special toxicology test must be ordered to detect the drug or its metabolites. Analgesia induced by a single injection of Ketamine begins in about 60 seconds when injected into a vein and lasts about 40 minutes although the patient might experience a dissociative state that lasts for hours after administration (Sadock & Sadock, 2007). During this dissociative state, the individual will have trouble forming memories, which makes this medication of value during the acute recovery stage following surgery. A common complication when it is used as a surgical anesthetic is a lack of concern for the environment, or personal safety (Sadock & Sadock, 2007).

It is possible to manufacture Ketamine in illicit laboratories, but it is rather difficult to do this and most commonly the Ketamine found on the streets is diverted, usually from veterinary supply companies (McDowell, 2005; Sadock & Sadock, 2007). It is a colorless and odorless compound, and can be abused by intranasal, oral, inhalation[26] or on rare occasions by intravenous injection (Sadock & Sadock, 2007). In a powdered form it might be intermixed with tobacco or marijuana, and then smoked (Gahlinger, 2004). The fact that it is odorless and colorless makes it an ideal "date rape" drug because it can be slipped into the victim's drink without arousing suspicion, whereas its ability to induce anterograde[27] amnesia will reduce the chance that the rapist will be identified by the victim.

The most common group of Ketamine abusers are 18- to 25-year-old adults (Lewis, 2011), who take advantage of the fact that the effects of an oral dose of Ketamine are dose dependent (Freese, Miotto, & Teback, 2002; Gahlinger, 2004). Dosage levels typically used by the Ketamine abuser is about one-half of that necessary to induce anesthesia, or about 1/60th of the LD50 for this compound (McDowell, 2004, 2005). Dosage levels commonly used by Ketamine abusers induce a sense of euphoria, visual hallucinations, a dissociative state, as well as vivid dreams (Freese et al., 2002; Gahlinger, 2004). Other effects of Ketamine when it is abused include (Gahlinger, 2004; McDowell, 2004, 2005; Sadock & Sadock, 2007; Walton, 2002) hypertension, tachycardia, respiratory depression, paranoia, apnea, anxiety, and "flashback" experiences in the

---

[24]Or, (2-o-chlorophenyl)-2-methylamine cyclohexanone), if you really must know.

[25]See Appendix three.

[26]This is referred to as a "bump" by abusers who use this method.

[27]See Glossary.

days or weeks after the last weeks of this compound. Long-term abuse can induce memory problems (Gahlinger, 2004; Morgan, Muetzelfeldt, & Curran, 2009). Frequent abusers experience deficits in the areas of spatial memory and pattern recognition on psychological tests, as well as delusional thought patterns that appear to resolve with abstinence (Morgan et al., 2009). Long-term abusers run the risk of bladder shrinkage, urinary incontinence, and damage to the kidneys and ureter (Bhattacharya, 2011).

Methoxetamine

Methoxetamine is a ketamine analog and at this time is not classified as a controlled substance (Troy, 2013). Abusers either "snort" methoxetamine powder or use it sublingually, although it might be injected. When used intranasally dosage levels range from 20 to 100 mg whereas intravenous doses range from 10 to 50 mg (Troy, 2013). When used intranasally the effects begin to manifest in 30–90 minutes and last 5–7 hours, but when injected the effects are first seen in 5 minutes and last for approximately an hour (Troy, 2013). The pharmacokinetics of this compound have not been explored but it is assumed that the side effects are similar to those of ketamine. Abusers report a sense of dissociation, visual hallucinations, and short-term elevation of mood, whereas some of the reported negative effects include confusion, agitation, depression, and catatonia (Troy, 2013). Further research into the mechanism of action and effects of methoxetamine is necessary.

Aminorex[28]

This compound was introduced in Europe as an aid to weight loss, and sold under the brand name of Menocil® (Karch, 2009; Rasmussen, 2008). It was rapidly withdrawn from the pharmaceutical market after it became apparent that this compound could induce fatal pulmonary hypertension, sometimes after just 4 weeks of use and there is currently no legitimate application for this medication (Karch, 2009; Rasmussen, 2008).

In the United States, it is occasionally sold to illicit drug abusers under the guise of methamphetamine (Karch, 2009). It is easily synthesized, thus making it an attractive compound to manufacture in illicit drug "labs," but was classified as a Schedule I[29] compound in April of 1989 and since then its use in the United

States has virtually ended (Karch, 2009). Unfortunately, a medication used by veterinarians to deworm livestock, levamisole, is biotransformed into aminorex in humans. It is a frequent adulterant in compounds such as illicit cocaine or amphetamines the drug is adulterated with this compound the levamisole will expose the user to the dangers inherent in aminorex abuse.

The effects of aminorex are not well documented, but do appear to be similar to those of the amphetamines or cocaine (Karch, 2009). Available evidence, based on research studies conducted before it was withdrawn from the market, suggest that aminorex is rapidly absorbed after an oral dose, with peak blood levels being seen approximately 2 hours after the drug was ingested. The reported half-life is approximately 7.7 hours (Karch, 2009), and it is excreted virtually unchanged by the kidneys. Because of its legal status and potential for harm to the user, all clinical research into the effects of this compound was discontinued when it was withdrawn from the market. Its potential to cause other medical complications beyond pulmonary hypertension remains unknown at this time (Karch, 2009).

Gamma Hydroxybutyric Acid

This compound was first identified in 1960 when scientists were doing research on the neurotransmitter gamma-aminobutyric acid (GABA). The chemical structure of gamma hydroxybutyric acid (GHB) is very similar to that of GABA itself, which is not surprising in that it is metabolized from GABA, the main inhibitory neurotransmitter in the brain (Flower, Mendelson, & Galloway, 2009). Initially, there was some interest in this compound as a presurgical agent because its effects were thought to be similar to those of GABA. However, the usefulness of this compound as a presurgical agent was very limited, because: (a) many patients experienced vomiting and seizures when recovering from its effects, (b) it has a rather narrow therapeutic window,[30] and (c) when used in a surgical setting other analgesics must still be administered to the patient (Tomb, 2008). These factors combined to make its use by physicians rather rare although it is sold under the brand name of Xyrem® in the United

---

[28]Technically, 2-amino-4-methyl-5-phenyl-2-oxazoline.

[29]See Appendix three.

[30]The LD50 is only five times the therapeutic dose, thus making it easy for the abuser to overdose on this compound. The therapeutic window is made even smaller if the abuser should be ingesting a CNS depressant such as alcohol simultaneously (Commission on Adolescent Substance and Alcohol Abuse, 2005; McDowell, 2005).

States for the treatment of narcolepsy[31] (Flower et al., 2009).

Small amounts of GHB are normally found in the human kidneys, heart, muscle tissues, and brain, and it is thought to function as a neurotransmitter in that organ (Drummer & Odell, 2001; McDowell, 2005). As a neurotransmitter, GHB helps mediate the sleep cycle, body temperature, cerebral glucose metabolism, and plays a role in the formation of memories, and possibly stimulates the release of the human growth hormone (Gahlinger, 2004; Karch, 2009; Weaver & Schnoll, 2008). This latter effect was what made GHB use so attractive to muscle builders after the anabolic steroids were banned. Because of its widespread abuse, GHB was classified as a Schedule II compound[32] by the Drug Enforcement Administration in 2000, a move that might have contributed to the decrease of GHB use observed in the United States (van Norden, van Dongen, Zitman, & Vergouwen, 2009). In response to this, body builders simply switched to any of a number of legal compounds that would be biotransformed into GHB after ingestion, or to illicit sources of this chemical. Instructions how to make it are available over the "Internet," but there are different formulas used and the potency and purity of the obtained product is often open to question. However, the majority of users report taking this compound for recreational purposes and not for body building purposes (Karch, 2009).

Clinically, it is well absorbed from the gastrointestinal tract following oral ingestion, but on occasion is also injected intravenously by abusers. When ingested orally, GHB's effects begin within 10–30 minutes. Peak blood plasma levels are seen in between 20 and 40 minutes following a single oral dose, and it has a half-life of approximately 20 minutes (Flower et al., 2009; Karch, 2009). During the process of biotransformation, most of a single dose of GHB is excreted from the body as carbon dioxide, and only 2–5% is excreted from the body unchanged. GHB's short half-life, combined with its ability to induce amnesia and escape detection by standard urine toxicology tests, are all characteristics that originally made it attractive as a "date rape" drug. However, a urine test has been developed to detect GHB in the first 12 hours after it was administered, thus limiting its attractiveness as a date-rape compound because law enforcement authorities now have the technique to identify its use (Gwinnell & Adamec, 2006; Karch, 2009).

Subjectively, the effects of GHB are similar to those of alcohol, producing effects such as drowsiness, a sense of euphoria, and disinhibition (Flower et al., 2009; van Norden et al., 2009). When used concurrently with alcohol at high doses, it is possible that high doses of GHB will inhibit the biotransformation of the alcohol. This increases the risk of a possible alcohol overdose, which may prove fatal (Karch, 2009). GHB may cause seizures if used simultaneously with methamphetamine (Smith, 2001). Patients with HIV infection who are protease inhibitors should not ingest GHB, as the antiviral agents alter the user's body to biotransform many compounds, including GHB (Drummer & Odell, 2001).

Table 36-2 outlines some of GHB's effects on the user. In addition to those listed in the table, reported side effects of GHB include nausea, vomiting, tunnel vision, ataxia, confusion, agitation, dizziness, hypersalivation, hypotonia, and amnesia (Commission on Adolescent Substance and Alcohol Abuse, 2005; Gahlinger, 2004). Conservative, supportive, medical care is the best treatment for a GHB overdose, although intubation and restraints might be necessary in extreme cases (Miro, Nogue, Espinoza, To-Figueras, & Sanchez, 2002).

Tolerance develops rapidly to GHB's effects. Long-term abusers can become physically dependent on GHB, and there is a characteristic withdrawal syndrome that includes symptoms such as: anxiety,

TABLE 36-2
Ghb's Effects on User

DOSAGE LEVEL	EFFECT
0.1 to 1.5 mg/kg	Sleep state with enhanced delta and REM sleep
10 mg/kg	Euphoria, lowered inhibitions, and amnesia (some reports of nausea, headache, itching, and vomiting reported at this dosage level)
20–30 mg/kg	In addition to above effects, light sleep and/or drowsiness
40–50 mg/kg	Deep sleep state
60–70 mg/kg	Deep coma, possible seizures
>70 mg/kg	Cardiopulmonary depression, seizures, respiratory depression, and possible death.

SOURCE: Based on Commission on Adolescent Substance and Alcohol Abuse (2005); Flower et al. (2009); Koesters, Rogers, and Rajasingham (2002); Rosenthal and Solhkhah (2005).

---

[31]See Glossary.

[32]See Appendix three.

tremor, insomnia, nausea, tachycardia, tremor, hypertension, and a delirium-tremens like syndrome in heavy abusers who suddenly discontinue the use of GHB (Freese et al., 2002; Klein & Kramer, 2004; Rosenthal & Solhkhah, 2005; van Norden et al., 2009). These symptoms usually begin within 12 hours of the person's last use of GHB, and can continue for up to 12–15 days. This withdrawal syndrome is potentially life threatening (van Norden et al., 2009). As the above information suggests, GHB is significantly more dangerous than was thought 20 or more years ago, and in spite of assurances from those who sell it should not be abused.

Phenethylamines[33]

There are more than 250 members of this family of compounds, including the natural compound mescaline that is found in the peyote cactus of the American southwest, the compound MDA, and the synthetic hallucinogen MDMA (Haroz & Greenberg, 2005; Strassman, 2005). Other compounds in this family include MMDA, DOET, DOB, 2C-I, and DOM, among others (Brust, 2007b; Shulgin & Shulgin, 2007).

Nexus[34]

Nexus is perhaps the best known synthetic member of the phenethylamines.[35] This compound is usually ingested orally, and a single dose of 10–20 mg will cause the user to experience intoxication, euphoria, and visual distortions or outright hallucinations for 6–8 hours. Doses above 50 mg result in extremely vivid, frightening, hallucinations and morbid delusions (Karch, 2009). Side effects include nausea, abdominal cramps, pulmonary problems, and cough. In the brain, the compound shows an affinity for the serotonin 5-HT receptor subtype. Clinical research into the pharmacokinetics of this compound is very limited because it was never intended for human use. Detection of this compound through urine toxicology tests is difficult, because it does not react with many reagents used to identify various drugs of abuse (Karch, 2009).

"Blue Mystic"

Another member of the phenethylamine family of compounds is 2C-T-7,[36] known as "Blue Mystic" (Boyer, 2005). It is thought that this compound is about 12 times as potent a hallucinogen as mescaline. This compound is often abused for its ability to induce visual hallucinations (Karch, 2009). Side effects can include nausea, cramps, seizures, and possible death from aspiration of material being regurgitated (Boyer, 2005). Beyond the fact that it has a narrow therapeutic window, and the difference between an effective dose and a toxic dose is only a matter of micrograms, very little is known about the pharmacokinetics of this compound.

DOB

The compound DOB[37] has effects similar to those of MDMA, but last longer. Its use is largely confined to Australia, although on occasion it is found as a contaminant or adulterant to MDMA, or as LSD (Karch, 2009). It is known that the effects begin 3–4 hours after the compound is ingested, and some of the symptoms might last for up to 24 hours (Karch, 2009; Shulgin & Shulkin, 2007). DOB use has been associated with blood vessel spasms, and seizures, both of which have the potential to be fatal (Karch, 2009). It is significantly more toxic than LSD, but specific pharmacokinetic studies are lacking at this time.

Paramethoxyamphetamine

This is a potent hallucinogen and its hallucinogenic potential appears to be approximately the same as LSD (Karch, 2009). It is very toxic and a number of deaths have been attributed to its use (Karch, 2009). Some of the adverse effects from the use of this compound include (Karch, 2009) tachycardia, hyperthermia, coma, seizures, arrhythmias, abnormal heart rhythm, and in isolated cases dangerously low blood sugar levels.

Tryptamines[38]

There are at least 200 compounds in this family of chemical agents, all of which have a chemical structure similar to that of the neurotransmitter serotonin (Brown, 2007). Some of the compounds in this family of chemicals include the hallucinogen psilocybin, DMT, DET, psilocin and bufotenine. These compounds enjoyed various

---

[33]Shulgin and Shulgin (2007) provide an excellent overview of this family of compounds for those readers interested in learning more about these compounds.

[34]Or, 2,5-Dimethoxyphenethylamine.

[35]In some communities it is sold under the name of Venus, Bromo, Erox, and XTC (Karch, 2009).

[36]Or, 2,5-dimethoxy-4-(n)propylthiophenethylamine

[37]Or, 4-Bromo-2,5-dimethoxyamphetamine

[38]Sometimes called the indolealkylamines.

degrees of popularity in the 1960s and 1970s, but were classified as Schedule I[39] compounds by the Drug Enforcement Administration (Brust, 2007b; Haroz & Greenberg, 2005). Little is known about the pharmacokinetics of these compounds, although it known that many of these compounds are extensively biotransformed by the "first pass" metabolism process, and must be "snorted" or smoked to be effective (Haroz & Greenberg, 2005; Mueller, 2005) All members of this family of compounds are able to induce the potentially lethal condition known as the "serotonin syndrome."[40]

One member of this family of compounds is known by a variety of names, including Foxy or Foxy Methoxy[41] (Boyer, 2005; Meatherall & Sharma, 2005; Mueller, 2005). This compound appeared in the 1990s and was quickly classified as a Schedule I compound (Mueller, 2005). Unlike the other tryptamines, "Foxy" is not significantly affected by the first-pass metabolism effect, and can be ingested orally. Although this compound has a different chemical structure than MDMA, the effects are very similar for the abuser, and it has the same potential for neurological damage as does Ecstasy. Little is known about the pharmacokinetics of this compound. It is known that when ingested orally the effects begin in about 20–30 minutes (Mueller, 2005). The main effects are thought to be the result of this compound's ability to act as a serotonin 5-HT2a receptor agonist. It can cause sexual stimulation and mild hallucinations, which are the desired effects. Side effects include (but are not limited to) (Meatherall & Sharma, 2005; Mueller, 2005) anxiety, restlessness, anxiety, insomnia, a fear of imminent death, and possible seizures. There is evidence suggesting a synergistic effect between "Foxy" and compounds such as PCP, Ketamine, and marijuana, but little is known about the pharmacokinetics of this compound either in isolation, or in combination with these substances.

Psilocybin

Psilocybin is a naturally occurring tryptamine compound found in the mushroom *Psilocybe mexicana*, which is found in the northern part of Mexico and the Southwestern United States. The Aztecs called psilocybin the "Flesh of the gods," suggesting that they were quite familiar with this compound and its ability to induce a mystical state of mind in the user (Griffiths, Richards, McCann, & Jesse, 2006). Research into the

pharmacokinetics of psilocybin ended in the 1960s for the most part, and there is little known about the pharmacokinetics of this compound. It is known that high doses can induce seizures, and confused states, but fatalities that occur after the ingestion of psilocybin are most often the result of accidents or suicide rather than the direct effects of this compound (Filley, 2004).

Fry

There have been isolated reports of this compound in the United States. Fry is essentially marijuana soaked in formaldehyde, and then laced with PCP (Klein & Kramer, 2004). Although euphoria is the desired effect of this mixture, it can produce a toxic psychosis, hallucinogens, delusional thinking, panic, paranoid, reduced attention span, loss of conscious, and brain and lung damage (Klein & Kramer, 2004).

Benzypiperazine (BZP)

This drug is abused for its euphoric and amphetamine-like effects. Available evidence suggests that it was originally considered as a compound to treat intestinal parasites in cattle, but its potent side effects made researchers lose interest in this compound. It is often abused for its MDMA-like effects, affecting both the serotonergic and dopaminergic receptor sites. Subjective effects are identified in Table 36-3.

TABLE 36-3
Some Side Effects of BZP Abuse

MILDER	SEVERE
Anxiety	Hyperthermia
Agitation	Psychosis
CNS stimulation	Renal toxicity
Confusion	Respiratory failure
Dilated pupils	Rhabdomyolysis
Dry mouth	Seizures
Headache	Serotonin syndrome
Hyperventilation	
Hypothermia	
Insomnia	
Nausea/vomiting	
Tachycardia	
Urinary retention	

© Cengage Learning

---

[39]See Appendix three.

[40]See Glossary.

[41]Or, 5-methoxy-N,N, diisopropyltryptamine.

Designer Narcotics

Fentanyl

Fentanyl is a synthetic opioid that is widely used in various medical procedures. The basic fentanyl molecule is one that can be manufactured from a few ordinary industrial chemicals, although this process is rather difficult and lends itself to errors in the production process (Karch, 2009). Still, on occasions, illicit drug chemists will attempt to manufacture fentanyl for sale. The high potency of fentanyl can result in unintentional drug overdoses, some of which might be rapidly fatal. For example, when smoked (a popular method of fentanyl abuse), it is possible for one inhalation to prove fatal to the abuser because of the potency of this compound ("Take time to smell the fentanyl," 1994).

By making just a minor change in the basic fentanyl molecule, it is possible to produce fentanyl analogs[42] with various psychoactive effects. At least 12 such compounds have been identified to date. One analog has been found to extend fentanyl's effects from the normal 30–90 minutes to 4–5 hours. Another fentanyl analog extends the effects to 4–5 days. The compound 3-Methyl fentanyl (or TMF) is thought to be about 6,000 times as potent as morphine, a characteristic that makes it a popular drug for "snorting." Although these fentanyl analogs can be produced using easily available industrial chemicals, a simple mistake in the production process can produce compounds that are toxic, and possibly fatal to the user.

Dextromethorphan (DXM)

This is a synthetic compound, which is a chemical cousin to codeine. It is not a controlled compound as of this time (Karch, 2009). Dextromethorphan was originally marketed in the 1960s as an antitussive compound for treatment of mild to moderate intensity coughs (Haroz & Greenberg, 2005). In this context, the user will ingest around 30 mg of dextromethorphan every 4–6 hours. It is a relatively effective cough suppressant, and more than 140 over-the-counter compounds are sold in the United States alone that contain dextromethorphan either as the primary, or one of the primary, ingredients (Bobo, Miller & Martin, 2005).

Dextromethorphan tends to concentrate in the brain, and the concentration of DXM in the brain is significantly higher than that found in the blood plasma (Karch, 2009). This is the site of its cough-suppressant effects. DXM is biotransformed in the liver and is a pro-drug with the active metabolite, dextrorphan, inducing its cough-suppressant effects (Karch, 2009). This compound is extensively deactivated by the "first-pass metabolism" effect (Karch, 2009). However, about 10% of the general population lack the ability to produce an enzyme[43] necessary to biotransform dextromethorphan, and are classified as "slow metabolizers" of this compound (Karch, 2009, p. 605). Where the effects of a typical dose of DXM last 4–6 hours in the average person, a single therapeutic dose will last 17–22 hours in a person deficient in this enzyme. The implications of this are especially important when one considers the dosage levels utilized by DXM abusers (discussed later).

DXM is frequently abused by adolescents. A powdered form of DXM is available over the Internet, and there are Web sites that will give step-by-step instructions on how to abuse DXM and what effects to look for at different dosage levels ("Escalating DXM abuse among teenagers," 2007). The peak age of DXM abuse is about 15–16 years of age (Bryner et al., 2006). However, in contrast to the dosage levels utilized when a person wishes to control a cough, DXM abusers routinely ingest doses of between 150 and 2,000 mg at one time (Brust, 2004).

In the brain, DXM functions as a NMDA[44] channel blocker and a serotonin reuptake blocker (Brust, 2004). At dosage levels of between 300 and 1,000 md/kg of body weight, the effects of DXM are similar to that of PCP (Bobo et al., 2005). The effects begin within 15–30 minutes, and last for 2–6 hours (Haroz & Greenberg, 2005). Adverse consequences of DXM when abused include disorientation, panic attacks, paranoia, slurred speech, ataxia, tremor, nausea, vomiting, and nystagmus (Bobo et al., 2005). A DXM overdose[45] might produce such symptoms as lethargy, slurred speech, hyperexcitability, ataxia, tremor, rigidity, tachycardia, hypertension, nystagmus, respiratory depression, acute psychosis, coma, and possible death from cardiovascular collapse. On rare occasions, DXM can also induce

---

[42]See Glossary.

[43]CYP2D6, which is part of the metabolic P-450 pathway of the liver.

[44]See Glossary.

[45]If the DXM was in a preparation that also included acetaminophen, which is common for many over-the-counter cough and cold medications, the abuser will be at risk for unknowingly ingesting an acetaminophen overdose (discussed in Chapter 18).

the Serotonin Syndrome.[46] As with any substance, all cases of possible dextromethorphan overdose should be assessed by a physician immediately. Another issue to consider when reviewing the toxic effects of DXM is the possibility that the agent in which it is mixed (cough syrup) might contain other compounds (acetaminophen, e.g.) that are also toxic if used in excess.

Hydromorphone[47]

Hydromorphone is a semisynthetic narcotic, which has strong cough suppressant effects. Research into the pharmacology of hydromorphone is limited, although it is known to bind at the *mu* opioid-receptor site and thus potentially can suppress the respiratory reflex and in extreme cases death by respiratory depression. Its abuse potential is approximately the same as that of oxycodone, and if extended-release tablets are crushed or chewed all of the medication is released into the body at once, possibly inducing a fatal overdose. Should the individual also be using another CNS depressant, the risk of overdose is markedly increased.

Medication Diversion

These persons know the physician's schedule, and know exactly when to come to the office, or the emergency room, with exaggerated signs of physical distress. They do so with the hope of obtaining a prescription from the overworked physician who is looking forward to the end of the shift/day. Such medical emergencies are often seen on Fridays, at 4 p.m., for example, and the narcotics addict hopes that the physician will just write out a prescription than spend time arguing with the person. Claims of physician abandonment are often intermixed with threats, and exaggerated complaints of physical illness are used to obtain desired prescriptions. These behaviors, plus reports that the person is "allergic" to less powerful narcotic analgesics such as tramadol, or that these compounds do not work for the person, should alert the physician to the possibility of drug-seeking behaviors. Still, because it is the end of the shift, there is a small mountain of paperwork waiting to be filled out, and the physician wants to go home, it is not uncommon for the physician to write out a prescription just to get the person to leave.

The diversion of prescribed narcotic analgesics has become a major problem in recent years, resulting in a larger number of overdose deaths than all of the other drugs of abuse combined. The individual's motivation for abusing prescribed narcotic analgesics, especially methadone, ranges from a desire to obtain narcotic-induced euphoria, to attempts to "taper" themselves from narcotic analgesics using illicit compounds (Davis & Johnson, 2008). Some individuals use illicit opioids to self-medicate pain, according to the authors. Seventy-two percent of the subjects in their study used methadone, and 65% sold it. Indeed, the authors found that methadone abuse was more common than that of OxyContin, Vicodin, or Percocet. The abuse of OxyContin has become so common that in some areas it is more commonly abused than is heroin. Recently, the author introduced a reformulated form of OxyContin that hopefully will make its abuse more difficult. Recently a toxic-synthetic narcotic by the name of krokodil has been found in the American southwest. The euphoric effects of this compound are similar to that of heroin, however it is extremely toxic to the body, often causing rapid necrosis of body tissues and the death of the user in a matter of weeks.

Chapter Summary

The relationship between criminal activity and substance use disorders (SUDs) is quite complex, and worthy of a book in its own right. The debate over whether those people most prone to criminal activity are drawn to SUDs as well, or if criminal activity is a consequence of the lifestyle forced on those who wish to engage in substance abuse, continues to rage. Currently, it appears that both are applicable, depending on the individual and his or her path toward addiction to a chemical.

At least some of the harm associated with SUDs is a direct result of society's efforts at supply reduction through the "war" on drugs. By making chemical abuse illegal, society has both generated a new class of criminals (the abusers), and helped the growth of a class of criminals associated with the sale and distribution of drugs. Because it is a closed, illegal, market, upper and middle-level drug dealers often add various adulterants to the product that ultimately is sold to the illicit drug abuser. These adulterants contribute to or cause various health consequences for the abuser, who then seeks medical assistance. This, in turn, places an additional burden on the health care system. There have been significant unanticipated consequences making drugs of abuse illegal.

---

[46]See Glossary.

[47]Although hydromorphone is a legitimate pharmaceutical, it is also frequently diverted to illicit markets, or abused by the individual taking the medication. For these reasons, it is included in this section.

Further, to avoid criminal prosecution, those involved in the drug sales/distribution industry have been searching for new "designer" drugs, which are yet to be banned. When these compounds are identified by law enforcement officials and then outlawed, the search for other "designer" compounds that have not been banned begins anew. This search is spurred by the criminal sanctions in place against the distribution and sale of illegal compounds. However, enforcement of these sanctions has resulted in a further demand on the overburdened court system, which will be discussed in the next chapter. Some of the more commonly encountered illicit drugs, and their effects are reviewed.

The diversion of prescribed narcotic analgesics has become a major problem in recent years. The individual's motivation for abusing prescribed narcotic analgesics, especially methadone, ranges from a desire to obtain narcotic-induced euphoria, to attempts to "taper" themselves from narcotic analgesics using illicit compounds (Davis & Johnson, 2008). Other persons use opioids to self-medicate pain, according to the authors. Seventy-two percent of the subjects in their study used methadone, and 65% sold it. Indeed, the authors found that methadone abuse was more common than that of OxyContin, Vicodin, or Percocet. The findings of this study underscore the problem of diversion of prescribed narcotic analgesics.

CHAPTER 37

The Debate Over Legalization[1]

When the United States is not invading some sovereign nation—or setting it on fire
from the air, which is more fun for our simple-minded pilots—we're usually busy
"declaring war" on something here at home. Anything we don't like about ourselves, we
declare war on it. We don't do anything about it, we just declare war. "Declaring war"
is our only public metaphor for problem solving. We have a war on crime, a war on
poverty, a war in litter, a war on cancer, a war on violence, and [President] Ronald
Reagan's ultimate joke, the war on drugs. More accurately, the war on the Constitution.

—Carlan (2001, p. 109)

Introduction

The comedian George Carlan was, in the opinion of many, at his best when he was poking fun at current
social and political trends. However, in a very real sense, the quote at the start of this chapter is more of a
joke than the general public realizes: It is the truth. The substance use disorders (SUDs) are the only
medical (or psychiatric) condition in which the manifestations of that illness (in this case alcohol misuse
or illicit drug use) are addressed through the legal system (Heyman, 2009). A person with diabetes, a seizure
disorder, or cancer does not need to fear arrest for experiencing a seizure, being diabetic, or for having
cancer. However, the person with an SUD such as heroin abuse is in danger of facing legal charges for
engaging in the very behaviors that define the disease!

Rational perspective about the problem of illicit drugs is "generally lacking" when the problem of illicit
drugs is considered ("Drugs drive politicians out of their minds," 2009, p. 5). In this chapter, we will briefly
explore the controversy surrounding the question of legalization of at least some of the current drugs of abuse.

Statement of the Problem

There are those in the United States who believe that
"[w]hat you do with your consciousness is your own
business" (Amanda Feilding, an early researcher
specializing in the study of psychoactive drugs, quoted
in Lawton, 2013, p. 37). In contrast to this rather tolerant view are those who have responded almost with a
military-like program of extermination. Those who

abuse substances classified as illegal are subject to
socio-legal sanctions that vary from one state to another
or from one country to another. In the United States, the
government has engaged in the deliberate use of false
information,[2] which in the case of the "war on drugs"
has become an almost unspoken official policy of entire
agencies on the local, state and federal levels (Szalavitz,
2005). "Alcohol and drug use will inevitably cause addiction," they scream from their bureaucratic fortresses.
The truth is somewhat different: About half of those
who begin to use an illicit substance discontinue it in

---

[1]It is not the purpose of this chapter to advocate the legalization of
compounds currently deemed illegal by law. Rather, it is the purpose
of this chapter to stir debate within the class as to the question of
legalization.

[2]Or disinformation.

the first year, suggesting that while drug addiction is a possible outcome, it is not inevitable (Center for Substance Abuse Research, 2008).

It is widely acknowledged that addressing SUDs through legal sanctions is not effective: The link between criminal penalties and the SUDs is weak, at best (Taverne, 2010). In spite of this, the governments of many countries have adopted an attitude to the effect that because they know that the drugs of abuse are terrible things, they do not need to look at evidence suggesting otherwise (Taverne, 2010). Where social scientists call for a more rational policy addressing SUDs, governments choose to listen to the loud, moralistic, special interest groups that warn that to change existing policies on illicit drugs is to be "soft on crime" ("Drugs drive politicians out of their minds," 2009; Taverne, 2010). However, in at least 21 other countries, decriminalization of at least limited substance use is being contemplated or has been enacted into law. This contrast between how legal policies in the United States and those of other countries illustrates how many social policy decisions are made on the basis of media reports that are biased toward one group or another. Recently, in England, for example, the compound mephedrone was classified as an illicit substance after the media reported that it was responsible for 27 deaths in that country. What was not reported was that the presence of mephedrone was confirmed in just 11 of those cases (40.74% of media reported cases) and was ruled a contributing factor in just 2 of the 27 deaths (0.074% of the total number of cases reported in the media). There is a dearth of clinical research into mephedrone's effects, toxicity, or pharmacokinetics, but loud calls in the popular media that the substance be outlawed. So, naturally, the substance was banned.[3] New, legal, substitutes were being advertised and sold by illicit drug dealers within a matter of days of this decision, a reflection of the resilience of the drug supply and distribution network that has evolved in the past half century.

When a government(s) bans a certain behavior/substance, it is attempting in effect to protect the citizens from the consequences of their choices. In the case of the drugs of abuse, the rewards for engaging in this behavior is rapid, and the "law can rarely reform a people who have already succumbed to the allures of immediate gratification"[4] (Woods, 2005, p. 212). That reality is ignored as law enforcement officials and politicians call for stronger and stronger draconian measures to "win the war on drugs." The logic behind this approach has repeatedly been criticized, but the leaders are unwilling to change their course of action. Further, as will be discussed later in this chapter, the problem of illicit drug use has been used as an excuse to negate many of the provisions of the U.S. Constitution and the Bill of Rights. In a sense, this country has been turned into a police state, a social change that is justified as necessary to help to end illicit substance use. To this end ever greater numbers of nonviolent offenders are sentenced to jail or prison on the pretense that this action will protect the public from illicit drug abusers.[5] To make room in the prison for these nonviolent drug abusers, individuals with violent criminal histories are of necessity released from prison before completion of their sentences.

The success of these tactics might be seen in the fact that at the beginning of the 21st century the United States consumes two-thirds of the world's illicit drugs (Dobbs, 2007). Globally, the illicit drug market has been estimated to be a $400 billion dollar per year industry (United Nations, 2011), and if the above estimate is correct, then our share of this illicit drug trade is $264 billion each year. The United States is also spending at least an additional $200 billion per year to fight the "war on drugs." Statistics such as those reviewed above hardly reflect a resounding success, especially in light of the fact that the relative levels of drug abuse have been stable around the world for the last decade (United Nations, 2011). In the next section, we will examine the impact that this expenditure has had on the illicit drug trade.

The "War" on Drugs: An Ongoing National Disaster

Future historians will view the "war" on drugs with disbelief. This "war" has raged for the better part of a century. It continues not because of the destructive

---

[3]It is not the author's intent to advocate for the legalization of mephedrone, but to demonstrate how drug policy is often set in response to social forces and not by the pharmacological properties of that compound.

[4]The quote referenced the immorality of Roman society under Caesar Augustus; however, it appears to be equally applicable in this setting.

[5]Heyman (2009) argued that the majority of those who are incarcerated are in prison for the crime of *drug sales* and not possession of a controlled substance. Although it is tempting to argue that this will reduce drug availability, evidence suggests that it is at most a temporary solution, because other drug dealers quickly move in to fill the void.

potential of the drugs of abuse, but because of the irrational beliefs of those in command. An example of this was the social movement to legalize marijuana in the United States in the early 1970s. Then President Richard M. Nixon refused to consider this possibility because of a personal belief that (a) people who consume alcohol do not use it for its intoxicating effects but for fun, whereas (b) people who used marijuana were mainly those who were protesting against the then-current Vietnam War whose substance use was part of the reason why they were protesting (Zeese, 2002).[6] There were also subtle racial undertones to the antidrug efforts of the Nixon Administration, which were only discovered in the early years of the 21st century (Zeese, 2002). For example, possession of powered cocaine (most prevalent in middle-class America) resulted in a much more lenient sentence than possession of an equal amount of "crack" cocaine (most prevalent in the inner cities).

The War on Drugs: The Fantasy

The "war" on drugs is based on four legs: (a) elimination of illicit compounds through destruction of raw materials, (b) the interdiction of drugs being shipped to this country, (c) legal sanctions against those who engage in the use of the substances deemed illegal by the government, and (d) treatment of individuals addicted to these compounds. We will examine each of these legs supporting the "war on drugs" in turn.

Elimination of Raw Materials

As a tactic, the elimination of the raw materials used to produce the illicit drugs makes sense. If you eliminate the raw materials, then the compound cannot be produced, and the problem is solved. The reality is far different. For example, during the administration of President George W. Bush,[7] a 5-year, multibillion dollar program to eradicate cocaine cultivation in Columbia by spraying the fields where the coca plant is cultivated with a herbicide proved to be a failure. The farmers just moved over to the next valley, and started to cultivate the coca plant there. The judicious use of bribes to prevent officials from targeting certain areas for attack also contributed to the failure of this program. Finally, much of the coca production was moved from Columbia to the neighboring countries

of Bolivia and Peru, where it might also be cultivated without fear of government eradication programs. It is doubtful that this program had any major effect on the production of cocaine. Indeed, having caused a glut of cocaine on the illicit drug market in the United States in the past decade, drug cartels targeted Europe as an untouched market, and now approximately 140 metric tons per year of cocaine (or a quarter of the world's annual production of illicit cocaine) is consumed there (Parenti, 2009).

Many compounds are manufactured from precursor chemicals, which are often legally obtained. An example of the failure precursor elimination might be seen in the ongoing battle over whether ephedrine should be outlawed or not. Ephedrine can be used in the production of methamphetamine and was briefly classified as a controlled substance in the United States. As a result of this decision, producers of illicit methamphetamine either (a) moved the production center to other countries where ephedrine is easily available or (b) changed the process of producing methamphetamine to use pseudoephedrine, and over-the-counter cold remedy. These (and a multitude of other) examples all suggest that the elimination of those products used in the production of illicit drugs has failed. However, this effort is necessary...

> because some of the plants that grow in the southern hemisphere are just plain evil. We know that because they're not stamped with labels like Bristol-Meyers, Squib, Eli Lilly or Pfizer. And it's vital that we understand that these southern hemisphere plants and their cultivators are to blame because the alternative is to believe that our national appetite for drugs is our own problem. And that's plain crazy talk. (Maher, 2002, p. 49, italics added for emphasis)

As should be readily apparent by now, efforts for elimination of the raw materials used to produce the world's illicit drugs have been a failure. We will examine each of the three social responses to the problem of the substance use disorders next.

1. Interdiction

The Lessons of History: Prohibition

The pages of history provide stunning evidence that the interdiction of illicit compounds is doomed to failure. The clearest example of this failure was the "Great Experiment" of Prohibition, or simply Prohibition,[8]

---

[6]Would it come as a surprise to learn that President Richard M. Nixon was known to drink liquor on many occasions? Go figure out ...

[7]2000–2008.

[8]Technically, the bill was called the "Volsted Act" of 1919.

which began in 1920 and ended in 1933.[9] This social experiment on the theory that many of society's ills were caused by alcohol (the "Demon Rum"), with the result being that the nonmedical use of alcohol was outlawed. Even when prescribed by physicians a patient might receive only one pint of liquor every 10 days (Pain, 2008). Because of this law, more than one physician concluded that his or her medical school education was negated by "a few farmers, lawyers, politicians and the like ... who have the audacity to say to the medical profession of this country that they can't prescribe this or that ..." (unknown physician, quoted in Pain, 2008, p. 45).[10]

Although Prohibition began in 1920, the per capita consumption of beer in the United States had reached its low point between 1911 and 1914 (Schweikart, 2008). The number of deaths from cirrhosis of the liver reached its lowest levels in 1921, just a year after the start of Prohibition.[11] Further, by the end of the Prohibition period, medical journal articles on alcohol had all but disappeared (Schweikart, 2008). One could argue that Congress willingly "closed the bar door after the horse was out," since Prohibition was passed after the problem began to resolve itself. Admittedly, the level of alcohol consumption continued to fall during the Prohibition years, but only by approximately 30% (Okrent, 2010; Schweikart, 2008).

So great was the demand for alcohol that at its height during Prohibition the distribution of illegal alcohol comprised 5% of the nation's Gross National Product (Schlosser, 2003). Faced with the demand for alcohol, enforcement of the Volstead Act of 1919[12] began to waver in the face of a tidal wave of illegal

alcohol. So, Congress passed what is known as the Jones Law to stiffen the penalties for violation of prohibition laws. In many cases, what were formerly misdemeanors were transformed into felonies under the Jones Law. An unintended consequence of this step, however, was that the small-time producer or transporter of alcohol was replaced by organized crime syndicates. Nor was this the only unanticipated consequence of Prohibition: Following the start of Prohibition, the homicide rate in the United States increased fourfold, whereas other forms of crime increased by 24% (McPherson, Yudko, Murray-Bridges, Rodriguez, & Lindo-Moulds, 2009). Arguably, Prohibition did little more than contribute to the staggering increase in corruption by elected officials and law enforcement officers, a decline in civil rights, and profits for what might loosely be called "organized crime" (Lessig, 2009). It also eliminated a source of tax revenue for the government.

Before the start of Prohibition, the activities of organized crime had mainly been limited to prostitution and illegal gambling. The emerging "organized crime" organizations, sensing huge profits in providing alcohol to those who wished to drink in spite of Prohibition, quickly took control of the emerging illicit distribution system (Gray, 1998). "Organized crime" was armed with bribery money and high powered attorneys to fight criminal charges should they be caught breaking the law (Okrent, 2010). These syndicates also rapidly started to fight among themselves to gain control of territories in which to distribute illegal alcohol. On occasion, these territorial negotiations were aided by the judicious use of explosives, or automatic weapons' fire from vehicles driving past a competitor's place of business.[13]

Another totally unanticipated consequence of Prohibition was that it forced those people who wanted to consume alcohol to switch from beer to hard liquor (Gray, 1998; McPherson et al., 2009). This is consistent with the theory that successful interdiction efforts might cause dealers to *increase* the potency of their product to encourage customer loyalty because of the difficulty of finding new customers during the time of increased police surveillance (Giles, 2009). For alcohol, liquor presented the appeal of having less bulk, a higher alcohol content, and it did not spoil as rapidly as did beer. Before the start of Prohibition, the typical drinker

---

[9]To his credit, Prohibition was passed over the veto of then President Woodrow Wilson. Many members of Congress, and Wilson's successor President Warren G. Harding were what Okrent (2010) called "dry-wets." In public, they espoused the benefits and goals of Prohibition, while openly flouting the law by maintaining bars well stocked from the best liquor captured by Federal agents who interdicted alcohol shipments into the United States. However, Congress often does exempt itself from laws passed to benefit the lowly citizens who voted for them.

[10]This is a charge that has been repeated when physicians encounter the federal ban against prescription of marijuana.

[11]As was discussed in Chapter 8, it takes a number of years of chronic alcohol use for liver cirrhosis to develop. The fact that cases of cirrhosis reached their lower point in 1921 is indirect evidence that alcohol use had been falling before the start of Prohibition in 1920.

[12]For better or worse, Andrew Volstead is the Congressman who is credited with writing the Prohibition laws.

---

[13]Which sounds vaguely like the current situation between gangs selling drugs on the street corners, or "crack" houses, does it not?

would "sip" their drink(s) over an extended period, without evidence of widespread intoxication (Barr, 1999; Gray, 1998). With the start of Prohibition, drinkers shifted to a pattern of "binge" drinking, with the goal of rapidly achieving a state of intoxication (Barr, 1999; Gray, 1998). At the same time, individuals who did drink switched from beer to liquor, which allowed them to achieve the highest level of intoxication in the least amount of time (Gray, 1998). When Prohibition ended, drinkers retained this pattern of alcohol consumption. In this manner, the "Great Experiment" helped shape the drinking habits of people for generations to come.

The World of Today

During the middle of the 20th century, a similar phenomenon to that seen in Prohibition evolved, although the parallels with the Prohibition era were not recognized until much later. Researchers believe that the interdiction efforts of law enforcement authorities encouraged drug smugglers to switch from bulky, low-profit, marijuana to cocaine. Pound-for-pound cocaine is less bulky, less smelly, more compact, and more lucrative to smuggle into the United States. Further, the interdiction efforts against cocaine dealers appears to have contributed to the development of drug gangs, and a wave of violence that swept across the country in the 1980s and 1990s. By arresting the older, established, drug dealers the way was opened for inner-city, violence-prone, younger drug dealers to move into the business of selling cocaine, and to fighting over "turf" (Brust, 2004).

Another example of the Law of Unanticipated Consequences might be seen in the efforts of law enforcement officials to interdict methamphetamine production in the United States. In the 1990s, much of the methamphetamine was produced in small "mom and pop" laboratories that produced small amounts of methamphetamine for local consumption. By making these facilities a focus for law enforcement, the manufacture of methamphetamine was switched to "superlabs" outside of the United States that are capable of producing large amounts of relatively pure methamphetamine to be smuggled into this country (McPherson, Afsarifard, Hall, Yudko, & Rodriguez, 2009; Smith, 2006).

Only a small percentage of the drugs that are produced and sent to be smuggled into this country are interdicted, and at best this only results in short-term, local reductions in drug availability. Given the level of profits involved, if one drug supplier is arrested,

another will step into the void to sell drugs to those who desire them. The interdiction policies ignore the facts that: (a) the more "effective" police activity is, the more [drug] prices rise, (b) increasing the profits of smuggling, and distribution of that product to meet demand. Further, (c) the more likely drug purity and concentration will also increase, and (d) to make importation more cost-effective and detection more difficult (Kleiman, 2011). This was a lesson that law enforcement officials and those who make policy could have learned from Prohibition had they but stopped to read the history books: Interdiction just does not work (Reuter, 2009). Frances (2013) rated the interdiction campaign as "... no more than a phony Whac-A-Mole charade" (p. 210), which has made many drug suppliers very wealthy. In return for taking the risk of criminal prosecution, high-level suppliers arrange for drugs to be manufactured or smuggled into this country (usually by surrogates), where they are delivered to major cities and then funneled to outlying regions by middle-level distributors (Furst, Herrmannk, Leung, Galea, & Hunt, 2004). The distributor at each level charges a high price for this service, which ultimately is passed on to the consumer. The product "mark-up" is rather high, for it is not a free-market economy, and is justified by the dealer's risk of arrest and prosecution. If one distributor arrested, another person interested in such profits will simply step into the void.

2. Criminalization

There is little evidence that criminalization reduces illicit substance use (Taverne, 2010). In spite of this fact, criminalization remains the cornerstone of the "war on drugs." The fact that it turns many otherwise law-abiding people into criminals is quietly ignored. However, because the abuse of illicit drugs is, by definition illegal, those who abuse an illicit drug are classified as a "criminal" for engaging in the very behavior used to define addiction as a disease. A person does not need to engage in the sale, manufacture, or distribution of illicit drugs. They are criminals just because they abuse a compound defined as illicit, and at best are pushed to the fringes of society.

Because the drugs of their choice are illegal, and not freely available, individuals with an SUD are then forced to use them under conditions that contribute to health care problems. Although the drugs can cause terrible damage to the user's body, the conditions under which the abuser must use these illicit compounds compound the damage causing health care problems becomes another indirect cost of the "war on drugs." Further, because by definition, the illicit drugs are illegal, the abuser must often resort to criminal activity to support his or her SUD. Paradoxically, these consequences of the criminalization of certain compounds are then used to justify keeping them illegal.

The methods used by law enforcement authorities involved in the "war on drugs" are hardly respectful of those who are addicted to these compounds. It has been suggested that the drug enforcement agencies in the United States, especially the Drug Enforcement Administration, have become "as cruel as the rapacious drug dealers who just try to make money" (Doblin, quoted in Frood, 2008, p. 43.). Most certainly, there is a definite lack of respect for those who, by definition, suffer from the medical disease known as addiction. In other words, to "win" the "war on drugs," we have become just as violent and indifferent as the "enemy."

Mandatory Sentencing

The "link between criminal penalties and drug use is weak" (Taverne, 2010, p. 26). On the basis of this dubious assumption, Congress authorized the execution of heroin dealers to stem the tide of narcotics abuse in the United States following World War II, and a few heroin dealers were executed (Walton, 2002). In spite of this drastic sanction, the number of narcotics abusers or addicts in the United States continued to increase (Walton, 2002). In the 1950s, Congress passed a new series of mandatory sentencing laws that dictated minimum sentences to be imposed on narcotics dealers. These laws met with almost universal acceptance, and were loosely called the "Boggs Act."[14] These laws were passed on the dubious assumption that it is possible to punish undesirable behaviors out of existence (Husak, 2004; Lundeen, 2002).

One dissenting voice to the Boggs Act was that of James V. Bennett, the Director of the United States Bureau of Prisons. He expressed strong reservations about the possible effectiveness of the Boggs Act, although he had not broken any laws in doing so. He was subsequently followed by agents of the Federal Bureau of Narcotics, who submitted regular reports to their superiors on the content of speeches that he made. In spite of the enthusiasm with which the Boggs Act was received and the reports filed by Federal Bureau of Narcotics agents on the content of

Mr. Bennett's views, it had become clear that Mr. Bennett was right: Mandatory minimum sentencing did little if anything to reduce the scope of narcotics abuse in the United States. Congress then replaced the Boggs Act with a set of sentencing guidelines that allowed the presiding judge to assign appropriate sentences based on the merits of each case. However, in one of the great reversals of all time, just 14 years later Congress again embraced mandatory prison sentences as part of then President Ronald Reagan's renewed "war on drugs."[15] The mandatory sentences were encoded in the Sentencing Reform Act of 1984, which denied even first-time drug offenders the promise of early parole.[16] As a result of this new law, the prison system was soon overwhelmed with nonviolent first-time offenders who were serving lengthy mandatory sentences for drug-related convictions.

Through this confluence of historical forces, the United States has a greater percentage of its population in a jail or prison than any other country in the world (Zakaria, 2012). In contrast to the incarceration rate of 90 per 100,000 persons in Germany or the 96 per 100,000 persons in France, the United States has 760 prisoners per 100,000 persons (Zakaria, 2012). Although the United States has just 5% of the world's population, this nation also holds the dubious honor of having 25% of the total number of people on earth who are incarcerated for one reason or another (Zakaria, 2012). Four-fifths of these people are incarcerated for simple possession of an illegal compound (Zakaria, 2012).

An often overlooked aspect of the criminal prosecution and incarceration of those convicted of drug-related offenses is that it is expensive to keep a person in prison. Zakaria (2012) reported that the cost of incarcerating one inmate in the California Dept of Corrections was $45,006 per year[17] (Zakaria, 2012). If approximately 1.32 million of the people incarcerated

---

[14]Named after the Congressmen who first proposed the legislation. This proposal became law in 1952.

[15]One has to wonder how many members of Congress voted in favor of these changes not because they thought that they might work, but because they were afraid of being accused of being "soft on crime" by their political rivals.

[16]Parole from prison was once a privilege offered only to a few offenders who demonstrated exceptional efforts toward rehabilitation. Now, it is expected, and is often viewed as a "right" of those being sentenced to prison. One will often hear the freshly convicted inmate state that although he was sentenced to prison for 10 years, for example, that his parole date is only 3 years away.

[17]A figure that includes the cost of salaries for the staff who work in the prison, the physical plant itself, construction costs, food, medical care, and so on.

in the United States simply for possession of a controlled substance, then this nation is spending $59.4 *billion* dollars for the cost of incarcerating these persons. Nor does the cost stop upon the inmate's release from the penitentiary: Individuals who have been incarcerated earn 40% less than those who have never been incarcerated, thus reducing the amount of state and federal income taxes that they pay, and increasing their subsequent dependence on state and federal supplementary funds for food stamps, and so on. Individuals convicted of drug-related offenses are barred from state and federal tuition assistance programs for college or vocational-technical school costs, making it virtually impossible for the individual to train for a better job (McPherson et al., 2009). This after-incarceration punishment contributes to the high recidivism rate for drug offenders who are released from prison. In many cases, they are pushed back into a life of crime because they can do little else to earn enough money to support themselves or their families.

In retrospect, the Boggs Act, and the Sentencing Reform Act of 1984 were both failures. In spite of the widespread knowledge of the legal sanctions against illicit drug use, "millions of people every year join the legions who have experimented with illegal substances" (Phillips & Lawton, 2004, p. 33). For virtually every action there is an unexpected consequence, a truism that has become enshrined as the "Law of Unintended Consequences." If you wish to "get tough on crime" by throwing first-time drug offenders into jail or prison, it will become necessary to release violent offenders from prison to make room for new convicted drug offenders. As a result of this unintended consequence, the average sentence served for a person convicted of homicide is approximately 9 years, whereas a person convicted of growing 100 marijuana plants could be sent to prison for up to 40 years[18] (Brust, 2004).

The Forfeiture Fiasco

During the administration of President Ronald Reagan, he pressured Congress to become "tough on crime" by enacting a series of "zero-tolerance" statutes. The possession of *any* amount of an illegal substance was a ground for criminal prosecution under these "zero-tolerance" statutes. People were prosecuted for offenses as innocuous as having money in their wallet tainted by traces of cocaine, as if this was proof of the individual's

cocaine abuse. Only later was it proven that a significant percentage of the dollar bills in circulation were tainted by traces of cocaine apparently by rubbing up against other paper currency that had traces of cocaine on it. It was also discovered that marijuana seeds blow in the wind, often alighting in a person's car or boat without their knowledge. By then, however, the damage had been done, and numerous people had been prosecuted under the guise of "zero tolerance."

Setting aside the constitutional provisions against unwarranted search and seizure, Congress also passed a law allowing law enforcement authorities to confiscate property on the simple *suspicion* that it had been purchased with money made from the illicit drug trade. Law enforcement agencies no longer had to *prove* that the property had been purchased with money made from the sale of illegal drugs. They only had to state their belief that this was the case. Not surprisingly, in the time since this law was passed they have been widely abused. Some police departments now *depend* on money and property seized under forfeiture laws for at least part of their operating budget. The level of abuse inherent in this law might be seen in the fact that up to 80% of the money seized by federal authorities comes from people who are *never* indicted for criminal activity, much less tried in a court of law and convicted (Leavitt, 2003). Police in at least two states (Florida and Louisiana) have been identified as using minor traffic offenses as justification to seize money from motorists who have committed no illegal act other than that traffic law violation because it *might* be drug money (Leavitt, 2003).

The "forfeiture" laws *do* provide a provision that allows the citizen whose property was seized to seek the return of the property. This process involves the individual filing a lawsuit against the agency that seized the property, then providing in a court that he or she did not obtain the money or property from the illegal drug trade. This process is expensive, time consuming, and the final cost of the process might be several times that of the property seized by authorities. Further, the agency that seized the property is not required to pay any form of interest on the material(s) seized. Few people are willing, or have the financial resources, to pay $4,000 in court costs to prove that the $1,000 that they had in their wallet for a vacation trip when stopped by the police was rightfully theirs, for example.

As should be obvious by now, the social experiment of trying to eliminate illicit drug trade through interdiction, incarceration, and punishment has been a

---

[18]Which, if you consider that the offender was 25 at the time of conviction, is essentially a life sentence.

failure. However, this does not stop law enforcement officials from trumpeting the minimal success of the past year, and from hinting that for just a few billion dollars more it might be possible to "win" the war on drugs. Unfortunately, law enforcement and incarceration of offenders, often touted as "a panacea for the problem of illicit drug use" (Fulde & Wodak, 2007, p. 334) have yet to prove effective. Indeed, the mandatory sentencing laws were intended to discourage upper- and middle-level dealers from engaging in drug distribution activities. However, these individuals are able to trade their knowledge for lighter prison sentences or even just probation! As a result of this process, only a minority of those incarcerated in the federal prison system are middle-level drug distributors, and more than half of those incarcerated are either drug abusers or low-level dealers who sold drugs on the street corners.

3. Treatment[19]

The treatment of people who are not involved in the distribution or sale of illegal substances but who have an SUD is a distant fourth when the funds for the "war on drugs" are distributed. The total expenditure for drug rehabilitation is estimated to be $15 billion from state and federal governments, and $5 billion from insurance companies[20] (Carey, 2008). Arguments that rehabilitation is not effective break down in the face of studies that have found that incarceration has been estimated to cost 2–10 times (Johnson, 2003) as much as rehabilitation. Other researches have suggested that for every dollar invested in treatment the community saves from $4 to 12 (Breithaupt, 2001; Brust, 2004; Dobbs, 2007; Mee-Lee, 2002; UKATT Research Team, 2009), to possibly as much as $50 (Garrett, 2000).[21] These figures do not mean that treatment is appropriate for every offender convicted of a drug-related crime. In spite of the claims of advocates:

> The addiction treatment field [has] not met either public expectations for reduction of addiction ... or

its own expectations to produce lasting abstinence. (McLellan, 2008, p. 94)

However, neither is incarceration the answer for every offender convicted of a substance-related crime. There should be an attempt to balance the application of legal sanctions against that of treatment, to find the appropriate response to the crime committed by each individual. In the year 2000, Portugal, for example, decriminalized drug use, placing emphasis on education and rehabilitation. In spite of dire warnings, the removal of criminal sanctions against substance abuse has not resulted in a major increase in drug use. Indeed, there has been a slow but steady decline in drug use (Taverne, 2010). This would argue that legal sanctions against drug use are apparently not effective, a lesson that historians have known ever since the Prohibition era of the 1930s.

The Reality of the War on Drugs

Simply stated, the "war on drugs" is a failure (Zakaria, 2012), although few outside of Washington, DC, dare accept this fact (Reuter, 2009). The worldwide effectiveness of this march of folly might be seen in the United Nations pledge in 1998 to win the "war on drugs" by the year 2008 (Room, 2009). The reality is that the drugs (or at least those who market and abuse them) have won ("Winning the War on Drugs?" 2007). In its efforts to "win" this war, the United States has gone so far as to attempt to interfere with the internal affairs of other countries. One of the many examples of this unwarranted, possibly illegal, interference was seen in 2003, when the then "drug czar" of the United States accused Canada of trying to poison American youth by relaxing its internal marijuana possession laws (Reuter, 2009). This intrusion into the internal affairs of another country does provide a fine example of how the weapons and tactics used in this "war" fail to work. For example, following the invasion of Afghanistan by the U.S. armed forces an estimated $800 million per year was spent to eliminate the problem of illegal opium poppy cultivation in that country, without any apparent benefit (United States Special Envoy for Afghanistan and Pakistan, Richard Holbrooke, quoted in Room, 2009).

In spite of the moralistic stance by those who argue against illicit drugs, the antidrug media campaigns launched with great fanfare, as well as attempts at interdiction by law enforcement agencies, the problem of illicit drug use has continued for over a century. In

---

[19]Discussed in more detail in Chapter 29.

[20]An amount that might increase now that the federal government has passed a "parity" law that now requires that insurance companies reimburse for drug rehabilitation on an equal level as for other health problems.

[21]These various estimates reflect, in part, different variables included from study to study. For example, one study might include long-term reductions in health care costs that another study does not include in its estimates of the savings that result from treatment.

the name of protecting all citizens from the drugs of abuse, Constitutional rights have been ignored, or, circumvented. Citizens are criminally prosecuted to save themselves from the scourge of illicit drug use, which, according to the American Medical Association, is a disease. Many of these prosecutions are based on weak or nonexistent evidence (English, 2009).

The effectiveness of the "war on drugs" might be seen in the fact that in the early 1950s, when the population of the United States was approximately half of its current level, only 60,000 people were estimated to be addicted to narcotics (Ropper & Brown, 2005). In the time since then the United States has spent $2.5 trillion[22] dollars on the "war on drugs" (Fleming & Grew, 2008). The population of the United States is a little more than double what it was in the early 1950s. Where one would expect that the number of heroin addicts were to double to 120,000 people based on the doubling of the population, 1 *million* opioid-dependent people in the United States are thought to be addicted to narcotics at this time (Hasemyer, 2006; Tinsley, 2005). In spite of the massive expenditure of time, energy, and personnel on the "war on drugs," substance abusers spend more money on illicit drugs now than they do for cigarettes in the United States each year (Debusmann, 2006; Dobbs, 2007; Schlosser, 2003). These statistics hardly reflect a resounding success.

The failure of the "war on drugs" should not come as a surprise: We are fighting the war on both fronts: (a) collectively we create the demand for illicit compounds, then (b) spend billions of dollars to interdict the compounds produced to meet this demand, and (c) spend even more money to prosecute those who abuse these compounds and are arrested. It does so in spite of the awareness that past legislative and legal efforts to control illicit substance use have all failed (McPherson et al., 2009). Rather than change a failed social policy, however, politicians blindly follow the same path, hoping for a different outcome.[23] This reflects, in part, the tendency for politicians to ignore scientific evidence in favor of "pander to public prejudice" (Nutt, 2009, p. 5).

A recent survey by the Hazelden Foundation revealed that 79% of those people sampled believe that the "war on drugs" has *not* been effective ("Americans want insurance to cover addiction; unsure if it does," 2009).

Interdiction efforts have been so successful that there are 66% *more* hardcore drug addicts at the start of the 21st century than there was at the start of the last decade of the 20th century (Falco, 2005). Incarceration has also proven to be a magnificent success: In 1972, it was estimated that there were 200,000 jail and prison cells[24] in the United States, and a quarter of a century later there are *2 million* jail and prison cells in this country (Pepper, 2004). In spite of this fact, ever growing numbers of people start to abuse drugs each year, and politicians continue to maintain that it is possible for society to arrest its way out of the drug abuse problem in spite of the facts reviewed above. Yet, the current policy continues.

The Drug War as Political Nonsense

The analogy between the fairy tale of the "Emperors' New Clothes" and the "war on drugs" is striking. The program has been shown to be a dismal failure, but nobody wants to say this publicly. Perhaps, this is because the "war on drugs" is designed to give the *illusion* that politicians are doing *something* about this social problem, without having to face reality: It is our *demand* for drugs that is the foundation for the illicit drug trade. As Delingpole (2009) noted, "in politics, unfortunately, fashion counts for rather more than integrity or ideology" (p. 9).

If politicians truly wanted to protect society from the dangers of substance abuse, then they would address the most destructive compounds being used today: cigarettes and alcohol. However, the focus of the "war on drugs" is on those mind-altering agents that do not make a profit for the large corporations who can hire lobbyists (Rasmussen, 2008). Collectively, alcohol and tobacco products cause or contribute to the deaths of almost one million people a year in the United States alone. Is it a coincidence that these industries also make lavish contributions to each political party on a regular basis? Cocaine, marijuana, heroin, and methamphetamine dealers do not make contributions to political parties, and their products are, by coincidence, classified as illegal.[25] It is not the purpose of this paragraph to argue that political contributions by what might loosely be called the "alcohol" or the "tobacco" industries are wrong. This is the political system in which we live. However, it *is* the purpose

---

[22]A trillion is a thousand billion, and a billion is a thousand million.

[23]One definition of insanity is doing the same thing over and over, hoping for a different outcome. Which says something about the current "war on drugs," does it not?

---

[24]*Jails* are usually incarceration facilities at the county level. *Prisons* are incarceration facilities at either the state or federal level.

[25]There is a lesson here, but I am not the one who suggested it!

of this paragraph (and the rest of this chapter) to make the reader question *why* the policies that are in place remain in place without question. A welcome voice of reason was offered by the U.S. Conference of Mayors, who publicly announced that the "war on drugs" was a failure (Curley, 2007). However, this announcement was an exception.

Politicians do not listen to the voice of reason. Rather, they use the "it will happen to everybody" approach to generate the hysteria necessary to allow them to justify the "war on drugs" (Delingpole, 2009; Reuter, 2009). Dissenting voices must be suppressed, just as they were when Adolf Hitler first came to power in Germany of the 1930s. For example, the original draft of the Federal Omnibus Crime Bill called for people who criticized the Federal government's anti-drug policies to be charged with *treason,* and for criminal prosecution for that offense (Leavitt, 2003). The Chairperson of the United Kingdom's Advisory Council on the Misuse of Drugs was dismissed in 2009 after voicing opinions that went counter to those of the government ("Drug Disarray," 2009). His "crime" was to point out that 1:350 attempts to ride a horse resulted in a serious injury, whereas 1:10,000 people who took MDMA suffered an adverse effect.

The "War on Drugs" as a Drain on National Resources

Remember that incarceration is one of the centerpieces of the "war on drugs." Having caught the drug distributor or user, prosecuted the individual, and convicted him or her, the question becomes one of what to do next? Incarceration is the answer, and it has been used with a vengeance: The expense of "treating" individuals with SUDs through the criminal justice system costs more than the SUD does to the individual, or society (King, 2006). Currently, many states are spending more on the construction of new jail or prison cells than they are for building college classrooms (Brust, 2004; Taylor, 2004).

An unintended consequence of the "war on drugs" is that the various states and communities become dependent on the salaries paid to those who staff the prisons built to house the influx of drug offenders. The same is true for construction companies that are contracted to build the new prisons. These agencies and states then maintain an impetus to maintain the current "war on drugs." This is clearly seen in the repeated efforts by the Drug Enforcement Administration (DEA) to keep marijuana classified as a controlled substance: If it were to be legalized, the number of "illicit drug users" would be reduced from approximately 13 million people[26] to 3 million, making it hard for the DEA to justify its large budget to Congress (Walton, 2002). This is an example of how various agencies come to depend on the grants handed out by the federal and state governments for funding.

Other Consequences of the Prohibition Against Drug Abuse

Medical sociologists have observed that, because of existing prohibitions against the use of illicit drugs, the abuser must use their limited supply of drugs under hazardous conditions. Some of the consequences include an increased risk of death for heroin abusers (6–20 times higher than for the general population) (Drummer & Odell, 2001). Some of the causes of death of intravenous drug abusers, for example, include drug overdose, infections (including AIDS), malnutrition, accidents, homicide, and suicide. The medical treatment of those who abuse illicit drugs and then develop associated illnesses is an indirect part of the health care crisis in this country, as are the social support(s) necessary for the families of those who are illicit drug abusers.

An interesting social experiment involving the effort to address the illicit drug problem was carried out in Portugal in 2001. The drug laws were revised so that they were less harsh and punishments were proportional to the crime. Although the level of illicit drug use remained approximately the same, the demand on the health care system for substance-related illness and deaths from illicit drug use dropped (Nutt, 2009). This is not to say that illicit drug use should be tolerated, but does illustrate the consequences of the application of legal sanctions to address this social problem.

The current legal structure in the United States also blocks research into potentially useful medical applications of, if not the drug of abuse itself at least a derivative of a chemical found in an abused substance. Nutt (2012) pointed out that in the 1960s, for example, research was being conducted into the application of lysergic acid diethylamide (LSD) in the treatment of alcoholism, with promising results. However, there has been no further research into possible medical applications of LSD or virtually any drug of abuse

---

[26]The number of "illicit drug abusers" if marijuana abusers are included, as opposed to the number of "illicit drug abusers" if marijuana abusers are no longer counted.

because of government sanctions against such research imposed in the mid-1960s.[27]

Section Summary

To date, each of the corner posts of the "war on drugs" has achieved some degree of success, and a significant degree of failure. It has been found that more successful interdiction efforts prove to be, the higher the profit margin for smugglers and the greater the incentive for others to enter the drug distribution or sales business. It has proven impossible for society to arrest its way out of the drug abuse problem, and although treatment holds some degree of promise, it is also not the ultimate answer to the problem of drug use disorders sweeping across this country. Further, society does not address the issue that it is the demand for illicit drugs that fuels the "crisis" in illicit drug use. Thus, the "war on drugs" does not really address the basic problems in society that help to cause the problem, and those who openly call the "war on drugs" a failure are ignored, or their views are called unrealistic by those already committed to the same policies that have proven to be such a dismal failure.

The Law and Morality: Where to Draw the Line?

In the modern "war on drugs," federal and state authorities have applied legal sanctions against individuals who wish to use any of a long list of chemicals, or, in the case of alcohol, to use it beyond certain established limits. If, as the American Medical Association argues, the SUDs are disease states, then these legal sanctions essentially turn these diseased people into criminal acts. However, the law is selective: Only certain substances, or certain euphoric states, are deemed worthy of criminal prosecution (Husak, 2004). Caffeine users, for example, achieve a drug-induced psychological state without fear of arrest or incarceration. Long-distance runners achieve the "runners high" without fear of legal consequences (Husak, 2004). The drinker, as long as he or she does not drive a motor vehicle while intoxicated or commit other crimes, can ingest alcohol to achieve a desired state of intoxication without fear of arrest.[28]

In the early 21st century, the line between legitimate medical purposes and recreational substance use, has become rather uncertain. Some people will use a prescribed medication (let us use diazepam as an example) to achieve a desired mood state, but if another person were to take the same medication without a prescription to achieve the same mood state he or she could be charged with a crime (Husak, 2004). Should this be the case? It has been argued that personal, recreational, drug use (as opposed to distribution of illicit chemicals to others) is a consensual crime. Are euphoric mood states grounds for legal sanctions? At what point does medical necessity blend into recreational drug use? If a man were to suffer from a clear case of erectile dysfunction, the prescribed use of a compound such as Viagra® would be appropriate. However, if a businessman were to ingest the same compound simply to enhance sexual performance, would this be grounds for criminal prosecution?[29] Both individuals may have obtained the same compound by prescription from a licensed physician, but where is the line between legitimate medical need, and recreational use of that compound? As Rasmussen (2008) observed:

> the myth of a sharp divide between medical and non-medical "recreational" drug use began to weaken. Some of the pharmaceuticals that people get from our modern medicine men suddenly began looking a lot like the illegal drugs that people take in alternative manners; perhaps some street "abusers" were actually self-medicating, and some legitimate patients were merely junkies hooked by the doctors and drug firms. (p. 175)

Imagine three hypothetical business executives. One will drink a martini(s) to relax after a hard day's work. The second will ingest a diazepam tablet for the same reason, whereas the last hypothetical person smokes marijuana at the end of the work day. The legal system tends to be exceptionally selective about where to draw the line, while failing to provide any rationale for this decision. If the person were to use the wrong chemical to achieve a desired state of mind, he or she could be ruined by the legal consequences of that decision. Thus, the "war on drugs" might be viewed as a "war" on those who attempt to alter their state of consciousness

---

[27]The researcher would be in possession of a controlled substance while conducting the research, which is a felony offense, for example.

[28]This assumes that the individual is not on bond, probation, or parole. In many cases, probation or parole agreements stipulate that the individual not ingest alcohol or illicit drugs as one of the conditions of the bond agreement, or of probation, or parole.

[29]Before you answer this question, there is evidence that sexual performance enhancement compounds are commonly abused by college students for recreational purposes. Should they be prosecuted for "criminal" activity?

in ways deemed inappropriate by segments of society. The understanding of this reality may have helped the "Drug Czar" to reexamine the manner in which the United States attempts to deal with the drug abuse problem in the country through referrals to treatment rather than incarceration (G. Fields, 2009).

The Debate Over "Medical Marijuana"

At the end of the first decade of the 21st century, the debate over whether marijuana use should be permitted for the treatment of medical disorders has resulted in a multitude of often conflicting state laws that prohibit all marijuana use, or allow its use for the control of symptoms of identified medical conditions. Detractors from the proposed use of marijuana as an adjunctive agent in the treatment of various medical disorders suggest that by allowing this initiative to pass, it will encourage marijuana abuse. This belief is not supported by the clinical evidence, which in fact finds the opposite: Authorizing the prescribed use of marijuana might reduce its attractiveness to others (Gorman & Huber, 2007).

For a number of reasons, including perhaps the fear identified, above, federal laws against marijuana possession have been aggressively enforced, making such state initiatives meaningless. The Department of Justice has recently issued instructions to the effect that federal resources should not be use in enforcing federal laws against marijuana use if the person using marijuana was doing so in a manner consistent with the "medical marijuana" law of that state (Hoffmann & Weber, 2010). However, the various state initiatives allowing for the medicinal use of marijuana has created a wide range of enforcement problems: The existing state laws do not regulate the potency or quality of the marijuana that is permitted for use in those states, and there is wide variation between states as to which conditions provide justification for the use of marijuana for medical purposes, the amount of marijuana that a person might have for such treatment, or a unified mechanism for distribution of marijuana to patients who qualify for marijuana use in that state (Hoffmann & Weber, 2010). The existing laws also do not address the issue of whether the physician who recommends the use of marijuana for a defined condition should discuss the potential risks and benefits of marijuana use, and whether such discussions

should be documented. As the above information would suggest, the use of marijuana for medical purposes is a process that is still evolving, and all of this work could be undone if the next President should rule that marijuana use for any reason should be suppressed by federal authorities.

The medicinal use of marijuana is not the same as the *legalization* of marijuana, although public perception often holds that they are one and the same. In reality, the medicalization of marijuana would simply place it on an equal footing with other accepted pharmaceuticals, and allow researchers to identify components in marijuana that might be of value to health care professionals. As is true today for the other pharmaceuticals, the possession of any of these compounds without a prescription would be grounds for legal prosecution. The relationship between medicalization and legalization might best be viewed as shown in Figure 37-1.

Unfortunately, the federal government has maintained a stance that even doing basic research into possible medical applications of marijuana is illegal. Currently, marijuana is classified as a Schedule 1 compound,[30] and as such research into possible medical applications of marijuana is prohibited. The American Medical Association has argued that marijuana should be reclassified as a Schedule II compound, which would then allow researchers to explore potential applications for the various chemicals found in marijuana smoke. However, as of this time, marijuana remains a Schedule I compound and this decision is defended on the

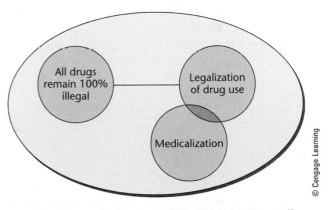

FIGURE 37-1 Medicalization and Legalization as Two Different Concepts.

© Cengage Learning

---

[30]See Appendix Three.

ground that: (a) there are no *proven* uses for marijuana, so (b) there is no need for research to possibly identify a legitimate application for marijuana in this country. The DEA recently threatened to suspend a physician's license to write prescriptions for supposedly writing prescriptions for certain illicit compounds, but the courts ruled that this was a violation of the physician's first Amendment rights under the Bill of Rights (Hoffmann & Weber, 2010). This is a complex issue, and the debate over the use of marijuana for medicinal purposes will continue well into the 21st century.

Legalization of Marijuana[31]

Should marijuana be legalized? Somewhere in the United States a person is arrested for a marijuana-related crime every 38 seconds (Raw Data, 2010b). In the Netherlands, by way of contrast, marijuana use is acceptable and the individual is allowed to have small amounts of marijuana for personal use if it were purchased in a government-approved coffee house. There is a tax placed on marijuana, providing a source of revenue. Illicit drug distributors are still subject to arrest and prosecution, however. Thus, the government-sanctioned use of marijuana is within strict limits, and the full power of the state is still applied to those who sell and distribute illicit marijuana.

In spite of the most draconian of legal measures, marijuana use has not been eradicated in the past half century, and arguably has made marijuana use even more attractive as a drug of abuse *because* it is illegal. A more reasonable approach might be an unbiased study into the possibility that legalization would be helpful, or at least less harmful to society than are current legal sanctions. If you but breathe the word "legalization," however, you are instantly engulfed by a multitude of political agendas, half truths, and illogical ideas, not the least of which is that you are "soft on crime"[32] (Taverne, 2010). Although the Obama administration's "drug czar, Gil Kerlikowske, said that that "we're not at war with the people in this country" (quoted in R.D. Fields, 2009), the military has been recruited to help law enforcement agencies stem the flow of drugs flowing into this country (Walton, 2002).

Proponents of the legalization of marijuana point out that the legalization of marijuana, even with strict controls such as those put into place in the Netherlands, would remove a source of income from what is loosely called "organized crime." The appropriate taxes might serve as a source of an additional $33 billion per year revenue for the government, which is hardly an insignificant matter[33] (Cafferty, 2009). Although there is a danger that legal access to marijuana might contribute to the potential adverse consequences inherent in marijuana use, one must ask whether these consequences are less costly both financially and in terms of human lives than the current draconian measures imposed on marijuana abusers.

Arguably, marijuana could soon lose its appeal to adolescents and young adults, many of whom currently use this compound as a form of rebellion (Barr, 1999). It has been argued that:

> If the appeal of drugs lies in their prohibited status, then we must expect that cannabis will soon be as fascinating as a new set of tax guidelines [if decriminalized]. (Walton, 2002, p. 137)

The author did admit that there would possibly be a short-term increase in the number of marijuana abusers, but as time passed the number of marijuana abusers would probably lose its appeal to many of those who are drawn to it now because it is illegal. This is a myth that perpetuates the continued application of repressive antidrug laws that have been shown not to work (Greenwald, 2009). In Portugal the antidrug laws were repealed or drastically revised recently without a major increase in drug abuse in that country. The legalization of at least marijuana has been tried in various countries in Europe with some success. However, those who set policy in this country have turned a blind eye to these social experiments to continuously reaffirm their belief in a failed policy of legal repression.[34]

Chapter Summary

Historically, the "war on drugs" in the United States is based on four legs: (a) elimination of illicit compounds through destruction of raw materials, (b) the

---

[31]Colorado's decision to decriminalize the possession of marijuana in 2014 will provide an interesting social experiment to determine the potential risks and benefits of the decriminalization of marijuana for personal use.

[32]As if, somehow, the two are synonymous.

[33]Or, giving the casual manner in which politicians in Washington toss around budgets of *trillions* of dollars (each $1 trillion is a thousand billion dollars) perhaps this figure is meaningless.

[34]It has been estimated that if marijuana use was legalized and taxed that it would generate between $2.4 and $6.2 billion dollars per year in new tax revenue (Raw Data, 2012b).

interdiction of drugs being shipped to the country, (c) legal sanctions against those who engage in the use of the substances deemed illegal by the government, and apparently if all else fails, and (d) treatment of those addicted to these compounds. These policies have failed miserably in spite of an expenditure of $2.5 *trillion* dollars since 1950 on the "war on drugs."

Future historians may well conclude that the only groups to benefit from the "war on drugs" are (1) those involved in the illicit drug trade, (2) street gangs involved in the daily distribution of the drugs and who profit from their sale, (3) the government employees whose job depends on the "war on drugs," (4) politicians who talk about "getting tough" on crime by stamping down on illicit drug abuser, (5) construction company employees, whose jobs depend on building the prisons to house those convicted of drug-related offenses, (6) people hired to staff the aforementioned prisons, (7) various police departments, who have come to be dependent on the federal and state subsidies to fight the "war on drugs," and (8) the terrorist groups who benefit from the sale of illegal drugs to fund their own activities.

The question of whether an illegal drug(s) should be legalized, and under what conditions, is a social issue, not a medical one (Brust, 2004). There are many who argue that society should blindly "stay the course" even if that course is toward the shoals of financial ruin and social upheaval. The last half century has demonstrated that society cannot arrest its way out of the current situation. However, it cannot provide enough treatment beds for those with SUDs.[35] There are no clear answers, nor is it clear which new social policies might be required to address this social dilemma. However, as has been demonstrated in this chapter, there is a need for a long, *honest,* examination of existing policies to find those that work and those that should either be modified or dismantled.

Are alcohol and the illicit drugs "evil"? The individual's response to this question is based on their perspective. The perspective is based both on personal experience and social feedback. To use an analogy, is a knife evil? Knives have been in use for thousands of years. If a person were to use a knife to slice a Thanksgiving turkey, is that an evil act? If that person were to use a knife to commit a murder,[36] is the knife an evil thing? It is important to remember that knives, alcohol, or drugs, are inanimate: *It is the manner to which they are used* that determines whether an object is helpful or harmful. As a topical anesthetic, cocaine might bring welcome relief from an injury.

In neither case, is the chemical itself "evil." It is the purpose to which that compound is used that society uses to classify it. The standards that society uses to make these judgments are subject to religious sanctions, legal regulations, information (and misinformation), political pressures, and so on. The antidepressant medication fluoxetine and the hallucinogen MDMA both cause select neurons in the brain to release the neurotransmitter serotonin and then block its reabsorption. Yet one is a recognized and accepted pharmaceutical, whereas the other is illegal.[37] Impact of social factors on the development of SUDs is perhaps best revealed during adolescence. This is not to say that social factors do not act during other periods of life. However, adolescence is such a dynamic phase of life with so many changes occurring over such a relatively short period of time providing a mirror against which social factors might be identified and measured. It should be kept in mind, however, that social development does not take place in a vacuum.

---

[35]This statement assumes that effective treatment methods can be developed which have a minimal risk of relapse, a complication of substance abuse rehabilitation programs that only complicates matters a hundredfold.

---

[36]"Jack the Ripper" comes to mind, here.

[37]The same point might be made about drugs used to treat "erectile dysfunction." A small but significant percentage of those who use such drugs do so not because they suffer from some degree of impotence, but because they find that it enhances sexual performance. Is this appropriate, or it is a form of medication misuse?

The *Diagnostic and Statistical Manual of Mental Disorders* (5th Edition) *(DSM-5)* and Substance Use Disorders[1]

The *Diagnostic and Statistical Manual of Mental Disorders* (5th edition) *(DSM-5)* (American Psychiatric Association, 2013) departs from the classification system used in earlier incarnations of the *Diagnostic and Statistical Manual of Mental Disorders* in a number of ways. First it is not assumed that substance *abuse* is a separate entity from substance *dependence*. Rather the more inclusive term *substance use disorder* is used to avoid the stigma terms such as "alcoholic" or the slightly less pejorative term "alcohol dependent" (for example) elicit in the general population.

The diagnostic criteria utilized in the *DSM 5* (American Psychiatric Association, 2013) are as follows:

Impaired control as evidenced by:

1. Taking more of a substance or taking it for longer than intended.
2. Unsuccessful attempts to cut down.
3. Spending a great deal of time in efforts to obtain, use, or recover from past episode of abuse.
4. "Craving" for drugs of abuse when not actively using drugs of abuse.

Social Impairment as evidenced by:

5. Failure to fulfill major life obligations due to substance use.
6. Continued use in spite of problems caused/exacerbated by the substance use.

7. Important obligations are given up or reduced in favor of substance use.

Risky use as evidenced by:

8. Recurrent use in dangerous situations.
9. Continued use despite of physical or psychological problems that are caused or exacerbated by continued substance use.

Pharmacological dependence, as evidenced by:

10. Tolerance to the effects of the substance.
11. Withdrawal symptoms when substance intake is either significantly reduced or discontinued.

The presence of two or more of these criteria was thought to identify a person with a substance use disorder (SUD). In contrast to its predecessor, the *DSM-5* does not include substance-related legal problems as a diagnostic sign of a SUD. Unlike its predecessor, the *DSM-5* diagnostic criteria substance an SUD included *craving* for a chemical, which was a welcome change. Other welcome changes include the modifier "in controlled environment" for individuals who claim being abstinent from alcohol or illicit drugs. Virtually every experienced substance abuse rehabilitation professional has encountered a client who claims to have abstained from all substance abuse for the past 3 months, 5 years, and so on, only to reveal later that they were incarcerated for part or all of that period of time. The modifier "in controlled environment" allows the reviewer to identify special cases in which the person's abstinence might have been motivated by external factors.

---

[1]This summary of the information in *DSM-5* provided in this appendix is provided for illustrative purposes only and should not be interpreted as nor function as a guide to patient care or diagnosis.

Another change from its predecessor is that the *DSM-5* attempts to classify the SUD as being mild, moderate, or severe in intensity. Persons who meet only two–three of the criteria were said to have a mild substance use disorder, while persons who meet three–six criteria are said to have a moderate intensity SUD. Those individuals who meet seven plus of the identified criteria are said to have a severe SUD. Yet another change from the predecessor to the *DSM-5* is a category known as the *substance-induced disorders*, where conditions that simulated a more traditional psychiatric disorder but are substance induced might be categorized. An example of a substance-induced disorder would be the depression seen when many cocaine abusers finish a period of intense cocaine use. Such a disorder would be separate from the primary depressive disorders that would have a similar appearance but a totally separate etiology.

A welcome change to the *DSM-5* is the categorization for SUD in early remission (<three months) as opposed to sustained remission (>twelve months). The definition of "early remission" or "sustained remission" allows the clinician to differentiate between an *active* SUD, say an ongoing cocaine addiction, and a cocaine addiction in early remission or in sustained remission. The *DSM-5* also allows for those individuals whose opiate use disorder is controlled because they are participating in an opiate agonist program to be identified.

As significant as these changes to the *DSM-5* (American Psychiatric Association, 2013) appear, the utility of this classification system has been challenged. Most insurance companies use the World Health Organization's *International Classification of Disease* (9th edition) manual for billing purposes.[2] Using two different classification systems opens the door for potential miscommunications and it probably would be most useful for psychiatric units to use the *ICD-9* system to minimize if not avoid opportunities for such problems.

---

[2]The author of this text was surprised to receive a telephone call from the billing department of the hospital where he once worked. The caller inquired why he, as a psychologist, was billing for a gynecological procedure. The author was somewhat surprised, asked the caller in the billing department for diagnostic code that had been submitted, and was provided with that information. The author of this text checked the current edition of the *Diagnostic and Statistical Manual of Mental Disorders* and saw that the diagnostic code for the patient's condition was correct. Then your author realized that the billing department used the *ICD-9* classification system, but that the psychiatric unit where he worked used the *Diagnostic and Statistical Manual of Mental Disorders-4*. The code number for major depression in the *DSM-4* was the same as the *ICD-9* code for the gynecological procedure.

Classes of Antiviral Drugs Currently in Use to Treat HIV Infection

Nucleoside/nucleotide analogs:	Compounds act as DNA chain termination agents, inhibiting the transcription of viral RNA into DNA in cells infected with the HIV-1 virus, thus inhibiting viral replication.
Non-nucleoside reverse transcriptase inhibitors:	Compounds that bind to and inhibit the action of the enzyme reverse transcriptase, which is essential for viral replication in infected cells.
Protease inhibitors:	Chemicals that block the action of a protein known as *viral protease*, which is necessary for viral replication.
Fusion inhibitors:*	Compounds that block the protein complex on the host cell that the HIV-1 virus uses to bind to the cell wall.
Integrase inhibitors:	New class of antiviral agents designed to block the process by which the HIV-1 virus inserts its RNA into host cell, forcing it to begin to manufacture copies of the HIV-1 virus to infect other cells.
Chemokine (C–C motif) inhibitors:	New class of antiviral agents that block effects of protein molecules in host cell wall (chemokine) that "pull" the molecular walls of the host cell and the virus together, allowing the virus then to "fuse" with the host cell.
Maturation inhibitors:	New class of antiviral agents under development. Maturation inhibitors interfere with the formation of a protein shell that normally surrounds the "daughter" virus particles, thus preventing full maturation and blocking the process by which new virus particles can be manufactured and released into the circulation.

*Sometimes referred to as *Entry inhibitors*.

The Comprehensive Drug Abuse Prevention and Control Act of 1970 provided for the classification of all compounds into one of five categories, depending on their abuse potential and medical applications. It is one of the most confusing aspects of drug rehabilitation work for health care and drug rehabilitation professionals. It is also the system by which drugs are identified for legal prosecution. This classification system is based not on the pharmacological properties of a compound, but on its perceived abuse potential and as noted all pharmaceuticals are classified as falling into one of five categories by the Drug Enforcement Administration (McPherson, Yudko, Murray-Bridges, Rodriguez, & Lindo-Moulds, 2009):

SCHEDULE	DEFINITION AND EXAMPLES
Schedule I compounds	Compounds with no recognized medical use. Examples: Marijuana, LSD, MDMA, heroin
Schedule II compounds	Compounds with a recognized medical use, but with a very high abuse potential. Examples: Morphine, amphetamine compounds
Schedule III compounds	Compounds with recognized medical use, but with a moderate abuse potential. Examples: Ketamine, codeine
Schedule IV compounds	Compounds with recognized medical use, but with a mild abuse potential. Examples: Phenobarbital, benzodiazepine compounds
Schedule V compounds	Compounds with recognized medical use, but with a low abuse potential. Example: Buprenorphine

The Twelve Steps of Alcoholics Anonymous[1]

STEP ONE: We admitted that we were powerless over alcohol—that our lives had become unmanageable.

STEP TWO: [We] came to believe that a power great than ourselves could restore us to sanity.

STEP THREE: Made a decision to turn out will and our lives over to the care of God as we understood Him.

STEP FOUR: Made a searching and fearless moral inventory of ourselves.

STEP FIVE: Admitted to God, to ourselves, and to another human being the exact nature of our wrongs.

STEP SIX: Were entirely ready to have God remove all these defects of character.

STEP SEVEN: Humbly asked Him to remove our shortcomings.

STEP EIGHT: Made a list of all persons we had harmed, and became willing to make amends to them all.

STEP NINE: Made direct amends to such people wherever possible, except where to do so would injure them or others.

STEP TEN: Continued to take personal inventory and when we were wrong, promptly admitted it.

STEP ELEVEN: Sought through prayer and meditation to improve our conscious contact with God as we understood Him, praying only for knowledge of His will for us, and the power to carry that out.

STEP TWELVE: Having had a spiritual awakening as a result of these steps, we tried to carry this message to alcoholics and to practice these principles in all our affairs.

APPENDIX FIVE
The "Jellinek" Chart for Alcoholism

Following the publication of earlier editions of *Concepts of Chemical Dependency*, questions were raised concerning my decision not to mention the so-called Jellinek chart in this text. This chart, which is viewed as gospel within the alcohol/drug rehabilitation industry, purports to show the progression from social drinking to alcoholism, then on to recovery. Since the time of its introduction, the chart has been used to illustrate the "unalterable" progression of alcoholism to countless patients who were in the earlier stages of alcohol use problems, as well as to browbeat reluctant individuals into accepting the need for help with their supposed drinking problem.

Variations of the chart have been developed for compulsive gambling, steroid abuse, compulsive spending, both heroin and cocaine addiction, and countless other disorders. An example of this chart is shown in Figure A5-1.

The problem is that Jellinek did *not* devise this chart! Even though it is often attributed to him, the chart is actually the work of Dr. Maxwell Glatt, a British physician who was so taken by Jellineks work that he operationalized the *gamma* subtype of alcoholism in chart form. The chart, which addresses *only* the gamma subtype of alcoholism as suggested by Jellinek (1960), has mistakenly been accepted by

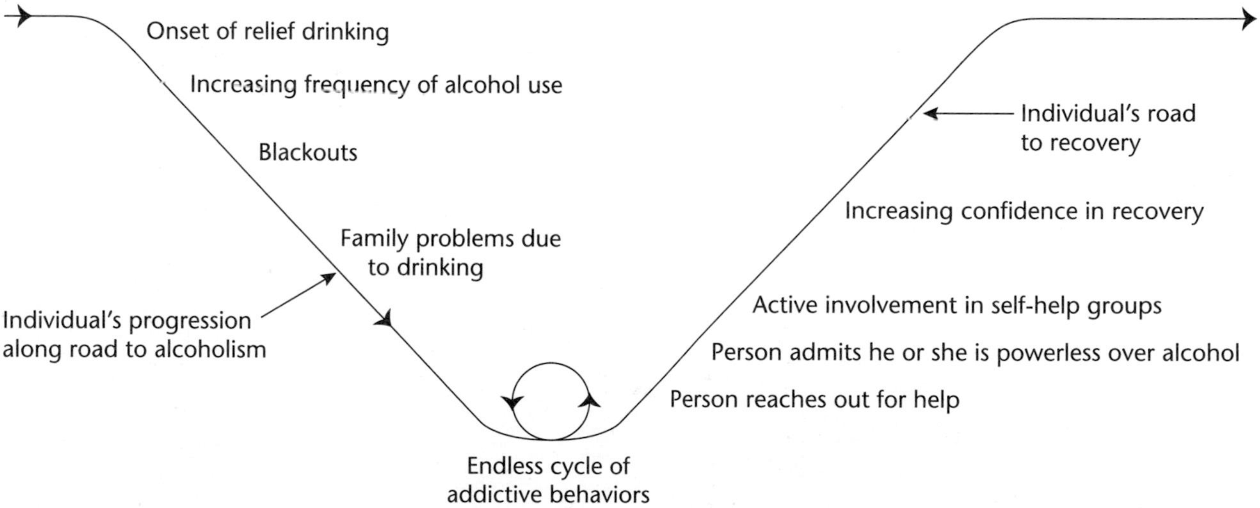

FIGURE A5-1 Alcohol Progression Chart Often Mistakenly Called the "Jellinek" Chart.

countless alcohol/drug rehabilitation professionals as *the* chart that identifies the progression of *all* forms of alcoholism. As a result of this mistake, many patients in rehabilitation programs, whose symptoms of alcohol use problems did not "fit" the progression of symptoms suggested in the chart, have been subjected to countless hours of confrontation because they were "in denial." Rather than perpetuate this misunderstanding, I decided not to make any reference to this chart in the text of *Concepts of Chemical Dependency*.

GLOSSARY

Acetaldehyde Toxic compound, possibly carcinogenic, that is produced during the process of alcohol biotransformation and cigarette smoking. The biotransformation of acetaldehyde is blocked by disulfiram, making the individual who has consumed alcohol feel ill, which in theory should reduce the desire to drink.

Acetylcholine One of the major excitatory neurotransmitters. Acetylcholine activates muscle cells in response to motor activation commands from the brain, and is also involved in anger, aggression, and sexual behaviors.

Acids (abbreviated to as the pH of a compound) A molecule that has eight (8) electrons and orbiting the nucleus is said to be neutral, or stable. It does not have an electrical charge to attract additional electrons.

However many compounds do have extra electrons orbiting the nucleus. This gives that molecule a small electrical charge. The greater the number of extra neutrons the greater the electrical charge and the stronger the potential for that molecule to attract other electrons in an attempt to achieve stability.

Compounds with large numbers of extra electrons are said to be acidic, or acids. The greater the number of extra electrons the more acidic a compound is said to be.

Activities of daily living (ADLs) There are two types of ADLs. The basic ADLs include basic activities such as grooming, getting dressed, feeding, bathing, and so on. *Instrumental ADLs* involve more complex tasks such as money management, shopping, medication management, and being able to arrange for transportation as needed.

Acute aortic dissection See: *aortic dissection.*

Adipose tissue Fat tissue.

ADLs Activities of Daily Living.

Agenesis Failure of development in, or damage to, a specific body organ during prenatal development.

Agonist A chemical that activates a receptor site in a cell wall.

Agranulocytosis A condition where there is an insufficient number of white blood cells (called *neutrophils* or *granulocytes*) that results when white blood cells are destroyed more rapidly than they are being produced.

Albumin One of the primary protein molecules found in the general circulation.

Alcohol use disorder A term that is applied to individuals whose use of alcohol is far in excess of the norms for his or her social or cultural group. This term is slowly gaining popularity over the older terms *alcohol abuse* and *alcoholism,* in part because it is more inclusive, and it lacks the social stigma of these other terms.

Allele A variation of a gene.

Alveolar Pertaining to the little pockets in the lungs where the process of oxygen/carbon dioxide exchange is carried out.

Amnesia See: *retrograde amnesia* or *anterograde amnesia.*

Amygdala A region in the brain that is shaped like an almond, located in each temporal lobe. This region is thought to be involved in the process of attaching emotional context to memory and modulating emotional responses to external reality. This includes behaviors centered on the process of obtaining reward(s), and on the anxiety and panic responses.

Analog, drug   A chemical that is a variation of the chemical structure of another compound, producing a "new" drug. The original compound is known as the *parent* compound, whereas the variation is known as an *analog* of the parent compound.

Anaphylaxis shock   Severe, potentially fatal whole body allergic reaction to a chemical that the body views as an allergen. Various tissues in the body release massive amounts of histamine, triggering the allergic reaction cascade. Some of the symptoms of anaphylactic shock include swelling of the mouth and throat causing the airway to constrict (and possibly close entirely), chest discomfort, hives, loss of consciousness, cardiac arrhythmias, and potential death in a short period of time. This is a medical emergency and persons who are experiencing, or believe that they might be experiencing, anaphylactic shock should immediately be transported to a hospital emergency room by ambulance.

Angina   Pain in the heart caused by the muscle tissue of the heart suffering damage through a reduction in blood flow to that tissue.

Anhedonia   Inability of a person to take pleasure in activities that she or he once enjoyed. This condition is a feature of some personality disorders, major depression, schizophrenia, and is seen in the drug withdrawal syndrome from various drugs of abuse.

Anorexia   Loss of desire to eat for an extended period of time, thus resulting in weight loss.

Anorexic   Agent that induces anorexia.

Anterograde amnesia   Inability to remember events after a specific point in time. This condition usually results from any of a wide range of forms of neurological trauma or a wide range of chemical compounds.

Alcohol-induced "blackouts" are a form of chemically induced state of anterograde amnesia. Other medications, such as Versed, a benzodiazepine often used in "conscious sedation" medical procedures, and Ketamine also can induce this same effect.

Traumatic brain injury may also induce anterograde amnesia. It is not uncommon for a patient who had been in a motor vehicle accident to assert that they could not remember events for the first few hours, or days, after the accident. It should be pointed out that anterograde and retrograde amnesia are not mutually exclusive, and may co-exist in the same patient.

Antidipsotrophic   An obsolete term used to identify compounds that would combat dipsomania, or chronic alcohol use.

Antitussive   Agent used to control cough.

Antipyretic   Against fever.

Anxiolytic   A compound that reduces the individual's subjective anxiety level.

Aortic dissection   A phenomenon in which the inner layer of the aorta separates from the outer layers. With each heart beat blood is forced into the dissection, forcing the tissues to rip apart even further. This condition is a surgical emergency and is frequently fatal.

Arteritis   Inflammation of an artery.

Aspiration pneumonia   A form of pneumonia that results when the individual aspirates stomach contents into the lungs during the process of vomiting. Bartlett (1999) identified two necessary components: (a) the aspiration of stomach contents into the lungs as a result of a breakdown of normal body defenses designed to prevent this and (b) damage to lung tissue from gastric juices or bacterial infection.

Astrocytes   A form of glial cell in the brain, which helps to provide physical support to the structure of the brain, as well as possibly play a role in the transfer of molecules from the blood to the neurons of the CNS.

Ataxia   Inability to properly coordinate muscle movements.

Attention deficit hyperactivity disorder (ADHD) Behavioral disorder in which the individual lacks the ability to focus attention on the task at hand. There are two subtypes: the *inattentive* variety and the *hyperactive* variety. The latter is more often diagnosed, because children with this disorder are more likely to be recognized. It has been estimated that 3% of the children with ADHD will "mature out" of this condition each year, with the result being that for many individuals ADHD continues well into adulthood.

AUD   Abbreviation for *Alcohol Use Disorder*.

Auto-amputation   A phenomenon in which the body essentially blocks the circulation to a limb so that the tissue dies. In the case of a limb, it will actually fall off. This is seen in cases of severe trauma, infection, or as a side effect of some chemicals.

Base   Opposite of Acid (above). Compounds that can absorb electrons are said to be alkaline, or base compounds. The greater the number of electrons that molecules can absorb the more basic that compound is said to be. Chemists often express this in terms of the "pH" of that compound.

Bibliotherapy   Use of assigned readings to help the client to better understand different concepts presented in individual or group therapy sessions.

Black market   System through which products are obtained outside of normal channels and then sold to those who are willing to pay for them for profit.

Blood–brain barrier   A structural component of blood vessels in the brain that blocks the passage of many toxins, bacteria, and other substances that might cause harm to the brain.

Body packer   Individual who will ingest a compound, usually cocaine, wrapped in multiple condoms, in an attempt to smuggle the compound into a country such as the United States within their body. If one of the packages should rupture, the "packer" will be exposed to massive amounts of cocaine, probably with terminal results.

Boost/boosting   This common process also increases the CNS depressant effect of each class of drugs to induce or reinforce drug-induced euphoria at the risk of potentially lethal results.

C-reactive protein   Protein molecule involved in inflammatory response.

Cannabinoids   Compounds that are manufactured and used in the brain to regulate neurotransmission, especially the *dopaminergic* neurons.

Cardiomyopathy   Technically any disease of the myocardium, or the muscle tissue of the heart.

Catecholamines   A family of compounds, including epinephrine, a compound normally produced by the adrenal glands, and the neurotransmitters norepinephrine and dopamine. These compounds help to regulate various body functions. Norepinephrine, for example, functions as a neurotransmitter in the brain.

Cerebellar ataxia   Loss of motor coordination and balance caused by damage to the cerebrum.

Cerebellar atrophy   Shrinkage in the overall size of the cerebellum because of death of neurons in this region of the brain.

Cerebellum   In terms of the total number of neurons, the cerebellum is the largest part of the brain, in spite of its relatively small size. It is involved in the process of coordinating motor activities in the body.

Certified Medical Review Officer (CMRO)   Physician who has been trained in the interpretation of urine toxicology test results. The CMRO is also responsible for the integrity of the urine toxicology testing procedures utilized for interpretation of unexpected test results, and is charged with maintenance of patient confidentiality in testing process.

Cilia   Microscopic hairlike projections from the wall of various body organs, including the lungs, where they help to propel mucus to the top of the lungs, helping to expel foreign particles from the lungs.

Conduct disorders   A childhood condition marked by behavioral dyscontrol, acting-out behaviors, and sometimes poor academic achievement, in a child of normal intelligence.

Confabulation   A neurological disorder in which the individual is (a) unable to remember part of his or her past and (b) will make up a history. Without collateral information, the individual's rendition of his or her past might actually seem plausible in many cases, making the need for collateral information imperative to detect such cases.

Causes of confabulation include (but are not limited to) the Korsakoff's syndrome. Thus, it is imperative that the assessor rule out other possible causes of confabulation before assuming that it is alcohol related.

Confounding variable   A variable in a research study that potentially can alter the outcome of that study. For example, not controlling for participant's age in a study of reaction time because our reaction time slows down as we age.

Contingency management   Process through which a person with a substance use disorder is trained to identify high risk situations in advance, and then practices coping mechanisms to avoid relapsing.

Corticogenesis   Production and maturation of new neurons in the cortex region of the brain.

Cortisol   Enzyme normally found in the body, which is found at higher levels during times of stress. It is often referred to as a *stress-fighting compound* because of this.

Creatinine   Waste product of muscle activity. This level is usually constant. Laboratories have established cutoff levels above or below which the urine is assessed as being suspicious because of the abnormal creatinine levels.

Cross-tolerance   Process through which an individual's tolerance to one compound, say alprazolam, is transferred to other compounds in the same class, such as diazepam, as well as to similar compounds such as ethyl alcohol (all of which, in the example provided, are CNS depressants).

Cyclooxygenase   An enzyme involved in the process of prostaglandin production. One form of cyclooxygenase (COX-1) is involved in the regulation of kidney and stomach functions, where it carries out a protective function.

The second form of cyclooxygenase (COX-2) is produced by body tissues when damaged. About 60% of the chemical structure of COX-1 and COX-2 is the same. Unfortunately, the shared elements of the molecule is what is blocked by NSAIDs, which function as nonselective COX inhibitors. By blocking the action of both forms of cyclooxygenase, the NSAIDs interfere with the normal function of COX-1 when it is the effect of COX-2 that prompted the use of the NSAID. It is for this reason that patients with hypertension are advised not to use an NSAID unless directed to do so by a physician, or why a patient taking aspirin for inflammation might suffer gastrointestinal damage, for example.

ΔFosB   A compound found in neurons that controls the process of manufacturing proteins within the neuron. ΔFosB is one of the *genetic transcription factors* that control when or if certain genes within the neuron become active. This compound is thought to be involved in the process of memory formation, although its exact role has not been delineated, and in the expression of resilience on the part of the person in the face of trauma or stress.

Delta FosB   See: *ΔFosB*.

Diagnostic inflation   Unfortunate outcome of the process where a poorly trained assessor or vague diagnostic criteria result in ever-growing number of people being diagnosed with a condition that in reality they do not have. This results in unnecessary referrals for treatment and blocks access to the available treatment resources for those who do need rehabilitation.

Diaphoresis   Perspiration, especially copious amounts.

Dimorphism   See: *sexual dimorphism*.

Discontinuance syndrome   The manifestations of the body's reaction when a compound regularly used as prescribed are either discontinued or markedly reduced. This is essentially a *withdrawal syndrome* from that compound, a term that offended many patients who were taking the compound as prescribed. To differentiate between the process of withdrawal from a prescribed as opposed to an illicit substance the term *discontinuance syndrome* is used if the person is withdrawing from a prescribed medication.

Dissimulation   A situation where the client provides false information in response to a question or test item.

Doctor making   See: *doctor shopping*.

Doctor shopping   Slang term for going to a number of different physicians until the substance abuser finds one who agrees that they might have a given condition and is willing to prescribe a desired substance for the treatment of a nonexistent or exaggerated condition.

Dopamine   Neurotransmitter utilized in the brain for such tasks as controlling behavior and mood, motivation reward, learning, as well as some psychomotor functions. It is also involved in the reward cascade.

Dopaminergic   Nerve cells that use dopamine as their primary neurotransmitter.

Dose-response curve   A graphic representation of the physiological response of the user's body to a given compound.

Down-regulation   Process in which a neuron reduces the number of neurotransmitter receptor sites. Paradoxically this increases the sensitivity of that neuron to a given neurotransmitter.

Dysentery   A painful infection of the lower intestinal tract, usually caused by the ingestion of contaminated water. The infected person will develop massive diarrhea, sometimes intermixed with blood and mucus. Unless the fluid loss caused by the diarrhea is rapidly controlled, dysentery can prove to be fatal after only a short period of time. Dysentery was common in the crowded, unsanitary, military camps of the 1700s and the 1800s, as well as in many cities throughout history, and major epidemics of dysentery were recorded throughout history before the cause of this disorder was identified.

Dysphoria   Feelings of sadness, sorrow, depression, and so on. The opposite of *euphoria.*

Dysthymia   The analogy to the former construct of "Depressive Neurosis" is not entirely inappropriate, here. Technically, the term *dysthymia* means "ill humored." Patients with dysthymia demonstrate depressed mood that lasts most of the day and that is continuously present. The individual will struggle with feelings of low self-esteem, guilt, inadequacy, irritability, and anger. They withdraw from others, lose interest in hobbies, and report that they have always felt depressed.

Unlike major depression, dysthymia begins early in life, often in childhood, and is most certainly present by young adulthood, although there is a subtype that does not manifest until middle age or even later in life. The symptoms must be present for at least 2 years prior to diagnosis, and the disorder has an intermittent course.

Edema   Swelling of tissues, usually seen immediately adjacent to injury.

Ejection fraction   The percentage of blood ejected from the heart's left ventricle each time the heart beats. In healthy individuals this is usually around 60–65%.

Endocannabinoid   One of a family of compounds bound within the brain or body where molecules of compounds found in marijuana bind. These natural, or endogenous, cannabis-like compounds carry out essential functions such as guiding the growth and neural cells in the cortex *in utero* and after birth, regulation of the immune system, and so on.

Enkephalins   One of the family of endogenous opioids, involved in the process of regulating pain.

Epigenesis   Process through which individual experiences alter the expression of the individual's genetic heritage. Although the experiences do not alter the actual genetic sequence, they do result in chemical markers being attached to the genes that alter the timing, strength, and manner in which they are expressed.

Epinephrine   (Also called adrenaline.) Major excitatory neurotransmitter, produced by the adrenal glands, that sits on top of the kidneys. It is produced and released when the individual requires a burst of energy (such as the fight-or-flight syndrome) and when the individual is under stress.

Euphoric recall   Tendency on the part of the person to remember past experiences in a positive light, while overlooking negative experiences associated with that event(s). For example, a heavy drinker might drive by a bar and turn to a companion and say "didn't we have a great time at the boss' birthday party?"—only to have the companion remind them that they were also arrested for driving while under the influence of alcohol on the way home, and had to both spend time in the county jail and pay a fine of over $1,000. These latter consequences are overlooked in favor of the positive memories of the night in question.

Executive functioning   Essentially the ability of the individual to plan ahead, anticipate the consequences of his or her actions, and so on.

Externalizing disorder   Cluster of psychiatric symptoms seen in the antisocial personality disorder in adults, conduct disorder in children, and/or attention deficit hyperactivity disorder (ADHD).

fMRI   See: *functional magnetic resonance imaging.*

"Fast" metabolizer   An individual whose body is, as a result of normal genetic variation(s), able to biotransform a compound more rapidly than average. This phenomenon is independent of those cases where the person is taking one compound that induces the biotransformation or metabolism of another through enzyme induction, for example.

Fentanyl analog   See analog, drug (above). A Fentanyl analog is a variation of the Fentanyl molecule.

Filler(s)   When prepared for oral administration, pharmaceutical companies will mix the active agent with compounds designed to give the pill or capsule shape and form. These compounds are designed to be destroyed by gastric juices (thus releasing the active compound for absorption), or to break down in the gastrointestinal tract and release the active agent so that it might be absorbed.

Intravenous drug abusers who crush a pill or capsule bypass the defenses of the gastrointestinal tract, and run the risk that these "fillers" might cause a blockage in a vein or artery.

First-pass metabolism   Over time, the body has developed a safety mechanism in which materials absorbed through the gastrointestinal tract are first carried to the liver, so that toxic compounds ingested might be subjected to detoxification before those compounds might injure the body. This is what is called the "first-pass metabolism" process.

Formication   The sensation of having unseen bugs crawling on, or just under, the skin. This sensation is often induced by large doses of some chemicals, such as the amphetamines or cocaine.

Free radicals   Molecules that, because of their ionic charge, are able to attach to and damage other molecules, thus disrupting the normal function of cells and possibly contributing to cellular death.

Free-radical molecules often contain an extra oxygen molecule, which will then "bind" to molecules found in cell walls, causing damage to them.

Functional magnetic resonance imaging (fMRI)
Modification of the *magnetic resonance imaging (MRI)* procedure designed to measure levels of energy released by hemoglobin molecules in the blood of a designated region of the body when the magnetic field utilized in the MRI process is switched off. This provides a measure of oxygenated blood being used by the identified tissues and thus is an indirect measure of the level of activity of that region of the body.

GABA   See: *Gamma-amino-butyric acid.*

Galactorrhea   Production of excess amounts of milk by the breast.

Gamma-amino-butyric acid (GABA)   This is the main inhibitory neurotransmitter in the brain. Approximately 20% of the receptor sites in the brain are thought to utilize GABA, including neurons in the *cortex, cerebellum, amygdala,* and the *nucleus accumbens*. It has been discovered that there are two main subtypes of GABA receptors in the brain: GABA-A and GABA-B. Scientists are mapping the distribution pattern and function of these subtypes to better understand GABA's function in the brain.

Gastritis   Inflammation of the stomach lining.

Gestalt   A German word that does not readily translate into English. The concept that the whole is greater than the sum of its individual parts conveys part of the meaning of this word. "Unity of being" also conveys part of the meaning of this word.

Glial cells   There are a number of subtypes of glial cells in the brain, including Schwann cells, Muller cells, epithelial cells, oligodendrocytes, and astrocytes, to name a few. Collectively, the glial cells make up 90% of the cells in the brain. Yet for a long time they were dismissed as providing only structural and metabolic support for the neurons, which comprise 10% of the brain's mass.

Some glial cells have been found to "monitor" the neurotransmission process between neurons and to modulate the process of neurotransmission at times. They have also been discovered to be capable of forms of intercellular communications that can utilize some of the same neurotransmitters as neurons, as well as distinctly separate forms of intercellular communications. Scientists are only now starting to understand that these cells are actively involved in the process of information processing, memory, and cellular repair following damage to the brain.

Glioma   Cancer arising from the glial cells in the brain.

Glossitis   A very painful inflammation of the tongue.

Glucocorticoids   Class of steroids involved in the stress response process, metabolism of sugar in the body, suppression of the inflammatory response, and suppression of the immune system response.

Glutamate   A major excitatory neurotransmitter that is found in much of the brain. It is also involved in the process of learning and memory. Excessive amounts of glutamate can prove to be neurotoxic, damaging or killing neurons in high doses.

Grave's disease   A dysfunction of the thyroid gland in which the thyroid produces too much thyroid hormone. This in turn interferes with the normal function of the thyroid.

Gray matter   The neurons in the cortex of the brain appear gray during an autopsy, hence the name. In the living brain they have a vivid, reddish brown color under normal conditions, a sight that is rarely seen except by neurosurgeons.

The cortex is the region of the brain where the so-called higher functions such as thought and planning take place. Some regions of the cortex are also responsible for planning and initiation of psychomotor activities, speech, and hearing.

Hectare   Unit of land measurement 100 m × 100 m square. This is an area about 2.471 acres in size.

H-P-A axis   The hypothalamus and pituitary regions of the brain, plus the adrenal glands are involved in the body's response to real (or perceived) threats, ultimately increasing the release of stress-fighting hormones such as cortisol in the body.

Hepatotoxicity   Toxic to the liver.

Hippocampus   A region of the brain that is thought to be involved in the process of processing sensory information, as well as the formation and retrieval of memories. In normal health adults it appears to shrink by 0.5% per year, although the importance of this data to the addictions is not clear at this time. The possibility exists that continuous exposure to alcohol or the drugs of abuse might exacerbate this shrinkage contributing to the development of depression seen in many alcohol or drug abusers, although this has not been proven.

Hyperthermia   Retention of body heat well above safe levels, which may prove fatal to the individual if not corrected before the brain is damaged by the abnormally high body temperature.

Hypnotic   A compound that can induce sleep or a sleep-like state.

Hypokalemia   Abnormally low blood potassium levels.

Hypothalamus   A region of the brain that controls behaviors such as eating, fighting, sleep, and mating.

Hypothermia   Abnormally low body temperature, which if not corrected in a timely manner might result in the individual's death.

Hypoxia   Reduced oxygen flow to the brain. This can result in organic brain damage if not rapidly corrected.

Iatrogenic   Literally, induced by a physician. This term is also often applied to conditions that are side effects of treatment of another disease, such as antibiotic-induced diarrhea where the antibiotic compound is used to treat a serious infection elsewhere in the body.

Isomer   One of two or more compounds with the same percentage of chemicals, but where the molecular structure of the chemical is slightly different.

Kindling   A process that has been called "reverse tolerance" by some scientists. Through the process of kindling, the brain becomes more and more sensitive to seizure triggers, which then initiates a seizure(s). Sometimes this process is called *sensitization.*

Law of unintended consequences   A rule that whenever a change is made, it alters the system in unforeseen ways, resulting in stressors and complications that were not expected when the original change was made.

   An excellent example of this law is the application of high cost, labor-intensive medical care to treat heart attack victims. This results in increased survival rates (the intended result), but also leaves a pool of heart attack survivors who require intensive medical monitoring afterward (unanticipated consequence), placing an unanticipated drain on the health care system.

mRNA   Also known as *messenger RNA.* A form of ribonucleic acid that carries directions from the DNA in the cell nucleus to the interior of the cell.

Macrophage cells   Generalist cells from the immune system that help to clean up cellular debris and attack foreign cells. Macrophages are also involved in some aspect(s) of the immune response.

Magnetic resonance imaging (MRI)   An imaging procedure in which a strong magnetic field is generated, forcing atoms with odd atomic weights to align with the magnetic field. Then the field is switched off and the energy generated when these atoms swing back to their normal position is measured.

Meconium   A thick, green, tar-like substance that lines the intestinal tract of the fetus. This substance is usually excreted by the infant in the first few days after birth.

   Occasionally, it is excreted before or during birth. If it is excreted prior to birth, physicians may try to dilute it by injecting sterile fluid into the uterus to dilute any meconium in that environment. If aspirated by the neonate during the birth process, it is called *meconium aspiration syndrome.* This is a medical emergency. Following birth it can prevent the infant's lungs from properly inflating and may cause pneumonia.

Medulla oblongata   Region of the brain, sometimes referred to as the *brain stem,* involved in the control of respiration and temperature regulation.

Melatonin   Hormone produced by the pineal gland in the brain, whose actions in the brain are still not well understood. It is thought that this compound plays a role in the regulation of human circadian rhythms.

Meningioma   A benign, slow growing, tumor of the central nervous system that is usually classified as a *space occupying lesion* rather than an invasive tumor. Because meningioma growth is so slow, the brain is often able to compensate for the tumor's presence. The meningioma is frequently found as an incidental discovery, such as when a patient has a C-T scan to rule out a fractured skull following a motor vehicle accident.

Meningiomas can grow over the years to an impressive size before producing symptoms that call attention to its presence. The symptoms produced by a meningioma depend on the specific location where it is located.

Mensch   A person with fortitude ("guts") and/or firmness of purpose. Strength of character.

Messenger RNA   A molecule that is formed within the cell nucleus by copying half of the DNA molecule, and then carrying these genetic instructions through the nucleus wall to the cell. This then "programs" the cell to follow the instructions on the messenger RNA molecule.

Methyl alcohol   Also known as *wood grain alcohol,* or *methanol, this* is one of the alcohol family of compounds. It is very toxic to the human body, with the estimated lethal dose being just two teaspoons for a child and a quarter of a cup for an adult.

During the Prohibition era, methyl alcohol was often mixed with industrial alcohol solvents to discourage the diversion of these chemicals to the illegal alcohol trade. The government ordered this on the theory that if the drinker knew of the dangers associated with drinking methyl alcohol he or she would not consume drinks made from diverted industrial solvents.

This theory was not supported by fact, and resulted in thousands of needless deaths in persons who might be unaware of the presence of methyl alcohol in their drink. The same enzymes that break down ethyl alcohol so easily struggle to biotransform methyl alcohol, producing formaldehyde and formic acid as intermediate metabolites. These compounds in turn destroy the retina, optic nerve, parietal cortex of the brain, and the lungs. Respiratory failure is the usual cause of death, although if the individual should survive there is the chance of permanent blindness.

Microcephaly   A condition in which the baby's head is below the 5th percentile for infant head circumference for that age group.

Mnemonic   To assist memory, or make recall easier.

Monoamine oxidase   Enzyme produced by the brain to break down members of the neurotransmitter family known as *monoamines.*

Monoamine oxidase inhibitor   Any of a number of compounds that will block the actions of the enzyme monoamine oxidase.

Myocardial infarction   The blockage of blood to the tissue of the myocardium, which is to say the tissues of the heart. If this blood flow is not restored in a short period of time, the tissue will die. Often called a "heart attack" by the layperson.

Narcolepsy   Very rare neurological condition in which the patient will experience sudden attacks of sleep.

Necrosis   Death of body tissues.

Nemonic   Something that aids memory. A nemonic device might be a series of letters that remind a person such as a health care professional to address certain issues. For example, the letters "A-B-C" remind the health care profession to check the patient's *airway, breathing,* and *circulation,* immediately.

Neuroadaptation   The process, once called "tolerance," by which the nervous system adapts to the constant presence of a foreign compound. This usually involves modification of the receptor sites on the neurons affected by that compound. This term is usually applied to the brain's adjustments to the constant presence of a prescribed chemical, whereas the term "tolerance" is applied to the same process when it involves an illicit compound.

Neurogenesis   Growth of new neurons.

Neuroplasticity   Ability of neurons to form new neural pathways in response to new experiences (what we call learning), and, to some degree, after neurological trauma.

Neurotoxin   A chemical that is toxic to the neurons in the brain.

Neurotransmitter   Any molecule that is released by one neuron to pass a chemical-electrical message on to the next neuron. This then causes the target neuron to respond to the chemical message passed on by the first neuron in a specific manner.

NMDA   See: *N-Methyl-D-aspartate.*

N-Methyl-D-aspartate   Protein that forms a receptor site in the neural wall for the excitatory neurotransmitter glutamate.

Norepinephrine   One of the catecholamine family of neurotransmitters. In the central nervous system, norepinephrine serves as a stimulatory function.

Nucleus accumbens   Region of the brain thought to be responsible for reward and motivation. At one point, the nucleus accumbens was thought to be *the* reward center in the brain. It has now been discovered that environmental stimuli (both reinforcing and aversive) stimulate a release of dopamine from the nucleus accumbens, suggesting that it signals that there is a change in external environment that requires attention.

It is known that this region of the brain is involved with the process of integrating the individual's conscious activities with sensory stimuli. It is most active when the body encounters an *unexpected* event, either positive or negative. When a reward becomes anticipated, other regions of the brain seem to become involved in the reward cascade and the nucleus accumbens becomes less active.

Obstructive sleep apnea   Condition in which the airway becomes blocked during sleep for longer than 10 seconds. The sleeping person must then struggle to reopen the airway, often through gasping, "snorting," or coughing. This is a medical problem that should be addressed by a physician if it is suspected to exist.

"Off-label" application   Medications are licensed to treat specific conditions after the pharmaceutical company conducts premarketing research to demonstrate that the compound is effective in treating those conditions. Occasionally new applications for that compound will be found which were not part of the original license application. These new applications are called "off label" for that compound. The Food and Drug Administration (FDA) will not approve an existing medication for a new use until its safety and effectiveness in treating that compound is proven, a process that might take months, or even years. During that time, physicians will often use the compound to treat a

disease(s) or condition(s) based on research data from Europe or antidotal data.

Oppositional defiant disorder   A behavioral disorder in which the child demonstrates temper outbursts, active refusal to comply with rules, and engage in annoying behaviors far in excess of what one would expect from the child on the basis of chronological age. There is an enduring pattern of negativistic, hostile, and defiant behaviors without the violations of social norms or rights of others.

Over pressure   Above the ambient atmospheric pressure. In the case of surgical anesthetics, pure oxygen must also be supplied to the patient at over pressure to avoid the danger of *hypoxia.*

Over-the-counter (medication)   There are more than 100,000 compounds that might be purchased without a prescription, thus earning the title of an over-the-counter compound.

Oxytocin   Functions both as a hormone and a neurotransmitter. It is involved in such functions as labor, production of breast milk, maternal love, romantic love, and the development of trust.

Peristalsis   Rhythmic muscle contractions of the muscles that surround the intestines, pushing the ingested material through.

PET scan   Abbreviation for positive emission tomography. This process produces three-dimensional images of specific organs after a molecule is "tagged" with a radioactive substance. Special detectors measure the regions that have absorbed most of the compound (usually glucose) allowing a computer to build a 3-D image of that region of the body and which regions have absorbed the most glucose "tagged" with the radioactive molecules.

Pharmaceuticals   (1) Compounds produced under supervision of various regulatory agencies, intended for the treatment of disease states in humans or (if veterinarian medications) animals. Such compounds are of a known potency, and purity. (2) Term applied to compounds intended for medical use that are diverted to the illicit drug market. As such, they are often prized by drug abusers, because they are known to be pure and not adulterated as illicit drugs often are.

Pharmacokinetics   The study of what happens to a compound and its effects after it is admitted into the human body. This includes the metabolites of that compound and their effect on the body as well.

Phrenology   A pseudo-science popular in the 1890s that asserted that you could deduce a person's character on the basis of the bumps in the skull. Proponents of this belief developed numerous maps and models of the skull, attributing various personality characteristics to these normal variations in skull structure.

Pituitary gland   Structure in the brain that has been called the "master gland" in the body. It activates a number of other glands in the body through the release of hormones through the blood, thus controlling growth, to cite one example.

Polypharmacology   Concurrent use of multiple agents. This may take place both in therapeutic settings and in the world of illicit drug use. One danger of this practice is the *potentiation* or *synergistic* effect between compounds in the same class of chemicals.

Polyphenols   Family of natural, semisynthetic, and synthetic compounds that have chemical similarities (essentially the phenol structures in the molecule). Some of these compounds are useful for humans, whereas others are harmful, depending on the exact chemical structure of that specific polyphenol molecule. Some of the nontoxic polyphenols are found in wine, helping to give that wine a specific flavor.

Potentiation   The pharmacological process through which the effects of one compound are reinforced by those of a second compound. This may prove to be fatal for the individual if the combined effects of these chemicals overwhelm the body's normal maintenance mechanisms.

Prefrontal cortex   Region of the brain that, among other things, is involved in complex cognitive and psychomotor processes including self-regulation of goal-directed behavior, working memory, problem solving, and response inhibition.

Presynaptic   Involving the "upstream" neuron, which is to say the neuron that releases neurotransmitters into the synaptic junction to activate the next neuron in the neural network.

Priapism   Extended, painful penile erection that may cause damage to the vasculature network of the penis and possibly resulting in permanent erectile dysfunction.

Prime effect (of a drug)   The desired effect of that compound. For example, a person who has a fever might take an aspirin tablet with the goal of reducing his or her fever to a more tolerable level. Compare this with the *side effect* of a compound. This is sometimes referred to as the *therapeutic effect* of that compound.

Prodrug (pro-drug)   Compound that must be biotransformed into another compound to have the desired effect.

Prostaglandin(s)   Any of a family of compounds found in the body, some of which are involved in normal maintenance of body organs and some of which are involved in the inflammatory response following injury. These compounds are active in very low concentrations.

Proteinuria   Presence of abnormal levels of protein in urine, which if found may indicate kidney damage or disease.

Pulmonary arteritis   See: *arteritis.*

REM rebound   Increase in the duration and frequency of the REM sleep stage, often with intense, vivid, imagery that might border on nightmares. This is thought to reflect the brain's attempt to "catch up" on lost REM sleep time from sleep deprivation or drug-induced suppression of this stage of the sleep cycle.

Reperfusion   Sudden restoration of blood flow to a region of the body that had been deprived of blood. The damage caused by the actual cessation of blood flow to that region of the body might be exacerbated by the sudden restoration of circulation to the affected cells.

Reticular activating system (RAS)   A small region of the brain, possibly only 100 neurons in size, that is responsible for the individual's ability to focus attention on the task at hand. Reticular activating system (RAS) Small concentration of cells in the brain that alters the individual's state of consciousness and allows the individual to concentrate on a specific task.

Retrograde amnesia   Inability of the individual to remember events prior to a specific time. This condition usually is the result of any of a number of forms of neurological trauma. It is not uncommon, for example, for patients to report that they were unable to remember having been in a motor vehicle accident or that they only have incomplete memories of the accident and what happened in the moments before the accident.

Each patient must be assessed individually to determine the degree to which his or her memory capacity has been affected. It should be pointed out that anterograde and retrograde amnesia are not mutually exclusive, and may coexist in the same patient.

Reuptake pump   Molecular structure located in the walls of a neuron that absorb molecules of a specific neurotransmitter after its release into the synapse, for recycling by the neuron.

Rhabdomyolysis   Destruction of muscle tissue on a massive scale. When muscle tissue(s) die, they release a compound known as *myoglobin*, which normally helps to store oxygen in the muscle cell. During rhabdomyolysis, massive amounts of myoglobin are released in the circulation at once, which interferes with normal kidney function. In extreme cases this can cause kidney failure, cardiac arrhythmias, and even death.

Rig   Slang term for device used for intravenous drug injection.

Selective androgen receptor modulators   Class of compounds first introduced in 1999 that are nonsteroidal selective agonists for mainly the androgenic receptor sites in the body. This class of medications does tend to lack the cardiovascular side effects of anabolic steroids, making them of particular interest to those who use "performance enhancing" compounds.

Sensitization effect   Almost a form of "reverse" tolerance, in which the brain becomes hypersensitive to the effects of or presence of a compound (such as cocaine), causing effects such as seizures or even death from doses once easily tolerated without ill effect(s). The concept of an allergy might not be entirely inappropriate, here.

Serotonergic   Pertaining to or using serotonin.

Serotonin   One of the major neurotransmitters found in the human brain. There are 19 known subtypes of serotonin, which are thought to control different functions in the brain. As a group, these subforms are involved in regulation of body temperature, memory, sleep, mood and appetite.

Serotonin syndrome   A potentially life-threatening drug-induced neurological condition. In spite of the best of medical care, up to 11% of patients who develop this condition will fail to survive. Behavioral symptoms of the serotonin syndrome include irritability, confusion, increased anxiety, drowsiness, *hyperthermia, sinus tachycardia,* dilation of the pupils, nausea, muscle rigidity, and seizures.

The serotonin syndrome might develop up to 24 hours after a patient started taking a medication that affects *serotonin*. In 50% of the cases, the patient begins to develop the disorder within 2 hours of when she or he started to take the medication.

All suspected cases of serotonin syndrome should be assessed by a physician immediately as this condition can be potentially fatal. There is no specific treatment for serotonin syndrome, and the only treatment is supportive care (Boyer, 2005).

Sexual dimorphism   Subtle differences between male and female.

Side effect (of a drug)   The unintended effects of a chemical on the body. For example, if a person were to take a dose of aspirin to reduce his or her fever, this is the primary effect. The ability of aspirin to also induce gastrointestinal bleeding is an undesired or side effect of that compound.

Sleep apnea   A breathing disorder in which the individual's ability to breathe normally during sleep is disrupted. Complications of sleep apnea can include hypertension, heart rhythm disturbance, and possible death.

Sleep latency   The period of time between when the person goes to bed and when she or he finally falls asleep.

"Slow" metabolizer   As a result of normal genetic variation(s) there are individuals whose body is unable to bio transform or metabolize a compound more slowly than the average person. This phenomenon is independent of those cases where the person is taking one compound that blocks the biotransformation or metabolism of another.

Stroke   Interruption of blood flow to a region of the brain. In *ischemic* strokes, a blockage in a blood vessel forms, cutting the neurons that rely on that vessel off from the cerebral vasculature. Unless these neurons are able to draw on other blood vessels (collateral circulation), they will die. Statistically, 85% of strokes are ischemic strokes.

In a *hemorrhagic* stroke a blood vessel in the cerebral vasculature ruptures. To prevent uncontrolled hemorrhage, the body then forms a blood clot in the damaged vessel, cutting off those neurons that depend on that vessel for access to the circulation off from oxygen and nutrients. In addition, free blood is very toxic to the neurons, so the blood that flows from the ruptured vessel causes additional damage to the brain. Statistically, about 15% of strokes are hemorrhagic strokes.

Synergistic response   A process through which two or more drugs of the same or similar mechanism of action reinforce the effects of the each other, causing a stronger-than-normal response to each compound. The synergistic effect can potentially be fatal. Often called *potentiation* between the two compounds.

Synesthesia   A phenomenon where information from one sensory modality slips over into another sensory interpretation system. Persons who possess this ability naturally will speak of how they are able to see colors in association with certain sounds, for example. This phenomenon, which can occur naturally in rare cases, can also be induced by some drugs of abuse.

Taper   A program in which gradually decreasing doses of a given compound are administered to a patient so that she or he might safely be taken off that compound.

Tardive dyskinesia   Condition resulting in abnormal movements of muscles. Technically, the term *tardive* means "late," and *dyskinesia* refers to the abnormal muscle movements. This condition was often seen as a late complication of Parkinson's disease.

However, certain compounds have been found to exacerbate the development of this condition. The abnormal muscle movements previously seen only as a late complication of Parkinson's disease are now seen in younger persons either as a side effect of medications or a side effect of some drugs of abuse.

Telescoping   A term applied to the accelerated progression from substance use through abuse to addiction.

Teratogen   A compound that permanently interferes with normal fetal growth and development.

Teratogenic   Harmful to the fetus.

Therapeutic window   The difference between the minimal effective dose of a medication and the level that will induce toxic effects. Alcohol, for example, has a "therapeutic" window of 1:3, which is to say that the amount of alcohol necessary to be ingested is about one-third of the amount necessary to induce toxic effects and possible death.

Thiamine   One of the "B" family of vitamins. The "B" vitamins are thought to be involved in the maintenance of the nervous system. These vitamins are water soluble, allowing the body to absorb the amount that it needs and then excrete the rest in the urine.

Thrombosis   A blood clot that has broken off from a larger clot and is blocking a blood vessel, thus starving the tissue that relies on that vessel for oxygen and nutrients.

Tinnitus   Loss of hearing, and a persistent "ringing" in the ears, which can be induced by loud noises, illness, or certain medications. This will gradually clear if the offending medications are discontinued immediately, but may become permanent.

Torsade de pointes   Cardiac arrhythmia that is potentially fatal.

Tourette's syndrome   A movement disorder in which the person will engage in repetitive, stereotypical movements, and often engage in repetitive vocalizations.

Trans-species jump   A process through which an infectious microbe will "jump" from its host species to another species. Glasser (2004) stated that of the more than 1,400 micro-organisms that can infect humans, approximately half originally caused infections in animals and subsequently "jumped" to the human population.

The AIDS virus (HIV-1) is one virus that made such a trans-species jump, moving from chimpanzees to humans in the 1950s. Another such virus is the one that causes measles. Measles killed 8 million people around the world in 1974, before the start of immunization programs around the world. By the year 2007 this figure dropped to approximately 300,000 measles-induced deaths around the globe (Oldstone, 2010).

Unfortunately people are becoming complacent about immunization against measles in the United States, where the virus once infected 500,000 people annually and killed about 500 of those infected. Lack of vaccination leaves children and uninfected individuals vulnerable to new waves of measles infection as evidenced by sporadic regional outbreaks of the disease.

Up-regulation   Process through which a neuron adds additional receptor sites for a given neurotransmitter, making that neuron less sensitive to the effects of the neurotransmitter.

Vasoconstriction   Constriction of blood vessels, especially veins. This condition can develop in the brain, the vessels around the heart, or the peripheral regions of the body.

Ventral striatum   Region of the brain involved in the integration of signals from the amygdala (emotional responses) with regions of the brain such as the hippocampus (memory functions) and cognitive/executive functions carried out by the prefrontal cortex regions of the brain.

Ventricular tachycardia   Cardiac arrhythmia in which the normal pattern of electrical discharge/repolarization in the ventricles of the heart is interrupted, disrupting the normal heart rhythm. This condition is potentially fatal if not immediately corrected.

Weak base   See base (above).

White matter   A region of the brain comprised of nerve cells responsible for relay of information. The cortex is often referred to as "gray matter" after its appearance after death. In contrast to this, the other neurons in different regions of the brain assume a white color following death.

Abnormalities in the white matter of the brain will make it difficult for the individual to consider multiple viewpoints when making decisions, and in adolescents will result in the "one track mind" so often seen during this phase of life.

REFERENCES

A very venerable vintage. (1996). *Minneapolis Star-Tribune,* *XV*(63), A16.

A tree shrew's favorite tipple. (2008). *New Scientist,* *199*(2667), 18.

Aanavi, M. P., Taube, D. O., Ja, D. Y., & Duran, E. F. (2000). The status of psychologists' training about and treatment of substance abusing clients. *Journal of Psychoactive Drugs, 31,* 441–444.

Abbey, A., Zawacki, T., Buck, P. O., Clinton, A. M., & McAuslan, P. (2001). Alcohol and sexual assault. *Alcohol Research and Health, 25*(1), 43–51.

Abrams, D. I., Hilton, J. F., Leiser, R. J., Shade, S. B., Elbeik, T. A., Aweeka, F. T., … Schambelan, M. (2003). Short-term effects of cannabinoids in patients with HIV-1 infections. *Annuals of Internal Medicine, 139,* 258–288.

Abrams, M. (2003). The end of craving. *Discover, 24*(5), 24–25.

Ackerman, J. (2012). The ultimate social network. *Scientific American, 306*(6), 36–43.

Ackerman, J. P., Riggins, T., & Black, M. M. (2010). A review of the effects of prenatal cocaine exposure among school-aged children. *Pediatrics, 125*(3), 554–465.

Acosta, M. C., Haller, D. L., & Schnoll, S. H. (2005). Cocaine and stimulants. In R. J. Frances, S. I. Miller, & A. H. Mack (Eds.), *Clinical textbook of addictive disorders* (3rd ed.). New York: Guilford.

Adamson, S. J., Heather, N., Morton, V., & Raistrick, D. (2010). Initial preference for drinking goal in the treatment of alcohol problems: II. Treatment outcomes. *Alcohol and Alcoholism, 45*(2), 136–142.

Adamson, S. J., & Sellman, J. D. (2008). Five-year outcomes of alcohol-dependent persons treated with motivational enhancement. *Journal of Studies on Alcohol and Drugs, 69,* 589–593.

Addiction and the problem of relapse. (2007). *Harvard Mental Health Letter, 23*(7), 4–7.

Adler, D. S., & Underwood, A. (2002). Aspirin: The oldest new wonder drug. *Newsweek, CXXIX*(21), 60–62.

Adolescent inhalant use and selected respiratory conditions. (2010). National Survey on Drug Use and Health. Washington, DC: Substance Abuse and Mental Health Services Administration.

Adolescents with insomnia are at risk for future substance abuse and depression. (2008). *Neuropsychiatry Reviews, 9*(11), 22.

Adult use of prescription opioid pain medications—Utah, 2008. (2010). *Morbidity and Mortality Weekly Report, 59,* 153–157.

Afdhal, N. H., & Curry, M. P. (2010). Early TIPS to improve survival in patients with cirrhosis and variceal bleeding. *New England Journal of Medicine, 362,* 2241–2222.

After 40 years, the basics of MMT are still valid. (2005). *Addiction Treatment Forum, 14*(4), 4–5.

Agalu, I. T., Ayo-Yusuf, O. A., Vardavas, C. I., Alpert, H. R. (2013). Use of conventional and novel smokeless tobacco products among US adolescents. *Pediatrics.* doi:10.1542/peds.2013-0843

Agency: More teens abusing inhalants. (2005). Retrieved from http://www.cnn.com.2005/HEALTH/03/22/drugs.inhalants.reut/index.html

Agrawal, A., Sartor, C. E., Lynskey, M. T., Grant, J. D., Pergadia, ML., Grucza, R., ... Heath A C. (2009). Evidence for interaction between age at first drink and genetic influences on DSM-IV alcohol dependence symptoms. *Alcoholism: Clinical and Experimental Research.* doi:10.1111/j.1530-0277. 2009.01044x

Aharonovich, E., Liu, X., Samet, S., Nunes, D., Waxman, R., & Hasin, D. (2005). Post-discharge cannabis use and its relationship to cocaine, alcohol, and heroin use: A new prospective study. *American Journal of Psychiatry, 162,* 1507–1514.

Ahrendt, D. M., & Miller, M. A. (2005). Adolescent substance abuse: A simplified approach to drug testing. *Pediatric Annals, 34,* 956–963.

Alati, R., Al-Manum, A., Williams, G. M., O'Callaghan, M. O., Najman, J. M., & Bor, W. (2006). In utero alcohol exposure and prediction of alcohol disorders in early adulthood: A birth cohort study. *Archives of General Psychiatry, 63,* 1009–1016.

Alattar, M. A., & Scharf, S. M. (2008). Opioid-associated central sleep apnea: A case series. *Sleep Breath.*

Albertson, T. E., Derlet, R. W., & van Hoozen, B. E. (1999). Methamphetamine and the expanding complications of amphetamines. *Western Journal of Medicine, 170,* 214–219.

Alcohol and minorities: An update. (2002). *Alcohol Alert, 43,* 1–2.

Alcohol and the liver. (1993). *Alcohol Alert, 29.* Washington, DC: National Institute on Alcohol Abuse and Alcoholism.

Alcohol and tobacco. (1998). *Alcohol Alert, 39.* Washington, DC: National Institute on Alcohol Abuse and Alcoholism.

Alcohol metabolism: An update. (2007). *Alcohol Alert, 72,* 1–5.

Aldhous, P. (2006). Breaking the cycle of drugs and crime. *New Scientist, 191*(2562), 6–7.

Aldhous, P. (2008). Beauty's in the eye of the beer holder. *New Scientist, 199*(2669), 12.

Aldhous, P. (2009). Shot keeps holiday drinkers on wagon. *New Scientist, 200*(2688), 12.

Aldhous, P. (2010). Prescription: Sobriety. *New Scientist, 205*(2742), 40–43.

Aldhous, P. (2013). The battle of the booze. *New Scientist, 217*(2899), 42–45.

Aldington, S., Williams, M., Nowitz, M., Weatherall, M., Pritchard, A., McNaughton, A., ... Beasley R. (2007). Effects of cannabis on pulmonary structure, function and symptoms. *Thorax.* doi:101136/thx.2006.077081

Alegria, A. A., Hasin, D. S., Nunes, E. V., Liu, S. M., Davies, C., ... Blanco, C. (2010). Comorbidity of generalized anxiety disorder and substance use disorders: Results from the national epidemiologic survey on alcohol and related conditions. *Journal of Clinical Psychiatry, 71*(9), 1187–1195.

Alfonso, R. (2008). *FAA bans anti-smoking drug Chantix for pilots, air controllers.* Retrieved from: www.latimes.com/news/nationworld/washingtondc/ lala-na-smokedriug22may,22,0, 5923950.story.

Ali, S., Patel, S., Avenidko, J., Bailey, R. K. (2011). Hallucinations: Common features and causes. *Current Psychiatry, 10*(11), 22–29.

Alpert, H. R., Connolly, G. N., & Biener, L. (2011). A prospective cohort study challenging the effectiveness of population-based medical intervention for smoking cessation. *Tobacco Control.* doi:10.1136/tobaccocontrol-2011-1

Alter, J. (2001, March 2). *Making marriage work: Communications in recovery.* Symposium presented to the Department of Psychiatry of the Cambridge Hospital, Boston, MA.

Alterman, A. I., McDermott, P. A., Cacciola, J. S., Rutherford, M. I., Boardman, C. R., ... Cook, T. G. (1998). A typology of antisociality in methadone patients. *Journal of Abnormal Psychology, 107,* 412–422.

Alquist, J. L., & Baumester, R. F. (2012). Self control and addiction. In H. J. Shaffer, D. A. LaPlante, & S. E. Nelson (Eds.), *A.P.A. addiction syndromes handbook* (Vol. 1, pp. 165–175). Washington, DC: American Psychological Association.

Ameling, A. I., & Povilonis, M. (2001). Spirituality, meaning, mental health, and nursing. *Journal of Psychosocial Nursing, 39*(4), 15–20.

American Academy of Pediatrics. (1998). Neonatal drug withdrawal. *Pediatrics, 101,* 1079–1089.

American Academy of Pediatrics. (2010). Policy statement—children, adolescents, substance abuse, and the media. *Pediatrics, 126,* 791–799.

American Psychiatric Association. (2013). *Diagnostic and statistical manual of mental disorders* (5th ed.). Washington, DC: American Psychiatric Press.

American Society of Addiction Medicine. (2001). *ASAM Patient Placement Criteria for the Treatment of Substance Related Disorders* (2nd ed., revised). Chevy Chase, MD: Author.

American Society of Health System Pharmacists. (2008). *AHFS drug information.* Bethesda, MD: Author.

Americans want insurance to cover addiction; unsure if it does. (2009). Retrieved from http://www.hazelden .org/web/public/pr090209healthinsurance.page

Ames, G. M., Duke, M. R., Moore, R. S., & Cunradi, C. B. (2009). The impact of occupational culture on drinking behavior of young adults in the U.S. navy. *Journal of Mixed Methods Research, 3.* doi:10.1177/1558689808328534

Aminoff, M. J., Greenberg, D. A., & Simon, R. P. (2005). *Clinical neurology.* New York: Lange Medical Books/McGraw-Hill.

Amtmann, D., Weydt, P., Johnson, K. L., Jensen, M. P., & Carter, G. T. (2004). Survey of cannabis use in patients with amyotrophic lateral sclerosis. *American Journal of Hospice & Palliative Care, 21*(2), 95–104.

Anacker, A. M. J., & Ryabinin, A. E. (2010). Biological contribution to social influence on alcohol drinking: Evidence from animal models. *International Journal of Environmental Research and Public Health, 7*(2), 473–493.

Anand, U., Otto, W. R., Sanchez-Herrera, D., Facer, P., Yiangou Y., … Anand, P. (2008). Cannabinoid receptor CB2 localisation and agonist-mediated inhibition of capsaicin response in human sensory neurons. *Pain, 138*(3), 667–680.

Ananth, K., Richeimer, S., & Durham, M. J. (2012). Managing chronic pain: Consider psychotropics and other non-opioids. *Current Psychiatry, 11*(2), 38–42.

Anczak, J. D., & Nogler, R. A. (2003). Tobacco cessation in primary care: Maximizing interventional strategies. *Clinical Medicine & Research, 1*(3), 201–216.

Anda, R. F., Whitfield, C. L., Felitti, V. J., Chapman, D., Edwards, V. J., Dube, S. R., … Williamson, D. F. (2002). Adverse childhood experiences, alcoholic parents, and later risk of alcoholism and depression. *Psychiatric Services, 53,* 1001–1009.

Anderson, C. E., & Loomis, G. A. (2003). Recognition and prevention of inhalant abuse. *American Family Physician, 68,* 869–874, 876.

Anderson, D. J. (1989). An alcoholic is never too old for treatment. *Minneapolis Star-Tribune, VIII*(200), 7EX.

Andersson, J. (2008). HIV after 25 years: How to induce a vaccine? *Journal of Internal Medicine, 263,* 215–217.

Angst, M., Lazzeroni, L. C., Phillips, G. N. S., Drover, D., Tingle, M., Ray, A., … Clark, J. D. (2012). Aversive and reinforcing opioid effects: A pharmacogenomic twin study. *Anesthesiology, 117*(1), 22–37.

Anthes, E. (2010). She's hooked. *Scientific American Mind, 21*(2), 14–15.

Antman, K., & Chang, Y. (2000). Kaposi's Sarcoma. *New England Journal of Medicine, 342,* 1027–1038.

Antoin, H., & Beasley, R. D. (2004). Opioids for chronic non-cancer pain. *Postgraduate Medicine, 116*(3), 37–44.

Anton, R. F. (1999). What is craving? Models and implications for treatment. *Alcohol Research & Health, 23,* 165–173.

Anton, R. F. (2005). Alcohol use disorders. In R. E. Rankel & E. T. Pope (Eds.), *Conn's current therapy, 2005.* Philadelphia: Elsevier Saunders.

Anton, R. F., O'Malley, S. S., Ciraulo, D. A., Cisler, R. A., Coupe, D., Donovan, D. M., Gastfriend, D. R., … Zweben, A. (2006). Combined pharmacotherapies and behavioral interventions for alcohol dependence. *Journal of the American Medical Association, 295,* 2003–2017.

Antonio, R. (1997). The use and abuse of ephedrine. *Muscle & Fitness, 58*(10), 178– 180.

Aquaro, G. D., Gabutti, A., Meini, M., Prontera, C., Pasanisi, E., Passino, C., … Lombari, M. (2011). Silent myocardial damage in cocaine addicts. *Heart, 97,* 2056–2062.

Arasteh, K., & des Jarlais, D. C. (2008). Injection drug use, HIV, and what to do about it. *The Lancet.* doi:10.1016/SO140-6736(08)613124

Arehart-Treichel, J. (2004). Homelessness does not lead to increased substance abuse. *Psychiatric News, 39*(12), 9.

Arehart-Treichel, J. (2008). Psychiatric genetic counseling: Don't expect easy answers. *Psychiatric News, 39*(12), 9.

Arkowitz, H., & Lilienfeld, S. O. (2011). Does alcoholics anonymous work? *Scientific American Mind, 22*(1), 64–65.

Armon, C. (2009). Smoking may be considered an established risk factor for sporadic ALS. *Neurology, 73,* 1693–1698.

Armstrong, M. A., Gonzales-Osejo, V., Liberman, L., Carpenter, D. M., Pantoja, P. M., Escobar, G. J. (2008). Perinatal substance abuse intervention in obstetric clinics decreases adverse neonatal outcomes. *Journal of Perinatology, 23,* 3–9.

Arria, A. M., & Wish, E. D. (2006). Nonmedical use of prescription stimulants among students. *Pediatric Annals, 35,* 555–571.

Aschwanden, C. (2012). The science of doping. *Smithsonian, 42*(4), 56–61.

Ashley, D. L., O'Connor, R. J., Bernert, J. T., Watson, C. H., Polzin, G. M., Jain, R. B., … McCraw, J. M. (2010).

Effect of differing levels of tobacco-specific nitrosamines in cigarette smoke on the levels of biomarkers in smokers. *Cancer Epidemiology, Biomarkers & Prevention, 19*(6), 1389–1398.

Asthma deaths blamed on cocaine use. (2007). *Forensic Drug Abuse Advisor, 9*(2), 14.

Athletes caught using a new steroid—THG. (2003). *Forensic Drug Abuse Advisor, 15*, 76–77.

Au, J. G., & Donaldson, S. I. (2000). Social influences as explanations for substance use differences among Asian-Americans and European-American adolescents. *Journal of Psychoactive Drugs, 32*(1), 15–23.

Aubin, H. J., Farley, A., Lycett, D., Lahmek, P., & Aveyard, P. (2012). Weight gain in smokers after quitting cigarettes: Meta-analysis. *British Medical Journal.* doi:10.1136/bmj.3349

Audo, I., Sahel, J. A., & Paques, M. (2010). Poppers-associated retinal toxicity. *The New England Journal of Medicine, 363*, 1583–1585.

August, G. J., Winters, K. C., Realmuto, G. M., Fahnhnorst, T., et al. (2006). Prospective study of adolescent drug use among community samples of ADHD and non-ADHD participants. *Journal of the American Academy of Child and Adolescent Psychiatry, 45*, 824–832.

Ayd, F. J., Janicak, P. G., David, J. M., & Preskor, S. H. (1996). Advances in the pharmacotherapy of anxiety and sleep disorders. *Principles and Practice of Psychopharmacotherapy, 1*(4), 1–22.

Azar, B. (2008). Better studying through chemistry. *Monitor on Psychology, 39*(8), 32–34.

Azar, B. (2011). Psychology is key to pain management. *American Psychologist, 42*(10), 25.

Baber, A. (1998). Addiction's poster child. *Playboy, 45*(5), 29.

Babor, T. F., Higgins-Briddle, J. C., Saunders, J. B., & Monterio, M. G. (2001). *The alcohol use disorders identification test: Guidelines for use in primary care* (2nd ed.). New York: World Health Organization.

Bacher, I., Rabin, R., Woznica, A., Sacco, K. A., & George, T. P. (2010). Nicotinic receptor mechanisms in neuropsychiatric disorders: Therapeutic implications. *Primary Psychiatry, 17*(1), 35–41.

Back, S. E., & Payne, R. (2009). Gender and prescription opioid addiction. In K. T. Brady, S. E. Back, & S. F. Greenfield (Eds.), *Women & addiction.* New York: Guilford.

Badon, L. A., Hicks, A., Lord, K., Ogden, B. A., Meleg-Smith, S., & Varner, K. J. (2002). Changes in cardiovascular responsiveness and cardiotoxicity elicited during binge administration of Ecstasy. *Journal of Pharmacology and Experimental Therapeutics, 302*, 898–907.

Bagnardi, V., Blangiardo, M., La Vecchia, C., & Corrao, G. (2001). Alcohol consumption and the risk of cancer. *Alcohol Research & Health, 25*, 263–270.

Bahr, S. J., & Hoffmann, J. P. (2010). Parenting style, religiosity, peers, and adolescent heavy drinking. *Journal of Studies on Alcohol & Drugs, 71*, 539–543.

Bai-Fang, X., Sobel, S. C., Sigmon, S. L., Walsh, R. E., Liebson, I. A., Nuwayser, E. S., ... Bigelow, G. E. (2004). Open label trial of an injection depot formulation of buprenorphine in opioid detoxification. *Drug & Alcohol Dependence, 73*(1), 11–22.

Baier, C. J., & Wright, B. R. E. (2001). "If you love me keep my commandments": A meta-analysis of the effect of religion crime. *Journal of Research in Crime and Delinquency, 38*(1), 3–21.

Bailey, B. A., & Sokol, R. J. (2011). Prenatal alcohol exposure and miscarriage, stillbirth, preterm delivery and sudden infant death syndrome. *Alcohol Research & Health, 34*(1), 86–91.

Bailey, C. P., & Connor, M. (2005). Opioids: Cellular mechanisms of tolerance and physical dependence. *Current Opinion in Pharmacology, 5*, 60–68.

Bailey, J. E., Campagna, E., Dart, R. C., & RADARS System Poison Center Investigators. (2008). The underrecognized toll of prescription opioid abuse on young children. *Annals of Emergency Medicine.* doi:10.1016/j.annerergmed.2008.07.015

Baker, S. (2009). Building a better brain. *Discover, 30*(4), 54–59.

Baker, T. E., Stockwell, T., Barnes, G., & Holroyd, C. B. (2011). Individual differences in substance dependence: At the intersection of brain, behavior and cognition. *Addiction Biology, 13*(3), 458–466.

Balamuthusamy, S., & Desai, B. (2006, June 21). MRI Changes in cocaine-induced toxic encephalopathy. *Psychiatry On-Line.* Retrieved from http://www.priory.com/psych/toxicencephelophy.pdf

Ballas, C. A., Evans, D. L., & Dinges, D. F. (2004). Psychostimulants in psychiatry: Amphetamine, methylphenidate and modfinil. In A. F. Schatzberg & C. B. Nemeroff (Eds.), *Textbook of psychopharmacology* (3rd ed.). Washington, DC: American Psychiatric Publishing, Inc.

Baltieri, D. A., Daro, F. R., Ribeiro, P. L., & de Andrade, A. G. (2008). *Addiction* (E-published ahead of print). Retrieved from http://www.ncbi.him.hih.gov/pubmed/1855810?ordinlalpos=1itool=EntrezSystem2.Pentrez.pubm

Bambico, F. R., Katz, N., Debonnel, G., & Gobbi, G. (2007). Cannabinoids elicit antidepressant-like behavior and activate serotonergic neurons through the medial prefrontal cortex. *Journal of Neuroscience, 27*(43), 11700–11711. doi:10.1523/JNEUROSCI.1636.2007

Bambico, F. R., Nguyen, N. T., Katz, N., & Gobbi, G. (2009). Chronic exposure to cannabinoids during adolescence but not during adulthood impairs emotional behavior and monoaminergic neurotransmission. *Neurobiology of Disease.* doi:10.1016/j.nbd.2009.11.020

Ban later, ask questions first. (2010). *New Scientist, 206*(2757), 3.

Bankole, A. J., & Alt-Daoud, N. (2005). Alcohol: Clinical aspects. In J. H. Lowinson, P. Ruiz, R. B. Millman, & J. G. Langrod (Eds.), *Substance abuse: A comprehensive textbook* (4th ed.). New York: Lipponcott, Williams & Wilkins.

Banta, J. E., & Montgomvery, S. (2007). How often are substance use disorders diagnosed in outpatient settings? *American Journal of Drug and Alcohol Abuse, 33*(4), 583–593.

Banta-Greene, C. J., Field, J. A., Chiala, A. C., Sudakin, D. L., Power, L., & de Montigny, L. (2009). The spatial epidemiology of cocaine, methamphetamine and 3,4-methylenedioxymethamphetamine (MDMA) use: A demonstration using a population measure of community drug load derived from municipal wastewater. *Addiction.* doi:10.1111/j.1360-0433/2002.20678

Barber, C. (2008). The medicated Americans. *Scientific American Mind, 19*(1), 44–51.

Barclay, T. R., Wright, M. J., & Hinkin, C. II. (2010). Medication management. In T. D. Marcotte & I. Grant (Eds.), *Neuropsychology of everyday functioning.* New York: Springer Publishing Co.

Bargh, J. A. (2014). Our unconscious mind. *Scientific American, 310* (1), 30–37.

Barki, Z. H. K., Kravitz, H. M., & Berki, T. M. (1998). Psychotropic medications in pregnancy. *Psychiatric Annals, 28,* 486–500.

Barnett, J. E. (2009). The pernicious influence of the pharmaceutical industry: Who's minding the store? *The Independent Practitioner, 29*(1), 12–14.

Barnes, A. J., Moore, A. A., Xu, H., Ang, A., Tallen, L., Mirkin, M., … Ettner, S. L. (2010). Prevalence and

correlates of at-risk drinking among older adults: The project SHARE study. *Journal of General Internal Medicine.* doi:20.1007/s11606-010-1341-x

Barnett, M. (2001). Alternative opioids to morphine in palliative care: A review of current practice and evidence. *Postgraduate Medical Journal, 77,* 372–378.

Baron, D., Garbely, J., & Boyd, R. L. (2009). Evaluation and management of substance abuse emergencies. *Primary Psychiatry, 16*(9), 41–47.

Baron, J. A., Cole, B. F., Sandler, R. S., & Haile, R. W. (2003). A randomized trial of aspirin to prevent colorectal adenomas. *The New England Journal of Medicine, 348,* 891–899.

Barr, A. (1999). *Drink: A social history of America.* New York: Carroll & Graf Publishers, Inc.

Barr, C. S., Schwandt, M., Lindell, S. G., Chen, S. A., Goldman, D., Suomi, S. J., … Heilig, M. (2007). Association of a functional polymorphism of the μ-opioid receptor gene with alcohol response and consumption in male rhesus macaques. *Archives of General Psychiatry, 64*(3), 369–376.

Barr, R. G., Kurth, T., Stamfer, M. H., Buring, J. E., Hennekens, C. H., Gaziano, J. M. (2007). Aspirin and decreased adult-onset asthma: Randomized comparisons from the Physician's Health Study. *American Journal of Respiratory and Critical Care Medicine, 175,* 120–125.

Barrera, S. E., Osinski, W. A., & Davidoff, E. (1949/1994). The use of Antabuse (tetraethylthiuraddisulphide) in chronic alcoholics. *American Journal of Psychiatry, 151,* 263–267.

Barry, C. E., & Cheung, M. S. (2009). New tactics against tuberculosis. *Scientific American, 300*(3), 62–69.

Barry, D. T., Beitel, M., Garnet, B., & Joshi, D. (2009). Relations among psychopathy, substance use, and physical pain experiences in methadone-maintained patients. *Journal of Clinical Psychiatry, 70*(9), 1213–1218.

Barth, A. (2012). Invasion of the marijuana clones. *Discover, 32*(9), 13.

Bartlett, J. G. (1999). *Management of respiratory tract infections* (2nd ed.). New York: Lippincott, Williams & Wilkins.

Bartsch, A. J., Homola, G., Biller, A., & Smith, S. M. (2007). Manifestations of early brain recovery associated with abstinence from alcoholism. *Brain, 130,* 36–47.

Barry, D. T., Beitel, M., Garnet, B., Joshi, D., Rosenblum, A., & Schottenfeld, R. S. (2009). Relations among psychopathology, substance use, and physical pain experiences in methadone maintained patients. *Journal of Clinical Psychiatry, 79*, 1213–1218.

Baselt, R. C. (1996). Disposition of alcohol in men. In J. C. Garriott (Ed.), *Medicolegal aspects of alcohol* (3rd ed.). Tuscon, AZ: Lawyers & Judges Publishing Co.

Batki, S. L. (2001, November 1). *Methamphetamine and MDMA*. Paper presented at symposium American Society of Addiction Medicine, Washington, DC.

Batzer, W., Ditzer, T., & Brown, C. (1999). LSD use and flashbacks in alcoholic patients. *Journal of Addictive Diseases, 18*(2), 57–63.

Bauernfeind, A. M., Dietrich, M. S., Blackford, J. U., Charboneau, E. J., Lillevig, J. G., Cannistraci, C. J., ... Cowan R. L. (2011). Human ecstasy use is associated with increased cortical excitability: An FMRI study. *Neuropsychopharmacology, 36*, 1127–1141.

Bauld, L., Chesterman, J., Ferguson, J., & Judge, K. (2008). A comparison of the effectiveness of group based and pharmacy led smoking cessation treatment in Glasgow. *Addiction, 104*, 308–318.

Bauman, M. H., & Rothman, R. B. (2007). Neorobiology of 3,4-methylenedioxymethamine (MDMA or Ecstasy). In S. B. Karch (Ed.), *Drug abuse handbook* (2nd ed.). New York: CRC Press.

Bayard, M., McIntyre, J., Hill, K. R., & Woodside, J. (2004). Alcohol withdrawal syndrome. *American Family Physician, 56*, 1443–1450.

Beasley, R., Clayton, T., Crane, J., von Mutius, E., Lai, C. K., Montefort, S., ... Stewart, A. (2008). Association between paracetamol use in infancy and childhood, and the risk of asthma, rhinoconjunctivitis and eczema in children aged 6-7 years: Analysis from phase three of the ISAAC programme. *The Lancet, 372*, 1039–1048.

Beattie, M. (2009). *The new codependency*. New York: Simon & Schuster.

Beauvais, F. (1998). American Indians and alcohol. *Alcohol Health & Research World, 22*, 253–259.

Beazley, H. (1998, March 3). *The integration of AA and clinical practice*. Paper presented to the "Treating the Addictions" seminar presented by the Department of Psychiatry of the Cambridge Hospital, Boston, MA.

Bechara, A. (2006, August 12). *Decision making, impulse control, and loss of will power to resist drugs: A neurocognitive perspective*. Symposium presented at the annual meeting of the American Psychological Association, New Orleans, LA.

Beck, A. T. (2004, March 5). *The cognitive-behavioral approach to addiction treatment*. Paper presented to the Department of Psychiatry of the Cambridge Hospital, Boston, MA.

Begley, S. (2007). *Train your mind, change your brain*. New York: Ballentine Books.

Behnke, M., Smith, V. C., Committee on Substance Abuse, & Committee on Fetus and Newborn. (2013). Prenatal substance abuse: Short and long term effects of the exposed fetus. *Pediatrics*. doi:10.1542/peds 2012-3931

Behrendt, S., Wittchen, H., Fofler, M., Lieb, R., Low, N. C., Rehm, J., & Beesdo, K. (2008). Risk and speed of transitions to first alcohol dependence symptoms in adolescents: A 10-year longitudinal community study in Germany. *Addiction, 103*(10), 1638–1647.

Belenko, S., Patapis, N., & French, M. T. (2005). *Economic benefits of drug treatment: A critical review of evidence for policy makers*. Retrieved from http//www.tresearch.org/resources/specials,2005Feb_economicbenefirts/pdf

Belhani, D., Fanton, L., Vaillant, F., Descotes, J., Manati, W., Tabib, A., ... Timour, Q. (2009). Cardiac lesions induced by testosterone: Protective effects of dexrazoxane and trimetazidine. *Cardiovascular Toxicology, 9*(2), 64–69.

Bell, H. (2009). Outwitting HIV. *Minnesota Medicine, 92*(10), 22–26.

Bell, R. A., Spangler, J. G., & Quandt, S. A. (2000). Smokeless tobacco use among adults in the southeast. *Southern Medical Journal, 93*, 456–462.

Bell, S. H., Stade, B., Reynolds, J. N., Andrew, G., Andrew, G., Hwang, P. A., ... Carlen, P. L. (2010). The remarkably high prevalence of epilepsy and seizure history in fetal alcohol spectrum disorders. *Alcoholism: Clinical & Experimental Research*. doi:10.1111/j.1530-0277.2010.01184.x

Bell, T. (1996). Abuse or addiction? *Professional Counselor, 11*(5), 12.

Bellack, A. S., Bennett, M. E., Gearon, J. S., Brown, C. H., et al. (2006). A randomized clinical trial of a new behavioral treatment for drug abuse in people with severe and persistent mental illness. *Archives of General Psychiatry, 63*, 426–432.

Bennett, A., & Golub, A. (2012). Sociological factors and addiction. In H. J. Shaffer, D. A. LaPlante, & S. E. Nelson (Eds.), *A.P.A. Addiction syndromes* handbook (Vol. 1, pp. 195–210). Washington, DC: American Psychological Association.

Bennett, P. N., & Brown, M. J. (2003). *Clinical pharmacology*. New York: Churchill Livingstone.

Benson, H. (2009, February 23–27). *Mind/body medicine: Components, research, techniques and application with the emphasis on the relaxation response*. Seminar presented by the Harvard Medical School Department of Continuing Education, Key Largo, Florida.

Benson, R. T., & Sacco, R. L. (2000). Stroke prevention. *Neurologic Clinics of North America, 19*, 309–320.

Bentall, R. P. (2009). *Doctoring the mind*. New York: New York University Press.

Benton, S. A. (2009). *Understanding the high-functioning alcoholic*. West Port, CN: Praeger.

Benyamina, A., Lecacheux, M., Blecha, L., Reynud, M., et al. (2008). Pharmacotherapy and psychothotherapy in cannabis withdrawal and dependence. *Expert Review in Neurotherapy, 8*(3), 479–491.

Berent, S., & Alberts, J. W. (2005). *Neurobehavioral toxicology* (Vol. 1). New York: Taylor & Francis.

Berg, J. E. (2003). Mortality and return to work of drug abusers from therapeutic community treatment 3 years after entry. *The Primary Care Companion to the Journal of Clinical Psychiatry, 5*(4), 164–167.

Bergamini, E., Demidenko, E., & Sargent, J. D. (2013). Trends in tobacco and alcohol placements in popular US movies, 1996 through 2009. *JAMA Pediatrics*. doi:10.1001/jamapediatrics.2013.393

Berger, J. S., Roncaglioni, M. C., Avanzini, F., Pangrazzi, I., et al. (2006). Aspirin for the primary prevention of cardiovascular events in women and men. *Journal of the American Medical Association, 295*, 306 313.

Berger, T. (2000). Nervous system. In G. Zernig, A. Saria, M. Kurz, & S. S. O'Malley (Eds.), *Handbook of alcoholism*. New York: CRC Press.

Berghuis, P., Rajnicek, A. M., Morozuv, Y. M., Ross, R. A., et al. (2007). Hardwiring the brain: Endocannabinoids shape neuronal connectivity. *Science, 316*, 1212–1216.

Bermani, S. M., Kuczenski, R., MaCracken, J. T., & London, E. D. (2009). Potential adverse effects of amphetamine treatment on brain and behavior: A review. *Molecular Psychiatry, 14*, 123–142.

Berry, J., & Mugford, G. (2007, April 28). *Addressing the epidemic of benzodiazepine over-prescribing*. Seminar presented at the 38th Annual Medical-Scientific

Conference of the American Society of Addiction Medicine, Miami, FL.

Bhattacharya, S. (2011). Ketamine warning of bladder damage. *New Scientist, 210*(2817), 12.

Bhattacharya, S., Fusar-Poli, P., Borgwardt, S., Martin-Santos, R., et al. (2009). Modulation of mediotemporal and ventrostriatal function in humans by Δ9-tetrahydrocannabinol. *Archives of General Psychiatry, 66*(4), 442–451.

Bhuvaneswar, C., & Chang, G. (2009). Substance use in pregnancy. In K. T. Brady, S. E. Back, & S. F. Greenfield (Eds.), *Women & addiction*. New York: Guilford.

Bialous, S. A., & Sarna, L. (2004). Sparing a few minutes for tobacco cessation. *American Journal of Nursing, 104*(12), 54–60.

Biller, A., Bartsch, A. J., Homola, L., & Bendszus, M. (2009). The effects of ethanol on human brain metabolites longitudinally characterized by proton MR spectroscopy. *Journal of Cerebral Blood Flow & Metabolism, 29*, 891–902.

Bini, E. J., Kritz, S., Brown, L. S., Robinson, J., et al. (2012). Hepatitis B virus and hepatitis C virus services offered by substance abuse treatment programs in the United States. *Journal of Substance Abuse Treatment, 42*(4), 438–445.

Biederman, J., Monuteaus, M. C., Spencer, T., Wilens, T. E., et al. (2008). Stimulant therapy and risk for subsequent substance use disorders in male adults with ADHD: A naturalistic controlled 10 year follow-up study. *American Journal Psychiatry*. doi:10.1176/appi.ajp.2007.07091486

Big tobacco's secret kiddie campaign. (1998). *Newsweek, CXXXI*(4), 29.

Bijttebier, P., Boethals, E., & Ansoms, S. (2006). Parental drinking as a risk factor for children's maladjustment: The mediating role of family environment. *Psychology of Addictive Behavior, 20*, 126–130.

Billoti de Gage, S., Begaud, B., Bazin, F., Verdoux, H., et al. (2012). Benzodiazepine use and risk of dementia: Prospective population based study. *British Medical Journal*. doi:10.1136/bmj.e6231

Bisaca, A. (2008). Benzodiazepines and other sedatives and hypnotics. In M. Galanter & H. D. Kleber (Eds.), *Textbook of substance abuse treatment*. Washington, DC: American Psychiatric Association, Inc.

Bisaga, A. (2008). Benzodiazepines and other sedatives and hypnotics. In M. Galanter & H. D. Kleber

(Eds.), *Textbook of substance abuse treatment.* Washington, DC: American Psychiatric Association, Inc.

Black, C. (1982). *It will never happen to me.* Denver, CO: MAC Printing and Publications.

Black, C. (2003, March 7). *The legacy of addictions: Looking at family patterns.* Symposium presented to the Department of Psychiatry of the Cambridge Hospital, Boston, MA.

Black, K., & Mann, A. (2009). *Brain surgeon.* New York: Wellness Central.

Black, R. A., & Hill, D. A. (2003). Over-the-counter medications in pregnancy. *American Family Physician, 160,* 2038–2045.

Blalock, J. A., Nyak, N., Wetter, D. W., Schreindorfer, L., et al. (2011). The relationship of childhood trauma to nicotine dependence in pregnant smokers. *Psychology of Addictive Behaviors, 25*(94), 652–663.

Bloch, S., & Pargiter, R. (2002). A history of psychiatric ethics. *Psychiatric Clinics of North America, 25,* 509–524.

Blondel, R. D. (2005). Ambulatory detoxification of patients with alcohol dependence. *American Family Physician, 71,* 495–502.

Blondell, R. D., & Ashrafioun, L. (2008). Treatment opioid dependency and coexisting chronic nonmalignant pain. *American Family Physician, 78*(10), 1132–1133.

Blow, F. C., Serras, A. M., & Barry, K. L. (2007). Late-life depression and alcoholism. *Current Psychiatry Reports, 9,* 14–19.

Blum, A. (2008). Alchemy, the safer cigarette, and Phillip Morris. *The Lancet, 371,* 1644–1647.

Blum, D. (1998). Finding strength. *Psychology Today, 31*(3), 32–38, 66–67, 69, 72–73.

Blum, D. (2010). *The poisoner's handbook.* New York: Penguin Press.

Blum, K. (2006). *Quitting early.* Retrieved from http//chicagotribune.com/business/bal_hs.smoke31mar31,1,880720.story?crack=1&cst=true

Blum, K., & Payne, J. E. (1991). *Alcohol and the addictive brain.* New York: Free Press.

Blume, A. W. (2005). *Treating drug problems.* New York: John Wiley & Sons, Inc.

Blume, A. W., & de la Cruz, B. (2005). Relapse prevention among diverse populations. In G. A. Marlatt & D. M. Donovan (Eds.), *Relapse prevention—maintenance strategies in the treatment of addictive behaviors* (2nd ed.). New York: Guilford.

Blume, S. B., & Zilberman, M. L. (2004). Addiction in women. In M. Galanter & H. D. Kleber (Eds.), *Textbook of substance abuse treatment* (3rd ed.). Washington, DC: American Psychiatric Press, Inc.

Blume, S. B., & Zilberman, M. L. (2005a). Alcohol and women. In J. H. Lowinson, R. B. Millman, & J. G. Langrod (Eds.), *Substance abuse: A comprehensive textbook* (4th ed.). New York: Lipponcott, Williams & Wilkins.

Blume, S. B., & Zilberman, M. L. (2005b). Addictive disorders in women. In R. J. Frances, S. I. Miller, & A. H. Mack (Eds.), *Clinical textbook of addictive disorders* (3rd ed.). New York: Guilford.

Boal, M. (2002). Designer drug death. *Rolling Stone, 888,* 44–49.

Bobo, W. C., Miller, S. C., & Martin, B. D. (2005). The abuse liability of dextromethorphan among adolescents: A review. *Journal of Child and Adolescent Substance Abuse, 14*(4), 55–75.

Boese, A. (2007). Did they really do that? *The Scientist.* Retrieved from http://www.the_scientist./news/home/53568

Boffeta, P., & Straif, K. (2009). Use of smokeless tobacco and risk of myocardial infarction and stroke: Systematic review with meta-analysis. *British Medical Journal.* doi:10.1136/bmj.b3060

Boffetta, P., Hecht, S., Gray, N., Gupta, P., et al. (2008). Smokeless tobacco and cancer. *The Lancet Oncology, 9*(9), 822.

Bohn, M. (2001, June 1). *Alcoholism pharmacotherapy.* Paper presented at the Contemporary Issues in the Treatment of Alcohol and Drug Use Symposium, Milwaukee, WI.

Boles, S. C. (2007, April 26). *Neurochemistry review: Advances in anti-relapse pharmacotherapy of alcoholism.* Paper Presented at the Ruth Fox Course for Physicians, 38th Medical-Scientific Conference of the American Society of Addiction Medicine, Miami, FL.

Bolla, K. I., & Cadet, J. L. (2007). Exogenous acquired metabolic disorders of the nervous system: Toxins and illicit drugs. In C. Goetz (Ed.), *Textbook of clinical neurology* (3rd ed.). Philadelphia: Saunders-Elsevier.

Bolnick, J. M., & Rayburn, W. F. (2003). Substance use disorders in women: Special considerations during pregnancy. *Obstetric and Gynecological Clinics of North America, 30,* 545–558.

Bombardier, C. H., Fann, J. R., Temkin, N. R., Esselman, P. C., et al. (2010). Rates of major depressive disorder and clinical outcomes following traumatic brain injury. *Journal of the American Medical Association, 303,* 1938–1945.

Bonanno, G. A. (2004). Loss, trauma, and human resilience. *American Psychologist, 59,* 20–28.

Bonar, E. E., Young, K. M., Hofmann, E., Gumber, S., et al. (2012). Quantitative and qualitative assessment of university students definitions of binge drinking. *Psychology of Addictive Behaviors, 26*(2), 187–193.

Bondesson, J. D., & Saperston, A. R. (1996). Hepatitis. *Emergency Medical Clinics of North America, 14,* 695–718.

Bongar, B. (1997, August 12). *Suicide: What therapists need to know.* Seminar presented at the 1997 meeting of the American Psychological Association, Chicago, IL.

Book, S. W., & Randall, C. L. (2002). Social anxiety disorder and alcohol use. *Alcohol Research & Health, 26,* 130–139.

Booth, M. (1996). *Opium: A history.* New York: St. Martin's-Griffin.

Borg, L., Kravets, I., & Kreek, M. J. (2009). The pharmacology of long-acting as contrasted with short-acting opioids. In R. K. Ries, D. A. Fiellin, S. C. Miller, & R. Saitz (Eds.), *Principles of addiction medicine* (4th ed., pp. 453–463). New York: Lippincott, Williams & Wilkins.

Borgwardt, S. J., Allen, P., Bhattacharyya, A., Fusar-Poli, P., et al. (2008). Neural basis of Δ-9-tetrahydrocannabinol and cannabidol: Effects inhibition. *Biological Psychiatry, 64*(11), 966–973.

Borowsky, I. W., Ireland, M., & Resnick, M. D. (2009). Health status and behavioral outcomes for youth who anticipate a high likelihood of earth death. *Pediatrics, 124.* doi:10.1542.1542ped.2008-3425

Borsook, D. (2010, May 1). *Understanding and approaching the co-occurrence of substance abuse and chronic pain.* Paper presented at the "Addictions in 2010" seminar, hosted by the Division of alcohol and Drug Abuse of the McLean Hospital, Boston, MA.

Boschert, S. (2010). Tailor therapy for GLBT substance abusers. *Clinical Psychiatry News, 38*(6), 19.

Botre, F., & Pavan, A. (2008). Enhancement drugs and the athlete. *Neurological Clinics of North America, 26,* 149–167.

Bowen, M. (1985). *Family therapy in clinical practice.* Northvale, NJ: Jason-Aronson.

Bowen, S. E., Batis, J. C., Mahammadi, M. H., & Hannigan, J. H. (2005). Abuse pattern of gestational toluene exposure and early postnatal development in rats. *Neurotoxicity & Teratology, 27,* 105–116.

Boyd, C. J., McCabe, S. E., & Morales, M. (2005). College students' alcohol use: A critical review. In J. J. Fitzpatrick, J. S. Stevenson, & M. S. Sommers (Eds.), *Annual review of nursing research, Vol. 23.* New York: Springer.

Boyer, E. W. (2005, March 5). *Emerging drugs of abuse.* Paper presented at the "Treating the Addictions" seminar hosted by the Department of Psychiatry of the Cambridge Hospital, Boston, MA.

Braden, J. B., Russo, J., Fan, M., Edlund, M. J., et al. (2010). Emergency department visits among recipients of chronic opioid therapy. *Archives of Internal Medicine, 170*(16), 1425–1432.

Bradley, K. A., Boyd-Wickizer, J., Powell, S., & Burman, M. L. (1998). Alcohol screening questionnaires in women. *Journal of the American Medical Association, 280,* 166–171.

Bradley, K. A., Bush, K. R., Epler, A. J., Dobie, D. J., et al. (2003). Two brief alcohol screening tests from the Alcohol Use Disorders Identification Test (AUDIT): Validation in a female veterans affairs patient population. *Archives of Internal Medicine, 163,* 821–829.

Brady, K. T., & Back, S. (2008). Women and addiction. In M. Galanter & H. D. Kleber (Eds.), *The American psychiatric publishing textbook of substance abuse treatment.* Washington, DC: American Psychiatric Publishing, Inc.

Brady, K. T., & Hartwell, K. (2009). Gender, anxiety and substance use disorders. In K. T. Brady, S. E. Back, & S. F. Greenfield (Eds.), *Women & addiction.* New York: Guilford.

Brady, K. T., Tolliver, B. K., & Verduin, M. L. (2007). Alcohol use and anxiety: Diagnostic and management issues. *American Journal of Psychiatry, 164,* 217–221.

Brain Trauma Foundation. (2000). Use of barbiturates in the control of intracranial hypertension. *Journal of Neurotrauma, 17*(6–7), 527–530.

Braithwaite, R. S., & Bryant, K. J. (2010). Influence of alcohol consumption on adherence to and toxicity of antiretroviral therapy and survival. *Alcohol Research & Health, 33*(3), 280–287.

Brambilla, C., & Colonna, M. (2008). Cannabis: The next villain on the lung cancer battlefield? *European Respiratory Journal, 31,* 227–228.

Bravo, G. (2001). What does MDMA feel like? In J. Holland (Ed.), *Ecstasy: The complete guide.* Rochester, VT: Park St. Press.

Breggin, P. R. (2008). *Brain-disabling treatments in psychiatry* (2nd ed.). New York: Springer Publishing.

Breggin, P. R. (1999). Letter to the editor. *Journal of the American Medical Association, 281,* 1490–1491.

Breithaupt, D. (2001). Why health insurers should pay for addiction treatment. *Western Journal of Medicine, 174,* 375–377.

Breiter, H. C. (1999, March 6). *The biology of addiction.* Symposium presented to the Department of Psychiatry of the Cambridge General Hospital, Boston, MA.

Brekke, J. S., Prindle, C., Woo Bae, S., & Long, J. D. (2001). Risks for individuals with schizophrenia who are living in the community. *Psychiatric Services, 52,* 1358–1366.

Brenhouse, H. C., & Anderson, S. L. (2008). Delayed extinction and stronger reinstatement of cocaine conditioned place preference in adolescent rats, compared to adults. *Behavioral Neuroscience, 122*(2), 460–465.

Brennan-Braden, J., Russo, J., Fan, M., Edlund, M. J., et al. (2010). Emergency department visits among recipients of chronic opioid therapy. *Archives of internal Medicine, 170*(16), 1425–1432.

Brennen, P. L., Schutte, K. K., & Moos, R. H. (2010). Patterns and predictors of late-life drinking trajectories: A 10 year longitudinal study. *Psychology of Addictive Behaviors, 24,* 254–264.

Brigham, G. S. (2003). 12-Step participation as a pathway to recovery: The Maryhaven experience and implications for treatment and research. *Science Practice & Perspectives, 2*(1), 43–51.

Brink, S. (2004). The price of booze. *U.S. News & World Report, 136*(4), 48–50.

Brister, H. A., Sher, K. J., & Fromme, K. (2011). 21st birthday drinking and associated physical consequences and behavioral risks. *Journal of Addictive Behaviors, 25*(6), 573–582.

Britt, J. P., & McGehee, D. S. (2008). Presynaptic opioid and nicotinic receptor modulation of dopamine overflow in the nucleus accumbens. *Journal of Neuroscience, 28,* 1672–1681.

Britton, A., Marmot, M. G., & Shipley, M. (2008). Who benefits most from the cardio- protective properties of alcohol consumption—health freaks or couch potatoes? *Journal of Epidemiology and Community Health, 62*(10), 905–908.

Brody, A. L., Mandelkern, M. A., London, E. D., Olmstead, R. E., et al. (2006). Cigarette smoking saturates brain a4ß2 niotinic acetylcholine receptors. *Archives of General Psychiatry, 63,* 907–915.

Brody, T. N. M. (1994). Clinical pharmacokinetics. In T. M. Brody, J. Larner, K. Minneman, & H. C. Neu (Eds.), *Human pharmacology molecular to clinical* (2nd ed.). St. Louis, MO: Mosby.

Bronisch, T., Hofler, M., & Lieb, F. (2008). Smoking predicts suicidally: Findings from a prospective community study. *Journal of Affective Disorders.* doi:10.10.16jad.2007.10.010

Brook, D. W. (2008). Group therapy. In M. Galanter & H. D. Kleber (Eds.), *Textbook of substance abuse treatment.* Washington, DC: American Psychiatric Association, Inc.

Brook, J. S., Pahl, K., & Rubenstone, E. (2008). Epidemiology of addiction. In M. Galanter & H. D. Kleber (Eds.), *The American psychiatric publishing textbook of substance abuse treatment.* Washington, DC: American Psychiatric Publishing, Inc.

Brooks, J. T., Leung, G., & Shannon, M. (1996). Inhalants. In L. Friedman, N. F. Fleming, D. H. Roberts, & S. E. Hyman (Eds.), *Source book of substance abuse and addiction.* New York: Williams & Wilkins.

Brower, K. J., Aldrich, M. S., Robinson, E. A. R., Zucker, R. A., et al. (2001). In somnia, self-medication and relapse to alcoholism. *American Journal of Psychiatry, 158,* 399–404.

Brown, A. (2007). Sensationalizing our drug and alcohol problems is failing public health. *Nursing Times, 103*(10), 12.

Brown, D. (2006). *Nicotine up sharply in many cigarettes.* Retrieved from http://www.washington post.com./wp/dyn/content/article/s006/08/30/AR2006083001418.html

Brown, D. J. (2007). Psychedelic healing? *Scientific American Mind, 18*(6), 60–65.

Brown, E. S. (2005). Bipolar disorder and substance abuse. *Psychiatric Clinics of North America, 28,* 415–425.

Brown, M. T. C., Bellone, C., Mameli, M., Labouebe, G., et al. (2010). Drug-driven AMPA receptor redistribution mimicked by selective dopamine neuron stimulation. *PLoS ONE, 5*(12), e15870. doi:10.1371/journal.pone.0015870

Brown, R. (2006). Speaking of "poppycock"... a reply to the Wall Street Journal. *ASAM News, 21*(3), 5–6.

Brown, R. L., Leonard, T., Saunders, L. A., & Papasoulioutis, O. (1997). A two-item screening test for alcohol and other drug problems. *The Journal of Family Practice, 44,* 151–160.

Brown, S., & Lewis, V. (1995). The alcoholic family: A developmental model of recovery. In S. A. Brown (Ed.), *Treating alcoholism.* New York: Josey-Bass.

Brown, S. A. (1985). *Treating the alcoholic: A developmental model of recovery.* New York: John Wiley & Sons, Inc.

Brown, S. A., McGue, M., Maggs, J., Schulenberg, J., et al. (2009). Underaged alcohol use. *Alcohol Research & Health, 32*(1), 41–52.

Brown, T. M., & Stoudemire, A. (1998). *Psychiatric side effects of prescription and over- the-counter medications.* Washington, DC: American Psychiatric Press, Inc.

Bruckner, J. V., & Warren, D. A. (2003). Toxic effects of solvents and vapors. In C. D. Klassen & J. B. Watkins (Eds.), *Casarett and Doull's essentials of toxicology.* New York: McGraw-Hill.

Bruinijnzeel, A. W., Repetto, M., & Gold, M. S. (2004). Neurobiological mechanisms in addictive and psychiatric disorders. *Psychiatric Clinics of North America, 27,* 661–674.

Brunton, L. L., Lazo, J. S., & Parker, K. L. (2006). *Goodman & Gilman's the pharmacological basis of therapeutics* (11th ed.). New York: McGraw-Hill.

Brunton, L. L., Parker, K., Blumenthal, D., & Buston, L. (2008). *Goodman & Gilman's manual of pharmacology and therapeutics.* New York: McGraw-Hill.

Brust, J. C. M. (1998). Acute neurologic complications of drug and alcohol abuse. *Neurological Clinics of North America, 16,* 503–519.

Brust, J. C. M. (2004). *Neurological aspects of substance abuse* (2nd ed.). New York: Elsevier Butterworth Heinemann.

Brust, J. C. M. (2007a). Alcoholism. In J. C. M. Brust (Ed.), *Current diagnosis and treatment in neurology.* New York: Lange Medical Books/McGraw-Hill.

Brust, J. C. M. (2007b). Drug abuse. In J. C. M. Brust (Ed.), *Current diagnosis and treatment in neurology.* New York: Lange Medical Books/McGraw-Hill.

Bryner, J. K., Wang, U. K., Hul, J. W., Bedodo, M., et al. (2006). Dextromethorphan abuse in adolescence. *Archives of Pediatrics and Adolescent Medicine, 160,* 1217–1222.

Bryson, C. L., Au, D. H., Sun, H., Williams, E. C., et al. (2008). Alcohol screening scores and medication nonadherence. *Annals of Internal Medicine, 149,* 795–803.

Buber, M. (1970). *I and thou.* New York: Charles Scribner's Sons.

Buckley, P. F. (2006). Prevalence and consequences of the dual diagnosis of substance abuse and severe mental illness. *Journal of Clinical Psychiatry, 67*(Suppl. 7), 5–9.

Buckman, J. F., Yusko, D. A., White, H. R., & Pandina, R. J. (2009). Risk profile of male college athletes who use performance-enhancing substances. *Journal of Studies on Alcohol & Drugs, 70,* 919–923.

Budney, A. J., Moore, B. A., Bandrey, R. G., & Hughes, J. R. (2003). The time course and significance of cannabis withdrawal. *Journal of Abnormal Psychology, 112,* 393–402.

Budney, A. J., Roffman, R., Stephens, R. S., & Walker, D. (2007). Marijuana dependence and its treatment. *Addiction Science & Clinical Practice, 4*(1), 4–16.

Budney, A. J., Sigmon, S. C., & Higgins, S. T. (2003). Contingency management in the substance abuse treatment clinic. In F. Rotgers, J. Morgenstern, & S. T. Walters (Eds.), *Treating substance abuse: Theory and technique* (2nd ed.). New York: Guilford.

Bufe, C. (1998). *Alcoholics anonymous: Cult or cure* (2nd ed.). Tuscon, AZ: See Sharp Press.

Buffenstein, A., Heaster, J., & Ko, P. (1999). Chronic psychotic illness from methamphetamine. *American Journal of Psychiatry, 156,* 662.

Buhrich, N., Weller, A., & Kevans, P. (2000). Misuse of anticholinergic drugs by people with serious mental illness. *Psychiatric Services, 51,* 928–929.

Buka, S. L., Shenassa, E. D., & Niaura, R. (2003). Elevated risk of tobacco dependence among offspring of mothers who smoked during pregnancy: A 30 year prospective study. *American Journal of Psychiatry, 160,* 1978–1984.

Bureau of Justice Statistics. (2008, June 6). *Slower growth in the nation's prison and jail populations.* Press release.

Buring, J., & Ferrari, N. (2006). Take an aspirin and … *Newsweek, CXLVII*(17), 71.

Burns, D. M. (2008). Nicotine addiction. In A. S. Fauci, E. Braunwald, D. L. Kasper, S. L. Hauser, D. L. Longo, J. L. Jameson, & J. Loscalzo (Eds.), *Harrison's principles of internal medicine* (17th ed.). New York: McGraw-Hill.

Burns, E. (2007). *The smoke of the gods.* Philadelphia: Temple University Press.

Busch, A. B., Weiss, R. D., & Najavits, L. M. (2005). Co-occurring substance use disorders and other psychiatric disorders. In R. J. Frances, S. I. Miller, & A. H. Mack (Eds.), *Clinical textbook of addictive disorders* (3rd ed.). New York: Guilford.

Butz, A. M., Pulsifer, M. B., Belcher, H. M. E., Leppert, M., et al. (2005). Infant head growth and cognitive status at 36 months in children with in-utero drug exposure. *Journal of Child & Adolescent Substance Abuse, 14*(4), 15–39.

By the numbers. (2013). *Monitor on Psychology, 44*(7), 12.

Byington, D. B. (1997). Applying relational theory to addictions treatment. In S. L. A. Straussner & E. Zelvin (Eds.), *Gender and addictions.* Northvale, NJ: Jason-Aronson.

Bynum, H. (2013). *Spitting blood.* New York: Oxford University Press.

Cabaj, R. P. (1997). Gays, lesbians and bisexuals. In J. H. Lowinson, P. Ruiz, R. B. Millman, & J. G. Langrod (Eds.), *Substance abuse: A comprehensive textbook* (3rd ed.). New York: Lipponcott, Williams & Wilkins.

Cabaj, R. P. (2005). Gays, lesbians and bisexuals. In J. H. Lowinson, P. Ruiz, R. B. Millman, & J. G. Langrod (Eds.), *Substance abuse: A comprehensive textbook* (4th ed.). New York: Lipponcott, Williams & Wilkins.

Caetano, R., Clark, C. L., & Tam, T. (1998). Alcohol consumption among racial/ethnic minorities: Theory and research. *Alcohol Health & Research World, 22*, 229–242.

Cafferty, J. (2009). *Commentary: War on Drug is insane.* Retrieved from http://www.cnn.com/2009/POLITICS/03/31/cafferty.legal.drugs/index.html

Cahill, T. (1998). *The gifts of the Jews.* New York: Doubleday.

Cahill, T. (2006). *How the Irish saved civilization.* New York: Bantam Doubleday Dell Publishing Group, Inc.

Calfee, R., & Fadale, P. (2006). Popular ergogenic drugs and supplements in young athletes. *Pediatrics, 117*, e557–e559.

California judges get tougher on science. (1997). *Forensic Drug Abuse Advisor, 9*(8), 61.

Callaway, J. C., & McKenna, D. J. (1998). Neurochemistry of psychedelic drugs. In S. B. Karch (Ed.), *Drug abuse handbook.* New York: CRC Press, Inc.

Cannabis booster. (2008). *New Scientist, 200*(2968), 6.

Cannabis chemical clue to colon cancer. (2008). *New Scientist, 199*(2668), 17.

Cape, G. S. (2003). Addiction, stigma and movies. *Acta Psychiatricia Scandinavica, 107*, 163–169.

Capretto, N. A. (2007, April 26). *ADDICTION: A family disease.* Paper Presented at the Ruth Fox Course for Physicians, 38th Medical-Scientific Conference of the American Society of Addiction Medicine, Miami, FL.

Carey, B. (2008). *Drug rehabilitation or revolving door?* Retrieved from http:www.nytimes.com/2008/12/23/health/23reha.html?pagewanted=1&_r=2&hy?8dpc

Carlan, G. (2001). *Napalm & silly putty.* New York: Hyperion.

Carmona, R. H. (2004). *The health consequences of smoking: A report of the surgeon general.* Washington, DC: Centers for Disease Control.

Carpenter, S. (2001). Research on teen smoking cessation gains momentum. *APA Monitor, 32*(6), 54–55.

Carpenter, S. (2012). That gut feeling. *Monitor on Psychology, 43*(8), 50–55.

Carol, C. (2012). Beer country. *National Geographic, 210*(5), 23.

Carol, G., Smelson, D. A., Losonczy, M. F., & Ziedonis, D. (2001). A preliminary investigation of cocaine craving among persons with and without schizophrenia. *Psychiatric Services, 52*, 1029–1031.

Carr, E. R., & Szymanski, D. M. (2011). Sexual objectification and substance abuse in young adult women. *The Counseling Psychologist, 39*(1), 39–66.

Carr, P., & Lynfield, R. (2009). Why HIV still matters in Minnesota. *Minnesota Medicine, 92*(10), 36–37.

Carrico, A. W. (2010). Elevated suicide rate among HIV-positive persons despite benefits of antiretroviral therapy: Implications for a stress and coping model of suicide. *American Journal of Psychiatry, 167*(2), 117–119.

Carroll, C. M., & Ball, S. A. (2005). Assessment of cocaine abuse and dependence. In D. M. Donovan & G. A. Marlatt (Eds.), *Assessment of addictive behaviors* (2nd ed.). New York: Guilford.

Carroll, K. M. (2003). Integrating psychotherapy and pharmacotherapy in substance abuse treatment. In D. M. Donovan & G. A. Marlatt (Eds.), *Treating substance abuse: Theory and technique* (2nd ed.). New York: Guilford.

Carroll, K. M., Smelson, D. A., Losonczy, M. F., & Ziedonis, D. (2001). A preliminary investigation of cocaine craving among persons with and without schizophrenia. *Psychiatric Services, 52*, 1029–1031.

Carter, L. (2013). Not smooth, not cool. *New Scientist, 220*(2939), 26–27.

Carter, R. C., Jacobson, J. L., Molteno, C. D., Jiang, H., et al. (2012). Effects of heavy prenatal alcohol exposure and iron deficiency anemia on child growth and body composition through age 9 years. *Alcoholism Clinical & Experimental Research.* doi:10.1111/j.1530-0227.2012.01810.x

Carvey, P. M. (1998). *Drug action in the central nervous system.* New York: Oxford University Press.

Casavant, M. J., Blake, K., Griffith, J., Yates, A., et al. (2007). Consequences of use of anabolic androgenic steroids. *Pediatric Clinics of North American, 54,* 677–690.

Casolla, B., Dequatre-Ponchelle, N., Rosse, C., Henon, H., et al. (2012). Heavy alcohol intake and intracerebral hemorrhage. *Neurology, 79,* 1109–1115.

Caspers, K., Amdt, S., Yucuis, R., McKirgan, L., et al. (2010). Effects of alcohol and cigarette use disorders on global and specific measures of cognition in middle age adults. *Journal of Studies on Alcohol and Drugs, 71,* 192–200.

Castro, F. G., Barrington, E. H., Walton, M. A., & Rawson, R. A. (2000). Cocaine and methamphetamine: Differential addiction rates. *Psychology of Addictive Behaviors, 14,* 390–396.

Centers for Disease Control and Prevention. (2004). *The health consequences of smoking: What it means to you.* Washington, DC: U.S. Government Printing Office.

Centers for Disease Control and Prevention. (2007). Types of alcoholic beverages usually consumed by students in 9th-12th grades—four states, 2005. *Morbidity and Mortality Weekly Report, 56*(29), 737–740.

Centers for Disease Control and Prevention. (2008). *HIV/AIDS in the United States. Centers for Disease Control and Prevention fact sheet* (August 2008 revision). Washington, DC: Author.

Centers for Disease Control and Prevention. (2009a). HIV-associated behaviors among injecting-drug users—23 cities, United States, May 2005–February 2006. *Morbidity and Mortality Weekly Report, 58,* 329–332.

Centers for Disease Control and Prevention. (2009b). Alcohol use among pregnant and nonpregnant women of childbearing age—United States, 1991–2005. *Morbidity and Mortality Weekly Report, 58*(19), 529–532.

Centers for Disease Control and Prevention. (2010a). Ecstasy overdoses at a new year eve's rave—Los Angeles, California, 2010. *Weekly and Morbidity Weekly Report, 59,* 677–681.

Centers for Disease Control and Prevention. (2010b). Emergency department visits involving nonmedical use of selected prescription drugs—United States, 2004-2008. *Morbidity and Mortality Weekly Report, 59,* 705–709.

Centers for Disease Control and Prevention. (2010c). Cigarette use among high school students—United States, 1991-2009. *Morbidity and Mortality Weekly Report, 59*(26), 797–801.

Centers for Disease Control and Prevention. (2012). More than half of young HIV-infected Americans are not aware of their status. *Morbidity and Mortality Weekly Report, 61*(early release).

Center for Substance Abuse Research. (2006). Alcohol, marijuana, Adderall, and Ritalin perceived to be most easily available drugs misused among undergraduates. *CESAR FAX, 15*(43), 1.

Center for Substance Abuse Research. (2008). Alcohol & marijuana have highest rates of continued use in the year after initiation: Heroin and Crack Cocaine have the highest rates of dependence. *CESAR FAX, 17*(15), 1.

Cepeda, M. S., Alvarez, H., Morales, O., & Carr, D. B. (2004). Addition of ultralow dose naloxone to postoperative morphine PCA: Unchanged analgesia and opioid requirement but with decreased incident of opioid side effects. *Pain, 107,* 41–46.

Ceren, S. L. (2003). Warning: Managed care may be dangerous to your health. *The Independent Practitioner, 23*(2), 77.

Cervero, F. (2012). *Understanding pain: Exploring the perception of pain.* Cambridge, MA: MIT Press.

Chaffin, M., Kelleher, M., & Hollenberg, J. (1996). Onset of physical abuse and neglect: Psychiatric, substance abuse and social risk factors from prospective community data. *Psychological Bulletin, 20*(3), 191–203.

Chaloupka, F. J. (2008). Smoking, food insecurity, and tobacco control. *Archives of Pediatric Medicine, 162*(11), 1096–1098.

Chambers, R. A., Sajdyk, T. J., Conrow, S. K., Lafuze, J. E., et al. (2007). Neonatal amygdala lesions: Co-occurring impact on social/fear related behavior and cocaine sensitization in adult rats. *Behavioral Neuroscience, 121,* 1316–1327.

Chan, A. T., Obino, S., & Fuchs, C. S. (2007). Aspirin and the risk of colorectal cancer in relationship to the expression of COX-2. *New England Journal of Medicine, 356,* 2131–2142.

Chan, A. T., Manson, J., Feskanich, D., Stampfer, M. J., et al. (2007). Long-term aspirin use and mortality in women. *Archives of Internal Medicine, 167,* 562–572.

Chang, G. (2006, October 8). *Screening instruments and brief interventions for prenatal alcohol use.* Symposium presented at the annual meeting of the American Psychological Association, New Orleans.

Chang, G. (2010, May 1). *Assessment and treatment of pregnant women with addiction.* Paper presented at the "Addictions in 2010" seminar, hosted by the Division of alcohol and Drug Abuse of the McLean Hospital, Boston, MA.

Chang, G., Chen, L., & Mao, J. (2007). Opioid tolerance and hyperalgesia. *Medical Clinics of North America, 91,* 199–211.

Chang, J. C., Dada, D., Frankel, R. M., Rodriguez, K. L., et al. (2008). When pregnant patients disclose substance use: Missed opportunities for behavioral change counseling. *Patient Education and Counseling, 72*(3), 394–401.

Chang, T. R., Kowalski, R. G., Caserta, F., Carmhuapoma, J. R., et al. (2013). Impact of acute cocaine use on aneurysmal subarachnoid hemorrhage. *Stroke, 4*(7), 1825–1829.

Chantix prescribing information. (2006). New York: Pfizer pharmaceuticals, Inc.

Chapman, C. R., & Okifuji, A. (2004). Pain: Basic mechanisms and conscious experience. In R. H. Dworkin & W. S. Brietbart (Eds.), *Psychosocial aspects of pain: A handbook for health care providers.* Seattle, WA: IASP Press.

Chapman, S., & MacKenzie, R. (2010). The global research neglect of unassisted smoking cessation: Causes and consequences. *PLoS Medicine.* doi:10.1371/journal/pmed.1000216

Chappel, J. N., & DuPont, R. L. (1999). Twelve-step and mutual help programs for addictive disorders. *Psychiatric Clinics of North America, 22,* 425–446.

Charney, D. S. (2004). Outpatient treatment of comorbid depression and alcohol use disorders. *Psychiatric Times, XXI*(2), 31–33.

Charney, D. S., Mihic, S. J., & Harris, R. A. (2006). Hypnotics and sedatives. In L. L. Bruntomn, J. S. Lazo, & K. L. Parker (Eds.), *The pharmacological basis of therapeutics* (11th ed.). New York: McGraw-Hill.

Chassin, L., Flora, D. B., & King, K. M. (2004). Trajectories of alcohol and drug use and dependence from adolescence to adulthood: The effects of familial alcoholism and personality. *Journal of Abnormal Psychology, 113,* 483–498.

Chartier, K., & Caetano, R. (2010). Ethnicity and health disparities in alcohol research. *Alcohol Research & Health, 33*(1), 152–160.

Chartier, K. G., Hesselbrock, M. N., & Hesselbrock, V. M. (2010). Development and vulnerability factors in adolescent alcohol use. *Child and Adolescent Psychiatric Clinics of North America, 19*(3), 493–500.

Cheatle, M. D., & Gallagher, R. M. (2006). Chronic pain and comorbid mood and substance use disorders: A biopsychosocial treatment approach. *Current Psychiatry Reports, 8*(5), 371–376.

Chen, C. M., Smith, G. D., Harbord, R. M., & Lewis, S. J. (2008). Alcohol intake and blood pressure: A systematic review implementing a Mendelian randomized approach. *PLoS Med, 5,* e52. doi:10.137/journal.pmed.0050052

Chen, C. M., Yoon, Y., Hi, H., & Lucas, D. L. (2007). Alcohol and hepatitis C mortality among males and females in the United States: A life table analysis. *Alcoholism: Clinical and Experimental Research, 31,* 285–292.

Chen, C. K., Lin, S. K., Sham, P. C., Ball, D., et al. (2003). Pre-morbid characteristics and co-morbidity of methamphetamine users with and without psychosis. *Psychological Medicine, 33,* 1407–1414.

Chen, I. (2013). Hidden Depths: Brain science is drowning in uncertainty. *New Scientist, 208*(2939), 32–35.

Chen, W., & Maier, S. E. (2011). Combination drug use and risk for fetal harm. *Alcohol Research & Health, 34*(1), 27–28.

Chen, W. Y., Rosner, B., Hankinson, S. E., Colditz, G. A., et al. (2011). *Journal of the American Medical Association, 306*(17), 1884–1890.

Cheng, A. T. A., Gau, S. F., Chen, T. H. H., Chang, J., et al. (2004). A 4 year longitudinal study of risk factors for alcoholism. *Archives of General Psychiatry, 61,* 184–191.

Cherny, N. I., & Foley, K. M. (1996). Nonopioid and opioid analgesic pharmacology of cancer pain. *Hematology/Oncology Clinics of North America, 10,* 79–102.

Cherpitel, C. J., & Ye, Y. (2008). Trends in alcohol and drug related ED and primary care visits: Data from the US national surveys (1995-2005). *American Journal of Drug and Alcohol Abuse, 34*(5), 576–583.

Chiauzzi, E. (1990). Breaking the patterns that lead to relapse. *Psychology Today, 23*(12), 18–19.

Chiauzzi, E. (1991). *Preventing relapse in the addictions.* New York: Pergamon.

China's healthcare woes. (2008). *New Scientist, 200*(2679), 11.

Chiva-Blanch, G., Urpi-Sarda, M., Ros, E., Arranz, S., et al. (2012). Dealcoholized red wine decreases systolic and diastolic blood pressure and increases plasma nitric oxide. *Circulation Research.* doi:10.1161/CIRCRCRESAHA. 112.272636

Chopra, D. (1997). *Overcoming addictions.* New York: Three Rivers Press.

Chou, R., Fanciullo, G. J., Fine, P. G., Adler, J. A., et al. (2009). Clinical guidelines for the use of chronic opioid therapy in chronic non-cancer pain. *The Journal of Pain, 10*(2), 113–130.

Chu, C., & Selwin, P. A. (2010). Diagnosis and initial management of acute HIV infection. *American Family Physician, 81,* 1239–1244.

Chung, P. J., Garfield, C. F., Elliott, M. N., Ostroff, J., et al. (2009). Association between adolescent viewership and alcohol advertising on cable television. *American Journal of Public Health.* doi:10.2105/ AJPH.2008.146423

Chugh, T., Socoteanu, C., Reinier, K., Walts, J., et al. (2008). A community based evaluation of sudden death associated with therapeutic levels of methadone. *The American Journal of Medicine.* doi:10.1016/j. amjmed.2007.10. 009

Cigarette package health warnings and interest in quitting smoking—14 countries, 2008–2010. (2011). *Morbidity and Mortality Weekly Report, 60*(20), 645–651.

Cigarette smoking among adults-United States, 2007. (2007). *Morbidity & Mortality Weekly Report, 57*(45), 1121–1126.

Cinciripini, P. M., Robinson, J. D., Karam-Hage, M., Minnix, J. A., et al. (2013). Effects of varenicline and bupropion sustained-release plus intensive smoking cessation counseling on prolonged abstinence from smoking and depression, negative affect, and other symptoms of nicotine withdrawal. *JAMA Psychiatry, 70*(5), 522–533.

Ciraulo, D. A. (2004, March 5). *A pharmacological approach to treatment.* Paper presented at the Treating the Addictions conference sponsored by the Department of Psychiatry of the Cambridge Hospital, Boston, MA.

Ciraulo, D. A., Ciraulo, J. A., Sands, B. F., Knapp, C. M., et al. (2005). Sedative-hypnotics. In J. H. R. Kranzler & D. A. Ciraulo (Eds.), *Clinical manual of addiction psychopharmacology.* Washington, DC: American Psychiatric Publishing.

Ciraulo, D. A., & Knapp, C. M. (2009). The pharmacology of nonalcohol sedative hypnotics. In R. K. Ries, D. A. Fiellin, S. C. Miller, & R. Saitz (Eds.), *Principles of addiction medicine* (4th ed., pp. 99–112). New York: Lippincott, Williams & Wilkins.

Ciraulo, D. A., & Nace, E. P. (2000). Benzodiazepine treatment of anxiety or insomnia in substance a use patients. *American Journal on Addictions, 9,* 276–284.

Ciraulo, D. A., Piechniczek-Buczek, J., & Iscan, E. N. (2003). Outcome predictors in substance use disorders. *Psychiatric Clinics of North America, 26,* 381–409.

Ciraulo, D. A., & Sarid-Segal, O. (2005). Sedative-, hypnotic-, or anxiolytic-related disorders. In B. J. Sadock & V. A. Sadock (Eds.), *Kaplan & Sadock's comprehensive textbook of psychiatry* (8th ed.). New York: Lippincott, Williams & Wilkins.

Ciraulo, D. A., Shader, R. I., Greenblatt, D. J., & Creelman, W. (2006). *Drug interactions in psychiatry* (3rd ed.). New York: Lippincott, Williams & Wilkins.

Clair, C., Rigotti, N. A., Porneala, B., Fox, C. S., et al. (2013). Association of smoking cessation and weight change with cardiovascular disease among adults with and without diabetes. *Journal of the American Medical Association, 309*(10), 1014–1021.

Clark, D. B., Martin, C. S., & Cornelius, J. R. (2008). Adolescent-onset substance use disorders predict young mortality. *Journal of Adolescent Health, 42*(6), 637–639.

Clark, D. B., Vanyukrov, M., & Cornelius, J. (2002). Childhood antisocial behavior and adolescent alcohol use disorders. *Alcohol Research & Health, 26,* 109–115.

Clark, R. E., Xie, H., & Brunette, M. F. (2004). Benzodiazepine prescription practices and substance abuse in persons with severe mental illness. *Journal of Clinical Psychiatry, 65*(2), 151–155.

Clark, R. E., Samnaliev, M. & McGovern, M.P. (2009). Impact of Substance Disorders on Medical Expenditures for Medicaid Beneficiaries With Behavioral Health Disorders. *Psychiatric Services* 2009; doi: 10.1176/appi.ps.60.1.35

Clausen, T., Anchersen, K., & Waal, H. (2008). Mortality prior to, during and after opioid maintenance treatment (OMT): A national prospective cross-registry study. *Drug and Alcohol Dependence, 94*(1–3), 151–157.

Clavel, F., & Hence, A. J. (2004). HIV drug resistance. *New England Journal of Medicine, 350,* 1023–1035.

Clay, S. W., Allen, J., & Parran, T. (2008). A review of addiction. *Postgraduate Medicine, 120*(2), EO1–EO7.

Cleveland, M. J., Feinberg, M. E., & Jones, D. E. (2012). Predicting alcohol use across adolescence: Relative strength of individual, family, peer, and contextual risk and protective factors. *Psychology of Addictive Behaviors, 26*(4), 703–713.

Cloak, C. C., Ernst, T., Fujii, L., Hedemark, B. A., et al. (2009). Lower diffusion in white matter of children with prenatal methamphetamine exposure. *Neurology.* doi:10.1212/01.wn1.0000346516.49126.20

Cloninger, C. R., Bohman, M., & Sigvardsson, S. (1981). Inheritance of alcohol abuse: Cross fostering analysis of adopted men. *Archives of General Psychiatry, 38,* 861–868.

Cloninger, C. R., Sigvardsson, S., & Bohman, M. (1996). Type I and type II alcoholism an update. *Alcohol Health & Research World, 20*(1), 18–23.

Cloos, J. M. (2010a). Benzodiazepines and addiction: Myths and realities (part 1). *Psychiatric Times, XXVII*(7), 26–29.

Cloos, J. M. (2010b). Benzodiazepines and addiction: Long-term use and withdrawal (part 2). *Psychiatric Times, XXVII*(8), 34–36.

Cloud, J. (2002). Is pot good for you? *Time, 160*(19), 62–66.

Cocaine and the brain. (2004). *Forensic Drug Abuse Advisor, 6*(9), 67.

Codependency. (1990). *The Wellness Letter, 7*(1), 7.

Coghlan, A. (2006a). Let's hear it again for red wine. *New Scientist, 190*(2551), 8.

Coghlan, A. (2006b). Trials for drug that gets to heart of HIV. *New Scientist, 190*(2555), 16–17.

Coghlan, A. (2008). Plans drawn up for a war on drink. *New Scientist, 198*(2652), 6–7.

Coghlan, A. (2009). Which way to turn on cannabis law? *New Scientist, 201*(2689), 6–7.

Coghlan, A. (2012). TB we can't treat is spreading in India. *New Scientist, 213*(2848), 8.

Coghlan, A., & MacKenzie, D. (2011). Daily pill can end HIV epidemic. *New Scientist, 211*(2822), 6–7.

Cohen, J. (2004). New TB drug promises shorter, simpler, treatment. *Science, 306,* 1872.

Cohen, J., Collins, R., Darkes, J., & Gwartney, D. (2007). A league of their own: Demographics, motivations and patterns of abuse of 1,955 male adult non-medical anabolic steroid users in the United States. *Journal of the International Society of Sports Nutrition, 4,* 12. doi:10:1186/1550-2783-4-12

Cohen, L. R., & Gordon, S. M. (2009). Co-occurring eating and substance use disorders. In K. T. Brady, S. E. Back, & S. F. Greenfield (Eds.), *Women & addiction.* New York: Guilford.

Cohen, L. R., & Hien, D. A. (2006). Treatment outcomes for women with substance abuse and PTSD who have experienced complex trauma. *Psychiatric Services, 57,* 100–106.

Cohen, M. (2000). *Counseling addicted women.* Thousand Oaks, CA: SAGE Publications.

Cohen, M. A. (2013). HIV: How to provide compassionate care. *Current Psychiatry, 12*(4), 19–23.

Coker, M. (1997). Overcoming sexism in A.A.: How women cope. In S. L. A. Straussner & E. Zelvin (Eds.), *Gender and addictions.* Northvale, NJ: Jason-Aronson.

Cole, J. Q., & Yonkers, K. A. (1995). Nonbenzodiazepine anxiolytics. In A. F. Shatzberg & C. B. Nemeroff (Eds.), *Textbook of psychopharmacology.* Washington, DC: American Psychiatric Press, Inc.

Coles, C. D. (2011). Discriminating the effects of prenatal alcohol exposure from other behavioral and learning disorders. *Alcohol Research & Health, 34*(1), 42–50.

Coleman, D. (2011). Challenging the second "A" in A.A. *New York Times,* p. ST1.

Coleman, E. D., & Balelt, R. C. (1997). Efficacy of two commercial products for altering urine drug test results. *Journal of Toxicology: Clinical Toxicology, 35*(6), 637–642.

Colfax, G. N., Santos, G. M., Das, M., McDermott-Santos, D., et al. (2011). Mirtazapine to reduce methamphetamine use. *Archives of General Psychiatry, 68*(11), 1168–1175.

Collins, E. D., & Kleber, H. D. (2004). Opioids. In M. Galanter & H. D. Kleber (Eds.), *Textbook of substance abuse treatment* (3rd ed.). Washington, DC: American Psychiatric Press, Inc.

Collins, E. D., Kleber, H. D., Whittington, R. A., & Heitler, N. E. (2005). Anesthesia-assisted vs buprenorphine- or clonidine-assisted heroin detoxification and naltrexone introduction: A randomized trial. *Journal of the American Medical Association, 294,* 903–913.

Collins, G. B., & Leak, B. C. (2008). Buprenorphine revolutionizes treatment for opiate dependence. *Cleveland Clinic Insights,* pp. 2–3.

Collins, J. A. (2009). Screening: Immunoassays. In J. D. Robero-Miller & B. A. Goldberger (Eds.), *Handbook of workplace drug testing* (2nd ed.). Washington, DC: AACC Press.

Collins, R. L., & McNair, L. D. (2002). Minority women and alcohol use. *Alcohol Research & Health, 26*(4), 251–256.

Colliver, J. D., Comptom, W. M., Gfroerer, J. C., & Condon, T. (2006). Projecting drug use among aging baby boomers in 2020. *Annals of Epidemiology, 16*(4), 257–265.

Comerci, G. D., Fuller, P., & Morrison, S. F. (1997). Cigarettes, drugs, alcohol & teens. *Patient Care, 31*(4), 57–83.

Evans, D. L., Foa, E. B., Gur, R. E., Hendin, H., et al. (2005). Commission on adolescent substance and alcohol abuse. In D. L. Evans, E. B. Foa, R. E. Gur, H. Hendin, C. P. O'Brien, M. E. P. Seligman, & B. T. Walsh (Eds.), *Treating and preventing adolescent mental health disorders*. New York: Guilford.

Committee on Addictions of the Group for the Advancement of Psychiatry. (2002). Responsibility and choice in addiction. *Psychiatric Services, 53,* 707–713.

Committee on Child Health Care Financing and Committee on Substance Abuse. (2001). Improving substance abuse prevention, assessment and treatment financing for children and adolescents. *Pediatrics, 108,* 1025–1029.

Committee on Secondhand Smoke Exposure and Acute Coronary Events. (2009). *Secondhand smoke exposure and cardiovascular effects: Making sense of the evidence*. Washington, DC: National Academy of Science.

Community Anti-Drug Coalitions of American. (1997, June 19). *The Meth challenge: Threatening communities coast to coast*. Interactive live national teleconference.

Comptom, P., & Athanasos, P. (2003). Chronic pain, substance abuse and addiction. *Nursing Clinics of North America, 38,* 525–537.

Comptom, W. M., Cottler, L. B., Jacobs, J. L., Ben-Abdallah, A., et al. (2003). The role of psychiatric disorders in predicting drug dependence treatment outcomes. *American Journal of Psychiatry, 160,* 890–895.

Compton, M. T., Kelly, K. E., Ramsay, C. E., Pringle, M., et al. (2009). Association of pre-onset cannabis, alcohol and tobacco use with age of prodrome and age of onset of psychosis in first-episode patients. *American Journal of Psychiatry, 166*(11), 1251–1257.

Compton, M. T., & Ramsay, C. E. (2009). The impact of pre-onset cannabis use on age at onset of prodromal and psychotic symptoms. *Primary Psychiatry, 16*(4), 35– 43.

Comptom, W. M., Thomas, Y. F., Stinson, F. S., & Grant, B. F. (2007). Prevalence, correlates, disability, and comorbidity of DSM-IV drug abuse and dependence in the United States: Results from the national epidemiologic survey on alcohol and related conditions. *Archives of General Psychiatry, 64,* 566–576.

Comtois, K. A., Schiff, M. A., & Grossman, D. C. (2008). Psychiatric risk factors associated with postpartum suicide attempt in Washington state, 1992-2001. *American Journal of Obstetrics & Gynecology, 199*(2), 120.e1–120.e5.

Concar, D. (1997). Deadly combination. *New Scientist, 155,* 2090–2091.

Concern at new "legal high" drugs. (2008). *BBC News.* Retrieved from http://news: bbc/cp/uk_news/politics/7670752.stm

Conen, D., Tedrow, U. B., Cook, N. R., Mororthy, M. V., et al. (2008). Alcohol consumption and risk of incident atrial fibrillation. *Journal of the American Medical Association, 21,* 2489–2496.

Congeni, J., & Miller, S. (2002). Supplements and drugs used to enhance athletic performance. *The Pediatric Clinics of North America, 49,* 435–461.

Connell, J. (2011). Effective drug policy. *New Scientist, 209*(2794), 24–25.

Conner, L. C., Le Fauve, C. E., & Wallace, B. C. (2009). Ethnic and cultural correlates of addiction among diverse women. In K. T. Brady, S. E. Back, & S. F. Greenfield (Eds.), *Women & addiction*. New York: Guilford.

Connor, K. R., Hesselrock, M. V. M., Schuckit, M. A., Hirsch, J. K., et al. (2006). Precontemplated and impulsive suicide attempts among individuals with alcohol dependence. *Journal of Studies on Alcohol, 67,* 95–101.

Connor, K. R., Li, Y., Meldrum, S., Duberstein, P. R., et al. (2003). The role of drinking in suicidal ideation: Analysis of project MATCH data. *Journal of Studies on Alcohol, 64,* 402–408.

Connors, G. J., Donovan, D. M., & DiClemente, C. C. (2001). *Substance abuse treatment and the stages of change*. New York: Guilford.

Conrad, P. J., O'Leary-Barrett, M., Newton, M., Topper, L., et al. (2013). Effectiveness of a selective, personality-targeted prevention program for adolescent alcohol use and misuse. *JAMA Psychiatry.* doi:19.1001/jamapsychiatry.2013.651

Conrod, P. J., Castellanos-Ryan, N., & Strang, J. (2010). Brief, personality-targeted coping skills interventions and survival as a non-drug user over a 2 year period during adolescence. *Archives of General Psychiatry, 67*(1), 85–93.

Conroy, D., Arnedt, J. T., & Brower, K. J. (2008). Insomnia in patients with addictions: A safer way to break the cycle. *Current Psychiatry, 7*(5), 97–109.

Constance, M. W., Campbell, C. I., Ray, G. T., Saunders, K., et al. (2009). Trends in prescribed opioid therapy for non-cancer pain for individuals with prior substance use disorders. *Pain, 145*(3), 267–268.

Copeland, L. (2011). Dangers of speed and alcohol not always seen. *USA Today, 29*(106), 6A.

Cook, K. (2010). Sleep is a battlefield. *Playboy, 57*(6), 52–54, 112–114.

Cooney, N. L., Kadden, R. M., & Steinberg, H. R. (2005). Assessment of alcohol problems. In D. M. Donovan & G. A. Marlatt (Eds.), *Assessment of addictive behaviors* (2nd ed.). New York: Guilford.

Cooper, D. A. (2008). Life and death in the CART era. *The Lancet, 372,* 266–267.

Cooper, J. R., Bloom, F. E., & Roth, R. H. (2003). *The biochemical basis of neuropharmacology* (8th ed.). New York: Oxford University Press.

Cooper, W. O., Habel, L. A., Sox, C. M., Chan, A., et al. (2011). ADHD drugs and serious cardiovascular events in children and young adults. *The New England Journal of Medicine, 365*(20), 1896–1904.

Cornwell, E. E., Blezberg, H., Belmahos, G., Chan, L. S., et al. (1998). The prevalence and effect of alcohol and drug abuse on cohort-matched critically injured patients. *The American Surgeon, 64,* 461–465.

Correia, C. J. (2005). Behavioral theories of choice. In M. Earlywine (Ed.), *Mind-altering drugs: The science of subjective experience.* New York: Oxford University Press.

Corrigan, J. D., Bonger, J., Lamb-Hart, G., Heinmann, A. W., et al. (2005). Increased substance abuse treatment compliance for persons with traumatic brain injury. *Psychology of Addictive Behavior, 19*(2), 131–139.

Corrigan, P. W., Lurie, B. D., Goldman, H. D., Slopen, N., et al. (2005). How adolescents perceive the stigma of mental illness and alcohol abuse. *Psychiatric Services, 56,* 544–560.

Science Daily. (2008). Retrieved from http://www.sciencedaily.com/releases/2008/10/081022222911.htm

Covey, L. W., Sullivan, M. A., Johnston, A., Glassman, A. H., et al. (2000). Advances in non-nicotine pharmacotherapy for smoking cessation. *Drugs, 59,* 17–31.

Covington, L. W. (2005). Update on antiviral agents for HIV and AIDS. *Nursing Clinics of North America, 40,* 149–165.

Cowan, D., Osselton, D., & Robinson, S. (2006). Drug testing. In D. Nutt, T. W. Robbins, G. V. Stimson, M. Ince, & A. Jackson (Eds.), *Drugs and the future* (pp. 315–336). New York: Academic Press.

Cox, S., Posner, S. F., Kourtis, A. P., & Jamieson, D. J. (2008). Hospitalizations with amphetamine abuse among pregnant women. *Obstetrics & Gynecology, 111*(2), 341–347.

Cozolino, L. (2002). *The neuroscience of psychotherapy.* New York: W.W. Norton & Co Inc.

Craig, R. J. (2004). *Counseling the alcohol and drug dependent client.* New York: WW Norton & Company, Inc.

Crawford, H. (2011). Why 30 years of AIDS is only the tip of the iceberg. *New Scientist, 210*(2808), 12.

Crego, A., Holguin, S. R., Prada, M., Mota, N., et al. (2009). Binge drinking affects attentional and visual working memory process in young university students. *Alcoholism Clinical and Experimental Research, 33*(11), 1870–1879.

Crews, F. T. (2008). Alcohol-related neurodegeneration and recovery. *Alcohol Research & Health, 31,* 377–388.

Croft, H. A. (2006). Physical handling of prescription stimulants. *Pediatric Annals, 35*(8), 86–97.

Crosby, A. E., Espitia-Hardeman, V., Hill, H. A., Ortega, L., et al. (2009). Alcohol and suicide among racial/ethnic populations—17 states, 2005-2006. *Morbidity and Mortality Weekly Report, 58*(23), 637–641.

Cross, C. L., & Ashley, L. (2007). Trauma and addiction. *Journal of Psychosocial Nursing, 45*(1), 24–31.

Crowley, T. J. (2007). Adolescents and substance-related disorders. In J. B. Saunders, M. A. Schuckit, P. J. Sirovatka, & D. A. Reiger (Eds.), *Diagnostic issues in substance use disorders.* Washington, DC: American Psychiatric Association Press, Inc.

Crowley, T. J., & Sakai, J. (2005a). Inhalant-related disorders. In B. J. Sadock & V. A. Sadock (Eds.), *Kaplan & Sadock's comprehensive textbook of psychiatry* (8th ed.). New York: Lippincott, Williams & Wilkins.

Crowley, T. J., & Sakai, J. (2005b). Neurobiology of alcohol. In M. Galanter & H. D. Kleber (Eds.), *Textbook of substance abuse treatment* (3rd ed.). Washington, DC: American Psychiatric Press, Inc.

Cruz, M. T., Bajo, M., Schweitzer, P., & Roberto, M. (2008). Shared mechanisms of alcohol and other drugs. *Alcohol Research & Health, 31*(2), 137–147.

Cunniff, C. (2003, May 28). *Fetal alcohol syndrome: Diagnosis, treatment, and public health.* Paper presented at the Continuing Medical Education Symposium Gundersen-Lutheran Medical Center, La Crosse, Wisconsin.

Cunningham, J. A., Sobell, L. C., Gavin, D. R., Sobell, M. B., et al. (1997). Assessing motivation for change: Preliminary development and evaluation of a scale measuring the benefits and costs of changing alcohol or drug use. *Psychology of Addictive Behaviors, 11*, 107–114.

Cunningham, J. K., Liu, L. M., & Callaghan, R. (2009). Impact of US and Canadian pre-cursor regulation on methamphetamine purity in the United States. *Addiction, 104*, 441–453.

Cupp, M. J. (1999). Herbal remedies: Adverse effects and drug interactions. *American Family Physician, 59*, 1239–1244.

Curley, B. (2007). *U.S. mayors declare drug war a failure.* Retrieved from http:www.jointogether.org/news/features/2007/us-mayors-declare-drug-war.html

Curran, H. V., Collins, R., Fletcher, S., Kee, S. C. Y., et al. (2003). Older adults and withdrawal from benzodiazepine hypnotics in general practice: Effects on cognitive function, sleep, mood and quality of life. *Psychological Medicine, 33*, 1223–1237.

Cutler-Triggs, C., Fryer, G. E., Miyoshi, T. J., & Weitzman, M. (2008). Increased rates and severity of child and adult food insecurity in households with adult smokers. *Archives of Pediatric and Adolescent Medicine, 162*(11), 1056–1062.

Daeppen, J. B., Gache, P., Landry, U., Sekera, E., et al. (2002). Symptom-triggered vs fixed-schedule doses of benzodiazepine for alcohol withdrawal. *Archives of Internal Medicine, 162*, 1117–1121.

Daghestani, A. N., Dinwiddie, S. H., & Hardy, D. W. (2001). Antisocial personality disorder in and out of correctional and forensic settings. *Psychiatric Annals, 31*(7), 441–446.

Dajer, T. (2005). Why is she so short of breath? *Discover, 26*(3), 21–22.

Dalen, J. T. (2007). Aspirin resistance: Is it real? Is it clinically significant? *The American Journal of Medicine, 120*, 1–4.

Daley, D. C., & Marlatt, G. A. (2005). Relapse prevention. In J. H. Lowinson, P. Ruiz, R. B. Millman, & J. G. Langrod (Eds.), *Substance abuse: A comprehensive textbook* (4th ed.). New York: Lipponcott, Williams & Wilkins.

Daley, D. C., & Marlatt, G. A. (2006). *Overcoming your alcohol or drug problem (therapist's guide).* New York: Oxford University Press.

Daling, J. R., Doody, D. R., Sun, X., Trabert, B. L., et al. (2010). Association of marijuana use and the incidence of testicular germ cell tumors. *Cancer, 115*, 1215–1223.

Daling, J. R., Doody, D. R., Traubert, B. L., Weiss, N. S., et al. (2009). Association of marijuana use and the incidence of testicular germ cell tumors. *Cancer, 115*(6), 1223–2009.

Dalley, J. W., Fryer, T. D., Brichard, L., Robinson, E. S., et al. (2007). Nucleus accumbens D2/3 receptors predict trait impulsivity and cocaine reinforcement. *Science, 315*, 1267–1270.

Danaei, G., Ding, E. L., Mozaffarian, D., Taylor, B., et al. (2009). The preventable causes of death in the United States: Comparative risk assessment of dietary, lifestyle and metabolic risk factors. *PLoS Medicine.* Retrieved from http:ww//www.plosmedicine.org/article/info%3Adoi%2F10.1317%Fjournal.Pmed.1000058

Dangers of benzodiazepine abuse during MMT. (2009). *Addiction Treatment Forum, 19*(2), 6–7.

Danjou, P., Paty, P., Fruncillo, R., Worthington, P., et al. (1999). A comparison of the residual effects of zaleplon and zolpidem following administration 5 to 2 h before awakening. *Analytical Chemistry, 45*(3), 777–780.

Dani, J. A., Kosten, T. R., & Benowitz, N. L. (2009). The pharmacology of nicotine and tobacco. In R. K. Ries, D. A. Fiellin, S. C. Miller, & R. Saitz (Eds.), *Principles of addiction medicine* (4th ed., pp. 179–191). New York: Lippincott, Williams & Wilkins.

Daniels, A. (2009). Is there a "right" to health care? *The Wall Street Journal.* Retrieved from http://online.wsj.com/article_email/sb10001424052970203517304574306170677645070

Danovitch, I., & Gorelick, D. A. (2012). State of the art treatments for cannabis dependence. *Psychiatric Clinics of North America, 35*(2), 309–326.

D'Arcy, Y. (2007). Conquering pain. *Nursing 2005, 35*(3), 36–41.

Darwin, J., & Reich, K. (2011, March 4). *Lessons from the waterfront: Crisis, PTSD and addiction.* Paper presented at the Treating the Addictions conference sponsored by the Department of Psychiatry of the Cambridge Hospital, Boston, MA.

Daubin, C., Quentin, C., Goulle, J., Guillotin, D., et al. (2008). Refractory shock and asystole related to tramadol overdose. *Clinical Toxicology, 45*(8), 961–964.

Dave, M. J., Miceli, K. P., & Modha, P. (2008). *Psychiatric medicine.* Philadelphia: Lippincot, Williams & Wilkins.

Davey, M. (2005). *Grisly effects of one drug: "Meth Mouth."* Retrieved from http:www.nytimes.com. /2005/06/11/national/11meth.hmtl?ex-1120104000en=82c41a6f61399c01&emc-etal)

Davidson, R. (1998). The transtheoretical model. In W. R. Miller & N. Heather (Eds.), *Treating addictive behaviors* (2nd ed.). New York: Plenum.

Davies, P. (2005). Long-dormant threat surfaces: Deaths from hepatitis C are expected to jump. *The Wall Street Journal, CCXLV*(105), D-1.

Davis, W. R., & Johnson, B. D. (2008). Prescription opioid use, misuse, and diversion among street drug users in New York City. *Drug & Alcohol Dependence, 92*(1–3), 267–276.

Davison, K. P., Pennebaker, J. W., & Dickerson, S. S. (2000). Who talks? *American Psychologist, 55,* 205–217.

Day, E., Bentham, P., Callaghan, R., Kuruvilla, T., et al. (2004). Thiamine for Wernicke-Korsakoff syndrome in people at risk from alcohol abuse. *The Cochrane Database of Systematic Reviews, 2.*

Day-Cameron, J. M., Muse, L., Hauenstein, J., Simmons, L., et al. (2009). Alcohol use by undergraduate students on their 21st birthday: Predictors of actual consumption, anticipated consumption and normative beliefs. *Psychology of Addictive Behaviors, 23,* 695–701.

Dayton, T. (2005). Discovering life after blame: A new model of the addicted/traumatized family system. *Counselor, 6*(1), 12–17.

Deadly drug adulterants. (2008). *Forensic Drug Abuse Advisor, 20*(6), 47–48.

"Deadly in Pink" report targets big tobacco. (2009). Retrieved from http://tobacco freekids.org/reports/wo,en_new/report/deadlyinpink_02182009_FINAL.pdf

de la Torre, R., Farre, M., Roset, P. N., Pizarro, N., et al. (2004). Human pharmacology of MDMA: Pharmacokinetics, metabolism, and disposition. *Therapeutic Drug Monitoring, 26*(2), 137–144.

De Bellis, M. D., Clark, D. B., Beers, S. R., Soloff, P. H., et al. (2000). Hippocampal volume in adolescent-onset alcohol use disorders. *American Journal of Psychiatry, 157,* 737–744.

DeBerardis, G., Lucisano, G., D'Ettore, A., Pelegrini, F., et al. (2012). Association of aspirin use with major bleeding in patients with and without diabetes. *Journal of the American Medical Association, 307,* 2286–2294.

Debusmann, B. (2006). *US war on drugs: Elusive victory, disputed statistics.* Retrieved from http://www.alertnet.org/thenews/newsdesk/NO371862.htm

Delaney-Black, V., Chiodo, L. M., Hannigan, J. H., Greenwald, M. K., et al. (2010). Just say "I don't": Lack of concordance between teen report and biological measures of drug use. *Pediatrics, 126*(5), 887–893.

DeLeon, G. (2008). Therapeutic communities. In M. Galanter & H. D. Kleber (Eds.), *Textbook of substance abuse treatment.* Washington, DC: American Psychiatric Association, Inc.

Delingpole, J. (2009). *Welcome to Obamaland—I have seen the future and it doesn't work.* Washington, DC: Regnery Publishing, Inc.

Demboski, A. (2009). Marijuana smoke is a carcinogen, California board rules. *Mercury News.* Retrieved from http://www.mercurynews.com/politics/ci_12644670?click_check=1

Department of Health and Human Services. (2010). *Results from the 2008 national survey on drug use and health: National findings.* Rockville, MD: Author.

Dervaux, A., Bayle, F. J., Laqueille, X., Bourdel, M. C., et al. (2001). Is substance abuse in schizophrenia related to impulsivity, sensation seeking, or anhedonia? *American Journal of Psychiatry, 158,* 494–494.

Deteriorating home life puts kids at risk. (2009). *New Scientist, 201*(2701), 14.

DeVane, C. L. (2004). Principles of pharmacokinetics and pharmacodynamics. In A. F. Schatzberg &

C. B. Nemeroff (Eds.), *Textbook of psychopharmacology* (3rd ed.). Washington, DC: American Psychiatric Publishing, Inc.

DeVane, C. L. (2009). Sex differences in pharmacokinetics and pharmacodynamics. In K. T. Brady, S. E. Back, & S. F. Greenfield (Eds.), *Women & addiction*. New York: Guilford.

DeVane, C. L., & Nemeroff, C. B. (2002). 2002 Guide to psychotropic drug interactions. *Primary Psychiatry, 9*(3), 28–51.

Devour, M. C. (1999). What is moderate drinking? *Alcohol Health & Research World, 23*(1), 5–14.

DeWilde, B., Dom, G., Hulstjn, W., & Wabbe, B. (2007). Motor functioning and alcohol dependence. *Alcoholism: Clinical and Experimental Research, 31,* 1820–1825.

Dheda, K., & Migliori, G. B. (2011). The global rise of extensively drug-resistant tuberculosis: Is the time to bring back sanatoria now overdue? *The Lancet.* doi:10.1016/S0140-6736(11)61062-3

Dickensheets, S. (2001). Roid rage. *Playboy, 48*(7), 128–129, 156–162.

Dickinson, A. (2000). Smoke screen. *Time, 155*(11), 92.

DiClemente, C. C., Bellino, L. E., & Neavins, T. M. (1999). Motivation for change and alcoholism treatment. *Alcohol Health and Research World, 23*(2), 86–92.

DiClemente, C. C., & Prochaska, J. O. (1998). Toward a comprehensive, transtheoretical model of change. In W. R. Miller & N. Heather (Eds.), *Treating addictive behaviors* (2nd ed.). New York: Plenum.

Dienstag, J. J. (2006). Hepatitis C: A bitter harvest. *Annuals of Internal Medicine, 144,* 770–771.

Dienstag, J. J. (2008). Acute viral hepatitis. In A. S. Fauci, E. Braunwald, D. L. Kasper, S. L. Hauser, D. L. Longo, J. L. Jameson, & J. Loscalzo (Eds.), *Harrison's principles of internal medicine* (17th ed.). New York: McGraw-Hill Medical.

Diercks, D. B., Gonarow, G. C., Kirk, J. D., Jois-Bilowich, P., et al. (2008). Illicit stimulant use in a United States heart failure population presenting to the emergency department (from the Acute Decompensated Heart Failure National Registry Emergency Module). *American Journal of Cardiology, 102*(9), 1216–1219.

DiFranza, J. R., Savageau, J. A., Fletcher, K., Pbert, L., et al. (2007). Susceptibility to nicotine dependence: The development and assessment of nicotine in youth 2 study. *Pediatrics, 120*(4), e-974–e983. doi:10.1542/peds.2007-0027

Dijkstra, B. J. M., De Jong, C. A. J., Krabbe, P. F. M., & van der Staak, C. P. F. (2008). Prediction of abstinence in opioid-dependent patients. *Journal of Addiction Medicine, 2*(4), 194–201.

Dill, P. L., & Wells-Parker, E. (2006). Court-managed treatment for convicted drinking drivers. *Alcohol Research & Health, 29*(1), 41–48.

Diller, L. H. (1998). *Running on Ritalin.* New York: Bantam Books.

Dilts, S. L., & Dilts, S. L. (2005). Opioids. In R. J. Frances, S. I. Miller, & A. H. Mack (Eds.), *Clinical textbook of addictive disorders* (3rd ed.). New York: Guilford.

Dimneff, L., & Marlatt, G. A. (1995). Relapse prevention. In R. K. Hester & W. R. Miller (Eds.), *Handbook of alcoholism treatment approaches* (2nd ed.). New York: Allyn & Bacon.

Disney, E. R., Elkins, I. J., McGue, M., & Iacono, W. G. (1999). Effects of ADHD, conduct disorder, and gender on substance abuse in adolescence. *American Journal of Psychiatry, 156,* 1515–1521.

Dixit, A. R., & Crum, R. M. (2000). Prospective study of depression and risk of heavy alcohol use in women. *American Journal of Psychiatry, 157,* 751–758.

D'Nofrino, G., & Degutis, L. C. (2004). Screening and brief intervention in the emergency department. *Alcohol Research & Health, 28*(2), 63–72.

Dobbs, D. (2011). Beautiful brains. *National Geographic, 200*(4), 36–59.

Dobbs, L. (2007). *The war within, killing ourselves.* Retrieved from http://www.cnn.com/2007/US/02/13/Dobbs.Feb14/index.html

Doble, A., Martin, I. L., & Nutt, D. (2004). *Calming the brain.* New York: Martin-Dunitz.

Doctors often skip health behavior conversations with teens. (2008, December 1). News release. Center for the Advancement of Health.

Does teen drug rehab cure addiction or create it? (2010). *Time.* Retrieved from http://www.time.com/time/health/article/0,8599,2003160-1,00.html

Doghramji, K. (2003). When patients can't sleep. *Current Psychiatry, 2*(5), 40–50.

Doidge, N. (2007). *The brain that changes itself.* New York: Viking.

Dokoupil, T. (2009). Can booze cure men's fashion phobia? Upscale stores hope spirits boost sales. *Newsweek.* Retrieved from http://blog.newsweek.comblogs/thehumancondition/archive/2009/07/08/can-booze-cure-men's-fashion-phobia?

Dolan, K., Rouen, D., & Kimber, J. (2004). An overview of the use of urine, hair, sweat and saliva to detect drug use. *Drug & Alcohol Review, 23*(2), 213–217.

Dole, V. P. (1988). Implications of methadone maintenance for theories of narcotic addiction. *Journal of the American Medical Association, 260,* 3025–3029.

Dole, V. P. (1989). Letter to the editor. *Journal of the American Medical Association, 261*(13), 1880.

Dole, V. P. (1995). On federal regulation of methadone treatment. *Journal of the American Medical Association, 274,* 1307.

Dole, V. P., & Nyswander, M. A. (1965). Medical treatment for diacetylmorphine (heroin) addiction. *Journal of the American Medical Association, 193,* 545–656.

Donaher, P. A., & Welsh, C. (2006). Managing opioid addiction with buprenorphine. *American Family Physician, 73,* 1573–1578.

D'Onofrio, B. M., Ricket, M. E., Langstrom, N., Donahue, K. L., et al. (2012). Familial confounding of the association between maternal smoking during pregnancy and offspring substance use and problems. *Archives of General Psychiatry, 69*(11), 1140–1150.

D'Onogrio, G., Rathlev, N. K., Ulrich, A., Rish, S. S., et al. (1999). Lorazepam for the prevention of recurrent seizures related to alcohol. *New England Journal of Medicine, 340,* 915–919.

Donovan, D. M. (2005). Assessment of addictive behaviors for relapse prevention. In D. M. Donovan & G. A. Marlatt (Eds.), *Assessment of addictive behaviors* (2nd ed.). New York: Guilford.

Donovan, J. E., Molina, B. S. G., & Kelly, T. M. (2009). Alcohol outcome expectancies as socially shared and socialized beliefs. *Psychology of Addictive Behaviors, 23,* 248–259.

Don't buy it. (2006). *New Scientist, 190*(2547), 15.

Dooldeniya, M. D., Khafagy, R., Mashaly, H., Browning, A. J., et al. (2007). Lower abdominal pain in women after binge drinking. *British Medical Journal, 335,* 992–993.

Doubeni, C. A., Li, W., Fouayzi, H., & DiFranza, J. R. (2008). Perceived accessibility as a predictor of youth smoking. *Annals of Family Medicine, 6,* 323–330.

Doubeni, C. A., Reed, G., & DiFranza, J. R. (2010). Early course of nicotine dependence in adolescent smokers. *Pediatrics.* doi:10.1542/ peds.2009-0238

Doweiko, H. E. (1999). Substance use disorders as a symptom of a spiritual disease. In O. J. Morgan & M. Jordan (Eds.), *Addiction and spirituality: A multidisciplinary approach.* St. Louis, MO: Chalice Press.

Doweiko, H. E. (2002). Dreams as an unappreciated therapeutic avenue for cognitive-behavioral therapists. *Journal of Cognitive Psychotherapy, 16*(1), 29–38.

Dowling, G. J., Weiss, S. R. B., & Condon, T. P. (2008). Drugs of abuse and the aging brain. *Neuropsychopharmacology, 33,* 209–218.

Drake, R. E. (2007). Management of substance use disorder in schizophrenia patients: Current guidelines. *CNS Spectrums, 12*(10), 27–32.

Drake, R. E., Essock, S. M., Shaner, A., Carey, A., et al. (2001). Implementing dual diagnosis services for clients with mental illness. *Psychiatric Services, 52,* 469–476.

Drake, R. E., & Mueser, K. T. (2002). Co-occurring alcohol use disorder and schizophrenia. *Alcohol Research & Health, 26,* 99–102.

Drake, R. E., Mueser, K. T., Brunette, M. F., & McHugo, G. J. (2004). A review of treatments for people with severe mental illnesses and co-occurring substance use disorders. *Psychiatric Rehabilitation Journal, 27*(4), 360–374.

Dregan, A., Stewart, R., & Guillford, M. C. (2012). Cardiovascular risk factors and cognitive decline in adults aged 50 and ove: A population based cohort study. *Age and Aging, 41*(6), 701.

Dreher, M. C., Nugent, K., & Hudgins, R. (1994). Prenatal marijuana exposure and neo-natal outcomes in Jamaica: An ethnographic study. *Pediatrics, 93,* 254–260.

Drew, S. M., Wilkins, K. M., & Trevisan, L. A. (2010). Managing medications and alcohol misuse by your older patients. *Current Psychiatry, 9*(2), 21–24, 27–28, 41.

Driessen, M., Meier, S., Hill, A., Wetterling, T., et al. (2001). The course of anxiety, depression and drinking behaviors after completed detoxification in alcoholics with and without comorbid anxiety and depressive disorders. *Alcohol & Alcoholism, 36,* 249–255.

Drinking and driving. (1996). *Alcohol Alert, 37.* Washington, DC: National Institute on Alcohol Abuse and Alcoholism.

Druesne-Peccolo, D., Tehard, B., Mallet, Y., Gerber, M., et al. (2009). Alcohol and genetic polymorphisms: Effect on risk of alcohol-related cancer. *The Lancet Oncology, 10,* 173–180.

Drug and Alcohol Services Information System. (2007). *Adolescent treatment admissions by gender: 2005.* Washington, DC: Substance abuse and Mental Health Services.

Drug disarray. (2009). *New Scientist, 204*(2733), 6.

Drug overdose deaths—Florida, 2003–2009. (2011). *Morbidity and Mortality Weekly Report, 60*(26), 869–872.

Drug Policy Alliance. (2011). *Drugs Courts are not the answer: Toward a health-centered approach to drug use.* Press release. Retrieved from http://222.drug policy.org/docUploads/DrugCourtsAreNotThe Answer.pdf

Drug war is lost. (2005). *New Scientist, 185*(1490), 4.

Drug war success claims challenged. (2006). Retrieved from http//www.jointogether.org./news/head-lines/ inthenews/2006/drug-war-success-claims.html

Drugs drive politicians out of their minds. (2009). *New Scientist, 201*(2695), 5.

Drugs in sports: New problems in doping detection. (2009). *Forensic Drug Abuse Advisor, 21*(9), 68–69.

Drummer, O. H., & Odell, M. (2001). *The forensic pharmacology of drugs of abuse.* New York: Oxford University Press.

Dube, C., Rostom, A., Lewin, G., Tsertsvandez, A., et al. (2007). The use of aspirin for primary prevention of colorectal cancer: A systematic review prepared for the U.S. prevention services task force. *Archives of General Medicine, 146,* 365–375.

Dube, S. R., Anda, R. F., Felitti, V. J., Chapman, D. P., et al. (2001). Childhood abuse, household dysfunction, and the risk of attempted suicide throughout the life span. *Journal of the American Medical Association, 286,* 3089–3096.

Dube, S. R., Asman, K., Malarcher, A., Carabollo, R., et al. (2009). Cigarette smoking among adults and trends in smoking cessation—United States, 2008. *Morbidity & Mortality Weekly Report, 58,* 1227–1232.

Dubovsky, S. (2005). Benzodiazepine receptor agonists and antagonists. In B. J. Sadock & V. A. Sadock (Eds.), *Kaplan & Sadock's comprehensive textbook of psychiatry* (8th ed.). New York: Lippincott, Williams & Wilkins.

Dudley, R. (2004). Ethanol, fruit ripening, and the historical origins of human alcoholism in primate frugivory. *Integrative and Comparative Biology, 44*(94), 315–323.

Dumais, A., Lesage, M., Alda, M., Rouleau, G., et al. (2005). Risk factors for suicide in major depression: A case controlled study of impulsive and aggressive behaviors in men. *American Journal of Psychiatry, 162,* 2116–2124.

Dunigan, R. (2009, March 6). *Addiction treatment with diverse populations.* Paper presented at the "Treating the Addictions" seminar hosted by the Harvard Medical School Department of Continuing Education, Boston, MA.

Dunlap, E., Johnson, B. D., Kotarba, J. A., & Fackler, J. J. (2010). Macro-level social forces and micro-level consequences: Poverty, alternate occupations and drug dealing. *Journal of Ethnicity in Substance Abuse, 9*(2), 115–127.

Dunn, K. M., Sauders, K. W., Rutter, C. M., Banta-Green, S. C., et al. (2010). Opioid prescriptions for chronic pain and overdose. *Archives of Internal Medicine, 152,* 85–92.

Dunn, R. (2013). The 10,000 year bender. *New Scientist, 217*(2901), 38–41.

Dyehouse, J. M., & Sommers, M. S. (1998). Brief intervention after alcohol-related injuries. *Nursing Clinics of North America, 33,* 93–104.

Eagleman, D. (2007). 10 Unsolved mysteries of the brain. *Discover, 28*(8), 54–59, 75.

Earlywine, M. (2005). Cannabis: Attending to subjective effects to improve drug safety. In *Mind altering drugs: The science of subjective experience* (pp. 240–258). New York: Oxford University Press.

Earnshaw, V. A., Bogart, L. M., Dovidio, J. F., & Williams, D. R. (2013). Stigma and racial/ethnic HIV disparities: Moving towards resilience. *American Psychologist, 68*(4), 225–236.

Eaton, D. K., Kann, L., Kinchen, S., Shanklin, S., et al. (2010). Youth risk surveillance—United States, 2009. *Weekly and Morbidity Weekly Report, 55*(SS05), 1–42.

Ebbert, J. O. (2009). Emerging drugs for the treatment of alcohol dependence. *Expert Opinion on Emerging Drugs, 14*(1), 23–32.

Eckholm, E. (2008). *Courts give addicts a chance to straighten out.* Retrieved from http://topics.nytimes .com/top/reference/timestopics/people/e/eckholm/ index.htmlinline=nyt-per

Echeburua, E., de Medina, R. B., & Aizpiri, J. (2005). Alcoholism and personality disorders: An exploratory study. *Alcohol & Alcoholism, 40*(4), 323–326.

Edenberg, H. J. (2007). The genetic of alcohol metabolism. *Alcohol Research & Health, 30,* 5–13.

Edlund, M. J., Booth, B. M., & Feldman, Z. L. (2009). Perceived need for treatment for alcohol use disorders: Results from two national surveys. *Psychiatric Services, 60,* 1618–1628.

Edlund, M. J., Martin, B. C., Devries, A., Fan, M. Y., et al. (2010). Trends in the use of opioids for chronic non-cancer pain among individuals with mental health and substance use disorders: The TROUP study. *Clinical Journal of Pain, 26*(1), 1–8.

Edlund, M. J., Steffick, D., Hudson, T., Harris, K. M., et al. (2007). Risk factors for clinically recognized opioid abuse and dependence among veterans using opioids for chronic, non-cancer pain. *Pain, 129*(3), 355–362.

Eggan, S. M., Hashimoto, T., & Lewis, D. A. (2008). Reduced cortical cannabinoid 1 receptor messenger RNA and protein expression in schizophrenia. *Archives of General Psychiatry, 65,* 772–784.

Egger, J. F., & Hebert, C. (2011). Buspirone: Anxiolytic, antidepressant, or neither? *Psychiatric Annals, 41*(3), 166–175.

Eisenberg, E. R., & Galloway, G. P. (2005). Anabolic-androgenic steroids. In J. H. Lowinson, P. Ruiz, R. B. Millman, & J. G. Langrod (Eds.), *Substance abuse: A comprehensive textbook* (4th ed.). New York: Lipponcott, Williams & Wilkins.

el-Guebaly, N. (2008). Cross-cultural aspects of addiction. In M. Galanter & H. D. Kleber (Eds.), *The American psychiatric publishing textbook of substance abuse treatment.* Washington, DC: American Psychiatric Publishing, Inc.

el-Guebaly, N., Cathcart, J., Currie, S., Brown, D., et al. (2002). Smoking cessation approaches for persons with mental illness or addictive disorders. *Psychiatric Services, 53,* 1166–1170.

Ellgren, M., Spano, S. M., & Hurd, Y. L. (2006). Adolescent cannabis exposure alters opium intake and opioid limbic neuronal populations in adult rats. *Neuropsychopharmacology.* (Advance publication online: doi:10.1038/sjnpp.1301127)

Ellickson, P. L., Martino, S. C., & Collins, R. L. (2004). Marijuana use from adolescence to young adulthood: Multiple developmental trajectories and their associated outcomes. *Health Psychology, 23*(3), 299–307.

Ellingrod, V. L. (2013). Drug interactions with tobacco smoke: Implications for patient care. *Current Psychiatry, 12*(1), 12–16.

Elliott, C. (2010). *White coat, black hat.* Boston: Beacon Press.

Elliott, F. A. (1992). Violence. *Archives of Neurology, 49,* 595–603.

Ellis, A., McInerney, J. F., DiGiuseppe, R., & Yeager, R. J. (1988). *Rational emotive therapy with alcoholics and substance abusers.* New York: Pergamon Press.

Ellison, J. M. (2012, March 5–9). *Mental health and mental illness in our aging population with treatment implications.* Symposium conducted by Harvard Medical School Department of Continuing Education, Key Largo, FL.

Elton, A., & Kilts, C. D. (2009). The role of sex differences in the drug addiction process. In K. T. Brady, S. E. Back, & S. F. Greenfield (Eds.), *Women & addiction.* New York: Guilford.

Encrenaz, G., Kovess-Masfethy, V., Jutand, M., Carmona, E., et al. (2009). Use of psychoactive substances and health care in response to anxiety and depressive disorders. *Psychiatric Services, 60*(3), 351–357.

Engel, G. (1977). The need for a new medical model: A challenge for biomedicine. *Science, 196,* 129–136.

Engels, R. C., & ter Bogt, T. (2004). Outcome expectancies and ecstasy use in visitors of rave parties in the Netherlands. *European Addiction Research, 10*(10), 152–162.

English, T. J. (2009). Dope. *Playboy, 56*(11), 66–68, 69, 150–156.

English, T. J. (2011). Narco Americano. *Playboy, 5*(2), 40–44, 119–120, 122–123, 126.

Epstein, J. A., Griffin, K. W., & Botvin, G. J. (2008). A social influence model of alcohol use for inner-city adolescents: Family drinking, perceived drinking norms, and perceived social benefits of drinking. *Journal of Studies on Alcohol and Drugs, 69,* 397–405.

Epstein, R. (2012). Sex and the society. *Discover, 33*(8), 56–58.

Epstein, R. (2013). Yet another stage of life? *Scientific American Mind, 23*(6), 18–19.

Erickson, C. K. (2007). *The science of addiction.* New York: W.W. Norton & Co.

Erlich, L. B. (2001). *A textbook of forensic addiction medicine and psychiatry.* Springfield, Illinois: Charles C. Thomas, Publisher, Ltd.

Erlich, P. F., Brown, J. K., & Drongowski, R. (2006). Characterization of the drug-positive adolescent trauma population: Should we, do we, and does it make a difference if we test? *Journal of Pediatric Surgery, 41*(5), 927–930.

Ernst, E. (2002). Complementary therapies for addictions: Not an alternative. *Addiction, 1,* 2–3.

Escalating DXM abuse among teenagers. (2007). *Forensic Drug Abuse Advisor, 19*(1), 2–3.

Espeland, K. E. (1997). Inhalants: The instant, but deadly high. *Pediatric Nursing, 23*(1), 82–86.

Estfan, B., Mahmoud, F., Shaheen, P., Davis, M. P., et al. (2007). Respiratory function during parenteral opioid titration for cancer pain. *Palliative Medicine, 21*(2), 81–86.

Eubanks, L. M., Rogers, C. J., Beuscher, I. V., Koob, G. F., et al. (2006). A molecular link between the active component of marijuana and Alzheimer's disease pathology. *Molecular Pharmaceutics.* doi:10.1021/mp060066mS1543-8384(06)00066-9

Europeans heaviest drinkers in the world. (2006). Retrieved from http://www.iol.co/za/index.php?et_id-31&art_id+vn20060604115400426c580480

Evans, K., & Sullivan, J. M. (2001). *Dual diagnosis* (2nd ed.). New York: Guilford press.

Ewart, R., Lausen, H., & Millian, D. (2009). Undisclosed changes in outcomes in randomized controlled trials: An observational study. *Annals of Family Medicine, 7,* 542–546.

Ewing, J. A. (1984). Detecting alcoholism: The CAGE questionnaire. *Journal of the American Medical Association, 252,* 1905–1907.

Ezzati, M., Henley, S. J., Lopez, A. D., & Thun, M. J. (2005). Role of smoking in global and regional cancer epidemiology: Current patterns and data needs. *International Journal of Cancer, 116*(6), 963–971.

Fadem, B. (2009). *Behavioral science* (5th ed.). New York: Wolters Kluwer, Lippincott, Williams & Wilkins.

Fahmy, V., Hatch, S., Hotopf, M., & Stewart, R. (2012). Prevalences of illicit drug use in people aged 50 years and over from two surveys. *Age and Aging.* doi:10.1093/ageing/ffs20 (First published online April 20, 2012).

Faith, C. H., Jiin-Cherng, Y., Chan, S. H. H., & Chang, A. Y. W. (2012). Bioenergetics failure and oxidative stress in brain stem mediates cardiovascular collapse associated with fatal methamphetamine intoxication. *PLoS One, 7*(1). doi:10.1371/journal.pone.0030589

Falco, M. (2005). US Federal drug policy. In J. H. Lowinson, P. Ruiz, R. B. Millman, & J. G. Langrod (Eds.), *Substance abuse: A comprehensive textbook* (4th ed.). New York: Lipponcott, Williams & Wilkins.

Fallon, J. H., Keator, D. B., Mbogori, J., Taylor, D., & Potkin, S. G. (2005). Gender: A major determinant of brain response to nicotine. *International Journal of Neuropsychopharmacology, 8*(1), 17–26.

Fauber, J., & Gabler, E. (2012). Chronic painkiller use booming among elderly. *Milwaukee Journal/Sentinel.* Retrieved from http://www.jsonline.com/watchdog/watchdogreports/narcotics-use-for-chronic-pain-soars-among-seniors-kg56kih-155555555.html

Fals-Stewart, W., O'Farrell, T. J., & Birchler, G. R. (2003). Family therapy techniques. In F. Rotgers, J. Morgenstern, & S. T. Walters (Eds.), *Treating substance abuse: Theory and technique* (2nd ed.). New York: Guilford.

Fals-Stewart, W., O'Farrell, T. J., & Birchler, G. R. (2004). Behavioral couple's therapy for substance abuse: Rationale, methods and findings. *Science & Practice perspectives, 2*(2), 30–40.

Fals-Stewart, W., Lam, W. K. K., & Kelley, M. (2009). Behavioral couple therapy. In K. T. Brady, S. E. Back, & S. F. Greenfield (Eds.), *Women & addiction.* New York: Guilford.

Farabee, D., Prendedrgast, M., & Carier, J. (2002). Alcohol, the "un-drug." *Psychiatric Services, 53,* 1375–1376.

Fatovich, D. M., McCourbrie, D. S., Song, S. J., Rosen, D. M., et al. (2010). Brain abnormalities detected on matnetic resonance imaging of amphetamine abusers presenting to an emergency department: A pilot study. *Medical Journal of Australia, 193*(5), 266–268.

Fauci, A. S., & Lane, H. C. (2008). Human immunodeficiency virus disease: AIDS and related disorders. In A. S. Fauci, E. Braunwald, D. L. Kasper, S. L. Hauser, D. L. Longo, J. L. Hameson, & J. Loscalzo (Eds.), *Harrison's principles of internal medicine* (17th ed.). New York: McGraw-Hill Medical.

Fauci, A. S., & Lane, H. C. (2010). HIV neurology. In S. L. Hauser & S. A. Josephson (Eds.), *Harrison's neurology in clinical medicine* (2nd ed.). New York: McGraw-Hill.

Fazel, S., Långstrom, N., Hjern, A., Grann, M., & Lichtenstein, P. (2009). Schizophrenia, substance abuse, and violent crime. *Journal of the American Medical Association, 301*(19), 2016–2023.

FDA revised guidelines, label warnings. (2004). *Forensic Drug Abuse Advisor, 16*(4), 26–27.

Feldman, H. S., Jones, K. L., Lindsay, S., Slymen, D., Klonoff-Cohen, H., Kao, K., Rao, & Chambers, C. (2012). Prenatal alcohol exposure patterns and alcohol-related birth defects and growth deficiencies: A prospective study. *Alcoholism: Clinical and Experimental Research.* doi:10.1111/j.1530-0277.2011.01664.x

Feilding, A., & Morrison, P. (2010). Safer skunk. *New Scientist, 205*(2774), 22–23.

Feldstein-Ewing, S. W., & Chung, T. (2013). Neuroimaging mechanisms of change in psychotherapy for addictive behaviors: Translational approaches that bridge biology and behavior. *Psychology of Addictive Behaviors, 27*(2), 329–335.

Felices, S. (2012). Out of the shadows. *Psychology Today, 45*(5), 38.

Feltstein, M. W., Alter, C. A., & See, R. E. (2007). Aripipazole blocks reinstatement of cocaine seeking in an animal model of relapse. *Biological Psychiatry, 61*(5), 582–590.

Fenton, M. C., Keyes, K. M., Martins, S. S., & Hasin, D. S. (2010). The role of a prescriptioon in anxiety medication use, abuse and dependence. *American Journal of Psychiatry, 167*, 1247–1253.

Fergusson, D. M., Boden, J. M., & Horwood, J. (2009). Tests of causal links between alcohol abuse or dependence and major depression. *Archives of General Psychiatry, 66*(3), 260–266.

Fetro, J. V., Coyle, K. K., & Pham, P. (2001). High risk behaviors among middle school students in a large majority-minority school district. *Journal of School Health, 71*(1), 30–37.

Fergusson, D. M., Horwood, J., Lunskey, M. T., & Madden, P. A. F. (2003). Early reactions to cannabis predict later dependence. *Archives of General Psychiatry, 60*, 1033–1039.

Fergusson, D. M., Boden, J. M., & Horwood, J. (2009). Tests of causal links between alcohol abuse or dependence and major depression. *Archives of General Psychiatry, 66*, 260–266.

Fernandez, H. H., Eisenschenk, S., & Okun, M. S. (2010). *Ultimate review for the neurology boards* (2nd ed.). New York: demosmedical.

Ferri, M., Amato, L., & Davoil, M. (2006). Alcoholics anonymous and other 12-step programs for alcohol dependence. *The Cochrane Database of Systematic Reviews, 3.*

Ferris, T. (2013). Planet fever. *Smithsonian, 43*(5), 32–36.

Feuillet, L., Mallet, S., & Sparad, M. (2006). Two girls with neurocutaneous symptoms cause by mothball intoxication. *New England Journal of Medicine, 355*, 423–424.

Field, A. E., Sonneville, K. R., Crosby, R. D., Swanson, S. A., Eddy, K. T., Camargo, C. A., Horton, N. D., & Micali, N. (2013). Prospective associations of concerns about physique and the development of obesity, binge drinking, and drug use among adolescent boys and young adult men. *JAMA Pediatrics, 168*(1), 34–39.

Fields, G. (2009). Why House Czar call for end to "war on drugs." *Wall Street Journal.* Retrieved from http://online.wsj.com/article/SB124225891527617397.html

Fields, R. D. (2009). Marijuana hurts some, helps others. *Scientific American Mind, 20*(5), 17.

Fiellin, D. A., Rosenheck, R. A., & Kosten, T. R. (2001). Office-based treatment for opioid dependence: Reaching new patient populations. *New England Journal of Medicine, 355*, 423–424.

Fiellin, D. A. (2008). Treatment of adolescent opioid dependence. *Journal of the American Medical Association, 300*, 1057–2058.

Figueredo, V. M. (1997). The effects of alcohol on the heart. *Postgraduate Medicine, 101*, 165–176.

Filley, C. M. (2004). Encephalopathies. In M. Rizzo & P. J. Elsinger (Eds.), *Behavioral neurology and neuropsychology.* Philadelphia: W.B. Saunders.

Fineschi, V., Riezzo, I., Centini, F., Sillingardi, E., et al. (2005). Anabolic steroid abuse and heart disease. *International Journal of Legal Medicine*, 1–6.

Finger, W. W., Lund, M., & Slagel, M. A. (1997). Medications that may contribute to sexual disorders: A guide to assessment and treatment in family practice. *Journal of Family Practice, 44*, 33–44.

Finnegan, L. P., & Kandall, S. R. (2008). Perinatal substance use. In M. Galanter & H. D. Kleber (Eds.), *Textbook of substance abuse treatment* (4th ed.). Washington, DC: American Psychiatric Press, Inc.

Finnegan, L. P., & Kandall, S. R. (2005). Maternal and neonatal effects of alcohol and drugs. In J. H. Lowinson, P. Ruiz, R. B. Miollman, & J. G. Langrod (Eds.), *Substance abuse: A comprehensive textbook* (4th ed.). New York: Lipponcott, Williams & Wilkins.

Fiore, M. C. (2006). *Tobacco use and dependence: Current recommendations and new treatment options.* Paper presented at the September 9th, 2006 Continuing Medical Education Symposium Gundersen-Lutheran Medical Center, La Crosse, Wisconsin.

Fiore, M. C., Hatsukam, D. K., & Baker, T. B. (2002). Effective tobacco dependence treatment. *Journal of the American Medical Association, 288*, 1768–1771.

Fiorillo, C. D., Tobler, P. N., & Schultz, W. (2003). Discrete coding of reward probability and uncertainity by dopamine neurons. *Science, 299,* 1898–1902.

First shots in the war on alcohol. (2009). *New Scientist, 204*(2730), 5.

Flaum, M., & Schultz, S. K. (1996). When does amphetamine-induced psychosis become schizophrenia? *American Journal of Psychiatry, 153,* 812–815.

Fleming, C. B., Mason, W. A., Mazza, J. J., Abbott, R. D., & Catalano, R. F. (2008). Latent growth modeling of the relationship bdtween depressive symptoms and substance use during adolescence. *Psychology of Addictive Behaviors, 22*(2), 186–197.

Fleming, N. (2010). The truth about mephedrone. *New Scientist, 206*(2757), 42–45.

Fisher, S., L., Bucholz, K. K., Reich, W., Fox, L., et al. (2006). Teenagers are right-parents do not know much: An analysis of adolescent-parent agreement on reports of adolescent substance use, abuse and dependence. *Alcoholism: Clinical and Experimental Research, 30*(10), 1699–1710.

Fleming, D. W., & Grew, J. P. (2008). *This is the U.S. on drugs.* Retrieved from http://www.latimes.com/news/opinion/commentry/la-oe-fleming5-2008julo5%2co%2C3205714.story

Fleming, M. F. (1997). Strategies to increase alcohol screening in health care settings. *Alcohol Health & Research World, 21,* 340–347.

Fleming, M., Mihic, S. J., & Harris, R. A. (2006). Ethanol. In L. L. Brunton, S. J. Lazo, & K. L. Parker (Eds.), *The pharmacological basis of therapeutics* (11th ed.). New York: McGraw-Hill.

Fletcher, A. M. (2013). *Inside Rehab.* New York: Viking Press.

Fletcher, M. (2003). *Sober for good: Variety of solutions for drinking problems.* Paper presented to the "Treating the Addictions" seminar hosted by the Dept. of Psych- iatry of the Cambridge Hospital, Boston, MA, March 8, 2003.

Flora, C. (2005). Tough love. *Psychology Today, 38*(6), 40–41.

Flower, K., Mendelson, N., & Galloway, G. P. (2009). GHB. In R. K. Ries, D. A. Fiellin, S. C. Miller, & R. Saitz (Eds.), *Principles of addiction medicine* (4th ed., pp. 113–115). New York: Lippincott, Williams & Wilkins.

Fogarty, M. (2003). Depending on cigarettes, counting on science. *The Scientist, 17*(6). Retrieved from http://www.the-scientist.com/yr2003/mar/feature_030324.html

Folks, D. G., & Burke, W. J. (1998). Sedative-hypnotics and sleep. *Clinics in Geriatric Medicine, 14,* 67–86.

Fonda, D. (2001). Why tobacco won't quit. *Time, 157*(26), 38–39.

Fong, T. W., Reid, R. C., & Parhami, I. (2012). Behavioral addictions—where to draw the lines? *Psychiatric Clinics of North America, 35,* 279–296.

Foroud, T., & Phillips, T. J. (2012). Assessing the genetic risk for alcohol use disorders. *Alcohol Research: Current Reviews, 34*(3), 266–272.

Fontana, R. J. (2008). Acute liver failure including acetaminophen overdose. *Medical Clinics of North America, 92,* 761–794.

Foote, J. (2006). *Evidence-based treatments meat reality: Misunderstandings, compromises, and promises.* Symposium presented by the Dept of Psychiatry at the Cambridge Hospital, Boston, MA, March 4, 2006.

Fored, C. M., Ejerblad, E., Linblad, P., Fryzek, J. P., et al. (2001). Acetaminophen, aspirin and chronic renal failure. *New England Journal of Medicine, 345,* 1801–1808.

Fortgang, E. (1999). Is pot bad for you? *Rolling Stone, 87,* 53, 101.

Forstein, M. (2002). *Sex, drugs and HIV: A clinician's nightmare.* Paper presented at the "Treating the Addictions" seminar presented by the Dept. of Psychiatry of the Cambridge Hospital, Boston, MA, February 2, 2002.

Forsyth, C. B., Tang, Y., Shaikh, M., Zhang, L., et al. (2009). Alcohol stimulates activation of snail, epidermal growth factor receptor signaling and biomarkers of epithelial-Mesenchymal transition in colon and breast cancers. *Alcoholism: Clinical and Experimental Research.* doi:10.1111/j.1530-0277.2009.01061.x

Fox, H., & Shina, R. (2009). Stress, neuroendocrine response and addiction in women. In K. T. Brady, S. E. Back, & S. F. Greenfield (Eds.), *Women & addiction.* New York: Guilford.

Frances, A. (2013). *Saving normal.* NewYork: William Morrow.

Franken, I. A. H., & Hendricks, V. M. (1999). Predicting outcome of inpatient detoxification of substance abusers. *Psychiatric Services, 50,* 813–817.

Franklin, D. (2012). Drug detectives. *Scientific American, 307*(4), 30, 32.

Franklin, J. E. (1989). Alcoholism among blacks. *Hospital & Community Psychiatry, 40,* 1120–1122, 1127.

Franklin, J., & Markarian, M. (2005). Substance abuse in minority populations. In R. J. Frances, S. I. Miller, & A. D. Mack (Eds.), *Clinical textbook of addictive disorders* (3rd ed.). New York: Guilford.

Frattaroli, E. (2001). *Healing the soul in the age of the brain*. New York: Penguin-Putnam, Inc.

Freedenthala, S., Vaugh, M. G., Jensona, J. M., & Howerd, M. O. (2007). Inhalant use and suicidality among incarcerated youth. *Drug and Alcohol Dependence, 90*(1), 81–88.

Freeborn, D. (1996). By the numbers. *Minneapolis Star-Tribune, XV*(94), D2.

Freedman, N. D., Silverman, D. T., Hollenbeck, A. R., Schatzkin, A., & Abnet, C. C. (2011). Association between smoking and risk of bladder cancer among men and women. *Journal of the American Medical Association, 306*(7), 729–736.

Freedman, R. (2008). Cannabis, inhibitory neurons, and the progressive course of schizophrenia. *American Journal of Psychiatry, 165*, 416–419.

Freese, T. E., Miotto, K., & Teback, C. J. (2002). The effects and consequences of selected club drugs. *Journal of Substance Abuse Treatment, 23*(2), 151–156.

Freiberg, M. S., & Samet, J. H. (2005). Alcohol and coronary heart disease: The answer awaits in a randomized controlled trial. *Circulation, 112*, 1379–1380.

Freiberg, M. S., Chang, C. C. H., Kuller, L. H., Skanderson, M., Lowy, E., Kraemer, K. L., Butt, A. A., Bidwell, G., Leaf, D., et al. (2013). HIV infection and the risk of acute myocardial infarction. *JAMA Internal Medicine.* doi:10.1001/jamainternalmed.2013.3278

Freimuth, M. (2005). *Hidden addictions*. New York: Jacob Aronson.

Fricchione, G. (2004). Generalized anxiety disorder. *New England Journal of Medicine, 251*, 675–682.

Friedman, L. F. (2012). Hello darkness, my new friend. *Psychology Today, 45*(6), 18.

Frierson, R. L., Melikian, M., & Wadman, P. C. (2002). Principles of suicide risk assessment. *Postgraduate Medicine, 112*(3), 65–71.

Froese, T., Woodward, A., & Ikegami, T. (2013). Turing instabilities in biology, culture and consciousness? On the enactive origins of symbolic material culture. *Addictive Behavior, 21*, 199–214.

Fromm, E. (1956). *The art of loving*. New York: Harper & Row.

Fromm, E. (1968). *The revolution of hope*. New York: Harper & Row.

Frood, A. (2008). The antagonism and the ecstasy. *New Scientist, 199*(2671), 42–43.

Fryer, S. L., Schweinburg, B. C., Bjorkquist, O. A., Frank, L. R., et al. (2009). Characterization of white matter microstructure in fetal alcohol spectrum disorders. *Alcoholism: Clinical and Experimental Research, 33*(3), 1–8.

Fudala, P. J., & O'Brien, C. P. (2005). Buprenorphine for the treatment of opioid addiction. In J. H. Lowinson, P. Ruiz, R. B. Millman, & J. G. Langrod (Eds.), *Substance abuse: A comprehensive textbook* (4th ed.). New York: Lipponcott, Williams & Wilkins.

Fulde, G. W. O., & Wodak, A. (2007). Ice: Cool drug or real problem? *Medical Journal of Australia, 186*, 334–335.

Fuller, P. G., & Sajatovic, M. (1999). *Drug information handbook for psychiatry*. Cleveland, OH: Lexi-Comp, Inc.

Furek, M. W. (2011). Deja vu: The war on drugs continued. *Counselor, 2*(3), 34–35.

Furstenberg, F. (2010). Passage to adulthood. *The Prevention Researcher, 17*(2), 3–7.

Furst, R. T., Herrmannk, C., Leung, R., Galea, J., & Hunt, K. (2004). Heroin diffusion in the mid-Hudson region of New York State. *Addiction, 99*(4), 431–441.

Fusar-Poli, P., Crippa, J. A., Bhattacharyya, S., Borgwardt, S. J., et al. (2009). Distinct effects of Δ-9-tetrahydrocannabinol and cannabidiol on neural activation during emotional processing. *Archives of General Psychiatry, 66*(1), 95–105.

Gahlinger, P. M. (2004). Club drugs: MDMA, gamma-hydroxybutyrate (GHB), Rohypnol, and Ketamine. *American Family Physician, 69*, 2919–2927.

Gahndi, N. R., Nunn, P., Kheda, K., & Schaaf, H. S. (2010). Multidrug-resistant and extensively drug-resistant tuberculosis: A threat to global control of tuberculosis. *The Lancet.* doi:10.1016/S0140-6736(10)60410-2

Gallagher, L. (2005). Stone age beer. *Discover, 26*(11), 54–59.

Galloway, G. P. (1997). Anabolic-androgenic steroids. In J. H. Lowinson, P. Ruiz, R. B. Millman, & J. G. Langrod (Eds.), *Substance abuse: A comprehensive textbook* (3rd ed.). New York: Williams & Wilkins.

Ganem, D., & Prince, A. M. (2004). Hepatitis b virus infection natural history and clinical consequencres. *New England Journal of Medicine, 350*, 1118–1129.

Garbutt, J. C., Kranzler, H. R., O'Malley, S., Gastfriend, D. R., et al. (2005). Efficacy and tolerability of long-acting injectable naltrexone for alcohol dependence. *Journal of the American Medical Association, 293,* 1617–1625.

Garbutt, J. C., Kapmov-Polevoy, A. B., Gallop, R., Kalka-Juhl, F., & Flannery, J. A. (2010). Efficacy and safety of baclofen for alcohol dependence: A randomized, double-blind, placebo-controlled trial. *Alcohol: Clinical & Experimental Research, 34*(11), 1849–1857.

Garfinkel, D., Zisapel, N., Wainstein, J., & Laudon, M. (1999). Facilitation of benzodiazepine discontinuation by melatonin. *Archives of Internal Medicine, 159,* 2456–2460.

Garrett, L. (1994). *The coming plague.* New York: Farrar, Straus Giroux.

Garrett, L. (2000). *Betrayal of trust.* New York: Hyperion.

Garriott, J. C. (1996). Pharmacology and tolicology of ethyl alcohol. In J. C. Garriott (Ed.), *Medioclegal aspects of alcohol* (3rd ed.). Tucson, AZ: Lawyers and Judges Publishing Co.

Garry, P. (1995). Oh, judge, can't you make them stop picking on me? *Minneapolis Star Tribune, XIV*(106), 10A.

Gastfriend, D. R. (2004a). *Patient treatment matching: What works for whom and why.* Paper presented to the Dept. of Psychiatry at the Cambridge Hospital, Boston, MA, March 8, 2004.

Gastfriend, D. R. (2004b). Patient placement criteria. In M. Galanter & H. D. Kleber (Eds.), *Textbook of substance abuse treatment* (3rd ed.). Washington, DC: American Psychiatric Press, Inc.

Gaysina, D., Fergsson, D. M., Leve, L. D., Horwood, J., Reiss, D., Shaw, D. S., Elam, K. K., Natsuaki, M. N., Neiderhiser, J. A., & Harold, G. T. (2013). Maternal smoking during pregnancy and offspring conduct problems. *JAMA Psychiatry.*

Gazzaniga, M. S. (2008). *Human.* New York: Harper Collins.

Gehricke, J. G., Potkin, S. G., Leslie, F. M., Loughlin, S. E., et al. (2009). Nicotine-induced brain metabolism associated with anger provocation. *Behavioral and Brain Functions, 5,* 5–19.

Gelernter, J., & Kranzler, H. R. (2008). Genetics of addiction. In M. Galanter & H. D. Kleber (Eds.), *The American psychiatric publishing textbook of substance abuse treatment.* Washington, DC: American Psychiatric Publishing, Inc.

Gemenetzidis, E., Bose, A., Riaz, A. M., Chaplin, T., et al. (2009). FOXM1 upregulation is an early event in human squamous cell carcinoma and is enhanced by nicotine during malignant transformation. *PLos One.* Retrieved from http://www.plosone.org/article/info2F10.1371%2Fjournal.pone.0004849

Gendel, M. H. (2006). Substance misuse and substance-related disorders in forensic psychiatry. *Psychiatric Clinics of North America, 29,* 649–673.

Genetics of drug addiction: The memory connection. (2009). *Addiction Treatment Forum, 18*(1), 6.

Genkinger, J. M., Spiegelman, D., Anderson, K. E., Bergkvist, L., et al. (2009). Alcohol intake and pancreatic cancer risk: A pooled analysis of fourteen cohort studies. *Cancer Epidemiology, Biomarkers & Prevention, 18,* 765–776.

George, R., & Brignard, C. (2007). Lethal opioids or dangerous prescribers? *Palliative Medicine, 21*(2), 77–80.

George, T. P., & Weinberger, A. H. (2008). Nicotine and tobacco. In M. Galanter & H. D. Kleber (Eds.), *Textbook of substance abuse treatment.* Washington, DC: American Psychiatric Association, Inc.

Geppert, C. M. A. (2008). Aristotle, augustine, and addiction. *Psychiatric Times, XXV*(7), 40–42.

Geppert, C. M., & Minkoff, K. (2004). Issues in dual diagnosis: Diagnosis, treatment and new research. *Psychiatric Times, XXI*(4), 103–107.

Gerada, C. (2005). Drug misuse: A review of treatments. *Clinical Medicine, 51,* 69–73.

Gerber, Y., Rose, L. J., Goldbourt, U., Genyamini, Y., et al. (2009). Smoking status and long-term survival after first acute myocardial infarction. *Journal of the American College of Cardiology, 54,* 2383–2387.

Gernstein, J. (2003). *SMART recovery: A group CBT approach to addictions.* Paper presented at the "Treating The Addictions" symposium hosted by the Dept. of Psychiatry of the Cambridge Hospital, Boston, MA, March 8, 2003.

Gessel, S. B., Tesdahl, & Ruchman, R. (2012). The distribution of physical activity in an after-school friendship network. *Pediatrics.*

Get over it. (2006). *New Scientist, 190*(2550), 5.

Getzfeld, A. R. (2006). *Essentials of abnormal psychology.* New York: John Wiley.

Ghaemi, S. N. (2011). Volkswagen psychopharmacology. *Psychiatric Times, XXVIII*(5), 9.

Ghaffar, O., & Feinstein, A. (2008). Multiple sclerosis and cannabis: A cognitive and psychiatric study. *Neurology, 2008.*

Ghoneim, M. M. (2004a). Drugs and human memory (part 1). *Anesthesiology, 100,* 987–1002.

Ghoneim, M. M. (2004b). Drugs and human memory (part 2). *Anesthesiology, 100,* 1277–1297.

Ghosh, D., Mishra, M. K., Das, S., Kumar, D., et al. (2009). Tobacco carcinogen induces microglial activation and subsequent neuronal damage. *Journal of NeuroChemistry.*

Giacchino, S., & Houdek, D. (1998). Ruptured varicies! *RN, 61*(5), 33–36.

Giancola, P. R., Levinson, C. A., Corman, M. D., Godlaski, A. J., et al. (2009). Men and women alcohol and aggression. *Experimental and Clinical Psychopharmacology, 17*(3), 154–164.

Giannini, A. J. (2000). An approach to drug abuse, intoxication and withdrawal. *American Family Physician, 61,* 2763–2774.

Gianoli, M. O., & Petrakis, I. L. (2013). Pharmaco-therapy for comorbid depression and alcohol dependence. *Current Psychiatry, 12*(1), 24–32.

Gibson, A., Degenhardt, L., Mattick, R. P., et al. (2008). Exposure to opioid maintenance treatment reduces long term mortality. *Addiction, 103*(3), 462–468.

Gilbert, L., El-Bassel, N., Chang, M., Wu, E., & Roy, L. (2011). Substance use and partner violence among urban women seeking emergency care. *Psychology of Addictive Behaviors, 26*(2), 226–235.

Gilbertson, R., Ceballos, N. A., Prather, R., & Nixon, S. J. (2009). Effects of acute alcohol consumption in older and younger adults: Perceived impairment versus psychmotor performance. *Journal of Studies on Alcohol and Drugs, 70* (2), 242–252.

Giles, J. (2009). Police crackdowns may encourage drug use. *New Scientist, 203*(2715), 9.

Giles, J. (2008). The immunity fix. *New Scientist, 199*(2667), 42–45.

Gilbertson, R., Caballos, N. A., Prather, R., & Nixon, S. J. (2009). Effects of alcohol consumption in older and younger adults: Perceived impairment versus psy-chomotor performance. *Journal of Studies on Alcohol and Drugs, 70,* 242–252.

Giles, J. (2009). Doubts raised over brain scan findings. *New Scientist, 201*(2691), 11.

Gillham, O. (2005). What happened to ACA adult children of alcoholics? *Counselor, 6*(1), 24.

Gilman, J. M., Bjork, J. M., & Hommer, D. W. (2007). Parental alcohol use and brain volumes in early and late onset alcoholics. *Biological Psychiatry, 62,* 607–615.

Gilliam, M. (1998). *How alcoholics anonymous failed me.* New York: William Morrow & Co., Inc.

Gilpin, N. W., & Kolb, G. F. (2008). Neurobiology of alcohol dependence. *Alcohol ReSearch & Health, 31*(3), 185–195.

Girls are abusing steroids too. (2005). Retrieved from http:cnn.com/2005/HEALTH/04/25/girls.dyrtpofd/ap/indexhtml

Gitlow, S. (2007). *Substance use disorders* (2nd ed.). New York: Lippinmcott, Williams & Wiltkins.

Gitlow, S. (2011). Addiction: The new definition. *Counselor, 12*(5), 14–15.

Glantz, S. A., Slade, J., Bero, L. A., Hanauer, P., & Barnes, D. E. (1996). *The cigarette papers.* Los Angeles: University of California Press.

Glasper, L. J., de Wet, C. J., Bearn, J., & Gossop, M. (2007). Comparison of buprenorphine and metha-done in the treatment of opiate withdrawal: Possible advantages of buprenorphine for the treatment of opiate-benzodiazepine codependent patients? *Journal of Clinical Psychopharmacology, 27,* 188–192.

Glasser, J. (2002). Cycle of shame. *U.S. News & World Report, 132*(17), 26–33.

Glasser, R. J. (2004). We are not immune. *Harper's Magazine, 309*(1850), 35–42.

Glatt, M. M. (1958). Group therapy in alcoholism. British Journal of Addiction, *54(2)*: 140.

Glazer, D. G., & Wu, L. T. (2009). The epidemiology of at-risk and binge drinking among middle-aged and elderly community adults: The national survey on drug use and health. *American Journal of Psychiatry.*

Glennon, R. A. (2004). Neurobiology of hallucinogens. In M. Galanter & H. D. Kleber (Eds.), *Textbook of substance abuse treatment* (3rd ed.). Washington, DC: American Psychiatric Press, Inc.

Glennon, R. A. (2008). Neurobiology of hallucinogens. In M. Galanter & H. D. Kleber (Eds.), *Textbook of substance abuse treatment.* Washington, DC: American Psychiatric Association, Inc.

Glick, S. D., & Maisonneuve, I. M. (2000). Development of novel medications for drug addiction. In S. D. Glick & I. Maisonneuve (Eds.), *New medications for drug abuse.* New York: New York Academy of Sciences.

Godwin, C. (2004). What's mew in the fight against AIDS. *RN, 67*(4), 46–52.

Going to pot. (2009). *Playboy, 56*(1), 22.

Gold, M. S., & Dupont, R. L. (2008). Teens + mari-juana: (still) a dangerous mix. *Clinical Psychiatry News, 36*(7), 14.

Gold, M. S., & Jacobs, W. S. (200). Cocaine and crack: Clinical aspects. In J. H. Lowinson, P. Ruiz, R. B. Millman, & J. D. Langrod (Eds.), *Substance abuse, a comprehensive textbook* (4th ed.). New York: Lipponcott, Williams & Wilkins.

Gold, M. S. (2005). From the guest editor. *Psychiatric Annals, 35*(6), 458, 460.

Gold, M. S., Frost-Pineda, K., & Jacobs, W. S. (2004). Cannabis. In M. Galanter & H. D. Kleber (Eds.), *Textbook of substance abuse treatment* (3rd ed.). Washington, DC: American Psychiatric Press, Inc.

Goldberg, I. J. (2003). To drink or not to drink? *New England Journal of Medicine, 348,* 163–164.

Goldkamp, J. S., White, M. D., & Robinson, J. B. (2002). *An honest chance: Perspectives on drug courts.* Washington, DC: U.S. Dept. of Justice.

Goldman, H., Frank, R. G., Burnam, A., Huskamp, H. A., et al. (2006). Behavioral health insurance parity for federal employees. *New England Journal of Medicine, 354,* 1378–1386.

Goldschmidt, L., Richardson, G. A., Cornelius, M. D., & Day, N. L. (2004). Prenatal marijuana and alcohol exposure and academic achievement at age 10. *Neurotoxicology & Teratology, 26*(4), 521–532.

Goldsmith, R. J., & Garlapati, V. (2004). Behavioral interventions for dual diagnosis patients. *Psychiatric Clinics of North America, 27,* 709–725.

Goldstein, D. (2005). Blunt instrument. *New Scientist, 185*(2492), 23.

Goldstein, R. Z., & Volkow, N. D. (2002). Durg addiction and its underlying neurobiological basis: Neuroimaging evidence for the involvement of the frontal cortex. *The American Journal of Psychiatry, 150,* 1642–1652.

Goler, N. C., Armstrong, M. A., Taillac, C. J., & Osejo, V. M. (2008). Substance abuse treatment liked with prenatal visits improves perinatal outcomes: A new standard. *Journal of Perinatology.*

Gomberg, E. S. L. (2004). Ethnic minorities and the elderly. In M. Galanter & H. D. Kleber (Eds.), *Textbook of substance abuse treatment* (3rd ed.). Washington, DC: American Psychiatric Press, Inc.

Gonzalez, R., Vasisileva, J., & Scott, J. C. (). Neuropsychological consequences of drug abuse. In I. Grnt & K. M. Adams (Eds.), *Neuropsychological assessment of neuropsychiatric and neuromedical disorders* (3rd ed.). New York: Oxford University Press.

Goodwin, R. S., Darwin, W. D., Chiang, C. N., Shih, M., et al. (2008). Urinary elimination of 11-nor-9-carbosy-?-tetrahydrocannabinol in cannabis users during continuously monitored abstinence. *Journal of Analytical Toxicology, 32*(8), 562–569.

Gordon, S. C. (2000). Antiviral therapy for chronic hepatitis b and c. *Postgraduate Medicine, 107,* 135–144.

Gordon, S. M. (2007). Women barriers to substance abuse treatment. *Counselor, 8*(3), 22–28.

Gore, A. (2013). What do we owe a difficult parent? *Psychology Today, 44*(6), 32–33, 35.

Gorelick, D. A. (2009). The pharmacology of cocaine, amphetamines and other stimulants. In R. K. Ries, D. A. Fiellin, S. C. Miller, & R. Saitz (Eds.), *Principles of addiction medicine* (4th ed., pp. 453–463). New York: Lippincott, Williams & Wilkins.

Gorman, D. (2003). The best of practices, the worst of practices: The making of science-based primary intervention programs. *Psychiatric Services, 54,* 1087–1089.

Gorman, D. M., & Huber, J. C. (2007). Do medical cannabis laws encourage cannabis use? *International Journal of Drug Policy, 18*(3), 160–167.

Gorter, R. W., Butorac, M., Cobland, E. P., & van der Sluis, W. (2005). Medical use of cannabis in the Netherlands. *Neurology, 64,* 917–919.

Goslawski, M., Plano, M. R., Bian, J. T., Church, E. C., Szczurek, M., & Phillip, S. A. (2013). Binge drinking impairs vascular function in young adults. *Journal of the American College of Cardiology, 62*(3), 201–207.

Gossop, M., Steward, D., & Marsden, J. (2007). Readiness for change and drug use outcomes after treatment. *Addiction, 102,* 301–308.

Gottleib, A. M. (1997). Crisis of consciousness. *Unte Reader, 79,* 45–48.

Goulding, E., & Fleming, M. (2011). Strategies to reduce alcohol use in problem drinkers. *Current Psychiatry, 10*(11), 30–42.

Gouzoulis-Mayfrank, E., Daumann, J., Tuchtenhagen, F., Pelz, S., et al. (2000). Impaired cognitive performance in drug-free users of recreational ecstasy (MDMA). *Journal of Neurology, Neurosurgery and Psychiatry, 68,* 719–725.

Graber, M. A. (2007). Identifying and treating the methamphetamine abuser. *Emergency Medicine, 39,* 12–16, 47.

Graedon, J., & Graedon, T. (1996). *The people's pharmacy.* New York: St. Martin's Griffin.

Graham, J. R. (1990). *MMPI-2 assessing personality and psychopathology.* New York: Oxford University Press.

Graham, N. A., Polles, A., & Gold, M. S. (2007). Performance enhancing, non-prescription use of erectile dysfunction medications. *Journal of Addictive Diseases, 25*(Supplement 1), 33–45.

Graham, S. (2009). A brief encounter. *The Independent Practitioner, 29*(1), 25.

Grahm, K., Massak, A., Demers, A., & Rehm, J. (2007). Does the association between alcohol consumption and depression depend on how they are measured? *Alcoholism: Clinical and Experimental Research, 31*(1), 78–88.

Grant, B. F., Dawson, D. A., Stonson, F. S., Chou, S. P., et al. (2006). The 12 month prevalence and trends in DSM-IV alcohol abuse and dependence: United States, 1991–1992 and 2001–2002. *Alcohol Research & Health, 29*(2), 79–93.

Grant, I., Heath, A. C., Bucholz, K. K., Madden, P. A. F., et al. (2007). Spousal concordance for alcohol dependence: Evidence for assortative mating or spousal interaction effect. *Alcoholism: Clinical and Experimental Research, 31*(5), 717–728.

Grant, J. E., Kushner, M. G., & Kim, S. W. (2002). Pathological gambling and alcohol use disorder. *Alcohol Research & Health, 26*, 143–150.

Grass is greener. (2007). *Playboy, 54*(4), 27.

Gray, J. D., Punsonim, M., Tabori, N. E., Melton, J. T., et al. (2007). Methylphenidate administration to juvenile rats alters brain areas involved in cognition, motivated behaviors, appetite and stress. *Journal of Neuroscience, 27*, 7196–7207.

Gray, M. (1998). *Drug crazy.* New York: Routledge.

Greely, H., Sahakian, B., Harris, J., Kessler, R. C., et al. (2008). Towards responsible use of cognitive-enhancing drugs by the healthy. *Nature.*

Green, C. A. (2006). Gender and use of substance abuse treatment services. *Alcohol Research & Health, 29*(1), 55–62.

Green, C. R., Munoz, D. P., Nikkel, S. M., & Reynolds, J. N. (2007). Deficits in eye movement control in children with fetal alcohol spectrum disorders. *Alcoholism: Clinical and Experimental Research, 31*(3), 500–511.

Green, J. (2002). *Cannabis.* New York: Thunder's Mouth Press.

Green, K. E., & Feinstein, B. A. (2012). Substance use in lesbian, gay, and bisexual populations: An update on empirical research and implications for treatment. *Psychology of Addictive Behaviors, 26*(2), 265–278.

Greenbaum, R. L., Stevens, S. A., Nash, K., Koren, G., et al. (2009). Social cognition and emotion processing abilities of children with fetal alcohol spectrum disorders: A comparison with attention deficit hyperactivity disorder. *Alcoholism Clinical and Experimental Research, 33*(10).

Greenberg, B. H., & Bernard, D. D. (2005). *Contemporary diagnosis and management of heart failure.* Newtown, PA: Handbooks in Health Care Co.

Greenberg, G. (2013). *The book of woe: The DSM and the unmaking of psychiatry.* New York: Blue Rider Press.

Greenberg, M. S. (2010). *Handbook of neurosurgery* (7th ed.). New York: Thieme Medical Publishers.

Greenfield, S. F. (2005). Is parity for the treatment of substance use disorders really sensible? *Psychiatric Services, 56,* 153–155.

Greenfield, S. F. (2010, May). *Gender differences in addiction and its treatment.* Paper presented at the "Addictions in 2010" seminar, hosted by the Division of alcohol and Drug Abuse of the McLean Hospital, MA.

Greenfield, S. F., & Hennessy, G. (2008a). Assessment of the patient. In M. Galanter & H. D. Kleber (Eds.), *Textbook of substance abuse treatment* (4th ed.). Washington, DC: American Psychiatric Press, Inc.

Greenfield, S. F. (2003, March). *Gender differences in addiction: Findings and treatment implications.* Symposium presented to the Dept. Of Psychiatry at the Cambridge Hospital, MA.

Greenfield, S. F. (2007). *Alcohol use and abuse.* Cambridge, MA: Harvard Health Publications.

Greenhill, L. L. (2006). The science of stimulant abuse. *Pediatric Annals, 35,* 552–558.

Greenwald, G. (2009). Viewfinder. *New Scientist, 202*(2704), 23.

Greenstein, M. (2012). The choice is yours. *Psychology Today, 45*(2), 24.

Grekin, E. R., Sher, K. J., & Wood, P. K. (2006). Personality and substance dependence symptoms: Modeling substance-specific traits. *Psychology of Addictive Behaviors, 20,* 415–424.

Grens, K. (2007). Scientists get hooked on a single transcription actor. *New Scientist.* Retrieved from http://www.the_scientist.com/article/come/53236

Greydanus, D. E., & Patel, D. R. (2005). The adolescent and substance abuse: Current concepts. *Disease a Month, 51,* 391–431.

Griffith, C. M., & Schenker, S. (2006). The role of nutritional therapy in alcoholic liver disease. *Alcohol Research & Health, 29*(4), 296–306.

Griffin, K. W., & Botvin, G. J. (2010). Evidence based interventions for preventing substance use disorders in adolescents. *Child and Adolescent Psychiatric Clinics of North America, 19*(3), 505–526.

Griffiths, R. R., Richards, W. A., McCann, U., & Jesse, R. (2006). Psilocybin can occasion mystical-type experiences having substantial and sustained personal meaning. *Psychopharmacology, 287*(3), 268–283.

Grinfeld, M. J. (2001). Decriminalizing addiction. *Psychiatric Times, 18*(3), 1, 5–156.

Grinspoon, L., Bakalar, J. B., & Russo, E. (2005). Marihuana: Clinical aspects. In J. H. Lowinson, P. Ruiz, R. B. Millman, & J. G. Langrod (Eds.), *Substance abuse: A comprehensive textbook*. New York: Lippincott, Williams & Wilkins.

Griswold, K. S., Arnoff, H., Kernan, J. B., & Khan, L. S. (2008). Adolescent substance use and abuse: Recognition and management. *American Family Physician, 77*, 331–336.

Grob, C. S., & Poland, R. E. (2005). MDMA. In J. H. Lowinson, P. Ruiz, & R. B. Millman (Eds.), *Substance abuse: A comprehensive textbook* (4th ed.). New York: Lippincott, Williams & Wilkins.

Gross, J. (2008). *New generation gap as older addicts seek help* (published online). Retrieved from http://www.nytimes.com/2008/03/06us/06abuse.html

Gruber, A. J., & Pope, H. G. (2002). Marijuana use among adolescents. *The Pediatric Clinics of North America, 49*, 389–413.

Gruber, A. J., Pope, H. G., Hudson, J. I., & Yurgelun-Todd, D. (2003). Attributes of long-term heavy cannabis abusers: A case-controlled study. *Psychological Medicine, 33*, 1415–1422.

Grucza, R. A., Norberg, K., Bucholz, K. K., & Bierut, L. J. (2008). Correspondence between secular changes in alcohol dependence and age of drinking onset among women in the United States. *Alcoholism: Clinical and Experimental Research, 32*(8), 1493–1501.

Grucza, R. A., & Bierut, L. J. (2006). Cigarette smoking and the risk for alcohol use disorders among adolescent drinkers. *Alcoholism: Clinical and Experimental Research, 30*, 2046–2054.

Grucza, R. A., Bucholz, J. P., Rice, L. J., & Bierut, L. J. (2008). Secular trends in the lifetime prevalence of alcohol dependence in the United States: A re-evaluation. *Alcoholism: Clinical and Experimental Reserach, 32*(5), 763–770.

Gual, A., & Lehert, P. (2005). Acamprosate during and after acute alcohol withdrawal: A double blind placebo-controlled study in Spain. *Alcohol and Alcoholism, 36*(5), 413–418.

Guilbert, H., & Krawiec, M. (2003). Natural history of asthma. *Pediatric Clinics of North America, 50*, 523–538.

Gullu, H., Caliskin, M., Ciftci, O., Erdogan, D., et al. (2007). Light cigarette smoking impairs coronary microvascular functions as severely as smoking regular cigarettes. *Heart.* Retrieved from http://heart.bmj.com/content/93/10/1274.full.pdf

Gunderson, E. W., & Stimmel, B. (2004). Treatment for pain in drug addicted persons. In M. Galanter & H. D. Kleber (Eds.), *Textbook of substance abuse treatment* (3rd ed.). Washington, DC: American Psychiatric Press, Inc.

Gunn, J. (2003). Psychopathy: An elusive concept with moral overtones. In T. Millon, E. Simonsen, M. Birket-Smith, & R. D. Davis (Eds.), *Psychopathy: Antisocial, criminal and violent behavior*. New York: Guilford.

Gunn, R. L., & Smith, G. T. (2010). Risk factors for elementary school drinking: Pubertal status, personality, and alcohol expectancies currently predict fifth grade alcohol consumption. *Psychology of Addictive Behaviors, 24*(4), 617–627.

Guo, J., Ibaragi, S., Zhu, T., Lou, L., et al. (2008). Nicotine promotes mammary tumor migration via a signaling cascade involving protein kinase c and cdc42. *Cancer Research, 68*, 8473–8481.

Gupta, S. (2007). Keg parties and cardiacs. *Time, 169*(19), 76.

Guttentag, M., & Secord, P. F. (1983). *Too many women? The sex ratio question*. New York: Sage Publications, Inc.

Gutstein, H. B., & Akil, H. (2006). Opioid analgesics. In L. L. Brunton, J. S. Lazo, & K. L. Parker (Eds.), *The pharmacological basis of therapeutics* (11th ed.). New York: McGraw-Hill.

Gwinnell, E., & Adamec, C. (2006). *The encyclopedia of addictions and addictive behaviors*. New York: Facts on File, Inc.

Haack, M. R. (1998). Treating acute withdrawal from alcohol and other drugs. *Nursing Clinics of North America, 33*, 75–92.

Haber, J. R. (2008). Alcohol and religion. *The Addictions Newsletter, 14*(3), 13–14.

Haghigi, A., Schwartz, D. H., Abrahamowicz, M., Lenard, G. T., Perron, M., Richer, L., Vettette, S., Gaudet, D., Paus, T., & Zdenka, P. (2012). Prenatal exposure to maternal cigarette smoking, amygdala volume and fat intake in adolescence. *Archives of General Psychiatry, 69*(5), 1–8.

Hale, T. W. (2003). Medications in breast feeding mothers of preterm infants. *Pediatric Annals, 32,* 337–347.

Halevy, A., & Shuper, A. (2009). Methylphenidate induction of complex visual hallucinations. *Journal of Child Neurology, 24*(8), 1005–1007.

Hahn, I. H., & Hoffman, R. S. (2001). Cocaine use and acute myocardial infarction. *Emergency Medical Clinics of North America, 19,* 493–510.

Hall, A. J., Logan, J. E., Toblin, R. L., Kaplan, J. A., et al. (2008). Patterns of abuse among unintentional pharmaceutical overdose fatalities. *Journal of the American Medical Association, 300*(200), 2613–2620.

Hall, H., McPherson, S. B., Towe, L., & Yudo, E. (2009). Effects and diagnosis of methamphetamine use. In S. B. McPherson, H. V. Hall, & E. Yudo (Eds.), *Methamphetamine use—clinical and forensic aspects.* New York: CRC Press.

Hall, W., & Solowij, N. (1998). Adverse effects of cannabis. *The Lancet, 352,* 1611–1616.

Hall, W., & Degenhardt, L. (2005). Cannabis-related disorders. In B. J. Sadock & V. A. Sadock (Eds.), *Kaplan & sadock's comprehensive textbook of psychiatry* (8th ed.). New York: Lippincott, Williams & Wilkins.

Hallas, J., Bjerrum, L., Støvring, H., & Andersen, M. (2008). Use of a prescribed ephedrine/caffeine combination and the risk of serious cardiovascular events: A registry-based case-crossover study. *American Journal of Epidemiology, 168*(8), 966–973.

Halpern, J. H., Sherwood, A. R., Hudson, J. I., Gruber, S., Kozin, D., & Pope, H. G. (2010). Residual neurocognitive features of long-term ecstasy users with minimal exposure to other drugs. *Addiction.*

Halushka, M. K., & Halushka, P. V. (2002). Why are some individuals resistant to the cardioprotective effects of aspirin?*Circulation, 105,* 1620–1622.

Hamer, M., Stamatakis, E., & Batty, G. D. (2010). Objectively assessed secondhand smoke exposure and mental health in adults. *Archives of General Psychiatry, 67*(8), 850–855.

Hamilton-Mason, J., & Melendez, M. P. (2011, March). *Women of color and addiction treatment.* Symposium conducted at the Treating The Addictions symposium, MA.

Hamilton, R., McGlone, L., MacKinnon, J. R., Russell, H. C., et al. (2010). Ophthalmic, clinical and visual electrophysiological findings in children born to mother prescribed substitute methadone in pregnancy. *British Journal of Ophthalmology.*

Hampson, A. J., Grimaldi, M., Lolic, M., Wink, D., Rosenthal, r, & Alexrod, J. (2002). Neuroprotective antioxidants from marijuana. *Annals of the New York Academy of Sciences, 939,* 274–282.

Hamzelou, J. (2011). Welcome to the exposome. *New Scientist, 208*(2793), 6–7.

Hamzelou, J. (2013). Global health report card. *New Scientist, 216*(2896), 6–7.

Han, B., Gofoerer, J. C., & Colliver, J. D. (2010). Associations between duration of illicit drug use and health conditions: Results from the 2005-2007 national surveys on drug use and health. *Annals of Epidemiology, 20*(4), 289–297.

Haney, M. (2008). Neurobiology of stimulants. In M. Galanter & H. D. Kleber (Eds.), *The American psychiatric publishing textbook of substance abuse treatment.* Washington, DC: American Psychiatric Publishing, Inc.

Hanley, M. (2004). Neurobiology of stimulants. In M. Galanter & H. D. Kleber (Eds.), *Textbook of substance abuse treatment* (3rd ed.). Washington, DC: American Psychiatric Press, Inc.

Hansen, J., Winzeler, S., & Topolinski, S. (2010). When death makes you smoke: A terror management perspective on the effectiveness of cigarette on-pack warnings. *Journal of Experimental Social Psychology, 46*(1), 226–228.

Hanson, G. R., & Finkenstein, A. E. (2009). Basic neuropharmacological mechanisms of methamphetamine. In J. R. Roll, R. A. Rawson, W. Ling, & S. Shoptaw (Eds.), *Methamphetamine addiction from basic science to treatment.* New York: Guilford.

Harmon, K. (2010). Renewed hope. *Scientific American, 302*(1), 15–16.

Harkness, A., & Bratman, S. (2003). *Mosby's handbook of drug-herb and drug-supplement interactions.* Philadelphia: Mosby.

Haroz, R., & Greenberg, M. I. (2005). Emerging drugs of abuse. *Medical Clinics of North America, 89,* 1259–1276.

Harper, C., & Matsumoto, I. (2005). Ethanol and brain damage. *Current Opinion in Pharmacology, 5,* 73–78.

Harrell, A., & Kleiman, M. (2002). Drug testing in criminal justice settings. In C. G. Leukefeld, F. Tims,

& D. Farabee (Eds.), *Treatment of drug offenders.* New York: Springer Publishing Co.

Harris, A. H. S., Kivlahan, D. R., Bowe, T., & Humphreys, K. N. (2010). Pharmacotherapy of alcohol use disorders in the veterans health administration. *Psychiatric Services, 61,* 392–398.

Harrison, P. A., Fulkerson, J. A., & Beebe, T. J. (1998). DSM-IV substance use disorder criteria for adolescents: A critical examination based on a statewide school survey. *American Journal of Psychiatry, 155,* 486–492.

Hart, C. L., & Smith, G. D. (2009). Alcohol consumption and use of acute and mental health hospital services in the west of Scotland collaborative prospective cohort study. *Journal of Epidemiology and Community Health.*

Hart, C. L., Marvin, C. B., & Smith, E. E. (2012). Is cognitive functioning impaired in methamphetamine abusers? A critical review. *Neuropsychopharmacology, 37*(3), 586–608.

Hart, K. E., & Fiissel, D. L. (2003). Do adult offspring of alcoholics suffer from poor mental health? A three-group comparison controlling for self-report bias. *Canadian Journal of Nursing, 35,* 52–72.

Hart, R. H. (1997). On the cannabinoid receptor: A study in molecular psychiatry. *Psychiatric Times, XIV*(7), 59–60.

Hartwell, K. J., Tolliver, B. K., & Brady, K. T. (2009). Biologic commonalities between mental illness and addiction. *Primary Psychiatry, 16*(8), 33–39.

Hashimoto, J. G., & Wiren, K. M. (2007). Neurotoxic consequences of chronic alcohol withdrawal: Expressing profiling reveals importance of gender over withdrawal severity. *Neuropsychopharmacology.*

Hasin, D. S., Stinson, F. S., Ogburn, E., & Grant, B. F. (2007). Prevalence, correlates, disability and comorbidity of DSM-IV alcohol abuse and dependence in the United States: Result from the national epidemologic survey on alcohol and related conditions. *Archives of General Psychiatry, 654,* 830–842.

Hasin, D. S., & Grant, B. F. (2002). Major depression in 6050 former drinkers. *Archives of General Psychiatry, 59,* 794–800.

Hassan, M. M., Donghui, L., el-Deeb, Wolff, R. A., et al. (2008). Association between hepatitis b virus and pancreatic cancer. *Journal of Clinical Oncology, 26*(28), 4457–4562.

Hatzipetros, T., Raudensky, J. G., Soghomonian, J. J., & Yamamoto, B. K. (2007). Haloperidol treatment after high dose methamphetamine administration is exictotoxic to GABA cells in substantia nigra para reticulata. *The Journal of Neuroscience, 27*(22), 5895–5902.

Hauck, F. R., Neese, B. H., Panchal, A. S., & El-Amin, W. (2009). Identification and management of latent tuberculosis infection. *American Family Physician, 79*(10), 879–886.

Haugh, R. (2006). Drunk denials. *Hospital & Health Networks, 80*(2), 1068–1069.

Haut, M. W., Moran, M. T., & Lonser, K. (2012). Toxic disorders and encephalopathy. In C. L. Armstrong & L. Morrow (Eds.), *Handbook of medical neuropsychology.* New York: Springer. (pp. 479–489).

Havens, P. L. (2009). *HIV in pregnancy: Delivery options and virus load* (Wisconsin HIV Providers teleconference, 11/09).

Hays, J. T., Croghan, I. T., Schroeder, D. R., Burke, M. V., Ebbert, J. O., McFadden, D. D., & Hurt, R. D. (2011). Residential treatment compared with outpatient treatment for tobacco use and dependence. *Mayo Clinic Proceedings, 86*(3), 203–209.

He, J., Whelton, P. K., Vu, B., & Klag, M. J. (1998). Aspirin and risk of hemorrhagic stroke. *Journal of the American Medical Association, 280,* 1930–1935.

ealy, B. C., Healy, B. C., Ali, E. N., Guttmann, C. R. G., Chitnis, T., et al. (2009). Smoking and disease progression in multiple sclerosis. *Archives of Neurology, 66*(7), 858–864.

Heavy drinkers "lie to doctors. (2008). *BBC News.* Retrieved from http://newsvote.bbc.uk/mpapps/pagetools/print/news.bbc.co.uk/2/hi/health/7737367.stm?ad=1

Hecht, S., & Hatsukami, D. (2005). Reducing harm caused by tobacco. *Minnesota Medicine, 88,* 40–43.

Hecht, S., Carmella, S. G., Murphy, S. E., Riley, W. T., et al. (2007). Similar exposure to a tobacco specific carcinogen in smokeless tobacco users and cigarette smokers. *Cancer Epidemiology Biomarkers & Prevention, 16,* 1657–1572.

Hefrich, Y. R., Yu, L., Ofori, A., Hamilton, T. A., et al. (2007). Effects of smoking on photoprotected skin. *Archives of Dermatology, 14*(3), 397–402.

Hegab, A. M., & Luketic, V. A. (2001). Bleeding esophageal varices. *Postgraduate Medicine, 109*(2), 75–76, 81–86, 89.

Heidbreder, C. A., & Hagan, J. J. (2005). Novel pharmacotherapeutic approaches to the treatment of drug addiction and craving. *Current Opinion in Pharmacology, 5,* 107–118.

Heil, S. H., & Subramanian, M. G. (1998). Alcohol and the hormonal control of lactation. *Alcohol Health & Research World, 22*(3), 178–184.

Heinemann, A. W., & Rawal, P. H. (2005). Disability and rehabilitation issues. In J. H. Lowinson, P. Ruis, R. B. Millman, & J. G. Langrod (Eds.), *Substance abuse: A comprehensive textbook* (4th ed.). New York: Lipponcott, Williams & Wilkins.

Heinlein, R. A. (1970). *I will fear no evil.* New York: G.P. Putnam's Sons.

Heller, A., Bubula, N., Lew, R., Heller, B., & Won, L. (2001). Gender dependent enhanced adult neuro-toxic response to methamphetamine following fetal exposure to the drug. *Journal of Pharmacology and Experimental Therapeutics, 298,* 1–11.

Heinz, A. (2006). Staying sober. *Scientific American MIND, 17*(2), 56–61.

Heinz, A., Ragan, P., Jones, D. W., Hommer, D., et al. (1998). Reduced Central serotonin transporters in alcoholism. *American Journal of Psychiatry, 155,* 1544–1549.

Henderson, L. A. (1994). Adverse reactions. In L. A. Henderson & W. A. Glass (Eds.), *LSD: Still with us after all these years.* New York: Lexington Books.

Hendricks, K., & Gorbach, S. (2009). Nutrition issues in chronic drug users living with HIV infection. *Addiction Science & Clinical Practice, 5*(1), 1623.

Henry, J., & Rella, J. (2001). Medical risks associated with MDMA use. In J. Holland (Ed.), *Ecstasy: The complete guide.* Rochester, VT: Park St. Press.

Henry, W. K., Alozie, O. K., & Bonham, S. (2009). Peering into the future. *Minnesota Medicine, 92*(10), 50–54.

Hernandez-Avila, C., Pierucci, & Lagha, A. (2005). Inhalants. In H. R. Kranzler & D. A. Ciraulo (Eds.), *Clinical manual of addiction psychopharmacology.* Washington, DC: American Psychiatric Publishing, Inc.

Herning, R. I., Better, W., & Cadet, J. L. (2008). EEG of chronic marijuana users during abstinence: Relationship to years of marijuana use, cerebral blood flow, and thyroid function. *Clinical Neurophysiology, 119,* 321–331.

Herzog, W., Aversano, T., & Atlantic CPORT Investigators and Coordinators. (2007). Gender differences in the effect of traditional cardiac risk factors on age of presentation with STEMI. *Circulation, 116,* II. 317.

Hesselbrock, V. M., & Hesselbrock, M. N. (2007). Are there empirically supported and clinically useful subtypes of alcohol dependence? In J. B. Saunders, M. A. Schuckit, P. J. Sirovatka, & D. A. Regier (Eds.), *Diagnostic issues in substance disorders.* Washington, DC: American Psychiatric Association Press.

Hester, T. (2008). *Study: NJH loses money through nonviolent drug sentences.* Retrieved from http://www.newsday.com/news/local/wire/newjersey/ny/-bc--nonviolentdrugoff0528may28,0,128334.story

Hester, R. K., & Squires, D. D. (2004). Outcome research. In M. Galanter & H. D. Kleber (Eds.), *Textbook of substance abuse treatment* (3rd ed.). Washington, DC: American Psychiatric Press, Inc.

Heyman, G. M. (2009). *Addiction: A disorder of choice.* Cambridge, MA: Harvard University Press.

Heyman, G. M. (2011, March). *Addiction and choice.* Paper presented at the "Treating the Addictions" seminar hosted by the Department of Psychiatry of the Cambridge Hospital, MA.

Heymann, P. (2008, March). *Narcotics, youth and the internet.* Paper presented at the "Treating the Addictions" seminar hosted by the Department Of Psychiatry of the Cambridge Hospital, MA.

Higgins, E. S. (2009). Do ADHD drugs take a toll on the brain? *Scientific American Mind, 20*(4), 38–43.

Hildebrandt, E. (2008). *$70 Billion a year for drug laws while predators remain free.* Retrieved from http://www.salem-news.com/articles/may242008/pot_culture_5-24-08.php

Hildebrandt, T., Langenbucher, J., Carr, S., Sanjuan, P., & Park, S. (2006). Predicting intentions for long-term anabolic-androgenic steroid use among men, a covariance structure model. *Psychology of Addictive Behaviors, 20,* 234–240.

Hilditch, T. (2000). Ya ba. *Gear2, 11,* 86–88.

Hill, P., Dwyer, K., Kay, T., & Murphy, B. (2002). Severe chronic renal failure in association with oxycodone addiction: A new form of fibillary glomerulopathy. *Human Pathology, 33,* 783–787.

Hill, D. B., & Kugelmas, M. (1998). Alcoholic liver disease. *Postgraduate Medicine, 103,* 261–275.

Hill, K., Goldstein, R. S., Guyatt, G. H., Blouin, M., et al. (2010). Prevalence and underdiagnosis of chronic obstructive pulmonary disease among patients at risk in primary care. *Canadian Medical Association Journal.*

Hill, K. G., Hawkins, J. D., Catalano, R. F., Abbott, R. D., & Guo, J. (2005). Family influences on the risk of daily smoking initiation. *Journal of Adolescent Health, 37,* 202–210.

Hill, S. Y., Steinhauer, S. R., Locke-Wellman, J., & Ulrich, R. (2009). Childhood risk factors for young adult substance dependence outcome in offspring from multiplex alcohol dependence families: A prospective study. *Biological Psychiatry, 66*(8), 750–757.

Hiller, M. L., Knight, K., Rao, S. R., & Simpson, D. D. (2002). Assessing and evaluating mandated correctional substance abuse treatment. In C. G. Leukefeld, F. Tims, & D. Farabee (Eds.), *Treatment of drug offenders*. New York: Springer.

Hilts, P. J. (1994). Labeling on cigarettes a smoke screen. *St Paul Pioneer Press, 146*(5), 1A, 6A.

Hilts, P. J. (1996). *Smoke screen*. New York: Addison-Wesley Publishing Co.

Hines, L. M., Stampfer, K. M. J., Ma, J., Gaziano, J. M., et al. (2001). Genetic variation in alcohol dehydrogenase and the beneficial effect of moderate alcohol consumption on myocardial infarction. *New England Journal of Medicine, 344,* 549–555.

Hines, S. C. (2002). Progress against hepatitis c infection. *Patient Care, 36*(3), 11–20.

Hingson, R. (2003, March). *College age drinking*. Symposium Presented to the Dept of Psychiatry at the Cambridge Hospital, MA.

Hingson, R. W. (2010). Magnitude and prevention of college drinking and related problems. *Alcohol Research & Health, 33*(1 and 2), 45–54.

Hingson, R. W., Heeren, T., & Winter, M. R. (2006). Age at drinking onset and alcohol dependence at age onset, duration and severity. *Archives of Pediatric and Adolescent Medicine, 160,* 739–746.

Hingson, R. W., Zha, W., & Weigzman, E. R. (2009). Magnitude of and trends in alcohol-related mortality and morbidity among US college students ages 18–24, 1998–2005. *Journal of Studies on Alcohol and Drugs,* 12–20.

Hingson, R. W. (2010). Magnitude and prevention of college drinking and related problems. *Alcohol Research & Health, 33*(1 & 2), 46–54.

Hitsman, B., Moss, T. G., Montoya, I. D., & George, T. P. (2009). Treatment of tobacco dependence in mental health and addictive disorders. *Canadian Journal of Psychiatry, 54*(6), 368–378.

HIV infection among injection drug users—34 states, 2004-2007. (2010). *Weekly Morbidity and Mortality Report, 303*(2), 1291–1295.

Hoag, H. (2008). Sex on the brain. *New Scientist, 199*(2665), 28–31.

Hobson, J. A. (1999). *Dreaming as delirium*. Cambridge, MA: MIT Press.

Hobson, J. A. (2001). *The dream drugstore*. Cambridge, MA: The MIT Press.

Hobson, J. A. (2005). *13 Dreams Freud never had*. New York: Pi Press.

Hoffman, R., & Hollander, J. E. (1997). Evaluation of patients with chest pain after cocaine use. *Critical Care Clinics of North America, 13,* 809–828.

Hoffmann, D. E., & Weber, E. (2010). Medical marijuana and the law. *New England Journal of Medicine, 362*(16), 1453–1347.

Hogan, M. J. (2000). Diagnosis and treatment of teen drug use. *Medical Clinics of North America, 84,* 927–966.

Holland, W. W., & Fitzsimons, B. (1991). Smoking in children. *Archives of Disease in Childhood, 66,* 1269–1270.

Holleran, R. S. (2002). The problem of pain in emergency care. *Nursing Clinics of North America, 37,* 67–78.

Holm, K. J., & Goa, K. L. (2000). Zolpidem. *Drugs, 59,* 865–889.

Holt, P. R. (2011). Changes in alcohol metabolism after gastric bypass surgery. *The Lancet, 378*(9793), 767–768.

Holzel, K. L., Weiser, A. K., Berner, M. M., & Harter, M. (2008). Meta analysis: Are 3 questions enough to detect unhealthy alcohol use? *Annuals of Internal Medicine, 149*(12), 878–888.

Hopfer, C. M., Mikulich, S. K., & Crowley, T. J. (2000). Heroin use among adolescents in treatment for substance use disorders. *Journal of the American Academy of Child and Adolescent Psychiatry, 39,* 1316–1323.

Hopson, J. (2013). Bad mix for the teen brain. *Scientific American Brain, 24*(3), 68–71.

Horgan, C. M., Garnick, D. W., Merrick, E. L., & Hoyt, A. (2007). Health care requirements for mental health and substance abuse screening in primary care. *Journal of General Internal Medicine, 22*(7), 930–936.

Horgan, J. (2005). The electric kool-aid clinical trial. *New Scientist, 185*(2488), 36–39.

Horney, K. (1964). *The neurotic personality of our time*. New York: W.W. Norton & Co.

Hornig, M. (2013). The role of microbes and autoimmunity in the pathogenesis of neuropsychiatric illness. *Current Opinion on Rheumatology, 25*(4), 48–495.

Horstman, J. (2010). *The scientific American brave new brain*. New York: Josey Bass.

Horvath, A. T. (2000). SMART recovery. *The Addictions Newsletter, 7*(2), 11.

Horvath, A. T. (2005). Alternative support groups. In J. H. Lowinson, P. Ruiz, R. B. Millman, & J. G. Langrod (Eds.), *Substance abuse: A comprehensive textbook* (4th ed.). New York: Lippincott, Wiliams & Wilkins.

Horvath, T. (2007). 9Th circuit rules government officials personally liable for mandated 12-step attendance. *The Addictions Newsletter, 14*(3), 16.

Horvath, T. (2013). Calming a turbulent mind. *Scientific American Mind, 24*(2), 58–66.

Howard, M. O., Bowen, S. E., Garland, E. L., Perron, B. E., & Baughn, M. G. (2011). Inhalant use and inhalant use disorders in the United States. *Addiction Science & Clinical Practice, 6*(1), 18–31.

How alcoholics anonymous works. (2007). *Harvard Mental Health Letter, 24*(1), 4–6.

How long does cocaine remain in the hair of former users? (2009). *Forensic Drug Abuse Advisor, 21*(7), 52–53.

How they smack up. (2005). *Playboy, 52*(4), 25.

Hser, Y., Anglin, M. D., & Powers, K. (1993). A 24 year follow-up of California narcotics addicts. *Archives of General Psychiatry, 50*, 577–584.

Hser, Y., Evans, E., Huang, D., & Anglin, D. M. (2004). Relationship between drug treatment services, retention and outcomes. *Psychiatric Services, 55*, 767–774.

Hser, Y., Hoffman, V., Grella, C. E., & Anglin, M. D. (2001). A 33 year follow-up of narcotics addicts. *Archives of General Psychiatry, 58*, 503–508.

Hsiao, E. Y., McBride, S. W., Hsien, S., Sharon, G., Embriette, R. H., McCue, T., Codell, J. A., Chow, J., … Reisman, S. E. (2013). Microbiota modulate behavioral and physiological abnormalities associated with neurodevelopmental disorders. Cell. doi:http://dx.doi.org/10.1016/j.cell.2013.11.024

Hubbard, J. B., Franco, sE, & Onaivi, E. S. (1999). Marijuana: Medical implications. *American Family Physician, 60*, 2583–2593.

Hudak, M. L., Tan, R. C., The Committee on Drugs, & The Committee on Fetus and newborn. (2012). Neonatal drug withdrawal. *Pediatrics.*

Huddleston, C. W., Freeman-Wilson, K., & Boone, D. L. (2004). *Painting the current picture: A national report card on drug courts and other problem solving court programs in the United States*. Alexandria, VA: National Drug Court Institute.

Hudziak, J., & Waterman, G. S. (2005). Buspirone. In B. J. Sadock & V. A. Sadock (Eds.), *Kaplan & sadock's comprehensive textbook of psychiatry* (8th ed.). New York: Lippincott, Williams & Wilkins.

Huestis, M. A. (2009). Cannabinoids. In J. D. Robero-Miller & B. A. Goldberger (Eds.), *Handbook of workplace drug testing* (2nd ed.). Washington, DC: AACC Press.

Huffing can kill your child. (2004). *CBS Evening News.* Retrieved from http://www.cbsnews.com/stories/2004/06/01eveningnews/main610508610528.html

Hughes, J. R. (2005). Nicotine-related disorders. In B. J. Sadock & V. I. Sadock (Eds.), *Comprehensive textbooks of psychiatry* (8th ed.). Baltimore: Lippincott, Williams & Wilkins.

Hughes, T. L., Wilsnack, S. C., Szalacha, L. A., Johnson, T., et al. (2006). Age and racial/ ethnic differences in drinking and drinking-related problems in a community sample of lesbians. *Journal of Studies on Alcohol, 67*, 579–590.

Humphreys, K. (2003). A research based analysis of the moderation management controversy. *Psychiatric Services, 54*, 621–622.

Humphreys, K., & Moos, R. H. (2007). Encouraging posttreatment self-help involvement to reduce demand for continuing care services: Two year clinical and utilization outcomes. *Alcoholism: Clinical and Experimental Research, 31*(4), 64–68.

Hunnault, C. C., Mensinga, T. T., de Vries, I., Hermien, H., et al. (2008). Delta-9-tetra-hydrocannabinol (THC) serum concentrations and pharmacological effects in males after smoking a combination of tobacco and cannabis containing up to 69 mg THC. *Psychopharmacology, 202*(2), 161–170.

Humphriss, R., Hall, A., May, M., Zuccolo, L., & Macleod, J. (2013). Prenatal alcohol exposure and childhood balance ability: Findings from a UK birth cohort study. *British Medical Journal.* doi:10.1136/bmjopen 2013-002718

Hung, J. (2003). Aspirin for cardiovascular disease prevention. *Medical Journal of Australia, 179*, 147–152.

Hunger leaves it mark on fetal DNA. (2008). *New Scientist, 200*(2680), 12.

Hunter, K., & Ochoa, r. (2006). Acamprosate (campral) for treatment of alcoholism. *American Family Physician, 74*, 645–646.

Hurcom, C., Copello, A., & Orford, J. (2000). The family and alcohol: Effects of excessive drinking and conceptualizations of spouses over recent decades. *Substance Use & Misuse, 35,* 473–502.

Hurt, R. D., & Robertson, C. R. (1998). Prying open the door to the tobacco industry's secrets about nicotine. *Journal of the American Medical Association, 280,* 1173–1181.

Hurt, R. D., Weston, S. A., Ebbert, J. O., McNallan, S. M., Croghan, I. T., Schrocder, D. R., & Roger, V. L. (2012). Myocardial infarction and sudden cardiac death in olmstead county minnesota before and after smoke-free workplace laws. *Archives of Interna Medicine.*

Hurwitz, B. E., Klaus, J. R., Llabre, M. M., Gonzalez, P. J., et al. (2007). Suppression of human immunodeficiency virus type 1 viral load with selenium supplementation: A randomized controlled trial. *Archives of Internal Medicine, 167,* 148–154.

Husak, D. N. (2004). The moral relevance of addiction. *Substance Use & Misuse, 39,* 399–436.

Hutchison, R. (2004). COX-2 selective NSAIDS. *American Journal of Nursing, 104*(3), 52–55.

Hyman, S. E. (2005, March). *Addictions and the brain: An update.* Seminar Presented at the Cambridge Department of Psychiatry, MA.

Hymowitz, N. (2005). Tobacco. In R. J. Frances, S. I. Miller, & A. H. Mack (Eds.), *Clinical textbook of addictive disorders* (3rd ed.). New York: Guilford.

Ilgen, M. A., Jain, A., Lucas, E., & Moos, R. H. (2007). Substance use-disorder treatment and a decline in attempted suicide during and after treatment. *Journal of Studies of Alcohol & Drugs, 68,* 503–509.

Ikehara, S., Iso, H., Toyoshima, H., Date, C., et al. (2008). Alcohol consumption and mortality from stroke and coronary heart disease among Japanese men and women. *Stroke.*

Illicit drug use among older adults. (2009, December 29). *The NSDUH Report.*

Insomnia in later life. (2006). *Harvard Mental Health Letter, 23*(6), 1–5.

Institute of Medicine of the National Academies. (2012). *Substance use disorders in the U.S. Armed forces.* Washington, DC: United States Government Printing Office.

International Narcotics Control Board. (2008). *Report of the international narcotics control board for 2008.* New York: United Nations.

Interlandi, J. (2013). Breaking the brain barrier. *Scientific American, 308*(6), 52–57.

Iqbal, M. M., Sobhan, T., & Ryals, T. (2002). Effects of commonly used benzodiazepines on the fetus, the neonate and the nursing infant. *Psychiatric Services, 53,* 39–49.

Ireland, T. (2001). The abuse connection. *Counselor, 2*(3), 14–20.

Irvin, J. E., Bowers, C. A., Dunn, M. E., & Wang, M. C. (1999). Efficacy of relapse prevention: A meta-analytic review. *Journal of Consulting and Clinical Psychology, 67,* 563–570.

Isaacson, J. H., & Schorling, J. B. (1999). Screening for alcohol problems in primary care. *Medical Clinics of North America, 83,* 1547–1563.

Ishida, J. H., Peters, M. G., Jin, C., Louie, D., et al. (2008). Influence of cannabis use on severity of hepatitis c disease. *Clinical Gastroenterology and Hepatology, 6,* 69–75.

Is there a genetic basis for drug addiction? (2008). *Forensic Drug Abuse Advisor, 20*(6), 44–46.

Is there a genetic basis for methamphetamine resistance? (2008). *Forensic Drug Abuse Advisor, 20*(6), 46–47.

Isaacson, J. H., & Schorling, J. B. (1999). Screening for alcohol problems in primary care. *Medical Clinics of North America, 83,* 1547–1563.

Isensee, B., Hns-Ulrich, W., Stein, M. B., Hofler, M., & Lieb, R. (2003). Smoking increases the risk of panic. *Archives of General Psychiatry, 60,* 692–700.

Ivanov, I. S., Schulz, K. P., Palmero, R. C., & Newcorn, J. H. (2006). Neurobiology and evidence-based biological treatments for substance abuse disorders. *CNS Spectrums, 11*(11), 864–877.

Ivanov, I. S., Schulz, K. P., Palmero, R. C., & Newcorn, J. H. (2006). Neurobology and evi-dence based treatments for substance abuse disorders. *CNS Spectrums, 11*(11), 864–877.

Iverson, L. (2005). Long-term effects of exposure to cannabis. *Current Opinion in Pharmacology, 5,* 69–72.

Iverson, L. L., Ivensen, S. D., Bloom, F. E., & Roth, R. H. (2009). *Introduction to neuropsychopharmacology.* New York: Oxford University Press.

Jackman, R. P., Purvis, J. M., & Mallett, B. S. (2008). Chronic nonmalignant pain in primary care. *American Family Physician, 78*(10), 1155–1162.

Jackson, D., Jackson, L. M., & Hawkey, C. J. (2000). COX-2 selective nonsteroidal antiinflammatory drugs. *Drugs, 59*(6), 1207–1216.

Jackson, V. A., Sesso, H. D., Buring, J. E., & Gasiano, M. (2003). Alcohol consumption and mortality in men with preexisting cerebrovascular disease. *Archives of internal Medicine, 163,* 1189–1193.

Jacobs, E. J., Thun, M. J., Bain, E. B., Rodriguez, C., et al. (2007). A large cohort study of long term daily yse of adult strength aspirin and cancer incidence. *Contemporary Nurse, 23*(2), 321–330.

Jacobus, J., McQueeny, T., Bava, S., Schweinsburg, B. C., et al. (2009). White matter integrity in adolescents with histories of marijuana use and binge drinking. *Neurotoxicity and Teratology.*

Jaffe, J. H. (2000). Opioi-related disorders. In H. I. Kaplan & B. J. Sadock (Eds.), *Comprehensive textbook of psychiatry* (7th ed.). Baltimore: Lippincott, Williams & Wilkins.

Jaffe, J. H., & Anthony, J. C. (2005). Substance-related disorders: Introduction and overview. In B. J. Sadock & V. A. Sadock (Eds.), *Kaplan & sadock's comprehensive textbook of psychiatry* (8th ed.). Baltimore: Lippincott, Williams & Wilkins.

Jaffe, J. H., & Jaffe, A. B. (2004). Neurobiology of opioids. In M. Galanter & H. D. Kleber (Eds.), *Textbook of substance abuse treatment* (3rd ed.). Washington, DC: American Psychiatric Press, Inc.

Jaffe, J. H., Ling, W. H., & Rawson, R. A. (2005). Amphetamine (or amphetamine-like) related disorders. In B. J. Sadock & V. A. Sadock (Eds.), *Kaplan & sadock's comprehensive textbook of psychiatry* (8th ed.). New York: Lipponcott, Williams & Wilkins.

Jaffe, J. H., Rawson, R. A., & Ling, W. H. (2005). Cocaine-related disorders. In B. J. Sadock & V. A. Sadock (Eds.), *Kaplan & sadock's comprehensive textbook of psychiatry* (8th ed.). New York: Lipponcott, Williams & Wilkins.

Jaffe, J. H., & Strain, E. C. (2005). Opioid-related disorders. In B. J. Sadock & V. A. Sadock (Eds.), *Kaplan & sadock's comprehensive textbook of psychiatry* (8th ed.). New York: Lipponcott, Williams & Wilkins.

Jaffe, J. H., Rawson, R. A., & Ling, W. H. (2005). Cocaine-related disorders. In B. J. Sadock & V. A. Sadock (Eds.), *Kaplan & sadock's comprehensive textbook of psychiatry* (8th ed.). New York: Lippincott, Williams & Wilkins.

Jaffe, W. B. (2010, April). *Validity and tampering in urine drug screening and testing.* Paper presented at the "Addictions in 2010" seminar, hosted by the Division of alcohol and Drug Abuse of the McLean Hospital, MA.

James, L. P., Farrar, H. C., Komoroski, E. M., Wood, W. R., et al. (1998). Sympathomimetic drug use in adolescents presenting to a pediatric emergency department with chest pain. *Journal of Toxicology: Clinical Toxicology, 36,* 321–329.

Jamison, R. N., Butler, S. F., Budman, S. H., Edwards, R. R., & Wasan, A. D. (2010). Gender differences in risk factors for aberrant prescription opioid use. *The Journal of Pain, 11*(4), 312–320.

Javitt, D., & Zukin, S. R. (2005). Phencyclidine (or phencyclidine-like) related disorders. In B. J. Sadock & V. A. Sadock (Eds.), *Kaplan & sadock's comprehensive textbook of psychiatry* (8th ed.). New York: Lippincott, Williams & Wilkins.

Jayaram-Lindstrom, N., Hammarberg, A., Beck, O., & Franck, J. (2008). Naltrexone for the treatment of amphetamine dependence: A randomized, placebo-controlled trial. *American Journal of Psychiatry, 165,* 1442–1448.

Jeffreys, D. (2004). *Aspirin: The remarkable story of a wonder drug.* New York: Bloomsbury.

Jellinek, E. M. (1952). Phases of alcohol addiction. *Quarterly Journal of Studies on Alcohol, 13,* 673–674.

Jellinek, E. M. (1060). *The disease concept of alcoholism.* New Haven, CN: College and University Press.

Jemionek, J. F., Copley, C. L., Smith, M. L., & Past, M. R. (2008). Concentration distribution of the marijuana metabolite ?-tetrahydrocannabinol-9-carboxylic acid and the cocaine metabolite benzoylecgonine in the department of defense urine drug-testing program. *Journal of Analytical Toxicology, 32*(6), 408–416.

Jenkins, A. J. (2007). Pharmacokinetics: Drug absorption, distribution and elimination. In S. B. Karch (Ed.), *Drug abuse handbook* (2nd ed.). New York: CRC Press.

Jenkins, A. J., & Cone, E. J. (1998). Pharmacokinetics: Drug absorption, distribution and elimination. In S. B. Karch (Ed.), *Drug abuse handbook.* New York: CRC Press.

Jenkins, S. C., Tinsley, J. A., & Van Loon, J. A. (2001). *A pocket reference for psychiatrists* (3rd ed.). Washington, DC: American Psychiatric Press, Inc.

Jernigan, T. L., Gamst, A. C., Archibald, S. L., Fennema-Notestine, C., et al. (2005). Effects of methamphetamine dependence and HIV infection on cerebral morphology. *American Journal of Psychiatry, 162,* 1461–1472.

Jerslid, D. (2001). *Happy hours.* New York: Harper-Collins.

Jha, P., Ramasundarahettige, C., Landsman, V., Rostron, B., Thus, M., Anderson, R. N., McAfee, T., &

Peto, R. (2013). 21St century hazards of smoking and benefits of cessation in the United States. *The New England Journal of Medicine, 368*, 341–350.

Johannes, C. B., Le, T. K., Zhou, X., Johnston, J. A., & Dworkin, R. H. (2010). The prevalence of chronic pain in United States adults: Results of an internet-based survey. *Journal of Pain, 11*(11), 1230–1239.

Johansen, P. O. (2012). Lysergic acid diethylamide (LSD) for alcoholism: Meta-analysis of randomized controlled trials. *Journal of Psychopharmacology*.

Johns, A. (2001). Psychiatric effects of cannabis. *British Journal of Psychiatry, 178*, 116–122.

Johnson, B. A., Rosenthal, N., Capece, J. A., et al. (2007). Topiramate for treatment alcohol dependece, a randomized controlled trial. *Journal of the American Medica Association, 298*(14), 1641–1651.

Johnson, B. A., Rosenthal, N., Capece, J. A., Wiegand, F., et al. (2008). Improvement of physical health and quality of life of alcohol-dependent individuals with topiramate treatment: US multisite randomized control trial. *Archives of Internal Medicine, 168*(11), 1188–1199.

Johnson, B. A., Devous, M. D., Ruiz, P., & Alt-Daud, N. (2001). Treatment advances for cocaine-induced ischemic stroke: Focus on diphdropyridine-class calcium channel blockers. *American Journal of Psychiatry, 158*, 1191–1198.

Johnson, B. A. (2010). Medication treatment of different types of alcoholism. *American Journal of Psychiatry, 167*, 639–639.

Johnson, B. A., Roache, J. D., Javors, M. A., DiClemente, C. C., et al. (2000). Ondansetron for reduction of drinking among bio;ogically predisposed alcohol patients. *Journal of the American Medical Association, 284*, 963–970.

Johnson, C., Drgon, T., Liu, Q., Walther, D., Edenberg, H., Rice, J., et al. (2006). Pooled association genome scanning for alcohol dependence using 104,268 SNPs: Validation and use to identify alcoholism vulnerability loci in unrelated individuals from the collaborative study on the genetics of alcoholism. *American Journal of Medical Genetics, 141B*(8), 844–853.

Johnson, J. L., & Hirsch, S. (2003). Aspiration pneumonia. *Postgraduate Medicine, 113*(3), 99–112.

Johnson, L. D., O'Malley, P. M., Bachman, J. G., & Schulenberg, J. E. (2012a). *National survey results on drug use from the monitoring the future study, 1975–2011 (vol i)*. Ann Arbor: Institute for Social Research, The University of Michigan.

Johnson, L. D., O'Malley, P. M., Bachman, J. G., & Schulenberg, J. E. (2012b). *National survey results on drug use from the monitoring the future study, 1975–2011 (vol II): College students and young adults*. Ann Arbor, MI: Institute for Social Research, The University of Michigan.

Johnson, S. (2006). *The ghost map*. New York: Riverhead Books.

Johnson, S. B. (2012a). Medicine's paradigm shift: An opportunity for psychology. *Monitor on Psychology, 43*(8), 3.

Johnson, S. B. (2012b). Treatment of adolescent alcohol abuse and dependence. *Child and Adolescent Psychopharmacology News, 17*(2), 1–5.

Johnson, S. L. (2003). *Therapist's guide of substance abuse intervention*. New York: Academic Press, Inc.

Johnson, V. E. (1980). *I'll quit tomorrow*. San Francisco: Harper & Row.

Johnson, V. E. (1986). *Intervention*. Minneapolis, MN: Johnson Institute Books.

Johnston, L. D., O'Malley, P. M., Backman, J. G., & Schulenberg, J. E. (2012a). *Monitoring the future: National survey results on drug use, 1975–2011: Volume 1, seconary school students*. Ann Arbor, MI: Institute for Social Research, University of Michigan.

Johnston, L. D., O'Malley, P. M., Backman, J. G., & Schulenberg, J. E. (2012b). *Monitoring the future: National survey results on drug use, 1975–2011: Volume 2, college students & adults ages 19–50*. Ann Arbor, MI: Institute for Social Research, University of Michigan.

Johnson, S. (2003). *Therapist's guide to substance abuse intervention*. New York: Academic Press.

Johnston, S. C., & Elkins, J. S. (2008). Neurological complications of hypertension. In M. J. Aminoff (Ed.), *Neurology and general medicine* (4th ed.). New York: Churchill-Livingstone.

Jones, A. W. (1996). Biochemistry and physiology of alcohol: Application to forensic sciences and toxicology. In J. C. Garriott (Ed.), *Medicolegal aspects of alcohol* (3rd ed.). Tuscon, AZ: Lawyers & Judges Publishing Co.

Jones, C. M. (2012). Frequency of prescription pain reliever nonmedical use: 2002–2003 and 2009–2010. *Archives of Internal Medicine*.

Jones, C. M., Mack, K. A., & Paulozzi, L. J. (2013). Pharmaceutical overdose deaths, United States, 2010. *Journal of the American Medical Society, 309*(7), 657–659.

Jones, E. M., Knutson, D., & Haines, D. (2004). Common problems in patients recovering from chemical dependency. *American Family Physician, 68,* 1971–1978.

Jones, G. R. (2009). Introduction. In J. D. Robero-Miller & B. A. Goldberger (Eds.), *Handbook of workplace drug testing* (2nd ed.). Washington, DC: AACC Press.

Jones, H. E., Kaltenbach, K., Heil, S. H., Stine, S. M., Coyle, M. G., Arria, A. M., et al. (2010). Neonatal abstinence syndrome after methadone or buprenorphine exposure. *New England Journal of Medicine, 363,* 2320–2331.

Jones, R. M., Lichtenstein, P., Grann, M., Långstrom, N., & Fazel, S. (2011). Alcohol use disorders in schizophrenia: A national cohort study of 12,653 patients. *Journal of Clinical Psychiatry, 72*(6), 775–779.

Jones, R. T. (2005). Hallucinogen-related disorders. In B. J. Sadock & V. A. Sadock (Eds.), *Kaplan & sadock's comprehensive textbook of psychiatry* (8th ed.). New York: Lippincott, Williams & Wilkins.

Jones, J. H., & Weir, W. B. (2005). Cocaine-associated chest pain. *Medical Clinics of North America, 39,* 1323–1342.

Jones, R. T., & McMahon, J. (1998). Alcohol motivations as outcome expectancies. In A. G. Eashton & M. S. Gold (Eds.), *Treating addictive behaviors* (2nd ed.). New York: The Guilford Press.

Jonnes, J. (2002). Hip to be high: Heroin and popular culture in the twentieth century. In D. F. Musto, P. Korsmeyer, & T. W. Maulucci (Eds.), *One hundred years of heroin.* Westbort, CN: Auburn House.

Jorgensen, E. D. (2001, March). *Dual diagnosis in treatment resistant adolescents.* Paper presented at the "Treating the Addictions" seminar hosted by the Dept of Psychiatry of the Cambridge Hospital, MA.

Jorgensen, E. D. (2008, March). *Adolescent addictions: What we can and can not do to help.* Paper Presented at the "Treating the Addictions" seminar hosted by the Dept. Of Psychiatry of the Cambridge Hospital, MA.

Joseph, H. (2004). Feedback/feedforward. *Addiction Treatment Forum, 13*(2), 3–4.

Joseph, H., & Langrod, J. (2005). The homeless. In J. H. Lowinson, P. Ruiz, R. B. Millmanm, & J. G. Langrod (Eds.), *Substance abuse: A comprehensive textbook* (4th ed.). New York: Lippincott, Williams & Wilkins.

Joubrt, B. R., Håberg, S. E., Nilsen, R. M., Wang, X., Vollset, E., Murphy, S. K., Huang, C. Y., Vopllset, E., ct al. (2012). 405K genome-wide scan identifies differential DNA methylation in newborns related to maternal smoking during pregnancy. *Environmental Health Perspective.*

Joyner, M. J. (2004). Designer doping. *Exercise and Sport Science Reviews, 32*(3), 81–82.

Juhnke, G. A. (2002). *Substance abuse assessment and diagnosis.* New York: Brunner-Routledge.

Juliana, P., & Goodman, C. (2005). Children of substance abusing parents. In J. H. Lowinson, P. Ruiz, R. B. Millman, & J. G. Langrod (Eds.), *Substance abuse: A comprehensive textbook* (4th ed.). New York: Lipponcott, Williams & Wilkins.

Julien, R. M. (2005). *A primer of drug action (10th ed.).* New York: Worth Publishers.

Justo, D., Gal-Oz, A., Paran, Y., & Seltser, D. (2006). Methadone associated torsades do pointes (polymorphic bentricular tachycardia) in opioid dependent patients. *Addiction, 101*(9), 1333–1338.

Kadehjian, L. J., & Crouch, D. J. (2009). Sweat testing. In J. D. Robero-Miller & B. A. Goldberger (Eds.), *Handbook of workplace drug testing* (2nd ed.). Washington, DC: AACC Press.

Kalantar-Zaden, K., Nguyen, M. K., Chang, R., & Kurtz, I. (). Fatal hyponatremia in a young woman after ecstasy ingestion. *Nature Clincal Practice Nephrology, 2*(5), 283–288.

Kalapatapu, R. J., Paris, P., & Neugroschl, J. A. (2010). Alcohol use disorders in geriatrics. *International Journal of Psychiatry in Medicine, 40*(3), 321–337.

Kalat, J. W. (2009). *Biological psychology (10th edition).* Belmont, CA: Wadsworth.

Kalivas, P. W. (2003). Predisposition to addiction: Pharmacokinetics, pharmacodynamics and brain circuitry. *American Journal of Psychiatry, 160*(3), 1–3.

Kallberg, H., Jacobsen, S., Bengtsson, C., Pedersen, M., et al. (2008). Alcohol consumption is associated with decreased risk of rheumatoid arthritis. Results from two scandinavian case-control studies. *Annals of the Rheumatic Diseases.*

Kalman, D. W. (2010, April). *Integrated treatment of smoking in the psychiatrically ill.* Paper presented at the "Addictions in 2010" seminar, hosted by the Division of alcohol and Drug Abuse of the McLean Hospital, MA.

Kamienski, M., & Keogh, J. (2006). *Pharmacology demystified.* New York: McGraw-Hill.

Kaminer, W. (1992). *I'm dysfunctional you're dysfunctional*. New York: Addison-Wesley Publishing Co, Inc.

Kaminer, Y. (1999). Addictive disorders in adolescents. *Psychiatric Clinics of North America, 22*, 275–288.

Kaminer, Y. (2001). Adolescent substance abuse treatment: Where do we go from here? *Psychioatric Services, 52*, 147–149.

Kaminer, Y. (2008). Adolescent substance abuse. In M. Galanter & H. D. Kleber (Eds.), *Textbook of substance abuse treatment*. Washington, DC: American Psychiatric Association, Inc.

Kaminer, Y. (2010). Been there, done that, and now what? Adolescent addictive behaviors from etiology to postvention. *Child and Adolescent Psychiatric Clinics of North America, 19*(3), xv–xvi.

Kaminer, Y., & Tarter, R. E. (2004). Adolescent substance abuse. In M. Galanter & H. D. Kleber (Eds.), *Textbook of substance abuse treatment* (3rd ed.). Washington, DC: American Psychiatric Press, Inc.

Kaminer, Y., & Buckstein, O. G. (2005). Adolescent substance abuse. In R. J. Frances & S. I. Miller (Eds.), *Clinical textbook of addictive disorders* (3rd ed.). New York: Guilford.

Kaminer, Y., & Goodley, M. (2010). From assessment reactivity to aftercare for adolescent substance abuse: Are we there yet? *Child and Adolescent Psychiatric Clinics, 19*(3), 577–590.

Kampman, K. M. (2005). New medications for the treatment of cocaine dependence. *Psychiatry, 2*(12), 44–48.

Kanayma, G., Cohane, G. H., Weiss, R. D., & Pope, H. G. (2003). Post anabolic-androgenic steroid use among men admitted for substance abuse treatment: An under-recognized problem? *Journal of Clinical Psychiatry, 64*, 156–160.

Kanayama, G., Barry, S., Hudson, J. I., & Harrison, G. P. (2006). Body image and attitudes towards male role models in anabolic-androgenic steroid users. *American Journal of Psychiatry, 163*(4), 697–703.

Kandel, D. B., & Chen, K. (2000). Types of marijuana users by longitudinal course. *Journal of Studies on Alcohol, 61*, 367–378.

Kandall, S. R. (1999). Treatment strategies for drug-exposed neonates. *Clinics in Perinatology, 26*, 231–243.

Kaner, E., Bland, M., Cassidy, P., Coiulton, S., Dale, V., Deluca, P., Gilvarry, E., Godfrey, C., Heather, N., Myles, J., et al. (2013). Effectiveness of screening and brief alcohol intervention in primary care (SIPS trial): Pragmatic cluster randomised controlled trial. *British Medical Journal.*

Kapadia, R. (2008). Get yourself some healthy profits. *Smart Money, XVII*(XI), 84–89.

Karam-Hage, N. M. (2004). Treating insomnia in patients with substance use/abuse disorders. *Psychiatric Times, XXI*(2), 55–56.

Karan, L. D., Haller, D. L., & Schnoll, S. H. (1998). Cocaine and stimulants. In R. J. Frances & S. I. Miller (Eds.), *Clinical textbook of addictive disorders* (2nd ed.). New York: Guilford.

Karch, D. L., Dahlberg, L. L., & Patel, N. (2010). Surveillance for violent deaths national violent death reporting system, 16 states, 2007. *Mobidity and Mortality Weekly Report, 59*, 1–50.

Karch, S. B. (2009). *The pathology of drug abuse* (4th ed.). New York: CRC Press.

Karch, D., Cosby, A., & Simon, T. (2006). Toxicology testing and results for suicide victims—13 states, 2004. *Morbidity and Mortality Weekly Report, 55*(46), 1245–1248.

Karlamangla, A. S., Sarkisian, C. A., Mako, D. M., Dedes, H., et al. (2009). Light to moderate alcohol consumption and disability: Variable benefits by health status. *American Journal of Epidemiology, 169*(1), 96–104.

Karsan, H. A., Rojter, S. E., & Saab, S. (2004). Primary prevention of cirrhosis. *Post Graduate Medicine, 115*, 25–30.

Kaskutas, L. A., Ammon, L., Delucchi, K., Room, R., et al. (2005). Alcoholics anonymous careers: Patterns of AA involvement five years after treatment entry. *Alcoholism: Clinical and Experimental Research, 29*(11), 1983–1990.

Katz, M. H., & Zolopa, A. R. (2009). HIV infection & AIDS. In S. J. McPhee & M. A. Papadakis (Eds.), *2009 Current medical diagnosis and treatment* (pp. 1176–1204). New York: Mc-Graw Hill.

Katz, N., & Fanciullo, G. J. (2002). Role of urine toxicology testing in the management of chronic opioid therapy. *The Clinical Journal of Pain, 18*, 576–582.

Katz, W. A. (2000). *Pain management in rheumatologic disorders*. USA: Drugsmartz Publications.

Katzung, G. B. (1995). Introduction. In B. G. Katzung (Ed.), *Basic & cinical pharmacology* (6th ed.). Norwalk, CT: Appleton & Lang.

Kauffman, J. F. (2003a, March). *Recovery and methadone treatment*. Paper presented at the "Treating the

Addictions" seminar sponsored by the Dept. Of Psychiatry of the Cambridge Hospital, MA.

Kauffman, J. F. (2003b). Methadone treatment and recovery for opioid dependence. *Primary Psychiatry, 10*(9), 61–64.

Kauffman, S. A. (2008). *Reinventing the sacred.* New York: Basic Books.

Kaufman, M. (2006). Smoking in US declines sharply. Retrieved from http://www.washingtonpost.com/wp-dyn/content/article/2006/03/08/AR2006030802368.html

Kaufman, M. J., Levin, J. M., Ross, M. H., Lang, N., et al. (1998). Cocaine-induced vasoconstriction detected in humans with magnetic resonance angiography. *Journal of the American Medical Association, 279,* 376–380.

Kavanagh, D. J., McGrath, J., Saunders, J. B., Dore, G., & Clark, D. (2002). Substance misuse in patients with schizophrenia. *Drugs, 62*(5), 743–756.

Kaye, A. D., Gevirtz, C., Bosscher, H. A., Duke, J. B., et al. (2003). Ultrarapid opiate detoxification: A review. *Canadian Journal of Anesthesia, 50*(7), 633–671.

Keany, L. (2011). 20 Things you didn't know about alcohol. *Discover, 32*(10), 80.

Keller, D. S. (2003). Exploration in the service of relapse prevention: A psychoanalytic contribution to substance abuse treatment. In F. Rotgers, J. Morgenstern, & S. T. Walters (Eds.), *Treating substance abuse: Theory and technique* (2nd ed.). New York: Guilford.

Keller, E. F. (2010). The sound of distant drumming. *New Scientist, 207*(2778), 28–29.

Keller, R. W., & Snyder-Keller, A. (2000). Prenatal cocaine exposure. In S. D. Glick & I. B. Maisonneuve (Eds.), *New medications for drug abuse.* New York: New York Academy of Sciences.

Kelly, J. F., Stout, R. L., Magill, M., Tonigan, J. S., & Pagano, M. E. (2010). Spirituality in recovery: A lagged mediational analysis of alcoholics anonymous principal theoretical mechanism of behavior change. *Alcoholism Clinical & Experimental Research*(), . Retrieved 1 7, 2011, from

Kelly, J. P., Cook, S. F., Kaufman, D. W., Anderson, T., Rosenberg, L., & Mitchell, A. A. (2008). Prevalence and characteristics of opioid use in the US adult population. *Pain, 138,* 507–513.

Kelly, J. F., Finney, J. W., & Moos, R. (2005). Substance use disorder patients who are mandated to treatment: Characteristics, treatment process, and 1 and 5 year outcomes. *Journal of Substance Abuse Treatment, 28*(3), 23–233.

Kelly, J. F., & Yeterian, J. D. (2011). The role of mutual-help groups in extending the framework of treatment. *Alcohol Research & Health, 33*(4), 350–355.

Kelly, V. A., & Saucier, J. (2004). Is your patient suffering from alcohol withdrawal? *RN, 67*(2), 27–31.

Kelly, Y., Iacovou, M., Quigley, M. A., Gray, R., Wolke, D., Kelly, J., & Sacker, A. (2013). Light drinking versus abstinence in pregnancy behavioral and cognitive outcomes in 7 year old children: A longitudinal cohort study. *BJOG.*

Kendler, K. S., Thorntonm, L. M., & Pederson, N. L. (2000). Tobacco consumption in Swedish twins reared apart and reared together. *Archives of General Psychiatry, 173,* 345–350.

Kendler, S., Sundquist, K., Ohlssom, H., Palmer, K., Maes, H., Winkleby, M. A., & Sundquist, J. (2012). Genetic and familial environmental influences on the risk for drug abuse. *Archives of General Psychiatry.*

Kenfield, S. A., Stampfer, M. J., Rosner, B. A., & Colditz, G. A. (2008). Smoking and smoking cessation in relation to mortality in women. *Journal of the American Medical Association, 299*(17), 2037–2047.

Kenneally, C. (2010). Talking heads. *New Scientist, 206*(2762), 32–35.

Kenny, P. J., Chen, S. A., Kitamura, O., Markou, A., & Koob, G. F. (2006). Conditioned withdrawal drives heroin consumption and decreases reward sensitivity. *Journal of Neuroscience, 26,* 5894–5900.

Kern, S., Skoog, I., Ostling, S., Kern, J., & Borjesson-Hanson, A. (2012). Does low-dose acetylsalicylic acid prevent cognitive decline in women with high cardiovascular risk? A 5-year follow-up of a nondemented population based cohort of Swedish elderly women. *British Medical Journal.*

Kerr, S., Woods, C., Watson, H., & Hunter, R. (2013). A qualitative exploration of barriers and facilitators to smoking cessation in people wiht enduring mental health problems. *BMCPublic Health, 13*(221).

Kertesz, S. G., Khodneva, Y., Richman, R. J., Tucker, J. A., Safford, M. M., Jones, B., Schumacher, J., & Pletcher, M. J. (2012). Trajectories of drug use and mortality outcomes among adults over 18 years. *Journal of General Internal Medicine, 27*(7), 808–816.

Kerrigan, M. (2008, 10). *Mothers issues after delivery.* Seminar presented at the Wisconsin State Methadone Providers Meeting, WI.

Kershaw, C. D., & Guidot, D. M. (2008). Alcoholic lung disease. *Alcohol Research & Health, 31*(1), 66–75.

Kessler, R. C., Aguilar-Gaxiola, S., Berglund, P. A., Caraveo-Anduaga, et al. (2001). Patterns and predictors of treatment seeking after onset of a substance use disorder. *Archives of General Psychiatry, 58,* 1065–1071.

Keyes, K. M., Martins, S. S., Blanco, C., & Hasin, D. S. (2010). Telescoping and gender differences in alcohol dependence: New evidence from two national surveys. *American Journal of Psychiatry, 167,* 969–976.

Keyes, M., Legrand, L. N., Iacono, W. G., & McGue, M. (2008). Parental smoking and adolescent problem behavior: An adoption study of general and specific effects. *American Journal of Psychiatry, 165,* 1338–1344.

Keyes, K. M., Hatzenbuehler, M. L., McLaughlin, K. A., Link, G., Olfson, M., Grant, B. F., & Hasin, D. (2010). Stigma and treatment for alcohol disorders in the United States. *American Journal of Epidemiology,* 1364–1372.

Khalsa, A. M. (2006). Prevention, counseling, screening, and therapy for the patient with newly diagnosed HIV infection. *American Family Physician, 73,* 271–280.

Khamsi, R. (2013). Going to pot. *Scientific American, 308*(6), 34, 36.

Khan, R., Morrow, L. J., & McCarron, R. M. (2009). How to manage complications of the 5 most abused substances. *Current Psychiatry, 8*(11), 35–47.

Khantzian, E. J. (2003a, March). *Introductory comments by moderator.* Symposium presented to the Dept of Psychiatry at the Cambridge Hospital, MA.

Khantzian, E. J. (2003b). The self-medication hypothesis revisited: The dually diagnosed patient. *Primary Psychiatry, 10*(9), 47–48, 53–54.

Khat calls. (2004). *Forensic Drug Abuse Advisor, 16*(3), 19–21.

Khurana, M., & Schubiner, H. (2007). ADHD in adults: Primary care management. *Patient Care Neurology and Psychiatry, 1*(1), 11–15, 27.

Khushalani, N. I. (2008). Cancer of the esophagus and stomach. *Mayo Clinic Proceedings, 83*(6), 712–722.

Kiefer, F., Jahn, H., Tarnaske, T., Helwig, H., et al. (2003). Comparing and combining naltrexone and acamprosate in relapse prevention of alcoholism. *Archives of General Psychiatry, 60,* 92–99.

King, M., Marston, L., McManus, S., Brugha, T., Melzer, H., & Bebbington, P. (2012). Religion, spirituality and mental health: Results from a national study of English households. *British Journal of Psychiatry.*

Kieser, R. J. (2005, 7). *Methadone and pregnancy.* Seminar presented at the Wisconsin State Methadone Providers Meeting, Wisconsin.

Kilbourne, J. (2002, February). *Deadly persuasion: Advertising and addiction.* Symposium presented to the Dept of Psychiatry at the Cambridge Hospital, MA.

Kilmer, J. R., Palmer, R. S., & Cronce, J. M. (2005). Assessment of club drug, hallucinogen, inhalant and steroid use and misuse. In D. M. Donovan & G. A. Marlatt (Eds.), *Assessment of addictive behaviors* (2nd ed.). New York: Guilford.

Kilts, C. (2004). Neurobiology of substance use disorders. In A. F. Schatzberg & C. B. Numeroff (Eds.), *Textbook of psychopharmacology* (3rd ed.). Washington, DC: American Psychiatric Publishing.

Kim, P. Y., Thomas, J. L., Wilk, J. E., Castro, C. A., & Hoge, C. W. (2010). Stigma, barriers to care, and use of mental health services among active duty and national guard soldiers after combat. *Psychiatric Services, 61,* 572–588.

Kim, Y., Teylan, M. A., Baron, M., Sands, A., et al. (2009). Methylphenidate-induced dendritic spine formation and ΔFosB expression in nucleus accumbens. *Proceedings of the National Academy of Sciences, 106,* 2915–2920.

King, A. C., deWit, H., McNamara, B. S., & Cao, D. (2011). Rewarding, stimulant, and sedative alcohol responses and relationship to future binge drinking. *Archives of General Psychiatry, 68*(4), 389–399.

King, G. R., & Ellinwood, E. H. (2005). Amphetamine and other stimulants. In J. H. Lowinson, P. Ruiz, R. B. Millman, & J. G. Langrod (Eds.), *Sub stance abuse: A comprehensive texboook* (4th ed.). New York: Lippincott, Williams & Wilkins.

King, R. S. (2006). *The next big thing? Methamphetamine in the United States.* Washington, DC: The Sentencing Project.

King, M., McKeown, E., Warner, J., Ramsay, A., et al. (2003). Mental health and quality of life of gay men and lesbians in England and Wales: Controlled, cross-sectional study. *The British Journal of Psychiatry, 183,* 552–558.

Kinsella, L. J., & Riley, D. E. (2007). Nutritional deficiencies and syndromes associated with alcoholism. In C. Goetz (Ed.), *Textbook of clinical neurology* (3rd ed.). Philadelphia: Saunders-Elsevier.

Kirisci, L., Mezzich, A., & Tarter, R. (1995). Norms and sensitivity of the adolescent version of the drug use screening inventory. *Addictive Behaviors, 20,* 149–157.

Kirisci, L., Vanyukov, M., & Tarter, R. (2005). Detection of youth at high risk for substance use disorders: A longitudinal study. *Psychology of Addictive Behaviors, 19,* 243–252.

Kirk, G. D., Mehta, S. H., Astemborski, J., Galai, N., Washington, J., Higgins, Y., Balagobal, A., & Thomas, D. L. (2013). HIV, age and the severity of hepatitis c virus-related liver disease: A cohort study. *Archives of Internal Medicine.*

Kirn, T. F. (2006). New alcohol test appears fallible. *Clinical Psychiatry News, 34*(6), 48.

Kishline, A. (1996). A toast to moderation. *Psychology Today, 29*(1), 53–56.

Klatsky, A. L. (2003). Drink to your health? *Scientific American, 288*(2), 74–81.

Klatsky, A. L., Morton, C., Udaltsova, N., & Friedman, G. D. (2006). Coffee, cirrhosis and transaminase enzymes. *Archives of Internal Medicine, 166*(11), 1190–1195.

Kleber, H. D. (2002). Methadone: The drug, the treatment, the controversy. In D. F. Musto, P. L. Korsmeyer, & T. W. Maulucci (Eds.), *One hundred years of heroin.* Westport, CN: Auburn House.

Kleiman, M. A. R. (2011). Material support how drug enforcement helps terrorists. *Playboy, 58*(9), 123–124.

Klein, M., & Kramer, F. (2004). Rave drugs: Pharmacological considerations. *AANA Journal, 72*(1), 61–67.

Kleinig, J. (2004). Ethical issues in substance use and intervention. *Substance Use & Misuse, 39*(3), 369–398.f.

Klesges, R. C., Johnson, K., & Somes, G. (2006). Varenicline for smoking cessation. *Journal of the American Medical Association, 296,* 94–95.

Klimstra, S., & Mahgoub, N. (2010). Alcohol and substance use disorders in the geriatric psychiatry inpatient. *Psychiatric Annals, 40*(6), 282–285.

Klotz, F., Garle, M., Granath, F., & Thiblin, I. (2006). Criminality among individuals testing positive for the presence of anabolic androgenic steroids. *Archives of General Psychiatry, 63,* 1274–1279.

Kluger, J. (2006). Balding, wrinkled, and stoned. *Time.* Retrieved from http://www.Time.com/time/magazine/article/0,9171,1149389,00.html?id=sphere-inline bot

Knapp, C. (1996). *Drinking: A love story.* New York: The Dial Press.

Knapp, C. M., Ciraulo, D. A., & Jaffe, J. (2005). Opiates: Clinical aspects. In J. H. Lowinson, P. Ruiz, R. Millman, & J. G. Langrod (Eds.), *Substance abuse: A comprehensive textbook* (4th ed.). New York: Lipponcott, Williams & Wilkins.

Knapp, C. M., Ciraulo, D. A., & Kranzler, H. R. (2008). Neurobiology of alcohol. In M. Galanter & H. D. Kleber (Eds.), *The American psychiatric publishing textbook of substance abuse treatment.* Washington, DC: American Psychiatric Publishing, Inc.

Knaresboro, T. (2011). A shot to end addiction. *Psychology Today, 44*(4), 16.

Knauer, S. (2002). *Recovering from sexual abuse, addictions, and compulsive behaviors.* New York: Halworth Social Work Practice Press.

Knight, J. R. (2005, March). *Adolescent substance abuse: New strategies for early identification and intervention.* Symposium presented to the Dept of Psychiatry of the Cambridge Hospital, MA.

Knight, J. R. (2000, February). *Adolescent substance use: New strategies for early identification and intervention.* Symposium presented to the Dept of Psychiatry of the Cambridge Hospital, MA.

Knight, J. R. (2003). No dope. *Nature, 426*(2963), 114–115.

Knight, J. R., Harris, S. K., Sherritt, L., et al. (2007). Prevalence of positive substance abuse screen results among adolescent primary care patients. *Archives of Pediatric and Adolescent Medicine, 16,* 1035–1041.

Knudson, H. K., Roman, P. M., & Ducharme, L. J. (2004). The availability of psychiatric programs in private substance abuse treatment centers, 1995-2004. *Psychiatric Services, 55,* 270–273.

Knudson, H. K. (2009). Adolescent-only substance abuse treatment: Availability and adoption of components of quality. *Journal of Substance Abuse Treatment, 36*(2), 195–204.

Kobeissy, F. H., O'Donoghue, M. B., Golden, E. C., Larner, S. F., et al. (2007). Performance enhancement and adverse consequences of MDMA. *Journal of Addictive Diseases, 25*(1), 47–59.

Kober, H., Mende-Siedlecki, P., Kross, E. F., Weber, J., Mischel, W., Hart, C. L., & Ochsner, K. N. (2010). Prefrontal-atriatal pathway underlies cognitive regulation of craving. *Proceedings of the National Academy of Sciences, 107*(33), 14811–14816.

Kober, H., Kross, E. F., Mischel, W., Hart, C. L., & Ochsner, K. N. (2009). Regulation of craving by cognitive strategies in cigarette smokers. *Drug and Alcohol Dependence.*

Kobor, M. S., & Weinberg, J. (2011). Focus on: Epigenetics and fetal alcohol spectrum disorders. *Alcohol Research & Health, 34*(1), 29–37.

Kodama, S., Saito, K., Tanaka, S., Horikawa, C., Saito, A., et al. (2011). Alcohol consumption and risk of atrial figrillation. *Journal of the American College of Cardiology, 57,* 427–436.

Koenig, L. B., Haber, J. R., & Jacob, T. (2011). Childhood religious affiliation and alcohol use and abuse across the lifespan in alcohol-dependent men. *Psychology of Addictive Behaviors, 25*(3), 381–389.

Koesters, S. C., Rogers, P. D., & Rajasingham, C. R. (2002). MDMA ("ecstasy") and other "club drugs": The new epidemic. *Pediatric Clinics of North America, 49,* 415–433.

Kolb, G. F. (2008). Neurobiology of addictio. In M. Galanter & H. D. Kleber (Eds.), *The American psychiatric publishing textbook of substance abuse treatment.* Washington, DC: American Psychiatric Publishing, Inc.

Kolla, B. P., Lovely, J. K., Mansukhani, M. P., & Morgenthaler, T. L. (2012). Zolpidem is independently associated with increased risk of inpatient falls. *Journal of Hospital Medicine.*

Kondro, W. (2003). Athlete's "designer steroid" leads to widening scandal. *The Lancet, 362,* 1466.

Konnikovam, M. (2012). Smells like old times. *Scientific American Mind, 23*(1), 59–63.

Konnor, M. (2010). *The evolution of childhood.* Cambridge, MA: Harvard University Press.

Konstan, M. W., Schluchter, M. D., Xue, W., & Davis, P. B. (2007). Clinical use of ibuprofen is associated with slower FEV1 decline in children with cystic fibrosis. *American Journal of Respiratory and Critical Care Medicine, 176,* 1084–1089.

Koob, A. (2009). *The rood of thought.* Upper Saddle River, N.J: FT Press.

Koob, G. F. (2008). Neurobiology of addiction. In M. Galanter & H. D. Kleber (Eds.), *Textbook of*
substance abuse treatment. Washington, DC: American Psychiatric Association, Inc.

Kosten, T. R., & George, T. P. (2002). The neurobiology of opioid dependence: Implications for treatment. *Science & Practice Perspectives, 1*(1), 13–20.

Kosten, T. R., & O'Connor, P. G. (2003). Management of drug and alcohol withdrawal. *New England Journal of Medicine, 348,* 1786–1795.

Kosten, T. R., & Sofuoglu, M. (2004). Stimulants. In J. H. Lowinson, P. Ruiz, R. B. Millman, & J. G. Langrod (Eds.). New York: Williams & Wilkins.

Kosten, T. R., Sofuoglu, M., & Gardner, T. J. (2008). Clinical management: Cocaine. In M. Galanter & H. D. Kleber (Eds.), *Textbook of substance abuse treatment.* Washington, DC: American Psychiatric Association, Inc.

Kovalesky, A. (2004). Women with substance abuse concerns. *Nursing Clinics of North America, 39,* 205–217.

Kraft, M. K., Rothbard, A., Hadley, T. R., McLellan, A. T., & Asch, D. A. (1997). Are supplementary services provided during methadone maintenance really cost effective? *American Journal of Psychiatry, 154,* 1214–1219.

Kraft, U. (2006). Natural high. *Scientific American Mind, 17*(4), 60–65.

Kraly, F. S. (2009). *The unwell brain.* New York: W.W. Norton & Co.

Krambeer, L. L., von McKnelly, W., Gabrielli, W. F., & Penick, E. C. (2001). Methadone therapy for opioid dependence. *American Family Physician, 63,* 2404–2410.

Kranzler, H. R., Covault, J., Pierucci-Lagha, A., Chan, G., et al. (2008). Effects of aripip-razole on subjective and physiological responses to alcohol. *Alcoholism: Clinical and Experimental Research, 32*(4), 573–579.

Kranzler, H. R., & Ciraulo, D. A. (2005a). Alcohol. In H. R. Kranzler & D. A. Ciraulo (Eds.), *Clinical manual of addiction psychopharmacology.* Washington, DC: American Psychiatric Publishing, Inc.

Kranzler, H. R., & Ciraulo, D. A. (2005b). Sedative-hypnotics. In H. R. Kranzler & D. A. Ciraulo (Eds.), *Clinical manual of addiction psychopharmacology.* Washington, DC: American Psychiatric Publishing, Inc.

Krasopoulos, G., Brister, S. J., Beattie, W. S., & Bushanan, M. R. (2008). Aspirin "resistance" and risk of cardiovascular morbidity: Systematic review and meta-analysis. *British Medical Journal.*

Kraus, J. F., & Chu, L. D. (2005). Epidemiology. In J. M. Siler, T. W. McAlister, & S. C. Yudofsky (Eds.), *Textbook of traumatic brain injury*. New York: CRC Press.

Kreeger, K. (2003). Inflammation's infamy. *The Scientist, 17*(4), 28.

Kreek, M. J. (1997, Septemper). *History and effectiveness of methadone treatment*. Paper presented at the NIDA "Heroin Use and Addiction" conference, DC.

Kreek, M. J. (2000). Methadone-related opioid agonist pharmacotherapy for heroin addiction. In S. D. Glick & I. B. Maisonneuve (Eds.), *New medications for drug abuse*. New York: New York Academy of Sciences.

Kreek, M. H. (2008). Neurobiology of opiates and opioids. In M. Galanter & H. D. Kleber (Eds.), *Textbook of substance abuse treatment*. Washington, DC: American Psychiatric Association, Inc.

Kreslake, J. M., Wayne, G. F., Alkpert, H. R., Hoh, H. K., & Connolly, G. N. (2008). Tobacco industry control of menthol in cigarettes and targeting of adolescents and young adults. *American Journal of Public Health*.

Kricechbaum, N., & Zernig, G. (2000). Adolescent patients. In G. Zernig, A. Saria, M. Kurz, & S. S. O'Malley (Eds.), *Handbook of alcoholism*. New York: CRC Press.

Kripke, D. F., Langer, R. D., & Kline, L. W. (2012). Hypnotics association with mortality or cancer: A matched cohort study.

Kruelwitch, C. J. (2005). Alcohol consumption during pregnancy. In J. J. Fitzpatrick, J. S. Stevenson, & M. S. Sommes (Eds.), *Annual review of nursing research (vol 23)*. New York: Springer Publishing Co.

Kubo, A., Levin, T. R., Block, G., Quesenberry, C. P., et al. (2009). Alcohol types and sociodemographic characteristics as risk factors for barrett's esophagus. *Gastroenterology, 136*(3), 806–815.

Kuhl, D. (2002). *What dying people want*. New York: Public Affairs.

Kuntsche, E., Simons-Morton, B., Fotiou, A., ter Bogt, T., et al. (2009). Decrease in adolescent cannabis use from 2002-2006 and links to evenings out with friends in 31 European and North American countries and regions. *Archives of Pediatrics and Adolescent Medicine, 163*(2), 119–125.

Kuper, H., Boffeta, P., & Adami, H. O. (2002). Tobacco use and cancer causation: Association by tumor time. *Journal of Internal Medicine, 252*, 206–224.

Kushner, M. G., Specker, S. M., & Maurer, M. (2011). Substance use disorders in patients with anxiety disorders. *Psychiatric Times, XXVIII*(9), 38–41.

Kurutz, S. (2003). Kill "em all. *Playboy, 50*(9), 49.

Kwok, M., Schooling, C. M., Ho, L., Leung, S., Mak, H. K., et al. (2008). Early life second hand smoke exposure and serious infectious morbidity during the first eight years: Evidence from Hong Kong's "children of 1997" birth cohort. *Tobbacco Control*.

Laaksonen, E., Vuoristo-Myllys, S., Koski-Jannes, A., & Alho, H. (2013). Combining medical treatment and CBT in treating alcohol-dependent patients effects on life quality and general well-being. *Alcohol & Alcoholism, 48*(6), 687–693.

Lack of funding for the war on drugs. (2008). *Forensic Drug Abuse Advisor, 20*(7), 55–56.

Lacson, J. C. A., Carroll, J. D., Tuazon, E., Castelao, E. J., Bernstein, L., & Cortessis, V. K. (2012). Population based case conrol study of recreational drug use and testis cancer risk confirms association between mariuana use and non-seminoma risk. *Cancer*.

LaGasse, L. L., Derauf, C., Smith, L. M., Newman, E., Shah, R., Neal, C., Arria, A., Huestis, M. A., Della-Grotta, S., Lin, H., Dansereau, L. M., & Lester, B. M. (2012). Prenatal methamphetamine exposure and childhood behavior problems at 3 and 5 years of age. *Pediatrics, 129*, 581–688.

Lai, S., Lima, J. A. C., Lai, H., Vlahov, D., et al. (2005). Human imunodeficiency virus 1 infection, cocaine, and coronary calcification. *Archives of Internal Medicine, 165*, 690–695.

Lakhan, S. E., & Rowland, M. (2009). Whole plant cannabis extracts in the treatment of spasticity in multiple sclerosis: A systematic review. *BMC Neurology, 9*(59). doi:10.1186/1471-2377-9-59

Lambert, N. M., Fincham, F. D., Marks, L. D., & Stillman, T. F. (2010). Invocations and intoxication: Does prayer decrease alcohol consumption? *Psychology of Addictive Behaviors, 24*, 209–219.

Lamon, B., Gadegbeku, B., Martin, J. L., Beicheler, M. B., et al. (2005). Cannabis intoxication and fatal road crashes in France: Population based case-control study. *British Medical Journal, 331*, 1371.

Landau, J., & Garrett, J. (2006). *Invitational intervention: A step by step guide for clinicians helping families engage resistant substance abusers in treatment*. New York: Halworth.

Larimer, M. E., & Kilmer, J. R. (2000). Natural history. In G. Zernig, A. Saria, M. Kurz, & S. S. O'Malley (Eds.), *Handbook of acoholism*. New York: CRC Press.

Larson, K. K. (1982). Birthplace of the "minnesota model." *Alcoholism, 3*(2), 34–35.

Lashley, F. R. (2006). Transmission and epidemiology of HIV/AIDS: A global view. *Nursing Clinics of North America, 41,* 339–354.

Latimer, W. W., Newcomb, M., Winters, K. C., & Stinchfield, R. D. (2000). Adolescent substance abuse treatment outcome: The role of substance abuse problem severity, psychosocial and treatment factors. *Journal of Consulting and Clinical Psychology, 68,* 684–696.

Lau, D., Berger, M. S., Khullar, D., & Maa, J. (2013). The impact of smoking on neuro-surgical outcomes—a review. *Journal of Neurosurgery.*

Latimer, W., & Zur, J. (2010). Epidemiologic trends of adolescent use of alcohol, tobacco and other drugs. *Child and Adolescent Psychiatric Clinics of North America, 19*(3), 451–464.

Lau-Barraco, C., Braitman, A. L., Leonard, K. E., & Padilla, M. (2012). Drinking buddies and their perspective influence on alcohol outcomes: Alcohol expectancies as a mediator. *Psychology of Addictive Behaviors, 26*(4), 747–758.

Laure, P., & Binsinger, C. (2007). Doping prevalence among preadolescent athletes: A four year follow up. *British Journal of Sports Medicine.*

Laurence, D. R., & Bennett, P. N. (1992). In D. R. Laurence & P. M. Bennett (Eds.), *Clinical pharmacology* (7th ed.). New York: Churchill Livingstone.

Lawton, G. (2009). If you party now, will you pay later? *New Scientist, 201*(2695), 8–9.

Lawton, G. (2012a). Turn on, tune in. *New Scientist, 215*(2883), 3.

Lawton, G. (2012b). On a high in an fMRI: My ecstasy brain scan. *New Scientist, 215*(2883), 11.

Lawton, G. (2013). The queen of consciousness. *New Scientist, 216*(2896), 36–37.

Le, A. D., Li, Z., Funk, D., Shram, M., Li, T. K., & Shaham, Y. (2006). Increased vulnerability to nicotine self-administration and relapse in alcohol-naive offspring of rats selectively bred for high alcohol intake. *Journal of Neuroscience, 26,* 1872–1879.

Leamon, M. H., Wright, T. M., & Myrick, H. (2008). Substance related disorders. In R. E. Hales, S. C. Yudofsky, & G. O. Gabbard (Eds.), *The American psychiatric publishing textbook of psychiatry* (5th ed.). Washington, DC: American Psychiatric Publishing, Inc.

Leavitt, F. (2003). *The real drug abusers.* New York: Rowman & Littlefield, Publishers.

Lee, C. C., Stolk, R. P., Adler, A. I., Patel, A., Chalmers, J., Neal, B., et al. (2010). Association between alcohol consumption and diabetic retinopathy and visual acuity the adrem study. *Diabetic Medicine, 27*(10), 1130–1137.

Lee, C. M., Geisner, I. M., Patrick, M. E., & Neighbors, C. (2010). The social norms of alcohol-related negative consequences. *Psychology of Addictive Behaviors, 24,* 342–348.

Lee, C. M., Lewis, M. A., & Neighbors, C. (2009). Preliminary examination of spring break alcohol use and related consequences. *Psychology of Addictive Behaviors, 23,* 689–694.

Lee, M. T., Garnick, D. W., Miller, K., & Horgan, C. M. (2004). Adolescents with substance abuse: Are health plans missing them? *Psychiatric Services, 55,* 116.

Lee, W., Jiang, Z., Liu, J., Haverty, P. M., et al. (2010). The mutation spectrum revealed by paired genome sequences from a lung cancer patient. *Nature, 465,* 473–477.

Lee, W. K., & Rega, T. J. (2002). Alcoholic cardiomyopathy: Is it dose-dependent? *Congestive Heart Failure, 8*(6), 303–306.

Leeds, J., & Morgenstern, J. (2003). Psychoanalytic theories of substance abuse. In F. Rotgers, J. Morgenstern, & S. T. Walters (Eds.), *Treating substance abuse: Theory and technique* (2nd ed.). New York: Guilford.

Leeman, R. F., Toll, B. A., Taylor, L. A., & Volpicelli, J. R. (2009). Alcohol-induced disinhibition expectancies and impaired control as prospective predictors of problem drinking in undergraduates. *Psychology of Addictive Behaviors, 23,* 553–563.

Le Foll, B., & Goldberg, S. R. (2005). Cannabinoid CB1 receptor antagonists as promising new medications for drug dependence. *Journal of Pharmacology and Experimental Therapeutics, 312*(3), 875–883.

Legrenzi, P., & Umilta, C. (2011). *Neuromania: On the limits of brain science* (F. Anderson, Trans.). New York: Oxford University Press.

Lehrman, S. (2004). Sobering shift. *Scientific American, 290*(4), 22, 24.

Lehrman, S. (2013). The diabolical genius of an ancient scourge. *Scientific American, 309*(1), 80–85.

Leinwand, D. (2000). New drugs, younger addicts fuel push to shift treatment from methadone clinics. *USA Today, 18*(179), 1–2.

Leistikow, B. N., Kabit, Z., Connolly, G. N., Clancy, L., & Alpert, H. (2008). Male tobacco smoke load and non-lung cancer mortality associations in massachusetts. *BMC Cancer, 8*(341). Retrieved from http://www.biomedcentral.com/ 1471-2407/8/341

Lembke, A. (2012). Why doctors prescribe opioids to known opioid abusers. *New Engl- and Journal of Medicine, 367*(9170), 1580–1581.

Lemonick, M. D., & Park, A. (2007). The science of addiction. *Time, 170*(3), 42–48.

Lender, M. E. (1981). The disease concept of alcoholism in the United States: Was jellinek first? *Digest of Alcoholism Theory and Application, 1*(1), 25–31.

Leonard, K. E., & Mudar, P. (2003). Peer and partner drinking and the transition to marriage: A longitudinal examination of selection and influence processes. *Psychology of Addictive Behaviors, 17,* 115–125.

Leri, F., Zhou, Y., Goddard, B., Levy, A. M., et al. (2008). Steady-state methadone blocks cocaine seeking and cocaine-induced gene expression alterations in the rat brain. *European Neuropsychopharmacology.*

Leshner, A. I. (2001a, March). *Addiction and the brain.* Paper presented to the Dept of Psychiatry of the Cambridge Hospital, MA.

Leshner, A. I. (2001b, November). *Recent developments in drug addiction research.* Paper presented to the American Society of Addiction Medicine symposium, DC.

Lessig, L. (2009). Our new prohibition. *Playboy, 56*(4), 115–116.

Lester, B. M., El-Sohly, M., Wright, L., Smeriglio, V. L., et al. (2001). The maternal lifestyle study: Drug use by meconium toxicology and maternal self-report. *Pediatrics, 107,* 309–317.

Leung, C. C., Lam, T. H., Ho, K. S., Yew, W. W., et al. (2010). Passive smoking and tuberculosis. *Archives of Internal Medicine, 170*(3), 287–292.

Levin, F. R., McDowell, D., Evans, S., Nunes, E., et al. (2004). Pharamacotherapy for marijuana dependence: A double-blind, placebo-controlled pilot study of dival- proex sodium. *American Journal on Addictions, 13,* 21–32.

Levin, J. D. (2002). *Treatment of alcoholism and other addictions.* Northvale, N.J: Jacob Aronson, Inc.

Levin, M. R. (2009). *Liberty and tyranny.* New York: Threshold Editions.

Levin, A. (2008). Might following your nose increase alcoholism risk? *Psychiatric News, 43*(1), 21.

Levis, J. T., & Garmel, G. M. (2005). Cocaine-related chest pain. *Emergency Medical Clinics of North America, 23,* 1083–1103.

Levisky, J. A., Karch, S. B., Bowerman, D. L., Jenkins, W. W., et al. (2003). False-positive RIA for methamphetamine following ingestion of an ephedra-derived herbal product. *Journal of Analytical Toxicology, 27*(3), 123–124.

Levitz, J. S., Bradley, T. P., & Golden, A. L. (2004). Overview of smoking and all cancers. *Medical Clinics of North America, 88,* 1655–1675.

Levy, T. M., & Orlans, M. (1998). *Attachment, trauma and healing.* Washington, DC: CWLA Press.

Levy, S., Harris, S. K., Sherritt, L., Angulo, M., & Knight, J. R. (2006). Drug testing of adolescents in ambulatory medicine. *Archives of Pediatric and Adolescent Medicine, 160,* 146–150.

Lewis, B. A., Singer, L. T., Short, E. J., Minnes, S., et al. (2004). Four year language outcomes of children exposed to cocaine in utero. *Neurotoxicology & Teratology, 26*(5), 617–627.

Lewis, D. C. (1997). The role of the generalist in the care of the substance-abusing abusing client. *Medical Clinics of North America, 81,* 831–843.

Lewis, M. (2011). *Memoirs of an addicted brain.* New York: Public Affairs Press.

Lewis, M. L. (1937). Alcohol and family casework. *Social Casework, 35,* 8–14.

Lezak, M. D., Hannay, H. J., & Fischer, J. S. (2004). Toxic conditions. In M. D. Lezak, D. B. Howieson, & D. W. Loring (Eds.), *Neuropsychological assessment* (4th ed.). New York: Oxford University Press.

Lezak, M. D., Howieson, D. B., Bingler, E. D., & Tranel, D. (2012). *Neuropsychological assessment* (5th ed.). New York: Oxford University Press.

Li, G., Baker, S. P., Smialek, J. E., & Soderstrom, C. A. (2001). Use of alcohol as a risk factor for bicycling injury. *Journal of the American Medical Association, 285,* 893–896.

Liang, Y., Mente, A., Yusuf, S., Gao, P., Sleight, P., Zhu, J., Fagard, R., Lonn, E., & Teo, K. K. (2012). Alcohol consumption and the risk of incident atrial fibrillation among people with cardiovascular disease. *Canadian Medical Association Journal.*

Lieber, C. S. (1998). Hepatic and other medical disorders of alcoholism: From pathogenisis to treatment. *Journal of Studies on Alcohol, 59*(1), 9–25.

Light cigarettes just as addictive as "full flavored." (2006). *ABC News.* Retrieved from http://abcnews.go.com/health/story?it=2135345&page=1

Lilienfeld, S. O., Lunn, S. J., Ruscio, J., & Beyerstein, B. L. (2010). *50 Great myths of popular psychology: Shattering widespread misconceptions about human behavior.* New York: Wiley-Blackwell.

Lillenfeld, S. O. (2012). Psychological treatments that cause harm. *Perspectives on Psychological Science, 2*(1), 53–70.

Lindsay, K. W., Bone, I., & Fuller, G. (2010). *Neurology and neurosurgery illustrated* (5th ed.). New York: Churchill Livingstone Elsevier.

Ling, W., Rawson, R., & Shoptaw, S. (2006). Management of methamphetamine abuse and dependence. *Current Psychiatry Reports, 8*(5), 335–354.

Ling, W., Mooney, L., & Wu, L. (2012). Advances in opioid antagonist treatment for opioid addiction. *The Psychiatric Clinics of North America, 35*(2), 297–308.

Lingamfelter, D. C., & Knight, L. D. (2010). Sudden death from massive gastrointestinal hemorrhage associated with crack cocaine use: Case report and review of the literature. *The American Journal of Forensic Medicine and Pathology, 31*(1), 98–99.

Lipman, J. J. (2010). Tranquilizer. *The Forensic Examiner, 19*(1), 17–32.

Lipman, J. J. (2008). The methadone poisoning "epidemic." *The Forensic Examiner, 17*(2), 38–46.

Lipton, B. H. (2008). Revealing the wizard behind the curtain. *Measuring the immeasurable: The scientific case for spirituality*. Bolder Colorado: Sounds True Press.

Lindman, R. E., Sjoholm, B. A., & Lang, A. R. (2000). Expectations of alcohol-induced positive affect: A cross-cultural comparison. *Journal of Studies on Alcohol, 61*, 681–687.

Ling, W., Rawson, R., & Shoptaw, S. (2006). Management of methamphetamine abuse and dependence. *Current Psychiatry Reports, 8*(5), 335–354.

Ling, W., Wesson, D. R., & Smith, D. E. (2005). Prescription drug abuse. In J. H. Lorenson, P. Ruiz, R. B. Millman, & J. G. Langrod (Eds.), *Substance abuse: A comprehensive textbook* (4th ed.). New York: Lipponcott, Williams & Wilkins.

Llewellyn, D. J., Lang, L. A., Langa, K. M., Naughton, F., & Matthews, F. E. (2009). Exposure to second-hand smoke and cognitive impairment in non-smokers: National cross sectional study with cotinine measurement. *British Medical Journal, 338*.

LoCastro, J. S., Potter, J. S., Donovan, D. M., Couper, D., & Pope, K. W. (2008). Chrateristics of first-time alcohol treatment seekers: The COMBINE study. *Journal of Studies on Alcohol & Drugs, 69*, 885–895.

London, E. D., Simon, S. L., Berman, S. M., Mandelkern, M. A., et al. (2004). Mood disturbances and regional cerebral metabolic abnormalities in recently abstinent methamphetamine abusers. *Archives of General Psychiatry, 61*, 74–84.

Longo, D. L., & Fauci, A. S. (2008). The human retroviruses. In A. S. Fauci, E. Braunwald, D. L. Kasper, S. L. Hauser, D. L. Longo, J. L. Hameson, & J. Loscalzo (Eds.), *Harrison's principles of internal medicine* (17th ed.). New York: McGraw-Hill Medical.

Longo, L. P., & Johnson, B. (2000). Addiction: Part i. *American Family Physician, 61*, 2401–2408.

Longo, L. P., Parran, T., Johnson, B., & Kinsey, W. (2000). Addiction: Part II. *American Family Physician, 61*, 2401–2408.

Longo, L. P. (2005, April). *Identification and management of alcohol dependence*. Paper presented at symposium Gundersen-Lutheran Medical Medical Center, Wisconsin.

Lopez, W., & Jeste, D. V. (1997). Movement disorders and substance abuse. *Psychiatric Services, 48*, 634–636.

Losing tolerance with zero tolerance. (2005). *The Lancet, 365*, 629–630.

Louie, A. K. (1990). Panic attacks when cocaine is the cause. *Medical Aspects of Human Sexuality, 24*(12), 44–46.

Lovasi, G. S., Roux, A. V. D., Hoffman, E. A., Kawut, S. M., et al. (2010). Association of environmental tobacco smoke exposure in childhood with early emphysema in adulthood among nonsmokers. *American Journal of Epidemiology, 171*(1), 54–62.

LoVecciho, F., Pizon, A., Riley, B., Sami, A., et al. (2007). Onset of symptoms after methadone overdose. *American Journal of Emergency Medicine, 25*(1), 57–59.

Lovinger, D. M. (2008). Communication networks in the brain. *Alcohol Research & Health, 31*, 196–214.

Luggen, A. S. (2006). Alcohol and the older adult. *Advice for Nurse Practitioners, 14*(1), 47–52.

Lukas, S. E. (2006, March). *The neurobiological basis of drug and alcohol abuse: How it directs treatment initiatives*. Paper Presented at the "Treating the Addictions" seminar, sponsored by the Dept of Psychiatry of the Cambridge Hospital, MA.

Lukas, S. E. (2009). The pharmacology of anabolic-androgenic steroids. In R. K. Ries, D. A. Fiellin, S. C. Miller, & R. Saitz (Eds.), *Principles of addiction medicine* (4th ed.) (pp. 251–264). New York: Lippincott, Williams & Wilkins.

Lundstrom, E., Kaillberg, H., Alfredsson, L., Klareskog, L., et al. (2009). Geneenvironmental interaction between the DRB1 shared epitope and smoking in the risk of anti-citrullinated protein antibody-positive arthritis: All alleles are important. *Arthritis & Rheumatism, 60*(6), 1597–1603.

Ly, K. N., Xing, J., Klevens, R. M., Jiles, R. B., Ward, J. W., & Holmberg, S. D. (2012). The increasing burden of mortality from viral hepatitis in the United States between 1999 and 2007. *Annals of Internal Medicine, 156*, 271–278.

Lybrand, J., & Caroff, S. (2009). Management of schizophrenia with substance use disorders. *Psychiatric Clinics of North America, 32*, 821–833.

Lynch, G., & Granger, R. (2008). *Big brain the origins and future of human intelligence*. New York: Palgrave Macmillan.

Lynch, W. J., Potenza, M. N., Cosgrove, K. P., & Mazure, C. M. (2009). Sex differences in vulnerability to stimulant abuse. In K. T. Brady, S. E. Back, & S. F. Greenfield (Eds.), *Women & addiction*. New York: Guilford.

Lynskey, M. T., & Hall, W. (2001). Attention deficit hyperactivity disorder and substance use disorders: Is there a causal link? *Addiction, 96*, 815–822.

Lundeen, E. (2002). On the implications of drug legalization. *The Independent Practitioner, 22*(2), 175–176.

Lungvist, T. (2005). Cognitive consequences of cannabis use: Comparison with abuse of stimulants and heroin with regard to attention, memory, and executive function. *Pharmacology, Biochemistry & Behavior, 81*(2), 319–330.

Lusthof, K. J., Oosting, R., Maes, A., Verschraggen, M., Dijkhuizen, A., & Sprong, A. G. A. (2011). A case of extreme agitation and death after the use of mephedrone in the Netherlands. *Forensic Science International, 120*(3), 195–203.

Lynskey, M., & Lukas, S. E. (2005). Cannabis. *Clinical manual of addiction psychopharmacology*. Washington, DC: American Psychiatric Publishing, Inc.

MacArthur, G. J., Minozzi, S., Martin, N., Vickerman, P., Deren, S., Bruneau, S., Degenhardt, L., & Hickman, M. (2012). Opiate substitution treatment and HIV transmission in people who inject drugs: Systematic review and meta-analysis. *British Medical Journal*.

Macgowan, M. J., & Engle, B. (2010). Evidence for optimism: Behavior therapies and motivational interviewing in adolescent substance abuse treatment. *Child and Adolescent Psychiatric Clinics of 527-545.North America, 19*(3).

MacKenzie, D. (2012). Parasite uses brain chemical to get host eaten. *New Scientist, 216*(2895), 38–42.

MacKenzie, K. (2007). The white plague. *New Scientist, 193*(2596), 17.

MacCoun, R. J., & Reuyter, P. (2001). Evaluating alternative cannabis regimes. *British Journal of Psychiatry, 178*, 123–128.

MacDonald, N., & MacLeod, S. M. (2010). Has the time come to phase out codeine? *Canadian Medical Association Journal, 182*, 1825.

MacParland, S. A., Pham, T. N. Q., Guy, C. S., & Michalak, T. K. (2009). *Hepatology, 49*(5), 1431–1441.

Madras, B. K. (2010, April). *Screening: Brief intervention, and referral to treatment: An idea whose time has come*. Paper presented at the "Addictions in 2010" seminar, hosted by the Division of alcohol and Drug Abuse of the McLean Hospital, MA.

Maher, B. (2002). *When you ride ALONE you ride with bin laden*. Beverly Hills, CA: New Millennium Press.

Mahoney, D. (2006). Teens and steroids: A dangerous mix. *Clinical Psychiatry News, 14*(6), 50–51.

Maisto, S. A., Clifford, P. R., Stout, R. L., & Davis, C. M. (2008). Factors mediating the association between drinking in the first year after alcohol treatment and drinking at three years. *Journal of Studies on Alcohol & Drugs, 69*, 728–737.

Malanga, C. J. (2009). Still no time for complacency. *Neurology, 72*, 2062–2063.

Maldonado, J. R. (2010). An approach to the patient with substance use and abuse. *Medical Clinics of North America, 94*(6), 1169–1205.

Malik, B., & Stillman, M. (2009). Pain syndromes. In S. I. Savitz & M. Ronthal (Eds.), *Neurology review for psychiatrists*. New York: Lippincott Williams & Wilkins.

Makki, T. (2003). Substance use, psychological distress and crime. *Medical Journal of Australia, 179*, 399–400.

Malinin, A. I., Callahan, K. P., & Serebruany, V. L. (2001). Paradoxical activation of major platelet receptors in the methadone-maintained patient after a single pill of aspirin. *Thrombosis Research, 104*, 297–299.

Malik, P., Gasser, R. W., Moncayo, R., Kemmier, G., & Fleischhacker, W. (2012). Markers of bone resorption and formation during abstinence im male alcoholic patients. *Alcoholism: Cliinical and Experimental Research.*

Mamer, M., Penn, A., Wildmer, K., Levin, R. I., & Maslansky, R. (2003). Coronary artery disease and opioid use. *American Journal of Cardiology, 93,* 1295–1297.

Mancall, E. (2008). Nutritional disorders of the nervous system. In M. J. Aminoff (Ed.), *Neurology and general medicine* (4th ed.). New York: Churchill Livingstone.

Manderson, D. R. A. (1998). Drug abuse and illicit drug trafficking. *Medical Journal of Australia, 12,* 588–589.

Mann, C. C., & Plummer, M. L. (1991). *The aspirin wars.* New York: Knopf.

Mann, J. (2000). *Murder, magic and medicine* (2nd ed.). New York: Oxford.

Mansvelder, H. D., Keath, J. R., & McGehee, D. S. (2002). Synaptic mechanisms underlie nicotine-induced excitability of brain reward areas. *Neuron, 33,* 905–919.

Marcotte, T. D., Scott, J. C., Kamat, R., & Heaton, R. K. (2010). Neuropsychology and the prediction of everyday functioning. In T. D. Marcotte & I. Grant (Eds.), *Neuropsychology of everyday functioning.* New York: Springer Publishing Co.

Marchetta, C. M., Denny, C. H., floyd, R. L., Cheal, N. E., Sniezek, J. E., & McKnight-Eily, L. (2012). Alcohol use and binge drinking among women of childbearing age United States, 2006–2010. *Morbidity and Mortality Weekly Report, 61*(28), 534–538.

Marcus, D. A. (2003). Tips for managing chronic pain. *Postgraduate Medicine, 113*(4), 49–50, 55–56, 59–60, 63–66, 98.

Marcus, G. (2008). *Kluge.* New York: Houghton-Mifflin.

Maremmani, I., Pacini, M., Lamanna, F., Pani, P. P., et al. (2010). Mood stabilizers in the treatment of substance use disorders. *CNS Sprectrums, 15*(2), 95–109.

Margolin, A., Kleber, H. D., Avants, S. K., Konefal, J., et al. (2002). Acupuncture for the treatment of cocaine addiction. *Journal of the American Medical Association, 287,* 55–63.

Mariani, J. J., & Levin, F. R. (2004). Pharmacotherapy for alcohol-related disorders: What clinicians should know. *Harvard Review of Psychiatry, 12,* 351–366.

Marijuana-related deaths? (2002). *Forensic Drug Abuse Advisor, 14*(1), 1–2.

Marijuana arrests. (2003). *Forensic Drug Abuse Advisor, 15*(1), 7.

Marik, pE. (2001). Aspiration pneumonitis and aspiration pneumonia. *New England Journal of Medicine, 344,* 665–671.

Markarian, M., & Franklin, J. (2005). Substance abuse in minority populations. In R. J. Frances & S. I. Miller (Eds.), *Clinical textbook of addictive disorders* (3rd ed.). New York: Guilford.

Markel, H. (2000). Easy answer might not be the right one. *New York Times, CL*(51551), D8.

Markel, H. (2004). *When germs travel.* New York: Pantheon Books.

Markel, H. (2011). *An anatomy of addiction: Sigmund freud, william halsted, and the miracle drug cocaine.* New York: Pantheon Books.

Marlatt, G. A., Baer, J. S., Kivlahan, D. R., Dimeff, L. A., et al. (1998). Screening and brief intervention for high risk college student drinkers: Results from a 2 year follow-up assessment. *Journal of Consulting and Clinical Psychology, 66,* 604–615.

Marlatt, G. A., & Donovan, D. M. (2005). Introduction. In G. A. Marlatt & D. M. Donovan (Eds.), *Relapse prevention: Maintenance strategies in the treatment of addictive disorders* (2nd ed.). New York: Guilford.

Marlatt, G. A., & Witkiewitz, K. (2005). Relapse prevention for alcohol and drug problems. In G. A. Marlatt & D. M. Doboban (Eds.), *Relapse prevention maintenance strategies in the treatment of addictive behaviors* (2nd ed.). New York: Guilford.

Marlowe, D. B., & DeMatteo, D. S. (2003). Drug policy by analogy: Well, it's like this. *Psychiatric Services, 54,* 1455–1456.

Marano, H. E. (2012). The cost of sobriety. *Psychology Today, 45*(6), 39–40.

Marsa, L. (2005). A generation out of control? *Ladies Home Journal, CXXI*(4), 162–164, 168, 173–174.

Marsch, L. A., Bickel, W. K., Badger, G. J., Stothart, M. E., et al. (2005). Comparison of pharmacological treatments for opioid dependent adolescents. *Archives of General Psychiatry, 62,* 1157–1164.

Marsicano, G., Wotjak, cT, Azad, S. C., Bisogno, T., et al. (2002). The endogenous cannabinoid system controls extinction of aversive memories. *Nature, 418,* 530–535.

Marsolek, M. R., White, N. C., & Litovitz, T. L. (2010). Inhalant abuse: Monitoring trends by using poison control data, 1993-2008. *Pediatrics, 125*(5), 906–913.

Martell, B. A., O'Connor, P. G., Kerns, R. D., Becker, W. C., Morales, K. H., et al. (2007). Systematic review: Opioid treatment for chronic back pain: Prevalence,efficacy, and association with addiction. *Annals of Internal Medicine, 146,* 116–127.

Martell, B. A., Orson, F. M., Poling, J., Mitchell, E., et al. (2009). Cocaine vaccine for the treatment of cocaine dependence in methadone maintained patients. *Archives of General Psychiatry, 66*(10), 1116–1123.

Martensen, R. L. (1996). From papal endorsement to Southern vice. *Journal of the Am-Erican Medical Association, 276,* 1615.

Martin, B. R. (2004). Neurobiology of marijuana. In M. Galanter & H. D. Kleber (Eds.), *Textbook of substance abuse treatment* (3rd ed.). Washington, DC: American Psychiatric Press, Inc.

Martin, N. M., Abu Dayyeh, B. K., & Chung, R. T. (2008). Anabolic steroid abuse causing recurrent hepatic adenomas and hemorrhage. *World Journal of Gastroenterology, 14*(28), 4573–4575.

Martin-Schild, S., Albright, K. C., Hallevi, H., Barreto, A. D., Philip, M., et al. (2010). Intracerebral hemorrhage in cocaine users. *Stroke, 41*(680).

Martins, S. S., Keyes, K. M., Storr, C. L., Zhu, H., & Grucza, R. A. (2010). Birth-cohort trends in lifetime and past-year prescription opioid use disorder resulting from nonmedical use: Results from two national surveys. *Journal of Studies on Alcohol & Drugs, 71*(4), 480–487.

Mash, D. C., Ouyang, Q., Pablo, J., Basile, M., et al. (2003). Cocaine abusers have an overexpression of synuclein in dopamine neurons. *Journal of Neuroscience, 23,* 2564–2571.

Maskell, P. D., De Paoli, G., Seneviratne, C., & Pounder, D. J. (2011). Case report: Mephedrone (4-methyl methcathinone) related deaths. *Journal of Analytical Toxicology, 3,* 188–191.

Mason, B. J., Salvato, F. R., Williams, L. D., Ritvo, E. C., & Cutler, R. B. (1999). A double-blind, placebo-controlled study of oral nalmefene for alcohol dependence. *Archives of General Psychiatry, 56,* 719–724.

Mason, W. A., & Spoth, R. L. (2011). Thrill seeking and religiosity in relation to adolescent substance use: Tests of joint, interactive and indirect influences. *Psychology of Addictive Behaviors, 25*(4), 683–696.

Masten, A. S. (2001). Ordinary magic: Resilience processes in development. *American Psychologist, 56,* 227–238.

Masten, A. S., Fade, V. B., Zucker, R. A., & Spear, L. P. (2009). A developmental perspective on underaged alcohol use. *Alcohol Research & Health, 32*(1), 3–15.

Matochik, J. A., Eldreth, D. A., Cadet, J. L., & Bolla, K. I. (2005). Altered brain tissue composition in heavy marijuana abusers. *Drug and Alcohol Dependency, 77,* 23–30.

Mattingley, J. S., & Groon, L. C. (2008). Wernicke's encephalophy: Is the gundersen lutheran alcohol detoxification protocol sufficient? *The Gundersen Lutheran Medical Journal, 5*(1), 13–16.

Max, T. D. (2010). The secrets of sleep. *National Geographic, 217*(5), 74–91.

Mayeda, S., & Sanders, M. (2007). Counseling difficult-to-reach adolescent male substance abusers. *Counselor, 8*(2), 12–18.

Mayer, K. H., Skeer, M., & Mimiaga, M. J. (2010). Biiomedical approaches to HIV prevention. *Alcohol Research & Health, 33*(3), 195–202.

Maze, I., Covington, H. E., Dietz, D. E., LaPlant, Q., et al. (2010). Essential role of histone methyltranserase g9a in cocaine-induced plasticity. *Science, 327*(5962), 213–216.

McAnalley, B. H. (1996). Chemistry of alcoholic beverages. In J. C. Garriott (Ed.), *Medicolegal aspects of alcohol* (3rd ed.). Tucson, AZ: Lawyers and Judges Publishing Co.

McCabe, S. E., Cranford, J. A., Morales, M., & Young, A. (2006). Simultaneous and concurrent polydrug use of alcohol and prescription drugs: Prevalence, correlates and consequences. *Journal of Studies on Alcohol and Drugs, 67*(4), 529–537.

McCabe, S. E., Cranford, J. A., & Boyd, C. J. (2006). The relationship between past-year drinking behaviors and nonmedical use of prescription drugs: Prevalence of cooccurrence in a national sample. *Drug & Alcohol Dependence, 84*(3), 281–288.

McCabe, S. E., West, B. Y., Morales, M., Cranford, J. A., & Boyd, C. J. (2009). Does early onset of nonmedical use of prescription drugs predict subsequent prescription drug abuse and dependence? Results from a national study. *Addiction, 102*(12), 1920–1930.

McCann, U. D., Sgambati, F. P., Schwartz, A. R., & Ricaurte, G. A. (2009). Sleep apneain young abstinent recreational MDMA ("ecstasy") consumers. *Neurology, 73,* 2011–2017.

McClain, C. (2006). Smoking 1 cigarette stiffens the heart. Retrieved from http://azstarnet.com/news/science/health-med-fit/smoking-cigarette-stiffens-the-heart/article_6de050a2-0d87-58fe-b667-393bb2d8a501.html

McClemon, F. J., Westman, E. C., Rose, J. D., & Lutz, A. M. (2007). The effects of food, beverages, and other factors on cigarette palatability. *Nicotine & Tobacco Research, 9*(4), 505–510.

McClure, J. B., Swan, G. E., Jack, L., Catz, S. L., et al. (2009). Mood side-effects and smoking outcomes among persons with and without probable lifetime depression taking verenicline. *Journal General Internal Medicine.* Retrieved from http://www.springerlink.com/content/77207452k3822r3v/full text.html

McCollister, K. E., & French, M. T. (2002). The economic cost of substance-abuse treat-ment in criminal justice settings. In G. G. Leukefeld, F. Tims, & D. Farabee (Eds.), *Treatment of drug offenders.* New York: Springer Publishing Co.

McCord, J., Jneid, H., Hollander, J. E., de Lemos, J. A., et al. (2008). Management of cocaine-associated chest pain and myocardial infarction. A scientific statement from the American heart association acute cardiac care committee of the counsel on clinical cardiology. *Circulation, 117,* 1897–1907.

McCrady, B. S. (2001). Alcohol use disorders. In D. H. Barlow (Ed.), *Clinical handbook of psychological disorders* (3rd ed.). New York: Guilford.

McCrady, B. S., & Irvine, S. (1980). Self-help groups. In R. K. Hester & W. R. Miller (Eds.), *Handbook of alcoholism treatment approaches.* New York: Pergamon Press.

McDargh, J. (2000, March). *The role of spirituality in the recovery process.* Paper presented at the "Treating the Addictions" seminar hosted by the Dept. Of Psychiatry of the Cambridge Hospital, MA.

McDonagh, M., & Peterson, K. (2006). *Drug class review on pharmaceutical treatments for ADHD: Final report, 2006.* Portland, OR: Evidence-Based Practice Center, Oregon Health and Science Center.

McDowell, A. K., Lineberry, T. W., & Bostwick, J. M. (2011). Practical suicide-risk assessment for the busy primary care physician. *Mayo Clinic Proceedings, 86*(8), 792–800.

McDowell, D. M. (2004). MDMA, ketamine, GHB and the "club drug" scene. In M. Galanter & H. D. Kleber (Eds.), *Textbook of substance abuse treatment* (3rd ed.). Washington, DC: American Psychiatric Press, Inc.

McDowell, D. M. (2005). Marijuana, hallucinogens and club drugs. In R. J. Frances, S. I. Miller, & A. H. Mack (Eds.), *Clinical textbook of addictive disorders* (3rd ed.). New York: Guilford.

McGillicuddy, N. B., Rychtarik, R. G., Morsheimer, E. T., & Burke-Storer, M. R. (2007). Agreement between parent and adolescent reports of adolescent substance use. *Journal of Child and Adolescent Substance Abuse, 16*(4), 59–78.

McGowan, L. M. E., Dekker, G. A., Chan, E., Stewart, A., et al. (2009). Spontaneous preterm birth and small for gestational age infanants in women who stop smoking early in pregnancy: Prospective cohort study. *British Medical Journal.*

McGovern, P. E. (2009). *Uncorking the past.* Los Angeles, CA: University of California Press.

McGowan, K. (2012). A census of your insides. *Discover, 34*(1), 21.

McGrath, J., Welham, J., Scott, J., Varghess, D., et al. (2010). Association between cannabis use and psychosis related outcomes using sibling pair analysis in a cohort of young adults. *Archives of General Psychiatry, 67*(5). doi:10.1001/archgenpsychiatry.2010.6

McGuinness, T. M. (2006). Nothing to sniff at: Inhalant abuse and youth. *Journal of Psychosocial Nursing, 44*(8), 15–18.

McGuinness, T. M., & Fogger, S. A. (2006). Hyperanxiety in early sobriety. *Journal of Psychosocial Nursing, 44*(1), 22–27.

McGuire, L. (1990). The power of non-narcotic pain relievers. *RN, 53*(4), 28–35.

McKay, A., Koranda, A., & Axen, D. (2004). Using a symptom-triggered approach to manage patients in acute alcohol withdrawal. *MEDSURG Nursing, 13*(1), 15–20, 31.

McKay, J. R. (2006). Continuing care in the treatment of addictive disorders. *Current Psychiatry Reports, 8,* 355–362.

McKee, S. A., Harrison, E. L. R., O'Malley, S. S., Krishnan-Sarin, S., et al. (2009). Verenicline reduces alcohol self-administration in heavy drinking smokers. *Biological Psychiatry.*

McKetin, R., Lubman, D. I., Baker, A. L., Dawe, S., & Ali, R. L. (2013). Dose-related psychotic symptoms in chronic methamphetamine users: Evidence from a prospective longitudinal study. *JAMA Psychiatry.*

McLellan, A. T. (2001, March). *Is addiction treatment effective: Compared to what?.* Symposium presented to the Department of Psychiatry of the Cambridge Hospital, MA.

McLellan, A. T. (2008). Evolution in addiction treat-ment, concepts and methods. In M. Galanter & H. D. Kleber (Eds.), *The American psychiatric publishing textbook of substance abuse treatment.*

Washington, DC: American Psychiatric Publishing, Inc.

McLellan, A. T. (2008). Evolution in addiction treatment concepts and methods. In M. Galanter & H. D. Kleber (Eds.), *The American psychiatric publishing textbook of substance abuse treatment.* Washington, DC: American Psychiatric Publishing, Inc.

McIlveen, J. W., Mullaney, D., Weiner, M. J., Diaz, N., & Horton, G. (2007). Dysthymia and substance abuse: A new perspective. *Counselor, 8*(2), 30–34.

McNichol, E., Horowicz-Mehler, N., Risk, R. A., Bennett, K., et al. (2003). Management of opioid side effects in cancer-related and chronic noncancer pain: A systematic review. *The Journal of Pain, 4P*(5), 231–256.

McPherson, S. B., Afsarifard, F., Hall, H. V., Yudko, E., & Rodriguez, P. (2009). Global perspective on methamphetamine. In S. B. McPherson, H. V. Hall, & E. Yudo (Eds.), *Methamphetamine use—clinical and forensic aspects.* New York: CRC Press.

McPherson, S. B., Yudko, E., Murray-Bridges, L., Rodriguez, P., & Lindo-Moulds, P. (2009). The history of drug control. In S. B. McPherson, H. V. Hall, & E. Yudo (Eds.), *Methamphetamine use—clinical and forensic aspects.* New York: CRC Press.

McPherson, S. B., Yudo, E., Afsarifard, F., & Freitas, T. (2009). Treatment. In S. B. McPherson, H. V. Hall, & E. Yudo (Eds.), *Methamphetamine use—clinical and forensic aspects.* New York: CRC Press.

McQueeny, T., Schweinsburg, G. B., Schweinsburg, A. D., Jacobs, J., et al. (2009). Altered white matter integrity in adolescent binge drinkers. *Alcoholism Clinical and Experimental Research, 21.* Retrieved from http://www3.interscience.wiley.com/journal/122343078

McRae-Clark, A., & Price, K. L. (2009). Women and marijuana dependence. In K. T. Brady, S. E. Back, & S. F. Greenfield (Eds.), *Women & addiction.* New York: Guilford.

McVoy, M., & Findling, R. (2009). Child and adolescent psychopharmacology update. *Psychiatric Clinics of North America, 32,* 111–133.

Meatherall, R., & Sharma, P. (2005). Fox, a designer tryptamine hallucinogen. *Journal of Analytical Toxicology, 25*(4), 313–317.

Medical reprieve. (2003). *Playboy, 50*(3), 60.

Medication-assisted treatment (MAT) during pregnancy—part 1. *Addiction Treatment Forum, 19*(3), 4–5.

Medication interactions. (2008). *Monthly Prescribing Reference, 12*(2).

Medina, K. L., Price, J., Harper, E., Logan, P., & Sheer, P. K. (2008). *Ecstasy consumption and executive functioning: Gender aspects.* Poster presentation American Psychological Association, Boston, MA, August 14, 2008.

Medina, K. L., Shear, P. K., & Schafer, J. (2006). Memory functioning in polysubstance dependent women. *Drug and Alcohol Dependence, 84*(3), 248–265.

Mee-Lee, D. (2002). *Clinical implications of four generations of addiction treatment: We've come a long way baby or have we?* Symposium presented to the Dept. Of Psychiatry at the Cambridge Hospital, Boston, MA, February 8, 2002.

Mee-Lee, D., & Gastfriend, D. R. (2008). Patient placement criteria. In M. Galanter & H. D. Kleber (Eds.), *The American psychiatric publishing textbook of substance abuse treatment.* Washington, DC: American Psychiatric Publishing, Inc.

Mehta, S. H., Astemborski, J., Kirk, J. D., Strathdee, S. E., Nelson, K. E., et al. (2011). Changes in blood-borne infection risk among injection drug users. *Journal of Infectious Diseases, 203*(5), 587–594.

Meier, B. (2003). *Pain killer: A "wonder" drug's trail of addiction and death.* New York: Rodale Press.

Meier, E. A., Troost, J. M., & Anthony, J. C. (2012). Extramedical use of prescription pain relievers by youth aged 12-31 years in the United States. *Archives of Oediatrics & Adolescent Medicine.*

Meier, M. H., Caspi, A., Amber, A., Harrington, H., Houts, R., Keefe, R. S. E., McDonald, K., Ward, A., Poulton, R., & Moffitt, T. E. (2012). Persistent cannabis users show neuropsychological decline from childhood to midline. *Proceedings of the National Academy of Science.*

Meldrum, M. L. (2003). A capsule history of pain management. *Journal of the American Medical Association, 290,* 2470–2475.

Melton, L. (2007). What's your poison? *New Scientist, 193*(2590), 30–33.

Mendelson, J. H., & Mello, N. K. (2008). Cocaine and other commonly abused drugs. In A. S. Fauci, E. Braunwald, D. L. Kasper, S. L. Hauser, D. L. Longo, J. L. Jameson, & J. Loscalzo (Eds.), *Harrison's principles of internal medicine* (17th ed.). New York: McGraw-Hill.

Mendelson, J. H., & Mello, N. K. (2010). Cocaine and other commonly abused drugs. In S. L. Hauser &

S. A. Josephson (Eds.), *Harrison's neurology in clinical medicine* (2nd ed.). New York: McGraw-Hill.

Mendelson, J. H., Mello, N. K., Schuckit, M. A., & Segal, D. S. (2006). Cocaine, opioids and other commonly abused drugs. In S. L. Hauser (Ed.), *Harrison's neurology in clinical medicine*. New York: McGraw-Hill.

Mendyk, S. L., & Fields, D. W. (2002). Acute psychotic reactions: Consider "dip dope" intoxication. *Journal of Emergency Nursing, 28,* 432–435.

Menegaux, F., Steffen, C., Bellec, S., Baruchel, A., et al. (2006). Maternal coffee and alcohol consumption during pregnancy, parental smoking, and risk of childhood acute leukemia. *Cancer Detection and Prevention, 29*(6), 487–493.

Mennella, J. A., & Pepino, M. Y. (2010). Breastfeeding and prolactin levels in lactating women with a family history of alcoholism. *Pediatrics, 125,* 1162–1170.

Merton, T. (1961). *New seeds of contemplation.* New York: New Directions Publishing.

Merton, T. (1978). *No man is an Island.* New York: New Directions Publishing.

Messing, R. O. (2008). Alcohol and the nervous system. In M. J. Aminoff (Ed.), *Neurology and general medicine* (4th ed.). New York: Churchill-Livingstone.

Messinis, L., Kyprianidou, A., Malefaki, S., & Papathanasoupoulos, P. (2006). Neuropsychological deficits in long-term frequent cannabis users. *Neurology, 66,* 737–739.

Methadone-cipro interactions. (2002). *Forensic Drug Abuse Advisor, 14*(1), 5–6.

Methadone overdose in MMT. (2007). *Addiction Treatment Forum, 16*(3), 1, 3–6.

Metzner, R. (2002). The role of psychoactive plant medicines. In C. S. Grob (Ed.), *Hallucinogens.* New York: Penguin Putnam, Inc.

Meyer, J. S., & Quenzer, L. F. (2005). *Psychopharmacology.* Sunderland, MA: Sinauer Associates.

Meyer, R. E. (1996). The disease called addiction: Emerging evidence in a 200 year debate. *The Lancet, 347,* 162–166.

Meyers, J. L., & Dick, D. M. (2010). Genetic and environmental risk factors for adolescent-onset substance use disorders. *Child and Adolescent Psychiatric Clinics of North America, 19*(3), 465–477.

Meyers, D. G., Neubrger, J. S., & He, J. (2009). Cardiovascular effect of bans on smoking in public places. *Journal of the American College of Cardiology, 54,* 1249–1255.

Migliori, G. B., De Laco, G., Besozzi, G., & Cirillo, C. R. (2009). First tuberculosis cases in Italy resistant to all tested drugs. *Eurosurveillance, 12*(20), 3194.

Mihic, S. J., & Harris, R. A. (2011). Hypnotics and sedatives. In L. L. Brunton, B. A. Chabner, & B. Knollman (Eds.), *Pharmacological basis of therapeutics* (12th ed., pp. 457–480). New York: McGraw-Hill.

Miles, H., Johnson, S., Amponsah-Afuwape, S., Cinch, E., Leese, M., & Thornicroft, G. (2003). Characteristics of subgroups of individuals with psychotic illness and a comorbid substance use disorder. *Psychiatric Services, 54,* 554–561.

Millar, H. (2009). The hidden epidemic of very young alcoholics. *San Francisco Chronicle.* Retrieved from http://www.sfgate.com/cgi-bin/article.cgl?f=/g/a/2009/07/16hearstmagfamily300674.DTL

Miller, G. M. (2008, Feb). *The neurobiology and genetic susceptibility of addiction.* Paper presented at the "Treating the Addictions" seminar hosted by the Dept. Of Psychiatry of the Cambridge Health Alliance, MA.

Miller, L., Davies, M., & Greenwald, S. (2000). Religiosity and substance use and abuse among adolescents in the national comorbidity survey. *Journal of the American Academy of Child and Adolescent Psychiatry, 39,* 1190–1197.

Miller, M. C. (2007). Drug diversion by adolescents. *Harvard Mental Health Letter, 24*(1), 8.

Miller, M. C. (2005). What are the dangers of methamphetamine? *Harvard Mental Health Letter, 22*(2), 8.

Miller, M. C. (2008). Songs, lyrics, stress, and substance abuse in adolescents. *Harvard Mental Health Letter, 24*(11), 8.

Miller, N. S. (2004). Prescription opiate medications: Medical uses, consequences, laws and controls. *Psychiatric Clinics of North America, 27,* 689–708.

Miller, N. S. & Adams, J. (2006). Alcohol and drug disorders. In J. M. Silver, T. W. McAllister, & S. C. Yudofsky (Eds.), *Textbook of traumatic brain injury.* Washington, DC: American Psychiatric Association Press, Inc.

Miller, N. S., & Werner, T. (2011). Alcohol and drug disorders. In J. M. Silver, T. W. McAllister, & S. C. Yudofsky (Eds.), *Textbook of traumatic brain injury* (2nd ed.) (pp. 461–474). Washington, DC: American Psychiatric Press.

Miller, N. S., & Brady, K. T. (2004). Preface. *Psychiatric Clinics of North America, 27,* xi–xviii.

Miller, W. R., & Brown, S. A. (1997). Why psychologists should treat alcohol and drug problems. *American Psychologist, 52,* 1269–1279.

Miller, W. R. (2003, March). *What really motivates change? Reflections on 20 years of motivational interviewing.* Symposium presented to the Dept of Psychiatry at the Cambridge Hospital, MA.

Miller, W. R., & Harris, R. J. (2000). A simple scale of gorski's warning signs for relapse. *Journal of Studies on Alcohol, 61,* 759–765.

Miller, N. S. (1999). Mortality risks in alcoholism and effects of abstinence and addiction treatment. *Psychiatric Clinics of North America, 27,* 371–383.

Miller, S. C., & Frankowski, D. (2012). Prescription opioid use disorder: A complex clinical challenge. *Current Psychiatry, 11*(8), 15–21.

Miller, T. R., Levy, D. T., Spicer, R. S., & Taylor, D. M. (2006). Societal costs of underaged drinking. *Journal of Studies on Alcohol and Drugs, 67,* 519–528.

Miller, T. R., Levy, D. T., Spicer, R. S., & Taylor, D. M. (2006). Societal costs of underaged drinking. *Journal of Studies on Alcohol, 67,* 519–528.

Miller, W. R., Andrews, N. R., Wilbourne, P., & Bennett, M. E. (1998). A wealth of alternatives. In R. K. Hester & W. R. Miller (Eds.), *Handbook of alcoholism treatment approaches* (2nd ed.). New York: Allyn & Bacon.

Miller, W. R., Walters, S., & Bennett, M. E. (2001). How effective is alcoholism treatment in the United States? *Journal of Studies on Alcohol, 62,* 211–220.

Miller, W. R., & Rollnick, S. (2002). *Motivational interviewing* (2nd ed.). New York: Guilford Press.

Miller, W. R., & White, W. (2007). Confrontation in addiction treatment. *Counselor, 8*(4), 12–30.

Milne, D. (2007). Perception of sleep quality linked to drinking relapse. *Psychiatric News, 42*(5), 29.

Milstein, J. M. (2008). Introducing spirituality in medical care. *Journal of the American Medical Association, 299,* 2440–2441.

Minkoff, K. (1997). Substance abuse versus substance dependence. *Psychiatric Services, 48,* 867.

Minkoff, K. (2008, October). *Changing the world: Welcoming, accessible recovery-oriented, culturally-fluent, comprehensive, continuous, integrates systems of care for individuals and families with psychiatric and substance use disorders.* Seminar presented at Gundersen-Lutheran Medical Center, WI.

Minnes, S., Lang, A., & Singer, L. (2011). Prenatal tobacco, marijuana, stimulant and opiate exposure: Outcomes and practice implications. *Addiction Science & Clinical Practice, 6*(1), 57–62.

Mintz, D. (2011). Psychodynamic psychopharmacology. *Psychiatric Times, XXVII*(9), 22–24.

Mir, A., Obafemi, A., Young, A., & Kane, C. (2011). Myocardial infarction associated with useof the synthetic cannabinoid k2. *Pediatrics.*

Mir, M. A., Amialchuk, A., & Dwyer, D. S. (2011). The social contagion effect of marijuana use among adolescents. *PLos ONE, 6*(1).

Miro, O., Nogue, S., Espinoza, G., To-Figueras, J., & Sanchez, S. (2002). Trends in illicit drug emergencies: The emerging role of gamma hydroxybutyrate. *Clinical Toxicology, 40,* 129–135.

Mitchell, J. M., O'Neil, J. P., Janabi, M., Marks, S. M., Jagust, W. J., & Fields, H. L. (2012, 01 15). Alcohol consumption induces endogenous opioid release in the human orbito-frontal cortex and nucleus accumbens. *Science Translational Medicine.*

Mithoefer, M., Mithoefer, A., & Wagner, M. (2008). *Methylenedioxymethamphetamine (MDMA)-assisted psychotherapy in subjects with chronic posttraumatic stress disorder: A phase II clinical trial completed 19 september, 2008.* Poster presented at the 24th Annual Meeting of the International Society of Traumatic Stress Studies, Chicago.

Mithoefer, M. (2011). Does MDMA have a role in clinical psychiatry? *Psychiatric Times, XXVIII*(5), 36–39, 49.

Mittleman, M. A., Lewis, R. A., Maclure, M., Sherwood, J. B., & Muller, J. E. (2001). Triggering myocardial infarction by marijuana. *Circulation, 103,* 2805–2809.

Moalem, D., & Prince, J. (2007). *Survival of the sickest.* New York: HarperCollins Publishers.

Mochly-Rosen, D., & Zakhari, S. (2010). Focus on: The cardiovascular system: What did we learn from the French (paradox)?*Alcohol Health & Research World, 33*(1), 76–86.

Modesto,-Lowe, V., & Fritz, E. M. (2005). The opioidergic-alcohol link: Implications for treatment. *CNS Drugs, 19*(8), 693–707.

Modesto-Lowe, V., & Kranzler, H. R. (1999). Diagnosis and treatment of alcohol dependent patients with comorbid psychiatric disorders. *Alcohol Research & Health, 23*(2), 144–149.

Moeller, F. G., & Dougherty, D. M. (2001). Antisocial personalty disorder, alcohol, and aggression. *Alcohol Research & Health, 25*(1), 5–11.

Moffett, S. (2006). *The three-pound enigma.* Chapel Hill, N.C: Algonquin Books of Chapel Hill.

Moir, D., Rickert, W. S., Levasseur, G., Larouse, Y., Maertens, R., White, P., & Desjardins, S. (2007). A comparison of mainstream and sidestream marijuana and tobacco cigarette smoke produced under two machine smoking conditions, *21*(2), 494–502.

Molina, P. E., Happel, K. I., Zhang, P., Kollsm, J. K., & Nelson, S. (2010). Focus on: Alcohol and the immune system. *Alcohol Research & Health, 33*(1), 97–108.

Mokdad, A. H., Marks, J. S., Stroup, D. F., & Gerberding, J. L. (2004). Actual causes of death in the United States, 2000. *Journal of the American Medical Association, 291*, 1238–1245.

Mone, G. (2012). Tracking the craving killer. *Discover, 32*(9), 12–13.

Monti, P. M., Kadden, R. M., Rohsenow, D. J., Cooney, N. L., & Abrams, D. B. (2002). *Treating alcohol dependence* (2nd ed.). New York: Guilford.

Montisci, M., El Mazioum, R., Cecchetto, G., Terranova, C., Ferrara, S. D., Thiene, G., & Basso, C. (2012). Anabolic androgenic steroids abuse and cardiac death in athletes: Morphological and toxicological findings in four fatal cases. *Forensic Science International*.

Montgomery, D. P., Plate, C. A., Jones, M., Jones, J., et al. (2008). Using umbilical cord tissue to detect fetal exposure to illicit drugs: A new multicentered study in utah and new jersey. *Journal of Perinatology, 28*, 750–753.

Moon, M. A. (2008a). Smoking associated with cognitive decline in middle age. *Clinical Psychiatry News, 36*(7), 37.

Moon, M. A. (2008b). Methylnaltrexone relieves opioid-induced constipation. *Clinical Psychiatry News, 36*(7), 44.

Mooney, L., Glasner-Edwards, S., Rawson, R. A., & Ling, W. (2009). Medical effects of methamphetamine use. In J. R. Roll, R. A. Rawson, W. Ling, & S. Shoptaw (Eds.), *Methamphetamine addiction from basic science to treatment*. New York: Guilford.

Moore, C. M. (2009). Drugs of abuse in oral fluid. In J. D. Robero-Miller & B. A. Goldberger (Eds.), *Handbook of workplace drug testing* (2nd ed.). Washington, DC: AACC Press.

Moore, T. J., Furberg, C. D., Glenmullen, J., Maltsberger, J. T., & Singh, S. (2011). Suicidal behavior and depression in smoking cessation treatments. *Plos ONE*.

Moore, T. J., Glenmullen, J., & Furberg, C. D. (2010). Thoughts and acts of aggression/ violence towards

others reported in association with verenicline. *The Annals of Pharmacotherapy, 44*, 1389–1394.

Moos, R. H. (2003). Addictive disorders in context: Principles and puzzles of effective treatment and recovery. *Psychology of Addictive Behaviors, 17*, 3–12.

Moos, R. H., & Moos, B. S. (2005). Paths of entry into alcoholics anonymous: Consequences for participation and readmission. *Alcoholism: Clinical and Experimental Research, 29*(10), 1858–1868.

Moos, R. H., & Moos, B. S. (2006). Treated and untreated indviduals with alcohol use disorders: Rates and predictors of remission and relapse. *International Journal of Clinical and Health Psychology, 6*(3), 513–526.

Moos, R. H., Moos, B. S., & Andrassy, J. M. (1999). Outcomes of four treatment approaches in community residential programs for patients with substance use disorders. *Psychiatric Services, 50*, 1577–1583.

Moos, R. H., & Moos, B. S. (2006). Participation in treatment and alcoholics anonymous: A 16 year follow-up of initially untreated individuals. *Journal of Clinical Psychology, 62*(6), 735–750.

Morasco, B. J., Gritzner, S., Lewis, L., Oldham, R., Turk, D. C., & Dobscha, S. K. (2010). Systematic review of prevalence, correlates, and treatment outcomes for chronic non-cancer pain in patients with comorbid substance use disorder. *Pain, 152*(3), 488–497.

Morean, M. E., Corbin, W. R., & Fromme, K. (2012). Age of first use and delay to first in-toxication in relation to trajectories of heavy drinking and alcohol-related problems during emerging adulthood. *Alcoholism Clinical & Experimental Research*.

Morgan, C. J. A., Muetzelfeldt, L., & Curran, H. V. (2009). Ketamine use, cognition and psychological wellbeing: A comparison of frequent, infrequent and ex-users and non-using controls. *Addiction, 104*(1), 77–87.

Morgan, P. T., Pace-Schott, E. F., Sahl, Z. H., Coric, V., et al. (2006). Sleep, sleep-dependent procedural learning and vigilance in chronic cocaine users: Evidence for occult insomnia. *Drug and Alcohol Dependence, 82*(3), 238–249.

Morgan, P. T., Pace-Schott, E., Pittman, B., Stickgold, R., & Malison, R. T. (2010). Normalizing effects of modafinil on sleep in chronic cocaine users. *American Journal of Psychiatry, 167*(3), 331–340.

Morgan, T. J. (2006). Behavioral treatment techniques for psychoactive substance use disorders. In

F. Rotgers, J. Morgenstern, & S. T. Walkers (Eds.), *Treating substance abuse: Theory and technique* (2nd ed.). New York: Guilford Press.

Morgenstern, J., Naqvi, N. H., Debellis, R., & Breiter, H. C. (2013). The contributions of cognitive neuroscience and neuroimaging to understanding mechanisms of behavior change in addictions. *Psychology of Addictive Behaviors, 27*(2), 336–350.

Morgenstern, M., Sargent, J. D., Isensee, B., & Hanewinkel, R. (2013). From never to daily smoking in 30 months: The predictive value of tobacco and non-tobacco advertising exposure. *British Medical Journal.*

Mortimer, J. T. (2010). The benefits and risks of adolescent employment. *The Prevention Researcher, 17*(2), 8–11.

Morton, J. (2005). Ecstasy: Pharmacology and neurotoxicity. *Current Opinion in Pharmacology, 5*, 79–86.

Mosier, W. A. (1999). Alcohol addiction: Identifying the patient who drinks. *Journal of the American Academy of Physician's Assistants, 12*(5), 25–26, 28–29, 35–36, 38, 40.

Moss, H. B., Chen, C. M., & Yi, H. (2007). Subtypes of alcohol dependence in a nationally representative sample. *Journal of the American Academy of Physician's Assistants, 12*(5), 25–26, 28–29, 35–36, 38, 40.

Moos, R. H., & Moos, B. S. (2006). Participation in treatment and alcoholics anonymous: A 16 year follow-up of initially untreated individuals. *Journal of Clinical Psychology, 62*(6), 735–750.

Moss, J., & Rosow, C. E. (2008). Development of opioid antagonists: New insights into opioid effects. *Mayo Clinic Proceedings, 83*(10), 1116–1130.

Motluk, A. (2004). Intemperate society. *New Scientist, 183*(2461), 28–33.

Motluk, A. (2006). To your good health. *New Scientist, 191*(2560), 31–34.

Motluk, A. (2008). Body's own drug damps down fear. *New Scientist, 198*(2657), 12.

Movig, K. L. L., Mathijssen, M. P. M., Nagel, P. H. A., van Egmondm, J., et al. (2004). Psychoactive motor use and the risk of motor vehicle accidents. *Accident Analysis and Prevention, 36*, 631–636.

Mozayani, A. (2009). Phencyclidine. In J. D. Robero-Miller & B. A. Goldberger (Eds.), *Handbook of workplace drug testing* (2nd ed.). Washington, DC: AACC Press.

Mueller, A. A. (2005). New drugs of abuse update: Foxy methoxy. *Journal of Emergency Nursing, 30*(5), 507–508.

Mueser, K. T., Noordsy, D. L., Drake, R. E., & Fox, L. (2003). *Integrated treatment for dual disorders.* New York: Guilford.

Muniyappa, R., Sable, S., Ouwerkerk, R., Mari, A., Gharib, A. M., Walter, M., Courville, A., Hall, G., Chen, K. Y., Volkow, N. D., Kunos, G., Huestis, M. A., & Skarulis, M. C. (2013). Metabolic effects of chronic cannabis smoking. *Diabetes Czre.*

Muggli, M. E., Ebbert, J. O., Robertson, C., & Hurt, R. D. (2008). Waking a sleeping giant: The tobacco industry's response to the polonium 210 issue. *American Journal of Public Health, 98*(9), 1643–1650.

Mukamal, K. J., Maclure, M., Muller, J. E., & Mittleman, M. A. (2008). An exploratory prospective study of marijuana use and mortality following acute myocardial infarction. *American Heart Journal, 155*(3), 465–470.

Muir, H. (2008). Science rules OK!. *New Scientist, 198* (2657), 40–43.

Mukamal, K. J., Maclure, N., Mueller, J. E., & Mittleman, M. A. (2008). An exploratory prospective study of marijuana use and mortality following acute myocardial infarction. *American Heart Journal, 155*(3), 465–470.

Mundt, M. P., & Zaletskalia, L. I. (2012). Prevention for college students who suffer alcohol-induced blackouts could deter high-cost emergency department visits. *Health Affairs, 31*(4), 863–870.

Mundt, M. P., Zakletskala, L. I., & Flemming, M. F. (2009). Extreme college drinking and alcohol-related injury risk. *Alcoholism: Clinical and Experimental Research, 33*, 1532–1538.

Mundle, G. (2000). Geriatric patients. In G. Zernig, A. Saria, M. Kurz, & S. S. O'Makketm (Eds.), *Handbook of alcoholism.* New York: CRC Press.

Mundt, M. P., Zakletskala, L. I., Brown, D. D., & Fleming, M. F. (2011). Alcohol-induced memory blackouts as an indicator of injury risk among college drinkers. *Injury Prevention.*

Mundt, M.P, Z., L. I. (2012). Prevention for college students who suffer alcohol-induced blackouts could deter high-cost emergency department visits. *Health Affairs.* Retrieved from http://content. healthaffairs.org/content/early/2012/03/13/ hlthaff.2010.11400.full

Muniyappa, R., Sable, S., Ouwerkerk, R., Mari, A., Gharib, A. M., Walter, M., Courville, A., Hall, G., Chen, K. Y., Volkow, N. D., Kiunos, G., Huestis, M. A., & Skarulis, M. C. (2013). Metabolic effects of chronic cannabis smoking. *Diabetes Care.*

Munsey, C. (2010). Marijuana potency a concern. *Monitor on Psychology, 41*(6), 53.

Murphy, S. (2012). Addictive personality. *New Scientist, 215*(2881), 36–39.

Murphy, T. D., Weldenbach, K. N., Van Houten, C., Gerona, R. R., Moran, J. H., Kirschner, R. I., Marraffa, J. M., Stork, C. M., Brkhead, G. S., Newman, A., Hendrickson, R. G., Vian, K., et al. (2013). Acute kidney injury associated with synthetic cannabinoid use multiple states, 2012. *Morbidity and Mortality Weekly Report, 62*(6), 93–98.

Musher, M. M. (2008). Pneumococcal infections. In A. S. Fauci, E. Braunwald, D. L. Kasper, S. L. Hauser, D. L. Longo, J. L. Hameson, & J. Loscalzo (Eds.), *Harrison's principles of internal medicine (17th ed.).* New York: McGraw-Hill Medical.

Musto, D. F. (1991). Opium, cocaine and marijuana in American history. *Scientific American, 265*(1), 40–47.

Myers, B. J., Dawson, K. S., Britt, G. C., Lodder, D. E., et al. (2003). Prenatal cocaine exposure and infant performance on the brazelton neonatal behavioral assessment scale. *Substance Use & Misuse, 38*(14), 2065–2096.

Mylonakis, E., Paliou, M., & Rich, J. D. (2001). Plasma viral load testing in the management of HIV infection. *American Family Physician, 63,* 483–490.

Myrick, H., & Wright, T. (2008). Clinical management of alcohol abuse and dependence. In M. Galanter & H. D. Kleber (Eds.), *Textbook of substance abuse treatment.* Washington, DC: American Psychiatric Association, Inc.

Nabi-Burza, E., Regan, S., Dreher, J., Ossip, D., Rigotti, N., Hipple, B., Dempsey, J., Hall, N., Friebely, J., Weiley, V., & Winickoff, J. P. (2012). Parents smoking in their cars with children present. *Pediatrics.*

Nace, E. P. (2003). The importance of alcoholics anonymous in changing destructive behavior. *Primary Psychiatry, 10*(9), 65–68, 71–72.

Nace, E. P. (2005a). Alcohlics anonymous. In J. H. Lowinson, P. Ruiz, R. B. Millman, & J. G. Langrod (Eds.), *Substance Abuse: A Comprehensive Textbook* (4th ed.). New York: Lipponcott, Williams & Wilkins.

Nace, E. P. (2005b). Alcohol. In R. J. Frances, S. I. Miller, & A. H. Mack (Eds.), *Clinical textbook of addictive disorders* (3rd ed.). New York: Guilford.

Naimi, T. S., Brewer, R. D., Mokdad, A., Denny, C., Serdula, M. K., & Marks, J. S. (2003). Binge drinking among US adults. *Journal of the American Medical Association, 289,* 70–75.

Najavits, L. M. (2010, May). *Integrated treatment of patients with co-occurring substance abuse and PTSD.* Paper presented at the "Addictions in 2010" seminar, hosted by the Division of alcohol and Drug Abuse of the McLean Hospital, MA.

Narcotics Anonymous. (1982). Van Nys, CA: Narcotics Anonymous World Service Office, Inc.

Nasrallah, H. A. (2010a). Treat the patient, not the disease. *Current Psychiatry, 8*(8), 13–14.

Nasrallah, H. A. (2010b). Out-of-the-box questions about psychotherapy. *Current Psychiatry, 9*(10), 13–14.

Nasrallah, H. A. (2011). Harnessing epigenetics for psychiatry. *Current Psychiatry, 10*(7), 12, 16.

National Center on Addiction and Substance Abuse at Columbia University. (2009a). *Shoveling up II: The Impact of Substance Abuse on Federal, State, and Local Budgets.*

Nazi meth on the rise. (2003). *Forensic Drug Abuse Advisor, 15,* 77–78.

Neergaard, L. (2004). Dieters, bodybuilders will lose ephedra: FDA ban takes effect april 12. *Milwaukee Journal Sentinel, 122*(84), 3A.

Neighbors, C., Pedersen, E. R., & Roberts, T. (2009). 21 Bottles of beer in my bloodstream: Extreme drinking on 21st birthdays among college students. *The Addictions Newsletter, 16*(3), 14–15.

Nelson, E. C., Heath, A. C., Bucholz, K. K., Madden, P. A., et al. (2004). Genetic epidemiology of alcohol-induced blackouts. *Archives of General Psychiatry, 61,* 257–273.

Nelson, R. (2007). Younger onset of alcohol dependence correlates with less help seeking. *CNS News, 9*(1), 19, 25.

Nelson, T. (2000, March). *Pharmacology of drugs of abuse.* Seminar presented by the Division of Continuing Studies, University of Wisconsin @ Madison, WI.

Nelson, T. F., Xuan, Z., Lee, H., Weitzman, E. R., & Wechsler, H. (2009). Persistence of heavy drinking and ensuing consequences at heavy drinking colleges. *Journal of Studies on Alcohol and Drugs, 70*(5), 726–734.

Nemeroff, C. B., & Putnam, J. S. (2005). Barbiturates and similarly acting substances. In B. J. Sadock & V. A. Sadock (Eds.), *Kaplan & Sadock's Comprehensive Textbook of Psychiatry* (8th ed.). New York: Lippincott Williams and Wilkins.

Nery, F. G., & Soares, J. C. (2011). Comorbid bipolar disorder and substance abuse: Evidence-based options. *Current Psychiatry, 10*(4), 57–66.

Nestler, E. J. (2005). The neurobiology of cocaine addiction. *Science & Practice Perspectives, 3*(1), 4–10.

Neto, D., Labaz, R., Agular, P., & Chick, J. (2008). *Effectiveness of sequential combined treatment in comparison with treatment as usual in preventing relapse alcohol dependence.* Retrieved from http://www.ncbi.him.hig.gov./pubmed/1885241?ordinalpos=1itool=EntrezSystem2Pentrez.com

Neubauer, D. N. (2005). *Insomnia.* Montvale, N.J: Thompson Healthcare, Inc.

Newberg, A., & Walkman, M. R. (2009). *How God Changes Your Brain.* New York: Random House.

Newcorn, J. H., & Ivanov, I. (2007). Psychopharmacological treatment of attentiondeficit/hyperactivity disorder and disruptive behavior disorders. *Pediatric Annals, 36,* 564–574.

Newman, T. B., Clay, C. M., Davis, G. L., McHutchison, J. G., & Liang, T. J. (2009). Combination therapy for hepatitis c infection. *New England Journal of Medicine, 340,* 1207.

Newsome, M. (2011). Twelve steps to nowhere. *Playboy, 58*(9), 125.

Newcomb, J. H., & Ivanov, I. (2007). Psychopharmacologic treatment of attention deficit/hyperactivity disorder and disruptive behavior disorders. *Pediatric Annals, 36,* 564–574.

Newman, J. L., & Mello, J. K. (2009). Neuroactive gonadal steroid hormones and drug addiction in women. In K. T. Brady, S. E. Back, & S. F. Greenfield (Eds.), *Women & Addiction.* New York: Guilford.

New York remains cocaine capital of the world. (2007). *Forensic Drug Abuse Advisor, 19*(1), 7.

Ngo, H. T. T., Tait, R. J., & Hulse, G. K. (2008). Comparing drug-related hospital morbitity following heroin dependence treatment with methadone maintenance or naltrexone implantation. *Archives of General Psychiatry, 65*(4), 457–465.

Nichol, P. E., Krueger, R. F., & Iacono, W. G. (2007). Investigating gender differences in alcohol problems: A latent trait modeling approach. *Alcoholism: Clinical & Experimental Research, 31,* 783–794.

Nicoll, R. A., & Alger, B. E. (2004). The brain's own marijuana. *Scientific American, 291*(6), 68–75.

Nichols, D. E. (2006). Commentary. *Psychopharmacology, 187,* 284–286.

Nichols, M., Scarborough, P., Allender, S., & Rayner, M. (2012). What is the optimal level of population alcohol consumption for chronic disease prevention in England? Modelling the impact of changes in average consumption levels. *British Medical Journal.*

Nielsen, S. F., Rygaard- Hjorthøj, C., Elangsen, A., & Nordentoft, M. (2011). Psychiatric disorders and mortality among people in homeless shelters in Denmark: A nationwide register-based cohort study. *Lancet.*

Nielson, S. J., Kit, B. K., Fakhouri, T., & Ogden, C. L. (2012). *Calories consumed from alcoholic beverages by U.S. adults, 2007-2010* (NCHS data brief # 110). Hyattsville, MD: National Center for Health Statistics.

Nielson, D. A., Virkkunen, M., Lappalainen, J., Eggert, M., et al. (1998). A tryptophanhydroxylase gene marker for suicidality and alcoholism. *Archives of General Psychiatry, 55,* 593–602.

Nierenberg, A. A. (2010). The perfect storm: CNS drug development in trouble. *CNS Spectrums, 15*(5), 282–283.

Nisbet, P. A. (2000). Age and the lifespan. In R. W. Maris, A. L. Berman, & M. M. Silverman (Eds.), *Comprehensive Textbook of Suicidology.* New York: Guilford.

Nishno, S., Mishma, K., Mignot, E., & Dement, W. C. (2004). Sedative-hypnotics. In A. F. Schatzberg & C. B. Nemeroff (Eds.), *Textbook of psychopharmacology* (3rd ed.). Washington, DC: American Psychiatric Publishing, Inc.

Niv, N., Pham, R., & Hser, Y. (2009). Racial and ethnic differences in substance abuse service needs and outcomes in california. *Psychiatric Services, 60,* 1350–1356.

No dope on dope. (2006). *New Scientist, 190*(2549), 6.

Noe, A. (2009). *Out of our heads.* New York: Hill and Wang.

Noonan, M. A., Bulin, S. E., Fuller, D. C., & Eisch, A. J. (2010). Reduction of adult hippocampal neurogenesis confers vulnerability in an animal model of cocaine addiction. *The Journal of Neuroscience, 30*(1), 304–315.

Nordahl, T. E., Salo, R., Natsuaki, Y., Galloway, G. P., et al. (2005). Methamphetamine users in sustained abstinence. *Archives of General Psychiatry, 62,* 444–452.

Nordgren, H. K., & Beck, O. (2004). Multicomponent screening for drugs of abuse: Direct analysis of urine by LC-MS-GS. *Therapeutic Drug Monitoring, 26*(1), 90–97.

Nordstrom, B. R. (2012). Drug treatment in criminal justice settings. *Psychiatric Clinics of North America, 35*(2), 375–391.

Nordstrom, B. R., & Williams, A. R. (2012). Drug treatments in criminal justice settings. *Psychiatric Clinics of North America, 35*(2), 375–392.

Northcutt, W. (2008). *The Darwin Awards: Next Evolution.* New York: The Plume Press.

Norris, K. (1996). *The Cloister Walk.* New York: Riverhead Books.

Norton-Hawk, M. (2009, March). *Social Class, dRugs, and Prostitution: Everything Old is New Again.* Paper presented at the "Treating the Addictions" seminar hosted by the Harvard Medical School Department of Continuing Education, MA.

Nowak, R. (2004). How our brains fend off madness. *New Scientist, 183*(2462), 13.

Nowak, R. (2008). Something for the pain. *New Scientist, 199*(2672), 13.

Nowinski, J. (2003). Facilitating 12-step recovery from substance abuse and addiction. In F. Rotgers, J. Morgenstern, & S. T. Walters (Eds.), *Treating Substance Abuse: Theory and Technique* (2nd ed.). New York: Guilford.

Noxon, C. (2002). The trouble with rehab. *Playboy, 49*(3), 86–88, 152, 154, 156–157.

Nunes, E. V., & Levin, F. R. (2006). Treating depression in substance abusers. *Current Psychiatry Reports, 8*(5), 363–370.

Nurnberger, J. I., & Bierut, L. J. (2007). Seeking the connections: Alcoholism and our genes. *Scientific American, 296*(4), 46, 48–53.

Nutt, D., Robbins, T., & Stimson, G. (2005). Drug futures 2025. In D. Nutt, T. W. Robbins, G. V. Stimson, M. Ince, & A. Jackson (Eds.), *Drugs and the future.* New York: Academic Press.

Nutt, D. (2009). A dangerous attitude to drugs. *New Scientist, 204*(2733), 5.

Nutt, D. (2012). One minute with david nutt. *New Scientist, 214*(2868), 29.

Nutt, D. J., King, L. A., & Phillips, L. D. (2010). Drug harms in the UK: A multicriteria decision analysis. *The Lancet, 376,* 1558–1565.

O'Brien, C. P. (2005). Benzodiazepine use, abuse and dependence. *Journal of Clinical Psychiatry, 66*(2), 28–33.

O'Brien, C. P. (2006). Drug addiction and drug abuse. In L. L. Bruxton, J. S. Lazo, & K. L. Parker (Eds.), *Pharmacological basis of therapeutics* (11th ed). New York: McGraw-Hill.

O'Brien, C. P. (2008). A 50-year-old woman addicted to heroin. *Journal of the American Medical Association, 300*(3), 314–321.

O'Brien, C. P. (2011). Drug addiction. In L. L. Brunton, B. A. Chabner, & B. Knollman (Eds.), *Pharmacological basis of therapeutics* (12th ed., pp. 649–667). New York: McGraw-Hill.

O'Brien, C. P., & McLellan, A. T. (1996). Myths about the treatment of addiction. *The Lancet, 347,* 237–240.

Oblora, E., Hubbard, R., Sanders, R. D., & Myles, P. R. (2012). The impact of benzodiazepines on occurrence of pneumonia and mortality from pneumonia: A nested case-control and survival analysis in a population-based cohort. *Thorax.*

O'Connor, P. G. (2000). Treating opioid dependence new data and new opportunities. *New England Journal of Medicine, 343,* 1332–1333.

O'Connor, P. G., Chang, G., & Shi, J. (1992). Medical complications of cocaine use. In T. R. Kiosten & H. D. Kleber (Eds.), *Clinician's Guide to Cocaine Addiction.* New York: Guilford.

O'Connor, P. G., Nyquist, J. G., & McCellan, A. T. (2011). Integrating addiction medicine into graduate medical education in primary care: The time has come. *Annals of Internal Medicine, 154*(1), 56–59.

O'Connor, A. D., Rusyniak, D. E., & Bruno, A. (2005). Cerebrovascular and cardiovascular complications of alcohol and sympathomimetic drug abuse. *Medical Clinics of North America, 89,* 1343–1358.

O'Farrell, T. J., & Fals-Stewart, W. (2008). Family therapy. In M. Galanter & H. D. Kleber (Eds.), *Textbook of substance abuse treatment.* Washington, DC: American Psychiatric Association, Inc.

O'Meara, A. (2009). *Chasing medical miracles.* New York: Walker & Co.

Oberg, M., Jaakkola, M. S., Woodward, A., Peruga, A., & Pruss-Ustun, A. (2010). Worldwide burden of disease from exposure to second-hand smoke: A retrospective analysis of data from 192 countries. *The Lancet.* Retrieved December 7, 2010, from http://www.thelancet.com/journals/lancet/article/PIIS0140-6736(10)61388-8/abstract

Oehmichen, M., Auer, R. N., & Konig, H. G. (2005). *Forensic Neuropathology and Associated Neurology.* New York: Springer-Verlas.

Oeltmann, J. E., Kammerer, J. S., Pevzner, E. S., & Moonan, P. K. (2009). Tuberculosis and substance abuse in the United States, 1997-2006. *Archives of Internal Medicine, 169,* 189–197.

Office of National Drug Control Policy. (2006). *National Drug Control Strategy*. Washington, DC: US Government Printing Office.

Ogawa, H., Nakayama, M., Morimoto, T., Uemura, S., et al. (2008). Low dose aspirin for primary prevention of atherosclerotic events in patients with type 2 diabetes. *Journal of the American Medical Association, 300*(18), 2134–2141.

Okrent, D. (2010). *Last call.* New York: Scribner.

Okuyemi, K. S., Nollen, N. L., & Akhluwalia, J. S. (2006). Interventions to facilitate smoking cessation. *American Family Physician, 74,* 262–271.

O'Leary, C. M., Nassar, N., Kurinczuk, J. J., deKlerk, N., Geelhoed, E., Elliott, E. J., & Bower, C. (2010). Prenatal alcohol exposure and risk of birth defects. *Pediatrics, 126*(4), e843–e850.

Oldstone, M. B. A. (2010). *Viruses, plagues & history.* New York: Oxford University Press.

Oliva-Marston, S. E., Yang, P., Mechanic, L. E., Bowman, E. D., et al. (2009). Childhood exposure to secondhand smoke and functional mannose binding lectin polymorphisms are associated with increased cancer risk. *Cancer Epidemiology Biomarkers & Prevention, 18*(12), 3375–3383.

Oliveto, A., Poling, J., Mancino, M. J., Feldman, Z., Cubells, J. F., Pruznsky, R., et al. (2010). Randomized, double blind, placebo controlled trial of disulfiram for the treatment of cocaine dependence in methadone-stabilized patients. *Alcohol & Drug Dependence, .* Retrieved November 30, 2010, from http://www.ncbi.nih.gov/pubmed/20828943

Olmedo, R., & Hoffman, R. S. (2000). Withdrawal syndromes. *Emergency Medical Clinics of North America, 18,* 273–288.

Olmstead, D. H., White, W. D., & Sindelar, J. (2004). The impact of managed care on substance abuse treatment services. *Health Services Research, 39*(2), 319–343.

Olson, J. (2006). *Clinical Pharmacology Made Rediculously Simple* (3rd ed.). Miami, FL: MedMaster, Inc.

Oncken, C. A., & George, T. P. (2005). Tobacco. In H. R. Kranzldr & D. A. Ciraulo (Eds.), *Clinical manual of addiction psychopharmacology.* Washington, DC: American Psychiatric Press, Inc.

Oquendo, M. A., Currier, D., Shang-Min, L., Hasin, D. S., Grant, B. F., & Blanco, C. (2010). Increased risk for suicidal behavior in cormorbid bipolar disorder and alcohol use disorders: Results from the national epidemiologic survey on alcohol and related conditions (NESARC). *Journal of Clinical Psychiatry, 71,* 902–909.

Oral fluid drug testing. (2005). *Forensic Drug Abuse Advisor, 17,* 27–28.

Ordorica, P. I., & Nace, P. E. (1998). Alcohol. In R. J. Frances & S. I. Miller (Eds.), *Clinical textbook of addictive disorders* (2nd ed.). New York: Guilford.

Orr, D. A. (2008). *Protecting high-risk adults against vaccine preventable hepatitis (VPH).* Seminar presented to the Madison, WI: Wisconsin State Methadone Providers Meeting

O'Shea, E., Escobedo, I., Orio, L., Sanchez, V., et al. (2005). Elevation of ambient room temperature has differential effects on MDMA induced 5-HT and dopamine release in striatum and nucleus accumbens of rats. *Neuropsychopharmacology, 30*(7), 1312–1323.

Osher, F. C., & Drake, R. E. (1996). Reversing a history of unmet needs: Approaches to care for persons with co-occurring addictive and mental disorders. *American Journal of Orthopsychiatry, 66,* 4–11.

Oshri, A., Rogoscu, F. A., Burnette, M. L., & Ciccette, D. (2011). Developmental pathways to adolescent cannabis abuse and dependence: Child maltreatment, emerging personality and internalizing versus externalizing psychopathology. *Journal of Addictive Behaviors, 25*(4), 634–644.

Ostacher, mJ, & Sachs, G. S. (2006). Update on bipolar disorder and substance abuse: Recent findings and treatment strategies. *Journal of Clinical Psychiatry, 67*(9), e10.

OTPs: Past, current, future part III. (2008). *Addiction Treatmentment Forum, 17*(3), 1, 4–5.

OTP liability and insurance claim trends an interview with richard J. Willetts. (2010). *Addiction Treatment Forum, 30*(3), 1, 6.

Otsuka, R., Watanabe, H., Hirata, K., Tokai, K., et al. (2001). Acute effects of passive smoking on the coronary circulation in healthy young adults. *Journal of the American Medical Association, 286,* 436–441.

Otto, R. K., Lang, A. R., Megargee, E. I., & Rosenblatt, A. I. (1989). Ability of alcoholics to escape detection by the MMPI. *Critical Items, 4,* 2, 7–278.

Outslay, M. G. (2006). Understanding ecstasy. *Journal of the American Association of Physician Assistants, 19*(7), 42–47.

Overman, G. P., Teter, C. J., & Guthrie, S. K. (2003). Acamprosate for the adjunctive treatment of alcohol dependence. *The Annals of Pharmacotherapy, 37,* 1090–1099.

Owen, F. (2007). The dark side of the summer of love. *Playboy, 54*(7), 56–60, 122–128.

Owen, F. (2008). The adderall effect. *Playboy, 55*(10), 50–52, 128.

Owen, F. (2013). The miami zombie. *Playboy, 60*(1), 78–80, 168–170.

Pagano, J., Graham, N. A., Frost-Pineda, K., & Gold, M. S. (2005). The physicians's role in recognition and treatment of alcohol dependence and cormorbid conditions. *Psychiatric Annals, 35*(6), 473–481.

Pagano, M. E., Friend, K. B., Tonigan, S., & Stout, R. L. (2004). Helping other alcoholics in alcoholics anonymous and drinking outcomes: Findings from project MATCH. *Journal of Studies on Alcohol, 65,* 766–773.

Page, J. (2001). Take two aspirin and call me in the morning. *Smithsonian, 32*(5), 96–105.

Pain, S. (2008). Two two pints, twice a day. *New Scientist, 200*(2680), 44–45.

Palmer, N. D., & Edmunds, C. N. (2003). Victims of sexual abuse and assault: Adults and children. *Victim Assistance.* New York: Springer.

Palmstierna, T. (2001). A model for predicting alcohol withdrawal delirium. *Psychiatric Services, 52,* 820–823.

Palmisano, S., Schwartzbaum, J., Prochazka, M., Pettersonn, D., Bergenhdim, T., Florentzson, R., Harder, H., Mathiesen, T., Nyberg, G., Siesjo, P., & Feychting, M. (2012). *Role of Tobacco Use in He Etiology of Acustic Neuroma.*

Pankiewicz, J. (2008, November). *Optimizing Clinical Outcomes Throughout the Course of Schizophrenia.* Eli Lilly & Co. Sponsored presentation in, Wisconsin.

Paparrigopoulos, T., Tzavellas, E., Karaiskos, D., Kouriaba, G., & Llappas, I. (2011). Treatment of alcohol dependence with low-dose topiramate: An open-label controlled study. *BMC Psychiatry.* Retrieved from http://www.biomedcentral.com/1471-244X/11/41

Papastefanou, C. (2007). Radiation dose from cigarette tobacco. *Radiation Protection Dosimetry, 123*(1), 68–73.

Papathanasopoulous, P., Messinis, L., Epameinondas, L., Kastellakis, A., & Panagis, G. (2008). Multiple sclerosis, cannabinoids and cognition. *The Journal of Neuropsychiatry and Clinical Neurosciences, 20*(1), 36–51.

Paradowski, J. (2008, 10). *Methadone, pregnancy and infant care.* Seminar presented at the Wisconsin State Methadone Providers Meeting, WI.

Parekh, R. (2006, March). *Adolescent substance use and abuse.* Paper Presented at the "Treating the Addictions" workshop, sponsored by the Dept. Of Psychiatry of the Cambridge Hospital, MA.

Parent, J. M., & Aminoff, M. J. (2008). Seizures and general medical disorders. In M. J. Aminoff (Ed.), *Neurology and General Medicine* (4th ed.). New York: Churchill-Livingstone.

Parenti, C. (2009). The drug coast. *Playboy, 56*(2), 38–40, 98, 100–105.

Pargament, K. I. (2007). *Spirituality Integrated Psychotherapy.* New York: Guilford.

Pargamet, K. I., & Sweeney, P. J. (2011). Building spiritual fitness in the army. *American Psychologist, 66*(1), 58–64.

Parini, S. (2003). Hepatitis c. *Nursing 2003, 33*(4), 57–63.

Park, A., Sher, K. J., & Krull, J. L. (2009). Selection and socialization of risky drinking during the college transition: The importance of microenvironments associated with specific living units. *Psychology of Addictive Behaviors, 23,* 404–414.

Parkinson-like symptoms linked to illicit khat use. (2008). *Forensic Drug Abuse Advisor, 20*(4), 27–28.

Parrott, A., Morinan, A., Moss, M., & Scholey, A. (2004). *Understanding Drugs and Behavior.* New York: John Wiley & Sons, Inc.

Patkar, A. A., Vergare, M. J., Batka, V., Weinstein, S. P., & Leone, T. (2003). Tobacco smoking: Current concepts in etiology and treatment. *Psychiatry, 66*(3), 183–199.

Patrick, D. D. (2003). Dual diagnosis' substance-related and psychiatric disorders. *Nursing Clinics of North America, 38,* 67–73.

Parrott, D. J., & Giancola, P. R. (2006). The effect of past-year heavy drinking on alcohol related aggression. *Journal of Studies on Alcohol, 67,* 122–130.

Pasic, J., & Ries, R. (2009). Treatment of methamphetamine addiction that co-occurs with serious mental illness. In J. R. Roll, R. A. Rawson, W. Ling, & S. Shoptaw (Eds.), *Methamphetamine Addiction From Basic Science to Treatment.* New York: Guilford.

Passie, T., Hartmann, U., Schnieder, U., Emrich, H. M., & Kruger, T. H. (2005). Ecstasy (MDMA) mimics the post-orgasmic state: Impairment of sexual drive and function during acute MDMA-effects may be due to increased prolactin secretion. *Medical Hypotheses, 64*(5), 899–903.

Patel, M., Belson, M. G., Wright, D., Lu, H., et al. (2005). Methylendioxy-N-methamphetamine (ecstasy)-related myocardial hypertrophy: An autopsy study. *Resuscitation, 66*(2), 197–202.

Patkar, A. A., Vergare, M. J., Batka, V., Weinstein, S. P., & Leone, F. T. (2003). Tobacco smoking: Current concepts in etiology and treatment. *Psychiatry, 66*(3), 183–199.

Patock-Peckham, J. A., & Morgan-Lopez, A. A. (2006). College drinking behaviors: Mediational links between parenting styles, impulse control, and alcohol-related outcomes. *Psychology of Addictive Behaviors, 20*(2), 117–125.

Paton, A. (1996). The detection of alcohol misuse in accident and emergency departments grasping the opportunity. *Journal of Accident & Emergency Medicine, 13*, 306–308.

Patrick, D. D. (2003). Dual diagnosis, substance-related and psychiatric disorders. *Nursing Clinics of North America, 38*, 67–73.

Patrick, S. W., Schumascher, R. E., Benneyworth, B. D., Krans, E. E., McAllister, J. M., & Davis, M. M. (2012). Neonatal abstinence syndrome and associated health care expdnditures, US 2000-2009. *Journal of the American Medical Association.*

Patrizi, R., Pasceri, V., Sciahbase, A., Summara, F., et al. (2006). Evidence of cocaine related coronary artery atherosclerosis in young patients with myocardial infarction. *Journal of the American College of Cardiology, 10*, 2120–2122.

Paula, C. A., Au, R., Fredman, L., Massaro, J. M., et al. (2008). Association of alcohol consumption with brain volume in the framingham study. *Archives of Neurology, 65*(10), 1363–1367.

Payer, D., & London, E. D. (2009). Methamphetamine and the brain. In J. R. Roll, R. A. Rawson, W. Ling, & S. Shoptaw (Eds.), *Methamphetamine addiction From Basic Science to Treatment.* New York: Guilford.

Payne, R. A., Back, S. E., Wright, T., Hartwell, K., & Brady, K. T. (2009). Alcohol dependence in women: Comorbidities can complicate treatment. *Current Psychiatry, 8*(6), 52–59.

Paynter, N. P., Chasman, D. I., Pare, G., Buring, J. E., Crook, N. R., et al. (2010). Association between a literature based benetic risk score and cardiovascular events in women. *Journal of the American Medical Association, 303*, 631–637.

Pearlman, B. L. (2004). Hepatitis c infection: A clinical review. *Southern Medical Journal, 97*, 365–373.

Pearson, A. (2009). *Addressing the challenges of substance abuse and brain injury.* Brooklyn Park, MN: Paper presented at the 10th Annual "Managing Challenging Situations in Brain Injury Care.

Peart, J., & Gross, G. (2004). Morphine-tolerant mice exhibit a profound and persistent cardioprotective phenotype. *Circulation, 109*, 1219–1222.

Pechnick, R. N., & Ungerleider, J. T. (2004). Hallucinogens. In M. Galanter & H. D. Kleber (Eds.), *Textbook of substance abuse treatment* (3rd ed.). Washington, DC: American Psychiatric Press, Inc.

Peck, M. S. (1997a). *The Road Less Traveled & Beyond.* New York: Simon & Schuster.

Peele, S. (2004a). The surprising truth about addiction. *Psychology Today, 37*(3), 43–46.

Peele, S. (2010). Blinded by biochemistry. *Psychology Today, 43*(5), 52–53.

Pele, S. (2004b). Is AA's loss psychology's gain? *Monitor on Psychology, 35*(7), 86.

Pegler, S., & Underhill, J. (2010). Evaluating the safety and effectiveness of new drugs. *American Family Physician, 82*, 53–57.

Pekekh, R. (2006, March). *Adolescent substance use and abuse.* Paper presented at the "Treating The Addictions" workshop, sponsored by the Dept of Psychiatry of the Cambridge Hospital, MA.

Pelander, A., Restimaa, J., Ilpo, R., Erkki, V., et al. (2008). Screening for basic drugs in hair of drug addicts. *Therapeutic Drug Monitoring, 30*(6), 717–724.

Peles, E., Hetzroni, T., Bar-Hamburger, R., Adelson, M., et al. (2007). Meltonin for perceived sleep disturbances associated with benzodiazepine withdrawal among patients in methadone maintenance treatment: A double-blind randomized clinical trial. *Addiction, 12*, 1947–1953.

Pell, J. P., Haw, S., Cobbe, S., Newby, D. E., et al. (2008). Smoke-free legislation and hospitalizations for acute coronary syndrome. *New England Journal of Medicine, 359*, 482–491.

Pendlebury, J. D., Wilsin, R. J. A., Bano, S., Lumb, K. J., Schneider, J. M., & Hasan, S. U. (2008). Respiratory control in neonatal rats exposed to prenatal cigarette smoke. *American Journal of Respiratory and Critical Care Medicine, 177*, 1255–1261.

Pennock, P. E. (2007). *Advertising Sin and Sickness.* DeKalb, IL: NIU Press.

Pepper, B. (2004). Responding to co-occurring disorders. *Psychiatric Services, 55*, 343.

Perkonigg, A., Goodwin, R. D., Fiedler, A., Behrendt, S., et al. (2008). The natural course of cannabis use, abuse and dependence during the first decades of life. *Addiction, 103*(9), 439–449.

Perry, P. J., Alexander, B., Liskow, B. I., & DeVane, C. L. (2007). *Psychotropic Drug Handbook* (8th ed.). New York: Lippincott Williams & Wilkins.

Pescosolido, B. A., Martin, J. K., Long, J. S., Medina, T. R., Phelan, J. C., & Link, B. G. (2010). A disease like any other"? A decade of change in public reactions to schizophrenia, depression and alcohol dependence. *American Journal of Psychiatry, 167,* 1321–1330.

Peteroy, D. (2012). Circuit builders. *Playboy, 59*(8), 112–113, 126, 128–132.

Peters, B. B. (2007, 4). *Fetal alcohol spectrum disorders: Its impact on the fetus to adults.* Paper presented at the Ruth Fox Course for Physicians. 38th medical-scientific conference of the American Society of Addiction Medicine, FL.

Peterson, A. M. (1997). Analgesics. *RN, 60*(4), 45–50.

Petrakis, I. L., Gonzalez, G., Rosenheck, R., & Krystal, J. H. (2002). Comorbidity of alcoholism and psychiatric disorders. *Alcohol Research & Health, 26*(2), 81–89.

Pettit, J. L. (2000). Melatonin. *Clinical Reviews, 10*(6), 87–88, 91.

Pferrerbaum, A., Sullivan, E. V., Rosenbloom, M. J., Mathalon, D. H., & Kim, K. Q. (1998). A controlled study of cortical gray matter and ventricular changes in alcoholic men over a 5 year interval. *Archives of General Psychiatry, 55,* 905–912.

Pferrerbaum, A., Rosenbloom, M., Deshmukh, A., & Sullivan, E. V. (2001). Sex differences in the effects of alcohol on brain structure. *American Journal of Psychiatry, 158,* 188–197.

Pfefferbaum, A., Rosenbloom, M. J., Serventi, K., & Sullivan, E. V. (2004). Brain volume, RBC status and hepatic function in alcoholics after 1 and 4 weeks of sobriety: Predictors of outcome. *American Journal of Psychiatry, 158,* 188–197.

Pharmacokinetics of MDMA (ecstasy) studied. (2008). *Forensic Drug Abuse Advisor, 20*(5), 35–36.

Phelps, D. Records suggest nicotine enhances. *Minneapolis Star-Tribune, XV*(5), 1A, 22A.

Phillips, H., & Lawton, G. (2004). The intoxication instinct. *New Scientist, 184*(2473), 32–39.

Piano, M. R., Benowitz, M. N. L., FitzGerald, G. A., Corbridge, S., Heath, J., & Hahn, E. Im pact of smokeless tobacco products on cardiovascular disease: Implications for policy, prevention and treatment. *Circulation, 122,* 1520–1544.

Pichini, S., Puig, C., Zuccaro, P., Marchel, E., et al. (2005). Assessment of exposure to opiates and cocaine during pregnancy in a mediterranean city: Prelimiary results of the "meconium project." *Forensic Science International, 153*(1), 59–65.

Pies, R. W. (2003, March). *Antidepressants and alcohol: How do they "mix"?* Symposium presented to the Dept of Psychiatry at the Cambridge Hospital, MA.

Pies, R. W. (2005). The top 10 adverse drug reactions in psychiatry. *Psychiatric Times, XXII*(11), 22–23.

Piette, J. D., Heisler, M., & Wagner, T. H. (2004). Cost-related medication underuse. *Archives of Internal Medicine, 164,* 1749–1755.

Pigott, T. A., Walker, M. H., Tietelbaum, S. A., & Lu, C. (2009). Sex differences and neurotransmitter systems in addiction. In K. T. Brady, S. E. Back, & S. F. Greenfield (Eds.), *Women & Addiction.* New York: Guilford.

Pihl, R. O. (1999). Substance abuse: Etiological considerations. In T. Millon, P. H. Blaney, & R. D. David (Eds.), *Oxford textbook of psychopathology.* New York: Oxford University Press.

Pinel, J. P. J. (2003). *Biopsychology* (5th ed.). New York: Allyn & Bacon.

Pinker, S. (2002). *The Blank Slate: The Modern Denial of Human Nature.* New York: Oxford University Press.

Pinsky, D. (2008). Playboy interview. *Playboy, 55*(7), 45–48, 120–122.

Piore, A. (2012). Chemists in the shadows. *Discover, 33*(2), 36–43.

Piper, M. E., Smith, S. S., Schlam, T. R., Fiore, M. C., et al. (2009). A randomized placebo controlled clinical trial of 5 smoking cessation pharmacotherapies. *Archives of General Psychiatry, 66*(11), 1253–1262.

Pirie, K., Peto, R., Reeves, G. K., Green, J., & Beral, V. (2012). The 21st century hazards of smoking and benefits of stopping: A prospective study of one million women in the UK. *The Lancet.*

Pletcher, M. J., Kiefe, C., Sidney, C., Carr, J. J., et al. (2005). Cocaine and coronary calcification in young adults: The coronary artery risk development in young adults (CARDIA) study. *American Heart Journal, 150,* 921–926.

Pletcher, M. J., Vittinghoff, E., Kalhan, R., Richman, J., Safford, M., Sidney, S., Lin, F., & Kertesz, S. (2012). Association between marijuana exposure and pulmonary function over 20 years. *Journal of the American Medical Association, 307*(2), 173–181.

Pliszka, S. R. (1998). The use of psychostimulants in the pediatric patient. *Pediatric Clinics of North America, 45,* 1085–1098.

Pohl, M. (2007). Chronic pain, opioids and addiction. *Counselor, 8*(4), 34–41.

Polivy, J., & Herman, C. P. (2002). If at first you don't succeed. *American Psychologist, 57,* 596–601.

Polydorou, S., & Kleber, H. D. (2008). Detoxification of opioids. In M. Galanter & H. D. Kleber (Eds.), *Textbook of Substance Abuse Treatment.* Washington, DC: American Psychiatric Association, Inc.

Pomerantz, R. J. (1998). How HIV resists eradication. *Hospital Practice, 33*(9), 87–90.

Pomerantz, R. J. (2003). Cross-talk and viral reservoirs. *Nature, 424,* 136–137.

Ponnappa, B. C., & Rubin, E. (2000). Modeling alcohol's effects on organs in animal models. *Alcohol Research & Health, 24*(2), 93–104.

Pope, C. A., Burnett, R. T., Krewski, D., Jerrett, M., et al. (2009). Cardiovascular mortality and exposure to airborne fine particulate matter and cigarette smoke. Shape of exposure-response relationship. *Circulation.*

Pope, H. G. (2010, May). *Update on anabolic steroids.* Paper presented at the "Addictions in 2010" seminar, hosted by the Division of alcohol and Drug Abuse of the McLean Hospital, MA.

Pope, H. G., & Brower, K. J. (2004). Anabolic androgenic steroids. In N. M. Galanter & H. D. Kleber (Eds.), *Textbook of Substance Abuse Treatment* (3rd ed.). Washington, DC: American Psychiatric Press, Inc.

Pope, H. G., & Brower, K. J. (2005). Anabolic-androgenic steroid abuse. In B. J. Sadock & V. A. Sadock (Eds.), *Kaplan & Sadock's Comprehensive Textbook of Psychiatry* (8th ed.). New York: Lipponcott, Williams & Wilkins.

Pope, H. G., & Brower, K. J. (2008). Of anabolic-androgenic steroid-related disorders. In M. Galanter & H. D. Kleber (Eds.), *Of Substance Abuse Treatment.* Washington, DC: American Psychiatric Association, Inc.

Pope, H. G., Gruber, A. J., Hudson, J. I., Huestis, M. A., et al. (2001). Neuropsychological performance in long-term cannabis abusers. *Archives of General Psychiatry, 58,* 909–915.

Pope, H. G., Kouri, E. M., & Hudson, J. I. (2000). Effects of supraphysiologic doses of testosterone on mood and aggression. *Archives of General Psychiatry, 57,* 133–147.

Pope, H. G., Phillips, K. A., & Olivardia, R. (2000). *The Adonis Complex: The Secret Crisis of Male Body Obsession.* New York: The Free Press.

Porcerelli, J. H., & Sandler, B. A. (1998). Anabolic-androgenic steroid abuse and psychopathology. *The Psychiatric Clinics of North America, 21,* 829–833.

Popovich, K. J., Weinstein, R. A., Aroutcheva, A., Rice, T., & Hota, B. (2010). Community associated methicillin-resistant staphylococcus aureus and HIV: Intersecting epidemics. *Clinical Infectious Diseases, 50,* 979–987.

Porreca, F., & Price, T. (2009). When pain lingers. *Scientific American Mind, 20*(5), 34–41.

Potent pot. (2008). *New Scientist, 198*(2661), 7.

Potenza, M. N., Kosten, T. R., & Rounsaville, B. J. (2001). Pathological gambling. *Journal of the American Medical Association, 286,* 141–144.

Potenza, M. N., Fiellin, D., Heninger, G. R., Rounsaville, B. J., & Mazure, C. M. (2002). Gambling: An addictive behavior with health and primary care implications. *Journal of General Internal Medicine, 17*(9), 721–732.

Predicting drug-related impairment. (2004). *Forensic Drug Abuse Advisor, 16*(3), 21–22.

Prem, S., & Uzoma, M. (2004). Marijuana-induced transient global amnesia. *Southern Medical Journal, 97*(8), 782–784.

Prenatal cocaine exposure not linked to bad behavior in kids. (2006). *Science Daily.* Retrieved from http://www.sciencedaily.com/releases/2006/05/06050222048.html

Prescribing information. (2006). Frazer, PA: Caphalon, Inc.

Preston, K. L., Epstein, D. H., Cone, E. J., Wesadik, A. T., et al. (2002). Urinary elimination of cocaine metabolites in chronic users during cessation. *Journal of Analytical Toxicology, 27,* 393–400.

Preston, R. (1999). The demon in the freezer. *The New Yorker, LXXV*(18), 44–61.

Preuss, U. W., & Wong, W. M. (2000). Comorbidity. In G. Zernig, A. Saria, M. Kurz, & S. S. O'Malley (Eds.), *Handbook of Alcoholism.* New York: CRC Press.

Preuss, U. W., Schickit, M. A., Smith, T. L., Danko, G. P., et al. (2003). Predictors and correlates of suicide attempts over 5 years in 1,237 alcohol-dependent men and women. *American Journal of Psychiatry, 160,* 56–63.

Preuss, U. W., & Wong, W. M. (2000). Comorbidity. In G. Zernig, A. Saria, M. Kurz, & S. S. O'Malley (Eds.), *Handbook of Alcoholism.* New York: CRC Press.

Price, L. H. (2009). Modafinil: A different kind of stimulus package. *The Brown University Psychophamracology Update, 20*(9), 9.

Primack, B. A., Dalton, M. A., Carroll, M. V., Agerwal, A. A., & Fine, M. J. (2008). Content analyss of tobacco, alcohol and other drugs in popular music. *Archives of Pediatrics & Adolescent Medicine, 162*(2), 169–175.

Primack, J. R., & Abrams, N. E. (2006). *The View From the Center of the Universe.* New York: Riverhead books.

Prochaska, J. O. (2002, February). *Stages of change: 25 years of addiction treatment.* Symposium presented to the Dept of Psychiatry of the Cambridge Hospital, MA.

Prochaska, J. O. (2011, March). *Addictions and stages of change.* Paper presented at the "Treating the Addictions" seminar hosted by the Dept. Of Psychiatry of the Cambridge Hospital, MA.

Prochaska, J. O. (1998, September). *Stage model of change.* Paper presented at Syposium Gindersen-Lutheran Medical Center, Wisconsin.

Prochaska, J. O., DiClemente, C. C., & Norcross, J. C. (1992). In search of how people change. *American Psychologist, 47,* 1102–1114.

Prochaska, J. J., Gill, P., Hall, S. E., & Hall, S. M. (2005). Identification and treatment of substance misuse on an inpatient psychiatry unit. *Psychiatric Services, 56,* 347–349.

Propoxyphene pharmacokinetics. (2009). *Forensic Drug Abuse Advisor, 21*(5), 37–38.

Prosser, A. T., Tang, T., & Hall, H. I. (2012). HIV in persons born outside the United States, 2007-2010. *Journal of the American Medical Association.*

Przekop, P., & Lee, T. (2009). Persistent psychosis associated with salvia divinorum use. *American Journal of Psychiatry, 166,* 832.

Pumariga, A. D., & Kilgus, M. D. (2005). Adolescents. In J. H. Lowinson, P. Ruiz, R. B. Millman, & J. G. Langrod (Eds.), *Substance abuse: A comprehensive textbook* (4th ed.). New York: Lipponcott, Williams & Wilkins.

Purow, D. B., & Jacobson, I. M. (2003). Slowing the progression of chronic hepatitis b. *Postgraduate Medicine, 114,* 65–76.

Pungpapong, S., Kim, W. R., & Poterucha, J. J. (2007). Natural history of hepatitis b infection: An update for clinicians. *Mayo Clinic Proceedings, 82,* 967–975.

Putnam, F. W. (1989). *Diagnosis and Treatment of Multiple Personality Disorder.* New York: Guilford.

Quednow, B. B., Jessen, F., Kuhn, K. U., Maier, W., et al. (2006). Memory deficits in abstinent MDMA (ecstasy) users: Neuropsychological evidence of frontal dysfunction. *Journal of Psychopharmacology, 20*(3), 373–384.

Quinn, P. D., & Fromme, K. (2012). Personal and contextual factors in the escalation of drinking after drinking across the college years. *Psychology of Addictive Behaviors, 26*(4), 714–723.

Qureshi, A., & Lee-Chiong, T. (2004). Medications and their effects on sleep. *Medical Clinics of North America, 88,* 751–766.

Qureshi, A. A., Dominguez, P. L., Choi, H. K., Jan, J., & Curhan, G. (2010). Alcohol intake and risk of incident psoriasis in US women. *Archives of Dermatology, 146,* 1364–1369.

Raby, W. N. (2009). Comorbid cannabis misuse in psychotic disorders: Treatment strategies. *Primary Psychiatry, 16*(4), 29–34.

RachBeisel, J., Scott, J., & Dixon, L. (1998). Co-occurring severe mental illness and substance use disorders: A review of recent research. *Psychiatric Services, 50,* 1427–1434.

Raj, A., & Sheehan, D. (2004). Benzodiazepines. In A. F. Schatzberg & C. B. Nemeroff (Eds.), *Textbook of Psychopharmacology.* Washington, DC: American Psychiatric Publishing, Inc.

Ramadan, M. I., Werder, S. F., & Preskorn, S. H. (2006). Protect against drug-drug interactions with anxiolytics. *Current Psychiatry, 5*(5), 16–28.

Ramcharan, S., Meenhorst, P. L., Otten, J. M. M. B., Koks, C. H. W., et al. (1998). Survival after massive ecstasy overdose. *Journal of Toxicology: Clinical Toxicology, 36,* 727.

Ramsay, J. R., & Newman, C. F. (2000). Substance abuse. In F. M. Dattilo & A. Freeman (Eds.), *Cognitve-Behavioral Strategies in Crisis Intervention* (2nd ed.). New York: Guilford.

Randle, K. D., Estes, R., & Cone, W. P. (1999). *The Abduction Enigma.* New York: Forge.

Rao, U., Hammen, C. L., & Poland, R. E. (2009). Mechanisms underlying the comorbidity between depressive and addictive disorders in adolescents: Interactions between stress and HPA activity. *American Journal of Psychiatry, 166*(3), 361–369.

Rasmussen, N. (2008). *On speed: The many lives of amphetamine.* New York: New York University Press.

Rational Recovery Systems, Inc. (2008). Organization web site.

Raviglione, M. C., & O'Brien, R. J. (2008). Tuberculosis. In A. S. Fauci, E. Braunwald, D. L. Kasper, S. L. Hauser, D. L. Longo, J. L. Jameson, & J. Loscalzo (Eds.), *Harrison's Principles of Internal Medicine* (17th ed.). New York: McGraw-Hill Medical.

Raw Data. (2008). *Playboy, 55*(9), 29.

Raw Data. (2009a). *Playboy, 56*(4), 22.

Raw Data. (2009b). *Playboy, 56*(6), 24.

Raw Data. (2010a). *Playboy, 57*(2), 23.

Raw Data. (2010b). *Playboy, 57*(6), 24.

Raw Data. (2010c). *Playboy, 57*(9), 28.

Raw Data. (2011). *Playboy, 58*(4), 27.

Raw Data. (2012a). *Playboy, 59*(8), 38.

Raw Data. (2012b). *Playboy, 59*(9), 36.

Raw Data. (2013a). *Playboy, 60*(2), 34.

Raw Data. (2013b). *Playboy, 60*(3), 32.

Rawson, R. A., Sodano, R., & Hillhouse, M. (2005). Assessment of amphetamine use disorders. In D. M. Donovan & G. A. Marlatt (Eds.), *Assessment of Addictive Behaviors* (2nd ed.). New York: Guilford.

Rawson, R. A., & Ling, W. (2008). Clinical management: Methamphetamine. In M. Galanter & H. D. Kleber (Eds.), *Textbook of Substance Abuse Treatment*. Washington, DC: American Psychiatric Association, Inc.

Reading, E. (2007). *Conscious contact: Religious experience in search of the spiritual.* Paper presented at the Ruth Fox Course for Physicians, 38th Medical-Scientific Conference of the American Society of Addiction Medicine, FL.

Reduced hospitalizations for acute myocardial infarction after implementation of a smoke free ordinance city of pueblo, colorado, 2002-2006. (2008). *Morbidity and Mortality Weekly Report, 57*(51), 1373–1377.

Redmond, E. M., Morrow, D., Kunkiml, S., Miller-Graziano, & Cullen, J. P. (2008). Acetaldehyde stimulates monocyte adhesion in a P-selectin-and THFa-dependent manner. *Circulation.*

Reed, S. C., & Evans, S. M. (2009). Research design and methodology in studies of women and addiction. In K. T. Brady, S. E. Back, & S. F. Greenfield (Eds.), *Women & Addiction*. New York: Guilford.

Rees, S., Silove, D., Chey, T., MAppSTAT, L. I., Steel, Z., Creamer, M., et al. (2011). Lifetime prevalence of gender-based violence in women and the relationship with mental disorders and psychosocial function. *Journal of the American Medical Association, 306*(5), 513–521.

Rehm, J., Patra, J., & Popova, S. (2007). Alcohol drinking cessation and its effects on esophageal and head and neck cancers: A pooled analysis. *International Journal of Cancer, 121*(5), 1132–1137.

Rehm, J., Mathers, C., Popova, S., Thavorncharoensap, M., et al. (2009). Global burden of disease and injury and economic cost attributable to alcohol use and alcohol-use disorders. *The Lancet, 373*(9682), 2223–2233.

Reichert, V. C., Folan, P., Bartscherer, D., Jacobsen, D., et al. (2007). A comparison of older smokers vrs younger smokers being treated for tobacco dependence. *Chest Meeting Abstracts 2007, 132*, 409b.

Reich, R. R., & Goldman, M. S. (2005). Exploring the alcohol expectancy memory network: The utility of free associates. *Psychology of Addictive Behavior, 19*, 317–325.

Reichert, V. C., Seltzer, V., Efferen, L. S., & Kohn, N. (2005). Women and tobacco dependence. *Medical Clinics of North America, 889*, 1467–1481.

Reiman, E. M. (1997). Anxiety. In A. J. Gelenberg & E. L. Bassuk (Eds.), *The Practitioners Guide to Psychoactive Drugs* (4th ed.). New York: Plenum.

Reisfield, G. M., Goldberger, B. A., Gold, M. S., & DuPont, R. L. (2012). The mirage of impaired drug concentration thresholds: A rationale for zero tolerance per se driving under the influence of drugs laws. *Journal of Analytical Toxicology, 36*(5), 353–356.

Rehm, J., Marmet, S., Anderson, P., Gual, A., Kraus, L., Nutt, D.J., Room, R., Samokhvalov, A.V., Scafato, E., Trapencieris, M., Wiers, R.W. & Gmel, G. (2013). Defining substance use disorders: Do we really need more than heavy use? Alcohol and Alcoholism, 48 (6), 633–640.

Rempel, M. (2005). *Recidivism 101: Evaluating the Impact of Your Drug Court.* New York: Center for Court Innovation.

Renner, J. A. (2004a). How to train residents to identify and treat dual diagnosis patients. *Biological Psychiatry, 56*, 810–816.

Renner, J. A. (2004b). Alcoholism and alcohol abuse. In T. A. Stern & J. B. Herman (Eds.), *Massachusetts general hospital psychiatry update and board preparation* (2nd ed.). New York: McGraw-Hill.

Repetto, M., & Gold, M. S. (2005). Cocaine and crack: Neurobiology. In J. H. Lowinson, P. Ruiz,

R. B. Millman, & J. G. Langrod (Eds.), *Substance Abuse: A Comprehensive Textbook* (4th ed.). New York: Lippincott, Williams & Wilkins.

Resilience. (2006). *Harvard Mental Health Letter, 23*(6), 5–6.

Reuter, P., & Pollack, H. (2006). How much can treatment reduce national drug problems? *Addiction, 101*(3), 341–347.

Rexrode, K. M., Buring, J. E., Glynn, R. J., Stampfer, M. J., et al. (2001). Analgesic use and renal function in men. *Journal of the American Medical Association, 286,* 315–321.

Reynolds, E. W., & Bada, H. S. (2003). Pharmacology of drugs of abuse. *Obstetrics and Gynecology Clinics of North America, 30,* 501–522.

Rhee, S. H., Hewitt, J. K., Young, S. E., Corley, R. P., Crowley, T. J., & Stallings, M. C. (2003). Genetic and environmental influences on substance initiation, use, and problem use in adolescents. *Archives of General Psychiatry, 60,* 1256–1264.

Renner, J. A. (2004a). Alcoholism and alcohol abuse. In T. A. Stern & J. B. Herman (Eds.), *Massachusetts General Hospital Psychiatry Update and Board Preparation* (2nd ed.). New York: McGraw-Hill.

Renner, J. A. (2004b). How to train residents to identify and treat dual diagnosis patients. *Biological Psychiatry, 56,* 810–816.

Repetto, M., & Gold, M. S. (2005). Cocaine and crack: Neurobiology. In J. H. Lowinson, P. Ruiz, R. Millman, & J. G. Langrod (Eds.), *Substance Abuse: A Comprehensive Textbook* (4th ed.). New York: Lippincott, Williams & Wilkins.

Reuter, P. (2009). Do no harm. *The American Interest, IV*(4), 46–52.

Reyna, V. F., & Farley, F. (2006/2007). Is the teen brain too rational? *Scientific American Mind, 17*(6), 58–65.

Rhame, F. (2009). Let's not forget the third world. *Minnesota Medicine, 92*(10), 38–39.

Rhee, S. H., Hewitt, J. K., Young, S. E., Corley, R. P., et al. (2003). Genetic and environmental influences on substance initiation, use and problems use in adolescents. *Archives of General Psychiatry, 60,* 1256–1264.

Ricaurte, G. A., Yuan, J., Hatzidimitriou, G., Branden, C., & McCann, U. D. (2002). Severe dopaminergic neurotoxicity in primates after a common recreational dose regimen of MDMA ("ecstasy"). *Science, 297,* 2260–2263.

Ricaurte, G. A., Langston, J. W., & McCannm, N. (2008). Neuropsychiatric complications of substance abuse. In M. J. Aminoff (Ed.), *Neurology and general medicine* (4th ed.). New York: Churchill Livingstone.

Ricaurte, G. A., Langston, J. W., & McCann, U. D. (2008). Neuropsychiatric complications of substance abuse. In M. J. Aminoff (Ed.), *Neurology and General Medicine.* New York: Churchill-Livingstone.

Richards, J. R. (2000). Rhabdomyolsis and drugs of abuse. *Journal of Emergency Medicine, 19,* 51–56.

Ries, R. K., Galanter, M., & Tonigan, J. B. (2008). Twelve step facilitation. In M. Galanter & H. D. Kleber (Eds.), *Textbook of Substance Abuse Treatment.* Washington, DC: American Psychiatric Association, Inc.

Rigler, S. K. (2000). Alcoholism in the elderly. *American Family Physician, 61,* 1710–1716.

Riggs, P. D. (2003). Treating adolescents for substance abuse and comorbid psychiatric disorders. *Science & Practice Perspectives, 2*(1), 18–28.

Rimsza, M. E., & Moses, K. S. (2005). Substance abuse on college campus. *Pediatric Medical Journal, 310,* 555–559.

Ringwald, C. D. (2002). *The Soul of Recovery.* New York: Oxford University Press.

Ritsher, J. B., Moos, R. H., & Finney, J. W. (2000). Relationship of treatment orientation and continuing care to remission among substance abuse patients. *Psychiatric Services, 53,* 595–601.

Rist, P. M., Berger, K., Buring, J. E., Kase, C. S., et al. (2010). Alcohol consumption and functional outcome after stroke in men. *Stroke, 41,* 141–146.

Roane, B. M., & Taylor, D. J. (2008). Adolescent insomnia as a risk factor for early adult depression and substance abuse. *Sleep, 31*(10), 1351–1356.

Roane, K. R. (2000). A scourge of drugs stsrikes a pious place. *US News & World Report, 128*(9), 26–28.

Robbe, D., Montbopmery, S. M., Thome, A., Rueda-Orozco, P. E., et al. (2006). Cannabinoids reveal importance of spike timing coordination in hippocampal function. *Nature Neuroscience, 9,* 1526–1533.

Roberts, S. (2004). Dual diagnosis. *Schizophrenia Digest, 2*(1), 30–34.

Robson, P. (2001). Therapeutic aspects of cannabis and cannabinoids. *British Journal of Psychiatry, 178,* 107–115.

Roberts, R. Q., Jacobson, D. J., Girman, C. J., Rhodes, T., et al. (2002). A population based study of daily nonsteroidal anti-inflammatory drug use and prostate cancer. *Mayo Clinic Proceedings, 77,* 219–225.

Robinson, D. J., Lazo, M. C., Davis, T., & Kufera, J. A. (2000). Infective endocarditis in intravenous drug users: Does HIV status alter the presenting temperature and white cell count. *Journal of Emergency Medicine, 19,* 5–11.

Robinson, E. A. R., Cranford, J. A., Webb, J. R., & Brower, K. J. (2007). Six-month changes in spirituality, religiousness, and heavy drinking in a treatment-seeking sample. *Journal of Studies on Alcohol and Drugs, 68*(2), 282–290.

Robson, D. (2009). Fuming. *New Scientist, 202* (2702), 34–37.

Rochester, J. A., & Kirchner, J. T. (1999). Ecstasy (3,4-methylenedioxymethamphetamine): History, neurochemistry and toxicity. *Journal of the American Board of Family Practice, 12,* 137–142.

Roden, D. M. (2004). Drug-induced prolongation of the QT interval. *New England Journal of Medicine, 350,* 1013–1022.

Rodriguez, J., Jiang, R., Johnson, W. C., MacKenzie, B. A., et al. (2010). The association of pipe and cigar use with cotinine levels, lung function, and airflow obstruction. *Annals of Internal Medicine, 152,* 1–28.

Rodriguez, S. C., Olguin, A. M., Miralles, C. P., & Valdrich, P. F. (2006). Characteristics of meningitis caused by ibuprofen. *Medicine, 85,* 214–220.

Roerecke, M., & Rehm, J. (2013). Alcohol use disorders and mortality: A systematic review and meta-analysis. *Addiction.*

Rogers, D., & Pies, R. (2008). General medical drugs associated with depression. *Psychiatry, 5*(12), 28–41.

Rogers, R. (2008). Detection strategies for malingering and defensiveness. In R. Rogers (Ed.), *Clinical Assessment of Malingering and Deception* (3rd ed.). New York: Guilford.

Rohde, P., Lewinsohn, P. M., Kahle, C. W., Seeley, J. R., & Brown, R. A. (2001). Natural course of alcohol use disorders from adolescence to young adulthood. *Journal of the American Academy of Child and Adolescent Psychiatry, 40,* 83–90.

Rohde, P., Lowinsohn, P. M., Seeley, J. R., Andrews, J. A., & Small, J. W. (2007). Psychosocial functioning of adults who experienced substance use disorders as adolescents. *Psychology of Addictive Behaviors, 21,* 155–164.

Rohenthal, R. N., & Solhkhah,, R. (2005). Club drugs. In H. R. Kranzler & D. A. Ciraulo (Eds.), *Clinical Manual of Addiction Psychopharmacology.* Washington, DC: American Psychiatric Publishing, Inc.

Rohrich, J., Schimmel, I., Zomtlein, S., Becker, J., Kaufmann, T., Kuntz, V., & Urban, R. (2010). Concentrations of ?-tetrahydrocannabinol and 11-nor-9-carboxytetrahydrocannabinol in blood and urine after passive exposure to cannabis smoke in a coffee shop. *Journal of Analytical Toxicology, 34*(4), 196–203.

Roiser, J. P., Cook, L. J., Cooper, J. D., Rubinsztein, D. C., & Sahakian, B. J. (2005). Association of a functional polymorphism in the serotonin transporter gene with abnormal emotional processing in ecstasy users. *American Journal of Psychiatry, 162,* 609–612.

Roldan, C. J., & Patel, M. M. (2008). Intracranial complications of cocaine abuse. *Emergency Medicine, 40*(10), 37–40.

Rollo, K. L., Sane, A., & Ewen, B. (2007). Meth: The crystal that kills. *Nursing 2007 Critical Care, 2*(1), 54–56.

Romach, M. K., Glue, P., Kampman, K., Kaplan, H. L., et al. (1999). Attenuation of the euphoric effects of cocaine by the dopamine d1/d5 antagonist ecopipam (SCH 39166). *Archives of General Psychiatry, 56,* 1101–1106.

Romano, E., & Voas, B. (2011). Drug and alcohol involvement in four types of fatal crashes. *Journal of Studies on Alcohol and Drugs, 72*(4), 567–576.

Ronksley, P. E., Brien, S. E., Turner, B. J., Mukamal, K. J., & Ghall, W. A. (2011). Association of alcohol consumption with selected cardiovascular disease outcomes: A systematic review and meta-analysis. *British Medical Journal.*

Room, B., Babor, T., & Rehm, J. (2005). Alcohol and public health. *The Lancet, 365,* 519–530.

Room, R. (2009). Get real, drug czars. *New Scintist, 202*(2709), 22–23.

Ropper, A. H., & Brown, R. H. (2005). *Adams and Victor's Principles of Neurology* (8th ed.). New York: McGraw-Hill.

Ropper, A. H., & Samuels, M. A. (2009). *Adams and Victors Principles of Neurology* (9th ed.). New York: Mc-Graw-Hill.

Rose, G. S. (2001, March). *Motivational Interviewing.* Symposium presented to the Dept. Of Psychiatry of the Cambridge Hospital, MA.

Rose, I. M. (1988). *The Body in Time.* New York: John Wiley & Sons, Inc.

Rose, J. E., Behm, F. M., Westman, E. C., Mathew, R. J., et al. (2003). PET studies of the influences of nicotine on neural systems in cigarette smokers. *American Journal of Psychiatry, 160,* 323–333.

Rosen, I. M., & Maurer, D. M. (2008). Reducing tobacco use in adolescents. *American Family Physician, 77,* 483–490.

Rosenbaum, R. (1999). *Zen and the heart of psychotherapy.* New York: Brunner/Mazel.

Rosenbloom, D. L. (2000, March). *The community perspective on addictions: Joining together.* Symposium presented by the Dept. Of Psychiatry at the Cambridge Hospital, MA.

Rosenbloom, D. L. (2005, March). *Cultural aspects of adolescent use and misuse of alcohol.* Symposium presented by the Dept. Of Psychiatry at the Cambridge Hospital, MA.

Rosenbloom, M. J., & Pefferbaum, A. (2008). Magnetic resonance imaging of the living brain. *Alcohol Research & Health, 31,* 362–376.

Rosenquist, J. N., Murabito, J., Fowler, J. H., & Christakis, N. A. (2010). The spread of alcohol consumption behavior in a large social network. *Annals of Internal Medicine, 152,* 426–433.

Rosenthal, R. N., & Solhkhah, R. (2005). Club drugs. In H. R. Kranzler & D. A. Ciraulo (Eds.), *Clinical manual of addiction psychopharmacology.* Washington, DC: American Psychiatric Press, Inc.

Roshsenow, D. J., Howland, J., Arnedt, J. T., Almeida, A. B., et al. (2009). Intoxication with bourbon versus vodka: Effects on hangover, sleep, and next-day neurocognitive performance in young adults. *Alcoholism: Clinical and Experimental Research.*

Ross, G. R. (2002, June). *Child and Adolescent Alcohol and Drug use.* Seminar presented by the Cross Country University, WI.

Ross, J., & Fuertes, J. (2010). Parental attachment, interparental conflict, and young adults' emotional adjustment. *The Counseling Psychologist, 38*(8), 1049–1077.

Ross, S. (2008). The mentally ill substance abuser. In M. Galanter & H. D. Kleber (Eds.), *Textbook of Substance Abuse Treatment.* Washington, DC: American Psychiatric Association, Inc.

Ross, S. (2012). Serotonergic hallucinogens and emerging targets for addiction pharmacotherapies. *Psychiatric Clinics of North America, 35*(2), 357–374.

Ross, V. (2010). Born into debt. *Scientific American Mind, 21*(3), 6.

Rostain, A. (2008). Attention-deficit/hyperactivity disorder in adults: Evidence-based recommendations for management. *Postgraduate Medicine, 20*(3), 27–38.

Roth, B. A., Benowitz, N. L., & Olson, K. R. (2007). Emergency management of drug abuse. In S. B. Karch (Ed.), *Drug Abuse Handbook* (2nd ed.). New York: CRC Press.

Roth, J. (2009). Evolutionary speculation about tuberculosis and the metabolic and inflammatory processes of obesity. *Journal of the American Medical Association, 301*(24), 2586–2588.

Rothenbergher, A., & Banaschewski, T. (2004). Informing the ADHD debate. *Scientific American Mind, 14*(5), 50–55.

Rothman, R. B., Vu, N., Partilla, J. S., Roth, B. L., et al. (2003). In vitro characterization of ephedrine-related stereoisomers at biogenic amine transporters and the receptorome reveals selective actions as norepinephrine transporters substrates. *Journal of Pharmacology and Experimental Therapeutics, 307,* 138–145.

Rothwell, P. M., Wilson, M., Elwin, C. E., Norrving, B., Algra, A., Warlow, C. P., & Meade, T. (2010). Long term effect of aspirin on colorectal cancer incidence and mortality: 20 year follow-up of five randomised trials. *The Lancet, 376*(9754), 1741–1750.

Rothwell, P. M., Price, J. F., Fowkes, F. G. R., Zanchetti, A., Roncaglioni, M. C., Tognoni, G., Lee, R., Belch, J. F. F., Wilson, M., Mehta, Z., & Meade, T. W. (2012). Shortterm effects of daily aspirin on cancer incidence, mortality, and non-vascular death: Analysis of the time course of risks and benefits in 51 randomised control trials. *The Lancet.*

Rounsaville, B. J. (2004). Treatment of cocaine dependence and depression. *Biological Psychiatry, 56,* 803–809.

Rounsaville, B. J. (2006, March). *Biopsychosocial Interventions for Addiction Treatment.* Paper presented at the Treating The Addictions workshop sponsored by the Dept. Of Psychiatry of the Cambridge Hospital, MA.

Rourke, S. B., & Grant, I. (2009). The neurobehavioral correlates of alcoholism. In I. Grnt & K. M. Adams (Eds.), *Neuropsychological Assessment of Neuropsychiatric and Neuromedical Disorders* (3rd ed.). New York: Oxford University Press.

Rouse, S. V., Butcher, J. N., & Miller, K. B. (1999). Assessment of substance abuse in psychotherapy clients: The effectiveness of the MMPI-s substance abuse scales. *Psychological Assessment, 11*(1), 101–107.

Roy, A. (2001). Characteristics of cocaine-dependent patients who attempt suicide. *American Journal of Psychiatry, 158,* 1215–1219.

Roy, A. (2003). Characteristics of HIV patients who attempt suicide. *Acta Psychiatrica Scandinavica, 107,* 41–44.

Ruben, D. H. (2001). *Treating Adult Children of Alcoholics.* New York: Academic Press.

Rubio, G., Martinez-Gras, I., & Manzanares, J. (2009). Modulation of impulsivity by topiramate: Implications for the treatment of alcohol dependence. *Journal of Clinical Psychopharmacology, 29*(6), 584–589.

Ruidavets, J.-B., Ducimetiere, P., Evans, A., Montaye, M., Haas, B., Bingham, A., Amouyel, P., et al. (2010). Patterns of alcohol consumption and ischaemic heart disease in culturally divergent countries: The prospective epidemiological study of myocardial infarction (PRIME). *British Medical Journal, 341,* c6077

Rumore, M. M., & Kim, K. S. (2010). Potential role of salicylates in type 2 diabetes. *The Annals of Pharmacotherapy, 44,* 1207–1221.

Russo, M. (2004). Hepatitis B. *Emergency Medicine, 36*(3), 18–19.

Russo, M. W. (2006). Acetaminophen overdose and acute liver failure. *Emergency Medicine, 38*(8), 15–17.

Rutherford, H. J. V., Mayes, L. C., & Potenza, M. N. (2010). Neurobiology of adolescent substance use disorders: Implications for prevention and treatment. *Child and Adolescent Psychiatric Clinics of North America, 19*(3), 479–492.

Rutherford, H. J. C., Mayes, L. C., & Potenza, M. N. (2010). Neurobiology of adolescent substance use disorders: Implications for prevention and treatment. *Child and Adolescent Psychiatric Clinics of North America, 19*(3), 479–492.

Rutkowski, B. A., & Maxwell, J. C. (2009). Epidemiology of methamphetamine use. In J. R. Roll, R. A. Rawson, W. Ling, & S. Shoptaw (Eds.), *Methamphetamine addiction from basic science to treatment.* New York: Guilford.

Ryan, A. M., Malboeuf, C. M., Bernard, M., Rose, R. C., & Phipps, R. P. (2006). Cyclyxygenase-2 inhbition attenuates antibody responses against human papilloma-virus like particles. *Journal of Immunology, 177,* 7811–7819.

Rylkova, D., Bruijnzeel, A. W., & Gold, M. S. (2007). Anabolic steroid abuse: Neurobiological substrates and psychiatric comorbidity. *Journal of Addictive Diseases, 25*(1), 33–45.

Rychtarik, R. G., Connors, G. J., Whitney, R. B., McGillicuddy, N. B., et al. (2000). Treatment settings for persons with alcoholism: Evidence for matching patients to inpatient versus outpatient care. *Journal of Consulting and Clinical Psychology, 68,* 277–289.

Sacks, O. (1970). *The Man Who Mistook His Wife for a Hat.* New York: Harper & Row.

Sacks, O. (2008). *Musicophilia: Tales of music and the brain.* New York: Vintage.

Sacks, O. (2010). Face blind. *The New Yorker, LXXXVI* (25), 36–43.

Sadeghejad, A., Ohar, J. A., Zheng, S. L., Sterling, D. A., et al. (2009). ADAM33 polymorphisms are associated with COPD and lung function in long term tobacco smokers. *Respiratory Research.*

Sadock, B. J., & Sadock, V. A. (2007). *Kaplan and Sadock's Synopsis of Psychiatry* (10th ed.). New York: Lippincott, Williams & Wilkins.

Sailloum, J. B., Ramchandani, V. A., Bodurka, J., Rawlings, R., et al. (2007). Blunder rostral anterior cingulate response during a simplified decoding task of negative facial expressions in alcohol patients. *Alcoholism: Clinical and Experimental Research, 31*(9), 1490–1504.

Saitz, R. (1998). Introduction to alcohol withdrawal. *Alcohol Health & Research World, 22*(1), 5–12.

Saitz, R. (2011, March). *Brief Intervention: Where the Evidence is.and Isn't.* Paper presented at the Treating the Addictions conference: hosted by the Division of alcohol and Drug Abuse of the McLean Hospital, MA.

Salazar, M., Carracedo, A., Salanueva, I. J., Hernandez-Tiedra, S., et al. (2009). Cannabinoid action induces autophagy-mediated cell death through stimulation of ER stress in human glioma cells. *Journal of Clinical Investigation.*

Salzer, M. S., & Kundra, L. B. (2010). Liability issues associated with referrals to selfhelp groups. *Psychiatric Services, 61*(1), 6–8.

Salerno, S. (2005). *Sham: How the Self-Help Movement Made America Helpless.* New York: Random House.

Salize, H. J., Jackie, C., Kief, S., Franz, M., & Mann, K. (2012). Treating alcoholism reduces financial burden on care-givers and increases quality adjusted years. *Addiction.*

Salo, R., Nordahl, T. E., Galloway, G. P., Moore, C. D., et al. (2009). Drug abstinence and cognitive control in methamphetamine-dependent individuals. *Journal of Substance Abuse Treatment.* Retrieved from http://www.journalofsubstanceabusetreatment.com/article/S0740-5472(09)00032-4

Salzman, S. (2008, February). *Essential Psychopharmacology: A Master's Class.* Seminar offered by the Harvard Medical School, Ocean Reef Club, Key, FL.

Samenuk, D., Link, M. S., Homoud, M. K., Contreras, R., et al. (2002). Adverse cardiovascular events temporally associated with ma huang, an herbal source of ephedrine. *Mayo Clinic Proceedings, 77,* 12–16.

Samet, S., Waxman, R., Hazenbuehler, M., & Hasin, D. S. (2007). Assessing addiction: Concepts and instruments. *Addiction Science & Clinical Practice, 4*(1), 19–30.

Sampson, H. W. (2002). Alcohol and other risk factors affecting osteoporosis risk in women. *Alcohol Research & Helath, 26*(4), 294–298.

San, L., Arranz, B., & Martinez-Rega, J. (2007). Antipsychotic drug treatment of schizophrenic patients with substance use disorders. *European Addiction Research, 13,* 230–243.

Sanchez, L. M., & Turner, S. M. (2003). Practicing psychology in the era of managed care. *American Psychologist, 58,* 116–129.

Sandhu, R. K., Jimenez, M. C., Chiuve, S. E., Fitzgerald, K. C., Kenfield, S. A., Tedrow, U. B., & Albert, C. M. (2012). Smoking, smoking cessation ad risk of sudden cardiac death in women. *Circulation: Arrhythmia and Electrophysiology.*

Sanna, P. P., & Koob, G. F. (2004). Cocaine's long run. *Nature Medicine, 10*(4), 340–341.

Santiago, P. M., Wilk, J. E., Milliken, C. S., Castro, C. A., et al. (2010). Screening for alcohol misuse and alcohol-related behaviors among combat veterans. *Psychiatric Services, 61,* 575–581.

Santora, P. B., & Hutton, H. E. (2008). Longitudinal trends in hospital admissions with co-occurring alcohol/drug diagnoses, 1994-2002. *Journal of Substance Abuse Treatment, 35*(1), 1–12.

Sattar, S. P., & Bhatia, S. (2003). Benzodiazepine for substance abusers: Yes or no? *Current Psychiatry, 2*(5), 25–34.

Satel, S. L. (2000, March). *The Limits of Drug Treatment and the Case for Coercion.* Symposium presented to the Dept of Psychiatry at the Cambridge Hospital, MA.

Satel, S. L., & Farabee, D. J. (2005). The role of coercion in drug treatment. In J. H. Lowinson, P. Ruis, R. B. Millman, & J. G. Langrod (Eds.), *Substance Abuse: A Comprehensive Textbook* (4th ed.). New York: Lipponcott, Williams & Wilkins.

Satel, S., & Lilienfeld, S. O. (2013). *Brainwashed: The Seductive Appeal of Mindless Neuroscience.* New York: Basic Books.

Satre, D. D., Mertens, J. R., Arean, P. A., & Weisner, C. (2004). Five year alcohol and drug treatment outcomes n older adults versus middle aged and young adults in a managed care program. *Addiction, 99,* 1286–1297.

Saum, C. A., & Inciardi, J. A. (1997). Rohypnol misuse in the United States. *Substance Use and Misuse, 32,* 723–731.

Sauret, J. M., Marinides, G., & Wang, G. K. (2002). Rhabdomyolysis. *American Family Physician, 65,* 907–912.

Savage, S. R., Kirsh, K. L., & Passik, S. D. (2008). Challenges in using opioids to treat pain in persons with substance use disorders. *Addiction Science & Clinical Practice, 4*(2), 4–25.

Sax, P. E. (2003). HIV infection. In B. A. Cunha (Ed.), *Antibiotic Essentials.* Royal Oak, MI: Physician's Press.

SBIRT Research Collaborative Group. (2007). The impact of screening, brief intervention, and referral for treatment on emergency department patients with alcohol use. *Annals of Emergency Medicine, 50,* 699–710.

Schaefer, M. R., Wonderlich, E. R., Roeth, J. F., Leonard, J. A., & Collins, K. L. (2008). HIV-1 ned targets MHC-I and CD4 for degradation via a common ß-COP dependent pathway in t cells. *PLos. Pathogens (published Online): PLos Pathogens 2008.*

Schaler, J. A. (2000). *Addiction is a Choice.* Chicago: Open Court.

Schanzer, B. M., First, M. B., Dominguez, B., Hasin, D. S., & Canton, C. L. M. (2006). Diagnosing psychotic disorders in the emergency department in the context of substance abuse. *Psychiatric Services, 57,* 1468–1473.

Scher, J. U., Sczesnak, A., Longman, R. S., Segata, N., Ubeda, C., Bielski, C., et al. (2013). Expansion of intestinal Prevotella copri correlates with enhanced susceptibility to arthritis. *Elife, 2,* e01202.

Schiffer, B., Muller, B. W., Scherbaum, N., Hodgins, S., Forsting, M., Wiltfang, J., Gizewski, E. R., & Leygraf, N. (2011). Disentangling structural brain alterations associated with violent behavior from those associated with substance use disorders. *Archives of General Psychiatr, 68,* 1039–1041.

Schirmer, M., Wiedermann, C., & Konwalinka, g. (2000). Immune system. In G. Zernig, A. Saria, M. Kurz, & S. S. O'Malley (Eds.), *Handbook of Alcoholism.* New York: CRC Press.

Schlit, T., de Win, M. L., Koeter, M., Jaker, D. J., et al. (2007). Cognition in novice ecstasy users with minimal exposure to other drugs. *Archives of General Psychiatry, 64,* 728–736.

Schlosser, E. (2003). *Reefer Madness.* New York: Houghton Mifflin Co.

Schlaepfer, T. E., Strain, E. C., Greenberg, B. D., Preston, K. L., et al. (1998). Site of opioid action in the human brain: Mu and kappa agonists subjective and cerebral blood flow effects. *American Journal of Psychiatry, 155,* 470–473.

Schlosser, E. (2003). *Reefer Madness.* New York: Houghton Mifflin Co.

Schmid, H., Bogt, T. T., Godeau, E., Hublet, A., Dias, S. F., & Fotiou, A. (2003). *Journal of Studies on Alcohol, 29*(1), 49–52.

Schmidt, L., Greenfield, T., & Mulia, N. (2006). Unequal treatment: Racial and ethnic disparities in alcoholism treatment services. *Alcohol Research & Health, 29*(1), 49–52.

Schmitt, M. M. (2003). *The role of unsupportive social relationships.* Unpublished doctoral dissertation Virginia Commonwealth University, Virginia.

Schmitz, J. M., & Delaune, K. A. (2005). Nicotine. In J. H. Lowinson, P. Ruiz, R. B. Millman, & J. G. Langrod (Eds.), *Substance Abuse: A Comprehensive Textbook* (4th ed.). New York: Lipponcott, Williams & Wilkins.

Schnoll, S. H., & Weaver, M. F. (2004). Phencyclidine and ketamine. In M. Galanter & H. D. Kleber (Eds.), *Textbook of Substance Abuse Treatment* (3rd ed.). Washington, DC: American Psychiatric Press, Inc.

Schomerus, G., Matschinger, H., & Angermeyer, M. C. (2006). Alcoholism: Illness beliefs and resource allocation preference of the public. *Drug & Alcohol Dependence, 82*(3), 204–210.

Schorling, J. B., & Buchsbaum, D. G. (1997). Screening for alcohol and drug abuse. *Medical Clinics of North America, 81,* 845–865.

Schottenfeld, R. S. (2008). Opioid maintenance treatment. In M. Galanter & H. D. Kleber (Eds.), *Textbook of Substance Abuse Treatment.* Washington, DC: American Psychiatric Association, Inc.

Schmitz, J. M., & Delaune, K. A. (2005). Nicotine. In J. H. Lowinson, P. Ruiz, R. B. Millman, & J. G. Langrod (Eds.), *Substance abuse: a comprehensive textbook* (4th ed.). New York: Lippincott, Williams & Wilkins.

Schuckit, M. A. (1994). Low level of response to alcohol as a predictor of future alcoholism. *American Journal of Psychiatry, 151,* 184–189.

Schuckit, M. A. (2005). Alcohol related disorders. In H. I. Kaplan & B. J. Sadock (Eds.), *Comprehensive Textbook of Psychiatry* (8th ed.). Baltimore: Williams & Wiltkins.

Schuckit, M. A. (2006a). *Drug and Alcohol Abuse: A Clinical Guide to Diagnosis and Treatment* (6th ed.). New York: Springer.

Schuckit, M. A. (2006b). Alcohol and alcoholism. In S. L. Hauser & editor in chief (Eds.), *Harrison's Neurology in Clinical Medicine* (5th ed.). New York: McGraw-Hill.

Schuckit, M. A. (2008a). Alcohol and alcoholism. In A. S. Fauci, E. Braunwald, D. L. Kasper, S. L. Hauser, D. L. Longo, J. L. Jameson, & J. Loscalzo (Eds.), *Harrison's Principles of Internal Medicine* (17th ed.). New York: McGraw-Hill.

Schuckit, M. A. (2008b). In A. S. Fauci, E. Braunwald, D. L. Kasper, S. L. Hauser, D. L. Longo, J. L. Jameson, & J. Loscalzo (Eds.), *Opioid Drug Abuse and Dependence. (in) Harrison's Principles of Internal Medicine* (17th ed.). New York: McGraw-Hill.

Schuckit, M. A. (2009). Alcohol-related disorders. In B. J. Sadock, V. A. Sadock, & P. Ruiz (Eds.), *Kaplan & Sadock's Comprehensive Textbook of Psychiatry* (9th ed.). New York: Lippincott, Williams & Wilkins.

Schuckit, M. A. (2010a). Alcohol and alcoholism. In S. L. Hauser & S. A. Josephson (Eds.), *Harrison's Neurology in Clinical Medicine* (2nd ed.). New York: McGraw-Hill.

Schuckit, M. A. (2010b). Opioid drug abuse and dependence. In S. L. Hauser & S. A. Josephson (Eds.), *Harrison's Neurology in Clinical Medicine* (2nd ed.). New York: McGraw-Hill.

Schuckit, M. A. (2011). Ethanol and methanol. In L. L. Brunton, B. A. Chabner, & B. Knollman (Eds.), *Pharmacological Basis of Therapeutics* (12th ed., pp. 629–647). New York: McGraw-Hill.

Schuckit, M. A., & Tapert, S. (2004). Alcohol. In M. Galanter & H. D. Kleber (Eds.), *Textbook of Substance Abuse Treatment* (3rd ed.). Washington, DC: American Psychiatric Press, Inc.

Schultz, C. H. (2002). Earthquakes. In D. E. Hogan & J. L. Burnstein (Eds.), *Disaster medicine*. New York: Lippincott, Williams & Wilkins.

Schurr, E. (2007). Is susceptibility to tuberculosis acquired or inherited? *Journal of Internal Medicine, 261*(2), 106–110.

Schwartz, J. M., & Beyette, B. (1996). *Brain lock: Free Yourself From Obsessive-Compulsive Behavior.* New York: Harper-Collins.

Schwartz, R. H., & Wirth, P. W. (1990). Potential substance abuse detection among adolescent patients. Using the drug and alcohol problem (DAP) quick screen, a 30-item questionnaire. *Clinical Pediatrics, 29,* 38–43.

Schweikart, L. (2008). *48 Liberal Lies About American History (that you Probably Learned in School).* New York: Sentinel books.

Scientists trace AIDS virus origin to 100 years ago. (2008). *CNN.* Retrieved from http://www.cnn.com/2008/TECH/science/10/01/aids.virus.origin.ap/index.html

Scott, C. G. (2000). Ethical issues in addiction counseling. *Rehabilitation Counseling Bulletin, 43*(4), 209–214.

Scott, J. C., & Marcotte, T. D. (2010). Everybody impact of HIV-associated neurocognitive disorders. In T. D. Marcotte & I. Grant (Eds.), *Neuropsychology of Everyday Functioning.* New York: Guilford.

Scientists call for stronger warnings for acetaminophen. (2002). *La Crosse Tribune, 99*(153), A1–A8.

Scott, I. (1998). A hundred-year habit. *History Today, 48*(6), 6–8.

Screening for alcohol problems-an update. (2002). *Alcohol Alert, 56,* 1–3.

Sekine, Y., Iyo, M., Ouchi, Y., Matsunaga, T., et al. (2001). Methamphetamine-related psychiatric symptoms and reduced brain dopamine transporters studied with PET. *American Journal of Psychiatry, 158,* 1206–1214.

Sekine, Y., Ouchi, Y., Takei, N., Yoshikawa, E., et al. (2006). Brain serotonin transporter density and aggression in abstinent methamphetamine abusers. *Archives of General Psychiatry, 63,* 90–100.

Segerstrom, S. C. (2008). *Doing Optimism. (in) Measuring the Immeasurable: The Scientific Case for Spirituality.* Bolder, CO: Sounds True Press.

Seife, C. (2012). Is drug research trustworthy? *Scientific American, 307*(6), 56–63.

Selzer, M. (1971). The michigan alcoholism screening test: The quest for a new diagnostic instrument. *American Journal of Psychiatry, 127,* 1653–1658.

Sepe, P., Kay, A., & Stober, K. (2012). QUIT: A mnemonic to help patients stop smoking. *Current Psychiatry, 11*(12), 41–42.

Seppa, N. (2010). Not just a high. *Science News, 177*(13), 16–20.

Seppala, M. D. (2004). Dilemmas in diagnosing and treating co-occurring disorders: An addiction professional's perspective. *Behavioral Healthcare Tomorrow, 13*(4), 42–47.

Sergio, P. (2008). New weapons against cocaine addiction. *Scientific American Mind, 19*(2), 54–57.

Sessa, B. (2005). Can psychedelics have a role to play in psychiatry once again? *British Journal of Psychiatry, 186,* 457–458.

Setlik, J., Gond, G. R., & Ho, M. (2009). Adolescent prescription ADHD medication abuse is rising along with prescriptions for these medications. *Pediatrics, 124,* 875–880.

Setola, V., Hufeisen, S. J., Grande-Allen, J., Vesely, I., et al. (2003). 3,4-Methyllenedioxymethamphetamine (MDMA, "ecstasy") induces fenfluramine-like proliferation actions in human cardiac valvular intertial cells in vitro. *Molecular Pharmacology, 63,* 1223–1229.

Shea, C. W. (2006). Alcohol dependence treatment. *Advances in Addiction Treatment, 1*(1), 12–14.

Shadel, W. G., & Scharf, D. (2012). Interactions and addiction. In H. J. Shaffer, D. A. LaPlante, & S. E. Nelson (Eds.), *A.p.a. Addiction syndromes handbook* (Vol. 1, pp. 211–228). Washington, DC: American Psychological Association.

Shader, R. I. (2003). *Manual of psychiatric therapeutics* (3rd ed.). New York: Lippincott, Williams & Wilkins.

Shaffer, H. J. (2001). *What is Addiction and Does it Matter?* Symposium presented to the Dept of Psychiatry of the Cambridge Hospital, Boston, MA.

Shakya, H. B., Christakis, N. A., & Fowler, J. H. (2012). Parental influence on substance use in adolescent social networks. *Archives of Pediatrics & Adolescent Medicine.*

Shalev, A. Y. (2009). Posttraumatic stress disorder and stress-related disorders. *Psychiatric Clinics of North America, 32,* 687–704.

Sharma, P. (2003). *Tylenol, the Wonder Drug*. Paper presented at the March 5th, 2003 Continuing Medical Education Symposium Gundersen-Lutheran Medical Center, La Crosse, WIsconsin.

Sharp, M. J., & Getz, J. G. (1998). Self-process in comorbid mental illness and drug abuse. *American Journal of Orthopsychiatry, 68,* 639–644.

Sharp, C. W., & Rosenberg, N. L. (2005). Inhalants. In J. H. Lowinson, P. Ruiz, R. B. Millman, & J. G. Langrod (Eds.), *Substance Abuse: A Comprehensive Textbook*. New York: Lipponcott, Williams & Wilkins.

Shea, S. C. (2002). *The Practical Art of Suicide Assessment*. New York: John Wiley & Sons, Inc.

Shea, S. C. (2006). *Improving Medication Adherence*. New York: Lippincott, Williams & Wilkins.

Shear, M. K. (2003). Optimal treatment of anxiety disorders. *Patient Care, 37*(5), 18–32.

Sheff, D., Warren, L., Ketcham, K., & Eban, K. (2007). In J. Hoffman & S. Froemke (Eds.), *Addiction: Why Can't they Just Stop?* New York: Rodale Press.

Shekelle, P. G., Hardy, M. L., Morton, S. C., Maglione, M., et al. (2003). Efficacy and safety of ephedra and ephedrine for weight loss and athletic performance. *Journal of the American Medical Association, 289,* 1537–1545.

Shelton, M. (2011). Treating gay men for substance abuse. *Counselor, 12*(1), 18–22.

Shem, S. (1978). *The house of god*. New York: Dell Publishing Co.

Shenk, J. W. (1999). America's altered states. *Harper's Magazine, 298*(1788), 38–52.

Shenouda, S. K., Lord, K. C., McIlwain, E., Lucchesi, P. A., & Varner, K. J. (2008). Ecstasy produces left ventricular dysfunction and oxidative stress in rats. *Cardiovascular Research, 79,* 662–670.

Shepard, D. S., Larson, M. J., & Hoffmann, N. G. (1999). Cost-effectiveness of substance abuse services. *Psychiatric Clinics of North America, 22,* 385–400.

Shepard, J. P., Sutherland, I., & Newcombe, R. G. (2006). Relation between alcohol, violence, and victimization in adolescence. *Journal of Adolescence, 29*(4), 239–253.

Sher, K. J. (1991). *Children of Alcoholics*. Chicago: University of Chicago Press.

Sher, K. J., & Wood, M. D. (2005). Subjective effects of alcohol II. In M. Earlywine (Ed.), *Mind-Altering Drugs: The Science of Subjective Experience*. New York: Oxford University Press.

Sher, K. J., Wood, M. D., Richardson, A. E., & Jackson, K. M. (2005). Subjective effects of alcohol: I. In M. Earlywine (Ed.), *Mind-Altering Drugs: The Science of Subjective Experience*. New York: Oxford University Press.

Sherer, R. A. (2006). Drug abuse hitting middle-aged more than Gen-Xers. Retrieved from http://www.psychiatrictimes.com/articles/drug-abuse-hitting-middle-aged-more-gen-xers

Sherman, C. (2008). Drug therapy for alcohol dependence. *Clinical Psychiatry News, 36*(7), 37.

Shermer, M. (2008). Why you should be skeptical of brain scans. *Scientific American Mind, 19*(5), 66–71.

Sherwood, B. (2009). *The Survivors Club*. New York: Grand Central Publishing.

Shih, R. A., Miles, J. N. V., Tucker, J. S., Zhou, A. J., et al. (2010). Racial/ethnic differences in adolescent substance use: Mediation by individual, family and school factors. *Journal of Studies on Alcohol & Drugs, 71*(5), 640–656.

Shinn, A. K., & Greenfield, S. F. (2010). Topiramate in the treatment of substance-related disorders: A critical review of the literature. *Journal of Clinical Psychiatry, 71*(5), 634–648.

Shipley, R., & Rose, J. (2003). *Quit Smart*. Durham, NC: QuitSmart Smoking Resources, Inc.

Shivani, R., Goldsmith, R. J., & Anthenelli, R. M. (2002). Alcoholism and psychiatric disorders. *Alcohol Research & Health, 26,* 90–98.

Siegel, B. (2009). No war on terror. *Scientific American Mind, 20*(1), 5.

Siegel, D. (2008). Reflections on the mindful brain. *Measuring the Immeasurable: The Scientific Case for Spirituality*. Bolder, CO: Sounds True Press.

Siegel, D. J. (2013). *Pocket Guide to Interpersonal Neurobiology*. New York: W.W. Norton & Company.

Shouse, R. L., Kajese, T., Hall, H. I., Valleroy, L. A., et al. (2009). Late HIV testing 34 states, 1996-2005. *Morbidity and Mortality Weekly Report*. Retrieved from http://www.cdc.gov/mmwr/preview/mmwrhtml/mm5824a2htm

Shulgin, A., & Shulgin, A. (2007). *Pihkal: A Chemical love Story*. Berkeley, CA: Transform Press.

Silvestri, N. J. (2009). Central nervous system infections. In S. I. Savitz & M. Ronthal (Eds.), *Neurology Review for Psychiatrists*. New York: Lippincott Williams & Wilkins.

Simkin, D. R. (2002). Adolescent substance use disorders and comorbidity. *Pediatric Clinics of North America, 49,* 463–477.

Simmons, L. A., Havens, J. R., Whiting, J. B., Holz, J. L., & Bada, H. (2009). Illicit drug use among women with children in the United States: 2002-2003. *Annals of Epidemiology, 19*(3), 187–193.

Simon, H. B. (2007). Old bugs learn new tricks. *Newsweek, CXLVIII*(24), 74, 77.

Simpson, D. D. (2004). A conceptual framework for drug treatment process and outcomes. *Journal of Substance Abuse Treatment, 27,* 99–121.

Simpson, T. L., Saxon, A. J., Meredith, C. W., Malte, C. A., et al. (2008). A pilot trial of the alpha adrenergic antagonist prazosin for alcohol dependence. *Alcohol Clinical and Experimental Research.*

Simpson, T. L., Stappenbeck, C. A., Varra, A. A., Moore, S. A., & Kaysen, D. (2012). Symptoms of posttraumatic stress predict craving among alcohol treatment seekers: Results of a daily monitoring study. *Psychology of Addictive Behaviors, 26*(4), 724–733.

Singer, E. A., Palapattu, G. S., & van Wjingarrden, E. (2008). Prostate-specific antigen levels in relation to consumption of nonsteroidal anti-inflammatory drugs and acetaminophen. *Cancer, 2002, 113.*

Singer, L. T., Minnes, S., Short, E., Arendt, R., et al. (2004). Cognitive outcomes of preschool children with prenatal cocaine exposure. *Journal of the American Medical Association, 291*(20), 2448–2546.

Sinha, R. (2000). Women. In G. Zernig, A. Saria, M. Kurz, & S. S. O'Malley (Eds.), *Handbook of Alcoholism.* New York: CRC Press.

Sirotin, Y. B., & Das, A. (2009). Anticipatory haemodynamic signals in sensory cortex not predicted by local neuronal activity. *Nature, 457,* 475–479.

Sklair-Tavron, L., Ski, W. X., Lane, S. B., Harris, H. W., et al. (1996). Chronic morphine induces visible changes in the morphology of mesolimbic dopamine neurons. *Proceedings of the National Academy of Sciences, 93,* 11202–11207.

Slade, J., Breo, L. A., Hanauer, P., Barnes, D. E., & Glantz, S. A. (1995). Nicotine and addiction. *Journal of the American Medical Association, 274,* 225–233.

Slutske, W. S., Hunt-Carter, E. E., Nabors, R. E., Sher, K. J., Bucholz, K. K., et al. (2004). Do college students drink more than non-college attending peers? Evidence from a population-based female twin study. *Journal of Abnormal Psychology, 113,* 530–540.

Slutske, W. S. (2005). Alcohol use disorders among US college students and their nondrinking peers. *Archives of General Psychiatry, 62,* 321–327.

Small, W., Fast, A., Krusi, A., Wood, E., & Kerr, T. (2009). *Substance Abuse Treatment, Prevention and Policy.*

Small, M. F. (2002). What you can learn from drunk monkeys. *Discover, 23*(7), 40–47.

Smith, A., Miles, I., Le, B., Finlayson, T., Oster, A., & DiNenno, E. (2010). Prevalence and awareness of HIV infection among men who have sex with men 21 cities, United States, 2008. *Morbidity and Mortality Weekly Report, 59*(37), 1201–1207.

Smith, B. H., Molina, B. S., & Pelham, W. (2002). The clinically meaningful like between alcohol use and attention deficit hyperactivity disorder. *Alcohol Research & Health, 26,* 122–129.

Smith, D. (1997). *Prescription Drug abuse.* Paper presented at the May, 1997, WisSAM Symposium: "Still Getting High: A 30 year perspective on drug abuse Gun dersen-Lutheran Medical Center, La Crosse, Wisconsin.

Smith, D. (2001, June). *All the Rave What's Pop in Substance Abuse.* Paper presented at the Contemporary Issues in the Treatment of Alcohol and Drug Abuse Symposium, WI.

Smith, D. M. (2007). Managing acute acetaminophen toxicity. *Nursing 2007, 37*(1), 58–63.

Smith, D. M., Wong, J. K., Hightower, G. K., Ignacio, C. C., et al. (2004). Incidence of HIV superinfection following primary infection. *Journal of the American Medical Association, 292,* 1177–1178.

Smith, G. E., & Wesson, D. R. (2004). Benzodiazepines and other sedative-hypnotics. In M. Galanter & H. D. Kleber (Eds.), *Textbook of Substance Abuse Treatment* (3rd ed.). Washington, DC: American Psychiatric Press, Inc.

Smith, G. R., Burnam, M. A., Mosley, C. L., Hollengerg, J. A., et al. (2000). Reliability and validity of the substance abuse outcomes module. *Psychiatric Services, 57,* 1452–1460.

Smith, G. S., Keyl, P. M., Hadley, J. A., Barlety, C. L., et al. (2001). Drinking and recreational boating fatalities. *Journal of the American Medical Association, 286,* 2974–2980.

Smith, J. E., Meyers, R. J., & Delaney, H. D. (1998). The community reinforcement approach with homeless alcohol-dependent individuals. *Journal of Consulting and Clinical Psychology, 66,* 541–548.

Smith, L. M., Chang, L., Yonekura, M. L., Gilbride, K., et al. (2001). Brain proton magnetic resonance spectroscopy and imaging in children exposed to cocaine in utero. *Pediatrics, 107,* 227–231.

Smith, L. M., Chang, L., Yonekura, M. L., Grob, C., et al. (2001). Brain proton magnetic resonance spectroscopy in children exposed to methamphetamine in utero. *Neurology, 57*(2), 255–260.

Smith, M. B. (2008). Chronic pain and psychotherapy: One psychiatrist's view. *Primary Psychiatry, 14*(9), 55–68.

Smith, P. C., Schmidt, S. M., Allensworth-Davies, D., & Saitz, R. (2010). A single question screening test for drug use in primary care. *Archives of Internal Medicine, 170*(13), 1156–1160.

Smith, P. H., Homish, G. G., Leonard, K. E., & Cornelius, J. R. (2012). Intimate partner violence and specific substance use disorders: Findings from the national epidemiologic survey on alcohol and related conditions. *Psychology of Addictive Behaviors, 26*(2), 236–245.

Smith, S. C., Benjamin, E. J., Bonow, R. O., Braun, L. T., Creater, M. A., Franklin, B. A., Gibbons, R. J., Grundy, S. M., Hiratzka, L. F., Jones, D. W., Lloyd-Jones, D. M., Minissian, M., Mosca, L., Peterson, E. D., Sacco, R. L., Spertus, J., Stein, J. H., & Taubert, K. A. (2011). AHA/ACCF secondary prevention and risk reduction therapy for patients with coronary and other atherosclerotic vascular disease: 2011 update. *Circulation, 124,* 2458–2473.

Smothers, B. A., Yahr, H. T., & Ruhl, C. (2004). Detection of alcohol use disorders in general hospital admissions in the United States. *Archives of Internal Medicine, 164,* 749–756.

Smucker, W. D., & Hedayat, M. (2001). Evaluation and treatment of ADHD. *American Family Physician, 64,* 817–829.

Smyth, B., Hoffman, V. I., Fan, J., & Hser, Y. (2007). Years of potential life lost among heroin addicts 33 years after treatment. *Preventative Medicine, 44*(4), 369–374.

Sneider, J. T., Pope, H., Silveri, M. M., Simpson, N. S., et al. (2006). Altered regional blood volume in chronic cannabis smokers. *Experimental and Clinical Psychopharmacology, 14,* 422–428.

Sobell, M. B., & Sobell, L. C. (2007). Substance use, health and mental health. *Clinical Psychology, 14*(1), 1–3.

Social networks show drug use follows lack of sleep. (2010). *New Scientist, 205*(2753), 11.

Sofuoglu, M., & Kosten, T. R. (2004). Parhmacologic management of relapse prevention in addictive disorders. *Psychiatric Clinics of North America, 27,* 622–648.

Sofuoglu, M., & Mooney, M. (2009). Subjective responses to intravenous nicotine: Greater sensitivity in women than in men. *Experimental and Clinical Psychopharmacology, 17*(2), 63–69.

Sokol, R. J., Delaney-Black, V., & Nordstrom, B. (2003). Fetal alcohol spectrum disorder. *Journal of the American Medical Association, 290,* 2966–2999.

Solis, M. (2012). A lifeline for addicts. *Scientific American Mind, 24*(1), 40–44.

Solomon, D. H., Glynn, R. J., LEvin, R., & Avorn, J. (2002). Nonsteroidal anti-inflammatory drug use and acute myocardial infarction. *Archives of Internal Medicine, 162,* 1099–1104.

Solomon, J., Rogers, A., Kate, P., & Lach, J. (1957). Turning a new leaf. *Newsweek, CXXIX*(13), 50.

Solotaroff, P. (2002). Killer bods. *Rolling Stone, 889,* 54–56, 58–59, 72, 74.

Solowij, N., Stephens, R. S., Roffman, R. A., Babor, T., et al. (2002). Cognitive functioning of long-term heavy cannabis users seeking treatment. *Journal of the American Medical Association, 287,* 1123–1131.

Solvent abuse puts teens at risk. (2003). *BBC News,* October 22, 2003. Retrieved from http://news.bbc.co.uk/2/hi/health/3205001.stm

Sommer, W. (2005, November). *Alcoholism and other addictions: Basic science and clinical applications.* Seminar presented at the Psychopharmacology & Neuroscience Course, Update 2005, MD.

Sommers, C. H., & Satel, S. (2005). *One Nation Under Therapy.* New York: St. Martin's Press.

Sonne, S. C., & Brady, K. T. (2002). Bipolar disorder and alcoholism. *Alcohol Research & Health, 26,* 103–108.

Sostre, S. O., & Tiu, G. (2013). Strategies for treating depression in patients with hepatitis c. *Current Psychiatry, 12*(4), 33–38.

Sorter, M. T. (2010). Adolescents in crisis: When to admit for self-harm or aggressive behavior. *Current Psychiatry, 9*(1), 35–39, 45–46.

South American drug production increases. (1997). *Forensic Drug Abuse Advisor, 9*(3), 18.

Southwick, S. M., & Charney, D. S. (2013). Ready for anything. *Scientific American Mind, 24*(3), 32–41.

Sowell, E. R., Leow, A. D., Brookheimer, S. Y., Smith, L. M., et al. (2010). Differentiating prenatal exposure to methamphetamine and alcohol fersus alcohol and not methamphetamine using tensor based brain morphometry and discriminant analysis. *Journal of Neuroscience, 30*(11), 3876–3885.

Soyka, M. (2000). Alcohol-induced psychotic disorders. In G. Zernig, A. Saria, M. Kurz, & S. S. O'Malley

(Eds.), *Handbook of alcoholism*. New York: CRC Press.

Spear, L. P. (2002). The adolescent brain and the college drinker: Biological basis of propensity to use and misuse alcohol. *Journal of Studies on Alcohol,* 71–81.

Spear, L. P. (2010). *The Behavioral Neuroscience of Adolescence*. New York: W.W. Norton & Sons, Inc.

Speck, P. M., Connor, P. D., Hartig, M. T., Cunningham, P. D., & Fleming, B. (2008). Vulnerable populations: Drug court program clients. *Nursing Clinics of North America, 43,* 477–489.

Spencer, T., Biederman, J., Wilens, T., Faraone, T., et al. (2001). Efficacy of a mixed amphetamine salts compound in adults with attention deficit/hyperactivity disorder. *Archives of General Psychiatry, 58,* 775–782.

SpencerT. J. (2008). Adult ADHD: Diversion and misuse of medicatios. *CNS Spectrums13*(10, 15), 9–15.

Spiegel, D. R., Kumari, N., & Petri, J. D. (2012). Safer use of benzodiazepines for alcohol detoxification. *Current Psychiatry, 11*(10), 10–15.

Spiller, H. A., & Krenzoelok, E. P. (1997). Epidemiology of inhalant abuse reported to two regional poison centers. *Journal of Toxicology: Clinical Toxicology, 35,* 167–174.

Spoth, R., Greenberg, M., & Turrisi, R. (2009). Overview of preventive interventions addressing underaged drinking. *Alcohol Research & Health, 32*(1), 53–66.

Squeglia, L. M., Spandoni, A. D., Infante, A., Myers, M. G., & Tapert, S. F. (2009). Initiating moderate to heavy alcohol use predicts changes in neuropsychological functioning for adolescent girls and boys. *Psychology of Addictive Behaviors, 23,* 715–722.

Srisurapanont, M., Marsden, J., Sunga, A., Wada, K., & Monterio, M. (2003). Psychotic symptoms in methamphetamine psychotic inpatients. *International Journal of Neuropsychopharmacology, 6*(4), 347–352.

Stahl, S. M. (2008). *Essential psychopharmacology* (3rd ed.). New York: Cambridge University Press, Inc.

Stahler, G. J., Mennis, J., Cotlar, R., & Baron, D. A. (2009). The influence of neighborhood environment on treatment continuity and rehospitalization in dually diagnosed patients discharged from acute inpatient care. *American Journal of Psychiatry, 166,* 1258–1268.

Stamp out drugs. (2003). *Playboy, 50*(7), 52.

Standridge, J. B., & DeFranco, G. M. (2006). The clinical realities of using drugs to fight alcoholism. *Patient Care, 40*(3), 13–20.

Standbridge, J. B., Adams, S. M., & Zotos, A. P. (2010). Urine drug screening: A valuable office procedure. *American Family Physician, 81,* 635–640.

Stanner, L., Boeijinga, P., Thierry, G. I., Muzet, M., et al. (2006). Effects of acamprosate on sleep during alcohol withdrawal: A double-blind, placebo-controlled polysomnographic study in alcohol-dependent subjects. *Alcoholism: Clinical & Experimental Research, 30,* 1492–1499.

Stanwood, G. D., & Levitt, P. (2007). Prenatal exposure to cocaine products produced unique developmental and long-term changes in dopamine d1 receptor activity and subcellular distribution. *The Journal of Neuroscience, 27*(1), 152–157.

Stark, M. J., Rhode, K., Maher, J. E., Pizacano, B. A., et al. (2007). The impact of clean indoor air exemptions and preemptive policies on the prevalence of a tobaccospecific lung carcinogen among nonsmoking bar and restaurant workers. *American Journal of Public Health.*

Starkman, B. G., Sakharkar, A. J., & Pandey, S. C. (2012). Epigenetics beyond the genome in alcoholism. Assessing the genetic risk for alcohol use disorders. *Alcohol Research: Current Reviews, 34*(3), 293–305.

Stauber, R. E., Trauner, M., & Fickert, P. (2000). Gastrointestinal system and pancreas. In G. Zernig, A. Saria, M. Kurz, & S. O'Malley (Eds.), *Handbook of Alcoholism*. New York: CRC Press.

Steele, T. E., & Morton, W. A. (1986). Salicylate-induced delirium. *Psychosomatics, 27*(6), 455–456.

Stein, L. A. R., & Rogers, R. (2008). Denial and misreporting of substance abuse. In R. Rogers (Ed.), *Clinical Assessment of Malingering and Deception.* New York: Guilford.

Stephens, M. (2008). Supplements and sports: Honest advice. *American Family Physician, 78,* 1025.

Stephens, R. S., & Roffman, R. A. (2005). Assessment of cannabis use disorders. In D. M. Donovan & G. A. Marlatt (Eds.), *Assessment of Addictive Disorders* (2nd ed.). New York: Guilford.

Stephens, A., Logina, I., Liguts, V., Aldins, P., et al. (2008). A parkinsonian syndrome in methcathinone users and the role of mangagese. *New Negland Journal of Medicine, 358,* 1000–1017.

Sterling, R. C., Weinstein, S., Hill, O., Gottheil, Gordon, S. M., & Shorie, K. (2006). Levels of spirituality and treatment outcome: A preliminary examination. *Journal of Studies on Alcohol, 67,* 600–606.

Steroids and growth hormones make users "really ripped." (2003). *Forensic Drug Abuse Advisor, 15,* 74–76.

Sternbach, H. (2003). Serotonin syndrome. *Current Psychiatry, 2*(5), 14–24.

Stevens, J. C., & Pollack, M. H. (2005). Benzodiazepines in clinical practice: Consideration of their long-term use and alternative agents. *Journal of Consulting and Clinical Psychology, 66*(2), 21–27.

Stevenson, J. S., & Sommers, M. S. (2005). The case for alcohol research as a focus of study by nurse researchers. In J. J. Fitzpatrick, J. S. Stevenson, & M. S. Sommers (Eds.), *Annual Review of Nursing Research* (Vol. 23). New York: Springer.

Stein, B., Orlando, M., & Sturm, R. (2000). The effect of copayments on drug and alcohol treatment following inpatient detoxification under managed care. *Psychiatric Services, 51,* 195–198.

Stein, S. M., & Friedmann, P. D. (2001). Generalist physicians and addiction care. *Journal of the American Medical Association, 286,* 1764–1765.

Steinhoff, K. W. (2008). ADHD in adolescents. *Postgraduate Medicine, 120,* 60–68.

Steinbrook, R. (2004). The AIDS epidemic in 2004. *New England Journal of Medicine, 351,* 115–117.

Steinhoff, K. W. (2008). Special issues in the diagnosis and treatment of ADHD in adolescents. *Postgraduate Medicine, 120*(3), 60–68.

Steinhubl, S. R., Bhatt, D. L., Brennan, D. M., Montalescot, G., et al. (2009). Aspirin to prevent cardiovascular disease: The association of aspirin dose and clopidogrel with thrombosis and bleeding. *Archives of Internal Medicine, 150,* 379–386.

Stelovich, S. (2011, March). *Working With the Dually Diagnosed.* Paper presented at the Treating the Addictions conference: hosted by the Division of alcohol and Drug Abuse of the McLean Hospital, MA.

Stephens, R. S., & Roffman, R. A. (2005). Assessment of cannabis use disorders. In D. M. Donovan & G. A. Marlatt (Eds.), *Assessment of Addictive Disorders* (2nd ed.). New York: Guilford.

Sterling, R. C., Weinstein, S., Hill, P., Gottheil, E., et al. (2006). Levels of spirituality and treatment outcome: A preliminary examination. *Journal of Studies on Alcohol, 67,* 600–606.

Sterling, S., Chi, F., & Hinman, A. (2011). Integrating care for people with co-occurring alcohol and other drug, medical, and mental health conditions. *Alcohol Research & Health, 33*(4), 338–349.

Stetter, F. (2000). Psychotherapy. In G. Zernig, A. Saria, M. Kurz, & S. S. O'Malley (Eds.), *Handbook of Alcoholism.* New York: CRC Press.

Stevens, J. C., & Pollock, M. H. (2005). Benzodiazepines in clinical practice: Consideration of their long-term use and alternative agents. *Journal of Consulting and Clinical Psychology, 62,* 92–99.

Stevenson, J. S. (2005). Alcohol use, misuse, abuse and dependence in later adulthood. In J. J. Fitzpatrick, J. S. Stevenson, & M. S. Somers (Eds.), *Annual Review of Nursing Research* (Vol. 23). New York: Springer.

Stevenson, J. S., & Somers, M. S. (2005). The case for alcohol research as a focus of study by nurse researchers. In J. J. Fitzpatrick, J. S. Stevenson, & M. S. Somers (Eds.), *Annual Review of Nursing Research* (Vol. 23). New York: Springer.

Stewart, M. T., & Horgan, C. M. (2011). Health services and financing of treatment. *Alcohol Research & Health, 33*(4), 389–394.

Stewart, S. A. (2005). The effects of benzodiazepines on cognition. *Journal of Medical Psychiatry, 66*(2), 9–13.

Sticherling, C., Schaer, B. A., Ammann, P., Maeder, M., & Osswald, S. (2005). Methadone induced torsade de pointes tachycardias. *Swiss Medical Weekly, 135* (19–20), 282–285.

Stillman, M. J., & Stillman, M. T. (2007). Choosing nonselective NSAIDS and selective COX-2 inhibitors in the elderly. *Geriatrics, 62*(22), 26–34.

Stimmel, B. (1997a). *Pain and its relief without Addiction.* New York: The Harworth Medical Press.

Stimmel, B. (1997b). *Drug Abuse and Social Policy in America: The War that must be Won.* Paper presented at the 1997 annual Frank P. Furlano, MD, memorial lecture: Gundersen-Lutheran Medical Center, La Crosse, Wisconsin.

Stitzer, M. (2003). *Nicotine Addiction and Tobacco Dependence.* Toronto, Canada: Seminar Presented at the 2003 meeting of the American Psychological Association.

Stix, G. (2009). Turbocharging the brain. *Scientific American, 301*(4), 46–55.

Stix, G. (2011). The neuroscience of true grit. *Scientific American, 304*(3), 28–33.

Stone, P., & Edwards, P. (1970). *1776*. New York: Penguin Books.

Stoschitzky, K. (2000). Cardiovascular system. In G. Zernig, A. Saria, M. Kurz, & S. S. O'Malley (Eds.), *Handbook of Alcoholism*. New York: CRC press.

Stott, D. J., Falconner, A., Kerr, G. D., Murray, H. M., et al. (2008). Does lot to moderate alcohol intake protect against cognitive decline in older people? *Journal of the American Geriatrics Society, 56*(16), 2217–2224.

Stout, P. R. (2009). Opioids. In J. D. Robero-Miller & B. A. Goldberger (Eds.), *Handbook of Workplace Drug Testing* (2nd ed.). Washington, DC: AACC Press.

Strandberg, A. Y., Strandberg, T. E., Pitkala, K., Salomaa, V., et al. (2008). The effect of smoking in midlife on health realted quality of life in old age. *Archives of Internal Medicine, 168*(18), 1968–1974.

Strassman, R. (2005). Hallucinogens. In M. Earlywine (Ed.), *Mind Altering Drugs: The Science of Subjective Experience*. New York: Doubleday.

Strauch, B. (2003). *The Primal Teen*. New York: Doubleday.

Stratton, R., & Hill, R. (2010). Grown in the USA. *Playboy, 57*(9), 44–46, 60, 124–127.

Steenrod, S. (2011, March). *Treatment Protocols: Recipe or Ingredient of Quality of Care?*. Paper presented to the Dept of Psychiatry of the Cambridge Hospital, MA.

Sturmi, J. E., & Diorio, D. J. (1998). Anabolic agents. *Clinics in Sports Medicine, 17*, 261–282.

Subbaraman, M. S., & Kaskutas, L. A. (2012). Social support and comfort in AA as mediators of "making AA easier" (MAAEZ), a 2-step facilitation intervention. *Psychology of Addictive Behaviors, 26*(4), 759–765.

Substance Abuse and Mental Health Services Administration. (2005a). *Results from the 2004 National Survey on Drug use and Health: National Findings*. Rockville, MD: Author.

Substance Abuse and Mental Health Services Administration. (2005b). *Substance abuse and dependence among women: National Survey on Drug use and Health*. Rockville, MD: Author.

Substance Abuse and Mental Health Services Administration. (2009). *Results from the 2008 National Survey on Drug use and Health: National Findings*. Rockville, MD: Author.

Substance Abuse and Mental Health Services Administration, Center for Behavioral Health Statistics and Quality. (2011). *Adults Represent Majority of Inhalant Treatment Admissions*. Retrieved from http:/// oas.samhsa.gov/spotlight024InhalantAdmissions.pdf

Substance Abuse and Mental Health Services Administration. (2011). *Results from the 2010 National Survey on Drug use and Health: Summary of National Findings*. Rockville, MD: Author.

Substance Abuse and Mental Health Services Administration, Office of Applied Studies. (July 29, 2010). *The DAWN report: Emergency department visits involving underage alcohol use: 2008*. Rockville, MD: Author.

Suddendorf, T. (2013). *The Gap*. New York: Basic Books.

Sukel, K. (2012). *Dirty Minds*. New York: The Free Press.

Sull, J. W., Sang-Wook, Y., Nam, C. M., & Ohrr, H. (2009). Binge drinking and mortality from all causes and crebrovascular disease in Korean men and women. *Stroke*.

Sullivan, M. G. (2007). Heavy alcohol use hastens death by up to 25 years: Neuropsychiatric patients at great risk. *Clinical Psychiatry News, 35*(8), 1.

Sundaram, R., Shulman, L., & Fein, A. M. (2004). Trends in tobacco use. *Medical Clinics of North America, 88*, 1391–1397.

Suppes, T., & Keck, P. E. (2005). *Bipolar disorder: Treatment and management*. Kansas City, MO: Compact Clinicals Medical Publishers.

Suris, J. C., Akre, C., Berchtold, A., Jeannin, A., & Michaud, P. (2007). Characteristics of cannabis users who have never smoked tobacco. *Archives of Pediatrics & Adolescent Medicine, 161*(11), 1042–1047.

Sussman, N., & Westreich, L. (2003). Chronic marijuana use and the treatment of mentally ill patients. *Primary Psychiatry, 19*(9), 73–76.

Sussman, N. (2009). Mental health parity act becomes the law on october 3, 2009. *Primary Psychiatry, 16*(10), 10–11.

Sutheimer, C. A., & Cody, J. T. (2009). Subversion of regulated workplace drug testing specimen adulteration and substitution. In J. D. Robero-Miller & B. A. Goldberger (Eds.), *Handbook of workplace drug testing* (2nd ed.). Washington, DC: AACC Press.

Svitil, K. A. (2003). What, me worry about SARS? *Discover, 24*(8), 19–20.

Swan, N. (1998). Drug abuse cost to society set at $97.7 billion, continuing steady increase since 1975. *NIDA Notes, 13*(4), 1, 12.

Swann, A. C. (2009). Behavioral neurochemistry and pharmacology. In S. I. Savitz & M. Ronthal (Eds.), *Neurology Review for Psychiatrists*. New York: Lippincott Williams & Wilkins.

Swartz, M. S., Wagner, H. R., Swanson, J. W., Stroup, T. S., et al. (2006). Substance use and psychosocial functioning in schizophrenia among new enrollees in the NIMH CATIC study. *Psychiatric Services, 57*, 1110–1116.

Swegle, J. M., & Logemann, C. (2006). Management of common opioid-induced adverse effects. *American Family Physician, 74*, 1347–1354.

Swift, R., & Davidson, D. (1998). Alcohol hangover. *Alcohol Health & Research World, 22*, 54–60.

Swift, R. M. (2005, January). *The Etiology of Alcohol abuse and Dependence: What Happens in the Brain?*. Seminar presented at the Four Seasons Hotel, Chicago.

Swift, R. M. (2010, May). *Update on Medication for Alcohol Dependence*. Paper presented at the "Addictions in 2010" seminar, hosted by the Division of alcohol and Drug Abuse of the McLean Hospital, MA.

Sylvestre, D. (2008). Hepatitis c for addiction professionals. *Addiction Science & Clinical Practice, 4*(1), 34–42.

Szabo, C., & MAndrekar, P. (2010). Focus on: Alcohol and the liver. *Alcohol Research & Health, 33*(1), 87–96.

Szalavitz, M. (2005). Give us the drugs. *New Scientist, 185*(2484), 19.

Szalavitz, M. (2006). *Help at Any Cost*. New York: Riverhead books.

Szalavitz, M. (2010). Is marijuana addictive? It depends on how you define addiction. *Time.com*. Retrieved November 10, 2010, from http://healthand.time.com/2010/10/19/is-marijuana-addictive-it-depends-how-you-define-addiction/

Szalavitz, M. (2012). Why the teen brain is drawn to risk. *Time Healthland*. Retrieved from http://healthland.time.com/2012/10/02/why-the-teen-brain-is-drawn-to-risk/.

Szasz, T. S. (1997). Save money, cut crime, get real. *Playboy, 44*(1), 121, 190.

Szasz, T. (2009). *The Medicalization of Everyday Life*. Syracuse, NY: Syracuse University Press.

Tabakoff, B., & Hoffman, P. L. (2004). Neurobiology of alcohol. In M. Galanter & H. D. Kleber (Eds.), *Substance abuse, a comprehensive textbook* (3rd ed.). Washington, DC: American Psychiatric Press, Inc.

Tacke, U., & Ebert, M. H. (2005). Hallucinogens and phencyclidine. In H. R. Kranzler & D. A. Ciraulo (Eds.), *Clinical manual of addiction psychopharmacology*. Washington, DC: American Psychiatric Publishing, Inc.

Take time to smell the fentanyl. (1994). *Forensic Drug Abuse Advisor, 6*(5), 34–35.

Talty, S. (2003). The straight dope. *Playboy, 50*(11), 89–92.

Taming drug interactions. (2003). *Addiction Treatment Forum, 12*(4), 1, 6.

Tan, J. S. L., Mitchel, P., Kifley, A., Flood, V., Smith, W., & Wang, J. J. (2008). Smoking and long-term incidence of age-related macular degeneration: The Blue Mountains Eye Study. *Archives of Ophthalmology, 125*, 1089–1095.

Tan, W. C., Lo, C., Jong, A., Xing, L., Fitzgerald, M. J., Vollmer, W. M., … Vancouver Burden of Obstructive Lung Disease (BOLD) Research Group. (2009). Marijuana and chronic obstructive lung disease: A population based study. *Canadian Medical Association Journal, 180*(8), 814–820. doi:10.1503/cmaj.081040

Tanhehco, E. J., Yasojima, K., McGeer, P. L., & Wang, J. J. (2000). Acute cocaine exposure up-regulates complement expression in rabbit heart. *Journal of Pharmacology and Experimental Therapeutics, 292*, 201–208.

Tannu, N., Mash, D. C., & Hemby, S. E. (2007). Cytosolic proteomic alterations in the nucleus accumbens of cocaine overdose victims. *Molecular Psychiatry, 12*, 55–73. doi:10.1038/sj.mp.4001914

Tapert, S. F., Caldwell, L., & Burke, C. (2004/2005). Alcohol use and the adolescent brain: Human studies. *Alcohol Research & Health, 28*(4), 205–212.

Tappert, S. F., Cheung, E. H., Brown, G. S., Frank, L. R., Paulus, M. P., Schweinsburg, A. D., … Brown, S. A. (2003). Neural response to alcohol stimuli in adolescents with alcohol use disorder. *Archives of General Psychiatry, 60*, 727–735.

Tarter, R. E., Vanyukov, M., Kirisci, L., Reynolds, M., & Clark, D. B. (2006). Predictors of marijuana use in adolescents before and after illicit drug use: Examination of the gateway hypothesis. *American Journal of Psychiatry, 163*, 2134–2140.

Tashkin, D. B. (2005). Smoked marijuana as a cause of lung injury. *Archives for Chest Disease, 63*(2), 93–100.

Tatro, D. S. (2009). *Drug interaction facts.* St. Louis, MO: Wolters Kluwer.

Tattersall, I. (2012). *Masters of the planet.* New York: Macmillan.

Tavakoli, H. D. (2009). A closer examination of current methods in psychiatric assessment. *Psychiatry, 6*(2), 25–30.

Taverne, D. (2010). See sense on drugs. *New Scientist, 208*(2788), 26–27.

Taylor, M. L. (2004). Drug courts for teenagers can be effective. *La Crosse Tribune, 101*(61), 16.

Taylor, S., McCracken, C. F. M., Wilson, K. C. M., & Copeland, J. R. M. (1998). Extended and appropriateness of benzodiazepine use. *British Journal of Psychiatry, 173*, 433–438.

Tebit, D. M., & Arts, A. J. (2010). Tracking a century of global expansion and evolution of HIV to drive understand and to combat disease. *The Lancet Infectious Diseases.* doi:10.1016/S1473-3099(10)70186-9

Teicher, M. H. (2002). The neurobiology of child abuse. *Scientific American, 286*(3), 433–438.

Tekin, S., & Cummings, J. L. (2003). Hallucinations and related conditions. In K. M. Heilman & E. Valenstein (Eds.), *Clinical neuropsychology* (4th ed.). New York: Oxford University Press.

Terplan, M., Smith, E., Kozloski, M., & Pollack, H. A. (2009). Methamphetamine use among pregnant women. *Obstetrics & Gynecology, 113*(6), 1285–1291.

Terry, M. B., Gammon, M. D., Zhang, F. F., Tawfik, H., Teitelbaum, S. L., Britton, J. A., … Neugut, A. I. (2004). Association of frequency and duration of aspirin use and hormone receptor status with breast cancer risk. *Journal of the American Medical Association, 291*, 2433–2440.

Tetrault, J. M., Crothers, K., Moore, B. A., Mehra, R., Concato, J., & Fiellin, D. A. (2007). Effects of marijuana smoking on pulmonary function and respiratory complications: A systematic review. *Archives of Internal Medicine, 167*(3), 229–235.

Thatcher, D. L., & Clark, D. B. (2008). Adolescents at risk for substance use disorders. *Alcohol Research & Health, 31*(2), 168–176.

The drug index. (1995). *Playboy, 42*(9), 47.

Thevis, M., Thomas, A., Kihler, M., Beuck, S., & Schanzer, W. (2009). Emerging drugs: Mechanism of action, mass spectrometry and doping control analysis. *Journal of Mass Spectrometry, 44*(4), 442–460.

Thomas, J. D., Waren, K. R., & Hewitt, B. G. (2010). Fetal alcohol spectrum disorders. *Alcohol Research & Health, 33*, 118–126.

Thombs, D. L., O'Mara, R. J., Tsukamoto, M., Rossheim, M. E., Weiler, R. M., Merves, M. L., & Goldberger, B. A. (2010). Event-level analysis of energy drink consumption and alcohol intoxication in bar patrons. *Addictive Behaviors, 35*(4), 325–330.

Thompson, J. P. (2004). Acute effects of drugs of abuse. *Clinical Medicine, 3*(2), 123–126.

Thompson, P. D. R. (2011). *2011 Physician's desk reference* (65th ed.). Montvale, NJ: Author.

Thomson, H. (2009). iSmoke. *New Scientist, 201*(2695), 32–35.

Thomson, W. M., Poulton, R., Broadbent, J. M., Moffit, T. E., Caspi, A., Beck, J. D., … Hancox, R. J. (2008). Cannabis smoking and periodontal disease among young adults. *Journal of the American Medical Association, 299*(5), 525–531.

Thorne, S., McClave, A., Rock, V., Asman, K., & Malarcher, A. (2010). Any tobacco use in 13 states behavioral risk factor surveillance system, 2008. *Morbidity and Mortality Weekly Report, 59*(30), 946–950.

Tildesley, E. A., & Andrews, J. A. (2008). The development of children's intentions to use alcohol: Direct and indirect effects of parent alcohol use and parenting behaviors. *Psychology of Addictive Behaviors, 22*, 326–339.

Tillich, P. (1957). *The dynamics of faith.* New York: Harper & Row.

Time to legalise marijuana. (2010). New Scientist, 208 (2784), 3.

Timko, C., Moos, R. H., Finney, J. W., & Lesar, M. D. (2000). Long-term consequences of alcohol use disorders: Comparing untreated individuals with those in alcoholics anonymous and formal treatment. *Journal of Studies on Alcohol, 61*, 529–540.

Timkok, C., DeBenedette, A., & Billow, R. (2006). Intensive referral to 12-step self-help groups and 6 month substance use disorder outcomes. *Addiction, 101*, 678–688.

Tinsley, J. A. (2005). Drug abuse. In R. E. Rakel & E. T. Pope (Eds.), *Conn's Current Therapy, 2005.* Philadelphia: Elsevier Sanders.

Tinsley, J. A., Finlayson, R. E., & Morse, R. M. (1998). Developments in the treatment of alcoholism. *Mayo Clinic Proceedings, 73*, 857–863.

Tobacco. (2009). *A to Z health guide how to live longer and better.* New York: Time, Inc.

Tobacco company tactics: lie for years, then blame victims for being deceived. (2007). Retrieved from http:www.jointogether.org/news/headlines/inthe-news/2007/ tobacco-company-tactics-lie.html

Todd, J., Green, G., Harrison, M., Ikuesan, A., Self, C., Pevalin, D. J., & Baldacchino, A. (2004). Social exclusion in clients with comorbid mental health and substance misuse problems. *Social Psychiatry and Psychiatric Epidemiology, 39,* 581–587.

Tolliver, B. K. (2010). Bipolar disorder and substance abuse. *Current Psychiatry, 9*(8), 32–38.

Tomb, D. A. (2008). *House officer series: Psychiatry* (7th ed.). New York: Lipponcott, Williams & Wilkins.

Tominga, G. T., Carcia, G., Dzierba, A., & Wong, J. (2004). Toll of methamphetamine on the trauma system. *Archives of Surgery, 139,* 844–847.

Toneatto, T., Sobell, L. C., Sobell, M. B., & Rubel, E. (1999). Natural recovery from cocaine dependence. *Psychology of Addictive Behaviors, 13,* 259–268.

Tong, E. K., & Glantz, S. A. (2007). Tobacco industry efforts undermining evidence linking secondhand smoke with cardiovascular disease. *Circulation, 116*(16), 1845–1854.

Tonigan, J. S., & Rice, S. I. (2010). Is it beneficial to have an alcoholics anonymous sponsor? *Psychology of Addictive Behaviors, 24*(3), 397–403.

Toombs, J. D., & Kral, L. A. (2005). Methadone treatment for pain states. *American Family Physician, 71,* 1353–1358.

Torregrossa, M. M., & Kalivas, P. W. (2009). Addictive processes. In G. G. Berntston & J. T. Cacioppo (Eds.), *Handbook of neuroscience for the behavioral sciences.* New York: John Wiley & Sons, Inc.

Tracy, E. M., Munson, M. R., Peterson, L. T., & Floersch, J. E. (2010). Social support: A mixed blessing for women in substance abuse treatment. *Journal of Social Work Practice in the Addictions, 10*(3), 257–282.

Trafton, J. A., & Gifford, E. V. (2008). Behavioral reactivity and addiction: The adaptation of behavioral response to reward opportunities. *Journal of Neuropsychiatry and Clinical Neurosciences, 20*(1), 23–35.

Trandon, K. (2007). Yoga: An excellent therapeutic adjunct for outpatient therapy. *Counselor, 8*(5), 12–17.

Traub, S. J. (2009). Substance abuse and neurotoxicity. In S. I. Savitz & M. Ronthal (Eds.), *Neurology review for psychiatrists.* New York: Lippincott Williams & Wilkins.

Treatment Episode Data Set. (2010). *Sociodemographic characteristics of substance abuse treatment admissions aged 50 or older: 1992 to 2008.* Washington, DC: Substance Abuse and Mental Health Services Administration.

Trell, S., Richenbach, S., Wandel, S., Hildebrand, P., Tschannen, B., Villiger, P. M., Egger, M., & Jüni, P. (2011). Cardiovascular safety of non-steroidal anti-inflammatory drugs: Network meta-analysis. *British Medical Journal, 342.* doi:http://dx.doi.org/10.1136/bmj.c7086

Tresch, D. D., & Aronow, W. S. (1996). Smoking and coronary artery disease. *Clinics in Geriatrics Medicine, 12,* 23–32.

Treweek, J., Wee, S., Kopob, G. F., Dickerson, T. J., & Janda, K. D. (2007, June 25). Self-vaccination by methamphetamine glycation products chemically links chronic drug abuse and cardiovascular disease. *Proceeds of the National Academy of Sciences.* doi:10.1073/pnas.0701328104

Trivedi, H. (2010). The elephant in the room. *Child and Adolescent Psychiatric Clinics of North America, 19*(3), xiii–xiv.

Tripodi, S. J., Bender, K., Litschge, C., & Vaughn, M. G. (2010). Interventions for reducing adolescent alcohol abuse. *Archives of Pediatric and Adolescent Medicine, 164*(1), 85–91.

Trocki, K. F., Drabble, L. A., & Midanik, L. T. (2009). Tobacco, marijuana, and sensation seeking: Comparisons across gay, lesbian, bisexual and heterosexual groups. *Psychology of Addictive Behaviors, 23,* 620–631.

Troy, J. D. (2013). New "legal" highs: Kratom and methoxetamine. *Current Psychiatry, 12*(8), 54–55.

Trudeau, D. L., Sokhadze, T. M., & Cannon, R. L. (2009). Neurofeedback in alcohol and drug dependency. In T. H. Budzynski, H. K. Budzynski, J. R. Evans, & A. Ararbanel (Eds.), *Introduction to quantitative EEG and neurofeedback* (2nd ed., pp. 241–268). New York: Academic Press.

Tsai, V. W., Anderson, C. L., & Vaca, F. E. (2010). Alcohol involvement among young female drivers in US fatal crashes: Unfavorable trends. *Injury Prevention, 16,* 17–20.

Tse, W., & Koller, W. C. (2004). Neurologic complications of alcoholism. In W. J. Weiner &

infeldt, J. A., & Kratz, L. M.
se attitudes, and alcohol
adolescents. *Psychology
*), 547–553.
abuse, medications,
Nursing Clinics of North

have misused ADHD
Retrieved from
t.com.wp-dyn/content/
2401733?htmareferrer=

ine, S. D. (2002). Intra-
evidence and clinical
Physician, 66(4), 601–608.
ofman, A., Launer, L. J.,
T., ... Stricker, B. H.
flammatory drugs and
ase. *New England Journal*
21.
R. I., & Greenblatt, D. J.
hanisms of drug disposi-
. In D. A. Ciraulo, R. I.
& W. Creelman (Eds.),
iatry (3rd ed.). New York:
ilkins.
Turner, C. E. (1998).
. Frances & S. I. Miller
f addictive disorders
lford.
D. M., van der Lugt, A.,
P., Stricker, B. H., &
se of antithrombotic
f cerebral microbleeds.
*(*6), 714–720.
.42
n, C., Berger, S., Blum, N.,
Heart Association Council
ng. (2008). Cardiovascular
nd adolescents with heart
ions for attention deficit/
irculation, 120(7), e55–e59.
ONAHA.107.189473
n, B. D. (2006). Neural
peutic change. *Psychiatric*

v, A., & Hedt, J. (2004).
substance use. *Psychiatric*
, 27, 97–109.

ed Nations. (2012). *UNAIDS world AIDS day
port|2012*. New York: United Nations Publications.
ed States Department of Health and Human
rvices. (2004). *Clinical guidelines for the use of
rprenorphine in the treatment of opioid addiction:
treatment improvement protocol*. Washington,
C: US Government Printing Office.
d States Department of Health and Human
rvices. (2012). *Preventing tobacco use among
th and young adults: A report of the surgeon
eral*. Atlanta, GA: US Department of Health and
man Services.
, B. K., Davis, M. K., & De Leeuw, J. B. (2000).
hological gambling. *American Family Physician,*
741–749.
yaya, H. P., & Gray, K. M. (2009). Adolescent
stance use and the role of gender. In K. T. Brady,
Back, & S. F. Greenfield (Eds.), *Women &
ction*. New York: Guilford.
e of drug abuse grows older*. (2006). Retrieved
http:www.msnbc.msn.com/id/128396/01/html
ns of "global meth threat." (2006). *BBC News*.
eved from http://news.bbc.co.uk/2/hi/
i-cas/4757179.stm
., & O'Brien, L. (2007). Fractured families:
tal perspectives of the effects of adolescent
abuse on family life. *Contemporary Nurse,*
321–330.
lge strikes down FDA van on ephedra*. (2005).
ved from http://www.cnn.com/2005/LAW04/
ephedra.suit.ap/index.html
., Salto, M., Gyetfal, B. M., Oros, M., Szakall,
acs, K. M., ... Toth, R. (2007). Glutamate
or metabotropic 7 is cis-regulated in the
brain and modulates alcohol drinking.
ics, 90*(6), 670–702.
. (2003). Antisocial personality disorder and
c addiction. In T. Millon, E. Simonsen,
etSmity, & R. D. Davis (Eds.), *Psychopathy:
ial, criminal and violent behavior*. New York:
l.
. E. (1990). We should retain the disease
of alcoholism. *The Harvard Medical School
Health Letter, 9*(6), 4–6.
. E. (1995). *The natural history of alcoholism
*. Cambridge, MA: Harvard University Press.
. E. (1996). A long-term follow-up of male
buse. *Archives of General Psychiatry, 53,*

Vaillant, G. E. (2000, March 4). *Alcoholics anonymous: Cult or magic bullet?* Symposium presented to the Department of psychiatry at the Cambridge hospital, Boston, MA.

Vaillant, G. E. (2005). Alcoholics anonymous: Cult or cure? *Australian and New Zealand Journal of Psychiatry, 39,* 431–436.

Vaillant, G. E., & Hiller-Sturmhofel, S. (1996). The natural history of alcoholism. *Alcohol Health & Research World, 20,* 152–161.

Valente, T. W., Gallaher, P., & Mouttapa, M. (2004). Using social networks to understand and prevent substance use: A transdisciplinary perspective. *Substance Use & Misuse, 39*(10–12), 1685–1712.

Vanable, P. A., King, A. C., & deWit, H. (2000). Psychometric screening instruments. In G. Zernig, A. Saria, M. Kurz, & S. S. O'Malley (Eds.), *Handbook of Alcoholism.* New York: CRC Press.

van den Bree, M., & Pickworth, W. B. (2005). Rick factors predicting changes in marijuana involvement in teenagers. *Archives of General Psychiatry, 62,* 311–319.

Vanderah, T. W. (2006). Pathohysiology of pain. *Medical Clinics of North America, 91,* 1–12.

Vandry, R. G., Budney, A. J., & Ligouori, A. (2008). A within-subject comparison of withdrawal symptoms during abstinence from cannabis, tobacco and both substances. *Drug and Alcohol Dependence, 92,* 48–54.

Van Dyke, R., & Chakraboety, R. (2013). Transitioning HIV-infected youth into adult health care. *Pediatrics.* doi:10.1542/peds.2013-1073

van Hook, S., Harris, S. K., Brooks, T., Careym, P., Kossack, R., Kulig, J., … New England Partnership for Substance Abuse Research. (2007). The "Six T's": Barriers to screening teens for substance abuse in primary care. *Journal of Adolescent Health, 40*(5), 456–461.

van Noorden, M. S., van Dongen, L. C., Zitman, F. G., & Vergouwen, T. A. (2009). Gamma-hydroxybutyrate withdrawal syndrome: Dangerous but not well known. *General Hospital Psychiatry, 4,* 394–396.

Varlinskaya, E. I., & Spear, L. P. (2006). Ontogeny of acute tolerance to ethanol induced social inhibition in Sprague-Dawley rats. *Alcoholism: Clinical and Experimental Research, 30,* 1833–1844.

Vaughan, E. L., Corbin, W. R., & Fromme, K. (2009). Academic and social motives and drinking behavior. *Psychology of Addictive Behaviors, 23,* 564–576.

Vaughan, E. L., de Dios, M. A., St̄ (2011). Religiosity, alcohol use in a national sample of *of Addictive Behaviors, 25(*

Vaughn, A. (2006). Substance HIV and the community. *America, 41,* 355–369.

Vedantam, S. (2006). *Millions stimulant drugs, study says* http: //www.washingtonpo article/2006/02/24ar200602 emailarticle

Vega, C., Kwoon, J. V., & Oa cranial aneurysms: Curren practice. *American Family*

Veld, B. A., Ruitenberg, A., F van Duijn, C. M., Stijnen, (2001). Nonsteroidal antiii the risk of Alzheimer's dise *of Medicine, 345,* 1515–15

Venkatakrishnan, K., Shader, (2006). Concepts and me tion and drug interactions Shader, D. J. Greenblatt, *Drug interactions in psych* Lippincott, Williams & W

Vereby, K., Buchan, B. J., & Laboratory testing. In R. (Eds.), *Clinical textbook* (2nd ed.). New York: Gu

Vernooij, M. W., Haag, M. Hofman, A., Krestin, G. Breteler, M. M. (2009). U drugs and the presence o *Archives of Neurology, 66* doi:1001/archneurol.2002

Vetter, V. L., Elia, J., Ericks Uzark, K., … American on Cardiovascular Nursi monitoring of children a disease receiving medica hyperactivity disorder. C doi:10.1161/CIRCULAT

Viamontes, G. I., & Beitma substrates of psychother *Annals, 36,* 238–246.

Vik, P., Cellucci, T., Jarcho Cognitive impairment ir *Clinics of North Americ*

Vilcheze, C., Hartman, T., Weinrick, B., & Jacobs, W. R. (2013). Macpbacteroi tuberculosis is extraordinarily sensitive to killing by a vitamin C-induced Fenton reaction. *Nature Communications, 4, 1881.* doi:10.1038/nomms 2898

Villalon, C. (2004). Cocaine country. *National Geographic, 206*(1), 34–55.

Villarreal, A. A. (2011). Role of cannabinoids in the management of chronic pain: A review of the clinical literature. *The Gundersen-Lutheran Medical Journal, 7*(1), 30–32.

Virani, A. D., Bezchlibnyk-Butler, K. Z., Jeffries, J. J., & Procyshyn, R. M. (2012). *Clinical Handbook of Psychotropic Drugs* (19th ed.). New York: Hogrefe publishing.

Visser, S. N., Bitsko, R. H., Danielson, M. L., Perou, R., & Blumburg, S. J. (2010). Increasing prevalence of parent-related attention deficit/hyperactivity disorder among children United States, 2003 and 2007. *Morbidity and Mortality Weekly Report, 59,* 1439–1443.

Vitacco, M. J. (2008). Syndromes associated with deception. In R. Rogers (Ed.), *Clinical assessment of malingering and deception* (3rd ed.). New York: Guilford.

Signs. (2007). *Clinical Psychiatry News, 35*(7), 1.

Vital signs: Drinking and driving among high school students aged 16 years United States, 1991-2011. (2012). *Morbidity and Mortality Weekly Report, 61* (early release), 1–6.

Vlad, S. C., Miller, D. R., Kowall, N. W., & Felson, D. T. (2008). Protect effects of NSAIDs on the development of Alzheimer's disease. *Neurology, 70,* 1672–1677.

Vocci, F., & Elkashef, A. (2009). Pharmacological treatment of methamphetamine addiction. In J. R. Roll, R. A. Rawson, W. Ling, & S. Shoptaw (Eds.), *Amphetamine addiction from basic science to treatment.* New York: Guilford.

Volkow, N. D. (2006a, August 12). *Addiction: The neurobiology of free will gone awry.* Symposium presented at the annual meeting of the American Psychological Association, New Orleans, LA.

Volkow, N. D. (2006b). Steroid abuse is a high-risk route to the finish line. *NIDA Notes, 21*(1), 2.

Volkow, N. D., Fowler, J. S., Logan, J., Alexoff, D., Zhu, W., Telang, F., … Apelskog-Torres, K. (2009). Effects of modafinil on dopamine and dopamine transporters in the male human brain. *Journal of the American Medical Association, 301*(11), 1148–1154.

Volkow, N. D., & Li, T. K. (2009). Drug addiction: The neurobiology of behavior gone awry. In R. K. Ries, D. A. Fiellin, S. C. Miller, & R. Saitz (Eds.), *Principles of addiction medicine* (4th ed., pp. 453–463). New York: Lippincott, Williams & Wilkins.

Volkow, N. D., & Swanson, J. M. (2003). Variables that affect the clinical use and abuse of methylphenidate in the treatment of ADHD. *American Journal of Psychiatry, 160*(11), 1909–1918.

Volkow, N. D., Wang, G. J., Fowler, J. S., Logan, J., Gatley, S. J., Gifford, A., … Pappas, N. (1998). Prediction of reinforcing responses to psychostimulants in humans by brain dopamine D2 receptor levels. *American Journal of Psychiatry, 156,* 1440–1443.

Vollmer, G. (2006). Crossing the barrier. *Scientific American Mind, 17*(3), 34–39.

Volpicelli, J. R. (2005). New options for the treatment of alcohol dependence. *Psychiatric Annals, 35*(6), 484–491.

Vonlaufen, A., Wilson, J. S., Pirola, R. C., & Apte, M. V. (2007). Role of alcohol metabolism in chronic pancreatitis. *Alcohol Research & Health, 30,* 48–54.

Vornik, L. A., & Brown, E. S. (2006). Management of comorbid bipolar disorder and substance abuse. *Journal of Clinical Psychiatry, 67*(Suppl. 7), 24–30.

Vozoris, N. T. (2012). Mentholated cigarettes and cardiovascular and pulmonary diseases: A population based study. *Archives of Internal Medicine, 172*(7), 590–591.

Vourakis, C. (1998). Substance abuse concerns in the treatment of pain. *Nursing Clinics of North America, 27,* 675–687.

Vuchinich, R. E. (2002). The president's column. *Addictions Newsletter, 10*(1), 1, 5.

Vul, E., Harris, C., Winkielman, P., & Pashler, H. (2009). *Puzzlingly high correlations in fMRI studies of emotion, personality and social cognition.* Retrieved from http://www.pashlet.com/Articles/Vul-etal-2008inpress.pdf

Wade, N. (2009). *The faith instinct.* New York: Penguin Press.

Wadland, W. C., & Ferenchick, G. S. (2004). Medical comorbidity in addictive disorders. *Psychiatric Clinics of North America, 27,* 675–687.

Wagner, E. F. (2009). Improving treatment through research: Directing attention to the role of development in adolescent treatment success. *Alcohol Research & Health, 32*(1), 67–75.

Wakefulness drug: New safety concerns. (2009). *A to Z health guide how to live longer and better*. New York: Time, Inc.

Walker, B. D. (2012). Secrets of the HIV controllers. *Scientific American, 307*(1), 44–51.

Walker, D. D., Venner, K., Hill, D. E., Myers, R. J., & Miller, W. R. (2004). A comparison of alcohol and drug disorders: Is there evidence for a developmental sequence of drug abuse? *Addictive Behaviors, 29*(4), 817–823.

Wallace, J. (2003). Theory of 12-Step oriented treatment. In F. Rotgers, J. Mordenstern, & S. T. Walters (Eds.), *Treating substance abuse: Theory and technique* (2nd ed.). New York: Guilford.

Walley, A. Y., Farrar, D., Cheng, D. M., Alford, D. P., & Samet, J. H. (2009). Are opioiddependence and methadone maintenance treatment (MMT) documented in the medical record? A patient safety issue. *Journal of General Internal Medicine, 24*(9), 1007–1011.

Walley, A. Y., Paasche-Orlow, M., Lee, E. C., Forsythe, S., Chetty, V. K., Mitchell, S., & Jack, B. W. (2012). Acute care hospital utilization among medical inpatients discharged with a substance use disorder diagnosis. *Journal of Addiction Medicine, 6*(1), 50–56.

Walsh, J. K., Pollak, C. P., Scharf, M. B., Schweitzer, P. K., & Vogel, G. W. (2000). Lack of residual sedation following middle of the night zaleplon administration in sleep maintenance insomnia. *Clinical Neuropharmacology, 23*(1), 17–21.

Walsh, K., & Alexander, G. (2000). Alcoholic liver disease. *Postgraduate Medicine, 76,* 280–286.

Walter, C. (2013). *Last ape standing*. New York: Walker & Co.

Walters, P. (2013). Risk takers. *National Geographic, 223*(1), 57–67.

Walters, S. T., Rotgers, F., Saunders, B., Wilkinson, C., & Towers, T. (2003). Theoretical perspectives on motivation and addictive behaviors. In F. Rotgers, J. Morgenstern, & S. T. Walters (Eds.), *Treating substance abuse: Theory and technique* (2nd ed.). New York: Guilford.

Walton, S. (2002). *Out of it: A cultural history of intoxication*. New York: Harmony Books.

Wannamethee, S. G., Camargo, C. A., Manson, J. A. E., Wllett, W. C., & Rimm, E. B. (2003). Alcohol drinking patterns and risk of type 2 diabetes mellitus among younger women. *Archives of Internal Medicine, 163,* 1329–1336.

Warner-Schmidt, J. L., Vanoverb, K. E., Chena, E. Y., Marshalia, J. J., & Greengardia, P. (2011). Antidepressant effects of selective serotonin reuptake inhibitors (SSRIs) are attenuated by antiinflammatory drugs in mice and humans. *Proceedings of the National Academy of Sciences, 108*(22), 9262–9267.

Washton, A. M., & Zweben, J. E. (2006). *Treating alcohol and drug problems in psychotherapy practice*. New York: Guilford.

Watkins, K. E., Burnam, A., Kung, F. Y., & Paddock, S. (2001). A national survey of care for persons with co-occurring mental and substance use disorders. *Psychiatric Services, 52,* 1062–1068.

Watson, S. J., Benson, J. A., & Joy, J. E. (2000). Marijuana and medicine: Assessing the science base. *Archives of General Psychiatry, 57,* 547–552.

Wattendorf, D. J., & Muenke, M. (2005). Fetal alcohol spectrum disorders. *American Family Physician, 72,* 279–282, 285.

Watters, E. (2006). DNA is not destiny. *Discover, 27*(11), 23–37, 75.

Wayne, G. F., & Connolly, G. (2009). Regulatory assessment of brand changes in the commercial tobacco market. *Tobacco Control, 18,* 302–309. doi:1136/fc2009.030502

Weafer, J., Fillmore, M. T., & Milich, R. (2009). Increased sensitivity to the disinhibiting effects of alcohol in adults with ADHD. *Experimental and Clinical Psychopharmacology, 17*(2), 113–121.

Weathermon, R., & Crabb, D. W. (1999). Alcohol and medication interactions. *Alcohol Research & Health, 23*(1), 40–54.

Weaver, M. F., Jarvis, M. A., & Schnoll, S. H. (1999). Role of the primary care physician in problems of substance abuse. *Archives of Internal Medicine, 159,* 913–924.

Weaver, M. F., & Schnoll, S. H. (2008). Hallucinogens and club drugs. In M. Galanter & H. D. Kleber (Eds.), *The American psychiatric publishing textbook of substance abuse treatment*. Washington, DC: American Psychiatric Publishing, Inc.

Webster, L. R., Cochella, S., Dasgupta, N., Fakata, K. R., Fine, P. G., Fishman, S. M., … Wakeland, W. (2011). An analysis of the root causes for opioid-related overdose deaths in the United States. *Pain Medicine, 12,* S26–S35.

Wedam, E. R., Bigelow, G. E., Johnson, R. E., Nuzzo, P. A., & Haigney, M. C. (2008). QT-interval effects of methadone, levomethadyl and buprenorphine in a randomized trial. *Archives of Internal Medicine, 167,* 2469–2475.

Wegscheider-Cruse, S. (1985). *Choice-making.* Pompano Beach, FL: Health Communications.

Wegscheider-Cruse, S., & Cruse, J. R. (1990). *Understanding co-dependency.* Pompano Beach, FL: Health Communications.

Weiden, P. J. (2011). The adherence interview: Better information, better alliance. *Psychiatric Annals, 41*(5), 279–285.

Weight loss and the release of THC from fat. (2009). *Forensic Drug Abuse Advisor, 21*(8), 58–59.

Weiner, D. A., Abraham, M. E., & Lyons, J. (2001). Clinical characteristics of youths with substance use problems and implications for residential treatment. *Psychiatric Services, 52,* 793–799.

Weiner, R. B., Kanayama, G., Hudson, J. I., Hutter, A. M., Picard, M. H., Pope, H. G., Jr., & Baggish, A. L. (2009). Abstract 3048: Chronic anabolic androgenic steroid use is associated with left ventricular systolic and diastolic dysfunction. *Circulation, 120(Suppl. S741).*

Weiss, C. J., & Millman, R. B. (1998). Hallucinogens, phencyclidine, marijuana and inhalants. In R. J. Frances & S. I. Miller (Eds.), *Clinical textbook of addictive disorders* (2nd ed.). New York: Guilford.

Weiss, F. (2005). Neurobiology of craving, conditioned reward and relapse. *Current Opinion in Pharmacology, 5,* 9–19.

Weiss, M. (2007). Drugs of abuse. In K. Z. Bezchlibnyk-Butler, J. J. Jeffries, & A. S. Virani (Eds.), *Clinical handbook of psychotropic drugs* (17th ed.). Ashland, OH: Hogrefe & Huber, Publishers.

Weiss, R. D. (2010, May 1). *Integrated treatment of patients with co-occurring substance abuse and bipolar disorder.* Paper presented at the "Addictions in 2010" seminar, hosted by the Division of alcohol and Drug Abuse of the McLean Hospital, Boston, MA.

Weiss, R. D., Griffin, M. L., Mazurick, C., Berkan, B., Gastfriend, D. R., Frank, A., … Moras, K. (2003). The relationship between cocaine craving, psychosocial treatment, and subsequent cocaine use. *American Journal of Psychiatry, 160,* 1320–1325.

Weiss, R. D., Jaffee, W. B., de Menil, V. P., & Cogley, C. B. (2004). Group therapy for substance use disorders: What do we know? *Harvard Review of Psychiatry, 12,* 339–350.

Weiss, R. D., Potter, J. S., & Iannucci, R. A. (2008). Inpatient treatment. In M. Galanter & H. D. Kleber (Eds.), *Textbook of substance abuse treatment.* Washington, DC: American Psychiatric Association, Inc.

Weitzman, M., Govil, N., Liu, Y. H., & Lalwani, A. K. (2013). Maternal prenatal smoking and hearing loss among adolescents. *JAMA Otolaryngology Head & Neck Surgery, 139,* 669–677. doi:10.1001/jamaoto.2013.3924

Welch, I. (2013). Dancing off the edge. *Playboy, 60*(3), 106–108, 132–133.

Welch, S. P. (2005). The neurobiology of marijuana. In J. H. Lowinson, P. Ruiz, R. B. Millman, & J. G. Langrod (Eds.), *Substance abuse: A comprehensive textbook* (4th ed.). New York: Lipponcott, Williams & Wilkins.

Welch, S. P. (2009). The pharmacology of cannabis. In R. K. Ries, D. A. Fiellin, S. C. Miller, & R. Saitz, (Eds.), *Principles of addiction medicine* (4th ed., pp. 193–214). New York: Lippincott, Williams & Wilkins.

Wells, J. E., Horwood, L. J., & Fergusson, D. M. (2006). Stability and instability in alcohol diagnosis from ages 18 to 21 and ages 21 to 25 years. *Alcohol & Drug Dependence, 81*(2), 157–165.

Wells, K. E., Paddock, S. M., Zhang, L., & Wells, K. B. (2006). Improving care for depression in patients with comorbid substance misuse. *American Journal of Psychiatry, 163,* 125–132.

Wells, S. K., Graham, K., & Purcell, J. (2009). Policy implications of the widespread practice of "pre-drinking" or "pre-gaming" before going to public drinking establishments are current prevention strategies backfiring? *Addiction, 104*(1), 4–9.

Welsby, P. D. (1997). An HIV view of the human condition. *Postgraduate Medicine, 73,* 609–610.

Wertz, M. S., Kyriss, T., Paranjape, S., & Glantz, S. A. (2011). The toxic effects of cigarette additives Phillip Morris' project MIX reconsidered: An analysis of documents released through litigation. *Plos Medicine, 8*(12). doi:10. 1371/journal.pmed.1001145

Wesson, D. R., & Smith, D. E. (2005). Sedative-hypnotics. In J. H. Lowinson, P. Ruiz, R. B. Millman, & J. G. Langrod (Eds.), *Substance abuse: A comprehensive textbook* (4th ed.). New York: Lipponcott, Williams & Wilkins.

Westermeyer, J. (1995). Cultural aspects of substance abuse and alcoholism. *The Psychiatric Clinics of North America, 18,* 589–620.

Westermeyer, J., Eames, S. L., & Nugent, S. (1998). Comorbid dysthymia and substance disorder: Treatment history and cost. *American Journal of Psychiatry, 155,* 1556–1560.

Westfall, T. C., & Westfall, D. P. (2006). Adrenergic agonists and antagonists. (2006). In L. L. Brunton, J. S. Lazo, & K. L. Parker (Eds.), *The pharmacological basis of therapeutics* (11th ed.). New York: McGraw-Hill.

Westover, A. N., McBride, S., & Haley, R. W. (2007). Stroke in young adults who abuse cocaine. *Archives of General Psychiatry, 64,* 495–502.

Westover, A. N., & Nakonezny, P. A. (2010). Aortic dissection in young adults who abuse amphetamines. *American Heart Journal, 160,* 315–321.

Westover, A. N., Nakonezny, P. A., & Haley, R. W. (2008). Acute myocardial infarction in young adults who abuse amphetamines. *Drug and Alcohol Dependence, 96,* 49–56.

Westphal, J., Wasserman, D. A., Masson, C. L., & Sorenson, J. L. (2005). Assessment of opioid use. In D. M. Donovan & G. A. Marlatt (Eds.), *Assessment of Addictive Behaviors* (2nd ed.). New York: Guilford.

Wetherill, R., & Tapert, S. F. (2013). Adolescent brain development, substance use, and psychotherapeutic change. *Psychology of Addictive Behaviors, 27*(2), 393–402.

What is moderation management? (2008). Retrieved from http://www.moderation.org/what ismm.shtml

Wheeler, K., & Malmquist, J. (1987). Treatment approaches in adolescent chemical dependency. *The Pediatric Clinics of North America, 158,* 86–95.

Whitaker, R. (2010). *Anatomy of an epidemic.* New York: Crown Publishers.

White, H. R., & Jackson, K. (2004/2005). Social and psychological influences on emerging adult drinking behavior. *Alcohol Research & Health, 28,* 182–190.

White, J. (2011). One minute with Mark Koska. *New Scientist, 212*(2838), 31.

White, M. P. (2009). Medication dosing in anxiety disorders: What the evidence shows. *Primary Psychiatry, 16*(10), 21–28.

White, N. E., & Richards, L. M. (2009). Alpha-theta neurotherapy and the neurobehavioral treatment of addictions, mood disorders, and trauma. In T. H. Budzynski, H. K. Budzynski, J. R. Evans, & A. Ararbanel (Eds.), *Introduction to Quantitative EEG and neurofeedback* (2nd ed., pp. 143–164). New York: Academic Press.

White, P. T. (1989). Coca. *National Geographic, 175*(1), 3–47.

White, W., & Nicolaus, M. (2005). Styles of secular recovery. *Counselor, the Magazine for Addiction Professionals, 6*(4), 58–61.

White, W. L. (2005). Fire in the family: Historical perspectives on the intergenerational effects of addiction. *Counselor, 6*(1), 20–23, 25.

Whitten, L. (2006). Study finds withdrawal no easier with ultrarapid opiate detox. *NIDA Notes, 21*(1), 4.

Whitten, L. (2008a). Basic sciences discoveries yield novel approaches to analgesia. *NIDA Notes, 22*(4), 1, 12–15.

Whitten, L. (2008b). Teen experiment confirms a suspected cocaine action. *NIDA Notes, 24*(1), 8–10.

Whitten, L. (2009). Studies link family of genes to nicotine addiction. *NIDA Notes, 22*(6), 1, 10–13.

Whitten, L. (2012a). Cognitive strategy reduces craving by altering brain activity. *NIDA Notes, 24*(2), 1, 6.

Whitten, L. (2012b). Physical activity reduces return to cocaine seeking in animal tests. *NIDA Notes, 24*(2), 9–11.

Wilson, B. A., Shannon, M. T., & Shields, K. M. (2011). *Pearson nurse's drug guide 2011.* New York: Pearson Education, Inc.

Winters, K. C., Botzet, A., Fahnhorst, T., Arria, A., Dykstra, L. G., & Oliver, O. (2012). Social factors and the addiction syndrome. In H. J. Shaffer, D. A. LaPlante, & S. E. Nelson (Eds.), *A.P.A. addiction syndromes handbook* (Vol. 1, pp. 229–250). Washington, DC: American Psychological Association.

Why confirmatory testing is always a necessity. (1997). *Forensic Drug Abuse Advisor, 9*(4), 25.

Why do the mentally ill die younger? (2008). Time Health & Science. Retrieved from http://www.time.com/time/article/0,8599,1863220,00.html

Wilcock, D. (2011). *The source field investigations.* New York: Dutton.

Wild, T. C., Cunningham, J., & Hobdon, K. (1998). When do people believe that alcohol treatment is effective? The importance of perceived client and therapist motivation. *Psychology of Addictive Behaviors, 12,* 93–100.

Wilens, T. E. (2006). Attention deficit hyperactivity disorder and substance use disorders. *American Journal of Psychiatry, 163,* 2059–2063.

Wilkins, T., Malcolm, J. K., Raina, D., & Schade, R. R. (2010). Hepatitis C: Diagnosis and treatment. *American Family Physician, 81*(11), 1351–1357.

Wilkinson, R. J., Liewelyn, M., Tossi, A., Patel, P., Pasvol, G., Lalvani, A., … Davidson, R. N. (2000). Influence of vitamin D deficiency and vitamin D receptor polymorphisms on tuberculosis among Gujarati Asians in West London: A case controlled study. *The Lancet, 355,* 618–621.

Willenbring, M. L. (2004). Treating co-occurring substance use disorders and hepatitis C. *Psychiatric Times, XXI*(2), 53–54.

Willenbring, M. L. (2010). The past and future of research on treatment of alcohol dependence. *Alcohol Research & Health, 33*(1), 55–63.

Willi, C., Bodenmann, P., Ghali, W. A., Faris, P. D., & Cornuz, J. (2007). Active smoking and the risk of type 2 diabetes. *Journal of the American Medical Association, 298,* 2654–2664.

Williams, B. R., & Baer, C. L. (1994). *Essentials of clinical pharmacology in nursing* (2nd ed.). Springhouse, PA: Springhouse Corp.

Williams, D. A. (2004). Evaluating acute pain. In R. H. Dworkin & W. S. Breitbart (Eds.), *Psychosocial aspects of pain: A handbook for health care providers.* Seattle, WA: IASP Press.

Williams, D. M., Whitely, J. A., Dunsiger, S., Jennings, E. G., Albrecht, A. E., Ussher, M. H., … Marcus, B. H. (2010). Moderate intensity exercise as an adjunct to standard smoking cessation treatment for women: A pilot study. *Psychology of Addictive Behaviors, 24*(2), 349–354.

Williams, H., Dratcu, L., Taylor, R., Roberts, M., & Oyefeso, A. (1998). "Saturday Night Fever": Ecstasy related problems in a London accident and emergency department. *Journal of Accident and Emergency Medicine, 15,* 322–326.

Williams, I. T., Bell, B. P., Kuhnert, W., & Alter, M. J. (2011). Incidence and transmission patterns of acute hepatitis C in the United States: 1982-2006. *Archives of Internal Medicine, 171*(3), 242–248.

Williams, T. (2000). High on hemp: Ditchweed digs in. *Utne Reader, 98,* 72–77.

Wills, T. A., Sandy, J. M., Yaeger, A. M., Cleary, S. D., & Shinar, Q. (2001). Coping dimensions, life stress and adolescent substance use: A latent growth analysis. *Journal of Abnormal Psychology, 110,* 309–323.

Wilson, B. A., Shannon, M. T., Shields, K. M., & Stang, C. L. (2007). *Prentice-Hall's Nurse's drug guide, 2007.* Upper Saddle River, NJ: Prentice Hall.

Wilson, C. (2005). Miracle weed. *New Scientist, 185* (2863), 40–43.

Wilson, C. (2008). Safer sex in a pill. *New Scientist, 200* (2683), 40–43.

Windle, M., Spear, L. P., Fuligni, A. J., Angold, A., Brown, J. D., Pine, D., … Dahl, R. E. (2009). Transitions into underaged and problem drinking. *Alcohol Research & Health, 32*(1), 3040.

Windle, M., & Zucker, R. A. (2010). Reducing underage and young adult drinking: How to address critical drinking problems during this developmental period. *Alcohol Research & Health, 33*(1 & 2), 29–44.

Winegarden, T. (2001, September 7). *Antipsychotic use in special populations.* Teleconference sponsored by Astra-Zeneca Pharmaceuticals, La Crosse, Wisconsin.

Winerman, L. (2013). Breaking free from addiction. *Monitor on Psychology, 44*(6), 30–34.

Winkelman, J. W. (2006). *Diagnosis and treatment of insomnia. Monthly Prescribing Reference.* New York: Prescribing Reference, Inc.

Winning the war on drugs? (2007). *Forensic Drug Abuse Advisor, 19*(7), 56.

Winslow, B. T., Voorhes, K. I., & Pehl, K. L. (2007). Methamphetamine abuse. *American Family Physician, 76*(8), 1169–1174.

Winters, K. C., Botzet, A., Fahnhopst, T., Arria, A., Dykstra, L. G., & Oliver, O. (2012). Social factors and the addiction syndrome. In H. J. Shaffer, D. A. LaPlante, & S. E. Nelson (Eds.), *A.P.A. addiction syndromes handbook* (Vol. 1, pp. 229–250). Washington, DC: American Psychological Association.

Winters, K. C., & Kaminer, Y. (2008). Screening and assessing adolescent substance use disorders in clinical populations. *Journal of the American Academy of Child and Adolescent Psychiatry, 47*(7), 740–744.

Wiseman, B. (1997). Confronting the breakdown of law and order. *USA Today, 125*(2620), 32–34.

Witkiewitz, K., Lustyk, M. K. B., & Bowen, S. (2013). Retraining the addicted brain: A review of hypothesized neurobiological mechanisms of mindfulness-based relapse prevention. *Psychology of Addictive Behaviors, 27*(2), 351–365.

Witkiewitz, K., & Marlatt, G. A. (2004). Relapse prevention for alcohol and drug problems. That was Zen, this is Tao. *American Psychologist, 59*(4), 224–235.

Witkiewitz, K., & Masyn, K. E. (2008). Drinking trajectories following an initial lapse. *Psychology of Addictive Behaviors, 22*(2), 157–167.

Woititz, J. G. (1983). *Adult children of alcoholics.* Pompano Beach, FL: Health Communications.

Wolf, M. E. (2006). Addiction. In G. J. Siegel, R. W. Albers, S. T. Brady, & D. L. Price (Eds.), *Basic neurochemistry* (7th ed.). New York: Elsevier Academic Press.

Wolfe, H. C. (2009, March 7). *Here's why you need to be aware of inhalant abuse: The hidden addiction.* Paper presented at the "Treating the Addictions" seminar hosted by the Harvard Medical School Department of Continuing Education, Boston, MA.

Wolin, S. J., & Wolin, S. (1993). *The Resilient Self.* New York: Villard Books.

Wolin, S. J., & Wolin, S. (1995). Resilience among youth growing up in substance abusing families. *Pediatric Clinics of North America, 42,* 415–429.

Woloshin, S., Schwartz, L. M., & Welch, H. G. (2008). The risk of death by age, sex, and smoking status in the United States: Putting health risks in context. *Journal of the National Cancer Institute, 100*(12), 845–853.

Wood, R. I. (2004). Reinforcing aspects of androgens. *Psychology & Behavior, 83*(2), 279–289.

Woods, A. R., & Herrera, J. L. (2002). Hepatitis C: Latest treatment guidelines. *Consultant, 42,* 1233–1243.

Woods, J. H., & Winger, G. (1997). Abuse liability of flunitrazepam. *Journal of Psychopharmacology, 17*(Suppl. 3), 1s–57s.

Woods, J. R. (1998). Maternal and transplacental effects of cocaine. *Annals of the New York Academy of Sciences, 846,* 1–11.

Woods, J. T. (2005). *How the Catholic Church built Western civilization.* Washington, DC: Regnery Publishing, Inc.

Woods, P. J., & Bartley, M. K. (2008). Improve pain management in patients with substance abuse. *Nursing 2008 Critical Care, 3*(1), 19–27.

Woodward, J. J. (2009). The pharmacology of alcohol. In R. K. Ries, A. Fiellin, S. C. Miller, & R. Saitz (Eds.), *Principles of addiction medicine* (4th ed.). New York: Lippincott, Williams & Wilkins.

Woody, G. E., Poole, S. A., Subramaniam, G., Dugosh, K., Bogenschutz, M., Abbott, P., … Fudala, P. (2008). Extended vs short-term buprenorphine-nalaxone for treatment of opiate-addicted youth: A randomized trial. *Journal of the American Medical Association, 300*(17), 2003–2011.

Worchester, S. (2006). Survey: Teens use inhalants more, worry about risks less. *Clinical Psychiatry News, 34*(6), 28.

Work Group on HIV/AIDS. (2000). Practice guidelines for the treatment of patients with HIV/AIDS. *American Journal of Psychiatry, 157*(Suppl. 11), 1–62.

Work Group on Substance Use Disorders. (2007). Treatment of patients with substance use disorders. *American Journal of Psychiatry, 164*(Suppl. 4), 5–123.

World Health Organization. (2006). *Tobacco-free initiative.* Retrieved from www.who.int/tobacco/research/cancer/en/

World Health Organization. (2008). *Anti-tuberculosis drug resistance in the world* (Report # 3). New York: Author.

Wright, R. (2009). *The evolution of god.* New York: Little-Brown& Co.

Wu, L. T., & Blazer, D. G. (2011). Illicit and nonmedical drug use among older adults: A review. *Journal of Aging and Health, 23*(3), 481–504.

Wu, L. T., & Ringwalt, C. L. (2005). Alcohol dependence and use of treatment services among women in the community. *American Journal of Psychiatry, 161,* 1790–1797.

Wu, L. T., & Ringwalt, C. L. (2006). Use of alcohol treatment and mental health services among adolescents with alcohol use disorders. *Psychiatric Services, 57,* 84–92.

Wuethrich, B. (2001). Getting stupid. *Discover, 22*(3), 56–63.

Wunsch, J. (2007, April 26). *Trends in adolescent drug use.* Paper presented at the Ruth Fox Course for Physicians, 38th Medical-Scientific Conference of the American Society of Addiction Medicine, Miami, Florida.

Wunsch, M. J., Boyd, C., & McMasters, M. G. (2009). Nonmedical use of prescription medications. In R. K. Ries, D. A. Fiellin, S. C. Miller, & R. Saitz (Eds.), *Principles of addiction medicine* (4th ed., pp. 453–463). New York: Lippincott, Williams & Wilkins.

Wyman, P. A., Moynihan, H., Eberly, S., Cox, C., Cross, W., Jin, X., & Caserta, M. T. (2007). Association of family stress with natural killer cell activity and frequency of illness in children. *Archives of Pediatrics & Adolescent Medicine, 161,* 228–234.

Wynn, G. H., Oesterheld, J. R., Cozza, K. L., & Armstrong, S. C. (2009). *Clinical manual of drug interaction principles for medical practice.* Washington, DC: American Psychiatric Publishing, Inc.

Xiong, G. L., & Kenedi, C. A. (2010). Aspirin to prevent cardiovascular events: Weighing risks and benefits. *Current Psychiatry, 9*(2), 55–56, 62–63.

Yeh, H. C., Duncan, B. B., Schmidt, M. I., Wang, N., & Brancati, F. L. (2010). Smoking, smoking cessation, and risk for type 2 diabetes mellitus: A cohort study. *Archives of Internal Medicine, 152*(1), 10–17.

Yeo, K., Wijetunga, M., Ito, H., Efird, J. T., Tay, K., Seto, T. B., … Schatz, I. J. (2007). The association of methamphetamine use and cardiomyopathy in young patients. *The American Journal of Medicine, 120,* 165–171.

Yi Wong, C. C., Mill, J., & Fernandes, C. (2010). Drugs and addiction: An introduction to epigenetics. *Addiction.* doi:10.1111/j.2360-0443. 2010.03321.x

Young adult drinking. (2006). *Alcohol Alert, 68,* 1–2.

Young, E. (2008). Strange inheritance. *New Scientist, 199*(2664), 28–33.

Young, E. (2012). Alimentary thinking. *New Scientist, 216*(2895), 38–42.

Young, S. Y. N., Hansen, C. J., Bigson, R. L., & Ryan, M. A. K. (2006). Risky alcohol use, age at onset of drinking and adverse childhood experiences in young men entering the US Marine Corps. *Archives of Pediatrics and Adolescent Medicine, 160,* 1207–1214.

Yu, Y., Ricciotti, E., Scalia, R., Tang, S. Y., Grant, G., Yu, Z., … Fitzgerald, G. A. (2012). Vascular cox-2 modulates blood pressure and thrombosis in mice. *Science Translational Medicine, 4*(132), 134–154.

Yu, K., & Daar, E. S. (2000). Primary HIV detection. *Postgraduate Medicine, 107,* 114–122.

Yucel, M., Solowij, N., Respondek, C., Whittie, S., Fornito, A., Pantelis, C., & Lubman, D. I. (2008). Regional brain abnormalities associated with long-term heavy cannabis use. *Archives of General Psychiatry, 65*(6), 694–701.

Yudko, E., Hall, H. V., & McPherson, S. B. (2009). Mechanisms of methamphetamine action. In S. B. McPherson, H. V. Hall, & E. Yudo (Eds.), *Methamphetamine use clinical and forensic Aspects.* New York: CRC Press.

Yudko, E., Hall, H. V., & Midson, P. (2009). Empirical evidence of the effects of methamphetamine on aggression. In S. B. McPherson, H. V. Hall, & E. Yudo (Eds.), *Methamphetamine use: Clinical and forensic aspects.* Boca Raton, FL: CRC Press.

Yudko, E., & McPherson, S. B. (2009). MDMA. In S. B. McPherson, H. V. Hall, & E. Yudo (Eds.), *Methamphetamine use clinical and forensic aspects.* New York: CRC Press.

Zahr, N. M., & Sullivan, E. V. (2008). Translational studies of alcoholism. *Alcohol Research & Health, 31*(3), 215–230.

Zajicek, J., Fox, P., Sandes, H., Wright, D., Vickery, J., Nunn, A., … UK MS Research Group. (2003). Cannabinoids for treatment of spasticity and other symptoms related to multiple sclerosis (CAMS study): Multicenter randomised placebo-controlled trial. *The Lancet, 362*(8), 1517–1526.

Zajicek, J., Hobart, J. C., Slade, A., Barnes, D., Mattison, P. G., & MUSEC Research Group. (2012). Multiple sclerosis and extract if cannabis: Results of the MUSEC trial. *Journal of Neurology, Neurosurgery & Psychiatry, with Practical Neurology, 83,* 1125–1132. doi:10.1136/jnnp-2012-302468

Zakaria, D. (2012). Incarceration nation. *Time, 179*(13), 18.

Zakhari, S. (2006). Overview: How is alcohol metabolized by the body? *Alcohol Research & Health, 29*(4), 245–254.

Zarkin, G. A., Bray, J. W., Aldridge, A., Mitra, D., Mills, M. J., Couper, D. J., … COMBINE Cost-Effectiveness Research Group. (2008). Cost and cost-effectiveness of the COMBINE study in alcohol-dependent patients. *Archives of General Psychiatry, 65,* 1214–1221.

Zarkin, G. A., Dunlap, L. J., Hicks, K. A., & Mamo, D. (2005). Benefits and costs of methadone treatment: Results from a lifetime simulation model. *Health Economics, 14,* 1133–1150.

Zax, D. (2008). Washington's boyhood home. *Smithsonian, 39*(6), 24–28.

Zealberg, J. J., & Brady, K. T. (1999). Substance abuse and emergency psychiatry. *Psychiatric Clinics of North America, 22,* 803–817.

Zeese, K. B. (2002). From Nixon to now. *Playboy, 49*(9), 49.

Zelvin, E. (1997). Codependency issues of substance-abusing women. In S. L. A. Straussner & E. Zelvin (Eds.), *Gender and addictions.* Northvale, NJ: Jason-Aronson.

Zemore, S. E., Kaskutas, L. A., & Ammon, L. N. (2004). In 12-step groups, helping helps the helper. *Addiction, 99*(8), 1015–1023.

Zerekh, J., & Michaels, B. (1989). Co-dependency. *Nursing Clinics of North America, 24*(1), 109–120.

Zernig, G., & Battista, H. J. (2000). Drug interactions. In G. Zernig, A. Saria, M. Kurz, & S. S. O'Malley (Eds.), *Handbook of Alcoholism.* New York: CRC Press.

Zevin, S., & Benowitz, N. L. (1998). Drug-related syndromes. In S. B. Karch (editor in chief), *Drug abuse handbook.* New York: CRC Press.

Zevin, S., & Benowitz, N. L. (2007). Medical aspects of drug abuse. In S. B. Karch (editor in chief), *Drug Abuse Handbook* (2nd ed.). New York: CRC Press.

Zhang, Y., Picetti, R., Butelman, E. R., Schussman, S. D., Ho, A., & Kreek, M. J. (2008). Behavioral and neurochemical changes induced by oxycodone differ between adolescent and adult mice. *Neuropsychopharmacology, 34,* 912–922. doi:10.1038/npp.2008.134

Zhang, Z., Infante, A., Meit, M., English, N., Dunn, M., & Bowers, K. H. (2008). *An analysis of mental health and substance abuse disparities & access to treatment services in the Appalachian region.* Washington, DC: Appalachian Regional Commission and the National Opinion Research Center.

Zhao, J., Stockwell, T., Martin, G., Macdonald, S., Vallance, K., Treno, A., … Buxton, J. (2013). The relationship between minimum alcohol prices, outlet densities and alcohol attributable deaths in British Columbia 2002-2009. *Addiction, 108,* 1059–1069. doi:101111/add.12139

Zhao, Z. Q., Gao, Y. J., Sun, Y. G., Zhao, C. S., Gereau, R. W., IV, & Chen, Z. F. (2007). Central serotonergic neurons are differentially required for opioid analgesia, but not for morphine tolerance or morphine reward. *Proceedings of the National Academy of Sciences, 104,* 14519–14524. doi:10.103/pnas.0705740104

Zhu, F., Zhang, J., Zhang, X., Zhou, C., Wang, A., Huang, S., … Xia, N. (2010). Efficacy and safety of recombinant hepatitis E vaccine in healthy adults: A large-scale, randomised, double-blind placebo-controlled phase 3 trial. *The Lancet.* Retrieved August 22, 2010, from http://www.thelancet.com/journals/lancet/article/PIIIS140-6736(10)6130-6/full text

Zhu, N. Y., LeGatt, D. F., & Turner, A. R. (2009). Agranulocytosis after consumption of cocaine adulterated with Levamisole. *Annals of Internal Medicine, 150*(4), 287–289.

Ziedonis, D., & Brady, K. (1997). Dual diagnosis in primary care. *Medical clinics of North America, 81,* 1017–1036.

Zilberman, M. L. (2009). Substance abuse across the lifespan in women. In K. T. Brady, S. E. Back, & S. F. Greenfield (Eds.), *Women & Addiction.* New York: Guilford.

Zimberg, S. (1995). The elderly. In A. M. Washton (Ed.), *Psychotherapy and substance abuse.* New York: Guilford.

Zimberg, S. (1996). Treating alcoholism: An age-specific intervention that works for older patients. *Geriatrics, 51*(10), 45–49.

Zimberg, S. (2005). Alcoholism and substance abuse in older adults. In R. J. Frances, S. I. Miller, & A. H. Mack (Eds.), *Clinical textbook of addictive disorders* (3rd ed.). New York: Guilford.

Zimmer, C. (2008). *Microcosm.* New York: Pantheon Books.

Zimmer, C. (2011). The brain. *Discover, 32*(2), 28–29.

Zisserman, R. N., & Oslin, D. W. (2004). Alcoholism and at-risk drinking in the older population. *Psychiatric Times, XXI*(2), 50–53.

Zucker, R. A., Donovan, J. E., Masten, A. S., Mattson, M. E., & Moss, H. B. (2009). Developmental processes and mechanisms: Ages 0-10. *Alcohol Research & Health, 32*(1), 16–29.

Zuckerman, B., Frank, D. A., & Mayes, L. (2002). Cocaine-exposed infants and developmental outcomes. *Journal of the American Medical Association, 287,* 1990–1991.

Zuckerman, M. (2012). Psychological factors and addiction: Personality. In H. J. Shaffer, D. A. LaPlante, & S. E. Nelson (Eds.), *A.P.A. addiction syndromes handbook* (Vol. 1, pp. 175–194). Washington, DC: American Psychological Association.

Zukin, S. R., Sloboda, Z., & Javitt, D. C. (2005). Phencyclidine. In J. H. Lowinstein, P. Ruiz, R. B. Millman, & J. G. Langrod (Eds.), *Substance abuse: A comprehensive textbook* (4th ed.). New York: Williams & Wilkins.

Zunz, S. J., Ferguson, N. L., & Senter, M. (2005). Post-identification support for substance dependent students in school based programs: The weakest link. *Journal of Child and Adolescent Substance Abuse, 14*(4), 77–92.

Zur, O. (2005). The psychology of victimhood. In R. H. Wright & N. A. Cummings (Eds.), *Destructive trends in mental health.* New York: Routledge.

Zweig, C., & Wolf, S. (1997). *Romancing the shadow.* New York: Ballantine Books.

Zylka, M. J., Sowa, N. A., Taylor-Blake, B., Twomey, M. A., Herrala, M. A., Voikar, V., & Vihko, P. (2008). Prostatis acid phosphatase is an ectonucleotidase and suppresses pain by generating adenosine. *Neuron, 60,* 111–122.

Zywiak, W. H., Stout, R. L., Longabaugh, R., Dyck, I., Connors, G. J., & Maisto, S. A. (2006). Relapse-onset factors in the project MATCH: The relapse questionnaire. *Journal of Substance Abuse Treatment, 31*(4), 341–354.

INDEX